THE MOJO COLLECTION

THIRD EDITION

THE MOJO COLLECTION

THIRD EDITION

The ULTIMATE Music Companion

EDITED BY

Jim Irvin & Colin McLear

CANONGATE

First published in the United Kingdom in
2000 by MOJO Books,
an imprint of Canongate Books Ltd, 14
High Street, Edinburgh EH1 1TE

This edition first published in 2003 by
Canongate Books

Published simultaneously in the United
States of America and Canada
by Canongate Books, 841 Broadway, New
York NY 10003

10 9 8 7 6 5 4 3 2 1

ISBN 1 84195 438 1

Typeset by Palimpsest Book Production Ltd,
Polmont, Scotland

Printed by Clays Ltd, St Ives, UK

www.canongate.net

Contents

We'd Love To Turn You On
An introduction to The Mojo Collection

"One good thing 'bout music, when it hits, you feel no pain."
– Bob Marley

Discussions about The MOJO Collection were initiated by the former editor of MOJO magazine Mat Snow and its former US Bureau chief Barney Hoskyns but both left before work could begin and in January 2000 the project was handed to Jim Irvin.

The editing of the book has taken the form of an "All back to ours" affair, where, in various rooms, you can discover new music, old sounds, hot hits and cool cuts, with plenty of, "Heard this?" "Check out this bit…!" and "Did you ever hear this story about…?" going on. We realise we couldn't include every decent record ever released, but we hope to have represented every taste to some degree.

We've interpreted "popular music" in its broadest possible sense. You'll find albums in many genres – folk, funk, jazz, punk and so on – from the 1940s to the middle of 2003, zillion-selling world-beaters to utterly obscure curiosities, hundreds of them written about in detail and many others recommended. We have been rigid about one criterion. All these records were conceived as albums. We've insisted on work that made the most of the form, in other words celebrating the best use of the format's wide possibilities rather than the tight pop nugget or the LP compiled from diverse sources. We have not rated the albums or ranked them, instead presenting them chronologically so you can see how the album has developed as both an art form and a mirror of music history.

It is an unashamedly biased selection, representing the collective enthusiasms of the contributors as they picked their way through their record collections and pulled out the albums they love and which matter to them.

The book was written by (in alphabetical order):

Phil Alexander, Mike Barnes, Angus Batey (AB), Johnny Black, Lloyd Bradley, Geoff Brown, Gly Brown, Jenny Bulley, John Bungey (JB), Andrew Carden, Rob Chapman, Richard Cook, Joe Cushley, Toni Davidson (TD), Fred Dellar, Bill De Main (BDM), Anuj Desai (AD), Dave Di Martino, Dawn Eden, Ben Edmonds, Mark Ellen, Tim Forster (TF), Pat Gilbert (PG), Andy Gill, Paul Gorman, Sid Griffin, Colin Harper, John Harris, Dave Henderson, Trevor Hodgett, Mick Houghton, Patrick Humphries, David Hutcheon (DH), Chris Ingham, Jim Irvin, Colin Irwin, Richard Morton Jack (RMJ) Al Kooper, Steve Lowe, James McNair, Andrew Male, Kenny Mathieson (KM), Merrell Noden, Sharon O'Connell, Peter Paphides, Mark Paytress, David Peschek, Alexis Petridis, Steve Rippon, Johnny Rogan, Kevin Sampson (KS), Harry Shapiro, Sylvie Simmons (SS), Neil Spencer (NS), Bob Stanley, Denise Sullivan, Phil Sutcliffe, Dave Thompson, Graeme Thomson, Paul Trnka, Jaa Uhelszki (JU), Douglas Wagner (DW), Helen Walsh (HW) and Lois Wilson.

There are also contributions from: Kingsley Abbott, Bill Brewster, Paul Du Noyer, Sophie Harris, Barney Hoskyns (BH), Cliff Jones, Mark Lewisohn, Steve Mailins, Eric Olsen, Steve Pafford, Edwin Pouncey, Neil Slaven, Robert Spellman, Steve Turner, Gianluca Tramontana, Ed Ward, Marc Weingarten, Mike White and Kevin Younger.

We have credited each entry where known. But, um, in the spirit of rock'n'roll, many of the contributions and their contributors have been forgotten (it was a long night . . .) but we are, of course, happy to rectify should anyone remember who did what.

Special mention to Sylvie Simmons, Phil Sutcliffe, Chris Ingham, Andy Gill, Fred Dellar, Merrell Noden, and Mark Paytress who did much, much more than simply supply material.

Thanks must also go to the following for their help, in varying degrees, in putting this book together:

Angelo Acanfora, Julian Alexander, Jenny Bulley, all at Canongate, Nadja Coyne, Clare Dowse, Sophie Harris, Dave Henderson, Susie Hudson, Sally Irvin, Sevil Miyhandar, Salmon Naqvi, David Peschek, Robert Spellman, Sheryl Stevoff, Paul Trynka, Henry Volans, Mark Wagstaff, and Lois Wilson.

Acknowledgment and thanks must also be given for the following reference works: The Great Rock Discography by Martin Strong (Canongate); The Complete Book Of The British Charts by Tony Brown, John Kutner and Neil Warwick (Omnibus); The Rock Record by Terry Hounsome (Hounsome); The Macmillan Encyclopedia Of Popular Music by Colin Larkin (Macmillan); The Q Book Of Rock Stars by Dafydd Rees and Luke Crampton; The Guinness Book of Hit Albums and The Guinness Book of Hit Singles (Guinness Books) and The Billboard Book Of Number One Hits by Fred Bronson, The Billboard Book Of Number One Albums by Craig Rosen, The Billboard Book Of Top 40 Albums by Joel Whitburn and The Billboard Book Of Top 40 Singles by Joel Whitburn (all Billboard).

It has been an incredibly daunting task putting this book together and not – as you can probably imagine – one without fierce debate and disagreement. Doubtless we've left out some of your favourite records – we've certainly had to leave out some of ours. We hope to include all such albums, and many more, in future expanded editions. So, without further ado... Welcome to The MOJO Collection...

The Editors, 2003

What have we here?

The albums are arranged chronologically by release date. At the rear of the book are indexes by artist and album title. This is a celebration of an art form – the pop album. We've selected hundreds of them from the very first vinyl pop album in 1946 to important releases from the first half of 2003 – and found out how they happened.

As well as the main text for each album, every entry of The MOJO Collection comprises the following information where available:

Artist

The Album Title
If an album is known by more than one name we've used that of the original issue.

Label
The label the album originally appeared on in the UK

Producer

Recording Information
Location and date recorded, if known

Release date
Date first issued in the UK

Chart Peaks
Highest album chart placing in the UK and US, if available

Personnel
The key players and technicians. Abbreviations as follows:

ae = assistant engineer
ag = acoustic guitar
ar = arranger
b = bass
bs = baritone sax
bv = backing vocals
c = cello
d = drums
db = double bass
e = engineer
ep = electric piano
g = guitar
hm = harmonica
k = keyboards
m = mixer
o = organ
p = piano

pc = percussion
ps = pedal steel guitar
rg = rhythm guitar
s = saxohpnoe
sg = steel guitar
syn = synthesiser
t = trumpet
tb = trombone
ts = tenor sax
v = vocals
va = viola
vn = violin

More esoteric instruments – zither, vibraphone, alpine horn etc – are listed in full

Track listing
Running order of the original UK release

Running Time
Total time of original album

Current CD
The catalogue number of the most recent CD edition of the album. If no label is shown the original label applies. If the album has been reissued on a different label, that's here, plus the details of any bonus tracks, omissions or alterations

Further Listening
Other albums by the same artist that best complement this one, interesting solo albums or side projects

Further Reading
The best biographies (whether or not they are still in print) and/or the most informative website

Like This?
Pointing you in the direction of another record you may enjoy if you like this one – not always the most obvious of choices, maybe even a different genre, it may simply be a similar attitude

The Beginning

Frank Sinatra
The Voice of Frank Sinatra
The Voice Of The Century pioneers the vinyl pop LP.

In 1946 you could buy these eight songs on four heavy, perishable, 10-inch, shellac 78rpm discs packaged together in a binder to resemble a book. It was a format known in the trade as an album.

It sold like crazy, for this was the period when "Swoonatra" was cresting his huge first wave of popularity. At the beginning of the decade, the skinny "kid" from Hoboken, New Jersey had made a phenomenal impact upon leaving the Tommy Dorsey Orchestra to go solo. A well-orchestrated publicity campaign attracted pop's first posse of screaming school-age girls. By the time of these recordings he'd crossed into the affections of adults too and made inroads into a creditable film career with the hit movie Anchors Aweigh. Not surprisingly, when Columbia began releasing 10-inch microgroove long-playing records in early 1949, this was the first pop item to appear in the new format. The collection found Francis Albert Sinatra – aged 30 when these songs were sung – in a romantic mode, interpreting eight standards with the aid of his long-term arranger and conductor, Axel Stordahl, a string quartet, a rhythm section and the oboe of Mitch Miller. They were songs that Sinatra loved, in simple settings – like chamber music – that allowed the singer's innate tenderness with a lyric to shine (a ploy that Frank would revisit over the years, in particular on the 1956 *Close To You sessions* with The Hollywood String Quartet). It added up to what is, in effect, the first concept album by a pop performer, a collection of songs about a helpless heart. No matter if a lyric suggested that a girl cared for him, Frank remained the little boy lost, requiring someone to watch over him, not standing a ghost of a chance with the one he cared for most, and reflecting, by means of a few foolish things, on a past attachment gone wrong, the perpetual victim of unrequited love.

Sinatra would record most of these songs again in the '50s, when he made his reputation as 'Voice Of The Century' and when his instrument had the timbre of a wise cello, a little more worldly, but no less susceptible to hopeless affairs of the heart. But here, still a creamy viola, he delivered performances that were simply the state of the post-Crosby pop singing art; passionate but gentle, sexy but vulnerable. Little wonder that an entire generation of adoring females experienced the simultaneous – and no doubt conflicting – arousal of their carnal and mothering instincts.

Record label:
Columbia
Produced
by Manny Sachs.
Recorded
in New York City; July 30 and December 7, 1945.
Released:
March 1946
Chart peaks:
None (UK) 1 (US)
Personnel:
Frank Sinatra (v) Axel Stordahl and his Orchestra
Track listing:
You Go To My Head; Someone To Watch Over Me; I Don't Know Why; These Foolish Things; Try A Little Tenderness; Ghost Of A Chance; Paradise; Why Shouldn't I
Running time:
22.35
Current CD:
CK 52868
Further listening:
Sing And Dance With Frank Sinatra (1950), the first album that Frank, with arranger George Siravo and producer Mitch Miller, shaped with a microgroove LP in mind. After that, take your pick from the wealth of mainly superb releases through Capitol and Reprise.
Further reading:
Sinatra – The Song Is You (Will Friedwald 1995) is the most detailed book on Sinatra's recording career; his daughter's Sinatra – An American Legend, (Nancy Sinatra, 1995) the most lavishly illustrated.
Like this?
Try . . . p.726

The 1950s

Peggy Lee
Black Coffee
Please welcome the fabulous Norma Deloris Egstrom!

Undoubtedly among the finest female singers to grace the world of popular music, Peggy Lee was vocally equipped to sing blues, jazz, Broadway standards or even cornball material, though she generally steered clear of the latter. She was also an accomplished songwriter; she fashioned the soundtrack for The Lady And The Tramp and picked up an Oscar nomination for her acting ability. All this and beauty too.

It was a long road to her debut album. Born Norma Jean Egstrom, she began as a teenage singer in 1936 with the Jack Wardlow Band, then joined Will Osborne (1940–41) before becoming part of vocal group The Four Of Us. Heard by King of Swing Benny Goodman, she became vocalist with his highly rated outfit, cutting her first records within days of taking the job and notching her first hit that same year with a cover of Duke Ellington's I Got It Bad And That Ain't Good. After several other hits with the Goodman outfit, she married the band's guitarist, Dave Barbour, whose own band featured on many of her initial solo recordings. Signed first to Capitol and then to Decca, Peg notched over 30 hit singles of varying quality (one was titled Bum, Bum, I Wonder Who I Am) between 1945 and 1953, when the opportunity arose to cut her first long-player.

It was released in ten-inch form with a mere eight tracks (four other songs, recorded at a Los Angeles session in April, 1956 were added when the record eventually appeared as a 12-inch). But with those original eight tracks the singer born Norma Deloris Egstrom established herself in the very top echelon, alongside Billie Holiday and Ella Fitzgerald. Though there was no outlet for her R&B talents, later manifest on such singles as The Comeback, *Black Coffee* allowed Peg the opportunity to swing effortlessly and phrase with dangerous abandon on such songs as I've Got You Under My Skin, faultlessly conjure a four-in-the-morning mood on the torchy title track, or interpret Johnny Mercer's superb lyric to When The World Was Young in such a manner that, to date, no one has yet managed to extract so much emotion from or bestow with such fragility.

Record label:
Decca
Producer:
unknown.
Recorded
in New York City; April 30, May 1 and 4, 1953.
Released:
1953
Chart peaks:
None (UK) None (US)
Personnel:
Peggy Lee (v); Pete Condoli (t); Jimmy Rowles (p); Wayne Bennett (b); Ed Shaughnessy (d)
Track listing:
Black Coffee; I've Got You Under My Skin; Easy Living; My Heart Belongs To Daddy (S); A Woman Alone With The Blues; I Didn't Know What Time It Was; When The World Was Young; Love Me Or Leave Me
Running time:
20.35
Current CD
MCLD 19363 adds: Sea Shells
Further listening:
The Man I Love, 1957 a bundle of string-laden ballads, recorded with an orchestra conducted by Frank Sinatra and containing a superlative The Folks That Live On The Hill.
Further reading:
Miss Peggy Lee (1990) an autobiography that fills many gaps without being entirely satisfactory; www.peggylee.com/
Like this?
Try . . . p.647

Julie London

Julie Is Her Name

Intimate and sensual torch song motherlode.

"The girl with the come-hither voice," said Bill Balance in his sleevenotes – never mind that she was a married woman with two children. Her voice, a husky instrument that lingered on syllables like honey oozing off a spoon, was the sexiest entreaty American music could offer in 1955. Elvis may have been knocking on the door, but the torch singers of the '50s – Holiday, Lee, Vaughan, Fitzgerald – still held American men spellbound, and the statuesque Miss London – already with a modest movie career behind her – came to represent the genre.

She had already done plenty of work as a nightclub singer, encouraged by her pianist husband Bobby Troup, but Liberty was the only label interested in taking a chance on recording her. Troup insisted that she be recorded in the same setting as her live act – no orchestra, not even a piano, and just the bare strings of guitar and acoustic bass in support. Every song a ballad and nothing uptempo. Kessel (who also played on some of The Coasters' records from the same period) offers trim accompaniments that introduce just a lick of jazz, but nothing to disturb the besotted listener. The mood had to be 'round midnight', and even though there are 13 songs on the record, it barely exceeds half an hour in length. Troup's instincts were right. Released as a single, Cry Me A River was a major hit, and suddenly everyone *knew* that her name was Julie. The other songs are similarly lonesome, but here and there Julie flirts with a sort of blues feel, particularly on Easy Street. There is a little vibrato at the end of each line, just enough to make a strong man's legs go weak, and when she disappears with Gone With The Wind, it's as if someone has opened a window and she has just drifted off, a copper-haired phantom. Julie made many more albums for Liberty, and many of them were gorgeous, but this one still says it all.

Record label:
Liberty
Produced
by Bobby Troup.
Recorded:
1955.
Released:
December 1955
Chart peaks:
None (UK) 2 (US)
Personnel:
Julie London (v); Barney Kessel (g); Ray Leatherwood (b)
Track Listing:
Cry Me A River; I Should Care; I'm In The Mood For Love; I'm Glad There Is You; Can't Help Lovin' That Man; I Love You; Say It Isn't So; It Never Entered My Mind; Easy Street; 'S Wonderful; No Moon At All; Laura; Gone With The Wind
Running time:
31.11
Current CD:
VCS010
Further listening:
Julie Is Her Name Vol 2 (1956)
Further reading:
www.autobahn.mb.ca/~agard/
Like this?
Try . . . p.685

The Four Freshmen

Four Freshmen And Five Trombones

Best album by vocal group that influenced The Beach Boys.

A four-piece vocal (and instrumental) group whose innovative harmonies completely changed the way such outfits sounded. Without them, there'd most likely have been no Beach Boys, no Jan And Dean. It could be argued that The Hi-Los were an even more inventive vocal group than the Freshmen, technically superior and, thanks to Clark Burrough's stratospheric flights of fancy, totally astounding to all raised on the traditional big-band harmony group sounds produced by artists like The Pied Pipers (with Tommy Dorsey) or Glenn Miller's Modernaires. But the Freshmen were warmer, somehow more human, able to reach a commercial market (something The Hi-Los were unable to do) without relinquishing their intricate way of things.

Voted Best Jazz Vocal Group of 1953, having earlier been dropped (and then reinstated) by Capitol – who initially failed to see the quartet's potential – they released their debut album, *Voices In Modern* the following year. But it was with *Four Freshmen And Five Trombones* that the breakthrough came. The format was hardly earth-shattering – just harmony interpretations of standards by such songwriters as Kern and Weill and lyricists who included Johnny Mercer, Ogden Nash and Oscar Hammerstein II, performed against a backdrop supplied by a team of Hollywood's top trombonists plus an equally stellar rhythm section. But the songs were sometimes delivered in surprising tempi, the traditionally romantic You Stepped Out Of A Dream virtually bursting out of its groove, Weill's Speak Low acquiring a Latin patina. And somehow, the album appealed to both those who tuned into the progressive jazz sounds of Stan Kenton and Woody Herman, and the family man who'd just cottoned onto hi-fi and wanted something spectacular but easy-on-the-ear.

When Brian Wilson heard the Freshmen, he became obsessed by their harmonies and contemporary arrangements. Claimed brother Carl: "Months at a time, days on end, he'd listen to Four Freshmen records." Later, the Beach Boys would even turn in an exact copy of the Freshmen's Graduation Day. No-one disputes that *Pet Sounds* started here.

Record label:
Capitol
Produced
by Dave Cavanagh and Pete Rugolo.
Recorded
at Capitol Studios, Hollywood; 1955.
Released:
February 1956
Chart peaks:
6 (UK) 6 (US)
Personnel:
Ross Barbour, Bob Flanigan, Ken Errair, Don Barbour (v); Frank Rosolino, Harry Betts Jr, Milt Bernhardt, Tommy Pederson, George Roberts (tb); Claude Williamson (p); Barney Kessel (g); Shelly Manne (d); Joe Mondragon (b)
Track listing:
Angel Eyes; Love Is Just Around The Corner; Mamselle; Speak Low; The Last Time I Saw Paris; Somebody Loves Me; You Stepped Out Of A Dream; I Remember You; Love; Love Is Here To Stay; You Made Me Love You; Guilty
Running time:
31.62
Current CD:
CCM0172 adds Four Freshmen And Five Trumpets
Further listening:
Tune in to The Hi-lo's Cherries And Other Delights (1994), a compilation of their radio appearances, to hear another exceptional array of harmonies and a sound that still resonates throughout contemporary vocal groups as Take 6.
Further reading:
American Singing Groups (Jay Warner, 1992)
Like this?
Try . . . p.49

Ella Fitzgerald

Sings The Cole Porter Songbook

Great American voice meets great American composer.

By 1955, Norman Granz, founder of Verve Records, had been trying to acquire Ella Fitzgerald as a recording artist for six years, though she'd been a valuable member of his touring jam-session-for-concertgoers – Jazz At The Philharmonic – since 1949. Her tenure at Decca under the canny A&R aegis of Milt Gabler had seen her juggle successful jukebox pop (My Happiness selling 500,000) with artistic successes (the 1950 and 1954 sessions with pianist Ellis Larkins) and a critical reputation that labelled her the First Lady Of Song (she also topped the Metronome and Downbeat polls for years). But Granz had sustained a campaign of public criticism about some of the fluff she was asked to record. "He used to have pieces in Downbeat saying how I was destroying her, giving her bad material," remembered Gabler.

By 1953 Granz was Ella's personal manager and announced a substantial Cole Porter songbook project for her. Recorded quickly with over thirty sides being cut in three sessions, there were "hardly any second takes," remembers pianist Paul Smith, "they were just sort of *ground* out." Clearly Granz was desperate for Ella to be associated with Porter's urbane blend of gently cynical romance (It's All Right With Me, Just One Of Those Things), sexy comedy (Too Darn Hot, Anything Goes) and elegant, witty sentiment (Ev'ry Time We Say Goodbye, From This Moment On). Ella's cool, clear delivery suited the material beautifully, although her personality was hardly the sort to overstate Porter's arch sophistication ("She is a simple person," judged massive fan and fellow jazz singer Mel Torme, "her approach to life is simple"), and the songs arrive in deceptively easy-going tones making for a subtle, rewarding listen.

The following few years saw Ella record songbooks of Rodgers And Hart, Duke Ellington and Irving Berlin, a five-album set of George Gershwin and sets of Kern and Mercer. Though some bemoaned the lack of jazz content in the series – and there remains critical dispute as to which songbook is the most artistically successful – *Cole Porter* was the most popular. "I don't actually like the man," said Mel Torme, "but I give Norman Granz great credit for saying to Ella, 'You are far more than a cult singer, you should be a national treasure,' and that's what he did for her."

Record Label:
Verve
Produced
by Norman Granz.
Recorded
in LA; February–March 1956.
Released:
Spring 1956
Chart peaks:
None (UK) 15 (US)
Personnel:
Ella Fitzgerald (v) with Buddy Bregman's Orchestra
Track Listing:
All Through The Night; Anything Goes; Miss Otis Regrets; Too Darn Hot; In The Still Of The Night; I Get A Kick Out Of You; Do I Love You; Always True To You Darling In My Fashion; Let's Do It; Just One Of Those Things; Ev'ry Time We Say Goodbye; Begin The Beguine; Get Out Of Town; I Am In Love; From This Moment On; I Love Paris; You Do Something To Me; Ridin' High; Easy To Love; It's All Right With Me; Why Can't You Behave; What Is This Thing Called Love; You're The Top; Love For Sale; It's Delovely; Night And Day; Ace In The Hole; So In Love; I've Got You Under My Skin; I Concentrate On You; Don't Fence Me In
Running time:
118.27
Current CD:
5372572
Further listening:
The following Songbooks are also indispensable: Sings The Rodgers And Hart Songbook (1956); Duke Ellington Songbook (1957); Irving Berlin Songbook (1958); Gershwin Songbook (1959)
Further reading:
Ella Fitzgerald (Stuart Nicholson, 1993)
Like this?
Try . . . p.497

Frank Sinatra

Songs For Swingin' Lovers

Sinatra's sophisticated cool peaks at the dawn of rock'n'roll.

When Capitol vice-president Alan Livingstone announced to their annual convention that he'd signed the down-and-out Sinatra (who had debt, depression and no career prospects), there was an audible groan. Livingstone: "My answer to them was, Look, I only know talent, and Frank is the best singer in the world." Though humble and grateful, Frank was having a hard time relinquishing his partnership with his '40s arranger Axel Stordahl. Livingstone was determined to put him together with burgeoning talent Nelson Riddle: "Nelson knew how to back up singers and make them sound great." Getting to know each other over a few sides, Sinatra was impressed with Riddle's 1953 treatment of World On A String, but upon hearing his polytonal ballad arranging told pianist Bill Miller, "Whew, we gotta be careful with him." Miller replied, "Hey, Frank, it's different, it's working."

By mid-'55 Sinatra was back on top (thanks to the movie *From Here To Eternity* and a series of confident albums) and Nelson was forging his distinctive heartbeat tempo, swing-band-plus-strings style that fitted the new Sinatra like a made-to-measure tux. Recasting the repertoire of a previous generation in exhilarating new light and creating new standard songs in the process, *Songs For Swingin' Lovers* was the epitome of the rejuvenated, finger-poppin' Sinatra. Full of lyrical playfulness ("Stars fractured 'bama last night") and exuberant re-phrasing (his second chorus of It Happened In Monterey), this music had a vitality and sexiness that made women want to bed him and men want to be him, nowhere more so than in the legend that is the Riddle/Sinatra take on Cole Porter's I've Got You Under My Skin. A brooding, sensuous groove that builds into an explosive, sputtering trombone solo (played by Milt Bernhart over the wrong chords, balancing on a box to get closer to the mike) and pushes on with a hearty ardour before the detumescent coda, it's one of the most thrilling three and a half minutes in popular music.

While Riddle recognised it as a "cornerstone recording for both him and me", Neal Hefti, the great Basie arranger said "no one has come close to what Nelson achieved with Sinatra. . . God! That enthusiasm just keeps going on and on and on!"

Record Label:
Capitol
Produced
by Voyle Gilmore.
Recorded
at Capitol Studios, Hollywood; June 1955–January 1956.
Released:
June, 1956
Chart peak:
8 (UK) 2 (US)
Personnel:
Frank Sinatra (v); Nelson Riddle (a, oa); orchestra including Milt Bernhart (tb); Harry Edison, Conrad Gozzo (t); Harry Klee (flute); Mahlon Clark (clarinet)
Track Listing:
You Make Me Feel So Young; It Happened In Monterey; You're Getting To Be A Habit With Me; You Brought A New Kind Of Love To Me; Too Marvellous For Words; Old Devil Moon; Pennies From Heaven; Love Is Here To Stay; I've Got You Under My Skin; I Thought About You; We'll Be Together Again; Makin' Whoopee; Swingin' Down The Lane; Anything Goes; How About You?
Running time:
44.51
Current CD:
CDP-746570-2
Further listening:
Swing Easy (1954); A Swingin' Affair (1957)
Further reading:
Sinatra! The Song Is You: A Singer's Art (Will Friedwald, 1995)
Like this?
Try . . . p.166

Johnny Burnette And The Rock'n'Roll Trio

Johnny Burnette And The Rock'n'Roll Trio

Neglected classic from the birth of rock'n'roll.

Brothers Johnny and Dorsey Burnette and guitarist Paul Burlison had been cutting up the Memphis area for a good five years before they entered Owen Bradley's famed Nashville studio in July 1956. A few months previously, former schoolmate and work colleague Elvis Presley had hit Number 1 in both the album and singles charts. The Trio were choking on his exhaust. Over the next few days, however, they laid down a series of tracks that hold their own with a lot of The King's best.

The Trio had signed to Coral on the strength of a string of wins on The Ted Mack Amateur Show in New York. "One of the reasons we signed with Coral instead of Capitol," Burlison remembers, "was that they gave us a free hand on the material we wanted to record." Burlison brought a Tiny Bradshaw track, Train Kept A-Rollin', to the band's attention; but more importantly he told Bradley about an accident he'd recently had with his Fender Deluxe amplifier. "I dropped it between the band-room and stage one evening. That night I got this weird, fuzzed-up sound from it. After the gig I took the back off and found I'd knocked a tube loose." Bradley was wise enough to employ this primitive, ear-grabbing tone on both Train Kept A-Rollin' and Honey Hush, while Johnny B. let rip over the top with a backwoods, rockabilly shout that made Presley sound positively tame.

"I played a 1952 Esquire with a treble sound that could kill crab-grass," recalls Burlison, "but I listened to and played everything. In fact, Latin music is one of my favourites." And there, on the self-penned Lonesome Tears In My Eyes you hear his Hispanic stylings, while Johnny exercises the melodic control that would later serve him as a teen idol – garnering hits with Dreamin' and You're Sixteen. Unfortunately, fraternal rows and a lack of will on the record label's part meant that this 10-incher never got off the ground, and the group would founder only a year later. Nevertheless, Burlison is still revered as a sonic pioneer by players as important as Clapton, Mick Green and Jeff Beck; and many of the riotous numbers included here (Lonesome Train, All By Myself) are staples to this day for any self-respecting roots rock'n'rollers.

Record label:
Coral
Produced
by Owen Bradley.
Recorded
at Quonset Studio, 16th Avenue South, Nashville; July 2–5, 1956.
Released:
Autumn 1956
Chart peaks:
None (UK) None (US)
Personnel:
Johnny Burnette (v, g); Paul Burlison (g); Dorsey Burnette (b); Buddy Harman Jr (d); Owen Bradley (p); Anita Kerr Singers (bv)
Track listing:
Honey Hush; Lonesome Train (On A Lonesome Track) (S); Sweet Love On My Mind; Rock Billy Boogie; Lonesome Tears In My Eyes; All By Myself; The Train Kept A-Rollin' (S); Just Found Out; Your Baby Blue Eyes; Chains Of Love; I Love You So; Drinking Wine Spo-Dee-O-Dee, Drinking Wine
Running time:
26.27
Current CD:
BGO CD177 adds: Tear It Up; You're Undecided; Oh Baby Babe; Eager Beaver Baby; Touch Me; Midnight Train; If You Want It Enough; Blues Stay Away From Me; Shattered Dreams; My Love, You're a Stranger; Rock Therapy; Please Don't Leave Me
Further listening:
Train Kept A-Rollin' (1997)
Further reading:
www.geocities.com/SunsetStrip/Palladium/9008/JohnnyBurnette.htm
Like this?
Try . . . p.175

Sonny Rollins

Saxophone Colossus

Saxophonist comes of age . . .

Sonny Rollins vied with John Coltrane for the title of top tenor saxophonist of his generation, including one meeting on disc (released as the title track of Rollins' *Tenor Madness*) only a month before this classic session was recorded. The two were highly individual stylists, and both are widely regarded as the ultimate exemplars of their instrument in jazz.

"I wasn't like the guy who started out, played for years and years, found a style, and then somebody heard him and got him a record date and everybody liked him," he insisted. "That's not my story. My story is that from the time I was a teenager, I was on records with great musicians."

In common with most of his peers on that scene, he began using heroin in 1948, and was jailed for a time in 1950, and again in 1952. He eventually kicked the habit in 1955, and resumed his career at a new level.

The previous years had allowed him to develop his ideas and musical understanding, work through some of his technical deficiencies, and take in invaluable lessons from musicians of the highest calibre (including Charlie Parker and Miles Davis). The shedding of his dependency on heroin can be seen as the final step in that process, leaving him ready to make the ascent to the next level of personal and artistic maturity.

He is notoriously self-critical of his playing, especially on record, but those recordings – from all points of his long career – contain some of the most brilliant and imperishable jazz ever committed to tape, and none more so than Saxophone Colossus.

The album's best known cut is 'St Thomas', an infectious calypso based on a traditional melody which became the most celebrated of his Caribbean-derived tunes, and has remained a trademark in his repertoire ever since.

Rollins approached all of the tunes through a coherent development of melodic fragments into spontaneous but logically extended improvised choruses. He employed a sophisticated degree of architectural development which was not simply a variation on the accepted bebop model of improvising on the harmonic material (chord changes) of the tune (a process often known as "running the changes"), but an alternative approach, employing a variety of patterns and devices, and much variation of rhythm, shape and texture.

The results impressed the critics, but *Saxophone Colossus* was also the record which really established Rollins as a major jazz name with the public, and remains an undisputed classic.

KM

Record Label:
Prestige
Produced
by Bob Weinstock
Recorded
at Van Gelder's Recording Studio, Hackensack, New Jersey, 22 June, 1956.
Released:
Autumn 1956
Chart peaks:
None (UK) None (US)
Personnel:
Sonny Rollins (ts); Tommy Flanagan (p); Doug Watkins (b); Max Roach (d).
Track listing:
You Don't Know What Love Is; St Thomas; Strode Road; Blue 7; Moritat
Running time:
39.31
Current CD:
OJC 291
Further listening:
Way Out West (1957); Live at the Village Vanguard (1959)
Further reading:
Sonny Rollins: The Cutting Edge (Richard Palmer, 1998); Open Sky (Eric Nisenson, 2000).
Like this?
Try . . . p.333

Miles Davis

Birth Of The Cool

Young bop trumpeter and hip arrangers invent cool jazz.

In the late '40s, Miles Davis was the trumpeter in the Charlie Parker Quintet in New York. Although in awe of the bebop genius of Bird, Miles was uncomfortable being a lesser instrumental virtuoso than his boss; bop's default style was that of Dizzy Gillespie, Parker's former partner, who Miles idolised but whose attack, speed or range he couldn't get near. Also, he was tiring of the theme-solos-theme structure of much bop and his ears had been tuning into Gil Evans' adventurous, unorthodox arrangements for the Claude Thornhill Orchestra, Anthropology and Thriving From A Riff.

Evans was something of a mentor to a New York group of young modern musicians (including Gerry Mulligan, John Lewis and John Carisi) and when he approached Davis to be allowed to arrange his tune Donna Lee, Davis asked to see the charts and became a regular part of the circle who gathered at Gil's flat to theorise and experiment. Recognising the ideas of Evans and Mulligan as an ideal vehicle for him to "solo in the style that I was hearing" – a nine-piece band with modern harmonic voicing and light textures – Davis "cracked the whip" as Mulligan put it; he organised rehearsals, got a live engagement at the Royal Roost and crucially, got Capitol (not a company particularly disposed toward modern jazz) to record the band. Released as singles in 1949 and 1950 and finally gathered as an album in 1957 (when the sides were first named Birth Of The Cool), the eleven original instrumentals (plus one vocal) featured a seamless integration of the arranged and the spontaneous; warm, dense ensembles unusually underpinned by tuba and French horn open up into characterful, smoothly-phrased improvised solos by Davis and the 19-year-old altoist Lee Konitz. The miniature masterpieces include Mulligan's perky but luminous Venus De Milo, Crisis altered minor blues Israel and the mysterious harmonic pea-souper that is Evans's Moon Dreams.

Though the band existed for mere months, the recordings were immeasurably influential on orchestral jazz and the West Coast cool school movement, cerebral and (to some) anaemic music played mainly by white musicians that Davis was quick to distance himself from. This was the first of several times in the coming 30 years that Miles Davis projects would profoundly affect the development of jazz.

Record label:
Capitol
Produced
by Pete Rugolo.
Recorded
in New York; January–April 1949 and March 1950.
Released:
February 1957
Chart peaks:
None (UK) None (US)
Personnel:
Miles Davis (t, a); Kai Winding, J.J. Johnson, Mike Zwerin (tb); Junior Collins, Sandy Sielgelstein (french horn); Bill Barber (tba); Lee Konitz (as); Gerry Mulligan (bs, a); Al Haig (p); John Lewis (p, a); Joe Schulman, Nelson Boyd, Al McKibbon (b); Max Roach, Kenny Clarke (d); Kenny Hagood (v); Gil Evans (a)
Track Listing:
Move; Jeru; Moon Dreams; Venus De Milo; Budo; Deception; Godchild; Boplicity; Rocker; Israel; Rouge; Darn That Dream
Running time:
35.57
Current CD:
CDP7928622
Further listening:
Miles Ahead (1957); Porgy And Bess (1958); The Complete Birth Of The Cool (1998), inc Live Sessions: Birth Of The Cool Theme; Symphony Sid Announces The Band; Move; Why Do I Love You; Godchild; Symphony Sid Introduction; S'il Vous Plait; Moon Dreams; Budo (Hallucinations); Darn That Dream; Move; Moon Dreams; Budo (Hallucinations)
Further reading:
Miles Davis (Ian Carr, 1999)
Like this?
Try . . . p.37

Nat 'King' Cole

Love Is The Thing

Gorgeous, moody and romantic in the extreme.

Nat 'King' Cole could be anything you wanted him to be – a vocal purveyor of pure pop able to apply his talents to the corniest material; a classy supper-club entertainer (known in his day as "the sepia Sinatra"); or even a poll-winning piano player able to jam with the best in jazz. He could deliver fine albums seemingly with the minimum of effort: swinging affairs, blues-hued wonders, country capers, lounge warmers filled with sly Latin licks, anything. But *Love Is The Thing* was the biggest of them all.

In October 1956, Nat was signed by NBC to host a TV show, the first black entertainer to have his own slot on a major network. Gordon Jenkins was brought in to provide the arrangements on Nat's first series and, despite problems with sponsors, it proved a winner with viewers, Nat's easy and relaxed style attracting a sizeable audience. When the time arrived for Cole to cut his next album, it made sense to continue the partnership with Jenkins, the creator of a distinctive string sound. The songs selected ranged from perhaps over-used standards such as Stardust and Ain't Misbehavin' through to the lovely When Sunny Gets Blue, previously a Johnny Mathis hit, and I Thought About Marie, a Jenkins original. There was also a link with Cole's past in When I Fall In Love, Where Can I Go Without You? and Love Letters, three songs penned by Victor Young, the composer responsible for Mona Lisa, one of Nat's most successful singles.

Love Is The Thing proved to be not only one of Cole's most moving albums – composer Hoagy Carmichael proclaimed Nat's version of Stardust the finest he'd ever heard – but also his best-selling LP, sitting at the peak of the US album charts for eight consecutive weeks. Among those who sat up and took notice was Capitol label-mate Frank Sinatra. He would turn to Jenkins to recreate the same mood on *Where Are You* and *No One Cares*, releases that followed in the path of *Love Is The Thing* but deliberately failed to offer the feeling of hope inherent in the Cole recording. An enormously influential record it, nevertheless, fails to gain a mention in Cole biographies.

Record label:
Capitol
Produced
by Lee Gillette.
Recorded
in Hollywood; December 19 and 28, 1956.
Released:
March 1957
Chart peaks:
None (UK) 1 (US)
Personnel:
Nat 'King' Cole (v); Gordon Jenkins And Orchestra
Track listing:
When I Fall In Love (S); Love Letters; Stardust; Stay As Sweet As You Are; Where Can I Go Without You?; Maybe It's Because I Love You; Ain't Misbehavin'; When Sunny Gets Blue; I Thought About Marie; At Last; It's All In The Game; Love Is The Thing
Running time:
35.47
Not currently available on CD
Further listening:
Where Did Everybody Go? (1963), a later Cole-Jenkins collaboration, is darker in tone, reflecting, perhaps, Nat's admiration for the Sinatra releases that followed in the path of his own.
Further reading:
Unforgettable: The Life And Mystique Of Nat 'King' Cole (Leslie Gourse, 1991).
Like this?
Try . . . p.100

Mose Allison

Back Country Suite

Debut album from a pianist/trumpeter/vocalist who would influence not only jazzmen but also The Who.

Mississippi born, Allison grew up in the bebop age and assimilated influences that ranged from blues and gospel through to the cool cabaret sounds of the Nat Cole Trio. A white boy raised in a largely black neighbourhood, he claims he absorbed a lot of blues from local jukeboxes. He played trumpet at high school, was a pianist in the army and later attended Louisiana State University. The last stint was to later cause him some embarrassment when a black magazine rang for an interview and asked if he was the first black student to graduate from LSU: "I think there's something you should know," began Mose.

He only needed one strike to make his mark and did so with *Back Country Suite*, an album that immediately established Mose as a musician who could be both down-home and city hip. The main thrust of the album is a series of vignettes, mainly instrumental, that depict his southern roots upbringing. Somehow Mose's amalgam of influences came together to produce a record that was totally original, and that would influence white blues practitioners throughout the '60s, The Who later pouncing on Mose's Young Man Blues and turning it into one of the highspots of *Live At Leeds*.

Though he's never made a poor record in his life, *Back Country Suite* remains Alison's most potent work, a record that provided the blueprint for what would become an extensive catalogue. "I regard a record as an expensive calling card. You have to have one in order to work," Mose once observed. *Back Country Suite* proved the ideal calling card and he's always found work easy to come by.

Record label:
Atlantic
Produced
by Rudy Van Gelder.
Recorded
in Hackensack, New Jersey; March 1957.
Released:
1957
Chart peaks:
None (UK) None (US)
Track listing:
Mose Allison (p, t, v); Taylor LaFargue (b); Frank Isola (d); Rudy Van Gelder (e)
Personnel:
New Ground; Train; Warm Night; Blues (Young Man); Saturday; Scamper; January; Promised Land; Spring Song; Highway 49; Blueberry Hill; You Won't Let Me Go; I Thought About You; One Room Country Shack; In Salah
Running time:
36.00
Current CD:
OJCCD0752
Further Listening:
Local Color (1958), a follow-up release that's virtually Back Country Suite part 2, and includes his highly personalised version of Parchman Farm.
Further Reading:
One Man's Blues (Patti Jones, 1998).
Like this?
Try . . . p.650

Nina Simone

Jazz As Played In An Exclusive Side Street Club

Neither, says the lady, jazz, nor her debut. Either way, it heralded a singular talent.

According to Nina, this was her second album. "The first album I ever made was a pirate that I never got paid for and knew nothing about." But *Jazz As Played In An Exclusive Side Street Club* – or *Little Girl Blue* as it is also known – which turned up in countless guises (and continues to do so) is the release that immediately established her as a unique performer, one who refused to be categorised – though record companies have repeatedly attempted to place Nina in 'file under' situations according to whichever trend is under scrutiny at the time.

Signed to Bethlehem, a jazz label, the singer-pianist born Eunice Waymon, found that her debut was initially sidelined into jazz racks. But a hit single, culled from the album, I Loves You Porgy, timed to coincide with the release of the film musical Porgy And Bess did provide her with a wider audience. Doubtless, those encountering the album for the first time experienced confusion. Certainly jazz pervaded several tracks, but Nina's instrumental version of Dizzy Gillespie's Good Bait proved as much Bach as bebop, while Duke Ellington might have faced difficulty recognising the intro to his Mood Indigo.

"I came to despise popular songs and I never played them for my own amusement," Nina claimed at the time. "Why should I when I could be playing Bach, Czeny or Liszt?" So things were hardly what they seemed on the track listing; even Little Girl Blue somehow mutated into Good King Wenceslas! But her late-night loner ballads – Don't Smoke In Bed and He Needs Me – are always moving, and Central Park Blues proves that she could provide a straightforward, heads-down, swinging instrumental if it took her fancy. In all probability, her now famous version of My Baby Just Cares For Me, with its rum-ti-tum rhythm and final lick nicked from Eddie Heywood's Begin The Beguine, was just Nina being perverse: "It was the last song we did and I spent the next three days playing Beethoven to get the recording session out of my system." Whatever she thought about it, it's an album that *still* reveals hidden facets.

Record label:
Bethlehem
Producer:
unknown.
Recorded
in New York City; 1957.
Released:
early 1958
Chart peaks:
None (UK) None (US)
Personnel:
Nina Simone (v, p); Jimmy Bond (b); Albert Heath (d)
Track listing:
Mood Indigo; Don't Smoke In Bed; He Needs Me; Little Girl Blue; Love Me Or Leave Me; My Baby Just Cares For Me; Good Bait; Plain Gold Ring; You'll Never Walk Alone; I Loves You Porgy (S); Central Park Blues
Running time:
45.73
Current CD:
CPCD8240-2 reissued by Charly as *Lady Blue*; adds concert album
Further listening:
Anthology: The Colpix Years (1996) a double-CD that features late '50s and '60s tracks taken from the diva's nine albums for the Colpix label.
Further reading:
I Put A Spell On You (Nina Simone with Stephen Cleary, 1991) an autobiography that, naturally enough, provides the Simone point-of-view.
www.boscarol.com/nina/
Like this?
Try . . . p.703

The Crickets

The 'Chirping' Crickets

First album by one of the giants of modern popular music.

"Even around the seventh or eighth grade I knew he had it. Buddy just had that rock'n'roll charisma." A handful of years later school and band-mate Jerry Allison co-wrote The Crickets first hit, That'll Be The Day. Holly and Allison initially recorded the song for Decca under the auspices of legendary country producer Owen Bradley. However, this liaison didn't work out, and the boys headed to Norman Petty's tiny Clovis studio to try the song again. The punchy result was infinitely superior to the Nashville take, though Allison points out it was only a demo. "We intended to record it again a bit slicker, later. We liked the song, but didn't think that version would even be released, much less be successful." But Bob Thiele at Coral Records liked it just so and the track became a slow-burning hit.

The band carried on recording with Petty for several good reasons. "The studio had really good equipment, it was cheap – seems like our first demos cost $15 each – there was no time limit, Petty was a good engineer, and Vi Petty was a great lady who made everyone feel comfortable."

Over the next few months Petty consistently coaxed the best from Holly's idiosyncratic, quavering tones – part country, part blues, sometimes vulnerable, often boyishly confident. The tracks could then be released by Buddy as a solo artiste or as a member of The Crickets – a good way to double airplay and income. "The atmosphere around the studio was pretty laid back at first. The process changed a lot after we got the record deal. Then we'd do a song twenty times and it got to be like work. And after we went on the road Petty dubbed on the backing vocals, which were not particularly thrilling to us."

Interestingly, the band also recorded four of the album tracks, including the melancholic mid-tempo rocker Maybe Baby, while out on that road – Petty dragging his gear up to Oklahoma for the purpose. Allison still jibs at the "schmaltzy" backing vox which characterise The Crickets as opposed to the Holly material, and justifiably complains about dodgy song-writing attributions: "I co-wrote Not Fade Away, and I'm still bitching about the lack of a credit!" But the eerie, spartan, Bo Diddley vibe of that very number, the raucous pop-rockabilly of Oh Boy and the R&B spice of Chuck Willis's It's Too Late helped send Holly and his band right to the front of rock music's early leading pack.

Record label:
Coral
Produced
by Norman Petty.
Recorded
at Norman Petty Studios, Clovis, New Mexico; February–March and May–July 1957; Tinker Air Force Base, Oklahoma City, Oklahoma; September 27–28 1957.
Released:
March 1958
Chart peaks:
None (UK) None (US)
Personnel:
Buddy Holly (g, v); Niki Sullivan (g, b, v); Joe Mauldin (b); Jerry Allison (d); Larry Welborn (b); June Clark (bv); Gary and Ramona Tollett (bv); The Picks: John Pickering, Bill Pickering, Bob Lapham (bv)
Track listing:
Oh Boy (S); Not Fade Away; You've Got Love; Maybe Baby (S); It's Too Late; Tell Me How; That'll Be The Day (S); I'm Looking For Somebody To Love; An Empty Cup (And A Broken Date); Send Me Some Lovin'; Last Night; Rock Me Baby
Running time:
25.27
Current CD:
MCAD31182
Further listening:
Buddy Holly (1958); difficult to find 6-LP box set The Complete Buddy Holly (1979).
Further reading:
Remembering Buddy (John Goldrosen and John Beecher, 1987); www.buddyholly.com/
Like this?
Try . . . p.805

Billie Holiday

Lady In Satin

The life of jazz's greatest singer, laid desperately bare.

Billie loved the Ray Ellis string sound and played Ray's *Ellis In Wonderland* album continuously. After getting together, the duo began selecting the songs for the three-day session, Ellis later observing: "I didn't realise that the titles she was picking at the time were really the story of her life." Billie was in poor shape and was about to face a trial for drug possession. The once beautiful woman had become one of the living dead, haggard, stooping, with a voice that cracked and failed to hold notes. Producer Townsend, who'd earlier worked with Mahalia Jackson, admitted: "Billie was closer to the end than most stars, but she was Billie Holiday with a style and a voice like no other woman ever had."

Ray Ellis revealed that the sessions were nothing if not problematic. The singer would turn up completely stoned – in the case of The End Of A Love Affair she professed not to know the song at all. Eventually the backing track for the side had to be recorded without a vocal, Billie adding a top line at a later date. But the juxtaposition of sandpaper on satin worked marvellously well. Though the voice had to be constantly lubricated by tots of gin, and the imperfections were apparent to all, somehow the result was beauty of an inestimable kind as Billie poured pain over careworn classics like Glad To Be Unhappy and I Get Along Without You Very Well: pure emotion expressed by a voice that virtually disintegrates before your ears.

When the record was released, Holiday-lovers became locked in conflict. Many voiced the opinion that *Lady In Satin* should never have been released because it was tantamount to recording someone in their death-throes. Others, including one-time Holiday accompanist Jimmy Rowles, felt it was the singer's greatest achievement, the most revealing album ever made. She would make one more album, again with Ray Ellis. But it would be her last: by July 17, 1959 the legend born Eleanora Fagan was dead.

Record label:
Columbia
Produced
by Irv Townsend.
Recorded
at CBS Studios, New York; February 18–20, 1958.
Released:
Autumn 1958
Chart peaks:
None (UK) None (US)
Personnel:
Billie Holiday (v); with the Ray Ellis Orchestra
Track listing:
I'm A Fool To Want You; For Heaven's Sake; You Don't Know What Love Is; I Get Along Without You Very Well; For All We Know; Violets For Your Furs; You've Changed; It's Easy To Remember; But Beautiful; Glad To Be Unhappy; I'll Be Around; The End Of A Love Affair
Running time:
44.32
Current CD:
CK65144 adds four previously unissued bonus takes.
Further listening:
Billie's Greatest Hits (1998) – the best of the singer's US Decca recordings, songs that formed the basis for the Lady Sings The Blues soundtrack, except that these are the originals and far superior to Diana Ross's interpretations.
Further reading:
The Life And Times Of Billie Holiday (Donald Clarke, 1995), the most thoroughly researched Lady Day biography; www.cmgww.com/music/holiday/
Like this?
Try . . . p.679

Mahalia Jackson

Live At Newport 1958

Maybe the most famous gospel album of all time.

It's said that when Mahalia Jackson began singing the jaunty spiritual Didn't It Rain during her Sunday morning slot at the '58 Newport Jazz Festival the soft summer drizzle suddenly stopped. We know from Mahalia's stage patter that it was actually still raining at the end of the concert, but it's testament to the truly unique spirit of her music that folks should insist some divine intervention took place. As her friend the Reverend Martin Luther King, Jr commented, a voice like hers came only "once in a millennium".

By 1958, Mahalia – then aged 46 – was a household name in America, following a string of crossover hits and a sensational performance on the Ed Sullivan Show two years earlier. Though she had made some recordings with Duke Ellington, she famously refused to sing pop or the blues, preferring to spread the word of the Lord through her beloved hymns and gospel music. She was far from a gospel 'snob', however; when musicologists from the Juilliard quizzed her about her extraordinary vocal technique in 1950, they discovered a woman who'd grown up listening to Enrico Caruso and blues queen Bessie Smith, as well as the maudlin jazz of New Orleans funeral marches and the religious music she heard in her father's church.

At 16, Mahalia, with $100 sewn into her underclothes, left the segregation and relentless poverty of New Orleans for the northern mecca of Chicago, where she'd heard that black and whites could sit together on the buses. Quickly recognised in her new church as an incredible talent, she was whisked away on gospel tours and to recording sessions, ever imploring the people around her to "make a joyful noise unto the Lord" and revel in the transcendental joy of religious singing. She also qualified as a beautician.

At Newport, Mahalia gave one of her finest ever performances, the rich, stirring rendition of An Evening Prayer kicking off a set of 19th century church music and 'modern' gospel innovations, all given a swinging jazz flavour by the backing of long-term accomplice Mildred Falls' piano, Lilton Mitchell's organ and Tom Bryant's bass. (In 1946, Mahalia had been one of the first gospel artists to use a Hammond organ on her records.) Three tracks – It Don't Cost Very Much, I'm Going To Live The Life I Sing About In My Song and Walk Over God's Heaven – were written by her favourite gospel composer, Thomas A. Dorsey, and her familiarity and identification with the material is clear in her mesmerising interpretations.

"I sing God's music because it makes me feel free," she once said. "It gives me hope. With the blues, when you finish, you still have the blues."

PG

Record label:
Philips
Produced
by Cal Lampley.
Recorded
at Newport Jazz Festival; July 6, 1958.
Released:
November 1958
Chart peaks:
(UK) None; (US) None
Personnel:
Mahalia Jackson (v); Mildred Falls (p); Lilton Mitchell (o); Tom Bryant (b)
Track listing:
Introduction; An Evening Prayer; A City Called Heaven; It Don't Cost Very Much; He's Got The Whole World In His Hands; The Lord's Prayer
Running time:
17.19
Current CD:
Legacy CK53629 adds: I'm On My Way; Didn't It Rain; When The Saints Go Marching In; I'm Goin' To Live The Life I Sing About In My Song; Keep Your Hand On The Plow; Walk Over God's Heaven; Joshua Fit The Battle Of Jericho; Jesus Met The Woman At The Well; His Eye Is On The Sparrow
Further listening:
Home in on the classic Columbia years with Mahalia Jackson's Greatest Hits (1988)
Further reading:
Just Mahalia, Baby (Laurrain Goreau, 1984)
Like this?
Try . . . p.619

Frank Sinatra

Come Fly With Me

Sinatra's first and best collaboration with Billy May.

As heaven-made as the Nelson Riddle/Frank Sinatra partnership was, Frank was unwilling to be too closely identified with one arranger and turned to Billy May for his travelogue album *Come Fly With Me*, the first of his themed records that weren't to do with love, loss or swingin'. Working with May was likened by Sinatra to having a "bucket of cold water thrown in your face" so vibrant was the Fat Man's presence. May was already famous for his albums of exotic orchestral work featuring trademark slurping saxes and elaborate percussion and some of that colourful stuff was imported none-too-seriously onto tracks like Isle Of Capri and Brazil on which arranger and singer are clearly having a ball. However, May had a reputation as the most versatile arranger in Hollywood and the range of his work on this one album is proof enough. Autumn In New York and Moonlight In Vermont rank among the best Sinatra ballads ever, with their sighing-for-exotic-lands arrangements and Frank in hyperaware interpretative form while Come Fly With Me is art-swing of a very high order, from the take-off expectancy of the intro to the mysterious shimmer-in-the-clouds of the final string colour. May's favourite was the Victor Young waltz Around The World: "That's a beautiful tune, and Frank sang the shit out of it too. Boy! He's really a good singer."

But perhaps the most startling piece is the Rudyard Kipling-inspired On The Road To Mandalay. Banned from the UK issue of the album by Kipling's daughter ("How dare she?" bitched Sinatra at a 1958 concert, "of course, she drinks a little bit so we'll forgive her"), it has a bizarre ending ("And the dawn comes up like thunder!") that sounds like someone has prematurely lifted the needle. Originally, there was a gong followed by another half-chorus but saxist Skits Herbert recalled that "Billy just kind of waved his hands to signal 'Don't say anything.' And instead of going on, Frank put on his hat and threw his coat over his shoulder, like he does, and walked out of the studio! We all laughed like mad. That was the way they put it out."

Record Label:
Capitol
Produced
by Voyle Gilmore.
Recorded
at Capitol Studios, Hollywood; Autumn 1957.
Released:
November 1958
Chart peaks:
2 (UK) 1 (US)
Personnel:
Frank Sinatra (v); Billy May (a, conductor). Orchestra includes Alvin Stoller (d); Skits Herbert (clarinet, s).
Track Listing:
Come Fly With Me; Around The World; Isle Of Capri; Moonlight In Vermont; Autumn In New York; On The Road To Mandalay; Let's Get Away From It All; April In Paris; London By Night; Brazil; Blue Hawaii; It's Nice To Go Trav'ling
Running time:
38.46
Current CD:
CDP7484692
Further listening:
Follow-up Come Dance With Me (1959) was doubly driving and almost as good but Come Swing With Me (1961) was contractual obligation work of an artist keen to leave Capitol. Francis A And Edward K, the 1967 May-Ellington collaboration on Reprise, however, was majestic.
Further reading:
Sinatra! The Song Is You: A Singer's Art (Will Friedwald, 1995)
www.sinatrafamily.com/
Like this?
Try . . . p.352

Frank Sinatra

Sings For Only The Lonely

The greatest of Sinatra's suicidal mood albums.

As well as the classic mid-tempo good-time swingers Songs For *Swingin' Lovers* (1955) and *A Swingin' Affair* (1956), in the renaissance Capitol years Frank Sinatra had already produced a classic torch album with arranger Nelson Riddle, *In The Wee Small Hours* (1955), and had even dallied with arranger Gordon Jenkins on the cloying deep gloom of *Where Are You?* (1957). But neither quite prepared the listener for the devastating tragic-romantic impact of *Only The Lonely*.

Set in sweepingly dramatic late-romantic/early-impressionist orchestral textures, Sinatra the actor-singer is at his absolute peak, in control of every technical and emotional nuance, entirely involving, completely believable. Riddle, regarding it as "the best vocal album I've ever done; because I had time to work on the arrangements – a week!" excelled himself with the beautiful intros alone. The Chopin-esque piano of the title track, the whispering dissonances in the violins on It's A Lonesome Old Town, the descending oboe line of Goodbye; Riddle attributed the tone of his work to the recent death of his daughter and imminent death of his mother – "if one can attach events like that to music, perhaps Only The Lonely was the result." Interestingly, though an astonishing arranger, Riddle was known as a vague conductor and Frank apparently contrived to have regular Sinatra concertmaster Felix Slatkin conduct the tricky, tempoless numbers while Riddle was out of town.

The album featured two of Sinatra's favourite boozy loser pieces, Angel Eyes and One For My Baby, one of which he would always perform in concert as the saloon song segment with just Bill Miller on piano accompaniment. He recorded Baby like that (available on *The Capitol Years* 4CD set) but returned the following day to cut it again with Riddle's discreet strings and Gus Bovine's delicious *alto obligatio* to create a masterpiece, the pinnacle – along with I've Got You Under My Skin from *Songs For Swingin' Lovers* – of the Sinatra/Riddle partnership.

Sinatra recalled the session: "Word had somehow got around, there were 60 or 70 people there, Capitol employees and their friends, people off the street, anyone. We had kept this song to the last track of the session. Dave Cavanaugh knew how I sang it in the clubs and he switched out all the lights bar the spot on me. The atmosphere in that studio was exactly like a club. Dave said 'Roll 'em', there was one take and that was that. The only time I've known it happen like that."

Record Label:
Capitol
Produced
by Dave Cavanaugh.
Recorded
at Capitol Studios, Hollywood; May–June 1958.
Released:
December 1958
Chart peaks:
5 (UK) 1 (US)
Personnel:
Frank Sinatra (v); Nelson Riddle (ac); Felix Slatkin (c); orchestra included Al Viola (g); Pete Condoli (t); Bill Miller (p); Gus Bivona (as); Ray Sims (tb)
Track Listing:
Only The Lonely; Angel Eyes; What's New; It's A Lonesome Old Town; Willow Weep For Me; Goodbye; Blues In The Night; Guess I'll Hang My Tears Out To Dry; Ebb Tide; Spring Is Here; Gone with the Wind; One For My Baby.
Running time:
54.35
Current CD:
CDP-7484471-2 adds Sleep Warm & Where Or When.
Further listening:
In The Wee Small Hours (1955); Close To You (1956)
Further reading:
Sinatra! The Song Is You: A Singer's Art by Will Friedwald (1995)
Like this?
Try . . . p.15

Marty Robbins

Gunfighter Ballads And Trail Songs

The first successful C&W concept album.

Glendale, Arizona's Marty Robbins was already successful with smash hits such as Singing The Blues (1956) and A White Sport Coat (And A Pink Carnation) a year later, though nothing could have prepared him for the reaction an album full of Zane Gray/Louis L'Amour-like gunslinger tales would bring him. Marty's grandfather was 'Texas Bob' Heckle, a one-time Texas ranger who told his grandson spellbinding tales of the Old West. Robbins' grew up a Gene Autry fan, seldom if ever missing a movie by The Singing Cowboy, and had bit parts in two Hollywood horse operas.

When his theme from a Gary Cooper western, The Hanging Tree, climbed the charts in early 1959, it put Robbins in a position where he could lobby his label for an entire album of cowboy ditties. They agreed and Robbins compiled a list of his favourite Old West songs including the Sons Of The Pioneers' Cool Water, his friends the Glasers' Running Gun, three traditional cowboy ballads and four of his own songs. And what songs they were; Big Iron, which became a hit C&W single; The Master's Call, an almost Biblical tale of a cowpoke's redemption; In The Valley, and El Paso, the Number 1 pop hit which earned the first Grammy ever awarded to a country song and fast became Robbins' signature tune. A tale of a foolish young cowboy's love for a forbidden maiden, El Paso remains one of the greatest C&W songs, and has been covered by everyone from Johnny Cash to the Grateful Dead. Produced with a cinematic viewpoint by Englishman Don Law (who had recorded blues legend Robert Johnson a quarter of a century earlier) and propelled by Grady Martin's bittersweet Mexican guitar flourishes, it was the album's centrepiece, becoming one of the most played songs on country radio, propelling the album to platinum sales.

Robbins would have many more country – and crossover – hits in his career, and he would win a second Grammy a decade later, but nothing could eclipse the bright burning lights of this album just as nothing could stop that foolish cowboy from returning to his love at Rosa's Cantina in El Paso.

Record label:
Columbia
Produced
by Don Law.
Recorded
at Bradley Film and Recording, Nashville; April 7, 1959.
Released:
June 1959
Chart peaks:
(UK) 20; (US) 6
Personnel:
Marty Robbins (v, g); Thomas Grady Martin (g); Jack H Pruett (g); Bob L Moore (b); Louis Dunn (d); The Glaser Brothers (bv)
Track listing:
Big Iron (S); A Hundred And Sixty Acres; They're Hanging Me Tonight; Cool Water; Billy The Kid; Utah Carol; The Strawberry Roan; The Master's Call; Running Gun; El Paso (S); In The Valley; The Little Green Valley
Running time:
44.42
Current CD:
4952472 adds: The Hanging Tree (S); Saddle Tramp; El Paso (S)
Further listening:
Marty's Greatest Hits (1958) his first hits collection, released before Gunfighter Ballads And Trail Songs and containing all the early smashes.
Further reading:
The Encyclopedia Of Country Music (OUP, 1998)
Like this?
Try . . . p.350

Ornette Coleman

The Shape of Jazz To Come

The influence of chaos . . .

Ornette Coleman was arguably the last musician to introduce a truly seismic shift in jazz styles. He ushered in the Free Jazz movement of the 1960s, a tag borrowed from one his albums (although he said it was a record company invention and claimed to dislike it). He grew up with the Texas tradition of tough, blues-rooted saxophonists, but from his earliest experiments evolved a singular and idiosyncratic approach to jazz and was regularly shunned from bandstands in his native state and later in California, where he finally made contact with musicians capable of empathy with his radical ideas.They included the members of what became his seminal quartet featured on this disc. They burst upon the New York jazz scene in 1959 as a fully fledged phenomenon. Their residence at The Five Spot was the talk of the town for months, their radically new sound polarising critics, musicians and jazz audience alike, continuing to do so even now.

Bass player Charlie Haden remembered hearing Ornette for the first time: "This guy came up on stage and asked the musicians if he could play, and started to sit in. He played three or four phrases, I couldn't believe it – I had never heard any sound like that before."

Atlantic Records had made its name as a rhythm and blues label, but was building up an impressive jazz roster, with Ray Charles and John Coltrane among its stars. The Ertegun brothers seized the opportunity to pick up on this new and controversial sensation, and launched with the defiantly titled *The Shape of Jazz To Come.*

It followed his debut for the California-based Contemporary label, *Something Else!!!,* and laid down a marker which he would develop across the ensuing decades. His new approach proved – and remains – crucially influential on subsequent generations of innovative musicians all around the world, but many listeners reared on jazz's well-defined rhythmic and harmonic relationships heard only chaotic polyphony.

"I play pure emotion," he claimed at the time. "Musicians should be free to play as they feel it, the way it's comfortable for them."

Coleman's music of this period sounds much more approachable today, to the point where it's hard to see why it was thought so untoward. Coleman's revolutionary notion centred on the abandonment of the harmonic structures which had been central to all previous jazz styles in favour of a musical system which he came to call Harmolodics. His approach was predicated on improvisation along melodic rather than chordal lines of development, with the traditional rhythm instruments of bass and drums being called upon to contribute equally with the two horns. A genuinely new sound had arrived in jazz.

KM

Record Label:
Atlantic
Produced
by Nesuhi Ertegun
Recorded
at Radio Recorders, Hollywood, 22 May, 1959
Released:
October 1959
Chart peaks:
None (UK) None (US)
Personnel:
Ornette Coleman (as); Don Cherry (p); Charlie Haden (b); Billy Higgins (d)
Track listing:
Lonely Woman; Eventually; Peace; Focus On Sanity; Congeniality; Chronology
Running time:
37.56
Current CD:
Atlantic 8122 72398-2
Further listening:
Free Jazz (1961); At the Golden Circle, Stockholm, Vols 1/2 (1965)
Further reading:
Ornette Coleman: A Harmolodic Life (John Litweiler, 1992); Ornette Coleman (Peter Niklas Wilson, 1999)
Like this?
Try . . . p.26

Miles Davis
Kind Of Blue
Masterclass in modal improvisation. Whatever that is.

The band that arrived at Columbia's 30th Street Studio in NYC on March 2, 1959 to record the album that became known as *Kind Of Blue* were barely a band at all anymore. Coltrane had left Miles in '57, only to return again following a period with Thelonious Monk, but his confidence and conception had skyrocketed and he was on the verge of leaving again. Cannonball had said he would only stay a year and was ready to go too; Bill Evans had left months before but Davis was so struck by the pianist's limpid, shifting-sands harmonic style, he devised the album around it and recalled him for the sessions.

Davis had made it clear in a 1958 interview that he was on the verge of a major shift in his musical thinking. "The music has gotten thick," he said. "I think a movement in jazz is beginning away from the conventional string of chords and a return to emphasis on melodic rather than harmonic variation. There will be fewer chords but infinite possibilities as to what to do with them." Influenced by composer George Russell's theory of Lydian tonality, Davis produced simple, slow-moving harmonic frameworks – devised only hours previously – and indicated the scales/modes to be used for improvisation.

The resulting music was a uniquely beautiful triumph of content over form; seeing the sketches for the first time, each player surpassed himself to create line after inspired line of improvised melody. "Everything was a first take," remembered Miles in his autobiography, "which indicates the level everyone was playing on. It was beautiful."

Immensely popular and influential, *Kind Of Blue* is a rarity among great works of art; a fashionable masterpiece whose stature is virtually undisputed. Amazingly, Miles claimed to have not quite nailed what he was after, which was the sort of interplay between the dancers, drummers and the finger piano he had witnessed at a performance of the Ballet Africaine. "When I tell people that I missed what I was trying to do, getting the exact sound of that African finger piano up in that sound, they look at me like I'm crazy," he remembered. "I just missed." The main players went swiftly on to blaze further trails of their own – artistic (Coltrane, Evans), commercial (Adderley) and both (Davis) – but for many, the essence of what these remarkable jazz musicians had to offer as improvising instrumentalists is to be found on *Kind Of Blue.*

Record label:
CBS
Produced
by Irving Townsend.
Recorded
at Columbia 30th Street Studio, New York City; March 2 and April 22, 1959.
Released:
1959
Chart peaks:
None (UK) None (US)
Personnel:
Miles Davis (t); John Coltrane (ts); Julian 'Cannonball' Adderley (as); Bill Evans (p); Wynton Kelly (p); Paul Chambers (b); Jimmy Cobb (d)
Track listing:
So What; Freddie Freeloader; Blue In Green; All Blues; Flamenco Sketches
Running time:
45.37
Current CD:
MILLEN101 adds: Flamenco Sketches 2
Further listening:
Milestones (1958); '58 Sessions Featuring Stella By Starlight (1958)
Further reading:
Miles The Autobiography (Miles Davis and Quincy Troupe, 1989); Miles Davis (Ian Carr, 1999)
Like this?
Try . . . p.48

Charles Mingus

Ah Um

Brawny, belligerent and beautiful, the jazz composer's rootsy modern masterpiece.

One of the all time great jazz composers, Mingus quickly found that writing out parts for the players of his Jazz Workshop was not quite achieving the vibrant synthesis of composed and improvised material he was after. He took to directing musicians from the piano, demonstrating the parts, encouraging an adventuresome attitude. One sideman remembered: "You had to keep stretching yourself while you were with Mingus. He just wouldn't let you coast. Even in public he'd yell at you in the middle of a solo to stop playing just licks and get into *yourself*. He had more confidence in what we were capable of than we had."

Though by 1959 this titan of jazz creativity was already a colossus of modern bass playing and composition, Mingus always had a respectful ear for the roots of the music. He had grown up with church music – Duke Ellington's Orchestra was the first secular musical sound he heard – and had cut his teeth with the Dixieland-style bands of Kid Ory and Louis Armstrong. Earlier that year he had already recorded *Blues And Roots* for Atlantic, a modernist album drenched in raucous Afro-American musical tradition. He was in the same broad bag by May 1959 – when it was time to record what became *Ah Um* – but this time he had more explicit references in mind. *Ah Um*, for all its Mingussy flavour (double-time passages, riffs bouncing off one another, ragged ensembles and free-spirited improvised solos) can be seen as a tribute to his ancestors. Sometimes generic (the gospel of the pulse-racing Better Git It In Your Soul, the deep blues of Pussy Cat Dues), there are also character-specific pieces; Goodbye Pork Pie Hat salutes saxophonist Lester Young who had died two months earlier; the dense, multi-tempo Open Letter To Duke is a gorgeous pastiche of his idol Ellington; Bird Calls was the latest of his tributes to Charlie Parker; Jelly Roll is for the great jazz composer of the '20s, Jelly Roll Morton).

Its head in the present and its heart in the past, there's a richness of spirit and expressiveness that makes *Ah Um* one of those rare jazz albums that can reach beyond jazz heads into the wider listening world.

Record Label:
CBS
Produced
by Teo Macero.
Recorded
at 30th St Studio, NYC; May 5 and 12, 1959.
Released:
1959
Chart peak:
None (UK) None (US)
Personnel:
Charles Mingus (b); John Handy (as, clarinet); Booker Irvin (ts), Shafi Hadi (as, ts); Jimmy Knepper (tb); Horace Parlan (p); Dannie Richmond (d); Willie Dennis (t)
Track Listing:
Better Git It In Your Soul; Goodbye Pork Pie Hat; Boogie Stop Shuffle; Self-Portrait In Three Colors; Open Letter To Duke; Bird Calls; Fables Of Faubus; Pussy Cat Dues; Jelly Roll
Running time:
45:56
Current CD:
Legacy CK 65512 adds Pedal Point Blues, GG Train, & Girl Of My Dreams
Further listening:
Blues And Roots (1959); Black Saint And The Sinner Lady (1963)
Further reading:
Mingus: A Critical Biography (Brian Priestley, 1984); Beneath The Underdog (Charles Mingus, 1995) www.mingusmingusmingus.com
Like this?
Try . . . p.632

The 1960s

Billy Fury

The Sound Of Fury

Driving debut from UK's only decent answer to Elvis, the man who had more hits in the '60s than The Beatles.

Only a handful of early British rockers merit favourable comparison with their maverick American cousins. Cliff Richard, Lonnie Donegan and Johnny Kid may have had their moments, but only Billy Fury could really be considered the English Elvis. In April 1960, after a reasonably successful run of singles, Decca sent 20-year-old Fury into the studio to record a 10-inch long-player and, unusually for the times, the songs were all penned by Fury himself. (Impresario Larry Parnes had signed Ronald Wycherley [as was] at least partly on the strength of his compositional ability.) Producer Jack Good had assembled the customary crew of sheet-music reading jazz musicians for the session, but had added the rocking young guitarist Joe Brown to the line-up. Brown had backed Eddie Cochran and Gene Vincent on tour, and remembers Good's instructions vividly: "The record was Jack's take on the Sun Studio sound. He had even hired electric and stand-up bass players to double up to get Bill Black's big slapped bass sound. He asked Reg Guest (piano) to play like Floyd Cramer and told me to do my Scotty Moore. We did a run through of each number and then a take. Practically everything was done in one go."

The result is a powerful, varied set with loud echoes of Memphis 1954 – Since You've Been Gone mirrors the tempo-change tomfoolery of Elvis's Milk Cow Blues. Elsewhere Fury's sweet, edgy tenor is often the spit of Cochran's. There are also hints, however, of something new. The ballad You Don't Know exudes a peculiarly British sense of vulnerability – Fury's Liverpudlian vowels resonating through the sparse arrangement. As Brown attests, "Even though we knew we were copying the Yanks, of course we brought something of our own upbringing to it as well."

The Four Jays (hired to imitate The Jordanaires) were later managed by Brian Epstein and gained success as The Fourmost. A curiously shy star, Fury continued to have hits well into the '60s and was charming as the self-parodic Stormy Tempest in the film *That'll Be The Day*. Unfortunately, he was chronically ill throughout the '70s and died in 1983. But amongst his many achievements was an album, which marks the moment when British rock'n'roll grew up.

Record label:
Decca
Produced
by Jack Good.
Recorded
at Decca Studio 3, West Hampstead, London; January 8, 1960 and April 4, 1960.
Released:
May 1960
Chart peaks:
18 (UK) None (US)
Personnel:
Billy Fury (v); Joe Brown (g); Reg Guest (p); Bill Stark (acoustic bass); Alan Weighell (b); Andy White (d); The Four Jays (bv)
Track Listing:
That's Love (S/UK); My Advice; Phone Call; You Don't Know; Turn My Back On You; Don't Say It's Over; Since You've Been Gone; It's You I Need; Alright, Goodbye; Don't Leave Me This Way
Running time:
21.53
Current CD:
8206272 known as The Sound of Fury +10 adds: Gonna Type A Letter; Margo (Don't Go), Don't Knock Upon My Door, Time Has Come, Angel Face, The Last Kiss, My Christmas Prayer, Baby How I Cried, I Got Someone, & Don't Jump Further listening: Halfway To Paradise (1961); The One And Only (1983). Joe Brown continues to record; On A Day Like This (1999) is a fine recent album.
Further reading:
www.billyfury.co.uk
Like this?
Try . . . p.46

Elvis Presley

Elvis Is Back!

The best rock'n'roll LP between Buddy Holly's death and the rise of The Beatles.

The omens were not good on March 20, 1960, when Presley, demob happy and shorn of sideburns, arrived for his first recording session since leaving the army. The Sun-era team of Elvis, Scotty and Bill was not an option. Scotty Moore had not spoken to Presley for two years but was willing to turn up, but Bill Black was pursuing a solo career. On the other hand, DJ Fontana, The Jordanaires and Floyd Cramer were still on board. The other musicians – most of whom were on the June 1958 date that was Elvis' most recent – were led to believe this was a Jim Reeves session. There was also a lot of business to be taken care of, not least a single (Stuck On You/Fame And Fortune) that had to be in the shops by the end of the week.

By 7am, that 45 plus four other tracks were in the can – Make Me Know It, the faintly biographical Soldier Boy, and two lascivious R&B songs, A Mess of Blues and It Feels So Right. With two weeks before the next date, Presley was whisked off to Miami for the Frank Sinatra TV Show. For the second recording date, April 3, Colonel Tom instructed that Elvis sing eight songs – all he was contractually obliged to give RCA for an LP – one of which was to be Are You Lonesome Tonight, a 1927 hit for Al Jolson, and his wife's favourite tune. By now Presley was back into his stride, with ideas that far outstripped his pre-draft capabilities. Fever featured just bass and two percussionists separated in the stereo mix; It's Now Or Never was mock-operatic, an adaptation of O Sole Mio; Like A Baby, Such A Night and Dirty, Dirty Feeling almost verged on the obscene. Recorded in the dark, Are You Lonesome Tonight was the ninth cut, although Elvis felt his voice wasn't suitable. The twelfth cut, Lowell Fulsom's bluesy Reconsider Baby, began as a jam and ended with everybody taking solos. By the time he left the studio, Stuck On You was Number 1 and Elvis had two weeks before starting work on GI Blues. A new beginning, but the end was already in sight.

Record Label:
RCA
Produced
by Steve Scholes and Chet Aktins.
Recorded
at RCA Studio B, Nashville; March–April 1960.
Release date:
July 1960 (UK); April 1960 (US)
Chart peaks:
1 (UK) 2 (US)
Personnel:
Elvis Presley (v, g); Scotty Moore (g); Bob Moore (b); Hank Garland (g, b); DJ Fontana (d); Buddy Harman (d); 'Boots' Randolph (s); Floyd Cramer (p); The Jordanaires (v); Bob Moore (e)
Track Listing:
Stuck On You (S); Fame And Fortune; Make Me Know It; Fever; The Girl Of My Best Friend (S); I Will Be Home Again; Dirty, Dirty Feeling; Thrill Of Your Love; Soldier Boy; Such A Night (S); It Feels So Right; Girl Next Door; Like A Baby; Reconsider Baby.
Running time:
31.29
Current CD:
07863677372 adds: Are You Lonesome Tonight (S); I Gotta Know (S), Mess Of Blues (S), & It's Now Or Never (S)
Further listening:
From Nashville To Memphis – The Essential '60s Masters Vol 1 (5 CD set)
Further reading:
Careless Love – The Unmaking Of Elvis Presley (Peter Guralnick, 1999)
Like this?
Try . . . p.233

Joan Baez

Joan Baez

As important as Dylan in popularising folk music in the '60s.

In 1960, Joan Baez (then 19) was exactly what the flat, dull and worthy folk scene needed. Unattractiveness was almost a mark of authenticity. That Joan was a striking, young raven-haired beauty with a sweet, pure voice certainly did not harm the prospects of her debut album.

She had been a huge hit at the Newport Festival in July the previous year, standing apart from a bill that included Bob Gibson (who invited her there), Pete Seeger, Odetta, Sonny Terry and Brownie McGhee. Unsurprisingly, *Joan Baez* was a folk revival landmark. No wonder Bob Dylan initially idolised her – his own rise would have been impossible without her. She turned a new younger generation onto folk music – kids who had no time for Pete Seeger singalongs and fresh-faced college boys singing Tom Dooley. It would have been enough if Joan Baez had simply given folk some sex appeal. Yet the content of her debut album also reflected what was happening on the campuses and in the coffee houses, and as one of the first folk soloists to achieve national (and later international) success, she brought the music into the mass market.

Joan Baez was recorded in a hotel ballroom in New York City and produced by Maynard Solomon, to whose label she signed – in preference to CBS – because Solomon was, like Joan, an idealist; he'd signed The Weavers, despite accusations that Pete Seeger was a Communist. She made her home at Vanguard for most of the decade, releasing a staggering 17 albums before a move to A&M. Despite her beautiful singing and the simple arrangements (she had to be persuaded to allow a second guitarist), the album may not be to current tastes; but at the time, its mixture of Carter Family songs (Wildwood Flower), the Negro spiritual All My Trials and a Spanish political song was quite captivating. The ballads – notably John Riley, Silver Dagger and Mary Hamilton – have lasted best.

In America, *Joan Baez* was an unlikely chart success. It eventually charted in the UK in July 1964, where she enjoyed a Top 10 single a year later with Phil Ochs' There But For Fortune.

Record label:
Vanguard
Produced
by Maynard Solomon.
Recorded
in New York City; autumn 1960.
Released:
October 1960
Chart peaks:
9 (UK) 15 (US)
Personnel:
Joan Baez (v, g); Fred Hellerman (second g)
Track listing:
Silver Dagger; East Virginia; Ten Thousand Miles; House Of The Rising Sun; All My Trials; Wildwood Flower; Donna Donna; John Riley; Rake And The Rambling Boy; Little Moses; Mary Hamilton; Henry Martin; El Preso Numero Nuevo
Running time:
37.30
Current CD:
VMD 2077-2
Further listening:
Farewell Angelina (1965)
Further reading:
www.baez.woz.org
Like this?
Try . . . p.140

Miles Davis

Sketches Of Spain

Trumpeter and arranger combine gloriously on timeless, impressionist orchestral jazz.

The Miles Davis/Gil Evans collaborations of the late '50s were era-defining statements of orchestral jazz that continue to inspire composers and arrangers of all persuasions.

Miles: "I loved working with Gil because he was so meticulous and creative, and I trusted his musical arrangements completely."

The Evans style – lugubrious, luminous brass, woodwind colours and modern shifting-sands harmony – was the ideal backdrop for the doleful splendour of Miles's horn and the music they made together spoke to an audience beyond jazz listeners. Indeed, some jazz lovers were openly sceptical about the balance between arrangement and spontaneity, though the reputation these days of the three albums they made between 1957 and 1960 is that of unassailable classics. It would have been a remarkable period for Davis with his sextet achievements alone (1958's *Milestones* and 1959's *Kind Of Blue*), but the artistic success of the *Birth Of The Cool* (1949/50) and the first full Evans collaboration *Miles Ahead* (1957), added to the commercial viability of their *Porgy And Bess* (1958), and assured Miles that "Gil and I were something special together musically."

When a friend played Miles Joaquin Rodrigo's guitar concerto, he excitedly shared it with Evans who ran with the Spanish idea, researching flamenco and the life of the Spanish gypsy, adapting Will O' The Wisp from Manuel de Falla's 1915 ballet El Amor Brujo and deriving Saeta from a religious Spanish march. Concept in place, the music proved elusive and difficult to play (Miles eventually instructed the ensembles to relax, creating a powerful raggedness). With awkward instrumental balances to record (several expensive sessions resulted in nothing being salvaged), it took fifteen 3-hour sessions and much editing to complete. The resulting record however, is perhaps the richest work that Davis and Evans had yet created; hypnotic percussive *ostinati*, drifting/hanging harmonic backdrops and Miles's floating, haunted meditations often on a single Spanish scale – music of ceremonial majesty.

There are resisters ("For the listener in search of jazz, there is mighty little of that commodity evident," observed the New York Times, "Inflated light music" maintains the respected Penguin Guide To Jazz On CD) but for generations of impartial listeners to come, *Sketches Of Spain* will continue to weave its spell.

Record Label:
CBS
Produced
by Teo Macero and Irving Townsend.
Recorded
at 30th St Studio, NYC; November 1959–March 1960.
Released:
1960
Chart peaks:
None (UK) None (US)
Personnel:
Miles Davis (t, flugelhorn); Gil Evans (a, oa); Ernie Royal, Bernie Glow, Louis Mucci, Taft Jordan (t); Dick Hixon, Frank Rehak (tu); Jimmy Buffington, John Barrows, Earl Chapin (french horn); Jimmy McAllister, Bill Barber (tuba); Al Block, Eddie Caine (flute); Romeo Penque (oboe); Harold Feldman (clarinet, oboe); Danny Bank (bass clarinet); Jack Knitzer (bassoon); Janet Putman (harp); Paul Chambers (bs); Jimmy Cobb (d); Elvin Jones (pc)
Track Listing:
Concierto De Aranjuez (Adagio); Will O' The Wisp; The Pan Piper; Saeta; Solea;
Running time:
41:24
Currently available CD:
Legacy CK 65142 adds: Song Of Our Country, Concierto De Aranjuez (Part One) & Concierto De Aranjuez (Part Two ending)
Further listening:
Miles Ahead (1957); Porgy And Bess (1958)
Further reading:
Miles The Autobiography (Miles Davis and Quincy Troupe, 1989); Miles Davis (Ian Carr, 1982)
www.milesdavis.com/
Like this?
Try . . . p.676

Oliver Nelson

Blues And The Abstract Truth

Jazz philospher creates a bracing new blend of musical colours to inaugurate the 1960s.

Talking to Melody Maker in 1993, Donald Fagen explained why this record had exerted an influential fascination upon him. "[It's] a very popular jazz record, kind of mainstrem big band. Nelson had a West Coast sound, and the contrast between Eric Dolphy's solos and that slick, swinging rhythm section was very interesting to me."

It often seemed that the music of master arranger Oliver Nelson was in search of a seamless blend of Ellington's thought and Coltrane's emotion. *Blues And The Abstract Truth*, rightly regarded by Nelson as his high water mark, was where he made that blend sound like nobody but himself.

He loved to mix 'n' match styles – as one of the great jazz synthesizers, there was little he couldn't envelop in his warm embrace. "Classical music of the 19th century, and contemporary music of our own 20th century," Nelson wrote in the album notes, "brought about the need for adopting a different perspective in order to create music that was meaningful and vital. One device which has always been successful and vital in both classical music and in present-day jazz is to let the musical ideas determine the form and shape of a musical composition. In effect, that is what I have tried to do here."

The musical ideas encompassed jazz (traditional and modern), blues, spirituals, Broadway scoring and even country music and classical flourishes. The all-star band included stellar soloists Freddie Hubbard, Bill Evens, Eric Dolphy and Nelson himself. You'll find the more fiery Dolphy elsewhere; here his playing is relatively restrained. But Nelson, whose renown was mostly for his arranging chops, shows himself to be a gifted, deceptively relaxed soloist.

He'd been prepared for this eclectic work by early stints with Louis Jordan, Erskine Hawkins and Wild Bill Davis, a college education in music theory and composition, and a trial-by-fire as the house arranger at the Apollo Theatre. Following the success of this album, he eventually settled in LA, working primarily in film and TV scoring until a heart attack claimed him prematurely in 1975. Though his Hollywood work was of extremely high calibre, it tended to diminish the jazz profile he'd established in New York. But as long as we have *Blues And The Abstract Truth*, his stature as a jazz giant will be indisputable.

Record label:
Impulse
Produced
by Creed Taylor.
Recorded
at Van Gelder Studio, Englewood, New Jersey; February 23, 1961.
Released:
May 1961
Chart peaks:
None (UK) None (US)
Personnel:
Oliver Nelson (as, ts); Eric Dolphy (as, flute); Freddie Hubbard (t); George Barrow (bs); Bill Evans (p); Paul Chambers (b); Roy Haynes (d); Rudy Van Gelder (e)
Track listing:
Stolen Moments; Hoe-Down; Cascades; Yearnin'; Butch and Bitch; Teenies Blues
Running time:
36.43
Current CD:
IMP11542
Further listening:
Soul Battle (1960) – wonderful blowing session with Jimmy Forrest and King Curtis; More Blues And The Abstract Truth (1964)
Like this?
Try . . . p.47

Jimmy Smith

Back At The Chicken Shack

Hammond-led groove that spawned soul-jazz and became one of Blue Note's biggest sellers.

By 1960, Jimmy Smith had already recorded a phenomenal 19 albums for Blue Note. That same year he recorded four more – two of them (Midnight Special and Back At The Chicken Shack) from the same session at Van Gelder's Recording Studio in Englewood Cliffs, New Jersey. Produced by Alfred Lion, the latter set the precedent for every Hammond organ-led record since with its instantly infectious, gutsy groove featuring Smith's trademark walking basslines and right hand solos. (Mention should also be made of the striking sleeve by Francis Wolff: "Let's get some pictures with 'grease'," said Smith – hence the shot of him on a friend's farm, in natty attire, with dog Elsie and a rooster.)

A pianist from the age of nine, Smith gigged in jazz and R&B groups around his home in western Pennsylvania. Then came the switch to organ. "I saw Wild Bill [Davis] in 1953 and took up the Hammond on the spot. I taught myself. I kept it in a shed so no one knew I couldn't play it. I battled with that beast every single day." Two years later Smith played his first gig with the Hammond at Jimmy's Jazz Club in The Village, New York. "It was a challenge. Nobody had thought about taking the Hammond into jazz and those jazz fans didn't like it, no way. But I went nuts. I went crazy."

As for *Back At The Chicken Shack*: "I just went in there and played my guts out. There was a lot of respect going down between those guys in the studio. Stanley [Turrentine] and Kenny [Burrell] were downright funky. Donald [Bailey] kept the rhythm ticking over." Recorded on 2-track analogue tape, Smith composed two of the four tracks – Messy BS, a funky blues inspired by Charlie Parker's Confirmation, and the title track, an effortlessly cool and sassy down-home number. The Romberg/Hammerstein standard When I Grow Too Old To Dream spotlights Turrentine's almost vocal sax style. Turrentine's own Minor Chant, written for his *Look Out!* album, is 32 bars and seven-and-a-half minutes of minor key sauntering with Stanley wailing centre stage.

The following year Smith recorded another two records for Blue Note. Then in 1962 he signed to Verve, successfully experimenting with a full big band sound and earning his nickname, The Cat.

Record label:
Blue Note
Produced
by Alfred Lion.
Recorded
at Van Gelder's Recording Studio, Englewood Cliffs, New Jersey; April 25, 1960.
Released:
summer 1961
Chart peaks:
None (UK) None (US)
Personnel:
Jimmy Smith (o); Stanley Turrentine (ts); Kenny Burrell (g); Donald Bailey (d)
Track listing:
Back At The Chicken Shack; When I Grow Too Old To Dream; Minor Chant; Messy Bessie
Running time:
38.04
Current CD:
7464022 adds: On The Sunny Side Of The Street
Further listening:
The Cat (1964) – more swinging organ tunes but this time arranged and conducted by Lalo Schifrin; Monster (1965) – Oliver Nelson big band arrangements and organ-led takes on classic theme tunes.
Further reading:
www.bluenote.com
Like this?
Try . . . p.824

Bill Evans Trio

Sunday At The Village Vanguard

An innovative pianist finds his niche and makes jazz history.

The choice of pianist Bill Evans to replace Red Garland in the Miles Davis group in 1958 was not a universally popular one. For one thing, he didn't appear to swing as hard as Red, for another he was white. But Miles responded to Evans's sound – detailed touch, limpid harmonies, emotional scalar lines – which Miles described as "like crystal notes of sparkling water cascading down from some clear waterfall." As for his time playing, "Bill underplayed it," said Miles, "which for what I was doing now with the modal thing, I liked what Bill was doing better."

Bill, though thrilled to be in a band with Coltrane, Cannonball, Miles and Philly Joe Jones, was stung by the audience's indifference-bordering-hostility to his contributions – which, in a live setting, were the antithesis of his hard-blowing colleagues – and quit after seven months. He was recalled for the seminal Davis album *Kind Of Blue* – which Davis admitted was "planned" around Bill's playing – but was keen to form his own trio which he had very clear ideas about.

"I'm hoping the trio will grow in the direction of simultaneous improvisation," he had said, "if the bass player, for example, hears an idea that he wants to answer, why should he just keep playing a 4/4 background?" After a few false starts (he lost several potential collaborators due to poor treatment at a club supporting Benny Goodman), Bill ended up with responsive drummer Paul Motian and a remarkable young bassist, Scott LaFaro, who was willing and more than capable to fulfil Bill's vision of concurrent invention. "Ideas were rolling out on top of each other," Evans said of LaFaro, "it was like a bucking horse."

The trio made two fine studio albums: December 1959's *Portrait In Jazz* and February 1961's *Explorations*, but with the tapes rolling all day Sunday, 25 June 1961 at New York club the Village Vanguard ("a relatively painless way to extract an album from the usually foot-dragging pianist" said producer Orrin Keepnews), two and a half hours of glorious, symbiotic music was taped. It was a rich, delicate summation of the trio's matured conception of interplay. Ten days later, 25-year-old LaFaro was killed in a car crash.

Shattered at the loss, Bill Evans stopped playing the piano for months. The sessions – emerging over three albums of which *Sunday At The Village Vanguard* is the first – are generally regarded as Evans's finest and among the most important recordings in all of jazz.

Record Label:
Riverside
Produced
by Orrin Keepnews.
Recorded
live at The Village Vanguard, New York; June 25, 1961.
Released:
September 1961
Chart peaks:
None (UK) None (US)
Personnel:
Bill Evans (p); Scott LaFaro (b); Paul Motian (d); Dave Jones (e)
Track Listing:
Gloria's Step; My Man's Gone Now; Solar; Alice In Wonderland; All Of You; Jade Visions
Running time:
40.11
Current CD:
OJC201402
Further listening:
Waltz For Debbie (1961); More From The Vanguard (1961)
Further reading:
How My Heart Sings (Peter Pettinger, 1998)
Like this?
Try . . . p.32

Ray Charles And Betty Carter

Ray Charles And Betty Carter

Masterly easy jazz vocal duets between the Genius Of Soul and Betty Bebop.

In the late '50s, Ray Charles was an R&B star with Atlantic records enjoying million-selling success with What'd I Say. ABC offered Charles better royalties, profit sharing, eventual ownership of his masters and, significantly, a production deal. Charles signed with them to the dismay of Atlantic. Given his own label to play with – Tangerine – Charles set about "trying to share something with his fellow man", as singer Jimmy Scott remembered. Scott himself got to record *Falling In Love Is Wonderful* ("the best record I ever made") under Ray's guidance but contractual difficulties prevented its release. No such problems for Ray's duet album with Betty Carter.

Carter was an uncompromisingly bold jazz singer whose inventive, musical way with a song had precluded wide appeal, but recommended to him by Miles Davis, Ray took her on tour and used his new entrepreneurial leverage to heighten her profile. The arranger Marty Paich was known for his super-hip, cool-school dektette work for Mel Torme but fashioned a more straightforward set of charts for the playful, romantic setting Charles had in mind. There were even the glutinous Jack Halloran Singers on a few of the cuts – much to the chagrin of some critics – but most of the resulting album bursts with relaxed, musicianly banter and sexual chemistry. Charles is growling and suggestive, Carter squirrelly and coy, and it remains one of the all-time great duet sets.

Baby It's Cold Outside was a massive hit and Charles went on to sustained popularity, starting with his huge-selling Hit The Road Jack. Carter enjoyed a degree of attention before temporarily retiring to bring up her family, re-emerging in the late '60s to build a reputation as the most fearsomely inventive singer in all of jazz, while admitting to "fond memories" of the easy listening album of duets with Brother Ray.

Record Label:
Atlantic
Produced
by Sid Feller.
Recorded
in Hollywood, California; June 1961.
Released:
1961
Chart peaks:
None (UK) None (US)
Personnel:
Ray Charles (p, v); Betty Carter (v); Jack Halloran Singers (bv); David 'Fathead' Newman (s); Marty Paich (a, oa)
Track Listening:
Ev'ry Time We Say Goodbye; You And I; Goodbye – We'll Be Together Again; People Will Say We're In Love; Cocktails For Two; Side By Side; Baby It's Cold Outside; Together; For All We Know; It Takes Two To Tango; Alone Together; Just You Just Me.
Running time:
67.17
Current CD:
5050042 adds Ray Charles's 1961 album Dedicated To You: Hardhearted Hannah; Nancy; Margie; Ruby; Rosetta; Stella By Starlight; Cherry; Josephine; Candy; Marie; Diane; Sweet Georgia Brown
Further listening:
Ray Charles: Modern Sounds In Country And Western (1962); An Audience With Betty Carter (1979)
Further reading:
Brother Ray (Ray Charles and David Ritz Da Capo, 1992); Ray Charles: Man and Music (Michael Lydon, 1999)
Like this?
Try . . . p.396

Charles Mingus

The Black Saint And The Sinner Lady

Some say it's the best jazz record ever made. Mingus thought it was folk music. Whatever it is, it's brilliant.

Charles Mingus decided in 1963 that henceforth his outfit would be known as the Charles Mingus New Folk Band. This rich, compelling work is closer to the metropolitan, symphonic jazz of Duke Ellington than anything a casual listener would recognise as folk music but, thinking about it, you can see his point – there's something very 'of the people' about this music, as sprawling, crowded and buzzy as a city, multi-faceted and teeming with life.

Superficially it has the sleazy, urban feel of an Elmer Bernstein film score; lots of conversational muted horns and slurring, *rubato* saxes, which, during recording, Mingus set in a V shape with the tenor at the fulcrum, furthest away from the mic. Such careful positioning gives the sound a theatrical sense of space – the brass interplay resembles dialogue. In this, though Mingus describes the music as a dance, it's more operatic. The use of overdubbing was unusual in jazz in the early '60s, but its employment here helps a modest-sized band sound busy and imposing.

Mingus, who'd spent some time as a patient in New York's Bellevue mental hospital, was never one for explaining himself rationally; his sleeve notes for the album were pell-mell. Starting to describe the action and then quickly digressing into a rant about critics, he asks the listener to "throw all other records of mine away except maybe one other". The track names weren't much help, and a review of the album by Mingus's psychiatrist tells us we're in the presence of mischief. Dr Edmund Pollock PhD, offers the following interpretation: "There are recurrent themes of loneliness, separateness and tearful depression, Mr Mingus cries of misunderstanding of self and people. Throughout he presents a brooding, moaning intensity about prejudice, hate and persecution." Cranky, stubborn and angry he may have been, but Mingus could not keep the intense pleasure that music brought him out of his work. Whatever the good doctor said, *The Black Saint And The Sinner Lady* drips with joy.

Record label:
Impulse
Produced
by Bob Thiele.
Recorded
in New York; January 20, 1963.
Released:
April 1963
Chart peaks:
None (UK) None (US)
Personnel:
Rolf Ericson, Richard Williams (t); Quentin Jackson (tb); Don Butterfield (tuba); Jerome Richardson (soprano sax, bs, flute); Dick Hafer (ts, flute); Charlie Mariano (as); Jaki Byard (p); Jay Berliner (g); Charles Mingus (b, p); Dannie Richmond (d)
Track listing:
Track A: Solo Dancer, Stop Look And Listen, Sinner Jim Whitney; Track B: Duet Solo Dancers, Hearts Beat And Shades In Physical Embraces; Track C: Group Dancers (Soul Fusion) Freewoman And Oh, This Freedom's Slave Cries; Mode D: Trio And Group Dancers, Stop! Look! And Sing Songs Of Revolutions!; Mode E: Single Solos And Group Dance, Saint And Sinner Join In Merriment On Battle Front; Mode F: Group And Solo Dance, Of Love, Pain And Passioned Revolt, Then Farewell, My Beloved, 'Til It's Freedom Day
Running time:
37.37
Current CD:
IMP11742
Further listening:
Mingus, Mingus, Mingus, Mingus, Mingus (1963);
Further reading:
Beneath The Underdog (Charles Mingus, 1971)
Like this?
Try . . . p.750

James Brown

Live At The Apollo (Vol. 1)

A benchmark for thrilling soul performance, and the first of Brown's enormous selection of live albums.

Some people can't recognise a good thing when it falls in their lap. Syd Nathan, the label boss of King Records in Cincinnati, wasn't convinced by James Brown. "The worst piece of shit I've ever heard" he declared in 1955 upon hearing Please, Please, Please. Released to embarrass Ralph Bass, the A&R man who had brought Brown to Nathan's attention, Please, Please Please – that contradiction in terms, a hard-driving ballad – gave King a Number 6 R&B hit in 1956. The nine 'failures' that followed only confirmed Nathan in his doubts. He had big reservations, too, about Try Me, a song getting great reactions on tour, and released it spitefully, to prove Brown's instincts wrong. It soared to Number 1 in the US R&B charts (48 pop). Henceforward, Brown charted as the seasons changed, at least four singles a year on the R&B charts and as many on the Hot 100. By 1962 "Mr Dynamite" was the biggest live draw in the R&B market, his physically athletic and dramatic performances matched by impassioned ballads, relentless uptempo numbers and a tightly-drilled band. All this, suggested Brown and his manager, Ben Bart, should be caught live on tape. Still surprisingly indifferent to his star's power, Nathan's reply was, in effect, Over my dead body.

Undaunted, Brown put up $5,700 of his own money to record a show at Harlem's black music mecca, the Apollo. His season there began on October 18, 1962 and by the night of the 24th the band was in blistering form, delivering a finely-honed set of their hits to date with Brown blasting from one song to the next with scarcely a pause for breath. For his core black audience it provided a vivid souvenir of Mr Dynamite in his pomp – and for whites it was an ear-boggling introduction to a thrilling kind of performance rarely seen or heard. As Brown (then still only 29) sails through the first five tracks, varying the pace but not the emotional intensity, you'd swear you can hear the sweat spraying out of his pores. With *Live At The Apollo* James Brown became – and would remain for many years to come – The Hardest Working Man In Showbusiness.

Record label:
Polydor
Produced
by James Brown.
Recorded
at Apollo Theater, New York; October 24, 1962.
Released:
May 1963
Chart peaks:
None (UK) 2 (US)
Personnel:
James Brown (v); Bobby Byrd, Bobby Bennett and Baby Lloyd Stallworth (v); Lewis Hamilton (t, MD); Roscoe Patrick and Teddy Washington (t); Dickey Wells (tb); St. Clair Pinckney and Clifford MacMillan (ts); Al 'Briscoe' Clark (bs); Lucas 'Fats' Gonder (o); Les Buie (g); Hubert Perry (b); Clayton Fillyau (d)
Track listing:
I'll Go Crazy; Try Me; Think; I Don't Mind; Lost Someone; Please, Please, Please; You've Got The Power; I Found Someone; Why Do You Do Me Like You Do; I Want You So Bad; I Love You Yes I Do; Why Does Everything Happen To Me; Bewildered; Please Don't Go; Night Train
Running time:
31.36
Current CD:
843 479-2
Further listening:
Say It Live And Loud/Live In Dallas (1998), a coruscating performance from August 26, 1968.
Further reading:
James Brown (Geoff Brown, 1996)
www.funky-stuff.com/jamesbrown/
Like this?
Try . . . p.547

Sam Cooke

Night Beat

A pivotal moment in soul history.

The sixth note in the musical scale is owned by Sam Cooke. No one has done more for that note in the history of recorded vocal music. While his peers were over-using the flatted seventh and flatted third notes, Sam was smoothly pinning his style right on that pure sixth interval. All the rest just rented their notes; Sam owned his. Many decades after his untimely death, he still does.

Cooke rose from a church background, the heartthrob lead singer of gospel superstars The Soul Stirrers, where he built his dizzying, flawless, effortless style. His transition to pop caused his former soulmates to berate him for converting to "the Devil's music". Cooke became massively famous as a pop singer and made an unprecedented step over the US colour line. By 1963, with several hits under his belt, Cooke was anxious to show the more mature side of his artistry. Prior to *Night Beat*, his LPs were filled with singles and weary fillers. Sam wanted an album that didn't pander to the radio audience, one where he could express what he was moving towards as he grew older. He had no compunction about covering blues shouter Howlin' Wolf (Little Red Rooster) or big band belter Joe Turner (Shake, Rattle And Roll).

A crack studio band was assembled around his long-time associates Rene Hall and Clifford White. Studio freshmen Billy Preston on organ and Hal Blaine on drums still count these sessions as some of their most mesmerising. On the opening track, Sam duets with double bass player Cliff Hils while the rest of the band takes five. It stands as one of Cooke's greatest vocal legacies. Elsewhere, blues and semi-gospel gems are addressed with real feeling, the musical perfection breathtaking.

Cooke's goal was realised, and the album, out of print for decades, was re-released in 1997 to a legion of new fans.

Record label:
RCA Victor
Produced
by Hugo and Luigi.
Recorded
at RCA Victor Studios, Hollywood; February 22–23 and 25, 1963.
Released:
September 1963
Chart peaks:
None (UK) None (US)
Personnel:
Sam Cooke (v); Ed Hall, Hal Blaine (d); Rene Hall, Cliff White, Barney Kessell (g); Clifford Hils (b); Raymond Johnson (p); Billy Preston (o); Dave Hassinger (e)
Track listing:
Lost And Looking; Mean Old World; Nobody Knows The Trouble I've Seen; Please Don't Drive Me Away; I Lost Everything; Get Yourself Another Fool; Little Red Rooster; Laughin' And Clownin'; Trouble Blues; You Gotta Move; Fool's Paradise; Shake, Rattle And Roll
Running time:
37.35
Current CD:
ABKCO 1124-2
Further listening:
The only other album that approaches this intensity is Live At The Harlem Square Club (1963).
Further reading:
You Send Me: The Life And Times of Sam Cooke (Daniel Wolff, 1996), a Cinderella story with a Tupac ending.
Like this?
Try . . . p.10

Koerner, Ray And Glover

Blues, Rags And Hollers

Lo-fi early '60s blues from influential American stylists.

Back in 1963 Paul Nelson, the editor of folk magazine The Little Sandy Review had been approached by Ed Nunn, a hobby-recordist and independent record label owner, who was looking for a folk act to record. Nelson suggested Koerner, Ray And Glover and for 300 bucks they recorded an album for his Audiophile label (his previous best seller was an album with one whole side devoted to a thunderstorm). Ensconced in an old Women's Club for a ten-hour session fuelled by a little speed and some good burgers, the trio cut 40 songs in a variety of set-ups; a cappella, accompanied, duets, solo and all three together playing live. "It wasn't exactly a comfortable situation," recalls Tony Glover. "We were on the edge about recording and the producer wouldn't allow us our usual lubrication."

Further reduction left a 20-track set, of raw and rattling blues – still an unusual pursuit among young white boys. A limited edition of 300 copies were pressed, including their spirited versions of Leadbelly's Hangman, Robert Johnson's Dust My Broom and Blind Lemon Jefferson's One Kind Favor, interspersed with suitably raucous rallying calls of their own making. It sold out immediately.

Glover: "We figured that this would be our only album, so we wanted to get as many tunes on as possible. But the tracks went right up to the label and cut out on some people's players." When Elektra's Jac Holzman heard it he lost no time in signing the trio and buying out the rights to re-issue their debut. Elektra removed four songs per side (which are re-instated on the Red House CD re-issue) in order to enhance the sound quality and *Blues, Rags And Hollers* helped establish it as the hippest of labels.

"Some years later, Love were being courted by every label on the scene," Holzman remembered. "But Arthur Lee insisted on Elektra because it was the label that released Koerner, Ray and Glover. The same thing happened with Paul Butterfield and The Doors." John Lennon was a fan too. What had impressed them all was the intense passion that Koerner, Ray And Glover displayed for the material. People had never heard anything like it before.

As The Lovin' Spoonful's John Sebastian noted: "It was played much faster than the originals because it was done by three excitable young white guys."

Record label:
Elektra
Produced
by Paul Nelson with Koerner, Ray And Glover.
Recorded
at The Woman's Club, Milwaukee, Wisconsin; March 24, 1963.
Released:
November 1963
Chart peaks:
None (UK) None (US)
Personnel:
'Spider' John Koerner (v, g); Dave 'Snaker' Ray (v, hm, bottleneck guitar, 12-string); Tony 'Little Sun' Glover (v, hm)
Track listing:
Linin' Track; Ramblin' Blues; It's All Right; Hangman; Down To Louisianna; Creepy John; Bugger Burns; Sun's Wail; One Kind Favor; Go Down Ol' Hannah; Good Time Charlie; Banjo Thing; Stop That Thing; Snaker's Here; Low Down Rounder; Jimmy Bel
Running time:
41.41
Current CD:
RHR CD 76 adds Ted Mack Rag; Dust My Broom; Too Bad; Mumblin' Word
Further listening:
Lots More Blues Rags And Hollers (1964); Koerner and Glover's Spider Blues (1965); Koerner and Willie Murphy's Running, Jumping, Standing Still (1994)
Further reading:
Follow The Music (Jac Holzman, 2000); the sleevenotes to the Red House re-issue of Blues, Rags And Hollers
Like this?
Try . . . p.225

The Holy Modal Rounders

The Holy Modal Rounders

America's first truly underground group blend old-time banjo music, bluegrass and traditional folk with a unique vision.

The Greenwich Village folk scene of the early '60s attracted the ambitious and talented, the ambitious but *talentless*, the right-on, the put-upon and the just plain weird. The Holy Modal Rounders were as weird as it got. Stampfel and Weber were talented and accomplished players, who first met up in Greenwich Village in March 1963. In the original sleevenotes, Stampfel attempted to pin down the fruit of their union: "Steve calls it rockabilly and I call it progressive old-timey. No-one has ever played music like us before."

They kicked their music *out of* shape by playing every theatre, book store, street gathering, festival, coffee house and folk club around the Village prior to recording *The Holy Modal Rounders* on December 11, 1963, for the Prestige Folklore imprint. The other key folk labels of the day, Elektra and Vanguard, had also approached them; they went with Prestige's Paul Rothschild because he smoked dope.

Opening with Blues In The Bottle – an obscure 1930 recording later brought to the wider world courtesy of The Lovin' Spoonful, the album's tone is set: the Rounders' personalised lyrics veering close to the edge: "I don't need nobody sniffin glue." Hesitation Blues features the first recorded use of the word 'psychedelic'; it's one of three brilliant Charlie Poole songs on the album, all '20s period pieces transformed into a kind of lysergic folk. Almost every song comes loaded with drug references and scatological rhymes: the Rounders made up new words for all the material they covered, and sang in unconventionally blended voices; Weber's like early Dylan on helium and Stampfel's a nasal twang. Ultimately, *The Holy Modal Rounders* is tremendous fun.

That the band ever got to make an album is remarkable; that there was a second later that year smacks of complete madness on the part of their record label. But there's a wit, originality and sense of joy – and a prescient, subversive intent – that sets these two records apart from everything else in their day. Unsurprisingly, they soon teamed up with beat activists The Fugs (on whose first two albums they play), though they're probably still best known for 1968's Bird Song, featured in the movie Easy Rider. The band continued into the '70s with augmented line-ups that included Michael Hurley and playwright Sam Shephard as drummer at different times. But none of their subsequent work approaches the inspired mayhem on offer here.

Record label:
Prestige
Produced
by Paul Rothschild.
Recorded
in New York City; December 11, 1963 and January 17, 1964.
Released:
February 1964
Chart peaks:
None (UK) None (US)
Personnel:
Peter Stampfel (fiddle, banjo, v); Steve Weber (g, v)
Track listing:
Blues In The Bottle; Fiddler A Dram; The Cuckoo; Euphoria; Long John; Hesitation Blues; Hey, Hey Baby; Reuben's Train; Mister Spaceman; Moving Day; Better Things For You; Same Old Man; Hop High Ladies; Bound To Lose
Running time:
35.13
Current CD:
Big Beat CDWIKD 176 adds: Flop Eared Mule; Black Eyed Susie; Sail Away Ladies; Clinch Mountain Backstep; Fishing Blues; Statesboro' Blues; Jumko Partner; Mole In The Ground; Hot Corn Cold Corn; Down The Old Plank Road; Chevrolet Six; Crowley Waltz; Bully Of The Town; Sugar In The Ground; Soldier's Joy
Further listening:
Everything you need is on the CD above.
Further reading:
Follow The Music (Jac Holzman and Gavan Daws, 1997)
Like this?
Try . . . p.76

Davy Graham And Shirley Collins

Folk Roots, New Routes

A seemingly bizarre pairing of folk song's English rose and an inventive young guitar genius.

Graham was always one of the British folk scene's maverick characters. While he was instantly lumped in with the scene because he played an acoustic guitar and worked London's Soho club circuit – so fashionable in the early '60s – he was forever in search of a broader canvas. A compulsive traveller and an avid musical adventurer (perhaps because his father came from the Isle Of Skye and taught Gaelic and his mother hailed from Guyana) he was heavily into blues, modern jazz, Indian and Arabic music, playing it all on guitar while barely out of his teens.

It was Shirley Collins's former husband Austin John Marshall who suggested that his inventive interpretations of Indian ragas might provide an intriguing accompaniment for one of Shirley's traditional tunes, Pretty Saro. Graham, it transpired, was a big Collins fan (he also loved Robert Johnson, Charlie Parker, Mary Wells and Rimsky-Korsakov) and joined her on-stage at a concert at London's Mercury Theatre in July 1964. The audience may have been baffled, but the results were extraordinary enough for the pairing to dive into the studio at the first opportunity. Many purist British folkies were appalled, but after a 2,000 mile journey trekking through the southern states of America collecting blues, gospel, jazz and folk songs with Alan Lomax, Shirley's ears were nothing if not open to different musical styles, and she threw herself into the project with a relish that startled many.

The fusion, light years ahead of its time, didn't sell particularly well but was massively influential, opening the way for other inventive guitarists such as John Martyn. Even now, in a time when world music is only a high street store away, the other-worldly settings of traditional warhorses like Nottamun Town, Love Is Pleasin' and Reynardine still sound extraordinary.

Record label:
Topic
Produced
by Ray Horricks.
Recorded
at Decca Studios, London; January 1964.
Released:
March 1964
Chart peaks:
None (UK) None (US)
Personnel:
Shirley Collins (v, g, banjo); Davy Graham (g); Gus Dudgeon (e)
Track listing:
Nottamun Town; Proud Maisrie; The Cherry Tree Carol; Blue Monk; Hares On The Mountain; Reynardine; Pretty Saro; Rif Mountain; Jane Jane; Love Is Pleasin'; Boll Weevil Holler; Hori Horo; Bad Girl; Lord Greggory; Grooveyard; Dearest Dear
Running time:
44.16
Current CD:
Topic CD819
Further listening:
The Graham album Folk, Blues And Beyond (1964) took folk guitar deeper into alien worlds of modern jazz, blues, Indian and even Arabic music. Further examples can be heard on the excellent compilation Fire In The Soul (1970).
Further reading:
www.daveygraham.org
Like this?
Try . . . p.16

The Rolling Stones

The Rolling Stones

British beat moves up a gear; Jagger wanted to make this LP "the best ever by a British group".

The time manager Andrew Loog Oldham walked in on Keith Richards revising Buddy Holly's Not Fade Away was the day he knew his Stones could write as well as roll; the time he locked Mick and Keith in the kitchen and wouldn't let them out until they'd finished a song was the night that they realized it too. And the January 1964 sessions which produced the Stones' debut album told the world that they weren't going to be a blues band forever. Stylistically, of course, The Rolling Stones is little more than a verbatim recounting of the band's live set of the period – Bobby Troup, Bo Diddley, Chuck Berry, American soul and R&B. One dramatic Jagger/Richard ballad, Tell Me, joined a couple of pseudonymous efforts which disguised the team's own early bashfulness – the instrumental Now I've Got A Witness, dedicated to Phil Spector and Gene Pitney (and rewriting the stage staple Everybody Needs Somebody To Love) and Little By Little, co-starring both, and co-written with Spector. On paper, the album is the sound of British beat 1964, pure and simple. It was what was done with the beat that mattered, though. Engineer Bill Farley recalls, "When they arrived, no one had any thought about arrangements. They just busked it until they got the feeling of the number," and that is what made the Stones as musicians, and Oldham as producer, so special.

The Rolling Stones emerged with a freshness and vitality which belied the rigidity of its repertoire and the sterility of the studio. There was no overdubbing, no gimmickry, no prima donna virtuosity. They played, they taped, they jammed, they relaxed, and when it felt right to everyone, it was finished.

Making a record, Oldham confirms, is not a craft, it's an art. "It's not something you know, it's something you feel, in your heart, in your gut, in every fibre of your instinct." *The Rolling Stones* is all heart, gut and instinct.

Record Label:
Decca
Produced
by Andrew Loog Oldham.
Recorded
at Regent Sound Studio; January 1964.
Release date:
April 17, 1964
Chart peaks:
1 (UK) 11 (US)
Personnel:
Mick Jagger (v); Keith Richard (g); Brian Jones (g, v); Bill Wyman (b, v); Ian Stewart (k); Charlie Watts (d); Gene Pitney (p on Little By Little); Phil Spector (maracas on Little By Little)
Track Listing:
Route 66; I Just Want To Make Love To You; Honest I Do; Mona (UK only); Now I've Got A Witness; Little By Little; I'm A King Bee; Carol; Tell Me (S, US only); Can I Get A Witness; You Can Make It If You Try; Walking The Dog; Not Fade Away (S, US only)
Not available on CD
in original form, current CD replicates US release England's Newest Hitmakers: The Rolling Stones
Running time:
31.12 (US)
Current CD:
LK 4605
Further listening:
Rolling Stones #2 (1964); Boxed Set Singles 1963–69 (1980)
Further reading:
Stoned (Andrew Loog Oldham, 2000)
Like this?
Try . . . p.637

Dusty Springfield

A Girl Called Dusty

The debut album, recorded only months after the split of The Springfields.

Very few British pop albums from 1964 were built to last: pop was still a singles form, and long-players seemed like little more than a couple of hits and ten other tracks. Dusty Springfield's debut was an amazing exception, though it followed the already familiar path of including covers of contemporary hits. Springfield created an album that bore almost no resemblance to the style she'd found success with as one of The Springfields, who'd played their farewell concert only six months before this album's release. She had already had a solo hit with I Only Want To Be With You – the first record ever to be played on Top Of The Pops – which suggested that the folky sound of The Springfields had been traded in for a zippier pop beat. But *A Girl Called Dusty* went much further than that. Several of the tunes were covers of black pop hits (or soon-to-be hits) which Springfield refused to mellow out in the normal manner of white cover acts. Her spirited rush at The Supremes' When The Lovelight Starts Shining Thru His Eyes, for instance, was just as effective as the original. She sings both parts on the treatment of the Inez and Charlie Foxx hit Mockingbird without neutering the result. On You Don't Own Me (a success for Lesley Gore in the US), she comes close to sounding like a blues mama. In tracks like these, Dusty's reputation as Britain's great soul voice was born. But that famous misnomer – bolstered further by the later and probably overrated *Dusty In Memphis* – conceals her greater talent, as a kind of ice queen of torch singing. The tracks which really stand out here are the Bacharach-David tunes: Twenty-Four Hours From Tulsa, Anyone Who Had A Heart, Wishin' And Hopin' and My Colouring Book, which approaches sheer desolation in feeling. Dusty was a great sufferer, and although even these songs would be surpassed by such monumental tearjerkers as I Close My Eyes And Count To Ten and All I See Is You, the record sows the seeds for her mastery of bathos. But that was some way off yet.

In 1964, this 25-year-old convent girl stared out from record racks and seemed an irresistible mix of country girl and pop diva.

Record Label:
Mercury
Produced
by John Franz.
Recorded:
1964.
Released:
April 1964
Chart peaks:
6 (UK) None (US)
Personnel:
Dusty Springfield (v); Ivor Raymonde (oa); The Breakaways (bv)
Track Listing:
Mama Said; You Don't Own Me; Do Re Mi; When The Lovelight Starts Shining Thru His Eyes; My Colouring Book; Mockingbird; Twenty Four Hours From Tulsa; Nothing; Anyone Who Had A Heart; Will You Love Me Tomorrow; Wishin' And Hopin'; Don't You Know
Running time:
56.33
Current CD:
534520-2 adds: I Only Want To Be With You (remix); He's Got Something; Every Day I Have To Cry; Can I Get A Witness; All Cried Out; I Wish I'd Never Loved You; Once Upon A Time; Summer Is Over
Further listening:
The Dusty Springfield Collection (1998)
Further reading:
www.dustyspringfield.co.uk/
Like this?
Try . . . p.490

The Beatles

A Hard Day's Night

Rock'n'roll grows up as the Fabs write all of their third album.

By March 1964, The Beatles had changed pop music forever, setting standards of cross-generational appeal that remain a wonder to this day. They were also getting nods of musical approval from the establishment about their song writing and for their third album – also serving as the soundtrack to their first movie – they decided to go for an unheard-of option, an all-originals set. In the end, side one of the LP comprised songs from the film while side two contained other new songs. (In America, side two used George Martin instrumentals, the other tracks creeping out on other albums.) John Lennon, perturbed by a recent Beatles single A-side being nabbed by the Paul McCartney-penned Can't Buy Me Love, took full advantage of Paul being relatively distracted (by his romance with Jane Asher) to reassert his domination of the band by lead-composing or singing on ten of the thirteen resulting tracks.

Inevitably, given that the songs were written in the pressure bubble that was Beatlemania, the band – however spirited – occasionally sounded formulaic (Any Time At All, I Should Have Known Better, When I Get Home) but the best tracks were the pinnacle of what rock-era pop songwriting had yet achieved. Lennon's ballad If I Fell encapsulates what Carr and Tyler called the "excellence-through-innocence" that characterises the whole album while McCartney's And I Love Her was instantly seized upon by adult pop merchants as a new standard. "I consider it his first Yesterday," Lennon reflected much later.

There was the bluesy title track with its unforgettable opening chord (written specifically as a startling opening to the movie), exotic guitar textures courtesy of George's new Rickenbacker 12-string (which would have such an effect on West Coast Beatle-freak Roger McGuinn) and a pair of delicious compositions (Lennon's I'll Be Back – based on Del Shannon's Runaway – and McCartney's Things We Said Today) that wallow in minor/major ambivalence, signposts toward future sophistication. The Dick Lester-directed black-and-white biographical fantasy film was described by US critic Andrew Sarris as "the Citizen Kane of juke box movies" while elsewhere Lennon and McCartney were hailed as the greatest songwriters since Schubert.

Record Label:
Parlophone
Produced
by George Martin.
Recorded
at Abbey Road, London; January–June 1964
Released:
July 10, 1964
Chart peaks:
1 (UK) 1 (US)
Personnel:
John Lennon (v, g); Paul McCartney (v, b); George Harrison (v, g); Ringo Starr (d); George Martin (p)
Track Listing:
A Hard Day's Night; I Should Have Known Better; If I Fell; I'm Happy Just To Dance With You; And I Love Her; Tell Me Why; Can't Buy Me Love; Any Time At All; I'll Cry Instead; Things We Said Today; When I Get Home; You Can't Do That; I'll Be Back
Running time:
30.30
Current CD:
CDP7464372
Further listening:
With The Beatles (1963); Help! (1965)
Further reading:
Revolution In The Head (Ian Macdonald, 1998); The Beatles As Musicians (Walter Everett, 1999); The Beatles: An Illustrated Record (Roy Carr and Tony Tyler, 1975)
Like this?
Try . . . p.535

The Animals
The Animals

Provincial British R&B, as dirty and sweaty as the group's ill-fitting suits.

By 1964, the Merseybeat boom had fizzled out. Only The Beatles and The Searchers proved to have staying power. The new boom on the block was tough, rootsy R&B, propagated by a network of clubs across the UK. Newcastle's Club Au Go Go was an essential stop on any American bluesman's tour itinerary. However, when elder statesmen such as Sonny Boy Williamson II hit town, they ran the risk of being blown off-stage by the toughest outfit of the British blues boom. The Animals majored on the musicianship of Alan Price on piano and Vox Continental organ and the secret weapon of the raw impassioned vocals of Eric Burdon and their repertoire, drawn from the rougher end of Muddy Waters, Bo Diddley, John Lee Hooker, et al.

They were signed to EMI by producer Mickey Most, and debuted during three one-day sessions in January 1964. A second date in February and third in July provided the material for this album, the first three singles and their B-sides. The second of these was The House Of The Rising Sun, which, released in July, quickly topped the charts on both sides of the Atlantic.

For the album, The Animals essentially played their live set and that was it. Burdon gave out true bottled soul on Bury My Body and I'm Mad Again (one of three John Lee Hooker songs), while the unsung Hilton Valentine (the final member to join) provided a great growling guitar solo. Alan Price contributed rolling piano to Hooker standard, Dimples. ("He was always better on piano," says Burdon, "I hated the sound of that fucking Vox Continental, but it was the only practical thing to use for live dates.")

Thanks to *The Animals* and two other eponymous, largely R&B-influenced albums by British bands the same year – *The Kinks* and *The Rolling Stones* – this music would remain the dominant form in the clubs and charts until the end of 1965, with the rise of the mod bands, soul and an increasing air of experimentation.

1965 also saw Alan Price's departure, officially citing "fear of flying". Burdon himself blames Price's sole arrangement credit on the band's biggest hit as the real reason: "When Alan Price walked off with the publishing for House Of The Rising Sun, well, what does that amount to in terms of finances? It would have given everybody a sense of success and achievement if the money had been distributed equally. So the band was always split into factions."

Record Label:
Columbia
Produced
by Mickey Most.
Recorded
at EMI Studios, London; 1964
Released:
October 1964
Chart peaks:
6 (UK) 7 (US)
Personnel:
Eric Burdon (v); Alan Price (k); Hilton Valentine (g); Chas Chandler (b); John Steel (d)
Track listing:
Story Of Bo Diddley; Bury My Body; Dimples; I've Been Around; I'm In Love Again; The Girl Can't Help It; I'm Mad Again; She Said Yeah; The Right Time; Memphis; Boom Boom (S/US); Around And Around
Running time:
38.52
Current CD:
EMI 16137
Further listening:
The Complete Animals (1990)
Further Reading:
I Used To Be An Animal – But I'm All Right Now (Eric Burdon, 1992)
Like this?
Try . . . p.264

Eric Dolphy

Out To Lunch

Tour de force of articulate free jazz.

When Eric Dolphy first arrived in New York in the late '50s with Chico Hamilton's West Coast group, AJ Spellman noted that he "played nice – pretty and all". The same writer noted that it was a different Dolphy who returned a year later with Charles Mingus: "This one was wild and woolly, played all kinds of unmentionable things you wouldn't say in front of your mother."

Stylistically, Eric Dolphy was somewhere between the slithery melodicism of Charlie Parker and the boundary-busting disorder of Ornette Coleman, of whom Dolphy said, "He taught me a direction." He had the energy and anarchy of a New Thing player but there was an instrumental virtuosity, melodic intelligence and tonal refinement that somehow set him apart from the centre of the avant-garde. Here, on his acknowledged masterpiece, Dolphy is majestic on bass clarinet on Hat And Beard (a witty nod to Monk in 9/4) and Something Sweet Something Tender (a gorgeous, Mingus-like semi-abstract reverie); lyrical and visceral by turns – sometimes within the same phrase – but always thoughtful and engaging.

"I play notes that would not ordinarily be said to be in a given key, but I hear them as 'proper'," Dolphy once explained. "I don't think I 'leave the changes' as the expression goes; every note I play has some reference to the chords of the piece."

While the chords on *Out To Lunch* are often not an issue (the quintet go 'free' on several occasions), there is pulse and rhythmic momentum throughout, though the rhythm section – especially vibist Hutcherson – are employed as equal contributors rather than time and harmony keepers.

"Everyone's a leader on this session," commented Dolphy, and how well they all lead; the lingering impression of this challenging, often beautiful work is far from the dense, cluttered argument that characterises much New Thing music, but is rather one of aerated, witty conversation. Leaving America soon after this date ("If you try and do anything different in this country, people put you down for it"), Dolphy died in Europe three months later of undiagnosed diabetes, aged 36. This tragedy, his musical boldness, and reputed personal charm have elevated his standing to nothing short of jazz saint.

Record Label:
Blue Note
Produced
by Alfred Lion.
Recorded
at Van Gelder Studio, Englewood Cliffs, New Jersey; February 25, 1964.
Released:
1964
Chart peaks:
None (UK) None (US)
Personnel:
Eric Dolphy (as, flute, bass clarinet); Freddie Hubbard (t); Bobby Hutcherson (vibes); Richard Davis (b); Anthony Williams (d)
Track Listing:
Hat And Beard; Something Sweet, Something Tender; Gazzelloni; Out To Lunch; Straight Up And Down
Running time:
42.18
Current CD:
CDP7465242
Further listening:
Far Cry (1960); Conversations (1963)
Further reading:
Eric Dolphy (Vladimir Simosko, 1979), www.farcry.neurobio.pitt.edu/Eric.html
Like this?
Try . . . p.24

John Coltrane

A Love Supreme

More than a jazz milestone, a landmark in music.

Few musicians have asked as much of music as John Coltrane. Fewer still have gotten as much out of it as Coltrane did with *A Love Supreme.* His musicians had only the sketchiest idea of what they would be recording that December day in 1964, but the tenor saxophone giant had been in preparation for years. After kicking a heroin habit in the late '50s, Coltrane's position as a fearless explorer of "new thing" jazz had been paralleled by a spiritual quest that embraced the wisdom of the Bible, Koran, Kaballah and other philosophical and mystical tracts.

"My goal is to live the truly religious life and express it in my music," Coltrane told Newsweek. "If you live it, when you play there's no problem because the music is just part of the whole thing. To be a musician is really something. It goes very, very deep. My music is the spiritual expression of what I am – my faith, my knowledge, my being ... When you begin to see the possibilities of music, you desire to do something really good for people, to help humanity free itself from its hang-ups. I think music can make the world better and, if I'm qualified, I want to do it. A musical language transcends words. I want to speak to their souls."

He did. From the gentle tenor invocation that opens this four-part suite, Coltrane is in command of something extraordinary – or perhaps *it* is commanding him. Neither as 'free' as the jazz he'd begin making the following year, nor as immediately accessible as *Giant Steps* or *My Favorite Things*, this music is distinguished by the spirit that moves through it. So complete was the moment that there is only one known instance of Coltrane attempting to play the piece live. (Another version of Acknowledgement, adding the sax of Archie Shepp and bassist Art Davis, was recorded the following day but is now lost.)

A Love Supreme is that rare thing: a work of exalted art that also touches the common consciousness. It was an immediate best-seller by jazz standards, indicating that there was a substantial audience for the new music. Certified gold in 1970, it has now sold more than a million copies.

Record label:
Impulse!
Produced
by Bob Thiele.
Recorded
at the Van Gelder Studio, Englewood Cliffs, New Jersey; December 9, 1964.
Released:
January 1965.
Chart peaks:
None (UK) None (US)
Personnel:
John Coltrane (ts); McCoy Tyner (p); Jimmy Garrison (b); Elvin Jones (d); Rudy Van Gelder (e)
Track listing:
Acknowledgement; Resolution; Persuance; Psalm
Running time:
33.03
Current CD:
IMP11552
Further listening:
Coltrane Live At Birdland (1963); Crescent (1964)
Further reading:
Ascension: John Coltrane and His Quest (Eric Nisenson, 1993); John Coltrane: His Life and Music (Lewis Porter, 1998)
Like this?
Try . . . p.254

The Beach Boys

The Beach Boys Today!

A teenage surf-band starts to grow-up strange.

Although no one could have known it when it was released, *The Beach Boys Today!* foreshadowed the end of the group's first era – the era of songs about cars, carefree love and surfing for which they remain most well known.

The first Beach Boys album of 1965 and their ninth studio album in three years (including a Christmas collection), *Today!* marked a critical point in Brian Wilson's development as a song-writer and producer. Perhaps as significantly, it was also when his lucidity was first brought into serious question.

Eager to better the artistic and commercial precedents set by The Beatles and Phil Spector, and increasingly insecure in his ability to do so, Wilson felt straitjacketed by the Boys' narrow – but winning – formula. His introduction to marijuana, and the bohemian community that supplied it to him, convinced him that the group's sound should expand as much as his mind if it was to remain relevant. Following an airborne breakdown en route to a Los Angeles live date on December 23, 1964, Wilson announced his retirement from the road to the horrified group, explaining that he would focus all of his creativity into the studio. "I told them I foresee a beautiful future for The Beach Boys, but the only way we could achieve it was if they did their job and I did mine," recalled Brian. "I felt I had no choice, I was run down mentally and emotionally."

Nothing looks amiss among the sweater-clad grinning boys beaming out from its cover, and the likes of Dance, Dance, Dance and Help Me, Ronda maintain the group's good-time reliability. Yet an air of delicate, desperate introspection bleeds from *Today*'s most beautiful songs (eight of the album's ten originals written by Brian alone), accentuated by complex orchestrations borne from Brian's new freedom. The album's entire second half, particularly, is regarded as the precursor to *Pet Sounds*' resolute, lush despair. Please Let Me Wonder (the first song Brian wrote stoned) and In The Back Of My Mind express love not as teenage paradise, but as a submission to paralysing vulnerability, the ultimate threat to childhood naiveté: "So happy at times that I break out in tears/In the back of my mind, I still have my fears." Even this side's cover version, The Students' doo-wop pearl I'm So Young, is equivocal. "I'm so young/ Can't marry no one."

Some of the group (can you guess who?) expressed concern over this break from custom, but to no avail. *The Beach Boys Today!* was the signpost to The Beach Boys' tomorrow.

Record label:
Capitol
Produced
by Brian Wilson.
Recorded
at Western Recording Studios and Gold Star Recording Studios, Hollywood; June 22, 1964, October 8 & 10, 1964, January 7, 19 1965
Released:
March 1965
Chart peaks:
13 (UK) 4 (US)
Personnel:
Mike Love (v, s); Carl Wilson (v, g, k); Alan Jardine (g, v); Brian Wilson (k, g, v); Dennis Wilson (v, d, k)
Track listing:
Do You Wanna Dance (S/US); Good To My Baby; Don't Hurt My Little Sister; When I Grow Up (To Be A Man); Help Me, Rhonda [LP Version] (S); Dance, Dance, Dance; Please Let Me Wonder; I'm So Young; Kiss Me Baby; She Knows Me Too Well; In The Back Of My Mind; Bull Session With 'Big Daddy'
Running time:
29.28
Current CD:
C18296321
Further listening:
Pet Sounds (1966), Summer Days (And Summer Nights!!) (1965)
Further reading:
Heroes And Villains: The True Story Of The Beach Boys (Stephen Gaines, 1986); www.beachboysfanclub.com/
Like this?
Try . . . p.564

The Sonics

Here Are The Sonics

Before they made The Sonics they broke the mould.

The secret behind the most visceral garage punk group of the '60s? "We wanted people to gasp, we wanted people to go 'oh my gawd!' And so that's how we approached it," reveals drummer Bob Bennett. "We wanted to blow people off their feet, not just with loudness, but with tightness, with music that made you want to dance." Hence their debut single The Witch. Originally intended as a simple dance number to rival The Twist and The Mashed Potato, the song gradually mutated into a raw, screaming horror show. On hearing the masters, the band were devastated. "All I did was pound my drums and I guess it just sounded like bashing when it was recorded," said Bob, "I remember the engineers arguing. One guy says, 'That doesn't even sound like drums,' and the other guy goes, 'Well what am I gonna do – look at this guy'?"

The Witch became the biggest selling single in America's Northwest and their record label Etiquette naturally demanded an album. The only problem was songwriter and singer Gerry Roslie's sloth. "I had to prod him," recalled Buck Ormsby, Etiquette's A&R man who had discovered the group, "The Sonics weren't great musicians, but they had this magic thing."

They eventually got it together at Audio Recording in Seattle. Twelve cuts were recorded live onto two-track tape. Six songs were covers, including a frenetic take on the Contours' Do You Love Me and their ferocious reading of Little Richard's Good Golly Miss Molly. Originals included Psycho, a deranged maelstrom propelled along by pounding drums, the fearsome Strychnine, which extols the virtues of guzzling poison and features Rob Lind's raucous, wailing sax, and their supercharged ode to a Ford Mustang, Boss Hoss.

What made The Sonics special was Gerry Roslie's fiendish, manic vocals, which some likened to Little Richard. "I always felt that somebody would have to come in and give him a blood transfusion," engineer Kearney Barton said, "I thought he was gonna tear his throat out – screaming from start to finish – amazing!"

Though influencing just about every band that came out of the North-west The Sonics were unable, despite their best efforts to break out nationally. Instead, at the end of the '60s, they broke up.

Record label:
Etiquette
Produced
as 'An Etiquette Production'.
Recorded:
Released:
March 1965
Chart peaks:
None (UK) None (US)
Personnel:
Gerry Roslie (v, p, o); Andy Parypa (b); Larry Parypa (g); Rob Lind (s); Bob Bennett (d)
Track listing:
The Witch (S/US); Do You Love Me; Roll Over Beethoven; Boss Hoss; Dirty Robber; Have Love Will Travel; Psycho (S/US); Money; Walkin' The Dog; Night Time Is The Right Time; Strychnine; Good Golly Miss Molly
Running time:
29.20
Current CD:
CNW903 adds Keep A Knockin'; Don't Believe In Christmas (S/US); Santa Claus; The Village Idiot
Further listening:
second album and more of the same, The Sonics Boom (1966)
Further reading:
www.history-of-rock.com/sonics.htm
Like this?
Try . . . p.313

Bert Jansch

Bert Jansch

Possibly the very first British singer/songwriter album.

"People saw him as a rival to Bob Dylan," says Martin Carthy. "When his first album came out it really was a big day." Along with Carthy, Bert was one of the kings of the folk music castle in 1965. The 'folk boom' looked like exploding on a national level and offbeat singer-songwriters were converging on London for its all-nighter folk scene. With an astonishingly original sound, blending Broonzy's blues with Mingus's jazz, Scottish trad and a flavour of English guitar exoticist Davy Graham, Bert had drifted down from Edinburgh.

"[Singer] Anne Briggs took me firmly by the throat and said, 'Look, for God's sake you must do this record,'" says freelance engineer Bill Leader. Bill had recorded Anne for trad label Topic, but there were no obvious outlets for the wayward Jansch. Not even owning a guitar, Bert recorded the album at Leader's flat on spec using a Revox and borrowed instruments. Anne was meanwhile lobbying Nat Joseph of Transatlantic, who finally agreed to a purchase of £100 and no royalties. It was the only option. "Perhaps if I'd sat on it for another six months," says Bill, "we might have done a better deal. But there comes a time when a record has to be released for an artist and if you miss that you bugger up his career."

Davy Graham's Angie, mischievously adopting Cannonball Adderley's Worksong as middle-eight, was the only cover – although Smokey River was essentially Jimmy Giuffre's Train And The River while Casbah had started life as Mingus's Better Get It In Your Soul. Mostly, though, these were intense, personal songs reflecting the lifestyle of its author, from his earliest composition Courting Blues through the swaggering imagery of Strolling Down The Highway – written in 1962 while hitch-hiking through France – to the more poignant reflections of Needle Of Death (the first anti-drugs song?) and Running From Home. Songs from the album were covered on record by Julie Felix, Marianne Faithful and Donovan while the moody cover shot of Bert with guitar in a bare flat completed the message that here was not only music to absorb but a way of life to acquire. "His work will touch youth with a force unknown to our present British artists," concluded Folk Scene. Another journal, Folk Music, nailed it: "It might be objected that this is not folk music, and of course it's not. But until our categories expand Bert must be included within folk in its broadest sense." Rightly or wrongly, he still is.

Record label:
Transatlantic
Produced
by Bill Leader.
Recorded
at 5 North Villas, Camden, London; September 1964–January 1965.
Released:
April 16, 1965
Chart peaks:
None (UK) None (US)
Personnel:
Bert Jansch (v, g)
Track listing:
Strolling Down The Highway; Smokey River; Oh How Your Love Is Strong; I Have No Time; Finches; Rambling's Going To Be The Death Of Me; Veronica; Needle Of Death; Do You Hear Me Now?; Alice's Wonderland; Running, Running From Home; Courting Blues; Casbah; Dreams Of Love; Angie
Running time:
38.52
Current CD:
ESM CD407 adds It Don't Bother Me
Further listening:
Jack Orion (1966); Rosemary Lane (1971); When The Circus Comes To Town (1995)
Further reading:
MOJO 80; Dazzling Stranger: Bert Jansch And The British Folk And Blues Revival (Colin Harper, 2000)
Like this?
Try . . . p.220

Jerry Lee Lewis

Live At The Star Club, Hamburg

The Killer invents garage punk with a little help from the Nashville Teens.

When Jerry Lee Lewis crashed into Hamburg in April of 1964 he was a pill-fuelled anachronism, a brilliant '50s rocker staring out at an audience of bowl-haired boy-girl Beatles kids. At just 28 years old he looked like an old man out of time. The past six years had not been kind. On May 22, 1958, a 21-year-old Lewis had arrived in England for his first tour outside the US, with his 13-year-old wife *née* cousin Myra Gale, in tow. Lewis told the press she was 15. "Back home," Myra explained, "you can marry at 10." It put an effective halt on his career for the next 10 years.

From 1958 to 1968 Jerry Lee toured constantly on a strict diet – Biphetamin to take him up, placidyls to bring him down, whiskey to bridge the gap. His regular $10,000 per night fee was knocked down to $250. "I couldn't care less," said Lewis. "Life is too short to worry your brains over making a buck." Then, on Easter Sunday 1962 – while Jerry was coming down from another amphetamine-wild gig in Minneapolis – his three-year-old child, Stevie Allen, wandered out into the garden of his Memphis home and drowned in the mud-filled family swimming pool. God had found him out and punished him and the Jerry Lee who toured Britain and Europe for the next four years, the one you hear on this record, played like a man with the Holy Ghost in his soul and the devil on his tail.

This date had no rehearsals. The Star-Club's house-band, The Nashville Teens – a mythic whippet-thin Scouse wrecking crew and no-argument best live band in Britain – spent the gig either struggling to keep up with Lewis or storming ahead – locked into a teeth-grindingly tense race to the end of each song. From the cavernous howl of Mean Woman Blues through to a final ragged Whole Lotta Shakin' the rhythm section sound like they've been remixed by Tom and Ed Chemical while Pete Shannon and John Allen's screwed-up jags of guitar and Jerry Lee's demonic growls, wails, yelps and piano stabs are sweat-soaked punk pre-history. He carried on playing like this for the next three years – The Greatest Live Show On Earth. No contest, true, but it nearly killed him. Then, in 1968, recording *Another Time, Another Place* for Mercury, Jerry Lee Lewis found country, dispensed with the pills and the booze, and a whole other kind of star was born.

Record label:
Phillips
Produced
by Siggi Loch.
Recorded
at The Star Club, Reeperbahn, Hamburg, West Germany; April 5, 1964.
Released:
April 1965
Chart peaks:
None (UK) None (US)
Personnel:
Jerry Lee Lewis (v, p); The Nashville Teens: Pete Shannon (g); John Allen (g); Ray Phillips (b); John Hanken (d)
Track listing:
Mean Woman Blues; High School Confidential; Money (That's What I Want); Matchbox; What'd I Say (Part 1); What'd I Say (Part 2); Great Balls Of Fire; Good Golly, Miss Molly; Lewis' Boogie; Your Cheatin' Heart; Hound Dog; Long Tall Sally; Whole Lotta Shakin' Goin' On
Running time:
37.12
Current CD:
Spectrum 554 195-2
Further listening:
The Golden Hits Of Jerry Lee Lewis (1964); listen to Jerry Lee's proper touring band speed through the hits on The Greatest Live Show On Earth (1964); check out his country resurrection on Another Time, Another Place (1968)
Further reading:
Killer (Jerry Lee Lewis and Charles White, 1995); Hellfire (Nick Tosches, 1982)
Like this?
Try . . . p.318

Them

Them

Future superstar Van Morrison arrives with an influential slice of garage blues.

Any listener only familiar with the sophisticated sounds of the middle-aged Van Morrison would be shell-shocked hearing *Them*, on which the Belfast bluesman, then only 19 years old, sings with a ferocity that's still startling. The album is a British blues boom classic and yet under-appreciated; rumours are that it was actually made by sessionmen having sabotaged its – and the band's – reputation. Morrison has never publicly refuted the allegations, but his colleagues are adamant that like contemporaries The Kinks and The Who, session men – including Jimmy Page – were occasionally imposed upon them, only to fill out the sound of the core band, not the featured roles. And aural evidence supports this, for, frankly, the ramshackle excitement of the playing is surely the sound of a bunch of rowdies from the bars, clubs and dives of Belfast, rather than the sound of professional sessionmen.

Sometimes known as *The Angry Young Them* after the slogan emblazoned on the back of the sleeve, the album begins electrifyingly, with the rampaging Mystic Eyes, an instrumental until near the end, when Morrison improvises some enigmatic, fragmentary lyrics. "Van was always good at ad libbing," enthuses guitarist Billy Harrison. "He could just conjure words as he was performing. And no one in Britain could phrase like him." *Them* includes Gloria, previously the B-side of the band's debut hit, Baby Please Don't Go, which became a US hit for the Shadows Of Knight and a rock standard, covered by Hendrix, Patti Smith, the Grateful Dead and countless others. Morrison had been the last to join the original band ("We brought him in to play saxophone, but he knew more blues songs than me so he began to sing," recalls Harrison) but Them's personnel never stabilised, which further undermined the band's status.

"If management had supported, instead of exploited, Them could have been on a level with the Stones," sighs founder member Eric Wrixon. "We were more extreme and musically in advance of them." But it wasn't to be and, to many, Them are now regarded as only a trivial, early footnote in the history of Van the Man, the absurdity of which is obvious to anyone who has ever thrilled to the raw power that throbs from this extraordinary album.

Record label:
Deram
Produced
by Tommy Scott, Bert Berns and Dick Rowe.
Recorded
at Decca Studios, West End Lane and Regent Studios, Denmark Street; July, September–October 1964 and January 1965.
Released:
June 1965
Chart peaks:
None (UK) 54 (US)
Personnel:
Van Morrison (v, hm, s); Billy Harrison (g); Eric Wrixon, Jackie McAuley, Peter Bardens (k); Ronnie Millings (d); Pat McAuley (d, k); Alan Henderson (b)
Track listing:
Mystic Eyes (S); If You And I Could Be As Two; Little Girl; Just A Little Bit; I Gave My Love A Diamond; Gloria (S/US); You Just Can't Win; Go On Home Baby; Don't Look Back; I Like It Like That; I'm Gonna Dress In Black (S/US); Bright Lights Big City; My Little Baby; (Get Your Kicks On) Route 66
Running time:
39.13
Current CD:
ABR00102
Further listening:
Them Again (1966), the band's second album.
Further reading:
MOJO 50; Van Morrison: Inarticulate Speech Of The Heart (John Collis, 1996).
Like this?
Try . . . p.154

Jackson C Frank

Jackson C Frank

American Troubadour Records Prototype Singer-Songwriter LP, influencing Nick Drake, Simon & Garfunkel, Sandy Denny and others in the process

Years before confessional singer-songwriting was in vogue, the enigmatic Jackson Carey Frank recorded an album that more or less defined the genre, describing it in his sleevenotes as 'the newspaper obituary of my inner self'. Yet whilst his acolytes achieved fame and fortune in his wake, his sad life bore out the words of his most famous song, the beautiful, prematurely world-weary 'Blues Run The Game': 'Maybe tomorrow honey, someplace down the line / I'll wake up older, and I'll just stop all my trying.'

Born in Buffalo, NY in 1943, Frank's entire life was blighted by a terrible fire that engulfed his school when he was 11, killing eighteen of his classmates and giving him third degree burns. Whilst he eventually recovered his mobility, physically and mentally he was scarred for life. After a slow convalescence during which he taught himself guitar, Frank gained access to a huge insurance payout when he turned 21 in 1964, and set sail for England in search of the high life, writing 'Blues Run The Game' en route.

He could not have arrived at a better time. The UK folk scene was blossoming and Frank largely abandoned his bacchanalian aspirations in favour of the bohemian club lifestyle, retaining only a dandified dress sense, an Aston Martin and a large collection of Martin guitars. He soon became romantically involved with Sandy Denny and moved in with Al Stewart and fellow expats Paul Simon and Art Garfunkel, all waiting for stardom. Simon was quick to appreciate Frank's talent and offered to produce an album for him. Recorded in a single three-hour session in mid-1965, it melds traditional sounds ('Kimbie') with protest ('Don't Look Back'), stream of consciousness ('My Name Is Carnival') and the more personal, melancholy songs ('Blues Run The Game', 'You Never Wanted Me') that were to have such an impact on the next generation of UK songwriters. Despite the extreme nerves that he experienced in the studio, where he insisted on recording behind a screen, his singing and picking are exceptional throughout. The album was rapturously received in folk circles and played to death by aspiring singers across the UK.

Despite this triumph, Frank found it hard to maintain his creativity. After abortive attempts at a follow-up, and having blown most of his money, in 1968 he fled homewards to an increasingly lonely and depressing existence. For much of the next 30 years he would be destitute, living either on the streets or in mental hospitals, too dispirited to contact old acquaintances and too infirm to perform. A broken man, Frank died in March 1999.

RMJ

Record label:
Columbia
Produced
by Paul Simon
Recorded
by CBS Studios, New Bond Street, London, Spring 1965.
Released:
Summer 1965.
Chart Peaks:
None (UK), None (US).
Personnel:
Jackson C. Frank (g, v) / Al Stewart (g, one track only).
Track listing:
Blues Run The Game / Don't Look Back / Kimbie / Yellow Walls / Here Come The Blues / Milk And Honey / My Name Is Carnival / Dialogue / Just Like Anything / You Never Wanted Me.
Further reading:
www.blueangel.demon.co.uk/jcfrank/
Like this?
Try . . . p.101

B.B. King

Live At The Regal

Widely regarded as the greatest ever live blues album.

"The world's greatest blues singer, the King Of The Blues – B.B. King", is how he is introduced on this seminal live album. If anyone doubted that King deserved such an introduction before hearing this performance, no one could doubt it afterwards.

The Regal Theatre was one of the major stops on the chittlin' circuit and King often played several residencies there in a year. "I don't think I played any better than I've played before, but the feedback from the audience was good," he has said of this performance. He's not kidding: the crowd shriek, scream and holler throughout as King plays with a white-hot intensity, his own voice as impassioned as his guitar Lucille's on songs such as Every Day (I Have The Blues), Sweet Little Angel and You Upset Me Baby, some of which he'd been playing for a decade or more and was to continue to play into the 21st century. On the witty How Blue Can You Get, King declaims: "I gave you seven children/And now you want to give them back," punching out the lyrics with an anger that still shocks.

"Because I play it every night like for the first time. I never go note for note on the melody – I play what I'm feeling now, not what I felt yesterday."

King's guitar playing throughout is articulate and thrillingly emotive, with never a hint of grandstanding or cliché. "You don't play a note simply because you can find one," explains King. "You do it because it makes sense. To me, every note is important." Apart from the irresistible power of the music, the album is also notable for signalling the end of blues music as an exclusively black form. It's a fair bet that there wasn't a single white member of the Regal audience. Soon, however, King would be playing gigs at which a black face would be a rarity.

Record label:
Chess
Produced
by Johnny Pate.
Recorded
at The Regal Theatre, Chicago, Illinois; November 21, 1964.
Released:
July 1965
Chart peaks:
None (UK) None (US)
Personnel:
B.B. King (g, v); other musicians uncredited.
Track listing:
Every Day (I Have The Blues); Sweet Little Angel; It's My Own Fault; How Blue Can You Get; Please Love Me; You Upset Me Baby; Worry, Worry; Woke Up This Mornin'; You Done Lost Your Good Thing Now; Help The Poor
Running time:
34.54
Current CD:
MCD11646
Further listening:
Another live album, Blues Is King (1967), recorded in a Chicago nightclub; King Of The Blues (1992) is a valuable 4-CD compilation.
Further reading:
The Arrival Of B.B. King (Charles Sawyer, 1980), a comprehensive biography; Blues All Around Me: The Autobiography of B.B. King (1996)
Like this?
Try . . . p.575

Bob Dylan

Highway 61 Revisited

Dylan's experiments with rock backings reach full fruition.

Mostly written in Dylan's new 31-room mansion (which he sold within a year, preferring not to write in the same place twice), *Highway 61 Revisited* was the fulfilment of the musical vision he had first developed on the electric side of *Bringing It All Back Home.* Using a studio band based partly on the Butterfield Blues Band musicians who had backed him at his notorious 1965 Newport Folk Festival appearance, the results were streamlined, sardonic, surrealistic, and bulging with raw blues power.

"I can't tell you how disorganised it was," recalled Al Kooper of the sessions. "*Highway 61* has a very raw edge to it, because half the people involved were studio musicians and half weren't, so it's got that rough thing which Dylan loves." Kooper had hustled his way into proceedings by seizing the chance to contribute organ (an instrument he had never played before!) to Like A Rolling Stone, the first track recorded for the new album. Dylan liked the effect, and Kooper became a staple of his studio band, eventually serving as musical director for the following year's *Blonde On Blonde.*

Dylan's new material was a quantum leap beyond the folk and pop clichés of the time, offering new possibilities for the subject matter and vocabulary of both genres, from the damning personal put-downs of Like A Rolling Stone and Ballad Of A Thin Man to the cultural critiques of Tombstone Blues and Desolation Row. In these songs, his former protest style was transmuted into a surreal stream of imagery; the protests were still there, but had become more a matter of implication and inference than direct address, as Dylan responded to the literary influence of French Symbolist poet Arthur Rimbaud and beat novelist William Burroughs.

The record outraged or baffled as many of his old fans as it impressed (the English poet Philip Larkin, for instance, felt that Desolation Row had "an enchanting tune and mysterious, possibly half-baked words"), though Dylan himself – usually his own harshest critic – was in no doubt about what he had achieved. "I'm never gonna be able to make a record better than that one," he said at the time. "[It's] just too good. There's a lot of stuff on there that *I* would listen to!"

Record label:
CBS

Produced
by Tom Wilson and Bob Johnston.

Recorded
at Columbia Studios, New York; June–August 1965.

Released:
August 1965

Chart peaks:
4 (UK) 3 (US)

Personnel:
Bob Dylan (v, g, k, hm); Mike Bloomfield (g); Charlie McCoy (g); Al Kooper (k); Paul Griffin (k); Russ Savakus (b); Harvey Brooks (b); Bobby Gregg (d); Sam Lay (d); Frank Owens (k, pc)

Track listing:
Like A Rolling Stone (S); Tombstone Blues; It Takes A Lot To Laugh, It Takes A Train To Cry; From A Buick 6; Ballad Of A Thin Man; Queen Jane Approximately; Highway 61 Revisited (S); Just Like Tom Thumb's Blues; Desolation Row

Running time:
51.40

Current CD:
4609532

Further listening:
The other core works of Dylan's electric period, Bringing It All Back Home (1965) and Blonde On Blonde (1966), form a triple pinnacle with Highway 61 Revisited.

Further reading:
My Back Pages: Classic Bob Dylan 1962-69 (Andy Gill, 1998); MOJO 60

Like this?
Try . . . p.158

Otis Redding

Otis Blue

The definitive Southern soul album.

It is rare – and usually accidental – for a '60s soul album to sit well as an entity, as a cohesive statement by the singer about his art. But *Otis Blue*, Redding's third album, subtitled Otis Redding Sings Soul is exactly that. His customary *modus operandi* was to arrive at the studio with an album's worth of ideas, often worked out in collaboration with guitarist Steve Cropper, rehearse for a day or two and then cut the tracks fast. For *Otis Blue* he had only three originals. Respect, which he said took a day to write, 20 minutes to arrange and one take to record, the ballad I've Been Loving You Too Long, co-written with Jerry Butler, and Ole Man Trouble, the churning soul-blues driven by Cropper's guitar, which opens the album.

Redding started work on the album in April 1965, three months after the death of his great idol, Sam Cooke, hence the three cover versions (Shake, Wonderful World, A Change Is Gonna Come). Cooke purists demur as to the quality of these covers but they clearly illustrate Otis's ability to grab a song and in the context of the album, make it his alone. He covers the Smokey Robinson-penned Temptations' hit My Girl, William Bell's You Don't Miss Your Water, the Solomon Burke soul-gospel hit Down In The Valley and B. B. King's Rock Me Baby: a catholic trawl. But the most audacious cover version for his core black market was Satisfaction, the Rolling Stones' hit. For years white rock bands had usurped black hits. Here was a rare instance of a black artist turning the tables. Cropper suggested the song while Otis was out of the studio, the MGs and Memphis Horns worked up an arrangement. When Redding heard the song he didn't care for it but tried using "a lot of words different – I made them up."

"There were no planning sessions, we just went in and did it," the Memphis Horns' trumpeter, Wayne Jackson, recalled. "All the really great stuff at Stax was done quick, a big group effort. It would start with bones that somebody brought and the muscle and sinew and flesh and skin would be put on it and the monster would rise and live!" *Otis Blue* took just two days to record.

Record label:
Atlantic
Produced
by Jim Stewart.
Recorded
at Stax Studios, Memphis; April and July 1965.
Released:
September 15, 1965
Chart peaks:
6 (UK) 75 (US)
Personnel:
Booker T. Jones and Isaac Hayes (k); Steve Cropper (g); Donald 'Duck' Dunn (b); Al Jackson Jr (d); Earl Sims (bv); Wayne Jackson, Gene 'Bowlegs' Miller (t); Andrew Love (ts); Tom Dowd (e)
Track listing:
Ole Man Trouble; Respect; A Change Is Gonna Come; Down In The Valley; I've Been Loving You Too Long; Shake; My Girl; Wonderful World; Rock Me Baby; Satisfaction; You Don't Miss Your Water
Running time:
32.54
Current CD:
7567 80318-2
Further listening:
The comprehensive 4CD box sets Otis! The Definitive Otis Redding (1993) or Dock Of The Bay – The Definitive Collection
Further reading:
MOJO 49; Sweet Soul Music (Peter Guralnick, 1998); www.otisredding.com
Like this?
Try . . . p.275

Herb Alpert And The Tijuana Brass

Going Places

Fifth album from MOR kings, six weeks at Number 1.

In the mid-'60s, while the kids were in thrall to the Fabs and their guitar wielding, hair-shaking contemporaries, there was a parallel music market that catered for the less spicy tastes of their parents. Unassailably dominant in that market was the phenomenally successful Herb Alpert and his Tijuana Brass.

Twenty-five-year-old Los Angeles ex-actor and trumpeter, Alpert had been keen to find a distinctive sound on his instrument and in 1962, fooling around on a tape recorder in his garage with a tune written by friend Sol Lake called Twinkle Star, he noticed that the melody worked well played in Mexican-style thirds – the Mariachi sound of the Tijuana bullfights Alpert occasionally frequented.

"I liked the Mariachi sound," said Alpert, "but it hadn't progressed much over the years and it seemed to me you could add an undercurrent of American sound, updating the bass-line and the guitars and timpani."

Forming a label with partner Jerry Moss – changing the title of Lake's tune to The Lonely Bull and naming the studio-creation (which soon became a real band) The Tijuana Brass – the ensuing single and album began a wave of popularity that saw The Tijuana Brass at their peak outselling the Beatles 2-to-1 and making A&M Records the most successful artist-owned label of all time.

Going Places was the fifth Tijuana Brass best-seller and typifies their exuberant, cheeky charm. Alpert's customised 'Ameriachi' style was by now so focused that the apparently incongruous, daringly juxtaposed material (Zorba The Greek, I'm Getting Sentimental Over You and The Third Man Theme on one album!) is vividly adapted, with the listener seduced into barely caring how these tunes originally sounded.

"It's a wild, happy sound, like the Mariachis," Alpert said, attempting to explain The Tijuana Brass's appeal. "It's good-natured and full of humour. It's not a protest and not a put-down. I think people were bugged with hearing music which had an undercurrent of unhappiness and anger, even sadism. But our music you can get with in a hurry, tap your feet and hum along." As The Tijuana Brass's popularity faded, Alpert, never a jazz player, continued making records in contemporary pop styles and on the back of A&M's success with The Carpenters, The Police and others, sold the label in 1990 to Polygram for $500 million.

Record Label:
A&M

Produced
by Jerry Moss.

Recorded
at Goldstar Studios, LA; 1965

Released:
September 1965

Chart peaks:
5 (UK) 1 (US)

Personnel:
Herb Alpert (t); Tonni Kalash (t); Julius Wechter (marimba/vibes); Bob Edmondson (tb); Pat Senatore (b); John Pisano (electric 12-string guitar); Lou Pagani (p); Nick Ceroli (d); Larry Levine (e)

Track Listing:
Tijuana Taxi; I'm Getting Sentimental Over You; More And More Amor; Spanish Flea; Mae; 3rd Man Theme; Walk, Don't Run; Felicia; And The Angels Sing; Cinco De Mayo; A Walk In The Black Forest; Zorba The Greek

Running time:
29.27

Current CD:
IMPT6402

Further listening:
The Lonely Bull (1963); Whipped Cream And Other Delights (1965)

Further reading:
www.tijuanabrass.com/

Like this?
Try . . . p.274

Vernon Haddocks

Vernon Haddock's Jubilee Lovelies

The most obscure album ever made.

Among the many obscure acts that recorded for major labels in the 1960s, perhaps the most extreme example was the memorably named Vernon Haddock's Jubilee Lovelies, who made one very peculiar album in 1965 before vanishing for good.

In 1965 Peter Eden and Geoff Stephens were hot property after discovering Donovan. Eager to produce as well as manage, they easily landed a four album deal with EMI. The first fruits, 'Songs For Swingin' Survivors' by Mick Softley and a folk album by Bob Davenport and the Rakes, both flopped. Unfazed, Eden and Stephens turned their attention homewards to Southend, where a group of their friends from school and art college were gigging as 'Vernon Haddock's Jubilee Lovelies'.

I'd always liked the word 'Lovelies'. Then I saw the word 'Jubilee' on a row of cottages and put them together', says their leader David Elvin of their bizarre moniker. 'Vernon was in the band. His name sounded good, so we added it - it's pure nonsense.'

Keen to capture their good-natured, inclusive atmosphere on record, Eden was glad to offer his friends a deal. 'I liked what they were doing' he says. 'They were having fun - the opposite of earnest folk.' And so it was that one summer's evening in 1965 the Lovelies made their way to London to make an album. 'We started at 5 and were done by midnight', says Elvin. The result is a charming, skilfully-played and very eccentric folk record, reflecting both their earlier influences and contemporary acts like Jim Kweskin's Jug Band, and the Bonzo Dog Doo/Dah Band.

Mainly comprising vigorous interpretations of standards like 'Coney Island Washboard', 'Viola Lee Blues' and 'Stealin'', the only original is 'Vickyandal', a belated tribute to Queen Victoria and Prince Albert. The percussion throughout is deft, and added atmosphere comes courtesy of a swanee whistle, surprisingly similar in sound to a theremin. Released in the autumn in an eye-catching red and blue sleeve, the album sold, um, 400 copies, all at gigs.

But Eden and Stephens had another album to make before fulfilling their obligation to EMI. When the well-regarded young guitarist Eric Clapton left the Yardbirds to pursue the blues more seriously, Eden immediately got in touch. Clapton readily agreed to make a solo acoustic recording, only to renege a few days later after joining John Mayall's Bluesbreakers. Frustratingly, the album was never made and the final quarter of Eden-Stephens's production contract remains unfulfilled. As for the Lovelies, all that remains today is a handful of extremely rare records and the members' fond memories.

RMJ

Record label
Columbia
Produced
Peter Eden / Geoff Stephens
Recorded
Summer 1965
Released:
Autumn 1965
Chart Peaks:
None (UK) None (US)
Personnel:
David Elvin (g, v, banjo, kazoo) / Vernon Haddock (mandolin, swanee whistle, jug) / Alan Woodward (g) / Alan 'Little Bear' Sutton (pc, washboard) / David Vaughn (hm, bv) / Sid 'Piles' Lockhart (v, 12 string guitar).
Track listing:
Coney Island Washboard / Don't Let Your Deal Go Down / Clementine / Coloured Aristocracy / Mandy, Make Up Your Mind / Boodle-Am Shake / Viola Lee Blues / Vickyandal / Stealin' / Little Whitewashed Chimney / I Wish I Could Shimmy Like My Sister Kate.
Not currently available on CD.
Further reading:
www.borderlinebooks.com/uk6070s/h1.html
Like this?
Try . . . p.191

Sun Ra

The Magic City

Pioneering big-band free jazz.

Following an apprenticeship as pianist and arranger for Fletcher Henderson's big band in the '40s, Sun Ra (*né* Herman Poole Blount) founded and led various line-ups of his own improvising big-band, Arkestra, until his death in May 1993, releasing literally hundreds of albums – mostly small editions in plain white (or hand-illustrated) covers on his own Saturn imprint – whose music ranged from manic swing and hard-bop outings to other-worldly solo synthesiser extravaganzas and bouts of collective improvisation.

Named after the promotional slogan of Ra's hometown Birmingham, Alabama, the 27-minute title-track of *The Magic City* is in the latter style, a breakthrough work contemporaneous with similar avant-garde explorations like Ornette Coleman's *Free Jazz* and John Coltrane's *Ascension*, but more fluid and obviously of a piece, the result of countless hours of development and rehearsal that enabled the Arkestra's musicians to play in each other's pockets even when they were navigating the most abstract sonic territory.

As producer Alton Abraham understood it, *The Magic City* was a city of fantasy, "a city without evil, a city of possibilities and beauty", whilst in a poem of the same title, Ra himself described it as "that city of all natural creation ... the magic of the Magi's thought".

The early parts find the mad-scientist whine of Ra's clavioline in cosmic dalliance with sprays of flute and piccolo over a bed of mournful bowed-bass, before bursting into volcanic new life as the horns take over, battling above the undergrowth of high-register wind parts. Also notable is the tape-delay effect (discovered by accident a few years earlier by Ra's recording engineer Thomas 'Bugs' Hunter, much to his boss's delight) that imposes its own semblance of order on one of the percussion parts.

The three pieces that make up the album's second side are further developments of the drum-choir style of his earlier *Nubians Of Plutonia*, with saxes trailing serpentine unison lines over complex polyrhythms of marimba, bongoes and tympani. Reissued several times by Ra's cottage industry through the late '60s, *The Magic City* eventually received its due acclaim when it formed part of an ambitious project which saw ABC/Impulse Records reissue ten Sun Ra albums in the early '70s.

Record label:
Saturn
Produced
by Alton Abraham.
Recorded
live at Olatunji's Loft, New York City; April 1965.
Release date:
1965
Chart peaks:
None (UK) None (US)
Personnel:
Sun Ra (clavioline, p, bass marimba, tympani, electronic celeste, Sun Harp, dragon drum); John Gilmore (ts); Pat Patrick (bs, flute, tympani); Marshall Allen (as, flute, oboe, piccolo); Ronnie Boykins (b); Danny Davis (as, flute); Robert Cummings (bass clarinet); Harry Spencer (as); Walter Miller (t); Chris Capers (t); Teddy Nance (tb); Ali Hassan (tb); Jimmi Johnson (pc); Roger Blank (pc)
Track listing:
The Magic City; The Shadow World; Absract Eye; Abstract "I".
Running time:
45.10
Current CD:
Evidence ECD 22069-2
Further listening:
Other Planes Of There (1964), The Heliocentric Worlds Of Sun Ra, Vols 1 & 2 (1966, 1967)
Further reading:
Space Is The Place: The Life And Times Of Sun Ra (John F. Szwed, 1997)
www.dpo.uab.edu/~moudry/
Like this?
Try . . . p.189

The Mamas And The Papas

If You Can Believe Your Eyes And Your Ears

The group who were the epitome of hippy become a commercial sensation musically, visually and commercially.

In his book Papa John, John Phillips described how he, Cass, Denny and Michelle auditioned for producer Lou Adler at Western Recording Studios in Hollywood while singing back-up vocals for Barry McGuire's This Precious Time. McGuire was an old pal from the group's Greenwich Village folk beginnings who was enjoying huge success with the protest pop of Eve Of Destruction. This was the summer of 1965 and the group was still using the name The New Journeymen. They sang California Dreamin' and Monday Monday for Adler, and he reputedly raved: "Wow, I can't believe my eyes and ears."

Within a month they were signed, had become The Mamas And The Papas and were back recording in the same studio. They looked and sounded like nothing else before or since. Along with The Byrds and The Lovin' Spoonful, also former folkies, The Mamas And The Papas were among the first American groups to present a challenge to the English Invasion: a year later, the whole California revival came along. By January 1966, California Dreamin' was all over the airwaves, anticipating the Summer of Love; Phillips also wrote that other Flower Power anthem, Scott McKenzie's San Francisco.

The Mamas And The Papas were the first public manifestation of hippiedom: their physical appearance, their flamboyant dress sense, and their moral stance anticipated the climate; outlandish rich kids living in Bel Air. All four of their albums are as strong as their debut, and each one maintained the high standard of John Phillips' songwriting. Cass usually pulled a favourite cover version out of her repertoire (Dedicated To The One I Love is, perhaps, the best known), but the crowning glory was the finest production that Los Angeles could offer, a clear and warm sound played by the same team of top flight session men on each record.

That The Mamas And The Papas' story ended in turmoil, strife, and eventually the death of Cass Elliot, after the group split in 1968 was almost inevitable given the love/hate tensions between them and an extraordinary drug intake. As is often the way, the sweetest music sprang from the darkest circumstances.

Record label:
RCA
Produced
by Lou Adler.
Recorded
at Western Recording Studios, Hollywood; late summer–autumn 1965.
Released:
January 1966
Chart peaks:
3 (UK) 1 (US)
Personnel:
John Phillips (v, g); Denny Doherty (v); Cass Elliot (v); Michelle Phillips (v)
Track listing:
Monday Monday (S); Straight Shooter; Got A Feelin'; I Call Your Name; Do You Wanna Dance; Go Where You Wanna Go (S); California Dreamin' (S); Spanish Harlem; Somebody Groovy; Hey Girl; You Baby; In Crowd
Running time:
34.58
Current CD:
MCAD-11739
Further listening:
Creeque Alley – The History Of The Mamas And The Papas (1991)
Further reading:
Papa John (John Phillips with Jim Jerome, 1987); www.mamasandpapas.com/
Like this?
Try . . . p.545

The Monks

Black Monk Time

Five GIs dressed as monks make garage rock in Germany. Strangely obscurity ensues.

Intentional squalling feedback rattles the control room windows as Polydor's genial producer struggles to protect Deutsche Gramophon's delicate equipment from the uber-beat onslaught of the Monks. The Velvet Underground will be bending VU needles in a couple of years time, egos bolstered by their art-world credentials. But now, in 1965, The Monks and their nihilist German mentors are forcing the issue in the rarefied atmosphere of the recording studio.

A year or so before, The Monks were a group of ex-GIs called The 5 Torquays, playing to Hamburg teens and US airbase personnel, until an alchemical reaction of boredom, experiment, and a pair of loopy existential visionaries called Walther and Karl brought about their miraculous transformation. Lovin' Spoonful bowlcuts and cuban heels give way to shaved tonsures, black shirts, and a bleakly realistic outlook. This was some of the hardest, most minimal and monochromatic rock'n'roll ever heard. Nobody in 1965 sang ferocious songs called things like I Hate You or Shut Up, stripped down to their fuzzed-up, screaming, percussive bones. Nowadays a lot of people do.

As bassist Eddie Shaw observes; "The Beastie Boys and Jello Biafra have said that our music had an effect on them. I really believe that music was evolving in this direction and we just stumbled across it early."

The album was never released by Polydor in the US; "They insisted we tone our music down ... or lose our contract" and The Monks disintegrated in a bitter flurry of impotent anger and disappointment. In retrospect, the album's unique appeal lies in the collision of naivety, rawness, and the utter pre-punk impossibility of its existence. Even its completely black cover-design, looking more Joy Division than Yellow Submarine, sounded a jarring note at the very dawn of flower-pop. They performed live shows with The Kinks, The Troggs and The Creation, but even these hardened outfits rarely got close to their live sound in the studio. Monk music – primal proto-punk, demented nursery rhymes – is all pounding drums, fuzztone bass, clattering electric banjo, gothic organ and histrionic vocals. As Shaw maintains, "Walther and Karl believed in having our music recorded as we played it. Studios, at that time, were not equipped to record our kind of music." They wouldn't be for some years to come.

Record label:
Polydor
Produced
by Jimmy Bowien.
Recorded
Polydor Studios, Koln, Germany; November 1965.
Released:
March 1966
Chart peaks:
None (UK) None (US)
Personnel:
Gary Burger (g, v); Larry Clark (o); Dave Day (banjo); Roger Johnston (d); Eddie Shaw (b)
Track listing:
Monk Time; Shut Up; Boys Are Boys And Girls Are Choice; Higgle-Dy Piggle-Dy; I Hate You; Oh, How To Do Now; Complication; We Do Wie Du; Drunken Maria; Love Came Tumblin' Down; Blast Off!; That's My Girl
Running time:
29.46
Currently unavailable on CD
Further listening:
Five Upstart Americans (1999) – sessions recorded before the album
Further reading:
Black Monk Time (Thomas Edward Shaw and Anita Klemke, 1994); www.the-monks.com
Like this?
Try . . . p.454

The Rolling Stones

Aftermath

The Stones take a quantum leap beyond recycled R&B.

Until *Aftermath*, the Stones were still largely thought of as Brit-blues recyclers of US R&B modes, although Jagger & Richards had already started to flex their compositional muscles with successes like Satisfaction and 19th Nervous Breakdown, the single which preceded the album's release. Featuring 14 of their own songs, *Aftermath* was recorded towards the end of a gruelling American tour, much of the material refelcting the band's frayed temperament in general and Mick Jagger's growing hostility towards girlfriend Chrissie Shrimpton in particular. Tracks such as Under My Thumb, Stupid Girl and Out Of Time revealed a deep vein of misogyny that dogged the Stones' reputation for years, while the contemptuous tone of Mother's Little Helper suggested an attitude towards drugs that was at best ambivalent – OK if you were a rich rock star, but cause for scorn if you were a hapless housewife.

"It was all a spin-off from our environment," Keith Richards explained later. "Hotels and too many dumb chicks. Not all dumb, by any means, but that's how one got. You got really cut off."

There was widespread speculation, meanwhile, regarding the inspiration for the song Lady Jane: their record label claimed it was about Henry VIII's wife Jane Seymour, and Jagger apparently allowed both Shrimpton and toff totty Lady Jane Ormsby-Gore to believe it was about them. It turned out to be derived from Lady Chatterley's Lover, being the gamekeeper's term for his mistress's vagina. Though manager Andrew Loog Oldham took the producer's credit, the album was effectively recorded by Richards with the group's American engineer Dave Hassinger. His job was not made any easier by Brian Jones' unreliability, which left Keith having to play most of the guitar parts by himself. Despite his growing drug and personality problems, however, Jones' contributions were crucial to the album's success. The band's most accomplished musician, he had begun seeking out new and unusual instruments to add to their sound: sitar on Mother's Little Helper, and marimba on Under My Thumb and Out Of Time, while Lady Jane and Waiting featured the sound of a dulcimer that had been given to him by the folk singer Richard Farina.

"Brian would be down on his back, lying around the studio with his guitar strapped around him," Richards told biographer Victor Bockris. "Then suddenly, from nine hours of lying there, he'd just walk in and lay some beautiful things down on a track (piano, harpsichord), something that nobody'd even thought of." Released as *Aftermath* after their record company rejected the "blasphemous" original title *Could You Walk On The Water?*, the LP quickly topped the album chart in Britain.

Record Label:
Decca
Produced
by Andrew Loog Oldham.
Recorded
at RCA Studios, Hollywood; December 1965.
Released:
April 1966
Chart peaks:
1 (UK) 2 (US)
Personnel:
Mick Jagger (v, p); Keith Richards (g, v); Brian Jones (g, k, sitar, dulcimer, marimba); Bill Wyman (b, pc); Charlie Watts (d, pc); Ian Stewart (p); Jack Nitzsche (k, pc); Dave Hassinger (e)
Track Listing:
Mother's Little Helper (S/US); Stupid Girl; Lady Jane; Under My Thumb; Doncha Bother Me; Goin' Home; Flight 505; High And Dry; Out Of Time; It's Not Easy; I Am Waiting; Take It Or Leave It; Think; What To Do
Running time:
52.48
Current CD:
8444662 adds Paint It Black (S)
Further listening:
The next two studio albums, Between The Buttons (1967) and Their Satanic Majesties Request (1967), failed to deliver on the promise of Aftermath, as the Stones paddled up a psychedelic backwater before regaining their bearings with Beggar's Banquet (1968).
Further reading:
The Stones (Philip Norman, 1984); Keith Richards – The Biography (Victor Bockris, 1992).
Like this?
Try . . . p.90

The Beach Boys

Pet Sounds

In 1995, MOJO contributors voted it the 'Greatest Album Of All Time'.

Tony Asher thought it was a joke when someone at his ad agency told him Brian Wilson was on the phone, one day late in 1965. He'd played some songs for Wilson several months earlier, but since then had dumped songwriting for a more profitable gig as a copywriter. But Wilson couldn't have been more serious. He'd just heard The Beatles' *Rubber Soul* and decided he wanted to make a meaningful album of his own – without the aid of The Beach Boys' resident sun-and-fun lyricist Mike Love, who was on tour with the rest of the Boys.

Recent exposure to heavy doses of LSD-25 had also boosted Wilson's interest in mind-expanding music that would affect people on a deeper level. Wilson remembered Asher and felt that he was a writer who could give a voice to his musical introspection. He couldn't have been more right.

"It's fair to say that the general tenor of the lyrics was always his and the actual choice of words usually mine," Tony Asher told Nick Kent. "Brian was constantly looking for topics that kids could relate to. Even though he was dealing with the most advanced arrangements, he was incredibly conscious of this commercial thing, this absolute need to relate."

As the fluffiest of all Beach Boys' hits, Barbara Ann, was topping the British and American charts, Brian began tinkering with a song called Good, Good Vibrations and another called God Only Knows. When Mike 'Don't Fuck With The Formula' Love returned from Japan to lay down his vocal tracks, he pronounced it "Brian's ego music". It's true that I Know There's An Answer was originally called Hang On To Your Ego (until Love insisted the lyrics be changed, and Brian's chauffeur Terry Sachen obliged) but what Love hated most about *Pet Sounds* was its LSD influence. He later asserted that "some of the words were so totally offensive to me that I wouldn't even sing 'em". Actually, Brian didn't need many of Love's vocals, because he could do all the parts himself. When Brian wasn't singing, he was arranging the orchestra creating dense, lush arrangements that owed at least as much to Nelson Riddle as they did to Jack Nitzsche.

With the notable exception of Sloop John B (a hit single that Capitol stuck on the album against Wilson's wishes), every song on *Pet Sounds* evinced a spiritual tenderness that opened new doors in rock. "I thought of it as chapel rock," Wilson later explained, "commercial choir music. I wanted to make an album that would stand up in ten years," Brian Wilson said.

Make that thirty-seven and counting.

Record label:
Capitol
Produced
by Brian Wilson.
Recorded
at Western, Sunset Sound, and Gold Star Studios, Los Angeles; July 1965 and November 1965–April 1966.
Released:
May 1966
Chart peaks:
2 (UK) 10 (US)
Personnel:
Brian Wilson (v); Carl Wilson (v); Mike Love (v); Bruce Johnston (v); Al Jardine (v); Dennis Wilson (v); Carol Kaye (b); Hal Blaine (d); Terry Melcher (v); Banana and Louie (dogbarking); Chuck Britz, Larry Levine, Ralph Balantin (e)
Track listing:
Wouldn't It Be Nice; You Still Believe In Me; That's Not Me; Don't Talk (Put Your Head On My Shoulder); I'm Waiting For The Day; Let's Go Away For A While; Sloop John B (S); God Only Knows (S); I Know There's An Answer; Here Today; I Just Wasn't Made For These Times; Pet Sounds; Caroline, No (S)
Running time:
36:24
Current CD:
5212412 adds: Hang On To Your Ego and features the album in both mono and stereo mixes.
Further listening:
Good Vibrations: 30 Years Of The Beach Boys (1993); 4CD box set Pet Sounds Sessions: Remastered (1997)
Further reading:
The Nearest Faraway Place (Timothy White, 1991)
Like this?
Try . . . p.314

John Mayall's Blues Breakers

Blues Breakers with Eric Clapton

The commercial breakthrough of British blues.

"I was arrogant, and I had an accelerator going," says Eric Clapton, explaining his dizzying ascent to star status in 1966. Eric Clapton quit The Yardbirds in March 1965; within a month, Mayall had sacked his guitarist Roger Dean, and persuaded Clapton to join up. Clapton describes Mayall as "a real father figure. I grew a hell of a lot in a short period of time with his help."

Mayall and producer Mike Vernon played Eric the latest records by Freddie King, Otis Rush and other Chicago greats. As well as copping their riffs, Clapton aimed for a similar density of sound. Seeing Freddie King photographed with a Gibson Les Paul, Clapton bought a second-hand Les Paul Sunburst and combined it with a newly-designed Marshall amp, to achieve a radically new sound; distorted, creamy and sustained: "I wanted some kind of thickness that would be a compilation of all the guitarists I'd heard, plus the sustain of a slide guitar," he remembers.

A June 1965 single, I'm Your Witchdoctor, demonstrated the band's raw power and helped Vernon persuade Decca to re-sign them. When they entered Decca's Studio 2 the following April they were all at their peak.

The songs included covers of Mose Allison, Little Walter, Ray Charles, some Mayall originals, and Robert Johnson's Rambling On My Mind – Clapton's vocal debut. "He was a little reticent about singing it," remembers Mayall, "but I had no doubts whatsoever."

There was one hurdle to clear. To achieve his sound, Clapton had to drive his Marshall amp to unprecedented volume levels. Freelance engineer (and future Elton John producer) Gus Dudgeon was staggered by his insistence on positioning the microphone – and refusing to turn down. Vernon let Clapton have his way. Mayall credits this as crucial: "Mike had the foresight not to mess with something that was happening live, to just get it down on tape, keeping all the spontaneity and feel."

Before the album ended its 17-week stay in the British charts, Eric Clapton had already left to form Cream. Mayall had the ideal replacement lined up in the shape of Peter Green. Neither party would ever look back.

Record label:
Decca
Produced
by Mike Vernon.
Recorded
at Decca Studio 2, London, April 1966.
Released:
July 1966
Chart peaks:
6 (UK) None (US)
Personnel:
John Mayall (v, g, hm); Eric Clapton (g, v); John McVie (b); Huey Flint (d); Gus Dudgeon (e)
Track listing:
All Your Love (S); Hideaway; Little Girl; Another Man; Double Crossing Time; What'd I Say; Key To Love; Parchman Farm (S); Have You Heard; Rambling On My Mind; Steppin' Out; It Ain't Right
Running time:
37.32
Current CD:
844827-2
Further listening:
A Hard Road (1967), with Peter Green shows band flourishing post-Clapton; Cream's Wheels Of Fire (1968) is Eric at his acid blues best.
Further reading:
MOJO 53; www.johnmayall.net
Like this?
Try . . . p.426

The Beatles

Revolver

The next great leap forwards for the Fab Four.

The progression from the zesty "yeah, yeah, yeah" of 'She Loves You to the mesmeric, acid-spiked Tomorrow Never Knows took four Liverpool kids just 33 months. Drugs, Eastern mysticism and fraternisation with their freakier peers (Dylan, Stones, Byrds, Brian Wilson) have traditionally been seen as the reason; yet one shouldn't underestimate the disorientating effects of a pop megastardom without precedent and the heady blend of fear and creative power that comes with it. *Rubber Soul* had been reasonably straightforward but, suddenly, instead of bashing down tightly-written songs within a few takes, The Beatles fancied new working methods. For the first session of their 1966 album, they oversaw a mad evening where engineers wrestled with six mono tape machines simultaneously running unwieldy loops of sound effects. Thus Lennon's 'recite the Tibetan Book Of The Dead on LSD' opus, The Void, took shape.

This was 20-year-old, newly promoted engineer Geoff Emerick's first session with The Beatles. "The group encouraged us to break the rules," he recalls. "[They told me] that every instrument should sound unlike itself: a piano shouldn't sound like a piano, a guitar shouldn't sound like a guitar, hence putting things through a Leslie speaker, and so on. When we were doing the horns on Got To Get You Into My Life we tried putting the mikes right into the bells of the trombones – treating mikes like camera lenses, in a way – and that hadn't been done before. I started moving the mike closer to the bass drum too. I was reprimanded for that, because, according to the technical staff [at Abbey Road], the air pressure from the drum would destroy the mikes! I got a special letter saying I could do it, but only on Beatles sessions."

John encouraged radical treatments on his voice. Paul experimented with his new Brennel tape recorder, George began mastering the sitar (and was awarded his first opening album cut with the punchy Taxman) and, on Tomorrow Never Knows (as The Void was renamed), Ringo's kit was split between two channels and fed into a limiter to achieve the famous 'backward' rush that propels the track. Every song came complete with some curious sonic innovation.

"I know for a fact that, from the day *Revolver* came out, it changed the way everyone else made records," says Emerick.

"It was a good point for us," agrees Paul McCartney. "It depends what you want from an album, but if you really look at it bluntly, most people just want good songs. There's a lot of good songs on *Revolver*. In fact, they're all good."

Record label:
Parlophone
Produced
by George Martin.
Recorded
at EMI Studios, Abbey Road, London;
April 6–June 21, 1966.
Released:
August 5, 1966 (UK); August 8, 1966 (US)
Chart peaks:
1 (UK) 1 (US)
Personnel:
John Lennon (rg, o, v); Paul McCartney (b, ag, v); George Harrison (g, v); Ringo Starr (d, v); Geoff Emerick (e); John Gilbert, Sidney Sax, John Sharpe, Jurgen Hesse (vn on Eleanor Rigby); Stephen Shingles, John Underwood (va); Derek Simpson, Norman Jones (c); Amil Bhagwa (tabla on Love You To); Anyana Deva Angadi (sitar); Eddie Thornton, Ian Hamer, Les Condon (t on Got To Get You Into My Life); Alan Branscombe, Peter Coe (ts); Brian Jones, Marianne Faithfull, Patti Harrison, Mal Evans, Neil Aspinall, Terry Condon, John Skinner (v on Yellow Submarine)
Track listing:
Taxman; Eleanor Rigby (S); I'm Only Sleeping; Love You To; Here, There And Everywhere; Yellow Submarine (S); She Said She Said; Good Day Sunshine; And Your Bird Can Sing; For No One; Dr Robert; I Want To Tell You; Got To Get You Into My Life; Tomorrow Never Knows
Running time:
34.59
Current CD:
CDP 7 46441 2
Further reading:
Revolution In The Head (Ian McDonald, 1995)
Like this?
Try . . . p.550

The Association

And Then ... Along Comes

Classy, harmony pop, and one of the most-played songs of all time.

If ever a group were sabotaged by their image, it was surely The Association. For on the sleeve of their classic 1966 debut, the sextet are pictured shamelessly togged out in matching three-piece suits, shirts and ties and proudly polished leather shoes. Naturally, all self-respecting rock fans dismissed them – a colossal shame, for the album is a delightful lite-psychedelic gem by one of rock's great harmony bands, produced with dazzling wit and flair by Curt Boettcher, with finger cymbals, electronic sound effects and crazily inspired harmonies that dart insanely in and around the lead vocals.

Boettcher, who died in 1987, did not remember the band fondly. "They were never able to handle their own success," he told Zigzag. "It really changed them as people." Despite the gushing sleeve notes improbably claiming that Terry Kirkman played 23 instruments, Boettcher also revealed that the music on the album was played by sessionmen. This fact isn't disputed, with Bluechel admitting to Goldmine that "all those tracks were recorded by studio musicians". Kirkman adds: "We had the same guys who played for The Beach Boys", although Alexander does assert that he played on all the sessions.

The album's most famous track is Along Comes Mary, credited to Tandyn Almer, although Boettcher always maintained he co-wrote the song. The song was rumoured to refer to marijuana, although the lyrics are impenetrable. Eight of the album's 12 songs were written by band members, the best of which is Kirkman's Cherish: one of the era's most beautiful love songs and an American Number 1 single, displaying the complex and striking multi-part harmonies typical of the band. Unfortunately, its success marked the end of their relationship with Boettcher.

"They informed me during the fourth week of Cherish being at the top that they no longer required my services and were going to produce themselves," recalled Boettcher bitterly. It was a catastrophic miscalculation by the band, who never sounded so enchanting again.

At the last count, Cherish had been played on US radio over four million times.

Record label:
Warner Brothers
Produced
by Curt Boettcher.
Recorded
at GSP Studios (aka Gary Paxton's garage) and Columbia Studios, Hollywood; June 1966.
Released:
August 1966
Chart peaks:
None (UK) 5 (US)
Personnel:
Gary Alexander (v, g); Terry Kirkman (v, woodwind, reeds); Russ Giguere (v, g, pc); Brian Cole (v, b); Ted Bluechel (v, d); Jim Yester (v, g, k); Gary Paxton (e); Pete Romano (e). The above musicians were mainly replaced by sessionmen including Mike Deasy (g); Ben Benay (g); Hal Blaine (d)
Track listing:
Enter The Young; Your Own Love; Don't Blame It On Me; Blistered; I'll Be Your Man; Along Comes Mary (S); Cherish (S); Standing Still; Message Of Our Love; Round Again; Remember; Changes
Running time:
31.24
Current CD:
WPCR-10074
Further listening:
Third album, Insight Out (1967), contains the classics Never My Love and Windy; Waterbeds In Trinidad! (1972), is outstanding.
Further reading:
http://theassociation.hyper-mart.net/
Like this?
Try . . . p.464

David Blue

David Blue

Unexpectedly caustic debut from former Dylan affiliate.

Hanging around with Bob Dylan in the early '60s can't have done much for your confidence. Aspiring folkie David S Cohen (later Blue) was part of the Bob in-crowd that included Eric Anderson, Dave Van Ronk, Phil Ochs and Tom Paxton. According to Anthony Scaduto's book Bob Dylan, he even strummed the chords while Bob pencilled in the lyrics for Blowin' In The Wind.

While Bob rallied the masses, Paxton and Ochs signed to Elektra and by 1965 Jac Holzman's label also had designs on a whole host of other regulars from the Greenwich Village scene. As David S Cohen, Blue's first recordings appeared on The Singer-Songwriter Project alongside tracks by Richard Farina, Patrick Sky and Bruce Murdoch and, within a year he was in the studio recording this self-titled album. It should have all been so easy. But it wasn't. For whatever reason, David Blue left David S Cohen's folky innocence in the closet. Instead, his debut became a strange mutation of influences – musical, social and otherwise. Dylan's *Highway 61 Revisited* had changed all the rules about electricity, while Love had just signed to Elektra and their first two albums bookended Blue's, changing the expectations of the label as the scene matured. Blue took up the challenge but to no avail.

Released alongside Tim Buckley's self-titled debut, this terrific album went on the missing list. At the time its phased guitars, swirling organ, quasi-classical motifs and jazz-paced breaks were part and parcel of a music scene that was encouraging experiment. But lyrically, Blue added yet another dimension, presenting a grubby insight into Village life. Indeed, the album rolls around the floors of bedsit Greenwich examining its inhabitants, like a Super-8 movie shot against a sub-psychedelic backdrop. Its failure signalled Blue's departure from the label and his slow decline into moody, morbid introversion. Certainly there's a sense of foreboding amid the cool and smoky jazz inflections. You kind of know it's all going to end in tears.

Record label:
Elektra
Produced
by Arthur Gorson
Recorded:
New York, 1966
Releases:
August 1966
Chart peaks:
None (UK) None (US)
Personnel:
Paul Harris (p, o, celeste); Harvey Brooks (b); David Blue (v, g); Monte Young (g); Herbert Lovelle; Buddy Salzman (d)
Track listing:
The Gasman Won't Buy Your Love; About My Love; So Easy She Goes By; If Your Monkey Can't Get It; Midnight Through The Morning; It Ain't The Rain That Sweeps The Highway Clean; Arcade Love Machine; Grand Hotel; Justine; I'd Like To Know; The Street; It Tastes Like Candy.
Running time:
41:57
Currently unavailable on CD
Further listening:
From his eponymous debut, David Blue became bleaker and more circumspect. The eventual follow-up These 23 Days In September (1968) is well worth locating as is Stories (1972) and Nice Baby And The Angel (1973), none of which are available on CD.
Further reading:
Follow The Music (Jac Holzman and Gavan Dawes, 1997); Bob Dylan (Anthony Scaduto, 1998)
Like this?
Try . . . p.478

Bob Dylan

Blonde On Blonde

Translucent poetic imagery and steaming Chicago blues – the single most convincing case for Dylan's genius.

Following some largely unsuccessful sessions in New York (from which only One Of Us Must Know, featuring Band members Rick Danko and Richard Manuel, eventually made the album), Dylan took producer Bob Johnston's advice and recorded the rest of *Blonde On Blonde* in Nashville, taking along only guitarist Robbie Robertson and organist Al Kooper to augment a crew of Tennessee's top session players. Used to recording three tracks in a typical three-hour session, the Nashville cats were surprised to find themselves left to their own devices for hours on end while Dylan finished writing the songs, whereupon Al Kooper – serving as musical director – would translate his ideas for the band.

"We would come in an hour late," explains Kooper, "and I would go in and teach the first song to the band. Then he [Dylan] would arrive, and the band would be ready to play." Compared to the more abrasive manner of New York players, the Nashville crew took everything in their stride as Dylan searched for what he called "that thin, wild, mercury sound", a more refined blend of the guitars/piano/organ/bass/drums/ harmonica set-up that had proved so effective on *Highway 61 Revisited*.

"Nobody bitched or complained or rolled their eyes," recalls Kooper. "Their temperaments were fabulous – they were the most calm, at-ease guys I'd ever worked with." They weren't even fazed when Dylan requested a marching band to play on Rainy Day Women #12 & 35, assuring him that if he was after a more ramshackle sound, they could "play pretty dumb if we put our minds to it". With a local friend, Wayne Butler, drafted in to play trombone, and Charlie McCoy playing bass and trumpet simultaneously, the track was cut in 20 minutes – so quickly that Robbie Robertson, who had nipped out to buy cigarettes, missed the session completely.

The album's string of love songs was generally found to be less esoteric than the texts of *Highway 61 Revisited*, though the dense, allusive imagery of Visions Of Johanna and Stuck Inside Of Mobile With The Memphis Blues Again, in particular, exercised the explicatory facilities of fans as much as anything in Dylan's oeuvre. At the time he considered the album's third epic, Sad Eyed Lady Of The Lowlands – amazingly, cut in one perfect 11-minute take – "the best song I've ever written".

"It's an amazing record, like taking two cultures and smashing them together with a huge explosion," reckons Al Kooper. "Dylan was the quintessential New York hipster – what was *he* doing in Nashville? But you take those two elements, pour them into a test-tube, and it just exploded."

Record label:
CBS
Produced
by Bob Johnston.
Recorded
at Columbia Studios, New York; January 1966; Columbia Music Row Studios, Nashville, Tennessee; February–March 1966.
Released:
August 1966
Chart peaks:
3 (UK) 9 (US)
Personnel:
Bob Dylan (v, g, k, hm); Robbie Robertson (g); Wayne Moss (g); Jerry Kennedy (g); Charlie McCoy (g, hm, t); Al Kooper (k); Hargus 'Pig' Robbins (k); Richard Manuel (k); Joe South (b); Henry Strzelecki (b); Rick Danko (b); Kenny Buttrey (d); Bobby Gregg (d); Wayne Butler (tb)
Track listing:
Rainy Day Women #12 & 35 (S); Pledging My Time; Visions Of Johanna; One Of Us Must Know (Sooner Or Later) (S); I Want You (S); Stuck Inside Of Mobile With The Memphis Blues Again; Leopard-Skin Pill-Box Hat (S); Just Like A Woman (S); Most Likely You Go Your Way (And I'll Go Mine); Temporary Like Achilles; Absolutely Sweet Marie; 4th Time Around; Obviously Five Believers; Sad Eyed Lady Of The Lowlands
Running time:
72.30
Current CD:
CD22130
Further listening:
Highway 61 Revisited (1965).
Further reading:
My Back Pages (1998)
Like this?
Try . . . p.714

The Byrds

Fifth Dimension

Splicing Dylan, jazz and quantum physics. And why not.

The Byrds faced some formidable obstacles during the recording of their third album. Their recent groundbreaking single Eight Miles High had been banned because of alleged drugs references in the title and, worse still, its composer, Gene Clark, had flown the nest. Clark had provided the key in-house songs on the first two albums prompting critics to wonder whether the Byrds could survive his loss. A policy decision to avoid relying on Bob Dylan as a song source meant that their troubles were doubled. The obvious answer lay with McGuinn and Crosby, who were forced to mature as singer-songwriters in order to fill the gap. McGuinn looked back to his folk roots and emerged with some tastefully orchestrated takes on Wild Mountain Thyme and John Riley. Crosby, eager to pursue the jazz direction pioneered on Eight Miles High, included the moody What's Happening?!?! and spacey I See You. The presence of Eight Miles High ensured that the album secured chart honours but McGuinn's hopes for a big hit with the title track 5D were scuppered as a result of further drugs allegations.

At the time of the record's release showbiz bible *Variety* featured the ominous headline: "Pop Music's Moral Crisis: Dope Tunes Fan DJ's Ire". As McGuinn ruefully observed: "I was talking about something philosophical and very light and airy with that song, and everyone took it down ... they took it down to drugs. They said it was a dope song and that I was on LSD, and it wasn't any of that, in fact. I was dealing with Einstein's theory of relativity, the fourth dimension being time and the fifth dimension not being specified so it's open, channel five, the next step. I saw it to be a timelessness, a sort of void in space where time has no meaning. All I did was perceive something that was there."

Record Label:
Columbia
Produced
by Allen Stanton.
Recorded
at CBS, Hollywood; January, April and May 1966.
Released:
September 22, 1966 (UK); July 18, 1966 (US)
Chart peaks:
27 (UK) 24 (US)
Personnel:
Jim McGuinn (g, v); David Crosby (g, v); Michael Clarke (d); Chris Hillman (b); Ray Gerhardt (e)
Track Listing:
5D (Fifth Dimension) (S); Wild Mountain Thyme; Mr Spaceman (S); I See You; What's Happening?!?!; I Come And Stand At Every Door; Eight Miles High (S); Hey Joe; Captain Soul; John Riley; 2-4-2 Fox Trot.
Running time:
28:34
Current CD:
Legacy 483707 2 adds: Why; I Know My Rider; Psychodrama City; Eight Miles High (RCA studio version); Why (RCA studio version); John Riley (instrumental)
Further listening:
Younger Than Yesterday (1967); The Notorious Byrd Brothers (1968)
Further reading:
MOJO 41; The Byrds: Timeless Flight Revisited (Johnny Rogan, 1997).
Like this?
Try . . . p.706

The Kinks

Face To Face

Ray Davies's satirical gaze – here turned on himself – finds its first full expression in album format.

Once the more important business of selecting their next hit single had been completed, The Kinks usually booked some studio time and rushed through a threadbare selection of uninspired material. By 1966, the pop aristocracy, inevitably led by The Beatles, was starting to use the album format for artistic expression, Ray Davies decided it was time to grasp the nettle and dazzle with 14 of his own compositions. A full year before *Sgt Pepper* he was planning an alluring montage in which tracks would be connected by sound effects. Davies's musical ambitions coincided with a dramatic turn in his life. Over the previous year, he had split with manager Larry Page and music publisher Eddie Kassner. A debilitating court battle lay ahead and Ray's nerves were frazzled. In the meantime, The Kinks had been banned in America and were fighting among themselves. Like Brian Wilson across the water, Davies was battling personal demons and simultaneously trying to push his group into fresh musical areas.

"I was a zombie," he admits. "I'd been on the go from when we first made it until then, and I was completely out of my mind. I went to sleep and woke up a week later with a moustache. I don't know what happened to me. I'd run into the West End with my money stuffed in my socks, I'd tried to punch my press agent, I was chased down Denmark Street by the police, hustled into a taxi by a psychiatrist, and driven off somewhere."

With Davies succumbing to a nervous breakdown, The Kinks had to complete a short European tour using a ringer. Meanwhile, Ray rested at home and composed this remarkable series of songs, many of which articulated his ambivalent feelings about wealth, fame and class. His pining for his sister, who'd emigrated just before The Kinks' formation, is behind Rosy Won't You Please Come Home. By contrast, the singalong Sunny Afternoon seems to centre around the life of a disillusioned young pop star with aristocratic pretentions; a memorable summer Number 1 single, it nestled comfortably here alongside other tales of nouveau riche overreaching – Most Exclusive Residence For Sale and House In The Country, the latter inspiring Blur's Number 1 single Country House thirty years on.

Record Label:
PYE
Produced
by Raymond Douglas Davies.
Recorded
at Pye Studios, London; October 1965 and April–June 1966.
Released:
October 1966
Chart peaks:
12 (UK) 135 (US)
Personnel:
Ray Davies (g, v); Dave Davies (g, bv), Mick Avory (d); Pete Quaife (b, bv)
Track Listing:
Party Line; Rosie Won't You Please Come Home; Dandy (S,US only); Too Much On My Mind; Session Man; Rainy Day In June; A House In The Country; Holiday In Waikiki; Most Exclusive Residence For Sale; Fancy; Little Miss Queen Of Darkness; You're Looking Fine; Sunny Afternoon (S); I'll Remember.
Current CD adds:
I'm Not Like Everybody Else; Dead End Street (S); Big Black Smoke; Mister Pleasant; This Is Where I Belong; Mr Reporter; Little Women
Running time:
59.44
Current CD:
ESM CD 4797
Further listening:
Something Else By The Kinks (1967); Arthur Or The Decline And Fall Of The British Empire (1969)
Further reading:
The Kinks: The Sound And The Fury (Johnny Rogan, 1984); The Kinks: The Official Biography (Jon Savage, 1984)
Like this?
Try . . . p.596

The Butterfield Blues Band

East-West

US blues rock pioneers. At the crossroads, but headed for the upper stratosphere.

In some ways The Butterfield Blues Band's second album didn't measure up to their electrifying debut, an unprecedented blues-rock blast from start to finish and as close as we're likely to get to a hot night in a bar on Chicago's South Side in 1964. *East-West* was more stylistically scattered, reflecting in part a piecemeal recording schedule necessitated by the tour demands of a hot underground following. But its enduring strength is its diversity, a reflection of a pop world looking to flex its new-found creative muscles.

East-West is known first and foremost for its two "long songs". The Butterfield crew's instrumental workouts on Nat Adderly's Work Song (7:53) and Mike Bloomfield's titanic title jam (13:10) featured the expanded canvas and solo virtuosity previously associated with jazz. Rock did a lot of growing up with these two songs. "*East-West* was such a radical departure, melodically, structurally and chordally from the rock and roll modes and licks at that time," Bloomfield explained to Tom Yates. "It was a long, long series of solos using scales that just had not been played by rock'n'roll guitar players. But believe me, I knew that they were not my scales. They were things I'd heard on John Coltrane records. I'd been listening to a lot of Ravi Shankar and guys who played modal music. These two tunes really broke a lot of ground for other guitar players. I think Carlos Santana still plays that way."

There are a couple of undistinguished blues fillers, almost as if the band was losing interest in the simple structures, but their versions of Robert Johnson's Walkin' Blues, Allen Toussaint's Get Out Of My Life Woman and Mike Nesmith's Mary Mary are all top drawer. And despite the epic performances, Mike Bloomfield's best demonstration of guitar wizardry may be the intro to I Got A Mind To Give Up Living, where he goes from a moan of despair to a howl of pain and then tears, all in the space of 42 seconds.

The Butterfield Band's take on virtuosity was markedly different from most of what it inspired. Bloomfield was the first real guitar hero of the 1960s, but he was part of a group that could soar with him. (Butterfield himself could match him solo for solo on harp.) Later, blues-rock bands became just rhythm sections there to keep the beat while some kid with no life experience would "jam the blues" past the threshold of annoyance. Therefore, we should revere the Butterfield Blues Band's version of blues rock, not blame them for the idiot children it spawned.

Record label:
Elektra
Produced
by Paul A. Rothchild, Mark Abramson and Barry Friedman.
Recorded
in NY and LA; spring–summer 1966.
Released:
December 1966
Chart peaks:
None (UK) 65 (US)
Personnel:
Paul Butterfield (v, hm); Mike Bloomfield (g); Elvin Bishop (g); Mike Naftalin (p); Jerome Arnold (b); Billy Davenport (d)
Track listing:
Walkin' Blues; Get Out Of My Life, Woman; I Got A Mind To Give Up Living; All These Blues; Work Song; Mary Mary; Two Trains Running; Never Say No; East-West
Running time:
44:55
Currently unavailable on CD
Further listening:
The Paul Butterfield Anthology (1998) (2-CD retrospective)
Further reading:
Mike Bloomfield (Ed Ward 1982)
Like this?
Try . . . p.344

Duke Ellington

Far East Suite

Jazz composer giant still hitting the heights 40-odd years into his career.

It's hard to overstate Duke Ellington's stature as a 20th century musician. Honoured by world leaders, respected by 'legit' cats and revered by jazz musicians of all styles and generations – Miles Davis once famously suggested that "all musicians should get down on their knees and thank Duke." His 2000-plus pieces of lovingly, compellingly crafted Negro Music (Ellington preferred the term to 'jazz') composed between 1923 and 1973, ranged from solo piano miniatures through art songs, pop novelties, tone parallels (his own term) and sprawling suites for jazz orchestra and choir, all characterised with discernible Ellingtonian wit, density and intelligence.

What makes his output doubly miraculous is that he kept an orchestra on the road his whole professional life. Financed by his own songwriting royalties, it was his travelling composer's workshop, enabling him to try things out as soon as he had written them. Rarely doing anything other than sleeping, eating, fornicating (he was a confessed "sexual intercourse freak"), performing, writing and travelling, he would compose on trains or at recording sessions and often rehearse after performances into the morning in an amazing sustained feat of unreasonable dedication. "It's our hobby," he would say, smiling.

Inspired by "that big, wonderful and beautiful world" the band visited the Middle East and Japan in 1963–64. Ellington and his friend and co-composer Billy Strayhorn fashioned first the four-movement Impressions Of The Far East, developing it into the nine-movement Far East Suite which ranks among their greatest achievements. Densely colourful and vividly exotic, it is at the same time archetypical Ellington with blues forms, impressionistic swing and characterful jazz solos, taking care not to over-utilise ethnic musical material. Ellington explained that other musicians had already copied the rhythms and scales of these places and he preferred to absorb the essence of an influence and "let it roll around, undergo a chemical change and then seep out on paper in a form that will suit the musicians who are going to play it." Those mighty players included tenorist Paul Gonsalves, serpentine and voluptuous on Tourist Point Of View, clarinetist Jimmy Hamilton fleet and playful on Blue Bird Of Delhi, and altoist Johnny Hodges magnificently sensual on Isfahan (where Ellington observed "all was poetry"), an unspeakably beautiful piece which must take its place within the top hour of all Ellingtonia. Strayhorn died months after the recording and though Ellington continued to produce rigorous work, the loss of his intimate musical confidant since 1941 signified the end of an era.

Record Label:
RCA Bluebird
Produced
by Brad McCuen.
Recorded
at RCA Victor, Studio A; December 19–21, 1966.
Released:
1967
Chart peaks:
None (UK) None (US)
Personnel:
Cootie Williams; William "Cat" Anderson; Herbie Jones; Mercer Ellington (t); Lawrence Brown, Charles "Chuck" Connors, Buster Cooper (tb); Johnny Hodges (as); Russell Procope (as, clarinet); Paul Gonsalves (ts); Jimmy Hamilton (clarinet, ts); Harry Carney (bs); Duke Ellington (p); John Lamb (b); Rufus Jones (d)
Track Listing:
Tourist Point Of View; Bluebird Of Dehli (Minah); Isfahan; Depk; Mount Harissa; Blue Pepper (Far East Of The Blues); Agra; Amad; Ad Lib On Nippon
Running time:
43.51
Currently available CD:
RCA 66552-2
Further listening:
Such Sweet Thunder (1957); Ella Fitzgerald Sings The Duke Ellington Songbook (1957); New Orleans Suite (1970)
Further reading:
Beyond Category: The Life And Genius Of Duke Ellington (John Edward Hasse, 1993); Duke Ellington Reader (Mark Tucker, 1993)
Like this?
Try . . . p.82

Bobby Darin

If I Were A Carpenter

Former teen idol reinvents himself for the third time with a Tim Hardin song.

Darin had one of rock'n'roll's most unfathomable careers. Listen to the records he made across a career cut short at the age of only 37 (he died of a heart attack in December 1973) and you have almost no clues to the man's identity. There are undoubted classic moments; his own Dream Lover (1959) is one of the era's classic teen ballads. But just a year later he was the finger-clicking swinger behind Mack The Knife.

There's some doubt, of course, that *If I Were A Carpenter* was truly Darin's own brainchild. The album's producers Charles Koppelman and Don Rubin brought the songs to the table, seven of which were by either Tim Hardin or John Sebastian, both of whom they also represented. Yet Darin was no stranger to folk or even folk rock. As early as 1963 he'd recorded the folk-based *Earthy* and *Golden Folk Hits*; James Burton, Jim McGuinn, Fred Neil and Phil Ochs allegedly attended the sessions. Darin was also the first to perform Dylan songs at Las Vegas around this time (a dubious honour, perhaps). But whatever the motives, *If I Were A Carpenter* and the similar *Inside Out*, which followed a few months later, are stylistic triumphs.

Darin recorded If I Were A Carpenter as a single in August 1966. Hardin's own released version would not appear for over a year, but his arrangement is clearly what Darin's treatment was based upon. Hardin complained bitterly that Darin had completely copied his phrasing. Susan Moore (Hardin's wife), later recalled: "Tim and I were out driving when it came on the radio. I thought it was him, it was so close. The brakes screeched. The door slammed. And Tim was stomping on the side of the road, screaming and swearing." Would Hardin's own version have met with the same success? Somehow it's doubtful.

There's further irony that Tim Hardin's only US chart hit (Number 50 in 1969) was Simple Song Of Freedom – penned by Bobby Darin. But 1967 was the last year that Bobby Darin himself was to grace the charts.

Record label:
Atlantic
Produced
by Charles Koppelman and Don Rubin.
Recorded
at Gold Star Studio, Los Angeles; August 15, November 31 and October 1, 1966.
Released:
January 1967
Chart peaks:
None (UK) 142 (US)
Personnel:
Bobby Darin (v); no other musicians credited
Track listing:
If I Were A Carpenter(S); Reason To Believe; Sittin' Here Lovin' You(S); Misty Roses; Until It's Time For You To Go; For Baby; The Girl That Stood Beside Me(S); Red Balloon; Amy; Don't Make Promises; Day Dream
Running time:
26.03
Current CD:
DIAB864 adds Inside Out
Further listening:
The 4-CD As Long As I'm Singing: The Bobby Darin Collection (1998)
Further reading:
www.bobbydarin.net
Like this?
Try . . . p.3

The Doors

The Doors

A great mess of an artist, Jim Morrison, captured in all his wild majesty.

Jim Morrison was the narcissistic stuff of rock legend. Shortly after graduating from the Theatre Arts department at UCLA in 1964, he met the classically trained keyboard player Ray Manzarek. In July the following year they got together with Robby Krieger and John Densmore – the drummer had shared a Transcendental Meditation class with Manzarek. Significantly, they took their name from Aldous Huxley's *The Doors Of Perception*, an account of a mescaline trip. They clicked immediately: Manzarek's alternately jittery and flowing organ identified a sound punctuated by Krieger's blues riffs, jazzy runs, and Spanish finger-picking, and Densmore's fluid sensitivity to the overarching personality of the frontman. Morrison was magnetic: wild, handsome and possessed of a rich baritone. When producer Paul Rothchild (who also recorded Paul Butterfield Blues Band, Janis Joplin and Love) saw The Doors live during a six-month residency at the Whisky A-Go-Go, Los Angeles, in July, 1966, he was so impressed by their presence that, according to his engineer Bruce Botnick, he at once proposed making a studio album as an "aural documentary" of their live set.

Remarkably, that is what he achieved with *The Doors*, capturing iconic songs propelled by an awe-inspiring sense of drama. Break On Through bounds in on Densmore's double-time bossa nova cymbal ride, Manzarek's charging organ bassline and Krieger's unison guitar; Morrison delivers his sermon with an evangelist's certain fervour. Light My Fire, a Krieger composition, rolls in on a majestic Manzarek organ line, stretches out on keyboard and guitar solos, but always returns to Morrison's sonorous vocal and the addictive chorus.

But, of course, there were problems inherent in Morrison's temperament, fuelled by his artistic wrestling bouts with the nature of order and chaos. His most extreme exploration occurred during the final session – appropriately, while working on The End. Comprehensively wrecked, the singer wound up lying on the floor mumbling the words to his Oedipal nightmare, "Fuck the mother, kill the father." Then, suddenly animated, he rose and threw a TV at the control room window. Sent home by Rothchild like a naughty schoolkid, he returned in the middle of the night, broke in, peeled off his clothes, yanked a fire extinguisher from the wall and drenched the studio. Alerted, Rothchild came back and persuaded the naked, foam-flecked Morrison to leave once more, advising the studio owner to charge the damage to Elektra; next day the band nailed the track in two takes. Morrison lived for only another five years.

Record label:
Elektra
Produced
by Paul Rothchild.
Recorded
at Sunset Sound Recorders, Los Angeles; September 1966.
Released:
January 1967
Chart peaks:
None (UK) 2 (US)
Personnel:
Jim Morrison (v); Ray Manzarek (o, p); Robby Krieger (g); John Densmore (d); Larry Knechtel (b); Bruce Botnick (e)
Track listing:
Break On Through (S/US); Soul Kitchen; The Crystal Ship; Twentieth Century Fox; Alabama Song (Whisky Bar) (S); Light My Fire (S); Back Door Man; I Looked At You; End of the Night; Take It As It Comes; The End
Running time:
43.25
Current CD:
7559740072
Further listening:
The Doors Box Set (1997); Waiting For The Sun (1968); LA Woman (1971)
Further reading:
Break On Through: The Life and Death of Jim Morrison (James Riordan and Jerry Prochnicky, 1991); No One Here Gets Out Alive (Jerry Hopkins and Danny Sugerman, 1981); www.thedoors.com
Like this?
Try . . . p.704

The Lovin' Spoonful

Hums Of The Lovin' Spoonful

Much-loved '60s hitmakers' finest album, packed with classic songs by John Sebastian.

Nowadays the Spoonful's chief songwriter, singer and all-round supremo John Sebastian plays in a jugband. And if he survives a gig without being constantly heckled to play Spoonful songs, he is prone to remarking, "Thank you for letting me outgrow my 20s". But if ever a songwriter had no reason to feel embarrassed by his early work it is surely Sebastian. He always wrote with a wit and care for language exceptional in rock, and with The Lovin' Spoonful he created jubilant music in a distinctive style influenced by rock-'n'roll, country, blues and folk.

His admirers included Clive James, who, in 1972, argued that, "Randy Newman is the only man who has outstripped his brilliant lyric technique". The Los Angeles Times described Sebastian as "one of the very select group of songwriters, including also John Lennon, Ray Davies and Brian Wilson, for which the term genius doesn't seem just a publicist's wild notion."

Listen, for example, to Nashville Cats, in which Sebastian declares, gloriously ungrammatically: "There's 1352 guitar pickers in Nashville and anyone who unpacks his guitar can play twice as better than I will!" His lyrics were nonchalantly fun-filled and quirky and irresistibly amusing. Consider Darlin' Companion, later covered by Johnny Cash, a virtuosic masterclass in rhyme, half-rhyme and assonance, or Summer In The City, a perfect evocation of New York, which Sebastian co-wrote with his brother Mark and bassist Steve Boone.

"It was a collaboration and the extra strength came out of that," asserts Sebastian of his most famous song. "We were putting out singles that sounded different all the time," he adds, a claim fully justified by this album's four diverse US hits, Summer In The City, the truly lovely and evocative Rain On The Roof, Nashville Cats and Full Measure.

Record label:
Kama Sutra
Produced
by Eric Jacobsen.
Recorded
at Columbia Studios, New York; 1966.
Released:
January 1967
Chart peaks:
None (UK) 14 (US)
Personnel:
John Sebastian (g, v, hm); Zal Yanovsky (g, banjo, v); Steve Boone (b, k, v); Joe Butler (d, v); Roy Hallee (e)
Track listing:
Sittin' Here Lovin' You; Bes' Friends; Voodoo In My Basement; Darlin' Companion; Henry Thomas; Full Measure (S/US); Rain On The Roof (S); Coconut Grove; Nashville Cats (S); 4 Eyes; Summer In The City (S)
Running time:
27.24
Currently unavailable on CD,
though many of the tracks are available on compilations.
Further listening:
All four of the Sebastian-era non-film soundtrack Spoonful albums are worth buying, but Daydream (1966) probably runs Hums closest. The Very Best Of (1996) is a good budget-priced compilation.
Further reading:
www.lovinspoonful.com
Like this?
Try . . . p.671

Fred Neil

Fred Neil

Recluse comes out of hiding long enough to leave indelible footprint in the sands of pop history.

The author of simple but affecting blues-stained folksongs Fred Neil was notoriously studio-shy, and a reluctant participant once coaxed there. Elektra producer Paul Rothchild had managed to squeeze two albums out of him, the excellent *Tear Down The Walls* (1964) and the exceptional *Bleecker And Macdougal* (1965). But when plans for a third Elektra album to be cut in Nashville fell through, producer Nik Venet signed him to Capitol in LA.

Venet had known Neil since their intersecting Brill Building experiences in the late '50s, and had a pretty good idea how to approach this difficult proposition. "I used three engineers and recorded directly to stereo," the late producer told Goldmine's Simon Wordsworth. "None of those songs are remixed; everything you hear on the albums I did with Fred are as they happened in the studio. What you hear there is all Fred Neil. There were no arrangements; no one rehearsed."

It was the East Coast folkie meeting the electric West Coast mob that Venet had used with Linda Ronstadt And The Stone Poneys. Fred was in superb, rumbling voice, and had what most would come to consider his best collection of songs, yet it remained difficult to pull them out of him.

"Getting Fred to even let you in on what songs he was going to record was damn near impossible," says then-manager Herb Cohen. "We went in and started putting down whatever songs he had. That was the way it was. We might have known a couple of titles ahead of time. We certainly *didn't* know Everybody's Talkin', because he didn't know it. We needed another song, and he said he might have one more. Matter of fact, I think he completed it in the toilet of the Capitol Records Studio. As you can tell by the lyric, all he wanted to do was finish the album and go back to Florida."

Though it originally fared little better than his Elektra albums, *Fred Neil* captures an elusive artist at the peak of his powers. It contains his two best-loved songs (Everybody's Talkin' and The Dolphins), and his loveliest blues rewrites (Shake Sugaree and Faretheewell) . By the time of the album's release, Neil had retreated to his Coconut Grove Sanctuary, from which he'd ventured forth only under duress. When Harry Nilsson's cover of Everybody's Talkin' was used as the theme for the Academy Award-winning 1969 film *Midnight Cowboy*, the duress factor, and Fred's stubbornness both went through the roof. Everybody's Talkin' would go on to become one of the most performed songs of all time (over five million performances!); the thing that drove him away for good was also what provided him his means of escape.

Record label:
Capitol
Produced
by Nik Venet.
Recorded
at Capitol Studios, Hollywood; autumn 1966.
Released:
January 1967
Chart peaks:
None (UK) None (US)
Personnel:
James E Bond (b); John T Forsha (g); Peter Childs (g); Al Wilson (hm); Billy Mundi; Cyrus Faryar (g, bouzouki); Rusty Faryar (finger cymbals); UFO (bv); Fred Neil (v, g); John Kraus (e); Pete Abbot (e)
Track listing:
The Dolphins; I've Got A Secret (Didn't We Shake Sugaree); That's The Bag I'm In; Everybody's Talkin'; Everything Happens; Sweet Cocaine; Green Rocky Road; Cynicrustpetefredjohn Raga
Running time:
38.27
Current CD:
The Many Sides Of Fred Neil compiles Fred Neil, Sessions and The Other Side Of This Life
Further listening:
Bleecker And Macdougal (1964); The Many Sides Of Fred Neil (1998), a 2-CD compilation including a batch of rare early cuts and unreleased stuff.
Further reading:
Mojo 75 (February 2000); feature by Simon Wordsworth in Goldmine 411 (1996)
www.fredneil.com/
Like this?
Try . . . p.638

The Left Banke

Walk Away Renee/Pretty Ballerina

Fey New York band combine pop with chamber music.

'Baroque-rock' this was the label attached to a young band who emerged in 1966 with a new sound on a Top 5 debut single. The Left Banke came together around keyboard player Michael Brown while he was working at the tiny Manhattan recording studio owned by his father, the arranger and producer Harry Lookofsky. The only trained musician in the group, Brown was just 16 when he wrote Walk Away Renee.

Inspired by his unrequited adoration of Renee Fladen, Tom Finn's girlfriend, the lyrical mixture of heartfelt yearning and salvaged pride displayed an astonishing maturity. As Brown later recalled: "It's not a love song about possession – it's about loving someone enough to set them free." The song's production was equally striking (amazing for 1965, when it was done): Lookofsky's unorthodox arrangement kept the guitars low in the mix, the string quartet allowed Martin's distinctive voice and Brown's mellifluous harpsichord to shine.

Defying the custom of its time, the subsequent album was far more than just a vehicle for the group's hits (follow-up single Pretty Ballerina, also inspired by Fladen and arguably even more beautiful had reached number 15 in the US charts), composed entirely of originals, were driven for the most part by Brown's old-master keyboards. Barterers And Their Wives was, perhaps, the most literally baroque, but the songs also encompassed slow ballads (the aching Shadows Breaking Over My Head), country (What Do You Know) and brash fuzz guitar (Lazy Day).

With a raft of catchy, if rather melancholy, pop tunes, 'English-style' long hair and a look that critic Lillian Roxon described as "almost too pretty for rock", The Left Banke looked destined for greatness. But the album, recorded piecemeal over a year, was released too late to capitalise on their early success and Brown, disillusioned with touring, left to form a rival outfit under the same name. When both Left Bankes released singles simultaneously, writs began to fly and radio stations quickly shunned the band. Subsequent recordings, including an enchanting second LP, produced diminishing returns and by 1969 the band had dispersed to other projects.

Record label:
Smash/Phillips
Produced
by Harry Lookofsky, Steve and Bill Jerome.
Recorded
at World United Studios, New York; December 1965, January, March and November 1966; Mercury Studios, New York; January 1967.
Released:
February 1967
Chart peaks:
None (UK) 67 (US)
Personnel:
Michael Brown (k, v); Steve Martin (v); Jeff Winfield (g); Tom Finn (v, b); George Cameron (v, g, d); Warren David (d); George Hirsch (g); Hugh McCracken (g); Rick Brand (g)
Track listing:
Pretty Ballerina (S); She May Call You Up Tonight (S); Barterers And Their Wives (S); I've Got Something On My Mind (S); Let Go Of You Girl; Evening Gown; Walk Away Renee (S); What Do You Know; Shadows Breaking Over My Head; I Haven't Got The Nerve (S); Lazy Day (S)
Running time:
28.50
Current CD:
Mercury 848 095-2.
Further listening:
Their work is collected on the CD There's Gonna Be A Storm: The Complete Recordings 1966–1969 (1992).
Further reading:
www.members.aol.com/bocad/lb_main.htm
Like this?
Try . . . p.512

Aretha Franklin

I Never Loved A Man The Way I Loved You

Breakthrough of a soul legend.

At 24 years old, Aretha Franklin could've been forgiven for thinking she had seen it all already. Daughter of a famous gospel preacher, already a mother and wife, a professional singer for some years and a much experienced performer, she had already rubbed shoulders with the greats from Sam Cooke and Ray Charles to boxer Joe Louis and more. After her deal with Columbia Records expired, Jerry Wexler wasted no time signing her to Atlantic in November 1966.

The soul music scene was rapidly growing with Wilson Pickett, Sam And Dave, Otis Redding, Carla Thomas and the more urbane Motown acts already achieving great chart success. But Wexler knew he had something special. Aretha's first six weeks with Atlantic were spent choosing the proper material. On January 24, 1967 Wexler, Franklin and her then husband Ted White flew to a tiny country airstrip outside of Florence, Alabama and drove over to Muscle Shoals. There Chips Moman had assembled what is now rightly considered a legendary band, but it was a legendary band with no black faces; Wexler had specifically asked for an *integrated* band. With Aretha on piano they cut I Never Loved A Man – Dan Penn: "Less than two hours and it was in the can and it was a killer, no doubt about it. That morning we knew a star had been born."

However, a drinking contest had begun between White and one of the horn section, degenerating into an ugly, name-calling argument, and work on the second song, Do Right Woman-Do Right Man, ground to an abrupt halt. Wexler pulled the plug and with White (who doubled as Aretha's manager) refusing to step foot in Alabama again, the sessions were rescheduled for New York City, where they were eventually completed in February.

"Of the hundreds of sessions I have participated in," Spooner Oldham recalls today, "I can honestly say those first few times with Aretha Franklin were simply and magically unforgettable."

Record label:
Atlantic
Produced
by Jerry Wexler.
Recorded
at Muscle Shoals Studios, Alabama; January 24, 1967 and Atlantic Studios, New York; February 8 and 14–16.
Released:
March 10, 1967
Chart peaks:
36 (UK) 2 (US)
Personnel:
Aretha Franklin (v, p); Spooner Oldham (k); Jimmy Johnson (g); Chips Moman (g); Tommy Cogbill (b); Roger Hawkins (d); Gene Chrisman (d); Melvin Lastie (cornet, t); Ken Laxton (t); Ernie Royal (t); David Hood (tb); Charlie Chalmers (ts); King Curtis (ts); Joe Arnold (ts); Willie Bridges (bs); Carolyn Franklin, Erma Franklin; Cissy Houston (bv); Tom Dowd (e); Arif Mardin (e)
Track listing:
Respect (S); Drown In My Own Tears; I Never Loved A Man (The Way I Loved You) (S); Soul Serenade; Don't Let Me Lose This Dream; Baby Baby Baby (S); Dr Feelgood (Love Is A Serious Business); Good Times; Do Right Woman-Do Right Man; Save Me; A Change Is Gonna Come
Running time:
41.26
Current CD:
8122719342 adds: Respect; I Never Loved A Man (The Way I Love You) (2); Do Right Woman-Do Right Man (2)
Further listening:
Lady Soul (1968).
Further reading:
Sweet Soul Music: (Peter Guralnick, 1986)
Like this?
Try . . . p.663

The Velvet Underground

Velvet Underground And Nico

New York's brutally realistic, genre-spawning riposte to the West Coast dream of psychedelia.

Now acknowledged as one of the most influential albums of all time, The Velvet Underground's 1967 debut barely limped into the Billboard chart at 197, then disappeared. New York's avant-garde art overlord Andy Warhol financed it, securing three days in Cameo-Parkway studios, Broadway, for $2,500. In return, the Velvets were obliged to use Warhol's latest 'superstar', Nico, as their vocalist, and to credit Warhol, who rarely visited the studio, as producer.

"The studio was still under construction," remembers Velvets' viola player John Cale. "The floorboards were up, the walls were out." Understandably, this did nothing to mitigate their open hostility to Nico. "We'd hear her go off-key or hit the wrong pitch. We would sit there and snigger." Nico's worst trial was I'll Be Your Mirror, which her relentless tormentors forced her to sing endlessly until she broke down in tears.

According to drummer Mo Tucker, time restrictions meant that most tracks were recorded live, virtually no overdubs and engineering limitations forcing the band to play unusually quietly. "Heroin is such a good song," says Tucker, "but it's a pile of garbage on the record. The guys couldn't have their amps up loud in the studio, so I couldn't hear anything."

Once the album was complete, the band began hawking it around. "We took it to Ahmet Ertegun (at Atlantic) and he said, 'No drug songs.'" remembered the late Sterling Morrison. "We took it to Elektra and they said, 'No violas.'"

They finally scored a deal with Dylan's producer Tom Wilson, who arranged for its release on Verve. But, like Warhol, Wilson's primary interest was Nico. He made Reed write another song for her, which he would produce and release as a single. Reed delivered Sunday Morning but, once in the studio, insisted on singing it himself. By the time the album hit the streets, Verve had lost interest and was concentrating instead on marketing another recent signing, The Mothers of Invention. Yet, despite the album's tortuous genesis, its patchy sound and the limited playing ability of its creators, for the few who did discover *The Velvet Underground And Nico*, it was like that first glimpse of a Fellini movie after a lifetime of Disney. In Lou Reed's songs, tenderness and violence were overpowering, the drugs were dangerous, and the music could scar you for life. The Record Mirror scribe who wrote, "It's solid and by no means freaky," was presumably one hell of a weird dude.

Record Label:
Verve

Produced
by Andy Warhol and Tom Wilson.

Recorded
at Cameo-Parkway, New York, and T.T.G., Hollywood; April 1966.

Chart peaks:
None (UK) 197 (US)

Released:
March 15, 1967

Personnel:
Lou Reed (g, v); Nico (v); John Cale (va, k, b); Sterling Morrison (g, b); Maureen Tucker (pc)

Track Listing:
Sunday Morning (S); I'm Waiting For The Man; Femme Fatale; Venus In Fur; Run Run Run; All Tomorrow's Parties; Heroin; There She Goes Again; I'll Be Your Mirror; The Black Angel's Death Song; European Son

Running time:
48.26

Current CD:
5312502

Further listening:
For the vicious side, White Light/White Heat (1968). For tuneful stuff, The Velvet Underground (1969)

Further reading:
Up-Tight – The Velvet Underground Story (Victor Bockris and Gerard Malanga,1983); What's Welsh For Zen (John Cale, 1999); www.velvetunderground.com

Like this?
Try . . . p.670

Merle Haggard And The Strangers

I'm A Lonesome Fugitive

All hail the first New Traditionalist.

Many country singers sang about a fantasy. Not Flossie Haggard's boy, who began running away from home when a young teen and who knew divorce, alcohol, railroads, even life behind bars. When people asked why he got himself into so much trouble, he'd tell them he just wanted to experience the kind of life he heard about in Jimmie Rodgers songs. Haggard was a New Traditionalist 20 years ahead of his time – and he sang about the classic country topics with authority and a tender, understanding grace.

Although he had had some success on his friend Fuzzy Owens's small Talley Records, it seemed like every song he released would be covered by a more established singer who would get the bigger hit. Fortunately, Capitol's country producer and A&R man Ken Nelson saw the pattern and called Owen in 1965 saying, "Why don't y'all cut out this baloney and get up here and let's take care of this thing." Which they did, signing to the label. Three albums later, Haggard's popularity was rising but he had still not made his mark in the eyes of the country music public. On the advice of a local agent he travelled to Liz Anderson's house to hear some songs she had written. Sitting down at a battered old pump organ, she performed the song that would become this album's title track.

Haggard was stunned as he listened. He felt the song defined him perfectly, outlining a persona he could quite comfortably colour in. His version of her song made Number 1 in the country singles charts – one of three hit singles he scored in 1966. Meanwhile, as demand for an album increased, Haggard set to writing (or, more precisely, dictating, or scribbling on used paper bags) some of the best material of his career – including classic honky tonk lament Drink Up And Be Somebody and the haunting Life In Prison, later covered by Gram Parsons on The Byrds' *Sweetheart Of The Rodeo* – augmenting them with a cover of Jimmie Rodgers's My Rough And Rowdy Ways. Haggard would go on to have better selling albums but he would never again be quite as raw and authentic.

Record label:
Capitol
Produced
by Ken Nelson.
Recorded
in Nashville; August 1–3, November 16 and December 16, 1966
Released:
March 1967
Chart peaks:
None (UK) None (US)
Personnel:
Merle Haggard (v, g); James Burton (g, dobro); Glen Campbell (bv, g); Lewis Talley (g); Shorty Mullins (g); Billy Mize (g, bv); Jerry Ward (b); Bonnie Owens (bv); Glenn D. Hardin (p); Ralph Mooney (ps); James Beck Gordon (d)
Track listing:
I'm A Lonesome Fugitive (S/US); All Of Me Belongs To You; House Of Memories; Life In Prison; Whatever Happened To Me; Drink Up And Be Somebody; Someone Told My Story (S/US); If You Want To Be My Woman; Mary's Mine; Skid Row; My Rough And Rowdy Ways; Mixed Up Mess Of A Heart
Running time:
31.16
Current CD:
CTS5547 adds: Mama Tried; Green Green Grass Of Home; Little Ole Wine Drinker Me; In The Good Old Days; I Could Have Gone Right; I'll Always Know; Sunny Side Of Life; Teach Me To Forget; Folsom Prison Blues; Run 'Em Off; You'll Never Love Me Now; Too Many Bridges To Cross Over
Further listening:
Branded Man (1967);
Further reading:
My House Of Memories: (Merle Haggard, 1999)
Like this?
Try . . . p.112

The Mothers Of Invention

Freak Out

Rock music's first double album takes in blues, R&B, doo-wop, rock, surrealist satire and La Monte Young.

When Frank Zappa gathered up his motley collection of bar band oddballs, LBJ "great society" rejects and bona fide freaks, and landed himself a major label record contract he alerted the world to the new American underground. *Freak Out* was a landmark that arguably has never been surpassed in scope and ambition. MGM hardly knew what they were getting.

"The first track we laid down was Any Way The Wind Blows," said Zappa. "The second was Who Are The Brain Police? I could see [producer] Tom Wilson on the phone through the control room window calling the head office in New York saying, Well you're not going to believe this."

Who Are The Brain Police? is one of the scariest songs ever to emerge from the rock psyche, a Kafka-esque vision of contemporary America where personal identity and individuality are erased. In context, it offers a nightmarish counterpoint to the more overt political polemic of Hungry Freaks Daddy and Trouble Every Day (the latter originally titled The Watts Riot Song). Although much of the music was played by the Mothers, Zappa was shrewd enough to augment *Freak Out* with the cream of LA's session musicians (credited as The Mothers Auxiliary). Go Cry On Somebody Else's Shoulder; You Didn't Try To Call Me; Any Way The Wind Blows; I'm Not Satisfied; How Could I Be Such A Fool – all later re-recorded for *Cruising With Ruben And The Jets* – are given full orchestral treatments and reveal Zappa's formidable talent as an arranger. Sure, the Mothers looked like Hell's Angels who'd come for your daughter, but there was also a good chance they'd take her home to play her Stravinsky and Charles Ives. Subsequently, Zappa tended to apportion his musical iconoclasm to specific albums: savage satire (*We're Only In It For The Money*); classical motifs and musique concrete (*Lumpy Gravy*) and doo wop (*Cruising With Ruben And The Jets*). Only the equally impressive *Uncle Meat* casts its net as wide as does this audacious debut.

Record Label:
Verve
Produced
by Tom Wilson.
Recorded
at Sunset Highland Studios of T.T.G. Inc.
Released:
March 1967 (UK); August 1966 (US)
Chart peaks:
None (UK) None (US)
Personnel:
Frank Zappa (g); Ray Collins (v); Jim Black (d); Roy Estrada (b); Elliot Ingber (g); various unknown LA sessioniers
Track Listing:
Hungry Freaks Daddy; I Ain't Got No Heart; Who Are The Brain Police?; Go Cry On Somebody Else's Shoulder; Motherly Love; How Could I Be Such A Fool; Wowie Zowie; You Didn't Try To Call Me; Any Way The Wind Blows; I'm Not Satisfied; You're Probably Wondering Why I'm Here; Trouble Every Day; Help I'm A Rock; It Can't Happen Here; The Return Of The Son Of Monster Magnet
Running time:
60.31
Current CD:
RCD 10501
Further listening:
Uncle Meat (1969); Mystery Disc (Rykodisc RCD 10580)
Further reading:
Waiting For The Sun (Barney Hoskyns, 1996); Frank Zappa In His Own Words (1993); The Negative Dialectics Of Poodle Play (Ben Watson, 1996)
Like this?
Try . . . p.678

Jimi Hendrix Experience

Are You Experienced?

Landmark debut from rock's original wild axe-man.

Are You Experienced? is best experienced in mono. With rock's involvement with stereo still confined to spacey panning and scattering vocals around either speaker – and period psychedelia only adding to the confusion – even the best realised record was a plague of distracting gimmickry. In mono, however, the full majesty of Hendrix's vision shatters the speakers, proof that this boy didn't need technology to make him ricochet round the room. He was doing it quite successfully, already – as engineer Eddie Kramer remembers. "He would come up with some kind of crazy sound, I would catch it on tape, then try and twist it around and make it even sillier." The freakish Third Stone From The Sun and the title track are the epics which paint Hendrix's future in screaming colours, but the title track is the brightest of the bite-sized rockers – Foxy Lady, Manic Depression, Fire – tracks whose success, Kramer insists, came down to manager/producer Chandler. "If you look at the first record, most of the tracks are three-and-a-half, four minutes long, and that was Chas's influence. He came from that whole pop vibe, keeping it to three and a half minutes, which was a bit frustrating for Jimi. But I think it was a good thing because it kept the improvising very intense and very compact."

It was this intensity which ensured the album's immortality. Dave Marsh has called *Are You Experienced?* "the greatest, most influential debut album ever released." Keith Altham described Hendrix as "a new dimension in electrical guitar music ... a one man assault upon the nerve cells." But Noel Redding laughs at the much-vaunted perfection of the album. "There's mistakes on the Experience albums ... I remember, I'd call over to Chas, 'Hey, I hit a wrong note,' and he'd go 'Don't worry, no one will fucking notice,' in that wonderful Geordie accent of his. Then Hendrix used to drop a couple of notes here or there, or miss a slight lyric, and Chas would say 'Don't worry, mate.' It was great, we paid a lot of attention to what we were doing, but it was the feel we were after, more than technical perfection." And that is what they got. An album which feels great and sounds just fine. Especially in mono.

Record Label:
Track
Produced
by Chas Chandler.
Recorded
at De Lane Lea, London; January–March 1967; Olympic Studios, London; February–April 1967.
Released:
May 12, 1967 (UK); August 23, 1967 (US)
Chart peaks:
2 (UK) 5 (US)
Personnel:
Jimi Hendrix (v, g); Noel Redding (b, v); Mitch Mitchell (d)
Track Listing:
Foxy Lady (S, US only); Manic Depression; Red House (UK only); Hey Joe (US only) (S); Can You See Me? (UK only); Love Or Confusion; I Don't Live Today; May This Be Love; Wind Cries Mary (US only) (S, UK only); Fire; Third Stone From The Sun; Remember (UK only); Purple Haze (S, US only); Are You Experienced?
Current CD adds:
Stone Free; 51st Anniversary; Highway Chile
Running time:
38.38 (US version)
Current CD:
MCD11608
Further listening:
Axis Bold As Love (1967); Electric Ladyland (1968)
Further reading:
Are You Experienced? (Noel Redding and Carol Appleby, 1990)
Like this?
Try . . . p.551

Tim Hardin

Tim Hardin 2

Second album by the errant young singer-songwriter, many of whose songs have become standards.

Susan Yardley was a young actress making a name for herself in the TV series The Young Marrieds when she first met Tim Hardin in Los Angeles. Hardin, already a hardened drug addict, had a bad record with women and may have had dishonourable intentions towards Susan, if the lyrics to The Lady Came From Baltimore are anything to go by. Instead he fell deeply and irrevocably in love with the actress – real name Susan Morss – who became his wife and inspired virtually all the songs that flooded out of him and formed the basis of *Tim Hardin 2*.

He set up a studio in his house and recorded a series of songs of poignant wonder which detail not only his intense love for Susan, but also the paranoia and neuroses that smothered him. Red Balloon is an anguished song about drugs; Black Sheep Boy confronts his sense of failure and alienation; Tribute To Hank Williams has him identifying strongly with the tragic, too-fast-to-live legend of the country icon. If I Were A Carpenter poetically relates his inferiority complex over his marriage to the well-connected Susan Morss, renamed as Susan Moore by Hardin for artistic purposes. If I Were A Carpenter went on to become his most celebrated song, a hit for Bobby Darin, Four Tops and many others. Not that it impressed Hardin, still unsuccessfully fighting his habit. It's said that when he first heard Bobby Darin's cover of Carpenter in the car, he screamed the car to a halt, jumped out and stamped on the ground in a rage.

There were no happy endings for Tim Hardin or Susan Moore. He eventually died of an OD, 13 years after the release of *Tim Hardin 2*. He had a long, difficult struggle with his own numerous demons, which included a terror of live performance, low self-esteem, constant writer's block, the emotional roller coaster of his on-off marriage and various attempts to escape the clutches of the drugs that ultimately killed him.

Record label:
Verve
Produced
by Charles Koppelman and Don Rubin
Recorded
at Hardin's home studio, Los Angeles; winter 1967.
Released:
May 1967
Chart peaks:
None (UK) None (US)
Personnel:
Tim Hardin (v, g, p); Artie Butler (strings); Felix Pappalardi (b); Sticks Evans (d); Phil Krauss (vibes)
Track listing:
If I Were A Carpenter; Red Balloon; Black Sheep Boy; Lady Came From Baltimore; Baby Close Its Eyes; You Upset The Grace Of Living When You Lie; Speak Like A Child; See Where You Are And Get Out; It's Hard To Believe In Love For Long; Tribute To Hank Williams.
Running time:
28.30
Current CD:
REP7030WP adds: Tim Hardin
Further listening:
Suite For Susan Moore And Damion (1969) is a disturbing confessional in song and poetry of a man whose life is falling apart. Of his later albums Nine (1973) is probably the best, though his magical songwriting had deserted him, he proved himself a sensual soul-blues singer.
Further reading:
www.zipcon.net/~highroad/hardin.htm
Like this?
Try . . . p.599

The Beatles

Sgt. Pepper's Lonely Heart's Club Band

The most famous rock album of all time.

While recording Sgt Pepper, Paul McCartney read an allegation that The Beatles had "dried up", so quiet were they from *Revolver* (August 1966) through the winter and spring of 1967. But he knew exactly what The Beatles had up their sleeves.

"I was sitting rubbing my hands, saying, You just wait!" he remembers. His arrogance is intriguing: The Beatles could not have known what the public's reaction to *Sgt Pepper* would be. It may have baffled the bulk of their fans, so great was its scale and ambition. But over the 129 days it took to record, the Fabs were following their noses, and no-one was going to tell them what could or couldn't be achieved. Their favourite expression in the studio at this time was "There's no such word as 'can't'."

The first song recorded (Strawberry Fields Forever) was quickly deemed too plain and a new, orchestral arrangement ordered. The next three songs recorded were When I'm Sixty Four, Penny Lane and A Day In The Life, a gauge of how different this record was intended to be from its predecessors. Their ambitions even stretched to plans for a TV special following the recording. (In the end only one session was filmed, the orchestra playing on A Day In The Life.) *Sgt Pepper* reeks of confidence and the desire to set new standards. It was a whole creation (and the first Beatles album to have the same sequence in Britain and America). McCartney – whose vision glued the project together – was especially daring, challenging Lennon to come up with sparkle to match. A Day In The Life was composed by them both, and the nods and winks that passed between the two as they put lyric onto paper belies the common misconception that they were worlds apart by this time. George Martin was urged to concoct brass, woodwind and orchestral parts, future Gary Glitter mastermind Mike Leander was commissioned to supply a string arrangement for She's Leaving Home and the engineers were encouraged to stretch Abbey Road's rather modest technology to its limits.

What they all came up with is arguably the reason for this book's existence, for it energised the album form, providing a high watermark for anyone with the chance to record 40 minutes of music and decorate twelve square inches of card. It may not be the best album ever made – it's not even the best Beatles album ever made – and in retrospect there's a lot that's gimmicky about it. It wasn't the first 'grown-up' rock album, the first to use an orchestra, the first themed album or the first psychedelic album, but it *was* by The Beatles, and consequently it became the first of these to be noticed by the wider public and to mark the moment where pop music simultaneously reflected and defined the times.

Record label:
Parlophone
Produced
by George Martin.
Recorded
at Studio Two, Abbey Road, London and Regent Sound Studio, Tottenham Court Road, London; December 6, 1966–April 21, 1967.
Released:
June 1, 1967
Chart peaks:
1 (UK) 1 (US)
Personnel:
Paul McCartney (b, k, v); John Lennon (g, k, v); George Harrison (g, sitar, v); Ringo Starr (d, pc, v); Geoff Emerick, Richard Lush, Phil McDonald, Keith Slaughter (e)
Track listing:
Sgt. Pepper's Lonely Hearts Club Band/With A Little Help From My Friends (S/released 1978); Lucy In the Sky With Diamonds; Getting Better; Fixing A Hole; She's Leaving Home; Being For The Benefit Of Mr. Kite; Within You Without You; When I'm Sixty Four; Lovely Rita; Good Morning Good Morning; Sgt. Pepper's Lonely Hearts Club Band (Reprise); A Day In The Life
Running time:
39.50 or, on vinyl, infinite
Current CD:
CDP 7 46442 2
Further listening:
Hear Pepper develop on Anthology II (1996)
Further reading:
MOJO 1, 24, 26, 35, 71; The Complete Beatles Chronicle (Mark Lewisohn, 1996); Revolution In The Head (Ian McDonald, 1995)
Like this?
Try . . . p.596

Donovan

Sunshine Superman

Donovan, at his peak, shakes off the junior plastic Dylan tag. Nobody shouts Judas.

Dismissed first as a Dylan imitator and then as a cosmic buffoon, Donovan Philip Leitch was nevertheless a bit of a trailblazer: the first pop star to be busted for drugs (jumping naked onto a policeman's back while high on LSD) and one of the first British solo stars to top the US charts – with the title track of this album.

Born in Glasgow, raised in Hatfield, at 18 he was already a seasoned itinerant musician when discovered playing in a St Albans folk club by songwriter Geoff Stevens. A deal was quickly struck with Southern Music and Stevens suggested covering Gale Garnett's American hit We'll Sing In The Sunshine. But the teenaged troubadour wanted to record a poem he'd just set to music, Catch The Wind. Stevens alerted Bob Bickford, a scout for Ready Steady Go!, and the unsigned singer was booked for the show in February 1965. "Two nights on from sleeping on somebody's floor I was on national television!" Donovan wore a denim Breton fisherman's cap, sat on a stool and made up a song in a Woody Guthrie style, Talking Pop Star Blues, which poked fun at the current acts in the charts. The show was flooded with positive mail and Donovan was quickly booked for the following week.

Catch The Wind was swiftly leased to Pye and by the end of March the song was at Number 4 and the teen magazines were full of advertisements for "The Donovan Cap". An American scout caught Ready Steady Go! and booked him for a slot on Shindig, still only weeks after that support slot in St Albans. Catch The Wind made 23 in the US. A few singles later, he signed up with hit-maker Mickie Most and at the end of 1965 they cut Sunshine Superman and aired it on the short-lived UK TV show A Whole Scene Going. However, legal problems held its release over until September 1966, when its mildly trippy, upbeat blues sound chimed perfectly with the emergent hippy movement and the single sailed to Number 1 in the US and Number 2 in Britian.

This marvellous album was, in fact, released late in the UK and compiled from two American releases *Sunshine Superman* and *Mellow Yellow*. Pye omitted three of the American version's most psychedelic tracks – The Trip (later released on the flip of the Sunshine Superman single), The Fat Angel (a tribute to Cass Elliot which namechecks Jefferson Airplane and was later covered by the band) and Ferris Wheel.

Whichever edition you hear, however, the album offers a daring musical blend of jazz, folk, rock, raga and Arabic influences, while lyrically exploring a combination of Celtic and Anglo-Saxon mythology, wry social satire and beat poetry.

Record label:
Pye
Produced
by Mickie Most.
Recorded
in Hollywood and London; 1965 (title track) and summer 1966.
Released:
June 1967 (UK); September 1966 (US)
Chart peaks:
(UK) 25 ; (US) 11
Personnel:
Donovan (v,g); Eric Ford (g); Jimmy Page (g); Bobby Rae (b); Spike Healey (b); Shaun Phillips (sitar); Bobby Orr (d); Fast Eddie Hoh (d); Tony Carr (pc); John Cameron (k, a); Harold McNair (f); Danny Thompson (db)
Track listing:
Sunshine Superman; Legend Of A Girl Child Linda; The Observation; Guinevere; Celeste; Writer In The Sun; Season Of The Witch; Hampstead Incident; Sand Of Foam; Young Girl Blues; Three Kingfishers; Bert's Blues.
Running time:
49.00 (UK) 41.22 (US)
Current CD:
Beat Goes On BGOCD68. US version also available: Sunshine Superman; Legend Of A Girl Child Linda; Three Kingfishers; Ferris Wheel; Bert's Blues; Season Of The Witch; The Trip; Guinevere; The Fat Angel; Celeste. Epic SLD 23562
Further listening:
Mellow Yellow (1967); A Gift From A Flower To A Garden (1967); Barabajagal (1969)
Further reading:
www.sabotage.demon.co.uk/donovan
Like this?
Try . . . p.452

The Monkees

Headquarters

TV's phoney-rockers prove they can make their own music.

The success of The Monkees, whose origins dated back to a September 1965 Variety ad for four "spirited" boys, had surpassed their corporate creators' dreams. While their public image was of a self-contained group, record mogul Don Kirshner, who chose their songs and oversaw their records, made no effort to hide his role in their fame. In January 1967, when their second album, *More Of The Monkees*, hit the stores, the group was on tour. As Peter Tork later recalled: "In Cleveland, we went across the street and bought the first copy of our record that we'd seen. The back liner notes were Don Kirshner congratulating all his boys for the wonderful work they'd done, and, oh, yes, this record is by The Monkees."

Thus began a rebellion by the prefab four, which climaxed in a legendary run-in with Kirshner at a Beverly Hills hotel, where Michael Nesmith reportedly put his fist through a wall. Nesmith proceeded to spill to TV Guide, "The music on our records has nothing to do with us. It's totally dishonest, tell the world we're synthetic, because, dammit, we are!" At the insistence of the TV show producers, Kirshner relaxed control and the group chose its own producer, Turtles bassist Chip Douglas. As the group-penned liner notes to *Headquarters* explained: "We aren't the only musicians on this album, but the occasional extra bass or horn player played under our direction, so that this is all ours."

Headquarters is indeed the work of a self-contained group, sounding closer to a garage band than the polished combos that cut The Monkees' previous records. The group's exhilaration at being let loose is obvious. The prevailing influence is folk-rock - it was rumoured for years that The Byrds played on the sparkling You Just May Be The One. Yet the album's most notorious track is, stylistically, all-but uncategorisable.

The Monkees' US label, Colgems, didn't deem any of *Headquarters* worthy of single release, but UK label, RCA, heard a song it thought perfect for the British market: Dolenz's absurdist rant Randy Scouse Git. (Dolenz had picked up the title watching 'Til Death Do Us Part while romancing British wife Samantha.) There was, however, the small problem of the title. An RCA rep wrote to The Monkees' US office, "You are no doubt aware that many English expressions have a totally different meaning in America and vice versa, and in this case it is a question of the versa being vice. To give you a perfectly straightforward translation of the title, you are referring to someone as being an 'oversexed illegitimate son of a prostitute from Liverpool.'" Hence The Monkees' second-biggest UK hit was known as Alternate Title.

Record label:
RCA
Produced
by Douglas Farthing Hatlelid, aka Chip Douglas.
Recorded
at RCA Victor Studios, Hollywood; February–April 1967.
Released:
June 1967
Chart peaks:
1 (UK) 2 (US)
Personnel:
Mike Nesmith (g, ps, o, v); Davy Jones (pc, v); Micky Dolenz (d, g, v); Peter Tork (k, 12-string guitar, b, banjo, v); Vince DaRosa (French horn); Fred Seykora (c); Chip Douglas (b)
Track listing:
You Told Me; I'll Spend My Life With You; Forget That Girl; Band 6; You Just May Be The One; Shades Of Gray; I Can't Get Her Off My Mind; For Pete's Sake; Mr. Webster; Sunny Girlfriend; Zilch; No Time; Early Morning Blues And Greens; Randy Scouse Git (S/UK – released as Alternate Title)
Running time:
28.56
Current CD:
450997662 adds: Girl I Knew Somewhere; All Of Your Toys; Nine Times Blue; Jericho; Peter Gunn's Gun; Pillow Time
Further listening:
The Monkees (1966); More Of The Monkees (1967); Pisces, Aquarius, Capricorn And Jones (1967)
Further reading:
Monkees sessionography site: www.monkees.net/
Like this?
Try . . . p.617

Pearls Before Swine

One Nation Underground

Ukelele protégé beats Dylan, signs to eccentric New York jazz label and records classic psychedelic-folk debut.

As a child Tom Rapp entered a Minnesota talent contest with his ukulele and came third ahead of a certain Bobby Zimmerman; years later it was hearing Dylan's Blowin' In The Wind that inspired him to take up folk guitar. In 1965 Rapp was still at High School in Florida when he put together a band under the somewhat provocative name of Pearls Before Swine. After sending a demo to the *avante-garde* ESP label (chosen because they had signed the Fugs) the group were summoned to New York where they cut their debut in just four days in a cramped but well-equipped 4-track studio.

The result is a timeless collage of evocative poetry and haunting melodies, performed with an eccentric array of mostly acoustic instruments. Another Time - Rapp's first serious venture into song writing and a blueprint for much of his later work – was inspired by his miraculous survival of a car crash, its meditative lyrics brooding upon the struggle of the individual within a wondrous, yet capricious, universe. Morning Song, with its striking recorder solo, and the aptly named Surrealistic Waltz, venture into darker territory reminiscent of J.R. Tolkein, while the spirit of the times is perfectly captured by songs like Drop Out! and Uncle John (the latter a scathing assault on the hypocritical alliance between religion, patriotism and politics). Yet there are also moments of delightful irreverence: (Oh Dear) Miss Morse apparently got a New York DJ into hot water after several boy scouts managed to crack its coded chorus - the dots and dashes spelt out F.U.C.K.!

According to Rapp the band's influences were diverse - "everything from Peter, Paul & Mary to the Velvet Underground" - but perhaps the Pearls' most intriguing quality was their ability to borrow from the distant past without losing sight of the present. I Shall Not Care quotes inscriptions from Roman tombs while the eastern modal patterns which trickle through Ballad Of An Amber Lady are a perfect evocation of a Pre-Raphaelite painting. The sleeve art featured a detail from Hieronymous Bosch's Garden Of Earthly Delights, the LP including a free poster of the painting.

Despite the album selling in excess of 100,000 copies, ESP's liberal attitude toward its artists sadly failed when it came to paying royalties. After one more record for the label Rapp moved to Reprise and later Blue Thumb, for whom he continued to record into the early seventies. Eventually he called it a day and qualified as a human rights lawyer, but after a revival of interest in his work he was persuaded to return to music and in 1999 released his first album in over 25 years.

TF

Record label:
ESP 1054
CD:
Get Back GET 1008
Produced
by Richard Alderson
Recorded
at 6 - 9 May 1967, Impact Sound Studios, New York
Chart Peak UK:
Not released in the UK
Chart Peak US: ?
Released:
June 1967
Total running time:
36.25
Personnel:
Tom Rapp (voc, gtr), Wayne Harley (b. voc, autoharp, banjo, mandolin, vibraphone, audio oscillator), Lane Lederer (voc, bs, gtr, English horn, swinehorn, sarangi, celeste, finger cymbals), Roger Crissinger (org, harpsichord, clavioline), Warren Smith (drms, perc), Richard Alderson (arrangements), Elmer J. Gordon (production aide).
Track listing:
Another Time / Playmate / Ballad To An Amber Lady / (Oh Dear) Miss Morse / Drop Out! (S) / Morning Song (S) / Regions Of May / Uncle John / I Shall Not Care / The Surrealist Waltz
Further listening:
Balaklava, also on ESP/ Get Back. Constructive Melancholy (Birdman Records BMR021, 1999) is an excellent compilation of the Reprise years.
Website at:
www.rockmuse.com/pearls.html
Like this?
Try . . . p.84

Small Faces

Small Faces

The Small Faces' second album proper took a subtle, organic approach to psychedelia.

Following their split with Decca and manager Don Arden at the end of 1966, the Small Faces signed to Immediate, an independent label run in a libertine spirit wholly in keeping with proprietor Andrew Oldham's day-job as The Rolling Stones' manager. With virtually unlimited access to Olympic's new 8-track facility, the Small Faces – under the auspices of virtuoso engineer Glyn Johns – began to experience a creative awakening akin to The Beatles' in '65, experimenting with multi-tracking and other studio trickery, while expanding their minds with copious acid and 'gear'.

The outcome was a rich, inventive and wonderfully cheery brew of folk, psychedelia, music hall, swing, soul and psychedelia, with a strong English baroque twist – McLagan often swapping his trademark Hammond for harpsichord. Congas, celeste and Mellotrons also enriched the sound, with brass (on the calypso-flavoured Eddie's Dreaming) courtesy of Georgie Fame's horn section.

"We really were ahead of our time," says Kenny Jones. "We were fortunate that we had Glyn Johns; he was in our opinion the best engineer in Britain. He got us some amazing sounds and he encouraged us to be experimental."

The contrast with the group's first album on Decca (confusingly also titled *Small Faces*) – a nervy but one-dimensional R&B outing – is abundantly clear. Complementing Steve Marriott's legendary lungs, Ronnie Lane sings on five tracks, while McLagan tackles his own utterly charming Up The Wooden Hills To Bedfordshire. Though *Small Faces* spawned no singles, and was soon eclipsed by the stellar success of their Summer Of Love Number 1, Itchycoo Park, it arguably captured better than any other contemporary British album the excitement, optimism and sheer fun of like-minded spirits journeying together through the acid era.

PG

Record label:
Immediate
Produced
by Steve Marriott and Ronnie Lane.
Recorded
at Olympic Studios, London; 1967.
Released:
June 1967
Chart peaks:
12 (UK) None (US)
Personnel:
Steve Marriott (g, v); Ronnie Lane (b, v); Ian McLagan (k, v); Kenny Jones (d); Glyn Johns (e)
Track listing:
(Tell Me) Have You Ever Seen Me; Something I Want To Tell You; Feeling Lonely; Happy Boys Happy; Things Are Going To Get Better; My Way Of Giving; Green Circles; Become Like You; Get Yourself Together; All Our Yesterdays; Talk To You; Show Me The Way; Up The Wooden Hills To Bedfordshire; Eddie's Dreaming
Running time:
28.26
Current CD:
ESMCD476 adds: Here Come The Nice; Itchycoo Park; I'm Only Dreaming; Tin Soldier; I Feel Much Better
Further listening:
Ogden's Nut Gone Flake (1968); posthumous compilation, The Autumn Stone (1969)
Further reading:
MOJO 12A; All The Rage: A Riotous Romp Through Rock'N'Roll History (Ian McLagan, 1998)
Like this?
Try . . . p.414

Albert King

Born Under A Bad Sign

Breakthrough album for an unorthodox blues giant.

King – a left-hander who finger-picked an upside-down, right-handed Flying V – was into his '40s with only a couple of R&B hits to his name when he signed to Stax. Admittedly, he already had a smokin' reputation, but the Stax house band were to help him reach his true soul-blues potential.

After a trio of unsuccessful singles, two studio stints in mid-'67 provided the bulk of an album which was to exert massive influence on other guitarists, and at the same time launch King as a darling of the white college and stadium circuit. Wayne Jackson, who played trumpet on these and literally hundreds of other hit-making sessions for the label: "Albert was the sweetest man you could imagine: a man of the Old South. He used to call me his whistle-tooter. It was a very happy studio. Steve Cropper and Al Jackson ran the recordings. Jim Stewart [company boss] wasn't a producer – Al knew all the chords and lyrics better than anyone. He would stop things if they were going wrong. Albert's guitar was always out of tune with everything else, but he was such a strong man he would just bend those notes back in! The band kept things simple because we were all young guys learning together. We didn't know how to play it any better!"

The 10-bar-blues smoulder of the title track opens proceedings ("Sometimes the funk got so thick you could spread it on bread and eat it"), and the bad-ass syncopations of Crosscut Saw keep the heat on. The jump-shuffle of Kansas City is a welcome throwback, and his rendition of The Very Thought Of You proves that King could sing. But ultimately the guitar's the thing. The stinging, howling, weeping solo on Personal Manager is, simply, one of the greatest ever: King may have played from a relatively small stock of phrases but he made every one of them count.

The following year, on the back of the album's artistic success, King opened for Hendrix at San Francisco's Fillmore. As a teenager Hendrix had worshipped King. He never stopped, even recording Born Under A Bad Sign in 1969.

Record label:
Stax
No producer credited.
Recorded
at Stax Studios, McLemore Avenue, Memphis, Tennessee; March 3, September 3 and November 2, 1966; May 17 and June 9, 1967.
Released:
July 1967
Chart peaks:
None (UK) None, (US)
Personnel:
Albert King (g, v); Steve Cropper (g); Booker T. Jones (p); Isaac Hayes (p); Donald 'Duck' Dunn (b); Al Jackson Jr (d); Wayne Jackson (t); Andrew Love (s, flute); Joe Arnold (s); Jim Stewart (supervision)
Track listing:
Born Under A Bad Sign (S); Crosscut Saw (S); Kansas City; Oh Pretty Woman (S/US); Down Don't Bother Me; The Hunter; I Almost Lost My Mind; Personal Manager; Laundromat Blues (S/US); As The Years Go Passing By; The Very Thought Of You
Running time:
34.41
Current CD:
SCD 723 – 2
Further listening:
Live Wire/Blues Power (1968), live recordings from the Fillmore shows mentioned above; Ultimate Collection (1983), a 2-CD round-up.
Further reading:
Soulsville, USA: The Story Of Stax Records (Rob Bowman, New York); www.bluesnet.hub.org/artists/albert.king.htm
Like this?
Try . . . p.104

The West Coast Pop Art Experimental Band

Part One

Drug-free psych made to satisfy the lusts of an eccentric millionaire.

If ever an album demonstrated the haphazard way in which much psychedelic music of the late '60s was recorded, *Part One* must surely be it. After going to see their heroes, The Yardbirds, play at a hip Hollywood party, teenage hopefuls Michael Lloyd and the Harris brothers found themselves locked into a Faustian pact with the host, eccentric millionaire Bob Markley. The deal? He would promote their band and buy expensive equipment if they let him bang a tambourine on stage. According to Lloyd, music was the last thing on Markley's mind: "He had seen the incredible amount of girls and that was his only motivation."

Coining the ludicrously cumbersome name, Markley used his society contacts to secure the group a three-LP deal with Reprise, but once in the studio his younger bandmates soon began to tire of their patron's increasing dominance. As Shaun recalls: "The part that was frustrating was that he had no musical aptitude of any kind and so what he was trying to do to be different and innovative ended up sounding contrived. It was an embarrassment."

Well, time can tell a different story. Recorded without the influence of drink or drugs, it is precisely the palpable tensions within the band – and the unexpected juxtapositions within the music – which make *Part One* so extraordinary. Alongside passionate, harmonic pop songs like Transparent Day and the cover of PF Sloan's Here's Where You Belong, lurk the hard-edged, distorted weirdness of Leiyla, Zappa's Help I'm A Rock and 1906. The latter, with Markley eerily reciting his lyrics, attempts to convey a dog's premonition of the San Francisco earthquake: "See the frightened foxes/See the hunchback in the park/He's blind and can't run for cover/I don't feel well."

Another of Bob's Tinseltown friends, Baker Knight (who had written for Elvis and Ricky Nelson) composed two of the album's highlights: a beautifully sparse arrangement of Shifting Sands and If You Want This Love. As Danny recalls, the latter was transformed by a driving time signature: "When Baker Knight first heard the playback he didn't know what to make of it and said: 'Hey! I thought this was a country song!'" These were balanced in turn by the delicate dreamy songs I Won't Hurt You (backed with a heartbeat) and the acoustic, post-apocalyptic Will You Walk With Me, complete with string quartet and celeste; the album closed with an energetic reading of Van Dyke Parks's High Coin. The group would go on to record another four albums, each as individual as the last, but none would quite capture the sound of their first Reprise LP – the sound of teenage dreams diverted.

Record label:
Reprise
Produced
by Bob Markley and Jimmy Bowen.
Recorded
at United Western Recording Studios, Los Angeles; late 1966.
Released:
July 1967
Chart peaks:
None (UK) None (US)
Personnel:
Bob Markley (v, p); Shaun Harris (v, b); Danny Harris (v, g); Michael Lloyd (v, g); Ron Morgan (g); Hal Blaine or Jim Gordon (d)
Track listing:
Shifting Sands (S); I Won't Hurt You; 1906 (S); Help I'm A Rock; Will You Walk With Me; Transparent Day; Leiyla; Here's Where You Belong; If You Want This Love; 'Scuse Me Miss Rose; High Coin
Running time:
30.36
Not currently available on CD
Further listening:
A Child's Guide To Good And Evil (1968); A Group (1970) Bob Markley 'solo' LP which reunited the original members.
Further reading:
www.members.ams.chello.nl/cvanderlely/wcpaeb.html I
Like this?
Try . . . p.549

The Electric Prunes

Underground

Dissolution around the corner, dark psychedelic visionaries – briefly – reach flashover.

Like many musicians of their time The Electric Prunes were not masters of their own destiny. The three albums they recorded in a mere nine months during 1967 tell a cautionary tale of what happens when a gifted band are subjected to the whims of an equally talented producer and brilliant, but erratic, songwriters. Although their debut album *I Had Too Much To Dream Last Night* contained material equally as powerful as the classic single from which it spawned its title, it had been marred by ill-judged gimmicks. By the time of the third LP, *Mass In F Minor*, the band would effectively be reduced to session musicians languishing under the weight of composer David Axelrod's quasi-religious visions. Between these two extremes, *Underground* comes closest to expressing the unique spirit of a group who will long be regarded as one of the finest exponents of psychedelic pop.

The stunning sleeve shows the Prunes charging out of the cover, a forlorn face looming above them – an image whose mystery and energy are reflected in opening cut The Great Banana Hoax. With pounding drums and a pulsing rhythm as irresistible as The Byrds' Eight Miles High, at its centre is one of the group's defining moments: a plaintive organ note rises from the maelstrom and seamlessly gives way to Williams' biting guitar solo.

Aided by producer Dave Hassinger, they created a collage of effects without swamping each individual contribution, and conjured an atmosphere of haunting melodrama. Lowe's vocals wavered between soft innocence and sneering malice while the band shifted between the soft, sparse arrangements of tracks like I and the electrical charge of Hideaway. Antique Doll and Children Of Rain explore dark corners of childhood and themes of emotional isolation. In the hyperactive Dr Do-Good, Lowe's demented cartoon voice was juxtaposed with a riot of distorted guitar; but the real treat comes at the album's climax where raw punk and eastern-tinged psychedelia blend perfectly in Long Day's Flight.

Sadly, however, the Prunes were running out of juice. The album sold poorly. They produced only one more single before losing control of both their name and their future.

Record label:
Reprise
Produced
by Dave Hassinger.
Recorded
at the American Recording Company, North Hollywood, California; mid-1967.
Released:
August 1967
Chart peaks:
None (UK) 172 (US)
Personnel:
James Lowe (v, autoharp, hm); Mark Tulin (b, o, p); Ken Williams (g, effects); James 'Weasel' Spangola, Mike Gannon (v, g); Preston Ritter, Michael 'Quint' Weakley (d); Richie Podolor, Bill Cooper (e)
Track listing:
The Great Banana Hoax (S); Children Of Rain; Wind-Up Toys (S); Antique Doll; It's Not Fair; I Happen To Love You; Dr Do-Good (S); I; Hideaway (S); Big City; Capt. Glory; Long Day's Flight (S)
Running time:
34.43
Current CD:
CCM133
Further listening:
I Had Too Much To Dream Last Night (1967)
Further reading:
www.electricprunes.com/
Like this?
Try . . . p.147

Etta James

Tell Mama

The toughest female soul voice of the '60s gets the full Muscle Shoals treatment.

Etta James began singing at the age of five, as little Jamesetta Hawkins belting out gospel at Los Angeles' St Paul Baptist Church. Discovered and re-christened by LA band leader Johnny Otis, the 16-year-old Etta James had her first hit in 1955 with Roll With Me Henry. For the next five years James' life was one of constant touring and full immersion in a rough on-the-road life – sex, drugs and real mean men. A voice of sweet'n'lowdown power, like a born-bad angel, James signed to Leonard Chess's Chess Records in 1960 and the hits soon followed: At Last, Something Got A Hold Of Me and Stop The Wedding. By 1967 she was a full-time soul star with painted-on cat eyes, tight cup dresses, a pistol in her purse, and a full-time heroin habit – "Working to get high, stay high, live high and, if the stuff was strong enough, die high."

James sang the life she lived. Leonard Chess was convinced that the only woman who did it like Etta was Aretha Franklin. So, after Jerry Wexler put Aretha in Rick Hall's Fame Studios in 1967 to cut the R&B heartache classic *I Never Loved a Man The Way I Love You*, Chess decided to do the same with Etta. The first track James cut with the Muscle Shoals team was I'd Rather Go Blind, a song ripped from the heart about loving someone so much that you "just don't want to be free." James knew all about that. At the time she was seeing a guy called Billy Foster. Sometimes they fought so hard that Etta would end up sticking Billy with a kitchen knife. Etta says *she* wrote I'd Rather Go Blind. The songwriting credit went to Billy Foster. James sang about Security as she saw it slipping through her fingers. "The same rope that pulls you up/sure can hang you," she hollers on The Same Rope.

What she ended up with was an album of pure pain and suffering, and drum-tight soul. Just don't expect Etta to love it in the same way. "They rant and rave about *Tell Mama*," says James, "how I sang the shit out of it. I wish I could agree. I don't like being cast in the role of the Great Earth Mother, the gal you come to for comfort and easy sex. Nothing was easy then. My career was building up but my life was falling apart."

Record label:
Chess
Produced
by Rick Hall.
Recorded
at Fame Studios, Muscle Shoals, Alabama; early 1967.
Released:
August 1967
Chart peaks:
None (UK) None (US)
Personnel:
Etta James (v); Albert Lowe Jr (g); Jimmy Ray Johnson (g); David Hood (b); Roger Dawkins (d); Dewey Oldham (p); Carl Banks (o); Gene 'Bowlegs' Miller (t); Charles Chalmers, Aaron Varnell, Floyd Newman (s); George Davis (p)
Track listing:
Tell Mama (S); I'd Rather Go Blind (S); Watch Dog; The Love Of My Man (S); I'm Gonna Take What He's Got; The Same Rope; Security (S); Steal Away; My Mother In Law; Don't Lose Your Good Thing; It Hurts Me So Much; Just A Little Bit
Running time:
30.10
Currently unavailable on CD.
Further listening:
Live album Etta James Rocks The House (1964); Etta James Sings Funk (1970); Chess Masters (1983)
Further reading:
Rage To Survive (Etta James and David Ritz, 1998)
Like this?
Try . . . p.10

Pink Floyd

The Piper At The Gates Of Dawn

London's underground goes overground with a mix of playpen pop and grown-up acid rock.

"*The Piper At The Gates Of Dawn was* Syd," declares Roger Waters, "and Syd was a genius." Having built up a keen underground club following, Pink Floyd went overgrown early in 1967. Despite their reputation, two singles – Arnold Layne and See Emily Play – were disarmingly melodic and surprisingly successful. However, the Floyd always saw themselves as an albums band. Some critics, notably Pete Townshend (who said the LP was "fucking awful"), doubted whether their live performances would work in the studio, but history proved them wrong: *Piper* virtually defines British psychedelia. It was completed in just 16 sessions at EMI's Abbey Road Studios over four months, several of those purely for over-dubs. It was long enough, though, for the group to push in two seemingly irreconcilable musical directions, a division that in retro-spect clearly mirrored Barrett's increasingly fractured mental state. Extended pieces born of onstage jamming (Astronomy Domini; Interstellar Overdrive; POW R To H; Take Up Thy Stethoscope And Walk), sat oddly alongside Barrett's nursery-rhyme fantasies (Matilda Mother; The Gnome; Bike; Scarecrow), a dichotomy emphasised by further contradictions (electric/acoustic; cosmic/rural; blissful/fearful; adult/child). Holding these extremes together inevitably led to conflicts, not least because EMI staff Norman Smith was keen to impress with his first production job. "Working with Syd was sheer hell and there are no pleasant memo-ries," he said later, citing Barrett's unpredictability and unwilling-ness to play songs (or even parts) the same way twice. Incredibly, despite Barrett's habit of handling the mixing controls as if he were painting a canvas, Smith turned in a remarkable job, capturing both dimensions of the band's work without sacrificing the edginess or the childlike innocence. "Gadzooks, it's foot-tapping stuff," wrote a puzzled Nick Jones in Melody Maker. "'Avant garde', I think it's called." It wasn't the last time the Floyd would baffle the critics, but with Barrett barely able to function within weeks of the album's release, it was a rather less extraordinary Floyd that re-emerged without him.

Record Label:
EMI Columbia
Produced
by Norman Smith.
Recorded
at Abbey Road Studios, London; March 15–July 5, 1967.
Released:
August 1967
Chart peaks:
6 (UK) None (US)
Personnel:
Syd Barrett (g, v); Roger Waters (b, v); Richard Wright (o, p); Nick Mason (d); Peter Brown (e)
Track Listing:
Astronomy Domine; Lucifer Sam; Matilda Mother; Flaming (S, US only); Pow R To H; Take Up Thy Stethoscope And Walk; Interstellar Overdrive; The Gnome; Chapter 24; Scarecrow; Bike
Running time:
41.57 (stereo); 42.13 (mono)
Current CD:
E21S31261 (stereo edition); 7243 8 59857 2 0 (mono edition box set). The mono mix was the one the band oversaw and is, in many respects, superior to the stereo master.
Further listening:
Relics (1971); the spectre of Syd Barrett looms large over Piper follow-up, A Saucerful Of Secrets (1968). Pink Floyd/1967 – The First Three Singles (1997)
Further reading:
MOJO 20, 31; Syd Barrett And The Pink Floyd (Julian Palacios, 1998)
www.pinkfloyd.co.uk/
Like this?
Try . . . p.633

Jefferson Airplane

Surrealistic Pillow

San Francisco's psychedelic secrets get their first airing.

Coffee-bar folkies energised by the British Invasion and The Byrds, Bob Dylan and Beat texts, free love and LSD, Jefferson Airplane were the mid-60s San Francisco scene's first fledglings. After headlining a series of druggy dances in autumn 1965, they secured a major deal with RCA and released a mild-mannered folk-rock album (*Takes Off*) in August 1966.

"We were unhappy with the results," remembered Paul Kantner, so he invited The Grateful Dead's Jerry Garcia along to the sessions for the follow-up, as a peacemaker between the band, whose working methods were increasingly rooted in improvisation, and the production team. More crucial still, was the arrival of singer Grace Slick, an ex-model who'd cut her teeth with Bay Area combo The Great Society. Slick brought a steely beauty, a scat singing style and, said Kantner, "an early punk attitude"; not to mention two breathtaking songs, Somebody To Love and White Rabbit, on which the album's reputation is largely based. Also in tow was new drummer Spencer Dryden (replacing the errant Skip Spence), whose free-flowing style liberated the rhythm section. Remarkably, sessions for *Pillow* began just two weeks after Slick's stage debut, yet her contribution was instantly felt. "A quantum leap" is how Jorma Kaukonen describes the record, though a surfeit of love songs, vogueish reverb and acoustic instruments tends to belie the album's acid reputation.

Writing in *Esquire*, Robert Christgau described it as "amplified Peter, Paul & Mary", and "competent, original folk-rock" at best; but to Garcia's ears it sounded "as surrealistic as a pillow". White Rabbit, with its "feed your head" pay-off, may have been an obvious paean to acid, inspired by Ravel's Bolero and Alice In Wonderland, but much of the album's countercultural clout was understated. A wistful "Too many days are left unstoned" (D.C.B.A.-25), sung in harmony over a gentle folk-rock backing, was more typical. White Rabbit aside, the moments of amplified abandon were reserved for each side's opening cuts, the Diddleyesque She Has Funny Cars, and 3/5 Of A Mile In 10 Seconds, with its memorable Balin rage, "Do away with people laughing at my hair". The singer's tear-stained vocals on Today and Comin' Back To Me sat uneasily beside the group's wayward image, but *Surrealistic Pillow* would have been far less enigmatic without him.

Record Label:
RCA
Produced
by Rick Jarrard.
Recorded
at RCA Studios, Hollywood; October 31–November 22, 1966.
Released:
September 1967
Chart peaks:
None (UK) 3 (US)
Personnel:
Grace Slick (v, p, k, recorder); Paul Kantner (g, v); Jorma Kaukonen (g, v); Jack Casady (b, g); Spencer Dryden (d); Marty Balin (v, g); Jerry Garcia (g, musical and spiritual adviser); Dave Hassinger (e)
Track Listing:
She Has Funny Cars; Somebody To Love (S); My Best Friend; Today; Comin' Back To Me; 3/5 Of A Mile In 10 Seconds; D.C.B.A.-25; How Do You Feel; Embryonic Journey; White Rabbit (S); Plastic Fantastic Lover
Running time:
34.26
Current CD:
PCD13766
Further listening:
After Bathing At Baxter's (1967)
Further reading:
Jefferson Airplane And The San Francisco Sound (Ralph J Gleason, 1969)
www.jeffersonairplane.com/
Like this?
Try . . . p.196

The Thirteenth Floor Elevators

Easter Everywhere

Alleged to get you high even when you're straight.

The Thirteenth Floor Elevators were the first band to describe or advertise their music as psychedelic, beating The Grateful Dead by two weeks. "I come out of Buddy Holly and then ran straight into Bob Dylan who then ran outta me," Roky Erickson said in 1996, "I was as Texas as I ever was, like a full dead creature could be." Which is about as articulate and succinct a statement about the Elevators as one could hope for today.

Producer Lelan Rodgers was a record business veteran – like famous brother Kenny – when he discovered the band playing in Houston. Signed to his optimistically named International Artists label, they hit Number 55 in the USA with Roky's You're Gonna Miss Me. Rodgers was convinced he had hit makers on his hands but jug player/chief lyricist/resident Owsley-type Tommy Hall kept the band pioneering psychedelia and they never troubled the charts again, becoming Lone Star state legends instead.

Hall, his wife Clementine, virtuoso guitarist Stacy Sutherland (more responsible for the style of those Fillmore West acid guitar solos than Jorma Kaukonen or Jerry Garcia) and Erickson wrote songs whose lyrics were laced with a stoned mysticism. Coupled with their hypnotic music, the lyrics were supposedly enough to give the listener the answer they were searching for, as well as provide him or her with a real high. Ya dig? Rodgers deliberately under-promoted the band because, he claimed, he wanted their growing mystique (they caused the authorities in Texas as much worry as the Sex Pistols would in the UK) to snowball. Which meant outside Texas relatively few heard the West Coast/Gulf Coast power of Slip Inside This House or Nobody To Love, the sweet folkish balladry of I Had To Tell You or Sutherland's stunning guitar leads or Erickson's manic vocals (he had one of the most earnest singing styles in pop).

By the end of these sessions they were already too far gone (Erickson would take acid over 300 times) and the authorities were waiting to pounce. The band began a slow dissolution. Yet ask any Texas musician over 40 about them and they'll tell you: the Elevators weren't mere prophets, they were Kings.

Record label:
International Artists
Produced
by Lelan Rodgers.
Recorded
in Houston; late spring 1967.
Released:
September 1967
Chart peaks:
None (UK) None (US)
Personnel:
Roky Erickson (v, g); Tommy Hall (jug, v); Dan Galindo (b); Stacy Sutherland (g); Danny Thomas (d)
Track listing:
Slip Inside This House (S/US); Slide Machine; She Lives (In A Time Of Her Own) (S/US); Nobody To Love; Baby Blue (S/US); Earthquake; Dust; Levitation (S/US); I Had To Tell You; Pictures (Leave Your Body Behind)
Running time:
43.15
Current CD:
CDGR 111 adds: Gettin' There; What's Your Movie?; Ever Since I Stole The Blues; Was; Gettin' Paid Waltz; My Backyard; Certified Senior Citizen; This Ain't Me; You Can't Push People Around; Earth Wants Me
Further listening:
The Psychedelic Sounds Of (1966), their first album.
Further reading:
There are several good Thirteenth Floor Elevators websites, try ex-Elevator Danny Thomas' www.ed.brocku.ca/~paul/favorite/elevators/
Like this?
Try . . . p.174

Bonzo Dog Doo-Dah Band

Gorilla

Debut from Britain's best comic-rock troupe.

The Bonzos tumbled out of the heady, early '60s art-school scene, an ever-changing troupe of eccentrics who delighted the college crowd with a riot of exploding wardrobes, archaic instruments, pre-war novelty songs and jazz-age pop. In 1966 they decided to get a bit more serious. Recalls Neil Innes, "The New Vaudeville Band had a hit with Winchester Cathedral, but as they were a studio creation we were asked to be the band. Bob Kerr was the only one who went. But Viv and I realised we had to write our own material. *Gorilla* is us in the throes of becoming modern."

Some of those songs from the '20s and '30s (Jollity Farm, Mickey's Son And Daughter) found their way onto the album, but now any idiom was fair game. Look Out, There's A Monster Coming is a calypsoed comment on personal vanity, the brassy Big Shot lampoons *film noir* gumshoes, while the quite brilliant The Intro And The Outro starts with the jazz tradition of introducing the band and, as Innes notes, takes it to absurd levels. "That was a collective effort. Amazingly enough it was done on four-track. We had a very good engineer – his name escapes me – who just kept bouncing things down." Lines such as "And looking very relaxed, Adolf Hitler on vibes" and "The Count Basie Orchestra on triangle", ooze comic greatness. Innes – later to write the songs for the superb Rutles mock-umentary – contributed a dollop or two of Fabs-derived fare. "*Sergeant Pepper* had just been released, and of course it was a great influence. We were actually driving to Liverpool when the idea for Equestrian Statue came to me. I was reading Jean Paul Sartre in the van, as you do, and there was some tosh about whether a lamp-post exists in the same way a human does so I thought, why not a statue.

"The whole recording process was very spontaneous. We never really discussed what we were doing. We just had a shared sense of community. We all had problems with our shirts." *Gorilla*, with patronage from The Beatles (the Bonzos performed Death Cab For Cutie in Magical Mystery Tour), established them as acerbic court jesters to the burgeoning rock business; an essential role they performed admirably, in various guises, on into the '70s.

Record Label:
Liberty
Produced
by Gerry Bron.
Recorded
at Regent Sound, Abbey Road and Landsdowne studios, London; May–July 1967.
Released:
October 1967
Chart peaks:
None (UK) None (US)
Personnel:
Viv Stanshall (v, brass, ukelele); Neil Innes (v, g, k); Roger Ruskin Spear (brass, xylophone, bells); 'Legs' Larry Smith (d, tuba, tap-dancing); Sam Spoons (b, p); Vernon Dudley Bohay-Nowell (b, brass, banjo); Rodney Slater (brass, wind)
Track Listing:
Cool Britannia; Equestrian Statue (S); Jollity Farm; I Left My Heart In San Francisco; Look Out There's A Monster Coming; Jazz, Delicious Hot,Disgusting Cold; Death Cab For Cutie; Narcissus; The Intro And The Outro; Mickey's Son And Daughter; Big Shot; Music For The Head Ballet; Piggy Bank Love; I'm Bored; The Sound Of Music
Running time:
34.38
Current CD:
BGOCD82
Further listening:
The Doughnut In Granny's Greenhouse (1968); Keynsham (1969)
Further reading:
MOJO 18, 67; www.bridge.anglia.ac.uk/~systimk/music/Bonzos/
Like this?
Try . . . p.91

Country Joe And The Fish

Electric Music For The Mind And Body

Pioneers of psychedelic-protest mix acid and satire.

Electric Music For The Mind And Body certainly sounds like an 11-song panegyric for LSD but, unusually for 1967, it also acknowledged the real world of Vietnam-era politics. That was largely due to activist/frontman Country Joe McDonald, who'd formed the group in 1965 to play jugband protest songs to Berkeley University beatniks. One, I-Feel-Like-I'm-Fixin'-To-Die-Rag, later became the counter-culture's key anti-war anthem, eclipsing the band's psychedelic reputation in the process.

A druggy mid-1966 EP, *Rag Baby*, enjoyed considerable success in and around San Francisco and later that year the Fish were signed to Vanguard.

"In many ways, *Electric Music* is fairly unrepresentative of what the band actually sounded like in concert," says Barry Melton. "When we played live, the amps had a typical overdriven sound that was much more rock'n'roll-ish. But (engineer) Bob DeSousa insisted we turn the amps down very low so that he could maintain separation between the instruments and balance them." The result was far more polished and rehearsed than the Fish had intended, but in spring 1967, *Electric Music* – dressed in one of the era's more evocative sleeves – was still way ahead of the competition. Taut, psychedelicised R&B (Flying High, Love) and waltz-time craziness (Porpoise Mouth, The Masked Marauder), were complemented by some extraordinary acid-rock excursions (Bass Strings, Section 43 and Grace), where Melton's highly-strung guitar, Cohen's asthmatic Farfisa and Joe's stoner vocals detonated over dreamlike, mock-Eastern rhythms. There was satire here too (Superbird, Flying High), but essentially *Electric Music* was about the politics of mind-altering drugs.

"It's hard to say who was right in the end," says the guitarist. "Bob may have come up with a more artistic recording, and cleaned us up enough to be commercial. But maybe we were cleaned up so much that we never had the smash success with our records that we had on stage." That said, *Electric Music* was a consistent seller throughout the Summer Of Love, and remains one of the few truly successful US psychedelic albums.

Record label:
Vanguard
Produced
by Samuel Charters.
Recorded
at Sierra Sound Laboratories, California; January–February 1967.
Released:
October 1967
Chart peaks:
None (UK) 39 (US)
Personnel:
Joe McDonald (v, g, hm, tambourine); Barry Melton (v, g); David Cohen (g, o); Bruce Barthol (b, hm); Chicken Hirsch (d); Bob DeSousa (e)
Track Listing:
Flying High; Not So Sweet Martha Lorraine; Death Sound Blues; Happiness Is A Porpoise Mouth; Section 43; Superbird; Sad And Lonely Times; Love; Bass Strings; The Masked Marauder; Grace
Running time:
44.15
Current CD:
VAN792444
Further listening:
Try I-Feel-Like-I'm-Fixin'-To-Die (1967) for more of the same, albeit with a little more bad-trip darkness.
Further reading:
www.well.com/~cjfish/
Like this?
Try . . . p.144

The Hollies

Butterfly

As close as they came to a classic.

By September 1967, the Indian Summer of Love was in full Technicolor bloom. If *Sgt Pepper* psychedelia's excesses had become public property, The Hollies – in particular Graham Nash – wanted in.

Butterfly, their fourth album of entirely self-penned songs in only two years (credited to the nucleus of Hicks/Clarke/Nash), represented all that was good and bad about British psychedelia. Although a typically well-crafted Hollies record, and blessed with their immaculate three-part harmonies, it features all the trademarks of its time – fairy tale lyrics (Pegasus), stuff about being "high as the sky" (Elevated Observations), full orchestral arrangements (Away Away Away) and, inevitably, Eastern instrumentation (Maker). High points include Nash's intricate Dear Eloise and Butterfly itself, in spite of its "lemonade lakes" and "candy floss snow" (a lower point is Clarke's embarrassing tale of two rag and bone men, Charlie And Fred). It is also largely Graham Nash's record: he sings most of the leads and his wistful, winsome qualities prevail.

In the US the album was known as *Dear Eloise/King Midas In Reverse* and included Nash's King Midas In Reverse, arguably The Hollies' finest recorded moment but a relative flop as a single and left off the UK edition. It had been released against the advice of the group's long-standing producer Ron Richards, who argued that it was too complex for Hollies fans. He was proved right.

Nash, however, wanted to reach beyond the limits of the band's fanbase. He met David Crosby while attending a Mamas And Papas recording session in LA at the end of 1967, and the seeds of a new collaboration were sewn. A follow-up to *Butterfly* was underway by March 1968 but was soon scrapped. Two new Nash songs (Marrakesh Express and Lady Of The Island) were not even attempted. For the rest of the year Nash's relationship with the band was increasingly strained. The appeal of the seaside cabaret circuit and a mooted album of Dylan covers led him to leave the band on December 8, whereupon he went straight into rehearsals with Crosby and Stephen Stills. Meantime, *The Hollies' Greatest*, their only Number 1 album, was still enjoying a 22-week run in the Top 10.

Record label:
Columbia
Produced
by Ron Richards.
Recorded
EMI Studios, London; September 1967.
Released:
October 1967
Chart peaks:
None (UK) None (US)
Personnel:
Allan Clarke (v, g); Tony Hicks (g); Graham Nash (v, rg); Bernie Calvert (b, k); Bobby Elliott (d)
Track listing:
Dear Eloise; Away Away Away; Maker; Pegasus; Would You Believe; Wishyouawish; Postcard; Charlie And Fred; Try It; Elevated Observations; Step Inside; Butterfly
Running time:
31.25
Current CD:
4997712
Further listening:
The Special Collection 3-CD box set (1997)
Further reading:
www.proweb.co.uk/~rhaywood/
Like this?
Try . . . p.31

Frank Sinatra

Francis Albert Sinatra and Antonio Carlos Jobim

The Voice Of The Century's last consistently great vocal performance.

Sinatra came relatively late to the bossa boom. The bewitching melodies of Brazilian composer Antonio Carlos Jobim and sensual slow-motion samba rhythms of the bossa nova had been common adult pop currency since Stan Getz, Joao and Astrud Gilberto had popularised them in 1962–63, but Sinatra had been trying different approaches to find a commercial foothold in "Beatleland", as he had it. There was the country rock of half of *Sinatra 65* and the Ray Charles-ish blues pop of the single That's Life that followed the commercial jackpot of Strangers In The Night. All this kept the blue-eyed one on the radio but the albums were lousy, either unsatisfying mish mashes (*Sinatra 65, That's Life*), or openly contemptuous of the material (*Strangers In The Night*). But by immersing himself in the bossa nova and programming seven of Jobim's elegant compositions along with three standards done Jobim-style (the closest he got to recording a songbook album, he didn't consider that the English lyrics were sufficiently good at the time to make it an all-Jobim set), Sinatra fashioned one of his most majestic recorded achievements.

With by far the gentlest singing of his career, Sinatra's tender-strong voice is a wonder, respectfully piping through the Brazilian's graceful, economic tunes, as if to acknowledge the greatness of this new generation of standards. Sinatra said "I haven't sang this soft since I had laryngitis"– it's the polar opposite approach of his bluesy snarling on That's Life.

Like a more minimalist version of Jobim's Verve recordings – arranger Claus Ogerman and Jobim's 'personal drummer' Dom Um Romao were key figures of those sessions – Sinatra kept urging Ogerman to remove elements of the arrangement until the air played its part. A magical ingredient was Jobim himself, picking at his gut guitar and murmuring a Portuguese counterpoint on four of the tracks, less a duet partner than a wise composerly appendage. Jobim described Sinatra as "Mount Everest for a songwriter" while Frank rated "Tone" (as he called him) "one of the most talented musicians I have ever met"; the album they made together outdid the praise they had for each other and is probably the last essential Sinatra record. An attempt to follow it up two years later was compromised by palpably lower grade performances and flip side rock-ballad programming.

Record label:
Reprise
Produced
by Sonny Burke.
Recorded
in Hollywood, LA; 1967
Released:
October,1967
Chart peaks:
28 (UK) 19 (US)
Personnel:
Frank Sinatra (v); Antonio Carlos Jobim (g, v); Claus Ogerman (a, conductor); orchestra including Dick Noel (tb); Dom Um Romao (d)
Track Listing:
The Girl From Ipanema; Dindi; Change Partners; Quiet Nights Of Quiet Stars; Meditation; If You Never Come To Me; How Insensitive; I Concentrate On You; Baubles Bangles And Beads; Once I Loved
Running time:
27.47
Current CD:
Reprise FS1021-2
Further listening:
Sinatra and Company (1969)
Further reading:
Sinatra! The Song Is You: A Singer's Art (Will Friedwald, 1995)
Like this?
Try . . . p.695

Tim Buckley

Goodbye And Hello

Landmark in the shift from folk to singer/ songwriting music.

Recorded in June 1967, the month the Beatles released *Sgt. Pepper*, Tim Buckley's second album is drenched in the musical freedom of that mythologized time. "We saw ourselves sailing along in the direction that Bob Dylan was taking lyrics and that The Beatles were taking instrumentation," says poet Larry Beckett, Buckley's old school friend, then creative collaborator and co-writer of half the songs on *Goodbye And Hello*. "That is, toward making rock'n'roll into art songs, where they're so beautifully made that they're meant to last in the culture."

According to producer Jerry Yester, "When Buckley and Beckett came to me, the only idea they had was that the album would be free of restraint or commercial consideration. There was to be no compromising on the songs or how they were presented. Working with Tim was a stretch. When someone says you can do anything you want, it's a little intimidating at first, and then it's totally exciting."

Though *Goodbye And Hello* feels like an orchestrated album, in fact only the ambitious title track was orchestrally sweetened. The album's broad spectrum of sound is suggested through the flexibility of relatively few instruments and Buckley's most diverse collection of songs: the topical folk-rock of No Man Can Find The War; a blistering dialogue with drug dependency in Pleasant Street; the cathartic I Never Asked To Be Your Mountain (addressed in part to his ex-wife Mary and son Jeffrey Scott). The tender, lamenting Once I Was ("Soon there'll come another/to tell you I was just a lie") is a cousin of Fred Neil's Dolphins (which Tim performed regularly); Morning Glory ("write me a song about a hobo" was the singer's entire instruction to his lyricist) became Buckley's most covered song, and closes the album with a brief, exquisite wave of choral harmony.

What holds *Goodbye And Hello* together, and animates its occasionally bombastic conceits, is a string of vocal performances of staggering authority for a young man not yet twenty one. The musical freedom trumpeted so clearly here was something Tim would insist on for the rest of his career, to the dismay of those who hoped he'd linger a little longer at some of the stops along the way.

Record label:
Elektra
Produced
by Jerry Yester.
Recorded
at TTG Studios, and mixed by Bruce Botnick at Sunset Sound, Los Angeles; June 1967.
Released:
November 1967
Chart peaks:
None (UK) 171 (US)
Personnel:
Tim Buckley (v, g, sg, kalimba, vibes); Lee Underwood (lead g); Brian Hartzler (g); John Forsha (g); Jimmy Bond (b); Jim Fielder (b); Eddie Hoh (d); Carter CC Collins (pc, congas); Dave Guard (kalimba, tambourine); Don Randi (p, hamonium, harpsichord); Jerry Yester (o, p, harmonium); Henry Diltz (hm)
Track listing:
No Man Can Find The War; Carnival Song; Pleasant Street; Hallucinations; I Never Asked To Be Your Mountain; Once I Was (S/UK); Phantasmagoria In Two; Knight-Errant; Goodbye And Hello; Morning Glory (S)
Running time:
42.53
Current CD:
740282
Further listening:
Happy Sad (1969) – jazz/folk lullabies; Blue Afternoon (1970) – his most focused songwriting; Starsailor (1972) – wild avant-jazz and Song To The Siren; Greetings From LA – soul-inspired and drenched in sweat; Dream Letter – Live In London 1968 (1990)
Further reading:
www.timbuckley.com
Like this?
Try . . . p.662

Buffalo Springfield

Buffalo Springfield Again

Landmark album recorded in the brief space between inventing West Coast rock and falling apart.

"A great group," said Neil Young. "Everybody was a fucking genius at what they did – but we just didn't get it on record."For such a short-lived outfit, Buffalo Springfield would have a huge influence: much of the '70s West Coast rock movement, from the Eagles on down, could trace its ancestry back to the stormy combo founded when Young, his folk-singing career in Canada going nowhere, jumped the border in a hearse with his friend Bruce Palmer and headed for Los Angeles in search of old acquaintance Stephen Stills.

Buffalo Springfield – named after the steamroller tearing up the road outside their house – found themselves in quick succession endorsed by The Byrds, made house-band at the Whisky A Go Go and given a major label deal. Just as quickly, its members were busy falling out. Even during the recording of their eponymous debut there were arguments over whose songs would be included. It gave them their first hit single – the Stills-penned Sunset Strip protest song For What It's Worth – and was critically acclaimed.

Tracks were recorded in New York and Los Angeles – several under the supervision of label boss Ahmet Ertegun – for an album to be called *Stampede*. But the record was abandoned amid squabbles over songs, arrangements and band leadership (the latter role increasingly nabbed by Stills, who had been to military school as a kid). Outside pressures didn't help: Bruce Palmer had been arrested on a dope charge and deported to Canada. Ken Koblun, Young's old friend from The Squires, came down to help out but went back to Canada when the tense atmosphere became too much. A summer single was released – two new songs, Steve's Bluebird backed with Neil's Mr Soul. Stills on one side, Young on the other, just as they were in reality – they were rarely in the studio at the same time, and Young was torn between quitting the band (which he did twice, over their decisions to appear on Johnny Carson's mainstream Tonight Show and at the Monterey Pop Festival) and asking to rejoin. Differences aside, the music they were coming up with in the rescheduled sessions (some of it reworked *Stampede* material) was often superb.

"We were just really discovering a lot of new things and experimenting," said Young but in May 1968 – barely four months after the second album's release – the band broke up. A third album appeared posthumously.

SS

Record label:
Atco
Produced
by Ahmet Ertegun and Buffalo Springfield.
Recorded
at Sunset Sound, Gold Star, Los Angeles; June–September 1967.
Released:
November 1967
Chart peaks:
None (UK) 44 (US)
Personnel:
Neil Young (v, g); Stephen Stills (v, g); Richie Furay (v, g); Bruce Palmer, Jim Fielder, Bobby West (b); Dewey Martin (d); Don Randi (p); Jack Nitzsche (electric piano, a); Jim Messina, Ross Meyering, Bruce Botnick, William Brittan, Bill Lazarus (e)
Track listing:
Mr Soul; A Child's Claim To Fame; Everydays; Expecting To Fly; Bluebird; Hung Upside Down; Sad Memory; Good Time Boy; Rock And Roll Woman; Broken Arrow
Running time:
33.56
Current CD:
756790391-2
Further listening:
Buffalo Springfield (1967)
Further reading:
The Story Of Buffalo Springfield: For What It's Worth (John Einarson and Richie Furay, 1997)
Like this?
Try . . . p.674

Country Joe And The Fish

I-Feel-Like-I'm-Fixin'-To-Die

San Francisco scenesters second, an essential acid rock milestone.

"Gimme an F ... Gimme an I ... Gimme an S ... Gimme an H ... What's that spell? FISH! What's that spell? FISH!" Country Joe's second album begins, bizarrely, in a stoned, subversive, demented parody of high school cheerleaders. But they actually had their roots in the traditional US jugband and folk scenes, before developing their sound to become the Bay Area's foremost psychedelic adventurers, dizzyingly blending acid rock, satire, revolutionary politics and mischief.

The rollicking title song, a satirical, anti-war masterpiece, was written as America's involvement in Vietnam deepened disastrously. "Be the first one on your block to have your boy come home in a box," is typical of the lyrics, sung to a disconcertingly jaunty tune while the band cheerily chant, "Psychedelic, psychedelic!" in the background. The song remains McDonald's personal favourite.

"It's affected so many people's lives and it's affected history. I don't know if I can claim writing it because it just popped out of my head one day, but I'm most proud of facilitating that."

Janis is a tender love song for McDonald's former girlfriend Janis Joplin, while unlisted between Thought Dream and Thursday, is The Acid Commercial, a jolly jingle advertising lysergic pursuits: "If you're tired or a bit rundown/Can't seem to get your feet off the ground/Maybe you ought to try a little bit of LSD!"

The outrageousness of The Acid Commercial still startles. "The Establishment weren't paying attention to what we were doing so we were able to do anything we wanted," reasons McDonald. "We were the best ever psychedelic band."

They certainly took their role as acid pioneers seriously. "I've taken LSD 300 times," boasted guitarist Barry Melton in 1968. In a truly hallucinatory twist the same Melton, in another life, was in 1985 named by the San Francisco Bar Association as Outstanding Lawyer In Public Service."

Record label:
Vanguard
Produced
by Samuel Charters.
Recorded
at Vanguard Records' 23rd Street Studio, New York City; June–September 1967.
Released:
November 1967
Chart peaks:
None (UK) 67 (US)
Personnel:
Joe McDonald (v, g, o); Barry Melton (g, v, kazoo); David Cohen (o, calliope, harpsichord, g, v); Bruce Barthol (bs, hm, v); Chicken Hirsh (d); Ed Friedner (e)
Track listing:
The Fish Cheer And I-Feel-Like-I'm-Fixin'-To-Die Rag; Who Am I (S/US); Pat's Song; Rock Coast Blues; Magoo; Janis (S/US); Thought Dream; Thursday; Eastern Jam; Colors For Susan
Running time:
45.03
Current CD:
VMD 79266-2
Further listening:
Electric Music For The Mind And Body (1967), the band's debut, which McDonald has proudly described as "the best psychedelic rock record ever made by anybody in the world".
Further reading:
www.countryjoe.com. Apart from being excellently informative, McDonald's website gives you the chance to be the first on your block to buy a Gimme An F... condom!
Like this?
Try . . . p.167

Cream

Disraeli Gears

The great virtuoso excess starts here.

On March 25, 1967, Cream arrived in New York for their first trip to America, performing I Feel Free and I'm So Glad five times a day for 10 days on Murray The K's pop show. With three days left on their visas, they went into Atlantic Studios to record their follow-up album to *Fresh Cream*.

Released in December 1966, *Fresh Cream* was a relatively straight-ahead homage to Eric Clapton's blues influences, covering the songs of Robert Johnson, Skip James and Muddy Waters. But *Disraeli Gears* was a very different proposition for three reasons. The first was the flowering of the Bruce/Brown co-writing partnership. Nearly half the album is credited to them, including enduring Cream classics such as Sunshine Of Your Love and Tales Of Brave Ulysses. Of the former, Jack Bruce recalls: "Pete and I had been up all night trying to write stuff and getting nowhere. I started playing this riff. Pete was looking out the window and said, 'It's getting near dawn, and lights closed their tired eyes ...'"

In addition, in Felix Pappalardi they found a producer who understood Cream in a way their manager and producer of *Fresh Cream*, Robert Stigwood, never would. Pappalardi's tasteful production and Tom Dowd's sensitive engineering brought Clapton's new Hendrix-inspired tone and effects to the fore. Pappalardi was also an excellent musician and writer himself, credited along with his wife Gail Collins with Strange Brew and World Of Pain (a tragically ironic title, as Collins was to shoot her husband dead in 1983).

Finally, there was the influence of LSD. Songs like She Was Like A Bearded Rainbow (SWLABR) weren't conceived on cups of tea. During a conversation about racing bikes, instead of saying "derailleur gears", roadie Mick Turner said something else. It became the title of Cream's landmark excursion into a sometimes whimsical interpretation of psychedelic blues, gift-wrapped in an equally famous riot of day-glo colour by Martin Sharp encapsulating its acid-drenched mood. Right album, right place, right time.

Disraeli Gears broke the band in the States, with Sunshine Of Your Love (its war dance rhythm suggested to Ginger Baker by Tom Dowd) becoming Atlantic's biggest selling single. The album reveals Cream at their most cohesive: from then on, the pressure of touring, resentments over writing royalties and the resurgence of animosities between Bruce and Baker led to their inevitable break-up just a year after this album's release.

Record label:
Reaction
Produced
by Felix Pappalardi.
Recorded
at Atlantic Studios, New York; May 8–19, 1967.
Released:
November 1967
Chart peaks:
5 (UK) 4 (US)
Personnel:
Eric Clapton (g, v); Ginger Baker (d); Jack Bruce (b, v); Tom Dowd (e)
Track listing:
Strange Brew (S); Sunshine Of Your Love; World Of Pain; Dance The Night Away; Blue Condition; Tales of Brave Ulysses (S); SWLABR; We're Going Wrong; Outside Woman Blues; Take It Back; Mother's Lament.
Running time:
31.00
Current CD:
Polydor 5318112
Further listening:
Fresh Cream (1966); Wheels Of Fire (1968); Goodbye (1969); or the whole shebang on Those Were The Days (1997).
Further reading:
Strange Brew (Chris Welch, 1988); Lost In The Blues (Harry Shapiro, 1992); Edge Of Darkness (Chris Sandford, 1994); www.whereseric.com and www.thecream.net
Like this?
Try . . . p.128

Kaleidoscope

Tangerine Dream

One of the very few genuine British psychedelic albums.

The clever money in early '67 was on a pioneering bunch of groups whose trade was neither R&B or hit parade pop, but something altogether odder, more visual, quite new. Pink Floyd, The Soft Machine and Kaleidoscope hogged the column inches but the latter – the ones with the nimblest melodies – were destined for a long run of near-misses.

Originally The Sidekicks, a beat group from Harrow, they became The Key in 1965 and, on signing to Fontana in late 1966, Kaleidoscope. As their line-up had remained constant, their debut 45 (Flight From Ashiya c/w Holidaymaker) sounded supertight. Replete with Pumer's nerve-jangling guitar line and exquisite vocal interplay, Flight was played to death by the pirates and, though not a hit, encouraged Fontana enough to proceed with the album.

Opening with plucked harp and ferocious drums, the self-titled signature tune sets the scene for *Tangerine Dream*. Like The Bee Gees or The Kinks, Peter Daltrey's songs are vignettes; pilots on their final flights, elderly watch repairers (prescient of Mark Wirtz's Teenage Opera), Dickensian murder scenes. Everywhere there are beautiful drones courtesy of Pumer, fine high harmonies. All is crisp. Ultimately there is Dive Into Yesterday – five minutes of ebbing and flowing, atonal scraped guitar and a dive-bombing Duane Eddy hookline – and The Sky Children which maintains beautiful fairytale imagery with an astonishingly simple and hypnotic arrangement for a full nine minutes.

"Their songs are the best since The Beatles," said that pop oracle The Daily Sketch. Radio One offered them session after session. Kenny Everett called them "incredible". *Tangerine Dream* exuded summertime optimism, but it was sadly misplaced. Three more albums followed (two as Fairfield Parlour, the last not obtaining a release until the '90s) but a place deep in the heart of psych fanatics is all Kaleidoscope earned after such a promising start.

Record label:
Fontana
Produced
by Dick Leahy and Jack Baverstock.
Recorded
at Stanhope Place Studios, London; mid-1967.
Released:
November 1967
Chart peaks:
None (UK) None (US)
Personnel:
Peter Daltrey (v, k); Eddie Pumer (g); Steve Clark (b); Danny Bridgman (d); John Cameron (oa); John Paul Jones (b); Clem Cattini (d); Dave Voyde (e)
Track listing:
Kaleidoscope; Please Excuse My Face; Dive Into Yesterday; Mr Small The Watch Repairer Man; Flight From Ashiya; The Murder Of Lewis Tollani; (Further Reflections) In The Room Of Percussion; Dear Nellie Goodrich; Holidaymaker; A Lesson Perhaps; The Sky Children
Running time:
36.20
Currently unavailable on CD
though most of its tracks appear on Dive Into Yesterday: A Kaleidoscope Anthology
Further listening:
as Fairfield Parlour, From Home To Home (1970)
Further reading:
http://hem.passagen.se/chla1014/Reviews.html
Like this?
Try . . . p.587

Moody Blues

Days Of Future Passed

Birmingham beat group turn into lush art-rockers.

When the Moody Blues recorded *Days Of Future Passed*, in October 1967, most of the record-buying public thought that the group's day had indeed passed. Their original lead singer, Denny Laine, was gone, and despite the addition of new members Justin Hayward and John Lodge, they hadn't managed a hit in over two years. Their label, Deram (a Decca subsidiary), was losing patience and had assigned staff producer Tony Clark to oversee the Moody Blues' recordings after Laine's departure, with a mandate to create hit singles that would recoup the group's £5,000 advance.

After two singles missed the charts entirely, the label gave the group an album project – of a sort. They were to make a demonstration record of the label's new 'Deramic Stereo' process to show the potential it held for rock and classical music. Specifically, they were to create a rock version of Dvorak's New World Symphony, augmented by Peter Knight's orchestrations. It is unclear if the group ever really intended to create the album Deram wanted. They requested one week of 'lockout time' at the label's studios so they could have them for 24 hours a day instead of just the usual morning sessions. Then they convinced Knight to allow them to record the stage act that they had been working on for the past year, a song cycle chronicling a day in the life of an Everyman called Moody Blue. (Yes, they beat a certain song cycle about Mr Pink Floyd by about 12 years.) They also sought to replicate the feel of what Hayward later called "the first concept album" – not *Sgt. Pepper* or, in fact, the work of a band, but a studio concoction – *The Zodiac* by Cosmic Sounds.

"That was the birth of that sound, the tinkling bells and weird effects," Hayward explained. "It was our oracle. It was a simple concept – 12 songs based on the signs of the zodiac."

The group debuted the album at a party for Decca's brass. According to Lodge, some of the label's staff didn't know what to make of it. "When it finished, initially, stunned silence reigned. The singles head didn't like it, neither did the managing director, who said, 'You can't dance to it. You can't play this at a party.'" Although Tuesday Afternoon was a reasonably-sized US hit, *Days Of Future Passed* is forever identified with Nights in White Satin. The wistful ballad made Number 19 in the UK in 1967 and became a surprise US smash five years later when it was rediscovered by a Seattle DJ. Hayward, while proud of the song's lyrical depth, would later confess that its inspiration was surprisingly prosaic: "Somebody had actually given me some white satin sheets. They were totally useless, especially if you've a decent growth of beard like I have. Dreadful things, satin sheets."

Record label:
Deram
Produced
by Tony Clarke and Michael Dacre-Barclay.
Recorded
at Decca Studios, West Hampstead; October 1967.
Released:
November 11, 1967
Chart peaks:
27 (UK) 3 (US)
Personnel:
Justin Hayward (g, v); John Lodge, (b, v); Michael Pinder (k, mellotron, v); Ray Thomas (hm, flute, v); Graeme Edge (d, pc); Hugh Mendl (executive producer). With the London Festival Orchestra; Peter Knight (conductor)
Track listing:
The Day Begins; Dawn: Dawn Is A Feeling; The Morning: Another Morning; Lunch Break: Peak Hour; The Afternoon: Forever Afternoon (Tuesday?); (Evening) Time To Get Away; Evening: The Sun Set; Twilight Time; The Night: Nights In White Satin
Running time:
41.47
Current CD:
Universal/Decca 8200062
Further listening:
The Moody Blues maintained a consistently high level of artistry through 1972's Seventh Sojourn.
Further reading:
www.moodyblues.co.uk/
Like this?
Try . . . p.584

Jimi Hendrix Experience

Axis Bold As Love

Hendrix gets trippier.

Given that he had to hit the UK for his talents to be appreciated, Jimi Hendrix relied heavily on English boffins; British Marshall and Sound City amps were an integral part of his sound, and when he felt the need to customise his electronic armoury, he called on Roger Meyer, a London electronics guru who modified Jimi's fuzzboxes and wah wahs, and invented entirely new effects pedals for him.

George Chkiantz, an employee at London's Olympic Studio, was another crucial influence: "George was a tape op who would hang around in the maintenance department," remembered Jimi's producer and co-manager, Chas Chandler. "He was very hung up on sound, and would work out new ways to bastardise the equipment." This spirit of experiment pervaded Jimi's second album, recorded on the run between live engagements. Material, such as opener EXP, with its then-fashionable UFO references, sound dated in hindsight, despite the still-thrilling guitar exploration. The ostensibly simple songs that would prove more durable, notably Little Wing, which opened with a gorgeously simple guitar intro, heavily influenced by Curtis Mayfield. Castles Made Of Sand also employed subtle soul guitar styles; indeed for many guitarists Hendrix's fluent use of guitar voicings, sliding 4ths and other techniques make *Axis Bold As Love* the album that most rewards constant listening.

Bassist Noel Redding points out that the album's finest moments see the band working at the limits of their powers: "On the last track, Bold As Love, there's one point where we're playing three different rhythms at the same time. Most of those things were worked out in the studio."

Ironically, given the intense work that had gone into the rushed recording, Jimi ended up losing the master reel for half of the album – possibly on purpose, because he was unhappy with the sound. Chandler and engineer Eddie Kramer heroically remixed the entire side in one night, with the exception of If 6 Was 9. The two couldn't match their lost, first mix, "But in the end we found that Noel had taken a copy on 7 ½ ips to play at home on his domestic machine," remembered Chandler. "His machine had chewed the tape up, so we had to iron it flat. Then we mastered from that copy."

Record label:
Track
Produced
by Chas Chandler.
Recorded
mainly at Olympic Studios, London; May–October 1967.
Released:
December 1, 1967
Chart peaks:
5 (UK) 3 (US)
Personnel:
Jimi Hendrix (v, g); Noel Redding (b, bv); Mitch Mitchell (d)
Track listing:
EXP; Up From The Skies; Spanish Castle Magic; Wait Until Tomorrow; Ain't No Telling; Little Wing; If 6 Was 9; You Got Me Floatin'; Castles Made Of Sand; She's So Fine; One Rainy Wish; Little Miss Lover; Bold As Love
Running time:
39.35
Current CD:
MCD11601
Further listening:
The Jimi Hendrix Experience, (2000) contains fascinating out-takes from the Axis sessions.
Further reading:
MOJO 23, 50, 72; Electric Gypsy (Harry Shapiro and Caesar Glebbeek, 1991); www.jimi-hendrix.com
Like this?
Try . . . p.725

Jefferson Airplane

After Bathing At Baxter's

A defiant statement of the possibilities of acid-rock.

The surprise success of *Surrealistic Pillow* and its two singles had transformed Jefferson Airplane into a Top 10 act. *After Bathing At Baxter's*, its title a euphemism for psychedelic drug-taking, hastily reaffirmed their underground credentials. Uprooted from their communal home in Haight-Ashbury, the band rented a mansion in the Hollywood Hills, complete with pool and underground bowling alley, where they held "parties, strange parties, and then weird parties". With rookie producer Al Schmitt manning the mixing-desk, the high-jinx continued in the studio.

"We took over the soundboard," remembered Kantner. "We had motorcycles in the studio, nitrous oxide tanks, marijuana everywhere. Smoke rose out of the boards with Jack's bass parts overloading. (We) experimented with every button."

"The material was being written as we were in the studio," remembered Grace Slick. Few bands had hitherto enjoyed such freedom. At the time, Marty Balin, the band's erstwhile leader and frontman, described *Baxter's* as "a whole new and different thing for the group". With Slick and Kantner emerging as the group's leading writers, and instrumentalists Kaukonen and Casady hell-bent on undermining pop song convention, it also marked the end of his influence, Balin by now reduced to one writer's co-credit and a single lead vocal.

Baxter's was single-mindedly dedicated to the pursuit of high art via hallucinogenics. Songs were grouped together as 'suites', the mix was unprecedentedly 'open', with the instrumental balance often throwing strange sounds to the fore, and the range of the material was huge. At its extremes were a silly stoned sound collage (A Small Package Of Value Will Come To You, Shortly) and an inspired power-trio jam (Spare Chaynge). Central to the album were Kantner's robust, harmony-drenched anthems (The Ballad Of You And Me And Pooneil; Wild Tyme; Watch Her Ride; Won't You Try). Meanwhile, Slick's rejoyce (a sharp-witted anti-war lament inspired by Joyce's Ulysses) and Two Heads were the album's brilliant, baffling, idiosyncratic wild cards. "It was sort of a progress report on how things were going," concluded Kantner.

Record label:
RCA
Produced
by Al Schmitt.
Recorded
at RCA Studios, Hollywood; June–October 1967.
Released:
December 1967
Chart peaks:
None (UK) 17 (US)
Personnel:
Grace Slick (v, k, recorder); Paul Kantner (g, v); Marty Balin (v, tambourine); Jorma Kaukonen (g); Jack Casady (s); Spencer Dryden (d, v); Richie Schmitt (e)
Track Listing:
Streetmasse: i. The Ballad Of You and Me and Pooneil; ii. A Small Package Of Value Will Come To You, Shortly; iii. Young Girl Sunday Blues. The War Is Over: i. Martha; ii. Wild Tyme. Hymn To An Older Generation: i. The Last Wall Of The Castle; ii. rejoyce. How Suite It Is: i. Watch Her Ride; ii. Spare Chaynge. Shizoforest Love Suite: i. Two Heads; ii. Won't You Try/Saturday Afternoon
Running time:
43.55
Current CD:
0786366798-2
Further listening:
Surrealistic Pillow (1967); Crown Of Creation (1968) replaces '67's heady vibe with more apocalyptic visions.
Further reading:
Jefferson Airplane And The San Francisco Sound (Ralph J Gleason, 1969)
www.jeffersonairplane.com/
Like this?
Try . . . p.187

Traffic
Mr Fantasy

Pastoral debut from the crushed velvet heart of hippie England.

By autumn 1966 Steve Winwood had outgrown his role as teenage prodigy with the Spencer Davis Group and become a restless 20-year-old keenly aware of the new mood sweeping through pop. That summer the Davis band had scored major hits with Keep On Running and Gimme Some Loving, but Winwood was tired of being the star of a group bearing another's name. Even as their *Autumn 66* album appeared, Winwood was jamming around his home town of Birmingham with younger, more adventurous spirits, among them the three future members of Traffic.

In February 1967 Winwood officially quit the Spencer Davis Group and swapped Birmingham for the Berkshire village of Aston Tirrold, where Island supremo Chris Blackwell had found him a cottage to rent. Blackwell, with whom Winwood had managerial ties, saw Winwood as a future mainstay of his label as it grew a rock roster from its reggae roots.

Winwood occupied the cottage alone, but there were numerous visitations from the band, and the blend of bucolic Berkshire and the intoxications of the Summer Of Love proved creatively invigorating. So began the myth of 'getting it together in the country', a notion that has trapped numerous bands into stoned, fruitless escapism (The Stone Roses' *Second Coming* is but one case in point). The cover of *Mr Fantasy* shows the group gathered in the candle-lit cottage. Rural tranquillity does pervade a portion of the record, though Berkshire Poppies is little more than an update of cockney music hall (various Small Faces are present on it).

Produced with striking clarity by Jimmy Miller, the record soared on Winwood's soulful voice and inventive keyboard and guitar playing. Behind the balmy moods of Coloured Rain and Heaven Is In Your Mind lay much bickering over whether the pastel psychedelia of Dave Mason's Utterly Simple was fit to sit alongside mournful Winwood creations like No Face No Name No Number. The schism between Mason and the others was there in the pair of singles that preceded the album's release at the close of '67, Paper Sun and Hole In My Shoe (both included on the US edition), the latter a sitar and patchouli confection from Mason which Winwood recorded only under pressure. Time has certainly been kinder to the questing spirit of the title track than Mason's surrealist escapades, yet *Mr Fantasy* would be a less endearing encapsulation of its era without them.

NS

Record label:
Island
Produced
by Jimmy Miller.
Recorded
at Olympic Sound Studios; April 1967.
Released:
December 1967
Chart peaks:
8 (UK) 17 (US)
Personnel:
Steve Winwood (o, g, b, p, harpsichord, pc, v); Dave Mason (g, Mellotron, sitar, tambura, shakkai, b, v); Chris Wood (flute, s, o, v); Jim Capaldi (d, pc, v); Eddie Kramer (e)
Track listing:
Heaven Is In Your Mind; Berkshire Poppies, House For Everyone, No Face No Name No Number; Dear Mr Fantasy; Dealer; Utterly Simple; Coloured Rain; Hope I Never Find Me There; Giving To You
Running time:
34.30
Current CD:
IMCD 264 adds: Paper Sun (S); Hole In My Shoe (S); Smiling Phases; We're A Fade You Missed This and the whole of the American edition of the album.
Further listening:
Traffic (1968)
Further reading:
Back In the High Life: A Biography of Steve Winwood (Alan Clayson, 1988); www.stevewinwood.com
Like this?
Try . . . p.40

The Appletree Theatre

Playback

Saturday Night Live meets Sergeant Pepper in an innovative - and irreverent - theatrical concept album.

After spending their early teens in England absorbing the influences of the Goon Show and Beyond The Fringe, brothers John and Terence Boylan returned to America to study drama at Bard College, near Woodstock. There they formed a band with fellow students Walter Becker and Donald Fagen, performed comedy skits with Chevy Chase and even got to hang out with their hero Bob Dylan. Vacations were spent playing the coffee house circuit in New York. One evening, confined to their apartment by illness, the brothers composed Hightower Square. If the song's staccato rhythm owed a conscious debt to The Beatles' Penny Lane, the bridge, which incorporates a spoken-word skit about smoking banana peel, pointed in a rather more light-hearted direction.

Having persuaded MGM to finance an album, the Boylans enlisted the services of the hottest session musicians they could find, while the presence of innovative engineers like Bill Szymczyk ensured that musical quality was never sacrificed to comic effect. As John recalls: "Because we were in the business we knew what these players could do – we felt like painters with an expensive new paint box." Structured like a play, the album intersperses musical burlesques with comedy sketches. A series of vignettes of Greenwich Village life send up weekend hippies (E-Train), druggies (Brother Speed) and squares (I Wonder If Louise Is Home) with equal relish. By contrast, side two has a rural focus, its ambitious centre-piece The Sorry State Of Staying Awake, in which a bored truck driver lazily turning his radio dial encounters fragments of hilariously over-blown Soul and Country music, spoof news bulletins and adverts. What A Way To Go, featuring a woodwind quintet and the late, great Zal Yanovsky on guitar, provides a beautiful, mournful coda to the preceding levity.

In a contemporary interview John Lennon cited *Playback* as one of his favourite albums, Time Magazine lauded the Boylans' sense of humour and satirical groups like the Firesign Theatre acknowledged them as an influence. Unfortunately, with MGM unsure how to promote the album and the material almost impossible to replicate live, the project remained a critical rather than commercial success. John became a highly-respected producer, notably with Rick Nelson and Boston, while Terence went on to release a number of solo albums, the first of which re-worked many of the songs from *Playback* with the help of the future members of Steely Dan. Yet as the Appletree Theatre the Boylan brothers had struck a balance between music and comedy which has seldom been equalled on record - and proved that rock musicians don't always have to take themselves too seriously.

TF

Record label:
MGM / Verve Forecast FTS 3042
Not currently available on CD

Produced
by John and Terence Boylan, Pete Spargo (executive producer)

Recorded
at 1967, Mirasound Studios, NYC

Chart peak UK:
None

Chart peak US:
None

Release date:
January 1968

Total running time:
33.28

Personnel:
J Boylan (voc, gtr, pno), T Boylan (voc, gtr, bs), CIsraels (bs), L Coryell (gtr), M Equine (drm), P Griffin (pno, org), C Rainey (bs), H Lovelle (drm), E Gale (gtr), B Saltzman (drm), Z Yanovsky (gtr), M Brown (cello), The NY Philharmonic

Track listing:
The Altogether Overture: In The Beginning / Hightower Square (S); Act 1: Lullaby / Saturday Morning / Nevertheless It Was Italy; Act 2: I Wonder If Louise Is Home / Chez Louise / E-Train / Meanwhile / Brother Speed / You're The Biggest Thing In My Life; Act 3: Don't Blame It On Your Wife / The Sorry State Of Staying Awake; Epilogue: Barefoot Boy / Lotus Flower (S) / What A Way To Go (S).

Further listening:
Terence Boylan: Alias Boona (MGM 1969)

Like this?
Try . . . p.485

Captain Beefheart And His Magic Band

Safe As Milk

Howlin' Wolf projected into the future. Extraordinary debut from one of rock's premier league eccentrics.

Perhaps impressed by the way in which Captain Beefheart's early singles Diddy Wah Diddy (a Bo Diddley cover) and Moonchild had paralleled contemporary blues-boom developments in Britain, A&M co-owner Jerry Moss was sufficiently encouraged to commission an album from the Los Angeles-based band. Upon hearing the demos, however, he refused to release the album on the grounds that it was too negative, and that songs like Electricity were not safe for his daughter to listen to. With their A&M contract finished, the first Magic Band broke up, leaving Beefheart free to sign with Buddah Records, where Bob Krasnow set to work polishing the songs that A&M had refused.

Beefheart reworked seven of the songs with bassist Herb Bermann – chosen because, as a professional songwriter already, he might lend a little more credence to the Captain's compositions in the eyes of the second Magic Band. This new aggregation retained guitarist Alex St Clair Snouffer and bassist Jerry Handley from the previous line-up, alongside two new players who would add distinctive elements to the band's sound: idiosyncratic drummer John "Drumbo" French, and 16-year-old slide-guitar virtuoso Ry Cooder, whose curling lines set the desert-dry tone of the album's opener Sure 'Nuff 'N Yes I Do, a modernised take on Muddy Waters' classic Rollin' And Tumblin' riff. This and a cover of Robert Pete Williams' Grown So Ugly provided the clearest connection with the Captain's blues roots, though already there were signs of Beefheart's burgeoning sonic ambitions, notably in the presence of the theremin in Electricity and Autumn's Child, and the addition of Milt Holland's log-drum and marimba to the grungey Dropout Boogie. Horns and backing vocals, meanwhile, brought an authentic Southern soul feel to Call On Me.

Though later albums would head for much weirder territory, the basic elements of the Magic Band sound were already in place on *Safe As Milk*: the rumbustious, jerky polyrhythms; the spindly, interlocking guitar lines; the abrupt changes in tempo; Beefheart's raw blues-harp; and most of all, Beefheart's voice, a fearsome multi-octave instrument capable of swooping mid-line from a high-pitched squawk to a subterranean bass growl. According to engineer Hank Cicalo, it was Beefheart's vocals that were responsible for destroying a $1200 Telefunken microphone – a feat he later repeated on The Woody Woodberry TV Show. Though the album caused few ripples on its American release, it became one of the most ubiquitous artefacts of UK hippiedom thanks to British DJ John Peel's assiduous championing.

Record label:
Buddah
Produced
by Bob Krasnow and Richard Perry.
Recorded
at RCA Studios and Sunset Studios, Hollywood, Los Angeles; April 1967.
Released:
February 1968
Chart peaks:
None (UK) None (US)
Personnel:
Don Van Vliet (v, hm, theremin, bass marimba); Alex St Clair Snouffer (g); Ry Cooder (g, b); Jerry Handley (b); Herb Bermann (b); John 'Drumbo' French (d); Milt Holland (pc); Taj Mahal (pc); Russ Titelman (g); Hank Cicalo, Gary Marker (e)
Track listing:
Sure 'Nuff 'N Yes I Do; Zig Zag Wanderer; Call On Me; Dropout Boogie; I'm Glad; Electricity; Yellow Brick Road (S); Abba Zabba (S); Plastic Factory (S); Where There's Woman (S); Grown So Ugly; Autumn's Child
Running time:
34.25
Current CD:
74321691752 adds: Safe As Milk; On Tomorrow; Big Black Baby Shoes; Flower Pot; Dirty Blue Gene; Trust Us; Korn Ring Finger
Further listening:
Clear Spot (1972)
Further reading:
www.beefheart.com
Like this?
Try . . . p.657

Leonard Cohen

The Songs Of Leonard Cohen

Definitive harbinger of bedsit melancholia.

Having made his reputation as a poet and novelist through the late '50s and '60s, Canadian songwriter Leonard Cohen originally intended to go to Nashville to become a country singer, but had been, as he put it, "hijacked" by New York, where he lived for a while in the mid-'60s at the notorious bohemian domicile, The Chelsea Hotel. His plan was to "make a record, make some money, and go back to writing books", although he found the ordeal of performance particularly gruelling to begin with.

Signed by legendary Columbia A&R man John Hammond after Judy Collins had featured his song Suzanne on her *In My Life* album, Cohen made an immediate impression with this debut album, whose sombre sepia cover hinted at the sometimes unflinching nature of the contents. Already well into his 30s by the time of its release, Cohen's work boasted a maturity and emotional intensity denied to the more youthful singer-songwriters that had appeared in Bob Dylan's wake. The album's songs dealt with personal issues, mostly this legendary ladies' man's relationships with women – particularly Norwegian girlfriend Marianne Jensen, whom he met during his time on the Greek island of Hydra, where he had spent much of the preceding decade (she's in the rear sleeve photo of his second album *Songs From A Room*). Both So Long Marianne and Hey That's No Way To Say Goodbye were responses to their gradually failing relationship, while Suzanne celebrated his subsequent partnership with Suzanne Elrod, who would bear Cohen's children Adam Nathan and Lorca Sarah.

Sung in his characteristic lugubrious baritone over rippling waves of fingerstyle acoustic guitar, Cohen's songs possessed a brooding intimacy which proved surprisingly erotic: *Songs Of Leonard Cohen* remains, along with Tim Buckley's *Happy Sad* and Tim Hardin's first two albums, one of the masterpieces of boudoir-folk-rock. At the time, however, critics like the Village Voice's Richard Goldstein castigated him for being a "Visceral Romantic ... who suffers gloriously in every couplet", crystallising a notion of Cohen as gloomily self-indulgent that would take years of wry drollerie to dispel.

Record label:
Columbia
Produced
by John Simon.
Recorded
at Columbia Records Studio E, New York; 1967.
Released:
February 1968
Chart peaks:
13 (UK) 83 (US)
Personnel:
Leonard Cohen (v, g)
Track listing:
Suzanne (S); Master Song; Winter Lady; The Stranger Song; Sisters Of Mercy; So Long Marianne (S); Hey That's No Way To Say Goodbye; Stories Of The Street; Teachers; One Of Us Cannot Be Wrong
Running time:
41.14
Current CD:
4686002
Further listening:
His debut's immediate successors Songs From A Room (1969) and Songs Of Love And Hate (1971) continued Cohen's soul-mining in similar manner. Later albums are less reliable, but 1988's superb I'm Your Man is one of rock's more notable comeback successes.
Further reading:
Leonard Cohen – A Life In Art (Ira Nadel, 1994)
www.leonardcohenfiles.com
Like this?
Try . . . p.762

Fleetwood Mac

Peter Green's Fleetwood Mac

Young Brit-blues master Green in excelsis. Not much to do with the Californian edition of Fleetwood Mac.

In the summer of 1967, Peter Green was wondering where to go next after leaving John Mayall's Bluesbreakers. He half thought about going to Chicago and hanging with the true blues guys. Then again, Mayall's producer, Mike Vernon, was starting a new label, Blue Horizon. Green wondered whether there might be a role for him as house guitarist, like Buddy Guy was for Chess. Vernon, however, keen to sign Green, encouraged him to form a band. By the autumn, Fleetwood Mac had come together and embarked on a hectic schedule of dates which left time only for sporadic recording. Vernon says the whole process was protracted, spread over five months with the end result being "a series of short stories rather than a novel".

Disenchanted with John Mayall's lurch towards jazz, Green wanted to record a no-nonsense 12-bar blues album. He provided the B.B. King stylings, Jeremy Spencer did a mean Elmore James and the whole thing was locked down by the Fleetwood and McVie rhythm engine. But they all had a very casual approach, didn't really believe the band would come to much, and were just out to have a good time. This did their recordings no harm, contributing to the louche, loose-limbed bounce of Shake Your Moneymaker and No Place To Go, which proved beyond all expectation that a British blues band could swing.

But their laid-back ways often drove Vernon to distraction. Spencer repeatedly sang all the wrong words to Hellhound On My Trail, and then, as the producer tried to get My Heart Beats Like A Hammer under way, the band subjected him to a barrage of raucous guitar intros until he rapped schoolmaster-like on the talk-back microphone to bring the urchins to order. The FM Blue Horizon box-set version of the album (see below) carries the full gamut of cock-ups Vernon had to put up with before he could patiently craft a final take.

Despite all the misdemeanours along the way, the "dog and dustbin" album – Chicago south side by way of the back streets of Battersea – proved a massive seller and an abiding testament to the stomping blues glory of swinging '60s London.

Record label:
Blue Horizon
Produced
by Mike Vernon.
Recorded
at CBS and Decca studios, London; November–December 1967.
Released:
February 1968
Chart peaks:
4 (UK) 198 (US)
Personnel:
Peter Green (g, v, hm); Jeremy Spencer (g, v); John McVie (b); Bob Brunning (b); Mick Fleetwood (d); Mike Ross (e)
Track listing:
My Heart Beat Like A Hammer; Merry Go Round; Long Grey Mare; Hellhound On My Trail; Shake Your Moneymaker; Looking For Somebody; No Place To Go; My Baby's Good To Me; I Loved Another Woman; Cold Black Night; The World Keep On Turning; Got To Move
Running time:
34.20
Current CD:
4773582
Further listening:
Fleetwood Mac: The Complete Blue Horizon Sessions 1967–1969 (1999).
Further reading:
Peter Green: The Biography (Martin Celmins, 1998) gives the most detail on the early days of Fleetwood Mac; www.fleetwoodmac.net
Like this?
Try . . . p.136

Love

Forever Changes

An unclassifiable trove of bittersweet pop.

A psychedelic masterpiece with neither lengthy jams nor studio wizardry; folk-rock with scant hint of protest or sweet harmonies: *Forever Changes* is an enigma wrapped in a web of contradictions – which hasn't harmed its impeccable cult credentials one bit. Starting life as a British Invasion-fixated bunch of Byrds acolytes, Love's primary weapon was Arthur Lee, a precocious songwriter reared on The Beatles, Beethoven and James Brown. "It was my name, my band, my music," Lee said, "and my music forever changes." It did, and rapidly, too. Besides Lee's dominating presence; Love's multi-racial mix juxtaposed Latin flavours with Lee's quirky R&B and Maclean's gentle folk-pop.

After releasing two albums (*Love* and *Da Capo*) in quick succession, the band retreated to Bela Lugosi's old mansion in the Hollywood hills, known as 'The Castle'. While they virtually fell apart, the acrimony magnified by paranoia-inducing quantities of heroin and acid, Love's Elektra rivals The Doors were succeeding fast. "The way I wrote music then was according to my lifestyle and environment," Lee later recalled. That certainly helps explain the disturbed, claustrophobic feel which undermines the album's deceptively blissful demeanour.

It was recorded in just seven sessions, over a period of four months. Neil Young produced the first day's work (The Daily Planet, Andmoreagain), with Phil Spector's 'Wrecking Crew' (Hal Blaine, Billy Strange and Carol Kaye) providing backing. After some tearful complaints, Young and the session players were banished and the band reclaimed the songs the following day by overdubbing new parts. David Angel's elegant string arrangements, so vital to the album's dreamlike charm, were added late in September at the end of the recordings. After Lee and Maclean grudgingly approved them, the results were mixed in a gruelling 17-hour session: "No coffee, a few cigarettes and a lot of cocaine", recalled Ken Forssi. Out of chaos came, according to Elektra at the time, "a vast study in moods". Maclean's Old Man and Alone Again Or were almost unbearably plaintive, but it was the nagging expressions of a seething irascibility (the contradictory voices on The Red Telephone, the spontaneous guitar duels on A House Is Not A Motel and Live And Let Live, Lee's alienated visions and sardonic delivery) that fortify the album's eggshell melodies with tough, impervious centres.

Record Label:
Elektra
Produced
by Arthur Lee and Bruce Botnick.
Recorded
at Sunset Sound Recorders, Los Angeles; June 9, 10 and 12; August 11–12; September 10 and 25, 1967.
Released:
February 1968 (UK); November 1967 (US)
Chart peaks:
24 (UK) 154 (US)
Personnel:
Arthur Lee (g, v); Bryan Maclean (g, v); John Echols (g); Ken Forssi (b); Michael Stuart (pc); David Angel (a); Hal Blaine (d); Billy Strange (g); Carol Kaye (b)
Track Listing:
Alone Again Or (S); A House Is Not A Motel; Andmoreagain (S); The Daily Planet; Old Man; The Red Telephone; Maybe The People Would Be The Times Or Between Clark And Hilldale; Live And Let Live; The Good Humor Man He Sees Everything Like This; Bummer In The Summer; You Set The Scene
Running time:
42.58
Current CD:
7559-60656-2
Further listening:
Da Capo for signs of incipient greatness, Love Story for the bigger picture.
Further reading:
MOJO 43; Try fanzine The Castle, edited by David P Housden, information on 01945 870065. The Delta Sweete Bobbie Gentry
Like this?
Try . . . p.616

Nirvana

The Story Of Simon Simonpath

Sumptuous soft-psych classic from the original UK Nirvana.

The brainchild of songwriters Patrick Campbell-Lyons and Alex Spyropoulos, Nirvana was originally conceived as a group but devolved into a duo by the time they signed to Chris Blackwell's Island Records.

"Blackwell said, 'You'll have to have an album' because he wasn't interested in singles as such," Lyons remembers. "It just evolved. We went back to a flat in Shepherd's Bush and used to work long days and long nights completing songs. This character Simon came out of the song Wings Of Love which also inspired the sleeve artwork." A lonely kid, living in a sixth dimensional city, is obsessed with the idea of sprouting wings and flying. After reaching the stars, he encounters an extra-terrestrial centaur and is taken to Nirvana where he meets and ultimately weds the impossibly beautiful mermaid creature Magdelena.

They dubbed their creation, "a science fiction pantomime". "To describe it as a concept album seems naff to me now," Lyons cautions. "We saw it as a musical pantomime for grown-ups with a slightly druggy undertone to it. I don't know if we really knew what psychedelia meant but we had our own feeling about it. Many people were living psychedelic lives in those days."

The musical backdrop was an oddly eclectic mix emphasising the schizophrenic divide between pop and rock in 1967. As ambitious songwriters, Lyons and Spyropoulos had one foot in Denmark Street's Tin Pan Alley but were also aspiring towards more adventurous studio experiments.

The album included upbeat singalongs like We Can Help You, the catchy Wings Of Love and even a bizarre trad jazz item, 1999. It says much for the interest in the album that these songs were covered by acts as diverse as Alan Bown, Herman's Hermits and Kenny Ball, respectively. The key track on the work was undoubtedly Pentecost Hotel, one of the finest pieces of orchestral pop ever released. "It really encapsulated the whole concept of the album," Lyons notes. "It was a journey somewhere out there. There was a lot of poetic licence in the whole concept. Maybe that's what makes it attractive, its naïveté, which is missing in a lot of things today."

Record label:
Island
Produced
by Chris Blackwell.
Recorded
at Pye Studios 1 and 2; early 1967.
Released:
February 1968
Chart peaks:
None (UK) None (US)
Personnel:
Patrick Campbell-Lyons (g, v); Alex Spyropoulos (k); Herbie Flowers (b); Frank Riccotti (g); Alan Parker (g); Alan Hawkes (k); Michael Coe (french horn); Sylvia Schuster (c); Barry Morgan (d); Clem Cattini (d); Sue & Sunny, Madeleine Bell, Lesley Duncan (bv); Brian Humphries (e); Syd Dale (a, oa)
Track listing:
Wings Of Love; Lonely Boy; We Can Help You; Satellite Jockey; In The Courtyard Of The Stars; You're Just The One; Pentecost Hotel (S); I Never Found A Love Like This; Take This Hand; 1999
Running time:
25.35
Current CD:
EDCD 465
Further listening:
All Of Us (1968)
Further reading:
Rainbow Chaser (Patrick Campbell-Lyons: unpublished manuscript extracted in liner notes to Nirvana's All Of Us)
Like this?
Try . . . p.718

bie Gentry
e Delta Sweete
Her great lost concept album.

"A perfect set of ivories, coffee-coloured eyes, a warm sensual face ... no-one would ever dream of throwing *her* off a bridge." So surmised Gordon Coxhill in his 1969 NME interview with Bobbie Gentry. In the two years since Ode To Billie Joe she'd had little in the way of a hit and journalists were apt to dismiss her as just another pretty face. Born Roberta Streeter in Chickasaw County, Mississippi, Gentry was, in fact, a self-taught musician who'd graduated from the Los Angeles Conservatory of Music, writing by day and spending her evenings as a Las Vegas chorus girl where she was discovered by Capitol A&R man Kelly Gordon.

"Kelly came into my office one night so choked he could hardly talk." remembers fellow A&R man David Axelrod. "He said, 'We've got a demo and I know it's real good.' It was Ode To Billie Joe. I said, 'This is terrific, what's the problem?' He said, 'General manager of A&R turned it down.' The guy who owned the song was Larry Shane, one of the biggest independent publishers. I dialled him and said 'What do you want for this?' He said 'Ten thousand dollars.' I said 'Done.' I hung up. Happy. Went over the general manager's head. Her stuff was too good *not* to hear."

Her second album, however, was roundly ignored. A concept album about white southern life in which all intros and outros are underscored by sad strings, each track flowing into the next, *The Delta Sweete* was a work of great emotional power. It ranged from the fractured Mississippi funk of Okolona River Bottom Band to Courtyard, the sparsely arranged tale of an imprisoned woman, and her most beautiful, tragic composition.

"No-one bought it but I didn't lose sleep over it," Gentry told NME, "I've never tried to pre-judge public taste."

After *The Delta Sweete* Gentry appears to have had difficulty deciding on a career path. Following a number of saccharine chart hits with Glen Campbell (Let it Be Me, All I Have To Do Is Dream), she returned with the hard country soul of *Fancy*, recorded with Rick Hall at Muscle Shoals. An astute businesswoman, by 1970 she also owned considerable property in California and had a large financial interest in the Phoenix Suns baseball team. She dropped out of the public eye altogether in 1976.

Record label:
Capitol
Produced:
by Kelly Gordon
Recorded:
winter 1967
Release date:
March 1968
Chart peaks:
None (UK) None (US:)
Personnel:
Bobbie Gentry (g, v); Jimmie Haskell and Shorty Rogers (a); other musicians not known.
Track listing:
Okolona River Bottom Band (S); Big Boss Man; Reunion; Parchman Farm; Mornin' Glory; Sermon; Tobacco Road; Penduli Pendulum; Jessye' Lisabeth; Refractions; Louisiana Man; Courtyard
Running time:
33.44
Currently unavailable on CD
Further listening:
Fancy (1970); Touch Em With Love (Capitol, 1969)
Further reading:
www.geocities.com/odetobobbiegentry/
Like this?
Try . . . p.79

The Incredible String Band

The Hangman's Beautiful Daughter

Celtic minstrels record their psychedelic masterpiece and copyright the concept of "getting it together in the country".

Fired by the success of their second album *The 5,000 Spirits*, Heron and Williamson repaired to a Chelsea studio to construct the album that would seal their reputation forever. With them they brought exotic instruments from a road-trip to Morocco and a collection of incandescent tunes requiring, for the most part, a single roll of the tape and a touch of embroidery.

"This was the first time multi-tracking was possible," Williamson remembers, "though it was still done in a pretty slap-dash, anarchic, have-a-go kind of way. The whole album was recorded in a few days. We didn't even stay for the mixes. The basic tracks were mostly one take, live vocal and guitar, and then the other instruments were put on top. Mercy I Cry City was pretty much live, with me playing two whistles and drums all at the same time. Waltz Of The New Moon had a harp player on it, and we had Dolly Simpson's flute organ on Water Song, but otherwise it was just us overdubbing the other parts." Williamson's contributions were written in a disused railway carriage in the garden of his friend Mary Stewart's house near Glasgow. It's Stewart's children who appear in the *Hangman*'s hugely influential cover picture, an image (taken on Christmas Day '67) that so perfectly captured the album's mystic appeal and sent kindred spirits scurrying for the hills in search of a rural retreat. There was instant critical acclaim, along with loud endorsements from Mick Jagger, John Lennon, Robert Plant and Jimmy Page.

"A very pleasant surprise," says Williamson, "but I felt it was something special even while we were making it. The whole of London had this fantastic atmosphere at the time, particularly Chelsea. A wonderful feeling of optimism after the 1950s, a tremendous flowering of the notion that the war was actually over and that life and love could be obtained. Hence the name of the album – The Hangman being the death in the war and The Beautiful Daughter being the coming age. Look at that misty gleam in our eyes on the cover: we were standing back and looking in amazement at what was going on!"

Record label:
Elektra
Produced
by Joe Boyd.
Recorded
at Sound Techniques Studios, London; December 1967.
Released:
March 1968
Chart peaks:
5 (UK) None (US)
Personnel:
Robin Williamson (v, g, gimbri, whistle, pc, pan pipe, p, oud, mandolin, Jews harp, chahanai, water harp, hm); Mike Heron (v, s, Hammond organ, g, dulcimer, harpsichord); Dolly Collins (flute, organ, harpsichord); Davis Snell (harp); Licorice McKechnie (v, finger-cymbals)
Track listing:
Koeeoaddi There; The Minotaur's Song; Witches Hat; A Very Cellular Song; Mercy I Cry City; Waltz Of The New Moon; The Water Song; There Is A Green Crown; Swift As The Wind; Nightfall
Running time:
49.55
Current CD:
7559-60835-2
Further listening:
Wee Tam And The Big Huge (1968); The 5,000 Spirits (1967); Liquid Acrobat As Regards The Air (1970)
Further reading:
MOJO 81
www.makingtime.co.uk/beglad/
Like this?
Try . . . p.407

Tom Rush

The Circle Game

Pivotal bedsit folk album that – though largely built around covers – helped herald the arrival of the singer/songwriter.

Exactly when folk singers became known as 'singer/songwriters' is hard to pinpoint, but this 1968 song cycle is certainly a milestone in that journey. *The Circle Game* was among folk rock's first fully orchestrated albums, recorded at roughly the same time as Phil Ochs' *Pleasures Of The Harbor* and Love's *Forever Changes* (though both beat it to the street by a couple of months). As a true concept album, it bettered the framing devices of *Sgt. Pepper* and *The Who Sell Out*; it also just happened to introduce the world to the work of no less than three singer/songwriter icons: James Taylor, Jackson Browne, and Joni Mitchell.

The seed was planted when Cambridge folk star Rush met the unknown Mitchell in a Detroit coffee house, and she taught him her song Urge For Going. A tape of Rush's moving six-minute demo of the song was played on Boston Top 40 powerhouse WBZ in the spring of 1967, where it became the radio station's most requested song for the next six months. Urge For Going would obviously be a centrepiece of his next album, but Mitchell's contribution didn't end there. "I got a package in the mail from Joni," Rush recalls. "It was a tape she'd made in her apartment, wonderful songs like Tin Angel and Moon In The Mirror. A the end she did this little spoken disclaimer: 'Gee, here's a song I just finished. I'm not sure if it's any good, but here it is.' That was The Circle Game."

Rush had always been an open-minded folkie – his previous album had featured a side of Al Kooper electric arrangements – and he conceived this record as an orchestrated song cycle that would trace the arc of a relationship from hello to goodbye; side one would be the upside, side two the down. Mitchell's tape had given him a title song (though The Circle Game was originally written for her old Toronto friend Neil Young), and a place to start in Tin Angel ("In a Bleecker Street café/She found someone to love today"). The narrative was fleshed out with songs from unknowns Taylor (Something In The Way She Moves and Sunshine Sunshine) and Browne (Shadow Dream Song), both still in their teens. And though Tom Rush was known primarily as an interpreter, the two songs that cap *The Circle Game* were his own: the melancholy instrumental Rockport Sunday running into supreme break-up song No Regrets, which The Walker Brothers would spin into gold six years later.

Record label:
Elektra
Produced
by Arthur Gorson.
Recorded
at Century Sound, New York and Sunset Sound, Los Angeles; autumn 1967.
Released:
March 1968
Chart peaks:
None (UK) 68 (US)
Personnel:
Tom Rush (v, ag); Bruce Langhorne (g); Hugh McCracken (g); Don Thomas (g); Eric Gale (g); Jonathan Raskin (classical guitar, b); Joe Mack (b); Bob Bushnell (b); Paul Harris (k, oa, a); Herbie Lovelle (d); Bernard Purdie (d); Richie Ritz (d); Joe Grimm (s); Buddy Lucas (s); Brooks Arthur, Bruce Botnick (e)
Track listing:
Tin Angel; Something In The Way She Moves; Urge For Going (S/US); Sunshine Sunshine; The Glory Of Love; Shadow Dream Song; The Circle Game; So Long; Rockport Sunday; No Regrets (S/UK)
Running time:
38.36
Current CD:
740182
Further listening:
The Very Best Of Tom Rush: No Regrets 1962–1999 (1999)
Further reading:
www.tomrush.com
Like this?
Try . . . p.40

The United States Of America

The United States Of America

The electronic rock revolution starts here.

A short-lived collective of experimental musicians, The United States Of America created one of the first successful marriages of electronic music and pop. Leader Joseph Byrd was a pivotal figure of "serious" modern music in the mid-'60s as a composer, conductor and producer. He moved to Los Angeles in 1967 to study at UCLA, but promptly got together with four other avant-gardiste students, started the band, tuned up and dropped out.

Every instrument they played was in some way treated through distorted amplifiers, ring modulators and other devices. Craig Woodson pioneered electronic drums, Gordon Marron played an electronically adapted violin. But what distinguished them was their distinctive sense of pop featuring the twisted lyrical intelligence of Dorothy Moskowitz.

Given its title, their only album had to aim high and it did. The opening track parodied *Sgt. Pepper's Lonely Hearts Club Band* with The American Metaphysical Circus which is loosely based on Being For The Benefit Of Mr Kite. The American Way Of Love observed homosexual prostitutes on New York's 42nd Street, while radio favourite I Won't Leave My Wooden Wife For You, Sugar adeptly sent up the straight suburban family cut off from the world in their "split-level house with a wonderful view" (this track became their best known via inclusion on CBS's key compilation/sampler album *The Rock Machine Turns You On*).

If some of *The United States Of America*'s enthusiastic phasing, echo and channel-swapping date-stamps it, it endures nonetheless through solid merit – musical verve and imagination, the melodic appeal of the trippy The Garden Of Earthly Delights and gentler pieces Love Song For The Dead Ché and Cloud Song. Thirty years on, Moskowitz, who moved on to Country Joe's All Star Band before becoming a music teacher, commented on the web: "I have no regrets about the electronic excess under which my voice was buried. It was part of the aesthetic and I was the one who insisted on singing through a ring modulator."

Byrd later worked with Phil Ochs and a relatively unimpressive band called The Field Hippies (1969) and also produced Ry Cooder's *Jazz* (1978).

Record label:
CBS
Produced
by Dave Rubinson.
Recorded
at CBS studios, autumn 1967.
Released:
March 1968
Chart peaks:
None (UK) 181 (US)
Personnel:
Joseph Byrd (electronic music, electric harpsichord, o, calliope, p); Dorothy Moskowitz (v); Gordon Marron (electric violin, ring modulator); Rand Forbes (bs); Craig Woodson (electric drums, pc)
Track listing:
The American Metaphysical Circus; Hard Coming Love; Cloud Song; The Garden Of Earthly Delights; I Won't Leave My Wooden Wife For You, Sugar; Where Is Yesterday; Coming Down; Love Song For The Dead Che; Stranded In Time; The American Way Of Love
Running time:
37.07
Current CD:
Edsel EDCD 541
Further listening:
There's not much out there that relates to this one-off delight, though Joseph Byrd did cut his own electronic LP of Christmas music, Xmas Yet To Come (1980).
Further reading:
www.freakemporioum.co.uk
Like this?
Try . . . p.555

The Byrds

The Notorious Byrd Brothers

Recorded amid group turmoil this unexpectedly emerged as their most gentle and reflective work.

The Byrds were at the peak of their artistic powers in 1967 and following the celebrated *Younger Than Yesterday* looked likely to climb new heights as a creative force. Unfortunately, they were also being eaten away from within. The rivalry between McGuinn and Crosby over leadership and direction continued to fester, most notably at the crucial Monterey festival where David Crosby played the counter-culture king, advocating LSD use and telling the world that the Kennedy assassination was a hushed-up conspiracy. To top it all, he appeared onstage with the Buffalo Springfield. "They were very upset when he played with them," manager Jim Dickson recalled. "There was a big dilemma. David seemed as if he was intent on destroying the group. I'm sure he didn't see it that way. It was compulsive behaviour."

In August, The Byrds commenced work on their new album, but friction in the studio threatened to overwhelm them. Apart from the bickering between McGuinn and Crosby, there was an ongoing battle with drummer Michael Clarke who responded to David Crosby's condescension with the priceless, "What do you know, man? You're not a musician." More problems ensued when McGuinn and Hillman rejected Crosby's *mènage á trois* ballad Triad as tasteless. He rebelled by declining to play on the Goffin & King number Goin' Back. With emotions running high, McGuinn and Hillman drove over to Crosby's house and told him he was fired. Gene Clark was recalled, but only lasted three weeks and contributed nothing to the album. By the end of the sessions, Michael Clarke had joined the ranks of ex-Byrds.

The final product should have been a disjointed mess but instead was breathtaking – evocative songs made otherworldly by Gary Usher's innovative use of phasing, reversed tapes, string sections and synthesizers. The Byrds survived destabilizing line-up changes during this period and would go on to record six more albums, but they would never again find the magic or mystery unveiled during this time of unprecedented internecine strife.

Record label:
Columbia
Produced
by Gary Usher.
Recorded
at CBS, Hollywood, August–December 1967.
Released:
April, 12 1968
Chart peaks:
12 (UK) 47 (US)
Personnel:
Roger McGuinn (g, v, syn); David Crosby (g, v); Michael Clarke (d); Chris Hillman (b); Roy Halee (e); Don Thompson (ae)
Track listing:
Artificial Energy; Goin' Back; Natural Harmony; Draft Morning; Wasn't Born To Follow; Get To You; Change Is Now; Old John Robertson; Tribal Gathering; Dolphin's Smile; Space Odyssey
Running time:
28.30
Current CD:
Legacy 4867512 adds: Moog Raga; Bound To Fall; Triad; Goin' Back; Draft Morning; Universal Mind Decoder
Further listening:
Younger Than Yesterday (1967)
Further reading:
MOJO 41; The Byrds: Timeless Flight Revisited (Johnny Rogan, 1997)
Like this?
Try . . . p.69

The Zombies

Odessey And Oracle

Gorgeous album, overlooked in UK, since acknowledged as a key example of British psychedelia.

The Zombies were hardly the stuff of teenage fantasy, carrying no aroma of danger or wild innovation. But beneath the tidy suits, nice jumpers and thick spectacles beat the hearts of five terrific musicians, more-than-merely-gifted writers who – in She's Not There and Time Of The Season – created two of the decade's most evocative and enduring hits.

They were almost classic one-hit wonders; the beautiful and timeless She's Not There proving impossible to follow. It hit around the world and provided them with plenty of experience on the road, but further singles performed poorly and their debut album was a disappointing, but typical, ragbag of blues covers and low-wattage originals. But chief writers Rod Argent and Chris White had a few ideas about ditching their old formula and making a proper album, and they took their plan to CBS Records. CBS liked it.

On June 1, 1967, the attention of the entire rock world was fixed upon the release of The Beatles' *Sgt Pepper's Lonely Hearts Club Band*, or so they say. The entire rock world *except*, that is, for five former beatsters holed up at Abbey Road, commencing the recording of *their* psychedelic masterpiece. At The Beatles' behest, the studio technicians had jerryrigged various 4-track recording machines so the group would have more tracks to work with; when The Zombies walked in to start recording, engineers Geoff Emerick and Phil MacDonald were busily disconnecting those same machines. Paul Atkinson later recalled, "We said, 'What are you doing? Plug those back in again.' And they said, 'No, no, please. We've had six months of this. It's been driving us crazy. We want to unplug all this stuff and get back to recording normally.'"

Odessey And Oracle (the title was misspelt by the sleeve designer) was a tightly arranged album that utilised their engineers' skills to the full. Despite cutting corners by using a mellotron instead of orchestra and flute, The Zombies still wound up having to spend £200 of their own money to pay for a stereo mixdown.

The record came out to almost universal indifference. A disheartened Paul Atkinson quit the band and Rod Argent took it as the final sign: "We may as well split then."

Within weeks, the angelic-voiced Blunstone was working at an insurance company. Meanwhile, CBS recording artist and A&R man Al Kooper persuaded his label to issue it stateside. Several extracted singles flopped before DJs unexpectedly picked up on Time Of The Season. In the spring of 1969 the song soared to Number 3 in the American charts. Nevertheless, Rod Argent resisted pressure from CBS to reform the band and The Zombies curious career, book-ended by two huge hits, was finally laid to rest.

Record label:
CBS
Produced
by Rod Argent and Chris White.
Recorded
at Abbey Road and Olympic Studios, London; June 1967.
Released:
April 19, 1968
Chart peaks:
None (UK) 95 (US)
Personnel:
Rod Argent (p, o, Mellotron, bv); Chris White (b, bv); Colin Blunstone (v); Paul Atkinson (bv, g); Hugh Grundy (bv, d)
Track listing:
Care Of Cell 44; A Rose For Emily; Maybe After He's Gone; Beechwood Park; Brief Candles; Hung Up On A Dream; Changes; I Want Her She Wants Me; This Will Be Our Year; Butcher's Tale (Western Front 1914); Friends Of Mine; Time Of The Season
Running time:
33.04
Current CD:
Ace CDWIKD 181 adds: A Rose For Emily (2); Time Of The Season (2); Prison Song
Further listening:
The all-killer/no-filler 4-CD box set Zombie Heaven (1997)
Further reading:
Alec Palao's fine liner notes to Zombie Heaven; also check out the Zombies Fan Page, w1.182.telia.com/~u18203287/music/zombies.htm
Like this?
Try . . . p.423

Johnny Cash

Johnny Cash At Folsom Prison

Cash's big-time comeback, after five years of declining sales and battles with pills and the law.

By 1968, Johnny Cash was a tired old C&W performer who seemed all washed up. Languishing on the Columbia label, he hadn't had a real hit in years and faced a middle age of playing two-bit roadhouses for declining audiences and diminishing returns. A live album might be his only salvation.

Cash had been held behind bars a number of times, and Columbia bosses agreed with him that an album recorded in one of the prisons where he'd done time might revive his moribund career. Cash chose Folsom Prison as the venue: he had several times enthralled inmate audiences there with his honest blue collar life stories and sympathetic banter. Cash returned to Folsom with high hopes, a full mobile recording crew and his future wife June Carter.

His music was the same as it always had been. Kicking off with his old Sun hit Folsom Prison Blues and following his usual formula of performing equal parts Cash originals and folk/country covers, he had the inmates of Folsom in the palm of his hand as his formidable storytelling abilities rose to the occasion. Lyrics about poverty, cocaine and whiskey abuse, about endless days of coalmining and the horror of life behind bars are stock-in-trade American folklore to Cash's many fans, but of course resonated even more strongly to the inmates he sang for on that chilly January evening.

Cash remains justifiably proud of this recording, which not only re-ignited his career in the States but signalled a turnaround in his previously chaotic private life: "(You) listen closely to this album and you hear the clanging of doors, the shrill of the whistle, the shouts of the men – even laughter from men who had forgotten how to laugh. There's some stuff here I'm proud of."

Record label:
CBS
Produced
by Bob Johnston.
Recorded
live at Folsom Prison, California; January 13, 1968.
Released:
April 1968
Chart peaks:
8 (UK) 13 (US)
Personnel:
Johnny Cash (v, g); June Carter (v); Carter Family (v); Marshall Grant (b); W.S. Holland (d); Carl Perkins (g); Luther Perkins (g); The Statler Brothers (v)
Track listing:
Folsom Prison Blues (S); Busted; Dark As The Dungeon; I Still Miss Someone; Cocaine Blues; 25 Minutes To Go; Orange Blossom Special; The Long Black Veil; Send A Picture Of Mother; The Wall; Dirty Old Egg-Suckin' Dog; Flushed From The Bathroom Of Your Heart; Joe Bean; Jackson (S); Give My Love To Rose; I Got Stripes; The Legend Of John Henry's Hammer; Green Green Grass Of Home; Greystone Chapel
Running time:
55.49
Current CD:
SNY659522
Further listening:
Johnny Cash At San Quentin (1969); American Recordings (1994)
Further reading:
The New Johnny Cash (Charles Paul Conn, 1973); Johnny Cash: The Autobiography (Johnny Cash with Patrick Carr, 1998)
Like this?
Try . . . p.689

Flat Earth Society

Waleeco

Teenage prodigies create Willy Wonka-style curio.

For some bands obscurity seems almost inevitable: for the Flat Earth Society it was assured. When the Boston-based F.B. Washburn Candy Company decided to promote their tasty new Waleeco candy bar by holding a competition amongst local groups to write a radio jingle, the prize they offered the winning band was the chance to cut an album. After submitting the chosen song, the Flat Earth Society, a group of talented teenagers from Lynn, Massachusetts, assembled at Fleetwood Studios. With no previous recording experience they found that they had only rehearsed enough songs for half the album and so the rest had to be written on the spot. Time was at a premium and the studio facilities were crude, but with considerable ingenuity the results were remarkable. Paul Carter recalls that in order to give his bass more definition he had to place his amplifier in the studio's bathroom: in Feelin' Much Better, a phasing effect was achieved by spraying an aerosol can into a bucket!

The band were heavily influenced by Jefferson Airplane and, of course, The Beatles, but also by folk music, which comes to the fore on When You're There and Prelude For The Town Monk. There's a beautiful electric piano rendition of Midnight Hour – the only non-original track – but it is on the second side that the group, forced to improvise, really show their talents; the atmospheric Dark Street Downtown; Portrait in Grey is an extended instrumental with haunting recorder playing; Satori, the album's mysterious, psychedelic climax, a wash of backwards piano spiked with sitar-like guitar. As the hype on the back cover put it: "Their bag is that they're in no particular bag at all."

Unfortunately, anyone who wished to hear the album was required to send off $1.50 together with six Waleeco wrappers. Few bothered and, with little else in the way of promotion, the record was destined to become a land-fill. Happily, now it's reissued on CD, everyone can hear it, without rotting any teeth.

Record label:
Fleetwood
Produced
by Quinn & Johnson, Inc. and Charlie Dreyer.
Recorded
at Fleetwood Studios, Revere, Massachusetts
Released:
April 1968
Chart peaks:
None (UK) None (US)
Personnel:
Jack Kerivan (p, o, v); Phil Dubuque (g, recorder, v); Rick Doyle (g, pc, v); Curt Girard (d); Paul Carter (b, v)
Track listing:
Feelin' Much Better; Midnight Hour; I'm So Happy; When You're There; Four And Twenty Miles; Prelude For The Town Monk; Shadows; Dark Street Downtown; Portrait In Grey; In My Window; Satori
Running time:
32.16
Current CD:
Arf-Arf AA-042
Further listening:
There's nothing at all, unfortunately. But the Arf-Arf label has lots of similar curiosities in its catalogue.
Like this?
Try . . . p.83

Magic Sam

West Side Soul

The record that announced a new generation of American electric blues.

In the early 1960s, no fresh African-Americans were breaking out from the Chicago blues bars, and it seemed that the music might one day become a museum piece until a young entrepreneur named Robert Koester began a talent hunt for his small label. He found it. Samuel Maghett was young yet already an experienced performer, easy on the eye, a gentleman in his dealings, charismatic, an incredible guitarist with his own style, a dramatic singer and the author of some bruising blues songs. Sam had already recorded for Cobra in 1957, Chief in 1960–61 and Crash in 1966 when Delmark signed him, but this time around he was promised a free hand. Thus, on a sticky summer's day, he entered a small Chicago studio to make blues history.

Sam knew to appeal to the young Caucasian college fan just discovering blues music as well as to his regular crowd: the album had to hang together musically, had to be of one piece like a rock album. Maghett lived on Chicago's West Side where he and his cohorts were much more ready to embrace music beyond the blues – rock'n'roll, soul and Latin – than his contemporaries on the South Side, the Chess Records crowd who were blues purists. It was this distinction that gave the album its uptempo drive and its title.

Sam's staccato lead guitar (he played with his fingers and thumb, forcefully plucking the strings) pushed through a Fender amp with reverb on full was a new sound in blues, and after *West Side Soul*'s release Sam briefly toured with The Grateful Dead, wowing Jerry Garcia when his Stratocaster was heard through a state-of-the-art PA system.

"Looking Good, his show-stopping boogie, blew guitar players' minds," remembers ex-manager Denny Bruce. "Ry Cooder came to my house to meet Sam and learn a few finger-picking tricks from him. Sam never showed him. He never got his due as a singer but his Mama Mama Talk To Your Daughter and Sweet Home Chicago are role models for so many out there."

Alas, it was not to last. After two years of growing fame, Magic Sam Maghett called to his wife one morning complaining of heartburn. It was a cardiac arrest, and within minutes Sam was dead. He was 32.

Record label:
Delmark
Produced
by Robert G. Koester
Recorded
at Sound Studios, Chicago; July 12 and October 25, 1967.
Released:
April 1968
Chart peaks:
None (UK) None (US)
Personnel:
Magic Sam Maghett (v, g); Mighty Joe Young (g); Stockholm Slim (p); Earnest Johnson (b); Odie Payne (d); Odie Payne III (d); Mack Thompson (b)
Track listing:
That's All I Need; I Need You So Bad; I Feel So Good (I Wanna Boogie); All Of Your Love; I Don't Want No Woman; Sweet Home Chicago; I Found A New Love; Every Night And Every Day; Lookin' Good; My Love Will Never Die; Mama Mama Talk To Your Daughter
Running time:
45.52
Current CD:
DD-615 adds: I Don't Want No Woman (alternate take)
Further listening:
follow-up Black Magic (1969); Easy Baby (1990), a collection of his early sides reissued by Charly.
Further reading:
Living Blues magazine, issues 125 (January–February 1996) and 127 (May–June 1996); www.bluesnet.hub.org/artists/magic.sam.html
Like this?
Try . . . p.824

Billy Nicholls

Would You Believe

Long-lost harmony-laden psych-pop rarity.

Immediate Records' head, Rolling Stones manager Andrew Loog Oldham was bowled over by the precocious talent of the 17-year-old singer/songwriter, who had been recommended to him by no less a person than George Harrison.

As Nicholls puts it, getting signed was a teenage dream; "Getting paid £20 a week, with my own room full of Revoxes, Mellotrons, and the Stones' guitars." Between writing songs for the album Oldham produced for Del Shannon, *Home And Away* (not released at the time, though tracks eventually turned up on various collections), and doing uncredited vocals on the Small Faces' classic *Ogden's Nut Gone Flake*, Nicholls got to make his own single, Would You Believe. Initially produced by Steve Marriott and Ronnie Lane, but an overambitious Oldham overlaid it with an orchestra, killing its commercial chances. (One wag called it "the most overproduced single of the '60s".)

While the ensuing *Would You Believe* album was comparatively modest, it fell foul of Immediate chaotic management and was left in the can, save for a few promo copies that became highly prized among collectors, some selling for over £1,000. Its reputation was enhanced by the knowledge that its credits included a veritable Who's Who of British late-'60s rockers: the Small Faces, John Paul Jones, Nicky Hopkins, Caleb Quaye, the great session guitarist Big Jim Sullivan, and Humble Pie drummer Jerry Shirley. Songs like the vibrant Girl From New York testify to what a great time Nicholls must have been having in the studio.

In 1998, Nicholls, by then a successful songwriter and musical director for The Who (and father to Morgan Nicholls of Senseless Things and Morgan), took pity on those lacking a large disposable income and made *Would You Believe* available to the masses for the first time, on his own Southwest label. It is greatly to his credit that the result was not a collective sigh of disappointment, as can be the case when long-hyped rarities are finally brought to light, but rather unanimous shouts of praise from critics and fans of song-oriented '60s pop.

Record label:
Immediate
Produced
by Steve Marriott, Ronnie Lane, and Andrew Loog Oldham.
Recorded
at Olympic Studios, Barnes, and IBC Studios, London; late 1967–early 1968.
Released:
April 1968
Chart peaks:
None (UK) None (US)
Personnel:
Billy Nicholls (ag, v, bv); Steve Marriott (g, bv); Ronnie Lane (b); Ian MacLagan (o); Kenny Jones (d); Big Jim Sullivan (g, ag); Caleb Quaye (p); Nicky Hopkins (k); John Paul Jones (b); Joe Moreti (g); Denny Gerrard (bv); Barry Husband (bv); Jerry Shirley (d); Arthur Greenslade, John Paul Jones, Denny Gerrard (oa)
Track listing:
Would You Believe; Come Again; Life Is Short; Feeling Easy; Daytime Girl; Daytime Girl Coda; London Social Degree; Portobello Road; Question Mark; Being Happy; Girl From New York; It Brings Me Down
Running time:
33.33
Current CD:
Sequel NENCD414 adds: Would You Believe (alternative take); Daytime Girl (alternative take)
Further listening:
Love Songs (1974); lone, self-titled album by a group that included Nicholls, White Horse (1976), both available on Nicholls's Southwest label.
Further reading:
www.nicholls.co.uk
Like this?
Try . . . p.204

Simon & Garfunkel

Bookends

Massively successful breakthrough album for former folkies.

Bookends was the fourth album from Simon & Garfunkel, but the first to reach a mass audience. Side One comprised a song-suite tracing the journey from birth to death – all original Simon compositions, aside from Voices Of Old People, drawn by Garfunkel from taped interviews with OAPs, which is the only jarring note in an otherwise seamless sweep.

Save The Life Of My Child reflects the raucous paranoia of America as the Vietnam war tore the nation apart, and parents everywhere scratched their heads and asked "What's become of the children?" It was also one of the first pop songs to use a synthesiser, and probably the first to use a sample – Simon & Garfunkel themselves can be heard singing Sounds Of Silence way down in the mix. America is timeless – a weary, disaffected odyssey – and its pristine production, blank-verse narrative and timely state-of-the-nation reflections, ensure that it sounds as fresh in the 21st century as it did in 1968. Overs is a bleak catalogue of marital breakdown, while the concluding Old Friends finds Simon reflecting: "How terribly strange to be 70" – not a sentiment shared, or cared-about, by many of his contemporaries at the time.

Never one to be rushed by a deadline, Simon didn't have enough new songs to complete *Bookends*, so the second side was padded out with previously released singles. Fakin' It was a dope-induced contemplation of an earlier life; Hazy Shade Of Winter had been a pounding, atmospheric single in 1967; while At The Zoo was an engaging, if none-too-subtle parable – human society symbolised by animals – but all matched Simon & Garfunkel's exacting standards. The two new songs were the quirky Punky's Dilemma – which director Mike Nichols rejected for *The Graduate* – and the song about that film's mature femme fatale, Mrs Robinson.

Simon & Garfunkel only had complete control of three of the five albums they recorded together, and in many ways *Bookends* stands as their finest moment. The duo stood in charge of the production and overall sound, and were eager to leave the formulas of pop-production and willing to experiment, which may help to explain the album's timeless quality. It was to be two years before there was another Simon & Garfunkel album, the all-conquering but, by comparison to *Bookends* a little sterile *Bridge Over Troubled Water.*

Record label:
CBS
Produced
by Paul Simon, Art Garfunkel, Roy Halee, Bob Johnson and John Simon.
Recorded
October 1967–February 1968.
Released:
April 1968
Chart peaks:
1 (UK) 1 (US)
Personnel:
Paul Simon (g, v); Art Garfunkel (v)
Track listing:
Bookends Theme; Save The Life Of My Child; America; Overs; Voices Of Old People; Old Friends; Bookends Theme; Fakin' It (S); Punky's Dilemma; Mrs Robinson (S); A Hazy Shade Of Winter (S); At The Zoo (S)
Running time:
29.45
Current CD:
Columbia CD 63101 P
Further listening:
Old Friends, Simon & Garfunkel box set (1997)
Further reading:
The Complete Guide To The Music Of Simon & Garfunkel (Chris Charlesworth, 1997); The Boy In The Bubble: The Paul Simon Story (Patrick Humphries, 1988); www.paulsimon.com www.artgarfunkel.com
Like this?
Try . . . p.182

Harper's Bizarre

The Secret Life Of . . .

A much underrated vocal group, smooth but perverse.

Marshmallow rock, soft and ultra-sweet. Maybe they shouldn't have added up to anything much – they didn't even boast a strong line in harmonies. But Harper's Bizarre possessed an indefinable something that set them apart from most other groups of the period.

Certainly everyone worthwhile at Warners thought so. Randy Newman pitched in to help them; so too did heavy-hitters Nick De Caro, Bob Thompson, Van Dyke Parks and Leon Russell. In their easy-on-the-ear way, Harper's Bizarre were ahead of the game, adventurous. They'd started out as The Tikis, a Santa Cruz band. Then, during 1966, they settled down as five-piece Harper's Bizarre (guitarist Eddie James having gone AWOL). They were still a young outfit – Scoppettone was 21 and Templeman 22 when they cut their debut album *Feelin' Groovy*, which gave them an immediate hit with a fizzy version of Simon and Garfunkel's 59th Street Bridge Song.

That first album set the mould. It included new songs from Parks and Newman, plus Happy Talk (from South Pacific) and, even dottier, a less-than-two-minutes-long rendition of Prokofiev's Peter And The Wolf. *Anything Goes* (1967) proved similarly diverse – Chattanooga Choo Choo, along with Van Dyke Parks' much-heralded High Coin. The stage was set for *The Secret Life*. This time around, the song selection was woven into a kind of Walter Mitty-ish dream sequence. Set against a recurring backdrop provided by Burton Lane and Yip Harburg's wistful Look To The Rainbow, the foursome sang of riding with cowboys, the battle of New Orleans, of building a stairway to paradise and other exploits that were hardly workaday and not exactly brimming with the radical spirit of '68.

The ultimate in melodic escapism, the album did little for the group's career and, in the wake of *Harper's Bizarre 4* (1970) – which featured contributions from Ry Cooder and Jack Nitzche – the group split, Templeton moving on to become an A&R mainman and significant producer at WEA. In 1976 the original line-up, minus Templeton, regrouped for a fifth album, *As Time Goes By*. But though some of the old idiosyncrasies remained – a theme from the New World Symphony rubbed shoulders with Back In The Saddle Again – the group's distinctive sound had, somewhere along the way, evaporated.

Record label:
Warner Brothers
Produced
by Lenny Waronker.
Recorded
in Hollywood; early 1968.
Released:
May 1968
Chart peaks:
None (UK) None, (US)
Personnel:
Dick Yount (b, v); John Peterson (d, v); Ted Templeman (g, t, v); Dick Scoppettone (g, v); Gloria Jones, Carolyn Willis, Sherlie Matthews (v, gospel choir)
Track listing:
Look To The Rainbow; Battle Of New Orleans; When I Was A Cowboy; Interlude; Sentimental Journey; Las Manitas; Bye Bye Bye/ Vine Street; Me Japanese Boy; Interlude; I'll Build A Stairway To Paradise; Green Apple Tree; Sit Down You're Rocking The Boat; Interlude; I Love You Mama; Funny How Love Can Be; Mad; Look To The Rainbow; The Drifter; Reprise
Running time:
33.52
Not currently available on CD
Further listening:
Feelin' Groovy: The Best Of Harper's Bizarre (1997), the only music by the group available in the UK, includes the magical Witchi-Tai-To.
Further reading:
There's next to nothing available, although the 16-page booklet enclosed with the above CD contains an informative interview with Lenny Waronker.
Like this?
Try . . . p.527

1968

Iron Butterfly

In-A-Gadda-Da-Vida

Herein the Iliad and Odyssey of heavy metal jamming.

Technically speaking, there was no Iron Butterfly on the night the band christened the glorified riff that would become its biggest hit and ticket to immortality. The band had already made one album, *Heavy*, but because of disputes between its producers and Atlantic and between members of the band, Iron Butterfly were no longer airborne. While the two remaining members, keyboardist Doug Ingle and drummer Ron Bushy, looked for new members, things grew so dire that Bushy was actually hawking pizza at a Sunset Strip nightclub. One night, upon returning to the apartment he shared with Ingle, Bushy found his roommate in a state of delirium. Not only had he been up for nearly two days, he had consumed almost a gallon of Red Mountain wine and possessed all the verbal dexterity of a caveman. He told Bushy he'd been writing a new song. Bushy could not make out the words, so he wrote them down phonetically: In-A-Gadda-Da-Vida. Only later did he learn that Ingle had been mumbling, "in the Garden of Eden".

Of course there is more to the song than its weird title. A classically trained keyboardist, Ingle needed constant reminders not to play bass with his left hand. Bass player Lee Dorman took one of those superfluous lines and simplified it to make what is arguably the most primal riff in all of rock. Though the other (surprisingly poppy) tunes on *In-A-Gadda-Da-Vida* were recorded in Hollywood, the famed 17-minute opus was recorded on Long Island, while the band took a break from touring with Jefferson Airplane.

When they turned up at Ultra-Sonic Studios, producer Jim Hilton had not yet driven out from New York City. To save time, studio owner Bones Howe asked if there was a song they could play to set volume levels. "We said, 'We have this really long song that we want to record and throughout it we have solos where each instrument is featured,'" says Dorman. Perfect. Off they went with what the band assumed was a sound check. For some reason, the engineers rolled tape, and they got virtually the entire song in one take. Though Atlantic first baulked at releasing the heavy epic (it had to be edited down to 2.52 for radio play), the label finally gave in and must be glad they did. The album sold 4 million copies in the US alone; until Led Zeppelin came along it was Atlantic's top seller.

Record label:
Atco
Produced
by Jim Hilton.
Recorded
at Gold Star Studios, Hollywood, California and Ultra-Sonic Studios, Hempstead, LI; spring 1968.
Released:
June 14, 1968.
Chart peaks:
None (UK) 4 (US)
Personnel:
Doug Ingle (k, v); Ron Bushy (d); Lee Dorman (b, v); Erik Brann (g, v)
Track listing:
Most Anything You Want; Flowers And Beads; My Mirage; Termination; Are You Happy; In-A-Gadda-Da-Vida
Running time:
36.00
Current CD:
7567903922
Further listening:
Rhino's deluxe re-release, Iron Butterfly: In-A-Gadda-Da-Vida (1996) includes three versions of the song – the original epic, the single and a live version – plus all original album tracks.
Further reading:
The Iron Butterfly website is at www.ironbutterfly.com
Like this?
Try . . . p.313

Ill Wind
Flashes
Boston hippie intellectuals make one-off psychedelic classic.

For every mediocre hippie band that sold a million records, another excellent one barely registered. Ill Wind had a sound of their own, irreproachable chops, excellent tunes and a major label record deal – but were scuppered by the catalogue of blunders that peppered their album's path to the few shops it ever appeared in.

The seeds of Ill Wind lay at MIT, the extremely competitive university in Boston where four of the band studied and threw themselves headlong into the counter-culture. 'We were into unusual music and unorthodox behaviour, and actively sought out marijuana and LSD' recalls Richard Griggs, their rhythm guitarist. Renaming themselves Ill Wind in late 1966, they were joined by the icy-voiced Connie Devanney, wife of one of their professors, and gigged solidly throughout the new year, supporting Fleetwood Mac, Moby Grape, Van Morrison, the Who and others.

By summer 1967 things were happening in earnest. Demos were cut at Capitol, but an untimely LSD bust put paid to that. Enter Tom Wilson, legendary producer of Bob Dylan, Simon & Garfunkel and the Velvet Underground, who promptly signed them to his fledgling production company. Having signed away their recording and publishing rights, they delightedly started work on an album - but were soon to be disappointed. For all his promises, Wilson made little effort in the studio. "We got to record an album', remembers Griggs, "but weren't at all happy with the recording process or the finished result".

Despite this, *Flashes* contains some of the finest psychedelia conceivable. People of the Night, for instance, centres on an epic five minute Eastern-tinged guitar solo that never stops gathering momentum over an ever more frantic rhythm section. The song also shows Devanney to have had one of the great female rock voices of the late 60s, cold yet surprisingly emotive. But the album's masterpiece is 'Dark World', one of the most personal and beautiful of all psychedelic recordings and graced with an unusual, sombre fuzz bass solo.

Recording complete, the band was unprepared for the volley of blows awaiting them. The album's tacky front cover, complete with incorrect song information and poorly reproduced photos on the rear, was injury enough. But adding insult was a pressing fault that necessitated the recall of the initial pressing. By the time it had been corrected, momentum was lost. No interviews were organised, so no airplay was arranged, so no reviews appeared. A promotional tour was cancelled and, trapped in a contract they resented, Ill Wind blew itself out at the end of 1968.

RMJ

Record label:
ABC
Produced
by Tom Wilson
Recorded
at Mayfair Studios, New York, Feb 1968.
Released:
Mid-1968.
Chart Peaks:
None (UK), None (US)
Personnel:
Connie Devanney (v) / Ken Frankel (g, banjo) / Richard Griggs (rg, v) / Carey Mann (b, v) / David Kinsman (d).
Track listing:
Walkin' and Singin' / People of the Night / Little Man / Dark World / L.A.P.D. / High Flying Bird / Hung Up Chick / Sleep / Full Cycle.
Further reading:
http://www.zvonar.com
Like this?
Try . . . p.658

Os Mutantes

Os Mutantes

Eccentric Brazilian trio invent Psouth American Psych.

The explosion of invention in mid-60s pop was startling enough to anyone listening on the Anglo-American axis. Imagine how it must have sounded in a place where music followed rigid traditional guidelines and "pop" was the province of fife and drum bands. When a particularly insane Brazilian rock trio called Os Mutantes (The Mutants) unveiled a mischievous, wayward hybrid of Pepper Beatles, Piper Floyd and Disraeli Cream having a bossa-nova jam – at a popular Brazilian music festival in September 1967, no one was too surprised when the crowd started booing and throwing things, or when the use of electric guitars was subsequently banned at the festival.

Originally from São Paolo, Os Mutantes became the adopted rock band of the Tropicalia movement, a group of artists from Bahia state who brought together music, pop art and concrete poetry to good-humouredly undermine conservative tradition and irritate the ruling military regime, taking pleasure in sending-up Brazilian sacred cows or appearing on TV in plastic trousers for a dada freak-out. Eccentric singer and percussionist Rita Lee, her loopy husband Arnaldo Baptista and his brother Sergio, all still in their teens, were guaranteed to delight or offend as required. A third Baptista brother remained off-stage building guitars for Sergio and creating fearsome musical devices out of electric sewing machines. There were also contributions from Tropicalia's pet orchestrator, the gifted Rogério Duprat.

This, the team's debut album was a lovely antic party in Portuguese, featuring wild versions of their contemporaries' songs. Tropicalia colleagues Caetano Veloso, Gilberto Gil and Jorge Ben were all present, as was a cover of The Mamas and Papas' Once Was A Time I Thought and an alkaline guitar sound which seared its way across Veloso's languid blues for the modern era, Baby.

Inspired by *Sgt Pepper* to experiment in the studio, their more peculiar inventions included using aerosol sprays in place of cymbals and serving a meal in the vocal booth and recording the prandial proceedings. One might assume that they were familiar with psychedelic drugs. In fact, the Baptista brothers were naturally bizarre enough not to need any chemical assistance, and didn't sample acid until they visited London in 1970.

Their crazy dream went sour in 1972 when Rita and Arnaldo split after a studio quarrel and she began a successful solo career. Relations between the two factions have been intensely awkward ever since. The brothers' subsequent albums went into the realms of prog-rock and Arnaldo descended into something akin to Brazil's answer to Syd Barret. But at their peak they were producing some of the '60s most vital music – in any language.

Record label:
Polydor
Produced
by Manuel Barenbeim.
Recorded
at Philips Studios, Brasil; 1967–1968.
Released:
June 1968
Chart peaks:
None (UK) None (US)
Personnel:
Rita Lee (v, pc, flute); Arnaldo Baptista (b, v); Sergio Dias Baptista (g); Rogerio Duprat (oa)
Track listing:
Panis Et Circencis; A Minha Menina; O Relogio; Adeus Maria Fulo; Baby; Senhor F; Bat Macumba; Le Premier Bonheur Du Jour; Trem Fantasma; Tempo No Tempo; Ave Genghis Khan
Running time:
36.01
Current CD:
Omplatten FJORD001
Further listening:
Mutantes (1969); A Divina Comedia Ou Ando Meio Desligado (1970); Technicolor (1970) recently released collection of highlights re-recorded in English, never issued at the time. Jardim Eléctrico (1971); Arnaldo Baptista's solo album tribute to his lost love, Rita (1974); Everything Is Possible: The Best Of Os Mutantes (1999)
Further reading:
www.luakabop.com/os mutantes/
Like this?
Try . . . p.553

Small Faces

Ogdens' Nut Gone Flake

Mods go prog on loveably nutty concept album in circular tobacco-tin sleeve.

1968 had started out bumpily for the Small Faces, first with organist Ian McLagan getting nicked for drug possession at Heathrow Airport and then a gruelling visit to Australia with The Who, which saw both groups herded around at gun-point after an ill-tempered slanging match with the tabloid press. A second album for Andrew Oldham's Immediate Records was due in the summer, and work on it had been slow so, around Easter time Oldham dispatched the band on a barging holiday up the Thames to replenish their creative juices and, more importantly, finish the new songs.

With dogs, girlfriends and guitars in tow, the group journeyed lazily from Henley to Maidenhead. In between visits to riverside pubs and several nautical disasters, a 'concept' for their new record was hatched, relating to the mystical *rite de passage* of a psychedelic chap called Happiness Stan and his quest to find where the moon went when it waned.

Soon their new Sony cassette machine was full of ideas for songs, the baroque, bombastic melodies and tragi-comic lyrics having strong echoes of the music hall of their native East End.

Throughout May, the band refined the tracks at Olympic Studios, fleshing them out with harpsichord, Mellotron and brass, under the watchful eye of legendary engineer Glyn Johns. "The idea was to let the group's imagination run wild," remembers Andrew Oldham. "It was like, You wanna go off and live on a barge for a month? Fine. You wanna spend months in the studio doing this record? Great. The most important thing was creating something new and exciting."

The band originally asked Spike Milligan to script and narrate the links between the Happiness Stan tracks on Side Two, but he was unavailable so Stanley Unwin was drafted in instead.

Already in the bag were a handful of rockier songs that eventually filled the first side, including the steely drive of Song Of A Baker (sung by Ronnie), the Foxy Lady-ish Rollin' Over – all throat-shredding Marriott vocals and heavy guitar – and Lazy Sunday, the Cockney sing-along which the band grew to regret after it was released as a single, thus further pigeonholing them as a novelty knees-up band.

On its release in June 1968, in the first ever circular album sleeve with artwork inspired by a tin of ready-rubbed tobacco, *Ogdens* shot straight to Number 1. They had undoubtedly produced one of the freshest and most unusual albums of the late '60s, with a joyous spirit few bands have ever matched since.

PG

Record label:
Immediate
Produced
by Steve Marriott and Ronnie Lane
Recorded
at Olympic, Pye, Trident, spring 1968
Release date:
June 1968
Chart peaks:
1 (UK) None (US)
Personnel:
Steve Marriott (g,v), Ronnie Lane (b,v), Ian McLagan (k,v), Kenny Jones (d), Stanley Unwin (narration). Glyn Johns (e)
Track listing:
Ogdens' Nut Gone Flake; Afterglow (Of Your Love) (S); Long Agos And Worlds Apart; Rene; Son Of A Baker; Lazy Sunday (S); Happiness Stan; Rollin' Over; The Hungry Intruder; The Journey; Mad John; Happydaystoytown
Running time:
38.31
Current CD:
Castle ORRLP001 adds Tin Soldier
Further listening:
their first Immediate album, Small Faces (1967), is a must-have and is currently available with extra tracks, while Autumn Stone (1969) mops up late-era rarities and hits.
Further reading:
McLagan's autiobiography All The Rage (Sidgwick & Jackson) and Quite Naturally: A Day-By-Day Guide by Keith Badman and Terry Rawlings (Complete Music Publications).
Like this?
Try . . . p.323

The Beach Boys

Friends

"I haven't talked to anyone who's discovered Friends," says Beach Boy Bruce Johnston. "They think it's a TV show."

Friends remains, perhaps, The Beach Boys' most misunderstood and underrated album. Upon its release in the early summer of 1968, it was thought to confirm the once mighty group's swift decline into commercial and cultural irrelevancy. Its American chart peak of 126 was profoundly lower than any of its 18 predecessors.

Friends is a polar opposite to the lushly orchestrated, hyper-emotional density of *Pet Sounds. Friends* also signifies the moment at which much of the group's remaining fanbase abandoned any hope that Brian Wilson would deliver a true successor to his 1966 masterwork. Spare, calm and "full of air", says Johnston, *Friends* was the result of the group's deliberate attempt to make "a really subtle album that wasn't concerned with radio". Indeed, the album's dozen shockingly brief tracks (five are under two minutes) rarely last long enough to anchor their delicate hooks before swiftly fading out. Only its lovely, waltz-time title track charted (and was, incidentally, the band's lowest charting single in six years).

It could be argued that virtually anything The Beach Boys might have released during the musical, cultural and political upheavals of 1968 would have failed. "The Beach Boys were just unfashionably unhip," admits Johnston. "*Friends* came out just after Hendrix and Cream.The whole country had discovered drugs, discovered words, discovered Marshall amplifiers, and here comes this feather floating through a wall of noise." Given distance and hindsight, however, *Friends* is a uniquely rewarding Beach Boys album that, excepting *Pet Sounds*, is the group's most sonically and thematically unified. Its 26 weightless minutes make up possibly the sweetest album ever to be filed under rock.

Significantly, *Friends* also marked the songwriting debut of drummer Dennis, whose beautifully fragile Be Still and Little Bird are highlights, signalling his development into a songwriter of major emotional reach. *Friends* has won many admirers since its initial humiliating launch. In his 1991 autobiography, Brian himself called it "my favourite Beach Boys album".

Record label:
Capitol
Produced
by The Beach Boys.
Recorded
at Brian Wilson's home studio, Bel Air, California; I.D. Sound Los Angeles; February–April 1968.
Released:
July 1968
Chart peaks:
6 (UK) 126 (US)
Personnel:
Mike Love (v, s); Carl Wilson (v, g, k); Alan Jardine (g, v); Brian Wilson (k, g, v); Dennis Wilson (v, d, k)
Track listing:
Meant For You; Friends; Wake The World; Be Here In The Morning; When A Man Needs A Woman; Passing By; Anna Lee, The Healer; Little Bird; Be Still; Busy Doin' Nothin'; Diamond Head; Transcendental Meditation
Running time:
25.58
Current CD:
CDP7936972 adds *20/20*
Further listening:
20/20 (1969); Sunflower (1970)
Further reading:
The Nearest Faraway Place (Timothy White, 1996); www.beachboysfanclub.com/
Like this?
Try . . . p.232

Dr John, The Night Tripper

Gris-Gris

The record that transformed session player Mac Rebennack into post-hippie psychedelic voodoo king Dr John.

Mac Rebennack had no intention of singing on this brooding underground classic; New Orleans belter Ronnie Barron had been designated for the job. But with Barron unavailable – "his manager thought it was a bad career move" – the man who had worked as a session keyboardist and guitar player (until a gunshot wound put paid to the picking) on albums by Professor Longhair, Joe Tex and Frankie Ford, morphed into his alter ego – mystical, menacing growler Dr John, The Night Tripper, a character he had learned about in the '50s from voodoo artist Prince LaLa.

"I figured it would be a one-off thing," recalls the Doctor.

Rebennack was familiar with the mystery and magic of Crescent City – his nightmarish 1965 *Zu Zu Man* borrowed liberally from the voodoo chants and incantations that were as prevalent as incense smoke in the tawdry French Quarter. But *Gris Gris* went further, grafting voodoo's dark, esoteric heart to a hypnotic groove with funky blues, sparse, repetitive minor chord melodies, funereal keyboards and Afro-Cuban syncopation shot through with feral noises, gibberish and metaphysical threats and boasts, creating an unwholesome witchy brew of sorcery and chicanery that fascinates as much as it disturbs.

"One thing I always did was believe. I used to play for gigs for the Gris-Gris church. I dug the music, and that's what I was trying to capture." Using left-over time at Gold Star from a Sonny and Cher session, Dr John and his fellow refugees did their best to turn the legendary studio into a voodoo church: "I remember Hugh Masekela was cutting next door to us and the engineers at Gold Star were nervous. They were used to Phil Spector and Sonny Bono and people like that coming in, and they saw my crew and next door they saw Hugh's crew and these guys didn't look like your regulation studio-looking kind of guys, and we were burning candles and incense to get into the mood and everything. But I got a kick out of that."

Centrepiece Walk On Gilded Splinters was based on a traditional voodoo church song. "It's supposed to be 'Splendors' but I turned it into 'Splinters'," said the Doctor. "I just thought splinters sounded better and I always pictured splinters when I sung it." And the ambling, subliminal title cut wormed its way into the nascent waves of American FM radio where it became a late night staple, catching the cresting wave of psychedelia and hippiedom. More than three decades on, the album retains its extraordinary power to cast a spell.

JU

Record label:
Atlantic
Produced
by Harold Battiste.
Recorded
at Gold Star Studio, Los Angeles, California; autumn 1967.
Released:
July 1968
Chart peaks:
None (UK) None (US)
Personnel:
Max Rebennack, (v, g, o); Steve Mann (g); Alvin 'Shine' Robinson (g, v); Ernest McLean (g); Harold Battiste (bs, clarinet); Ron Johnson (b); David West (b); Richard 'Didimus' Washington (d, pc); John Boudreaux (d); Dave Dixon (v, pc); Jessie Hill (v); Shirley Goodman (v); Tami Lynn (v); Joanie Jones (v); Sonny Raye (v); Ronnie Barron (v, o); Morris Bachamin (ts); Plas Johnson (s)
Track listing:
Gris-Gris Gumbo Ya Ya; Danse Kalinda Ba Boom; Mama Roux (US/S); Danse Fambeaux; Croker Courtbullion; Jump Sturdy (US/S); I Walk On Gilded Splinters
Running time:
33.32
Current CD:
CCM 131-1 R2 7508
Further listening:
Babylon (1969); Gumbo (1972); Dr John Plays Mac Rebennack (1982); Anutha Zone (1998)
Further reading:
Under A Hoodoo Moon: The Life of the Night Tripper (Mac Rebennack with Jack Rummel, 1994)
Like this?
Try . . . p.383

J.K. & Co.

Suddenly One Summer

Dreamy psychedelia from Canada! Now a cult classic.

One of those treasured items record collectors occasionally stumble across and pick up merely because they find the cover to be interestingly tacky, *Suddenly One Summer* has proven to be a jewel of a record, albeit a mystifying one. Canadian in origin, and issued in the US on White Whale Records – a label with a bizarrely eclectic artist roster that included The Turtles, Nino Tempo And April Stevens, and British under-achievers John's Children – the record is a whooshing, floating trip.

As its cover credits only three humans to speak of – and anonymously named ones at that – one is left to ponder whether J.K. & Co was in fact a band or a psychedelic predecessor of the Alan Parsons Project. In some ways it indeed seems a producer's record: opening vocal track Fly boasts a drum sound lifted straight off The Beatles' A Day In The Life; a sitar can be heard on The Magical Fingers Of Minerva; Little Children features the inevitable sound effect of children at play and actually breaks into a few bars of Frere Jacques; and, most appropriately, album closer Dead includes the voice of a clergyman invoking burial rites, and – nice touch, this – the sound of someone shovelling actual dirt.

But what holds *Suddenly One Summer* together throughout is the voice and song of one Jay Kaye, who has crafted a rather special song cycle. From its whirling beginning – in which Kaye in lazy reverie sings, "If you want to fly ..." – through the troubled lyrics of Nobody ("My happiness is a needle/I will escape for another day"), which recalls Love's Signed D.C. – to the cheery sound of that gravedigger's shovel, there's a story of some sort being told here.

Consider this one of those late '60s psychedelic concept albums – Ford Theatre's *Trilogy For The Masses* and Mandrake Memorial's *Puzzle* are two others – that in their ambition to tell some sort of life parable emerge with an oddly open-ended suite that can be interpreted in any manner the listener finds appropriate. In the end, the big question is less the matter of J.K.'s identity and more the motivation of the people who made the record – not to mention the expectations of the label that decided to release it. Stranger still is how Fly manages to anticipate Radiohead's *OK Computer*, a mere 30 years beforehand. What goes around ...

Record label:
White Whale
Produced
by RH Spurgin.
Recorded
at Vancouver Recording, Canada, dates unknown.
Released:
July 1968
Chart peaks:
None (UK) None (US)
Personnel:
Jay Kaye; (all instruments, v); RW Buckley (a)
Track listing:
Break Of Dawn; Fly; Little Children; Christine; Speed; Crystal Ball; Nobody; O.D; Land Of Sensations & Delights; The Times; Magical Fingers Of Minerva; Dead
Running time:
33.03
Currently unavailable
on legitimate CD, though bootlegs exist.
Further listening:
Ford Theatre, Trilogy For The Masses (1968)
Further reading:
You just read it!
Like this?
Try . . . p.186

The Millennium

Begin

Ambitious, avant-garde, but accessible West Coast genius from a legendary cult figure

The Millennium were the brainchild of LA-based producer Curt Boettcher (1943–1987), whose work on The Association's 1966 debut album had yielded the hits Along Comes Mary and Cherish. Seeing himself as an auteur in the Phil Spector mould, Boettcher sought a broad canvas for his outpouring of ideas. His production partner was Keith Olsen, a whiz-kid engineer who quit his gig as bass player in the Music Machine to follow Boettcher's lead. (Olsen would later become a hit producer himself for Fleetwood Mac, The Grateful Dead, and others.)

Armed with a concept and a partner, all Boettcher needed was an angel. He found one in the form of Brian Wilson's former writing partner, Gary Usher. A staff producer at Columbia, Usher first learned of Boettcher in 1966, when he heard strange sounds wafting down the hall at Studio Three West. As Usher (who died in 1990) later recalled, he was not the only one who was impressed; "Brian Wilson said, 'What is *that*?'" It was Boettcher doing a single with future Millennium member Lee Mallory. "That record stunned Brian. He's doing little surfer music, and here comes this kid who is light years ahead of him. I had never seen Brian turn white. All he could talk about for a week was that song and that kid. Brian sensed that that was where it was at, that's where it was going."

Although The Millennium was conceived as a studio group, its line-up was solid. In addition to Mallory, Salisbury, and Boettcher, it included former Music Machine members Ron Edgar and Doug Rhodes, newcomer Joey Stec, and future Crabby Appleton leader Michael Fennelly.

Begin was recorded on two jerryrigged 8-track machines, making it only the second album to use 16-track technology. (Simon And Garfunkel's *Bookends* was the first.) The sound is dense; Boettcher's philosophy could be summed up as, 'Sixteen tracks and every one of them has to be filled!' At the same time, it escapes being a Wall of Mush; in fact, it sounds strikingly modern, rendering the West Coast vocal-harmony sound of the time with a lush intricacy. The songs are as strong as the production, too: Fennelly-Stec composition It's You presages '70s power pop, while Boettcher's The Island sparkles like beach glass in the sun. It's no surprise that the album is a favourite of contemporary pop confectioners such as Belle And Sebastian, Saint Etienne, and The High Llamas. Even in 1968, when *Begin* died a commercial death, there were people who knew that it pointed towards the sound of the next millennium. And then, there were also those who didn't want to know. "I sent Brian [Wilson] a copy of The Millennium album," Usher recalled. "Freaked him out. He never called me back."

Record label:
Columbia
Produced
by Curt Boettcher and Keith Olsen.
Recorded
at Columbia Studios, Los Angeles; early 1967 to mid 1968.
Released:
July 1968
Chart peaks:
None (UK) None (US)
Personnel:
Curt Boettcher (v, g); Lee Mallory (v, g); Doug Rhodes (b, tuba, p, o, harpsichord, v); Ron Edgar (d, pc, v); Michael Fennelly (v, g); Joey Stec (v, g); Sandy Salisbury (v); Michelle O'Malley (v); Red Rhodes (ps); Mike Deasy (g); Toxie French (d); Jerry Scheff (b); Pat Shanahan (d) Paulinho DaCosta (pc)
Track listing:
Prelude; To Claudia On Thursday; I Just Want To Be Your Friend; 5am; I'm With You; The Island; Sing To Me; It's You; Some Sunny Day; It Won't Always Be The Same; The Know It All; Karmic Dream Sequence #1; There Is Nothing More To Say; Anthem (Begin)
Running time:
43.15
Current CD:
Rev-Ola CREV052 adds: Just About The Same; Blight
Further listening:
The album made by Curt Boettcher and various Millenium personnel as Sagittarius, Present Tense (1968)
Further reading:
www.geocities.com/Hollywood/3218 (The Millennium Home Page)
Like this?
Try . . . p.294

The Band

Music From Big Pink

Astonishing debut from Dylan's backing band, a soulful throwback completely against the grain of the times.

Following a gruelling period backing Bob Dylan on his 1966 world tour, the musicians later christened "The Band" by Capitol Records (in preference to the more controversial "Crackers") re-grouped at their Woodstock hideaway Big Pink, where the informal sessions that resulted in Dylan's *Basement Tapes* also gave rise to the material that made up their own debut album. Recorded with the imaginative young producer John Simon at sessions in New York and Los Angeles, these songs favoured the wisdom and values of a shared tradition over the transitory upheavals of the youth movement.

"The songs were more like buried treasure from American lore than new songs by contemporary artists," claims John Simon. "They were playing out of what I called their 'Appalachian scale', a pentatonic, five-note scale like the black keys on the piano. That was the palette from which those melodies came."

Lyrically, the band's main songwriter Robbie Robertson had clearly learnt much from his time with Dylan, whose hand was initially believed by many to be behind the mythopoeic single The Weight. Dylan did, however, collaborate with Rick Danko and Richard Manuel on This Wheel's On Fire and Tears Of Rage respectively (as well as providing the surreal-naïve cover painting), while The Band's version of his I Shall Be Released became the definitive version of this modern liberation anthem.

"The music was the sum of all the experiences we'd shared for the past ten years, distilled through the quieter vibe of our lives in the country," believes Levon Helm. Yet for all its traditional virtues, the album featured several innovatory musical strategies, notably from inventive organist Garth Hudson.

The album kick-started the "country-rock" trend – a term they hated – and was an immediate critical success. Reviewers in *Time, Life* and *Rolling Stone* acclaimed it as a work which presciently articulated contemporary doubts and uncertainties about the direction of American "progress", while musicians such as George Harrison and Eric Clapton also garlanded it with praise. Appropriately enough, it is one of the few recordings from its era whose power remains immune to the passage of time.

Record Label:
Capitol
Produced
by John Simon.
Recorded
at A&R Studios, New York; Capitol Studios, Los Angeles; January–March 1968.
Release date:
August 1968
Chart peaks:
25 (UK) 30 (US)
Personnel:
Jaime Robbie Robertson (g, v); Rick Danko (b, v); Richard Manuel (k, v); Garth Hudson (k, s); Levon Helm (d, v); John Simon (horns); Shelly Yakus (e); Rex Updegraft (e)
Track Listing:
Tears Of Rage; To Kingdom Come; In A Station; Caledonia Mission; The Weight (S); We Can Talk; Long Black Veil; Chest Fever; Lonesome Suzie; This Wheel's On Fire; I Shall Be Released
Running time:
42.03
Current CD:
CDP 7 46069 2
Further listening:
Follow-up The Band (1969) is, if anything, even better. Stage Fright (1970), Northern Lights – Southern Cross (1975) and live triple Rock Of Ages (1972) are the best of their other albums. Robbie Robertson, Rick Danko and Levon Helm each subsequently released several solo albums.
Further reading:
Across The Great Divide (Barney Hoskyns, 1993); This Wheel's On Fire: Levon Helm And The Story Of The Band (Levon Helm with Stephen Davis, 1993); http://theband.hiof.no/
Like this?
Try . . . p.95

Blue Cheer

Outsideinside

Second album by San Francisco lysergic hard rock outfit who sowed the seeds of punk and grunge.

Blue Cheer's fearsome reputation as one of the founding fathers of the metal genre is largely due to the ferocity of their bombastic *Vincebus Eruptum* debut. A fine example of cro-magnon hard rock, it featured a deranged re-working of Eddie Cochran's Summertime Blues along with a similarly crazed cover of Mose Allison's Parchment Farm. While *Vincebus* can be seen as reflecting the growing sense of social unrest and violence fuelled by the escalation of the Vietnam conflict, it also happens to sound one-dimensional when placed alongside Blue Cheer's second effort, *Outsideinside.*

The album's intriguing title is down to the fact that the threesome of Dickie Peterson, Leigh Stevens (as he's credited on the sleeve, despite spelling his surname Stephens) and Paul Whaley elected to record half of the album outdoors. Rock mythology suggests that this occured after the band's use of excessive volume caused too much damage to assorted studios.

The result adds a melodic edge to Blue Cheer's patented sonic assault. Tracks like Sun Cycle and Gypsy Ball, for instance, both bear testimony to Jimi Hendrix's influence on the trio, the latter nodding in the direction of The Wind Cries Mary and making the most of the newfound joys of stereo panning.

High-octane tracks like Come And Get It point the way forward for the likes of the MC5, Just A Little Bit boasts a similar feel to Hendrix's re-working of Fire, while the fantastically titled Magnolia Caboose Babyfinger is an instrumental piece of proto-grunge which Mudhoney would later cover. Elsewhere, Blue Cheer attempt to emulate the success of their Summertime Blues cover by turning their hand to a version of the Stones's (I Can't Get No) Satisfaction, delivering it at double the speed. Album closer Babylon is a further slice of funky, cowbell-banging hard rock.

Virtually ignored on its release (most UK publications didn't even bother to review the album), *Outsideinside* just about managed to sneak into the Billboard 100 in the US. A remarkable dip in form when you consider that *Vincebus...* managed to peak at Number 11 less than 12 months earlier.

Outsideinside remains a criminally under-rated second effort from a band whose legacy is substantial but who have yet to receive the credit for embarking on what Leigh Stevens describes as "a violent and frightening trip".

Record label:
Mercury
Produced
by Abe 'Voco' Kesh.
Recorded outside
at Gate 5, Sausalito, and Muir Beach, California; Pier 57 (Department Of Marine And Aviation), New York City; studio sessions recorded at Pacific Recorders, San Mateo, California; A&R Studios, Olmstead Studios and The Record Plant, New York City; early 1968.
Released:
August 1968
Chart peaks:
None (UK) 90 (US)
Personnel:
Dickie Peterson (b, v); Leigh Stevens (g, v); Paul Whaley (d, v); Ralph Burns Kellogg (k); Eric Albronda (v); Eddie Kramer, Hank McGill, Jay Snyder, Tony May (e)
Track listing:
Feathers From Your Tree (S); Sun Cycle (S); Just A Little Bit; Gypsy Ball; Come And Get It; (I Can't Get No) Satisfaction; The Hunter; Magnolia Caboose Babyfinger; Babylon
Running time:
33.10
Current CD:
Line AK012
Further listening:
Vincebus Eruptum (1968); New! Improved! (1969)
Further reading:
the official Blue Cheer site at: http://bp.bpcwsb.com/inet.files/fo01.htm#bluecheer15
Like this?
Try . . . p.533

Nilsson

Aerial Ballet

The Beatles' favourite songwriter and group.

"I always thought," mused Harry Nilsson, "I was a street cat who could pass for someone who went to college." *Aerial Ballet*, his second album, perfectly showcases his unique, utterly charming blend of earthiness and airiness. In an era bloated with confessional songwriters, Nilsson was a contradiction. His lyrics often seemed extraordinarily intimate, yet he bristled when fans attempted to read too much meaning into them. He was accommodating enough to explain the album's title – Nilsson's Aerial Ballet was a name his grandparents used for their trapeze act. However, when asked the meaning of one of his songs, he was likely to give an answer like the one he gave Hugh Hefner on TV's Playboy After Dark. Hef had inquired as to the inspiration behind *Aerial Ballet*'s Good Old Desk. With a straight face, Nilsson replied that the song's meaning was in its initials: G.O.D.; "I bullshitted him," Harry admitted later. "I thought it was funny. Nobody else thought it was funny!"

Shortly before the release of *Aerial Ballet*, Nilsson's career received the kind of boost most performers can only dream of. Derek Taylor, The Beatles' close friend and former press agent, had given the group a copy of Nilsson's first album, *Pandemonium Shadow Show*. At an Apple press conference, when asked to name their favourite singer, The Beatles said "Nilsson". Asked about their favourite group, they gave the same reply. Nilsson subsequently met the Fabs during a trip to England, where he played Lennon *Aerial Ballet*. Lennon especially liked Mr. Richland's Favorite Song (named after record promoter Tony Richland). Recalling those times with Lennon, Nilsson told Rolling Stone, "I really fell in love with him. I knew he was all those things you wanted somebody to be."

Although it was largely Nilsson's songwriting that impressed The Beatles, it was *Aerial Ballet*'s lone non-original that would catapult him to fame. According to legend, it was the inexhaustible Taylor who turned director John Schlesinger on to Nilsson's version of Fred Neil's Everybody's Talkin', which had an unsuccessful run as a single on *Aerial Ballet*'s release. When it emerged in August 1969 as a single from the film's soundtrack, it became an international smash. Everybody's Talkin' won Nilsson his first Grammy: Best Contemporary Vocal Performance, Male.

Record label:
RCA
Produced
by Rick Jarrard.
Recorded
at RCA Victor's Music Center of the World, Los Angeles; late 1967–early 1968.
Released:
August 1968
Chart peaks:
None (UK) None (US)
Personnel:
Harry Nilsson (v); Larry Knechtel (b, p); Lyle Ritz (b); Al Casey (g); Dennis Budimir (g); Michael Melvoin (harpsichord, o, p). With orchestra; George Tipton (a)
Track listing:
Good Old Desk; Don't Leave Me; Mr Richland's Favorite Song; Little Cowboy; Together; Everybody's Talkin'; I Said Goodbye To Me; Little Cowboy (reprise); Mr. Tinker; One; The Wailing Of The Willow; Bath
Running time:
25.15
Current CD:
74321 757422 2CD set includes Pandemonium Shadow Show and Aerial Pandemonium Ballet, the 1971 remixed compilation of the two albums.
Further listening:
Nilsson said that his albums came in trilogies. Aerial Ballet could be said to be the middle of a trilogy that began with his debut, Pandemonium Shadow Show (1967), and ended with Harry (1969), both highly recommended.
Further reading:
www.harrynilsson.com/
Like this?
Try . . . p.422

David Ackles

David Ackles

A former toilet-factory security guard taps into the American heartland on classic debut.

Born into a showbiz family, at the age of four David Ackles was half of a song-and-dance act with his sister, and in his early teens was a Hollywood B-movie child actor. Contracted to Elektra purely as a songwriter in the late '60s, label boss Jac Holzman soon realised that compositions as idiosyncratic as The Road To Cairo, about a man immobilised by fear, or His Name Is Andrew, detailing the pain of lost faith, would best be served if Ackles sang them himself. Partnered with his old school-friend David Anderle as producer, he set to work recording and orchestrating his poignant story-songs.

"We had to make that album twice to get what I wanted," explained Ackles later. The second attempt came when Ackles was introduced to Rhinoceros, another recent Elektra signing. "We sat around and I played the songs and they filled in, and we just had such a good time. We knew that was the right thing to do."

The album offered the intelligence and imagery of Leonard Cohen without the self-pity, as it stumbled along on Ackles' curious piano rhythms, augmented with Michael Fonfara's whistling organ and Doug Hastings' empathetic guitar filigrees. These collaborative arrangements tended towards stagey structures, as if written for some half-realised off-Broadway musical, ideal for tracks like Down River, an ingeniously plotted, semi-autobiographical, one-sided conversation with a sting in its tail. Ackles later recalled the sessions as "an easy-going, friendly affair", but the atmosphere was shot through with the singer's world-weary aching and loneliness. On release, *Rolling Stone* complimented his voice but reckoned his melodies were "almost no melodies at all" while the nearest *Record Mirror* got to a positive comment was "a plaintive sort of collection". After four unsuccessful albums, Ackles became variously a lecturer, TV scriptwriter and scorer of ballets. As if he was becoming a character in one of his own songs, various accidents left him with an all-but crippled arm and a steel hip before he had his first encounter with cancer. Tracked down in 1994, Ackles said, "I'm really enjoying my life, which will no doubt come as a shock to fans of my first two albums, in whose angst they swim." On March 2, 1999, David Ackles died of lung cancer, leaving a legacy of four of the most beautiful but rarely heard albums of his era.

Record Label:
Elektra
Produced
by David Anderle and Russ Miller.
Recording
location unknown.
Released:
September 3, 1968
Chart peaks:
None (UK) None (US)
Running time:
37.54
Personnel:
David Ackles (p, v); Michael Fonfara (o); Danny Weis (g); Douglas Hastings (g); Jerry Penrod (b); John Keliehor (pc)
Track Listing:
The Road To Cairo (S); When Love Is Gone; Sonny Come Home; Blue Ribbons; What A Happy Day; Down River (S); Laissez-Faire (S); Lotus Man; His Name Is Andrew; Be My Friend
Currently unavailable on CD
Further listening:
American Gothic (1972)
Further reading:
MOJO 57; http://www.mathie.demon.co.uk/da/
Like this?
Try . . . p.577

The Byrds

Sweetheart Of The Rodeo

The Byrds unintentionally kickstart the country rock boom of the early '70s.

Streamlined to a trio at the start of 1968, The Byrds were reduced to playing small club dates and support slots. "We really needed somebody," Roger McGuinn recalls. Three months later, he was auditioning for a jazz keyboard player and improbably chose Gram Parsons. It rapidly transpired that Parsons knew nothing about jazz but was a promising country singer and songwriter. A Harvard dropout with a Southern background that would not have been out of place in the tortured pages of a Tennessee Williams play, Parsons was thrusting and ambitious enough to replace the recently fired David Crosby as The Byrds' resident troublemaker. After allying himself with fellow country enthusiast Chris Hillman, Parsons successfully deflected McGuinn from pursuing his dream concept of a double album chronicling the history of 20th century music. McGuinn had intended to tackle traditional country, move on to folk, R&B and rock, then conclude the work with some snatches of jazz and synthesizer experimentation. Once Parsons arrived, they never got beyond the country.

"Chris, Gram and producer Gary Usher just didn't want to go along with the electronic music idea, so I was outvoted," McGuinn explains. The Byrds certainly played the country angle to perfection. First they cut their hair, then moved to Nashville and even risked their lives playing before a staunch redneck audience at the Grand Ole Opry. The new line-up appeared at the Royal Albert Hall in July and sounded highly accomplished with a neat combination of country-style material and Byrds classics. The future looked bright but on the day they were due to set forth on a controversial tour of South Africa, Parsons quit.

The following month, his four months as a Byrd was validated with the release of this groundbreaking and innovative album. At a time when rock was in danger of suffocation by the overblown excesses of hard rock and stale psychedelia *Sweetheart* offered a sense of place and respect for tradition. Like Dylan's *John Wesley Harding* and The Band's *Music From Big Pink*, it evoked an America before the fall, articulated most vividly in Parsons' Hickory Wind and the Woody Guthrie classic Pretty Boy Floyd. The sales were disappointing – hardly surprising considering Gram was now gone – but in challenging their audience, The Byrds had shown a courage that was commendable.

Record label:
Columbia
Produced
by Gary Usher.
Recorded
in Nashville; March–April 1968.
Released:
September 27, 1968
Chart peaks:
27 (UK) 24 (UK)
Personnel:
Roger McGuinn (g, v, banjo); Kevin Kelley (d); Chris Hillman (b, v, mandolin); Gram Parsons (g, v); Earl P. Ball (p); Jon Corneal (d); Lloyd Green (sg); John Hartford (banjo, g); Roy M. Huskey (b); Jaydee Maness (sg); Clarence J. White (g); Roy Halee (e); Charlie Bragg (e)
Track listing:
You Ain't Going Nowhere (S); I Am A Pilgrim (S); The Christian Life; You Don't Miss Your Water; You're Still On My Mind; Pretty Boy Floyd; Hickory Wind; One Hundred Years From Now; Blue Canadian Rockies; Life In Prison; Nothing Was Delivered
Running time
58.55
Current CD:
Legacy 4867522 adds: You Got A Reputation; Lazy Days; Pretty Polly; The Christian Life (rehearsal); Life In Prison (rehearsal); You're Still On My Mind (rehearsal); One Hundred Years From Now (rehearsal); All I Have Is Memories
Further listening:
Younger Than Yesterday (1967)
Further reading:
MOJO 41; The Byrds: Timeless Flight Revisited (Johnny Rogan, 1997)
Like this?
Try . . . p.324

The Jeff Beck Group

Truth

A great band built on shifting sand, export the blues back to America.

Jeff Beck always meant more in America than on his home turf, and *Truth* (released in the US as a Jeff Beck solo album), has a reputation in America as a seminal '60s heavy rock album that laid the foundations for what would become heavy metal.The band gained notoriety through their clever reworking of blues, embellished with Beck's visionary guitar. They sounded lighter and more fluid than any other British blues contenders, with a dramatic element other bands didn't possess – Rod Stewart's gritty and resolute singing, trading guitar and vocal lines – which would become the blueprint for hard rock bands in years to come.

But the band's dynamics – both musically and politically – often seemed to be underpinned by the interplay of grace *and* attack. At the time, Stewart would complain that fans and even record company executives would come up to him, slap him on the back, and say, "Great show, Jeff!" – automatically assuming that the band was named after the singer. Beck remembers it a little differently. "No, we were getting on pretty well then. The fact was that they all began to see the method in my madness when they heard the playbacks, and that I was prepared to put my own money into getting really good players, like John Paul Jones. On Ol' Man River we used John Paul, Nicky Hopkins and Moonie on timpani."

Though *Truth* occupies an important place in the evolution of rock, Beck had a few reservations. "We had a great sound," he remembers, "but nobody had written any songs. Rod wrote folk songs then, which wouldn't have worked out for us, so he suggested we do [The Yardbirds'] Shapes Of Things." The band also did a version of the Willie Dixon's seductive classic You Shook Me. Unknown to Beck at the time, former bandmate Jimmy Page's new outfit Led Zeppelin would also record the song for their own debut album; but to Beck's delight, theirs was released the next year.

"I took that as a compliment, because that album was already second-hand. And we both did You Shook Me in a slightly different style. It was a flattering thing, but the flattery went out the window when they began to be known for it and we weren't." While not the closest of friends, Beck did allow that Stewart was behind the album's title: "Whenever Rod and I used to go on-stage, he'd say, 'Shall we tell them the truth tonight?' It was a great thing to say. It was his way of saying, 'Are we going to pull out every bit of emotion we can?' When we were on speaking terms, we used to use that as a measuring stick, that we gave them the truth tonight. And so I said, 'Why don't we call the album that?' He went misty-eyed on me. There was a good vibe about the whole record."

JU

Record label:
Columbia
Recorded
at Abbey Road Studios, London; May 14–16 and May 25, 1968.
Produced
by Mickie Most and Jeff Beck.
Released:
September 28, 1968
Chart peaks:
None (UK) 15 (US)
Personnel:
Jeff Beck (g, b); Rod Stewart (v); Ron Wood (b, g); Nicky Hopkins (k, p); Keith Moon (d); Aynsley Dunbar (d); Mickey Waller (d); Ken Scott (e)
Track listing:
Shape Of Things; Let Me Love You, Morning Dew; You Shook Me; Ol' Man River; Greensleeves; Rock My Plimsoul; Beck's Bolero; Blues De Luxe; I Ain't Superstitious
Running time:
40.26
Currently unavailable on CD
Further listening:
Beckology, the 3-disc, 55-track set released in 1998 spanning Beck's entire career includes three unreleased tracks and a 64-page booklet encased in a guitar-shaped box.
Further Reading:
In Session With Jeff Beck: Guitar-Tab Book and CD (1997)
Like this?
Try . . . p.63

Whistler, Chaucer, Detroit And Greenhill

The Unwritten Works Of Geoffrey, Etc.

Showcase of the sophisticated scene in Ft. Worth, Texas.

Anyone picking up this nondescript 1968 Uni Records album expecting to glean any information about the performers within were confronted with period liner notes reading: "I predict Benjamin Whistler, Geoffrey Chaucer, Nathan Detroit and Phillip Greenhill will be the next big thing, and I'm sure after you dig this album you'll agree they have what it takes to be just that."

Anyone reading the songwriting credits, though, would note that producer Joseph Burnett – soon known as T-Bone – penned four of the album's 11 tracks, and that the real names of the mysterious 'next big thing' were nowhere to be seen. In fact, WCD&G were not a band, but a loosely based, non-performing group of musicians "just learning to use the studio, really," says T-Bone Burnett today. With Houston's John Carrick the only non-Ft. Worth homeboy, Burnett, David Bullock, Scott Fraser, Phil White, and Eddie Lively were just making it up as they went along.

"We were hanging out recording stuff down in the basement of this radio station in Ft Worth. We did the Legendary Stardust Cowboy at that time, then we recorded a bunch of tunes – mostly staying up all night taking a lot of speed or something, staying up for five days at a time making music. And that group of tunes somehow ended up being a record. And I don't know how that name came about."

The music from those non-stop recording sessions is surprisingly coherent rock'n'roll that comes from all directions and provided this "group" with the same sort of varied sound that made bands like Buffalo Springfield and Moby Grape so worthy. With notably different singing and writing styles, the lingering impression was of vast untapped talent waiting to come to further fruition on follow-up or solo albums yet unmade. Much of this crew would end up recording a memorable, Byrdsy classic for Epic as Space Opera in 1973, then disappear.

"I was by far the least talented of all these people," says Burnett, "and – this just shows you that life is tricky – I think it's funny that that I've managed to stay doing it all these years."

Record label:
Uni
Produced
by Joseph Burnett.
Recorded
at Sound City Studios, Forth Worth, Texas and United Audio Studio, Santa Ana, California.
Released:
September 1968.
Chart peaks:
None (UK) None (US)
Personnel:
David Bullock; Scott Fraser; John Carrick; Phil White; Eddie Lively; T-Bone Burnett; George J Fernandez (m, special effects)
Track listing:
The Viper (What John Rance Had To Tell); Day Of Childhood; Upon Waking From The Nap; Live 'Til I Die; Street In Paris; As Pure As The Freshly Driven Snow; Tribute To Sundance; House Of Collection; Just Me And Her; On Lusty Gentlemen; Ready To Move
Running time:
28.12
Currently unavailable on CD
Further listening:
J Henry Burnett, The B-52 Band And The Fabulous Skylarks (1972); Space Opera (1973)
Like this?
Try . . . p.374

Jimi Hendrix Experience

Electric Ladyland

Mould-busting double disc set, notorious in UK for its gratuitous naked lady-lined gatefold.

"We call our music Electric Church Music," said Hendrix. "It's like a religion to us. Some ladies are like the church to us too. Some groupies know more about music than the guys. People call them groupies but I prefer the term 'electric ladies'. My whole *Electric Ladyland* album is about them." Physically, eight months and the Atlantic Ocean divided the first and last sessions for *Electric Ladyland*; spiritually, a lifetime sundered the set. The soft soul of the title track was only the first of the surprises in store, as Hendrix pulled away from the visceral sex-rock of his first two albums and began daubing from the broader, expressionist palette of subsequent experience. The sessions could have produced two great single albums. But blended together, they were heart-stopping. Wild experimentation blurred into solid rocking grooves. All Along The Watchtower not only reinvented Dylan's original for the audience, it reinvented it for Dylan as well – he subsequently performed the song as a *de facto* Hendrix cover. The two Voodoo Chiles offer first, a funkadelic jam with Winwood and Cassidy; then a screaming guitar exorcism (based around Cream's Sunshine Of Your Love riff, played backwards); and Burning Of The Midnight Lamp is spectral moodiness grafted to a mid-period Stones' arrangement.

Yet bassist Redding recalls, "The stuff we did in America, apart from Midnight Lamp, didn't work as well. I'd say we all preferred working in London. While we were at Olympic, the Stones were next door. We used to go and hang out, have a smoke, all that stuff, and it was a good atmosphere. If Chas wanted to do a bit of mixing, he'd go 'alright lads, go down the pub,' and we'd troop off. It was very relaxed. Whereas American studios were always so clinical. It wasn't such a good environment to be working in."

Chandler's withdrawal from the sessions, sick of constantly rowing with Hendrix, only exacerbated the discontent. Indeed, says Redding, "By the time we recorded Little Miss Strange (on April 20/21), the band had already broken up." They would carry on gigging for another year, but only because their work schedule was already mapped out that far in advance.

Record label:
Track
Produced
by Jimi Hendrix (and Chas Chandler)
Recorded
at Olympic, London; December 20, 1967–January 28, 1968; Record Plant, New York; April 18–August 27, 1968.
Released:
October 25, 1968 (UK)
Chart peaks:
6 (UK) 1 (US)
Personnel:
Jimi Hendrix (g, v); Noel Redding (b, v); Mitch Mitchell (d); Rainy Day; Still Raining: Mike Finnigan (o); Freddie Smith (horn); Larry Faucette (congas); Buddy Miles (d); Stevie Winwood (o on Voodoo Chile); Jack Cassidy (b); Al Kooper (p)
Track listing:
... And The Gods Made Love; Have You Ever Been (To Electric Ladyland); Crosstown Traffic (S); Voodoo Chile; Little Miss Strange; Long Hot Summer Night; Come On (Let The Good Times Roll); Gypsy Eyes; Burning Of The Midnight Lamp (S, UK only); Rainy Day Dream Away; 1983 ... (A Merman I Should Turn To Be); Moon Turn The Tides ... Gently Gently Away; Still Raining, Still Dreaming; House Burning Down; All Along The Watchtower (S); Voodoo Child (Slight Return) (S, UK only)
Running time:
75.29
Current CD:
MCD 11600
Further listening:
Experience Hendrix: The Best Of (1997)
Further reading:
www.jimi-hendrix.com/
Like this?
Try . . . p.449

The Outsiders

Dutch psychedelic beast touches on love, murder, revenge - and space travel.

It's easy to forget that at the height of the 60s, rock and roll was alive and kicking in the most unexpected places. And arguably nowhere outside the UK and the US had a more fertile scene than Holland, home of the now- legendary 'Nederbeat' scene, where great bands like Q65, Group 1850, Sandy Coast and the Motions were churning out high quality records that were barely released abroad. Few would dispute, though, that the greatest Dutch band of all was The Outsiders, who never recorded a song they hadn't written and in 1968 produced the mighty *CQ*.

Led by the androgynous Wally Tax, they'd been playing the dives up and down the seafront of the Hague for years, honing their musicianship in front of a transient audience largely comprised of rowdy sailors. In this period they grew impressively hard-hitting, their magnificent, adrenaline-filled set captured on their live March 1967 debut - such was their power that they reportedly blew the Stones off stage when supporting them in 1966. Releasing a string of punchy hit singles like the raunchy 'Touch', the melodic 'Monkey On My Back' and the gritty 'That's Your Problem', in the summer of 1967 they had a Dutch smash with the uncharacteristically fey 'Summer Is Here'. This success encouraged Polydor to grant them total freedom in recording their second album early the following year.

Closeted in the studio for months on end, the Outsiders experimented with new instruments and sounds, massively expanding their repertoire without losing any of the focus or drive displayed on their singles. The crunching opener, 'Misfit', announces itself with an ominous bass riff before dementedly energetic drums and guitar crash in. Its unusual, jerky structure typifies the unconventional approach of the album. On the spacey, claustrophobic title track (which could be mistaken for Can or even Radiohead) waves of static wash from speaker to speaker as Tax increasingly desperately cries 'do you receive me?' over a mesmerising groove.

Few releases of the time could boast such varied fare or ferocious delivery, but when *CQ* appeared in 1968 (in a striking yellow pop art sleeve) it bombed and the band disintegrated. Less than 1000 copies are thought to have been sold, making the recent reissue especially welcome. Though the Outsiders can be compared superficially to the Stones or the Pretty Things, on *CQ* they developed a sound all of their own and proved that they could hold their own alongside anyone – and that means *anyone*.

RMJ

Record label:
Polydor
Produced
by The Outsiders
Recorded
at GTB Studios, The Hague, spring / summer 1968.
Released:
October 1968.
Chart Peaks:
n/a (UK) / n/a (US).
Personnel:
Wally Tax (v, g, hm, o, pc, flute, vibes, balalaika) / Ronny Splinter (g, b, bv) / Frank Beek (b, g, o, p, bv, vibes) / Buzz (d, pc, bv, mouthharp).
Track listing:
Misfit / Zsarrahh / C.Q. / Daddy Died On Saturday / It Seems Like Nothing's Gonna Come My Way Today / Doctor / The Man On The Dune / The Bear / Happyville / You're Everything On Earth / Wish You Were Here With Me Today / I Love You no. 2 / Prisonsong.
Current CD:
Pseudonym.
Like this?
Try . . . p.317

Pentangle

Sweet Child

The UK's folk-rock supergroup make their definitive work.

Including two celebrated solo recording artists in Jansch and Renbourn, and a second-to-none rhythm section drafted in from previous spells with Alexis Korner and Duffy Power's Nucleus, the Pentangle were a supergroup from day one – and uniquely so in fusing together individuals and repertoire from both the folk and jazz/blues scenes of the day.

The group existed initially as a spare-time concern, playing almost exclusively at their own Sunday night club at the Horseshoe Hotel in Tottenham Court Road throughout 1967. At the start of that year Bert Jansch had filled a series of thousand-seater city halls on his own and many people, record label included, viewed his commitment to developing the group project bewildering.

It could indeed have been a disaster. There were a number of blown opportunities and false starts in trying to move beyond the Horseshoe before the arrival of New York publicist Jo Lustig, who became the group's manager in early 1968. He immediately oversaw the release of a first album, *The Pentangle*, secured substantial print, radio and TV coverage, and curtailed all group and solo live appearances, invariably in small clubs, to allow for their relaunch as a concert hall act – a scam that worked perfectly.

The Festival Hall concert on June 29 was thus widely anticipated and, as Melody Maker's review concluded, 'Will go down on record as a great success and a highlight in the group's career'. This was literally correct: the show was recorded for this, the second album, and featured an extraordinarily wide-ranging repertoire, utilising the quintet's virtuosic membership in a whole range of solo, duo, trio, quartet and full band combinations. Never again would the balance between them be so perfect or the interplay so fresh and dynamic. Traditional and contemporary folk songs shared space with modern jazz covers, medieval dance pieces, blues, and group originals closer to the folkish end of the rock underground than the whimsical style of their perceived rivals, the Incredible String Band.

The live half of the set includes most of the concert bar first-album material (pointless to issue at the time), a couple of solo tracks and a failed crack at Sweet Child – a complex piece which was subsequently done full justice for the equally eclectic studio half. Conversely, Haitian Fight Song was tried in the studio but the live version retained. The group reached a commercial peak with the UK No 5 LP *Basket Of Light* the following year, but creatively and critically *Sweet Child* was the apogee.

Record label:
Transatlantic
Produced
by Shel Talmy.
Recorded
at the Royal Festival Hall; June 29, 1968; and IBC Studios, London; September, 1968.
Released:
November 1, 1968
Chart peaks:
None (UK) None (US)
Personnel:
Jacqui McShee (v); Bert Jansch (v, g); John Renbourn (v, g); Danny Thompson (db); Terry Cox (v, d, glockenspiel); Damon Lyon-Shaw (e)
Track listing:
Live: Market Song; No More My Lord; Turn Your Money Green; Haitian Fight Song; A Woman Like You; Goodbye Pork-Pie Hat; Three Dances: i. Brentzel Gay; ii. La Rotta; iii. The Earle Of Salisbury; Watch The Stars; So Early In The Spring; No Exit; The Time Has Come; Bruton Town Studio: Sweet Child; I Loved A Lass; Three Part Thing; Sovay; In Time; In Your Mind; I've Got A Feeling; The Trees They Do Grow High; Moondog; Hole In The Coal
Running time:
84.48
Current CD:
ESMCD354
Further listening:
Basket Of Light (1969); Reflection (1971)
Further reading:
Dazzling Stranger: Bert Jansch And The British Folk And Blues Revival (Colin Harper, 2000)
Like this?
Try . . . p.437

The Beatles

The Beatles

The White Album.

Following a particularly relaxing and fertile meditation break in India, The Beatles presented over 30 songs for consideration for the follow-up to Sgt. Pepper, deciding to record as many as possible for a double.

The normal state of Beatles sessions was soon disrupted by the presence of Lennon's constant companion, avant-garde artist Yoko Ono. "Once I found *the* woman, the boys became of no interest whatsoever," Lennon would explain later. "The old gang of mine was over the moment I met her." It was the first time anyone had been allowed access to the band's inner working process and McCartney, Harrison and Starr were naturally thrown by both Lennon's distraction and Yoko's vocal opinions on their music. Things were further aggravated by Lennon's extreme mood swings, caused by his recently acquired heroin habit. Tired of the tension, long-time engineer Geoff Emerick quit. Equally sick of the atmosphere (and disheartened by McCartney's drumming instructions), Ringo walked out for two weeks. McCartney pragmatically (and skilfully) took over on drums for a few tracks and later took to recording on his own in an adjacent studio, which Lennon later confessed to being stung by: "I can't speak for George but I was always hurt when Paul knocked something off without involving us." But then, McCartney had felt equally excluded by Lennon and Yoko contriving the nine-minute sound collage Revolution 9 without him.

With the breakdown of both communication and the old team spirit, the tormented sessions actually produced a rich, amazing record encompassing an incredibly wide stylistic range. From the compellingly visceral (Helter Skelter, Yer Blues, Birthday) to the comically whimsical (Honey Pie, Goodnight, Martha My Dear); from the obscured confessional (Julia, Everybody's Got Something To Hide) to political commentary (Revolution, Blackbird), the whole is rated by some as the pinnacle of The Beatles' genius, by others as disappointingly indulgent.

Producer George Martin famously tried to persuade the band to trim the fat and make it a "really super" single album, starting a debate that continues to this day. McCartney's having none of it: "Come on, it's The Beatles' White Album."

Record Label:
Apple
Produced
by George Martin.
Recorded
at Abbey Road, London; June–October 1968.
Released:
November, 22 1968
Chart peaks:
1 (UK) 1 (US)
Personnel:
John Lennon (v, g, p, o); Paul McCartney (v, b, p, g, d); George Harrison (v, g); Ringo Starr (d); George Martin (p); Chris Thomas (harpsichord); Eric Clapton (g)
Track Listening:
Back in the USSR.; Dear Prudence; Glass Onion; Ob-La-Di, Ob-La-Da; Wild Honey Pie; The Continuing Story Of Bungalow Bill; While My Guitar Gently Weeps; Happiness Is A Warm Gun; Martha My Dear; I'm So Tired; Blackbird; Piggies; Rocky Raccoon; Don't Pass Me By; Why Don't We Do It In The Road?; I Will; Julia; Birthday; Yer Blues; Mother Nature's Son; Everybody's Got Something to Hide Except Me And My Monkey; Sexy Sadie; Helter Skelter; Long, Long, Long; Revolution 1; Honey Pie; Savoy Truffle; Cry Baby Cry; Revolution 9; Good Night
Running time:
93.15
Current CD:
CDS 7 46443 8
Further listening:
Let It Be (1970); Anthology 3 (1997)
Further reading:
www.getback.org/bwhite.html
Like this?
Try . . . p.485

The Kinks

The Kinks Are The Village Green Preservation Society

Chart success on the wane, Ray Davies conceives one of the quintessentially English pop albums.

True to its title, *Village Green Preservation Society* eschewed the wide-eyed psychedelia and studio experiment of its contemporaries. Which may be why it was grossly overlooked at the time. Instead, it focused on the wistful, sharp social commentary of Davies's writing and it's the fulcrum on which his deserved reputation as a songsmith pivots.

While Davies's peers on *Village Green* are not from the rock and pop world, neither are they – despite the claims of many a pop historian – the kitchen sink dramatists of the early '60s. If anything, Davies alludes to the short stories of Harold Nicholson, the Bloomsbury essays (rather than novels) of E.M. Forster, George Orwell's Coming Up For Air, and the mundane urbanity of Philip Larkin. What Davies seemed to crave was certainty and stability, the bastion of the familiar. The title track speaks of saving everything from "strawberry jam to variety, china cups and virginity", but Picture Book anticipates the bleaker Shangri-La (from *Arthur*) and Last Of The Steam Powered Trains hints at something darker and more directionless.

The album contains at least two bona fide classics (three if you include the subsequent hit single Days, withdrawn from the original LP but restored to the CD). Do You Remember Walter updates David Watts, the hero-emulation of schooldays replaced by sentiments that seesaw between fondness and regret and a sad denouement in which the narrator talks himself out of a reunion, realising that memories are all that he and Walter have. People Take Pictures Of Each Other, with its weary refrain "Don't show me no more please" offers a cameo of human beings validating a transitory existence and also serves as a metaphorical postscript for the swinging '60s. Musically, the band complement Davies's lyrical concerns majestically, illustrating a similar disregard for contemporary musical fashion, and Nicky Hopkins provides wonderfully ornate touches on celeste and harpsichord throughout. Not a phased guitar in sight.

Record Label:
PYE
Produced
by Ray Davies.
Recorded
at Pye Studios; February 1967–August 1968.
Released:
Original 12 track stereo version released and withdrawn September 1968. Revised 15 track mono album released November 1968.
Chart peaks:
None (UK) None (US)
Personnel:
Ray Davies (v, g, k); Dave Davies (v, g); Pete Quaife (b, v); Mick Avory (d); Nicky Hopkins (k); Rasa Davies (v); Alan Mckenzie, Brian Humphries (e)
Track Listing:
15 track mono album: The Village Green Preservation Society; Do You Remember Walter; Picture Book; Johnny Thunder; Last Of The Steam Powered Trains; Big Sky; Sitting By The Riverside; Animal Farm; Village Green; Starstruck; Phenomenal Cat; All My Friends Were There; Wicked Annabella; Monica; People Take Pictures Of Each Other. 12 track stereo album: The Village Green Preservation Society; Do You Remember Walter; Picture Book; Johnny Thunder; Monica; Days; Village Green; Mr Songbird; Wicked Annabella; Starstruck; Phenomenal Cat; People Take Pictures Of Each Other
Running time:
36.15
Current CD:
Essential ESM CD 481
Further reading:
Kinks: The Official Biography (Jon Savage, 1984)
Like this?
Try . . . p.594

The Smoke

The Smoke

Forgotten American psych-pop in thrall to The Beatles and dedicated to Stuart Sutcliffe.

Michael Lloyd was a precocious 12-year-old when he first decided to be in a band. It was 1962 and he was swimming with a friend. "We were far out from the shore and we heard music coming from the beach. It sounded great. So we paddled in and there were these local guys playing Ventures songs – they were very good – and that started us thinking. We've got to have a band!"

A couple of bands later, Lloyd started at the Hollywood Professional School. where he met Shaun and Danny Harris. Together they formed The West Coast Pop Art Experimental Band and made an album in Michael's bedroom. (He left before they signed to Reprise.) Still only 17, he was next handed a number of projects by young executive Mike Curb, under names such as The Laughing Wind and The Rubber Band and for Epic Records he produced a group of fresh-faced teenagers called October Country. Although it flopped, that album gave him a taste of what he could achieve with good studio facilities at his disposal and he persuaded Curb to give him some studio time. Thus was born The Smoke.

Michael poured all he had learnt into the album, he produced, arranged, sang lead vocals and played bass and keyboards while Stan Ayeroff, who co-wrote three of the songs, handled guitar and Steve Baim played drums. The record opens with the organ-driven Cowboys and Indians, echoing Brian Wilson's Heroes and Villains. There are overt Beatles references throughout, too. The chorus of Lucy In the Sky With Diamonds is quoted in the fade to Fogbound and its influence is clear in Gold Is The Colour of Thought.

"I didn't really think of what I was doing as psychedelic," says the undoubtedly clean-cut Lloyd. "There may have been drug references in Beatles songs, but in my naive way it just seemed to be some brilliant creative thing they were doing."

Despite a wide release, nothing ever happened with the album. Curb subsequently appointed Lloyd Vice-President of MGM, where he finally achieved commercial success as a producer and composer, with The Osmonds, Lou Rawls and Debbie Boone (he produced You Light Up My Life) and the multi-million selling soundtrack to Dirty Dancing. But this non-moneyspinning nugget from his psych-pop roots is still one of his favourites.

Record label:
Tower
Produced
by Michael Lloyd
Recorded
at Hollywood Boulevard Studios, LA, summer 1968.
Released:
November 1968
Chart peaks:
None (UK) None (US)
Personnel:
Michael Lloyd (v, k, g, b, horn and string ar), Stan Ayeroff (g), Steve Baim (d).
Track listing:
Cowboys And Indians; Looking Thru The Mirror; Self-Analysis, Gold Is The Colour Of Thought, Hobbit Symphony; Daisy-Intermission; Fogbound; Song Thru Perception; Philosophy; Umbrella; Ritual Gypsy Music Opus 1; October Country, Odyssey.
Currently unavailable on CD
Further listening:
October Country (1967). In a similar vein, try The Millennium Begin.
Further reading:
The West Coast Pop Art Experimental Band Story by Tim Forster, published in Ptolomeic Terrascope magazine, 1999.
Like this?
Try . . . p.617

The Beau Brummels

Bradley's Barn

Psychedelic San Franciscan pop outfit turns up in Nashville. With creamy results.

The Beau Brummels had spent the early '60s interpreting the British invasion from the safety of their San Francisco home. Impressed by the Fabs and The Searchers, they'd hit on an angular version of beat music which songwriter Ron Elliott perfected for the deep, country-toned voice of singer Sal Valentino. Their early records on the Autumn label (some produced by hip young house producer Sylvester Stewart AKA Sly Stone) were state-of-the-art pop-rock and they enjoyed several American hits, but Autumn crumbled in 1966 and members of the band started to peel off.

Moving to Warners they cut *Beau Brummels '66* and then in 1967 hit on a folk vein which they mined for the moderately successful, but quite exquisite album *Triangle*. Their Warners contract demanded another album forthwith, and the last remaining original members, Valentino and Elliott, decided to decamp to Nashville to come up with the goods. It was to prove a real culture shock for them. "To be sure, Dylan and Ian And Sylvia had recorded there, sleeve note compiler Stan Cronyn pointed out. But this was The Beau Brummels who flew down to meet the younger Nashville musicians on common ground."

"We arrived in a Chrysler and all the Nashville guys had Cadillacs," recalled Sal. Musical differences were also on the cards when they sat down with the local musicians and unveiled their songs. "It was a 180 degree shift from what Nashville was about."

The venue for the showdown was, of course, Bradley's Barn and the resultant collection, although not the style-shattering opus the press and public at the time were led to believe, is an exceptional example of roomy country playing which envelops Valentino's rich, resonant voice. Cronyn's notes conclude that "In Bradley's Barn a pop album was created in a hush!" and indeed the far-reaching effects of this mild-mannered country rock can't be under-rated. *Bradley's Barn* is as much about the ambience of its setting, as anything else. In that, it's a quiet classic.

Record label:
Warner Brothers
Produced
by Lenny Waronker.
Recorded
at Bradley's Barn, Wilson County, Tennessee; 1968.
Released:
1968
Chart peaks:
None (UK) None (US)
Personnel:
Sal Valentino (v); Ron Elliott (g); Jerry Reed (g); Wayne Moss (g); Harold Bradley (g); Billy Sanford (g); Norbert Putnum (b); David Briggs (k); Kenny Buttrey (d)
Track listing:
Turn Around; An Added Attraction; Deep Water; Long Walk Down To Misery (S); Little Bird; Cherokee Girl (S); I'm A Sleeper; The Loneliest Man In Town; Love Can Fall A Long Way Down; Jessica; Bless You California
Running time:
31.50
Not currently available,
though it has been reissued on CD but is currently deleted.
Further listening:
The Brummels' Triangle (1967) is well worth casting back over and there's a good Rhino retrospective Best Of The Beau Brummels (1981) if you want to scan their whole career from Mersey to flower power and beyond.
Further reading:
http://www.beaubrummels.com/
Like this?
Try . . . p.326

The Insect Trust

The Insect Trust

Hippie visionaries who deserve to be in the dictionary under 'eclectic'.

Even by the standards of an era that constantly broke down musical boundaries, the Insect Trust were quite extraordinarily unusual, being described in Rolling Stone at the time as 'absolutely original and unique'. Combining elements of rock, jazz, bluegrass, soul, Dixieland, folk, raga, blues and – well, practically every genre of music there is - they made two visionary, under-appreciated albums that still sound truly unlike anything else.

Every member of the band had a varied and scholarly musical background. Forming in New York in the mid 1960s, after spending time soaking up influences in Memphis they decamped to Hoboken, New Jersey and moved into a large tenement together. After landing an unexpected $25,000 advance from Capitol Records through contacts, they set about synthesising their extraordinary range of experience into an album. This classic debut, recorded in 1968, shows up one major difference between them and almost all other major US bands of the time. While the majority were in thrall to Eastern sounds, the Insect Trust sound resolutely homegrown. Banjos, clarinets and saxophones were of far greater interest to them than sitars or tablas. Their obviously deep love of traditional American music shines through in the beautiful bottleneck guitar on 'Going Home', and the fiddle and banjo exchanges on 'Foggy River Bridge Fly'. But that is not to say for a moment that they sound old-fashioned: whilst rooted in their country's musical heritage, the Insect Trust sounded contemporary.

Take the opening track, 'The Skin Game' for example. Starting with a mellow acoustic guitar and Nancy Jeffries's delightful voice, it unexpectedly veers off into squalling guitar and avant-garde saxophone, anchored only by echoing cowbell - and then, as abruptly as this interlude has begun, it ends. The acoustic guitar fades back up, Jeffries resumes her glorious singing, and the listeners are left to ponder whether or not they *actually* heard what they just heard.

Tuneful, intelligent and highly musical, the Insect Trust truly forged something new out of the past -. and what makes the success of their experiment particularly extraordinary is that they had no permanent rhythm guitarist, bassist or drummer, instead employing a variety of session players. In fact, that was one of the major factors in their split. Despite universal critical acclaim, when few bought their records it became increasingly hard to support the cost of a hired rhythm section capable of keeping up with them, especially for their sporadic concerts. Coupled with certain members' overly enthusiastic drug use, they finally called it a day in 1971, leaving behind them two of the most beguilingly strange and original rock albums ever recorded - a claim that few of their far more successful contemporaries can make.

RMJ

Record label:
Capitol
Produced
by Steve Duboff
Recorded
in 1968
Released:
1968
Chart Peaks:
None (UK) / ? (US)
Personnel:
Bill Barth (electric, acoustic, knife and bottleneck guitars, Swiss warbler, pc) / Bob Palmer (alto sax, alto & soprano recorders, clarinet, pc) / Trevor Koehler (baritone sax, piccolo, sewer drum, thumb piano, upright bass, ar) / Nancy Jeffries (v, pc) / Luke Faust (banjo, banjo guitar, v, pc) / Buddy Saltzman (d) / Bernard 'Pretty' Purdie (d) / Hugh McCracken (g) / Joe Mack (b) / Chuck Rainey (b) / Steve Duboff (conga drums, pc).
Track listing:
The Skin Game / Miss Fun City / World War I Song / Special Rider Blues / Foggy River Bridge Fly / Been Here And Gone So Soon / Declaration of Independence / Walking On Nails / Brighter Than Day / Mountain Song / Going Home
Further listening:
Hoboken Saturday Night (Atco, 1970).
Further reading:
www.furious.com/perfect/insecttrust.html
Like this?
Try . . . p.184

Open Mind

The Open Mind

London hippies make the world's first heavy metal album.

As the Beatles bowed out and Led Zeppelin took off, many other excellent bands slipped between the cracks. Amongst them The Open Mind are prominent - and some would say pre-eminent. In 1969 they released a thunderously heavy psychedelic album and a legendary 45, both of which vanished so completely that mint copies now fetch truly terrifying sums on the collectors' market.

Their roots lay in London's fertile blues scene, where they gigged for years as the Drag Set before embracing the emerging psychedelic scene in 1966 and becoming a fixture in underground clubs such as the Middle Earth, the UFO and The Marquee. "Bluesy bands started to go psychedelic, and we were no exception", says Tim du Feu, their bassist. In keeping with the changing times, they rethought both their name and image. Far from the standard hippie threads on show all around them, the Open Mind opted to reflect their proto-metal psychedelia in the leather suits they always wore. "It was very unusual at the time", he continues. "You could say that we started the look that people like Iron Maiden took up later."

Their music was evolving as well. "The later it got at gigs, the wilder things became, and we'd experiment", says Tim. Playing alongside such legends as Jimi Hendrix, Pink Floyd and the Electric Prunes, by 1968 they were red hot and ready to record. Landing a deal with Philips, they made their sole album that summer.

Standing today as an unquestionable high point of UK psychedelia, it's arguably the first album in the style that came to be known shortly afterwards as 'heavy metal'.

Album completed, the band returned to the live circuit and eagerly awaited its release. They were to be disappointed, though. Too heavy for hippies and too snappy for progressive rock fans, *The Open Mind* vanished at once when it appeared in early 1969, though du Feu believes it went to number one in Japan. Resisting disillusionment, they returned to the studio shortly afterwards to record the mighty 'Magic Potion', a single whose frantic riff, demented drumming and furious guitar solos make many consider it to be the finest heavy psychedelic rock 45 ever produced in Britain. If anything was going to break them, it was this. John Peel put his weight behind it and it seemed reasonable to expect a breakthrough, especially give the heavier direction that rock was starting to take. Fate, however, intervened again. The censorious British media panicked at the song's unabashed celebration of the joys of acid, and the single was swiftly banned. In the wake of this blow, a split became inevitable. The Open Mind was closed for business, leaving some of the heaviest music of the decade in their wake.

RMJ

Record label:
Philips
Produced
by John Franz
Recorded
by Stanhope Place Studios, London, summer 1968.
Released:
1969.
Chart Peaks:
None (UK), None (US).
Personnel;
Terry Martin (g, v) / Mike Brancaccio (g) / Timothy du Feu (b, p) / Philip Fox (d) / Kiki Dee & Maggie Bell (bv).
Track listing:
Dear Louise / Try Another Day / I Feel The Same Way Too / My Mind Cries / Can't You See / Thor The Thunder God / Horses and Chariots / Before My Time / Free As The Breeze / Girl I'm So Alone / Soul and My Will / Falling Again.
Current CD:
(adds Magic Potion / Cast A Spell).
Like this?
Try . . . p.205

Euphoria

A Gift From Euphoria

Two musical nomads fuse psychedelic rock, bluegrass and the Los Angeles Philharmonic to create an extravagant musical travelogue, then follow their sole album into lasting obscurity.

Even for an era renowned for eclectic musicianship, *A Gift From Euphoria* treads a particularly fine line between grandeur and folly. This extraordinary record was the culmination of a musical odyssey that had begun five years earlier, when Bill Lincoln and Wesley Watt met while playing in rival groups in West Hollywood. They went on to cut singles under a variety of names, and worked with hit vocal group the Platters (they shared a manager). Success, however, remained elusive and by 1966 the two friends were on different continents. Watt headed for the thriving music scene in Houston, Texas while Lincoln had married an English girl and was living with her family above a greengrocer's shop on the outskirts of Manchester. The experience would later inspire one of his most memorable songs: "Docker's Son was written about her brother - their father was a watchman on the docks at the Salford shipyards just down the street. I used to hear the rag-bone man come by daily. It was a poor, working class area, but it was full of interesting things to a young American."

When Lincoln returned to the States he and Watt conceived their ambitious new project. The entire album was funded without any record company involvement after a family friend arranged a bank loan. Recording followed four distinct stages, beginning at Western Studios, Hollywood, where the orchestral tracks were laid down with the help of a young arranger named Irwin Webb and over 60 musicians from the Los Angeles Philharmonic. For the country songs they enlisted the help of a trio of session veterans in Nashville before travelling to London's Pye Studios to complete the remainder and overdub vocals. Finally, they returned to Hollywood to add sound effects and sweetening and record one exuberant final track, Suicide.

Now all they had to do was find a record deal. Pitched unsuccessfully to the Apple label, the album eventually found favour with staff producer Nik Venet at Capitol Records. However, the band became caught in a power struggle within their new label: "It all got very ugly, Nik lost his job, we lost our album and the rest is non-history".

Still friends today, Watt now runs a country music saloon in Sheboygan, Wisconsin while Lincoln works as an administrative assistant for a Community College in Oregon. Until recently both were completely unaware that their album had been reissued.

Record label:
Capitol SKAO 363
See For Miles SEE CD 465

Produced
by Hamilton Wesley Watt Jr., William D. Lincoln, Nik Venet ("with additional direction from Nikolas Venetoulis")

Recorded
at 1967 – 8, Western Studios & Sunset Sound Recorders, Hollywood, Nashville & Pye Studios, London,

Chart peak UK:
None

Chart peak US:
None

Release date:
1969

Total running time:
43.05

Personnel:
Wesley Watt (voc, gtr, drms), William Lincoln (voc, gtr, bs, pno, harmonica), David Briggs (pno), Bobby Thompson (banjo), Lloyd Green (steel gtr), Irwin Webb (orch arrangements), musicians of the Los Angeles Philharmonic Orchestra.

Track listing:
Lisa / Stone River Hill Song / Stone River Hill Song (Reprise) / Did You Get The Letter / Through A Window / Young Miss Pflugg / Lady Bedford / Suicide On The Hillside Sunday Morning After Tea / Sweet Fanny Adams / I'll Be Home To You / Sunshine Woman / Hollyville Train / Docker's Son / Something For The Milkman / Too Young To Know / World.

Like this?
Try . . . p.98

Gandalf

Gandalf

Bar band record hypnotic one-off psychedelic classic.

In the explosion of record company interest occasioned by flower power, many excellent groups were treated shamefully. Take the Rahgoos. Having paid their dues for years in the bars and clubs of New York and New Jersey, they were offered a regular gig at the legendary Night Owl Cafe in Greenwich Village. Refining their set night after night at the centre of a scene including such luminaries as Fred Neil, the Lovin' Spoonful and Tim Hardin, they were excellently placed for signing - and so it proved to be. Their friends Bonner and Gordon (writers of 'Happy Together' amongst other hits) urged their managers Charlie Koppelman and Don Rubin to catch the band live in the summer of 1967. Blown away, they swiftly added The Rahgoos to their impressive roster, and a deal to release albums on Capitol via their own production company had just been struck. It all seemed too good to be true – and it was.

Firstly, they were made to rename themselves Gandalf, which they resented but agreed to. After a month of intensive rehearsals, they entered the studio at the end of 1967. The sessions were swift, and the band felt increasingly sidelined. 'Don Rubin and Brooks Arthur, the engineer, were great to work with initially, but when they got what they needed, we were cut out of the sessions', says their leader Peter Sando today. Cover versions dominate the album, including three by Tim Hardin, two by Bonner & Gordon and a magnificent rendition of Eden Ahbez's much-loved 'Nature Boy', featuring a gut-wrenching, heavily distorted solo from Sando, whose own songwriting confidence was not yet fully developed. This is a great shame as, wonderful though the covers are, the group's finest performances are reserved for his mere two originals - the wistful 'Can You Travel In The Dark Alone?' and the thundering 'I Watch The Moon'. The former features a dizzying blend of electric sitar, vibes and organ and the latter ends with a full-on psychedelic jam, complete with great swathes of fuzz guitar.

With such strong performances on tape, the group was understandably excited about its prospects – but as quickly as opportunity had beckoned them, they were spurned. Unbeknownst to them, the deal with Capitol was collapsing. When the record finally appeared in early 1969, in a glorious psychedelic sleeve, yet another blow was to befall them. Shipped with the wrong disc inside, all copies were recalled, and any momentum it may have gathered was lost. Barely promoted, it sank without trace – but its reputation and price tag have never stopped growing since. As Sando puts it today, 'it's great to get a little credit- even after 35 years!'

RMJ

Record label:
Capitol
Produced
by Koppelman-Rubin
Recorded
by Century Sound Studios, NY, late 1967.
Released:
1969.
Chart Peaks:
None (UK), None (US).
Personnel:
Peter Sando (g, v) / Frank Hubach (p, ep, o) / Bob Muller (b) / Davy Bauer (d)
Track listing:
Golden Earrings (s) / Hang Onto A Dream / Never Too Far / Never Too Far / Scarlet Ribbons / You Upset the Grace Of Living / Can You Travel In The Dark Alone? / Nature Boy / Tiffany Rings / Me About You / I Watch The Moon.
Current CD:
Sundazed.
Like this?
Try . . . p.54

The MC5
Kick Out The Jams

Bucking tradition, these Motor City rock revolutionaries released a live album as their debut.

Detroit's MC5 fuelled their vision of revolution by grafting it onto high-octane garage rock, using their guitars as assault weapons against a lethargic status quo. Under the guiding hand of poet and activist John Sinclair, The MC5 created the soundtrack for the nascent White Panther Party, promulgating the incendiary ethos of "Rock'n'roll, dope and fucking in the streets".

Over the years, the leftist politics may have become quaint, but *Kick Out The Jams* remains a fine blast of serrated rock rage. In addition to polemics, the "5" established their own religion, Zenta, and it was on the Zenta New Year in1968 – Halloween weekend – that the band planned to record their debut record at Detroit's Grande ballroom, where they'd been gigging weekly for two years, opening up for better known bands. In fact, the band dubbed their album after a phrase they used to heckle the star attractions.

"More often than not, the bands were really tired,' explains guitarist Wayne Kramer. "They'd come from San Francisco and play all this kind of electric folk music. I mean they were wimpy, they had no passion, they were posers, slackers, and we were young and aggressive fellows and so we used to harass them. We'd scream at them from the wings, 'Kick out the jams or get off the stage.' Or, 'Get down, brother or get the fuck out!'"

MC5 were offering up a gritty, cacophonous rock show, complete with atonal industrial din of the Detroit factories and unapologetic distortion that was best experienced live, so it was not a surprise that they chose to debut with a live album.

"We really worked hard at perfecting a performance that on a bad night would be great and on a good night would be unbelievable," remembers Kramer. "The MC5 were a mercurial band. All of a sudden this was "the" night, we were making "the" record, the posters were up, the fans were there and the recording truck was in from California, and the record company was there, and it was a lot of pressure for us to be under. In fact it rattled us. I hear it every time I listen to the record." Though he admits it's not the band's best work, Kramer acknowledges, " Our power is concentrated in that record in a way that you can't deny. *Kick Out The Jams* is a powerful statement of a time."

JU

Record label:
Elektra
Produced
by Jac Holzman and Bruce Botnick.
Recorded
at the Grande Ballroom, Detroit, Michigan; October 30 and 31, 1968.
Released:
February 1969
Chart peaks:
None (UK) 30 (US)
Personnel:
Rob Tyner (v); Fred 'Sonic' Smith (g, v); Wayne Kramer (g, v); Dennis Thompson (d, v); Michael Davis (b); Bruce Botnick (e)
Track listing:
Ramblin' Rose; Kick Out The Jams; Come Together; Rocket Reducer No. 62 (Rama Lama Fa); Borderline; Motor City Is Burning; I Want You Right Now; Starship
Running time:
36.17
Current CD:
AMCY2563
Further listening:
High Time (1971) – the band's final studio album was a return to their rough and tumble roots, after the more sanitized "commercial" sounds of 1970's Back In The USA; Babes In Arms (1973) rarities and never released tracks; The Big Bang Beat: The Best Of The MC5 (2000) a well-chosen collection of the 5's grittiest tracks and free jazz masterworks.
Further reading:
MOJO 27; www.ourworld.compuserve.com/homepages/rauk/mc-5.htm
Like this?
Try . . . p.559

Silver Apples
Contact

Second album from pioneers of loops and ambience. Now active again after belated recognition.

In 1967, Simeon Coxe III began to spice up the performances of his conventional rock band by adding electronic effects. "One of my best buds then was a serious composer called Harold Rodgers. He had an old Second World War oscillator. He used to get loaded on vodka and try to play along with Beethoven, Bartok, etc. One day I put on a Stones record and played along. I was hooked!"

The band quickly became a duo, based around Simeon's rapidly multiplying and interlinked battery of audio-generators and Danny Taylor's massive, carefully tuned drum kit. Their 1968 debut introduced the maverick coupling, but *Contact* marks the apotheosis of their sound. "The first album was a recording studio project, whereas *Contact* was recorded during and after a three-month tour and my pipes were road-toughened," says Coxe. It's a harder record than their debut – titles such as A Pox On You and the harsh, edgy wailings of Cox's electrickery speak volumes.

"I was fortunate enough to know Hendrix [Danny Taylor had drummed with Jimi's Blue Flames]. We traded gear and talked about new sound distortions. He called me Mr Apple and I called him Mr Experience." The influence is apparent on the bucking, electro-ballistics of You're Not Foolin' Me and Gypsy Love, while Taylor's urgent, human-drum-machine beats provide the perfect underpinning. Coxe: "By 1969 a lot of the hippy dream had faded. I'm not sure the world had become dystopian, but I was sure feeling the darker side." This finds a perfect expression in the dissonant flower-power anthem I Have Known Love, a perfectly curdled pop song. And if things didn't sound weird enough, Simeon – who was raised in the Tennessee mountains – found time to play banjo on Ruby and Confusion, to create a sort of techno-bluegrass.

Unfortunately, Kapp had no money to promote *Contact*, and Silver Apples went into cold storage for almost 25 years. "At the time," Coxe notes ruefully, "electronics as a musical concept had not yet been embraced by musicians and fans as something that could stand on its own, other than in universities and laboratories. We embraced that concept."

Record label:
Kapp
Produced
by Silver Apples, co-produced by Barry Bryant.
Recorded
at Universal Studios, Los Angeles and Apostolic Studios, New York; late 1968.
Release date:
February 1969
Chart peaks:
None (UK) None (US)
Personnel:
Simeon Coxe III (oscillators [often known as 'The Simeon'], banjo, v); Danny Taylor (pc, v); Jack Hunt (e)
Track listing:
You And I (S); Water; Ruby; Gypsy Love; You're Not Foolin' Me; I Have Known Love; A Pox On You; Confusion; Fantasies
Running time:
40.21
Current CD:
MCD 11680 adds Silver Apples: Oscillations; Seagreen Serenades; Lovefingers; Program; Velvet Cave; Whirly-Bird; Dust; Dancing Gods; Misty Mountain
Further listening:
Long-lost third album The Garden (1970) is now available; two recent albums, Beacon (1997) and Decatur (1998). See also the collaborations The Alchemysts And Simeon (2000) and A Lake Of Teardrops (1998, with Sonic Boom from Spaceman 3).
Further reading:
long interview with Simeon in Ptolemaic Terrascope 22, February 1997 (www.terrascope.org); www.silverapples.com
Like this?
Try . . . p.680

Bee Gees

Odessa

Red velvet-covered double which almost killed them.

Beautifully sung, delicately orchestrated and filled with highly individual songs about lost love, electric light and sinking ships, *Odessa* was the culmination of a burst of creativity which almost destroyed the Bee Gees before the '70s had begun. Returning to the UK from Australia in early 1967 the Gibb brothers followed their breakthrough New York Mining Disaster 1941 with a further six hit singles and three highly-successful albums in just sixteen months. It was hardly surprising that by the time they re-entered the studio in 1968 some strain was beginning to show. While working titles such as *Masterpeace* and *American Opera* might suggest some grand artistic design, Barry Gibb recalls that the real motivation came from manager Robert Stigwood: "I think it was basically a financial deal. If we do a double album everyone makes more money – except the group. So we were doing something that we weren't motivated to do and it became full of all this stuff that didn't necessarily blow me away."

Yet the finished work justified Stigwood's faith in his young protegés. Opening with a dramatic swirl of strings, acoustic guitar and cello and the line "14th of February 1899, the British ship Veronica was lost without a sign," the dense, melancholy title track set the tone. Bill Shepherd's sympathetic orchestration, which went far beyond mere sweetening – three of the tracks were instrumental – allowed the melodies to shine and in Sound Of Love and the Eleanor Rigby-influenced Melody Fair the Bee Gees produced two of their finest ballads. Less predictably, there were also nods towards American country-rock: Marley Purt Drive was a deliciously languid number complete with electric piano, slide guitar and banjo.

Unfortunately, discord arising over the choice of the album's single precipitated Robin's departure to pursue a solo career: it would be another eighteen months before all three brothers were reunited on one record. Yet *Odessa* remains one of the Bee Gees finest albums, a work of extraordinary depth of feeling and a fitting end to an important chapter in their career. With little nostalgia, Barry suggests the key to its success: "Maybe it's because there was so much trouble and strife going on at the time. I think there's probably a little bit of that in every song."

Record label:
Polydor
Produced
by Robert Stigwood and the Bee Gees.
Recorded
in New York, August–December 1968; De Lane Lea and IBC Studios, London; early 1968.
Released:
March 1969
Chart peaks:
10 (UK) 20 (US)
Personnel:
Barry Gibb (v, g); Robin Gibb (v, o); Maurice Gibb (v, b, p, g); Colin Petersen (d); Paul Buckmaster (c); Bill Shepherd (MD); P Wade, E Sharp, A Barber (e)
Track listing:
Odessa (City On The Black Sea); You'll Never See My Face Again; Black Diamond; Marley Purt Drive; Edison; Melody Fair; Suddenly; Whisper Whisper; Lamplight (S); Sound Of Love; Give Your Best; Seven Seas Symphony; With All Nations (International Anthem); I Laugh In Your Face; Never Say Never Again; First Of May (S); The British Opera
Running time:
64.22
Current CD:
825 451-2 omits: With All Nations
Further listening:
Horizontal (1968); Idea (1968)
Further reading:
www.beegeesonline.com/
Like this?
Try . . . p.126

Quicksilver Messenger Service

Happy Trails

Hippies get heavy, live and loud.

Anyone who has ever sneered at drippy, wimpish hippies should have their attention forcibly drawn to *Happy Trails*, on which Quicksilver play with a visceral, crunching power that is the absolute antithesis of drippiness or wimpiness.

As acid rock adventurers Quicksilver were peers of the Grateful Dead and Jefferson Airplane, but, unlike those bands, their roots weren't in the folk, bluegrass or jugband scenes. The band's John Cippolina, raunchiest of the great '60s psychedelic guitarists, has explained: "I cut my teeth in blues and hard rock. My biggest influence was Link Wray . . . the grandfather of punk. I heard that sound and thought, 'God, you can swear without using four letter words!'"

Much of the album comprises various live tapes from the Fillmores East and West, spliced together. "We were always better live," Cipollina later told Zigzag magazine. "We found the [studio] atmosphere a little strange when we cut our first album and we decided to cut the follow-up live in a familiar setting and with a familiar audience, so we could really cook and let ourselves go."

The album's highlight is an improvisation, comprising the whole of the first side of the original album, on Bo Diddley's Who Do You Love, an exuberant deconstruction and exploration of the song's every nuance, described by critic Greil Marcus as "One of the best rock'n'roll recordings to emerge from San Francisco [and] some of the finest hard rock ever recorded."

Throughout the track, Cipollina's distinctive, quivering, vibrato-heavy playing, with its surprising hint of flamenco, is massively exciting, while one section of the performance features the Fillmore audience exchanging yelps and howls with the band, an interlude that Marcus describes as "a beautiful example of the kind of communication rock'n'roll is all about." With the exception of the title track, a brief and amusingly straightfaced rendition of the corny old Roy Rogers ditty, Side Two also comprises one, extended piece of music, the most thrilling element of which is Calvary, recorded live in the studio and described by Cipollina as "our interpretation of the Crucifixion: it starts with the condemnation, goes through the journey to the cross and ends with the angels coming." Full of ideas these hippies, huh?

Record label:
Capitol
No producer credited.
Recorded
at Fillmore East and West; Calvary recorded live at Golden State Recorders, San Francisco; November 19, 1968.
Released:
March 1969
Chart peaks:
None (UK) 27 (US)
Personnel:
John Cipollina (g); Gary Duncan (g, v); David Freiberg (b, v); Greg Elmore (d, v)
Track listing:
Who Do You Love Suite: Who Do You Love [Part 1] (S/US); When You Love; Where You Love; How You Love; Which You Love; Who Do You Love [Part 2]; Mona; Maiden Of The Cancer Moon; Calvary; Happy Trails
Running time:
50.18
Current CD:
Beat Goes On BGOCD151
Further listening:
The band's previous album, their self-titled debut (1968), is also worth hearing, as is Anthology (1973), which compiles 1968–1971 tracks.
Further reading:
www.penncen.com/quicksilver/
Like this?
Try . . . p.424

Flying Burrito Brothers

The Gilded Palace Of Sin

Gram Parsons' finest work: fusing soul, country and R&B in one package.

When the Byrds teetered on the brink of collapse at the end of 1968, founding member Chris Hillman decided to join erstwhile member Gram Parsons in a new venture – the Flying Burrito Brothers. 'Country rock' was still a neologism at the time they pushed forward with this groundbreaking record. Holed up in a house together, Parsons and Hillman wrote some of the best songs of their lives.

"When I was living with Parsons I woke up one day and said, This old town's filled with sin, it'll swallow you in," Hillman remembers. "Gram then finished the second part. As far as lyrics and melody went, we shared it all the way."

Parsons spoke of his vision of 'Cosmic American Music' fusing soul, R&B and traditional country alongside a distinctive rock beat. Image was also a part of the equation. Inspired by the Stones, Parsons took to wearing make-up and on the cover of the album the group were dressed in garish, floral suits adorned with cannabis leaves, the creation of the famous Nashville tailor Nudie.

The music was both inspired and confrontational, brazenly mixing steel guitars and mandolins with advanced studio effects, phasing and synthesized brass. It was a potent concoction. The compositions were righteous assaults on LA life, with riveting tales of groupies (Christine's Tune), drug abuse (Juanita), draft evasion (My Uncle) and lost innocence (Hippie Boy). Parsons' vocals displayed a remarkable range of emotion, sometimes forthright, occasionally vulnerable and, most famously, cracking with emotion on the heart-rending Hot Burrito #1, which Elvis Costello later revived using the less impressive title I'm Your Toy. Parsons' finest work was featured on this album but only the cognoscenti were listening. Lost in the gap between the country and rock markets the Burritos never received the acclaim they deserved. It was left to successors like the Eagles to reap the benefits of their pioneering work.

Record label:
Asylum
Produced
by The Burritos, Larry Marks and Henry Lewy.
Recorded
at A&M Studios, Los Angeles; February 1969.
Released:
April 21, 1969
Chart peaks:
None (UK) 164 (US)
Personnel:
Gram Parsons (g, v); Chris Hillman (g, v, mandolin); Chris Ethridge (b, p); Sneeky Pete Kleinow (sg); Jon Corneal (d); Eddie Hoh (d); Sam Goldstein (d); Popeye Phillips (d); Henry Lewy (e)
Track listing:
Christine's Tune; Sin City; Do Right Woman; Dark End Of The Street; My Uncle; Wheels; Juanita; Hot Burrito # 1; Hot Burrito # 2; Do You Know How It Feels; Hippie Boy
Running time:
37.33
Current CD:
Edsel EDCD 191
Further listening:
Burrito Deluxe (1970); Gram Parsons, GP (1973) and Grievous Angel (1974)
Further reading:
MOJO 41; The Byrds: Timeless Flight Revisited (Johnny Rogan, 1997)
Like this?
Try . . . p.241

Tommy James And The Shondells

Cellophane Symphony

Bubblegum pin-up becomes psychedelic pop composer.

A child prodigy at 13, Tommy James spent the early '60s fusing garage rock with bubblegum pop. A second incarnation of his group The Shondells charted with I Think We're Alone Now in 1967 and Mony, Mony in 1968 before the psychedelic bug bit and the album and single Crimson And Clover introduced a new phase for the group. Still with songwriting partner Richie Cordell, James moved into new, less formulated territory. Influenced by *Sgt Pepper*, the group changed garb and paid lip service to musical fashion while retaining their pert pop sound. However, by the end of 1968 James had seized full control of proceedings and *Cellophane Symphony* became his most ambitious project yet.

The opening title track was a nine-minute-plus instrumental, some way from the three-minute slices of pop he was renowned for, sounding more like an atmospheric Pink Floyd outtake complete with Farfisa organ. The mood generally is one of irreverence: plenty of tongue-in-cheek wordplay and even, at one point, a John Wayne impersonation, before side one closes with the vaudevillian Papa Rolled His Own. In the spirit of Zappa's *We're Only In It For The Money*, *Cellophane Symphony* climaxes with James's very own attack on the establishment, On Behalf Of The Management And Staff, a spoof party singalong where James is presented with a gold watch for services rendered. The mood takes an even more bizarre twist when James starts squealing "It doesn't work, it doesn't work/the watch doesn't even work/I hate you." Perhaps it was a refutation of the futility of playing the pop game. Whatever, James is seen seated in an empty auditorium on the reverse of the original UK version of the album with an expression that seems to be asking "What the hell was all that about?"

Record Label:
Roulette

Produced
by Tommy James.

Recorded
in New York City, summer 1968–January 1969.

Released:
April 1969

Chart peaks:
None (UK) None (US)

Personnel:
Tommy James (v, g); Eddie Gray (g); Ronnie Rossman (k); Mike Vale (b); Pete Lucia (d)

Track Listing:
Cellophane Symphony; Makin' Good Time; Evergreen; Sweet Cherry Wine (S); Papa Rolled His Own; Changes; Loved One; I Know Who I Am; The Love Of A Woman; On Behalf Of The Entire Staff And Management.

Running time:
41.55

Current CD:
NEMCD647 (with Crimson And Clover)

Further listening:
Crimson And Clover (1968) is well worth tracking back to and it's available on one CD with Cellophane Symphony. Of course, the early singles are ace.

Further reading:
www.tommyjames.com

Like this?
Try . . . p.625

1969

Dusty Springfield

Dusty In Memphis

Landmark white-soul session that almost didn't happen.

They may have sent Dusty South, but the South had to meet her halfway. When this beautiful album first appeared, the general feeling among record buyers was that barge-poles just weren't long enough. But they were in good company: Dusty loathed it too. She confessed to MOJO 20 that it took over a year before she could bear to play the record at all.

Atlantic's idea had been a great one. Send Dusty down South with Jerry Wexler, just as they'd done with Aretha Franklin. After all, despite the West Hampstead background, the blonde bouffant and the history of pneumatic Euro-pop melodrama, here was a soulful vocalist whose subtlety was combined with impressive fire-power. But, whether it was fear, fastidiousness or just cussedness, Dusty took an age to agree on material – though the eventual selections were impeccable, with Randy Newman, Goffin/King and Bacharach/David to the fore – and sessions in Muscle Shoals had to be cancelled.

Once actually in Memphis, Dusty's painstaking way of working was at odds with Wexler's, and she froze. Tension filled the air (as did a flying ashtray, at one point) in the absence of Dusty's vocals. In fact she didn't sing until she'd left Memphis, cutting the final vocals in Atlantic's New York studios. Despite all the problems, the music was gorgeous. Clipped and slinky Memphis funk complements the easy-going material with great sophistication. Son Of A Preacher Man became the key track, but even more seductive were Breakfast In Bed and Just A Little Lovin'. Even in Wexler's exalted company it is Springfield's intuitive feel for each song's emotional possibilities that remains the record's ultimate virtue.

Record label:
Philips
Produced
by Jerry Wexler, Tom Dowd and Arif Mardin.
Recorded
at American Studios, Memphis; September 1968. Vocals overdubbed at Atlantic Studios, New York City.
Released:
April 1969
Chart peaks:
None (UK) 99 (US)
Personnel:
Bobby Wood (p); Bobby Emmons (o); Reggie Young (g); Gene Chrisman (d); Tommy Cogbill (b); The Sweet Inspirations (bv); Ed Kollis (e)
Track listing:
Just A Little Lovin'; So Much Love; Son Of A Preacher Man (S); I Don't Want To Hear It Anymore; Don't Forget About Me; Breakfast In Bed; Just One Smile; The Windmills Of Your Mind; In The Land Of Make Believe; No Easy Way Down; I Can't Make It Alone
Running time:
33.36
Current CD:
5286872-2 adds: Willie And Laura Mae Jones; That Old Sweet Roll (Hi-De-Ho); What Do You Do When Love Dies
Further listening:
A Girl Called Dusty (1964); Everything's Coming Up Dusty (1965)
Further reading:
MOJO 20; Dusty (Lucy O'Brien, 1997); www.dustyspringfield.co.uk/
Like this?
Try . . . p.93

The Youngbloods

Elephant Mountain

New York quartet go West to make sprawling Sgt. Pepper-inspired masterpiece.

In 1967, two years before a television ad promoting brotherhood turned it into a national smash, The Youngbloods' Get Together had been a regional hit on the West Coast. Excited by its success, the New York City-based quartet headed west, settling in bucolic Inverness, California, 30 miles up the coast from San Francisco. The dominant feature of the landscape was Black Mountain, which resembled an elephant's back, so when it came time to name the ambitious album they seemed to have been working on for ever (two years, in fact), The Youngbloods did not hesitate: it was *Elephant Mountain.*

"Recording actually began in New York," says Lowell Levinger, who played just about every instrument on it except bass and drums, and also wrote arrangements. "When we were all living out here, we would fly down to LA for two or three weeks at a time to work on it. We'd stay at the Tropicana Hotel and go to the studio every night." The commute cost them their second guitar player, Jerry Corbitt.

"Just about when we first began flying down to Los Angeles, Jerry developed an aversion to flying," says Levinger. "Then he developed an aversion to a lot of other things." The Youngbloods' sound was always distinguished by the soft, airy tenor of founder Jesse Colin Young "the Golden Throat", as Levinger calls him. But they were actually one of the more eclectic, adventuresome bands of their time, with a repertoire of styles ranging from folk and upbeat country to jazz, blues and even ragtime. Inspired by the ambitiousness of *Sgt Pepper* and their own live shows, which often sprawled over three hours, the band conceived *Elephant Mountain* as an organic whole. Its 13 tracks flow into one another with the help of short instrumental segues and studio banter.

"We used to do a lot of improvising in the studio with the tape running," says Levinger. "Joe spent a lot of time going through those tapes and finding good snippets." One amusing snippet is Turn It Over: an obsolete 12 seconds since no one needs to be reminded to turn a record over in the CD age. The album's centrepiece is Darkness, Darkness, a minor-key meditation on the seductiveness of oblivion. "Producing that song took forever," says Levinger. "I played the echo on Jesse's voice the same as I would any other musical instrument." Levinger's raw, intense guitar solo is just one high point of this beautiful, ambitious record.

Record label:
RCA
Produced
by Charles E. Daniels with Bob Cullen and The Youngbloods.
Recorded
at RCA Studios, New York City; RCA's Music Center of the World, Hollywood; autumn 1967–winter 1968.
Released:
April 1969
Chart peaks:
None (UK) 113 (US)
Personnel:
Jesse Colin Young (v, b); Lowell Levinger, aka 'Banana' (g, ps, p, k, o, harpsichord, v); Joe Bauer (d, pc); David Lindley (fiddle); Victor Feldman (vibes); Plas Johnson (s); Joe Clayton (t); Richie Schmidt, Hank Cicalo, Mickey Crofford (e)
Track listing:
Darkness, Darkness (S/US); Smug; On Sir Francis Drake; Sunlight; Double Sunlight; Beautiful; Turn It Over; Rain Song; Trillium; Quicksand; Black Mountain Breakdown; Sham; Ride the Wind
Running time:
39.51
Current CD:
EDCD 276
Further listening:
The Youngbloods contains the band's two biggest hits, Get Together and Grizzly Bear, while Best Of The Youngbloods is a good introduction despite being a little thin at 10 tracks.
Further reading:
Jesse Colin Young raises coffee in Kona, Hawaii. The web page for his business – www.jessecolinyoung.com – also has some music information.
Like this?
Try . . . p.305

The Who

Tommy

Huge double concept-album, the first rock opera, spawning a movie, an orchestral spin-off and a stage musical.

Early in 1968, Pete Townshend had emerged from an encounter with Indian mystic Meher Baba with a growing sense of frustration at the limitations of rock in general, and The Who in particular, he announced to the NME that on their next record he wanted The Who to "preach", a notion he'd first approached in an aborted song called You've Gotta Have Faith In Something Bigger Than Yourselves. However, he recognised that Roger Daltrey might not look convincing singing that one, so he went back to work on their fourth album – provisionally titled *Who's For Tennis* – and started coming at the idea from a different direction.

Townshend had often been musically ambitious. A Quick One was an unprecedented nine-minute song cycle, *The Who Sell Out* packaged itself as a pirate radio show devoted to the band. But that was primitive stuff compared to the scope of what he eventually unveiled: *Tommy* – the seemingly bizarre idea of a thematic double album telling how a deaf, dumb and blind boy found salvation in his genius on a pinball machine and became the leader of a reclusive religious cult. It still sounds mad, but in an age when rock heroes were taking on the persona of prophets, *Tommy* was both credible and captivating, orchestral links lending gravitas to The Who's characteristically colourful pulsating rock which swung from the proto-prog grandeur of Amazing Journey to the music hall jauntiness of Tommy's Holiday Camp and the searing rock of Acid Queen.

"I wanted the story of *Tommy* to have several levels, a rock singles level and a bigger concept level," Pete wrote later. "I wanted it to appeal as a fairy story to young kids and also be intellectually entertaining. And I wanted it have a spiritual message too."

Not everyone bought it. "It's sick!" denounced horrified Radio 1 DJ Tony Blackburn and plenty of critics shared his view.

"*Tommy* wasn't as big a success as people now imagine," says Roger Daltrey, "not when it was released anyway. It wasn't particularly big at all – it was only after we'd flogged it on the road for three years and played Woodstock and things like that it got back in the charts. Then it stayed in the charts for a year and took on a life of its own."

Record label:
Track
Produced
by Kit Lambert.
Recorded
at IBC Studios, London; October 1968–March 1969.
Released:
May 23, 1969
Chart peaks:
2 (UK) 4 (US)
Personnel:
Roger Daltrey (v, hm); Pete Townshend (v, g, k); Keith Moon (v, d); John Entwistle (v, b, k); Damon Lyon-Shaw (e); Chris Stamp (executive producer)
Track listing:
Overture/It's A Boy; 1921 (You Didn't Hear It); Amazing Journey; Sparks; Eyesight To The Blind (The Hawker); Christmas; Cousin Kevin; Acid Queen; Underture; Do You Think It's Alright?; Fiddle About; Pinball Wizard; There's A Doctor I've Found; Go To The Mirror Boy; Tommy Can You Hear Me?; Smash The Mirror; Sensation; Miracle Cure; Sally Simpson; I'm Free; Welcome Tommy's Holiday Camp; We're Not Gonna Take It
Running time:
74.00
Current CD:
8411212
Further listening:
The Who's other classic rock opera, Quadrophenia (1973)
Further reading:
A good place to start might be The Who In Print: An Annotated Bibliography, 1965 Through 1990 (Stephen Wolter and Karen Kimber, 1992); www.thewho.net
Like this?
Try . . . p.340

Richie Havens

Richard P. Havens 1983

Double folk apocalypse from the Woodstock Freedom man.

It's been said about a lot of albums recorded between 1967 and 1971, but what *were* they on when they made this?

Thanks to that landmark performance at 1969's Woodstock Festival – hollering "Freedom!", hammering away at a battered acoustic guitar – and such albums as 1967's *Mixed Bag* and 1971's *The Great Blind Degree*, the common perception of Richie Havens is of a rough-edged folk shouter dealing in ten-cent peace 'n' love. His background *was* a folk one, growing up in the Bedford-Stuyvesant district of New York, hanging out with street-corner harmony groups and watching the legendary Dino Valente and Fred Neil harmonise at The Cafe Wha? He studied the songs of Neil, Hardin and Gene Michaels and perfected his trademark open tuning technique (playing all six strings and using his thumb to make different chords at every fret stop). However, his first two albums for Jerry Schoenbaum's MGM offshoot, Verve Folkways pushed that 'folk' definition to the limits. It was a new label with free reign and on *Mixed Bag* and 1968's *Something Else Again* producer John Court told Havens to try everything.

"He said we should avoid songs of any one type" says Havens. "He told me I could sing opera if I wanted." It all made for a distinctive combination of Village folk, New York pop and a rumpled psychedelia which sold over a million copies. Richie became a valuable commodity and MGM gave him the freedom to set up his own Stormy Forest production company and make the *Richard P Havens 1983* double album.

It was a stunning, labyrinthine achievement – combining the fractured hippie visions of Leonard Cohen, Donovan, The Beatles and Dylan with such cryptic Havens folk puzzles as Indian Rope Man and Just Above My Hobby Horses's Head.

"The year was 1969," he explains. "The title *1983* was based on the idea that I thought we were already in the world created in George Orwell's 1984, which warned about the dangers of a monolithic society. My album said there was still time brother, but not much..."

After Woodstock, Richie Havens was set for life, securing a $650,000 deal with MGM that included his own office on the 20th floor. Apocalyptic urgency went out of the window. He would make other great records but nothing ever approached the bewitching insanity of this one.

Record label:
Verve Forecast
Produced
by Richie Havens and Mark Roth
Recorded
at RKO Sound Studios, New York City, early 1969
Released:
May 1969
Chart peaks:
None (UK) 80 (US)
Personnel:
Richie Havens (v, g), Arnie Moore, Carol Hunter, Brad Campbell and Stephen Stills (b), Skip Prokop and Don MacDonald (d), Weldon Myrick (sg), Paul Williams (g), Jeremy Steig (flute), Colin Walcott (sitar), Paul Harris (p), Warren Bernhardt (k), John Ord (p, o), Carter C.C. Collins (congas)
Track listing:
Stop Pulling And Pushing Me; For Haven's Sake; Strawberry Fields Forever; What More Can I Say, John; I Pity The Poor Immigrant; Lady Madonna; Priests; Indian Rope Man; Cautiously; Just Above My Hobby Horse's Head; She's Leaving Home; Putting Out The Vibration And Hoping It Comes Home; The Parable Of Ramon; With A Little Help From My Friends; Wear Your Love Like Heaven; Run Shaker Life; Do You Feel Good?
Running time:
69.37
Currently unavailable on CD
Further listening:
Mixed Bag (1967); Alarm Clock (1971)
Further reading:
They Can't Hide Us Anymore (Richie Havens and Steve Davidowitz, 1999)
Like this?
Try . . . p.586

Neil Young

Everybody Knows This Is Nowhere

First electric album with Crazy Horse blueprinted the guitar-driven sound that would later inspire grunge.

Neil Young was in search of something new. Freed from the burning intensity of Buffalo Springfield he had signed to Reprise as a solo artist and issued a lavishly arranged, predominantly acoustic album which gained solid reviews but sold poorly. His voice had been buried in the mix which briefly caused him to disown the album. Now, he was determined to start afresh. His new direction owed much to a debilitating bout of flu which had rendered him helpless but simultaneously unleashed his imagination. High with fever, he'd written three songs – Cinnamon Girl; Cowgirl In The Sand; Down By The River. The lyrics were understandably vague and dreamy and the chords simple yet arresting. In his mind, Young began to hear a hypnotic beat that cried for electric instrumentation. He could have assembled a crack team of LA session players but instead he chose a bar band that he knew from the Springfield days. The Rockets had made one album for White Whale but weren't exactly setting Hollywood alight. "He took the rhythm section, which was me, Billy Talbot and Danny Whitten," drummer Ralph Molina recalls. "It evolved into Crazy Horse. We hadn't played many shows as the Rockets anyway."

Crazy Horse was one of Young's most inspired moves. They provided him with the same excitement he remembered from the heyday of Buffalo Springfield, albeit without the mind games and rivalry that characterised his dealings with the fiery Stephen Stills. Although the partnership would drift at various points in his career, Young would always return to Crazy Horse in search of renewal. This album proved one of the best electric guitar albums of its era and established Young's reputation as a player of great passion and unrestrained intensity.

"I still think that us being with Neil was fate," Molina concludes. "We were just four guys. That Crazy Horse sound came from all four of us. Neil wouldn't have found that sound with anybody else. That was the way we played – with raw emotion."

Record Label:
Reprise
Produced
by David Briggs and Neil Young.
Recorded
in Los Angeles; March 1969.
Released:
May 1969
Chart peaks:
None (UK) 34 (US)
Personnel:
Neil Young (g, v); Danny Whitten (g, bv); Ralph Molina (d, bv); Billy Talbot (b, bv); Robin Lane (v); Bobby Notkoff (vn)
Track Listing:
Cinnamon Girl (S/US); Everybody Knows This Is Nowhere (S/US); Round And Round; Down By The River (S); The Losing End; Running Dry (Requiem For The Rockets); Cowgirl In The Sand
Running time:
40.32
Current CD:
87599272422
Further listening:
Tonight's The Night (1975); Zuma (1976); Rust Never Sleeps (1979); Arc/Weld (1991)
Further reading:
MOJO 10, 25, 44; Neil Young: Here We Are In The Years (Johnny Rogan, 1982); http://hyperrust.org
Like this?
Try . . . p.558

Euphoria

A Gift From Euphoria

Two musical nomads take psychedelic rock, bluegrass and orchestral ballads into lasting obscurity.

From the cover of their only album, Wesley Watt and Bill Lincoln stare out moodily like an odd couple in an old master, beneath them a pseudo-biblical text ending: "For I am the music, the instrument of God". Well, the music certainly moves in mysterious ways.

Little is known about Euphoria, but how they secured a deal with Capitol allowing them to record this ambitious album is perhaps the greatest puzzle of all. The culmination of a musical journey between California and Texas, Nashville and London – encountering such disparate bands as the Thirteenth Floor Elevators, Love and the Bee Gees – *A Gift from Euphoria* is a work of startling diversity and eccentric charm. After the lushly orchestrated opening, which is sung partly in French, a crash of tympani heralds the first of a series of sudden, disorientating transitions, as Lisa surrenders to the Stone River Hill Song – a slice of banjo bluegrass and bar-room piano.

The album's defining moment follows with the exhortation: "Jesus knew life is changing/So take my hand/To change this land/*Change it*!" whereupon the band burst raucously into Did You Get The Letter and any remaining preconceptions are swept away in a blaze of distorted guitar. The remainder is a roller-coaster ride of laid-back psychedelia (Through a Window), unabashed country (I'll Be Home To You), atmospheric sound effects (Young Miss Pflugg) and whispered voices over delicate harpsichord (Lady Bedford). The crowning moment is the achingly beautiful Sunshine Woman: "Ice cream palace in your eyes/Paper horses racing by", which heralds a subtle, splendid climax of strings, French horns and female chorus. With its quintessentially English references to chips and tea, it is tempting to suggest that Docker's Son was one of the tracks recorded in London. It was here that Euphoria may have crossed paths with the Bee Gees (given "special thanks" on the inside cover) who, in the same year, brought an unexpected Nashville influence to their double album, *Odessa*. Benefiting from Nik Venet's sympathetic production, *A Gift From Euphoria* exemplifies the bravado and folly of an era that was rapidly approaching its close. It must have cost a small fortune to record, yet its scope was probably too ambitious for most people to comprehend. The present whereabouts of Watt and Lincoln are unknown.

Record label:
Capitol
Produced
by Hamilton Wesley Watt Jr, William D Lincoln, Nik Venet (credited as 'Nikolas Venetoulis').
Recorded
in Hollywood, Nashville and London; 1968.
Released:
spring 1969
Chart peaks:
None (UK) None (US)
Personnel:
Hamilton Wesley Watt Jr (v, g); William D Lincoln (v, g); Irwin Webb (oa)
Track listing:
Lisa; Stone River Hill Song; Did You Get The Letter; Through A Window; Young Miss Pflugg; Lady Bedford; Suicide On The Hillside Sunday Morning After Tea; Sweet Fanny Adams; I'll Be Home To You; Sunshine Woman; Hollyville Train; Docker's Son; Something For The Milkman; Too Young To Know; World
Running time:
43.05
Current CD:
SEE CD 465
Like this?
Try . . . p.156

Burt Bacharach

Make It Easy On Yourself

Having conquered the Brill Building, Broadway and movies, Burt becomes a reluctant pop star.

As a composer, producer and arranger of hits by Dionne Warwick, Dusty Springfield, Cilla Black, Tom Jones, Herb Alpert and scores of other eminent '60s popsters, it was only a matter of time before Burt Bacharach stepped into the spotlight himself. Especially given his twinkling good looks and soft-spoken charisma. But he insists he had to be coaxed into his star turn.

"I was very insecure about singing," he says. "It's one thing to do it in a live performance on stage. It's like yesterday's newspaper. It's forgotten. It wasn't so good, okay. But when you go onto tape, it's there forever. I try to sing the songs not as a singer, but just interpreting it as a composer and interpreting a great lyric that Hal [David] wrote."

On his second solo LP, he surrounds his voice (the liner notes called it a "rumpled, earnest baritone") with all the energetic components of what became known as the "Bacharach Sound" – honey-dipped flugelhorns, bossa-nova sidesticks, breezy flutes, molto fortissimo strings and cooing female voices – and interprets hits such as I'll Never Fall In Love Again, Promises, Promises and Make It Easy On Yourself.

"I didn't want to make the songs the same way as they'd been done," Bacharach says, "so I'd split vocals and instrumentals and try to make it interesting to me, and hopefully interesting to the listener. 'For me, it's about the peaks and valleys of where a record can take you. You can tell a story and be able to be explosive one minute then get quiet as kind of a satisfying resolution."

His co-producer and engineer Phil Ramone recalls how the dynamics originated from Burt himself: "The whole room would come to life with his conducting – the way he would look over at the drummer and with just the flick of his finger, things could happen. Once the groove was happening in the room, forget it, there was nothing like it. And everything, including the strings, responded to the kind of body movement that Burt had. He brings an incredible amount of life to the studio. He's probably one of the most amazing musicians in the world."

Record label:
A&M
Produced:
by Burt Bacharach and Phil Ramone.
Recorded:
at A&M Studio, New York; 1968.
Released:
June 1969
Chart peaks:
None (UK) 51 (US)
Personnel:
Burt Bacharach (v, a, oa); Phil Ramone (e); with orchestra
Track listing:
Promises, Promises; I'll Never Fall In Love Again; Knowing When To Leave; Any Day Now; Wanting Things; Whoever You Are I Love You; Make It Easy On Yourself; Do You Know The Way To San Jose; Pacific Coast Highway (S); She's Gone Away; This Guy's In Love With You
Running time:
35.32
Current CD:
Universal 394188
Further listening:
The Look Of Love: The Burt Bacharach Collection (1998)
Further reading:
MOJO 28; www.bacharachonline.com
Like this?
Try . . . p.180

Creedence Clearwater Revival

Bayou Country

Second album from San Francisco's own Southern boys.

In 1964, the Californian, Berkeley-based jazz label Fantasy decided the time had come to cash in on the beat craze and auditioned local instrumental group Tommy Fogerty and the Blue Velvets. Encouraged by A&R man Hy Weiss to sound more British, they became The Visions and then The Golliwogs, releasing singles on the label's Scorpio subsidiary without much success. Then in 1966, key personnel John Fogerty and Doug Clifford were drafted. 18 months later, Fogerty returned home determined to quit trying to sound British and do something a little truer to his roots.

"Rock'n'roll is Southern," he says today, "and that's why I'm Southern. Because what I learned from was Southern. I rest my case." And there are few Southern rock tracks greater than the joyful, folksy chug of Proud Mary, with its utopian vision of Mississippi river life, the kind of song that sounds as if it has always been there. Freshly discharged from the army, Fogerty wrote the song as an expression of his overwhelming sense of freedom.

The group's new style needed a new name and they became Creedence Clearwater Revival. A cover version of Dale Hawkins' Suzie-Q attracted attention as a welcome antidote to the pretensions of acid rock and the sterility of bubblegum pop, and Fantasy switched them to the parent label. John Fogerty has since maintained that he steered the group every inch of the way from that moment on. "This stuff is hardly rocket science," says bassist Stu Cook, rebutting such claims. "It's not as if we had two-and-a-half brain cells and needed a guiding light to lead us through the key of E. We'd been together 10 years already. We learned how to play together. The Proud Mary bassline is mine for a start – I could go on."

"*Bayou Country* is my favourite album because we had played those songs live and because we were still a band," continues Cook. "We still had an input at the mix, welcomed or not. Hank McGill got a great sound from my Rickenbacker on tape and it survived all sabotage attempts!"

The album is bookended by the two tracks that opened and closed the band's sets: Born On The Bayou is a rocking, funky thing that announces Fogerty's long-running obsession with Southern pop, while Keep On Chooglin' is a rumbling, good-time salute to blue-collar pleasures. Vocally, Fogerty is superb throughout. His wonderfully rugged rendition of Little Richard's Good Golly Miss Molly tips a nod to one mentor and the hypnotic Graveyard Train does the same to bluesman Howlin' Wolf. *Bayou Country* represents the start of CCR's golden period.

Record label:
Fantasy
Produced
by John Fogerty.
Recorded
at RCA Studios, Hollywood
Released:
June 1969
Chart peaks:
None (UK) 7 (US)
Personnel:
John Fogerty (g, v); Tom Fogerty (g); Stu Cook (b); Doug 'Cosmo' Clifford (d); Hank McGill (e)
Track listing:
Born On The Bayou; Bootleg; Graveyard Train; Good Golly Miss Molly; Penthouse; Proud Mary (S); Keep On Chooglin'
Running time:
34.07
Current CD:
FCD24 8387-2
Further listening:
Green River (1969); Willy And The Poor Boys (1970); Cosmo's Factory(1970): The Blue Ridge Rangers: Blue Ridge Rangers (1973), essentially a John Fogerty solo album of Country covers, lovingly rendered.
Further reading:
Bad Moon Rising: The Unofficial Story Of Creedence Clearwater Revival (Hank Bordowitz, 1998); Up Around The Bend: The Oral History Of Creedence Clearwater Revival (Craig Werner, 1998); www.creedence-revisited.com/
Like this?
Try . . . p.833

Crosby, Stills And Nash

Crosby, Stills And Nash

One moment of harmony beget a roller-coaster career.

Disillusioned by the commerciality of his work with The Hollies, and increasingly beguiled by the burgeoning underground music scene in the States, Graham Nash was spending more and more time with ex-Byrd David Crosby and former Buffalo Springfield kingpin Stephen Stills. The three were already united by a love of dope and good music, when they discovered the flawless compatibility of their voices. Crosby and Stills were working out one of the latter's compositions, You Don't Have To Cry, when, as an experiment, Nash added an irresistible third harmony.

"It was," Stills reflected, "one of those moments."

Crosby, Stills & Nash were, on paper, an unbeatable combination, and much was riding on their debut album. They began rehearsing together at Notting's Hill's Moscow Road in late 1968, with The Beatles' Blackbird as an early vocal try-out, and all three brought their best material to the sessions. Nash, who had been chafing at what he saw as The Hollies' musical conservatism, supplied the drug-infused Marrakesh Express and Pre-Road Downs; Crosby contributed the beguiling Guinevere and timely Long Time Gone; but it was Stills who felt he had most to prove, and his were the lengthy opening (Suite: Judy Blue Eyes) and closer (49 Bye-Byes), as well as the inimitable Helplessly Hoping – the one song on the album that indicated the trio's potential for true greatness.

Harmonically intricate and musically potent, the album was more than just a calling card for Messrs Crosby, Stills & Nash; it was an album very much of its time, an Us vs Them broadside across the Hippie-Straight divide. The album spoke directly to the millions of young people who, while disillusioned by a society they saw as without values and despairing of inequality, were also terrified of getting drafted to fight in the war that was raging in Vietnam. Besides the knowing drug innuendoes and heavy emphasis on "ladies", there was Stills' Spanish coda to Suite: Judy Blue Eyes – a plea to President Nixon to let US citizens visit Cuba.

Short of a fourth member for touring, Neil Young, Stills' old sparring partner from Buffalo Springfield was recruited, and within three months of this album's release, Crosby, Stills, Nash & Young were playing at Woodstock – it was only their second gig, but the world had got its first supergroup.

Record label:
Atlantic
Produced
by Crosby, Stills and Nash.
Recorded
at Wally Heider's Studio III, Los Angeles
Released:
June 1969
Chart peaks:
25 (UK) 6 (US)
Personnel:
8David Crosby (v, rg); Stephen Stills (g, b, o, v); Graham Nash (v); Dallas Taylor (d); Bill Halverston (e)
Track listing:
Suite: Judy Blue Eyes (S); Marrakesh Express (S); Guinevere; You Don't Have To Cry; Pre-Road Downs; Wooden Ships; Lady Of The Island; Helplessly Hoping; Long Time Gone; 49 Bye-Byes
Running time:
40.57
Current CD:
WEA 7567-82651-2
Further listening:
The Best Of Crosby Stills And Nash box set (1991)
Further reading:
The Complete Guide To The Music Of Crosby, Stills, Nash And Young (Johnny Rogan, 1998); Crosby, Stills, Nash And Young: The Visual Documentary (Johnny Rogan, 1996); www.crosbystillsnash.com
Like this?
Try . . . p.576

Judy Henske & Jerry Yester

Farewell Aldebaran

The definitive space-blues-Arthurian-bubblegum album.

Signed to Frank Zappa former Lovin' Spoonful member Jerry Yester and his singer/songwriter wife Judy Henske, created a forgotten classic. Its ten songs range from surreal rock (Snowblind) and spoof bubblegum (Horses On A Stick) to Arthurian folk rock (Three Ravens) and, on the title track, full blown avant-garde composition, owing more to Stockhausen or Sun Ra than the pop psych of the Spoonful.

The couple got together in 1962 when Henske was in vogue as a pop singer with a distinctive, lusty voice and Yester was her accompanist. Jerry then joined the Modern Folk Quartet and Judy signed to Elektra where she made several albums with Herb Cohen as producer, scoring a hit with High Flying Bird (later recorded by Jefferson Airplane). When Jerry was invited to join The Lovin' Spoonful the couple moved to New York and started writing together. When the Spoonful finally split, Cohen suggested they move back to California and record for Straight.

With help from Jerry's Spoonful comrade Zal Yanovsky, began to graft musical flesh onto the songs they'd written. Powerful opening track Snowblind, was a testament to the skills of this experienced line-up.

"We wrote the song kind of as we did it," reveals Yester. "I was playing rhythm guitar, Zal was playing lead, Judy was singing and Larry Beckett [ex Tim Buckley] was playing drums. The whole thing just took shape in an hour." Another stellar moment is the closing, title track, which leaves pop and rock trajectories to enter another musical orbit.

"I loved the idea of a huge asteroid burning up in our atmosphere and telling its story," says Jerry. Creating the apocalyptic voice of this imagined invader involved some unusual techniques. "For the voice of the asteroid, we put Judy's voice through a series of ring modulators, took all the actual tone out and just made it all overtones."

Despite some rave critical response, *Farewell Aldebaran* crashed to earth. Henske and Yester went on to form the short-lived Rosebud until their marriage collapsed and they went their separate ways.

Record label:
Straight
Produced
by Jerry Yester and Zal Yanovsky.
Recorded
Feb–March1969.
Released:
June 1969
Chart peaks:
None (UK) None (US)
Personnel:
Judy Henske (v); Jerry Yester (k, Moog, g, banjo, zither); Zal Yanovsky (g, b); Ry Cooder (rhythm mandolin); David Lindley (bowed banjo); Solomon Feldthouse (dulcimer); Toxey French (d); Larry Beckett (d); Jerry Scheff (b); Joe Osborn (b); Dick Rosmini (g)
Track listing:
Snowblind; Horses On A Stick; Lullaby; St. Nicholas Hall; Three Ravens; Raider; One More Time; Rapture; Charity; Farewell Aldebaran
Running time:
33.48
Currently unavailable on CD
Further listening:
Judy Henske's solo LPs, High Flyin' Bird (1963) and Little Bit Of Sunshine (1965)
Further reading:
www.tctv.ne.jp/members/m-site/jerryyester/JHJY6901.html
Like this?
Try . . . p.322

Kaleidoscope (US)

Incredible

Apogee of these undervalued American avatars of acid-rock comes with Middle-Eastern spice.

Jimmy Page once described the American band called Kaleidoscope as, "My favourite band of all time, my ideal band. Absolutely brilliant"; the influential critic Robert Shelton, who crucially boosted Dylan's early career, enthusiastically called them "super-eclectic"; and pioneering FM disc jockey Tom Donahue hailed them as, "one of the best groups in the country". And much good did such acclaim do the band, for *Incredible*, like the other three albums they released during their original career (they reformed in the late '70s), sold negligibly. And yet in their adventurousness and their eclecticism, Kaleidoscope were an archetypal '60s band, creators of cutting edge acid-rock and trailblazers of world and fusion musics, who by rights should now be regarded as legends.

"We wanted to experiment with a music which could combine various other musical areas with rock . . . to see if we could come up with something new and interesting," asserts guitarist David Lindley.

And *Incredible*, their third album, triumphantly demonstrates how they achieved their ambition, for the music sweeps up rock, blues, country, folk, cajun and Near and Middle Eastern musics, all linked by an unmistakeably psychedelic consciousness. Timid souls should however be warned that this is not the whimsical, cutesy psychedelia of the "Let's all go and blow our minds down in Toytown" variety. Much of the album is possessed by a unnerving strangeness. Cuckoo, for example, the band's reinvention of a traditional folk song, is permeated with a sense of evil, singer Feldthouse chillingly snarling the line, "Let's make love now," an invitation that never sounded less enticing. Or consider Petite Fleur, which ends with a sinister cackle. Or the near 12-minute Seven-Ate Suite, where the cymbals sound like knives being sharpened, assorted exotic instruments solo eerily, and suddenly, after more than five intense minutes, Feldthouse starts wailing in tongues.

"He's singing Turkish obscenities," explains Lindley, more prosaicly. "We didn't want to be a conventional band."

Record label:
Epic
Produced
by Jackie Mills.
Recorded
1969.
Released:
June 1969
Chart peaks:
None (UK) None (US)
Personnel:
David Lindley (g, vn, banjo, v); Solomon Feldthouse (g, o, clarinet, caz, jumbus, v); Templeton Parcely (vn, o, v); Stuart A Brotman (b, v); Paul Lagos (d, v); Max Buda (hm); Bob Breault (e)
Track listing:
Lie To Me; Let The Good Love Flow; Tempe Arizona aka Killing Floor (S/US only); Petite Fleur; Banjo; Cuckoo; Seven-Ate Sweet
Running time:
30.58
Current CD:
Edsel EDCD 533
Further listening:
Side Trips (1967) and A Beacon From Mars (1968) have the same killer combination of acid rock and fearless eclecticism. Do not confuse them with the British psych-pop band of the same name – as record shops often do.
Further reading:
very little exists except the booklets that accompany the CD reissues.
Like this?
Try . . . p.699

Jeff Beck

Beck-Ola

Career high-point for mercurial guitar genius.

In retrospect, *Beck-Ola* is clearly the soundtrack of a band in the midst of disintegration. By 1969, The Jeff Beck Group was barely intact. The seeds of discontent had been sown after the release of *Truth*, when other band members complained that their credits were too small. To ensure his visibility this time, vocalist Rod Stewart insisted that the credits for *Beck-Ola* read: "Rod Stewart, vocalist extraordinaire".

On *Beck-Ola*, Beck's guitar is more combative and flinty than the sinuous sounds of *Truth*, but that is perhaps because the band members were constantly at odds. Prior to the band's second tour of America in February 1969, Beck had fired and rehired Ron Wood twice and, having shown drummer Mickey Waller the door, replaced him with Sounds Incorporated stickman Tony Newman. Only Rod Stewart seemed beyond Beck's compulsive changes. During the band's second US tour, Beck collapsed after a concert in Minneapolis and cancelled the rest of the dates, hastening home to make another record.

"The world was ready for the Jeff Beck Group in a way much bigger than I had imagined," he says. "I suddenly realised I had to go home and do something about it. So in four days, we nailed together *Beck-Ola*. The whole damn album was pretty much dreamt up on the spot. It was made in desperation to get product out. We just got vicious on it, because we were all in bad moods, and it came out quite wild."

In the brief liner notes, Beck became an apologist for the material: "Today, with all the hard competition in the music business, it's almost impossible to come up with anything totally original. So we haven't. However, this album was made with the accent on heavy music."

To drive the point home, the former art student chose a Magritte print of an oversized green apple for the album cover. "The painting had something heavy and weighty about it. Ron Wood and I were looking through this book of Magritte, and I said, 'Let's just open the book at random and see what happens'."

Beck sees *Beck-Ola* today as "a good reference point for where serious metal started. It may not be up to scratch sound-wise, but the riffs, the notes, the whole attitude was vicious."

JU

Record label:
Columbia
Produced
by Mickie Most.
Recorded
at Kingsway Recorders, London; May 1969.
Released:
July 1969
Chart peaks:
39 (UK) 15 (US)
Personnel:
Jeff Beck (g, b); Rod Stewart (v); Ron Wood (b, g); Tony Newman (d); Nicky Hopkins (k, p); Martin Birch (e)
Track listing:
All Shook Up; Spanish Boots; Girl From Mill Valley; Jailhouse Rock; Plynth (Water Down The Drain) (S/withdrawn); Hangman's Knee; Rice Pudding
Running time:
30.29
Current CD:
TOCP6318
Further listening:
Truth (1968), the band's sparkling debut; Blow By Blow(1975), an all-instrumental effort where Beck teamed up with Beatles producer George Martin; Beckology 3-CD box set.
Further reading:
www.jeffbeck.com/-
Like this?
Try . . . p.426

Fairport Convention

Unhalfbricking

The record that sowed the seeds of British folk-rock

In its long, chequered history, Top Of The Pops has screened many bizarre TV moments. Few, perhaps, quite as mad as the sight in 1969 of Fairport Convention performing the Bob Dylan song If You Gotta Go, Go Now – Cajun style. Richard Thompson on accordion, Ashley Hutchings playing double bass with a French loaf, Dave Mattacks on washboard the song leapt to the dizzy heights of Number 21 in the British charts, their only hit. "We were," mused Hutchings, "very impetuous in those days, very sparky. There was certainly a feeling of experimentation, great energy then."

Unhalfbricking played a crucial role in the Fairport story, marking the arrival of Dave Swarbrick on fiddle and the first hint of their epochal step into serious folk music territory. It was also the album they'd just finished when drummer Martin Lamble was killed on the M1 in May, '69 as roadie Harvey Branham drove their transit van near Scratchwood Services on the way back from a gig in Birmingham. The band were still in shock when the album was compiled by Boyd and released, and they almost split completely. Eventually they opted to regroup with Swarbrick as a full time member and Dave Mattacks as drummer. (It was this line-up that cut *Liege & Lief.*)

Unhalfbricking stands as a folk rock benchmark; Thompson believes it's better than its more celebrated successor. While there was a real sense of fun about the Cajun influence of Million Dollar Bash, Cajun Woman and If You Gotta Go (which they translated into French), Thompson weighed in with a dramatic composition which provided a signpost to his songwriting future, Genesis Hall, and singer Sandy Denny contributed her greatest song, Who Knows Where The Time Goes? But most profound of all was their epic arrangement of A Sailor's Life. "Sandy used to sing Scots ballads in the bus or dressing room, and that's really what got them intrigued by British traditional music," explains producer and manager Joe Boyd. "She specifically played them A Sailor's Life, which she used to do in the clubs. I went to see them in Bristol and heard them do it for the first time and it was wonderful. How do you put a rock'n'roll attitude to a traditional ballad? There it is."

Record label:
Island
Produced by
Joe Boyd and Simon Nicol.
Recorded
at Olympic Studios, London; March–April 1969.
Released:
July 1969
Chart peaks:
12 (UK) None (US)
Personnel:
Dave Swarbrick (fiddle, mandolin, v); Sandy Denny (v, g); Richard Thompson (v, g); Marc Ellington (v); Ashley Hutchings (b, v); Trevor Lucas (g, pc, triangle, v); Simon Nicol (v, g); Martin Lamble (d, vn); Ian Matthews (v); Marc Wellington (v); John Wood (e)
Track listing:
Genesis Hall; Si Tu Dois Partir (S); Autopsy; A Sailor's Life; Cajun Woman; Who Knows Where The Time Goes?; Percy's Song; Million Dollar Bash
Running time:
35.42
Current CD:
IMCD61
Further listening:
What We Did On Our Holidays (1968); Liege & Lief (1969); Sandy Denny: The North Star Grassman And The Ravens (1970). Hear an alternative take of A Sailor's Life on Watching The Dark, a 3-CD retrospective of Richard Thompson. Other favoured Fairport albums are Full House and Rising For The Moon.
Further reading:
MOJO 9, 55; Meet On The Ledge: Fairport Convention, The Classic Years (Patrick Humphries, 1997)
Like this?
Try . . . p.117

Procol Harum

A Salty Dog

Procol Harum remain a greatly undervalued band, and this was undoubtedly their finest hour.

For most people, the story of Procol Harum began, and ended, with Whiter Shade Of Pale. After that one era-defining single, the band simply skipped the light fandango right out of the frame. But that, as with so many rock'n'roll clichés, is only half the picture. Procol Harum actually went on to record a further ten albums, and this, their third, is generally regarded among fans as their best.

A Salty Dog was their fourth single, released in June 1969 – a swirling, Gothic epic, drenched in salt spray, it was progressive rock at its very best, Procol Harum *in excelsis*. The subsequent album built on the band's strengths – Trower's guitar flowed freely (he was yet to be subsumed by his Hendrix infatuation); Brooker had rarely sung better; Fisher's production was '69 rock in Cinerama; and Barrie Wilson's thunderous drumming (he was Jimmy Page's original choice for the Led Zeppelin drumstool) underpinned the whole album. As well as the title track, the music was ambitious on Matthew Fisher's epic Pilgrim's Progress and Wreck Of The Hesperus. They got all heavy on The Devil Came From Kansas, folkie on Milk Of Human Kindness, and slipped into a Latin rumba groove on Boredom; while All This And More took Procol Harum into a stratospheric place all of its own.

The 1999 reissue added the single's B-side – the robust Long Gone Geek – which found Procol trying to sound like the Small Faces; some out-takes; and a real gem, in the shape of the only existing take of McGregor.

In its day, *A Salty Dog* received respectful reviews, and helped cement Procol's position as critics' favourites – particularly in America where they toured pretty much non-stop during the late 60s; but increasing apathy at home led to their split in 1977. Posthumously, Procol Harum began to receive the respect they had always deserved. Latterly, A Salty Dog has been covered by Marc Almond and, ahem, Sarah Brightman; while Pete Townshend and Brian May have testified to Procol's influence on The Who and Queen. Unfortunately, in the aftermath of *A Salty Dog*, the band let slip the one gig that could really have lifted them up another notch: by declining to appear at a rock festival in upstate New York – reputedly because the Trower family had already booked their summer holidays – Procol Harum missed out on Woodstock.

Record label:
Regal Zonophone
Produced
by Matthew Fisher.
Recorded
at Abbey Road, London; January–February 1969.
Released:
July 1969
Chart peaks:
27 (UK) 32 (US)
Personnel:
Gary Brooker (p, v, hm, celeste, recorder); Matthew Fisher (o, g, marimba, recorder); Dave Knights (b); Barrie Wilson (d, pc); Robin Trower (g, tambourine); Kellogs (bosun's whistle); Ken Scott; Ian Stuart, Henry Lewy (e)
Track listing:
A Salty Dog (S/UK); The Milk Of Human Kindness; Too Much Between Us; The Devil Came From Kansas (S/US); Boredom; Juicy John Pink; Wreck Of The Hesperus; All This And More; Crucifiction Lane; Pilgrim's Progress
Running time:
43.07
Current CD:
WESM534 adds Long Gone Geek; All This And More (Alt take); The Milk Of Human Kindness (Alt take); Pilgrim's Progress (Alt take) McGregor; Still There'll Be More
Further listening:
Procol Harum: 30th Anniversary Collection (1997). For the excellent later incarnation of the band seek out the mighty Grand Hotel (1973), a real forgotten gem.
Further reading:
Procol Harum; Beyond The Pale (Claes Johansen, 2000); www.procolharum.com
Like this?
Try . . . p.163

Jethro Tull

Stand Up

Featured a pop-up likeness of the group in the gatefold. Sadly, a marketing wheeze that never caught on.

There was a time when Jethro Tull were kings of the British rock underground. Hard to imagine, perhaps, given the perception of many that they're purveyors of music-hall buffoonery in monstrously unfashionable clothing, but they came second only to The Beatles in the Melody Maker poll of 1969, streets ahead of more conventionally swaggering rock behemoths like Led Zeppelin or The Who. Having worked their way up by constant gigging and a reputation founded largely on Ian Anderson's uniquely charismatic and eccentric stage persona (shabby raincoat, hair, flute, standing on one leg), Tull would enjoy a good two or three years as rock aristocracy before slipping gently down to a more sustainable level. As Anderson was quick to realise, being "top of the second division" has its advantages, not least in longevity. Thirty years later the Tull brand would still be shifting a dependable half-million worldwide units per annum.

Though America would always prefer *Aqualung* (1971) and *Thick As A Brick* (1972), for the Brits the flute-dominated *Stand Up* is the fondest memory – a triumph of youthful imagination, drive, wit and naïveté with just a little dash of melancholy, where later there would be cleverness, cod-pieces and concepts.

"When we did *Stand Up*," Anderson recently recalled, "I thought, Hey, we're on our second album – there could be a third! That's about as far as I saw it going. I can remember writing the material for it and really struggling for ideas. If you get one, firstly it's a relief and secondly, if it's a good one then you're jumping up and down. That excitement was there then and it's still there now. Mind you, it would be difficult for me to write Jeffrey Goes To Leicester Square now. It would seem a bit silly."

As on Tull's debut, the influences were "black American blues, which it all started with when I was 16 years old and, from growing up in Scotland, Scottish folk music, as well as the English folk heritage which I started getting aware of later. I don't think you could call it folk rock, although it's one of the many terms that have been applied to it. I can only say we're sort of a rock band, but with a lot of different influences."

Record label:
Island
Produced
by Terry Ellis and Ian Anderson.
Recorded
at Morgan Studio, London; April 1969.
Released:
August 1, 1969
Chart peaks:
(UK) 1, (US) 20
Personnel:
Ian Anderson (v, g, flute, k, mandolin, balalaika, hm); Martin Barre (g, flute); Glen Cornick (b); Clive Bunker (d, pc); Andy Johns (e)
Track listing:
A New Day Yesterday; Jeffrey Goes To Leicester Square; Bouree; Back To The Family; Look Into The Sun; Nothing Is Easy; Fat Man; We Used To Know; Reasons For Waiting; For A Thousand Mothers
Running time:
38.18
Current CD:
CDP3210422
Further listening:
Aqualung (1971); LP/singles compilation, Living In The Past (1972)
Further reading:
Flying Colours: The Jethro Tull Reference Manual (Greg Russo, 2000) From Elvis In Memphis Elvis Presley
Like this?
Try . . . p.109

Elvis Presley

From Elvis In Memphis

Hot from his TV comeback, the King exorcises the frustration of his wasted years in Hollywood

Elvis's output in the '60s is unfairly maligned: whenever Presley was inspired, the results were phenomenal: *Elvis Is Back!*, the TV special, two religious albums – *His Hand In Mine* (1960) and *How Great Thou Art* (1967) – and a handful of great flop singles; but all anybody remembers are the movies. When the 34-year-old singer arrived at 827 Thomas Street, Memphis, he knew he was as good as washed-up. Chips Moman wanted the kudos of producing The King; Memphis Horn Wayne Jackson was fairly enthusiastic, "it wasn't like doing Neil Diamond," he admitted; but others were more concerned about the lack of decent material – publishers no longer needed Presley to sing their songs and take a cut. After a heated fight over Suspicious Minds (never part of any album), which Moman owned, Presley broke rank – get the songs, to hell with the percentages. Then the sessions began.

From the hoarse, autobiographical howl – "I had to leave town for a little while" – that opened Wearin' That Loved On Look, it was obvious Elvis was for real. The band, the hottest in the States in '69, fused gospel, soul and rock perfectly – though country was beyond their reach (particularly obvious on It Keeps Right On A-Hurtin'). In nine days, 20 tracks were completed; 14 more were recorded in February. Everybody knew the songs were the business, but would they sell? Deciding to keep the best track until they'd tested the water, RCA stuck out In The Ghetto. It was his first Top 10 hit since Crying In The Chapel; *From Elvis In Memphis* – "unequivocally the equal of anything he has ever done", according to Rolling Stone – recorded a respectable 13 in the US charts, then Suspicious Minds propelled him back to the top, the first time he'd been there in America since Good Luck Charm.

By this time, he'd returned to live performance, at the International Hotel in Las Vegas. A live album was welded to a second selection from Memphis: the studio set is disappointing, but the Vegas disc is essential, especially a seven-minute run at Suspicious Minds. For two more years, Presley was on top of his game again, creating a mature brand of rock that crossed the generation gap.

Record label:
RCA
Produced
by Lincoln 'Chips' Moman.
Recorded
at American Studios, Memphis; January–February 1969.
Released:
August 1969
Chart peaks:
1 (UK) 13 (US)
Personnel:
Elvis Presley (v, g, p); Reggie Young (g); Mike Leech (b); Gene Chrisman (d); Bobby Emmons (o); Tommy Cogbill (b); Bobby Wood (p); The Memphis Horns (brass); Ed Hollis (hm); Al Pachuki (e)
Track listing:
Wearin' That Loved On Look; Only The Strong Survive; I'll Hold You In My Heart (Till I Can Hold You In My Arms); Long Black Limousine; It Keeps Right On A-Hurtin'; I'm Movin' On; Power Of My Love; Gentle On My Mind; After Loving You; True Love Travels On A Gravel Road; Any Day Now; In The Ghetto (S)
Running time:
36.51
Current CD:
ND 90548
Further listening:
5-CD box-set, From Nashville To Memphis (2000); The '68 Comeback Special – the entire TV show (1992); Elvis In Person (At The International Hotel) (1970); Suspicious Minds (1999) – the whole session plus outtakes.
Further reading:
MOJO 63; Careless Love: The Unmaking Of Elvis Presley (Peter Guralnick, 1998)
Like this?
Try . . . p.18

Fleetwood Mac

Then Play On

The last and greatest recording of the Mac's first phase.

By the time Fleetwood Mac came to record *Then Play On*, they'd scored hit singles with the languid Albatross and the heartbreakingly beautiful Man Of The World, giving notice that their blue horizons were ever broadening. Danny Kirwan was now on board: his songwriting skills and his folk leanings edged an increasingly detached Jeremy Spencer further to the margins and emphasised the new directions the band were taking.

Sessions began in April 1969 with two Kirwan songs, Coming Your Way and Although The Sun Is Shining. Engineer Martin Birch recalled how he would work individually with Green and Kirwan; "Peter would come in and show me the feel and structure, lay down the basic track and when we were happy with the drums, the bass and two guitars, the others would disappear and I would work on his song until it was completely recorded . . . Then I would do the same with one of Danny's songs and it would alternate like that until the album was done."

While great music emerged, this way of working was indicative that the band was in the early throes of fragmenting. There were disputes over Oh Well, with Fleetwood and McVie almost convincing Peter not to release this magnificent work as a single.(neither was the song on the original UK version of the album).

Producing the album themselves was a mistake, according to Green. "We should have had a producer, then it might have sold better . . . we weren't completely aware of what the producer's job was."

In hindsight, you can also hear it in the songs. Green has often noted that Show-Biz Blues, "says it all about why I left Fleetwood Mac". Musically, it was a homage to Bukka White's percussive slide guitar, but "Now tell me anybody, do you really give a damn for me" is the cry of a band leader in the spotlight and under pressure. Even now, 30 years after the event, Peter Green complains, "They could have helped me more, but they just stayed in the background."

Then Play On delivered symphonic, elegiac rock, so far removed from the rough hewn white-blooze of only 18 months previous. Green was rightly proud of the album upon completion and remains so. "I love it, every minute of it. There is nothing I feel I could have done better."

A Californian aesthetic was already looming – the wave-washed beaches and rolling highways suggested by Danny and Peter's wistful guitar sounds and Mick Fleetwood 's tyres-on-the road thump. Americans loved it. One can only wonder what Fleetwood Mac might have achieved had Peter stayed and created a fourth album. Oh well . . .

Record label:
Reprise
Produced
by Fleetwood Mac.
Recorded
in London; April 1969.
Released:
September 9, 1969
Chart peaks:
6 (UK) 109 (US)
Personnel:
Peter Green (g, v, hm); Jeremy Spencer (p); Danny Kirwan (g, v); John McVie (b); Mick Fleetwood (d); Martin Birch (e)
Track listing:
Coming Your Way; Closing My Eyes; Show-Biz Blues; My Dream; Underway: Oh Well (S); Although The Sun Is Shining; Rattlesnake Shake (S/US); Searching For Madge; Fighting For Madge; When You Say; Like Crying; Before The Beginning
Running time:
54.16
Current CD:
927448-2
Further listening:
The Vaudeville Years Of Fleetwood Mac 1968-1970 (1998). A spiffing two CD set which contains unreleased and extended versions of tracks on Then Play On plus unissued versions of Man of the World and Green Manalishi.
Further reading:
Peter Green: The Founder Of Fleetwood Mac (Martin Clemens, 1998); My 25 Years In Fleetwood Mac (Mick Fleetwood, 1992); www.fleetwoodmac.net/penguin
Like this?
Try . . . p.122

The Beatles
Abbey Road
Glorious almost-swan-song for the ultimate pop group.

The Beatles were falling apart in 1969. The January Get Back sessions (temporarily shelved but later Spectorised and released as *Let It Be* in May 1970) had been even more miserable than those for the White Album, John Lennon appeared more interested in promoting himself and Yoko as avant-garde peacenik performance artists than his old band, and a dispute over who should take control of The Beatles' finances saw the group that had represented such an explosion of artistic and spiritual possibilities in the '60s ending the decade as bitter, feuding businessmen. Even their remarkable producer, the normally unruffled George Martin had stayed away from the Get Back sessions: "I thought, oh gosh, I don't want to be a part of this anymore." So, he was surprised to be asked by Paul to produce a Beatles record "like we used to" but agreed on the condition that he be allowed to produce a polished studio album, which is exactly what he did. With excellent group performances, slick programming and high production values (it's the best *sounding* Beatles album) giving the impression of a unified whole, in fact the sessions were as disparate as ever, the band personally uncomfortable with each other, rarely attending the overdubbing sessions of each other's songs.

"On Come Together I would have liked to sing harmony with John," McCartney said later, "but I was too embarrassed to ask him." Paul wanted the songs linked together while John wanted each song separate, preferably with all of his on one side; the compromise of separate songs on side one and a medley taking up much of side two was reached. Although Lennon would later talk of he and Paul "cutting each other down to size to fit into some kind of format" as the main artistic reason why The Beatles could no longer continue as a group, it's also the reason why *Abbey Road* is such a success. Excesses are mostly curbed, strengths are emphasised. This, combined with Harrison's two offerings – for the first time, comparable to Lennon's and McCartney's (Frank Sinatra sang Something throughout the '70s, famously calling it "the greatest love song of the last fifty years") – make *Abbey Road* a heartbreakingly fitting epitaph. Get a certain kind of music fan of a certain age in a certain mood and he'll tell you that pop music was all downhill from here.

Record label:
Apple
Produced
by George Martin.
Recorded
at Abbey Road;
February–August 1969.
Released:
September, 26 1969
Chart peaks:
1 (UK) 1 (US)
Personnel:
John Lennon (v, g, p, o); Paul McCartney (v, b, p, g, d); George Harrison (v, g, syn); Ringo Starr (d); Billy Preston (o)
Track Listing:
Come Together; Something; Maxwell's Silver Hammer; Oh! Darling; Octopus's Garden; I Want You (She's So Heavy); Here Comes The Sun; Because; You Never Give Me Your Money; Sun King; Mean Mr Mustard; Polythene Pam; She Came In Through The Bathroom Window; Golden Slumbers; Carry That Weight; The End; Her Majesty
Running time:
47.26
Currently available CD:
CDP 7 46446 2
Further listening:
Let It Be (1970); Anthology 3 (1997)
Further reading:
Revolution In The Head (Ian Macdonald, 1998); Many Years From Now (Barry Miles, 1997); The Beatles As Musicians (Walter Everett, 1999)
Like this?
Try . . . p.565

Jack Bruce

Songs For A Tailor

Ex-member of world's biggest band boldly follows his muse into the realms of jazz-rock.

Only a rock superstar at the peak of his power, as Bruce was after the success of Cream, could have taken a record like *Songs For A Tailor* into the charts, for the music on the album is uncompromising, uncommercial, contemporary jazz fusion. Bruce recruited some of Britain's most creative young jazz musicians, all of whom play scintillatingly, with techniques light years ahead of the average rock musician. The songs were all co-written by Bruce and lyricist Pete Brown.

"My songs are usually written using the piano and the music tends to come first," explains Bruce. "It's a question of getting into Jack's mind," offers Brown. "Some of the songs took an awfully long time – The Clearout and Weird Of Hermiston took two and a half years before we got what we wanted."

One of the album's most acclaimed songs is the cryptic Theme From An Imaginary Western.

"The words were about the Graham Bond band," clarifies Brown, referring to one of Bruce's early outfits. "I saw them as a mob of cowboys and pioneers. I was always amazed at the camaraderie between the early groups but now and then you'd get explosive situations between them, just like in the Westerns."

There is no title song, the album title being a dedication to clothing designer Jeannie Franklyn, who died in the Fairport Convention van crash.

"The day she was killed I got a letter from her which said all the little things she always used to say, like, 'Sing some high notes for me,'" recalls Bruce.

Colosseum drummer Jon Hiseman, who plays on the album, still enthuses about it. "It was the best album I ever made. Jack was a genius: he plays the best bass in the world, he's a magnificent singer and he writes wonderful music. But I think the reason he never was a major star after Cream was Pete Brown's lyrics are too obscure for a popular audience." Bruce seems unconcerned. "I've never wanted extreme commercial success. Cream was an accidental thing that was such a huge success I don't have to worry about money, so I've been able to concentrate on what I want to do."

Record label:
Polydor
Produced
by Felix Pappalardi.
Recorded
at De Lane Lea, London; April–June 1969.
Released:
September 1969
Chart peaks:
6 (UK) 55 (US)
Personnel:
Jack Bruce (v, p, b, o, c, g); Harry Beckett (t); Henry Lowther (t); Dick Heckstall-Smith, Art Themen (s); Chris Spedding (g); Jon Hiseman (d); John Marshall (d); Felix Pappalardi (v, pc, g); John Mumford (tb); L'Angelo Misterioso (g); Andrew Johns (e)
Track listing:
Never Tell Your Mother She's Out Of Tune; Theme For An Imaginary Western; Tickets To Water Falls; Weird Of Hermiston; Rope Ladder To The Moon; The Ministry Of Bag; He The Richmond; Boston Ball Game, 1969; To Isengard; The Clearout
Running time:
31.47
Current CD:
835 242-2
Further listening:
Of the three jazz-influenced albums Bruce released after Cream, his own favourite is Harmony Row (1971), "I just sat down at the piano, with a joint, and there it was," he declared.
Further reading:
MOJO 18; www.jackbruce.com
Like this?
Try . . . p.58

Chicago Transit Authority

Chicago Transit Authority

A benchmark for brass and guitar-fuelled jazz-rock.

At the tail end of the '60s rock big-band Chicago Transit Authority were peers and label mates with Santana, Janis Joplin, and Sly And The Family Stone. The band had honed their craft playing up to six sets a night on the bar band circuit. Based in Chicago and its suburbs, they had begun as Big Thing, changing their name to Chicago Transit Authority in May, 1967. In August they were spotted by manager James William Guercio, who was producing local Top 40 band The Buckinghams and would cut the break-through second album by Blood Sweat And Tears. Robert Lamm did most of the writing and Jim Pankow most of the arranging on their debut album, but Guercio played a crucial role, imposing tightness and economy.

For all the indulgence soon to be associated with rock LPs – not least Chicago's – their first album was recorded in just two weeks. It contains some great musical moments: the *Forever Changes*-style latin brass coda at the end of Beginnings, Kath's guitar sustain as he comes in after the lengthy percussion break in I'm A Man – his guitar runs are exemplary throughout when he's augmenting, not soloing. Then there's the "The whole world is watching" chant recorded from the demonstration at the 1968 Democratic Convention in Chicago. No band that learned its chops at the same time as Mayor Daly's law enforcers were cracking heads could have emerged from that bloody environment without comment – a great McLuhanesque soundbite from the days when it really did look like the revolution might be televised.

It hasn't all worn so well. Kath and Lamm's mannered rock growls and Cetera's wavery upper register do, in truth, grate a bit over the four sides. Strange to consider that their harmonies sounded sublime at the time. In essence that's Chicago. A greater-than-the-sum-of-their-parts outfit who, in their early days at least, soared majestically. Their second album was equally inspired, but dedicating it 'to the revolution' whilst being promoted with the big bucks of the CBS rock machine merely aroused the ire of the rock press and the band's early critical acclaim rapidly wilted. Bludgeoning a fresh and inventive formula to death by issuing three consecutive double albums, and a live quadruple, in the space of two years didn't help matters either – so remember them this way.

Record Label:
Columbia
Produced
by James William Guercio.
Recorded
at CBS studios, New York
Released:
September 1969
Chart peaks:
9 (UK) 17 (US)
Personnel:
Peter Cetera (v); Terry Kath (g, v); Robert Lamm (k, v); James Pankow (tb); Daniel Seraphine (d); Walter Parazaider (woodwind; v) Lee Loughnane (t, v); Fred Catero (e)
Track Listing:
Introduction; Does Anybody Really Know What Time It Is?; Beginnings; Questions 67 And 68; Listen; Poem 58; Free Form Guitar; South California Purples; I'm A Man; Prologue August 29, 1968; Someday August 29, 1968; Liberation
Running time:
77.43
Current CD:
CRD3001
Further listening:
Chicago II
Further reading:
'Chicago At Carnegie Hall', from Psycotic Reactions And Carburetor Dung (Lester Bangs, 1988)
Like this?
Try . . . p.215
Like this?
Try . . . p.215

Scott Walker

Scott 4

Former heartthrob sheds last remaining fans with only entirely self-written album.

No career trajectory in pop matches Scott Walker's. As leader of the unrelated Walker Brothers, he was a teen idol with an audience even more hysterical than the Beatles' but by 1967 he'd grown heartily sick of performing for frenzied girls and recording for a largely unadventurous audience. Upon completing a mismatched and increasingly fraught tour with Jimi Hendrix and Engelbert Humperdinck in April 1967, the reclusive Walker went it alone.

His first solo albums, *Scott* and *Scott 2*, combined heavily orchestrated cover versions with a handful of originals that hinted at the complex, cryptic persona that would reach its fullest expression on *Scott 4*. Songs like 'Montague Terrace (In Blue)' and 'The Amorous Humphrey Plugg' indicated a writer drawn to the darker sides of human nature, more intrigued by psychological detail than was common in chart music. With *Scott 2* lodged at number one in the Spring of 1968, Walker was free to pursue his own inclinations further on *Scott 3*, which appeared in early 1968. Alongside his own increasingly wistful and elliptical material, on this classic Walker covered several songs by his hero Jacques Brel, the wry Belgian chronicler of continental low life whose blunt and darkly sexual songwriting was increasingly influencing his own material.

Scott 3 sold less well, but Walker had no intention of surrendering any of his newfound artistic freedom in order to regain chart supremacy. The sessions for *Scott 4* took place in Philips's Stanhope Place studios in mid-1969, produced (like its predecessors) by industry veteran Johnny Franz. The first track, 'The Seventh Seal', immediately establishes not only the record's mysterious, enigmatic mood, but also just how far Walker had come since his teen idol days. Over an insistent beat, ominous bells, jaunty castanets, prominent classical guitar, a ghostly choir and spaghetti Western strings, his voice is more resonant than ever as he asks 'Anyone seen a knight pass this way? / I saw him playing chess with death yesterday…'

Throughout the album his lyrics tread a fine line between abstruseness and romance, with one notable foray into politics, 'The Old Man's Back Again', a funky number which the sleeve tells us is 'dedicated to the Neo-Stalinist regime'. The arrangements are immaculate throughout, encompassing flourishes from various traditions – morose balalaika on 'Boy Child', pedal steel on the aching closer 'Rhymes of Goodbye' or the Hispanic swing of 'The Seventh Seal' – without being as overblown as before.

Walker's refusal to tour or give interviews to promote the record, and his insistence on its being released under his real name, Scott Engel, combined to ensure that it was barely promoted. Its failure to chart, though, still represented a shocking fall from grace. Walker had embarked on a path of his own, one that continues to baffle and confound to this day.

Record label:
Philips
Produced by
John Franz
Recorded
in Summer 1969
Released:
Autumn 1969
Chart Peaks:
None (UK) None (US)
Personnel:
Scott Walker (g, v); n/a.
Track listing:
The Seventh Seal; On Your Own Again; The World's Strongest Man; Angels of Ashes; Boy Child; Hero of the War; The Old Man's Back Again; Duchess; Get Behind Me; Rhymes of Goodbye.
Running Time:
32.36
Current CD:
available…
Further listening:
Scott 3 (1969); 'Til The Band Comes In (1970).
Further reading:
Scott Walker – A Deeper Shade of Blue (Watkinson / Anderson, 1994).
Like this?
Try . . . p.166

The Stooges

The Stooges

Debut from Michigan misfits, regarded by most as the world's punk pioneers

Rock music distilled down to its barest essentials, *The Stooges* still sounds fresher and more contemporary than most of the punk, alternative, glam and thrash-metal material it allegedly spawned in the ensuing decades. Fittingly, its recording was a perfect combination of planning and serendipity. Signed by Elektra as a kind of adjunct to leading Detroit band the MC5, The Stooges hit New York intent on capturing their live set, which comprised around four songs: "We had I Wanna Be Your Dog, 1969 and No Fun, along with We Will Fall," says guitarist Ron Asheton. "[Label boss Jac] Holzman goes, 'You got any more songs?' and we said, 'Oh yeah.' So we sat down in the Chelsea Hotel, came up with Little Doll, Real Cool Time and Not Right, we rehearsed it one time and did it all the next day, one take for each tune."

The Stooges' simplistic, gonzoid sound did not derive from mere stupidity; the minimal lyrics, mostly taken from Stooge in-house slang, were meant to echo the stripped down couplets of the bluesmen Iggy had heard in Chicago. The slow pace at which the band attack the songs adds a monumental, menacing undertone: "The tempos were a little slow because we were all constantly on pot," says Iggy. "When there was an audience the tempos would come up because we were shitting our collective little pants. But without the audience the dope took over!"

The day after their writing stint, The Stooges stacked up their Marshalls in the Hit Factory: "We stick our Marshalls on 10 and start doing our thing, and Cale's shouting 'No no no, you can't play this loud!'" says Asheton. "This was the only way we knew how to play, because the sound of the instruments, the power, was the catalyst to drive us on. So we went on strike. They couldn't believe it, we went into the sound booth, sat down and started smoking hash." Producer John Cale engineered a compromise, the band turned down one notch to 9, and the songs were recorded with minimal decorum. Iggy claims that Cale's "bizarre art mix" of the album was dumped after the singer staged a tantrum in Jac Holzman's office; Iggy supervised the mix heard on the final version. Released to widespread indifference outside the band's Detroit stronghold, *The Stooges* scraped into the lower reaches of the American charts, and was deleted just a couple of years before every aspiring British punk guitarist started learning the iconic riffs to No Fun, 1969, and I Wanna Be Your Dog.

Record label:
Elektra
Produced
by John Cale.
Recorded
at Jerry Ragavoy's R&B Studio (later the Record Plant), New York; June 19–21 1969.
Released:
September 1969
Chart peaks:
None (UK) 106 (US)
Personnel:
Iggy Stooge (v); Ron Asheton (g); Scott Asheton (d); Dave Alexander (b)
Track listing:
1969; I Wanna Be Your Dog (S); We Will Fall; No Fun; Real Cool Time; Ann; Not Right; Little Doll
Running time:
34.24
Current CD:
EKS 47051
Further listening:
Fun House (1970) takes the basic blueprint one step further.
Further reading:
MOJO 29; www.rawiguana.com
Like this?
Try . . . p.842

Van Morrison

Astral Weeks

Van's first official solo album went beyond blues rock to a magical place many have tried to revisit since.

Released from his contract with Bert Berns's Bang Records, Van was free at last to explore his musical vision. With a handful of songs he went into Century Sound Studios in Manhattan and created a recording of such breathtaking originality that it sounded like a career pinnacle rather than a beginning.

He'd told his new managers Lewis Merenstein and Robert Schwaid that he was aiming for a "jazz feel". So jazz buff Schwaid recruited a quartet of crack New York sessionmen that included his bassist friend Richard Davis and drummer Connie Kay from The Modern Jazz Quartet. Shortly after Van's 23rd birthday, on the September 25 session, from 7–11pm they recorded Cyprus Avenue, Madame George, Beside You and Astral Weeks. Three weeks later the same musicians returned to record Sweet Thing, Ballerina, Young Lovers Do and Slim Slow Slider. String overdubs and the harpsichord on Cyprus Avenue were added by arranger Larry Fallon during mixing sessions, adding an unexpected texture to the basic tracks' jazz lilt, heightening the album's eerie, nostalgic mood.

Guitarist Jay Berliner hadn't heard of Van Morrison before the September 25 session and wasn't to hear the album until the late '70s when younger friends pointed out to him that he had contributed to a classic. "In those days I was so busy that I had no idea what I was playing on," recalls Berliner. "I played classical guitar [which] was very unusual in that context. We were used to playing to charts, but Van just played us the songs on his guitar and then told us to go ahead and play exactly what we felt." Although the finished tracks were essentially live takes, both Schwaid and John Payne remember the material being much longer during recording. "About five minutes of improvisational sax playing was cut from Slim Slow Slider," says Payne. "I was just jamming. It made me sick that they cut it out." (Tapes of the jams were given to Warner Brothers by Schwaid in the '70s but have never featured on any reissues.)

Although production was credited to Lewis Merenstein, Robert Schwaid and engineer Brooks Arthur (who owned Century Sound Studios), all played an important part in the sound. "In all fairness to Van, he was the one who was directing the taping," admits Schwaid. "Lew and I were in the control room but Van was the real producer." No one involved in the sessions can boast that they knew they were making a masterpiece. "I thought it was a great record at the time," says Schwaid, "but initially it was a failure. I don't think we did 20,000 copies. It wasn't until years later that people started to come up to me and tell me that their lives had been changed by *Astral Weeks*."

Record label:
Warner Brothers
Produced
by Lewis Merenstein.
Recorded
at Century Sound Studios, New York City; September 25 and October 15, 1968.
Released:
September 1969
Chart peaks:
None (UK) None (US)
Personnel:
Van Morrison (v, g); Jay Berliner (ag); Richard Davis (b); Connie Kay (d); John Payne (flute, soprano s); Warren Smith Jr (pc, vibraphone); Larry Fallon (oa); Brooks Arthur (e)
Track listing:
Astral Weeks; Beside You; Sweet Thing; Cyprus Avenue; Young Lovers Do; Madame George; Ballerina; Slim Slow Slider
Running time:
47.14
Current CD:
7599271762
Further listening:
Tupelo Honey (1971); St. Dominic's Preview (1972); Veedon Fleece (1974)
Further reading:
Van Morrison: Too Late To Stop Now (Steve Turner 1993); Celtic Crossroads: The Art Of Van Morrison (Alan Clayson and Brian Hinton, 1997); Van Morrison (John Collis, 1998)
Like this?
Try . . . p.477

King Crimson

In The Court Of The Crimson King

A bunch of unknown British jazz-rock virtuosos and their pet wordsmith define prog rock with their ambitious debut.

This intense brew of classical melodies, jazz and hard rock, matched with fantastical lyrics – and housed in an intriguing, lurid sleeve – created the template for progressive rock. All the more remarkable, then, that the music was created in a week.

Michael Giles and Robert Fripp had briefly been together in a band called Brain and moved in a folky direction as a trio, Giles, Giles & Fripp (with Michael's brother Peter), cutting one poor-selling album *The Cheerful Insanity Of . . .*, and a single which featured former Army bandsman Ian McDonald as a guest. Greg Lake, a schoolfriend of Fripp's and former member of The Gods, joined, Peter Giles left and the new quartet scored a management deal, a John Peel session and a three-month residency at the Marquee Club in London under the name King Crimson. Pete Sinfield, an associate of McDonald's, was recruited as a roadie and lyricist. They began work on the album shortly after appearing in front of 600,000 people at The Rolling Stones free concert in Hyde Park.

Because of Robert Fripp's subsequent takeover of the group, *In The Court Of The Crimson King* is often wrongly assumed to be largely his record. But it was a collective effort. A session with Moody Blues producer Tony Clark fell apart and the band quickly concluded they could work better by themselves. Ian McDonald, who wrote much of the music, recalls: "We recorded it in eight days, very quickly. There was no argument about anything. We just knew if an idea was usable and if it wasn't there was no fighting." They employed whatever came to hand in the studio: all the keys on an ancient pipe organ were jammed down to create the wheezy industrial noises that open the record. A Mellotron was used for the grandiose backdrop to the title track. McDonald grabbed a set of vibes for Illusion, the last segment of Moonchild. This meandering trilogy – which Fripp now admits should probably have been edited – was improvised when they realised they'd used all their original material but were reluctant to record a cover version.

The album was released to wide acclaim, Pete Townshend declaring it "an uncanny masterpiece". But some pundits (and anyone who liked to dance) were suspicious; critic Lester Bangs condemned it as an unholy mix of "myth, mystification and Mellotrons". Nonetheless, the album quickly climbed the charts. But within four months the line-up had fallen apart, exhausted by touring and the pressure of sudden success. Says Fripp, "Some of the musical vocabulary may seem dated now, but there's still something remarkable there waiting for listeners."

Record Label:
Island
Produced
by King Crimson.
Recorded
at Wessex Sound Studios, London; July 1969.
Released:
October, 10 1969
Chart peaks:
5 (UK) 28 (US)
Personnel:
Robert Fripp (g); Ian McDonald (reeds, woodwind, vibes, k, v, Mellotron); Greg Lake (b, v); Michael Giles (d, pc, v); Peter Sinfield (words, illumination)
Track Listing:
21st Century Schizoid Man (S) (including Mirrors); I Talk To The Wind; Epitaph (including March For No Reason; Tomorrow And Tomorrow); Moonchild (including The Dream; The Illusion); The Court Of The Crimson King (S) (including The Return Of The Fire Witch; The Dance Of The Puppets)
Running time:
43.54
Current CD:
EGCD1
Further listening:
Fripp and Sinfield taped the rest of the line-up's material on In The Wake Of Poseidon (1970). Cirkus (1999) is a good two CD round-up of 30 years of Crimson.
Further reading:
MOJO 73; Robert Fripp (Eric Tamm, 1990); www.elephant-talk.com; www.disciplineglobalmobile.com/kingcrimson/
Like this?
Try . . . p.37

Frank Zappa

Hot Rats

Instrumental, jam-heavy fusion masterpiece.

The arrival of *Uncle Meat* in the spring of 1969 made Zappa's frustrations abundantly clear: his love of satire and talent for outrage were clearly denying him recognition as a composer. Its comparative simplicity, downplayed lyrics and a sleeve note advertising the joys of something called "overdubbing", set the stage for its immortal successor six months later. The almost entirely instrumental *Hot Rats* was the perfect Zappa release for those intrigued by his music but bored – or possibly repulsed – by his wit and somewhat twisted worldview. It remains his biggest seller in the UK where its cover – GTO stalwart Christine Frka in an abandoned swimming-pool – so perfectly captured the progressive mood of the period. Lured by the possibilities of its 16-track desk, Zappa repaired to Sunset Sound and installed the most accomplished collection of West Coast veterans that money could buy – Paul Humphrey had drummed with Wes Montgomery and Lee Konitz, bassist Max Bennett was a Hollywood studio legend who'd worked with Quincy Jones and Peggy Lee, Sugarcane Harris had pioneered R&B hits in the late '50s as part of the duo Don & Dewey. Together they cut a series of superbly drilled compositions combining a fiercely hip (and uniquely American) technical proficiency and a peerless ability to improvise, much of its ornate embroidery the result of Zappa and Underwood's jazz and classical influences.

"It was extremely interesting because the music was interesting," Underwood reflects. It took two months of relentless multi-tracking to perfect, with many of Underwood's original parts eventually erased by the composer. "*Hot Rats* was more about overdubbing than anything else," Zappa remembered. It also made much of that sonic device du jour, the wah-wah pedal, of which Zappa was the absolute master. The only vocal on the entire album – the growling blues delivery of Willie The Pimp – was supplied by fellow art-rock alchemist and former schoolfriend Captain Beefheart. The lyrics coming from an interview conducted by Zappa with a New York-based groupie called Annie. "It was kind of a turn from the way the (earlier) band had been," Underwood remembers. "It was a chance just to use a few studio musicians and try other routines out."

Record label:
Reprise
Produced
by Frank Zappa.
Recorded
at Sunset Sound Studio, Los Angeles; August–September 1969.
Released:
October 10, 1969
Chart peaks:
9 (UK) 173 (US)
Personnel:
Frank Zappa (g, octave b, pc); Ian Underwood (p, organus maximus, flute, clarinet, s); Captain Beefheart (v on Willie The Pimp); Don 'Sugarcane' Harris, Jean Luc Ponty (vn); Max Bennett, Shuggy Otis (b); John Guerin, Paul Humphrey, Ron Selico (d); Cliff Goldstein, Jack Hunt, Dick Kunc (e)
Track Listing:
Peaches En Regalia; Willie The Pimp; Son Of Mr Green Genes; Little Umbrellas; The Gumbo Variations; It Must Be A Camel
Running time:
47.17
Current CD:
Ryko RCD 10508
Further listening:
Uncle Meat (1969); Mystery Disc (1998)
Further reading:
MOJO 4; Waiting For The Sun (Barney Hoskyns, 1996); Frank Zappa In His Own Words (1993); The Negative Dialectics Of Poodle Play (Ben Watson, 1996); The Complete Guide To The Music Of Frank Zappa (Ben Watson, 1998
Oar Alexander Spence
Like this?
Try . . . p.412

Alexander Spence

Oar

Among the most enigmatic solo albums in all of pop music.

The man who walked into Columbia studios in Nashville in December 1968 to make *Oar* was a man with a troubled history. Alexander "Skip" Spence had fallen out of Moby Grape in New York earlier that year, soon after the release of *Wow*, their excessive (but mostly superb) second album. He did not have a good time in the Big Apple; the large quantities of psychedelic drugs Spence consumed took their toll on the man. Following a violent studio incident in July 1968 in which he went after his fellow Grapesters with an axe – truly, rock criticism of the harshest sort – Spence was arrested and eventually committed to New York's Bellevue Hospital for six months. When he emerged, Columbia – amazingly – gave him the opportunity to record again and bankrolled the Nashville sessions that would comprise *Oar*. And what very weird sessions they were.

Among *Oar*'s major claims to fame is its status as one of the very first true solo, multi-tracked rock recordings. Spence indeed played and sang every note on the album – guitar, bass, drums and unforgettably intimate vocals included – in a series of sessions that in fact took several days, despite the album's back-cover claim of a one-day affair. Still, the looseness of the songs, the haphazard rhythms and fade-in/fade-out guitar overdubs, made that claim believable, which only added to the album's mystique. Then again, there were the songs themselves. One could easily imagine him making them up while staring at the walls of the mental hospital he had just spent a half-year in.

"I remember him," says Mike Figlio, the Columbia engineer most intimately involved in the making of the record. "He was kind of a way-out cat, creative, knew what he wanted. He just did one instrument at a time, just kept building it – and once we got it all down as far as instruments, he and I sat in the studio and decided how we wanted to mix it and how we wanted to make it sound."

"I think it's genius," Moby Grape guitarist Jerry Miller now says of *Oar*. But at the time, Columbia Records didn't agree – which might be a major reason the album sold minimally and was (despite favourable reviews) quickly deleted. "I think they humoured him. Not that they didn't promote it – but I don't know how they could've ever thought it was mainstream enough to *do* anything with."

Record label:
CBS
Produced
by Alexander Spence.
Recorded
at Columbia Studios, Nashville, Tennessee; December 16, 1968.
Released:
October 1969
Chart peaks:
None (UK) None (US)
Track listing:
Alexander Spence (all instruments); Charlie Bradley, Mike Figlio, Don Meehan (e)
Track listing:
Little Hands; Cripple Creek; Diana; Margaret-Tiger Rug; Weighted Down; War In Peace; Broken Heart; All Come To Meet Her; Books Of Moses; Dixie Peach Promenade; Lawrence Of Euphoria; Grey; Afro
Running time:
60.39
Current CD:
SC 11075 adds: This Time He Has Come; It's The Best Thing For You; Keep Everything Under Your Hat; Furry Heroine (Halo Of Gold); Givin' Up Things; If I'm Good; You Know; Doodle; Fountain; I Think You And I
Further listening:
Moby Grape, Moby Grape (1967); Oar tribute album, More Oar (1999)
Further reading:
The official Moby Grape website www.mobygrape.net/
Like this?
Try . . . p.601

The Mandrake Memorial

Puzzle

Psychedelic delight from Philadelphia.

A stunning set upon its 1969 arrival – both because of its gorgeous packaging (Escher graphic, Milton Glaser design) and the even more beautiful music within – *Puzzle* is unlike any album you've likely heard. The final LP by this highly regarded Philadelphia-based band, it smoothly blends slightly trippy, ballad-laced rock with full orchestration and chorale and seduces with every listen. With vague lyrics that pop in and out of focus intermittently, including such snippets as "my dolphin friend and I", and the recurring reality check Just A Blur, one is left with the impression that the LSD has unexpectedly, suddenly, just kicked in.

Actually the second attempt at making the same album – the first, much more acoustic version had been recorded in the UK months earlier with producer Shel Talmy but didn't work out – *Puzzle* is notably juiced by the participation of onetime Melanie producer Frangipane.

"He was actually the guy who wanted to add all the orchestral things," notes Mandrake's guitarist and prescient electronics whiz, Craig Anderton. "He saw us play live a couple of times, and he always felt that we were pushing for something grander and bigger in our onstage thing, which we always were. For three people, we made a lot of noise."

Conspicuously impressed was famed classical conductor Seiji Ozawa – so much so that his quote calling *Puzzle* a musical masterpiece appeared in several ads Poppy Records took out in the pop press at the time.

"Actually, there's a terrible story about that," says Anderton. "We were supposed to do a promotional appearance with him, and I had come down with this horrible, horrible flu, and so had our bass player – so the only person who got to meet him was the drummer. I had to call up and cancel, which was just horrible because I really wanted to meet this guy – you know, Seiji Ozawa, *wow*. And I think he was kind of offended that only one of us showed up. But I didn't want to be responsible for reading in the paper 'Seiji Ozawa cancels concert tour owing to flu.' It was kind of unfortunate."

The band would follow-up the album with a final single, a relatively unnecessary cover of Thunderclap Newman's Something In The Air. One listen to *Puzzle*, and you'll suspect something was indeed.

Record label:
Poppy
Produced
by Ronald Frangipane.
Recorded
at Century Sound Recording Studios, New York; 1969.
Released:
autumn 1969
Chart peaks:
None (UK) None (US)
Personnel:
Kevin Lally (d); Randy Monaco (b, v); Craig Anderton (g); Brooks Arthur (e)
Track listing:
Earthfriend Prelude; Earthfriend; Just A Blur (Version 1); Hiding; Just A Blur (Version 2); Tadpole; Kyrie; Ocean's Daughter; Volcano Prelude; Volcano; Whisper Play; Bucket Of Air; Children's Prayer; Puzzle; Just A Blur (Version 3)
Running time:
47.30
Current CD:
Collectables MMCD 013 adds Something In The Air
Further listening:
Mandrake Memorial (1968); Medium (1969)
Further reading:
M.C. Escher: His Life And Complete Graphic Work (Harry N Abrams, 1992)
Like this?
Try . . . p.150

The Grateful Dead

Live/Dead

The Dead at their improvisational best.

In the autumn of 1969, having spent eight months in the studio recording *Aoxomoxoa*, The Grateful Dead were deep in debt to Warner Bros. No one was so stoned or unrealistic as to believe that the highly experimental *Aoxomoxoa* was going to recoup all that money, so someone had a bright idea: put out a live album, easily culled from the many shows the band was playing in the Bay Area. Not only would such an album finally showcase the band at its spacey, jamming best, it would be incredibly cheap to make.

The Dead took a state-of-the-art 16-track recorder to gigs at the Avalon and Carousel ballrooms, and from those shows came *Live/Dead*, a double album that, according to Lenny Kaye's review in Rolling Stone, "explains why the Dead are one of the best performing bands in America, why their music touches on ground that most other groups don't even know exists." The album kicks off with a great version of Dark Star, 23 minutes of jazzy jamming. "They'd usually only play Dark Star if they were pretty high," said Caroline 'Mountain Girl' Garcia. Not just high: this is music from deepest space, as if someone had recorded the sound of a star exploding then slowed it down to its dreamy, pulsing elements. The song's great appeal was that no one – neither audience nor band – knew where it was headed.

"People loved it for the mystery of it," said manager Rock Scully. Robert Hunter's first lyrics for the Dead speak volumes about where the band was coming from at the end of the '60s: "Shall we go, you and I while we can?/Through the transitive nightfall of diamonds." While clearly this was music for altered states, the band were always quick to point out that pulling it off required plenty of rehearsal time. Phil Lesh's The Eleven, named for its highly unusual 11/4 time signature, was based on the rhythmic calisthenics the band performed during practice, in which part of the band played 11 beats while the rest played 33 or even 66. "It was really designed to be a rhythm trip," said Lesh. "It wasn't designed to be a song."

The Dead were genuinely experimental, following each other down strange paths and hoping they'd find their way back, as on the frenzied storm of noise that is Feedback. "It was like somebody tossing a bloody chicken into a school of pirhanas," marvelled Mickey Hart. "For a few minutes you'd be out on the edge with the roaring animal all around you, and it was always an open question whether it was going to go back into its cage or not."

Record label:
Warner Bros
Produced
by The Grateful Dead, Bob Matthews and Betty Cantor.
Recorded
at Avalon and Carousel ballrooms, San Francisco; summer of 1969.
Released:
November 10, 1969
Chart peaks:
None (UK) 64 (US)
Personnel:
Jerry Garcia (g, v); Bob Weir (g, v); Phil Lesh (b, v); Mickey Hart (pc); Bill Kreutzmann (pc); Pigpen, aka Ron McKernan (o, congas, v); Tom Constanten (k)
Track listing:
Dark Star; Saint Stephen; The Eleven; Turn On Your Lovelight; Death Don't Have No Mercy; Feedback; And We Bid You Tonight
Running time:
73.05
Current CD:
7599271812
Further listening:
Anthem of the Sun (1968); the two-CD Fillmore East: 2/11/69 (1997); or the five-CD So Many Roads (1965–95) (1999).
Further reading:
There are almost literally more books, fanzines and websites than you can count. The American Book Of The Dead: The Definitive Grateful Dead Encyclopedia (Oliver Trager, 1997) is a start. Also, Dead to the Core: An Almanack Of The Grateful Dead (Eric Wybenga, 1994) and Garcia, by the editors of Rolling Stone (1999). www.dead.net/
Like this?
Try . . . p.766

Kevin Ayers

Joy Of A Toy

Urbane ex-Soft Machine chap goes to Majorca and pens a slice of classic 'anglodelica'.

Taking its name from a track on Soft Machine One, which in turn had been taken from an Ornette Coleman composition, *Joy Of A Toy* evocatively captured its performer before he was burdened with the trappings of cultdom or the requirements of trying to be a pop star. Although he'd retreated to Majorca to write the songs for this album only the singalong title track, The Clarietta Rag, and Oleh Oleh Bandu Bandong convey any sense of carefree sunny climes (and the latter was mainly a legacy of Ayers' colonial upbringing in Malaya, at that). In fact *Joy Of A To* is an unmistakably English, at times (as on the sombre Town Feeling) resolutely urban record full of drizzly streets and hungover memories of last night's party.

Song For Insane Times, a bittersweet freeze frame full of astute cameos, perfectly captures the post-Summer Of Love spirit of ennui, disillusion and detachment that was abroad in the late-'60s. Both lyrically and musically it would have sat easily on Soft Machine Two had Ayers stayed with the band he helped form. (Incidentally, the voice captured in a snatch of studio dialogue at the beginning of Song For Insane Times, for a long time rumoured to be Syd Barrett, is in fact Robert Wyatt.) Lady Rachel, a mainstay of Ayers' live set, was written for his daughter. Girl On A Swing shimmers like heat haze on a summer's day with some beautifully delicate piano played by arranger David Bedford (soon to join Ayers' band The Whole World). Stop This Train (Again Doing It) was, like Why Are We Sleeping? on Soft Machine One, inspired by the teachings of Gurdjieff, the mystic and philosopher who has also inspired the music of Robert Fripp, Kate Bush, and Keith Jarrett, among others.

"Gurdjieff's teachings were the lightening bolts that formulated my later ideas," Ayers told MOJO. "You develop a fairly comfortable little story and then slip something startling in as if nothing had happened." *Joy Of A Toy* is full of such moments. As the man once said, "Banana".

Record label:
Harvest
Produced
by Peter Jenner.
Recorded
at EMI Studios, London; 1969
Released:
November 1969
Chart peaks:
None (UK) None (US)
Personnel:
Kevin Ayers (g, v); Robert Wyatt (d); Mike Ratledge (k); Hugh Hopper (b); Rob Tait (d); David Bedford (k, p); Peter Mew (e); Sean Murphy (e); Ian Knight (e)
Track listing:
Joy Of A Toy; Town Feeling; Clarretta Rag; Girl On A Swing; Song For Insane Times; Stop This Train (Again Doing It); Eleanor's Cake (Which Ate Her); Lady Rachel; Oleh Oleh Bandu Bandong; All This Crazy Gift Of Time
Running time:
41.30
Current CD:
Beat Goes On BGOCD 78
Further listening:
Whatevershebringswesing (1970)
Further reading:
Why Are We Sleeping fanzine; www.users.globalnet.co.uk/~marwak/
Like this?
Try . . . p.51

Captain Beefheart And His Magic Band

Trout Mask Replica

The most radical-sounding record of the 1960s.

In 1968, a revamped Magic Band moved into a rented house in Woodland Hills, near Los Angeles, and set about rehearsing the music for *Trout Mask Replica. Safe As Milk* and the full-blown acid rock of *Strictly Personal* had made the group's reputation, but now signed to Frank Zappa's new Straight label, Beefheart – aka Don Van Vliet – was about to make his art statement. To avoid any confusion arising from his musical instructions and whistled lines, he set about composing on the piano. Technically, he couldn't really play the instrument, but at this point he had confidence to spare.

Beefheart had put the brakes on his voracious consumption of LSD but was convinced the house was built on a native American burial ground, and claimed he talked to the spirits. Meanwhile the group spent six months in grinding poverty learning John (Drumbo) French's transcriptions of Don's piano outpourings – which were often overlaid in different keys and metres; a feat of superhuman dedication. Beefheart had given all the musicians new names and was becoming increasingly tyrannical. Problems like noise complaints from the neighbours were minor compared to elongated 'brainwashing' sessions, fist fights breaking out in the fractious atmosphere, and the group getting arrested during a shoplifting spree. By spring 1969 they were ready to make a 'field recording' in the house with Dick Kunc – a near neighbour, occasional house guest, and regular engineer on Zappa's music – bringing over his portable two-track Uher reel-to-reel.

"They were certainly well rehearsed. I seem to recall it was pretty much controlled chaos, with Don very much in command," he says. After a few tracks had been recorded, Beefheart insisted they use a proper studio, and they decamped to Whitney, in nearby Glendale. Although Kunc was "ready for anything" he admits that "as a neophyte to that galaxy of music at the time, I wondered how to tell the difference between good and not-so-good performances."

The album was recorded at breakneck speed and emerged as a massive scrapbook of free jazz, blues, rock and surreal poetry. Lester Bangs waxed rhapsodic in Rolling Stone, while others found it incomprehensible. In Britain, largely thanks to the patronage of John Peel's Top Gear, *Trout Mask Replica* almost broke into the top twenty and remains surprisingly popular for such an extreme record. In an HMV poll of customers' favourite albums in 1998, it ambled in at number 42, one place above Bowie's *Hunky Dory.*

Record label:
Straight/Reprise
Produced
by Frank Zappa.
Recorded
at Whitney Studios, Glendale, California and Ensenada Drive, Woodland Hills, California; March–April 1969.
Released:
November 1969
Chart peaks:
21 (UK) None (US)
Personnel:
Zoot Horn Rollo (g, flute); Antennae Jimmy Semens (g); Captain Beefheart (bass clarinet, ts, soprano sax, simran horn, musette, v); The Mascara Snake (bass clarinet, v); Rockette Morton (b, narration); Drumbo (d); Doug Moon (g); Dick Kunc (e)
Track listing:
Frownland; The Dust Blows Forward 'N The Dust Blows Back; Dachau Blues; Ella Guru; Hair Pie: Bake 1; Moonlight On Vermont; Pachuco Cadaver (S/France); Bills Corpse; Sweet Sweet Bulbs; Neon Meate Dream Of A Octafish; China Pig; My Human Gets Me Blues; Dali's Car; Hair Pie: Bake 2; Pena; Well; When Big Joan Sets Up; Fallin' Ditch; Sugar 'N Spikes; Ant Man Bee; Orange Claw Hammer; Wild Life; She's Too Much For My Mirror; Hobo Chang Ba; The Blimp (mousetrapreplica); Steal Softly Thru Snow; Old Fart At Play; Veteran's Day Poppy
Running time:
79.08
Current CD:
7599271962
Further listening:
Lick My Decals Off (1970)
Further reading:
MOJO 2; www.beefheart.com
Like this?
Try . . . p.401

Creedence Clearwater Revival

Green River

Third album from archetypal roots-rockers. Internal schisms forming.

Green River was CCR's second album of 1969 and John Fogerty, their driven front-man, assumed even more power during its making – banning the rest of the band from the studio during the mix. Drummer Doug Clifford remembers: "It was like, 'Turn in your key'. It was a lock-out. We were allowed back in for 10 minutes to do the 'wah doo days' on The Night Time Is The Right Time!"

"I just refused to let them be there because it was so disruptive," explains Fogerty. "It was a go-around I had with Tom for the whole three years we were Creedence. He kept saying, 'My part's not loud enough.' The truth is, I would write the song, and then the producer in me would take over and write the arrangement, and I would show everyone *exactly* how it went." Clifford recollects things differently. "The good news was that I was the only drummer in the band, and he was less stringent with me than with the other guys. All the groovy little things I put in got to stay." Such as the spine-tingling high-hat work at the end of the Mephistophelean swamp-rock of Sinister Purpose? "That was pure instinct; it was just a natural process."

The tension between the players is also manifest in the subject matter of several tracks. The titles shout for themselves – Commotion, Tombstone Shadow, Bad Moon Rising.

"If there wasn't a demon there John would invent one," bassist Stu Cook reckons, "which was great when he was writing!" And in the writing *Green River* is almost faultless. From the churning, nostalgic Country R&B of the title track to the Sun-era rockabilly bounce of Cross-Tie Walker, Fogerty assimilated his influences perfectly and the band did him proud.

"The circumstances weren't exactly pleasant," muses Clifford, "but we did a job. We laid down the basic tracks in two days or so, and then waited to hear the record!"

"Some of the initial playback tapes sounded better than the final product," remembers Stu Cook, "but I suppose it was partly our fault for letting him get away with it." Despite these problems, the album represents the pinnacle of Creedence's achievement, and thus one of the high-points of late '60s American Rock. Fogerty agrees. "My favourite album is *Green River*. That's the soul of where I live musically, the closest to what's in my heart."

Record label:
Fantasy
Produced
by John Fogerty.
Recorded
at Wally Heider Studio, San Francisco
Released:
December 1969
Chart peaks:
20 (UK) 1 (US)
Personnel:
John Fogerty (v, g); Tom Fogerty (g, bv); Stu Cook (b, bv); Doug Clifford (d); Russ Gary (e)
Track listing:
Green River (S); Commotion; Tombstone Shadow; Wrote A Song For Everyone; Bad Moon Rising (S); Lodi; Cross-Tie Walker; Sinister Purpose; The Night Time Is The Right Time
Running time:
29.20
Current CD:
FCD24 8393-2
Further listening:
Bayou Country (1969); Willy And The Poor Boys (1970); Cosmo's Factory (1970); The Blue Ridge Rangers: Blue Ridge Rangers (1973), essentially a John Fogerty solo album of country covers, lovingly rendered.
Further reading:
Bad Moon Rising: The Unofficial Story Of Creedence Clearwater Revival (Hank Bordowitz, 1998); Up Around The Bend: The Oral History Of Creedence Clearwater Revival (Craig Werner, 1998)
Like this?
Try . . . p.622

Fairport Convention

Liege And Lief

The first British electric folk album.

"The thing is," said Dave Swarbrick in that informal, matey way he has of cutting right to the chase, "if you're singing about a bloke having his head chopped off or a girl screwing her brother and having a baby and the brother cutting her guts open, stamping on the baby and killing his sister, that's a fantastic story by anybody's standards. Working with a storyline like that with acoustic instruments wouldn't be half as potent as saying the same things electrically."

Applying rock arrangements to traditional ballads which so outraged folk purists when Fairport first tried it. It was bass player Ashley Hutchings, the Fairport member with the least folk credentials, who pushed hardest for the unequivocal move into traditional song, courting Sandy Denny and Dave Swarbrick for the band and driving even them to distraction with his obsessive fascination with the potential of folk song. It still didn't sway everyone. Despite the contributions of Sandy and Swarb the folk world still regarded them as chancers, while rock fans frowned in confusion at their move away from more commercial West Coast roots. Rolling Stone dismissed the album as "boring".

Even Richard Thompson later conceded that he felt it was artificial and contrived, yet *Liege And Lief* left an indelible mark on both the folk and rock worlds, providing a reference point for Steeleye Span, the Albion Band and many others to follow. The recording sessions were stormy, and rifts over the controversial new direction went so deep the group was in tatters even before the album was released. Hutchings and Denny, both quit in the wake of quarrels in the studio. Denny had already had her fill singing ballads in folk clubs and was more interested in writing her own material. Hutchings was concerned his dream wouldn't materialise with Fairport, especially with Thompson also keen to develop his own writing, and he resolved to form Steeleye Span with musicians more entrenched in the folk world. So *Liege And Lief*'s often thrilling amalgam of ancient and modern was both a beginning and an end.

Record label:
Island
Produced
by Joe Boyd.
Recorded
at Sound Techniques, London; June-July 1969.
Released:
December, 1969.
Chart peaks:
17 (UK) None (US)
Personnel:
Dave Swarbrick (v, mandolin, v, va); Sandy Denny (v, g); Richard Thompson (g); Ashley Hutchings (g, b, v); Simon Nicol (g, v); Dave Mattacks (d); John Wood (e)
Track listing:
Come All Ye; Reynardine; Matty Groves; Farewell Farewell; The Deserter; The Lark In The Morning; Tam Lin; Crazy Man Michael
Running time:
36.33
Current CD:
IMCD60
Further listening:
For a similar excursion into folk-rock check out Unhalfbricking (1969), or Fotheringay, the band formed by Sandy Denny following her departure.
Further reading:
Meet On The Ledge: A History Of Fairport Convention (Patrick Humphries, 1997)
Like this?
Try . . . p.239

The 1970s

Simon & Garfunkel

Bridge Over Troubled Water

A generation-defining, multi-platinum farewell to the '60s.

By the time Simon & Garfunkel came to make *Bridge Over Troubled Water*, they were drifting apart. Art was preoccupied with his acting career and, consequently, Paul felt he was no longer pulling his weight.

"It was a tough album to make," Garfunkel has admitted, "but tough is one of the words that leads to great results." That it still stands as their definitive statement is a measure of Simon's tendency to shine brightest in adversity.

According to Simon, "I knew the minute I wrote, 'Like a bridge over troubled water I will lay me down,' that I had a very clear image. The whole verse was set up to hit that melody line. With certain songs you just know it." Even so, he remembers the original demo as "a much less grandiose thing than the record. In fact, it wasn't grandiose at all. It was a humble, little gospel hymn song with two verses and a simple guitar behind it." Embellished with a Spector-ish production and a staggering arrangement, it has since made its presence felt in virtually every poll of best-ever singles.

The Boxer emerges as another astonishing achievement and, in some ways, a more satisfying song than Bridge, with its rippling guitar soaring into the 'lie-la-lie' hook (written because Simon couldn't think of any words) set against Roy Halee's brilliantly engineered percussion effects (the signature explosive snare crack was recorded in an echoing CBS stairwell, one night when the building had been vacated), rising towards the haunting, primitive, synthesiser solo, climaxing with celestial strings and synth-bass drones before fading finally into Simon's lonesome acoustic picking.

Fellow musicians were blown away. "It's a great record," declared Sandy Denny, "fantastically produced." Some critics, however, were less perceptive. "Their music has gotten stale," opined Rolling Stone's Gregg Mitchell. "Everything they play, someone else has played before." Joe Public disagreed. On February 21, 1970, the album entered the UK chart at Number 1, a position it held for a staggering 35 weeks topping both UK and US charts. Ironically, just as the duo had split before their first hit Sounds Of Silence in 1965, by the time Bridge Over Troubled Water scooped six Grammys, on March 16, 1971, Paul Simon was a solo artist.

Record Label:
CBS
Produced
by Paul Simon, Arthur Garfunkel and Roy Halee.
Recorded
in New York and Los Angeles; June 13, 1968–November 19, 1969.
Chart peaks:
1 (UK) 1 (US)
Released:
January 26, 1970
Personnel:
Paul Simon (g, v); Art Garfunkel (v); Larry Knechtel (k); Fred Carter Jr (g); Hal Blaine (d); Joe Osborn (b); Jimmy Haskell, Ernie Freeman (oa)
Track Listing:
Bridge Over Troubled Water (S); El Condor Pasa (If I Could) (S); Cecilia (S); Keep The Customer Satisfied; So Long, Frank Lloyd Wright; The Boxer; Baby Driver; The Only Living Boy In New York; Why Don't You Write Me; Bye Bye Love; Song For The Asking
Running time:
837.26
Current CD:
Columbia 4624882
Further listening:
Any hits compilation, or their second greatest album, Parsley, Sage, Rosemary & Thyme (1966)
Further reading:
MOJO 50; Simon And Garfunkel: The Definitive Biography (Victoria Kingston, 1997)
Like this?
Try . . . p.506

The Band
The Band
The definitive Americana classic.

A consistently high scorer in polls of the greatest albums of all time – especially amongst fellow musicians – The Band's second album had the peculiar quality of sounding as if it had existed for decades, the very first time you heard it. This impression was partly due to the richly-textured arrangements, which employed mandolin, fiddle, accordion and various arcane wind instruments alongside the group's basic instrumentation; partly to the distinctive vocal harmonies, whose soulful bluegrass intervals contravened the smooth West Coast close-harmony style of the times; and partly to the evocative lyrics, which seemed to traverse the entire course of American history in a dozen songs, relating events through the voices of ordinary working-class folk at work, rest, play and war.

Relocating to Los Angeles in February 1969 to record the songs they had been developing since their debut *Music From Big Pink*, the group rented Sammy Davis Jr's house in the Hollywood Hills, living in the various suites and converting the pool-house into a studio. When Capitol Records were a month late installing the recording equipment, the band used what Richard Manuel called "them high-school fat-girl diet pills" to help them meet the tight schedule, though they still had to finish three songs back in New York. Levon Helm found a set of drums with wooden rims in a Hollywood pawnshop – "old-fashioned instruments, but they read well on the microphones" – which added their own distinctive flavour to the album, and Garth Hudson was as diligent as ever in his search for the appropriate sound, frequently staying late "sweetening" the tracks with extra layers of horns, keyboards, "whatever was needed to make that music sing".

Flashy solos were a rarity, each instrumental part being sublimated to a song's overall feel. They made an even bigger break with the era's virtuosic tendencies by swapping instruments around amongst themselves and making a virtue of their limitations. Rag Mama Rag – a Top 20 UK hit in 1970 – featured the drummer playing mandolin, the pianist playing drums, the bassist playing fiddle, the organist playing piano, and co-producer John Simon playing tuba (for the first time in his life!). Rarely has an album been greeted with quite as much acclaim as *The Band*, as critics marvelled at its musical depth and range of styles, with the Village Voice claiming it was "beyond anything in rock except some of The Beatles' best work."

Record label:
Capitol
Produced
by The Band and John Simon.
Recorded
at Sammy Davis Jr's pool house, Sunset Plaza Drive, Los Angeles; February–April 1969; and The Hit Factory, New York; April 1969.
Released:
January 1970
Chart peaks:
25 (UK) 9 (US)
Personnel:
Garth Hudson (k, s, acc, slide trombone); Richard Manuel (v, k, d, s, mouth harp); Levon Helm (v, d, g, mandolin); Rick Danko (vn, b, v, tb); Jaime Robbie Robertson (g, e); John Simon (tuba, k, high school and peck horns, e); Joe Zagarino (e)
Track listing:
Across The Great Divide; Rag Mama Rag (S/UK); The Night They Drove Old Dixie Down; When You Awake; Up On Cripple Creek (S); Whispering Pines; Jemima Surrender; Rockin' Chair; Look Out Cleveland; Jawbone; The Unfaithful Servant; King Harvest (Has Surely Come)
Running time:
43.58
Current CD:
CDP 746493 2
Further listening:
The Band's debut Music From Big Pink (1968) remains a classic; of their other albums, Stage Fright (1970), Northern Lights – Southern Cross (1975) and the live triple-album Rock Of Ages (1972) are all worth investigating.
Further reading:
Across The Great Divide (Barney Hoskyns, 1993); This Wheel's On Fire (Levon Helm with Stephen Davis, 1993)
Like this?
Try . . . p.835

Syd Barrett

The Madcap Laughs

Pink Floyd's usurped frontman makes his first solo album. Somehow.

Listening to *The Madcap Laughs* is like watching a man fooling around on a cliff-edge. Evidence of Barrett's original musical genius and exquisite painterly lyricism ("Pussy willow that smiled on this leaf") is shaded by evidence of his impending mental collapse ("My head touched the ground/I was half the way down"). This makes for some distinctly uneasy, at times voyeuristic, listening.

The album was painstakingly put together in three stages. Floyd manager Peter Jenner produced the first sessions between May and July 1968, which were largely fruitless. Silas Lang, Swan Lee and Lanky weren't pursued further, Clowns And Jugglers became Octopus, a wonderfully off-kilter attempt to emulate Green Grow The Rushes O. Syd frittered away the next few months, occasionally turning up unannounced backstage at Top Of The Pops, where he liked to hang out. Finally Harvest's head Malcolm Jones appointed himself producer in April 1969 and drafted in Soft Machine to help out on No Good Trying, but Syd was beginning to lose his grip. "Every time he played a tune through, the bars before the chord change were different," says Soft Machine's keyboard player Mike Ratledge. "You had to watch his hands. It was the only way you could follow what was going on."

Exasperated, Jones asked Dave Gilmour and Roger Waters to help out in June 1969. They finished the album in a matter of days. The haste of those sessions is exemplified by the sequence of She Took A Long Cold, Look, Feel and If Its In You which include Syd's audibly agitated studio chatter and wildly out-of-tune first takes. But glimpses of the Barrett genius linger in Late Night, with its gossamer-light slide guitar and tender lyric, the brooding menace of Dark Globe, the starkly beautiful adaptation of James Joyce's poem Golden Hair, Octopus and No Good Trying. Syd was upbeat upon its release, promoting the album with interviews and a session for John Peel's Top Gear, before going into the studio with Gilmour to record a follow-up, *Barrett,* which was even more chaotic. In his 1973 NME appraisal, The Cracked Ballad Of Syd Barrett, journalist Nick Kent accurately called these thirteen songs, "exercises in distance". They make up a strange, poignant album, so tangential it refuses to yield up its inner logic.

Record label:
Harvest
Produced
by David Gilmour, Roger Waters and Malcolm Jones.
Recorded
at Abbey Road Studios, May 1968 – June 1969
Released:
January 1970
Chart peaks:
40 (UK) None (US)
Personnel:
Syd Barrett (g, v); Willie Wilson (b); Jerry Shirley (d); Hugh Hopper (b); Robert Wyatt (d); Mike Ratledge (k); Jeff Jarratt, Pete Mew, Mike Sheady, Phil Mcdonald (e)
Track listing:
Terrapin; No Good Trying; Love You; No Man's Land; Dark Globe; Here I Go; Octopus (S); Golden Hair; Long Gone; She Took A Long Cold Look; Feel; If It's In You; Late Night
Running time:
39.00
Current CD:
CDGO 2053
Further listening:
The even more hard-won follow-up Barrett (1970); the subsequent collection of outtakes and fragments, Opel. Both form part of Crazy Diamond boxed set.
Further reading:
MOJO 34; The Dark Stuff: Selected Writings On Rock Music 1972–1993 (Nick Kent, 1995)
Like this?
Try . . . p.546

Miles Davis

Bitches Brew

Davis's first full-blown excursion into jazz-rock.

While Miles Davis had already broached the idea of jazz melding into rock with *In A Silent Way*, *Bitches Brew* was the real thing. It doesn't sound like other rock music, but it stood a country mile away from the post-bop and soul-jazz which Davis's contemporaries had been creating as their response to rock's take-over. Miles liked the style and the energy of rock, but he couldn't entertain any dumbing-down in his own music. So he sought players like McLaughlin, the young British bassist Dave Holland, and Chick Corea; spirits fresh enough to inject something new into his own outlook, but virtuosos in their own right. The previous record had been put together with a lot of post-production work, but for this set, Davis simply took his men into the studio for three days and set them off.

"It was just like one of them old-time jam sessions we used to have up at Minton's back in the old bebop days," enthused the leader. "Everybody was excited when we all left there each day." Teo Macero's main job was simply to let the tapes run and call the tunes.

The result was an album of six tracks, two of them breaking the 20-minute barrier, and all of them (bar the brief John McLaughlin) by turns spacey, frenetic, ferocious and even whimsically funky (Miles Runs The Voodoo Down). It sounds like a recipe for commercial disaster, but an audience that had grown used to the trance-like jamming of The Grateful Dead ate it up and put Miles in the charts. These were early days for recording this kind of thing, and although Columbia have since released an extensively cleaned-up set – *The Complete Bitches Brew Sessions* – much of it still sounds almost primitive, with its wayward guitar tone and clanking electric keyboards. Davis himself, though, always cuts through; the most modern sound on the record.

Not everyone saw *Brew* as an epiphany: many long-time Davis admirers were scathing in their condemnation. Perhaps the best summary was the sympathetic one offered some years later by Jack Bruce: "Miles wants to be Jimi Hendrix, but he can't work it out on trumpet".

Record label:
CBS
Produced
by Teo Macero.
Recorded
in New York City, August, 1969.
Released:
July 1970
Chart peaks:
71 (UK) 35 (US)
Personnel:
Miles Davis (t); Wayne Shorter (s); Bennie Maupin (bass clarinet); Chick Corea, Larry Young, Joe Zawinul (p); John Mclaughlin (g); Harvey Brooks, Dave Holland (b); Jack DeJohnette, Charles Alias, Lenny White (d); Jim Riley (pc)
Track listing:
Pharoah's Dance; Bitches Brew; Spanish Key; John McLaughlin; Miles Runs The Voodoo Down; Sanctuary
Running time:
93.57
Current CD:
C2K65774, adds: Feio
Further listening:
Jack Johnson (1970); Live-Evil (1970); On The Corner (1972)
Further reading:
The Penguin Guide To Jazz On CD (1999)
Like this?
Try . . . p.188

Little Milton

If Walls Could Talk

Highpoint of this giant of soul blues.

John Lee Hooker has described Little Milton Campbell as "One of the finest blues singers and guitar players there ever was", but unlike his great contemporary B.B. King, Milton has failed to achieve significant crossover success. And yet for nearly 50 years he has been one of the most powerful and emotive performers in American blues, his talents at least recognised by Greg Allman, for one, who has declared, "Milton has been one of the biggest influences on my life. B.B. King and Little Milton are tied for first in my book. But when it comes to power, Little Milton has the edge over everybody."

If Walls Could Talk splendidly showcases Milton's prowess, with magnificent soulful singing, excellent songs, impressive ensemble work and glorious horn arrangements. One of the best moments is Your Precious Love, a touching declaration of the redeeming power of love, with Milton humbly acknowledging, "Your love has made me a better man."

"When I got into what music was all about I discovered I catered for women in my songs," he explains. "I sing about the goodness women have done for me, how important the woman is to me and how much I love her. I know if I draw twenty women, I'm going to draw forty men, see?"

Another powerfully emotive performance is Let's Get Together, on which Milton implores his ex for a second chance, alleging of her new lover that, "He's treating you twice as bad as I used to!"

For all these riches, Milton's distinctive playing is heard sparingly on the album. "Les Paul influenced me with that little plucking thing. I took that same sound, added my own feel and transformed it into a blues thing." Milton is philosophical about his failure to cross over. "I'm not a superstar and I don't know if I want to be. I want to be free to go where I want, and not worry about being kidnapped and every time I go to bed somebody got to pull my clothes off and tuck me in. Or I go to the bathroom and they're there with some toilet paper to wipe my butt. I'm doing OK and I love what I do and I'll be doing it till I die."

Record label:
Chess
Produced
by Calvin Carter.
Recorded
in Chicago; spring 1969 and 15–16 October 1969.
Released:
January 1970
Chart peaks:
None (UK) None (US)
Personnel:
Little Milton (v, g); Gene Barge (oa); Donny Hathaway (p); David Purple (e)
Track listing:
If Walls Could Talk; Baby, I Love You (S/US); Let's Get Together (S); Things I Used To Do; Kansas City; Poor Man's Song; Blues Get Off My Shoulder; I Play Dirty (S/US); Good To Me As I Am To You; Your Precious Love; I Don't Know
Running time:
32.21
Currently unavailable on CD
Further listening:
Raise A Little Sand and We're Gonna Make It compile tracks from the '50s and '60s respectively. Since the mid-'80s Milton has released a number of terrific, soul-drenched albums on Malaco.
Further reading:
http://www.littlemilton.com
Like this?
Try . . . p.795

The MC5

Back In The USA

The band's taut, foot-to-the-floor second LP; a precursor to punk adrift in a climate of hippy rock.

The MC5 had much to live up to with their second album, and almost as much to live down. '69's *Kick Out The Jams* had been one of the most electrifying debuts of 1969. But their rabble-rousing had got them kicked off Elektra, and their White Panther rhetoric got them branded a "revolutionary hype". Typical was a savaging in Rolling Stone at the hands of first-time contributor Lester Bangs, which wrote them off as a musically regressive joke. (Bangs later recanted, but the tone of the backlash had been set.) "I wanted to make a note-perfect record," guitarist Wayne Kramer states. "I was still stinging from Lester Bangs' remarks, and wanted to answer the criticism that we used excessive volume to hide the fact that we couldn't play. I knew what bullshit that was, and we wanted people to know that we were the best band in the world. The guitars are gonna be in tune, the tempos are gonna be right on. No excuses for nothing."

Initial sessions in June with first-time producer Jon Landau were unproductive. When Landau returned to Detroit a month later, the change was astonishing. They'd worked out physically as if they were a sports team, jogging and eating a high protein diet, and had rehearsed relentlessly. "There was discipline and a return to basics," said late singer Rob Tyner. "We got back to the kind of straight-ahead band we'd been in the early days. We focused our energy. We tried to make it sound like – whoosh! – it was racing right past you. Total velocity. Our souls got psychedelicized there for a while, so it felt good to be back in the pocket."

Bookended by Little Richard and Chuck Berry, *Back In The USA* is an affirmation of the root values of rock'n'roll. Most songs stay well south of the three minute mark, the solos are sharp and to the point. Throughout, the guitars of Kramer and Fred 'Sonic' Smith are so perfectly meshed that they often sound like a single instrument (though there may not be a single track where the five members all played together). Despite some of their most overtly political material (American Ruse and Human Being Lawnmower) and the creative emergence of Smith (Tonight and Shakin' Street), the radical revamping of their sound bewildered their Detroit constituency, and failed to connect with a national audience more interested in rock operas and drum solos.

Record label:
Atlantic
Produced
by Jon Landau.
Recorded
at GM Studios, Detroit; July–September 1969.
Released:
January 1970
Chart peaks:
None (UK) 137 (US)
Personnel:
Rob Tyner (v); Wayne Kramer (g, b); Fred 'Sonic' Smith (g); Michael Davis (b); Dennis Thompson (d); with Danny Jordan (p); Jim Bruzzese (e)
Track listing:
Tutti Frutti; Tonight (S/US only); Teenage Lust; Let Me Try; Looking At You; High School; Call Me Animal; The American Ruse; Shakin' Street (S/US); The Human Being Lawnmower; Back In The USA
Running time:
28.30
Current CD:
8122710332
Further listening:
The Big Bang! Best Of The MC5 (2000)
Further reading:
MOJO 27
Like this?
Try . . . p.53

Laura Nyro

New York Tendaberry

The second in a classic trilogy from a highly individual singer and songwriter.

At once a reclusive and an almost overpoweringly frank artist, Nyro records are a strange legacy of a talent that never quite found its best expression. She is often still more remembered for her failures: the disastrous appearance at Monterey in 1967, where she was booed offstage, or the feeble *Mother's Spiritual*, her last studio album.

"She was born 150 years too late," opined Robert Christgau, dismissive of her romantic tendencies. But here was a singer-songwriter who aspired to a sophisticated, metropolitan pop-soul at a time when most of her peers preferred gentrified folk. Her third record, *New York Tendaberry*, was the centrepiece of what came to be seen as a three-part cycle – *Eli And The 13th Confession* and *Christmas And The Beads Of Sweat* came either side. Common to all three is the feeling that they pivoted around Nyro singing by herself at the piano: there are rhythm sections and strings and brass which break in from time to time, but these are more like framing devices for the rise and fall of Nyro's voice, swelling into an ecstatic high passage on Captain For Dark Mornings and falling away into a whisper in the next few bars.

All her music has a stop-start feel to it, something which she only surrendered when in her most facile pop-tune mood (and some would say that's what she should have stuck to, on the basis of such three-minute glories as Wedding Bell Blues and Stoney End). At its most eccentric, as on the murderous Tom Cat Goodbye, she sounds like she's making a *grand guignol* opera. But the texture of the record, engineered by Roy Halee, soundtracks a great, dangerous city in darkness: it actually *feels* like New York at night. There is a heart-stopping moment in Gibson Street, where the horns blare in over the gorgeous harmonies, and the music seems to be soaring past skyscrapers. Beyond its setting, *New York Tendaberry* is also a treatise on damned love, and one that suggests disturbing depths. Among countless chilling lines are these: "I wish my baby were forbidden/I wish my world be struck by sleet/I wish to keep my mirror hidden/To hide the eyes that looked on Gibson Street".

Record label:
Columbia
Produced
by Laura Nyro and Roy Halee.
Recorded
in New York; 1969.
Released:
January 1970
Chart peaks:
None (UK) 32 (US)
Personnel:
Laura Nyro (p, v); Roy Halee (e)
Track listing:
You Don't Love Me When I Cry; Captain For Dark Mornings; Tom Cat Goodbye; Mercy On Broadway; Save The Country; Gibson Street; Time And Love; The Man Who Sends Me Home; Sweet Lovin' Baby; Captain Saint Lucifer; New York Tendaberry
Running time:
46.22
Current CD:
XUSK019737
Further listening:
Christmas & The Beads Of Sweat (1970); Gonna Take A Miracle (1971)
Further reading:
www.LauraNyro.net; www.lauranyro.com
Like this?
Try . . . p.614

oneybus

Story

Ditched by their leader, classic neglected pop band produce their only album - and it's a stunner.

With three top-notch singer-songwriters, a sound of their own and major label support, it should all have gone so differently for Honeybus. Instead they're remembered for their sole hit, the charming 'I Can't Let Maggie Go', written like the bulk of their early material by the great Pete Dello, who (along with fellow guitarist Ray Cane) had been busy throughout the 60s as a jobbing session musician, arranger and writer. In 1967 they decided to focus fully on their own talents with, as Cane says today, 'the express intention of producing music that did not have a mind-numbing bass drum going four beats to the bar'.

Accordingly the instantly recognisable Honeybus sound was conceived, a whimsical, highly melodic brand of pop with intricate harmonies and frequent use of woodwind and strings. After two excellent but unsuccessful singles, they hit the jackpot third time around. 'Maggie' hit the top ten in April 1968 and the future seemed assured. But then the unthinkable happened. Without warning or explanation, Dello quit in August. To this day Colin Hare, their rhythm guitarist, doesn't understand precisely why.'We were completely wrong-footed', he says. As job offers flooded in from all over the world, the band was left reeling and unsure as to what to do next.

Salvation came in the form of Cane. As Hare puts it 'we were at sea and Ray took the helm.' Determined not to lose the opportunity that had come the group's way, and with an album deal from Deram on the table, he set about writing songs that would maintain the momentum given by their hit. Hare also contributed exceptional songs, well aware that they had an uphill struggle on their hands. 'The public perception was that without Pete, Honeybus were finished', he says. 'We were determined to prove that wrong.'

Having found a very able replacement for Dello in Jim Kelly, the band worked on *Story*, their sole album, throughout 1969. As Hare says, 'Ray and I really grafted. We all put in an awful lot of work, even though the album was done in fragments, at different times, under different circumstances.' Despite this, it's remarkably coherent and inventive, spanning straight harmony ('She's Out There'), upbeat pop ('Black Mourning Band'), folk rock ('Scarlet Lady') and harder, more psychedelic work ('Under The Silent Tree').

Story slipped out in early 1970, by which time the band's moment had truly passed. Reluctantly, they split. But interest in them has never wavered, largely owing to that evergreen hit. As Cane says, 'we had the ability to produce good songs. Producing hit records is something else. Perhaps we just didn't have a sufficiently overwhelming desire to be pop stars!'

RMJ

Record label:
Deram
Produced
by Ivor Raymonde / Honeybus
Recorded
by Central Sound Studios, London, 1969.
Released:
February 1970.
Chart Peaks:
None (UK) None (US)
Personnel:
Ray Cane (g, v, p, b, mellotron) / Colin Hare (b, v) / Jim Kelly (g, v) / Pete Kitcher (d)
Track listing:
Story / Black Mourning Band / Scarlet Lady / Fresher Than The Sweetness In Water / He Was Columbus / Ceilings No. 1 / Under The Silent Tree / She's Out There / She Said Yes / I Remember Caroline / How Long / Ceilings No. 2
Running Time:
?
Current CD:
She Flies Like A Bird: The Honeybus Anthology - Sequel, 2002. An exhaustive retrospective, containing the entire album and much more.
Further listening:
Pete Dello – Into Your Ears (1971) / Colin Hare – March Hare (1971). Hare is still active in music. Details of recordings and gigs can be found at the website below.
Further reading:
http://www.angelfire.com/pop2/honeybus.
Like this?
Try . . . p.153

Van Morrison

Moondance

For the follow-up to the legendary Astral Weeks, Van changed direction, and not for the last time.

Much as he might dislike it now, Brown Eyed Girl was the song that saved Van Morrison's skin. In New York following the split of Them, Morrison let producer Bert Berns lead him to the pop charts. When the song was a hit in 1967, Warner Bros signed Morrison, and the result was the 1968 album which is regularly voted among the best ever made. But *Astral Weeks* had yet to be cemented into the rock pantheon when Van came to record *Moondance.*

Astral Weeks was a mesmerising song suite – an acoustic journey – in which Morrison, in exile in America, recalled his distant hometown of Belfast. During 1969 Morrison had moved to an artistic hamlet in upstate New York but, following the famous festival, Woodstock had become in Van's words "a joke". While he was there though, Van – like so many of his peers – had become mesmerised by The Band. By the beginning of the new decade, The Band had long moved on from simply being Bob Dylan's backing group, and were fashioning their own brand of rural rock'n'roll: gritty and lived-in, it was a sound which Van Morrison found particularly enticing. The over-riding sound of *Astral Weeks* had been acoustic, with its feet in folk and jazz; *Moondance* is brass-based, harder-edged, rooted in jazz and R&B. While *Astral Weeks* meandered, *Moondance* had a more disciplined song structure, with only Brand New Day edging over the five minute mark. The original album's first side was as strong as any in rock's 15 year history. And It Stoned Me and Into The Mystic are enchanting, inscrutable souvenirs of the era; Crazy Love and Caravan display Morrison's peerless blue-eyed soul; while the title track, which had begun life as "a saxophone solo", would go on to become one of Van's best-loved songs.

The other outstanding song on *Moondance*, the anthemic Brand New Day, was inspired by Morrison hearing The Band's version of Dylan's I Shall Be Released on a Boston radio station.

Upon its release, Rolling Stone called *Moondance* "an album of musical invention and lyrical confidence". It gave Van Morrison his solo chart debut. Following the dispiriting split of Them, the unrepresentative Brown Eyed Girl and the unsuccessful *Astral Weeks*, the man was on his way.

Record label:
Warner Brothers
Produced
by Van Morrison.
Recorded
at Century Recording, New York; 1969
Released:
February 1970
Chart peaks:
32 (UK) 29 (US)
Personnel:
Van Morrison (g, pc); Jack Schrorer (s); Collin Tillton (s, flute); Jeff Labes (k); John Platania (g); John Klingberg (b); Garry Malabar (d); Guy Masson (d); Emily Houston, Judy Clay & Jackie Verdell (bv); Tony May, Elliot Schierer, Shelly Yakus, Steve Friedberg, Neil Schwartz (e)
Track listing:
And It Stoned Me; Moondance; Crazy Love; Caravan; Into The Mystic; Come Running (S); These Dreams Of You; Brand New Day; Everyone; Glad Tidings
Running time:
39.17
Current CD:
7599-27326-2
Further Listening:
The Best of Van Morrison (1990); The Philosopher's Stone (1998)
Further Reading:
It's Too Late To Stop Now (Steve Turner, 1993); Wavelength, The Unofficial Van Morrison Magazine, PO Box 80, Winsford, Cheshire, CW7 4ES, UK
www.wavelengthltd.co.uk; www.harbour.sfu.ca/~hayward/van
Like this?
Try . . . p.692

Rodriguez

Cold Fact

Downbeat debut from modest Detroit singer-songwriter finds a warm reception down under.

Born in 1942 to Mexican immigrant parents, his working class, Spanish-speaking upbringing gave Sixto ("sixth child") an early insight into life as an outsider. It was a theme that would inform much of his song writing – tales of social alienation, drug-induced paranoia and doomed relationships. Asked how he started his career in music he shrugs: "I started playing when I was about 17. I think it was a way to escape and get out into the world." An early folk-rock single for the local Impact label, I'll Slip Away, was doomed by the company's bankruptcy, but in 1969 Rodriguez signed to the newly formed Buddha off-shoot, Sussex and *Cold Fact* emerged as its first release.

Skilfully overseen by Mike Theodore and Dennis Coffey (later of the Detroit Guitar Band), the album's sparse production gives prominence to Sixto's acoustic guitar and haunting vocals, its tone set by the distinctly bitter-tasting Sugar Man. Over a subtle backing of guitar, brass and electronic effects the singer reels off a pharmaceutical shopping list - silver magic ships, jumpers, coke, sweet Mary Jane - before delivering a stark message: "Sugar man, met a false friend on a lonely dusty road. Lost my heart, when I found it, it had turned to dead black coal."

That *Cold Fact* is short on happy endings is hardly surprising, yet Rodriguez recalls a certain amount of pressure to make the LP still more controversial: "Mike Theodore said: 'Can you add these two songs (Gommorah and Hate Street Dialogue) to it?' And I said: 'Sure!' But I fixed the words. I said: 'I cannot say *that*. If I talked like that I couldn't even go back home (laughs)!' How could I refuse? I was just getting out there..."

Despite a favourable review in Billboard the album never troubled its chart and although Sussex did finance one further album they preferred to throw their promotion behind smooth sounding Bill Withers. Rodriguez quit music to raise a family and, apart from a brief foray into local politics, just seemed to disappear. Yet, halfway across the world, the most extraordinary phase of his career had only just begun. A few boxes of *Cold Fact* were shipped to Australia where they rapidly sold out. The LP was picked up by A&M the following year and steadily acquired a cult following amongst the country's disaffected youth, as well as in New Zealand and South Africa. When finally issued on CD it went platinum and Rodriguez was so well known by the beginning of the 1980s that he toured with Midnight Oil. After slipping into temporary obscurity once more - during which increasingly bizarre rumours circulated about his 'demise' - he recently travelled to South Africa for two sell-out stadium tours. A subsequent live album became his first release in almost 30 years.

TF

Record label:
Sussex SXBS 7000
CD release:
RCA Victor VPCD 6745 (Australian import)
Produced
by Mike Theodore and Dennis Coffey.
Recorded
at August - September 1969, Tera-Shirma Studios, Detroit. Re-mixed at RCA, New York.
Chart peak UK:
None
Chart peak US:
None
Released:
March 1970
Total running time:
31.38
Personnel:
Sixto Rodriguez (acoustic gtr, voc), Dennis Coffey (electric gtr), Mike Theodore (keyboards, orch arrangements, engr), Bob Babbitt (bs), Andrew Smith (drms), children of Joyce Vincent and Telma Hopkins (choir on Gommorah).
Track listing:
Sugar Man / Only Good For Conversation / Crucify Your Mind / This Is Not A Song, It's An Outburst: Or, The Establishment Blues / Hate Street Dialogue / Forget It (S) / Inner City Blues (S) / I Wonder / Like Janis / Gommorah (A Nursery Rhyme) / Rich Folks Hoax / Jane S. Piddy
Further listening:
At His Best (RCA Victor VPCD 6748), a compilation from both albums and 3 unreleased tracks, is an excellent starting point.
Further reading:
http://www.new.co.za/~currin/rodriguez.html
Like this?
Try . . . p.574

Black Sabbath

Black Sabbath

The smelting house of Heavy Metal.

The sound of the industrial factory floor fed through an amp and turned up to 11, *Black Sabbath* lays more claim than any record before or since to having invented heavy metal. Its occult imagery, slow, menacing songs and murky, Sensurround production made to be played at previously unheard-of volume, were to have a widespread, lasting influence.

With a grass-roots following amassed by solid touring, Sabbath comprised four working class men from Birmingham who had played together in various blues- and jazz-rock combos with names like Earth and Polka Tulk before bassist Butler's interest in Dennis Wheatley novels and the band's discovery of a '30s horror film gave them both a winning name and a gimmick. They were sent into the studio with producer Rodger Bain and a £600 budget from Phillips' new progressive rock label Vertigo.

"We were given just two days to record," said Tony Iommi. "In those days we didn't know if two days was a long time or short", so they finished it in a day.

Said Ozzy Osbourne, "We were just kids. We were coming out with a new thing and we knew fuck all about recording, so we just went in and played it innocently and it was really raw and earthy. It sounded like a live record without the audience.

Aggressive, ponderous, dripping black-country doom and gloom from the opening track, *Black Sabbath* was one of the final nails in the coffin of hippy rock – or would have been but for the quasi-psychedelic noodlings into which Sabbath occasionally launched during the long instrumental jams. Mostly, though, it was basic and unfussy: Ozzy Osbourne's piercing, cheerless but affecting vocals, Butler's rumbling bass, Ward's aggressive drums and Iommi's much-imitated guitar.

"A lot of the songs had an aggressive mood, Satanic if you like, but that was the way we felt," said Iommi, "so that was the way we played." The record attracted immediate attention, the band's supposedly satanic stance won them some controversy. They were even interviewed on Radio 4's Today programme. If it was intended to scare off the kids it, naturally, had the opposite effect. The album was an instant Top 10 hit, and was followed just six months later with the equally-enduring *Paranoid*.

SS

Record label:
Vertigo
Produced
by Rodger Bain with Geezer Butler and Tony Iommi.
Recorded
at Trident Studios; February 1970.
Released:
April 1970
Chart peaks:
8 (UK) 23 (US)
Personnel:
Ozzy Osbourne (v); Tony Iommi (g); Terry 'Geezer' Butler (b); Bill Ward (d); Barry Sheffield, Bill Freesh, Lee DeCarlo, Tom Allom (e)
Track listing:
Black Sabbath; The Wizard; Behind The Wall Of Sleep; N.I.B; Evil Woman Don't Play Your Games With Me (S/UK); Sleeping Village; Warning
Running time:
30.16
Current CD:
Essential/Castle ESMCD301 adds: Wicked World
Further listening:
Paranoid (1970); Sabbath Bloody Sabbath (1973); 3CD box set The Ozzy Osbourne Years (1991)
Further reading:
Wheels Of Confusion: The Story Of Black Sabbath (Steven Rosen, 1996); www.black-sabbath.com
Like this?
Try . . . p.707

The Who

Live At Leeds

What the rock opera pioneers really sounded like. One of rock's live milestones.

1970 was a heady time for The Who. They'd been performing their celebrated rock opera *Tommy* in front of classical music critics and European royalty in opera houses, and the talk was of maturation of rock music, deepening of insight and extension of form. All this for a band who in live performance also represented the pinnacle of freeform rock. The inspired lunacy of Keith Moon's whirlwind percussion style, the huge-sounding, restlessly exploratory basslines of John Entwistle and the chopping, plangent power-chording of Pete Townshend's guitar could turn Mose Allison's Young Man Blues – originally a two minute aside on his rural-cool *Back Country Suite* (1957) – into an electrifying one-chord work-out of immense power and dynamic control. They were a unique live band and they knew it.

Entwistle: "When we go on stage we all try and upstage one another. We play full tilt from the very start. Then at the end of the set we have to pull something extra out of the bag as a climax. It's as simple as that."

So a live album would serve both as a handy stop-gap before the next Big Idea and present another side to The Who. With Pete Townshend unable to face listening through the hours of material recorded on a US tour – he instructed the tapes to be destroyed on a bonfire to foil bootleggers – the Pye mobile was enlisted to record the Leeds University Valentine's Day set. The musical chemistry of the band could be volatile; if Moon wasn't on top form, they could sound like they were limping from one sloppy drum fill to the next – but this day Moon was crisp and alert and the band responded accordingly, delivering a boiling set.

Recorded with great immediacy by Jon Astley and packaged like a bootleg, the original *Live At Leeds* featured a pair of old singles, a couple of rock'n'roll covers, the remarkable Young Man Blues and the legendary 14 minute 45 seconds of My Generation which incorporated Tommy themes, blues hollering, glorious finger-picking, slap-back guitar interludes and a range of tensions and climaxes that leaves the listener breathless. Influential on many up-and-coming volume-heavy combos, *Live At Leeds* still has the edge on other fine live Who recordings of the period, standing proud as a landmark live rock album. Though the CD issue more than doubles the original playing time, the real magic remains most vivid on the originally released tracks.

Record label:
Track
Produced
by Jon Astley.
Recorded
at Leeds University, England; February 14, 1970.
Released:
May 1970
Chart peaks:
3 (UK) 4 (US)
Personnel:
Roger Daltrey (v, hm); Pete Townshend (g, v); John Entwistle (b, v); Keith Moon (d)
Track listing:
Young Man Blues; Substitute; Summertime Blues; Shakin' All Over; My Generation; Magic Bus.
Running time:
37.10
Current CD:
Polydor 527 169-2 adds: Heaven And Hell; I Can't Explain; Fortune Teller; Tattoo; Happy Jack; I'm A Boy; A Quick One, While He's Away; Amazing Journey/Sparks
Further listening:
Live At The Isle Of White (1970); Woodstock (1969); The Kids Are Alright (1978)
Further reading:
Hope I Die Before I Get Old (Dave Marsh, 1995); Maximum R&B (Richard Barnes, 1996)
Like this?
Try . . . p.595

Free

Fire And Water

Young, British R&B band craft song that echoes round the world for 30 years. Fortunately, it's on their best album.

At the height of the British blues boom, on April 19 1968 four boys, aged 15-18, got together in a London pub for their first rehearsal. From disparate backgrounds – Paul Kossoff's father a famous actor, Paul Rodgers's an unknown Teesside shipyard worker – but all steeped in R&B, they clicked, wrote at least four songs that night, and hit the road for six-gigs-a-week. With Kossoff a follicle-shivering guitarist, Rodgers a hard yet mellifluous singer, Andy Fraser a remarkably original, melodic bass player, and Kirke the adamantine drummer required to keep these young guns firing in the same direction, Free built a strong live reputation. Even so, their first two albums, *Tons Of Sobs* and *Free* sold only 20,000 apiece. But then, in autumn 1969, after a rare bad gig, according to Kirke, "In the dressing-room I said, We've got to have a song people can dance to!, and Andy and Paul Rodgers started bopping around, going, All right now, all right now." Free had the song that changed their lives.

All Right Now accentuated their gradual shift of emphasis from blues to soul stylings – for instance, Fraser and Rodgers deliberately wrote Fire And Water with Wilson Pickett in mind and, to prove their point, in 1971 he covered it. The first six tracks of the album are dark, sparse and powerful. Then comes the explosive relief of All Right Now. "We were *allowed* to be happy!" enthuses Kirke. "We all picked up maracas and tambourines and sang back-ups together. Then Andy and me got down on our hands and knees and hammered the bass pedals on the Hammond organ with our fists."

They recorded quickly, but only on the odd day when they didn't have a gig. Then, confusingly, a row with Blackwell led to two mixes of the album being released and marketed ever since – plus a conflict over the single edit of All Right Now which Free objected to on purist grounds. But, in UK and America, the charts endorsed Blackwell's view. At every gig they were mobbed. By girls!

Yet, inconceivably, the following May Free broke up – exhausted, disappointed with follow-up album *Highway*'s abysmal sales, and rather disgusted with the pop reputation All Right Now brought them. They did reunite and had more hits before their final separation and Kossoff's sorry decline into drug-induced death at 25. But All Right Now and *Fire And Water* left one glorious summer to remember them by.

Record label:
Island
Produced
by Free.
Recorded
at Trident Studios, Island Studios, London, January–April 1970.
Released:
June 26, 1970
Chart peaks:
2 (UK) 17 (US)
Personnel:
Paul Rodgers (v, g); Paul Kossoff (g); Andy Fraser (b); Simon Kirke (d); Roy Thomas Baker (e)
Track listing:
Fire And Water; Oh I Wept; Remember; Heavy Load; Mr Big; Don't Say You Love Me; All Right Now (S)
Running time:
35.33
Current CD:
IMCD 80 842 556 (the UK CD comes from Chris Blackwell's remix of the album, originally released on the second pressing of the vinyl album; the US CD retains some of Free's original mixes as released on the first vinyl pressing in UK – the difference is most evident on the title track)
Further listening:
Free (1969) – earlier, more R&B Free (with the famous "girl full of stars" cover)
Further reading:
MOJO 54; Heavy Load (2000); www.allrightnow.com
Like this?
Try . . . p.248

Deep Purple

Deep Purple In Rock

The UK's proto-heavy metal scene spawns a monster.

"Quite simply," says bassist Roger Glover, "there was nothing to lose." Deep Purple were already on a hiding to nothing; they'd had a taste of fame in the US with Hush, but the departure of original vocalist Rod Evans and bassist Nick Simper meant that the line-up convening to record the band's fourth album was almost completely unknown. Right at the start, guitarist Blackmore told his bandmates, "If it's not dramatic or exciting, it has no place on this album," and the band took him at his word.

"If I had to pick one image which sums up *In Rock*," Glover says, "it would be the VU meters on the consoles bent hard over to the right." It *is* a deafening record – the opening Speed King, co-opting a clutch of Gillan's favourite rock'n'rollers, sees to that. But it also contains one of their most powerful numbers, the anti-war tract Child In Time, rewritten from It's A Beautiful Day's Bombay Calling, but taken to a new dimension by Gillan's near-supernatural screams. Indeed, with sessions squeezed in between gigs, one can almost trace the band's evolution, from proto-prog tinged sellers of psych to classically tinted merchants of mayhem as the album progresses – Flight Of The Rat even exploded out of an extemporised romp through Flight Of The Bumblebee.

Though the album would soon be established as Purple's first classic, not everyone in the band was immediately keen on it. Glover concludes, "We were on a train going up to Scotland for a gig. We'd just come out of the studio the previous night, and I said, Ah, it's not as good as it could have been if we'd been more together, and Jon Lord turned round, gave me a sharp look . . . he was much more of a senior member in those days . . . and he says 'Roger, you're wrong.' And that stopped me in my tracks. Then he said, 'If it could have been better, it would have been better. It is what it is and that's it. So shut the fuck up.'" Consider yourself told.

Record label:
Harvest
Produced
by Deep Purple.
Recorded
at IBC, London; De Lane Lea, London; Abbey Road, London; October 14, 1969–April 13, 1970.
Release date:
June 1970
Chart peaks:
4 (UK) None (US)
Personnel:
Ian Gillan (v); Ritchie Blackmore (g); Roger Glover (b); Jon Lord (k); Ian Paice (d); Andy Knight, Martin Birch, Philip McDonald (e)
Track listing:
Speed King; Bloodsucker; Child In Time; Flight Of The Rat; Into The Fire; Living Wreck; Hard Lovin' Man
Running time:
43.17
Current CD:
7243 8 34019 2 5
Anniversary Edition adds Black Night (S); Speed King (piano version); Cry Free (Roger Glover remix); Jam Stew; Flight Of The Rat (Roger Glover remix); Speed King (Roger Glover remix); Black Night (unedited Roger Glover remix)
Further listening:
Fireball (1971); Machine Head (1972)
Further reading:
Child In Time (Ian Gillan with David Cohen, 1994)
www.deep-purple.com
Like this?
Try . . . p.355

John Phillips

John, The Wolfking of LA

Papa goes solo.

Sometimes an artist can totally undervalue his own work. Such is surely the case with John Phillips, who, after The Mamas And The Papas disbanded, recorded this wonderful solo album – which he clearly loathes.

"I never had the front man's ego and that LP proved it," he wrote dismissively in his autobiography. "I sounded seriously depressed. The songs were fine, the backup vocalists and musicians were fine, but the lead singer seemed groggy. That work sounded lethargic." Well, what to Phillips seems like lethargy is perceived by the album's admirers as being soothing and attractively restrained; and the vocals which Phillips thought groggy, seem warm and intimate. Certainly the music has nothing of the sunny sparkle of The Mamas And The Papas and there are few moments where anyone breaks sweat, but the music is exquisitely crafted.

"Do it to me, James," Phillips instructs James Burton on Mississippi and sure enough, Burton does it to him, and to us, with a wonderful dobro solo, while the piano of Larry Knechtel and the steel guitars of Buddy Emmons and Red Rhodes, are also scintillating throughout the record.

Drummer Hal Blaine remembers it fondly. "John was a fine musician, always a gentleman. There are no studio credits because the studio was an attic. John had bought the Jeanette MacDonald estate in Bel Air, which was like a fairyland, and in this beautiful attic he built the most magnificent studio in the world. There was magnificent woodwork throughout this home and one secret panel. When you touched the secret button this door opened and you entered the secret world of John Phillips." The songs are wonderfully appealing but undeniably less commercial than those Phillips had written for The Mamas And The Papas, and their meanings are elusive, although they often seem to be describing Phillips' debauched, rich hippie lifestyle. However the album flopped and within a year or two Phillips' life began to spiral out of control. He was convicted of trafficking in narcotics in 1981, and spent a considerable amount of time in rehabilitation. Finally, in 1989, he resurrected The Mamas And The Papas as a touring attraction, though he was the only original member.

And the house? Well, that, as it happens, was flogged, studio and all, to Sly Stone, who famously recorded *There's A Riot Going On* in it.

Record label:
Stateside
Produced
by Lou Adler.
Recorded
at 783 Bel Air Road; 1969–70.
Released:
June 1970
Chart peaks:
None (UK) None (US)
Personnel:
John Phillips (v, g, hm); Hal Blaine (d); Larry Knechtel (p); Joe Osborne (b); David Cohen (g); Dr Hord (g); Darlene Love, Jean King, Fanita James (bv); James Burton (g, dobro); Buddy Emmons, Red Rhodes (sg); Gordon Terry (fiddle); Chuck Britz (e)
Track listing:
April Anne; Topanga Canyon; Malibu People; Someone's Sleeping; Drum; Captain; Let It Bleed, Genevieve; Down The Beach; Mississippi (S); Holland Tunnel
Running time:
32.42
Current CD:
Edsel EDCD372
Further listening:
addictions to heroin, barbiturates and alcohol sapped Phillips' creativity and he recorded little of note after Wolfking. But The Mamas And The Papas' best, such as If You Can Believe Your Eyes And Ears (1966) are always worth hearing.
Further reading:
Papa John: An Autobiography (John Phillips with Jim Jerome, 1986) is a grim rock-'n'roll horror story. Sadly there is much more on Phillips' addictions than on his music.
Like this?
Try . . . p.168

Soft Machine

Third

London underground mavericks journey into jazz-rock.

The Soft Machine's early career was plagued by personal acrimony, musical differences and record company apathy. Consequently, the UK underground's second sons (behind Pink Floyd) only got round to recording their debut in 1968 while touring the States with Jimi Hendrix. Before the second album Kevin Ayers left and was replaced by Hugh Hopper, Wyatt and Ratledge had stopped speaking to each other.

Volume Two maintained the psych-pop vision, fortified with Hopper's fuzz bass and Ratledge's increasingly sophisticated, jazz-inflected compositions. After supporting Hendrix and Traffic at the Albert Hall early in 1969, the trio on Wyatt's suggestion, briefly experimented with a four-piece brass section. "This hastened the demise of our commitment to songs," says Hopper, "because the brass tended to play Robert's vocal parts."

By the time work began on *Third*, in spring 1970, the group had advanced considerably. "We weren't consciously playing jazz-rock," Hopper insists. "It was more a case of not wanting to sound like other bands; we certainly didn't want a guitarist." Rock was now a dirty word. "We'd got into that John Coltrane Quartet sound, mainly modal things, rather than the tricky bebop timings."

Third, a double album consisting of just four side-long pieces, was daringly ambitious, turned around the band's fortunes, and even prompted an appearance at that year's Proms. Yet the intra-band tensions remained.

"We worked round it by each looking after different chunks of the record," maintains Hopper. "If we hadn't had done that, we might never have finished it." The bassist's extraordinary Facelift, a live/studio concoction of assault-style keyboards, Zappa-like riffs and squealing tape loops was in marked contrast to Ratledge's smoother contributions. Most idiosyncratic was Wyatt's Moon In June, a hugely affecting, largely solo piece that features what's probably the longest coda in rock and – gulp – vocals. A little over a year later Wyatt was fired. "I loved playing their music, and I admired them enormously," he claims, "but one day I got a phone call from the organist and I was out."

Record label:
CBS
Produced
by Soft Machine.
Recorded
at IBC Studios, London; spring 1970. Facelift recorded live at Fairfield Hall, Croydon; January 4, 1970 and Mothers Club, Birmingham; January 11, 1970.
Released:
June 1970
Chart peaks:
18 (UK) None (US)
Personnel:
Mike Ratledge (o, p); Hugh Hopper (b); Robert Wyatt (d, v); Elton Dean (s, saxello); Rab Spall (vn); Lyn Dobson (flute, s); Nick Evans (trombone); Jimmy Hastings (flute, b, clarinet); Andy White (e); Bob Woolford (e)
Track listing:
Facelift; Slightly All The Time; Moon In June; Out-Bloody-Rageous
Running time:
75.19
Current CD:
Legacy XUSK0230339
Further listening:
Fourth (1971) refines the sound; The Peel Sessions (1990) includes contemporaneous reworkings of Third material.
Further reading:
MOJO 64; Wrong Movements: A Robert Wyatt History (Mike King, 1994)
Like this?
Try . . . p.664

Traffic

John Barleycorn Must Die

Pop band's curious folk-soul experiment.

By 1970 Steve Winwood was barely out of his teens, yet he had already seen service in The Spencer Davis Group, Traffic and Blind Faith. The world was waiting for the solo album – and there are tantalising tales of just what remains in Island's vaults from those sessions, including a rumoured 20 minute version of Dylan's Visions Of Johanna. In the event, what began life as Winwood's solo debut – to be called *Mad Shadows* and produced by Guy Stevens – became instead Traffic's third studio album.

True to both his talent and the spirit of the times, Winwood started out playing every instrument himself; and two tracks – Stranger To Himself and Every Mother's Son – were recorded with Stevens. But Winwood wanted more musicians, and it was only a matter of time before old band-mates Capaldi and Wood were recruited and Traffic were back. Thanks to his lustrous pedigree, it was inevitably Winwood on whom all eyes focused – and *John Barleycorn Must Die* was a remarkable showcase.

But this was Winwood the former member of Blind Faith at work, not a return to Traffic's former guise as a pop group, and he allowed the six songs to meander, kicking off with the instrumental Glad, before finding a groove on Freedom Rider and the haunting Stranger To Himself. But, for many, the highlight of the album was its title track – following on from Fairport Convention's pioneering *Liege & Lief* the previous December, in Traffic's hands this centuries-old traditional folk song seemed to confirm a strong folk-rock fusion for the new decade. To promote the album, Traffic toured America where they had enjoyed a loyal following from the beginning and – again true to the spirit of the times – an in-concert album was recorded. Sadly though, *Live-November 70* never saw the light of day – although two tracks from the album do appear as bonus tracks here. Traffic were always a band who promised more than they actually delivered. But, from the complexity and confusion that characterised the band at the end of the '60s, they did at least summon up the stamina to record this magnificent album, before spiralling downhill during the '70s.

Record label:
Island
Produced
by Chris Blackwell, Steve Winwood and Guy Stevens.
Recorded
at Island and Olympic Studios, London; 1969.
Released:
July 1970
Chart peaks:
5 (UK) 11 (US)
Personnel:
Steve Winwood (k, g, v); Jim Capaldi (d, bv); Chris Wood (s, flute); Andy Johns, Brian Humphries (e)
Track listing:
Glad; Freedom Rider; Empty Pages (S/US); Stranger To Himself; John Barleycorn Must Die; Every Mother's Son
Running time:
34.38
Current CD:
IMCD266 adds: I Just Want To Know; Sittin' Here Thinkin' Of My Love; Who Knows What Tomorrow May Bring (Live); Glad (Live)
Further listening:
Heaven Is In Your Mind: An Introduction To Traffic (1998)
Further reading:
Keep On Running: The Steve Winwood Story (Chris Welch, 1989);
www.stevewinwood.com
www.azstarnet.com/~bobbieg/winwood.htm
Like this?
Try . . . p.705

The Carpenters
Close To You

The unfashionably sunny brother-sister duo truly arrives, platinum sales result.

For their second album, A&M honcho Herb Alpert advised The Carpenters to cover (They Long To Be) Close To You, an obscure 1963 album track written by Bacharach & David for Dionne Warwick. "Dionne's had a straight eighths feel. I was the first one to put it into a slow shuffle, and then the bit at the end was mine," Richard Carpenter says. "We cut two early versions of Close To You, one where Karen tried to sing it like Nilsson. Herb hated it. The third time was a charm. We brought in Hal Blaine. As fine a drummer as Karen was, she couldn't lay into them the way – and I'm going to sound like a chauvinist pig – a man can. Everyone was excited as hell about the song. Even the people around A&M who didn't much care for us were pushing open the door to the studio, saying, 'What is that? We've never heard anything like it.' Herbie was ecstatic. He played it over the phone for Burt. Burt was ecstatic. Herb asked me, 'What do you think it's going to do?' and I said, 'It's either going to be Number 1 or a complete stiff.'

"So we've got six songs complete, then out comes Close To You. You could tell within a week that it was going Top 5. That's when the phone rang and it was, 'Get your album done!'. All of a sudden we had no time."

Thirty years later, Richard still marvels at his sister's poise under pressure. "Karen didn't need to warm up. She didn't give a damn what time of day it was. She didn't need a special headphone mix. They took her right into the board. She was a marvel. Everything about her – the phrasing, the timbre, the diction." The only sore spot for Richard remains the cheesy cover photo. "We protested but were told, 'Learn to live with it.' I learned to live with it in that I haven't committed suicide! It's good to know that we're still so popular that the album is in release 30 years later – but there it is around the world, as we speak, with that awful, *awful* cover. That was the whole beginning of that image thing that so many writers have gone on about – where you were in camps when it came to The Carpenters. That cover started the whole thing."

Record label:
A&M
Produced
by Jack Daugherty.
Recorded
at A&M Studios, Los Angeles; January–May 1970.
Released:
August 19, 1970
Chart peaks:
23 (UK) 2 (US)
Personnel:
Karen Carpenter (v, d); Richard Carpenter (k, v, o); Hal Blaine (d); Joe Osborn (b); Danny Woodhams (b); Jim Horn, Bob Messenger, Doug Strawn (woodwind); Ray Gerhardt, Dick Bogert (e)
Track listing:
We've Only Just Begun (S); Love Is Surrender; Maybe It's You; Reason To Believe; Help; (They Long To Be) Close To You (S); Baby It's You; I'll Never Fall In Love Again; Crescent Noon; Mr Guder; I Kept On Loving You; Another Song
Running time:
38.35
Current CD:
3931842
Further listening:
A Song For You (1972)
Further reading:
MOJO 29; The Carpenters: The Untold Story (Ray Coleman, 1994)
Like this?
Try . . . p.851

The Moody Blues

A Question Of Balance

The finest hour of the forgotten emperors of portentous pop.

When The Moody Blues entered the studio to record what became their fourth album, they had no finished songs.

"It was a deliberate intention to get back to something that was very playable on stage – almost a live recording," says Justin Hayward.

Ray Thomas adds, "We found that with *Children's Children*, it was one thing putting layer upon layer on tape but, at the end of the day, even with the Mellotron, there was only five of us and some tracks literally couldn't be reproduced on stage. So we arranged *A Question Of Balance* so the songs were easier for us, because it's very hard to promote your album if you can't play it live."

For five weeks, the band jammed, developed ideas and committed hours of music to tape. "The sharing was fabulous," recalls John Lodge, "because when any one of us had written something, we'd put it on the table and say this is my song. But as soon as we'd played it for everyone in the band, it became a Moody Blues song, and you sort of relinquished ownership in a spiritual way. Everyone had suggestions and that's what you wanted to happen."

Though they saw it as a back to basics, their penchant for heady lyrics still came through, from the war protest of Question (a song Hayward stitched together from two unfinished fragments the night before it was recorded) to the invitations to self-discovery on Dawning Is The Day and The Balance.

"We were still very young, in our early 20s," says Lodge, "so I think *Question Of Balance* was us questioning who we were again. Also, were we doing the right things? This is where the album came from, trying to get a perspective, a balance on our own lives – as people, as human beings and as very successful musicians, with all that brings. By reflecting on who we were, we were able to make *A Question Of Balance*, which then everyone else could relate to. Because whatever level you're at, there is always a question of balance of everything."

Record label:
Threshold
Produced
by Tony Clarke.
Recorded
at Decca Studios, London; spring 1970.
Released:
August 1970
Chart peaks:
1 (UK) 3 (US)
Personnel:
Justin Hayward (g, v); John Lodge (b, v); Ray Thomas (flute, v); Graeme Edge (d, v); Mike Pinder (k, v); Derek Varnals (e)
Track listing:
Question (S); How Is It (We Are Here); And The Tide Rushes In; Don't You Feel Small; Tortoise And The Hare; It's Up To You; Minstrel's Song; Dawning Is The Day; Melancholy Man; The Balance
Running time:
38.32
Current CD:
Universal 844771-2
Further listening:
Days Of Future Passed (1967); On The Threshold Of A Dream (1969)
Further reading:
index of Moody Blues sites at www.frisk.org/mbindex/pages/
Like this?
Try . . . p.336

Black Sabbath

Paranoid

It defined them, and heavy metal, for all time.

You don't hear the riff so much as feel it, like a distant mudslide slowly moving your way or the last few seconds before the bus hits the school gates, when everything seems to slow down and a second lasts for ever. And then the voice cuts in with "generals gathered in their masses . . ." and it doesn't even matter that the next rhyme is "masses" too because, one minute and three seconds into the opening War Pigs, you're not looking to Sabbath for subtlety or art. You're looking for them to rip the top of your head off, and you know they're going to do it.

Following on from their eponymous debut, *Paranoid* not only gave Black Sabbath a chart-topping album, but the title track came close to topping the singles chart too. They never followed it up, but, as journalist Andrew Wiener remarked two years later, if they had "they could have established themselves as the biggest singles band since the Stones. Think of that – Sabbath on Top Of The Pops, month after month, churning out their Awful Warnings. How could Gary Glitter hope to follow that?"

That's how big Sabbath were – and how potent their Satanic imagery was. Chief lyricist Geezer Butler disagrees. "Even at the beginning, when everyone was calling us devil worshippers, I didn't think we had a Satanic image. I was brought up an incredibly strict Catholic, and though I'd been taught about God and Jesus no one ever went into what the Devil was all about. So when I was 16 or 17, I went about trying to find out. And because I wrote most of Black Sabbath's lyrics, some of that ended up in the songs. It was a dark name, Black Sabbath, but the songs were *never* advocating Satanism. It was warning against evil."

Indeed, ol' Beelzebub doesn't get a mention on *Paranoid*. Rather, the album is pure science fiction and, from the drifting oddity of Planet Caravan and the robotic apocalypse of Electric Funeral, to the future conflict wickedness of War Pigs and the tragedy of Iron Man, *Paranoid* has more in common with Asimov. The difference was, Isaac's Armageddon always took place in space. Sabbath's was an earthbound experience. And it started with the riff.

Record label:
Vertigo
Produced
by Roger Bain.
Recorded
at Regent Sound, Island Studios; July 1970.
Released:
September 1970
Chart peaks:
1 (UK) 12 (US)
Personnel:
Ozzy Osbourne (v); Tony Iommi (g); Terry 'Geezer' Butler (b); Bill Ward (d)
Track listing:
War Pigs; Paranoid (S); Planet Caravan; Iron Man (S/US); Electric Funeral; Hand Of Doom; Rat Salad; Fairies Wear Boots
Running time:
42.09
Current CD:
ESMCD 302
Further listening:
Black Sabbath (1970), Master Of Reality (1971) and try and find the quadrophonic mix of Paranoid, for a brain-peeling remix of War Pigs.
Further reading:
Wheels Of Confusion (Steven Rosen, 1998); www.black-sabbath.com
Like this?
Try . . . p.511

Santana

Abraxas

Santana take in jazz alongside staple Latino-blues-rock. The first world-music crossover success?

By the time the '60s drew to a close, Santana had built up a reputation as an awesome live outfit whose brand of fiery Latin-streaked blues-rock was guaranteed to get audiences on their feet. Much of their early set, however, was made up of covers they had adapted to their own jamming needs – such as a version of Chim Chim Cheree done in the style of Coltrane's My Favourite Things (!) – and by the time they came to record the follow-up to their Top 5 debut album, they realised they needed to develop more of their own material.

"Bill Graham made us aware that we needed songs to get on the radio," says Carlos Santana. "But it wasn't until *Abraxas* that we started hearing our own babies. For me, one of the first ones was Samba Pa Ti, where I just heard a voice singing. Once we learned how to do that, it gave us confidence to find our own place." Accordingly, all bar two of the album's nine tracks were penned by band members, though ironically it would be the two covers that would bring the band their biggest single hits.

Dissatisfied with the sound of their debut, the group brought in as co-producer the veteran jazz engineer Fred Catero, whose skills proved invaluable in balancing the new range of musical flavours Santana were bringing into their sound: the result was a giant step on from their debut. Incident At Neshabur prefigures the group's subsequent move towards jazz, while their core Latin-blues style reached a new level of sophistication with a gorgeous version of Fleetwood Mac's Black Magic Woman, transformed into an elegant samba and served with a side-order of Hungarian jazz guitarist Gabor Szabo's Gypsy Queen. The album's other big hit was an infectious version of Tito Puente's Oye Como Va, which Carlos Santana believed would strike a universal chord.

"I thought, this is a song like Louie Louie or Guantanamera," he said, "a song that when you play it, people are going to get up and dance, and that's it". *Abraxas* remains Santana's most accomplished record, a landmark release which spent over a year on the UK charts and eventually went quadruple platinum, cementing the band's position as one of the most vibrant, fertile units of the era, and bearing out Rolling Stone reviewer Jim Nash's contention that Santana "...might do for Latin music what Chuck Berry did for the blues."

Record label:
CBS
Produced by
Fred Catero and Santana.
Recorded
at Wally Heider Studios, San Francisco; June–July 1970; Pacific Recording, San Mateo; May 1970.
Released:
October 1970
Chart peaks:
7 (UK) 1 (US)
Personnel:
Carlos Santana (g, v); Gregg Rolie (k, v); Dave Brown (b, e); Mike Shrieve (d); Jose Areas (timbales, conga); Mike Carabello (conga); John Fiore (e)
Track listing:
Singing Winds, Crying Beasts; Black Magic Woman/Gypsy Queen (S); Oye Como Va (S); Incident At Neshabur; Se A Cabo; Mother's Daughter; Samba Pa Ti (S); Hope You're Feeling Better (S); El Nicoya
Running time:
51.13
Current CD:
489543 2 adds tracks recorded live at Royal Albert Hall, April 4, 1970: Se A Cabo; Toussaint L'Ouverture; Black Magic Woman/Gypsy Queen
Further listening:
2-CD compilation Viva Santana! (1988) and 1999 comeback Supernatural.
Further reading:
MOJO 70; www.santana.com
Like this?
Try . . . p.771

Lindisfarne

Nicely Out Of Tune

Geordie folk-rockers arrive with a debut of charismatic, rough-hewn magic.

In the late '60s, songwriter and mental nurse Alan Hull was having trouble relating to the trend in heavy rock on the north eastern club scene so he played his songs at folk clubs, eventually starting his own in 1969 at the Rex Hotel, Whitley Bay. His interests at the time revolved around madness ("In that mental hospital I met about three extraordinary poets and they were locked up in that place just because they saw too much and it scared me a little bit"), Buddhism ("Buddhism proper, nothing flash like Zen") and Edgar Allen Poe's Tales Of Mystery And Imagination. His material – like the dream-inspired Lady Eleanor ("I wrote it almost in a trance") – reflected those interests, but, faced with folk club audiences, he found himself inclined to write lighter, more communal fair like We Can Swing Together, a song about an erroneous drug bust at a Newcastle party.

One of the bands that played at his club were a bunch of blues-cum-folk musicians looking for a direction, called Brethren. Hull heard them "doing exactly the same things as I was" and mutually impressed, they joined forces. "The first time it really happened we played Lady Eleanor – we'd just arranged it and I've never had such a tremendous feeling. There were only about a hundred people there but they were friends and it really happened. And afterwards I came off feeling great and Ray Laidlaw came up and said, 'Heeeey, Alan' with a big smile on his face, 'I think we've got it.' And I knew what he meant." Lady Eleanor was a magical, otherworldly number with misty acoustic guitar and haunting harmonies, but in the end it was Ray Jackson's earthy harmonica playing (Jackson would do a whole spot of drinker-pleasing tunes including Blaydon Races and Z-Cars) that convinced Tony-Stratton Smith to sign them to Charisma. Changing their name to Lindisfarne (Brethren had already been nabbed by a US band) their debut album was an endearingly ragged reflection of their live style, combining knees-up (Jackhammer Blues) with plaintive introspection (Scarecrow Song) and droning folk-rock (Turn A Deaf Ear, Things We Should Have Said).

Amid talk of Hull being "one of the finest songwriters this country has produced since the emergence of the patriarchs Lennon and McCartney" (Roy Carr, NME), their best-selling follow-up *Fog On The Tyne* established Lindisfarne as one of the most popular bands in the UK. For many, though, the band's charm is best heard on their debut.

Record label:
Charisma
Produced
by John Anthony.
Recorded
at Trident Studios, Soho; 10–14, August, 1970.
Released:
November 1, 1970
Chart peaks:
8 (UK) None (US)
Personnel:
Alan Hull (v, g); Ray Jackson (v, hm, mandolin); Si Cowe (g); Rod Clements (bs, vn); Ray Laidlaw (d)
Track listing:
Lady Eleanor; Road To Kingdom Come; Winter Song; Turn A Deaf Ear; Clear White Light Part 2; We Can Swing Together; Alan In The River With Flowers; Down; Things I Should Have Said; Jackhammer Blues; Scarecrow Song.
Running time:
53.00
Currently available CD:
CASCD1025 adds: Knacker's Yard Blues; Nothing But The Marvellous Is Beautiful.
Further listening:
Fog On The Tyne (1971); Dingly Dell (1972)
Further reading:
The Official History Of Lindisfarne (1998); www.lindisfarne.de
Like this?
Try . . . p.697

Spirit

The 12 Dreams Of Dr Sardonicus

A surreal trip, potent as purest California Sunshine.

Measured in sales, Los Angeles' psychedelic pioneers Spirit never meant much. And, even compared to the minor chart placings of their previous albums, *Dr Sardonicus* was the low watermark, stalling well outside the US Top 50. Still, the departure of Spirit's first producer/mentor Lou Adler, prompted guitarist Randy California to stroll up Topango Canyon and seek neighbour Neil Young's advice, one spring morning in 1970. When Young recommended his own producer, David Briggs, California proceeded to Briggs' house, at the bottom of the canyon, and introduced himself. In Randy's assessment, Briggs transformed Spirit from a great band into a transcendently great band.

"David became a sixth member – guided us to our very best studio performances – this album could not have happened without David." Indeed, *Dr Sardonicus* is the nickname the band bestowed on the studio mixing desk. Sardonicus' songs ranged across the concerns of the era – racism, ecology, war, pornography – but the weighty topics never edged out catchy hooks and an astonishing assortment of mind-tickling new noises. Taught by Hendrix, Randy California's guitar work varied from proto-metal on Nothin' To Hide to delicate finger-picking on Why Can't I Be Free, and the unlikely juxtaposition of his coruscating licks with Cassidy's meaty big-band drumming and John Locke's jazzy keyboards, further added to this kaleidoscopic sonic palette. But to achieve all this, California assumed control, and other members felt sidelined. Vocalist Jay Ferguson recalls how

"The fights we were having were so bitter and people were threatening to quit all the time," vocalist Jay Ferguson recalls. In California's version, Ferguson plotted to betray Spirit by forming a new band, Jo Jo Gunne, with bassist Mark Andes. "Jay and Mark were sneaking off rehearsing and not telling anybody, and so a lot of the mixing and finishing up for *Sardonicus* was just left with me and David." On release, Nick Tosches of Rolling Stone had reservations but still rated it "a blockbuster", while Record Mirror's Lon Goddard reckoned "Spirit have excelled themselves – beautifully blown and precisely picked." One month later, the original Spirit line-up played its last ever concert, on New Year's Eve at the Fillmore East. Once again, the work of birthing a classic album had torn a band apart.

Record label:
Epic
Produced
by David Briggs.
Recorded
at Sound City Studios, Los Angeles; April–September 1970.
Chart peaks:
None (UK) 63 (US)
Released:
November 25, 1970
Running time:
39.13
Personnel:
Randy California (g, v); Ed Cassidy (d); Jay Ferguson (v, pc); John Locke (k); Mark Andes (b)
Track listing:
Prelude – Nothin' To Hide; Nature's Way; Animal Zoo; Love Has Found A Way; Why Can't I Be Free; Mr Skin; Space Child; When I Touch You; Street Worm; Life Has Just Begun; Morning Will Come; Soldier
Current CD:
Epic 476603 2
Further listening:
The double CD Time Circle (1991) compiles Spirit's early high points, while the sprawling Spirit Of '76 (1977) is a flawed masterwork.
Further reading:
Hot Wacks, special edition, Issue 16, June 1978; http://www.lls.se/~johanb/spirit/
Like this?
Try . . . p.60

Family

Anyway

Turning point from prog rock to unlikely pop stardom for early '70s style-straddlers.

Family were not obvious pop stars. Hailing from Leicester, this unkempt, beardy bunch inhabited a curious musical backwater all their own and became a staple on the college rock circuit. Their sound centred around the gritty, almost operatic vibrato of stick-thin vocalist Roger Chapman. It was an odd, warbling voice which could sour milk, but Chapman (a man with LOVE and HATE tattooed on his knuckles) could also provide a richly emotive foil for the intricate guitar and tricky arrangements of Charlie Whitney and the instrumental adventures of their band.

Family's first recordings had dabbled in psychedelia – 1967's truly oddball single, Scene Through The Eye Of A Lens – then added jazz, neo-classical and folk influences to form a unique but quite serious brand of rock for boys. Family's thoughtful sound eventually came to the fore in August 1970, when a three track EP, Strange Band, took them to Number 11 in the singles chart. Startled by commercial success, the group hurriedly shelved plans to make their fourth album a double live affair, and released *Anyway* instead. On paper it was a dangerous half-way house – their heavier live sound showcased on four songs and their intended future path on four studio takes. It could have easily alienated all-comers but, instead, it sounded audaciously eclectic, littered with violin figures, tinkling piano and the roar of a band on stage. Family had become pin-sharp through incessant touring and the studio songs were full of innovation. "Because Olympic was used for film music there would always be tons of gear waiting to be collected the next day," recalls multi-instrumentalist Poli Palmer. "So in the middle of the night, you'd have a good look through, pull out bits of percussion or a harpsichord and have a go."

The result was housed in a suitably unusual sleeve, with a Leonardo Da Vinci illustration printed in gold upon a textured plastic bag, which apart from its eccentricity, did little to prepare the listener for Family life within. Family songs functioned as playlets; there was always something gritty and resolutely English about them. They really don't make records like this any more.

No one followed in Family's footsteps.

Record label:
Reprise
Produced
by Family for Bradgate Bush Ltd.
Recorded:
Tracks 1–5 recorded live at Fairfield Hall, Croydon; tracks 6–11 recorded at Olympic Studios, London.
Released:
November 1970
Chart peaks:
7 (UK) None (US)
Personnel:
Charlie Whitney (g, b); Roger Chapman (v); Rob Townsend (d, p); John Weider (v, b); Poli Palmer (p, pc, vibes, d, f)
Track listing:
Good News – Bad News; Willow Tree; Holding The Compass; Strange Band (S); Part Of The Load; Anyway; Normans; Lives And Ladies. Current CD adds: Today (S); Song For Lots; Today (edit)
Running time:
52.40 (includes extra tracks)
Current CD:
Essential ESMCD615
Further listening:
The three previous Family albums, Music In A Doll's House (1968); Entertainment (1969) and A Song For Me (1970) are all excellent, and Anthology: Best Of (2000) is a very useful 2CD collection.
Further reading:
MOJO 33
Like this?
Try . . . p.258

Vashti Bunyan

Just Another Diamond Day

Ex-starlet makes poignant record of her horsedrawn odyssey to the Hebrides, finally finding an audience thirty years on.

After spending several musically frustrating years contracted to Andrew Oldham, during which a mere two singles were made and many promises broken, Vashti Bunyan had had enough. While other hippies pontificated about the joys of nature without ever properly experiencing them, she left London early in 1968 for the Scottish islands, where Donovan was supposedly establishing an artistic commune. Accompanied only by her partner Robert, Bess the horse, Blue the dog, an old wagon and a guitar, she fully lived the romantic life evoked on this glorious album.

"The days were long, and the industrial parts we travelled through were very grimy - but the grimier they were, the more dreamlike and longing were the songs I wrote. Maybe that optimism is what catches people now", she says today. Having reached the outer Hebrides and survived the exigencies of a Celtic winter, she returned to London in late 1969 at the urging of Joe Boyd, eager to capture the spirit of her voyage while it remained fresh.

The sessions took about a month, much of which Vashti spent dazed at the sheer fact of being recorded at all. "I was about as unconscious as it's possible for a songwriter to be since I wasn't writing the songs with a thought to ever recording them", she says. Avoiding both the trappings of traditional folk and contemporary peace and love clichés, the album is strongly melodic and immaculately arranged by Robert Kirby, best known for his exceptional work with Nick Drake. The supporting cast, including members of Fairport Convention and the Incredible String Band, contribute magnificent touches such as the soaring recorders on 'Rainbow River' and the disembodied piano on 'Timothy Grub', but it's her own performances that mesmerise. From the unearthly beauty of 'Diamond Day' to the a capella introduction to 'Window Over The Bay', the whimsy of 'Glow Worms' and Jog Along Bess' and the austere intimacy of 'Iris's Song For Us' and 'Where I Like To Stand', she casts an unforgettable spell, evoking with immediacy both the hardships and glories of life on the road, her fragile, whispering delivery perfectly suiting her sincere, poetic lyrics.

Although *Just Another Diamond Day* can seem overwhelmingly precious on a first listen, its quiet joys soon seep through. Sadly, though, when it 'blushed and shuffled' out (as Vashti puts it) in 1970, the only review she saw was dismissive, leading her to abandon music in favour of family. Having almost forgotten about the album, when she first went online she was astounded to see how much interest it had generated. A recent reissue has reached a far greater audience than ever anticipated originally.

RMJ

Record label
Philips
Produced
at Joe Boyd
Recorded
at Sound Techniques, London, November / December 1969.
Released:
November 1970.
Chart peaks:
None (UK) / n/a (US).
Personnel:
Vashti Bunyan (g, v) / Christopher Sykes (p, o) / John James (dulchichord) / Robin Williamson (fiddle, penny whistle, Irish harp) / Dave Swarbrick (fiddle, mandolin) / Simon Nicol (banjo) / Robert Kirby (ar).
Track listing:
Diamond Day / Glow Worms / Lily Pond / Timothy Grub / Where I Like To Stand / Swallow Song / Window Over The Bay / Rose Hip November / Come Wind Come Rain / Hebridean Sun / Rainbow River / Trawlerman's Song / Jog Along Bess / Iris's Song For Us.
Running time:
31.24 (current CD adds 4 bonus tracks, 40.02).
Currently available:
Spinney CD 001 (July 2001).
Like this?
Try . . . p.641

Carole King

Tapestry

Brill Building contract songwriter makes successful transition to solo artist, and sells 10 million albums in two years.

Superficially, with *Tapestry*, King seemed to be coat-tailing contemporaries like Joni Mitchell or Laura Nyro. In fact she had been a working songwriter, and occasional artist, for a decade, composing over 100 Top 40 hits with lyricist Gerry Goffin, eight of which reached Number 1. As the '60s ended, however, King had to change her *modus operandi*. The success of Dylan and The Beatles, she explained, meant that "the need for outside writers was less. The only way to get my songs heard was to sing them myself." Most of *Tapestry*'s songs were done as demos, intended for other artists, but as her producer Lou Adler noted, "When she was writing for other people, Carole was, in effect, impersonating somewhat the sound and feel of an artist's hit." To become a singer-songwriter, she had to find her own identity, and Adler knew how to help. "I had a definite theme in mind, to have that lean, almost demo-type sound, with a basic rhythm section and Carole on piano, playing lots of her figures."

Partly because King's friend James Taylor was recording *Mud Slide Slim And The Blue Horizon* nearby, he provided another valued presence on *Tapestry*, contributing ideas, backing vocals and guitar. Although It's Too Late gave King her only US Number 1 single, the core of *Tapestry* is probably You've Got A Friend, which King says, "was as close to pure inspiration as I've ever experienced. The song wrote itself. It was written by something outside of myself, through me." Unfortunately, she couldn't release it as a single, because Taylor got there first.

"*Tapestry* maybe cost $15,000, but I doubt it was that much," says Adler. "I remember the first ad, Honesty Is Back." The timing was perfect. The simple veracities of King's lyrics and her understated performances came as soothing balm to listeners who, for the past five years had been subjected to the excesses of psychedelia and prog. Indeed, asked why it became such a huge success, King has said, "Right time and the right place." Even so, it's hard to disagree with Jon Landau of Rolling Stone whose review called it "an album of surpassing personal intimacy and musical accomplishment, and a work infused with a sense of artistic purpose." On June 19, 1971, it hit Number 1 in Billboard, and stayed put for 15 weeks, ultimately spending 302 weeks in the chart – the longest-charting album by any female solo artist. At the Grammys, she collected Best Album, Best Song, Best Record and Best Female Vocalist.

Record Label:
Ode
Produced
by Lou Adler.
Recorded
at A&M Studios, Hollywood; January 4–15, 1971.
Chart peaks:
4 (UK) 1 (US)
Released:
November 1970
Personnel:
Carole King (k, v); James Taylor (g, v); Danny "Kootch" Kortchmar (g); Charles Larkey (b); Jim Gordon (d); Ralph Shuckett (k); Curtis Amy (s, flute); Perry Steinberg (b); Terry King (c); Barry Socher (vn); Joni Mitchell (bv); Merry Clayton (bv); Julia Tillman (bv); David Campbell (oa)
Track Listing:
I Feel The Earth Move; So Far Away (S); It's Too Late (S); Home Again; Beautiful; Way Over Yonder; You've Got A Friend; Where You Lead; Will You Love Me Tomorrow; Smackwater Jack; Tapestry; (You Make Me Feel Like) A Natural Woman
Running time:
43.30
Current CD:
Sony Legacy 4931802, adds: Out In The Cold; Smackwater Jack (live)
Further listening:
The Ode Collection 1968–1976 contains all of Tapestry, plus the best of King's other work, while The Goffin & King Songbook collects versions of her Brill Building hits.
Further reading:
members.home.net/caroleking/
Like this?
Try . . . p.361

James Taylor

Sweet Baby James

Sophomore disc by the unassuming bard of bedsitter-land that begat the singer-songwriter movement.

Shy, retiring James Taylor was only 22 when *Sweet Baby James* broke. He had recorded an album in London in 1968 for The Beatles' Apple label, but it was only back in Los Angeles, with former Apple executive Peter Asher as manager, that he hit pay-dirt. "The album was made fast, back when music was still my hobby," said Taylor. But although the album was barely half an hour long, he still had a job finishing it. The last – and longest – track, Suite For 20G, was made up of several unfinished songs pieced together and named "somewhat cynically" after the fact that "we were getting twenty grand for delivering the album."

The title track is a poignant narrative of a young cowboy alone on the range, thinking about "women and glasses of beer", while the album's best-known song, the captivating Fire And Rain, is a tragic recollection of a girlfriend's suicide, couched in accessibly poetic lyrics. "Other than Fire And Rain, much of the record is very whimsical, very un-self-important, and not taken very seriously," Taylor reflects, "which is probably why it still comes off fresh. After *Sweet Baby James* things changed, and I became professional, which meant a loss of innocence and a shift of motivation."

Peter Asher handled the clean, crisp production; Carole King helped out on piano (just prior to recording her own landmark *Tapestry*) and Taylor's teenage friend Danny Kortchmar (they had been together in the band The Flying Machine, which features in Fire And Rain's lyrics) played guitar. "I joke that I knew James before he was sensitive," chuckles Kortchmar, "but the truth is that James is the archetypal singer-songwriter – *the* mould. He's a guitar virtuoso who subverted folk forms with a lot of major 7ths and higher inversion chords and he mixed influences like Stephen Foster, Pete Seeger, Aaron Copland, Lightnin' Hopkins and The Beatles, so they disappeared into the James Taylor stew. His songs sound like blues, like Christmas carols and like a church choir too, yet it all essentially comes only from him."

Sweet Baby James's loose-limbed charm and Taylor's easy way with a song – not to mention the to-die-for cheekbones – would quickly make him a college pin-up, a Time magazine cover-boy and a reluctant superstar.

Record label:
Warner Brothers
Produced
by Peter Asher.
Recorded
at Sunset Sound, Los Angeles; December 1969.
Released:
November 1970
Chart peaks:
7 (UK) 3 (US)
Personnel:
James Taylor (g); Danny Kootch (g); Carole King (p); Russ Kunkel (d); Randy Meisner (b); Bobby West (b); John London (b); Red Rhodes (ps); Chris Darrow (vn); Jack Bielan (a); Bill Lazerus (e)
Track listing:
Sweet Baby James; Lo And Behold; Sunny Skies; Steamroller; Country Road (S/US); Oh Susannah; Fire And Rain (S); Blossom; Anywhere Like Heaven; Oh Baby, Don't You Loose Your Lip On Me; Suite For 20G.
Running time:
31.53
Current CD:
7599-27183-2
Further Listening:
(Live) (1993)
Further Reading:
MOJO 46;
www.james-taylor.com
Like this?
Try . . . p.287

John Lennon

John Lennon/Plastic Ono Band

He kicks the '60s into touch and invents angst-rock.

Exorcising one's torment through rock music was still a relatively new idea when John Lennon made his first proper solo album. There had always been the blues, of course, but the transatlantic white rock aristocracy had tended to avoid all but the most oblique soul-baring. Lennon had occasionally made an exception – cf Help! and Yer Blues – but *John Lennon/Plastic Ono Band* saw him reaching new heights of confessional honesty.

The reason lay in his and Yoko's trip to America on April 23, 1970. They flew to Los Angeles to begin a course of Dr Arthur Janov's 'primal scream' therapy; but the stay, meant to last well over a year, was cut short by the US immigration authorities on August 1. John and Yoko duly returned to their Tittenhurst Park mansion, and Lennon began writing a new batch of songs. They dealt explicitly with Janov's treatment, and found Lennon attempting to clear out his psyche in preparation for a new phase of life. Thus, he dealt with the loss of his mother (in Mother and the mini-song My Mummy's Dead), the delusions of hippydom (I Found Out), and the roots of his own inner dislocation in the British class system (Working Class Hero). Most spectacular of all was God, his scattershot rejection of religion, Dylan, Elvis and life as a Beatle.

The group he used was deliberately tiny – indeed, on Mother and God, there is little more than piano, bass, drums and vocals – and though the involvement of Phil Spector might have suggested a detour into polish and embellishment, Lennon ensured that he attended only the last three days of the sessions, employing him as a mixer rather than an old-style producer. "We never gave him his head," said Lennon. "But we used his amazing ear for pop music and sound without it becoming *Spector*."

"They said it was simplistic and self-indulgent," said Lennon in 1980. "Now, self-indulgent means you talk about yourself, right? If we'd have used pseudonyms and called it *Tommy, The Rock Opera* or *Ziggy Stardust*, or sung in the third person, it might have been more acceptable. But we prefer to not wear make-up."

Record label:
Apple
Produced
by John Lennon, Yoko Ono and Phil Spector.
Recorded
at Abbey Road, London; September 26–October 5, 1969.
Released:
December 11, 1970
Chart peaks:
11 (UK) 6 (US)
Personnel:
John Lennon (v, g, p); Klaus Voorman (b); Ringo Starr (d); Billy Preston (p); Phil Spector (p); Phil McDonald, Richard Lush, John Leckie (e)
Track listing:
Mother (S); Hold On; I Found Out; Working Class Hero; Isolation; Remember; Love; Well Well Well; Look At Me; God; My Mummy's Dead
Running time:
39.48
Current CD:
Parlophone CDFA3310
Further listening:
The John Lennon Anthology (1998)
Further reading:
We All Shine On (Paul Du Noyer, 1999); The Lives Of John Lennon (Albert Goldman, 1989)
Like this?
Try . . . p.77

James Brown

Sex Machine

The refining of bass-heavy funk, and definitive evidence of the rapid evolution of Brown's music.

"Recorded live at home in Augusta Georgia with his bad self" claimed the sleeve. Actually, only tracks 6–14 were cut in concert. And there were two different bands. The second half of *Sex Machine* captures the Fred Wesley-Maceo Parker band recorded live and at its peak in Augusta, Georgia in 1969, shortly before a dispute over money led them to walk out/be sacked. Tracks 1–5 and 8 were studio-recorded with audience brouhaha dubbed afterwards. On four of these, Brown uses the youthful vigour and enthusiasm of his new rhythm section to recast old material. Bassist Bootsy Collins, authoritative beyond his years (hear him fly on Give It Up Or Turn It A Loose), his elder brother guitarist Catfish Collins and long-serving drummers Jabo Starks and Clyde Stubblefield are at the eye of this particular storm, with Brown audibly enthused by their propulsive drive. He revisits the title track (its older version was a hit single at the time), and reins in the horn section, making it an adjunct of the rhythm section, a process heard more obviously on another of the remakes, the brief I Got The Feelin'.

The second track, Brother Rapp, was cut with the older, more-seasoned troupe and melodically makes more use of the horns, while the guitars of Nolen and Kellum have richer, thicker tones. Brown veterans also drive the genuine in-concert recordings and they are in exceptional form. The horn players even get solos! I Don't Want Nobody bounces along on the beat, and the punishing pace of Licking Stick makes it little wonder these guys pulled fines for mistakes. When, in Man's Man's Man's World – which, incidentally, is a terrific example of his rapport with his audience – Brown says "Give the band a hand for being so together," you can't quite work out if he's fining them in code or not; when he quietly admonishes, "Don't play so much jazz," you know they're in trouble. Still, they sound great to these ears. Two superb bands for the price of one and a 36-year-old musical revolutionary marching forward with a different drum ringing in his ears. It's soul history in the making.

Record label:
Polydor
Produced
by James Brown.
Recorded
at King Studios, Cincinnati, Ohio and Bell Auditorium, Augusta, Georgia.
Released:
December 1970
Chart peaks:
None (UK) 29 (US)
Personnel:
James Brown (v, k); Clayton 'Chicken' Gunnels, Darryl 'Hasaan' Jamison, Richard 'Kush' Griffith, Joseph Davis (t); Maceo Parker (ts, o, MC); St. Clair Pinckney (ts, bs); Robert 'Chopper' McCullough, Eldee Williams (ts); Alfred 'Pee Wee' Ellis (as); Fred Wesley (tb); Bobby Byrd (o, v); Phelps 'Catfish' Collins, Jimmy Nolen, Alphonso 'Country' Kellum, Kenny Poole (g); William 'Bootsy' Collins, 'Sweet' Charles Sherrell (b); John 'Jabo' Starks, Clyde Stubblefield, Melvin Parker (d)
Track listing:
Sex Machine; Brother Rapp; Bewildered; I Got The Feelin'; Give It Up Or Turn It A Loose; I Don't Want Nobody To Give Me Nothing; Licking Stick; Lowdown Popcorn; Spinning Wheel; If I Ruled The World; There Was A Time; It's A Man's Man's Man's World; Please, Please, Please; I Can't Stand Myself; Mother Popcorn
Running time:
65.00
Current CD:
517 984-2
Further reading:
James Brown: The Autobiography (1996)
Like this?
Try . . . p.542

Derek And The Dominos

Layla And Other Assorted Love Songs

A flop when first released: now widely regarded as the height of Clapton's achievement.

During 1969–1970, Eric Clapton had at least one monkey on his back; like both Hendrix and Peter Green, he was tired of being regarded as a guitar hero. He sought refuge with white soul singers Delaney and Bonnie, revelling in their laid back style and rootsy authenticity. By May 1970, their musicians had become Eric's, while he in turn had become Derek, a half-joking, half-serious attempt to become anonymous again.

August saw the band camped out at the Criteria Studios in Miami trying to turn bits of songs and half-formed ideas into an album. *Layla* came together through endless jamming; "We really didn't know what we were going to do," says Bobby Whitlock. "Tom and the engineers' job was just to make sure they hit those faders as soon as we started playing. That fade in on Key To The Highway was the only time they missed."

Among the new songs was the surging and lyrical title track, Eric's cry of unrequited love for George Harrison's wife Patti. Clapton and Whitlock formed a fertile writing and vocal partnership, but the ante soared with the arrival of Duane Allman who took the music to another place. The musicians themselves were already there, thanks to copious amounts of drugs. Though ultimately highly destructive, there seems little doubt that the chemicals played an important part in the magic of the Dominos. Eric has never played any less; the gorgeous runs, fills and solos were present, but it was all so much more measured and restrained. It was a unique situation which could never be repeated; the closeness of the musicians interlocking with each other on several levels, the womb-like environment of Criteria, the sympathetic production of Tom Dowd, the freedom and space to create.

As engineer Karl Richardson put it, "You couldn't not know that the music flying out of Studio B was phenomenal. You'd have to be deaf." But this was not the view of the music-buying public; the initial critical and commercial failure of the album when first released just added to the problems piling up for the band both as a group and as individuals. Indeed, if Eric originally entered the project to take it easy, he ended up making things infinitely harder for himself, becoming addicted to heroin.

After tours of Britain and America, the Dominos broke up in acrimony after only a year, in May 1971. Drugs and madness did for them all in one way or another. Whitlock survives but Allman and Radle are both dead, Jim Gordon is serving a life sentence for murdering his mother. Derek eventually became Eric again – not just a cult guitar hero, but a musician and songwriter of international repute – though at some cost.

Record label:
Polydor
Produced
by Tom Dowd.
Recorded
at Criteria Studios, Miami; August–September 1970.
Released:
December 1970
Chart peaks:
None (UK) 16 (US)
Personnel:
Eric Clapton (g, v); Duane Allman (g); Bobby Whitlock (p, o, v); Carl Radle (b, pc); Jim Gordon (d, pc, p); Ron Albert, Chuck Kirkpatrick, Howie Albert, Karl Richardson, Mac Emmerman (e)
Track listing:
I Looked Away; Bell Bottom Blues (S/US); Keep On Growing; Nobody Knows You When You Are Down And Out; I Am Yours; Anyday; Key To The Highway; Tell The Truth; Why Does Love Got To Be So Sad (S/UK); Have You Ever Loved A Woman; Little Wing; It's Too Late; Layla (S); Thorn Tree In The Garden
Running time:
77.09
Current CD:
Polydor 5318202
Further listening:
3 CD 20th Anniversary box set Derek and the Dominos: the Layla Sessions (1990) comprising not only the album, but also all the alternative version, long jams plus the tracks from the abortive second album.
Further reading:
Midnight Riders: The Story Of The Allman Brothers Band (Scott Freeman, 1995); www.whereseric.com
Like this?
Try . . . p.372

The Grateful Dead

American Beauty

Minimalist rootsy opus from mellowing masters of the elongated jam.

Having visited their country roots on *Workingman's Dead* earlier in the year, The Grateful Dead delved even deeper with *American Beauty*. The heady days of psychedelia and guiltless freedom had swiftly passed and their search for a context in the subsequent months of political unrest and Vietnam war protest, not to mention a slew of drug busts, led them to flee to the country, where they explored folkloric melody, subdued storytelling and three-part harmony. The latter was a direct influence of Crosby Stills & Nash, whose first album they'd paid homage to on *Workingman's Dead*, but who, in the subsequent months, they actually visited at work on *Deja Vu*. Seeing how CS&N recorded vocals – all three around a 360° mic plus an identical overdub mixed at three-quarters of the level – really turned the Dead's heads.

"It amazed them," recalled Graham Nash in MOJO 67. "They'd been used to doing individual voices. [That's why] *Workingman's Dead* didn't sound anywhere near *American Beauty* vocally. Whatever they'd learned from us they put into good practice." FM radio noticed and began to give the album's great ballads, Box Of Rain and Ripple, unexpected support, which in turn won the Dead new fans. The key was simplicity. The songs were extracted from fruitful back-porch jams (Jerry Garcia and lyricist Robert Hunter were sharing a house by this time) that not only spawned this album but also a Garcia side project, The New Riders Of The Purple Sage. Among the many friends invited along to these pick-a-thons was mandolin player Dave Grisman: "The original recordings were built out of endless sessions where Jerry and I would play off against each other, with the rest of the New Riders crew sitting in too. The end result was a far more stripped down version of what we were doing."

In fact, it's the paring-down and editing of the material that was the making of *American Beauty*. At times, it is utterly bare, just the harmonies of Garcia, Weir and Lesh melding into a kind of gothic choir. And, in places it's truly moving, too, as in the beautiful melodies of Sugar Magnolia and Friend Of The Devil, the sound of America shaking itself awake to a challenging new decade. And if that weren't enough definitive Dead, there's also the more prosaic Truckin', their road-jockey's anthem that quickly became part of their legend, mainly because it included their most memorable line: "What a long, strange trip it's been."

Record label:
Warner Brothers
Produced
by The Grateful Dead.
Recorded
at Wally Heider Studios, San Francisco; autumn 1969.
Released:
December 1970
Chart peaks:
None (UK) None (US)
Personnel:
Jerry Garcia (v, g, ps, p); Bob Weir (rg); Ron 'Pigpen' McKernan (v, hm); Phil Lesh (b, g, p, v); Bill Kreutzman (d); Mickey Hart (pc); David Nelson (g); David Grisman (mandolin); Dave Torbert (b); Howard Wales (o, p); Ned Lagin (p)
Track listing:
Box Of Rain; Friend Of The Devil; Sugar Magnolia; Operator; Candyman; Ripple; Brokedown Palace; Till The Morning Comes; Attics Of My Life; Truckin' (S/US)
Running time:
42.28
Current CD:
7599271902
Further listening:
Workingman's Dead (1970) was composed in the same period. "I think of those as being really one record, in a way," said Jerry Garcia. Hear also the closely related New Riders Of The Purple Sage's self-titled first album (1971).
Further reading:
for a comprehensive Grateful Dead bibliography, try www.sfmuseum.org/hist1/deadbib.html
Like this?
Try . . . p.60

George Harrison

All Things Must Pass

A chart-topping triple set that sounds better and better as time goes by.

When promo copies of Paul's solo album, *McCartney* were sent out in April 1970, the press release inadvertently tipped off the tabloids that The Beatles were finished.

It was a messy finish that didn't seem conclusive. As months went by, though, it began to dawn on the public that their favourite pop group really had gone for good. Suddenly, George – of all people – came to the rescue with a bountiful triple boxed set accompanied by the first solo Beatle US Number 1 single, My Sweet Lord (not released in the UK until January). A bumper Christmas treat with a little religion thrown in – perfect. George certainly announced his arrival as a solo artist in grand style.

"I've always looked at *All Things Must Pass* like someone who's had constipation for years and then finally they get diarrhoea," he explained helpfully to Billboard's Craig Rosen. Indeed, he'd acquired a backlog of material while with The Beatles and one or two of the songs had been, by necessity, road-tested elsewhere. My Sweet Lord and All Things (Must) Pass appeared on Billy Preston's Apple album, *Encouraging Words*. Tapes also exist of George demoing songs with engineer Phil Macdonald, including titles like Everybody, Nobody; Window, Window and Mother Divine, none of which made it onto this record. George was clearly enjoying a creative burst.

On May 1, 1970 he'd jammed with Bob Dylan during sessions for the *New Morning* album, played slide guitar on Bob's version of If Not For You and written I'd Have You Anytime with him. By late May, George was ready to record his own album and backing tracks were laid at Abbey Road with an all-star cast of heavy session friends, including an uncredited Eric Clapton audible on many tracks, and Phil Spector joining George at the controls. Overdubbing was done at Trident Studios and Abbey Road from June and mixes were completed in New York.

The third disc – Apple Jam, featuring Harrison, Clapton, Billy Preston, Bobby Keys and Klaus Voormann – included an impromptu 30th birthday greeting to John Lennon, It's Johnny's Birthday, sung to the tune of Congratulations. This "free gift" inevitably hiked the price of the album and now spoils its overall mood on CD. It is perhaps the unwieldy (and costly) nature of the whole package that has prevented *All Things Must Pass* from being more popular down the years. The two main albums are superb, the best George ever produced, concise and filler-free. Spector's warm, pillowy sound provides an epic grace and an engaging habitat; George's sense of freedom is audible and many of the songs outshine his contributions to Beatles albums. work.

Record label:
Apple
Produced
by George Harrison and Phil Spector.
Recorded
at Abbey Road and Trident Studios, London.
Released:
December 1970
Chart peaks:
4 (UK) 1 (US)
Personnel:
George Harrison (g, v); Eric Clapton (g); Dave Mason (g); Pete Ham, Tom Evans (rg); Ringo Starr, Jim Gordon, Alan White (d, pc); Klaus Voormann, Carl Radle (b); Gary Wright, Bobby Whitlock, Billy Preston, Gary Brooker (k); Bobby Keys (ts); Jim Price (t); Pete Drake (psg); Mal Evans (tea, sympathy, tambourine); John Burnham (oa); Ken Scott, Phil Macdonald (e)
Track listing:
I'd Have You Anytime; My Sweet Lord; Wah-Wah; Isn't It A Pity (One); What Is Life; If Not For You; Behind That Locked Door; Let it Down; Run Of The Mill; Beware Of Darkness; Apple Scruffs; Ball Of Sir Frankie Crisp; Awaiting On You All; All Things Must Pass; I Dig Love; Art Of Dying; Isn't It A Pity (Two); Hear Me Lord; Out Of The Blue; It's Johnny's Birthday; Plug Me In; I Remember Jeep; Thanks For The Pepperoni
Running time:
105.11
Current CD:
EMI CDS 7 46688 8
Further listening:
Extra Texture (1975), specifically the single You.
Further reading:
The Beatles After The Break-Up 1970–2000 (1999)
Like this?
Try . . . p.812

The Stooges

Fun House

Stooges sophomore album anticipated the dense metallic sound of punk, goth and industrial music.

The plan behind *Fun House* was simple. It was to be a faithful reproduction, in sequence, of The Stooges' live set. First, however, the band needed a sympathetic producer. Elektra boss Jac Holzman selected one-time Kingsman Don Gallucci.Gallucci went to see the band and turned down the job: "I said, 'Jac, it's a performance band, it's got a lot of vitality and energy, but there is nothing musical here.'" Holzman, relishing the creative tension, told Gallucci he was doing the job anyway. His confidence was repaid; realising the importance of retaining the band's live energy, Gallucci, aided by the staid but inspired British enginer Brian Ross-Myring, stripped Holzman's elegant studio of all its carpeting and sound baffling and had the band set up as if playing live; lead singer Iggy roamed the floor with a basic hand mic.

Fortunately, the band already had everything nailed before recording commenced. As Iggy puts it, "It had a unity and a reality before we ever got on the studio. I knew exactly what I wanted it to be." New Stooge Steve Mackay, recruited shortly before the session, concurs: "Iggy's already got *Fun House* written in his head and knows there's gonna be sax on it, so he invites me for a coffee and already knows he wants to take me to Los Angeles to record." Mackay's saxophone fitted in perfectly with The Stooges' stripped-down ethos, distilled from a musical diet of James Brown, Hendrix, and Harry Partch.

By now, Ron Asheton's guitar playing had progressed from the charming primitivism of the band's debut, to something much more powerful and concise: "There is not one solo that is overdubbed; the only thing I went back and overdubbed was little picking pieces, rhythms here and there."

The results were unique in musical history, an aggressive rock band packing in high-density musical ideas, captured with the natural freedom of a jazz recording. Iggy describes it as "Osterberg's fifth symphony". The rest of the world, however, was unmoved. Lester Bangs' epic Creem review, run over two weeks, didn't prevent the album sinking without trace. Its most immediate consequence for The Stooges would be a collective heroin habit, acquired in LA's low-spots.

Record label:
Elektra
Produced
by Don Gallucci.
Recorded
at Elektra Sound Recorders, Los Angeles; May 11–24, 1970.
Released:
December 1970
Chart peaks:
None (UK) None (US)
Personnel:
Iggy Pop (v); Dave Alexander (b); Ron Asheton (g); Scott Asheton (d); Steve Mackay (ts); Brian Ross-Myring (e)
Track listing:
Down On The Street (S); Loose; TV Eye; Dirt; I Feel Alright; Fun House; LA Blues
Running time:
36.28
Current CD:
7559-60669-2
Further listening:
Funhouse Sessions (2000) a 6-CD box set containing session out-takes.
Further reading:
MOJO 29; www.rawiguana.com
Like this?
Try . . . p.261

Emitt Rhodes

Emitt Rhodes

The best LP that Paul McCartney never made.

Poor Emitt Rhodes was as ill-fated in business as he was blessed with musical talent. He had two golden opportunities, both of which began promisingly and ended in disappointment. Rhodes' first proper band The Merry Go Round secured an A&M deal in 1967 and released a first single Live that was a huge regional hit and made it to Number 63 nationally. Packed off to make an album, Rhodes discovered a talent for inventiveness in the studio and got the bug; the band disintegrated and he became a one-man studio-bound band instead.

Purchasing a 'washing machine type four track' he shut himself away in his parents' garage., recording a good half of the material on *Emitt Rhodes* there before doing a deal with Dunhill. The album was completed with the mix-down assistance of Keith Olsen (who would later produce Fleetwood Mac) and Curt Boettcher, already something of a soft-pop legend for his work with The Association, Millennium and Sagittarius.

Things began like a dream. A single, Fresh As A Daisy, ascended the charts and the album reached as high as 29 by the beginning of 1971. Then the music business corrupted it all. Firstly A&M cobbled together a spoiler album *The American Dream* which ate into sales of *Emitt Rhodes* and then Dunhill suspended him for not delivering a second album on time. His career started to disintegrate and the whole affair left a bitter taste. Yet *Emitt Rhodes* is a true delight and far more than a mere footnote in pop history. At least the equal of other Beatles inspired records by Badfinger or Todd Rundgren. Rhodes took classic Beatles motifs and made them his own: *Abbey Road* guitar, McCartney upper register bass lines, and the familiar call and response harmonies of Hello Goodbye. And it anticipates each wave of Fabs-obsessed powerpop that followed, from The Raspberries to Jellyfish to Matthew Sweet.

Neither of his two final Dunhill albums quite measured up, *Mirror* in 1971 and the prophetic *Farewell to Paradise* in 1973. By the '80s, in his own words, he was washed up, putting his decline down to "demos, debauchery and drugs". All in all, a tragedy, made more poignant by the wide-eyed exuberance of this lovely record.

Record label:
Dunhill
Produced
by Emitt Rhodes and Harvey Bruce.
Recorded
at Homes Studios, Hawthorne, California.
Released:
winter 1970
Chart peaks:
None (UK) 29 (US)
Personnel:
Emitt Rhodes (all instruments, v, e)
Track listing:
With My Face On The Floor; Somebody Made For Me; She's Such A Beauty; Long Time No See; Lullaby; Fresh As A Daisy; Live Till You Die; Promises I've Made; You Take The Dark Out Of The Night; You Should Be Ashamed; Ever Find Yourself Running; You Must Have
Running time:
32.05
Current CD:
Edsel EDCD569
Further listening:
Further reading:
Power Pop: Conversations With The Powerpop Elite (Ken Sharp and Doug Sulp, 1997)
Like this?
Try . . . p.177

Fela Kuti

Fela's London Scene

Funky music, sho' nuff turns Africa on.

As the 1960s turned into an angrier, uglier decade, Nigeria's Fela Kuti hit top gear, taking the funk and politics of America's Black Panthers and offering it back to its homeland. In 1969, Fela and his band, the Koola Lobitos, arrived in Los Angeles, where Sandra Isidore, a black activist (and later a member of the Hummingbirds) introduced him to Black Power. His eyes opened, he renamed the band The Nigeria 70 and dreamt up Afrobeat. They scraped together enough money to record – *The '69 Los Angeles Session*, an uneven collection of soul and funk pastiches – then headed home.

Back in Lagos, the speed of development of Afrobeat was startling, with live shows and regular singles increasing his fan base, fleshing out the politics and breathing life into the music. His record company decided to support a visit to London, where Fela had been a student at the Royal College of Music in 1958. This time, he was feted as a star of Africa: living in a luxury hotel and recording at Abbey Road. He also had A-list celebrity pals – Ginger Baker had made friends with Kuti in Lagos in 1969, and was on hand to help the band acclimatise to Britain. Keeping their hand in, Nigeria 70 gigs were scheduled around London, but the real action was taking place in the studio.

J'Ehin J'Ehin attacks fools (people who "eat their own teeth"); Buy Africa is a nationalistic anthem encouraging pan–Africanism; and the centrepiece, the 13-minute Egbe Mi O (recorded live with Baker) uses dancing as metaphor, warning the overindulgent that "all your underwear drop". Fela's development was not complete – he would soon use pidgin English rather than Yoruba, to increase his audience – but the musical blueprint was there.

Almost immediately, he changed the band's name again – to Africa 70 – and started getting heavy. EMI refused to release his next LP, the two-song *Why Black Man Dey Suffer*, but Fela was on a roll, with a torrent of singles and albums that would grow increasingly political. In 1977, the army retaliated, attacking his home, fracturing his skull and murdering his mother. But the band played on.

NS

Record label:
Barclay
Produced
by Fela Kuti.
Recorded
at Abbey Road Studios, London; 1970.
Released:
1970
Chart peaks:
None (UK) None (US)
Personnel:
Fela Kuti (v, k, s); Ginger Baker (d); Tony Allen (d); Igo Chico (s); Lekan Animashaun (s); Tony Njoku (t); Tutu Sorunmu (g)
Track listing:
J'Ehin J'Ehin; Egbe Mi O; Who're You; Buy Africa; Fight To Finish
Running time:
43.24
Current CD:
STERNS3007 adds: Shakara Oloje; Lady
Further listening:
Open And Close (1971); He Miss Road (1974); Expensive Shit (1975); Confusion (1975); The Best Best Of: Black President (1999)
Further reading:
Fela: The Life And Times Of An African Musical Icon (Micheal E Veal, 2000)
Like this?
Try . . . p.607

1970

vk

overs

by former Frank Zappa protégé; rave ales, cult legend.

In a parallel world, Essra Mohawk's name would be so familiar no one would confuse it with an unfortunate hairstyle. But in this world, she remains a largely overlooked figure, famous more for her associations with an almost laughably impressive number of significant '60s pop music icons than her ability as a record maker. Had more people believed what they read about *Primordial Lovers* – the five-star review in Downbeat, or Rolling Stone's lauding it as "one of the best 25 albums ever made" – that likely wouldn't be the case.

Discovered in the mid-'60s by producer Shadow Morton and introduced to the pop world as Sandy Hurvitz via a debut album bearing Frank Zappa's picture on its cover – 1969's *Sandy's Album Is Here At Last* – Mohawk spent a brief period with the Mothers Of Invention before being offered a deal by Reprise Records' Mo Ostin. *Primordial Lovers* would be the eventual result, but not before she married the album's producer Frazier Mohawk, whose name can be found on Nico's *The Marble Index* as well. ("Of course his real name was Barry Friedman," she'd later note, "but Danny Kortchmar gave Barry the choice of Frazier Mohawk or Gabriel Roughweather. I think it's fortunate for me that he chose Frazier Mohawk.")

With its impressive cast of backing musicians, including members of San Francisco's Jerry Hahn Brotherhood and Tim Buckley's longtime guitarist Lee Underwood, the LP is firstly a sonic marvel, providing Mohawk's songs a beautiful setting she'd never capture again. And as for the songs themselves – an intimate collection of one-to-one lyrics addressed to a lover (presumably primordial) – they are magnificently, almost erotically, sung. When the raves came – and there were many – nobody listened. Was it a lack of promotion? Was it merely a question of cover art?

"They came up with a mostly black album," Mohawk recalls, "which does not draw light, does not draw eyes. And my idea was to have one set of bodies across the front and back – instead of the Rorschach effect that you have – and that would've been mostly white. And then superimposed over that a sunset and the earth – so it would be heaven and earth, primordial lovers. The horizon would be made by the meeting of the bodies." But back in black, it stayed in the rack.

Record label:
Reprise
Produced
by Frazier Mohawk.
Recorded
at Elektra Sound Recorders, Los Angeles and Pacific High Recording Co., San Francisco; 1969.
Released:
1970
Chart peaks:
None (UK) None (US)
Personnel:
Essra Mohawk (k, v); Doug Hastings (g); Jerry Hahn (g); Lee Underwood (g); Mel Graves (b); Jerry Penrod (b); Dalls Taylor (d); George Marsh (d); Phil Sawyer, Brian Ross-Myring (e)
Track listing:
I Am The Breeze; Spiral; I'll Give It To You Anyway; I Have Been Here Before; Looking Forward To The Dawn; Thunder In The Morning; Lion On The Wing; It's Up To Me; It's Been A Beautiful Day
Running time:
41.46
Currently unavailable on CD
Further listening:
Essra Mohawk (1975); Essra (1977)
Further reading:
When The Music Mattered (Bruce Pollock, 1984); www.rockersusa.com/EssraMohawk/
Like this?
Try . . . p.7

Eugene McDaniels

Headless Heroes Of The Apocalypse

Lost masterpiece of funky social commentary from "the black Bob Dylan".

Headless Heroes Of The Apocalypse stands as one of the most disarming and accessible albums of the black power era, but it's taken the best part of thirty years for the record to reach anywhere near audience it deserved.

Eugene McDaniels arrived at Atlantic as something of an enigma. The accidental creator of the Number One hit 100 Pounds Of Clay, he was perceived as a pop artist, but his roots lay in jazz. He also wrote songs, and had a hit with Compared To What, recorded by Les McCann and Eddie Harris on their Atlantic LP Swiss Movement. When McCann brought Roberta Flack to Atlantic, she put a version on her debut LP, and McDaniels went on to pen her massive '74 hit Feel Like Making Love. Atlantic's staff producer Joel Dorn, who worked with McCann and Flack at Atlantic and remembered 100 Pounds Of Clay, naturally suggested McDaniels record some of his own songs.

The band McDaniels assembled was staffed by jazz greats, and the album's eight songs reflect both his compact and direct style of writing and Dorn's famously stripped-down approach. While Alphonse Mouzon's insistent, shuffling drum work powers the tracks along the album is characterised by a delicate intimacy. It doesn't so much shine as glow; a sonic bonfire in a forest at night, themes and moods first flickering then roaring into view before disappearing back into the shadows. At the heart of the flame, McDaniels looks around at a world of skewed values and hypocrisy, calling out the liars and the cheats, prophesying the wrath of a vengeful god.

The title track is politically explicit, but it was the epic closer, The Parasite, that probably sealed the album's doom. McDaniels spoke of the genocide of native Americans and described the USA's first European settlers as "hoodlums and jailbirds".

"Richard Nixon's people called and asked [Atlantic founder] Ahmet Ertegun 'What the hell's going on over there?'," McDaniels remembers. "It really embarrassed him, so he fired me off the label." Ironically, Ertegun's compatriot, Jerry Wexler, had phoned Dorn on hearing the album to say he thought McDaniels was "the black Bob Dylan," and that the album would be a hit.

With promotion halted, the album languished in obscurity until a revival of interest in the 1990s, sparked initially by A Tribe Called Quest and the Beastie Boys sampling from it. Finally, in 2001, Dorn's Label M gave Headless Heroes its first CD release.

AB

Record label:
Atlantic
Produced
by Joel Dorn
Recorded
at Regent Sound Studio, NY; Atlantic Recording Studio, NY
Released:
1971
Chart peaks:
Personnel:
Eugene McDaniels (vocals, guitar): Harry Whitaker [mistakenly credited on both original and reissue sleeves as Dhitaker] (piano): Gary King (electric bass): Miroslav Vitous (acoustic bass): Alphonse Mouzon (drums): Richie Resnikoff (guitar): Carla Cargill (female vocals): the Welfare City Choir (backing vocals)
Track listing:
The Lord Is Back: Jagger The Dagger: Lovin' Man: Headless Heroes: Susan Jane: Freedom Death Dance: Supermarket Blues: The Parasite (For Buffy)
Running time:
38 mins 01 secs
Current CD:
Label M 485733
Further listening:
Outlaw (Atlantic, 1971)
Like this?
Try . . . p.580

Yoko Ono

Yoko Ono/Plastic Ono Band

Companion set to Lennon's solo debut that could have been recorded tomorrow.

John Lennon was once asked to explain why people didn't understand Yoko: "She is a woman and she's Japanese – it's as simple as that." He neglected to mention that she was also a former member of Fluxus, the '60s art movement dedicated to ridiculing the establishment, and to blurring the distinction between art and life. She had inspired Lennon to do likewise, but with much public recrimination. By 1970, the lives of the "two gurus in drag" had indeed become inseparable from their work, just as Lennon's separation from The Beatles had finally become public knowledge. The wranglings over the group's demise left deep scars; The Primal Scream author Arthur Janov was called on to help the pair confront their pain using a radical healing therapy based on catharsis. Lennon responded in singer-songwriterly fashion by recording the most revealing songs of his career; Ono opted to recreate the treatment's howling exorcisms on this extraordinary album which only really began to make sense after punk. (Appropriately, Lennon had dubbed it "1980s music".) But the decision to release both records on the same day, and in matching sleeves, didn't exactly help Yoko's cause. "Yoko is as important to me as Paul and Dylan rolled into one," Lennon insisted. Cynics assumed he was either joking or, more likely, hopelessly in love.

The real folly was in mistaking dazzling originality for gimmickry; as far back as 1961, Yoko envisaged "a 'New Music', a fusion of avant-garde jazz rock and East and West". Earlier collaborations with Lennon – *Two Virgins*, *Life With The Lions*, *Wedding* Album – may have been prankish excursions into the pair's private world, and gave little hint of what to expect on this improvised, exhilarating solo debut, made all the more remarkable for its swift execution: "Yes, it was recorded in one afternoon, and we mixed it that evening," Ono confirms.

The Starr/Voormann rhythm section used on Lennon's album remained but the transformation, particularly on the uptempo cuts (Why; Touch Me), was breathtaking. Lennon's abrasive guitar playing wouldn't have disgraced PiL's Metal Box, while the insistent rhythms evoke Can or early '70s Miles Davis. Elsewhere (Greenfield Morning; Paper Shoes), Yoko utilised tape loops and layers of heavily reverbed vocals reminiscent of mid-'70s dub. Lennon compared her to Spector. And the Stones and Townshend. And no, he wasn't joking.

Record label:
Apple
Produced
by John and Yoko.
Recorded
at Abbey Road Studios, London; one day in October 1970, except AOS, recorded in rehearsal for Albert Hall show; February 1968.
Released:
January 1971
Chart peaks:
11 (UK) None (US)
Personnel:
Yoko Ono (v); John Lennon (g); Ringo Starr (d); Klaus Voormann (b); Ornette Coleman (t on AOS); Edward Blackwell (d on AOS); Charles Haden (b on AOS); Phil MacDonald, John Leckie, Andy Stevens, 'Eddie' (e)
Track listing:
Why; Why Not; Greenfield Morning I Pushed An Empty Baby Carriage All Over The City; AOS; Touch Me; Paper Shoes. CD bonus tracks: Open Your Box; Something More Abstract; The South Wind
Running time:
40.37
Current CD:
Apple 10414
Further listening:
Fly (1971) is marginally more subdued than its predecessor but, being a 2-LP set, has more room to roam.
Further reading:
www.yoko.com
Like this?
Try . . . p.184

Serge Gainsbourg

Histoire De Melody Nelson

French master of outrage crafts mould-breaking suite for rock band and orchestra. Nobody notices.

It was while Jane Birkin – her acting career blossoming – was in the South of France making a film (the not-quite-classic Mustard Goes Up My Nose) that Gainsbourg started work on his masterpiece. Its plot revolves around a middle-aged Frenchman running into a teenage redhead cyclist in his Rolls Royce. He and the "délicieuse enfant" Melody fall in love and go off to a hotel for sex (the sound effects in L'Hotel Particulier feature Jane, being tickled by her brother Andrew). But she soon becomes homesick – for Sunderland! – and flies back home. The plane crashes, the distraught narrator becomes a crazed obsessive.

"When I first met him he had given me a nice little leather-covered book called Chansons D'Aujourdhui," recalls Jane, "and in it he wrote: 'To Jane Mallory' – my maiden name – 'for whom I shall write the story of Melody Nelson. Je T'Aime,' and on the next page he wrote 'Moi non plus'. Therefore he had already got the idea in 1968 when he met me to write about a girl who came, like my father did, from the North of England – which is why she's going back to Sunderland."

The recordings took place in Philips' London studios with a 50-piece orchestra and a large choir, plus a basic rock rhythm section of guitars, bass and drums. "We were ecstatic," recalls Birkin. "My brother was so enthusiastic that he got a demo and ran to every English disc jockey he knew to have it played. But no-one wanted to play it. Even in France it wasn't a hit."

Discerning French critics hailed its seven tracks, two of them nearly eight minutes long, as "the first true symphonic poem of the pop age"; "One of my favourite albums," said Françoise Hardy. "Musically completely new, extremely refined, and utterly, inimitably original."

It *was* incredibly unusual for its time and it still sounds thoroughly modern. "There's an ambition, a conceptual depth to *Melody Nelson* that's incredibly hard to pull off but which he does completely," says contemporary fan, Beck Hanson. "One of the best marriages of rock band and orchestra that I've ever heard. It's a very cool record, and the dynamic of it is genius – there's this band that's completely rocking on this almost acid tangent, but they're buried in the mix with him whispering on top, and he's the loudest thing on it."

Jane, four months pregnant with daughter Charlotte Gainsbourg, was photographed for the cover. "He wanted Melody to have red hair, so they bunged a wig on my head and put on a lot of freckles. I'm holding my monkey – which I buried with Serge because he always wanted it, so it will keep him safe now."

Record label:
Philips
Produced
by Jean-Claude Desmarty.
Recorded
at Philips Studios, Marble Arch, London; 1970.
Released:
March 1971
Chart peaks:
None (UK) None (US)
Personnel:
Serge Gainsbourg (v); Jane Birkin (v); JC Vannier (oa); Jean-Claude Charvier (e); Rémy Aucharles (ae)
Track listing:
Melody; Ballade De Melody Nelson; Valse De Melody; Ah! Melody; L'Hotel Particulieur; En Melody; Cargo Culte
Running time:
28.02
Current CD:
532 073-2
Further listening:
L'Homme A Tete De Chou (1976)
Further reading:
Serge Gainsbourg: View From The Exterior (Alan Clayson, 1996); www.francevision.com/nsltr/vf14/gains.htm; www.geocities.com/Paris/Musee/1489/gainsbourg/serge.html
Like this?
Try . . . p.723

Elvis Presley

Elvis Country (I'm 10,000 Years Old)

His last truly great album.

The first half of 1970 had been kind of a drag for Elvis. There'd been the Vegas rehearsals and karate lessons to occupy his mind but there was a whole bunch of dead time as well. With no big movie or TV special to lose weight for it was easy to just sit around, gobbling pills, scarfing burgers, shooting stuff, getting bored. Even the live shows, as evidenced on the *On Stage – February 1970* album weren't really doing it. Then, when the time came to do another album, Elvis just didn't want to go back to Memphis. Despite the success of the recordings at American Studios, Elvis felt that producer Chips Moman hadn't accorded him enough respect. Instead he went back to his official producer Felton Jarvis in Nashville. Ever since first working with Elvis in 1966, Felton had wanted to assemble a band who could really keep up with the King. The original Muscle Shoals rhythm section, wrestled from Rick Hall's studio, Elvis' new band were as sharp as anything. They were also frightened to death. As bassist Norbert Puttnam tells it "I was scared, staring at my reflection and saying 'Dear God, don't let me be the one to screw up the session...don't let me be the first guy to ruin it . . .'"

Elvis was thoroughly inspired by the new band. He insisted that they group around him, watch his moves, shifting gears at the slightest sign. They worked well, cutting seven masters on the first night and another 12 over the next couple of nights with Elvis constantly open to suggestion, taking each song by the scruff of the neck, singing ahead of the beat, attacking tracks like Whole Lotta Shakin' for all he was worth. Over five nights the band cut 35 masters. The true broken heart of the album can be found in such deep gospel ballads as Tomorrow Never Comes, Funny (How Time Slips Away) and I Really Don't Want to Know, tracks invested with a soul power lost to Elvis for the previous 15 years. Passionate, wild, dynamic, *Elvis Country* sounds like it's tapped straight from the true soul of that once and future King. He'd never sing like this again.

After those five days, Elvis returned to Memphis to prepare for more Vegas shows. In no time he was back on a diet of burgers.The only way was down.

Record label:
RCA
Produced
by Felton Jarvis
Recorded
at RCA's Nashville Studios, June 4–8, 1970
Released:
March 1971
Chart peaks:
6 (UK) 12 (US)
Personnel:
Elvis Presley (v); James Burton (g); Charlie McCoy (g, b, d, hm); Chip Young (g); David Briggs (k); Jerry Carrigan (d); Norbert Puttnam (b); the Jordonaires (v); The Imperials Quartet (v); Don Tweedy (ar); Cam Mullins (ar); Bergen White (ar)
Track listing:
Snowbird; Tomorrow Never Comes; Little Cabin On The Hill; Whole Lotta Shakin' Goin' On; Funny How Time Slips Away; I Really Don't Want To Know; There Goe My Everything; It's Your Baby, You Rock It; The Fool; Faded Love; I Washed My Hands In Muddy Water; Make The World Go Away
Running time:
38.54
Current CD:
74321 146922
Further listening:
From Elvis In Memphis (RCA 1969)
Further reading:
Careless Love: The Unmaking Of Elvis Presley – (Peter Guralnick 1999). Indispensable.
Like this?
Try . . . p.240

Anne Briggs

Anne Briggs

Belated debut from singer who exiled herself to obscurity.

"To hear the elusive Anne Briggs on her first solo album is an opportunity not to be missed," opined the Melody Maker. Already by 1971 a mythical figure in British folk, Anne had existed on the fringes of the commercial recording world – with a handful of a cappella releases between 1963–66 – as a singer of magical beauty and pursuer of a truly alternative, nomadic lifestyle. Mostly travelling in Ireland, her five-year silence had been tantalisingly broken in August 1969 by a BBC radio session for John Peel. This subsequent album captured Anne at the point where her confidence in songwriting and in using accompaniment was perfectly balanced with her mostly dark traditional repertoire. A moody silhouette of the loping young lass and her faithful hound adorned the cover while eight traditional songs – as stunning as any previous work – and two originals were featured. The most extraordinary piece, Living By The Water, had been written on bouzouki during a period of solitude on Bull Island, off western Ireland.

"Very profound time that," says Anne of this lonely episode. "Focuses the mind wonderfully on priorities. I've always felt totally at one with the natural environment – the landscape, the wildlife. What is. It's only people that make life difficult."

Along with Go Your Way, co-written with Bert Jansch in 1965, it typifies a strain of nature-driven writing that remains a hallmark of her work. Anne's boyfriend of the time, Johnny Moynihan, in between stints with Sweeney's Men and Planxty, cameos on Willy O'Winsbury.

The album would be a virtual source book for the Fairport generation. Indeed, Sandy Denny recorded The Pond And The Stream in 1970 in awe of Anne – free to come and go while peers like herself, Bert Jansch and others were tied to the commercial treadmill. "I assumed they were all having a great time," says Anne, "making a great deal of money and travelling all over the world. There was me, happy to wander around. Sandy made her choice and I made mine."

Anne disappeared from music in 1973, surfacing sporadically for a few gigs and a duet with Bert Jansch in the BBC film *Acoustic Routes*. Her aborted final album appeared in 1997.

Record label:
Topic
Produced
by A L Lloyd.
Recorded
in London, probably City Of London Recording Studios; late 1970.
Released:
April 1971
Chart peaks:
None (UK) None (US)
Personnel:
Anne Briggs (v, g, bouzouki); Johnny Moynihan (bouzouki)
Track listing:
Blackwater Side; The Snow It Melts The Soonest; Willie O'Winsbury; Go Your Way; Thorneymoor Woods; The Cuckoo; Reynardine; Young Tambling; Living By The Water; Ma Bonny Lad
Running time:
41.53
Current CD:
TSCD 504 reissued as Anne Briggs: A Collection adds: Recruited Collier; Doffin Mistress; She Moves Through The Fair; Let No Man Steal Your Thyme; Lowlands; My Bonny Boy; Polly Vaughan; Rosemary Lane Gathering Rushes In The Month Of May; Whirly Whorl; Stonecutter Boy; Martinmas Time
Further listening:
The Time Has Come (1971); Sing A Song For You (1973)
Further reading:
MOJO 52; Colin Harper's sleevenote to Anne Briggs: A Collection (1999)
Like this?
Try . . . p.419

Caravan

In The Land Of Grey And Pink

The quintessential Canterbury album.

Caravan started life on Decca, but they were a progressive lot, and in 1971 the classically-slanted label decided the band's third album would be a better bet for new offshoot Deram. Bands worked quickly in those days: it was only a few months after they'd released their second set, *If I Could Do It All Over Again, I'd Do It All Over You*. David Hitchcock made his debut as the group's producer, but otherwise it was the same line-up as before, with British jazzman Jimmy Hastings – older brother to guitarist Pye – guesting on sax, flute and piccolo.

The key members of Caravan in this period, however, were the Sinclair cousins. Richard had been in the original line-up of The Wilde Flowers, the semi-legendary early '60s group which never released a record but spawned the idea of a "Canterbury" movement in English rock, since out of it came Kevin Ayers and the Whole World, Soft Machine, Gong and Caravan. Canterbury isn't much different to any other provincial cathedral town, but the music associated with the name came to possess a particularity which Caravan embodied perhaps better than any other group. Light, slightly wayward vocals; whimsical lyrics; long, vaguely jazz-inflected solos played over a driving but not overpowering rock pulse; and the indefinable sense of something poised between an English meadow and outer space. Richard Sinclair's Home Counties voice and Dave Sinclair's energetically meandering fuzztone organ and piano solos dominate this record, which most Caravanners still hold up as their finest hour.

Golf Girl, with an uncredited trombonist echoing the melody line, is as sweet-natured as English rock would ever be, but the centre is Nine Feet Underground, which runs almost 23 minutes and took up side two of the album. A seamless integration of a string of themes, this oddly mournful but spirited suite is a timeless memento of Canterbury's legacy. As time went on, "we spent less time getting stoned and playing music together", as Richard Sinclair ruefully remembered, "and Caravan became more and more like an orthodox touring band, turning out pleasant but uneventful records.

Record label:
Deram
Produced
by David Hitchcock.
Recorded
at AIR and Decca Studios, London; November 1970–January 1971.
Released:
April 1971
Chart peaks:
None (UK) None (US)
Personnel:
Richard Sinclair (b, g, v); Pye Hastings (g, v); Dave Sinclair (o, p, mellotron, v); Richard Coughlan (d); Jimmy Hastings (f, ts, piccolo); David Grinsted (cannon, bell wind)
Track listing:
Golf Girl; Winter Wine; Love To Love You; In the Land Of Grey And Pink; Nine Feet Underground: i. Nigel Blows a Tune; ii. Love's a Friend; iii. Make It 76; iv. Dance of the Seven Paper Hankies; v. Hold Grandad By The Nose; vi. Honest I Did!; vii. Disassociation; viii. 100% Proof
Running time:
43.18
Current CD:
820520-2
Further listening:
Waterloo Lily (1972)
Further reading:
perso.club-internet.fr/calyx/cantdisco/C.html
Like this?
Try . . . p.202

David Crosby

If I Could Only Remember My Name

With CSN&Y at their commercial zenith, Crosby cuts controversial experimental mood piece.

The sense of community in the rock world was still strong in the wake of Woodstock and few typified its ideals more than David Crosby. A firm believer in the dictum 'Peace, Love and Music', he saw his first solo album as a gathering of the tribes and invited the cream of the West Coast community to join him for a musical love-in. On paper it looked like another case of hippie superstar indulgence but the results were both unexpected and extraordinary: a striking and experimental mood piece. Neil Young produced an expressive guitar solo on the conspiratorial What Are Their Names and Jerry Garcia excelled himself on the CSN&Y allegory Cowboy Movie; Joni Mitchell added a wonderful vocal flourish on Laughing, while various Dead and Jefferson Airplane personnel brought further depth to the arrangements. Crosby masterminded the entire proceedings and his underlying melancholy cut through the stoned beatitude. Prior to the recording his girlfriend Christine Hinton had been killed in a car accident leaving the singer distraught.

"Crosby went to see her body and he's never been the same since," Graham Nash confided. The album closed on an eerie note with the disturbing I'd Swear There Was Somebody Here, a Gregorian-styled requiem to his lost love. "I was in the studio and I felt like she was there," Crosby remembers. "I was singing and just started feeling she was there, which hadn't happened before and hasn't happened since." Engineer Stephen Barncard was astounded by the results. "I've rarely seen anything that intense," he recalls. "It just happened. I witnessed the creation of the song in real time and recorded it as we went along. It was probably the most remarkable event in my entire life." Critical reaction was divided at the time of the album's release. Both Rolling Stone and Melody Maker were particularly harsh in their assessments but the album still went gold. In the UK, Melody Maker was bombarded with letters and phone calls railing against Richard Williams's negative review. It was one of biggest public backlashes against a reviewer in the long history of the music paper.

Record label:
Atlantic
Produced
by David Crosby.
Recorded
at Wally Heiders, San Francisco, California; autumn 1970.
Released:
April 24, 1971 (UK); March 8, 1971 (US)
Chart peaks:
12 (UK) 12 (US)
Personnel:
David Crosby (g, v); Jerry Garcia (g, b,v); Phil Lesh (b); Mickey Hart (d); Bill Kreutzmann (tambourine); Jorma Kaukonen (g); Joni Mitchell (v); Neil Young (g, v); Laura Allan (autoharp); Greg Rollie (p); Michael Shrieve (d); Jack Casady (b); Paul Kantner (b, v); David Freiberg (b, v); Grace Slick (b, v); Graham Nash (b, v); Stephen Barncard (e); Ellen Burke (e)
Track listing:
Music Is Love (S, US only); Cowboy Movie; Tamalpais High (At About 3); Laughing; What Are Their Names; Traction In The Rain; Song With No Words (Tree With No Leaves); Orleans; I'd Swear There Was Somebody Here
Running time:
37.54
Current CD:
7567814152
Further listening:
Crosby, Stills & Nash (1969); Deja Vu (1970)
Further reading:
MOJO 62; Crosby, Stills, Nash And Young: The Visual Documentary (Johnny Rogan, 1996)
Like this?
Try . . . p.230

1971

The Flamin' Groovies

Teenage Head

Fashion-disdaining San Francisco rock'n'rollers third, and most influential album.

The Flamin' Groovies were in a spot. It seemed like they were always in a spot, but this time fate was really having a laugh. Their guitarist Tim Lynch was fighting the draft – at a time when the draft meant Vietnam – and their other guitarist Cyril Jordan and vocalist Roy Loney were increasingly in conflict – *Teenage Head* would be the singer's last album with the band. And although the band had one of the world's great rock'n'roll producers on board for *Teenage Head*, they'd employed him to *play piano*, giving the production job to a writer and talented magician who, although indisputably a music-lover, was not a musician at all.

If that wasn't enough, although they had signed to Kama Sutra the previous year and made one of the best albums of their career (*Flamingo*), other San Francisco bands continued to look down on them, and promoter Bill Graham was still reluctant to book them. In end-of-the-'60s San Francisco the Groovies stuck out like a sore thumb, playing short, catchy, greasy, garage rock'n'roll in an era dominated by the complex, freak-outery of Jefferson Airplane and the Dead.

Galvanised by seeing the MC5 kick out the jams in Detroit one night on a trip to the Midwest they abandoned their jug band influences and decided to crank up to 11 – which is exactly what can be heard on this session.

Arguably, the blueprint for *Teenage Head* is The Rolling Stones' *Sticky Fingers*. Yet while Yesterday's Numbers is certainly Stonsey and Whiskey Women recalls John Lennon, Evil Hearted Ada sounds like an unreleased Elvis Sun side. As for the title track, Jordan's own description – "the Mothers Of Invention doing Led Zeppelin" – is spot on, although like everything else on this album it sounds more like the Groovies, putting pedal to the metal and unapologetically side-swiping the hippie zeitgeist. *Teenage Head*, once again shunned by West Coasters, was a favourite among hip New Yorkers and a cult hit in Europe – indeed, when Loney left for a solo career the mark II band decamped to Europe for several years, hooking up with fan Dave Edmunds before releasing their next album *Shake Some Action* some five years later. *Teenage Head* stands as a barometer of contemporary hip and a signpost on the way to punk.

Record label:
Big Beat
Produced
by Richard Robinson.
Recorded
at Bell Sound Studio, New York City; January 1971.
Released:
May 1971
Chart peaks:
None (UK) None (US)
Personnel:
Cyril Jordan (g, v); Roy Loney (v); Danny Mihm (d); George Alexander (b); Tim Lynch (g); Jim Dickinson (p); Jeff Hanna, Jim Fadden, Jimmy Ibbotsen (bv)
Track listing:
High Flying Baby; City Lights; Have You Seen My Baby?; Yesterday's Numbers; Teenage Head; 32-20; Evil Hearted Ada; Doctor Boogie; Whisky Woman
Running time:
47.38
Current CD:
74321716902 adds: Shakin' All Over; That'll Be The Day; Louie Louie; Walkin' The Dog; Scratch My Back; Carol; Going Out Theme
Further listening:
Flamingo (1970); Shake Some Action (1976)
Further reading:
Issues 3, 4 and 6 of Greg Shaw's late, great fanzine Who Put The Bomp?
Like this?
Try . . . p.687

Bert Jansch

Rosemary Lane

Released at the height of electric folk-rock in Britain, Bert's stripped-down masterpiece was criminally ignored.

Although immersed in the frantic international touring of the Pentangle era, the making of *Rosemary Lane* was, for Bert, a throwback to more carefree times. It was recorded simply, on portable equipment, by his first producer Bill Leader over the course of periodic visits to his rustic home. "We'd set the gear up and then we'd go for a pint, discuss it, and if I felt like recording we did it," says Bert. "The songs were just wherever my head was at the time. I was losing interest in the band, wishing for other things to do."

Fuelled by a sense of longing for times past, *Rosemary Lane* was romantic, pastoral and daringly stark. The dearth of tangible contemporary references – save for a glimpse of America, a place he now loathed, and the undateable nature of Bert's instrumental technique – he produced a work of timeless quality. With his unmistakably rough-hewn voice displaying a new poise and clarity, the material here – traditional songs, baroque vignettes and a clutch of singer-songwriter originals – was accompanied by an open invitation to the mind's eye. And the view was breathtaking. When Bert sings on the traditional English title track one hears something straight from a fireside storyteller in some indeterminate place and time. The same is true of Reynardine: the accompaniment a masterful distillation of Bert's guitar vocabulary.

"The thing with Jansch is that you cannot compare him with anyone else, you can only draw the comparison between the man as he was and the man as he is today," wrote Jerry Gilbert in Sounds, establishing a truism that still stands. Jansch's solo career was effectively on hold during the Pentangle era and bar one solitary concert at the Festival Hall in June 1971, with guests Anne Briggs and Clive Palmer (who had both influenced *Rosemary Lane*'s content), there were no opportunities to air this material onstage. Only a few tracks have re-entered his repertoire since, although stunning versions of Rosemary Lane and Reynardine were performed, by request, for the Channel 4 documentary Dream Weaver. It remains his greatest work.

Record label:
Transatlantic
Produced
by Bill Leader.
Recorded
at Bert's home in Ticehurst, Sussex; June 1970–January 1971.
Released:
May 1971
Chart peaks:
None (UK) None (US)
Personnel:
Bert Jansch (v, g)
Track listing:
Tell Me What Is True Love?; Rosemary Lane; M'Lady Nancy; A Dream, A Dream, A Dream; Alman; Wayward Child; Nobody's Bar; Reynardine; Silly Woman; Peregrinations; Sylvie; Sarabanda; Bird Song
Running time:
37.40
Currently unavailable on CD
Further listening:
When The Circus Comes To Town (1995)
Further reading:
MOJO 80; Dazzling Stranger: Bert Jansch And The British Folk And Blues Revival (Colin Harper, 2000)
Like this?
Try . . . p.142

Paul And Linda McCartney

Ram

Bruised ex-Beatle comes out of hiding with his new missus.

Ram, his second post-Beatles album, was the midpoint in McCartney's nervous re-integration with the outside world. *McCartney* had been a determinedly upbeat DIY construction, assembled in his remote Scottish hideaway. The third, Wings' *Wildlife*, would find him nostalgically touring the UK with a minibus and the security of another band around him. But the autumn of 1970 found McCartney renting a New York hotel suite and a block of time at Manhattan's A&R Studios, and signing up session drummer Denny Seiwell (who later joined Wings) and guitarist Dave Spinoza (who turned the chance down). Locked in the control room for hours on end working up the basic compositions, he was acutely aware of his need for another sounding-board.

"Obviously I was used to having a collaborator and I felt the pinch after John," McCartney reflects today. "I was used to writing solo stuff too, of course, but some of them I'd get a bit stuck on – like I would with John – and Linda would change some of the words, alter a little piece here and there, write a line or two, give me ideas. It was just me and her in the studio most of the time, there together all day, so it would have been churlish not to credit her really." Paul's publisher, Lew Grade, who refused to believe that Linda – who wasn't part of their deal – had collaborated on the songs and threatened to sue, wasn't the only one to give the project a cool reception; but, apparently unfazed, McCartney opted to mine this whimsical seam for most of his solo career. And the public seemed to approve; the decidedly odd Uncle Albert/Admiral Halsey even topped the US singles chart.

Arriving in the middle of the very public John/Paul spat, *Ram* was scrutinized for Lennon references – and didn't disappoint (the photo of the copulating beetles on the back cover was also subject to some imaginative interpretation). Monkberry Moon Delight descends gloriously into primal scream pastiche; Too Many People ("Too many people preaching practices"), he now admits, "was about John and Yoko telling people what to do. I thought, Bollocks to that." The couple even expressed their ire in the backing vocals, 'piece of cake' rendered as "piss off cake". "Just mad!" Paul chuckles. "You had to get your feelings out one way or another."

Record label:
Apple
Produced
by Paul and Linda McCartney.
Recorded
at A&R Studios, New York; October–November 1970 and February–March 1971.
Released:
May 1971
Chart peaks:
1 (UK) 2 (US)
Personnel:
Paul McCartney (g, bs, v); Linda McCartney (k, pc, v); Denny Seiwell (d); Hugh McCracken (g); Dave Spinoza (g)
Track listing:
Too Many People; 3 Legs; Ram On; Dear Boy; Uncle Albert – Admiral Halsey (S); Smile Away; Heart Of The Country; Monkberry Moon Delight; Eat At Home; Long-Haired Lady; Ram On; The Back Seat Of My Car (S)
Running time:
50.51
Not currently available on CD
Further listening:
McCartney (1970); Band On The Run (1973)
Further reading:
Many Years From Now (Barry Miles, 1998)
Like this?
Try . . . p.661

The Rolling Stones

Sticky Fingers

The centrepiece of the great Stones triptych found them at their most rootsy and American.

Recorded in a period when the Stones were beset by financial problems, contemplating tax exile, and experiencing an ever-widening palette of influences, *Sticky Fingers* turned out to be one of the band's most consistent works. The reason lay back in 1966, when Keith Richards started a new educational regime: "I started getting into different blues tunings, Fred McDowell, 12-string and slide. Then I met Ry Cooder in '68, when he was hanging around with Taj Mahal and Jesse Ed Davis. And Clarence White was around too. You'd just pick stuff up."

Those new influences made their debut on 1969's Honky Tonk Women single; by 1970, Richards was still pushing forward the boundaries of the 'Open G' tuning he had learned from Cooder. As he puts it, "It restricts you so much, five strings, three notes, two fingers . . . one asshole! And there's something about being restricted that opens up the possibilities."

Richards' delving into Americana was complemented by the band's two-day stay at Muscle Shoals, Alabama to record Brown Sugar, Wild Horses and You Gotta Move (the other songs were mainly recorded at Mick Jagger's home, Stargroves). Appropriately, given the surroundings, Keith's new trademark tuning suggested country music, but as album opener Brown Sugar demonstrated, it was a vehicle to take the Stones somewhere entirely new. The song's basic two-chord rock'n'roll strut obviously derived from Chuck Berry, but the sudden swerve eight bars in (as Keith modulates from G to an utterly unexpected E flat) show the Stones suddenly liberated by Richards' self-imposed restrictions.

Wild Horses, probably the Stones' tenderest, most perfectly-formed ballad, demonstrated the other extreme of the possibilities thrown up by Keith's new style. It has been incorrectly claimed that The Flying Burrito Brothers' own version, released in May 1970, was a crucial influence, but the Stones had already laid down their basic track in December 1969. In any case, the chordal structure fits so snugly within the limits of Richards' tuning that the melody must be his alone, for as Richards points out, "Gram taught me a lot, but he was strictly a standard tunings guy."

Ironically, given that the world's stadiums were beckoning, *Sticky Fingers* would prove the Stones' mastery of small-scale, minority music. A rousing critical reception preceded its ascent to the top of the UK charts on May 8 1971; a couple of weeks later it topped the charts in the US, demonstrating that, in a brand new decade, the Stones sounded anything but dated. Once again they had managed the enviable feat of selling America's culture back to its country of origin.

Record label:
Rolling Stones Records
Produced
by Jimmy Miller
Recorded
at Muscle Shoals Sound Studios Alabama; Rolling Stones Mobile, Stargroves Newbury; Olympic Studios, London, December 1969–May 1970.
Release date:
May 1971
Chart peaks:
1 (UK) 1 (US)
Personnel:
Mick Jagger (v); Bill Wyman (b); Charlie Watts (d); Keith Richards (g); Mick Taylor (g); Bobby Keyes (s); Ian Stewart Nicky Hopkins (p); Ry Cooder (sg)
Track listing:
Brown Sugar; Sway, Wild Horses; Can't You Hear Me Knocking; You Gotta Move; Bitch, I Got the Blues; Sister Morphine; Dead Flowers; Moonlight Mile
Running time:
46.27
Current CD:
Further listening:
Let It Bleed (1969) spans a similar mix of styles to its successor; Ry Cooder's Into The Purple Valley (Reprise 1972) shows Keith's one-time guitar guru constructing his own parallel version of Americana.
Further reading:
Blown Away: The Rolling Stones & The Death Of The Sixties (AE Hotchner, 1990)
Like this?
Try . . . p.572

Bridget St John

Songs For The Gentle Man

Exquisitely arranged folk album by unheralded contemporary of John Martyn and Nick Drake.

Responsible for the very first album on John Peel and Clive Selwood's quirky Dandelion label, folk singer Bridget St. John was a unique talent that, in her understated way, occupied the same creative space as her better known male contemporaries (and friends) John Martyn, Nick Drake and Michael Chap man. That album, *Ask Me No Questions*, was a bare-bones production that introduced to the world a quiet, thought-provoking singer/song-writer with a deep voice not unlike an on-key Nico; part of its minimalist charm was the simple fact that it was recorded in 10 consecutive hours at CBS Studios.

"I don't know if that was the time I was given, but that's the time it took," says St. John today, now in New York, a resident there since 1976. "That was my first ever thing in the recording studio, so I wouldn't have known how to do anything differently. John Peel was producing it, and he really just made it sound like I *was* at that time, and that was a very honest recording."

But by no means was its follow-up, *Songs For The Gentle Man*, dishonest on any level. A simply gorgeous album, the 1971 disc paired Bridget with producer/arranger Ron Geesin, whose work with Pink Floyd (*Atom Heart Mother*) and Roger Waters (*Music From The Body*) had brought him significant critical success. Unrestrained and inventive, Geesin provided the gentle singer a context that was extremely alluring.

"I did a lot of work with Ron on that," she says. "I remember going to his house, where he had his own studio and we did a lot of preparation there." Filled with cellos, violas, flutes, bassoons, a "celestial organ" and St. John's own guitar and harmonium, *Gentle Man* is a quiet jewel of a record that sounds surprisingly contemporary 30 years on.

A final Dandelion album would come, then a brief move to Chrysalis for *Jumble Queen* in 1974, but in 1976, Bridget departed for New York to be with boyfriend Gordon Edwards of American band Stuff (who once backed Fred Neil) and has lived there since. One is tempted to say "in obscurity", but every one of her albums has been reissued on CD since (though as we went to press they were currently out of print). "It absolutely amazes me," she says. "My boyfriend is Gordon from Stuff, and I think of them as a massive band – and yet Warner Brothers has never re-released their albums over here. It's incredible to me."

Record label:
Dandelion
Produced by
Ron Geesin.
Recorded
at Sound Techniques Ltd., London.
Released:
May 1971.
Chart peaks:
None (UK) None (US)
Track listing:
Bridget St. John (v, g, hm); Ron Geesin (g, oa); Rick Sanders (g); Jerry Boys (e)
Track listing:
A Day A Way; City-Crazy; Early-Morning Song; Back To Stay; Seagull-Sunday; If You'd Been There; Song For The Laird Of Connaught Hall – Part Two; Making Losing Better; The Lady And The Gentle Man; Downderry Daze; The Pebble And The Man; It Seems Very Strange
Running time:
38.21
Currently unavailable on CD
Further listening:
Ask Me No Questions (1969); Thank You For . . . (1972)
Like this?
Try . . . p.556

Loudon Wainwright III

Loudon Wainwright III

Debut by Canadian folk-singing specialist in social commentary and wry observation.

Back in 1971, Loudon Wainwright III came to the UK to support the release of his debut album. He played BBC2's American-oriented rock show The Old Grey Whistle Test. He also opened for The Everly Brothers at the Albert Hall, where he was bottled off by Teddy Boys; undoubtedly, the wit and wisdom of this clever singer/songwriter from North Carolina went way above their quiffs. Previously, Wainwright had honed his act on the live circuit where he'd gained a reputation as a "new Bob Dylan", and as the '60s came to a close he signed to Atlantic and produced this stark and moving album. Almost 30 years on it still sounds pointed and pertinent, even if Wainwright himself is long since tired of the set.

"I'm fed up of the generation of people who are hung up on those early records," he said back in the '80s. "People want you to stay the way they were in 1971 because it just so happens they were 20 then, were having fun and weren't divorced yet, so they say, 'Ah man, that first album, that's the best album.'" According to Wainwright, "some of those songs like School Days and Central Square Song are great, but others like Black Uncle Remus and I Don't Care are very marginal."

Certainly subsequent albums have songs that rank alongside the likes of School Days, Glad To See You've Got Religion and Four Is A Magic Number, but it's the uneasy minor chords, and this virginal introduction to Loudon's distinctive singing style that makes the album special. In 1971 this album had all the social realism that was needed for people looking for something to believe in after the frivolity of the '60s. Songs such as the rite-of-teenage-passage School Days linked the angst of the post-hippy era with another, presumably survivable, period of confusion and loss.

Fan and friend Pete Fallon, in his sleevenotes on a recent Rhino limited reissue, concludes: "He should be better known. He should be richer and more famous. He should be a legend. The best of these songs, they've lasted already. And they will last."

Record label:
Atlantic
Produced
by Milton Kramer and Loudon Wainwright III.
Recorded
at Media Sound, A&R Studios, and Atlantic Recording Studios, New York.
Released:
May 1971
Chart peaks:
None (UK) None (US)
Personnel:
Loudon Wainwright III (g, v)
Track listing:
School Days; Hospital Lady; Ode To Pittsburgh: Glad To See You've Got Religion; Uptown; Black Uncle Remus; Four Is A Magic Number; I Don't Care; Central Square Song; Movies Are A Mother To Me; Bruno's Place
Running time:
38.02
Not currently available on CD, bar a Rhino Handmade limited edition, available via the internet, which adds Album II, and Drinking Song.
Further listening:
Album II (1971) featuring Motel Blues is essential, while Album III (1973) and Attempted Moustache (1974) are both worthy of investigation.
Further reading:
http://lwiii.com/
Like this?
Try . . . p.716

Link Wray

Link Wray

Guitar godfather takes acoustic guitars and dobros on a journey up country.

In 1958 Link Wray changed the face of electric guitar playing with his ominous, power-chord driven instrumental, Rumble – a track which persuaded Pete Townshend, among others, to take up the instrument. Wray continued to record in-yer-face guitar rockers for smaller and smaller labels, until the late '60s found him in semi-retirement on the family farm. Link's brother, who had played with him in various bands over the years, moved his three track recorder into one room and a chicken coop was coverted into a studio. Thus, The Shack – perhaps the most basic arrangement ever to record a major label release – came into being.

In a contemporary interview Link outlined the problems: "The two rooms were never connected so we still have to yell back and forth, 'Is it running Ray?' every time we want to start." At this time producer Steve Verocca saw Wray performing in a local club. "I was overwhelmed. Here was a man singing out his soul. I asked him about recording an album, and I suggested we do it at The Shack. I believe The Shack has a soul. You can hear people burping on the record, and that's great. It's real."

The music produced at The Shack is a beautiful but raggedy quilt sewn from blues, country, soul, folk and patterns from a deeper past – Wray is after all half Shawnee Indian. This last element is most evident in the anything-to-hand percussion which rattles the bones of songs such as Fire And Brimstone: a title which also contributes to the album's rich gospel atmosphere. (The seemingly infinite backing vocals on Take Me Home Jesus and the fuzz-guitared, revivalist vim of God Out West would make the Devil testify.) But Link has always been as much about the dark side; and his version of Willie Dixon's Tail Dragger is a throwback to his earlier, leathered-up incarnation. Other groups, notably The Band, have explored similar territory, but even they cannot match the backwoods glory that Wray's tortured, reedy vocals summon up. Polydor's executives heard the magic, but after releasing this bare-arsed masterpiece put Wray into a studio with Jerry Garcia et al. The result, *Be What You Want To Be*, isn't a bad album, but for authentic roots-rock, head to The Shack.

Record label:
Polydor
Produced
by Steve Verroca and Ray Vernon in association with Bob Feldman.
Recorded
at Wray's Shack Three Track, Accokeek, Maryland; October 1970.
Released:
May 1971
Chart peaks:
None (UK) None (US)
Personnel:
Link Wray (v, g, b, dobro); Billy Hodges (k, v); Bobby Howard (mandolin, k); Doug Wray (d, pc, v); Steve Verocca (d, pc, v)
Track listing:
La De Da; Ice People; Take Me Home Jesus; Black River Swamp; Rise And Fall Of Jimmy Stokes; Fallin' Rain; Fire And Brimstone; God Out West Crowbar; Juke Box Mama; Tail Dragger
Running time:
43.52
Currently unavailable on CD.
Further listening:
Guitar Preacher: The Polydor Years (1995) includes all of Link Wray as well a plethora of tracks from the other albums Wray recorded for the label; there's an excellent accompanying booklet by Colin Escott. Rocking '50s and '60s guitar instrumentals available on Norton's fine Missing Links series.
Like this?
Try . . . p.196

Michael Hurley And Pals

Armchair Boogie

Second album from the folk troubadour, the ultimate outsider.

The term maverick might have been invented for Pennsylvania-born, Ohio-based Hurley, an American one-off whose devoted cult following includes many musicians half his age. While his music borrows from Depression-era folk, blues, country, railroad songs, swing, ragtime, even '50s doo wop, the songs' subject matter makes them unique.Hurley's 1965 debut *First Songs* – recorded by American musicologist Fred Ramsey Jr for the Folkways label – was, despite some pretty unconventional moments, a tense and earnest record. By follow-up *Armchair Boogie*, some six years later, Hurley had loosened up a little – almost to the point of falling apart. By now he had found a more sympathetic home – The Youngbloods' label Raccoon – although even *they* baulked at releasing songs with titles like Your Monkey Pissed In My Beer And Your Dick Is Hanging Out Of Your Pants. Mainstream acceptance was never one of Hurley's considerations, and it was this indifference rather than a lack of songs that brought about the long gap between the first and second albums.

"I don't normally intend to write songs," he once said. "I always seem to happen upon them or they happen upon me. There was never a time when I experimented with putting out my music in any way other than I felt it."

Armchair Boogie was recorded in Hurley's house with Jesse Colin Young handling the production, which mostly required rolling the tapes then switching them off. "It just saunters along in the buff," is how Hurley's sleevenote writer described it. "It recalls a time when quaintness was one of American regional music's most valuable elements."

The record also marked the first appearance of Hurley's cartoon paintings of Boone and Jocko, a pair of Bohemian wolves. They have graced the sleeve of every subsequent Hurley album, a singular link to his world of sentiment and sorrow, the real and the surreal.

Record label:
Raccoon
Produced
by Jesse Colin Young.
Recorded
at Hurley House, Brookline, Massachusetts; May–June 1970.
Released:
spring 1971
Chart peaks:
None (UK) None (US)
Personnel:
Michael Hurley (v, g); Maggie Hurley (bv, tambourine); Robin Remailly (fiddle, mandolin); Michael Kane (cornet, b); Jeff Myer (d); Earthquake (hm); Scott Lawrence (p); Jesse Young (b)
Track listing:
The Werewolf; Grand Canyon Line; English Noblemen; Be Kind To Me; Troubled Waters; Red Ravagers Reel; Sweedeedee; Open Up; Jocko's Lament; Light Green Fellow; Get The Best Of Me; Biscuit Roller; When The Swallows Come Back To Capistrano; Penguins
Running time:
41.35
Currently unavailable on CD
Further listening:
Long Journey (1976)
Further reading:
www.snock.com
Like this?
Try . . . p.662

1971

…ers

… I Am

… while he was still working in a factory ma… g toilet seats for jet planes.

Born in tiny Slab Fork, West Virginia, Withers spent nine years in the US Navy then worked at a number of factory jobs before finally launching his music career in his mid-30s. Indeed, when he began making *Just As I Am* in 1970, he was still working at the Lockheed factory in Los Angeles, manufacturing toilet seats and airstairs for 747 jets. The cover photo, which shows him in dungarees, carrying a lunch bucket, was shot during his lunch hour at the plant. Withers was laid off in the course of making the album but, as he coyly puts it, "As things turned out, I didn't have to go back." Ain't No Sunshine went to number 3 and won the Grammy for Best R&B Song, though that too was something of a surprise since the intended single was Harlem, with Ain't No Sunshine as its B-side.

Bill had been using his own money to make demos since 1967, but had gotten nowhere. It was Ray Jackson of the Watts 103rd Street Rhythm Band who started things moving for Withers. Jackson passed one of those demo tapes on to Forrest Hamilton, son of jazz drummer Chico Hamilton, who in turn passed it on to Clarence Avent of Sussex Records, who liked what he heard. Originally Jackson was going to produce the album, but when touring commitments made that impossible, Avent introduced Withers to Booker T. Jones, of the MGs.

It is hard to imagine that Jackson – or anyone else for that matter – could have done a better job than Jones of creating such perfect settings for Withers's warm voice, which manages to convey endurance while perching right on the edge of breaking. The music was unmistakably R'n'B, but Jones's use of acoustic guitars and strings gave it a whiff of gospelly country right out of Slab Fork. Nowhere was that more true than on Grandma's Hands, Withers' tribute to the woman who raised him and his five brothers and sisters after his father died when Withers was very young.

For the early sessions, Jones used the MGs, with Stephen Stills subbing for Steve Cropper. But Sussex Records ran out of money, halting recording for six months, and when work resumed, Dunn and Jackson had been replaced by Chris Ethridge and Jim Keltner. The relaxed atmosphere Jones encouraged in the studio also helped relax Withers.

"Graham Nash, who was a fun guy because he was drinking then, was hanging out," recalls Withers. "When I'd get frustrated Graham would sit in front of me and offer encouragement. All these people who had established careers were going out of their way to help me. It was reassuring, because hearing yourself played back for the first time can be a sobering moment."

Record label:
Sussex
Produced
by Booker T. Jones.
Recorded
at Sunset Sound Recorders and Wally Heider Recording Studio, Hollywood, California; throughout 1970.
Released:
June 1971
Chart peaks:
None (UK) 39 (US)
Personnel:
Bill Withers (v,g); Booker T. Jones (k,g); Stephen Stills (g); Donald 'Duck' Dunn (b); Chris Ethridge (b); Al Jackson (d); Jim Keltner (d); Bobbie Hall Porter (pc)
Track listing:
Harlem (S); Ain't No Sunshine (S); Grandma's Hands; Sweet Wanomi; Everybody's Talkin'; Do It Good; Hope She'll Be Happier; Let It Be; I'm Her Daddy; In My Heart; Moanin And Groanin; Better Off Dead
Running time:
35.39
Currently unavailable on CD
Further listening:
Still Bill (1972) contained the evergreen Lean On Me. Written while at Lockheed, the song was, according to Withers, a song of gratitude for all the support he'd received from his co-workers.
Further reading:
The Billboard Book Of Soul (1992)
Like this?
Try . . . p.20

The Beach Boys

Surf's Up

A career-saver and the boys' best post-Brian achievement.

Recent years had delivered a series of body blows to The Beach Boys and by 1970 they were reeling. The psychological fragility of their creative core, Brian Wilson, had left them struggling to find a voice in the acid-rock era. To make matters worse, an ex-hanger-on and Dennis Wilson collaborator – Charles Manson – had been revealed as head of a cult that had perpetrated the Sharon Tate murder; singer Mike Love became temporarily deranged, spending time in a clinic; their last album, *Sunflower* (1970) – a gorgeous, elegantly mature set – had been their worst selling record ever.

Jack Rieley, an "aspiring broadcast journalist", gained their confidence with positive ideas about career and artistic direction and they set about recording an album to be called *Landlocked.* Al Jardine pursued his penchant for folk with Rieley-inspired social concern and eco-overtones, Bruce Johnson had his finest Beach Boys moment with the intelligent nostalgia of Disney Girls, Carl Wilson and Rieley co-wrote two magnificent pieces of spiritual yearning (Feel Flows and Long Promised Road): the boys were finding their feet. Brother Brian's offering, 'Til I Die, was coolly received ("What a fucking downer", Brian recalled Mike Love saying). He also co-wrote with Rieley a bizarre little song (Day In The Life Of A Tree) which Jack was allowed to croakily sing.

"I was tricked into that," Rieley told MOJO in 1995. "It was going to be sung by Brian. I went over to produce the vocal, guide him through it. He said "Jack, I just don't get it. You gotta explain to me how I'm going to sing this," and went up into the control room. I put on the cans and sang it a half-a-dozen times to show how it went. He came out roaring with laughter saying, "It's done! The vocal's done!" I thought it was just a quick joke of Brian's but it turned up on the record. It was a long-term joke. For a brief moment I felt flattered, but it wasn't what I intended for the song. There's one argument that it does indeed sound like a dying tree!"

Still short of material, the band once more unearthed a remnant of Brian's aborted 1967 masterpiece-that-never-was *Smile* (elsewhere they had revived Cabinessence and Our Prayer), the mysterious and deeply beautiful Surf's Up, building the track around Brian's piano and voice performance on a 1967 Leonard Bernstein TV special. Initially opposed to the idea ("I was superstitious about the *Smile* material"), Brian attempted a new vocal but Carl finally delivered the mellifluous lead. Constructed without Brian's input, the by-now title track was a masterpiece showing – along with the other successes of *Surf's Up* – that with or without Brian, The Beach Boys were big boys now.

Record label:
Brother/Reprise
Produced
by the Beach Boys.
Recorded
at Brother Studio, Santa Monica; 1970.
Release date:
July 25, 1971
Chart peaks:
15 (UK) 29 (US)
Personnel:
Carl Wilson (g, v); Alan Jardine (g, v); Dennis Wilson (d, v); Mike Love (v); Bruce Johnson (k, v); Brian Wilson (k, v); Jack Rieley (v)
Track listing:
Don't Go Near The Water; Long Promised Road; Take A Load Off Your Feet; Disney Girls (1957); Student Demonstration Time; Feel Flows; Lookin' At Tomorrow (A Welfare Song); A Day In The Life Of A Tree; 'Til I Die; Surf's Up
Running time:
32.46
Current CD:
ZK46951
Further listening:
Sunflower (1970); Holland (1973)
Further reading:
Heroes And Villains (Steven Gaines, 1986); The Nearest Faraway Place (Timothy White, 1994); Wouldn't It Be Nice (Brian Wilson with Todd Gold, 1991) www.beachboys.com
Like this?
Try . . . p.52

The Allman Brothers Band

At Fillmore East

It made them national stars and launched the Southern rock movement.

Veteran producer Tom Dowd was sitting in a mobile production truck outside Fillmore East taping the first of four weekend shows from which the classic album *The Allman Brothers Band at Fillmore East* would be taken. Dowd knew the band well, having already worked with them on the album that would become *Eat A Peach*. With one eye on the stage video monitor and one on his set list, Dowd was cuing the engineers through a set that showed the band at their bluesy, blistering peak.

"Everything is sweet as a nut," says Dowd, "when one of the engineers says, 'What track do I put the horns on?'" Dowd, knowing there should be no horns, told him precisely where he could stick those horns. "The guy says, 'No, look.' I look at the monitor and I see two horns and a harp coming on. I heard them play like, two bars, I jumped off the chair, ran through the backstage door and grabbed Duane. I screamed, 'Don't ever, *ever* put them on stage with your band as long as you live!' I was livid. These horn players were wasted. That was the norm for the day, fine. But they were out of tune and not even playing the right parts." Dowd made a key decision. "For the rest of the night I made sure we had rough mixes of every song," he says. "After the last set I went backstage and said, 'I want you to come uptown to go over what you did.'"

So at three o'clock in the morning Dowd and the band raced uptown to Atlantic Studios on West 60th Street. "We're sitting there listening and they're saying stuff like, 'Don't use that,' or 'Well, we don't have to do that again. That's as well as we can play it.'" They cringed on hearing the horns, but kept Thom Doucette's harmonica.

Some call *Fillmore* the finest live album ever made. Certainly it launched the band from regional to national fame, showcasing the brilliant interplay between Duane Allman and Dicky Betts on guitar. When Duane died in a motorcycle crash seven months after the Fillmore shows and bass player Berry Oakley followed in 1972, *At the Fillmore East* acquired a terrible poignancy.

Record label:
Capricorn
Produced
by Tom Dowd.
Recorded
at Fillmore East, New York City; March 12–13, 1971.
Released:
July 1971
Chart peaks:
None (UK) 13 (US)
Personnel:
Duane Allman (g); Gregg Allman (v, o, p); Dickey Betts (g); Berry Oakley (b); Jai Johanny Johanson (d, congas, timbales); Butch Trucks (d, tympani); Thom Doucette (hm)
Track listing:
Statesboro Blues; Done Somebody Wrong; Stormy Monday; You Don't Love Me; Hot 'Lanta; In Memory of Elizabeth Reed; Whipping Post
Running time:
78.38
Current CD:
823 273-2
Further listening:
Eat A Peach (1972), with three tracks taken from the Fillmore shows, and *The Fillmore Concerts* (1992), a 2-CD collection remastered by Tom Dowd, who says it features better takes than the original.
Further reading:
Midnight Riders: The Story of the Allman Brothers Band, (Scott Freeman and Michael Pietsch, 1996); www.allmanbrothersband.com
Like this?
Try . . . p.652

The Move

Message From The Country

Heavy, genre-busting pop music bearing the seeds of the Electric Light Orchestra.

Message From The Country was created under some duress. The Move made it, essentially, to keep their record labels happy. In the UK, Harvest had signed Roy Wood and Jeff Lynne's new idea for a 'serious' band The Electric Light Orchestra, whose concept, the pair leaked to the press, was to pick up from where The Beatles' I Am The Walrus left off and integrate classical instrumentation into rock'n'roll. All well and good, but when Harvest realised that Wood and Lynne intended to take their own sweet time making the first ELO album, they tried to talk them into making a Move album to keep their name alive. At the same time, US label Capitol insisted that they were *committed* for one more Move album, following which the label would *then* decide if it wished to release the Electric Light Orchestra's debut.

Perhaps it was a certain Dunkirk spirit that resulted in *Message From The Country* having more humour than any of the group's other works. There are several out-and-out parodies – the Johnny Cash-style Ben Crawley Steel Company; the Elvis rip Don't Mess Me Up; the megaphonic My Marge. Even many of the 'straight' numbers – It Wasn't My Idea To Dance; Until Your Mama's Gone – are done in an ironic style that prompted Rolling Stone to compare the group favourably to the Bonzo Dog Band, adding that *Message From The Country* "ranks right up there with Procol Harum's *Broken Barricades* as a prime contender for 1971's best album". What takes *Message From The Country* out of jokey territory is Wood and Lynne's eagerness to experiment. On the two most irony-free cuts – the haunting title track and the delicate No Time – the band created a gorgeous, ethereal sound more felt than heard, while on the melodramatic It Wasn't My Idea To Dance, Wood's ranging cello calls up dark, forboding, atonal notes worthy of a Bernard Hermann soundtrack. It was the kind of experimentation that they would bring to fruition later that same year on ELO's eponymous debut.

Record label:
Harvest
Produced
by Roy Wood and Jeff Lynne.
Recorded
early 1971, location unavailable.
Released:
July 1971
Chart peaks:
None (UK) None (US)
Personnel:
Roy Wood (g, v); Rick Price (b); Bev Bevan (d); Jeff Lynne (v, k, g)
Track listing:
It Wasn't My Idea to Dance; The Minister; Message from the Country; The Words of Aaron; Ben Crawley Steel Company; Until Your Mama's Gone; No Time; Ella James; Don't Mess Me Up; My Marge
Running time:
38.28
Currently unavailable on CD
Further listening:
Movements (1997), a three-CD set, compiles practically all the Move's pre-Message recordings.
Like this?
Try . . . p.296

Joni Mitchell

Blue

Spare. Tender. Moving. Perfect.

Joni Mitchell, singer, poet and devout smoker, regards herself first and foremost as a painter. She maintains that had her training at Calgary Art College in Canada been stimulating enough, she'd never have drifted towards music. Claiming she first picked up a ukulele "with the intention of accompanying dirty drinking songs at weiner roasts", she found she could make pin money by singing in coffeehouses while at college in the early '60s. A visit to the Mariposa Folk Festival in 1964 alerted her to the Yorkville folk scene in Toronto and she decided to stay there, marrying singer Chuck Mitchell in 1965. They toured as a duo while Joni's original songs found favour with American singers Tom Rush and Judy Collins. When the marriage fell apart in 1967, Joni planned to settle in New York and paint. However, making her rent on the folk scene once again, she was spotted by manager Elliot Roberts, who introduced her to David Crosby. The two singers became lovers and Crosby "pretended to produce" her first album with engineer Henry Lewy, who stayed with Joni for 13 albums. *Blue*, her fourth, consolidated her reputation as queen of the Californian singer-songwriters. Aptly, this suite of solitude found her almost entirely alone. "Only Henry and I were in there," she recalls. The closed-set atmosphere reflected the extent to which she was baring her soul on the 10 songs she had chosen. From the naked desire of All I Want to the more scornful The Last Time I Saw Richard, *Blue* offered self-examination, vulnerability and a sharp, railing cynicism still pretty new to rock.

"I perceived a lot of hate in my heart," Mitchell has said of the mood behind *Blue*, adding that the album is "probably the purest emotional record I will ever make." Throughout the sessions she felt defenceless to the point of hallucination: "Everything became transparent . . . I was so thin-skinned, just nerve endings." Loneliness, grief and infatuation were just three themes of an album which has become a sacred text of nostalgic introspection and a source of almost healing power.

"I have felt that it was perhaps my role on occasion," says Joni, "to pass on anything I learned that was helpful to me on the route to fulfilment or a happy life." It's the honesty and unmediated emotion of *Blue* that still resonate with anyone who has ever lost sleep over lost love.

Record label:
Reprise
Produced
by Joni Mitchell (uncredited)
Recorded
at A&M studios, Los Angeles; spring 1971.
Released:
August 1971
Chart peaks:
3 (UK) 15 (US)
Personnel:
Joni Mitchell (g, p, dulcimer, v); James Taylor (g); Stephen Stills (b); "Sneaky" Pete Kleinow (psg); Russ Kunkel (d); Henry Lewy (e)
Track listing:
All I Want; My Old Man; Little Green; Carey; Blue; California; This Flight Tonight; River; A Case Of You; The Last Time I Saw Richard
Running time:
36.16
Current CD:
7599271992
Further listening:
Follow-up For the Roses (1972) was less intimate, but full of good songs. After the excellent Court And Spark (1973), Mitchell turned to a more oblique, cerebral mode, fruitfully explored on the superb Hissing Of Summer Lawns (1975), and to jazz for Hejira (1976) and the largely overlooked Mingus (1977).
Further reading:
www.jonimitchell.com
Like this?
Try . . . p.221

The Who

Who's Next

A classic album snatched from the ashes of a conceptual Tower Of Babel.

"I thought it was a huge technical magnum opus," says Pete Townshend of The Who's aborted *Lifehouse* project. "It was an extraordinary moment of visionary imagination from me, and it seemed to have been wasted."

Lifehouse was a brave attempt to go one better than *Tommy*, via the creation of an integrated movie and album. But it was hampered by one key problem: the inability of its author to explain exactly what it was all about. The new compositions were bound up with a story involving a society in which individuals are dependent on a government-controlled "grid" for their entertainment, until a group of "savages" who've been keeping rock'n'roll alive in the woods turn up to battle with the forces of evil.

In February 1971, The Who began a series of shows at the Young Vic Theatre in South London, aimed at road-testing the new material. Meanwhile, attempting to tie up a movie script, a stage show and a song cycle simultaneously, Townshend was tumbling into a nervous breakdown.

"People thought I was raving mad," Pete recalled. "Until, constantly trying to tell this, I thought, really simple story to people in a number of different ways – film producer, record producer, theatre director, and so on, in a language each would understand – I actually did start to go completely mad."

Finally, manager/producer Kit Lambert persuaded Pete to just try recording some songs. He and the band took up residence at New York. The sessions, some of which included work with Cream and Mountain producer Felix Pappalardi, produced some good raw material. But Townshend was still having trouble letting go of *Lifehouse* and, going through "a prim phase", was appalled that Lambert was using heroin. Townshend finally agreed to let Glyn Johns who'd be angling to work on the record have a go at salvaging the sessions. In the early summer, they began work at Mick Jagger's country house, Stargroves. They then moved to Olympic in Barnes where Johns had recorded much of his work with the Stones. By this time well-rehearsed (there had even been a few *Lifehouse* try-out gigs), the songs practically flew onto tape, six complete within a week. Such was the group's bafflement about what exactly to do with the material that they simply handed Johns the tapes and instructed him to come up with a single album. *Who's Next* was the result. Still, Townshend considered the album a partial failure.

"It has tremendous merits, and it sounds fantastic, but it could have been the musical 2001," he says. "That's why on the cover, we're pissing over the obelisk. The band didn't get it, but that was the idea."

Record label:
Polydor
Produced
by The Who and Glyn Johns.
Recorded
at Olympic Studios, Barnes; The Record Plant, New York; 1971.
Released:
August 1971
Chart peaks:
1 (UK) 4 (US)
Personnel:
Roger Daltrey (v); John Entwistle (b, brass, v, p); Pete Townshend (g, VCS3 organ, ARP syn,v, p); Nicky Hopkins (p); Dave Arbus (vn); Glyn Johns (e)
Track listing:
Baba O'Riley; Bargain; Love Ain't For Keeping; My Wife; The Song Is Over; Getting In Tune; Going Mobile; Behind Blue Eyes (S/US); Won't Get Fooled Again (S)
Running time:
43.27
Current CD:
527 760-2 adds: Pure And Easy; Baby Don't You Do it; Naked Eye; Water; Too Much Of Anything; I Don't Even Know Myself; Behind Blue Eyes (original version)
Further listening:
The Lifehouse Chronicles (1999), Pete Townshend's boxed set of the development of Lifehouse
Further reading:
MOJO 32, 82; Before I Get Old: The Story Of The Who (Dave Marsh, 1983); www.thewho.net
Like this?
Try . . . p.596

Beaver and Krause

Gandharva

Synthesiser pioneers employ the acoustics of a San Francisco cathedral for cultish ambient jazz suite.

The unique nature of this "score for a non-existent film" reflects the diverse backgrounds of its creators: Paul Beaver was a jazz organist who met Bernie Krause through a shared interest in electronic music; Krause had performed with the Weavers folk group and produced for Motown. Together they became pioneers of the Moog synthesiser, working with The Doors, The Byrds, The Rolling Stones and George Harrison, among others. Krause was also interested in the sounds of the natural world and the pair's previous record, *In A Wild Sanctuary*, is claimed to be the first to use environmental sounds as a central part of the composition. "*Gandharva* was an attempt to continue in that vein," says Krause, "but we wanted to explore our own music – to take the chaos of rock'n'roll on the opening track and bring it down to a more spiritual level on side two." The music finally fades into long, pure notes that echo slowly around the walls of Grace Cathedral – the "sound" of the building itself. Side one features clattering blues-rock, a gospel choir plus synthesiser and vocal experiments. But it is for side two, recorded in the cathedral with its seven-second sound decay, that the disc is remembered.

"It's an unbelievable cavern," explains Krause. "It allowed you to use the whole space as an instrument, which was our intent."

In this slow, contemplative music Gerry Mulligan and Bud Shank star on saxophones with Krause playing Moog and Beaver at the cathedral organ. The record was the first to be recorded live in quadraphonic sound and the musicians were encouraged to wander among the four sets of mics. *Gandharva* was premiered at a San Francisco film theatre using sound equipment lent by the Grateful Dead and distributed in stereo and three competing quad formats (ever wonder why the system failed?). Paul Beaver died in 1975, but Krause has forged a career in bioacoustics and soundscaping.

"I couldn't tell you what the music is on *Gandharva*," he says. "It was categorised all over the place; it was pop, it was jazz. I don't like to be too specific. It just was what it was."

Record label:
Warner Bros
Produced
by Beaver and Krause.
Recorded
at various studios in Los Angeles and Grace Cathedral San Francisco; January–February 1971.
Released:
September 1971
Chart peaks:
None (UK) None (US)
Personnel:
Paul Beaver (Moog, o); Bernard Krause (Moog); Mike Bloomfield, Ronnie Montrose, Rik Elswit, Howard Roberts (g); Gerry Mulligan (sax); Bud Shank (s, flute); Lee Charlton, George Marsh (pc); Gail Laughton (harp); Clydie King, Patrice Holloway, the Beaver and Krause choir (v)
Track listing:
Soft; White; Saga Of The Blue Beaver; Nine Moons In Alaska; Walkin'; Walkin' By The River; Gandharva; By Your Grace; Good Places; Short Film For David; Bright Shadows. US CD also includes In A Wild Sanctuary (1970)
Running time:
34.36
Current CD:
Warner Bros. 456632
Further listening:
In A Wild Sanctuary (1970). Try also Paul Horn, Inside (1968), a flautist explores the astonishing acoustics of the Taj Mahal. One of the first, and best, "New Age" ambient recordings.
Further reading:
www.wildsanctuary.com
Like this?
Try . . . p.567

Funkadelic

Maggot Brain

Eco-friendly funkateers marry psychedelic rock to a whacked-out soul groove.

Funkadelic's previous two records – their self-titled debut and its follow-up *Free Your Mind And Your Ass Will Follow* – saw funk as the road to redemption and transcendental experience. *Maggot Brain* was no exception. With a screaming black woman's head rising out of the earth on the album sleeve, liner notes that quoted the teachings of the Process Church Of Final Judgement and eerie, foreboding lyrics that informed the listener: "I have tasted the maggots in the mind of the universe/And I was not offended/For I knew I had to rise above it all/Or drown in my own shit!", their third album was a frighteningly frazzled trip.

Fourteen years on from his innocent beginnings as singer in doo wop group The Parliaments, George Clinton was on a mission centred around LSD-inspired liberation and black consciousness and pride. Fusing the R&B of James Brown, Sly Stone and Curtis Mayfield with trippy acid-rock riffs, Funkadelic confounded both critics and listeners, despite reaching Number 14 in the US R&B chart.

"Back then people said, 'You just can't do that sorta thing on a record, George,'" explains Clinton. "And I was sayin' right back, 'You bet yo' ass I can.'"

Little is remembered about the actual recording sessions that gave birth to *Maggot Brain*. Clinton admits the album was produced while he was on acid. "I just got in there and turned the knobs," Clinton said. "It was such a vibe. I didn't know any better – you can only do that stuff when you don't know any better." Despite Clinton's unusual approach to producing, *Maggot Brain* successfully mixed politically charged comment (You And Your Folks, Me And My Folks tackled racism, Wars Of Armageddon dealt with the horrors of Vietnam) with gospel music (Can You Get To That) and cosmic funk rock stomps (Super Stupid).

But the finest moment has to be the haunting, transcendental title track. Rumour has it that Clinton had discovered his brother's decomposed body lying in a Chicago apartment with a cracked skull – hence the Maggot Brain – and he locked guitarist Eddie Hazel alone in the studio with the brief to "play like your mother just died". Hazel did just that producing an anguished, fragile, nine-minute guitar solo that rivalled Hendrix and was a world away from Funkadelic's next project, the more conventional funk sound of *America Eats Its Young*.

Record label:
Westbound
Produced
by George Clinton.
Recorded
at Universal Studios, Detroit; late 1970–early 1971.
Released:
September 1971
Chart peaks:
None (UK) 108 (US)
Personnel:
George Clinton (v); Eddie Hazel (g); Tawl Ross (g, v); Bernie Worrell (k, v); Billy 'Bass' Nelson (b); Tiki Fullwood (d); Clarence 'Fuzzy' Haskins (v, d); Ray Davis, Rose Williams, Pat Lewis, Diane Lewis, Grady Thomas, Calvin Simon, Gary Schider (v); McKinley Jackson (tb); Eddie Bongo (bongos); James Wesley Jackson (Jew's Harp)
Track listing:
Maggot Brain; Can You Get To That; Hit It And Quit It; You And Your Folks, Me And My Folks; Super Stupid; Back In Our Minds; Wars Of Armageddon
Running time:
36.58
Current CD:
CDSEWM002
Further listening:
Funkadelic (first album, spaced-out psychedelic funk 1970)
Further reading:
Funk (Rickey Vincent, 1996), For The Record: George Clinton And P-Funk (Dave Marsh, 1998); www.gnofn.org/~1nation
Like this?
Try . . . p.774

Marvin Gaye

What's Going On

The last great Motown record from Detroit and their first overtly political soul album.

What's Going On, the song, had been written by Renaldo 'Obie' Benson of The Four Tops with lyricist Al Cleveland. The Four Tops wouldn't do it and an attempt to sell it to Joan Baez had failed, so Benson offered it to Gaye. Marvin, now fancying himself as a producer, tried to give it to unsung Motown band The Originals, but Benson offered him a share of the publishing if Marvin cut it himself. "We measured him for the suit and he tailored it," Benson told MOJO 64. "He fine-tuned the tune and added spice to the lyrics." To cut the song Marvin assembled a large band of percussionists and his buddies from the Detroit Lions football team to provide a party atmosphere, then got everybody stoned.

"My first thought was that it was never gonna fly," says arranger and conductor David Van DePitte of these sessions. "Then after we both got into a 'to hell with the company' mode, whatever happened, happened."

Berry Gordy was appalled by the results, and was mad at Motown president Barney Ales when What's Going On was mooted as a single, reportedly calling it the worst record he'd ever heard. Put it out or I walk," Gaye demanded. The single sold 100,000 in its first day and Motown was forced to run with whatever Marvin wanted for the resultant album.

That's when Van DePitte's headaches began. Marvin hadn't finished any songs and kept missing sessions, and when he did show, work was inconclusive and slow. It was only when Gordy bet him a substantial sum that he couldn't finish it in 30 days, that Marvin was energised to complete the album. He worked on songs with Benson, Cleveland and veteran Motown switchboard operator Jamie Nyx, who supplied lyrics to Inner City Blues. The rhythm tracks were recorded and edited into one long piece over which the string, brass and vocal overdubs were laid.

Meanwhile, Marvin refined his new approach to the vocals, having chanced upon his trademark dual-vocal style after hearing two separate takes being played back at once. "I'd been studying the microphone for years," he said, "and I realised what I'd been doing wrong. I'd been singing too loud. One night, listening to a record by Lester Young it came to me. Relax, just relax." Apparently, Marvin's patent relaxation techniques included hours of masturbating before attempting a vocal take.

What's Going On signalled great changes in the label's music. The happy-go-lucky Motown sound was doomed. By the following year, Berry Gordy had taken Motown to LA to become just another Californian record company. The unique spirit of Hitsville was left behind.

Record label:
Tamla Motown
Produced
by Marvin Gaye.
Recorded
at Motown Studios and Golden Studios, Detroit; June–July 1970 and March 1971.
Released:
September 1971
Chart peaks:
None (UK) 6 (US)
Personnel:
Marvin Gaye (p, v); Eli Fontaine (as); Bill Moore (ts); Joe Messina, Robert White, Earl Van Dyke (g); Bob Babbit, James Jamerson (bs); Chet Forest (d); Jack Ashford (pc); Eddie Brown (bongos); Earl De Rouen (congas); Jack Brockensha (vibes); David Van DePitte (oa); Ken Sands, Steve Smith (e)
Track listing:
What's Going On (S); What's Happening Brother; Flyin' High (In The Friendly Sky); Save The Children (S); God Is Love; Mercy Mercy Me (The Ecology) (S); Right On; Wholly Holy; Inner City Blues (Make Me Wanna Holler) (S)
Running time:
35.30
Current CD:
5308832
Further listening:
Marvin's orchestral tour-de-force was the Trouble Man soundtrack (1973). The politics of sex were explored on Let's Get It On (1973), explored even further on I Want You (1976) and followed, perhaps inevitably, by the politics of divorce on Here, My Dear (1979).
Further reading:
MOJO 64; Troubleman (Steve Turner, 1999); Divided Soul (David Ritz, 1991)
Like this?
Try . . . p.761

John Lennon

Imagine

Lennon's greatest solo success, produced amid domestic harmony before he and Yoko fled the UK for ever.

The primal screaming *John Lennon/Plastic Ono Band* had alienated critics and fans alike. *Imagine* – released exactly a month after John and Yoko took up permanent residence in the US – proved to be Lennon's greatest solo commercial and critical success, causing his controversial chronicler Albert Goldman to note sourly: "Which doesn't speak well of the tastes of the public or reviewers." *Imagine* was a product of the genial atmosphere in which it was recorded in late spring 1971. "It was great," recalls drummer Alan White. "We'd all sit around the long table in the kitchen with the builders building around us. John had that sound in his head. He wanted Phil Spector to do it and he loved everything that was turning out, so he was very happy."

Contributions from such long-term associates as George Harrison and Klaus Voorman, as well as Joey Molland and Tom Evans from the Apple-signed Badfinger and Mike Pinder from beat rivals The Searchers, further lent to the harmonious feel. Not that all is sweetness and light. Lurking beneath the "chocolate-coated" surface, the same dark themes festered: self-disgust (Crippled Inside, Jealous Guy), hatred (How Do You Sleep?) and paranoia (Gimme Some Truth). Even the idealistic title track had a dark side.

"It's Working Class Hero with sugar on for conservatives like yourself," Lennon spat at McCartney, so roundly and famously lambasted on How Do You Sleep? "The only thing you done was Yesterday," sang Lennon, who would later withdraw the attack. "It's like Dylan says, often these things are really about yourself," he muttered.

The song reached Number 3 in the US, but Lennon abruptly nixed a single release in Britain, preferring instead to concentrate on the hastily assembled Happy Xmas (War Is Over) campaign. This was indicative of how quickly his life had changed since the recording of *Imagine* in England's Green Belt. His politics had attained a militant edge, fuelled by his fascination for the frantic pace of life in New York. "I'm just sort of fascinated by it, like a fucking monster," he confessed. "it's where I belong." But he was more than aware of the dangers which lurked in the city. Spector had persuaded one of Lennon's musical heroes, the legendary King Curtis, to overdub a contribution after the main sessions were finished. A month later Curtis was stabbed to death by a vagrant outside his house in New York, in a disturbing portent of the fate of the creator of this beautiful, sardonic and, above all, human masterpiece.

Record label:
Apple
Produced
by John Lennon and Yoko Ono with Phil Spector.
Recorded
at Ascot Sound Studios; late spring 1971.
Released:
October 3, 1971
Chart peaks:
1 (UK) 1 (US)
Personnel:
John Lennon (v, g, p, mouth organ, whistling); Klaus Voorman (b); Alan White (d); George Harrison (dobro); Nicky Hopkins (p); Jim Gordon (d) King Curtis (s); Joey Molland, Tom Evans (g); Mike Pinder (tb)
Track listing:
Imagine (S); Crippled Inside; Jealous Guy; It's So Hard; I Don't Wanna Be A Soldier Mama; Gimme Some Truth; Oh My Love; How Do You Sleep?; How; Oh Yoko!
Running time:
39.31
Current CD:
5 24858 2
Further listening:
Mind Games (1973)
Further reading:
MOJO 42; We All Shine On: The Stories Behind Every John Lennon Song (Paul Du Noyer, 1997)
Like this?
Try . . . p.630

Shirley Collins And The Albion Country Band

No Roses

Perhaps the single best English electric folk set.

Shirley Collins seemed the least likely of the established folkies to get involved with electric folk – a genteel Sussex artist who took her vocal style directly from the old singers and could scarcely have been more immersed in traditional song, having travelled around Britain and America collecting material with the researcher Alan Lomax. Yet she'd already broken a few barriers with her multicultural *Folk Roots, New Routes* album with Davey Graham in 1964 and the conceptual early music themes of *Anthems In Eden* with sister Dolly Collins in 1969 while the simple, understated depth of her 1970 album *Death And The Lady* had given direction to many bands of the day, notably Pentangle.

She was dubious when her husband Ashley Hutchings spoke of his plans to create a relevant, modern band exploring the spirit of English country dance bands of old but found she got a great kick out of fronting the Albion Country Band venture without remotely compromising her distinctively relaxed rural style.

"I remember talking to Ashley about what a dance band was," says one-time Albion Band member John Tams. "I said I thought it should sound like Joe Loss with Anne Shelton singing while people danced. Not long afterwards there was this big band with Shirley Collins doing Anne Shelton while people danced." It led to a lifetime of Albion Bands in different formats with hugely varying line-ups pursuing contrasting goals – and Collins was an early departure when her marriage to Hutchings broke up.

But *No Roses* remains appealing as an album that brilliantly matched a singer and musical style of apparently sharp contrast, driven by natural, inventive interpretations of some of the finest songs produced by the British tradition, notably the Coppers' Claudy Banks, Joseph Taylor's White Hare and, best of all, a spectacular theatrical treatment of The Murder Of Maria Marten.

Record label:
Mooncrest
Produced
by Sandy Robertson and Ashley Hutchings.
Recorded
at Sound Techniques, Morgan and Air Studios, London; summer, 1971.
Released:
October 1971
Chart peaks:
None (UK) None (US)
Personnel:
Shirley Collins (v, ag, banjo, a); Nic Jones (v, vn); John Kirkpatrick (acc); Maddy Prior (v); Richard Thompson (ag, g); Lol Coxhill (s); Ashley Hutchings (b); Simon Nicol (v, ag, g); Roger Powell (d); Tim Renwick (ag, g); Roy Wood (v); Francis Baines (g, hurdy gurdy); Dave Bland (dulcimer, concertina); Alan Cave (bassoon); Dolly Collins (v, p); Barry Dransfield (vn, v); Tony Hall (melodeon); Alan Lumsden (s); Dave Mattacks (d); Lal Waterson (v); Mike Waterson (v); Ian Whiteman (p); Royston Wood (v); Jerry Boys (e)
Track listing:
Claudy Banks; The Little Gypsy Girl; Banks Of The Bann; Murder Of Maria Marten; Van Dieman's Land; Just As The Tide Was A'Flowing; The White Hare; Hal-An-Tow; Poor Murdered Woman
Running time:
41.00
Current CD:
CRESTCD011
Further listening:
Battle Of The Field (1976)
Further reading:
www.folkicons.co.uk
Like this?
Try . . . p.577

The Master Musicians Of Jajouka

Brian Jones Presents The Pipes Of Pan At Jajouka

"The menace of darkness outside the circle of firelight," according to Rolling Stone.

Unwanted by Mick and Keef ("I have the feeling my presence is not required," was how Jones described the early *Let It Bleed* sessions), hounded by the fuzz in Britain, no longer able to play his guitar and mentally crumbling, Brian Jones fled to Morocco in the summer of 1968. Earlier in the year he had taken the producer Glyn Johns to record Gnaoua musicians, but had been unhappy with the results. In the Rif mountains near Tangiers, the artist Brion Gysin had taped Berber music for him, and he wanted more. When Jones arrived, the musicians happily re-enacted part of the 4,000-year-old Rites Of Pan for him. The musicians (all men) played pipes and drums, making unearthly sounds that whipped the participants into trances, seemingly possessed and unable to stop for hours. "I don't know if I possess the stamina to endure the incredible constant strain of the festival," Jones wrote in the sleevenotes, "such psychic weaklings has Western civilisation made of so many of us."

Jones returned to London certain he had uncovered a link between Africa and American music – a concept outside the scope of most pop musicians in the 1960s. Filled with enthusiasm, he turned tyro producer, swamping parts in electronic effects, adding keyboards and guitar wherever he felt they were required. Take Me With You sounds as if it's running backwards in parts, Your Eyes is scarily intense, and I Am Calling Out could be an Afro-Caribbean voodoo chant. "What exists here is a specially chosen representation of the type of music which is played and chanted during the festival," he wrote. "We apologise for the virtual inaudibility of the lead singer during the chanting of the women, but they are chanting an incantation to those of another plane. It was not for our ears."

The two sides were unbroken single tracks (the titles were not added until a 1995 re-release) and the total cost was more than £20,000. On the positive side, it was unquestionably unique – no other Moroccan music was commercially available in Britain. But then again, neither was Brian's LP – at least, not until two years after his death.

Record label:
Rolling Stones Records
Produced
by Brian Jones.
Recorded
in Morocco; 1968.
Released:
October 1971
Chart peaks:
None (UK) None (US)
Personnel:
Brian Jones (v, g, k); The Master Musicians Of Jajouka (v, d, pipes)
Track listing:
55; War Song; Standing And One Half; Take Me With You My Darling, Take Me With You; Your Eyes Are Like A Cup Of Tea; I Am Calling Out; Your Eyes Are Like A Cup Of Tea (Reprise)
Running time:
46.00
Currently unavailable on CD
Further listening:
Jajouka Between The Mountains (1996)
Further reading:
www.eyeneer.com/World/Nawa/Profiles/Jajouka
Like this?
Try . . . p.700

Van Der Graaf Generator

Pawn Hearts

The sound of the underground at its most unpredictable.

"The times were intense, and we were an intense, even scary band," remembers frontman/songwriter Peter Hammill. Back in 1971, things rarely got scarier than *Pawn Hearts*, VDGG's most traumatic album. Hammill's odyssey blurred searching, bad-trip visions with moments of blissful revelation; the complex arrangements owed much to 20th century classical music, contemporary jazz and psychedelia; the manic, end-of-tether results belied the progressive tag that's often been attached to the band. Unusually, there were few showy displays of virtuosity.

Emerging from the late '60s underground scene, VDGG's previous albums had won them keen college and continental followings. "Things were extremely open," says Hammill, "and that's the attitude we went in with. We were given more time than before, and we were aware that it was going to be an epic production. In the writing, I was trying to push things as far as they could go, and in the playing we were trying to pull many influences into one cohesive mess."

After rehearsals at a haunted house in Crowborough (where the inner sleeve photo was shot), the group spent around four weeks between July and September 1971 stretching Trident's studio technology. "A lot of effects had to be invented," says Hammill. Phasing involved running two stereo machines slightly out of sync by balancing a heavy ashtray on one of the reels. "At one stage during the mixing, we were using every tape-machine that Trident had in order to cope with the phasing, delays and repeats." While the basic structure of the album's three pieces was pre-planned, the VDGG ethos allowed room for improvisation. "We were a touring band at the time and we trusted each other to do the business when the red light went on." Some bridging sections were completely improvised, notably the start and finish of Lemmings and the Pictures segment of Plague Of Lighthouse Keepers, a complex, side-long segue of ten parts cross-faded together. "The mixing, which often involved six pairs of hands, was effectively a live performance," Hammill adds.

Pawn Hearts compelling, claustrophobic, carefully-hewn chaos is practically unique in pop.

Record label:
Charisma
Produced
by John Anthony.
Recorded
at Trident Studios, London; July–September 1971.
Released:
October 1971
Chart peaks:
None (UK) None (US)
Personnel:
Peter Hammill (v, g, p); David Jackson (s, flute, v); Hugh Banton (k, o, p, Mellotron, syn, b, v, psychedelic razor); Guy Evans (d, pc, p); Robert Fripp (g); Robin Cable (e); David Hentschel (e); Ken Scott (e)
Track listing:
Lemmings (including Dog); Man-Erg; A Plague Of Lighthouse Keepers: i. Eyewitness; ii. Pictures/ Lighthouse; iii. Eyewitness iv. SHM; v. Presence Of The Night; vi. Kosmos Tours; vii. (Custard's) Last Stand; viii. The Clot Thickens; ix. Land's End (Sineline); x. We Go Now
Running time:
45.06
Current CD:
1704616392
Further listening:
Hear the band limber up on H To He, Who Am The Only One (1970)
Further reading:
www.vub.ac.be/STER/KoenWWW/Ph/RefHome.html
Like this?
Try . . . p.560

Mickey Newbury

'Frisco Mabel Joy

Gritty songwriter crafts dark, stormy songs to the sound of the rain.

Mickey Newbury had a reputation as a composer of chirpy hits for the likes of Willie Nelson, Tom Jones and Kenny Rogers (the evocative psychedelia of I Just Dropped In To See What Condition My Condition Was In, later on the soundtrack of The Big Lebowski) when he landed a deal with Elektra to make his own records and, between 1969 and 1971, cut three albums of intensely personal music that bore little resemblence to his pop work. "I never really liked those early songs," he now admits.

Holed-up on a barge in Nashville, he'd often write while rain tumbled onto the roof and its melancholy rhythm soon began to permeate his work, so much so that all three albums – *Looks Like Rain*, *'Frisco Mabel Joy* and *Heaven Help The Child* – feature the sounds of those stormy nights.

"It seemed to be raining all the time back then. And I just seemed to turn it into sad songs," Newbury confirms. These were stories of loss, missed opportunity and road-weary misadventure, on *'Frisco Mabel Joy* they languish in a strange orchestral haze of minor chords, choirs, peeling bells, distant steel guitars and a gathering storm just in earshot. Although the album was recorded in Nashville, the only link to country music is Newbury's groggy twang of a voice, and the songs owe more to the blackest of gothic stories.

Opening with An American Trilogy, a medley of three Civil War songs fused to underline their gloominess, the mood is set for this study in despair. Elvis Presley's subsequent cover added drum rolls and whistles to play up the patriotic element. "I thought Elvis kinda missed the point," Newbury said later. "The idea was to emphasise that they were real folk songs, talking about real people." Newbury simply relied on the lyrics' inherent pain and poignancy to carry the weight. And his self-penned tunes mined a similarly dark vein; recurring orchestral themes enhancing their grandiose, weather-beaten feel. These tales of unfaithful lovers, a fondly-remembered past and a future that can't compete make *'Frisco Mabel Joy* a mood piece that aches to be wallowed in.

Record label:
Elektra
Produced
by Dennis Linde.
Recorded
at Cinderella Sound Studios, Nashville, Tennessee; 1970.
Released:
Autumn 1971
Chart peaks:
None (UK) None; (US)
Personnel:
Mickey Newbury (v,p); Dennis Linde (g); Wayne Moss (g); Charlie McCoy (hm); Weldon Myrick (s,g); Charles Navarro (c); Don Grant (vn); Norman Spicher (d); Farrell Morris (pc); Bobby Thompson (g, banjo); Beegie Cruser (k); James Isbell; James Capps and the Nashphilharmonic; with Dr John Harris; John Moss; Walter Sill and Bob Beckham
Track listing:
An American Trilogy; How Many Times (Must The Piper Be Paid For His Song); Interlude; The Future's Not What It Used To Be; Mobile Blue; Frisco Depot; You're Not My Same Sweet Baby; Interlude; Remember The Good; Swiss Cottage Place; How I Love Them Old Songs
Running time:
36.05
Currently unavailable on CD
Further listening:
Though not available as individual CDs, the ten albums Newbury released between 1969 and 1981 are compiled on eight CDs as The Mickey Newbury Collection.
Further reading:
No Depression (Grant Allen and Peter Blackstock,1999)
www.mickeynewbury.com
Like this?
Try . . . p.201

Led Zeppelin

IV

Their fourth, untitled, album – also known as "Four Symbols" – turned them into untouchable superstars.

Led Zeppelin's blues-rock origins as The New Yardbirds were a little misleading. Both Page and Plant were as influenced by British folk music as they were by American blues and had begun to explore their fascination in earnest on their third album which was coolly received by critics.

Jimmy Page took it badly, Robert Plant got on the defensive. "Plant Denies Soft Charge", trumpeted Record Mirror. "Now we've done *Zeppelin III* the sky's the limit," Plant declared. They'd been making full use of the emerging mobile studio technology, hiring The Rolling Stones' truck-mounted facility and parking it in the Hampshire countryside outside a former Victorian workhouse known as Headley Grange. Here, they'd cut some of *Led Zeppelin III* and after they'd got used to the damp and draughty accommodation, had grown to like the relaxed creative atmosphere it afforded.

"It gave us a chance to work at our own pace," recalls Jimmy Page. "It was a three-storey house with a huge hallway where we miked the drums. We'd have the amplifiers in other rooms and cupboards. It was an unconventional way to record but it certainly worked." The gargantuan sound of John Bonham's drums on When The Levee Breaks – captured by one microphone hanging down the house's central stairwell – has been imitated and sampled countless times. "We always wanted the drums to sound like real drums," Page proclaims, "but that hall made them sound like cannons."

The sound, indeed the whole album, became a benchmark for the future of heavy rock, as Page, Plant, Bonham and Jones definitively wove together their individual influences for the crunching riff of Rock And Roll, the sword and sorcery lyric of Battle Of Evermore and all points in between. But over the years, the record's wider pleasures have been overshadowed by rock radio's most-played album track of all time, Stairway To Heaven. It was begun in Island's Basing Street Studios in December 1970, Page having planned it as a 25-minute fusion of all their various styles, (although Plant has claimed, perhaps fancifully, that it started out as a reggae number). The mini-symphony was refined at the Grange, Page spending days on the solos and Plant coming up with the lyrics one evening in front of the fire.

"Stairway crystallised the essence of the band," says Page. "It was a milestone for us." The band's anti-marketing seemed geared to scupper their milestone's chances. No singles, no band name or even title on the muted, very un-rock sleeve. But all of that simply added to the record's mystique and majesty. Zeppelin ascended into the loftiest realms of the rock gods. This was the record that made them untouchable.

Record label:
Atlantic
Produced
by Jimmy Page.
Recorded
at Headley Grange, Hampshire; Island and Olympic Studios, London; Sunset Sound, Los Angeles; December 1970 to June 1971.
Released:
November 1971
Chart peaks:
1 (UK) 2 (US)
Personnel:
Jimmy Page (g); Robert Plant (v, hm); John Paul Jones (b, k, syn); John Bonham (d); Sandy Denny (v)
Track listing:
Black Dog; Rock And Roll; The Battle Of Evermore; Stairway To Heaven; Misty Mountain Hop; Four Sticks; Going To California; When The Levee Breaks
Running time:
42.37
Current CD:
7567826382
Further listening:
Houses Of the Holy (1973); Physical Graffiti (1975)
Further reading:
MOJO 12A, 77; Led Zeppelin: The Definitive Biography (Ritchie Yorke, 1994); Hammer Of The Gods (Stephen Davis, 1985)
www.led-zeppelin.com
Like this?
Try . . . p.50

Sly & The Family Stone

There's A Riot Goin' On

Drug-addled weirdness and tuneful hits combine on one of pop's most perplexing records.

"Two years is a short time to wait for a work of genius," declared manager David Kapralik when the follow-up to his band's smash-hit 1969 album, *Stand!* was finished. Once scheduled as *The Incredible And Unpredictable Sly And The Family Stone*, the edgy and inscrutable record he delivered wasn't what anyone was expecting. "Unpredictable" was right enough. In 1970, the band had missed 26 out of 80 shows. Things were obviously awry chez Stone, a mock-Tudor mansion at 783 Bel Air, overrun by hangers-on, groupies, drug dealers and a psychotic pit-bull terrier named Gun, who'd attack anyone wearing a hat. In the small attic studio, Sly Stone (who used his real name, Sylvester Stewart, when producing) was trying to cut his masterpiece. But he'd also discovered PCP – a drug not so much mind-altering as brain-damaging – and added it to a frightening pharmaceutical shopping list. Riot sounds like it was recorded haphazardly. In fact, it was painstakingly compiled from hours of tape. There was constant overdubbing. Sly would sometimes work three days without sleep. Bobby Womack, Miles Davis, Billy Preston and others dropped by, but no one's too sure who made it to the final mixes (Preston almost certainly plays electric piano on Family Affair). Even long-serving drummer Gregg Errico is only certain he's on the spaced-out jam Africa Talks To You. (Family Affair marks one of the first recorded appearances of a drum machine.)

Jerry Martini recalls that Sly also used the sessions to get laid. "He'd ask women if they wanted to be on his album. They'd lay down some terrible vocal. Sly would get the goods and then erase [their voice]." That's why the $1m-budgeted Riot sounds murky. "The tape was worn out."

Though it topped the American charts, few who purchased this dense brew of stoned grooves and crazed voices could have known exactly what Sly was on about. Were the lyrics militant tirades or whacked-out paranoia? Was the irresistibly funky Family Affair wistful or pessimistic, the beautiful Running Away disturbed or playful? And what's with the yelling of "Timber!" or the yodelling on Spaced Cowboy? Why was an invisible title track listed at 0 minutes and 0 seconds? "It's so complex, words get in the way," offered the original liner notes, unhelpfully. Whatever, the all-positive, good-time Family Stone was over.

Record label:
Epic
Produced
by Sylvester Stewart.
Recorded
at Record Plant and 783 Bel Air, Los Angeles; Spring/Summer, 1971.
Released:
November 1971
Chart peaks:
31 (UK) 1 (US)
Personnel:
Sly Stone (v, k); Rose Stone (v); Freddie Stone (g); Bobby Womack (g, v); Larry Graham (b); Gregg Errico (d); Jerry Martini (ts); Cynthia Robinson (t); Billy Preston, Miles Davis, Johnny "Guitar" Watson, Herbie Hancock, James Conniff (e)
Track Listing:
Luv'N'Haight; Just Like A Baby; Poet; Family Affair (S); Africa Talks To You (The Asphalt Jungle); There's A Riot Goin' On; Brave & Strong; (You Caught Me) Smilin' (S/US); Time; Spaced Cowboy; Runnin' Away (S); Thank You For Talkin' To Me Africa
Running time:
47.40
Current CD:
4667770639 CD DIGIPACK
Further listening:
Fresh (1973); the Sly Stone solo album *High On You* (1975).
Further reading:
Sly And The Family Stone (An Oral History) – For The Record (1999); www.slyfamstone.com
Like this?
Try . . . p.605

Wings

Wildlife

McCartney's forgotten folly.

Just 18 months after the Beatles split, and Paul McCartney was up the proverbial creek. *Ram* was ridiculed, and perhaps Paul felt the need for the security of a band again. In August 1971 he announced that he had formed Wings with a drummer he'd met during the New York *Ram* sessions and one of his old heroes, Denny Laine (real name Brian Hines) once of The Moody Blues, and intended to undertake an old-fashioned tour by funky bus. The new band had cut their first album within days of first meeting. McCartney proudly unveiled the result at a lavish Come Dancing-style album launch. "Bip Bop," announced Paul tenderly on the opening track, "Bip bop-a-bip-bip-bop a-bip-bop bip-bop-bay." Or some nonsense to that effect. Critics could barely contain their contempt. *Wildlife* quickly became the most reviled record in any Beatle's canon. Plans to extract a single (the, ahem, reggae cover of Micky And Sylvia's Love Is Strange) were hastily dropped. Paul has barely mentioned the album since, and even Linda later conceded, "We could have done it better."

Ah, but "could have" is not the same as "should have", and time has shown that the McCartneys' misguided experiment in off-the-cuff simplicity wasn't so mad, after all. For *Wildlife*'s weaknesses back then are the very same factors that make it fascinating today, a sparse, bare-bones defiance reaching back into the infancy of rock-'n'roll and forward to the lo-fi boom of the '90s. Nonsense it may have been, but Bip Bop is a big groove – Paul's meaty bass right up in the mix – and absurdly catchy. Mumbo emerges as an archetypal McCartney rocker, somewhere between Helter Skelter and Soily; and Tomorrow – one of Paul's most surprsingly overlooked songs – could have slipped into the *Abbey Road* medley. Dear Friend is a first-class, Paul-at-piano heart-render, while the title track is an intricately constructed six minute mantra awash with some utterly lovely Linda harmonies. Indeed, comparisons between *Wildlife* and the pre-Spector mix of the Beatles' *Let It Be* demonstrate that everything McCartney was now attempting with Wings, he had first envisioned during those last, fraught months of The Beatles; and would be bringing to fruition as the '70s developed. In other words, Wings may have made some bigger albums, but they never made a more distinctive one.

Record label:
Apple
Produced
by Paul McCartney.
Recorded
at Abbey Road, London; August, 1971.
Released:
December 7, 1971
Chart peaks:
8 (UK) 10 (US)
Personnel:
Paul McCartney (v, b); Denny Laine (g); Linda McCartney (k, v); Denny Seiwell (d)
Track listing:
Mumbo; Bip Bop; Love Is Strange; Wild Life; Some People Never Know; I Am Your Singer; Bip Bop Line (uncredited on LP); Tomorrow; Dear Friend; Mumbo Link (uncredited on LP).
Running time:
39.41
Current CD:
CDP7892372 adds: Oh Woman Oh Why; Mary Had A Little Lamb (S); Little Woman Love
Further listening:
Band On The Run (1974); Wings At The Speed Of Sound (1976)
Further reading:
The Paul McCartney Story (George Tremlett, 1975)
Like this?
Try . . . p.493

David Bowie

Hunky Dory

The birth of a superstar

In mid-1971, 24-year-old David Bowie was being berated by his manager Tony Defries for dragging his heels. Mercurial of temperament and ambition – Bowie would announce variously at the time that he was a washed up old rocker or about to be bigger than Elvis – and distracted by the birth of his son, Bowie was taking his time over the follow-up to his under-noticed, futuristic proto-metal album *The Man Who Sold The World.* Spurred by the news from Defries that he had a mere £27 in the bank and freshly inspired by his recent acquaintanceship with New York's decadent art-rock crew (Messrs Pop, Reed and Warhol), within weeks Bowie had written and recorded enough material for two albums.

The first was the schizophrenic *Hunky Dory.* Side one was an attractive set with a misleadingly sunny, acoustic sound – all guitars and undulating piano – and remains among Bowie's most extravagantly melodic achievements. Both Changes and Oh! You Pretty Things were built on a reassuringly bouncy descending bass line, Life On Mars? (with what Wilfred Mellors called "near-lunatic shifts" of key, as the movie-going heroine dissolves into the film she watches) was Bowie's concerted effort to re-write My Way and Kooks was a Kinksy slice of optimism for his new-born son. The haunted self-examination of Changes and announcement of the obsolescence of the older generation (if not the human species) in Oh! You Pretty Things barely impacts upon a listener in thrall to the music's tunefulness, but side two adopts a grimmer tone and the darkness of Bowie's imagination (images of madness, drugs and cross-dressing abound) becomes more vivid. His nods to Warhol (on, erm, Andy Warhol), Dylan (Song For Bob Dylan) and The Velvet Underground (Queen Bitch) are snarling, ambiguously critical homages, while Bewlay Brothers is a remarkably evocative and impenetrably personal meditation on Bowie's schizophrenic half-brother Terry Burns.

Though a New York critic was sufficiently moved by the album to state that Bowie was "the most intelligent person to have chosen rock music as his medium of communication", Bowie's attention-grabbing "I'm gay" announcement and launch (only six months after *Hunky Dory*) of his career-changing alter-ego Ziggy Stardust meant it took a while for *Hunky Dory* to build its reputation as a classic. For many – despite a further 30 years of astonishingly disparate Bowie music – it remains his finest songwriting hour.

Record label:
RCA Victor
Produced
by David Bowie and Ken Scott
Recorded
at Trident Studios, London summer 1971
Release date:
December 1971
Chart peaks:
3 (UK) 93 (US)
Personnel:
David Bowie (g, p, v, s); Rick Wakeman (p); Mick Ronson (g, v); Trevor Bolder (b, t); Mick "Woody" Woodmansey (d)
Track listing:
Changes; Oh! You Pretty Things; Eight Line Poem; Life on Mars?; Kooks; Quicksand; Fill Your Heart; Andy Warhol; Song for Bob Dylan; Queen Bitch; Bewlay Brothers
Running time:
51.24
Current CD:
EMI 5218990
Further listening:
The Man Who Sold The World (1970); The Rise & Fall Of Ziggy Stardust And The Spiders From Mars (1973)
Further reading:
Loving The Alien by (Christopher Sandford, 1996), www.bowie.com; www.home-users.prestel.co.uk/neukoln/
Like this?
Try . . . p.829

Faces

A Nod's As Good As A Wink

The quintessential lad rock knees-up.

By 1971, The Faces had an outlandish live reputation: boozy, boisterous and brash, they brought the house down in America but still hadn't got it together in the studio. Their debut *First Step* had reached Number 45 and then disappeared after a week, and the follow-up *Long Player* didn't fare much better. To make matters worse, Rod Stewart's solo career was skyrocketing: *Every Picture Tells A Story* and Maggie May had given him his first Number 1 album and single respectively. The fans were clamouring for more – and if they couldn't buy another Rod solo record, then the Faces were the next best thing.

"That's really when we came good," recalled Stewart. "The Faces as a band never surpassed *A Nod's As Good As A Wink*. Incredible album." Few would disagree. The Faces' third album broke their familiar recording pattern. Usually they'd meet in the pub before a session, stay until closing time and then wonder why the album took so long to complete. This time, with producer Glyn Johns bullying them into action, first takes were the order of the day.

"Glyn pulled us together and kept us focused," recalls organist Ian McLagan. "Rod and Kenny would start rattling their car keys about 10 o'clock because they couldn't wait to get out of the studio and go clubbing, while the two Ronnies and I were happier getting high and playing music all night. Glyn was the referee – he could vote a song in or out. We were quite happy to let him be the judge," explains McLagan. Of the nine tracks, four were Wood/Stewart compositions. Rod would sing an idea to Wood, who'd tinker with it and lay down a basic track. Rod would write the lyrics at home – a task he didn't relish: "I hate writing words, that's the hardest part. I'm not really a natural songwriter."

Stay With Me is the album's pinnacle. Their first hit single, an instantly catchy yell-along anthem with Stewart casting himself as a bog-brush haired misogynist demanding: "Just don't be here in the morning when I wake up." The strutting Miss Judy's Farm is a comic tale of sexual slavery, while the McLagan/Lane-penned You're So Rude is more tongue-in-cheek sleaze-rock. But the two Ronnie Lane compositions are more downbeat, Last Orders Please and the beautifully bleak, reflective folk ballad Debris – rumoured by Lester Bangs to be directed at Stewart: "Now we both know you got the money/And I wonder what you would've done/Without me hanging around."

Record label:
Warner Brothers
Produced
by Glyn Johns and the Faces.
Recorded
at Olympic Studios, London; summer 1971.
Released:
December 1971
Chart peaks:
2 (UK) 6 (US)
Personnel:
Rod Stewart (v); Ron Wood (g); Ronnie Lane (b); Ian McLagan (p, o); Kenny Jones (d)
Track listing:
Miss Judy's Farm; You're So Rude; Love Lived Here; Last Orders Please; Stay With Me (S); Debris; Memphis; Too Bad; That's All You Need
Running time:
36.11
Current CD:
7599259292
Further listening:
Good Boys When They're Asleep, a comprehensive 'best of' featuring the previously unissued Open To Ideas (1999).
Further reading:
All The Rage (Ian McLagan, 1998); MOJO 18; Smiler fanzine, online at http://members.aol.com/smilerfrg/rod/sminfo.htm
Like this?
Try . . . p.600

Terry Callier

What Color Is Love

Magisterial jazz/folk/soul meisterwerk from the lost genius of Chicago soul.

Terry Callier made records in the 1970s to virtually no acclaim that, two decades later, had devotees so ardent they travelled halfway round the world to persuade him to give up his day job progamming computers and come back to music. How many records are *that* powerful?

Callier's masterpiece is a spiritual experience, rich in wisdom, texture and import. Amid swirling orchestral arrangements and delicately plucked guitar lines, brimming with beauty and intelligence, his voice seems almost supernatural. You feel that if trees, mountains or rivers could sing, they would sound like Terry Callier.

A contemporary of Curtis Mayfield and his Impressions cohort Jerry Butler, Callier grew up in Chicago's north side. Liberated by John Coltrane's A Love Supreme and energised by the songwriting of Bob Dylan, he cut a debut, The New Folk Sound Of Terry Callier, and joined Butler's songwriter's workshop. In 1971, Chess/Cadet producer Charles Stepney asked him to record some of his own compositions.

What Color... and its follow-up, Occasional Rain, were intended as a double album, but financial worries meant they were split into two single LPs showcasing Callier's unique fusion of soul, blues, folk and jazz. Recording was fast, both artist and producer preferring single takes, even with complex arrangements. Three of the four tracks on side two – the gorgeous ballad Just As Long As We're In Love, political love song Ho Tsing Mee (A Song Of The Sun) and the closer You Don't Care – were recorded in a single session, Callier singing alongside the 20-piece orchestra Stepney had secretly arranged.

But it's the startling opener, Dancing Girl, and the delicate title track that have become Callier's calling cards. The latter is a simple, almost fragile song, Callier musing on eternal questions over a delicate filigree of acoustic guitar, while the former is a nine-minute epic of metaphysical social commentary, the Dancing Girl pirouetting "through time and space" between junkies and poverty-stricken mothers.

"What Color Is Love took about 20 minutes to write, but Dancing Girl was about two years in the making," he recalls. "It's something people can relate to straight away. They know that these things happen in your life."

When he played it in London's Jazz Café, almost three decades on from its writing, it hit everyone; people wept. Callier's career was reborn, and he has gone on to make several fine albums of pertinent, patient, powerful music; but What Color Is Love, a connoisseur's classic, is a record to treasure.

AB

Record label:
Cadet
Produced
by Charles Stepney
Recorded
at RCA Studios, Chicago, Illinois
Released:
1972
Chart peaks:
Personnel:
Terry Callier (v, gtr): Louis A Satterfield (b): Alfred Nalls (congas & bongos): Fred Walker (congas & perc): Donny Simmons (drums): Morris Jennings (drums): Charles Stepney (piano & e piano): W. Zlatoff-Mirsky (violin): Jerry Sabransky (violin): Elliot M Golub (violing): Ruth Goodman (violin): Joseph Golan (Violin): Theodore Silavin (violin): William Faldner (violin): Irving Kaplan (violin): Sol A Bobrov (violin): Harold Kupper (viola): Harold Klatz (viola): Arthur Ahlman (viola): Bruce Hayden (viola): Roger Moulton (viola): Karl B Fruth (cello): Leonard Chausow (cello): Edward Druzinsky (harp): Cyril Touff (harmonica): Phil Upchurch (gtr): Donald Myrick (alto sax and flute): Ethel Merker (French horn): Paule Tervelt (French horn): Arthur Hoyle (Trumpet): John Howell (trumpet)
Track listing:
Dancing Girl: What Color Is Love: You Goin' Miss Your Candyman: Just As Long As We're In Love: Ho Tsing Mee (A Song Of The Sun): I'd Rather Be With You: You Don't Care
Further listening:
Occasional Rain (1972):
Like this?
Try . . . p.743

D.R. Hooker

The Truth

Connecticut hippie philosopher concocts homemade psych-funk masterpiece.

In the late 60s and early 70s, long before 'lo-fi' became a hip credential for unit-shifting, many frustrated musicians funded and produced their own records, despairing of being offered a deal. These private pressings tended to appear in issues of 99 copies, the cheapest run possible. As today's collectors forage ever more desperately for lost classics, these often poor albums are frequently pounced upon and erroneously pronounced to be lost classics. Occasionally, though, the hype is justified. These include such legends as the Rising Storm, Anonymous, the Dark, Zerfas and the Lazy Smoke, groups who could conceivably have made it, if only they'd received proper backing. Foremost among them is Connecticut's mighty D. R. Hooker.

Tempting though it is to exaggerate the worth of such obscurities, *The Truth* deserves every compliment that comes its way, making it even more surprising that there was no real band to speak of. Instead, ten musicians are credited alongside the mysterious Donald Hooker, who wrote, sang and played lead on the album. Culled from the local music scene, they rehearsed only briefly before entering the studio. Tom Kobela, who plays dobro on *The Truth*, remembers that Hooker 'was a very likable, long-haired fellow' with a most unusual appearance. Heavily bearded and very thin, Hooker looks messianic on the front cover. Kobela recalls that 'D.R. wore robes, which was pushing the dress code conventions even then.'

Heralded by an eerie whoosh, the first track, 'The Sea', exemplifies the album's sound: a strong melody, funky drumming and percussion and piercing guitar underpin oddly philosophical, quasi-Christian lyrics. Some songs are extremely mellow (the eerie 'Weather Girl' and soporific 'Falling Asleep'), whilst others rock hard ('I'm Leaving You' and 'The Truth'). But the album's masterpiece is the unforgettable 'Forge Your Own Chains', whose smouldering groove, enlivened by delicate synth and atmospheric brass, provides the backing for Hooker's admonitory lyrics about the iniquities of substance abuse.

Despite the profusion of musicians involved, *The Truth* has a remarkably intimate, uncluttered feel - no small achievement. Kobela, however, admits that 'at the time I thought D.R. overestimated his own talents. I've since learnt not to judge people so quickly.' The group, such as it was, split as soon as the recording was complete and that was that. 'I never heard the final mix of the album or even saw the cover art', Kobela continues, only learning of its cult status when, to his amazement, he stumbled across it on the internet, where limited reissues are occasionally available. In fact, he hasn't seen or heard of Hooker since the sessions for this atmospheric classic. Has anyone? Are you out there, D.R.? RMJ

Record label
n/a (private pressing)
Produced
by D.R. Hooker
Recorded
by Dynamic Recording Studios, New Haven, Connecticut, 1972.
Released:
1972.
Chart Peaks:
None (UK) / None (US)
Personnel:
D.R. Hooker (g, v, b, bv) / Vincent de Paul Linus Pasternak (g) / George Sheck (b) / Nick Oliva (o, p) / Tom Kobela (dobro) / Rick Sanders (syn) / Art Ryerson (ep, bv, ar) / Dave Masson (bv) / Buddy Santori (bv) / Haywood Sheck (d) / Ken Lovelett (pc, vibes) / Samot Arikos & Paul Saffioti (e).
Track listing:
The Sea / Fall In Love / A Stranger's Smile / Weather Girl / This Thing / Forge Your Own Chains / I'm Leaving You / The Truth / The Bible / Falling Asleep.
Further listening:
Armageddon (1979) allegedly consists of outtakes from sessions for The Truth; Rain On The Moon (1987, cassette only).
Like this?
Try . . . p.656

Bread

Baby I'm-A Want You

The fourth, most polished and best-selling of the soft-rock kings' five albums.

Although they delivered five albums, with enough world-class material to justify endless recompiling for decades to come, the original Bread recording era was remarkably succinct: 1969–72. Trailered by its feather-light title track, *Baby I'm-A Want You* was the apex of Bread's ascendency in the soft-rock pantheon and also the album debut of the group's finest line-up.

Originally conceived as a harmony-based pop-rock group, with an emphasis on quirky, three-minute songwriting in The Beatles vein – and specifically as an alternative to the lengthy indulgences of the West Coast acid rock acts – Bread began life as a trio. Spending most of the '60s in Los Angeles as successful session players and songwriters-for-hire, David Gates and James Griffin met during album sessions for Robb Royer's Pleasure Faire. Subsequently tiring of session work the pair, with Royer as Griffin's writing partner, embarked on their own project.

A superb first album, *Bread* failed to secure the sales it deserved, but shortly afterwards Gates' schmaltzy ballad Make It With You became a smash hit in both US and UK charts. Not necessarily representative of the group, it set the agenda – certainly for public expectations, and to an extent for group direction. In the subsequent battle for whose songs became singles, Griffin (essentially responsible for Bread's raunchier material) tended to lose out – a situation that would contribute, along with simple creative burn-out, to Bread's demise in 1973. But, as Gates has wisely observed: "Ultimately, soft rock was what we did best, and you can't really argue with success."

Baby I'm-A Want You opened with Mother Freedom, a disarmingly funky slab of heavy rock written by Gates in a style he christened "Bread Zeppelin". Inevitably, it fared weakly as a single. In an album brimming with exquisitely crafted material from all concerned – one, Down On My Knees, a rare and dynamic Griffin/Gates co-write – once again the biggest hits were by Gates alone: "Everything I Own was written for my dad, who had then just passed away. Diary was just a fictitious thing – it disappointed a lot of people who were hoping there really was a diary, but there never was!" Within a year, there was no more Bread either.

Record label:
Elektra
Produced
by David Gates.
Recorded
at Sound Recorders, Hollywood, California and Sound Labs, Hollywood, California; late 1971.
Released:
January 1972
Chart peaks:
9 (UK) 3 (US)
Personnel:
David Gates (v, g, b, Moog, vn); James Griffin (v, g, p); Larry Knechtel (k, b, hm, g); Mike Botts (d); Armin Steiner (e); James Griffin (associate producer)
Track listing:
Mother Freedom (S/US); Baby I'm-A Want You (S); Down On My Knees; Everything I Own (S); Nobody Like You; Diary (S/US); Dream Lady; Daughter; Games Of Magic; This Isn't What The Governmeant; Just Like Yesterday; I Don't Love You
Running time:
34.19
Current CD:
7559606782
Further listening:
Manna (1971); The Guitar Man (1972); David Gates And Bread: Essentials (1996)
Further reading:
Waiting For The Sun: Strange Days, Weird Scenes And The Sounds Of Los Angeles (Barney Hoskyns, 1996)
Like this?
Try . . . p.585

J.J. Cale
Naturally
Magical debut from the man who came to epitomise the term "laid back".

"John had an amazing local reputation," recalled Leon Russell. "When he played a black club in Tulsa called The Rose Room, it was just like Jackie Wilson or somebody, and then when he started making his own records it's kind of like he turned into Miles Davis or someone. Very odd!"

Jean Jacques Cale had been a stalwart of Tulsa, Oklahoma's music scene for several years before getting the chance to record his solo debut for his friend Leon Russell's new label Shelter Records. Already the wrong side of 32, Cale had led a chequered career which saw him try his hand at whatever musical mode was currently in fashion, starting with western swing in the '50s and taking in rock'n'roll (Johnnie Cale & The Valentines), country and even garage psychedelia as the '60s progressed, eventually releasing a tongue-in-cheek "hippie" album (A Trip Down Sunset Strip by The Leathercoated Minds) during a spell as studio engineer and session musician in Los Angeles.

It was an earlier recording that triggered his subsequent solo career, however, when Eric Clapton covered Cale's 1965 single After Midnight on his own 1970 debut solo album. "It was like discovering oil in your own backyard," Cale later commented, while Clapton explained, "I was tired of gymnastic guitar-playing, and when I listened to J.J. Cale records, I was impressed by the subtlety, by what wasn't being played." Clapton's interest prompted Cale's manager Audie Ashworth to invite him down to Nashville to make an album. Recorded at fabled country studio Bradley's Barn, *Naturally* showcased Cale's smoky murmur and liquid guitar style on his own country, blues and rockabilly grooves, with opener Call Me The Breeze, another version of After Midnight, and the album's first single Crazy Mama (US No.22, 1972) quickly becoming rock standards.

"'Mellow' and 'laid-back' are the two terms most applied to my style and I guess I go along with that," said Cale. "Most of it is medium-, slow-tempo, not really an aggressive in-your-face kind of thing. When I was a real young fellow and played in bands, just as a guitar player, I played a lot more rock 'n'roll, but when I got into songwriting and had to sing, since I only have about a two-note range it was easier to do mellow stuff and grooves."

Despite his backwoods image and the album's title, Cale – who has an engineering background – has always been a devoted techie. *Naturally* even featured an early model of a drum machine. "I'm sure it wasn't the first," said Cale, "but it was in a very infant stage at that time. The deal is, in those days people didn't know about it, so they didn't realise what it was."

Record label:
A&M
Produced
by Audie Ashworth.
Recorded
at Bradley's Barn, Mt. Juliet, Tennessee; September 29–October 4, 1970.
Released:
January 1972
Chart peaks:
None (UK) 51 (US)
Personnel:
J.J. Cale (v, g); Karl Himmel (d); Chuck Browning (d); Tim Drummond (b); Carl Radle (b); Norbert Puttnam (b); Bob Wilson (k); David Briggs (k); Jerry Whitehurst (k); Weldon Myrick (sg); Shorty Lavender, Buddy Spicher (fiddle); Walter Haynes (dobro); Mac Gayden (slide g); Ed Colis (hm); Diane Davidson (bv); Joe Mills (e); Jim Williamson (e)
Track listing:
Call Me The Breeze; Call The Doctor; Don't Go To Strangers; Woman I Love; Magnolia; Clyde; Crazy Mama (S); Nowhere To Run; After Midnight (S); River Runs Deep; Bringing It Back; Crying Eyes
Running time:
40.08
Current CD:
830042-2
Further listening:
His sophomore effort Really was a little funkier than his debut, while Okie achieved a near-perfect blend of low-key soul and country elements. Of the later albums, Travel-Log and Ten are the closest in quality to the earlier ones.
Further reading:
J.J. Cale interview in Q38; www.jjcale.com
Like this?
Try . . . p.298

Nilsson

Nilsson Schmilsson

A less whimsical, more gruff Nilsson has his first big success.

At the start of 1971, Nilsson went back into the recording studio after almost a year's absence to make the album that would become his all-time best-seller, *Nilsson Schmilsson*. His first album of mostly original, non-soundtrack material in the two years since *Harry*, it was also his first recorded in London, and his first with producer Richard Perry. Perry, who was almost exactly a year younger than Nilsson and, like him, born in Brooklyn, NY, had a colourful resumé that included Tiny Tim's first two albums and Captain Beefheart's *Safe As Milk*. He was also a talented arranger – he'd worked on Nilsson's friend Ringo Starr's *Sentimental Journey*.

From its (to say the least) informal cover photo – Harry, unshaven and dishevelled in a dressing gown – to its tongue-in-cheek title, *Nilsson Schmilsson* was a surprising change from Nilsson's previous albums. Most surprising was that he had made such a great artistic leap. "What do you say to a man who writes The Puppy Song," he said later, "and then writes Jump Into The Fire? I really needed [to make that change], too, that was exactly what I was hoping would happen. That album was a great meeting [of minds]. I was so glad to meet Richard Perry, because he was thinking the same thing I was thinking at the same time: now let's go to work and do some rock'n'roll and get down!"

It was while in England that Nilsson heard and recorded the Badfinger's Without You. While the Badfinger version (on their 1970 album *No Dice*) still stands up, there is no question that Nilsson's version remains definitive. It topped the charts for four weeks in the US and five weeks in the UK, selling well over one million copies and earning Nilsson his second Grammy.

Nilsson Schmilsson spent nearly a year on the charts, spawning two more US hit singles, Jump Into The Fire and the Top 10 hit Coconut. The hard-rocking Jump Into The Fire was a completely left-field choice for a follow-up to Without You; "I wanted to do a fast song," Nilsson shrugged later. Fortunately, fans took it on its own merit and sent it up to Number 27. To this day, it is the only hit to feature a bass detuning, courtesy of legendary session man Herbie Flowers. Presented with the contrast between Jump Into The Fire and his earlier work, Nilsson countered "My earlier stuff had the same soul in it, only it was more subtle."

Record label:
RCA
Produced
by Richard Perry.
Recorded
at Trident Studios, London; between January and June, 1971.
Released:
January 1972
Chart peaks:
4 (UK) 3 (US)
Personnel:
Harry Nilsson (v, p, Mellotron); Richard Perry (Mellotron, pc); Roger Coolen (o); Gary Wright (p); Ian Duck (g); Caleb Quaye (g); Chris Spedding (g); John Uribe (g); Herbie Flowers (b); Klaus Voormann (b); Jim Gordon (d); Roger Pope (d); Jim Price (horns)
Track listing:
Gotta Get Up; Driving Along; Early In The Morning; The Moonbeam Son; Down; Without You; Coconut; Let The Good Times Roll; Jump Into the Fire; I'll Never Leave You
Running time:
35.48
Current CD:
ND83464
Further listening:
For the rocking Nilsson, the aptly-named follow-up, Son Of Schmilsson (1973); for the more delicate Nilsson, Harry (1969).
Further reading:
www.jadebox.com/nilsson
Like this?
Try . . . p.244

Isaac Hayes
Black Moses
Fourth album of seductive self-indulgent soul with a bittersweet undertow.

By 1971 Isaac Hayes was a cultural icon – a renowned writer and producer with David Porter for Stax, an esteemed solo artist and a Grammy and Academy Award winner for his third album, the soundtrack to Shaft. With the difficult prospect of writing the follow-up, he entered the recording studios in March of that year and emerged with this sprawling epic. Lavishly packaged with a fold out sleeve that formed a cross four feet high by three feet wide, it pictured Hayes as Moses, resplendent in a robe by the water.

It was Stax minder Dino Woodard who had dubbed Hayes with the Black Moses moniker. "I had nothing to do with it," admits Isaac, "I was kicking and screaming all the way. But when I saw the relevance and effect that it had on people, it wasn't a negative thing." With Hayes' increasing popularity and success however, came a downside. Production and presentation became more extravagant and more often than not completely over the top.

"There's a difference in his music from what he produced when he took a bus to the studio," explains Larry Shaw, Stax's creative editor and man behind the sleeve artwork, "as opposed to when he took a limousine". Yet *Black Moses* is arguably Hayes' most personal and emotionally intense work. He would often write about a love gone bad, but this time he was writing about it from experience. "I was going through the break-up of my marriage. I was heartbroken. That's the only way I could express myself," says Isaac. As a result, he doesn't remember the sessions with particular affection, they weren't much fun. At one point he had to call his secretary into the studio so that he could focus on her while singing, "I was at the mic, tears running down my face. I needed somebody to just hold on to at the time".

Of the 14 songs, three are extended Ike Raps – long, spoken narratives – and 12 are covers. Hayes had a knack of using a familiar song as the starting block for something new. The Jackson 5's Never Can Say Goodbye is stripped bare of its pop origins and reborn as a mammoth tear-jearker, A Brand New Me becomes sheer sensual celebration and Your Love Is Doggone Good completely overshadows The Whispers' original. And if all that wasn't enough, fans could also send off for their very own hand-woven Black Moses robe for a mere $24.95.

Record label:
Stax
Produced
by Isaac Hayes.
Recorded
at Stax Studios, Memphis; spring 1971.
Released:
February 1972
Chart peaks:
38 (UK) 10 (US)
Personnel:
Isaac Hayes (p, vibes, o, electric piano, v); Lester Snell (electric piano); Charlie Pitts (g, rg); Willie Hall (d, tambourine); Gary Jones (bongos, congas); Ronald Hudson (b); Hot Buttered Soul (bv); Sidney Kirk (p); The Bar-kays (bv); Pat Lewis (backing vocal arrangement)
Track listing:
Never Can Say Goodbye; (They Long To Be) Close To You; Nothing Takes The Place Of You; Man's Temptation; Never Gonna Give You Up; Medley: i. Ike's Rap II; ii. Help Me Love; Need To Belong To Someone; Good Love; Medley i. Ike's Rap III ii. Your Love Is So Doggone Good; For The Good Times; I'll Never Fall In Love Again; Part Time Love; Medley i. Ike's Rap IV ii. A Brand New Me; Going In Circles
Running time:
95.00
Current CD:
CDSXE2 033
Further listening:
Hot Buttered Soul – his debut album, including the epic By The Time I Get To Phoenix (1969).
Further reading:
Soulsville USA: The Story Of Stax Records (Rob Bowman)
Like this?
Try . . . p.709

Don McLean

American Pie

Anyone for money-spinning albatross.

Just weeks before the single American Pie topped the US charts in January 1972, Don McLean was a virtual unknown outside the coffee houses and college campus bars of the US folk circuit. Yet before winter was out, there were very few record-buyers in the Western hemisphere who weren't wondering whether the States had finally found a "new Bob Dylan" for the '70s. The song had all the hallmarks of a truly epochal recording, somehow managing in the era of Nixon and Vietnam to both celebrate that nation's down-home values – whisky-drinking good ol' boys, Chevvies taken to the levee, rock'n'roll dances, high-school romances – while strongly suggesting that the age of post-war innocence had long since passed. The references to Buddy Holly's death in 1959 ("The day the music died"), and veiled allusions to Elvis, Bob Dylan and the Stones, add to the song's deeply symbolic undertow: but as he refuses to shed any light on the lyrics himself, it's left to being mostly a *feel* thing. Triumphant, elegiac, happy, sad – American Pie is all these things and more.

Two years before American Pie's breakthrough, McLean had been picked by Pete Seger to join a crew of folkies on The Hudson River Sloop restoration benefit (sailing up the Hudson river by day, singing and writing songs by night). The experience was invaluable, but McLean had to wait until his recording contract with the Mediarts label was bought up by United Artists for his big break. American Pie would probably have made him famous just by itself, but the parent album of the same name showed he was no one-trick pony. Most of the tracks were set to a sparse backing of acoustic guitar and piano, with songs like Winter Wood, Crossroads and Empty Chairs offering quiet, reflective and profoundly felt meditations on a screwed-up, morally bankrupt world, where birds still sing despite the gloom; yet there were also occasional rock combo arrangements – as on the title track and the chilling, anti-'Nam statement The Grave – to give *American Pie* some rock muscle.

It was, though, McLean's ruminations on Van Gogh that provided the album's second enduring triumph, his gentle, precise picking and clean, arresting tenor ensuring that "Starry, starry night, paint your palette blue and grey" is up there with some of the most memorable opening lines of all time.

PG

Record label:
United Artists
Produced
by Ed Freeman
Recorded
in New York, autumn 1971
Released:
February 1972
Chart peaks:
3 (UK) 1 (US)
Personnel:
Don McLean (v, ag), Lee Hays (a)
Track listing:
American Pie (Parts 1 & 2); Till Tomorrow; Vincent; Crossroads; Winterwood; Empty Chairs; Everybody Loves Me, Baby; Sister Fatima; The Grave; Babylon
Running time:
36.10
Current CD:
EMI CDFA3023
Further listening:
Tapestry (1971) is his belatedly recognised debut and home to Castles In The Air; American Pie – The Greatest Hits is exactly what it says on the tin.
Further reading:
John Tobler's sleeve note on American Pie – the Greatest Hits sketches out the basics of his career; Billboard's book of Number 1 singles offers an insightful look into his craft. Also check out www.don-mclean.com
Like this?
Try . . . p.661

1972

Al Green

Let's Stay Together

Secular or sacred, he was soul's most seductive singer.

Willie Mitchell, mastermind of the unmistakable soft soul sound of Memphis's Hi Records, was pushing his protégé Al Green pretty hard during the recording of *Let's Stay Together*. As the hours wore on towards the 100 they would spend on just the title track, Green was growing increasingly frustrated.

"Al's like my son, but he objected a lot," recalls Mitchell in a soft drawl. "He said, 'Well, what you want?' I said, I want *YOU*. He's got a pretty voice and I wanted him to put that prettiness in it. Well, we got it. I think I captured everything I wanted to on that record."

Twenty-five years old at the time, Green was a rising star. He'd met Mitchell in 1969, and after flopping with Beatles covers and having a minor R&B hit with the Temptations' I Can't Get Next To You, the two men had refined their style, tapping both Green's gospel roots and Mitchell's background in jazz. In 1971 Tired Of Being Alone reached Number 11 on the pop charts, but Mitchell believed there was more room for Green to cross over to the white pop audience. The song he pinned his hopes on was Let's Stay Together, a gorgeous plea for love he'd co-written with Green and Al Jackson, drummer for the MGs.

"This was a transition record," recalls Mitchell. "Softer, more melodic, with more jazzy chords." Let's Stay Together would eventually top both the R&B and pop charts, making it the only Number 1 song of Green's long career. Over Mitchell's gently pulsing arrangement of strings, horns and vocals floats Green's ethereal voice, perhaps the most intimate in the music world. The lyrics sound like a lover's plea, but Green insists he was writing also about the social upheavals of the '60s.

"I was trying to figure out where we were all going. You know, 'Whether times are good or bad, happy or sad.'" Brotherhood was treasured at Hi. Situated in gritty south Memphis, the company was smaller than its crosstown rival, Stax, and, as run by Mitchell, very much a family affair. The core of the house band were the Hodges brothers, Teenie on guitar, Leroy on bass and Charles on keyboards. In a sweet if risky nod to brotherhood, Mitchell invited the neighbourhood winos in for this session.

Record label:
Hi Records
Produced
by Willie Mitchell.
Recorded
at Royal Recording Studios, south Memphis; summer and autumn of 1971.
Released:
March 1972
Chart peaks:
None (UK) 8 (US)
Personnel:
Al Green (v); Teenie Hodges (g); Charles Hodges (o, p); Leroy Hodges (b); Al Jackson (d); Howard Grimes (d); Wayne Jackson (t); Andrew Love (ts); Ed Logan (ts); James Mitchell (bs); Jack Hale (t); Willie Mitchell (k, a); Charles Chalmers (oa, bv); Sandra Rhodes (bv); Donna Rhodes (bv)
Track listing:
Let's Stay Together (S); La-La For You; So You're Leaving; What Is This Feeling; Old Time Lovin; I've Never Found A Girl; How Can You Mend A Broken Heart; Judy; It Ain't No Fun To Me
Running time:
34.05
Current CD:
HIL0152
Further listening:
Green Is Blues (1969); I'm Still In Love With You (1972); Call Me(1973)
Further reading:
Sweet Soul Music: Rhythm and Blues and the Southern Dream of Freedom (Peter Guralnick, 1986) has a good chapter; Take Me To The River, Al Green's Autobiography (2000)
Like this?
Try . . . p.606

Neil Young

Harvest

It transformed him into a singer-songwriter superstar, a role he has been systematically dismantling ever since.

1971 should have been the biggest year in Neil Young's recording life. The combined success of CSN&Y's *Deja Vu* and his own *After The Goldrush* had transformed him into the hottest property among the new breed of LA-based singer-songwriters. Unfortunately, he was in no position to take advantage of his new-found fame. Back problems made it difficult for him to even hold an electric guitar, and doctors warned that he might well be confined to a wheelchair unless he underwent an operation to remove some damaged discs. During a slow convalescence, Young was allowed to remain on his feet for only a few hours a day. A laid-back musical style had been forced upon him quite literally: much of the album was written while under sedation, and recorded in a surgical back-brace. As the months passed demand for new product became all the more intense.

He already had a backlog of songs, some of which had been premiered in concert. The grandiose A Man Needs A Maid – featuring an arrangement by Young's longtime friend, Spector side-kick Jack Nitzsche, and recorded with the London Symphony Orchestra during a UK visit – contained some straightforward auto-biography: laid up at his northern California ranch, he was watching a movie with a friend and fell in love with the actress, Carrie Snodgress, who would become the mother of his first child, Zeke. During a visit to Nashville, Young met producer Elliot Mazer who assembled a hand-picked team of local musicians. "They just learned the essence of the songs," Mazer recalls. "With somebody like Neil playing acoustic guitar and singing a song the complete vibe is out there. Those guys heard that and we got those tracks in one or two takes."

The album quickly topped the charts on both sides of the Atlantic. Critics accused him of dumbing down at the time - Rolling Stone accusing him of "invoking most of the LA variety of super-stardom's weariest clichés in an attempt to obscure his inability to do a good imitation of his earlier self" – and there was no denying that the album contained its share of saccharine. But *Harvest* can now be seen as simply another facet of Young's musical person-ality, representing the acoustic, pastoral idyll that usually preceded another barrage of electric howl. Fears that he would take the easy road to MOR blandness, were unfounded. Having a chart-topping single was "empty", Young found. "I thought the record was good, but I also knew that something else was dying." As he would later write, "the middle of the road became a bore"; he much preferred the ditches on either side.

Record label:
Reprise
Produced
by Elliot Mazer, Neil Young, plus Jack Nitzsche and Henry Lewy; 1972.
Recorded
at Quadrafonic Studios, Nashville; Broken Arrow Studio no. 2, San Francisco; Barking Town Hall, London; Royce Hall, UCLA
Released:
March 1972 (UK); February 20, 1972 (US)
Chart peaks:
1 (UK) 1 (US)
Personnel:
Neil Young (g, v, banjo); Ben Keith (sg); Kenny Buttrey (d); Tim Drummond (b); Jack Nitzsche (p, slide g); John Harris (p); James Taylor (bv); Linda Ronstadt (bv); David Crosby (bv); Graham Nash (bv); Stephen Stills (bv); Danny Whitten (g, bv); Ralph Molina (d, bv); Billy Talbot (b, bv)
Track listing:
Out On The Weekend; Harvest; A Man Needs A Maid; Heart Of Gold (S); Are You Ready For The Country?; Old Man (S); There's A World; Alabama; The Needle And The Damage Done; Words (Between The Lines Of Age)
Running time:
37.38
Current CD:
7599272392
Further listening:
Comes A Time (1978); Harvest Moon (1992)
Further reading:
MOJO 10, 25, 44; Neil Young: Here We Are In The Years (Johnny Rogan, 1982)
Like this?
Try . . . p.629

Manassas

Manassas

CSN&Y renegade forms crack team whose legacy is this exemplary double.

Double albums were regarded as something of an indulgence by critics in the early '70s, but few complained about this one. Burning with creative zeal and egomaniacal ambition, Stephen Stills assembled the top players in his orbit and soon realized that their combined talents could not be contained within the context of a single album. Having already impressed with two solo albums, Stills seemed determined to display the full range of his abilities over four sides, pointedly titled The Raven, The Wilderness, Consider and Rock'n'Roll Is Here To Stay. The package proved the ultimate artistic CV, embracing bluegrass, country, pop, rock, R&B, blues and Latin. Remarkably, Stills sounds equally comfortable in each genre – a tribute to his canny choice of players, who include ex-Byrd Chris Hillman, country steel guitarist Al Perkins and Jamaican bassist Fuzzy Samuels.

Premiering the new band, Stills announced: "It's not totally a partnership but it's enough of a partnership that everyone's satisfied. It's better than *Crosby, Stills And Nash*, *Deja Vu* and my two solo albums. I'm really proud of it." Echoing the musical diversity, Stills displayed his abilities as a lyricist covering favourite themes like starcrossed love in the Judy Collins tribute So Begins The Task, ecology in Fallen Eagle and a quirky stab at philosophy in Move Around – "What do we do given life? We move around." Bill Wyman was on hand to co-write the bluesy Love Gangster and was supposedly so smitten with the septet that he briefly considered leaving the Rolling Stones to join their ranks. "I nearly jumped off a bridge when I found out about this," Stills roared.

Manassas embarked on a world tour, including appearances in the UK that are still spoken of with reverence by those lucky enough to have attended. Alas the group's unwieldiness ensured that they split after recording a less impressive second album. Unlike other superstar aggregations, they would never reform. Chris Hillman still regards their double album as a seamless piece of work. "A lot of people have said it should have been a single album, but I think it's a great double," he insists. "It's very rare for me to come from a project and say, 'That's wonderful'. Manassas had some really good players in it. It had the capacity to do anything from bluegrass to Latin. It was very rewarding and stimulating for the period it lasted."

Record label:
Atlantic
Produced
by Stephen Stills, Chris Hillman and Dallas Taylor.
Recorded
at Criteria Sound Studios, Miami, Florida; January–February 1972.
Released:
April 12, 1972
Chart peaks:
12 (UK) 12 (US)
Personnel:
Stephen Stills (g, v, p); Chris Hillman (b, v, mandolin); Al Perkins (sg, bv); Dallas Taylor (d); Joe Lala (congas, pc, bv); Paul Harris (p, k); Calvin Samuels (b); Byron Berline (fiddle); Bill Wyman (b); Sydney George (hm)
Track listing:
Song Of Love; (a) Rock'n'Roll Crazies (b) Cuban Bluegrass; Jet Set (Sigh); Anyway; Both Of Us (Bound To Lose); Fallen Eagle; Jesus Gave Love Away For Free; Colorado; So Begins The Task; Hide It So Deep; Don't Look At My Shadow; It Doesn't Matter; Johnny's Garden; Bound To Fall; How Far; Move Around; The Love Gangster; What To Do; Right Now; The Treasure (Take One); Blues Man
Running time:
72.00
Current CD:
7567828082
Further listening:
Déjà vu (1970); Down The Road (1973)
Further reading:
Crosby, Stills, Nash And Young: The Visual Documentary (1996).
Like this?
Try . . . p.477

Big Star

#1 Record

Debut by legendary underachievers whose influence can be heard in R.E.M., Teenage Fanclub and The Replacements.

Big Star's *#1 Record*? Ironic, of course. But few bands abandon hope before they begin. Although group member Alex Chilton had already experienced fame at its most fickle as the singer of '60s pop-soul hitmakers The Box Tops, the irony he applied to naming his new outfit and their debut album wasn't intended to be damning. Having grown up during the glory days of AM radio, that Beatles-fuelled age when great records often happened to be hits and vice versa, Big Star naturally believed that their own sparkling tunes might likewise rule the airwaves.

Chilton has become acutely uncomfortable with his reputation as a pop avatar. He tends to characterise himself as a fan of Memphis soul and blues who just happened to join a pop/rock group led by that city's biggest Anglophile. "I was joining Chris Bell's band and all I did was to fit in with his concept of the group," he claimed recently. In a 1987 interview, however, he admitted that his relationship with Bell, who co-wrote most of *#1 Record* with him, was one of shared sensibilities: "I loved British music myself. When I first got interested in rock'n'roll, it was when all the British stuff first started coming out. [From] '64 through '66, I thought music was great. But then in '67, when all this psychedelic Californian music started happening, people got more pretentious, but '64 to '66 was still three-minute songs and everything was fairly understandable."

Formed in 1971, Big Star were together only a few months before they went into Ardent Studios to record *#1 Record*. The intense chemistry between Bell and Chilton resulted in a clutch of original songs, none of which sounded like anything else out of Memphis – or anywhere, for that matter.

"After our first run-through of The Ballad Of El Goodo, I thought there was really something magic here," recalls drummer Jody Stephens. "I was so inspired by the songs, by what Alex and Chris were singing and how they sang it. It was a great feeling. For me, recording with Big Star was a Magical Mystery Tour, a trip to Disneyland." The transcendent longings of high-decibel rocker Feel and harmony-draped anthems like My Life Is Right, justified Stephens' enthusiasm, but the album was a flop and, by the end of 1972, Bell had quit to go solo.

Record label:
Ardent
No producer listed.
Recorded
at Ardent Studios, Memphis, Tennessee, late 1971–early 1972.
Released:
April 1972
Chart peaks:
None (UK) None (US)
Personnel:
Chris Bell (g, v); Alex Chilton (g, v); Andy Hummel (b, p, v); Jody Stephens (d, v); John Fry (executive producer) .
Track listing:
Feel; The Ballad Of El Goodo; In The Street; Thirteen; Don't Lie To Me; The India Song; When My Baby's Beside Me; My Life Is Right; Give Me Another Chance; Try Again; Watch The Sunrise
Running time:
37.03
Current CD:
ACE AK028
Further listening:
Radio City (1974); Third (1978)
Further reading:
MOJO 75; http://frontlinearts.com/bigstar
Like this?
Try . . . p.564

Deep Purple

Machine Head

The album which brought us Smoke On The Water, the alma mater of every other '70s school rock band.

It's a story that's entered rock'n'roll myth: on December 6, 1971, Deep Purple arrived at the Montreux Casino, intending to take over the venue for two weeks and record their next album live. But the night before the sessions began, as the Casino hosted its last show of the season, a flare-gun-toting Zappa fan fired into the ceiling. The roof went up, the Casino burned down and Purple were suddenly homeless. A few alternatives presented themselves – a bank vault and a fall-out shelter among them – but the band eventually rented space at the Grand Hotel. They also had a day or so at the nearby Pavilion, and it was there that Purple made history. "We were kicked out because of the noise," bassist Glover recalls. "The only thing we recorded there was a riff of Ritchie's which we called Title #1, and the police were actually outside banging on the doors, the roadies were holding the doors shut while we recorded it – one can almost hear the banging as the song fades out. So we finished the track, but we really didn't think much of it. When we went back to it a week later it was, 'Oh, what are we going to write over this?' So we wrote something, put it on the album, and that was it." "It" just happened to be Smoke On The Water.

The sessions were tight. "What you get is what we did," says Glover. "There were no out-takes, no alternate versions. When I came to remaster *Machine Head* for the anniversary edition, that was the challenge. All there was were those eight songs and a little bit of banter – right at the end of Lazy you hear somebody, I think it's me, going 'wooh!' And that speaks volumes because there's so little else." Nevertheless, Purple wound up with what would be instantly proclaimed a hard rock classic, home to at least four future Purple live staples (Lazy, Smoke, Highway Star and Space Truckin' all reappear on the seminal *Made In Japan*) and, of course, repository of one of the most instantly recognisable riffs in rock.

"The funny thing is, when *Machine Head* came out the song we thought was going to be big was Never Before. We put a lot of work into that, a nice middle eight, polished performances, properly mixed. No-one ever expected Smoke to take off."

Record label:
Harvest
Produced
by Deep Purple.
Recorded
at Grand Hotel, Montreux; December 6–21, 1971.
Released:
April 1972
Chart peaks:
1 (UK) 7 (US)
Personnel:
Ian Gillan (v); Ritchie Blackmore (g); Roger Glover (b); Jon Lord (k); Ian Paice (d)
Track listing:
Highway Star; Maybe I'm A Leo; Pictures Of Home; Never Before; Smoke On The Water; Lazy; Space Truckin'
Running time:
37.44
Current CD:
31002
Further listening:
Deep Purple In Rock (1970); Made In Japan (1973)
Further reading:
Child In Time (Ian Gillan and David Cohen, 1994); www.deep-purple.com
Like this?
Try . . . p.344

Mellow Candle

Swaddling Songs

Overlooked folk classic. Yours for upwards of £500.

Had Clodagh Simonds and Alison O'Donnell been to a more permissive school, it's hard to say whether Mellow Candle's small legacy would have been so remarkable. But at the Holy Child Convent School in Killiney, Dublin, the '60s didn't get much of a look-in among all the Bible-reading and talking to God. As a result, the girls were forced to conduct their discourse with pop music beneath the bedsheets, covertly listening to Radio Luxembourg. These two very different lives – one for the days, the other at nights – finally started seeping into each other when Simonds, aged only 12, began to write a whole succession of baroque, hymnal pop songs on her parents' piano. One of them, *Lonely Man* featured lyrics that went, "Lonely man looking for the day/Damns the night whose stars have left him cold." This much we know because, amazingly, it was good enough to end up on *Swaddling Songs.*

By the time Simonds and O'Donnell formed their first band, briefly called The Gatecrashers, aged 15, their musical vision was complete. But it was four years before *Swaddling Songs* emerged. Events in the interim almost killed off Mellow Candle's appetite for music. They released just one single on Simon Napier-Bell's SNP label before it folded, forcing the girls to return to Dublin and complete their studies. This at least allowed Mellow Candle the time to expand into practitioners of peerlessly explosive psychedelic folk. John Peel caught them at the 1971 Wexford Festival and came away a fan: "The seeds of something good are there," he proclaimed.

A year later, now living in London, Mellow Candle had gathered the makings of an extraordinary album. Medieval pop gems like Heaven Heath and Reverend Sisters set the tone, punctuated by almost operatic excursions like The Poet And The Witch. Simonds and Williams' lyrics often depicted a merciless world, free of spiritual comforts. On paper, Mellow Candle's realm of "bold bright-eyed saints", "shadows of unicorns", "sailing angels", ravens crying "Beware!" and "Solstice [that] brings the chill winds to an end" should have amounted to the most enormous folly. Indeed, according to the CD reissue notes, Simonds is now "reluctant to consider the Mellow Candle album as anything other than an old if charming skeleton in the closet." A shame, because despite the indifferent reception that caused Mellow Candle to disband, *Swaddling Songs* repays repeated listening.

Record label:
Deram
Produced
by David Hitchcock.
Recorded
at Decca Studios, Tollington Park, London; December 1971.
Released:
April 1972
Chart peaks:
None (UK) None (US)
Personnel:
Clodagh Simonds (v, p); Alison Williams (v); David Williams (g, v); Frank Boylan (b, v); William A Murray (d)
Track listing:
Heaven Heath; Sheep Season; Silver Song; The Poet And The Witch; Messenger Birds; Dan The Wing (S); Reverend Sisters; Break your Token; Buy Or Beware; Vile Excesses; Lonely Man; Boulders On My Grave
Running time:
43.14
Current CD:
See For Miles (import) SEECD 404
Further listening:
The Virgin Prophet: Unreleased Sessions 1969–71 (1996) – unofficial collection of demos and unreleased recordings
Further reading:
http://website.lineone.net/~geoff.burton/mellowc/mellowc.html
Like this?
Try . . . p.172

The Rolling Stones

Exile On Main Street

The record that distilled the Stones mystique, often hailed as the greatest rock album ever made.

The album which holds pride of place in the Stones' mythology has a shambling, expansive feel on the surface, but is underpinned by a brooding, barbarous quality which reflects the trying conditions in which it was recorded. Having left Britain to avoid paying their taxes, the band set up shop for the summer in the basement of Keith Richards's villa in the south of France, recording on their 16-track mobile. The house had been the headquarters of the Gestapo during the Nazi occupation of France. The sessions turned into what's been described as "the biggest house party of Keith's hospitable career."

"It was a right sodding pain in the arse, actually," Mick Taylor recalls. "We bloody hated it almost from the moment we started work on it – thought it was crap. Keith wanted to trash it all and start again." In the makeshift studio there was barely room to accommodate the instruments. Engineer Andy Johns vividly remembers the swastika-shaped air-conditioning ducts, and overdubs being done in the kitchen while people were "sitting at the table talking; knives, forks, plates clanking."

"It was party time all the fucking time," agrees Taylor. "It's a wonder we got anything done, the place was so overrun with people. Plus it was damp and cold. Keith and I got boils. Very unpleasant." After some weeks, with no end in sight, Keith's wife Anita became volubly peeved about the occupying forces who'd invaded their home. Meanwhile, to the evident chagrin of Richards, Mick Jagger was away for much of the time with his heavily pregnant bride Bianca.

"Jagger came in and did a bit of poncing about as usual, but Keith guided that one to completion," confirms Taylor. "It was ideal for Keith because all he had to do was fall out of his bed, roll downstairs and voila, he was at work."

Material left in the can from *Sticky Fingers*, such as Sweet Black Angel (known to Keith as Bent Green Needles), was reworked and, though its looseness would suggest otherwise, work on every aspect of the album was fastidious. Tumbling Dice alone took almost two weeks to nail, with over 150 takes before one captured the groove Keith was seeking. In all, the sessions lasted for six months. A further six were spent mixing in Hollywood. Chaotic it may have been, but the group's chemistry was never again so strong.

Record label:
Rolling Stones Records
Produced
by Jimmy Miller.
Recorded
at Rolling Stones Mobile, Nellcôte, France; May–September 1971.
Released:
May 12, 1972
Chart peaks:
1 (UK) 1 (US)
Personnel:
Mick Jagger (v, g, hm); Keith Richards (g, v, b, p); Bill Wyman (b); Charlie Watts (d); Mick Taylor (g, b); Nicky Hopkins (p); Ian Stewart (p); Bobby Keyes (s); Jim Price (t, tb); Bill Plummer (db); Jimmy Miller (pc); Al Perkins (psg); Mac Rebennack (o, bv); Tammi Lynn, Kathi McDonald, Clydie King, Jerry Kirkland, Shirley Goodman, Joe Green, Vanetta Fields (bv)
Track listing:
Rocks Off; Rip This Joint; Hip Shake; Casino Boogie; Tumbling Dice; Sweet Virginia; Torn & Frayed; Black Angel; Loving Cup; Happy; Turd On The Run; Ventilator Blues; Just Wanna See His Face; Let It Loose; All Down The Line; Stop Breaking Down; Shine A Light; Soul Survivor
Running time:
69.16
Current CD:
CDV 2731
Further listening:
Goat's Head Soup (1973)
Further reading:
The True Adventures Of The Rolling Stones (Stanley Booth, 1975)
Like this?
Try . . . p.500

Rory Gallagher

Live In Europe

Gallagher was the first real Irish rock star, this his only UK Top 10 album.

Live In Europe was Rory's third solo album, recorded during a frenetic and extraordinarily creative 18-month period after splitting psychedelic power trio Taste at the height of their popularity. The two studio albums from 1971, *Rory Gallagher* and *Deuce*, chronicled Rory's maturing as an artist and introduced a more crafted and varied aspect to his work.

Gallagher had created his own sound on these albums, drawing from modern jazz, urban and Delta blues, hillbilly flat-picking, heads-down rock and Celtic folk. On slide and acoustic there was a passing affinity with Jimmy Page; his use of the guitar's volume controls, feedback and sublime tone was more akin to Free's Paul Kossoff; while quirky power-pop classics like Laundromat – along with In Your Town, one of only two previous recordings reprised on *Live In Europe* – doffed a cap to Pete Townshend. It was a potent, and very popular, concoction. "A lot of groups get annoyed with audiences that are too rowdy, but I think I know where the line is," said Rory in 1971. "You don't see the old greats on the blues scene preaching about sitting still."

With two posthumous Taste in-concert sets to compete with, *Live In Europe* had to be good, and it was: a definitive snapshot of what made Gallagher great on-stage. Two more concert albums appeared before his untimely death in 1995, but neither has the masterfully channelled energy nor breadth of palette as *Live In Europe* – purportedly the album that inspired future U2 members Adam Clayton and The Edge to form a band. This period marked the height of Rory's public and critical popularity. He did sessions for old heroes Muddy Waters and Jerry Lee Lewis, turned down serious invitations to join The Rolling Stones and Deep Purple, and ousted Eric Clapton as Best Guitarist in 1972's Melody Maker poll. The following year the title went to another non-Brit, Jan Akkerman from Dutch band Focus. They were both 'outsiders' who won.

"I never had the pleasure to meet him," says Akkerman, "but I knew his playing and I admired it. He was the king of the white blues players as far as I'm concerned." Many others have since agreed.

Record label:
Polydor
Produced
by Rory Gallagher.
Recorded
at various European shows; February–March 1972.
Released:
May 1972
Chart peaks:
9 (UK) None (US)
Personnel:
Rory Gallagher (v, g, mandolin, hm); Gerry McAvoy (b); Wilgar Campbell (d)
Track listing:
Messin' With The Kid; Laundromat; I Could've Had Religion; Pistol Slapper Blues; Going To My Home Town; In Your Town; Bullfrog Blues
Running time:
45.31
Current CD:
74465996852 adds: What In The World; Hoodoo Man
Further listening:
Rory Gallagher (1971); Deuce (1971)
Further reading:
MOJO 59; Irish Rock (Mark J Prendergast, 1987)
Like this?
Try . . . p.488

Spring

Spring

Brian Wilson borrows the immaculate sound and emotional focus of The Beach Boys' late '60s work for a girl group gem.

Brian Wilson's first non-Beach Boys production job was Shoot The Curl for The Honeys – Marilyn and Diane Rovell and their cousin Ginger Blake – released in May 1963. Brian produced three other Honeys singles, the last and best, Tonight Belongs To Me, recorded in late 1968. Like all Brian's extra-curricular production work, the tracks echoed The Beach Boys' style but were all commercial failures. Marilyn Rovell (Brian's future wife) and Diane would go on to sing backing vocals on Beach Boys albums well into the '70s. But in November 1971, the two of them – minus cousin Ginger – were reborn as Spring, and released a debut single, Carole King's Now That Everything's Been Said. They retained the Honeys' girl group sound but displayed a greater sophistication, and the evocation of wonder and loss in their vocals echoed *Pet Sounds*.

For Brian, Spring was an outlet for his talents unhampered by the commercial pressures of The Beach Boys, and recording at the Wilsons' home studios made for a relaxed and creative ambience. Marilyn, speaking at the time, explained: "The idea was to record all the songs that we ever loved. Brian helped out in all departments – he sang, arranged most of the backgrounds, wrote some of the songs and picked the material. He was very emotional throughout and would cry at the sessions because he liked a song so much he couldn't believe it." Most intriguing is Thinking About You, originally produced by Brian for Sharon Marie in 1964 but *Spring* also benefits from the presence of *Sunflower* tracks This Whole World and brother Dennis Wilson's lovely ballad Forever. This Whole World is a real high point, adding a bridge ("starlight, starbright") with a stunning harmony between Brian and the girls which tops the Boys' own version. Marilyn and Diane imbue these songs with extraordinary emotion and innocence.

Dynamic and expansive, *Spring* is an uncomplicated, unpretentious – and largely unheard – record, as fine as anything Brian Wilson ever produced.

Record label:
United Artists
Produced
by Brian Wilson, Stephen Desper and David Sandler.
Recorded
at Brian Wilson's studio; throughout 1970.
Released:
May 1972
Chart peaks:
None (UK) None (US)
Personnel:
Marilyn Rovell, Diane Rovell (v); Brian Wilson (v, all instruments, a)
Track listing:
Tennessee Waltz; Think 'Bout You Baby; Mama Said; Superstar; Awake; Sweet Mountain; Everybody; This Whole World; Forever; Good Time; Now That Everything's Been Said (S); Down Home
Running time:
40.33
Current CD:
REP4472WP
Further listening:
The Beach Boys, Sunflower (1970)
Further reading:
www.geocities.com/Heartland/8303/brian/honeys.htm
Like this?
Try . . . p.87

Wishbone Ash

Argus

"The British Allman Brothers" surprise themselves by recording a classic.

Formed in 1969 when Martin Turner and Steve Upton, remnants of a West Country beat group, advertised in Melody Maker for a new guitarist – and couldn't decide between Andy Powell and Ted Turner – Wishbone Ash became and remain, however fluctuating latterday line-ups have been, owners of a most distinctive 'sound'. Initially the British answer to the Allman Brothers – a twin lead guitar blues/boogie outfit – by their second album *Pilgrimage* (1971) influences of a decidedly more pastoral and English nature had been absorbed. Pentangle and Fairport Convention, for example, were of equal importance to guitarist Andy Powell as The Who, and by this stage the group were finding their feet as writers.

Incessant road work and the fearless door-openings achieved by their young American manager Miles Copeland had resulted in the group claiming Melody Maker's Brightest Hope award for 1971. *Argus*, their third album, would not only be their best-selling release but also, beyond question, their best work. It had been the happy combination of youthful energy, two weeks between touring to write the songs and a little convenient geography: "We were all living in the same street in the Ladbroke Grove area," says Andy Powell, "and I can remember the influences just tumbling out. Most of it was written on acoustic guitars, in each others bedsits – running from one bedsit to the next, exchanging ideas for guitar melodies, Martin feverishly writing out lyrics . . . There also was a lot of Bible-reading going on at the time. It was just a good spirit. But perhaps *Argus* promised a lot more than we delivered afterwards. I think we felt that we'd tapped into a spiritual vein and that we were opening our hearts out and maybe we got a bit self-conscious and didn't want to sound too pretentious."

In a way, Argus was Wishbone's *Led Zeppelin IV* – powerful, mystical, dynamic. Conversely, 1973's *Wishbone Four* was more akin to *Led Zeppelin III* (right down to its conception in a Welsh cottage). Not a bad record, it just wasn't strong enough to build on *Argus*' surprise success. Ted Turner retired with exhaustion and the band effectively moved to America – filling stadiums, but rarely recapturing what had made *Argus* so special. One curious footnote: the entire album was remixed by Martin Turner in 1989, though the tracks are only available dotted over two compilations, *Time Was* (1993) and *Distillation* (1997).

Record label:
MCA
Produced by
Derek Lawrence.
Recorded
at De Lane Lea Studios, London; January–February 1972.
Released:
May 1972
Chart peaks:
3 (UK) None (US)
Personnel:
Martin Turner (v, b); Andy Powell (g, v); Ted Turner (g, v); Steve Upton (d); Martin Birch (e)
Track listing:
Time Was; Sometime World; Blowin' Free (S); The King Will Come; Leaf And Stream; Warrior; Throw Down The Sword
Running time:
45.08
Current CD:
MCLD 19085 adds: No Easy Road
Further listening:
4-CD box set of classic, live and rare Ash, Distillation (1997).
Further reading:
The Illustrated Collector's Guide To Wishbone Ash (Andy Powell, 1989); www.wishboneash.com
Like this?
Try . . . p.840

Stevie Wonder

Music Of My Mind

Stevie meets Tonto for electro.

At the age of 18, after six years of writing and singing big hits for Motown Records and Jobete Publishing, Stevie Wonder downed tools. He stopped recording and composing, fed up with his role on the Motown assembly line, and waited out his contracts for three years. In May 1971, he turned 21, came into the vast sum of royalties sitting in his trust fund, and was free from the shackles of the Motown machine. Determined to prove himself, he ignored Motown's urgings to work with their house producers and, instead, chose Bob Margouleff and Malcolm Cecil, who made records under the name Tonto's Expanding Headband. Stevie was taken by his bass player, Ronnie Blanco, to Tonto's studio in the Mediasound complex in mid-town NYC. Cecil recalls looking out the window and seeing Blanco standing there with some guy in shades and a pistachio green cape on. When Cecil realised it was Stevie, he dialled his partner Margouleff, imploring him to come over immediately. It was Memorial Day Weekend (the last weekend in May). Stevie sat down in the studio that Saturday afternoon, and by Monday night they'd recorded an amazing 17 tracks. Six of them became part of *Music of My Mind.*

Out of gratitude to Berry Gordy and Ewart Abner, owner and president of Motown, respectively, Stevie re-signed to Motown, delivering his first new album at the signing in December 1971. When Abner did not hear a traditional Stevie single on the album he was angry. But when the record was released in the first quarter of 1972 to critical raves, he changed his tune. *Music Of My Mind* started to sell to an across-the-board audience, a fact which was not wasted on Motown's marketing people. Three months into the release, they finally got behind the album with Superwoman, Happier Than The Morning Sun and Keep On Running garnering consistent airplay. It took two years before Motown sweetened the pot enough to re-sign Stevie to Jobete as a writer. It cost them $13 million and half the publishing which stayed with Stevie's Black Bull Music company.

Record label:
Motown
Produced
by Stevie Wonder.
Recorded
at Media Sound NYC, Electric Lady NYC, and Crystal Studios LA, California; May 1971–December 1971.
Released:
May 1972
Chart peaks:
None (UK); 21 (US)
Personnel:
Stevie Wonder (all instruments, v); Buzzy Feiten (g); Art Baron (tb); Lani Groves, Jim Gilstrap (bv); Malcolm Cecil; Bob Margouleff (e, syn programming)
Track listing:
Love Having You Around; Superwoman; I Love Every Little Thing About You; Sweet Little Girl; Happier Than The Morning Sun; Girl Blue; Seems So Long; Keep On Running; Evil
Running time:
48.06
Current CD:
Motown/Universal 5300282
Further listening:
The albums that followed belong together as a listening experience: Talking Book (1973), Innervisions (1973) and Songs In The Key Of Life (1976) complete a quartet that few, if any, artists might equal in a lifetime.
Further reading:
Stevie Wonder (John Swenson, 1994)
www.insoul.com/stevie
Like this?
Try . . . p.501

David Bowie

The Rise And Fall Of Ziggy Stardust And The Spiders From Mars

The alter-ego has landed.

"A star is born," proclaimed Melody Maker when Ziggy emerged. But it had been a helluva gestation, from Marquee R&B nights via Buddhism and the Beckenham Arts Lab to avant-garde mime. Now Bowie's moment had finally arrived and, under the wing of tough New York manager Tony DeFries and his MainMan set-up, he seized every opportunity to realise long-held dreams of fame.

The attention garnered by *Hunky Dory* – released just six months earlier – helped set the scene, as had the "confession" to the music press at the start of 1972 that he was "gay and always have been, even when I was David Jones".

Then came the first single, Starman, which revealed an androgynous glam creation to a generation of young dudes eager for flamboyant imagery and hard-edged pop. The new fans lapped up such gestures as the key Top Of The Pops appearance when Bowie, vermilion-haired in a skintight jumpsuit and painted nails, camply slung a provocative arm around Mick Ronson during the guitarist's solo.

Ziggy, an amalgam of Bowie's heroes Marc Bolan, Iggy Pop and Vince Taylor, is an apocalyptic rock star whose rise and fall comes just in time for the end of the world. Arguably pop's first post-modern construct, the album enabled Bowie to simultaneously explore and flaunt his own hunger for stardom. "No one has seen anything like this before," he boasted to pop pot-boiler George Tremlett in 1972. "That's what's missing in pop music now, entertainment. There's not much outrageousness left."

On *Ziggy*, the trusty Ronson marshalls the Spiders into providing a tough and concise musical backdrop which allows every song to shine. Highlights include remarkable scene-setter Five Years, the pre-punk hysteria exhibited on Star, magical bi-ballad Lady Stardust and the overwrought beauty of Rock'n'Roll Suicide. "Bowie has arrived – a worthy pin-up with such style," declared Melody Maker's Ray Coleman.

With DeFries at the controls, Bowie willed his stardom into existence. Journalists were flown in from the US to witness a Ziggy showcase at Friars Club, Aylesbury and the British press were granted short interviews at the Dorchester. In reality, the Bowie were still ensconced in his £7 a week abode in Beckenham.

But not for long. *Ziggy* worked as well live as on record and Bowie's career obligingly went supernova. US music biz magazine Cashbox described *Ziggy* as "an album to take you into the 1980s". And many a decade beyond.

Record label:
RCA
Produced
David Bowie and Ken Scott.
Recorded
at Trident Studios, London; September 1971–January 1972.
Released:
June 9, 1972
Chart peaks:
5 (UK) 75 (US)
Personnel:
David Bowie (g, s, v); Mick Ronson (g, p, v); Trevor Bolder (b); Mick Woodmansey (d)
Track listing:
Five Years; Soul Love; Moonage Daydream; Starman (S); It Ain't Easy; Lady Stardust; Star; Hang Onto Yourself; Ziggy Stardust; Suffragette City; Rock'N'Roll Suicide
Running time:
38.48
Current CD:
EMI CDP7944002 adds: John I'm Only Dancing; Velvet Goldmine; Sweet Head; Ziggy Stardust (2); Lady Stardust (2)
Further listening:
Aladdin Sane (1973)
Further reading:
MOJO 49; David Bowie's The Rise And Fall Of Ziggy Stardust And The Spiders From Mars (Mark Paytress, 1999)
Like this?
Try . . . p.782

Aphrodite's Child

666

A double helping of Greek rock opera.

Born Evangelos Odyssey Papathanassou in March 1943. As early as 1963 he was anxious to express his classical keyboard chops in a pop format and devised Aphrodite's Child, which – like much later UK equivalent The Nice – was a neo-classical rock trio: bass and drums providing the foundation while the Athenian wizard flew around a bank of keyboards.

They quickly became Greece's most extraordinary band and began to look further afield, moving to France in 1967. The bass player and singer was Egyptian born Demis Roussos, possessor of a remarkable, high sob of a voice, which was put to good use on their single, Rain And Tears, a hit all over Europe (making Number 27 in the UK) in 1968. An album *The End Of The World*, provided further European hits.

Feeling that wider acceptance was eluding them, the group disbanded and Vangelis returned to Greece to write with poet Costas Ferris. They came up with an extravagant vision of the apocalypse and the group reformed to record this ambitious rock opera complete with a Greek chorus, a posh English narrator, five minutes of female orgasm (Irene Pappas gasping "I am to come, I was" over and over, years before Clare Torry's throes of ecstasy on *Dark Side Of The Moon*), the massive 19 minute rock-out montage, All The Seats Were Occupied, and a charming, puzzling closing song Break (sung by drummer Lucas Sideras) which, when released as a single some time after the group had disbanded, almost made the British charts.

The album's lush arrangements were as startling as any of the progressive era and it have aged better than most, Vangelis having the vision not to lard the record with keyboard noodling but to use an appropriately broad and dark palette and to highlight the excellent playing of guitarist Silver Koulouris. Taxing and costly to make, when *666* failed to fanfare them world-wide, Aphrodite's Child split for the final time. Roussos soon found fame as a bizarre, rotund purveyor of lachrymose ballads that were avidly consumed by Europe's housewives. Vangelis later composed the popular and evocative soundtracks to Chariots Of Fire and Blade Runner.

Record label:
Vertigo
Produced
by Vangelis Papathanassou.
Recorded
at Europasonor Studios, France; 1971.
Released:
June 1972
Chart peaks:
None (UK) None (US)
Personnel:
Vangelis Papathanassou (o, syn, flute, pc, vibes, bv); Demis Roussos (b, v); Lucas Sideras (d, v); Silver Koulouris (g, pc); Harris Halkitis (b, ts, conga, bv); Michel Ripoche (tb, ts); John Forst (narration); Yannis Tsarouchis (Greek text); Irene Pappas (v); Roger Roche (e)
Track listing:
The System; Babylon; Loud Loud Loud; The Four Horsemen; The Lamb; The Seventh Seal; Aegean Sea; Seven Bowls; The Wakening Beast; Lament; The Marching Beast; The Battle Of the Locusts; Do It; Tribulation; The Beast; Ofis; Seven Trumpets; Altamont; The Wedding Of The Lamb; The Capture Of The Beast; *f*; Hic And Nunc; All The Seats Were Occupied; Break (S)
Running time:
78.10
Current CD:
838-430-2
Further listening:
It's Five O'Clock (1970); Vangelis's Earth (1974)
Like this?
Try . . . p.743

Everly Brothers

The Stories We Could Tell

Rock'n'roll duo retrace their upbringing on this countrified super-harmony excursion.

By 1970, the musical landscape the Everly Brothers had helped shape in the '50s had changed beyond all recognition. For the brothers themselves, successful records had become elusive and, apart from TV guest slots and some routine live work, their career was almost at a standstill. Don made the first break, cutting a truly unusual solo album for A&M that featured Ry Cooder, Spooner Oldham and various Flying Burrito Brothers among its guest players. Inspired by the experience, and enjoying playing with a new crowd brought together by their love of country music, Don saw a way forward for the Everly brand and reunited with Phil in 1972 to make this album, steeped in the emerging new-country sound.

Don and Phil created beautifully poignant arrangements that pointed at a whole new audience, using accomplices which included ex-Byrds, Burritos, Lovin' Spoonfuls and Delaney And Bonnie. Their 1968 album *Roots* had taken the brothers' back-porch past at face value, *Stories* married down-home earthiness to ultra-loose hippie idealism on a selection of songs by contemporary figures like Kris Kristofferson, Rod Stewart, Jessie Winchester, John Sebastian (in whose home the album was recorded) and multi-instrumentalist Dennis Linde. The Everlys themselves turned in breathtaking performances. Set against brooding, churchy keyboards and high, lonesome guitar, their close harmony work was spellbinding. There were tear-drenched ballads, melancholy tales of bar-room regret, Western rock opera in the David Crosby mould and the kind of Nashville gloom that comes with a spoonful of syrup. A timeless slice of Americana, a – mostly unheard – gem.

The following year's *Pass The Chicken And Listen* took the sound a stage further, but neither album revived the Everlys' career and their chronic sibling rivalry, which had spilled over into their love lives, finally exploded on stage in 1973, initiating a split which lasted for 10 years.

Record label:
RCA
Produced by
Paul A Rothchild.
Recorded
at the home of John Sebastian, California; 1972.
Released:
June 1972
Chart peaks:
None (UK) None (US)
Personnel:
Don Everly, Phil Everly, Dennis Linde (g,b,k,v); Geoff Muldaur (g); Wayne Perkins (g); John Sebastian (g, v, hrm); Waddy Watchel (g); Danny Weiss (g); Chris Ethridge (b); Clarence White (g); Ry Cooder (g); Buddy Emmons, Jerry McGee (slide g); Barry Beckett, Michael Fonfara (k); Spooner Oldham (k); Warren Zevon (k); Johny Barbata, Jim Gordon (d); Russ Kunkel (d); George Bohanon, Tommy Johnson (brass); Jeff Kent (v); Bonnie Bramlett (v); David Crosby (v); Delaney Bramlett (v); Graham Nash (v)
Track listing:
All I Really Want To Do; Breakdown; Green River; Mandolin Wind; Up In Mabel's Room; Del Rio Dan; Ridin' High (S); Christmas Eve Can Kill You; Three-Armed Poker-Playin' River Rat; I'm Tired Of Singing My Song In Las Vegas; The Brand New Tennessee Waltz; Stories We Could Tell.
Running time:
37.15
Current CD:
CAMDEN 74321 432552.
Further listening:
Roots (1968)
Further reading:
www.everly brothers.com
Like this?
Try . . . p.168

Alice Cooper
School's Out

Cooper's commercial breakthrough included an instant teen rebellion anthem.

Prior to the release of *School's Out*, Alice Cooper, the band, was regarded as a novelty act: grown men dressing up in women's clothes, churning out badly-played blasts of abrasive rage. But to their credit, they invented the horror hard rock genre, with their mutilation of rubber baby dolls, mock executions and, er, pillow fights. The onstage theatrics outstripping their musical ability earned them the title of 'worst band in Los Angeles' from some pundits. After moving to a farm outside Detroit and hooking up with 21-year-old Canadian producer Bob Ezrin, the band underwent a transformation, honing their musical skills by practising for up to 12 hours a day under his uncompromising tutelage. The iron-fisted work ethic paid off, with contemporary reviewers claiming that "Alice Cooper has finally found their voice".

"Bob Ezrin wasn't the sixth member of Alice Cooper, he was our George Martin," explained Alice Cooper. "Bob made us stop touring, made us stop writing. He put us in a barn in Detroit for seven months and said, 'We work from 10 in the morning until 10 at night, and all we do is relearn how to be Alice.' He was taking us to another level."

Heralded as a concept album, the entire record was inspired by old movies on late-night television. "We were really affected by West Side Story, but I don't know why. People connected us more with Clockwork Orange than West Side Story – the more modernistic kind of gang thing. But the track Gutter Cats Vs The Jets is a total tribute to West Side Story. If there's a theme in the album, it's gang mentality. The '50s and '60s gang were actually very much part of our life, and we identified with it."

Bob Ezrin concurs. "*School's Out* was recorded when the band was the happiest being Alice Cooper and working together and were the most respectful of what they were doing – and they were doing their best work. *Billion Dollar Babies* might have been better from an artistic point of view, but in terms of spirit *School's Out* was fabulous. This was the first time that they had ever used a big orchestra, which was fun for me – and kind of goofy and fun for the guys, because it was so incongruous."

"When we wrote [the song] *School's Out* we always said, 'What's the greatest three minutes in your life?'" Alice remembers. "There's two times during the year. One is Christmas morning, when you're just getting ready to open your presents. The greed factor is right there. The next one is the last three minutes of the last day of school when you're sitting there and it's like a slow fuse burning. I said, 'If we can catch that three minutes in a song, it's going to be so big.'"

JU

Record label:
Warner Brothers
Produced
by Bob Ezrin.
Recorded
at the Record Plant, New York and Alice Cooper Mansion, Greenwich, Connecticut; spring 1972.
Release date:
July 1972
Chart peaks:
1 (UK) 2 (US)
Personnel:
Alice Cooper (v); Michael Bruce (g, k); Glen Buxton (g); Dennis Dunaway (b); Neal Smith (d); Dick Wagner (g); Roy Cicala, Shelly Yakus (e)
Track listing:
School's Out (S); Luney Tune; Gutter Cat Vs The Jets; Street Fight; Blue Turk; My Stars; Public Animal #9; Alma Mater; Grande Finale
Running time:
35.59
Current CD:
7599272602
Further listening:
Love It To Death, (1971); Killer (1971), considered by aficionados to be Cooper's best studio album; Greatest Hits (1974)
Further Reading:
Me, Alice (Alice Cooper with Steven Gaines, 1976); www.netfx.com/~mansion/cooper.html
Like this?
Try . . . p.380

Randy Newman

Sail Away

The world's most sardonic liberal debunks God and America, and nearly charts.

"The feel's good. We don't care if we hit all the notes do we?" That was Randy Newman's cry whenever a melody started to elude him and the producers demanded take 23. "You see I have a real good ear, but I don't have absolute control over my voice," he would assert-confess.

Yet he made those wobbly tones a crucial part of his act. He came from a family of topnotch musicians; uncles Lionel and Alfred scored movies, while uncle Emil conducted the orchestra on *Sail Away*. Serving a songwriting apprenticeship at the legendary Brill Building – and much covered long before he began recording – Newman became an expert pianist and arranger, precise in every detail. But his voice carried the load of human frailty implied by his pithy lyrics. When, for instance, he failed pathetically to hit the high note at the end of Simon Smith And The Amazing Dancing Bear, it was only appropriate.

On his fifth album, *Sail Away*, he was as usual abetted by a friend since childhood in co-producer Lenny Waronker, and top-of-the-range session allies. His ambivalent playlets and in-character monologues lean more to big issues than before. But, like no other, he can handle it, touching every verbal subtlety with a moan of woodwind, a sigh of strings, or his own oblique little piano figures. Then the scratchy front-porch voice delivers the shocks. The 18th-century adman scamming Africans into slavery: "In America you'll get food to eat/Won't have to run through the jungle/And scuff up your feet" (Sail Away). The redneck advising on defence policy: "They don't respect us – so let's surprise them/We'll drop the big one and pulverize them/Boom goes London and boom Paree/More room for you and more room for me" (Political Science). God telling the human race where to get off: "[Man] chases round this desert/Cause he thinks that's where I'll be/How we laugh up here in heaven at the prayers you offer me" (God's Song (That's Why I Love Mankind)).

As often happened to Newman, some told him he was going too far with this last one, debunking people's faith. An atheist, Newman just thought it one of the best pieces he had ever written: "It all clicks together. Those are real good big jokes. I think believers will disagree with me, that's all. I don't wanna hurt anybody's feelings – except assholes and bigots maybe, but that's an extreme case."

Record label:
Reprise
Produced
by Lenny Waronker and Russ Titelman.
Recorded
at Amigo, Western and Poppi Studios, Los Angeles, Jan–Feb 1972.
Released:
July 1972
Chart peaks:
None (UK) 193 (US)
Personnel:
Randy Newman (v, p); Ry Cooder, Russ Titelman (g); Jim Keltner, Gene Parsons, Earl Palmer (d); Chris Ethridge, Wilton Felder, Jimmy Bond (b); Milt Holland (pc); Lee Herschberg (e)
Track listing:
Sail Away (S); It's Lonely At The Top; He Gives Us All His Love; Last Night I Had A Dream; Simon Smith And The Amazing Dancing Bear; Old Man; Political Science (Let's Drop The Big One); Burn On Big River; Memo To My Son (S/US); Dayton, Ohio, 1903; You Can Leave Your Hat On; God's Song (That's Why I Love Mankind)
Running time:
30.38
Current CD:
7599272032
Further listening:
12 Songs (1970); Good Old Boys (1974); Little Criminals (1977); Land Of Dreams (1988); Bad Love (1999) – best of a life's work; always witty, acerbic and joli laid.
Further reading:
MOJO 57
Like this?
Try . . . p.291

Jorge Ben

Ben

Peak for Brazilian superstar who energised the bossa nova.

Jorge Ben, the son of a Brazilian fishmonger and an Ethiopian immigrant mother, was a former choirboy and an aspirant footballer thwarted by injury when he began hanging out with a trendy crowd on Brazil's Copacabana beach. To entertain his new friends he started composing his own songs and, in 1963, was signed to Philips after just one appearance at The Bottle Club, a hot spot at the epicentre of the bossa nova boom. A&R man Armando Pittigliani was impressed by the young man's versatile voice – sometimes seductively gritty, sometimes sweetly falsetto (as in the brilliant early single Menina) – and his propulsive, compulsive guitar playing. Ben was an overnight sensation, selling over 100,000 copies of his debut Mas Que Neda (But It's Nothing) – which has since become a standard worldwide. He popularised a new strain of high-energy bossa nova, based around the Bantu tribe's maracatu rhythm. His distinctive acoustic guitar style – strumming rhythm parts while simultaneously picking out basslines – which he has described as "the beat of a samba school on its way out the door", was self-taught and hugely influential, particularly when he won the disapproval of bossa nova purists by plugging in his guitar and adding electric R&B feels to the Afro-Brazil-ian blend.

He has experimented with Afro, carnival, jazz and funk and made records with huge percussion-driven bands, small trios, lush, brassy orchestras and once even improvised an entire double album for guitar and voice with Gilberto Gil. He's sung about the Black Panthers (Take It Easy My Brother Charlie), Dostoyevski (As Rosas Eram Todas Amarelas) and his homeland's soccer stars (notably the masterful Umbabaraumba, included by David Byrne on the excellent *Beleza Tropical* compilation).But for this 1972 release he utilised a small band and extracted the maximum effect from his acoustic guitar playing and foot-stamping, creating sexy, irresistible dance music that's richly melodic too. The album's most famous song, the rousing Taj Mahal, had its chorus appropriated by Rod Stewart and Carmine Appice for D'Ya Think I'm Sexy (now co-credited to Ben). But practically every track is a corker.

The man who now "researches into alchemy" in his spare time was forced to adopt the recording name Jorge Ben Jor in 1989 for legal reasons, but still makes good music. However, it's his work of the '70s that's commonly held to be his career best, and has been cited as an influence by non Brazilian pop artists such as Beck and The Beastie Boys.

Record label:
Philips
Produced
by Paulinho Tapajös.
Recorded
at the Phonogram Studios, Brazil; 1972.
Released:
summer 1972
Chart peaks:
None (UK) None (US)
Personnel:
Jorge Ben (g, ag, 12-string guitar, v); Osmar Milto (a); Luigi Taninho (e)
Track listing:
Morre O Burro Fica O Homem; O Circo Chegou; Paz E Arroz; Moiça; Domingo 23; Fio Maravilha; Quem Cochicha O Rabo Espicha; Caramba; Que Nega É Ess; As Rosas Eram Todas Amarelas; Taj Mahal
Running time:
37.16
Currently unavailable on CD
Further listening:
Jorge Ben – excellent 4-CD box set selected from all his Polygram recordings; O Bidu (Silencio No Brooklin) (1968) his one non-Polygram album of the '60s & '70s has the most peculiar, recorded in a wheelie-bin sound, but is good stuff too.
Further reading:
The Billboard Book Of Brazilian Music (1992)
Like this?
Try . . . p.695

Yes

Close To The Edge

Yes pull together their influences – pop, jazz, classical – to deliver one of progressive rock's most convincing extended pieces.

Close To The Edge may sound like the most carefully conceived of concept albums, but its creation owed more to chance and deft tape editing. Yes's method of working up new material at the time involved everyone playing live in the rehearsal studio until the music either ground to a halt or someone made a mistake. The band would then go back a few bars and start again. With the tapes rolling, Eddie Offord or a tape operator would be feverishly taking notes. Thus the title piece was patched together from possibly 30 or 40 edits. According to Rick Wakeman, the take of the closing section had to be retrieved from a dustbin full of tape after Offord, working overnight on the master, had spliced on the wrong edit. "When we finally found the right section we were horrified because the sound did not match, there was lots more echo," Wakeman recalls. "But after a few listens it seemed to work, sort of opened the music out, so we reproduced the change when we played the piece live."

The arrival of the classically trained Wakeman had started to "professionalise" the band's methods of composition. On And You And I, Wakeman took Jon Anderson's tune and developed it into an 11-minute opus by varying the chord structure and tempo. Treatises have been written about Anderson's hippy-mystic lyrics, teasing out which lines exactly are inspired by Hesse, Hinduism or Bilbo Baggins. But Wakeman is dismissive: "It's a bit like McCartney's first words for Yesterday were 'scrambled eggs'. Jon used to just make up words in the studio, only he'd keep them if they sounded good." For all the "amateurism and shamateurism" that Bruford, the soon-to-depart drummer later complained of, *Close To The Edge* still holds together impressively as a work of sustained creativity and inspired playing. "Every element is utilised to enhance or modify mood," noted Rolling Stone, "and you never get the impression that a particular passage was included because Wakeman just found a hot new sound on his Moog and they had to get it in there." The tedium of *Tales From Topographic Oceans* may have followed, but *Close To The Edge* was a moment of greatness.

Record label:
Atlantic
Produced
by Eddie Offord and Yes.
Recorded
at Advision Studios, London; early summer, 1972.
Released:
September 13, 1972
Chart peaks:
4 (UK) 3 (US)
Personnel:
Jon Anderson (v); Chris Squire (b, v); Steve Howe (g, v); Rick Wakeman (k); Bill Bruford (d)
Track listing:
Close To The Edge: i. The Solid Time Of Change; ii. Total Mass Retain; iii. I Get Up I Get Down; iv. Seasons Of Man; And You And I: i. Cord Of Life; ii. Eclipse; iii. The Preacher And The Teacher; iv. Apocalypse; Siberian Khatru
Running time:
37.51
Current CD:
7567826662
Further listening:
Fragile (1972); Yessongs (1973)
Further reading:
Yes: The Authorized Biography (Dan Hedges, 1981); for an insight into the obsessive US fan's mind, read Music Of Yes (Professor Bill Martin, 1996); www.yesworld.com
Like this?
Try . . . p.258

Black Sabbath

Vol 4

Birmingham's heaviest sons record in a blizzard.

By the time Black Sabbath rented a mansion in Bel Air early in '72 to write their fourth album they'd been on the road for three years straight.

"We were completely fried," admits bass player Geezer Butler. "When we got to LA we had six million groupies, booze, coke and heroin – which we sniffed, we never shot up – everything. We were still pretending to enjoy it, but you could feel everyone changing." For drummer Bill Ward in particular, Los Angeles was not a good place to be. "I was getting a bad cocaine addiction. When we decided to try and kick back in LA things got worse because things were so available. Things started to sound different behind that wall of cocaine," states Ward. Such was their infatuation with cocaine that Sabbath decided to call the album Snowblind in tribute to their drug of choice. Their US label, Warner Brothers, baulked at the prospect. "They made us change the name of the album but we left a load of references to coke all over it!" laughs Ozzy Osbourne. "If you listen to the track Snowblind itself you can hear the word 'cocaine' being whispered in those quiet bits. I don't know why they didn't object to that. Maybe they didn't bother listening to it."

But there's a pervading sense of paranoia and self-loathing in songs such as Wheels Of Confusion, the brooding Cornucopia and the semi-acoustic ballad Changes. "Musically it's a good album," says Butler, "but, on a personal level, I think we all have mixed feelings about it." The strength of material like Tomorrow's Dream and the cantering Supernaut (resplendent with Ward's soulful drum break), hides the fact that *Vol 4* marked the beginning of the end for Sabbath. While it would take another seven years for the original line-up to finally split, their own excesses were causing the four friends from Aston to drift apart. "It was easy not to bother talking to each other because we were so fucked," states Ozzy.

"We went totally mad making that album," concludes Geezer. "The album cost around $65,000 dollars to make and we'd spent about $75,000 on coke. We also managed to wreck the house in Bel Air, with Ozzy having water fights with hose pipes inside the house all the time. I didn't realise how nuts we'd gone until I went home and the girl I was with at the time couldn't recognise me!"

"We wish to thank the great COKE-Cola Company of Los Angeles," states the sleeve.

Record label:
Vertigo
Produced
by Patrick Meehan and Black Sabbath.
Recorded
at The Record Plant, Los Angeles; spring 1972.
Released:
September 1972
Chart peaks:
(UK) 8; (US) 13
Personnel:
Ozzy Osbourne (v); Tony Iommi (g); Geezer Butler (b); Bill Ward (d); Colin Caldwell, Vic Smith (e)
Track listing:
Wheels Of Confusion; Tomorrow's Dream (S); Changes; FX; Supernaut; Snowblind; Cornucopia; Laguna Sunrise; St Vitus Dance; Under The Sun
Running time:
43.23
Current CD:
Essential ESM CD 304
Further listening:
The first six Black Sabbath albums – Black Sabbath (1970); Paranoid (1970); Master Of Reality (1971); Vol 4 (1972); Sabbath Bloody Sabbath (1973) and Sabotage (1975) – are described by Henry Rollins as "albums that you can't live without".
Further reading:
Mick Wall's None More Black feature, MOJO 49; live album Reunion (1998) also features a detailed biography written with the band's approval; www.black-sabbath.com
Like this?
Try . . . p.205

Sandy Denny

Sandy

Sandy's second solo album after quitting Fairport Convention.

Right from the start *Sandy*, with its lavishly glamorous David Bailey cover photo, was the one that Sandy Denny and Island Records believed would establish her as a solo act in her own right. Sandy will always be linked inextricably with Fairport Convention, even though she was with the band for barely 18 months before quitting in late 1969, immediately after the release of the landmark *Liege & Lief*. But, against all advice, Sandy decided to put her solo career on hold and instead formed Fotheringay – who broke-up after one album in 1970. Her engaging but ill-conceived solo debut, *The North Star Grassman & The Ravens*, sold to Fairport fans but did little to expand her audience beyond the university circuit. Sandy did win Melody Maker's prestigious Best Female Vocalist award two years running, and Robert Plant, who met her at the 1970 MM awards ceremony, later admitted: "Sandy (was) my favourite singer out of all the British girls that ever were." She was subsequently invited to sing on Battle Of Evermore for Led Zeppelin's fourth album in 1971, and also appeared in the ill-fated but star-studded stage version of *Tommy*.

So when it came to recording *Sandy* during the spring of 1972, it seemed – with the current vogue for female singer-songwriters such as Carole King, Carly Simon and Joni Mitchell – that the timing couldn't be better for Sandy Denny. The strength of *Sandy* lay in its diversity. Songs like It Suits Me Well, Sweet Rosemary and Bushes And Briars obviously drew on her enthusiasm for, and knowledge of, traditional folk music; while other original compositions – It'll Take A Long Time and Listen, Listen (Tony Blackburn's Radio 1 single of the week!) – displayed Sandy's more commercial side. Even her choice of covers was impeccable and distinctive – Dylan's Tomorrow Is A Long Time was given a rich country tinge; while Richard Farina's Quiet Joys Of Brotherhood (which she had earlier attempted with Fairport) was vividly a cappella, with only Dave Swarbrick's violin for added poignancy at its conclusion.

It remains a mystery why *Sandy* didn't sell. The original compositions were probably the best and most accessible of Sandy's whole career and, perhaps more significantly, her standing was at its highest. But within two years she was back with Fairport. *Sandy* was her crack at the title. And she should have been a contender.

Record label:
Island
Produced
by Trevor Lucas.
Recorded
at Sound Techniques and Island Studios, Basing Street, London; spring 1972.
Released:
September 1972
Chart peaks:
None (UK) None (US)
Personnel:
Sandy Denny (g, v, p); Richard Thompson (g, mn); Pat Donaldson (b); Timi Donald (d); Dave Swarbrick (vn); Pete Kleinow (ps); John Bundrick (p, o); Linda Peters (bv); John Wood (e)
Track listing:
It'll Take A Long Time; Sweet Rosemary; For Nobody To Hear; Tomorrow Is A Long Time; Quiet Joys Of Brotherhood; Listen, Listen (S); The Lady; Bushes And Briars; It Suits Me Well; The Music Weaver
Running time:
40.40
Current CD:
IMCD 132
Further Listening:
Who Knows Where The Time Goes (1985) 3-CD box set; Listen, Listen: An Introduction To Sandy Denny (1999)
Further Reading:
MOJO 55; Meet On The Ledge: Fairport Convention, The Classic Years (Patrick Humphries, 1997)
Like this?
Try . . . p.51

Genesis

Foxtrot

Prog-rock mavericks reach early creative peak.

The Charterhouse old boys Banks, Rutherford and Gabriel had imported ex-Flaming Youth drummer Collins and Fripp-freak guitarist Hackett for their third album, *Nursery Cryme*, and – though stuffed with bright-eyed invention, charming acoustic whimsy and black humour – it failed to grab the imagination of an England more drawn to the blues rock of Deep Purple and Led Zeppelin. Buoyed by interest in Europe, Genesis jammed, rehearsed, argued and arranged their music into a new set of pieces to be recorded as *Foxtrot*. Hackett describes them as a "songwriting collective" though Banks remembers "my tastes controlled the group more than the others, perhaps because I got the most unpleasant if people didn't agree with me."

Indeed, one producer lasted only a week, with the band even by-passing usual man David Hitchcock in favour of engineer John Burns. There was the archetypical Ancient Kings mythology of Time Table and Can-Utility And The Coastliners, the Mellotron-drenched sci-fi Watcher Of The Skies with its maddening 12/8 rhythmic motif and a fantastic satirical mini-opera Get 'Em Out By Friday. Gabriel's increasing sense of theatre had made Musical Box and Harold The Barrel the highlights of the previous album, and his multi-voiced characterisations in the evil-property-developer drama of Friday were even more vivid. The centre-piece, however, was the 23-minute Supper's Ready, a seven-part work of extraordinary power and imagination. Inspired in-part by a real-life supernatural encounter experienced by Gabriel and his wife, Supper's Ready was a remarkable patchwork achievement. It ran the gamut of Genesis textures from bass pedal pomp to enchanting acoustic passages to psychedelic music hall back to anthemic, soulful rock in an exhaustingly rich exposition on the forces of good and evil.

Gabriel remains close to and proud of it: "I felt like I was singing from my soul – almost like singing for my life." *Foxtrot* represented a turning point for the band's commercial and artistic fortunes.

Openly disappointed by *Nursery Cryme*, manager Tony Stratton-Smith was bowled over upon hearing their follow-up; "I remember I had to wipe a tear from my eye. Everything that one had believed about the band had come through."

Record label:
Charisma
Produced
by David Hitchcock.
Recorded
at Island Studios, London; August–September 1972.
Released:
October 1972
Chart peaks:
12 (UK) None (US)
Personnel:
Tony Banks (o, mellotron, p, syn, 12 string, v); Steve Hackett (g, 12 string-g, 6 string solo); Phil Collins (d, v, pc); Peter Gabriel (v, flute, bass d, tambourine, oboe); Michael Rutherford (b, bass pedal, 12 string-g, v, c)
Track listing:
Watcher Of The Skies; Get 'Em Out By Friday; Time Table; Can-Utility And The Coastliners; Horizons; Supper's Ready (i. Lover's Leap, ii. The Guaranteed Eternal Sanctuary Man, iii. Ikhnaton And Itsacon And Their Band Of Merry Men, iv. How Dare I Be So Beautiful, v. Willow Farm, vi. Apocalypse In 9/8 (Co-starring The Delicious Talents Of Gabble Ratchet), vii. As Sure As Eggs Is Eggs (Aching Mens' Feet)
Running time:
51.09
Current CD:
CASCDX1058
Further listening:
Nursery Cryme (1971); Selling England By The Pound (1973)
Further reading:
www.genesis-path.com
Like this?
Try . . . p.289

Can

Ege Bamyasi

A more questing but approachable music from Germany.

In December 1971, Can left Schloss Norvenich, the castle in which they had recorded double-album *Tago Mago* and their astonishing debut *Monster Movie*, and moved their studio into an old cinema in Weilerswist, some 20 kilometres from Köln, nailing 1,500 army-surplus mattresses to the walls as soundproofing, and renaming the location Inner Space in memory of the band's original name.

The first music recorded there was Spoon, which was used as the theme music for a popular television thriller, *Das Messer*. Released as a single, it became the group's only Number 1 hit (in Germany). It would be some while before the accompanying album could capitalise on its success, however, due to injunctions taken out by Abi Ofarim (yes, of Cinderella Rockefella fame), the group's former manager, which delayed its release until much later that year.

Recorded between December 1971 and the following June, the dark, rather bleak tone of *Ege Bamyasi* reflects the rainy weather and the onset of Michael Karoli's illness (he was hospitalised shortly after its completion with a perforated ulcer), Can being a band peculiarly sensitive to environmental conditions. For all that, it remains one of their most rewarding albums, an engaging blend of structure, improvisation and sensitivity ranging from the spirited abstraction of I'm So Green to the slow, sensuous waltz of Sing Swan Song, a Damo Suzuki piece to which Holger Czukay added an overture of babbling-brook water. Jaki Liebezeit's trademark cyclical drumming and Suzuki's impassioned vocal made a particular success of Vitamin C, which was also used as theme music, for the Sam Fuller thriller *A Dead Pigeon In The Beethovenstrasse*.

"I can't sing, so I use the voice as an instrument," explains the Japanese singer. "I'm not so much interested in anything in particular, that's why I sing about nothing. I improvise melody and texture too... Sometimes it sounds like English, French or German, but really it is the language of the Stone Age."

The album was completed bang on deadline by the inspired improvisation of Soup, which Irmin Schmidt describes as "one of the most spontaneous pieces we've ever done". The title derived from a can of okra (ladies' fingers) which they encountered in a Turkish restaurant; "it was the name of the manufacturer in Istanbul!"

Record label:
United Artists
Produced
by Can.
Recorded
at Inner Space Studio, Weilerswist, nr. Köln; 1971–72.
Released:
November 1972
Chart peaks:
None (UK) None (US)
Personnel:
Holger Czukay (b, e); Michael Karoli (g); Jaki Liebezeit (d); Irmin Schmidt (k); Damo Suzuki (v)
Track listing:
Pinch; Sing Swan Song; One More Night; Vitamin C; Soup; I'm So Green; Spoon (S)
Running time:
40.08
Current CD:
SPOON CD 008
Further listening:
All of Can's albums offer manifold delights, though those featuring vocalist Damo Suzuki (Tago Mago (1972), Ege Bamyasi and Future Days (1973)) have the most pleasing similarity of sound and purpose.
Further reading:
The Can Book (Pascal Bussy and Andy Hall, 1989); MOJO 41
Like this?
Try . . . p.380

Captain Beefheart And The Magic Band

Clear Spot

His most accessible offering. Includes ballads!

Legend had it that Captain Beefheart wrote the entire *Clear Spot* album in the course of an eight-hour car journey from Boston to Yale, and "transmitted" it to The Magic Band via harmonica (just as the parts for *Trout Mask Replica* had been painstakingly transcribed by John "Drumbo" French from Beefheart's piano demos), though in actual fact, several of the songs – including Low Yo Yo Stuff, Circumstances, Sun Zoom Spark and Clear Spot itself – were held over from the previous album *The Spotlight Kid*.

Clear Spot is a much slicker affair than its grumpy predecessor, in large part due to the more professional approach imposed on the band by producer Ted Templeman (once of Harper's Bizarre) – and the better studio afforded by their newly-enlarged budget. "Of course, there were still all the usual band blow-ups and fights, the same old shit," recalls Bill Harkleroad (Zoot Horn Rollo) in his book *Lunar Notes*. "This time, however, I got the feeling that Ted had taken Don to one side and said something along the lines of, 'I'm not going to put up with this.'" Whatever the reason, the end results offer the most rewarding rapprochement between the artistic and commercial imperatives of Beefheart's career – and thanks also to the general emphasis on love and sex, it became his biggest seller.

Driven along by the idiosyncratic engine-room of Artie Tripp and Oréjon – both refugees from Zappa's Mothers Of Invention – *Clear Spot* has a flexible muscularity lacking in some of the earlier albums, enabling Beefheart to carve his most elegant wrinkles yet on the R&B format. Also unlike previous recordings, overdubbing was employed extensively. "In some places there are actually tons of guitar parts," explains Harkleroad, "yet the actual parts themselves are so sparse, it doesn't feel like that."

As throughout The Magic Band's existence, Beefheart's solo composer credits remain a sore point with the other musicians. Zoot Horn Rollo, for instance, recalls creating "two mandolin parts, three electric guitar tracks, and two or three acoustic [guitar] tracks" on the beautiful Her Eyes Are A Blue Million Miles, which along with My Head Is My Only House Unless It Rains found Beefheart's lyricism at its most romantically inventive.

Record label:
Reprise
Produced
by Ted Templeman.
Recorded
in Los Angeles; 1972.
Released:
November 1972
Chart peaks:
None (UK) 191 (US)
Personnel:
Don Van Vliet (v, hm, wings on Singabus); Zoot Horn Rollo (solo g, steel appendage g, glass finger, mandolin); Rockette Morton (g, b); Ed Marimba aka Art Tripp (d, tattoos, pc); Oréjon aka Roy Estrada (b); Milt Holland (pc); The Blackberries (b, v); Russ Titelman (g); Donn Landee (e)
Track listing:
Low Yo Yo Stuff; Nowadays A Woman's Gotta Hit A Man; Too Much Time (S); Circumstances; My Head Is My Only House Unless It Rains; Sun Zoom Spark; Clear Spot; Crazy Little Thing; Long Neck Bottles; Her Eyes Are A Blue Million Miles; Big Eyed Beans From Venus; Golden Birdies
Running time:
37.16
Current CD:
7599-26249-2
Further listening:
Safe As Milk (1967)
Further reading:
Zoot Horn Rollo's Captain Beefheart Experience (Bill Harkleroad, 1998)
www.beefheart.com
Like this?
Try . . . p.82

Bobby Charles

Bobby Charles

Enigmatic teenage writer of rock'n'roll standards resurfaces after years in the wilderness to jam with The Band.

The word was that Bobby Charles was on the run when he showed up in Woodstock in 1971. The FBI was very interested in his whereabouts, apparently. Nevertheless, the 33-year-old "outlaw" was made to feel very welcome in the musical community that circulated around Bob Dylan and The Band. And no wonder, for Bobby Charles (born Robert Charles Guidry in February 1938), was well-respected among rock'n'roll cognoscenti as the composer and originator of (See You) Later Alligator, one of rock's defining songs.

Charles, a Louisiana cajun boy, had written the tune, aged only 17, in 1955 with Fats Domino in mind. Fats turned it down so Bobby stayed in New Orleans and cut it himself for Chess. Decca's Milt Gabler seized on the song while scouting for material for Bill Haley. Their version sold millions worldwide; Bobby's died on the American R&B charts soon after record buyers discovered he was white. But he found acceptance as a writer, penning such classics as But I Do (Clarence Frogman Henry) and Walking To New Orleans (Fats Domino).

How he spent the '60s is a bit of a mystery, but when he decamped to Woodstock in the summer of 1971 he soon ran into old friend, guitar player Ben Keith. Ben introduced him to The Band and their manager, Albert Grossman, who promptly signed Bobby to his Bearsville label and put him in the studio with Rick Danko and producer John Simon, for some ramshackle, star-packed sessions that meandered well into the following year.

They cut a profoundly laid-back record, bound to appeal to fans of The Band – all of whom, apart from Robbie Robertson, appear on it. Charles's voice is relaxed, even a little careworn, and the playing is loose as a goose. One song sticks out, the beautiful Small Town Talk, a Charles/Danko collaboration that's as coolly mellow and gently groovy as anything by, say, J.J. Cale or Little Feat. It was released as a single in 1973, by which time Bobby had fallen out with Grossman. His album was allowed to languish in obscurity and its follow-up was never released. However, fans of easy-living Woodstock music hold this album up as a classic example. Charles later turned out to sing at The Band's Last Waltz show. But he was a reluctant live performer and his unwillingness to promote his music may be why he's currently only known to a lucky few.

Record label:
Bearsville

Produced
by Bobby Charles, Rick Danko and John Simon.

Recorded
at Bearsville Studios, Woodstock; December 1971–July 1972.

Released:
November 1972

Chart peaks:
None (UK) None (US)

Personnel:
Bobby Charles (v, g); Rick Danko (b, v); Levon Helm (bv, d), Garth Hudson (p, o, acc); Amos Garrett (g); Billy Mundi (d); Buggsy Maugh (b); Jim Colgrove (b); Ben Keith (g, sg); Mac Rebennac (p, pc); Geoff Muldaur (g); Richard Manuel (p, v); David Sanborn (s); Joe Newman (t); Bob Neuwirth (bv); Mark Harmon (e)

Track listing:
Street People; Long Face; I Must Be In A Good Place Now; Save Me Jesus; He's Got All The Whiskey; Small Town Talk; Let Yourself Go; Grow Too Old; I'm That Way; Tennesse Blues

Running time:
41.72

Current CD:
Essential ESM CD675

Further listening:
Bobby Charles (1983); Chess compilation of his '50s hits; Fats Domino Million Sellers (1970)

Further reading:
For the lowdown on The Band in Woodstock: Across The Great Divide (Barney Hoskyns, 1994)

Like this?
Try . . . p.447

Focus

Focus III

Look mum, virtuoso Euro classical-prog fusion!

The origins, discography and family tree of Focus are complex. Essentially formed when guitar whizz Jan Akkerman was kicked out of Dutch hard rockers Brainbox in late 1969 for jamming with the classically trained Van Leer's cabaret trio. A first single, House Of The King – thereafter assumed by everyone to be either Jethro Tull or some TV theme – was a European hit and subsequently appeared on the debut album *In And Out Of Focus* and later on this, their third. Akkerman claimed to have written it in five minutes to vent some angst the very night he left Brainbox.

Happening to have a generator on their first UK tour, in 1972, proved their making: the trip coincided with an electricity strike. The first of several legendary appearances on TV's Old Grey Whistle Test ensued and album two, *Moving Waves* – featuring the bizarre heavy-metal yodel-fest Hocus Pocus – was a cult hit.

By January 1973 Focus had two albums in the UK Top 30, two singles – Hocus Pocus and Sylvia – in the singles Top 20, and an even more frenzied version of Hocus Pocus heading for the US Top 10. Akkerman was voted that year's Best Guitarist in the Melody Maker poll, but a concert at the Rainbow Theatre, London – filmed and recorded for album number four – marked the end of an era. Musical differences had emerged and the eccentric Akkerman appeared to have become a part-time member. Living in England during 1972, he had become enamoured of renaissance lute music, glimpsed here on the beautiful Elspeth Of Nottingham – a love which was indulged further on his 1974 solo set *Tabernakel*. Like Eric Clapton, he seemed content to move away from guitar herodom, and later brushed aside an offer to work with Sting "because I didn't like his music".

Focus III, a luxuriant double set brimming with energy, improvisational brilliance, catchy tunes and exquisite taste, remains the moment of perfect balance between the ultimately uncontainable influences and aspirations at work.

Record label:
Polydor
Produced by
Mike Vernon.
Recorded
at Olympic Studios, Barnes; July 1972.
Released:
November 1972
Chart peaks:
6 (UK) 35 (US)
Personnel:
Thijs van Leer (v, k, alto flute, piccolo); Jan Akkerman (g, lute); Bert Ruiter (b); Pierre Van der Linden (d); George Chkiantz (e)
Track listing:
Round Goes The Gossip; Love Remembered; Sylvia (S); Carnival Fugue; Focus III; Answers? Questions! Questions? Answers!; Anonymous II; Elspeth Of Nottingham; House Of The King
Running time:
70.00
Currently unavailable on CD
Further listening:
Moving Waves (1971); the Akkerman solo albums Profile (1973) and 10,000 Clowns On A Rainy Day (1997), a live double featuring Focus material revisited for the first time in 20 years.
Further reading:
www.janakkerman.com (the official Akkerman site).
Like this?
Try . . . p.174

The Nitty Gritty Dirt Band

Will The Circle Be Unbroken

Great down-homers meet their country heroes.

The Dirt Band started out as a kind of zany jug band, good-timey, with more than a sprinkling of country influence. The line-up and the direction appeared to change almost weekly and members such as Jackson Browne and Chris Darrow soon moved on. Odd as it may seem, the band even turned up in a Hollywood musical during 1968, performing in Paint Your Wagon. That same year, The Byrds arrived in Nashville to record *Sweetheart Of The Rodeo*, while Dylan, who'd been working in the city since the mid-'60s, created *Nashville Skyline*. Bluegrass performers got in on the trend – Earl Scruggs made an album titled *Nashville's Rock* in 1970. It was in the wake of such activity that the long-hairs arrived in Music City to record with any country legends who would enter the studio with them. John McEuen, the band's banjo picker, was a bluegrass enthusiast. He talked Earl Scruggs into becoming involved, after which everything else fell into place, though some of the Nashville aristocracy remained suspicious. Jim Ibbotson later recalled auditioning for Wesley Rose, Roy Acuff's publisher. "We sat around his office and it was like 'Well, do you rape babies? Are you actually actively selling narcotics right now?'"

Ibbotson speculated on the use of heavy drums and wah wah pedals – real country rock. But, he later informed writer William Ruhlmann: "I realised my job on the record was to hold the door for Mother Maybelle and sing a little harmony here and there." In the event, each of the six main guest stars (Mother Maybelle, Acuff, Travis, Martin, Scruggs and Watson) performed four or five songs or instrumentals associated with them and what was regarded as a Nashville 'happening' veered increasingly towards the traditional side of things, while retaining just a mild hint of the Woodstock Nation. The title song, which opens and closes Circle encapsulated the event, with the whole cast – including wives, kids and anyone else who happened to be around – joining in for a final touch of spontaneity. The album quickly went gold, remarkable for a triple set. Robert Christgau hailed as "an instant classic – an intensely agreeable way into mountain music".

Record label:
United Artists
Produced
by William E McEuen.
Recorded
in Nashville; 1971.
Released:
November 1972
Chart peaks:
None (UK) None (US)
Personnel:
J Fadden (hm); JHanna (v, washboard, d); J Ibbotson (v, g, d); J McEuen (mandolin); L Thompson (v); M Carter (v, g, a-harp); E Scruggs (g); D Watson (g, v); JMartin (g); R Acuff (v); M Travis (v, g)
Track listing:
Grand Old Opry Song; Keep On The Sunny Side; Nashville Blues; You Are My Flower; The Precious Jewel; Dark As A Dungeon; Tennessee Stud; Black Mountain Rag; The Wreck On The Highway; The End Of The World; I Saw The Light; Sunny Side Of The Mountain; Nine Pound Hammer; Losin' You; Honky Tonkin'; You Don't Know My Mind; My Walkin' Shoes; Lonesome Fiddle Blues; Cannonball Rag; Avalanche; Flint Hill Special; Togary Mountain; Earl's Breakdown; Orange Blossom Special; Wabash Cannonball; Lost Highway; First Meeting; Way Downtown; Down Yonder; Pins And Needles; Honky Tonk Blues; Sailin' On To Hawaii; I'm Thinking Tonight Of My Blue Eyes; I Am A Pilgrim; Wildwood Flower; Soldier's Joy; Will The Circle Be Unbroken; Both Sides Now
Running time:
118.47
Current CD:
CDPB7465891/2
Further reading:
www.nittygritty.com
Like this?
Try . . . p.671

1972

Lou Reed

Transformer

Reed's commercial breakthrough was powered by this irresistible broadside from the Wild Side.

On leaving the Velvet Underground in 1970, Lou Reed clerked for his accountant father and made a solo album which sold just 7,000 copies. Then David Bowie saved his career by offering to produce him.

In July 1972, Reed flew to London, rented a Wimbledon flat and set about making one of the quintessential New York albums. He had some brilliant material ready. Andy Warhol had offered the initial stimulus via the boggling suggestion that Reed write a musical with himself and Parisian couturier Yves St. Laurent. Oddly, Walk On The Wild Side emerged from a completely different, misconceived Broadway proposal. Candy [Darling], who "never lost her head even when she was giving head" was hardly the stuff of family entertainment but, as Reed leered: "I always thought it would be kinda fun to introduce people to characters they maybe hadn't met before, or hadn't wanted to meet."

But *Transformer* wasn't all scuzz. New York Telephone Conversation and Goodnight Ladies recall Noel Coward, re-creating waspish Manhattan gossip, while the brief, brilliant Make Up depended on unexpected, but undeniable, *charm*: "The gay life at the moment isn't that great," Reed remarked. "I wanted to write a song which made it terrific." Perfect Day, bizarrely adopted by the BBC as an institutional anthem 25 years later, further baffled expectation with sweet sincerity but tempered it with a hint of self-loathing ("I thought I was someone else/Someone good"). Reflecting its lyrical scope, *Transformer* delivered equal parts Velvet Underground dirt rock and cute-to-comic oompah, with Herbie Flowers' virtuosity evident as much in the tubby tuba of New York Telephone Conversation as in the slinky bass of Walk On The Wild Side.

Despite extreme tantrums en route – Reed screaming, Bowie retiring to the studio toilet to curl himself around the pedestal in the foetal position – *Transformer* gave Reed his lifetime best chart placings in on both sides of the pond, and Bowie's choice, Walk On The Wild Side, proved his biggest hit single too (UK 10, US 16). Even so, Reed could often be heard lamenting the sham nature of his successful persona: "I mimic me probably better than anybody else. I created Lou Reed. I have nothing faintly in common with that guy, but I can play him well."

Record label:
RCA
Produced
by David Bowie and Mick Ronson.
Recorded
at Trident Studios, London; summer 1972.
Released:
November 1972
Chart peaks:
13 (UK) 29 (US)
Personnel:
Lou Reed (v, g); Mick Ronson (g, p, recorders); David Bowie (bv); Klaus Voorman (b); Herbie Flowers (b, string bass, tuba); Ronnie Ross (bs); John Halsey (d); Barry DeSouza (d); Ritchie Dharma (d)
Track listing:
Vicious (S/US); Andy's Chest; Perfect Day; Hangin' Round; Walk On The Wild Side (S); Make Up; Satellite Of Love (S); Wagon Wheel; New York Telephone Conversation; I'm So Free; Goodnight Ladies
Running time:
37.09
Current CD:
74321601812
Further listening:
Berlin (1973); Rock 'N' Roll Animal (1974)
Further reading:
Transformer: The Lou Reed Story (1995)
Like this?
Try . . . p.263

Bob Marley And The Wailers

African Herbsman

The conjunction of Lee Perry and The Wailers results in a definitive moment in reggae history.

As the 1960s dribbled to a close, Bob Marley and his two cohorts in The Wailers were in a state of vexation. The stream of Jamaican hits they had enjoyed since the middle of the decade had all but dried up, they had fallen out with several producers, and attempts to establish themselves as an independent production force had foundered. In the small pool of the Jamaican music industry, their options were limited.

Help arrived from an unexpected source in the wiry, querulous shape of Lee 'Scratch' Perry, a 27-year-old producer who had amazed the island by scoring a major hit in Britain with a jaunty instrumental called Return of Django. Perry agreed to produce the troubled trio, immediately giving them a hit with Small Axe, a Marley song threatening to chop down Jamaica's 'big t'ree' record studios. Over the next year Perry coached the group in the back of his Beeston Street record store, frequently recording them at Randy's Studio a block across town. Under Scratch's inspired tutelage, the group's style mutated, leaving behind the doo-wop gymnastics of their early years in favour of a more visceral approach.

Marley, a ceaseless songwriter, found material to match; among his creations were the joyous Trench Town Rock and Lively Up Yourself, the fiercesome Duppy Conqueror (in which the singer casts himself as ghost-buster), the dreamy ganja song Kaya, and the cryptic, anguished reverie of Sun Is Shining. The partnership was at times stormy – the three Wailers beat Perry savagely when they suspected he was cheating them of royalties – but it produced reggae of a different order to almost anything else emerging from Jamaica, its soulful vocals and lyrical intricacy wound round the sparse but heavy rhythms conjured up by the young rhythm section of the Barratt brothers. The sides were, in effect, the template on which the group's subsequent success was built, many of the songs becoming cornerstones of Marley's live shows. Their release on 1971's *Soul Revolution* and this album in the following year, mark a turning point not just in Marley's career, but in the evolution of reggae music.

NS

Record label:
Trojan
Produced
by Lee Perry.
Recorded
at Randy's Studio, Kingston, Jamaica; 1969–70.
Released:
December 1972
Chart peaks:
None (UK) None (US)
Personnel:
Bob Marley (v); Peter Tosh (v); Bunny Livingstone (v); Aston 'Family Man' Barrett (b); Carlton Barrett (d); Glen Adams (k); Alva Lewis (g); Lee Perry (e)
Track listing:
Lively Up Yourself (S/UK); Small Axe (S/UK); Duppy Conqueror (S/UK); Trenchtown Rock (S/UK); African Herbsman; Keep On Moving; Fussing and Fighting; Stand Alone; All In One; Don't Rock the Boat; Put It On; Sun Is Shining; Kaya (S/UK); Riding High; Brain Washing; 400 Years
Running time:
35.22
Current CD:
TRL62
Further listening:
The Complete Upsetter Collection, a six CD set gathers all known vocal, instrumental and DJ sessions resulting from these sessions (113 in all!). The Perry tracks are much anthologised elsewhere.
Further reading:
MOJO 16; Catch A Fire (Timothy White, 1983); Bob Marley: Conquering Lion Of Reggae (Stephen Davis, 1983); Bob Marley: Songs of Freedom (Chris Salewicz and Adrian Boot, 1995); Bob Marley (Scotty Bennett, 1997)
Like this?
Try . . . p.743

Michael Viner's Incredible Bongo Band

Bongo Rock

The most important record in late 20th century pop? Quite possibly. Read on …

Sometimes revolutions happen without anyone knowing. This was certainly the case with Bongo Rock, possibly the most influential album in the history of post-'60s popular music.

The record itself seemed unremarkable even to its creators. MGM soundtrack executive Michael Viner had inaugurated his Incredible Bongo Band when 1972 B-movie The Thing With Two Heads required music to accompany a chase scene. Roping in producer and Oscar-winning songwriter Perry Botkin, Jr., they put together two instrumental tracks of propulsive, drum-driven funk-rock. Played entirely by session hands who've probably forgotten they were even there, Bongolia and Bongo Rock ended up on the soundtrack album, and were also released as a 7" single which topped the Canadian pop chart. MGM decided a Bongo Band album would be a shrewd commercial move and so, taking advantage of rules governing radio broadcast of home-made music, Viner decided to record in Vancouver.

Botkin says the session was "a pretty professional deal. We just went bang, bang, bang and knocked these things off." Musicians came and went, but legendary Traffic drummer and co-author of Layla, Jim Gordon, and bongo maestro King Errisson were ever-presents. The overall sound and structure of the music – funky, drum-laden and elongated – was simply down to Viner and Botkin feeling that this was the fun way to go. "I just enjoyed it – there was no more to it than that," Viner shrugs.

And that was that. The record came out, and did good enough business for MGM to commission a follow-up. But by 1974 all concerned had pretty much forgotten about the Bongo Band.

But in New York in 1975, a Jamaican expatriate used Bongo Rock to make musical history. DJ Kool Herc realised that his crowds particularly enjoyed the percussion breakdown sections of the tunes he was spinning, and decided to prolong their ecstasies by using a second copy of the record. The first disc he played in this way was Bongo Rock.

Nowadays, Herc's '70s parties – at which he played the IBB's Apache, too – are acknowledged as the birthplace of hip hop culture, and the records he spun are revered as the foundation stone upon which all sample-based dance musics have been based. Viner and Botkin didn't hear about any of this until much later, when rap records were made sampling their album, and Viner still finds it "hilarious" that Bongo Rock, recorded for a laugh, went on to change the world. Hilarious, yes, but undeniable, too.

Record label:
Pride/MGM
Produced
by Michael Viner: Perry Botkin, Jr.
Recorded
at MGM Studios, LA, USA: Can Base Studios, Vancouver, Canada
Released:
1973
Chart peaks:
Personnel:
Michael Viner (drums, bongos, bass): Perry Botkin, Jr. (drums, bongos): Jim Gordon (drums): King Errisson (bongos): Steve Douglas (horn arrangements): Michael Omartian (kbds – possibly: neither Viner nor Botkin are sure whether he is on this record or not): all other personnel unkown
Track listing:
Let There Be Drums: Apache: Bongolia: Last Bongo In Belgium: Duelling Banjos: In-A-Gadda-Da-Vida: raunchy '73: Bongo Rock '73
Running time:
33 mins 17 secs
Current CD:
Bongo Rock: The Story Of The Incredible Bongo Band (Strut, 2001, STRUTCD017)
Further listening:
Return Of The Incredible Bongo Band (Pride 1974)
Like this?
Try . . . p.501

Steely Dan

Can't Buy A Thrill

Wryly cynical songs buffed to an impeccable shine.

When Gary Katz moved to Los Angeles to take up an A&R position with ABC Records, the first thing he did was persuade his employers that they should also hire a young songwriting duo he'd met in New York. Accordingly, Walter Becker and Donald Fagen soon found themselves on the West Coast, vainly trying to write songs to fit ABC artists like Three Dog Night, whilst secretly using the company's money to fund their own project, which became Steely Dan.

"We realised that to succeed, we would have to do these songs ourselves," recalled Walter Becker. "They were too odd, too out of context for the time. On the one hand, they expressed an odd sensibility lyrically, and they were musically unusual, because of the jazz and other harmonic elements."

With their old friend Denny Dias brought over from the East Coast, and Katz's acquaintances Jeff "Skunk" Baxter and Jim Hodder drafted in from Boston, they set about rehearsing their new material after hours in an accountant's office at ABC, before recording it at the Village Recorder studio in West LA.

"Before we did the first album," says Becker, "we presented pretty much finished arrangements to the musicians." Though Fagen had sung on the demos, he was unsure of his vocal capabilities, so Jim Hodder (on the rare debut single Dallas) and subsequently David Palmer (on Dirty Work and Brooklyn)were featured as singers, before Fagen was persuaded that the songs required his peculiar pipes.

"They have to be performed with a certain attitude," Fagen acknowledged, "I became singer by default, because I was the only one with the right attitude, even though I didn't consider myself a singer at the time." Proof of Fagen's capabilities came when the album's two hit singles established his sardonic nasal sneer as the band's characteristic trademark. The slinky mambo rhythm and electric sitar solo of Do It Again proved surprisingly irresistible over the airwaves, as did the rockier Reeling In The Years. The parent album has since become recognised as a genuine pop landmark, recorded with peerless clarity by their brilliant engineer Roger "The Immortal" Nichols, while the post-hippy cynicism of songs like Only A Fool Would Say That has come to be regarded as prefiguring the pervasive disillusion of the mid- to late-'70s.

Record label:
ABC
Produced
by Gary Katz.
Recorded
at Village Recorder, Los Angeles; 1972.
Released:
January 1973
Chart peaks:
None (UK) 17 (US)
Personnel:
Donald Fagen (v, k); Walter Becker (b, v); Denny Dias (g, electric sitar); Jeff 'Skunk' Baxter (g, sg); Jim Hodder (d, pc, v); David Palmer (v); Elliot Randall (g); Victor Feldman (pc); Jerome Richardson (s); Snooky Young (flugelhorn); Clydie King King, Shirley Matthews, Venetta Fields (bv); Roger Nichols (e)
Track listing:
Do It Again (S); Dirty Work; Kings; Midnite Cruiser; Only A Fool Would Say That; Reelin' In The Years (S); Fire In The Hole ; Brooklyn (Owes The Charmer Under Me); Change Of The Guard; Turn That Heartbeat Over Again
Running time:
41.02
Current CD:
MCA118862
Further listening:
The follow-up Countdown To Ecstasy (1973) bore evidence of hard touring, longer solos illuminating the songs; Pretzel Logic added jazzy touches to the classy pop songwriting, Katy Lied and The Royal Scam refined the formula further within a strictly studio/sessionman milieu; the hugely successful Aja delved even deeper into jazz.
Further reading:
www.steelydan.com
Like this?
Try . . . p.207

Stevie Wonder
Talking Book
Second instalment of Stevie's purple patch.

On May 13 1971, Stevie Wonder inherited a million dollar trust fund. Unlike most heirs to such fortunes, he'd earnt it all himself from the many hits he'd scored since the age of 12. By now, however, he was keen to break from the Motown production line. "I wasn't growing," he said in 1972. "I just kept repeating the Stevie Wonder sound, and it didn't express how I felt about what was happening out there." Instead, he set up his own autonomous company Taurus Productions and forced Motown to give him total artistic control. He then embarked on a mammoth solo recording session, sealing himself inside Greenwich Village's legendary Electric Lady Studios with his new toys, some Arp and Moog synthesisers. He'd often forget to eat or sleep attempting to get all the music bursting from his astonishingly fertile, newly unleashed mind down on tape.

Friend and publicist Ira Tucker recalls, "He'd call me at four in the morning and say 'Hey, we gotta go to the studio, right now.'" From the 40-ish songs he demoed, six appeared on *Music Of My Mind*. A succulent ballad suite, its meandering psychedelia was too introspective for the public. *Talking Book*, released just eight months later and drawing from the same song stock, revealed a more confidently extrovert figure. At the same time, after only a year, his marriage to Syreeta Wright was ending and *Talking Book* (aside from the brazenly political Big Brother) is essentially a meditation on love's closure and new beginning, complicated by the fact that Syreeta wrote the lyrics to wondrous break-up odes Blame It On The Sun and Lookin' For Another Love.

"I was too young, and I also dug another person," Stevie explained. That other person was Gloria Barley, the female vocalist on and subject of the soon-to-be-standard You Are The Sunshine Of My Life (and the reason it was tactfully held over from the previous year). Influenced by Billy Preston's keyboard work on 1972 hit Outa-Space, the album's distinctive fluttering keyboard sound was achieved by wiring a clavinet to the Arp synth. The two singles, You Are The Sunshine Of My Life and the devastating Superstition represented the polar opposites of his craft – generous spirited pop-soul and blaring street-funk – and both became among the biggest hits of the year. Constantly touching on jazz, Latin and rock music but settling on none, *Talking Book* revealed a teeming, unconstrained creative impulse that could do little wrong.

Record label:
Tamla
Produced
by Stevie Wonder, Malcolm Cecil and Robert Margouleff.
Recorded
at Air Studios, London; Electric Lady Studios, New York; Crystal Studios, Los Angeles; Record Plant, LA; summer 1971–autumn 1972.
Released:
January 1973
Chart peaks:
16 (UK) 3 (US)
Personnel:
Stevie Wonder (v, k, p, b, g, d, pc); Scott Edwards (b); David Ben Zebulon (pc); Jim Gilstrap, Lani Groves, Loris Harvin, Shirley Brewer, Gloria Barley and Debra Wilson (bv); Ray Parker Jnr, Jeff Beck, Buzzy Feton (g); Dave Sanborn, Trevor Lawrence (s); Steve Madaio (tp)
Track listing:
You Are The Sunshine Of My Life (S); Maybe Your Baby; You And I; Tuesday Heartbreak; You've Got It Bad Girl; Superstition (S); Big Brother; Blame It On The Sun; Lookin' For Another Love; I Believe (When I Fall In Love)
Running time:
43.30
Current CD:
1573542
Further listening:
Music Of My Mind (1972); Innervisions (1973)
Further reading:
Stevie Wonder – Written Musiquarium: 41 Hits Spanning His Career (Hal Leonard, 1999); www.insoul.com/stevie
Like this?
Try . . . p.39

Nick Drake

Pink Moon

Beyond folk, beyond singer/songwriterly convention, a stark, redemptive – and final – missive from an elusive talent.

Nick Drake's third and last album is, "far from bleak and ghoulish, it is a stark, sparingly beautiful meditation on redemption through spiritual trial," wrote Ian MacDonald in MOJO 74. Of the three albums that Drake recorded in his short lifetime, the debut, *Five Leaves Left*, represents the first flourish of promise, *Bryter Layter*, its full fruition. *Pink Moon* is the portent, the lingering remnant of a soul – and its muse – in retreat. This view is, of course, almost entirely retrospective, bolstered by the artist's tragically early death and the myths that have sprung up subsequently. Drake had in fact indicated immediately after the recording of *Bryter Layter* that his next album was going to feature just him and his guitar, and at least one of *Pink Moon*'s songs, Things Behind The Sun had been written years earlier.

But Drake's crushing depression began exerting its grip after *Bryter Layter*. He started to take the anti-depressants that eventually killed him, and he became increasingly withdrawn. Later in 1971, Island Records' head Chris Blackwell offered him the use of his villa in Portugal for a change of scene. On his return, Drake called engineer John Wood and announced he wished to record. He completed the record in two nights, took the tapes and left them – without telling anyone – in the reception of Island Records.

It was his masterpiece. The one that draws deserved comparisons with Van Gogh and Robert Johnson. More than merely the product of a troubled mind, it is a confident record delivered with clarity and singularity of vision. Apart from the delightful eight bars of overdubbed piano which grace the title track, *Pink Moon* is just Nick Drake's voice and guitar. It leaves you no choice but to listen to what he has to say. Drake had never before written anything as apocalyptic and judgmental as the title track, while Parasite, with a four note melody which evokes church bells peeling, is an astoundingly specific cry of self-loathing and alienation. (Commentators rarely note Drake's black humour, evident in Parasite's "Changing a rope for a size too small/people all get hung".) Two tracks, Road and Know, have four lines of lyric and last for less than two minutes, yet both speak volumes. On Place To Be, Drake sang of a newfound maturity and reflective understanding of the nature of things. He was 23. Within months of the album's completion Drake plunged into the depression from which he never re-emerged. He cut only a few more songs in his life. His mother found him dead in his bedroom on November 25, 1974. In *Pink Moon* he left behind the perfect testimony to his greatness.

Record label:
Island
Produced
by John Wood.
Recorded
at Sound Techniques, November 1971.
Released:
February 25, 1972
Chart peaks:
None (UK) None (US)
Personnel:
Nick Drake (g, v, p); John Wood (e)
Track listing:
Pink Moon; Place To Be; Road; Which Will; Horn; Things Behind The Sun; Know; Parasite; Ride; Harvest Breed; From The Morning
Running time:
28.00
Current CD:
IMCD 94 / 842 923-2
Further listening:
Five Leaves Left; Bryter Layter; the posthumous compilation Time Of No Reply. All are collected on the Fruit Tree boxed set (1991). Way To Blue: An Introduction To Nick Drake (1994) is an effective Best Of.
Further reading:
MOJO 74; Nick Drake: The Biography (Patrick Humphries, 1998)
www.algonet.se/~iguana/DRAKE/DRAKE.html
Like this?
Try . . . p.672

John Martyn

Solid Air

Weightless, melancholy folk-jazz never bettered by its maker.

John Martyn had two ways of making records in this period. He'd either take his time, think each track through with producer/engineer John Wood, who had a magical touch with Martyn's music, and put together an album, or he'd go in with a bunch of musical pals, lock the doors and create what was effectively a jam session, picking out the best of it at the end. The stormy *Inside Out* is an example of the latter; *Solid Air*, his masterpiece, was done by the first method.

It's such a harmonious record it's hard to see how it could ever have been improved. Martyn, a tempestuous Glaswegian who'd been on the London folk circuit since 1967, had darkened his music without surrendering its acoustic base or the innate virtuosity of his playing and singing. Previous entries such as *Bless The Weather* or *Stormbringer* (the latter with wife Beverly), were stepping slowly but steadily away from folk and into singer-songwriter rock. A tougher feel was cautiously imported into this record, although it came via Fairport Convention's Dave Pegg and Dave Mattacks, who were hardly heavy metal merchants. Jazz-directed players such as saxophonist Tony Coe and acoustic bassist Danny Thompson, with whom Martyn enjoyed a long relationship, added an improvisatory feel. Martyn's own snapping guitar work was expanded by his new fascination with fuzz and echo units, used to formidable effect on the long, hallucinatory version of Skip James's blues I'd Rather Be The Devil. Martyn's concerts with this set-up were *the* place to hear him, though. Anyone who heard him live during this period, particularly in the trio with Thompson and drummer John Stevens, will never forget that music. The second half of *Solid Air* is similarly memorable, with the sexy lilt of Go Down Easy, John Bundrick's spellbinding chords on Dreams By The Sea and Martyn's signature wish-you-well May You Never, which was subsequently butchered by Eric Clapton. But one always goes back to the title track, the vocals slipping in over Thompson's long sliding notes, the vibraphone glinting in the background, Coe's tenor sax drifting in like smoke, to catch the essence of *Solid Air*. It was Martyn's tender tribute to his friend Nick Drake, whose passing, 18 months after *Solid Air* was released, he still refuses to discuss.

Record label:
Island
Produced
by John Martyn and John Wood.
Recorded
at Island and Sound Techniques Studios; Nov–Dec 1972.
Released:
February 1973
Chart peaks:
None (UK) None (US)
Personnel:
John Martyn (g, v, syn); John Bundrick (p, o, clavinet); Tony Coe (ts); Richard Thompson (mandolin); Sue Draheim (vn); Simon Nicol (autoharp); Neemoi Acquaye (vibes); Danny Thompson (b); Dave Pegg (b); Dave Mattacks (d); Tristan Fry (vibraphone)
Track listing:
Solid Air; Over The Hill; Don't Want To Know; I'd Rather Be The Devil; Go Down Easy; Dreams By The Sea; May You Never; The Man In The Station; The Easy Blues
Running time:
34.53
Current CD:
IMCD585
Further listening:
Sunday's Child (1975); One World (1977)
Further reading:
come.to/johnmartyn
Like this?
Try . . . p.117

Pink Floyd

The Dark Side Of The Moon

A cult band goes stellar. At 30 million copies and rising, it's still the biggest selling album ever by a British band.

By late November 1971, Floyd watchers were complaining that the band had been coasting during live shows, and their albums had been high on ambition but only superficially entertaining. Most recent release *Meddle*, however, pointed a way out of this creative trough; the epic, side-long Echoes, though assembled from assorted fragments of music, approached the cohesion they'd been lacking.

After an American tour, the band convened at their London rehearsal studios. Using the methods employed on Echoes, they began to work up some scraps – Roger's song Breathe, Rick's unused tune for the *Zabriski Point* soundtrack (Us & Them), and his chord sequence which was destined to become Great Gig In the Sky. But an adhesive concept was missing. It was Roger who provided it. "When [he] walked in with the idea of putting together one piece with this linking theme he'd devised, that was a moment," recalls Dave Gilmour. Roger's theme? Insanity and its catalysts – the demands of modern life: work, money, deadlines.

Gilmour admits that Waters did the majority of the subsequent writing, "while the rest of us went home to enjoy our suppers" on what was originally called *Eclipse: A Piece For Assorted Lunatics*. The new work was first road-tested in Brighton in January 1972. After a four-day stint at London's prestigious Rainbow theatre in February, a live bootleg of the piece – since retitled *The Dark Side Of The Moon* – appeared under record shop counters. Recording of the real thing began in earnest in June and was completed seven months later, though only 38 days were spent in Abbey Road while the Floyd undertook various obligations (tours, the La Valée film soundtrack, a ballet). They stretched the studio's resources to its limits, creating new reverb and delay effects, experimenting with the nascent Quadraphonic technology and mastering the VCS suitcase synthesiser.

With just six songs linked by instrumental interludes and sonic collage, the result was the Floyd's most succinct and approachable album, crammed with hooks and episodes of simple beauty. In places it's remarkably soulful too.

Though some elements may seem crass now, moments like Time's pivotal lines: "No-one told you when to run, you missed the starting gun" and "Hanging on in quiet desperation is the English way" retain their power and On The Run is surely acid-house 15 years before the fact. But it was the album's directness, in songs like Money and Us & Them, which won it unprecedented global approval. In America it remained in the Billboard 200 for an astounding 741 weeks – over 14 years.

Record label:
Harvest
Produced
by Pink Floyd.
Recorded
at Abbey Road, London; June 1972–January 1973.
Released:
March 25, 1973
Chart peaks:
2 (UK) 1 (US)
Personnel:
Roger Waters (b, v, VCS3 synthesiser, tape effects); David Gilmour (g, v, VCS3); Richard Wright (k, v, VCS3); Nick Mason (p, tape effects); Dick Parry (s); Clare Torry (v on Great Gig In The Sky, bv); Les Duncan, Lisa Strike, Barry St. John (bv); Alan Parsons (e); Peter James (ae)
Track listing:
Speak To Me; Breathe; On The Run; Time; The Great Gig In The Sky; Money; Us & Them; Any Colour Your Like; Brain Damage; Eclipse
Running time:
42.57
Current CD:
CDEMD 1064 digitally remastered
Further listening:
Hear The Dark Side... sound evolve on the under-rated soundtrack Obscured By Clouds (1972).
Further reading:
MOJO 6, 20, 52, 73; Echoes (Cliff Jones, 1997); www.pinkfloyd.com
Like this?
Try . . . p.691

Mahavishnu Orchestra

Birds Of Fire

John McLaughlin's virtuoso heavy-hitters deliver fusion's most explosive moment.

If fusion later noodled off into high-brow muzak, for a few years in the early '70s this heady collision of jazz and rock was one of the most exciting styles on the block. Of the three great fusion bands – Weather Report, Return To Forever and the first Mahavishnu Orchestra – it was McLaughlin's outfit who came on loudest and fastest.

Their house style was a kind of heavy metal jazz, and their three soloists, propelled by Cobham's rolling thunder, could outgun any band on the planet. But *Birds Of Fire* is not all clatter, the Mahavishnus could also play with extreme delicacy, as on Thousand Island Park. According to McLaughlin, the band was at the top of its form after several long tours when it embarked on the second album. "We were on a wave, we were experiencing a success that was unforeseen, and we were making light-year jumps in terms of playing together, developing new ways of playing." The guitarist worked out most of the music with Billy Cobham in a New York rehearsal studio, with the others adding their parts later. McLaughlin says: "The album was recorded in two or three days, quite simply. It was a 24-track machine: we'd mike up the amps, mike up the drums, one, two, three, go. There would be two or three takes but invariably it would be the first take that had the magic. We always worked fast – we didn't have the budget to go and live in the studio like pop bands do."

Birds Of Fire possessed the same fierce, occasionally exhausting, intensity as its predecessor, *The Inner Mounting Flame*. But if the debut was for jazzers, the second record was more accessible to a rock audience, with its snatches of skewed blues, Hendrix-tinged guitar and strong tunes. Cobham's extraordinary drum attack stems in part from his belief that the band needed a second percussionist and he opted to do the work of two men. The album's visceral brew was given further mystique by McLaughlin's quaintly exotic song titles, inspired by his guru of the time, Sri Chinmoy.

McLaughlin believes the band's golden period lasted another year after the recording before personal clashes led to the break-up. Evidence of how much more this line-up had to offer came with the 1999 release of the band's shelved third studio album as *The Lost Trident Tapes*."

Record label:
CBS
Produced
by John McLaughlin.
Recorded
at Trident Studios, London; Electric Lady and CBS Studios, New York; August 1972.
Released:
March 1973
Chart peaks:
20 (UK) 20; (US) 15
Personnel:
John McLaughlin (g); Jan Hammer (k); Jerry Goodman (vn); Rick Laird (b); Billy Cobham (d); Ken Scott, Jim Green (e)
Track listing:
Birds Of Fire; Miles Beyond; Celestial Terrestrial Commuters; Sapphire Bullets Of Pure Love; Thousand Island Park; Hope; One Word; Sanctuary; Open Country Joy; Resolution
Running time:
40.29
Current CD:
CK66081
Further listening:
Live album Between Nothingness And Eternity (1974).
Further reading:
Go Ahead: The Music Of John McLaughlin (Paul Stump, 2000)
Like this?
Try . . . p.161

Roxy Music

For Your Pleasure

Roxy's crowning glory, created as Ferry's autocratic style clashed with Eno's urge to experiment.

For Your Pleasure exudes confidence, it is a record that brims with bravado. After all, by the time Roxy Music (minus original member Graham Simpson, who was replaced by John Porter, the first in a series of revolving-door bass players) convened at Air Studios, they had good reason to feel upbeat. The success achieved in the few months since the release of their self-titled debut had overcome initial critical suspicion, and was consolidated by striking appearances on Top Of The Pops promoting non-album single Pyjamarama and sell-out tours all over the UK and Europe. But *For Your Pleasure*'s sheen masked a deepening and ultimately unbridgeable gap between mainman Bryan Ferry and the band's increasingly mischievous electronic sprite Brian Eno.

Eno's limelight-grabbing stage antics had certainly not endeared him to Ferry, but at the heart of the matter was a major difference of musical opinion. Ferry favoured a structured approach to recording, one which had been achieved on the band's debut since songs had been written and rehearsed meticulously over a number of years. Eno, by contrast, was (and continues to be) a keen advocate of randomness, and the lack of preparation for album two allowed him to flourish.

"We did have some material, like For Your Pleasure, which was one of our first songs," says Eno. "But there weren't a lot of new tracks, and that suited me fine, because it meant we could invent the sound. The studio is my instrument. I didn't play the guitar or the oboe so I came into my own there. What resulted wasn't just the transmission of pre-existing ideas."

The spontaneity gave rise to one of Roxy's most extraordinary conceits, In Every Dream Home A Heartache. Here Ferry's cool reflections on materialism are matched by an electronic backdrop which boils over as the track becomes a paean to an inflatable rubber doll. "In Every Dream Home came to life in the studio," confirms Eno. "What happened was that I was allowed to become a random element which stopped the rest of the band working in a traditional way." But therein lay Eno's fate. The conflict with Ferry spilled over into the dates to promote the album, with Eno deliberately extending synthesiser solos and increasing the volume to swamp out the singer. Within a couple of months Eno had quit the band.

"What Roxy Music lacks for me is one of the most important elements of my musical life, which is insanity," Eno told Geoff Brown of the Melody Maker. Ferry restricted his comments to the pithy: "Two non-musicians in a band is one too many."

Record label:
Island
Produced
by Chris Thomas and Roxy Music.
Recorded
at Air Studios, London; spring 1973.
Released:
March 1973
Chart peaks:
3 (UK) 193 (US)
Personnel:
Bryan Ferry (v, p); John Porter (b); Andrew Mackay (oboe, s); Brian Eno (syn, tapes); Paul Thompson (d); Phil Manzanera (g)
Track listing:
Do The Strand; Beauty Queen; Strictly Confidential; Editions Of You; In Every Dream Home A Heartache; The Bogus Man; Grey Lagoons; For Your Pleasure
Running time:
42.21
Current CD:
Virgin ROXYCD2
Further listening:
Brian Eno, Here Come The Warm Jets (1974); Bryan Ferry, These Foolish Things (1973)
Further reading:
MOJO 21, 25; Unknown Pleasures: A Cultural Biography Of Roxy Music (Paul Stump, 1998); The Bryan Ferry Story (Rex Balfour, 1976)
Like this?
Try . . . p.283

Terry Reid

River

Downbeat and dreamy curio from an unrequited next big thing.

Terry Reid was the man most likely to succeed as the '60s spiralled to a close. He was first noticed as a member of Peter Jay And The Jaywalkers. When Jimmy Page was recruiting for The New Yardbirds (later Led Zeppelin), it was Reid – clean-cut, cool and only 19 – who was first offered the role of vocalist. Recommending Robert Plant, Reid turned down the job. At first it seemed he'd made the right decision: his acclaimed solo debut with producer Mickie Most, *Bang Bang You're Terry Reid*, was followed by gigs opening for Cream, and a cover of his song Friends was a sizeable hit for British band Arrival. But after that, very little went as planned and a string of business and personal problems hobbled his career.

By 1973, Reid had moved to Atlantic Records. A quick scan of his bedraggled state on the gatefold of *River* is worth a thousand words: bearded, unkempt, far-away eyed and with a serious trouser problem, he's hardly the stuff of stardom. The music, however, is excellent. *River* progresses from pristine early '70s rock – with Reid's searing rock voice in full effect – to deep Southern fried soul (with accompanying slide from David Lindley), before it spins into outer space for side two's awesome trio of songs. The band dissolve from the title track on, until Reid is accompanied only by percussion. His voice swoops and floats, a strange amalgam of Tim Buckley and Dino Valente, his unplugged guitar drives the mesmeric backing. By Dream, the percussion is gone too and multi-tracked guitars drift by. Then, for the lengthy closer Milestones, Reid's vocal is reduced to a plaintive cry, a series of wordless, emotive sounds coaxed from deep within.

River functions as a kind of journey, the story of a man travelling inward and reaching the inarticulate core of his soul. Sadly, the album didn't work as a therapeutic self-exorcism, it reaped little attention at the time, has never been issued on CD and only occasionally turns up at record fairs, but it is a treasure; for just over half an hour you'd swear you were listening to a superstar.

Record label:
Atlantic
Produced
by Eddie Offord and Tom Dowd.
Recorded
in London, 1971 and Los Angeles, 1973.
Released:
April, 1973
Chart peaks:
None (UK) None (US)
Personnel:
Terry Reid (g, v); David Lindley (sg, slide g); Leo Miles (b); Conrad Isidore (d); Willie Bobo (pc)
Track listing:
Dean; Avenue; Things To Try; Live Life; River; Dream; Milestones
Running time:
36.26
Currently unavailable on CD
Further listening:
Nothing in Reid's sporadic output resembles River, but the promise is evident on Bang Bang You're Terry Reid (1968) and some fans swear by the mellow, Graham Nash-produced Seed Of Memory (1976)
Further reading:
Sleevenotes to BGO's 1992 reissue of Rogue Waves (1978).
Like this?
Try . . . p.563

The Wailers

Catch A Fire

The first crossover reggae album announces a new force in world pop.

The music industry thought Chris Blackwell had taken leave of his senses. Not only had he signed an unknown Jamaican group, The Wailers, he had paid handsomely for them; £4,000 handed to the group to cut an album, £5,000 to prise Bob Marley from a previous deal with CBS and a cut of future profits. And for what? A reggae act? In 1972, reggae was regarded by most of the business with a disdain that verged on racism.

"Everyone told me I was mad, that I'd never see the money again," said Blackwell. The Island boss was confident he'd prove his critics wrong. A Jamaican himself, he had built his label by selling the island's hits to Britain's black community, had stayed in tune with what was happening back a yard, and saw the potential of the charismatic and prolific Marley. When writer Richard Williams, then working for Island, visited Kingston to check on progress at Harry J's Kingston studios, he was astonished: "I was prepared to find someone talented, but it quickly became obvious that Bob simply was Marvin Gaye, Bob Dylan or both."

The appearance of *Catch A Fire*, lavishly packaged as a giant Zippo lighter and promoted with the same fuss as, say, Roxy Music, confounded conceptions of reggae. Partaking of the same blighted urban romanticism as Gaye and Curtis Mayfield, its mix of militancy and mysticism helped lay bare the pomposity of a rock scene long since drained of the fervour of the '60s. Not that *Catch A Fire* didn't borrow some licks from rock. Once Blackwell had its master tapes, he secreted himself in Island's Notting Hill studios to sweeten and polish the sound of Trench Town for western ears. US guitarist George Perkins and keyboard player Rabbit Bundrick were among the uncredited names adding sheen. But the album remained the work of the group, or band, as they'd now become, with live appearances at London's chic Speakeasy club and on BBC TV to prove it. If all this succeeded in raising media eyebrows, and shifted The Wailers from Caribbean hitmakers to international cult, it didn't yet make them, or Marley, into superstars. That was to come.

NS

Record label:
Island
Produced
by Bob Marley and Chris Blackwell.
Recorded
at Dynamic Sound Studios, Harry J Studios and Randy's Studios, Kingston, Jamaica; spring 1972.
Released:
April 1973
Chart peaks:
None (UK) None (US)
Personnel:
Bob Marley (v, g); Peter Tosh (v, g, k); Bunny Linvingstone (v, congas); Aston 'Family Man' Barrett (b); Carlton Barrett (d); Rabbit Bundrick (k); Carlton Lee, Stu Barrett, Tony Platt (e)
Track listing:
Concrete Jungle (S); Slave Driver; 400 Years; Stop That Train (S); Rock It Baby (UK/S); Stir It Up; Kinky Reggae; No More Trouble; Midnight Ravers
Running time:
33.51
Current CD:
Tuff Gong TGLCD1
Further listening:
Though 1973's Burnin' was a lesser work than its predecessor, it expanded the Marley canon and contained I Shot The Sheriff, whose cover by Eric Clapton did much to raise Marley's profile.
Further reading:
MOJO 16; Catch A Fire (Timothy White, 1983); Bob Marley: Conquering Lion Of Reggae (Stephen Davis, 1983); Bob Marley, Songs of Freedom (Chris Salewicz and Adrian Boot, 1995); Bob Marey (Scotty Bennett, 1997)
Like this?
Try . . . p.742

Mike Oldfield

Tubular Bells

Teenage social misfit's debut expands the horizons of the electric guitar like no-one since Hendrix.

"Record companies looked at me as if I was mad," says Mike Oldfield. "They all said, because there were no vocals, no words, no drums or anything, that it was not marketable." And who could blame them? Confronted by a hesitant, gawky, unself-confident teenager touting a 20 minute demo of multi-tracked guitar riffs cheaply recorded on a Bang & Olufsen tape machine borrowed from Kevin Ayers, any experienced A&R man would show him the door. And if the Arthur Lewis Band, for which Oldfield played guitar, hadn't been sent by chance to make test recordings at the soon-to-open Virgin Manor studio in Oxfordshire, Oldfield wouldn't have played his demo for studio boss Tom Newman.

"He was just a funny little hippie," recalls Newman, who nevertheless championed Oldfield's cause to reluctant Virgin boss Richard Branson, and won him some recording time.

In late 1972, Oldfield set to work in earnest, playing virtually all the instruments himself, cobbling *Tubular Bells* together from what Newman had first heard as "half a dozen little unconnected pieces", beginning with a motif inspired by US minimalist composer Terry Riley.

"It was very fashionable not to have everything in 4/4," points out Oldfield, "so I made one bar 7 beats and one bar 8 and then later realised that it had the complexity of Eastern music, the repetitiveness of Terry Riley and the technique of Bach. It just turned out by accident that it was a very nice listenable thing."

But, on hearing the completed masterwork, Branson was far from convinced. According to Newman, getting his hip capitalist boss to release the record "was like dragging stuff uphill through treacle." Ultimately though, it did become the first album released by Virgin. In the course of the '70s, it was outsold in the UK only by Simon And Garfunkel's *Bridge Over Troubled Water* and found American success after the theme was used in the soundtrack for The Exorcist. It was unquestionably the massive sales Oldfield generated which established not only the Virgin label (sold to EMI in March 1992 for £560 million) but, by extension, the entire Branson empire. By the dawn of the new millennium *Tubular Bells* had easily surpassed 25 million sales, not to mention spawning two sequels and an orchestral version. Not bad for a funny little hippy.

Record label:
Virgin
Produced
by Mike Oldfield, Simon Heyworth and Tom Newman.
Recorded
at The Manor, Shipton-on-Cherwell, Oxfordshire; November 1972.
Chart peaks:
2 (UK) 3 (US)
Released:
May 25, 1973
Running time:
48.47
Personnel:
Mike Oldfield (g, k, p, pc, v, b, taped motor drive amplifier organ chord, mandolin-like guitar, flageolet, Lowrey organ, glockenspiel, Farfisa organ); Jon Field (flutes); Lindsay Cooper (db); Mundy Ellis (bv); Sally Oldfield (bv); Steve Broughton (d); Viv Stanshall (Master of Ceremonies)
Track listing:
Tubular Bells Part One; Tubular Bells Part Two
Current CD:
CDV2001
Further listening:
The subsequent Hergest Ridge is pretty much an anagram of Tubular Bells. Tubular Bells II (1996) and Tubular Bells III (1999) didn't move the story on much, but Songs Of Distant Earth (1994) is arguably Oldfield's most intriguing full-length instrumental composition after Tubular Bells.
Further reading:
The Making Of Mike Oldfield's Tubular Bells (1993); http://tubular.net
Like this?
Try . . . p.180

Planxty

Planxty

The band who changed the face of Irish music.

Christy Moore, long established as one of Ireland's most beloved icons, still can't quite grasp his fortune in finding the magic that dropped into his lap with Planxty. An old schoolfriend of Donal Lunny, Moore – from Newbridge, County Kildare – had quit his safe job in a bank to chance his luck on the English folk circuit playing a mixture of standard fare, rousing sing-alongs, comedy songs and the odd protest number. His instinctive, intimate way with an audience was such that he swiftly became one of the scene's biggest draws, even if a lifestyle of heavy drinking and sleeping on people's floors did him no favours. He was loved in a roustabout, Dubliners sort of way and nobody – least of all Christy himself – could have anticipated the consequences of his return to Ireland.

He gravitated to the infamous sessions in the village of Prosperous which had become a magnet for the better young Irish folk musicians of the day, and it was there he met up again with Donal Lunny. Moore decided that his next album wouldn't be the standard song collection, and that he would instead utilise the vibrant new Irish sounds of pipes he was now hearing at home. His next album – titled *Prosperous* – heavily featured the brilliant young uilleann piper Liam Og O'Flynn, the dextrous guitarist/mandolin player Andy Irvine and Lunny pulling all the rhythmic strings. All four of them were so enthused and invigorated by the sounds they were creating that there was never much doubt that they'd put the relationship on an official basis. The band Planxty came out of it and – released on the back of lone Irish hit single Cliffs Of Dooneen – made the album that still stands as modern Irish folk's primary landmark.

"It was an amazing feeling to be part of it all," says Moore. "I think we did know we were doing something special, although it did seem very natural at the time." They were young guys with energy and ideas to burn, and instantly pulled in a new young audience to give the music a new impetus; but with Liam Og O'Flynn in particular revered as one of the finest pipers in the country, they retained the respect of the purists with a total understanding and love of the roots of traditional music. "I always felt that traditional music could be expanded in the same way as contemporary music because people were used to hearing a rhythm section," said Lunny. "But it was still hard accompanying a piper as good as Liam in a way that didn't dilute the music or affect its character."

Record label:
Polydor
Produced
by Phil Coulter.
Recorded
at Escape Studios, Kent; January 1973.
Released:
May 1973
Chart peaks:
None (UK) None (US)
Personnel:
Christy Moore (v, g, hm, bodhran); Andy Irvine (v, g, mandolin, mandola, hm, hurdy gurdy); Donal Lunny (v, g, bouzouki, bodhran); Liam Og O'Flynn (uilleann pipes, tin whistle); Barry Ainsworth (e)
Track listing:
Raggle Taggle Gypsy/Tabhair Dom Do Lamh; Arthur McBride; Planxty Irwin; Sweet Thames Flow Softly; Junior Crehan's Favourite/Corney Is Coming; West Coast Of Clare; Jolly Beggar; Only Our Rivers; Sí Bheag Sí Mhór; Follow Me Up To Carlow; Merrily Kissed The Quaker; The Blacksmith
Running time:
41.20
Current CD:
SHANCD79009
Further listening:
After The Break (1979) is especially recommended. Check also the first self-titled albums by the Bothy Band and Moving Hearts. There's also a direct lineage to the Riverdance soundtrack, composed by Planxty member Bill Whelan.
Further reading:
Bringing It All Back Home: The Influence Of Irish Music (Nuala O'Connor, 1991); Folk Roots 43 (www.froots.co.uk)
Like this?
Try . . . p.279

Can

Future Days

A chill-out classic long before the term was coined.

Compared to the somewhat bleak tone of its predecessor *Ege Bamyasi*, the ethereal ambience of *Future Days*, particularly the shimmering Bel Air suite which takes up the whole of side two, is like balm: the perfect accompaniment to a summer's day, as close to rustic bliss as technology gets. Appropriately enough, it was recorded (on twin two-track Revox machines) during the balmy summer of 1973, with the band on particularly empathic form. "Nothing is planned, both in the studio and on stage," explains Irmin Schmidt. "It sounds strange, but everybody in this group is a telepath. We never called it improvising, that was a very misleading term. What we improvised were forms, which we called 'instant composition'. It needs some time to come together: you've got to learn to listen to others, rather than just playing. We played every day, hours and hours, for years."

"We created a spiritual universe between us which allowed this kind of music," adds Michael Karoli. "If you take a mistake as a mistake, you don't get very far with improvisation. If you take a mistake as music as well, you get your ideas from the mistakes. I think our greatest strength was to let things happen."

Appropriately enough, the album's front cover contains both the I-Ching hexagram Ting (The Cauldron) and the Greek letter psi, representative of ESP. For Holger Czukay, Bel Air in particular represented the culmination of what he was trying to do with the bass: "I love it when Can gets the symphonic feeling that Bel Air has. It's when Michael and Irmin are just getting somewhere, and I put the counterpoint to it. That's something which Jack Bruce did so well with Cream."

Not all of the band were as convinced about the album's worth, however. Jaki Liebezeit, for instance, preferred the band's earlier work, when "...everybody just had a few notes he could play, so it stayed simple. But later our technical abilities increased...And then it really went off with *Future Days*, I think, it became too symphonic." Damo Suzuki, too, was disenchanted enough to leave the group: "It was really boring," he said later. "*Future Days* was musically very good, but it was really distant music for me, and more elemental than at the beginning, not so much of a freak out."

For all that, *Future Days* was widely acclaimed as Can's finest work yet, with NME's Ian MacDonald describing it as containing "more positive energy to the square centimetre than three barrels of brown rice".

Record label:
United Artists
Produced
by Can.
Recorded
at Inner Space Studio, Weilerswist, near Köln; 1973.
Released:
June 1973
Chart peaks:
None (UK) None (US)
Personnel:
Holger Czukay (b, e); Michael Karoli (g); Jaki Liebezeit (d); Irmin Schmidt (k); Damo Suzuki (v)
Track listing:
Future Days; Spray; Moonshake (S); Bel Air
Running time:
40.08
Current CD:
SPOON CD 009
Further listening:
All of Can's albums offer manifold delights, though those featuring vocalist Damo Suzuki (Tago Mago (1972), Ege Bamyasi (1972) and Future Days) have the most pleasing similarity of sound and purpose.
Further reading:
The Can Book (Pascal Bussy and Andy Hall, 1989); MOJO 41
Like this?
Try . . . p.641

Iggy Pop & The Stooges

Raw Power

The Stooges' last gasp, this time with new patron David Bowie.

"I felt doomed at the time, very doomed. No one was listening to me so I thought if we're going down then it's going to be very beautiful," says Iggy today.

Raw Power represented an astonishing comeback for The Stooges, who'd disappeared into junkie oblivion after being dropped by Elektra in 1971. Iggy had bounced back after a fateful meeting with David Bowie and Bowie's manager Tony DeFries while exiled to New York. Ignoring DeFries's plans for a transatlantic, *Transformer*-style collaboration with English sessioneers, Iggy brought over new Detroit hotshot guitarist James Williamson to London, and then the Asheton brothers, with Ron now grudgingly demoted from guitar to bass.

After rehearsing and demoing songs at various London studios, the revamped Stooges discovered a whole new work ethic: "There wasn't a lot of conflict at the time," says James Williamson. "We would just go into CBS studios every single night right after dinner, and just work pretty much until we were too tired to work any more. That was pretty much it. We weren't really doing drugs at that time."

Williamson's guitar style – firmly in the tradition of MC5-style Detroit metal – brought a new brutal muscle to the sound; counterpointed with Iggy's paeans to becoming a good-looking corpse: "I was singing about death trips way before any metal band got into that," he points out, "although that wasn't the whole story."

More conventional in structure than any other Stooges album, *Raw Power* was also bursting with memorable anthems. The album's mix, however, became a source of friction, when Tony DeFries rejected the original Williamson and Pop mix (which was subsequently bootlegged after being previewed on a Detroit radio station). Instead, The Stooges were forced to wait months until Bowie completed a live tour and had a day and a half free to mix the album. Making heavy use of a then-fashionable delay device called The Time Tube, Bowie's version lost much of the punch of the original. A 1997 remix by Iggy himself was far more brutal, VU meters firmly locked in the red, and it's this edition which is most widely available today.

Record label:
CBS
Produced
by James Williamson and Iggy Pop.
Recorded
at CBS Studios, London, September 10–October 6, 1972; mixed March 1973, Western Sound Recorders, Los Angeles.
Released:
June 1973
Chart peaks:
None (UK) 182 (US)
Personnel:
Iggy Pop (v, m); Ron Asheton (b); Scott Asheton (d); James Williamson (g); David Bowie (m)
Track listing:
Search And Destroy; Gimme Danger; Hard To Beat; Penetration; Raw Power; I Need Somebody; Shake Appeal; Death Trip
Running time:
33.57
Current CD:
4851762 Hard To Beat replaced by Your Pretty Face Is Going To Hell
Further listening:
Kill City (1978); live album Metallic KO (1977)
Further reading:
MOJO 29; www.sonymusic.com/artists/IggyPop
Like this?
Try . . . p.707

Sly & The Family Stone

Fresh

Long-awaited follow-up to Riot revealed that even an incapacitated Sly could be more alive than most.

The two years since *There's A Riot Goin' On* had not proved any more peaceful. Drug busts, financial hassles, royally wasted TV appearances and rumours of dead bodies at his Bel Air home had accompanied the increasingly haunted figure of Sly Stone. When the new album was titled *Fresh*, few found its claim believable.

Lines like "I switched from coke to pep and now I'm a connoisseur" from opener In Time stretched credibility further. But it was supposed to mark a new beginning. Sly had finally split from manager David Kapralik and signed a new deal with CBS as Fresh Productions. "Sly was developing what he thought was the next step in music," says Robert Joyce who, at 19, had just been made the Family's new production manager at that time. "We were leaders in the field of what we were doing, but the pressure all fell back on him to keep it going. Keep it going. Keep everybody paid."

So Sly attempted to return to sunnier times. The album's a convincing stab at allying his previous album's sprawling, fragmentary voodoo (the mantric closer Babies Makin' Babies) with the upbeat pulse of his early work (witness the straight-ahead pop of If It Were Left Up To Me). Keep On Dancin' even explicitly reprises their first hit Dance To The Music.

Despite losing key members, legendary bassist Larry Graham and drummer Greg Errico, Sly still managed to coax brilliant performances from the Family. Tracks like Thankful 'N' Thoughtful took the funk to such new heights of complex syncopation, it almost appeared as though they'd mastered telepathy. The bass duties are mixed between Graham (who laid down some tracks before his exit), Rusty Allen and Sly himself. It was Sly who performed the stealthily creeping bassline on the outstanding single If You Want Me To Stay. In his usual self-referential mode, this song offered a message to his public claiming he would stick around on the scene as long as they realised that, "I've got to be me...".

Sadly, this 'me' proved to be a singularly unknowable entity. The single went to Number 12 in the US charts – it was to be his last hit. The epically swaying, end-of-night take on Que Sera, Sera got some radio play after rumours of an unlikely romance between Sly and Doris Day. And Sly was still influential: Miles Davis was taken with In Time, using it as the blueprint for his own voodoo funk album, *On The Corner*.

But he was on his way to the point of no return. The cover shot, taken by Richard Avedon, portrayed Sly as full of high-kicking vitality. The effect was achieved by laying him out on a glass table and shooting from underneath.

Record label:
Epic
Produced
by Sly Stone, Hamp 'Bubba' Banks and Bro Fred.
Recorded
at Record Plant, and 783 Bel-Air, Los Angeles
Released:
June 1973
Chart peaks:
None (UK) 7 (US)
Personnel:
Sly Stone (g, k, v); Freddie Stone (g); Rose Stone (p, v); Jerry Martini (s); Rusty Allen (b); Andy Newmark (d); Little Sister (bv); Pat Rizzo (s); Cynthia Robinson (t); Larry Graham (b); Bob Gratts, Willie Greer, George Engfer, Tom Flye aka 'Superfly', Mike Fusaro, James Green, Chris Henshaw, Don Puluse, Roy Segal, Bill Schruggs, Richard Tilles (e)
Track listing:
In Time; If You Want Me To Stay; Let Me Have It All; Frisky; Thankful 'N'Thoughtful; Skin I'm In; I Don't Know; Keep On Dancin'; Que Sera, Sera; If It Were Left Up To Me; Babies Makin' Babies
Running time:
39.40
Current CD:
485170 2 A remastering mix-up means that this CD contains inferior test mixes that Sly had abandoned in 1972. Thus the only version currently available in Europe amounts to an anthology-style alternative version.
Further listening:
There's A Riot Goin' On (1971)
Further reading:
Sly And The Family Stone, An Oral History (J Selvin, 1997)
Like this?
Try . . . p.302

Todd Rundgren

A Wizard, A True Star

Blue-eyed soul man takes a trip.

An essential navigational aid for all astral travellers. Tucked between the sweet-scented sattiva vibe of his 1972 double album *Something/Anything* and the sprawling eponymous 1974 masterwork *Todd* came this, Rundgren's acid home-movie, his Fantasia for one. Famously shy of the drug culture during his time with The Nazz in the '60s, by the early '70s Todd had finally taken the lysergic plunge. "Psychedelics brought me to an awareness of myself that I'd no comprehension of previously," said Rundgren. "You don't know you're 'you' until you've had your ego stripped away and you realise you're all that stuff."

The 'Wizard side', is a microcosmic encapsulation of an acid trip, from take-off to landing and all stratospheric stop-offs between. The trip begins and ends with interstellar anthem International Feel ("Here we are again/The start of the end/But there's more"), skims across the interplanetary terrain of Disney's Never Never Land (Todd always was a shrewd and iconoclastic judge of cover versions), gets horny and disintegrates into tiny molecules on Tic Tic Tic It Wears Off, You Need Your Head, Rock and Roll Pussy and Dogfight Giggle, glams up and gender-bends on You Don't Have To Camp Around, glides majestically across the universe on Zen Archer, gets the giggles again on Just Another Onion Head and Dada Dali, before crashing and burning gloriously, emerging only slightly singed by the multi-coloured flames on When The Shit Hits The Fan.

Part two showcases Todd, the singer-songwriter, the "True Star". Sometimes I Don't Know What To Feel and I Don't Want To Tie You Down are emotionally raw ballads that Carole King might have written. The sublime medley of I'm So Proud, Ooh Baby Baby, and La La La Means I Love You pays homage to his blue-eyed soul heritage, his heroes, and his home town of Philadelphia. Cool Jerk and Is It My Name are Todd, the unreconstructed cosmic buffoon, peeling off power chords and goofing off at the same time. He was a self-promoting, self-producing, self-sufficient polymath, ten years before Prince and this was his finest hour.

Record label:
Bearsville
Produced
by Todd Rundgren.
Recorded
at Secret Sound, USA, 1972–1973.
Released:
June 1973
Chart peaks:
None (UK) 86 (US)
Personnel:
Mark 'Moogy' Klingman (k); John Seigler (c, b); Randy Brecker (t); Dave Sanborn (s); John Siomos (d); Ralph Shuckett (b); Mike Brecker (s); Tom Cosgrove; Jean Yves Lebout; Rick Deringer (g); Barry Rogers (tb); Buffalo Bill Gelber (b)
Track listing:
International Feel; Never Never Land; Tic Tic Tic It Wears Off; You Need Your Head; Rock And Roll Pussy; Dogfight Giggle; You Don't Have To Camp Around; Flamingo; Zen Archer; Just Another Onionhead; Dada Dali; When The Shit Hits The Fan – Sunset Boulevard; Le Feel Internationale; Sometimes I Don't Know What To Feel (S/US); Does Anybody Love You?; I'm So Proud/Ooh Baby Baby/La La La Means I Love You/Cool Jerk; Hungry For Love; I Don't Want To Tie You Down; Is It My Name?; Just One Victory
Running time:
53.04
Current CD:
ESM CD 673
Further listening:
Something/Anything (1972)
Further reading:
www.tr-i.com
Like this?
Try . . . p.269

Stevie Wonder

Innervisions

Mid-point of his great creative eruption.

The ultimate natural, an accomplished multi-instrumentalist by the time he was 10, by the early '70s Stevie Wonder was demanding new challenges which did not include compliance with his label's plan to make him "Stevie Wonder the entertainer, another Sammy Davis". Intrigued by new developments in electronic instruments, he asked for a tutorial from Tonto's Expanding Head Band synthesiser masters Malcolm Cecil and Robert Margouleff.

According to Cecil, he walked into the studio brandishing Tonto's *Zero Time* album, saying "'I don't believe all this was done on one instrument. Show me.' So we dragged his hands all over the Moog and he thought he'd never be able to play it."

Wonder remembered no such doubt: "It was definitely a lot of knobs to turn and push and levers to twist and pull up and down. But my concern was not as great as my eagerness to learn it."

Within weeks, he embarked on one of music's more magisterial tides of creativity. Often working 48 hours solid, in the course of a year he completed tracks that formed the basis of his next five albums.

The third of the sequence, *Innervisions*, confirmed his quality MOR side with love ballads Golden Lady and All In Love Is Fair, but really grasped lapels with the unrestrained anger and political punch of Living For The City. Hard-driving funk rams home the rage behind such lines as "To find a job is like a haystack needle/'Cause where he lives they don't use coloured people". Halfway through, it breaks off to run a highly compressed playlet in which the innocent boy "born in hard time Mississippi" is arrested and jailed for a drugs offence.

The joy was that Wonder took control of the machines and made them express his emotions, warm or raging, and follow his startling sense of where a limber melody or hip-jolting syncopation might lead. Playing almost everything on synthesisers, he powered through Higher Ground, Latin-swayed Don't You Worry 'Bout A Thing, set his anti-drug song Too High pulsing with tension (his 48-hour days ran on adrenaline, his first joint having put him off drugs forever).

The feeling is cornucopia.

Record Label:
Motown
Produced
by Stevie Wonder.
Recorded
at Record Plant, Los Angeles and Media Sound, New York; autumn 1971–spring 1973.
Released:
August 3, 1973
Chart peaks:
8 (UK) 4 (US)
Personnel:
Stevie Wonder (v, Arp & Moog synthesisers, p, electric piano, d); Malcolm Cecil, Scott Edwards, Willie Weeks (b); Dean Parks, David 'T' Walker, Ralph Hammer (g); Clarence Bell (o); Larry 'Nastyee' Latimer (congas); Yusuf Roahman (shaker); Sheila Wilkerson (pc); Lani Groves, Tasha Thomas, Jim Gilstrap (bv); Robert Margouleff, Malcolm Cecil (e, programming); Dan Barbiero, Austin Godsey (e)
Track Listing:
Too High; Visions; Living For The City (S); Golden Lady; Higher Ground (S); Jesus Children Of America; All In Love Is Fair; Don't You Worry 'Bout A Thing (S); He's Misstra Know-It-All (S, UK only)
Running time:
44.15
Current CD:
157 355-2
Further Listening:
Music Of My Mind, Talking Book (1972); Fulfillingness' First Finale (1974); Songs In The Key Of Life (1976)
Further reading: Stevie Wonder (Constance Elsner, 1977); Stevie Wonder (John Swenson, 1986)
Like this?
Try . . . p.824

New York Dolls

New York Dolls

Rough-hewn punk primer.

"Get the glitter out of your asses and play," barked the producer to the New York Dolls from the safety of his side of the studio glass. That Todd Rundgren himself had hair in four garish colours not found in nature's rainbow is an indication of the bizarre spectacle that was the recording of the Dolls' debut album.

To the band, the sessions were just one more show. They dressed in their finest thrift-shop flash, and always had enough of an entourage present to constitute an audience for every take. Fortunately, there was plenty of music too.

"We'd been working on songs for a solid year," singer David Johansen says. "Once we started going out on the road and being rock stars, we got kind of lax in that department. That's not a terribly unique story, is it?"

Perhaps not, but few bands have delivered a debut this brash and assured. There was no basis for it: the Dolls had been turned down by every major label, finally winding up on Mercury, and even producer Rundgren admitted that their unschooled clatter wasn't his musical cup of tea. The Dolls noticed none of this, rocking on as if they were the center of the universe. They were a rough and raucous extension of the line that ran through The Rolling Stones to the MC5, adding the then-modern touch of sexual confusion to the mix. They more than compensated in energy and style what they lacked in musical grace. Johansen was no Jagger or Tyner vocally, but his attitude was dead-on. The self-taught Johnny Thunders let loose with jagged bursts of stun guitar, playing off the steady rhythm guitar of Sylvain Sylvain and (depending on his liquid/chemical consumption on the day) Arthur Kane's bass. Curiously, Rundgren chose to minimise the band's most powerful and accomplished musician – drummer Jerry Nolan – in the final mix.

Highlights include Personality Crisis, Looking For A Kiss, Trash and Jet Boy, but every other song (excepting a regrettable acoustic number) displays gloriously sloppy excellence. Johansen describes it as "a little jewel of urban folk art", but he's being modest. The album didn't make them the stars they imagined themselves to be but all the right people heard it as a call to arms. *New York Dolls* lit the fuse to punk, and contains enough attitude, enthusiasm and excess to incite more revolutions in the future.

Record label:
Mercury
Produced
by Todd Rundgren.
Recorded
at the Record Plant, New York; April 1973.
Released:
August 1973
Chart peaks:
None (UK) 116 (US)
Personnel:
Johnny Thunders (g); Sylvain Sylvain (g); David Johansen (v, hm); Arthur Kane (b); Jerry Nolan (d); Todd Rundgren (p, Moog); The Fantastic Buddy Bowser (s); Jack Douglas, Ed Sprigg
Track listing:
Personality Crisis; Looking For A Kiss; Vietnamese Baby; Lonely Planet Boy; Frankenstein; Trash (S/US); Bad Girl; Subway Train; Pills; Private World; Jet Boy (S/UK)
Running time:
42.42
Current CD:
Polygram 832-7522
Further listening:
In Too Much Too Soon (1974), second Polygram album; Lipstick Killers (1981) early demos; Red Patent Leather: Live In NYC 1975 (1984) end of the road.
Further reading:
From The Velvets To The Voidoids (Clinton Heylin, 1993); In Cold Blood: The Johnny Thunders Story (Nina Antonia, 1987)
Like this?
Try . . . p.515

Elton John

Goodbye Yellow Brick Road

The second of seven consecutive US number one albums underlined his status as a global superstar without peer.

From the pomp of the anticipation-building overture Funeral For A Friend, it was clear that this hulking masterwork betrayed a new set of concerns far removed from the country comforts and suburban dreams conjured up previously by lyricist Bernie Taupin: a growing obsession with the travails of fame (Candle In The Wind), excitement for primal rock 'n' roll energy (Saturday Night's Alright For Fighting); nostalgia (Goodbye Yellow Brick Road) and a decidedly confused attitude towards sexuality (All The Girls Love Alice). However the album's epic nature was achieved by accident. But for The Rolling Stones, everything would have been very different, according to producer Gus Dudgeon who points out that Mick Jagger recommended Byron Lee's Dynamic Studios in Kingston, Jamaica to Elton after a happy sojourn recording the Stones' *Goats Head Soup*.

But Dudgeon soon encountered problems. "It sounded amazing when I'd previously been there," says Dudgeon. "It had exactly what we were looking for, this massive bottom end [which adds bass to a recording]. Things were looking great until we set all the equipment up." The bottom end had inexplicably vanished. After days of dickering, the team taped just one track, a rough run-through of Saturday Night's Alright..., before repairing to trusted standby the Château d'Herouville in France. Here the tight band of musicians raced through the 21 songs John had stockpiled while holed up in his Kingston hotel room waiting for the studio problem to be resolved.

"That's how it came out a double," says Dudgeon. "Elton just had more time to write than usual. None of us was particularly into doing a double, but the stuff he had was just too good." Although the impact of the fragile Candle In The Wind may now be forever dissipated by overfamiliarity in the wake of the mawkish Diana tribute, *Goodbye Yellow Brick Road* is stacked full of winners, including several hidden gems such as This Song Has No Title, which, combined with The Ballad Of Danny Bailey, apparently provided Billy Joel with an entire career template.

As the release of the album was being finalised, Elton played the Hollywood Bowl, introduced in jokey style by Deep Throat star Linda Lovelace and a cast of royal and film star lookalikes. He trailed the album by playing many of its songs there and by selling out two nights at the historic venue. Within weeks *Goodbye Yellow Brick Road* had confirmed him as the biggest British star in the US since The Beatles.

Record label:
DJM
Produced
by Gus Dudgeon.
Recorded
at Château d'Herouville, France; summer 1973.
Released:
October 1973
Chart peaks:
1 (UK) 1 (US)
Personnel:
Elton John (v, p, o, farfisa, mellotron); Dee Murray (b, v); Davey Johnstone (g, v); Nigel Olsson (d, v); David Henstchel (ARP synth); Del Newman (a); Prince Rhino (v); Kiki Dee (v); Ray Cooper (pc); Leroy Gomez (s)
Track listing:
Funeral For A Friend (Love Lies Bleeding); Candle In The Wind (S/UK); Bennie And The Jets (S); Goodbye Yellow Brick Road (S); This Song Has No Title; Grey Seal; Jamaica Jerk-Off; I've Seen That Movie Too; Sweet Painted Lady; The Ballad Of Danny Bailey (1909–34); Dirty Little Girl; All The Girls Love Alice; Your Sister Can't Twist (But She Can Rock'N'Roll); Saturday Night's Alright For Fighting (S); Roy Rogers; Social Disease; Harmony
Running time:
76.23
Current CD:
MCA 528159-2
Further listening:
Elton's other double album Blue Moves (1976)
Further reading:
Elton: The Definitive Biography (Philip Norman, 1992); www.eltonjohn.com
Like this?
Try . . . p.397

Emerson, Lake And Palmer

Brain Salad Surgery

The master showmen of prog rock reach their creative and commercial zenith.

Emerson, Lake And Palmer's torrid brew of keyboard savagery, wistful balladry and hot-wired classicism may seem an unaquirable taste to modern ears, but in 1973–74 they were the cat's knackers, the cutting edge, and stadium giants. Only Led Zeppelin, The Rolling Stones and The Who were bigger live draws, and none of them offered a set that took in Mussorgsky, Copland, Dave Brubeck and boogie-woogie. Here was a band cocky enough and clever enough to record William Blake and the astringent music of Argentine classical composer Alberto Ginastera for their fourth hit album.

Most of *Brain Salad Surgery* (working title was *Whip Some Skull on You*) was assembled at the band's Manticore Studios, an abandoned Odeon cinema in Fulham, London they had turned into a rehearsal and production centre. They worked in the upstairs foyer while the downstairs area was rented out to bands including Zeppelin and Jethro Tull.

Greg Lake remembers *Brain Salad Surgery* as a group effort, whereas previous albums were very much a question of each person thinking of ideas in solitude. Emerson had wanted to have a crack at Jerusalem since his Nice days, but only with Lake had he found an arrangement that worked. For Toccata, Emerson adapted a piece by Ginastera; but there was panic when, close to release, it was discovered that the venerable composer's approval was required. Emerson flew to his Swiss home with a tape, where, to his relief, Ginastera declared the adaptation diabolical. This was meant as a compliment: he gushed that Emerson had captured the malevolent essence of the music.

The album is dominated by the sci-fi suite Karn Evil 9, whose technical complexities built on their hit album *Tarkus*. The title was suggested by lyricist Pete Sinfield as a corruption of "carnival". A former IBM tape operator, Sinfield was also responsible for the 3rd Impression's theme of computers taking over humanity. A carnival of bombast and grungy early Moogs, there's a furious energy about this record and a real spirit of adventure: a couple of minutes of Toccata sound like prototype drum'n'bass.

Greg Lake says that the album came out of the band's "healthy days – as opposed to when everything became fragmented, ego-driven. Our creativity was at its very best."

Record label:
Manticore
Produced
by Greg Lake.
Recorded
at Olympic and Advision Studios, London; 1973.
Released:
November 19, 1973
Chart peaks:
2 (UK) 11 (US)
Personnel:
Keith Emerson (k); Greg Lake (v, b, g); Carl Palmer (d, drum synthesiser); Geoff Young (e)
Track listing:
Jerusalem; Toccata; Still You Turn Me On; Benny The Bouncer; Karn Evil 9 (1st Impression – Part 1); Karn Evil 9 (1st Impression – Part 2); Karn Evil 9 (2nd Impression); Karn Evil 9 (3rd Impression)
Running time:
45.04
Current CD:
ESM CD344
Further listening:
The eponymous first album (1970) and Tarkus (1971) stand up better than bloated later works.
Further reading:
www.dynrec.com/elp/ – the official site; www.brain-salad.com is a good fan site.
Like this?
Try . . . p.289

The Isley Brothers

3+3

Two generations of a great soul band come together.

During the '50s and '60s The Isley Brothers – Ronald, Rudolph and O'Kelly – had left an indelible mark on soul music with Shout, Twist And Shout and This Old Heart Of Mine, and influencing white pop from The Beatles on down. Then, self-producing and running their own label, T-Neck, they turned the tables by covering the likes of Stephen Stills, Jackie De Shannon, James Taylor and Bob Dylan.

Hearing the possibilities engineer/programmers Bob Margouleff and Malcolm Cecil opened up by introducing Stevie Wonder to synthesisers on *Music Of My Mind* (1972), the Isleys the duo to produce their next album. It was to be titled *3+3* because the three veteran brothers were joined officially by a triumvirate from the next generation, Ernie, Marvin, and 'cousin' Chris Jasper (they had appeared uncredited on the T-Neck albums while finishing college).

Led by the burly O'Kelly, patriarch of the clan, they came punctually to each session, as Margouleff notes: "They arrived prepared, knowing exactly what they wanted. They were a hard-working industrious group, no drugs or alcohol." If any Isley made a mistake, they had to endure O'Kelly's wrath.

With Ronald's timeless tenor in the lead, they tackled Seals and Crofts' Summer Breeze, the Doobie Brothers' Listen To The Music and James Taylor's ballad Don't Let Me Be Lonely Tonight. But their own That Lady (a new version of 1964 hit Who's That Lady) really served notice that The Isleys were back – and that there was a new guitar in town. His name was Ernie Isley, 17 and almost a reincarnation of Jimi Hendrix. At nine, he had stood transfixed when Hendrix was employed in the Isleys' backing band and begged guitar lessons from him. "Ernie's playing on That Lady was all done in one take and he was only rehearsing!" recalls Marvin proudly. "He'd play with the lights off facing the wall so he couldn't see anybody's expression. What he didn't see was us screaming, Ernie, don't stop! Keep it going! By the end we were jumping up and down and giving each other five. To us it was some of the baddest stuff we'd ever heard." Ernie himself remembers that, when he had finished, "Kelly looked at me for about 15 minutes straight without blinking. I felt like I had one foot on the ground and the other on Mount Olympus." That Lady and Summer Breeze were all over American radio in 1973–74 and ushered in the funky family's golden era, which endured well into the '80s.

Record label:
Epic
Produced
by The Isley Brothers.
Recorded
at Record Plant Studios Los Angeles, CA; 1973.
Released:
November 1973
Chart peaks:
None (UK) None (US)
Personnel:
Ron Isley (v); O'Kelly Isley (bv); Rudy Isley (bv); Ernie Isley (g); Marvin Isley (b); Chris Jasper (k); Truman Thomas (o); George Moreland (d); Bob Margouleff (e); Malcolm Cecil (e)
Track listing:
That Lady; Don't Let Me Be Lonely Tonight; If You Were There; You Walk Your Way; Listen To the Music; What It Comes Down To; Sunshine (Go Away Today); Summer Breeze; The Highways Of My Life
Running time:
38.56
Current CD:
4879372
Further listening:
It's Your Thing: The Story Of The Isley Brothers – a comprehensive, well-compiled 3-CD anthology.
Further reading:
www.isleybrothers.com
Like this?
Try . . . p.443

Tangerine Dream

Atem

One giant step for ambient music.

Tangerine Dream's 1971 album *Alpha Centauri* was dedicated "to those obliged to space"; its successor, the rhythmless double album *Zeit*, was almost all space. These predominantly keyboard-based, *kosmische* albums – "like Pink Floyd without the tunes" was how one commentator summed them up – sounded as if they had been conceived at the point where psychedelia had run its course. But the group were drug-free and Edgar Froese has a different explanation.

"We rather came from a background of painting, sculpting and graphic design, and viewed music as a sort of extension of our creativity – which was limited to concrete form and images in the other art forms," he says. "Music has a sense of abstraction, which has always fascinated us." If its predecessors had read like galactic charts set to music, *Atem* sounds as if Tangerine Dream had landed on one of those far-off worlds and were beaming back musical information. Although the results were more melodic, the group created a series of shifting, semi-fathomable atmospheres where individual instruments were often unrecognisable as they morphed together into new textures and timbres.

Live, the group had used backing tapes since the '60s to "increase the surreal atmosphere for the audience", as Froese puts it. Here the title track begins with a treated recording of breathing ("atem" means "breath" in German) and, taking the Pink Floyd comparison further, the Mellotron fanfares and tympani that usher in the track are reminiscent of that group's Sysyphus from their 1969 album *Ummagumma*. But former jazz drummer Chris Franke's tom-toms soon cut loose, whipping the processional into a cacophony that suddenly implodes, then drifts into a lengthy soundscape of sublime austerity, with keyboard notes hanging like sheets of mist. Fauni-Gena finds Froese's eerie, Debussyesque Mellotron in an alien glade surrounded by teeming, twitching animal life. "We made our own sound recordings at the coast of the North Sea and the bird houses of the Berlin Zoo," he explains. The echo repeats on Circulation Of Events, meanwhile, point towards the sequencer patterns that would become their trademark on their next album, the big-selling *Phaedra*. The band created potent music before and after, but *Atem* still stands as a unique world of sound, an evocative album of seductive strangeness.

Record label:
OHR
Produced
by Tangerine Dream.
Recorded
at Dierks Studios, Stommelen and Cologne; December 1972–January 1973.
Released:
November 1973
Chart peaks:
None (UK) None (US)
Personnel:
Chris Franke (o, VCS3, pc, v); Edgar Froese (Mellotron, g, o, v); Peter Baumann (o, VCS3, p); Dieter Dierks (e)
Track listing:
Atem; Fauni–Gena; Circulation Of Events; Wahn
Running time:
41.54
Current CD:
ESMCD 348
Further listening:
Green Desert, Edgar Froese and Chris Franke's extension of the Atem sound in this appetiser for Virgin Records, recorded in 1973 but not released until 1986.
Further reading:
MOJO 41; Digital Gothic: A Critical Discography Of Tangerine Dream (Paul Stump, 1997) www.tangerinedream.de
Like this?
Try . . . p.170

The Who

Quadrophenia

Another four-sided enigma from Pete & Co.

Hugely frustrated by the short-circuiting of his *Lifehouse* project (eventually released on six CDs in 2000) in 1973 Pete Townshend turned his ever conflicted creative emotions towards another grand concept, his to Mod, the movement which gave The Who identity.

The title did allude to the ultimately useless technology of quadraphonic sound, but more significantly to the four sides of the personality of central character Jimmy as he struggles to assert his identity in the face of peer pressure, drug confusion, family condemnation and sexual disappointment. To Townshend, it also reflected the split personality of The Who, "Roger the fighter, John the romantic, Keith the lunatic and Pete the self-dubbed 'beggar and hypocrite'".

Structurally, said Townshend, "It's a series of impressions, of memories. You see a kid on a rock in the middle of the sea, and this whole thing explains how he got there."

The band were less than enamoured with the whole idea. While Moon's alcoholism took its toll on his abilities, Daltrey remained staunchly unimpressed, complaining that his voice had been buried in the mix, and Entwistle growled that all the songs sounded the same to him.

But the quartet produced peak performances on songs such as 5.15, Dr Jimmy and Love Reign O'er Me. The adolescent frustration evoked by songs such as Sea And Sand and Cut My Hair proved that Townshend was still in touch with both his own generation and the teenage angst of any era. Moon was instructed to play every percussion instrument to hand, and as the album ends he hurls the tubular bells at his drumkit which noisily collapses in what one critic called "his last great moment on record".

"*Quadrophenia* is about The Who and what happens to us," Townshend explained at the time. "I left it open-ended on a note of spiritual desperation because we're in the middle of nowhere, not sure where we're going." He would tell concert audiences, "It's about growing up. At the end of the album the hero is in grave danger of maturing."

Not so The Who, though. On tour, technical problems resulted in more feuding. Townshend responded to Daltry's complaints by hitting him over the head with a guitar. The singer's response was one mighty right hook which put his old friend in hospital with concussion. *Quadrophenia* was never played live again until 1996.

Record label:
Polydor
Produced
by The Who.
Recorded
at The Kitchen, Battersea, London and Ronnie Lane's Mobile; June 1972 and June 1973.
Released:
November 1973
Chart peaks:
2 (UK) 2 (US)
Personnel:
John Entwistle (b, horns, v); Roger Daltrey (v); Keith Moon (pc, v); Pete Townshend (g, v, syn); Chris Stainton (p); Chris Stamp, Pete Kameron and Kit Lambert (executive producers)
Track listing:
I Am The Sea; The Real Me (S/US); Quadrophenia; Cut My Hair; The Punk Meets The Godfather; I'm One; The Dirty Jobs; Helpless Dancer; Is It In My Head?; I've Had Enough; 5:15 (S); Sea And Sand; Drowned; Bell Boy; Doctor Jimmy; The Rock; Love Reign O'er Me (S/US)
Running time:
81.44
Current CD:
531 971-2
Further listening:
The Who Sing My Generation (1965)
Further reading:
MOJO 32, 82; Before I Get Old: The Story Of The Who (Dave Marsh, 1983); www.thewho.net
Like this?
Try . . . p.355

Paul McCartney And Wings

Band On The Run

The fraught fifth post-Beatles release that restored McCartney's worldwide reputation.

The critical gush that greeted *Band On The Run* was a sigh of relief that the man who'd helped set an unmatchable standard for pop music in the '60s hadn't completely lost it. Even John Lennon, who'd blown raspberries at earlier efforts, called it "a great album – you can call them Wings but it's McCartney music." Perhaps the key to its charms was the duress it was made under. A week before the five-piece Wings were to fly to Lagos to record, guitarist Henry McCullough stormed out of the Mull Of Kintyre rehearsals, and six days later drummer Denny Seiwell followed suit. Paul pushed on with just Linda and ex-Moody Blues pal Denny Laine. Arriving in Nigeria, the McCartneys were robbed at knife point and relieved of, among other things, the sole demo tape of the songs they were about to record. Paul was accused by irate locals of intending to exploit Africa's music and musicians and, later still, a doctor was called when it was thought McCartney was suffering a heart-attack.

"It was a challenge to be in Lagos," he charmingly understates, "and very uphill."

Work began at a ferocious lick once the fabulously outmoded Studer 8-track desk had been dusted down and some microphones were located in a cardboard box. It was, Laine remembers, "like a home studio; nobody knew what we were doing but us". The MO was basic in the extreme: "Normally me and Denny would start it off with a couple of acoustics, like you would for a demo," McCartney recalls, "then it would be me on drums, and then we'd build it up like a sculpture." Back at AIR in London, the tapes were transferred to 16-track for the overdubs and Tony Visconti's sax, brass and orchestral scores.

The result was a jewel. *Band On The Run* has a tangible vibe, McCartney's customary breezy confidence at last matched by his inspiration. The title track is an irresistible statement of buoyant defiance, Jet is his best rocker since Back In The USSR, Bluebird is almost a parody of McCartney-esque beauty. Even the question mark over his might-mean-something-probably-don't lyrics is answered by the delightfully sustained paean to rainfall, Mamunia, a pearl of naïve wisdom. The fun he has with Picasso's Last Words shows him not letting the absence of a proper song (he wrote it at a party to impress Dustin Hoffman) get in the way of a great track. Laine co-wrote the glorious slab of Wings harmony No Words with his husky tones a discernible part of the fabulous vocal arrangements throughout, but his suggestion that "the contribution of the three people was, you know, very equal" sounds a touch hopeful, with even McCartney regarding the resulting work as "nearly a solo album".

Record label:
Parlophone
Produced
by Paul McCartney.
Recorded
at Arc and EMI Studios, Lagos, Nigeria; September 1973.
Released:
December 1973
Chart peaks:
1 (UK) 1 (US)
Personnel:
Paul McCartney (v, b, d, g, k); Denny Laine (g, v); Linda McCartney (v, pc); Howie Casey (s); Tony Visconti (a); Geoff Emerick (e)
Track listing:
Band On The Run; Jet; Bluebird; Mrs Vanderbilt; Let Me Roll It; Mamunia; No Words; Picasso's Last Words; 1985
Running time:
41.09
Current CD
CDP7892402 adds second, documentary CD
Further listening:
Mauled at the time but undergoing reassessment, Ram (1971); Flaming Pie (1997).
Further reading:
Beatles After The Break Up (Keith Badman, 1999); Mark Lewisohn's sleeve notes to the Band On The Run 25th Anniversary Edition
Like this?
Try . . . p.474

Dan Penn

Nobody's Fool

Debut solo album from stellar back-room boy, one of the decade's great songwriters.

"I made the record because I didn't have anything else to do," Penn explains with characteristic modesty. "There was no-one to cut, so I thought, cut you." Penn had composed his first hit by the age of 18 (for Conway Twitty) and spent the '60s helping invent country-soul as sessionman, producer and songwriter, first at Muscle Shoals and then at the American Sound studios in Memphis. By the end of the decade Penn had used some of his song-writing royalties (from hits such as the Box Tops' Cry Like A Baby, James Carr's Dark End Of The Street and Percy Sledge's Out Of Left Field) to establish his own studio, Beautiful Sounds; certainly an apposite name. This independence allowed Penn to step into the spotlight himself, but though – for example – I Hate You boasts one of the great soul vocals, Penn, typically, downplays the majesty of the performance ("I put too much echo on that one. I've never been real big on echo"). Elsewhere his voice is "dry" and typically laid-back: on the Mississippi symphony Raining In Memphis he resembles a mellow Elvis – though Penn insists he shares with The King a tendency to "waller" vocally – and on Ain't No Love he indulges in some splendid Otis Redding-style bravura. The album closes with three tracks which form a Southern white man's *What's Going On?* in miniature: "I guess I was a bit political at that point," Penn deadpans. Prayer For Peace is a plea to end racial disharmony, complete with gospel choruses winging in from every point of the stereo picture. If Love Was Money is a rich girl/poor boy story zinging with sophisticated strings, while the extraordinary Skin returns to the problem of race. "I was working at Ardent (Memphis studio) and just found this two-track tape in my briefcase, I'd never seen it before in my life." The tape had a combination of distorted '40s film soundtrack and "backwards Christmas music" on it. Over this Penn dubbed his underplayed but emotive spoken vocal; an idiosyncratic coda to a beautifully played and often surprisingly experimental album.

"We didn't have synthesisers back then so we had to do things with tape speeds and editing," Penn recalls, "We were just having fun." That's what it sounds like, and at the time the album received good reviews but did next-to-nothing commercially. Only now is Penn being paid his true due as a performer, his recent tours with cohort Spooner Oldham (and a superb live album) attracting plaudits and many new converts.

Record label:
Beautiful Sounds
Produced
by Dan Penn.
Recorded
at Beautiful Sounds Studios, Memphis, Tennessee, "and some other nice places"; 1969–1971
Released:
1973
Chart peaks:
None (UK) None (US)
Personnel:
Dan Penn (v, g); Spooner Oldham (k); Mike Utley (k); Greg Redding (k); Jay Spell (k); Bill Phillips (k); Bergen White (vibes); Tommy Richards, Charlie Freeman, Tony Oterri, Marlin Greene (g); John Huey, Leo LeBlanc (steel gtr); Jim Johnson, David Hood (b); Dulin Lancaster, Roger Hawkins, Sammy Creason (d); Wayne Jackson (t); Andrew Love (s); Cargo, Jeanie Green, Mary Holiday, Ginger Holiday, Susan Dotson, Susan Coleman (bv); Nashville Strings & Horns; Memphis Horns; Memphis Strings; Bergen White (a)
Track listing:
Nobody's Fool (S/US); Raining In Memphis; Tearjoint; Time; Lodi; Ain't No Love; I Hate You; Prayer For Peace; If Love Was Money; Skin
Running time:
30.17
Current CD:
EE 4622
Further listening:
Do Right Man (1994). Moments From This Theatre (1999)
Further reading:
Say It One Time For The Brokenhearted (1998); It Came From Memphis (1995)
Like this?
Try . . . p.709

Eno

Here Come The Warm Jets

Patenting glam punk on rush-recorded solo debut.

It's said that the day Brian Eno left Roxy Music – June 21, 1973 – he wrote this album's standout track, the nagging and nasty pre-punk classic Baby's On Fire. At this distance, Eno can't confirm the story, but he does recall the sense of freedom after the acrimonious fall-out with Bryan Ferry during the recording of the band's second album *For Your Pleasure*.

"I was absolutely euphoric," he says. "I remember leaving my management offices on the King's Road the day I resigned and skipping and leaping down the road in delight. I felt so liberated." He quickly began recording at the very economical Majestic Studios in Clapham, south London, the total recording costs were £5,600.

"I was flat broke, having not been a songwriter with Roxy," he says. "It was very cheap but served its purpose – I needed a place where I could feel comfortable making mistakes. If a day was wasted it didn't cost me a fortune." Musicians included Chris Spedding, his Sharks bandmate Busta Cherry Jones – who Eno would later recall to help funkify Talking Heads – and all of Roxy Music except, of course, Ferry.

"I wanted to make a hard-sounding record, one that didn't try and hide its artifice and pretend it was a recording of a performance." To that end he ruled that there should be no reverb simulating a live sound, though producer Chris Thomas snuck it onto a couple of tracks. *Here Come The Warm Jets* (among the jumble on the cover's mantelpiece is a charming Victorian picture of a micturating maiden) retains a brittle, synthetic and thoroughly modern ring. Eno's playfulness is evident in his wordplay (The Paw Paw Negro Blowtorch) and while he sticks in the main to traditional song structure, they're interlaced with doo-wop harmonies, sub-Velvets white noise, stop-start rhythms, Beach Boys pastiche and faux-Roxyisms (during Dead Finks Don't Talk's jokey attack on Ferry he breaks into a spot-on parody of the Roxy mainman's braying vocal style).

However, once recording was over, Eno lost interest in the album, moving onto to the experimental collaboration with Fripp, *No Pussyfooting*. He even tried to persuade Island to abandon its release. "It seemed full of lost opportunities. This often happens though – I suffer from post-partum depression!" he says. "But fortunately they wouldn't listen to me and went ahead. I'm glad they did."

Record label:
Island
Produced
by Eno.
Recorded
at Majestic Studios, London; September 1973.
Released:
January 1974
Chart peaks:
26 (UK) 151 (US)
Personnel:
Brian Eno (v, k, snake guitar, syn, treatments); Andy Mackay (s, k); Robert Fripp (g); Phil Manzanera (g); Paul Rudolph (g, b); Chris Spedding (g); Busta Cherry Jones (b); John Wetton (b); Paul Thompson (pc)
Track listing:
Needles In The Camel's Eye; The Paw Paw Negro Blowtorch; Baby's On Fire; Cindy Tells Me; Driving Me Backwards; On Some Faraway Beach; Blank Frank; Dead Finks Don't Talk; Some Of Them Are Old; Here Come The Warm Jets
Running time:
41.40
Current CD:
ILPS 9268
Further listening:
Taking Tiger Mountain By Strategy (1974)
Further reading:
Paul Morley's sleevenotes to Enobox 2: Vocal (1993); enoweb at www.hyperreal.org
Like this?
Try . . . p.307

Gram Parsons

Grievous Angel

A touchstone of alternative country.

In his last year, the young man born into a wealthy family as Cecil Ingram Conner III had realised it was time to turn his life around. A paid up member of the Brian Jones Physical Abuse Programme, he tasted many of the Devil's most insidious pleasures in his quarter century. But, invigorated by the way his first solo tour and album (1973's *GP*) were received, Gram Parsons was now itching to mend his no-good ways and continue his winning streak. To do so would require a certain amount of sobering up.

When the *GP* tour ended in spring '73, he was already assembling songs for the follow-up. He was particularly enthused by his new singing partner, Emmylou Harris from Birmingham, Alabama (previously resident songstress in a Washington, DC bar until discovered by The Flying Burrito Bros). The ache in Parsons' cracked voice dovetailed perfectly with Emmylou's clear soprano. Although eyebrows were raised when Gram chose himself as the album's sole producer, by all accounts the sessions were magical. "There was a real sense of exhilaration, such an excitement," recalls Harris. "He would go back at the end of the day's recording just to listen to the songs we did and talk about the band we would put together, the tour we would do. There were so many plans. Because he loved that record. It just seemed like he was so strong, that's why his death was such a shock to me."

Parsons had come up with his most enduring songs: a heartfelt ballad to his deceased mother called Brass Buttons, the gorgeous left-at-the-altar tale of $1000 Wedding, the rockin' Ooh Las Vegas, and the poignant In My Hour Of Darkness which recounted the deaths of three close friends and subsequently seemed an omen for Parsons' own demise a few weeks after it was recorded. Add to this the terrifically cinematic Return Of The Grievous Angel and you have five country-rock standards. Supported by strong covers of Tom T. Hall and The Everly Brothers and with crisp, inventive playing from a band largely on hire from Elvis Presley's Vegas crew, this was the album Parsons had dreamed of.

Then, when he finished recording, he decided to go to the town of Joshua Tree in the Californian desert to celebrate. He celebrated himself to death, overdosing in his hotel room on a narcotic cocktail which stopped his heart. He was 26.

Record label:
Reprise
Produced
by Gram Parsons.
Recorded
at Wally Heider Studio 4 and Capitol Recording Studios, Hollywood; summer 1973.
Released:
January 1974
Chart peaks:
None (UK) None (US)
Personnel:
Gram Parsons (v, g); Emmylou Harris (v); Glen D Hardin (k); James Burton (g); Emory Gordy (b); Ronnie Tutt (d); Herb Pederson (g); Al Perkins (sg); Bernie Leadon (g, dobro); Byron Berline (fiddle, mandolin); ND Smart II (d); Steve Snyder (v); Linda Ronstadt (bv); Hugh Davies (e); Phil Kaufman, Kim Fowley, Ed Tickner, Jane & Joe Doe ("background blah blah on Northern Quebec Medley")
Track listing:
Return Of The Grievous Angel; Hearts On Fire; I Can't Dance; Brass Buttons; $1000 Wedding; Medley Live From Northern Quebec: Cash On The Barrelhead/Hickory Wind; Love Hurts; Ooh Las Vegas; In My Hour Of Darkness
Running time:
36.12
Current CD:
7599261082 adds: GP
Further listening:
Parsons first solo album, GP (1973); Gram Parsons & the Fallen Angels, Live, 1973 featuring Emmylou Harris and crew in concert.
Further reading:
Hickory Wind: (Ben Fong-Torres, 1991); www.gram-parsons.com
Like this?
Try . . . p.241

Tangerine Dream

Phaedra

With one bound, the guitar becomes obsolete.

Nothing much prepared the record-buying public for *Phaedra*. Sure, rock stars had been dabbling with synthesisers since the late '60s, Terry Riley had composed works using layers of minimalist keyboards, and Tonto's Expanding Head Band had begun devising ways to give electronic music a rhythmic pulse. With *Phaedra*, though, it all came together into an accessible ambient brew, sending reviewers scrurrying to their thesauruses in search of alternative ways to say 'cosmic'.

It had started when German rock guitarist Edgard Froese formed The Ones in 1965. They played traditional rock instruments, quite contentedly, until May 15, 1967 – when they supported Hendrix and were stunned by him. Convinced they could never match Hendrix on guitars, switched to primitive synthesisers as soon as they became available, and started devising their own futuristic instrumental music.

In 1973 mindful that the unlikely success of Mike Oldfield's long-form instrumental *Tubular Bells* had established his Virgin label, Richard Branson offered them a five-year contract. Until they entered Manor Studios, Tangerine Dream's music had all been improvised. Now, however, the complexity of the latest synths and sequencers required them to impose some pre-arranged shape on their compositions. "Just tuning the instruments took several hours each day," recalls Froese. Working daily from 11am until 2am, they completed six and a half minutes of music in 11 days, before finally mastering the machines and finishing the rest in a frenzied week. Musical inspiration (and titles) were drawn largely from Greek, Egyptian and Indian mythology, but the swirling electronic dreamscapes with their constantly shifting patterns, gradual changes of pace and vast blocks of seemingly orchestral/choral sound, could be interpreted uniquely by every listener. Gordon Fletcher of Rolling Stone hailed the "three visionary German kids" and their "amazing record" as "an immensely enjoyable experience". Before long, *Phaedra* was the only album cover on which any self-respecting head would be seen rolling a joint. Despite its lack of similarity to anything preceding it, *Phaedra* earned gold discs in seven countries, and (along with their fellow-countrymen, Kraftwerk) paved the way for modern electronic music.'

Record label:
Virgin
Produced
by Edgar Froese.
Recorded
at The Manor, Shipton-on-Cherwell, Oxfordshire; November 20–December 11, 1973.
Chart peaks:
15 (UK) None (US)
Released:
February 20, 1974
Running time:
37.57
Personnel:
Edgar Froese (Mellotron, b, syn); Chris Franke (syn); Peter Baumann (k, syn, flute); Phil Becque (e)
Track listing:
Phaedra; Mysterious Semblance At The Strand Of Nightmares; Movements Of A Visionary; Sequent C'
Current CD:
TAND5
Further listening:
Stratosfear (1976), the point at which Tangerine Dream reached a perfect balance between innovation and proficiency.
Further reading:
http://www.tangerinedream.de/
Like this?
Try . . . p.321

Lamont Dozier

Black Bach

Euphoric, string-powered soul from revered Motown writer and producer.

Anyone who takes the mantle of a classical icon and has an illustration of himself as a weathered bust on the cover of their album might well be accused of being a little full of himself. But Lamont Dozier's unusual mid-'70s album does just that and he gets away with it.

Still only 32, Dozier had already had hits in his own right, written and produced dozens for Motown, formed his own labels and worked with everyone from The Four Tops and Supremes through to Chairmen Of The Board and Freda Payne. His lengthy relationship with Brian and Eddie Holland had made the Holland/Dozier/Holland writing and production team a household name. What else was there left to do but leave it all and start again?

He broke up the partnership, abandoned their HDH label and started to record for ABC Records. His 1973 solo album, *Out Here On My Own* had concentrated on simple narrative mixed with a little politics (the single Fish Ain't Bitin'*). Black Bach*, on the other hand, was a grand act of hubris, a lushly orchestrated soul symphony, silky, sweet and simmering with emotion.

He called in a huge band of seasoned players to fill out the sound. At times there was a cast of hundreds in attendance, choirs of angels accompanying Lamont's ruminations on life and love, as he stood centre stage hamming it up. Dark and brooding in places, euphoric elsewhere, it indicated his distance from the mini-soap operas he'd helped create at Motown. And set in among all this swirling grandeur is Dozier's solitary, rather plain voice commanding all of the attention. It many ways it could be viewed as a folly, exactly the kind of record one would expect from a proven writer of hits not known for his own vocal prowess, but with a lavish budget to play with – not dissimilar in many ways from Jimmy Webb's solo albums of the same period. Even so, that mix of conceit and wing-and-a-prayer experiment makes it fascinating too. Naturally it didn't sell and, like much on the ABC label, hasn't made it onto CD, so this classic soul folly has receded into myth.

Record label:
ABC
Produced
by McKinley Jackson.
Recorded
at ABC Recording Studio, Los Angeles, California; 1973.
Released:
February 1974
Chart peaks:
None (UK) None (US)
Personnel:
Lamont Dozier (v); Ray Parker Jr (g); Melvin 'Wah Wah' Ragin (g); Dean Parks (g); Greg Poree (g); Rick Straviski (g); Scott Edwards (b); Ronald Brown (b); Ed Greene (d); Sylvester Rivers, Sonny Burkes, McKinley Jackson, Ernest Vantrese (p); Clark E Sprangler (s); Eddie 'Bongo' Brown, Leslie Bass (pc); Jessica Smith, Patricia Hodges, Myrna Matthews, Edna Wright, Darlene Love, Julia Tillman, Maxine Willard, Oren Waters, Luther Waters, Marti McCall (v)
Track listing:
Shine; Put Out My Fire; Let Me Start Tonite (S/US); All Cried Out; Intermission; Prelude; Rose; Thank You For The Dream; I Wanna Be With You; Blue Sky And Silver Bird
Running time:
39.52
Currently unavailable on CD
Further listening:
While Out Here On My Own (1973) and the following Love And Beauty (1975) have some excellent songs, they lack the carefully-tempered power of Black Bach. They're certainly worth a listen as are any of his earlier Motown, Invictus and Hot Wax sides.
Further reading:
www.lamontdozier.com
Like this?
Try . . . p.289

Roy Harper
Valentine
Folk-rocker's most vivid and enduring collection.

A singular mix of hardcore hippy and unrepentant chauvinist, Harper is a folk singer who effected a superbly bloody-minded rapprochement with rock. Friends like Jimmy Page, Robert Plant, Keith Moon and Ian Anderson crop up on his various records from the early to middle '70s – his great period – and lend a little muscle to music which already had plenty of gristle in it. Harper could write effective protest-cum-political songs, such as the haunting South Africa, but his love songs – battered, intoxicated and helplessly personal – are his finest work. He made clever use of the studio, too: the earlier *Stormcock* was a soloistic tour de force, and his deployment of multi-tracking and reverb, in some ways similar to some of John Martyn's work of the same period, made the records intriguingly individual. But *Valentine* is his warmest and most affecting set.

"I don't know, man, I've listened to a lot of other singers," he said around this time, "but none of them have the burning intensity of my own work." Fair comment, except that Roy's intensity could as easily spill over into embarrassing wrong-headedness. "Equality yes, but when it comes to breast feeding, I just can't make it," he says about the preposterously nasty Magic Woman (Liberation Reshuffle), a completely daft demolition of women's lib; Forbidden Fruit is about sex with 13-year-old schoolgirls ("Sing it smiling with gentle integrity and a knowledge of the real world"). Small wonder that his personal kind of outrage fell out of sight when punk swept in, and although he has continued to make occasional records, he is a tough subject for rehabilitation. Better to remember him for his gorgeous elegies to a pastoral England which was already slipping quickly from view in 1974: Twelve Hours Of Sunset, Commune and above all his astonishingly lovely rendition of North Country, which effortlessly cuts Bob Dylan's version.

Record label:
Harvest
Produced
by Peter Jenner and Roy Harper.
Recorded
in 1974.
Released:
March 1974
Chart peaks:
27 (UK) None (US)
Personnel:
Roy Harper (g, v); Max Middleton (p); Tim Walker, Jimmy Page (g); Pete Sears (b); Keith Moon, Marty Simon (d) John Leckie (e)
Track listing:
Forbidden Fruit; Male Chauvinist Pig Blues; I'll See You Again; Twelve Hours Of Sunset; Acapulco Gold; Commune; Magic Woman (Liberation Reshuffle); Che; North Country; Forever.
Running time:
42.04
Current CD:
Science Friction HUCD015 adds: Home (studio); Too Many Movies; Home (live)
Further listening:
HQ (1998); Flashes From The Archives Of Oblivion (1974)
Further reading:
www.royharper.com
Like this?
Try . . . p.427

Richard And Linda Thompson

I Want To See The Bright Lights Tonight

His emergence as the major folk-rock artist of his generation and hers as the finest interpreter of his songs.

Linda Peters originally met Richard Thompson when she was recording a Kelloggs Cornflakes TV commercial at Sound Techniques studio at the same time Fairport Convention were recording Liege & Lief. She was already a close friend and big fan of Sandy Denny and, always insecure about her own singing, and desperately nervous in front of an audience, reluctant to assume duo status with Richard after they were married.

"I was always amazed by Richard's writing," said Linda. "He was very focused and constantly came up with these incredible songs. People sometimes said I should write more but how could I write when there's Richard in the house turning out all this amazing stuff?"

In fact, the fragile emotions she exuded provided the perfect foil for Richard's songwriting as it took on a new personality, rooted in a cinematic storytelling style and built around vivid, heart-breaking scenarios. If Richard's initial steps into a solo career with *Henry The Human Fly*'s modern take on the folk tradition were tentative and uneasy, he was audibly growing in confidence and flair with Linda as the conduit for his songs. Certainly the title track is a superior kind of pop song – covered as a single by Julie Covington – and the album is full of tracks that have long been accepted as classics by Thompson aficionados, brooding master-pieces like Down Where The Drunkards Roll, The Great Valerio and, most desperate of all, The End Of The Rainbow. Richard had invented a new, thoroughly English style of social commentary. You could see its roots in folk, but ever ready to launch into a blistering guitar solo, this was a modern rock album with a difference. The public didn't quite know what to make of it, setting Richard off on a familiar path of critical acclaim dampened by marketing confu-sion and commercial disappointment. It's been the story of his career ever since.

Record label:
Island
Produced
by John Wood and Richard Thompson.
Released:
April 1974
Chart peaks:
None (UK) None (US)
Personnel:
Richard Thompson (v, g); Linda Thompson (v); John Kirkpatrick (acc, concertina); Richard Harvey (horn, krummhorn); Trevor Lucas (v); Simon Nicol (g, k, v, dulcimer); Roy Wood (v); Timi Donald (d); Pat Donaldson (b); Brian Gulland (v, horn, krummhorn); Royston Wood (v); CWS Silver Band (horns); John Wood (e)
Track listing:
When I Get To The Border; The Calvary Cross; Withered And Died; I Want To See The Bright Lights Tonight; Down Where The Drunkards Roll; We Sing Hallelujah; Has He Got A Friend For Me; The Little Beggar Girl; The End Of The Rainbow; The Great Valerio
Running time:
36.45
Current CD:
IMCD160
Further listening:
Pour Down Like Silver (1975) an awesome study in bleak-ness. Richard's most rounded solo albums, Rumor And Sigh (1991) and Hand Of Kindness (1983).
Further reading:
Richard Thompson: Strange Affair (Patrick Humphries, 1997)
Like this?
Try . . . p.239

10cc

Sheet Music

Clever pop-single craftsmen make great album.

It looked like a novelty. In the glittery early '70s a decidedly unglamorous, denim-clad quartet of pasty-faced Manchester studioniks appeared with Donna, a doo-wop pastiche that sounded like The Beatles' Oh Darling; cartoon falsetto juxtaposed with dark brown bass vocals, limp hair, squinty drummer, moderate hit, goodbye surely? But no: Rubber Bullets, a cheery shuffle about the suppression of prisoners, complete with sadistic jokes ('I love to hear those convicts squeal/It's a shame these slugs ain't real') and super-dumb chorus, was a monster hit. But it was the follow-up – The Dean And I – that pointed the way; hook-stuffed but with an unpredictable structure and a pervading sense of the smarts, it signalled musicians of extraordinary gifts. Their second album, *Sheet Music*, proved they could also riff big, jump-cut into a rumba, harmonise like angels and make awful puns. "The Beach Boys of Good Vibrations; the Beatles of Penny Lane" gushed the Melody Maker, "[It] defies you to label it mere eclecticism, something akin to musical Dada," raved the NME.

The four writers, singers and multi-instrumentalists happily cross-fertilised in various co-composer permutations, attempting to impress each other. Later, it became clearer that this art-pop combo were really Godley/Creme (art) and Gouldman/Stewart (pop) but on *Sheet Music* the union was seamless.

"We had tremendous fun, we couldn't go wrong," remembers Gouldman. "We had to keep ourselves entertained and being the people we were, you couldn't get away with anything. No cliché was allowed unless it was so obvious, we wanted it like that."

The Worst Band In The World, a knowing satire on pop mediocrity, packed more invention into its two and a half minutes than could be found in the entire output of their glam contemporaries. Significantly, that particular Godley/Creme track failed as a single but Stewart/Gouldman's lighter though still relentlessly clever Wall Street Shuffle did the trick.

Gouldman: "We came close to sixth-form humour but it was too smart. Kevin and Loll were better at that than me and Eric but we got infected with it." Though 10cc went on to more elaborate recordings and bigger commercial success, *Sheet Music* represents their artistic peak.

Record label:
UK
Produced
by 10cc.
Recorded
at Strawberry Recording Studios, Stockport, Cheshire; winter 1973–1974.
Released:
May 1974
Chart peaks:
9 (UK) 81 (US)
Personnel:
Lol Creme (v, g, gizmo, p, k); Kevin Godley (v, d, pc); Graham Gouldman (v, b, g); Eric Stewart (v, g, p, k, e, m)
Track listing:
The Wall Street Shuffle; The Worst Band In The World; Hotel; Old Wild Men; Clockwork Creep; Silly Love; Somewhere In Hollywood; Baron Samedi; The Sacro-iliac; Oh Effendi.
Running time:
37.44
Current CD:
Repertoire REP4843WY, adds 18 Carat Man Of Means; Gismo My Way
Further listening:
Original Soundtrack (1975); How Dare You (1976)
Further reading:
The 10CC Story (George Tremlett, 1975); http://welcome.to/10cc www.page27.co.uk/tencc
Like this?
Try . . . p.318

Robert Wyatt
Rock Bottom

His second solo album, and debut for Richard Branson's burgeoning hippy-rock label.

You'd think the title referred, ironically or otherwise, to Wyatt's state of mind following the tragic accident on June 1 1973 – he fell from a fourth-storey window – which left him paraplegic. However, the way Wyatt tells it, the mood was one of euphoria: "One of the things about lying around hospital for a year was that I was free to dream," he remarks today. "I was able to really think through the music. Most musicians are busy thinking about trying to pay their bills. If anything, the title alluded to the sea bed, to sleep and dreams."

Wyatt, to his eternal distress, had been expelled from The Soft Machine in 1970, shortly after cutting *The End Of An Ear*, a patchy avant-garde solo album. He subsequently made two excellent records under the name Matching Mole. But none of those records quite prepared the listener for the vivid inventiveness of this album.

It began life as the third Matching Mole record – and was mostly composed on the Venetian island of Guidecca while Wyatt's partner Alfreda Benge (who drew the cover image) worked as an assistant on director Nic Roeg's thriller Don't Look Now. Wyatt was "spending all day watching lizards on the walls of the house. To keep me occupied Alfreda bought me a basic little keyboard with a particular vibrato that shimmered like the water around us." Returning to London, Wyatt began rehearsing a new band and asked Pink Floyd's drummer, Nick Mason, to produce the record because he wanted to repay a favour. "I had a card from Robert asking me to produce the album about two days before he had his accident," says Mason. "It's one of the things I'm most proud of doing in 30 years of music, and I still find it very moving to listen to." After the accident Wyatt realised that he'd never drum or tour again, but neither would he be tied to one band of musicians. "In a way it gave me a new freedom," he reflects.

The next summer, the Virgin Mobile was tethered in a field outside a borrowed Wiltshire cottage and recording began. "I loved working with Robert," says Mason. "I remember one piece where he played the rhythm on an old tea tray. He was very focused, full of ideas. It's an important album, so personal, with some beautiful songs." Guided by Wyatt's plaintive Olde-England croon, the album's impressionistic drift had no precedent in the art-rock canon and has remained inimitable.

Record label:
Virgin
Produced
by Nick Mason.
Recorded
at The Manor, Oxfordshire and Mobile studio at Delphina's Farm, Little Bedwyn Wiltshire; February–March 1974.
Released:
July 26, 1974
Chart peaks:
None (UK) None (US)
Personnel:
Robert Wyatt (v, k, g, "James's drum"); Richard Sinclair (b); Laurie Allan (d); Hugh Hopper (b); Ivor Cutler (v); Mongezi Feza (t); Alfreda Benge (v); Gary Windo (bass clarinet tenor); Fred Frith (va); Mike Oldfield (g)
Track listing:
Sea Song; A Last Straw; Little Red Riding Hood Hit The Road; Alifib; Alife; Little Red Robin Hood Hit The Road
Running time:
39.34
Current CD:
HNCD 1426
Further listening:
Ruth Is Stranger Than Richard (1975); Nothing Can Stop Us – compilation (1982)
Further reading:
MOJO 64; www.strongcomet.com/wyatt
Like this?
Try . . . p.406

Average White Band

Average White Band

Average? Not hardly.

By early 1974 Average White Band seemed to have blown it. Their first album for MCA, *Show Your Hand*, had bombed. Their second was handed back to them unreleased. It looked grim. For about a week. Then they met Atlantic Records co-founder Jerry Wexler. He loved the songs on their MCA tape and by April they were at Criteria Studios, Miami, looking on bemused while soul immortals Wexler, Tom Dowd and Arif Mardin decided which of them should produce the revamped album. Eventually, they decamped to New York with Mardin. Seasoned pros permanently enraptured by James Brown, Donny Hathaway, Marvin Gaye and other soul greats, they responded eagerly.

"Arif was lovely, the bee's knees, he cared so much about what we were doing," says Hamish Stuart. "Even the engineer Gene Paul (Les Paul's son) got right behind us." Duly encouraged, they nailed it: the discipline, the ease, the funk. Although the songs on the second vinyl side were less strong, the band were all firing – viz Stuart's soaring falsetto on Person To Person, the booty-shaking architecture of Onnie McIntyre's guitar solo on The Isley Brothers' Work To Do, the judder of Alan Gorrie's bass on Got The Love, the saxmen's moan-and-thrust riffs and Robbie McIntosh's snap-crackle drumming throughout. However, to general surprise, the instrumental Pick Up The Pieces stood out. "The MCA version was like The JBs' Pass The Peas," says Stuart. "But we dug deeper, found an innovative groove. The moment we finished it we were all hysterically dancing round the room. Playing it back we just thought, 'God, that's us!'" But Stuart reckons it took him 20 years to digest subsequent events: "A surreal time. I've only recently started writing some songs about it." That September, at a showbiz party after a Los Angeles Troubadour gig, McIntosh died of "a strychnine-based heroin overdose" thinking he was snorting cocaine. Then, with the band in a hopeless spin, Pick Up The Pieces took off via black radio, crashing straight through the "blue-eyed soul" jibes. They all moved to the States and prospered until the early '80s. And if they needed further vindication the sampling era provided it as their records were repeatedly plundered by rap-R&B artists including TLC, Ice Cube and Utah Saints – an enduring tribute to McIntosh.

"Robbie strapped us to the groove," says Stuart. "He understood it better than any of us. He had an arranger's mind. He was the catalyst. It wouldn't have happened without him."

Record label:
Atlantic
Produced
by Arif Mardin.
Recorded
at Criteria Sound Studios, Miami, Florida; Atlantic Recording Studios, New York; April–May, 1974.
Released:
July 1974
Chart peaks:
6 (UK) 1 (US)
Personnel:
Alan Gorrie (v, b, g); Hamish Stuart (v, g, b); Roger Ball (k, s); Onnie McIntyre (g); Malcolm 'Molly' Duncan (s); Robbie McIntosh (d); Gene Paul (e)
Track listing:
You Got It; Got The Love; Pick Up The Pieces (S); Person To Person; Work To Do; Nothing You Can Do (S); Just Wanna Love You Tonight; Keepin' It To Myself; I Just Can't Give You Up; There's Always Someone Waiting
Running time:
40.24
Current CD:
CCSCD438
Further listening:
Soul Searching (1976) – decent follow-up
Further reading:
www.averagewhiteband.com
Like this?
Try . . . p.639

Neil Young
On The Beach

Young dreamily combines personal and political horror and creates his masterpiece. But nobody gets it.

In 1974, Crosby, Stills, Nash & Young reformed for one of the biggest arena tours of the decade. Halfway through, cunning plan or not, with no new CSNY album available Young put out his own LP. *On The Beach*, he told Rolling Stone, was "probably one of the most depressing records I've ever made", a statement with which most of the reviews at the time (NME – "It's a downer") concurred. Then, as he pointed out some years later, "It was only a reflection of what I was going through at the time." Things like divorce, death, dealing with celebrity, and the demise of the hippy dream.

Though closer examination would reveal more positive, cathartic aspects and even sparks of dark humour, this was as raw an album as Young had made. Since separating from actress Carrie Snodgress, Young had moved south from his Northern California ranch to his house in Malibu, on the beach, before making this record, on which neighbours Rick Danko and Levon Helm helped out. It wasn't just the estrangement that was occupying his thoughts, nor the fact that their son Zeke had been diagnosed as suffering from cerebral palsy, though these no doubt added to the prevalent feeling of paranoia and decay.

One theme – somewhat incongruous, perhaps, given his decision to rejoin the mammoth CSNY – was the hollowness of stardom, in addition to the decline of American culture – although unnamed, Charles Manson (whom Young knew prior to the Family murder, having met the budding singer-songwriter at Beach Boy Dennis Wilson's house) and kidnapped heiress-turned-revolutionary Patty Hearst feature in the songs Revolution Blues and Ambulance Blues.

When Young tried to add some of these songs to the CSN&Y set he met resistance – outright refusal when it came to the Manson-inspired number; what David Crosby would have called "a bummer". Vampire Blues had more of a note of resigned optimism: "Good times are coming," Young sang, "but they sure are coming slow," while the epic title track was a lament for Young as much as a lament for his adopted country.

It was a therapeutic album, signalling Young's emergence from a dark night of the soul, and analysing his past like a man three times his age, offering a fresh perspective on his future. Thankfully, the album was critically "rediscovered" quite soon. One month after the NME's negative review, assistant editor Ian MacDonald wrote: "*On The Beach* isn't, as previously interpreted, the fag-end of Neil Young's romance with rejection but actually a quite positive piece of work in the Merciless Realism bracket of Lennon's primal-scream period."

Record label:
Reprise
Produced
by Neil Young with co-production from David Briggs, Mark Harman and Al Schmitt.
Recorded
at Sunset Sound, Hollywood and Broken Arrow Studios, San Francisco; 1974.
Released:
July 1974
Chart peaks:
42 (UK) 16 (US)
Personnel:
Neil Young (g, v, banjo, hm); Ben Keith (sg, p, bv); Billy Talbot (b); Ralph Molina (d); Tim Drummond (b, pc); Levon Helm (d); David Crosby (g); Rick Danko (b); George Whitsell (g); Graham Nash (p, hm, tambourine); Rusty Kershaw (sg)
Track listing:
Walk On (S); See The Sky About To Rain; Revolution Blues; For The Turnstiles; Vampire Blues; On The Beach; Motion Pictures; Ambulance Blues
Running time:
39.00
Currently unavailable on CD
Further listening:
Tonight's The Night (1975); Sleeps With Angels (1995)
Further reading:
MOJO 10, 25, 44; Neil Young: Here We Are In The Years (1982);
www.bosco.net/human-highway
www.neilyoung.com
Like this?
Try . . . p.512

Blue Öyster Cult

Secret Treaties

'Heavy-metal' before it got speedy. The working title was Power In The Hands Of Fools.

Think Blue Öyster Cult and you inevitably think Don't Fear The Reaper. Great as that track was, there was much more to this inventive troupe. As this fine album attests.

"Personally, *Secret Treaties* is my favourite BÖC album," says Eric Bloom. "I was the only one who was single, so I did a lot of writing on it."

In 1974, the Blue Öyster Cult had a communal house/rehearsal den on Long Island, New York where Bloom composed the music for Subhuman and ME 262. By the time recording started at Columbia's 30th Street studio, though, BÖC's third album was shaping-up as the usual team-effort: outside influences included Lanier's girlfriend Patti Smith, whose *Poem Of Isadore Ducasse* inspired Career Of Evil, and Richard Meltzer, a former scribe for music magazine Crawdaddy, who supplied the Dada-esque lyric for Harvester Of Eyes. Co-producer Sandy Pearlman was BÖC's Svengali-figure. Like Meltzer, he'd written for Crawdaddy, but he'd also been instrumental in BÖC's inception, coined the term 'heavy-metal' to describe their music, and given 'Buck Dharma' his nickname.

"Sandy would basically be the judge," says Donald Roeser. "There were a lot of ideas flying around for the album, so we needed somebody to be the Fuhrer."

The album's undoubted stand-out was Astronomy, its music written and arranged by the Bouchard brothers. The lyrics came from Imaginos, an epic poem Pearlman had written back in the '60s, and according to the fanzine Morning Final, the song's memorable chorus riff was inspired by Mick Ronson's work on Bowie's Panic In Detroit. When Metallica were looking for a BÖC song to cover on 1998's *Garage Inc.*, Astronomy was the obvious choice.

Upon its release, the album's sado-masochistic lyrics and a sleeve which pictured BÖC with a German ME 262 fighter-jet drew allegations of neo-Nazism. Bloom and Pearlman – both Jewish – thought this unlikely. Melody Maker's readers voted *Secret Treaties* Top Rock Album Of All Time in 1975. *Agents Of Fortune* would catapult the band to stadium-status.

Record label:
Columbia
Produced
by Murray Krugman and Sandy Pearlman.
Recorded
at Columbia Studios, New York
Released:
September 1974
Chart peaks:
None (UK) 53 (US)
Personnel:
Donald 'Buck Dharma' Roeser (g,v); Eric Bloom (g, v, k); Albert Bouchard (d,v); Joe Bouchard (b,v); Alan Lanier (k, g); Tim Geelan (e)
Track listing:
Career Of Evil (S/US); Subhuman; Dominance And Submission; ME262; Cagey Cretins; Harvester Of Eyes; Flaming Telepaths; Astronomy
Running time:
38.28
Current CD:
468 018 2
Further listening:
Tyranny And Mutation (1973)
Further reading:
www.blueoystercult.com; http://members.aol.com/bocfaqman/
Like this?
Try . . . p.359

Supertramp

Crime Of The Century

Pop-prog rockers regroup, rethink and create a concept album that propels them towards stadium stardom.

By 1973 Supertramp had made two lacklustre albums and spent their time "bombing up and down the M1 in a Transit and playing Johnny B. Goode as an encore," according to Rick Davies. The band's financial backer, a Dutch millionaire called Stanley Miesegacs, announced he wanted to cut his losses. Their label, A&M, was also losing faith, but after Davies and Hodgson replaced the other band members, the company agreed to fund a stay at a Somerset farm where a new album would be created.

"This was the first time something had clicked," recalls Hodgson. "We knew we had a band, not just a hotch-potch of styles, and the music was working." Many of the players remember *Crime Of The Century* as the most enjoyable Supertramp record to make. An unknown and uncredited street musician played saw on Hide. For Rudy the band went to Paddington Station to tape the sound of trains, and to Leicester Square for crowd noises.

The album addresses the same themes of loneliness and lunacy that the Pink Floyd had tackled on *Dark Side Of The Moon* the year before. But it is only a concept album "in the loosest sense", says Hodgson. "There was a link from School to the opening line of Bloody Well Right, 'So you think you're schooling's phoney', and that's about as far as we took it. Listeners could take it further if they wanted." The music mixed the ambition and scale of prog rock with Hodgson's instinctive feel for a poppy melody, which drew in listeners who steered well clear of King Crimson or Gentle Giant's knottier constructions.

When Supertramp toured that year they played the first side in order, then newer songs that would later appear on *Crisis? What Crisis?* before ending with side two and no encore. "It was like a house catching fire, it just clicked with audiences," says Davies. "It was a magical time because before then we had only known absolute failure." With Dreamer becoming a British hit single, Supertramp's rise to the top had begun and their Dutch uncle, somewhat to his surprise, would soon get his £60,000 investment back.

Record label:
A&M
Produced
by Ken Scott and Supertramp.
Recorded
at Trident, Ramport Studios and Scorpio Sound, London; February–June 1974.
Released:
September 1974
Chart peaks:
4 (UK) 38 (US)
Personnel:
Roger Hodgson (v, g, p); Rick Davies (v, k, hm); John Helliwell (s, clarinet, v); Dougie Thomson (b); Bob Siebenberg (d); Ken Scott and John Jansen (e)
Track listing:
School; Bloody Well Right (S/US); Hide In Your Shell; Asylum; Dreamer (S/UK); Rudy; If Everyone Was Listening; Crime Of The Century
Running time:
44.10
Current CD:
393 647-2
Further listening:
Crises? What Crises? (1975); Even In The Quietest Moments (1977); Breakfast In America (1979) sees the band hit commercial peak.
Further reading:
MOJO 44; www.supertramp.com
Like this?
Try . . . p.459

Millie Jackson

Caught Up

Potent combo of lubricious talk and deep soul.

By 1973, Millie Jackson had tired of the men directing her recording career. She'd moved to Spring Records, had R&B hits with My Man Is A Sweet Man (a 1972 UK Number 50) and Hurt So Good (taken from the film Cleopatra Jones), but the positive reaction to her live performances – where she told down'n'dirty real-life stories between songs – suggested her audience could take something stronger, more in keeping with that saltier stage self.

"I had been doing If Loving You Is Wrong [with a long, spoken intro] for quite some time. So I just recorded what I had been doing live." Introducing material with a rap, in its pre-hip hop meaning of dialogue, had been a strong staple of soul music since the '60s, with Joe Tex and Isaac Hayes being particularly adept. In her rap on this song, Jackson sets up the story of a woman who realises that her relationship with a married man is at a critical stage: Will he or won't he leave his wife and kids for a life with her?

On the album's second side, Jackson reverses the viewpoint and takes the role of the 'wronged' wife in It's All Over But The Shouting, Bobby Womack's I'm Through Trying To Prove My Love To You and, an unexpected but effective choice, Bobby Goldsboro's Summer (The First Time), in which she sets up the sequel by reminiscing about the good times. Jackson had been impressed by the way Marvin Gaye segued tracks on *What's Going On*. She took the device further to build two complete stories for soul's first truly effective concept album.

Though *Still Caught Up*, the follow-up, is at least as good (and Jackson herself preferred it), the element of groundbreaking surprise gives *Caught Up* the slight advantage. Soon, raps by women soul singers from the point of view of wife or mistress or aimed at philandering male, proliferated. Millie's own style coarsened down the years, expletives went undeleted and the pursuit of outrage seemed to outweigh her pursuit of good material (*Back To The Sh*t* which pictured her on the lavatory, panties round her ankles, was a bit of a low point). But at her peak Jackson was one of the most distinctive and inventive of all soul performers, someone whose music really connected with its audience.

Record label:
Polydor
Produced
by Brad Shapiro and Millie Jackson.
Recorded
at Muscle Shoals Sound, Alabama and Criteria Studios, Miami.
Released:
October 1974
Chart peaks:
None (UK) 21 (US)
Personnel:
Jimmy Johnson, Pete Carr (g); Barry Beckett (k); David Hood (b); Roger Hawkins (d); Tom Roady, Brad Shapiro (pc); Mike Lewis, Brad Shapiro (oa)
Track listing:
If Loving You Is Wrong I Don't Want To Be Right; The Rap; If Loving You Is Wrong I Don't Want To Be Right (Reprise); All I Want Is A Fighting Chance; I'm Tired Of Hiding; It's All Over But The Shouting; It's Easy Going; I'm Through Trying To Prove My Love To You; Summer (The First Time)
Running time:
33.23
Current CD:
CDSEWM003
Further listening:
The rest of her "cheatin' trilogy": Still Caught Up (1975) and Free And In Love (1976). She starts to get saucier on Feelin' Bitchy (1978)
Further reading:
www.davidnathan.com/millie.htm
Like this?
Try . . . p.647

King Crimson

Red

Studio swansong from the most radical Crimson line-up.

Of the '70s Crimson albums, *Red* has endured best, even resonating with some of the pioneers of grunge – Kurt Cobain among them. But the record was made in what Bill Bruford remembers as "excruciating" circumstances. The original five-piece line-up had shrunk after the departures of, firstly, percussionist Jamie Muir, then violinist David Cross, worn down by the rigours of a punishing touring schedule and a live show that relied heavily on intense improvisation.

As the trio entered the studio morale was mixed; both Wetton and Bruford believed that the band was about to make a quantum leap into Top 10 success, as the Floyd had just done. Fripp, however, had been growing tired of trying to play intricate rock-jazz fusions to arena crowds who had come to boogie. He also felt that his free-wheeling rhythm section was crowding him out. Then, the night before the sessions, the guitarist read a text by the mystical thinker J.G. Bennett that plunged him into spiritual turmoil.

"I had a glimpse of something – the top of my head blew off," he recalled later. In the studio the band leader found himself unable to function normally. Bruford says: "Robert had 'decided to withhold the passing of my opinion' which meant you'd do a take and you'd say, 'What did you think, Robert?' Nothing, nothing at all. He had decided the way to Nirvana was not to express an opinion – and it seemed to me that John Wetton and I more or less moved his hand about on the fretboard."

Fripp's head blown off or not, the results are remarkable. The angular guitar of the title track defined an avant-metal style that Fripp would come to revive years later. Providence gives a glimpse of the band's live power, while the epic Starless with its furious instrumental section and soaring reprise recalls the grandeur of the first line-up. But with the sessions over, Fripp unilaterally declared the band was finished. Announcing his disillusionment with the rock musician's lifestyle he went to a spiritual retreat – to the exasperation of fellow band members. But maybe Fripp's timing was right – *Red* is that rarest of records, the sound of a line-up quitting while ahead.

Record label:
Island
Produced
by King Crimson.
Recorded
at Olympic Sound Studios, London; July–August 1974. Providence recorded live at Palace Theatre, Providence, Rhode Island; June 30, 1974.
Released:
October 1974
Chart peaks:
45 (UK) None (US)
Personnel:
Robert Fripp (g, Mellotron); John Wetton (b, v); Bill Bruford (d); David Cross (vn), Mel Collins, Ian McDonald (s); Robin Miller (oboe); Marc Charig (cornet); George Chkiantz (e)
Track listing:
Red; Fallen Angel; One More Red Nightmare; Providence; Starless
Running time:
40.05
Current CD:
EGCD15
Further listening:
The posthumous Great Deceiver (1989) box set is the best document of the line-up's live ingenuity.
Further reading:
MOJO 73
Like this?
Try . . . p.387

The Raspberries

Starting Over

Last and greatest album by terminally misunderstood US power popsters.

When The Raspberries converged upon New York's Record Plant with longtime producer Jimmy Ienner to record *Starting Over*, they sported a new line-up and a new direction. Bassist Dave Smalley and drummer Jim Bonfanti were out, replaced, respectively, by Scott McCarl and Michael McBride. Musically, although their obsession with classic '60s pop raged unabated, they were out to shed their teenybopper image. Gone were the matching white suits, likewise the gimmicky album covers (which had contained raspberry puns, photos of raspberries, even a raspberrry-scented scratch'n'sniff sticker).

The effort to assume a more mature face was driven at least in part by lead guitarist Wally Bryson. He had almost followed Smalley and Bonfanti out of the group, but Ienner convinced him to stay. "My condition was that Eric had to be real," Bryson later recalled. "What had always been happening was that Eric would want our songs to sound like The Beach Boys, The Who or The Beatles. He'd say, 'Play a Who drum roll there, or play a Townshend guitar riff here.' I wanted us to be The Raspberries."

Perhaps Bryson was still smarting from the distant indignity of having to get two haircuts before Carmen would let him join the group. Carmen, for his part, felt persecuted, as he told a reporter in 1975: "When you're trying to write to please four people instead of yourself, it's very strange. It's very difficult to convince the public that you believe in yourself when half the band doesn't even believe in what you're doing."

The album is a shining example of what evangelists call 'the sandpaper ministry': the opposing forces sanded down one another's imperfections to a heavenly sheen, creating a result that was probably finer than any of them had in mind. Not that the group's intentions were purely artistic. They laid out their ambitions on the album's leadoff track, Overnight Sensation (Hit Record). The song barely made it into the US Top 20, however, and *Starting Over* sold poorly.

The Raspberries disbanded less than six months after the album's release, leaving a gap on hit radio that would not be filled until the power pop movement that they helped inspire took flight. McCarl spoke for many fans when he later told a reporter, "I see The Raspberries as the American Badfinger, carrying on soon after The Beatles when it really wasn't in vogue to do it with that same three minute pop song thing."

Record label:
Capitol
Produced
by Jimmy Ienner.
Recorded
at The Record Plant, New York City; April 1974.
Released:
October 1974
Chart peaks:
None (UK) 143 (US)
Personnel:
Eric Carmen (k, g, v); Wally Bryson (g, v); Scott McCarl (b, v); Michael McBride (d, v)
Track listing:
Overnight Sensation (Hit Record) (S); Play On; Party's Over (S); I Don't Know What I Want; Rose Coloured Glasses; All Through The Night; Cruisin' Music; I Can Hardly Believe You're Mine; Cry; Hands On You; Starting Over
Running time:
40.05
Current CD:
RPM 163 re-released as Power Pop, Volume 2; includes Starting Over and its predecessor, Side 3
Further listening:
The Raspberries' first two albums, The Raspberries (1972) and Fresh (1972), are available on a single disc, Power Pop, Volume One.
Further reading:
www.raspberries.net
Like this?
Try . . . p.384

Queen

Sheer Heart Attack

Imaginative third album triumph for over-the-top pop rockers.

The first couple of albums-worth of Queen's brand of densely layered, fantastical, post-Zeppelin heavy pop had met with vicious critical resistance ("the dregs of glam rock" went one review, "a bucket of stale urine" another), though the band were gradually finding a loyal audience. Their sonically flamboyant, elaborately arranged *Queen II* had yielded a Number 10 hit with Seven Seas Of Rye, but Brian May later admitted the album had perhaps "dished up too much for people to swallow". Having already cancelled a US tour due to May's arm infection, when he fell ill again during the initial sessions for *Sheer Heart Attack*, he worried that the band would replace him with another guitarist. However, with May's unique multi-layered contributions an intrinsic part of Queen's signature, the band carried on recording leaving space for his guitar parts which, when recuperated, he filled with powerful relish in an intense two week solo session – the guitar part on Killer Queen alone taking several days and 12 overdubs.

Much of the album continued to effectively combine and juxtapose extreme bombast (Brighton Rock – May's tour-de-force of stereo echo, Flick Of The Wrist – classic Mercury bile, Now I'm Here – May's parade of chunky riffs) with melodic delicacy (Lily Of The Valley – Mercury in mythological quest mode, Dear Friends – May's funeral hymn). However, the humour – whether heavy rock'n'roll (Stone Cold Crazy), ingenious banjo-driven '30s pastiche (Bring Back That Leroy Brown) – introduced a lighter touch that opened many ears, not least in Mercury's Killer Queen, a delightfully camp and amazingly inventive piece about a high-class whore.

"You almost expect Noel Coward to sing it," said Freddie. "It's one of those bowler hat, black suspender belt numbers – not that Noel would wear that." Suffering from restrictive management and deep suspicion from the press (they had a resistance to Freddie's showiness which an outrageous chest wig on the album's cover probably didn't assist in overcoming), reaching Number 2 in the UK with Killer Queen was a serious boost for the band.

May: "It was the turning point. It was the song that best summed up our kind of music and a big hit. And we desperately needed it as a mark of something successful happening to us."

Record label:
EMI
Produced
by Roy Thomas Baker and Queen.
Recorded
at Trident, Wessex, Rockfield and Air Studios; July–September 1974.
Released:
November 8, 1974
Chart peaks:
2 (UK) 12 (US)
Personnel:
Roger Taylor (d, v); Freddie Mercury (v, p); John Deacon (b, ag); Brian May (g, p, banjo)
Track listing:
Brighton Rock; Killer Queen; Tenement Funster; Flick Of The Wrist; Lily Of The Valley; Now I'm Here; In The Lap Of The Gods; Stone Cold Crazy; Dear Friends; Misfire; Bring Back That Leroy Brown; She Makes Me (Stormtrooper In Stilettos); In The Lap Of The Gods (Revisited)
Running time:
39.09
Current CD:
CDPCSD129
Further listening:
Queen II (1974); Night At The Opera (1975); Day At The Races (1976)
Further reading:
MOJO 69; Mercury (1996); Good Vibrations: A History Of Record Production (1996); www.queen-fip.com
Like this?
Try . . . p.829

Genesis

The Lamb Lies Down On Broadway

Eccentric English prog-rockers hit NYC.

Genesis's 1973 offering *Selling England By The Pound*, along with the minor hit I Know What I Like (In Your Wardrobe), had further established them as a vital and creative unit but they remained maverick outsiders of the progressive scene because of their continued focus on songwriting. For the next project, however, they wanted to pursue a concept and Peter Gabriel's idea of the semi-autobiographical, allegorical adventures of Puerto Rican New York street punk Rael was voted best idea. Gabriel has admitted that band democracy at this stage was "bullshit on my part, as there was only one story I was going to pursue", and further insisted on writing all the lyrics himself.

The band decamped to Led Zeppelin's rat-infested rehearsal cottage. Collins: "It was horrible, we spent three months in there driving each other crazy." Meanwhile, Gabriel, already feeling stifled by group life and suffering from his wife's infidelity with a close friend, temporarily left the band to pursue a vague film offer from William "The Exorcist" Friedkin but when it came to nothing "returned to a very murky reception," as he remembered. The band, by this time, had written a double album's worth of good music and Gabriel was way behind with the lyrics. Banks: "I felt we were separated at that point really." Hackett was not happy either: *The Lamb* happened despite me, not with me. I really felt it was indulgent and I couldn't get to grips with it or contribute something great in the guitar sense."

The ensuing double album remains Genesis's most controversial. Melody Maker's Chris Welch complained that they should "learn the importance of self-editing", but though extravagantly detailed, dense and difficult to follow, *The Lamb* is much more fun than it's often given credit for. The music is playful. Gabriel is a compelling central presence, the whole bubbles with good things, some (In The Cage, Carpet Crawlers) among the highest achievements in the Genesis oeuvre. After 102 live performances Gabriel left, sick of the rock life and the internal resentment (as he perceived it) of the attention he received as front man. Genesis went on to conquer the world with Phil Collins as lead vocalist.

Record label:
Charisma
Produced
by John Burns and Genesis.
Recorded
at Glosspant, Wales with the Island Mobile, mixed at Island, London; August–October 1974.
Release date:
November 1974
Chart peaks:
10 (UK) 41 (US)
Personnel:
Tony Banks (k); Steve Hackett (g); Phil Collins (d, v, pc); Peter Gabriel (v, flute); Michael Rutherford (b, 12 string); Brian Eno ('Enossification'); David Hutchins (e)
Track listing:
The Lamb Lies Down On Broadway; Fly On A Windshield; Broadway Melody Of 1974; Cuckoo Cocoon; In The Cage; The Grand Parade Of Lifeless Packaging; Back In N.Y.C; Hairless Heart; Counting Out Time; Carpet Crawlers; The Chamber Of 32 Doors; Lilywhite Lilith; The Waiting Room; Anyway; Here Comes The Supernatural Anaesthetist; The Lamia; Silent Sorrow In Empty Boats; The Colony Of Slipperman (Arrival, A Visit To The Doktor, Raven); Ravine; The Light Dies Down On Broadway; Riding The Scree; In The Rapids; It
Running time:
94.12
Current CD:
CGSCDX1
Further listening:
For a terrific 1975 live version, check Archive (1998)
Further reading:
www.genesis-path.com
Like this?
Try . . . p.499

Dr Feelgood

Down By The Jetty

Scorching live act's debut gives pub rock a good name, inspiring punk along the way.

By the early '70s the blues seemed to have run out of puff. After a decade of civil rights activity, young blacks were turning their backs on an idiom associated with slavery days, while white bands had sentenced the music to death by guitar solo. In late 1974 four distinctly seedy looking saviours swaggered off their Canvey Island home on the Thames Estuary, to produce a back to basics R&B album which helped revitalise the form, and at the same time laid the foundations of a further revolution. After a year of garnering rave gig reviews at the vanguard of the pub rock movement, Dr Feelgood went into the studio with The Who's *Live At Leeds* engineer Vic Maile.

"A beautiful guy," recalls guitarist and songwriter Wilko Johnson. "He was the only person who called to ask how I was after the band bust-up in 1977. But we had terrible arguments during the recording. I was inexperienced and a bit cocky and I said, 'Can't we all play and you stick up a microphone?'"

Drummer, John 'The Big Figure' Martin remembers: "I was a bit disappointed. I was a struggling musician and wanted the whole studio bit, but Wilko wouldn't do any overdubs, so the tracks seemed a bit thin on stereo playbacks."

"It was never our intention to be deliberately Luddite releasing it as a mono mix," claims Wilko. "In fact I thought we were a very forward looking band, it just sounded better that way." Lee Brilleaux's gritty vocalisms and Sparks' and Martin's solid but agile rhythm section played their part. But it was Johnson's extraordinary, cubist, simultaneous rhythm and lead playing which provided the main thrust. ("I tried to copy The Pirates' Mick Green, but got it wrong!") The inexorable drive of She Does It Right, the industrial, quasi-bluebeat of Roxette, the choppy, soul-funk of Keep It Out Of Sight each possessed a visceral impetus which seemed to point a way ahead. Gary Valentine of Blondie confirms this: he recalls attending a 1975 New York party with Johnny Thunders, Richard Hell, Talking Heads and the Ramones among others. "*Down By The Jetty* was played over and over. Dr Feelgood inspired everyone there that night to go on."

Record label:
United Artists
Produced
by Vic Maile.
Recorded
at Rockfield Studios, Monmouth; August 26–September 1 and November 25–27, 1974; Jackson's Studios, Rickmansworth; September 23, 1974; Dingwall's, London; July 8, 1974 (live recording).
Released:
December 1974
Chart peaks:
None (UK) None (US)
Personnel:
Lee Brilleaux (v, hm); Wilko Johnson (g, v, k); John B 'Sparko' Sparks (b); John 'The Big Figure' Martin (d, pc); Barry Andrews (k, s); Brinsley Schwarz (s)
Track listing:
She Does It Right (S/UK); Boom Boom; The More I Give; Roxette (S/UK); One Weekend; That Ain't The Way To Behave; I Don't Mind; Twenty Yards Behind; Keep It Out Of Sight; All Through The City; Cheque Book; Oyeh; Bonie Moronie; Tequila
Running time:
40.51
Current CD:
GRANDCD05
Further listening:
Malpractice (1975); Stupidity (1976) (a superb live album, Number 1 in Britain); Solid Senders by Wilko Johnson's Solid Senders (1978); Going Back Home (Wilko Johnson, 1998); Wilko was also with Ian Dury And The Blockheads for the album Laughter.
Further listening:
Down By The Jetty (1997)
Like this?
Try . . . p.839

Gene Clark

No Other

Taking singer-songwriter rock to its logical extreme, one of the most extravagant productions of the era.

Despite his wonderful work with The Byrds, Gene Clark was always one of rock's most frustrating underachievers. He quit The Byrds just as they were reaching new peaks with his composition Eight Miles High, completed one of the first LA singer-songwriter albums and pioneered country rock, but never received the recognition he deserved.

Maybe it was his reluctance to tour, but his solo albums failed to sell, leaving him in a precarious position in the early '70s. The Byrds' 1973 reunion album provided a much-needed spotlight for his songwriting talents, and although the work was panned on release most critics acknowledged the quality of Clark's contributions. Asylum founder and starmaker David Geffen was sufficiently impressed to offer Clark the chance of a lifetime with a big budget album. Producer Thomas Jefferson Kaye approached the project like a man possessed and boasted of recording an album that resembled a cross between The Beatles' *Sgt. Pepper* and Brian Wilson's *Pet Sounds/Smile*. Clark was living in pastoral bliss in Mendocino and, while looking over the ocean, composed a series of strange but arresting songs, quite unlike anything he had previously written.

"I was strongly influenced at that time by two other artistes," he explained. "Stevie Wonder's *Innervisions* and The Rolling Stones' *Goat's Head Soup*. When I was writing *No Other* I concentrated on those albums a lot, and was very inspired by the direction of them – which is ironic because *Innervisions* is a very climbing, spiritual thing, while *Goat's Head Soup* has connotations of the lower forces as well. But somehow the joining of the two gave me a place to go with *No Other*, and I wanted it to go in a powerful direction."

Clark crafted an intriguing fusion that includes gospel, country and choral, music and has a rich, cinematic feel. It should have elevated Clark to a new standing in the rock marketplace, but sales were disastrous. Thereafter, Clark was consigned to the cult fringe and increasingly dependent on questionable money-spinning reunions with former Byrds colleagues. He was bitterly disappointed by the commercial failure of *No Other*. Some reckon he never fully recovered from the blow. The great album remains scandalously unavailable on CD in either the US or UK and cries out for reappraisal.

Record label:
Asylum
Produced
by Thomas Jefferson Kaye.
Recorded
at The Village Recorder, West Los Angeles; early 1974.
Released:
January 1975
Chart peaks:
None (UK) None (US)
Personnel:
Gene Clark (v, g); Lee Sklar (b); Butch Trucks (d); Russ Kunkel (d); Michael Utley (p); Craig Doerge (k); Joe Lala (p); Richard Greene (vn); Chris Hillman (mandolin); Ted Machell (c); Bill Cuomo (o); Jerry McGee (g); Danny Kootch (g); Jesse Ed Davis (g); Steve Bruton (g); Buzzy Feiten (g); Tony Reale (e); Joe Tuzen (ae)
Track listing:
Life's Greatest Fool (S); Silver Raven; No Other; Strength Of Strings; From A Silver Phial; Some Misunderstanding; The True One; Lady Of The North
Running time:
39.00
Current CD:
AMC Y6066
Further listening:
Gene Clark With The Gosdin Brothers (1967); White Light (1971); Two Sides To Every Story (1976)
Further reading:
The Byrds: Timeless Flight Revisited (1997)
Like this?
Try . . . p.334

Led Zeppelin

Physical Graffiti

Led Zeppelin's first for their nascent label, Swan Song, was preceded by over one million advance orders.

Almost eighteen months in the making, *Physical Graffiti* began life in November 1973, when the band moved en masse into Headley Grange in Hampshire. They started work just as Jimmy Page was finishing up his music for Lucifer Rising, a film by Kenneth Anger, who shared Page's interest in the occult. Then, after a bout of illness, John Paul Jones announced to manager Peter Grant that he was seriously thinking about giving it all up to be the choirmaster at Winchester Cathedral. Grant told him to take a few weeks off to think it over. Recording was postponed until the following February, a month after the band announced the formation of Swan Song Records.

Finally, after the delays, and skirmishes over the album's sleeve art – which originally sported images of Aliester Crowley, Lee Harvey Oswald and two photos of the band in drag – Led Zeppelin returned to rock's frontlines with their most ambitious work ever, spanning genres, tempos, and once again contrasting bombastic, rock-solid tunes alongside folksy spiritual quests. Page had been contemplating putting out a double-disc for some time and went on a scavenger hunt in the band's vaults, unearthing outtakes from their previous albums and grafting them to the band's more recent compositions, giving a sprawling view of what they were capable of.

At the height of their powers, and already wearing the thorny crown of rock legends, Graffiti exposes Led Zeppelin's more human side. For instance during the recording of In My Time of Dying you can hear drummer John Bonham coughing and then saying, "That's going to be the one, isn't it?" Also left in the mix are the sounds of a supersonic jet in Black Country Woman, and then the phrase "We gotta leave the airplane in."

Jimmy Page simply explains it by saying, "We were in that frame of mind in those days. That album's really good because we were having a long run working as a band, and it really shows. We had this beautiful freedom that we could try anything, do anything, which was what the beauty of how the band was, and how the music was made as opposed to how things are today. A band today has to constantly try to keep its head above water."

Within two weeks of its release *Graffiti* was perched at the top of the US charts, (reportedly selling over 500 copies an hour at one point), pulling all of the band's previous five albums in its wake, back onto the Billboard album charts, making them the first band ever to have six albums on the Top 200. In the UK it was a more modest success, enjoying just one week at the top.

JU

Record label:
Swan Song/Atlantic
Produced
by Jimmy Page.
Recorded
at Ronnie Lane's Mobile at Headley Grange, the Rolling Stones' Mobile and Olympic Studios, London; November1973–July 1974.
Released:
February 25, 1975
Chart peaks:
1 (UK) 1 (US)
Personnel:
Jimmy Page (g); Robert Plant (v, hm); John Paul Jones (b, k, mellotron); John Bonham (d); Ian Stewart (p); Eddie Kramer, George Chkiantz, Andy Johns, Ron Nevison (e); Peter Grant (executive producer)
Track listing:
Custard Pie; The Rover; In My Time Of Dying; Houses Of The Holy; Trampled Underfoot (S/US); Kashmir; In The Light; Bron-Yr-Aur; Down By The Seaside; Ten Years Gone; Night Flight; Wanton Song, The; Boogie With Stu; Black Country Woman; Sick Again
Running time:
82.15
Current CD:
7567924422
Further listening:
Led Zeppelin Remasters (1990) – the 54-track compilation pulls material from the nine studio albums, with some previously unreleased stuff.
Further reading:
Hammer Of The Gods: The Led Zeppelin Saga (Stephen Davis, 1985); www.led-zeppelin.com
Like this?
Try . . . p.448

Bob Dylan

Blood On The Tracks

Dylan's astonishing 1975 return to form, a suite of songs prompted by the emotional fallout of his failing marriage.

Commonly regarded as the only one of his later albums able to stand comparison with his innovative '60s work, *Blood On The Tracks* finds the songwriter in a series of emotionally-charged narratives and reflections that defies simple assessment. As so often in Dylan's career, uncertainty and procrastination presaged the eventual appearance of the album with it being scrapped a few weeks before its delivery date, as he hurriedly re-recorded some tracks with a scratch band in Minneapolis. The sudden change came so late in the production schedule that early copies of the album came with not only the wrong musician credits, but also liner notes by journalist Pete Hamill which quoted lyrics that had since been changed. It is typical of Dylan's unreliable judgement concerning his own output that when the out-takes appeared shortly after on the *Joaquin Antique* bootleg, most hardcore Dylan aficionados (including close friends like Robbie Robertson and Joni Mitchell) preferred the abandoned original versions of some songs – particularly Idiot Wind, which is transformed from an eerie, reflective piece into something altogether more scathing and strident at the Minneapolis sessions. (With customary contrariness, the out-take eventually released on *The Bootleg Series* is not the one originally scheduled for release, either!)

Seeking a more acoustic sound after the rock-band settings of *Planet Waves*, Dylan employed Eric Weissberg's folk group Deliverance for the New York sessions, though ultimately only bassist Tony Brown appeared on the record. The band's three guitarists were apparently expected to follow Dylan's fingering largely by instinct, a situation not helped by his open D tuning. "If it was anybody else," said Weissberg later, "I would have walked out." For all that, the songs recorded by Dylan and Brown (with overdubs added later by organist Paul Griffin and pedal-steel guitarist Buddy Cage) are amongst the album's more affecting, particularly Shelter From The Storm and the concluding Buckets Of Rain. But when Dylan played a test-pressing of the album to his brother David, he was persuaded that some of the songs sounded too thin and bare, and ought to be re-done with a group of local Minneapolis musicians. Accordingly, a few days after Christmas Dylan went into a local studio to re-cut half the tracks, of which only Tangled Up In Blue really matched the emotional acuity of the earlier version. The results were rush-released a few weeks later, and despite the circuitous nature of its development, the two sessions' material meshed together well enough to form one of Dylan's most attractive and purely enjoyable albums.

Record Label:
CBS

Produced
by Bob Dylan.

Recorded
at Columbia A&R Studios, New York, September 1974 and Sound 80 Studios, Minneapolis, December 1974.

Released:
February 1975

Chart peaks:
4 (UK) 1 (US)

Personnel:
Bob Dylan (v, g, hm); Chris Weber (g); Ken Odegard (g); Tony Brown (b); Bill Peterson (b); Paul Griffin (k); Greg Imhofer (o); Bill Berg (d); Buddy Cage (sg); Phil Ramone (e)

Further Listening:
Tangled Up In Blue (S); Simple Twist Of Fate; You're A Big Girl Now; Idiot Wind; You're Gonna Make Me Lonesome When You Go; Meet Me In The Morning; Lily, Rosemary And The Jack Of Hearts; If You See Her, Say Hello; Shelter From The Storm; Buckets Of Rain.

Running time:
51.53

Current CD:
4678422

Further listening:
Of his other albums dealing in matters of the heart, Blonde On Blonde (1966) and Time Out Of Mind (1997) are to be preferred to the comparatively dismal Empire Burlesque (1985).

Further reading:
Dylan Behind The Shades (Clinton Heylin, 1991)

Like this?
Try . . . p.633

Neil Young

Tonight's The Night

Young's painful, personal requiem to Crazy Horse guitarist Danny Whitten and roadie Bruce Berry.

Desperate, bleak and emotionally cathartic, the wasted vocals and ragged production of *Tonight's The Night* were the antithesis of the consumer-friendly *Harvest*. It took two years to release it, and nobody, his record company thought, would buy it. That they did bears testament to Young's post-CSNY marketability as much as to the album's undoubted brilliance – the best part of the 'doom trilogy' that encompassed *Time Fades Away* and *On The Beach*.

In November '72 Danny Whitten, friend and Crazy Horse guitarist, died of a dose of heroin bought with the $50 Young gave him when he fired him. It was, said Young, "traumatic". It didn't help when the following summer, while working in a Hawaii with Crosby, Stills And Nash on an aborted album, he learned that his roadie Bruce Berry had also OD-ed.

Back in LA, Young got together with the remains of Crazy Horse, Nils Lofgren, Ben Keith and several crates of tequila in a Hollywood rehearsal room. In two live, loud, late-night sessions-come-wakes they recorded nine of the album's 12 songs. Trying to capture their late friends' states of mind they got wasted "right out on the edge, where we knew we were so screwed up that we could easily just fall on our faces" and waited "until the middle of the night until the vibe hit us and just did it," Young told Rolling Stone.

The label might have stopped its release but they couldn't stop him doing the songs live. A month later a dishevelled Young wearing a white jacket and sunglasses stumbled onstage at LA's Roxy, launching the *Tonight's The Night* tour. The band shared the stage with a palm tree, wooden Indian, old piano and silver glitter platform boots. A similar set-up came to Britain. Audiences who had no idea of the provenance of this furious, fucked up, moving music – among its highlights a raw cover of Crazy Horse's Downtown, the poignantly lovely New Mama (inspired by the birth of his son) and the agonizing Borrowed Tune (whose melody the lyrics confess were stolen from the Stones, Young being "too wasted to write my own") were often hostile or confused. Said manager Elliot Roberts, "Neil was sort of dribbling out of the side of his mouth on that tour, the mood was so down." Finally appearing in 1975, the album still stands up as one of the most honest and harrowing in rock.

SS

Record label:
Reprise
Produced
by David Briggs and Neil Young, with Tim Mulligan, Gabby Garcia and Elliot Mazer.
Recorded
at Studio Instrument Rentals Rehearsal Hall, Hollywood; Broken Arrow; and live at Fillmore East, San Francisco, August and September 1973.
Released:
June 1975
Chart peaks:
48 (UK) 25 (US)
Personnel:
Neil Young (v, g, p, hm); Nils Lofgren (g); Billy Talbot (b, v); Ralph Molina (d); Ben Keith (sg, v)
Track listing:
Tonight's The Night; Speakin' Out; World On A String; Borrowed Tune; Come On Baby Let's Go Downtown; Mellow My Mind; Roll Another Number (For The Road); Albuquerque; New Mama; Lookout Joe; Tired Eyes; Tonight's The Night Part II
Running time:
44.58
Current CD:
7599272212
Further listening:
Time Fades Away (1973); On The Beach (1974)
Further reading:
Neil Young: The Rolling Stone Files (1994); Neil And Me (Scott Young, 1997); www.hyperrust.org/
Like this?
Try . . . p.343

Guy Clark

Old No. 1

A Lone Star answer to Nashville's Outlaw movement, possibly the best country-folk album of the 1970s.

If there was a theme to Guy Clark's music it was Texas.

Not the Texas of cattle drives and shoot-outs, but the Texas whose citizens work hard and drink cases of Lone Star beer while arguing about whose chilli is the hottest and whose woman is the sweetest.

Clark's first album was named *Old No. 1* with real foresight and no little accuracy. Texas music. Clark, whose photos graced albums by the psychedelic pioneers The 13th Floor Elevators, came from the same Texan circuit as Townes Van Zandt and fresh-faced San Antonio youngster Steve Earle. *Old No. 1* wove together several threads of Texan sound and hasn't a duff cut on it.

"The album wasn't meant to have a theme, and it didn't really occur to me it had one till I went back and looked at it later as a solid body of work," recalled Clark recently. "Now I can appreciate how all the pieces fell together. It's a collection of songs about life as I knew it in Monahans, in Rockport and later on in Houston and Austin."

Rightly considered a classic today, the album represents the sympathetic Lone Star state response to the country establishment, drawing Dixie's folk and country audiences closer together, and gave the contemporary alt-country crowd another icon. These days, Clark lives off his substantial songwriting royalties.

Record label:
RCA
Produced
by Neil Wilburn.
Recorded
at RCA Studios, Nashville; spring 1975.
Released:
August 1975
Chart peaks:
None (UK) None (US)
Personnel:
Guy Clark (g, v); Mike Leech (b); Jerry Kroon (d); Jerry Carrigan (d); Larrie London (d); Chip Young (g); Pat Carter (g, bv); Steve Gibson (g); Dick Feller (g); Jim Colvard (g); Reggie Young (g); Hal Rugg (ps, dobro); Jack Higgs (dobro); David Briggs (p); Chuck Cochran (p); Shane Keister (p); Lea Jane Berinati (p, bv); Johnny Gimble (fiddle); Mickey Raphael (hm); Rodney Crowell (bv); Emmylou Harris (bv); Gary B White (bv); Florence Warner (bv); Steve Earle (bv); Sammi Smith (bv)
Track listing:
Rita Ballou; L.A. Freeway; She Ain't Goin' Nowhere; A Nickel For The Fiddler; That Old Time Feeling; Texas 1947; Desperados Waiting For The Train; Like A Coat From The Cold; Instant Coffee Blues; Let Him Roll
Running time:
36.20
Current CD:
74321588 132 adds Texas Cooking
Further listening:
Texas Cooking (1976)
Further reading:
Who's Who In Country Music (Hugh Gregory, 1993)
Like this?
Try . . . p.398

Curtis Mayfield

There's No Place Like America Today

The former Impression brings biting social commentary, messages of hope and love songs.

In his Impressions days, Mayfield had written with a sharp eye for social injustice, a keen ear for striking melody and an optimistic heart for the future of mankind. Quitting the group in 1970, he ploughed much the same furrow as a solo act and crossed over to the mass market with the Superfly soundtrack. Thereafter he strode on boldly with the somewhat darker *Back To The World*, but by the time he settled to record *There's No Place Like America Today*, disco had become a prime mover in the market place. He would not follow that trend just yet.

The scene is set by the striking album-sleeve painting – in front of a huge billboard whose poster depicts an All-American WASP family grinning hugely and heading off for the sunshine in their shiny automobile, a line of black Americans queue dejectedly. For what? Welfare? A soup kitchen? The American Dream? The specifics do not matter. The sharp disparity in potential happiness and actual comfort of the characters is plainly stated.

Starting with the tough, cautionary tale of Billy Jack, victim of a casual shooting, and When Seasons Change (there is no difference for the hard-up, victimised and oppressed), thereafter Mayfield seamlessly shifts between the reality of Blue Monday People and Hard Times to the more tender passages of the exquisite So In Love and the positive note on which he ends, Love To The People.

Long since dubbed the 'gentle giant of soul', Mayfield's well-attuned sensitivity as a singer of his own material is matched by the simple and subtle promptings of the band. But the album's tone and content were at odds with the commercial successes of the day.

"One of my favourite albums was one that didn't sell at all – *America Today*," Mayfield told Black Music magazine in 1979. "I felt a need to say those things. This is the way it's just got to be."

Never exactly a superstar, but always hugely respected and admired, Mayfield was still working hard, enjoying his music and delivering his message of hope when, on stage in August 1990 he was crushed by a falling lighting rig and paralysed from the neck down. While he was in hospital his house burnt to the ground. Despite it all, Curtis kept as active in music as possible but missed being able to play his guitar, though he found he could sing for short periods and started occasional work on a new album, *New World Order* which was finally released in 1997. In 1998 he lost a limb due to diabetes, which had been triggered by his accident. Finally, this brave, noble king of soul music died on the morning of December 26, 1999 at North Fulton Regional Hospital in Roswell, Georgia, a suburb of Atlanta.

Record label:
Buddah
Produced
by Curtis Mayfield
Recorded
at Curtom Studios, Chicago. February 1985
Release Date:
August, 1975
Chart Peaks:
None (UK) None (US)
Personnel:
Curtis Mayfield (v,k,g); Rich Tufo (k); Lucky Scott (b); Quinton Joseph (d); Gary Thompson, Phil Upchurch (g); Henry Gibson (congas, bongos)
Track listing:
Billy Jack; When Seasons Change; So In Love; Jesus; Blue Monday People; Hard Times; Love To The People
Running Time:
35.30
Current CD:
NEMCD401 adds Give Get Take Have
Further Listening:
Curtis (1970); Roots (1971); Superfly (1972); Back To The World (1973); People Get Ready: The Curtis Mayfield Story (1996)
Further Reading:
www.curtismayfield.cjb.net.
Like this?
Try . . . p.316

Eno

Another Green World

Instrumental-dominated release which provided Bowie with his Berlin trilogy template.

Until *Another Green World*, Brian Eno's post-Roxy Music card had been marked as that of an arch dilettante.

But Eno's serious side had already begun to emerge with the establishment of the world's first ambient imprint Discreet Music. Eno had also immersed himself in the work of soundtrack maestros such as Nino Rota and Ennio Morricone resulting in the cinematic lushness of this excellent collection.

The dandified glam piss-taker of solo debut *Here Come The Warm Jets* had been replaced by a short-haired fellow of studious demeanour. "I'd worked out that I was interested in building picture landscapes, soundscapes," he says now. "The impressionistic soundtrack music I was listening to was made to complement visuals, and I wanted to make similar music which was less personality-based, more evocative of times or places."

Eno created the soundbeds for the tracks at his home studio before presenting them to musicians he had assembled from the ranks of regular collaborators (Fripp, Cale) and selected fellow travellers (Collins, Rudolph, Melvin). Each was encouraged to play as awkwardly as possible as Eno and producer Rhett Davies whittled away at a total of 36 tracks.

"I had these sonic experiments and then tried to see what we could do with them to make music in the studio," says Eno, who rejects the opinion that this album is where he started to flex his minimalist muscles. "I like unfinished things – a musical idea seems to be more powerful if you are operating on the cusp because you start a picture and create a proposition which lets the listener fill in the rest. So these songs are actually minimalist by accident. I'd also been listening to a lot of music by the Mahavishnu Orchestra, I really liked their singularity – they didn't sound like anything else. Each piece of music could be like a jewel."

Which is exactly what is achieved here – an album full of jewels, from the opening squall of Sky Saw to the baroque of St Elmo's Fire, the motorik of In Dark Trees and the exotica of Zawinul/Lava, the beautiful Becalmed and the somnolent Spirits Drifting. Decades after its release *Another Green World* continues to live up to its title, offering the listener entry to an opulent aural plain.

Record label:
Island
Produced
by Brian Eno and Rhett Davies.
Recorded
at Island Studios, London; July–August 1975.
Released:
September 1975
Chart peaks:
None (UK) None (US)
Personnel:
Brian Eno (v, snake guitar, syn, treatments); Phil Collins (d); Percy Jones (b); Rod Melvin (p); Paul Rudolph (g, anchor bass); John Cale (va); Robert Fripp (g)
Track listing:
Sky Saw; Over Fire Island; St Elmo's Fire; In Dark Trees; The Big Ship; I'll Come Running; Another Green World; Sombre Reptiles; Little Fishes; Golden Hours; Becalmed; Zawinul/Lava; Everything Merges With The Night; Spirits Drifting
Running time:
41.10
Current CD:
EGCD21
Further listening:
Before And After Science (1977)
Further reading:
Paul Morley's sleevenotes to Enobox 2: Vocal (1993); http://noc.pue.udlap.mx/eno/
Like this?
Try . . . p.292

Glen Campbell

Rhinestone Cowboy

Precise, multi-million-selling MOR.

By the mid-'70s, Glen Campbell's career as a bankable recording artist seemed over. It was several years since his interpretation of Jimmy Webb's tryptich of haunting, ballads – By The Time I Get To Phoenix, Galveston, Wichita Lineman, all located in the South – had made him a worldwide superstar, and his time was now spent on the golf course, making movies or cutting lacklustre religious and country albums. Even a much-anticipated collaboration with Webb, 1974's *Reunion*, had nose-dived spectacularly. Then, while driving home one evening in late 1974, Campbell heard a song on the radio that he thought might revive his chart fortunes. Capitol A&R chief Al Coury agreed to hear it on the condition that Campbell first listen to a song *he* believed would do the same trick: as it turned out, they'd both picked the same tune, Rhinestone Cowboy.

A flop for its author Larry Weiss the previous year, the song seemed tailor-made for Campbell, its story of a jaded country star pounding "the dirty sidewalks of Broadway" as unnervingly autobiographical as Jimmy Webb's late '60s songs. "With that record, I was determined that the lyrics call attention to themselves," recalls Campbell. "This was the first time I had ever made a record in which the words needed to shine above my singing. I recorded the vocal melody, then overdubbed my voice harmonising with myself. I thought this duet would compel listeners to focus on the words."

Teaming up with pop producers/writers Dennis Lambert and Brian Potter, an album was constructed around the concept of a compromised, 40-something country star at odds with the fruits of his fame. From the conviction and fluidity of his honey-sweet tenor, you could tell that Campbell – then having drink, drug and marital problems – felt a rare affinity with the material: on Comeback, Count On Me, Miss You Tonight and the delightful Country Boy ("Looking back, I can remember a time when I sang my songs for free!"), it seemed as if Glen was confiding the infernal woes of his own life, then a well-kept showbiz secret. Side two had a looser collection of covers, Johnny Cunningham's subtly melancholic Pencils For Sale, Randy Newman's gorgeous Marie and, as a fitting finale, Mann and Weil's We're Over.

Rhinestone Cowboy resurrected Campbell's global profile in one fell swoop.

PG

Record label:
Capitol
Produced
by Dennis Lambert and Brian Potter.
Recorded
at Sound Labs, Hollywood; summer 1975.
Released:
October 1975
Chart peaks:
38 (UK) 1 (US)
Personnel:
Glen Campbell (v, ag); Dean Parks, Ben Benay (g); Scott Edwards (b); Michael Omartian, Dennis Lambert (k); Ed Greene, Dave Kemper (d)
Track listing:
Country Boy (s); Comeback; Count On Me; I Miss You Tonight; My Girl; Rhinestone Cowboy (S); I'd Build A Bridge; Pencils For Sale; Marie; We're Over
Running time:
33.25
Currently unavailable on CD
Further listening:
The 2-CD selection The Capitol Years (1999) anthologises his career to 1977, and includes the near-legendary, Brian Wilson-penned and produced Guess I'm Dumb from 1966.
Further reading:
It's all in the great man's own, brutally honest account of his life, Rhinestone Cowboy (Glen Campbell with Tom Carter, 1994)
Like this?
Try . . . p.74

Dion

Born To Be With You

Both born in the Bronx, Dion DiMucci and Phil Spector team for a mouth-watering album.

At the end of the '60s, John Lennon had coaxed Phil Spector out of retirement to produce Instant Karma and doctor The Beatles' Let It Be. Spector went on to greater things, producing George Harrison's *All Things Must Pass* and Lennon's *Imagine.* Two near fatal car crashes later, Spector decided to set up another label, Phil Spector International in the UK in 1975.

Dion had had his problems too. Drug addiction had almost caused his career to falter completely in 1964, but by the end of the '60s he had re-emerged as a singer-songwriter. At Christmas 1968, he even hit the US Top 10 with Abraham, Martin And John. Though they were raised in the same part of New York, Spector didn't really know Dion until they worked together on this LP. On the liner notes he writes: "As kids, we probably threw rocks at the same gangs, at each other. We fought the same wretched battles rooted in boredom and bigotry. And it was the same music that saved us from (destroying) ourselves."

With its dedication to Lenny Bruce, Spector's close friend who died in 1968, *Born To Be With You* has also taken on a reputation as music to take drugs to. But it's not a bleak work, it's an uplifting record, five of the six Spector productions being quite magnificent. The Wall Of Sound orchestra – featuring many of Spector's regular musicians: drummers Hal Blaine and Frank Kapp, guitarists Barney Kessel and Dennis Budimir, horn players Steve Douglas, Jay Migliori and Nino Tempo among them – is as sharp as ever. The songs have pedigree too, best of all being Barry Mann and Cynthia Weil's pleading Make The World Love Me, where Dion's voice somehow manages to soar above the towering mix. Two songwriting collaborations with Spector stalwart Gerry Goffin continue the mood of introspection, Only You Know and In And Out Of Showers. Finally, there's the Phil and Dion collaboration He's Got The Whole World In His Hands: a strange hybrid of gospel and pop which sounds modern enough to have been recorded 20 years later.

Born To Be With You was Phil Spector's last great record. Meanwhile, Dion continued to make well received albums like 1978's *Return Of The Wanderer* and 1989's *Yo Frankie.* As Spector claimed in his liner notes: "He is also a GREAT artist. I hope I've done justice to his talent."

Record label:
Phil Spector International
Produced
by Phil Spector.
Recorded
at A&M Studios, Los Angeles; September 1975.
Release date:
October 1975
Chart peaks:
None (UK) None (US)
Personnel:
Dion DiMucci (v, g); The Wall Of Sound Orchestra; Nino Tempo (a)
Track listing:
Born To Be With You (S); Make The World Love Me; Your Own Backyard; He's Got The Whole World In His Hands; Only You Know; New York City Song; In And Out Of Showers; Good Lovin' Man
Running time:
35.20
Currently unavailable on CD
Further listening:
Runaround Sue (1998)
Further reading:
http://yodion.com
Like this?
Try . . . p.18

Al Green

Al Green Is Love

Green's comeback album after serious injury.

Choosing between any of Al Green's '70s albums is a tough task, and it might seem perverse to pick the most misanthropic and idiosyncratic of all of them. But *Al Green Is Love* crystallises the dilemma at the heart of Green's music, and at the core of soul itself: the conflict between the sacred and the profane. On The Love Sermon, six and a half minutes of near-madness, preacher Green seems to be berating some of the more wayward members of his flock, but he still manages to sneak through the line "I want to do everything for you that all the married men won't do." It comes as no surprise his father sacked him from the family gospel quartet after catching young Al listening to Jackie Wilson.

Green was coming off the back of a period of both astonishing success and personal turmoil. He had already scored 12 gold records in the US, but less than a year earlier had suffered terrible burns after an attack by an ex-girlfriend (who then shot herself). What was going through his mind when he started these sessions is open to conjecture, but the results range from child-like lyrics (Rhymes) to classic pop-soul (L-O-V-E, later covered in a memorable mismatch by Edwyn Collins' Orange Juice) to stream-of-consciousness confession (The Love Sermon) and pure rhythmic grooving (Love Ritual). As always, producer Willie Mitchell covers the music in the dusty patina of the Hi Records sound, and sometimes Green seems to be disappearing into a box. But there is always that peerless voice. Nobody else really comes close to Green's gentle, musing tenderness on a ballad. I Didn't Know is close to eight minutes as he goes through his repertoire of voices, from mewling, bird-like falsetto to half-spoken growl, and presents himself for our mercy. As with all Green's records, there is a lot of barefaced machismo here, but it dissolves in the cracks of his shape-changing artistry. As MOJO's Barney Hoskyns put it, he is "the jester of soul, a meta-singer, a cat narcissistically chasing its own tail". This is one of Green's last performances before he committed more fully to the gospel over soul, and it's an amazing transition.

Record label:
Hi Records
Produced
by Willie Mitchell and Al Green.
Recorded
at Royal Recording Studios, Memphis; 1975.
Released:
October 1975
Chart peaks:
None (UK) 28 (US)
Personnel:
Al Green (v); Teenie Hodges, Larry Lee (g); Charles Hodges (o, p); Archie Turner, Michael Allen (p); Leroy Hodges (b); Howard Grimes (pc); Congo Lou (congas); Wayne Jackson (t); Jack Hale (tb); Andrew Love, Lewis Collins (ts); James Mitchell (bs); The Memphis Strings; Rhodes, Chalmers & Rhodes, Duncan Sisters (bv)
Track listing:
L-O-V-E (Love); Rhymes; The Love Sermon; There Is Love; Could I Be The One; Love Ritual; I Didn't Know; Oh Me, Oh My (Dreams In My Arms); I Gotta Be More (Take Me Higher); I Wish You Were Here
Running time:
41.12
Current CD:
HIL0157
Further listening:
Call Me (1973)
Further reading:
From A Whisper To A Scream (1991) and autobiography Take Me To The River (2000)
Like this?
Try . . . p.348

Jade Warrior

Waves

Obscure British instrumental duo cut sonic hymn to oceans, whales, truth and beauty.

"Whale sounds from recording all notes of organ, splicing them together then running tape through by hand + sine wave generator." On the inner sleeve of *Waves*, Jade Warrior decided to explain how their music was made. It revealed their painstaking methods – such as recreating whale calls as their own music rather than borrowing a library recording – but it hardly conveyed their emotional and aesthetic intensity. Friends for 15 years since they met as forklift truck drivers and discovered a shared love of jazz, Tony Duhig and Jon Field had wandered in the penumbra of rock's glory years until, in the early '70s, they formed Jade Warrior as a prog rock band. They sounded a bit like Jethro Tull and recorded for Vertigo. When that folded, they dropped the vocals, kept the name – triggered by their own passion for Japanese culture and Kurosawa movies in particular – and betook themselves to Island (Steve Winwood recommended them to label owner Chris Blackwell). At which they became an "exclusive club of two and did our floaty stuff", as Field puts it. Through four widely ignored albums, they strove to capture the pristine notions of ideal beauty inspired in them by years of chewing over matters Oriental and philosophical.

Waves found them tense with one another, abraded by the impossibility of commercial success with the music they longed to make. But still, says Field, they could resolve their differences into "complete musical harmony. We were push-and-pull, that's how it worked, that's how we reached the golden road". Boundlessly imaginative-cum-happy-accidental, they reached for the heavenly sound they imagined. At night in the Oxfordshire countryside, they would park speakers in the fields, the microphones 400 yards away, so that Duhig's "distant" guitar solos really were just that. The birdsong at the start of side two (as was) arose from Duhig flinging open the studio window at 4am to take a leak, as musicians will, and being overwhelmed by the dawn chorus.

Wordless *Waves* is a drama, a meditation, a composition of entrancing grace. Even so, Field still views it with some rue: "Really, we always made the same album under different names and the number of albums we made is the extent of our failure to get it right." He recalls a '70s interview in which his late friend Duhig was asked whether he would describe Jade Warrior as a pop group. "No, it's not popular music," he said. "It's more *un*popular music." But great.

Record label:
Island
Produced
by Jon Field and Tony Duhig.
Recorded
at The Manor, Shipton-on-Cherwell, Oxfordshire; The Argonaut, Little Venice, London; May–August 1975.
Release date:
October 1975
Chart peaks:
None (UK) None (US)
Personnel:
Jon Field (flute, oboe, clarinet, c, p, pc, bv); Tony Duhig (g, bv); Steve Winwood (Moog, p); Dave Duhig (g); Graham Morgan (d); Nick Glossop, Tom Newman (e)
Track listing:
The Whale; The Sea; Section See; Caves; Wave Birth; River To The Sea; Groover; Breeze; Sea Part Two.
Running time:
42.46
Current CD:
314524140-2
Further listening:
Floating World (1974), Kites (1976), The Way Of The Sun (1978), or complete Island CD anthology Jade Warrior: Elements (1995) – the isolated striving for elegance and grace continues.
Further reading:
www.feghoot.ml.org; www.radagast.org/jade-warrior
Like this?
Try . . . p.507

Paul Simon

Still Crazy After All These Years

The summit of Simon's post-Garfunkel creative surge.

Effectively, this album covered the continuing aftermath of two divorces. In 1970, Simon and Garfunkel had separated to go solo musically. In 1975, Simon and Peggy, his wife of six years, were formalising their break-up while he wrote and recorded *Still Crazy After All These Years.*

Naturally, this shaped the songs. "That's what was happening," he said, ruefully. "I guess I have an easier time expressing myself in song than in real life." But the marital divorce stirred him to seek reconciliation in his fractured friendship with Garfunkel by offering him a song – even if he proposed My Little Town as something 'nasty' to offset the sugary nature of his former partner's solo repertoire.

The domestic emphasis in Simon's life may have contributed to the ethnic explorations of his first two solo albums being put on hold. But he stayed with producer Phil Ramone who shepherded him through nine months of sporadic progress until he emerged with his most consistent, coherent and profoundly communicative album – the Brill Building musical craftsmanship acquired in his youth, sharpened by inquisitive imagination and matched by lyrics which were subtle yet clear, never blurred by his tendency to run for cover behind poetic obfuscation.

Unusually, this was a successful album built on a prevailing sense of doubt. Gone At Last, the glorious gospel track driven by the late Richard Tee's piano, is the only unbridled expression of happiness. The other songs all carry questions and hints of sour irony in either the lyrics or acidic musical comments; in the hit single 50 Ways To Leave Your Lover the turmoil of breaking up is set against a rigid military beat (the "You just slip out the back, Jack" chorus inspired by a rhyming game Simon played with his son).

Significantly, the only track which didn't work well was Silent Eyes. A Jew wanting to write about the Holocaust, he drifted into the fatal trap for artists dealing with history and politics of expressing how *he felt* about the Holocaust, calling for attention to himself rather than the event. But that was just one (well-meant) false step. Simon advertised the temporary rapprochement with Garfunkel by singing with him on American TV's Saturday Night Live. The album a huge hit, he stopped recording for five years.

Record label:
CBS
Produced
by Paul Simon and Phil Ramone (except My Little Town produced by Simon, Art Garfunkel, Ramone)
Recorded
January–September 1975.
Release date:
October 1975
Chart peaks:
6 (UK) 1 (US)
Personnel:
Paul Simon (v, g); Pete Carr, Joe Beck Jerry Friedman, Hugh McCracken (g); Barry Beckett, Leon Pendarvis (p); David Hood, Tony Levin, Gordon Edwards (b); Roger Hawkins, Steve Gadd, Grady Tate (d); Mike Brecker, Phil Woods (s); Ralph McDonald (pc); Bob James (electric p); Toots Thielemans (hm on Night Game); Richard Tee (p on Gone At Last); Art Garfunkel (duet v on My Little Town); Phoebe Snow, Valerie Simpson, Patti Austin, The Jessy Dixon Singers, The Chicago Community Choir (bv); Burt Szerlip, Glen Berger (e)
Track listing:
Still Crazy After All These Years; My Little Town; I Do It For Your Love; 50 Ways To Leave Your Lover; Night Game; Gone At Last; Some Folks' Lives Roll Easy; Have A Good Time; You're Kind; Silent Eyes
Running time:
34:33
Current CD:
Warner Bros 7599-25591-2
Further listening:
Graceland (1986)
Further reading:
http://paul.simon.org
Like this?
Try . . . p.496

Queen

Night At The Opera

The pinnacle of Queen's achievements, a monstrous, marvellous magnum opus.

Freddie Mercury was playing a powerful ballad from the point of view of someone who had 'just killed a man' for producer Roy Thomas Baker when he suddenly stopped, saying "this is where the opera section comes in." Baker fell about laughing but knew what he meant.

Baker: "I had worked with the D'Oyly Carte Opera at Decca so I knew a lot about vocals and the way vocals are stressed, so I was probably one of the few people in the pop world who knew what he was talking about."

There ensued a series of marathon sesssions overdubbing, bouncing-down (the resulting distortion accidentally contributes to Queen's 'saturated' sound) and splicing to realise Mercury's grandiose vision. Baker: "Every time Freddie would come up with another Galileo I would add another piece of tape to the reel which was beginning to look like a zebra crossing whizzing by." The band didn't mind spending so much time on Freddie's baby, they knew it was a monster and were united in insisting that the unedited six-minute track should be the single (though Baker remembers Roger Taylor locking himself in a cupboard until his I'm In Love With My Car was allowed on the B-side). Meeting managerial and record company resistance, the band got a white label to Kenny Everett who 'accidentally' played it 14 times in one weekend creating huge interest and it went on to be, along with the groundbreaking promo film, a milestone in pop music, revered and reviled in equal extremes. Wisely, it was placed at the end of an album which, though rigorous and resourceful, couldn't hope to top Mercury's ludicrous masterpiece.

Beautifully paced and programmed, the album opens with the remarkably sustained viciousness of Mercury's revenge-in-song Death On Two Legs that brickwalls into the hilariously carefree Lazing On A Sunday Afternoon. Further highlights include Deacon's delightfully breezy You're My Best Friend (showing he was the only one in Queen who could write a straightforward pop song), May's sprawling, atmospheric Prophet's Song, the cheeky pastiches Seaside Rendezvous and Good Company (May combining George Formby with an astounding guitar-created swing band) and Mercury's gorgeous ballad Love Of My Life. Freddie said Queen would be "the Cecil B De Mille of rock, always wanting to do things bigger and better." With *Night At The Opera* they achieved it.

Record label:
EMI

Produced
by Roy Thomas Baker and Queen.

Recorded
at Sarm, Roundhouse, Olympic, Rockfield, Scorpio and Lansdowne; August–November 1975.

Released:
November 21, 1975

Chart peaks:
1 (UK) 4 (US)

Personnel:
Roger Taylor (d, v); Freddie Mercury (v, p); John Deacon (b, ag); Brian May (g, p, ukelele, harp)

Track listing:
Death On Two Legs; Lazing On A Sunday Afternoon; I'm In Love With My Car; You're My Best Friend; '39; Sweet Lady; Seaside Rendezvous; The Prophet's Song; Love Of My Life; Good Company; Bohemian Rhapsody; God Save The Queen

Running time:
43.11

Current CD:
CDPCSD130

Further listening:
Queen II (1974); Sheer Heart Attack (1974); Day At The Races (1976)

Further reading:
Mercury (Laura Jackson, 1996); Good Vibrations: A History Of Record Production (Mark Cunningham, 1996); www.queen-fip.com

Like this?
Try . . . p.160

Peggy Lee
Mirrors

Autumn-years rumination makes high art of high camp.

Having sold-out their interests in Red Bird records, songwriters Jerry Lieber and Mike Stoller moved on to a pet project of philosophy-drop-out Jerry Lieber's, a song adaptation of Thomas Mann's story Disillusionment.

"It's an example in existentialist thinking, like Heidegger and Camus," said Leiber, "and I was fascinated by it." Lieber presented Stoller with spoken vignettes voicing nonchalant disappointment with a fire, a circus, a love affair and encroaching death but in the absence of a sung linking passage to bind the vignettes together, Stoller composed some music and Leiber some lyrics, separately. When they compared them "we didn't have to change one syllable or anything," remembers Stoller. "It's the only time that's ever happened."

Peggy Lee loved the song – Is That All There Is? – and recorded it; a further cry from Leiber/Stoller's rock'n'roll songs of the '50s like Hound Dog and Yakety Yak could hardly be imagined. With something of Irving Berlin and Kurt Weill in the song's tenor, it was arranged by Randy Newman – having a similar elliptical orchestral ebb and flow to his early work – and Lee's performance was adult and heady. Her record company, Capitol, hated it, refusing to issue it. So she traded an appearance on a TV show she didn't want to do for the record's release. It became a nationwide hit, winning Lee a Grammy and revitalising her career.

Six years later, the same team – minus Newman but plus brilliant arranger Johnny Mandel – fashioned a series of similarly toned songs for *Mirrors*, which combined new tunes with numbers from failed Lieber/Stoller musicals into a kind of concept. Lee explained: "It's like a voyage of the mind, a vehicle for moving from thought to thought, place to place, person to person. You can make up your own endings. There's a sort of question mark – on purpose, not by accident."

Mauled by rock critics at the time, to some ears it remains camp and pretentious – a smokey-voiced blonde wordily straining for profundity amongst banjo-punctuated oom-pah grooves, and a trancelike life's-a-circus atmosphere. To others it's a rich, alluring piece of mature cabaret whose complex musical palette is matched by resonant, psychologically dense lyrics and wise, world-weary performances.

Record label:
A&M
Produced
by Jerry Leiber and Mike Stoller.
Recorded
at A&M Studios, Hollywood; Record Plant, New York; 1975.
Released:
November 1975
Chart peaks:
None (UK) None (US)
Personnel:
Peggy Lee (v); Johnny Mandel (oa, conductor); Hank Cicalo, Bob Ludwig (e)
Track listing:
Ready To Begin Again (Manya's Song); Some Cats Know; I've Got Them Feelin' Too Good Today Blues; A Little White Ship; Tango; Professor Hauptmann's Performing Dogs; The Case Of M.J.; I Remember; Say It; Longings For A Simpler Time
Running time:
39.07
Currently unavailable on CD
Further listening:
Is That All There Is? (1969)
Further reading:
Miss Peggy Lee (Peggy Lee, 1989); www.geocities.com/Broadway/Stage/2481/home.html
Like this?
Try . . . p.8

Bob Marley & the Wailers

Live

Transcendent, career-defining show caught on record.

The 1975 tour that launched *Natty Dread* turned the year into an *annus mirabilis* for Marley. The last tour, with Peter and Bunny still in the group, had been a disaster – playing shabby venues amid a biting winter. Marley had realised that to succeed in a world defined by slick rock and soul acts, his live shows had to be honed into a sharper force. Bass player Family Man Barrett became his musical lieutenant, tightening up a band in which American guitarist Al Anderson now had a role, while Marley himself developed a shamanic stage presence. Floundering for a description of the phenomenon, the Village Voice called him "the Mick Jagger of reggae" when he played New York in June. By the time the tour arrived in Britain, Marley fever had begun to break out. Demand for tickets to his concerts exceeded availability several times over, with the two London Lyceum shows mobbed by people trying to get in. Inside, the atmosphere resembled a muggy night in Kingston.

"The first night, the intensity and the vibe were just nuts," said Steve Smith, who helped Chris Blackwell record the second night's show on The Rolling Stones' Mobile for what is widely regarded as one of the handful of truly great live albums. "They opened up the roof because it was so hot."

The sweaty passion of the occasion is palpable on *Live*, where the audience's waves of emotion surge from the speakers along with the band's music. "The recording would never have been as good as it was if it hadn't been for Dave Harper, who mixed the live sound out front," said Smith. "So much of the mix is to do with those live hall mikes, and you can hear that in No Woman, No Cry."

No Woman No Cry was one of the night's surprises – transformed from a slight piece on *Natty Dread* (where it was mysteriously speeded up) to become what Smith described as "the ultimate singalong." When the live version was released as a single, it became Marley's first UK hit ("the damn thing just jumped off the radio," said Smith) and one of his enduring anthems. "At the Lyceum it was, like, 50-50 black and white", said Dennis Morris. "And those 2,000 people spread the word to 20,000 people, who then spread it to another 50,000. No-one had ever seen a performer like that before." No small thanks to that concert, Bob Marley – 30 years old when he stepped onto the Lyceum stage – would become a legend.

NS

Record label:
Island
Produced
by Steve Smith and Chris Blackwell.
Recorded
at the Lyceum, London; July 1975.
Released:
November 1975
Chart peaks:
38 (UK) None (US)
Personnel:
Bob Marley (v, g); Aston 'Family Man' Barrett (b); Carlton Barrett (d); Al Anderson (g); Tyrone Downie (k); Rita Marley (v); Judy Mowatt (v); Marcia Griffith (v); Dave Harper, Phill Brown (e)
Track listing:
Trenchtown Rock; Burnin' And Lootin'; Them Belly Full; Lively Up Yourself; No Woman No Cry (S); I Shot The Sheriff; Get Up, Stand Up
Running time:
35.44
Current CD:
Further listening:
Natty Dread (1975); Rastaman Vibration (1976). A lesser, but still entertaining live album was Babylon By Bus (1978).
Further reading:
Catch A Fire (Timothy White, 1983); Bob Marley (Stephen Davis, 1983); Bob Marley: Songs of Freedom (Chris Salewicz and Adrian Boot, 1995); Bob Marley (Scotty Bennett, 1997); MOJO 16; www.bobmarley.com
Like this?
Try . . . p.737

Joni Mitchell

The Hissing Of Summer Lawns

Joni stays two steps ahead.

Bizarrely, Rolling Stone critics declared *Hissing Of Summer Lawns* Worst Album Of The Year. In mitigation, Mitchell was too musically fleet of foot for many a '70s pundit. After David Crosby 'discovered' her in 1968, she recorded a sequence of pristine, confessional, acoustic albums. But with the naked exposure of *Blue* (1971), she said, "I felt at the end of that phase. I was still lonely at moments, but I was damned if I was going to write about it any more."

Her next three albums saw her working rather rowdily with Tom Scott's brass-based LA Express, and following well publicised romances with Graham Nash, Leonard Cohen and James Taylor – at the end of her 1974 tour she set up home in a Bel Air hacienda with the band's drummer, John Guerin. Apparently, they spent their time playing cribbage and backgammon – while casting a beady eye over the svelte suburbs around them. Dropping the horn section, she gathered up her big box of Camels, crate of red wine, some classy session friends, and set off for the neighbourhood mega-studio to transport her sound to a supple, subtle jazziness beyond genre definition. Her observations focused on women, as in the film Diary Of A Mad Housewife, women trapped in rooms full of furniture: "There must be something more! What's missing?" These characters populate the title track (co-written by Guerin), Don't Interrupt The Sorrow, Shades Of Scarlett Conquering and, by implication, Harry's House/Centrepiece. The obvious eyebrow-raiser is Jungle Line's concatenation of Burundi drums, Moog, gymnastic voice and bloody clever lyrics: "In a low-cut blouse she brings the beer/Rousseau paints a jungle flower behind her ear" (Henri Rousseau the Impressionist, that is). It laid out her theme of man's innate primitivism, the well-watered lawn as a delusion of civility, Los Angeleno sophistication as an almighty bluff. But the final track, Shadows And Light, went even further, proffering elegant reflections on "blindness and sight, wrong and right" drenched in whole choirs of harmonised minor-key Mitchells.

Twenty-five years on, *Hissing of Summer Lawns* is said to be Prince's all-time favourite album. Mitchell thought rather well of it herself, remarking in her sleevenote that "This is a total work conceived graphically, musically, lyrically and accidentally – as a whole."

Record label:
Asylum
Produced
by Joni Mitchell.
Recorded
Burbank Studios, Los Angeles, summer 1975.
Released:
November 1975
Chart peaks:
14 (UK) 4 (US)
Personnel:
Joni Mitchell (v, g, k, p); Robben Ford, Jeff Baxter, Larry Carlton (g); Victor Feldman (p); Joe Sample (electric piano); John Guerin (d); Max Bennet, Wilton Felder (b); Chuck Findley (horn); Bud Shank (s, flute); Graham Nash, David Crosby (bv); James Taylor (bv, g); Henry Lewy (e); Ellis Sorkin (ae)
Track listing:
In France They Kiss On Main Street; The Jungle Line; Edith And The Kingpin; Don't Interrupt The Sorrow; Shades Of Scarlett Conquering; The Hissing Of Summer Lawns; The Boho Dance; Harry's House/Centerpiece; Sweet Bird; Shadows And Light
Running time:
42.26
Current CD:
7559-60332-2
Further listening:
Her acoustic apogee, Blue (1972); Chalk Mark In A Rainstorm (1988) – eccentric highlight: Mitchell duets with Billy Idol; Both Sides Now (2000), smoky club jazz covers gloriously sung.
Further reading:
MOJO 12A, 57; The Complete Poems And Lyrics (Joni Mitchell, 1997); www.JoniMitchell.com/
Like this?
Try . . . p.221

Patti Smith

Horses

Rimbaud goes garage, a new way forward with a poet's debut album.

"Five crazed neo-punks" – according to guitarist Lenny Kaye – played CBGB's club on the Bowery in New York, four to five nights a week for nine straight weeks, then rehearsed in Times Square behind a huge billboard before decamping to Electric Lady to make a debut album almost christened *Land*. Smith, a rock lover who'd had several volumes of poetry published in the early '70s, had been experimenting with music as a vehicle for some time, and had cut a stirring single, Hey Joe/Piss Factory, with Kaye and Richard Sohl in 1972. Joined by Ivan Kral and Dee Daugherty they began to develop into a popular act and were spotted by Clive Davis and signed, rather incongruously, to his rather mainstream Arista label. The album they made was a splurge of garage abandon, pop hooks and high-wire improvisation around Smith's wildcard role as Baudelaire's kid sister – a record embracing "the sea of possibilities", as she sings on Land.

Kaye's abiding memory is combating John Cale's will to make a more traditionally arranged record. "It was strange to us because we'd chosen him for his artistic ability, but he was into The Beach Boys at the time. He made us stand for what we believed, to challenge our artistic notions of who we wanted to be, which pushed us out onto the edge."

Unleashed upon a moribund music scene, the effect of *Horses* was startling. This and The Ramones' first album are the records most often cited as the catalysts for punk: raw examples of how music might have been. But it's maybe not too surprising that few who were inspired by it subsequently took up Patti's model of tumbling free-form beat poetry declaimed over semi-improvised garage rock. It was a daring, complex trick to pull off. Even Smith herself couldn't really repeat the recipe.

"All we were trying to do," she reflected in 1995, "was to rekindle people's spirit and motivate new people to keep going. We really looked at it as our prime mission, so when people say good things about it, it really does make me feel good. It makes me feel like we achieved what we set out to do."

Record label:
Arista
Produced
by John Cale and Alan Lanier.
Recorded
at Electric Lady Studios, New York City; September–October 1975.
Released:
November 1975
Chart peaks:
None (UK) 47 (US)
Personnel:
Patti Smith (v, g); Lenny Kaye (g); Ivan Kral (g, b); John Cale (b); Richard Sohl (p); Jay Dee Daugherty (d); Bernie Kirsh (e)
Track listing:
Gloria (In Excelis Deo) (S); Redondo Beach; Birdland; Free Money; Kimberly; Break It Up; Land: Horses/Land Of A Thousand Dances/La Mer; Elegie
Running time:
43.07
Current CD:
07822188272
Further listening:
Radio Ethiopia (1976) was less focused, less appealing. After an extended hiatus due to a broken back, Patti returned with Easter (1978), a more conventional, radio-friendly sound.
Further reading:
MOJO 33; The Complete Poems And Lyrics (Patti Smith, 1999)
Like this?
Try . . . p.365

Keith Jarrett

The Køln Concert

At three million copies, this improvised live recording is the biggest selling piano record ever.

Few great albums have been made by artists apparently on the verge of falling asleep: *The Køln Concert* is one of them. Jarrett, in the midst of a European solo tour, reckons he hadn't slept for 24 hours when he arrived at the Cologne concert hall to tackle an audibly substandard piano. Avoiding the instrument's tinny high notes, he concentrates on pulsing rhythmic patterns in the middle register whose hypnotic repetition may have had something to do with his exhaustion. The resulting album – a musical triumph over adversity – contains fewer harmonic adventures than normal but a simplicity and passion that resonated far beyond Jarrett's jazz following.

The pianist, a Miles Davis veteran, had been performing improvised solo shows for about two years before the Cologne date, conjuring up music that see-sawed between his classical training and the jazz, gospel and blues he loved. Before the Cologne show, however, Jarrett was feeling less than inspired. With Manfred Eicher, manager of the fledgling ECM label, driving, he had spent a long day travelling by car from a Lausanne date, trying fruitlessly to catnap. The pair arrived exhausted and at the hall discovered that of the two Bosendorfer pianos in the city, the wrong one had been delivered. There was a row but the removal team's lorry had already left. Jarrett went back to his hotel and tried again to sleep without success. A late meal at an overheated Italian restaurant was bolted down while Jarrett and Eicher discussed whether to scrap plans to tape the sold-out show. Eventually they decided that since the engineers had already been paid, they might as well have a document of the gig.

Jarrett says he was fighting off waves of fatigue as he headed for the stage. "When I finally had to play it was a relief because there was nothing more of this story to tell. It was 'I am now going out here with this piano . . . and the hell with everything else.'" Listening to the tape later on the tour, the pair decided that, dodgy piano or no, the performance had something special – and the resulting record duly received rave reviews. The album's sales helped turn the tiny ECM label into a major European force and won Jarrett the kind of across-the-board recognition that only a handful of living jazzmen have achieved.

Record label:
ECM
Produced
by Manfred Eicher.
Recorded
in Oper der Stadt, Cologne; January 24, 1975.
Released:
1975
Chart peaks:
None (UK) None (US)
Personnel:
Keith Jarrett (p); Martin Wieland (e)
Track listing:
Part I; Part IIa; Part IIb; Part IIc
Running time:
67.33
Current CD:
8100672
Further listening:
The world is not short of solo Jarrett, veering from the transcendental to the predictable. Solo Concerts (1973) and Concerts (1981) are among the very best.
Further reading:
Keith Jarrett: The Man And His Music (Ian Carr, 1992); www.bruchez.org/olivier/music/keith
Keith Jarrett discussion group
Like this?
Try . . . p.318

June Tabor

Airs And Graces

Tabor's first serious album release established her as England's premier female interpreter of traditional song.

Tabor, a former Oxford University student, worked in a library and was (by choice) only a part-time singer when she made this album on a shoestring budget. Many years later she was still hanging on to her day job, fearful that turning professional and singing on a daily basis would blunt her desire and commitment to her music. To this day she becomes so emotionally immersed in her performance she will end a particularly emotional song in tears: "I sang The Band Played Waltzing Matilda at Inverness Folk Festival and I couldn't finish it because I was crying and the whole audience was crying," she remembers. In the end she stopped performing the song – written by Scotsman Eric Bogle after watching in despair the Anzac Day parades in Australia – altogether, because she felt that singing it on a regular basis would diminish its importance, but it still has an enormous impact and must rank as one of the greatest anti-war songs ever written.

The album also includes a powerful version of John Tams' melancholy song about funfairs, Pull Down Lads – which put him on the map as a major songwriter. But dominant is Tabor's icily moving a cappella voice performing serious child ballads like Waly Waly, Young Waters and Bonny May. It gave her the platform to move on to greater things, but despite recording the high profile *Silly Sisters* duet album and touring with Maddy Prior she stayed true to her roots in the folk clubs and stuck to her strict beliefs about the sanctity of traditional song. Her music subsequently evolved to include a partnership with Martin Simpson, an album and tour with the Oyster band, an album of jazz standards, work with the Creative Jazz Orchestra and a natural move towards French *chansons*.

As a landmark for English folk music and pure traditional singing, however, *Airs And Graces* remains a must.

Record label:
Topic
Produced
by Paul Brown.
Recorded
at Sound Techniques Studios, London; November 1975.
Released:
March 1976
Chart peaks:
None (UK) None (US)
Personnel:
June Tabor (v); Nic Jones (g, fiddle); Jon Gillaspie (p, o, bassoon); Victor Gamm (e)
Track listing:
While Gamekeepers Lie Sleeping; Plains Of Waterloo; Bonny May; Reynardine;The Band Played Waltzing Matilda; Young Waters, Waly Waly; The Merchant's Son; Queen Among The Heather; Pull Down Lads
Running time:
38.53
Current CD:
TSCD298
Further listening:
The upbeat, fun partnership with Maddy Prior, Silly Sisters (1986); hitting another vocal peak with demanding, rewarding mostly contemporary material on Aqaba (1988); her celebrated collaboration with the Oyster band, Freedom And Rain (1990)
Further reading:
Folk Roots magazine, www.froots.co.uk
Like this?
Try . . . p.291

Thin Lizzy

Jailbreak

The record that established Lizzy as the rockers who even the punks could love.

"We knew we had to get it right with *Jailbreak*," Phil Lynott reflected almost a decade after the album's release. "Because if we didn't, we'd be stuck playing Whiskey In The Jar for the rest of our lives."

Almost three years had elapsed since Thin Lizzy burst into the British chart with their epic rearrangement of a traditional Irish drinking song and, since that time, their reputation as one of the hardest rocking bands on the circuit had soared towards the heavens. Their vinyl appeal, however, remained locked in the past, and Lynott continued, "we knew we were moving in the right direction with *Fighting* (#60 the previous summer); and to be honest, I think Springsteen helped – suddenly there was this Yank writing the same kind of songs as we were, the romantic street-fighting thing, and maybe people started looking around for something similar, a little closer to home."

The Boys Are Back In Town, the first single from this new album, set the stage effortlessly – swaggering, lawless, mercilessly punched along by Gorman and Robertson's twin guitars. But as the hottest summer in living memory unfolded over the UK, the song's own mood of impending menace captured more than the meteorological heat – punk was taking its first, tentative steps in the *barrio* bars of the capital and, is it simply hindsight talking or did Lynott really zap a social mood which even its practitioners had yet to fully comprehend?

"I don't know," he admitted. "Of course we were going out to the clubs, we were aware of the bands coming up behind us, but what you have to remember is, before *Jailbreak* took off, we were still playing the same places they were, the Greyhounds and Nashvilles and Dingwalls. Who were the boys? We all were." *Jailbreak* is Lizzy's masterpiece, but it wasn't to be the final word on the subject. Two years later, the double *Live And Dangerous* readdressed five of the album's finest moments; both singles, the rebellious thunder of Emerald, the seething Warriors and the rollicking Cowboy Song ("lonesome trail" rhymed with "certain female" – how can anybody resist?), and imbibed them all with even greater meaning. Not only were the boys back in town, they'd stuck around as well. And what they had wrought would never be undone.

Record label:
Mercury
Produced
by John Alcock.
Recorded
at Ramport Studios, London; winter 1975.
Released:
March 1976
Chart peaks:
10 (UK) 18 (US)
Personnel:
Phil Lynott (v, b, acoustic g), Scott Gorman (g), Brian Robertson (g), Brian Downey (d)
Track listing:
Jailbreak (S); Angel From The Coast; Running Back; Romeo And The Lonely Girl; Warriors; The Boys Are Back In Town (S); Fight Or Fall; Cowboy Song; Emerald
Running time:
36.16
Current CD:
532294-2
Further listening:
Dedication: The Very Best Of (1991)
Further reading:
MOJO 2; Phil Lynott – The Rocker (Mark Putterford, 1998); www.thinlizzyfan.com
Like this?
Try . . . p.279

Kiss

Destroyer

Fourth studio album by stack-heeled New York cartoon rockers is their first to top the million mark in the US.

Between January 1974 and mid-'75 Kiss allegedly relied on then-manager Bill Aucoin to overload his credit cards in order to obtain the necessary tour support to keep the band on the road. By the end of '75, however, their legwork had paid off forcing the double album *Alive!* set to crash into the US Top 10. In a bid to raise the stakes for that all-important fourth album, Kiss recruited Bob Ezrin whose work included several Alice Cooper albums including the chart-topping *Billion Dollar Babies* set. Sharing the songwriting on seven of the nine *Destroyer* tracks, Ezrin added a suitably grandiose edge to the proceedings – the overblown pomp of Great Expectations and the keyboard interlude on Flaming Youth, an otherwise typical chest-beating Kiss number.

Opener Detroit Rock City, a tribute to Kiss's Motor City stronghold, boasts a lengthy intro which catalogues the death of a drink-driver in Pontiac, Michigan – the newscast and subsequent sound of the wreckage being cleared from the road. Ominous, brooding but anthemic, the track sets the tone for the entire album. Paul Stanley's King Of The Night Time World is pure machismo, while the thumping God Of Thunder allows Gene Simmons to unleash his demonic persona to full effect. Anthems such as Shout It Out Loud and Do You Love Me are dumb-ass glam nuggets furnished with a layer of production gloss courtesy of Ezrin. Top 10 single Beth, a weepy ballad about life on the road penned and sung by drummer Peter Criss in his best *faux* Rod Stewart rasp, is the album's biggest track, providing Kiss with a wave-your-lighters-in-the-air live showstopper. *Destroyer* was one of Kiss's most accomplished and ambitious albums, and their first million-seller, kick-starting the second phase of the band's career.

In the next two years, just as punk broke in the UK, Kiss became America's hottest live attraction, developing a larger-than-life stageshow (see the inside sleeve of *Alive II*) alongside a range of merchandise that extended from lunchboxes to lawnmowers and, later, even cars. In short, Kiss – *literally* – sold their audience a rock-'n'roll dream, and reaped considerable financial benefits. Their influence upon the next generation of American rock bands should not be underestimated.

Record label:
Casablanca
Produced
by Bob Ezrin.
Recorded
at The Record Plant, New York; summer 1975.
Released:
May 1976
Chart peaks:
22 (UK) 11 (US)
Personnel:
Paul Stanley (v, g); Gene Simmons (v, b); Ace Frehley (g, v); Peter Criss (d, v)
Track listing:
Detroit Rock City; King Of The Night Time World; God Of Thunder; Great Expectations; Flaming Youth (S); Sweet Pain; Shout It Out Loud (S); Beth (S); Do You Love Me
Running time:
34.06
Current CD:
824 149
Further listening:
Alive II (1977)
Further reading:
Kiss And Sell: The Making Of A Supergroup (CK Lendt, 1997) – the band's former business manager spills the beans on Kiss's marketing strategies.
Like this?
Try . . . p.424

Steve Miller Band

Fly Like An Eagle

Charisma-free, but classy, the cosmic hippy/downhome R&B crossover.

Brought up in Texas and San Francisco, Steve Miller benefited from his doctor father's fondness for having star musicians round for tea. With house guests ranging from Les Paul through T-Bone Walker to Charlie Mingus, he grew up usefully apprised that "musicians had funny manners and funny habits", but also believing it would do no harm to learn how to play a bit.

In '60s San Francisco, his skill distinguished him from the run of hippy bands while his fondness for peace-and-love lyrics linked him handily to the new cosmic mainstream. Astutely, in 1967 he secured from Capitol the best contract any artist had achieved up to that time. Then, less cleverly, he slave-drove himself through eight albums in six years. But after *The Joker* (1973) sold a million, already 30 and having finally "snapped" on the road, he took a break. It turned out that he could sneak away from the public eye very easily because, according to Rolling Stone, he was rock's "most faceless top-ranked performer". Miller knew it and liked it that way. "I don't want to be a personality," he said. "I like to slip in and out of other characters." So, playfully, in his songwriting he had concealed himself behind personas like The Gangster Of Love on *Sailor* (1968) and the sleazeball Maurice (that's Maureece) on *Recall The Beginning . . . A Journey From Eden* (1972).

For two years he worked mostly at home, creating *Fly Like And Eagle* (1976) and *Book Of Dreams* (1977), both seductively coherent mergers of late-blooming psychedelia with grunty R&B. The rough and the smooth – juxtaposed by Miller's pithy guitar and whipped-cream vocals – work like rye bread with honey. There's an irresistible slippiness to cool rockers Mercury Blues, Take The Money And Run and Rock 'N Me and a sense of airiness, flight even, to his insouciant digressions into hoedown with Dance, Dance, Dance, soul with Sam Cooke's You Send Me and spooky blues with Sweet Maree (abetted by Muddy Waters' harmonica player James Cotton). Developing into a careful planner, Miller promoted the album with a break-even theatre tour when he could have played arenas for big money: "The show will start at eight sharp – hopefully it'll be the ultimate rational concert." And he got a result: more than 4 million American sales each for *Fly Like An Eagle* and its successor. With which he bought a farm in Oregon and withdrew to conduct sporadic musical activities as the mood took him.

Record label:
Mercury
Produced
by Steve Miller.
Recorded
at Steve Miller's home in Marin County and CBS Studios, San Francisco, California; June 1974–December 1975.
Released:
May 1976
Chart peaks:
11 (UK) 3 (US)
Personnel:
Steve Miller (v, g, Roland, sitar, g); Gary Mallaber (d, pc); Lonnie Turner (b); James Cotton (hm); Mike Fusaro (e)
Track listing:
Fly Like An Eagle (S, US only); Space Odyssey; Wild Mountain Honey; Serenade; Dance, Dance, Dance; Mercury Blues; Take The Money And Run (S); Rock 'N Me (S); You Send Me; Blue Odyssey; Sweet Maree; The Window
Running time:
37.44
Current CD:
EAM CD 041
Further listening:
Sailor (1968), The Joker (1973), Abracadabra (1982) – the other times when Miller's sleek self-confidence opened out to become really seductive.
Further reading:
Clippings-zines on Steve Miller (available direct from David Housden, tel 00 44 (0)1945 870065); www.stevemillerband.com or www.gangster-of-love.com
Like this?
Try . . . p.248

Ramones

Ramones

Four skinny jerks from New York tear down rock music and start again.

Clocking in at under 30 minutes and sounding the death knell for flares, Ramones is one of the most exciting and influential records in rock'n'roll. Though it seemed to have come of the blue, the band had been honing their sound for two years.

"It was born out of a chemical imbalance between me, Dee Dee and Johnny," says Joey Ramone. "Rock'n'roll had got so bloated and lost its spirit. We stripped it down and reassembled it under the influence of The MC5, The Beatles and the Stones, Alice Cooper and T Rex. We had all the songs worked up before we went in, we were always good like that. The Ramones was always about having fun. Fun disappeared in 1974, there were too many serious people out there at that time."

Joey remembers that they tried putting the bass and drums through one channel, with guitars and vocals through the other, but neither method worked.

"That approach was far too retro," states producer Craig Leon (also the scout who'd brought the group to Sire). "[*Ramones*] was recorded on the graveyard shift, very quickly, then we mixed and remixed the whole thing in one night. Each song was recorded slower than its live counterpart because the studio metronome would only go up to 208 beats per minute!"

Of course, the band's "dumb" image was just an act: the subtlety and intelligence at work evidenced in the application of a joyous Brill Building pop instinct to a compressed metal wall of sound.

The Ramones went on to even greater glory with Leave Home and Rocket To Russia, but their debut was the crucial broadside, a defining statement, a wake-up call.

Record label:
Sire
Produced
by Craig Leon and Tom Erdelyi (aka Tommy Ramone).
Recorded
at Plaza Sound, Radio City Music Hall, New York City;
Released:
May 1976
Chart peaks:
None (UK) 111 (US)
Personnel:
Johnny Ramone (g); Joey Ramone (v); Dee Dee Ramone (b); Tommy Ramone (d)
Track listing:
Blitzkrieg Bop; Beat On The Brat; Judy Is A Punk; I Wanna Be Your Boyfriend; Chain Saw; Now I Wanna Sniff Some Glue; I Don't Wanna Go Down In The Basement; Loudmouth; Havana Affair; Listen To My Heart; 53rd & 3rd; Let's Dance; I Don't Wanna Walk Around With You; Today Your Love, Tomorrow The World
Running time:
29.14
Current CD:
7599-27421-2
Further listening:
Try the exhilarating double It's Alive (1979), effectively a live greatest hits.
Further reading:
The Ramones, An American Band (Jim Bessman, 1993); www.officialramones.com
Like this?
Try . . . p.690

Aerosmith

Rocks

Their sex-and-drugs-fuelled fourth album is the nearest thing yet to a rock festival on record.

Inspired and honed by an increasingly successful three years on the road, with all the lurid sex-and-drugs excesses that encompassed, this sinewy, horny, heavy rock album found Aerosmith at the peak of their powers – and of their drug intake. If the previous year's *Toys In The Attic* had marked the Boston band's shift from wannabe British blues-rockers (the Stones, Yardbirds and Zeppelin were critics' usual comparisons) to all-American, superstar stadium-rockers, *Rocks* marked the shift, according to Joe Perry, "from a bunch of musicians dabbling in drugs to a bunch of addicts dabbling in music."

In early 1976, when they backed a mobile recording truck into The Wherehouse to start preproduction, Aerosmith were one of the biggest bands in America. *Toys* was gold, all three of their albums were in the charts, and sales had topped three million. This accounts for *Rocks*' confident swagger, from the metal-funk of Get The Lead Out, the Black Sabbathy power of Nobody's Fault and the lighter-wielding ballad Home Tonight to the punch-along, powerhouse opening anthem Back In The Saddle, which aimed for "this larger-than-life vibe, to bring the band right into the middle of the kid's head when he put on his phones in his bedroom at night."

The album, Jack Douglas said, "had to make a big statement about how loud and hard they were, how unapologetic they felt about being who they were – this brash, rude, sexual, hardcore rock band." The band's two core obsessions – sex and drugs – were both well represented; Rats In The Cellar inspired by the death of their dealer during the recording, and Back In The Saddle by a discussion in the studio about Gene Autry whom Tyler was convinced was referring to "fucking". *Rocks* shipped platinum, an immediate hit, and would become probably the biggest influence on the next generation of US stadium-rockers such as Van Halen and Guns N'Roses, whose Slash cites it as the album that made him pick up a guitar. A review in American rock magazine Creem summed it up: "Coming after a brief era when rock'n'roll fans were bombarded with the exaggerated sexual ambiguity of Alice, Bowie and Reed, it must be reassuring to have a band that knows everything we've wanted to know about sex all along: it's dirty."

SS

Record label:
CBS
Produced
by Jack Douglas and Aerosmith.
Recorded
at the Wherehouse, Waltham, Massachusetts; Record Plant, New York; February–March 1976.
Release date:
June 1976
Chart peaks:
None (UK) 3 (US)
Personnel:
Steven Tyler (v); Joe Perry (g); Brad Whitford (g); Tom Hamilton (b); Joey Kramer (d); Jay Messina (e)
Track listing:
Back In The Saddle; Last Child; Rats In The Cellar; Combination; Sick As A Dog; Nobody's Fault; Get The Lead Out; Lick And A Promise; Home Tonight
Running time:
34.25
Currently available CD:
4749652
Further listening:
Toys In The Attic (1975); Pump (1989); Get A Grip (1993); Nine Lives (1997)
Further reading:
Walk This Way: The Autobiography Of Aerosmith (Stephen Davis, 1998)
www.aerosmith.com
Like this?
Try . . . p.515

Parliament

Mothership Connection

The Parliafunkadelicment thang goes universal as Clinton marries serious funk to a comic-book tale.

In 1974 the wildly prolific and continually inventive George Clinton, tired of trying to make Funkadelic a commercial success and unsure about their immediate direction, reactivated the name of his former vocal group, The Parliaments, and signed them as Parliament to Neil Bogart's new label, Casablanca.

Classically trained keyboard player Bernie Worrell had brought a greater sense of order to the arrangements, the Horny Horns from James Brown's band meant a sharp new colour in the mix, and the younger recruits, Bootsy and Phelps Collins and Frank Waddy, infused the band with a fresh energy, just as they had James Brown's orchestra. The new sound was called P-Funk. The final ingredient was lyrics, written by Bootsy and Clinton, that set up an unlikely tale of intergalactic struggle for the funk which unravelled like some particularly perverse soap opera over two subsequent albums.

Typically, Clinton played it to the hilt, laying inspiration for the songs at the door of extraterrestrial intervention. He and Bootsy, he said at the time, were driving along a highway in Canada when a solid beam of light hit their car. "I told Bootsy to step on it . . .ever since then things have really begun to happen. It was like somebody out there saying they were hip to the Mothership and approve."

More likely is the confluence of great dance music honed after years of touring and studio work, Clinton's innate sense of cool, copious amounts of drugs and a visual flair far removed from the mohair suits and slick dance steps associated with virtually every top male black act. P-Funk (Wants To Get Funked Up) and Give Up The Funk (Tear The Roof Off The Sucker), were Parliament anthems to set alongside Funkadelic's Get Off Your Ass And Jam, while Handcuffs introduced new singer Glen Goins and the title track unveiled Star Child, leading character in the space battle for funk and dance that would evolve between Dr Funkenstein and Sir Nose D'Voidoffunk. Dense, freewheeling, goodtiming music with its crazy head in the stars. It might have been baffling to outsiders but the hip bought it by the truckload, P-Funk stormed the charts.

Record label:
Casablanca
Produced
by George Clinton.
Recorded
at United Sound, Detroit, Hollywood Sound, Hollywood; Autumn 1975.
Released:
June 1976
Chart peaks:
None (UK) 13 (US)
Personnel:
George Clinton (v); Calvin Simon, Fuzzy Haskins, Raymond Davis, Grady Thomas (bv); Bootsy Collins (v, b, g, d, pc); Fred Wesley, Maceo Parker, Michael Brecker, Boom, Joe Farrell (horns); Cordell Mosson (b); Gary Shider (g, bv); Michael Hampton (g); Glen Goins (bv, g); Tiki Fulwood, Jerome Brailey, Gary Cooper (d, pc); Bernie Worrell (k, syn)
Track listing:
P-Funk (Wants To Get Funked Up) (S); Mothership Connection (Star Child); Unfunky UFO; Supergroovalistic-Prosifunkstication; Handcuffs; Give Up The Funk (Tear The Roof Off The Sucker) (S); Night Of The Thumpasorus Peoples
Running time:
38.19
Current CD:
AA8245022
Further listening:
The Clones Of Dr Funkenstein (1977); Funkentelechy Vs The Placebo Syndrome (1977); Parliament Live: P-Funk Earth Tour (1977); Funkadelic's One Nation Under A Groove (1978)
Further reading:
MOJO 34
Like this?
Try . . . p.839

Rush

2112

Half hard rock, half concept album that spawned numerous sci-fi metal imitations. Side one features Alex Lifeson tuning-up in a cave.

Some collective consciousness has decreed that Rush be eternally unhip, but the Toronto band's fourth album was an instantly intriguing gambit. Side one – the concept side – was heavily-influenced by the novelist and philosopher Ayn Rand, and imagined a futuristic society ruled by priests who had banned musical instruments as the setting for an examination of human freewill.

Lyricist Neil Peart's penchant for extended ruminations had been established on 1975's *Caress Of Steel*, but if this was a poor-seller which left the band with everything to prove, *2112* was a brilliantly-executed riposte.

"I grew up in the suburbs and it was all very prosaic and dull," said Peart of the sci-fi fascination he shared with a large portion of his audience, "so I started getting interested in all those kinds of things just in the belief that there must be a more interesting world out there. Consequently you get tied up in all that, and whether you believe it or not really doesn't matter. It becomes an escape. I can understand it from the kids' point of view, having been that way myself. And as a writer, fantasy is really an excellent vehicle for expressing ideas in their purest sense, without any preconceptions. There's nothing better than having your own made-to-order extra-terrestrial world."

Much of side two offered more traditional fare. The lyrics of A Passage To Bangkok – later a live favourite – read like a hash menu at an Amsterdam cafe, and Something For Nothing – the kind of song which would later prompt Pavement's Steven Malkmus to wonder how Geddy Lee's voice got so high – works its magic with little more than a few power-chords. Lifeson's lead-guitar work is at its best on The Twilight Zone, where he makes spine-tingling use of the false-harmonic technique which was becoming his trademark. Only the slush-laden ballad Tears let the side down.

Showcasing the kind of chops that would regularly see them top "best musician" polls, Lee, Lifeson and Peart – "I don't know about numerology or anything mystical but there's something good about three people," he said – created a spirited galaxy of riffs which eclipsed their Zeppelin-esque roots.

The album also saw them lay the foundations of a sound which would establish them as one of the premier hard rock acts of the '80s and '90s. Fans of *2122* include Beck, who used to play live with a sticker of the Rush star logo on his guitar. By November 1977, the album was certified gold, and by November 1995 triple platinum.

Record label:
Mercury
Produced
by Rush and Terry Brown.
Recorded
at Toronto Sound Studios, Ontario, Canada; 1975–1976.
Released:
June 1976
Chart peaks:
None (UK) 61 (US)
Personnel:
Geddy Lee (b, v); Alex Lifeson (g); Neil Peart (d); Hugh Syme (k); Terry Brown (e)
Track listing:
2112: I Overture; II The Temples of Syrinx; III Discovery; IV Presentation; V Oracle: The Dream; VI Soliloquy; VII Grand Finale; A Passage To Bangkok; The Twilight Zone; Lessons (S); Tears; Something For Nothing
Running time:
38.52
Current CD:
534 626-2
Further listening:
A Farewell To Kings (1977)
Further reading:
Rush Visions: The Official Biography (Bill Banasiewicz, 1988); www.oceanrush.com www.blarghnet.com/supper/rush/index.html#top
Like this?
Try . . . p.305

Boz Scaggs

Silk Degrees

Slick and soulful music for satin-sheet-sliding. Allegedly caused hump(!) in the US population graph.

When William Royce (Boz) Scaggs began work on his *Slow Dancer* album in 1974, he forsook recording with his road band in favour of studio musicians for the first time since his debut album in the late '60s. A lot of Detroit/Motown expatriates turned up at those Los Angeles sessions including famed bassist James Jamerson. Scaggs knew he was on the right track, but was prevented from artistic closure by the total-control tactics of producer/writer/artist Johnny Bristol.

So, for his next effort, Scaggs dumped Bristol and turned to Columbia staff producer Joe Wissert, who had been doing wonderful things with Earth, Wind & Fire. Together, they assembled a rhythm section of studio up-and-comers including drummer Jeff Porcaro, bassist David Hungate and keyboardist/arranger David Paitch (the three soon to become the nucleus of the band Toto). The chemistry between the musicians and Scaggs' material was inspiring. Wissert wisely stepped back and let magic take place, offering only the occasional suggestion or tie-breaking vote in a musical "discussion". Along with guitarists Fred Tackett and Louie Shelton, and the cream of LA's horns-for-hire, they produced a slick, uptown, soulful goo that slid right down inside your best dancin' shoes.

The resultant collection, named after a discarded Scaggs lyric, was immediately embraced by American radio. Lowdown, We're All Alone, What Can I Say and Lido Shuffle billowed creamily out of car speakers and pumped out of the dance clubs. Scaggs vocals moved up a notch as he essayed the material in the manner of an authoritative, yet laid-back white-boy Al Green. Later artists, such as Bobby Caldwell or middle-period Robert Palmer, built careers on the musical foundation of *Silk Degrees*. Photographer Moshe Brakha's evocative cover shot showed an apparently-despondent Scaggs sitting on a seaside park-bench facing left, while a glimpse of a woman's nicely manicured hand indicates her exit stage right. On the back, Scaggs is nowhere to be seen, but the woman's hand remains on the right, apparently frozen in time by the proceedings. Lowdown was awarded a Grammy for best R&B song in 1976, and album sales soared to four million. The following year, when work began on the follow-up, *Down Two, Then Left*, squabbles from the past year over who wrote what, availability, and scheduling prevented the same line-up from being reprised. So it was for one time only that Scaggs delivered the goods with a great batch of songs and sympathetic studio stringers who perfectly matched his muse.

Record label:
CBS
Produced
by Joe Wissert.
Recorded
at Dav-Len Studios and Hollywood Sound, Los Angeles; 1975.
Released:
September 1976
Chart peaks:
37 (UK) 2 (US)
Personnel:
Boz Scaggs (g, v); David Paitch (k, arr); David Hungate (b); Jeff Porcaro (d); Fred Tackett (g); Louie Shelton (g); Tom Perry (e)
Track listing:
What Can I Say (S); Georgia; Jump Street; What Do You Want The Girl To Do; Harbor Lights; Lowdown (S); It's Over (S); Love Me Tomorrow; Lido Shuffle (S); We're All Alone
Running time:
41.33
Current CD:
Columbia 4719682
Further listening:
The album before, Slow Dancer (1974); the album after, Down Two Then Left (1977); a sprinkling from all 13 solo albums on two CDs: My Time: A Boz Scaggs Anthology (1999).
Like this?
Try . . . p.57

Stevie Wonder

Songs In The Key Of Life

Only the third album ever to enter the US charts at Number 1 (after two by Elton John), where it stayed for 14 weeks.

Back in the mid-'70s, a two-year gap between albums seemed interminable. Two years after *Fulfillingness' First Finale*, Stevie was seen around LA in a T-shirt that proclaimed "We've nearly finished". It had been made for him by engineer Gary Olazabal, who was, according to Stevie, "very patient."

After signing his first contract with Motown as an adult, Wonder had produced an astonishingly sustained run of four excellent albums in a creative partnership with programmers and arrangers Malcolm Cecil and Bob Margouleff. Having signed a new seven-year deal for $13 million in 1975, he began, then aborted, two albums, *Fulfillingness' Second Finale* and *Let's See Life The Way It Is* and severed his ties with Cecil and Margouleff before delivering this double-plus masterpiece.

This was the first album where Stevie called all the shots. The sweep of styles, from the big-band jazz of the Ellington tribute Sir Duke, via the string-driven street opera of Village Ghetto Land through the driving polemic of Black Man, is the broadest of any Wonder album. Bursting with inspiration, Stevie would spend literally days on end recording, up to 72 hours at a stretch without food or sleep.

Many things held up recording: new songs that simply had to be included; a chase around Los Angeles maternity wards to obtain the first cries of a new-born baby for Isn't She Lovely; experimenting with new gadgets like the Yamaha Electrone Polyphonic Synthesizer GX10 (which produced the most convincing synthesized strings anyone had heard to that date); even – it was reported at the time – Stevie's dissatisfaction with the cover art! If Wonder's tardiness would become a matter of legend, few could dispute that the delays paid off here. "I wanted it to be the very best I can do," declared Stevie with a note of triumph in his voice. Released on a tidal wave of hype, it was kept from the UK peak by Abba's *Greatest Hits*.

Record label:
Motown
Produced
by Stevie Wonder.
Recorded
at Crystal Industries Inc., Los Angeles; Hit Factory, New York City; Record Plant, Los Angeles; Record Plant, Sausalito, California; 1975–76.
Released:
October 16, 1976
Chart peaks:
2 (UK) 1 (US)
Personnel:
All instruments played by Stevie Wonder. Additional parts by: Mike Sembello, Ben Bridges, Dean Parks, George Benson, WG 'Snuffy' Walden (g); 'Sneaky Pete' Kleinow (sg); Nathan Watts (b); Ray Pound, Greg Brown (d); Greg Philinganes, Herbie Hancock (k); Ronnie Foster (o); Gary Olazabal, John Fischbach (e)
Track listing:
Love's In Need Of Love Today; Have A Talk With God; Village Ghetto Land; Contusion; Sir Duke (S); I Wish (S); Knocks Me Off My Feet; Pastime Paradise; Summer Soft; Ordinary Pain; Isn't She Lovely; Joy Inside My Tears; Black Man; Ngiculela/Es Una Historia/I Am Singing; If It's Magic; As; Another Star (S)
Running time:
86.53
Current CD:
1573572 adds: Saturn; Ebony Eyes; All Day Sucker; Easy Goin' Evening (My Mama's Call)
Further listening:
Hotter Than July (1980) includes such great pop moments as Masterblaster and Lately.
Like this?
Try . . . p.532

Abba

Arrival

Abba's fourth album irrevocably transformed them from Swedish pop curiosity to worldwide phenomenon.

In the summer of 1976 Abba were invited to perform at the most exclusive Swedish social event of the year – a Stockholm ball celebrating the wedding of King Carl Gustaf and Silvia Sommerlath. Dressed in bizarre medieval costumes they decided to perform a new song Björn and Benny had written six months earlier, Dancing Queen. The reaction was extraordinary. Sweden, which had been coolly sceptical of their success thus far, elevated them to musical royalty, erroneously assuming they'd written the song in honour of the new ruler and Dancing Queen embarked on a startling journey of its own, becoming Abba's first and only American chart-topper, and eventually becoming a front-line gay anthem.

"I hope," said Björn when *Arrival* was finally released six months behind schedule, "people will stop assuming we're one hit wonders." The NME didn't, dismissing it as "patent rubbish", but for most other commentators it was the album that finally earned them respect, albeit grudging. Björn and Benny had all but eradicated the trashier influence of manager Stig Anderson from the songwriting and provided a vindication for pure pop song as a valid art form. "Our difficulty was always to get rid of the Eurovision stamp and it was especially hard in England where they were used to groups coming over from the continent and not lasting very long, but with *Arrival* we were finally accepted," said Bjorn.

It also, briefly, cracked America. Partly due to Agnetha's terror of live audiences, an even greater terror of flying and a hatred of being parted from daughter Linda, Abba were reluctant to spend time in the States, and once announced they'd never tour the US until they had a chart-topper. When Dancing Queen hit Number 1 there in April '77 they ran out of excuses, but there remained something half-hearted about their American adventure and they never enjoyed the success there that they knew in the rest of the world.

Arrival also included the classic Knowing Me Knowing You (a-ha!) and Money Money Money which apart from showing Björn and Benny's willingness to poke fun at themselves, also hinted at musical ambitions beyond a three-minute pop format into the world of musicals. Years later they achieved it, working with Tim Rice on Chess, but for most people in the late '70s Abba's vindication of the three-minute format and their search for the perfect pop record was enough. Here's where they found it.

Record label:
Epic
Produced
by Benny Andersson and Björn Ulvaeus.
Recorded
at Metronome Studios, Stockholm; January–February 1976.
Released:
November 5, 1976
Chart peaks:
1 (UK) 20 (US)
Personnel:
Agnetha Fältskog (v); Anni-Frid Lyngstad (v); Benny Andersson (syn, p, accordion, k, marimbas, chimes, v); Björn Ulvaaeus (ag, g, v, a); Janne Schaffer (ag, g); Ola Brunkert (strings, d); Lars Carlsson (horn); Anders Dahl (strings); Malando Gassama (pc); Anders Glenmark (ag, g); Roger Palm (strings, d); Lasse Wellander (ag, g); Michael B Tretow (e); Sven-Olof Walldoff (a)
Track listing:
When I Kissed The Teacher; Dancing Queen (S); My Love My Life; Dum Dum Diddle; Knowing Me Knowing You (S); Money Money Money (S); That's Me (S); Why Did It Have To Be Me?; Tiger; Arrival
Running time:
33.16
Current CD:
Polydor 5339812
Further listening:
The massively successful compilations Abba Gold (1992) and More Abba Gold (1993) tell the complete story, but for deeper intrigue try the thematic, moody The Visitors, (1981).
Further reading:
www.abbasite.com
Like this?
Try . . . p.177

The Eagles

Hotel California

Erstwhile proponents of that Peaceful Easy Feeling get real and metaphorical too.

"We wanted it all. Peer respect, Number 1 singles and albums, great music and a lot of money," said Glenn Frey, summing up The Eagles shortly after they recorded *Hotel California*. His co-frontman and rival Don Henley added: "I was driven, a man possessed." But weren't they the epitome of '70s soft rock's slumberous laid-back genre? Frey elucidated: "The only difference between boring and laid-back is a million dollars."

Before *Hotel California* they had shuffled their citified country rock – exemplified by vapid hits Take It Easy, Peaceful Easy Feeling and so on – across to the rockier sound of *One Of These Nights* (1975). This and US chart-topping compilation, *Their Greatest Hits 1971-1975*, left their blatant greed satiated, their longing for esteem less so because critics still scorned them. So, with original member Bernie Leadon replaced by Joe Walsh, just when The Eagles might have succumbed to complacency they were fired up as never before.

Aiming a touch high, they decided "the Eagles' Bicentennial album" should express everything they felt about America post-'60s, post-Vietnam, post-Watergate. With the title track and Life In The Fast Lane they had songs which slicked their way into the singles charts while bearing durable, era-defining metaphors. "The Hotel California is something that was elegant, but now is decadent – we think this album represents the whole world, not just California," Henley proclaimed.

Although Victim Of Love came on like *faux* Bad Company, the key songs were well supported by tough-tender tales of innocence and experience in New Kid In Town and Wasted Time, while the seven-minute final track, The Last Resort, was at least a valiant sacrifice on the altar of saying it all in one song about the state of the world and the world of the state.

Personally the antithesis of their cool image, The Eagles effectively burned themselves out making *Hotel California*. Recording between tour dates, for weeks on end their daily timetable read "gig, airport, fly to Miami, record all night, airport, fly to next gig, gig, airport." At the end of it, Henley boasted of chalking up his first stomach ulcer at 29 and Frey simply insisted, "We've tried harder than we ever tried before."

Henley argued that their concept extended to satirising "the kind of limbo we are experiencing in the music business while we are waiting for the next big surge of inspiration". Then came punk and, as it happened, The Eagles never made another good record.

Record label:
Asylum
Produced
by Bill Szymczyk.
Recorded
at Criteria Studios, Miami, and The Record Plant, Los Angeles, March–October 1976.
Release date:
December 1976
Chart peaks:
2 (UK) 1 (US)
Personnel:
Don Henley (v, d, pc, syn); Glenn Frey (v, clavinet, p, g); Don Felder (v, g, ps); Joe Walsh (g, v, p, organ, syn); Randy Meisner (v, guitarone); Bill Szymczyk, Allan Blazek, Ed Mashal, Bruce Hensal (e)
Track listing:
Hotel California (S); New Kid In Town (S); Life In The Fast Lane (S); Wasted Time; Wasted Time (reprise); Victim Of Love; Pretty Maids All In A Row; Try And Love Again; The Last Resort
Running time:
43.28
Current CD:
7559-60509-2
Further listening:
One Of These Nights (1975) – big step on the way from LA dudes posing as desperadoes to self-discovery as ironic rockers.
Further reading:
To The Limit: The Untold Story Of The Eagles (Marc Eliot,1999).
www.eaglesfans.com
Like this?
Try . . . p.207

Johnny 'Guitar' Watson

Ain't That A Bitch

Smash-hit disco comeback by veteran bluesman.

When disco started cutting a swathe through black American music in the early '70s, it put a whole generation of musicians out of work. But while scores of his blues and soul contemporaries were consigned to obsolescence, one-time Texas bluesman Johnny 'Guitar' Watson hit paydirt with one of the biggest dance albums of the '70s, winning a Grammy nomination as best new vocalist – at the age of 41: "I'm saying to myself, is this a joke? But better late than never is what I always say."

Watson had scored several small hits in a staggeringly eclectic career, but the big time eluded him until British blues producer Mike Vernon suggested an unlikely partnership.

"He tells me this guy Dick James is looking to start a new label. I found out later they didn't really expect a big success, it was possibly a tax write-off."

If Dick James, publisher of The Beatles and mentor of Elton John, was really hoping for a tax write-off, he met with failure of Producers-size proportions. Given *carte blanche* in the studio, Watson crafted an outrageously over-the-top epic, combining synth bass, Vocoders, spiky funk guitar, and outrageously witty lyrics.

"Man, when I recorded that album I had a serious ego problem, I felt like I could do anything – and somehow it all worked, it was the strangest thing. I did all the horns on studio time, said to the musicians, bring your manuscript and your horn and play what you want when you get there! Then when I told the promotion people what the title of the album was they were going 'Jeez, this man is crazy.' But Dick [James] was great, he was saying 'if that's what Mr Watson wants, that's what we'll do!'"

The wit and timeliness of the writing helped *Ain't That A Bitch* crossover into R&B and Pop markets, going gold in the process; the recording quality would help make it a favourite for shop assistants demonstrating hi-fi systems, while his pristine but organic grooves would later see him sampled by Snoop Doggy Dogg, Dr Dre and others.

Record label:
DJM
Produced
by Johnny 'Guitar' Watson.
Recorded
in Los Angeles, 1976.
Released:
1976
Chart peaks:
None (UK) None (US)
Personnel:
Johnny 'Guitar' Watson (v, g, b, k); Emry Thomas (d); Tommy Roberson (tb); Paul Dunmall (s); Peter Martin (tp)
Track listing:
I Need It; I Want To Ta-Ta You Baby; Superman Lover; Ain't That A Bitch; Since I Met You Baby; We're No Exception; Won't You Forgive Me Baby
Running time:
34.28
Current CD:
NEMCD774
Further listening:
A Real Mother (1977) and Funk Beyond The Call Of Duty (1978) repeat the irresistible funk formula; Ace compilation Hot Like TNT (1996), of early single sides like Gangster Of Love shows how far ahead of his time Watson was.
Further reading:
MOJO 80; Portrait Of The Blues (Paul Trynka, 1997)
Like this?
Try . . . p.579

Boston

Boston

Super-melodic AOR, custom-built for US radio, sold zillions.

Until it was overtaken by Whitney Houston's efforts in 1986, *Boston* was the fastest-selling debut album in history. Band lynchpin Tom Scholz – inventor of the Rockman micro-amp – was a studio boffin who'd graduated from the Massachusetts Institute Of Technology. When he married guitars reminiscent of an airbrushed Thin Lizzy with Brad Delp's gymnastic yet emotive vocals, America melted.

Scholz was a perfectionist: every note here is just how he wanted it. The band re-recorded several tracks on the West Coast with producer John Boylan, but much of the album consists of the original 12-track demos recorded at Scholz's home studio in Watertown.

The undoubted stand-out was More Than A Feeling, the ultimate AOR anthem. Slick as the song is, it has surprising links with grunge: Kurt Cobain later acknowledged that its chorus riff had partly inspired Smells Like Teen Spirit. Hitch A Ride and Peace Of Mind aired contrasting views on the American Dream, but most of the album's lyrics chewed the familiar fat of sex (Let Me Take You Home Tonight), drugs (Smokin'), and rock'n'roll (Rock'N'Roll Band).

Three US Top 40 singles set Boston's ball rolling, and *Boston* eventually sold over 15 million copies.

When Scholz laboured for two years over the follow-up, CBS grew impatient. The company rush-released the new record as soon as Scholz released the tapes, and it went on to shift six million units. The title was a misnomer: *Don't Look Back* was a virtual re-write of its predecessor.

Record label:
Epic
Produced
by John Boylan and Tom Scholz.
Recorded
at Foxglove Studios, Watertown, Massachusetts; winter 1975; Mastered at Capitol Studios, Hollywood, and The Record Plant, Los Angeles; spring 1976.
Released:
January 1977
Chart peaks:
11 (UK) 3 (US)
Personnel:
Brad Delp (v, g); Tom Scholz (g, k); Barry Goudreau (g); Fran Sheehan (b); Sib Hashian (d)
Track listing:
More Than A Feeling (S); Peace Of Mind (S); Foreplay; Long Time (S); Rock'N'Roll Band; Smokin'; Hitch A Ride; Something About You; Let Me Take You Home Tonight
Running time:
37.47
Current CD:
4894122
Further listening:
Don't Look Back (1978)
Further reading:
www.boston.org
Like this?
Try . . . p.459

David Bowie

Low

The first of Bowie's "Berlin" trilogy of collaborations with Brian Eno.

After the Neu!-influenced motorik of *Station To Station*, Bowie delved deeper into his Krautrock influences for *Low*, collaborating with Eno on this breakthrough work which brought the notion of "industrial music" experimentation to a mainstream audience. Using a basic group of Carlos Alomar, George Murray and Dennis Davis, Bowie decamped to Berlin, where he and Eno worked in complementary ways to open up exciting new paths for mainstream pop. "There was a very clear separation of jobs," recalls Eno. "Mine was to make musical settings in which something could happen, which suited me fine – I love being the scene-painter – and David, of course, is just great at stepping into things like that and becoming the actor. It suited both of our temperaments." Bowie was so charged-up by the experience that he employed the widest instrumental palette of any of his albums, while Eno added his distinctive patina of synths, tapes and treatments to the songs. At the time, however, Bowie was away from the studio for long stretches dealing with a protracted court case, so Eno worked on some tracks alone, intending to use them himself if they weren't deemed appropriate for *Low*. "A couple of those things on the second side, like Warszawa, started out of that process," he says. "As soon as David heard it he said, 'Get me a mic,' and just did this whole thing. He's very fast when he gets going, really a brilliant singer – I don't think people realise how finely he can tune his singing, in terms of picking a particular emotional pitch: it's really scientific, the way he does it. He'll say, 'I think that's slightly too theatrical there, it should be more withdrawn and introspective,' and he'll go in and sing it again, and you'll hear this point four of a degree shift which makes all the difference. That's what he's good at: he picks up the mood of a musical landscape, such as the type I might make, and he can really bring it to a sharp focus, both with the words he uses and the style of singing he chooses."

Balancing one side of angular electronic pop with one of more experimental tone poems, the album was a striking reaffirmation of the power of musical imagination at a time of Luddite retrenchment in rock, enabling Bowie to be one of the few glam-rock stars to successfully withstand the onslaught of punk with his reputation intact. It remains one of the pinnacles of his career.

Record label:
RCA
Produced
by David Bowie and Tony Visconti.
Recorded
at Château d'Herouville, France, and Hansa By The Wall; West Berlin; October 1976.
Released:
January 1977
Chart peaks:
2 (UK) 11 (US)
Personnel:
David Bowie (v, g, k, s, syn, tapes, c, pump bass, hm, vibes, xylophone, pc, Chamberlain); Eno (syn, k, Chamberlain, treatments, v); Carlos Alomar (g); George Murray (b); Dennis Davis (pc); Roy Young (p, Farfisa organ); Ricky Gardener (g); Iggy Pop (v); Mary Visconti (v); Eduard Meyer (c); Peter & Paul (k)
Track listing:
Speed Of Life; Breaking Glass; What In The World; Sound And Vision (S); Always Crashing In The Same Car; Be My Wife (S); A New Career In A New Town; Warszawa; Art Decade; Weeping Wall; Subterraneans
Running time:
38.54
Current CD:
5219070
Further listening:
The subsequent Heroes (1977) further developed the Bowie/Eno association, though by Scary Monsters (and Super Creeps) (1980) their joint inspiration was getting somewhat thinner on the ground.
Further reading:
www.davidbowie.com
Like this?
Try . . . p.418

The Damned

Damned Damned Damned

The first British punk album.

Speed – in both senses of the word – was of the essence. The first UK punk band to release a single (New Rose, October 1976), the first to hit daytime television (performing Neat Neat Neat on Supersonic), the first to visit America, it was inevitable The Damned would also be first to release an album, and what a little monster it was. With (as Brian James succinctly puts it) "a honkful of toot" to sustain them and six months of gigging behind them, even producer Nick Lowe later confessed that he did little more than watch while The Damned slammed through their live set.

"We treated it like a gig," explains James. "We went in and just bashed it down – I know that was Nick's nickname, Basher Lowe, 'Bash it down and tart it up in the mix' – but that's what we did. There were one or two numbers we had to do a second take on like Feel The Pain, because we weren't playing it live so much, and a couple of minuscule guitar bits on top – like on New Rose, there was a little guitar overdub on the middle eight. But that was it. It was just like a gig."

Written in haste, the songs represented punk's first public steps, with a couple – Stab Yor Back, So Messed Up – trailing the obligatory hail of gob. Yet for every slobbering three-chord blur in the Ramones mould, there was a genuine gem: Fish, which dated back to James' days with legendary rehearsal-room heroes, London SS; New Rose, of course; Feel The Pain – described by James as "our Jonathan Richman number" – and Fan Club, one of rock's most honest examinations of its audience, with a classic riff thrown in. Who said these punks couldn't write or play? Not that The Damned themselves went along with the punk-rock tag. Rat Scabies insists, "They were pop songs that were there to be played today and thrown away. That was the whole point." The Damned's brand of anarchy was resolutely playful, as the pie-fight sleeve-art attests. Neither was there any thought of longevity. "We never expected anything to last fucking 20 years," muses Rat. "The point was simply to do it."

Record label:
Demon
Produced
by Nick Lowe.
Recorded
at Pathway Studios, London; late 1976.
Released:
February 1977
Chart peaks:
36 (UK) None (US)
Personnel:
Dave Vanian (v); Brian James (g); Captain Sensible (b); Rat Scabies (d)
Track listing:
Neat Neat Neat (S); Fan Club; I Fall; Born To Kill; Stab Yor Back; Feel The Pain; New Rose (S); Fish; See Her Tonite; 1 Of The 2; So Messed Up; I Feel Alright
Running time:
31.34
Current CD:
FIENDCD91
Further listening:
Neat Neat Neat (Demon 3-CD box, 1997); The Dripping Lips (fronted by Brian James) Ready To Crack? (1998)
Further reading:
The Light At The End Of The Tunnel by Carol Clerk (1987)
Like this?
Try . . . p.392

Fleetwood Mac

Rumours

Internal romantic fall-out creates an AOR milestone, and Fleetwood Mac's first trans-Atlantic chart-topper.

Unity was never Fleetwood Mac's strongest point. Twelve musicians in eight years – 15 if you include the ersatz Mac sent on tour by a former manager in 1974 – ensured a family tree which was more of a small forest. But the discord they were accustomed to was as nothing to what was unleashed here: it was the stuff of soap opera. Stevie was breaking up with Lindsey, Christine was breaking with John, Mick and his first wife were separating and he was becoming close to Stevie, with liberal quantities of coke on hand to further fuel the paranoia. *Rumours* was less a collection of songs, more a bag of emotional crutches for the members to batter one another with.

"It was crucifyingly difficult at certain points," Mick Fleetwood admits, describing the frosty atmosphere in the studio. Compared to the three months it took to record their previous album, *Rumours* took a year, as private heartache became public property and every lyric, it seemed, became a source for further conflict. Buckingham took his rage out on his guitar, turning in a couple of solos (Go Your Own Way and Don't Stop) of soul-searing intensity; Christine McVie buried hers in the sonorous delicacy of Songbird; Nicks draped hers in the tragedy of Dreams and the vicious Gold Dust Woman. Fleetwood smashed hell out of the drums. "Stevie did her first take of Gold Dust Woman in a fully lit studio and, as take followed take, she began withdrawing into herself," recalls Mick. "So we dimmed the lights, brought her a chair, a supply of tissues, a Vicks inhaler, a box of lozenges for her sore throat and a bottle of mineral water. And on the eighth take, at four in the morning, she sang the lyric straight through to perfection."

The key to *Rumours*, however, lay in The Chain, the one song which turned all the betrayal and bitterness around and pinpointed what Fleetwood remembers as the sole unifying factor in all the turmoil. "We were so engrossed in what we were doing, realizing that we'd been given an opportunity, as individuals and as a band, that may only come once in a lifetime. And to throw it away would have been a sin. That's how we looked at it. That's how we got round all the other stuff, the bedroom stuff." Self-explanatory and, ultimately, self-fulfilling, the brooding, mantric Chain was the album's only band composition and became the creed which has since been woven into the musical and personal fabric of Fleetwood Mac: no matter what happens, you must never break the chain.

Record label:
Warners
Produced
by Fleetwood Mac, Richard Dashut and Ken Caillat.
Recorded
at Record Plant, Sausalito and LA; Wally Heider Recording Studios, LA; Criteria Studios, Miami FL; Davlen Recording Studio; North Hollywood; Zellerback Auditorium, UC Berkeley (Songbird).
Released:
February 1977
Chart peaks:
1 (UK) 1 (US)
Personnel:
Christine McVie (v, k, syn); Stevie Nicks (v); Lindsey Buckingham (g, v); John McVie (b); Mick Fleetwood (d)
Track listing:
Second Hand News; Dreams (S); Never Going Back Again; Don't Stop (S); Go Your Own Way (S); Songbird; The Chain; You Make Loving Fun (S); I Don't Want To Know; Oh Daddy; Gold Dust Woman
Running time:
39.58
Current CD:
7599 27313 2
Further listening:
The previous year's Fleetwood Mac, the calm before the storm.
Further reading:
Mick Fleetwood: My Life And Adventures With Fleetwood Mac (1990); www.repriserec.com/fleetwoodmac
Like this?
Try . . . p.113

Television

Marquee Moon

Not quite art rock but not quite prog or punk, the cult US outfit produce one of rock's most accomplished debuts.

By the mid-'70s, Television had became a focal point of the New York scene and were instrumental in persuading CBGB's manager Hilly Kristal to give a platform to some of the city's more *outré* musical units – themselves included. Malcolm McLaren was so impressed by the group – not least by bass player Richard Hell's ripped T-shirt – that he offered to manage them. The group recorded demos with Brian Eno (which Island were keen to release as an album) and with Blue Öyster Cult's Allen Lanier, but the group turned down a number of major label offers while waiting for the right deal. Hell left in 1975 and was replaced by ex-Blondie bassist Fred Smith, who added both a solidity and rhythmic flexibility. The group developed rapidly as a unit, in a collective style which reflected their musical influences: Smith and Richard Lloyd came from a more rock'n'roll background, Billy Ficca was a jazz enthusiast, while Tom Verlaine was interested in all points between The 13th Floor Elevators and Albert Ayler.

"Television rehearsed for six to seven days a week for four to six hours a day," Lloyd explains. "So we were both really roughshod musicians on one hand and desperadoes on the other, with the will to become good." Once Television signed to Elektra, Verlaine was keen not to have a name producer tell them what to do in the studio. So the job went to engineer Andy Johns who had worked in conjunction with producer brother Glyn, most famously with The Rolling Stones. "He had got some of the great guitar sounds in rock," says Lloyd.

Marquee Moon captured the group's new-found chemistry in action, sounding like nothing else around at the time. The tension generated between Lloyd and Verlaine's guitars was crucial, the players swapping between rhythm and melodic lines, sometimes several times per song. The soloing is superb, from Verlaine's dive-bombing runs on Friction to Lloyd's sublime cameo on Elevation.

Press reaction was ecstatic in the UK (though less so in the US), with NME immediately putting Television on its front cover. Lloyd: "There was a certain magic happening, an inexplicable certainty of something, like the momentum of a freight train. That's not egoism but, if you cast a spell, you don't get flummoxed by the results of your spell."

Record label:
Elektra
Produced
by Andy Johns and Tom Verlaine.
Recorded
at A&R Studios, New York City; September 1976.
Released:
February 1977
Chart peaks:
28 (UK) None (UK)
Personnel:
Tom Verlaine (v, g, k); Richard Lloyd (g, v); Fred Smith (b, v); Billy Ficca (d)
Track listing:
See No Evil; Venus; Friction; Marquee Moon (S/UK); Elevation; Guiding Light; Prove It (S/UK); Torn Curtain
Running time:
45.54
Current CD:
7559-60616-2
Further listening:
Adventure (1978), the group's untimely swansong; hear them cut loose live in the same year on double CD set, The Blow-Up.
Further reading:
http://www.slip.net/~rivethed/tvsite.htm
Like this?
Try . . . p.446

The Clash

The Clash

Soundtrack to 1977's 'Summer of Hate' and the totemic album of the English punk insurrection.

Mick Jones' claim that "I was so into speed I don't even recall making the first album" was undoubtedly an exaggeration, but by February 10, 1977, when the The Clash arrived at CBS Studios (where five years earlier Iggy and The Stooges had recorded *Raw Power*) things were certainly moving fast. The group had played their first show a mere eight months earlier, had inked their £100,000 contract with CBS just weeks before, and still hadn't written enough songs to fill their first long-player. As they swaggered into the Soho studios in their artfully paint-spattered clothes – causing the receptionist to mistake them for workmen – The Clash brought more attitude than expertise.

Engineer Simon Humphrey recalled that "They wouldn't shake my hand because I was a hippy."

The sessions, which took place over three, four-day weekends, proved imponderable to producer Mickey Foote and his engineer. None of the group liked to be first to arrive; if they were, they would vanish for an hour or two, each thereby missing the others. An entire session could vanish through this competition in cool. "There was a rivalry between Mick and Joe," said Humphrey. "One of them would turn up and say, 'Who else is here?' and I'd say, 'Actually Mick you're the first one.' He'd say 'Fuck that!' and bugger off. Then Joe would turn up and say 'Where's Mick?' and I'd say, 'He was here earlier but left.' So Joe would say 'Bloody hell!' and storm off. Then they'd all reconvene later on." There were other problems; drummer Terry Chimes (derisively named 'Tory Crimes' on the cover) had already been flung out of the group, but since they could find no replacement, he played on the album anyway.

From this muddle of inexperience, ideological posturing and amphetamine overload, a magnificent record somehow emerged, one which distilled punk rock's intoxicating brew of anger, boredom and excitement better than any other. To go with its barking vocals, leering choruses and ram-a-lam guitar (all much copied) was snappy sloganeering; the dole queue moan of Career Opportunities, the confrontation of White Riot, the anti-Americanism of I'm So Bored With The USA (ironic given the band's later infatuation with the country). Its two-minute songs zipped past, requiring six minutes of clumsy white reggae on Police And Thieves for padding. In America Rolling Stone hailed it as "the definitive punk album" but CBS were nonetheless loath to release it there, relenting only after 100,000 import copies were sold. They had realised what Jones had claimed all along: "It ain't punk, it ain't new wave. Call it what you want, all the terms stink. Call it rock'n'roll."

NS

Record label:
CBS
Produced
by Micky Foote.
Recorded
at CBS Studios, London; February 1977.
Released:
April 1977
Chart peaks:
12 (UK) 100 (US)
Personnel:
Joe Strummer (g, v); Mick Jones (g, v); Paul Simonon (b); 'Tory Crimes' Terry Chimes (d); Simon Humphrey (e)
Track listing:
Janie Jones; Remote Control (S); I'm So Bored With The USA; White Riot (S); Hate And War; What's My Name; Deny; London's Burning; Career Opportunities; Cheat; Protex Blue; Police And Thieves; 48 Hours; Garageland
Running time:
34.00
Current CD:
4687832. The American edition of the album had a different track listing, adding Clash City Rockers, Complete Control, I Fought The Law, Jail Guitar Doors and (White Man) In Hammersmith Palais and removing Deny, Protex Blue and 48 Hours. Cat. no: EK63883
Further listening:
The mini-album Black Market Clash (1980) and The Story of The Clash (1991) include out-takes from '77.
Further reading:
MOJO 71; The Last Gang In Town by Marcus Gray (1996); The Illustrated History (Chris Salewicz and Adrian Boot, 1996)
Like this?
Try . . . p.435

1977

Kraftwerk

Trans-Europe Express

Landmark Euro-electronica. The future starts here.

Trans-Europe Express marked the culmination of the "romantic impressionist" style which Kraftwerk had initially developed a few years earlier with their hit transport tribute Autobahn. The idea for the new album came from a friend, Paul Alessandrini, who took Ralf Hütter and Florian Schneider to lunch in a restaurant in the Gare De Lyon station in Paris. As they watched the trains arriving and departing beneath them, Alessandrini told them: "With the kind of music you do, which is kind of like an electronic blues, railway stations and trains are very important in your universe – you should do a song about the Trans-Europe Express."

Back at their Kling Klang Studio a short distance from Düsseldorf Station, Kraftwerk set about devising the electronic analogues of train sounds that would power their new work. Both Arthur Honegger's 1923 symphonic poem Pacific 231 and Pierre Schaeffer's 1948 proto-sampling piece Étude Aux Chemins De Fer had previously featured train noises sculpted into musical shape – but this was the first time that synthesisers had been employed to mimic the metronomic click-clack of railways. "We were fascinated with train sounds and machine sounds," explained Ralf Hütter. "They create certain rhythm patterns that are very dynamic and stimulating, and at the same time monotonic, repetitive. We called it Electronic Ballet."

The melodies were better than any Kraftwerk had come up with before, particularly on the wryly self-deprecatory Showroom Dummies and the opening track Europe Endless, which developed the theme of trans-European cultural unity, serenading the "parks, hotels and promenades" of the continent's great cities. This theme was emphasised in the superb packaging, which presented Ralf, Florian and their two electronic drummers as ultra-bourgeois sophisticates at a time when punk was the height of fashion. The album has stood the test of time significantly better than their punk contemporaries' work, becoming the single most important influence on future developments in techno from Detroit to Tokyo, and revolutionising the course of black American music courtesy of Afrika Bambaataa's sampling of the Metal On Metal section of the title track on his seminal hip hop cut Planet Rock. It remains one of the most affectionately regarded works of electronic music.

Record label:
Capitol
Produced
by Ralf Hütter & Florian Schneider.
Recorded
at Kling Klang Studio, Düsseldorf and the Record Plant, Los Angeles; 1976–77.
Released:
April 1977
Chart peaks:
49 (UK) None (US)
Personnel:
Ralf Hütter (v, electronics); Florian Schneider (v, electronics); Karl Bartos (electronic pc); Wolfgang Flur (electronic pc); Peter Bollig (e); Bill Halverson (e)
Track listing:
Europe Endless; The Hall Of Mirrors; Showroom Dummies (S); Trans-Europe Express (S); Metal On Metal; Franz Schubert; Endless Endless (S)
Running time:
42.44
Current CD:
CDP 7 46473 2
Further listening:
The ensuing albums The Man-Machine and Computer World further refine the formula. The earlier Autobahn and Radio-Activity are like preparatory sketches, while their very earliest albums are more experimental and improvisatory.
Further reading:
Kraftwerk: Man, Machine And Music (Pascal Bussy, 1999); MOJO 41; comprehensive links site at: web.bham.ac.uk/busbykg/kraftwerk/links.html
Like this?
Try . . . p.312

The Beatles

Live At The Hollywood Bowl

Sounds like a beat group inside one of Concorde's engines. Fantastically exciting.

Recorded for possible release at the height of Beatlemania by Voyle Gilmore – one of the house producers for The Beatles' American label Capitol – but turned down by the band and label as poor quality, the Hollywood Bowl concert tapes weren't seriously considered until Phil Spector (so the legend goes) – fresh from his contentious salvage job on *Let It Be* – took the 3-track recordings to the acetate stage in readiness for release on Apple in 1971.

With The Beatles in litigation, the project was shelved until 1977 when George Martin was asked to prepare the tapes for release. He wasn't keen: he remembered the '64 show as an unsatisfactory performance ("the boys didn't sing too well during the shows: they had no foldback speakers so they couldn't hear themselves") and was further dismayed to find the mixing on the 3-track tapes hadn't isolated the vocals: "I found guitar and voices mixed on the same track and the recording seemed to concentrate more on the wild screaming of 18,700 kids than on The Beatles on-stage." Having trouble finding a 3-track machine that worked ("Eventually we found an old one which we prevented from overheating by having a vacuum cleaner in reverse blowing cool air into it"), Martin and Geoff Emerick transferred the recordings to 24-track and edited the best of two shows a year apart into a continuous concert record.

Appearing 11 years after the Beatles had given their last concert, it wasn't the most refined live recording but it certainly countered the myth that The Beatles were actually not very good on-stage ("Good in the studio, rubbish live," Charlie Watts was heard to mutter as recently as 1997). As well as conveying a palpable excitement, there's a musical fervour and commitment that entirely fails to convey the tiredness and growing cynicism the band later admitted to feeling about the shows of the period. And with the absence of vocal foldback, that anything of musical value occurred in the face of the wall of hysteria that overwhelmed them (and, on the record, us) is miraculous.

It was deleted from the catalogue in the mid-'90s to make way for the live cuts on the *Anthology* releases.

Record label:
Parlophone
Produced
by Voyle Gilmore and George Martin.
Recorded
at the Hollywood Bowl; August 1964 and August 1965.
Released:
May 6, 1977
Chart peaks:
1 (UK) 2 (US)
Personnel:
John Lennon (g, v, o); Paul McCartney (b, v); George Harrison (g, v); Ringo Starr (d, v); Hugh Davies (concert engineer 1964); Pete Abbott (concert engineer 1965); Geoff Emerick (remixing)
Track listing:
Twist And Shout; She's a Woman; Dizzy Miss Lizzy; Ticket To Ride; Can't Buy Me Love; Things We Said Today; Roll Over Beethoven; Boys; A Hard Day's Night; Help!; All My Loving; She Loves Me; Long Tall Sally
Running time:
28.30
Not currently available on CD
Further listening:
Anthology 1 (1996), Anthology 2 (1996)
Further reading:
Beatles: An Illustrated Record (Roy Carr and Tony Tyler, 1978)
Like this?
Try . . . p.43

Tom Waits
Small Change

Recorded live in the studio, the jazziest of Waits' records.

Tom Waits was discovered at the Troubadour Club's amateur night by manager Herb Cohen (Frank Zappa/Tim Buckley) and quickly established himself as one of LA's most peculiar singer-songwriters. He would write about, and live, a bohemian, flophouse lifestyle, taking on the persona of a sentimental, grizzly-voiced barfly and motel poet howling at the moon.

Small Change sums up Waits' chequered relationship with jazz and beat poetry. Meticulously written and spontaneous in feel, it is the closest any artist has come to making a jazz record that the jazz audience never heard or cared about. Waits wanted to use Zoot Sims for the saxophone role, but the ever-busy Sims was double-booked, and instead he got the marvellous Lew Tabackin, a pro's pro among session men and the perfect choice for the date. The greatest single track Waits has ever created is Step Right Up, a seemingly improvised flow of street barking – actually carefully planned – which Tabackin and the superlative team of Jim Hughart and veteran West Coast drummer Shelly Manne underscore and elevate with the most exciting playing imaginable. Even Waits is taken out of himself: listen to the way he suddenly spills out the line "Change into a nine-year-old Hindu boy/Get rid of your wife!" – an explosive piece of surrealism which his subsequent albums, no matter how accomplished, have rarely matched.

In some ways *Small Change* is a farewell to a tradition of West Coast musicianship. Shelly Manne, who had already been a fixture of Californian jazz and session work for three decades, probably played the stripper-music beat on Pasties And A G-String with a nostalgic grin on his face. The work which these musicians had enjoyed in Californian studios for the past 20 years was drying up, and Waits's decision to use these masters of their craft was already quaint. The studied poetry of his previous records – and his carefully nurtured gravelly timbre – was by now sufficiently lived-in to give this album an entirely plausible feel, even though in 1976 this kind of music was as idiosyncratic as his more out-there later work. But for now, Waits sticks with the woozy romanticism which makes this period of his music so affecting. Bad Liver And A Broken Heart is a sodden unrequited valentine; Small Change is pure reportage, something he would later come at much more obliquely; I Can't Wait To Get Off Work is a blue-collar farewell that would melt the heart of the sternest boss. The Piano Has Been Drinking is a delicious comic gem. While Waits' subsequent records deal with similar territory (albeit in different ways), he never made more humane and moving music than this. Some years later Tom Traubert's Blues was pilfered by Rod Stewart, to the dismay of many.

Record label:
Asylum
Produced and engineered
by Bones Howe.
Recorded
at Wally Heider Recording, Hollywood 15–20 July 1976.
Released:
May 1977
Chart peaks:
None (UK) 89 (US)
Personnel:
Tom Waits (v, p); Lew Tabackin (ts); Jim Hughart (b); Shelly Manne (d)
Track listing:
Tom Traubert's Blues; Step Right Up; Jitterbug Boy; I Wish I Was In New Orleans; The Piano Has Been Drinking (Not Me); Invitation To The Blues; Pasties And A G-String; Bad Liver And A Broken Heart; The One That Got Away; Small Change; I Can't Wait To Get Off Work
Running time:
50.02
Current CD:
7559-60612-2
Further listening:
Foreign Affairs (1977)
Further reading:
www.officialtomwaits.com
Like this?
Try . . . p.674

Muddy Waters

Hard Again

A career-defining masterpiece of Chicago blues in one great – and final – burst of creativity.

When recording his earlier, legendary sides for Chess Records the man born McKinley Morganfield was usually alotted only enough studio time for cutting four songs. Singles were the order of the day at Chess, as elsewhere then, and when enough singles had been issued a few were collected for an album release. The label's initial forays into the LP market for Muddy resulted in psychedelic blues misfires like *Electric Mud* (1968). When Muddy Waters signed to Blue Sky at the behest of Johnny Winter he was assured that things would be different. They were.

With Winter producing and playing guitar, Muddy recorded four fine albums in a row before his death in 1983. *Hard Again* is the best, a culmination of everything he stood for and a personal triumph for both him and Winter, who'd been battling a heroin addiction. Recorded in a small studio – Muddy and his band were set up downstairs with the mics bleeding into one another for a rich ambient sound – there were few overdubs. Winter was upstairs with no window or video monitor to see the band and had to keep running up and down the stairs to help adjust the mics or play guitar.

"The sessions for *Hard Again* were my favourite we did," recalled Pine Top Perkins, "they proved we still had it as a band and that Muddy still had it as a singer. The blues hadn't left us." Winter wisely chose a selection of old and new Muddy material. They returned to old chestnuts like Mannish Boy (a thumping great version that opens the album and sets the agenda), I Want To Be Loved (the Stones' first ever B-side) and I Can't Be Satisfied. Muddy also wrote new tunes – his hilarious The Blues Had A Baby And They Named The Baby Rock'n'Roll (co-written with Brownie McGhee) and the powerful punch of Bus Driver. *Hard Again* was named by a proud Waters who claimed that that's what this music made him.

Record label:
Blue Sky
Produced
by Johnny Winter.
Recorded
at The Schoolhouse, New York; winter 1977.
Released:
May 1977
Chart peaks:
None (UK) None (US)
Personnel:
Muddy Waters (v, g); Johnny Winter (g, miscellaneous screaming); James Cotton (harp); Pine Top Perkins (p); Bob Margolin (g); Charles Calmese (b); Willie "Big Eyes" Smith (d)
Track listing:
Mannish Boy (S); Bus Driver; I Want To Be Loved; Jealous Hearted Man; I Can't Be Satisfied; The Blues Had A Baby And They Named The Baby Rock'N'Roll (#2) (S); Deep Down In Florida; Crosseyed Cat; Little Girl
Running time:
45.66
Current CD:
SNY344492
Further listening:
The best of Muddy's Blue Sky years Hoochie Coochie Man (1993); Muddy Waters: The Chess Box (1989)
Further reading:
www.muddywater.com; Bluesland: Portraits Of Twelve Major American Blues Masters (Pete Welding and Toby Byron, 1992)
Like this?
Try . . . p.55

Cheap Trick

In Color

Boisterous, hook-laden missing link between '60s British pop and American arena.

When the first Cheap Trick album came along it confused the hell out of people. Here was a band with no apparent history, just a reputation for having played every bar-room across the Midwest of America. Cheap Trick's black and white sleeve added to the puzzlement. Were they New Wave and, if so, why did they look more like Queen? Add to that the sound of the record itself; stylish high-power pop but noisily mixed – it was too harsh and too fast to be pop, too pop and too lyrically weird to be metal and, too heavy *and* too pop to be New Wave.

In Color came along just six months later. Producer Steve Douglas, whose Aerosmith connections had helped clinch their deal with Epic, was gone, along with his blitzkrieg live/studio sound. He was replaced by Tom Werman, another heavy rock producer but with a cleaner sound that emphasised their melodies and hooks – of which there were plenty – and their up-close-and-personal vocals. The band have subsequently suggested they'd have preferred their natural sound – "The way we sound in person when you come to see the band," as bassist Petersson put it – but this was Cheap Trick *In Colour* and bright, bold colours at that. Despite the slicker production, the guitars still fizz and the energy level is still off the scale. The 10 songs, all written by guitar player Rick Nielsen – "I'm not sure what the reason is; they like to go out more than I do" – are shoe-horned into 30 boisterous minutes littered with Anglophilia: The Move, The Beatles and The Who, and even more notably Gary Glitter and The Sweet. Picking up early on the glam connection, Kim Fowley had once advised Nielsen to put his colleague Bun E. Carlos on a diet and dress him like David Bowie.

Thanks to incessant touring – no great sacrifice; Cheap Trick were always a touring band, spending three years on the road before recording their first album – the album nudged into the lower reaches of the American charts, though failed to ignite UK audiences. Japan, however, was a different matter. The Rockford, Illinois band were fast becoming superstars. Two years later their live-in-Japan album *Cheap Trick at Budokan* – recorded amidst scenes like The Beatles at Shea Stadium – would be their breakthrough, making a UK hit single of a beautifully tinny live version of I Want You To Want Me.

Record label:
Epic
Produced
by Tom Werman.
Recorded
at Kendun Recorders, Los Angeles; early summer 1977.
Released:
August 1977
Chart peaks:
None (UK) 73 (US)
Personnel:
Robin Zander (v, rg); Tom Petersson (b, v); Bun E Carlos (d); Rick Nielsen (g, v)
Track listing:
Hello There; Big Eyes; Downed; I Want You To Want Me (S); You're All Talk; Oh Caroline; Clock Strikes Ten; Southern Girls; Come On, Come On; So Good To See You
Running time:
31.05
Current CD:
491230 2 adds: Oh Boy; Southern Girls (2); Come On, Come On (2); You're All Talk (2); Goodnight
Further listening:
Heaven Tonight (1978)
Further reading:
Reputation Is A Fragile Thing: The Story Of Cheap Trick (Mike Hayes with Ken Sharp, 1998); www.cheaptrick.com
Like this?
Try . . . p.374

Dennis Wilson

Pacific Ocean Blue

The Beach Boy least-likely-to delivers the band's first solo masterpiece.

Dennis Wilson was never allowed the level of involvement in the early Beach Boys' successes he might have liked. Indeed, he'd only been grudgingly allowed into the band at the insistence of his mother. His role of drummer and band heart-throb established, such was Dennis' unreliable nature, the others became increasingly happy to keep him at arm's length. But when big brother Brian became unreliable too, The Beach Boys needed any decent songs they could get. With poet and lyricist Steve Kalinich, Dennis' increasingly emotional and epic contributions suggested that Brian wasn't the only great mind in the group after all.

While his singing wasn't as sweet as his brothers', there was a distinctive, tender quality to his voice, suggesting that under the rakish exterior lurked a sensitive soul.

"Dennis and I used to sit up in his tree-hut and talk about how we would like to change and help influence the world towards peace, and helping all the sick kids," Kalinich recalls. "Despite all the things you read about Dennis, there was that side of him that wanted to give."

Finally, in 1977, he recorded something exactly the way he wanted it. *Pacifc Ocean Blue* allowed Dennis to bear his soul. The songs were given expansive, dreamy settings in delicately complex arrangements. The musical landscape was oceanic too: powerful, motive and uplifting.

The bulk of the songs dealt with the theme of love, though from a more wistful, almost metaphysical viewpoint than The Beach Boys' optimistically adolescent take. The Dennis version of romance was fatalistic, mordant even. Two of the album's most chillingly lovely songs – Time and You And I – were written with his wife, Karen Lamm Wilson, most of the others were composed with co-producer and long-standing friend Gregg Jacobson.

It's quite easy to imagine that the warm critical reception which welcomed *Pacific Ocean Blue* would have given rise to mixed emotions within The Beach Boys' camp. Its release came only five months after the official band album, *The Beach Boys Love You* and in terms of coherence, sound and a mature sense of purpose, it beat that album hands down. Dennis was suitably buoyed to begin preparing tracks for a second album with the working title of *Bamboo* which never made it to the finishing line. Two of the best songs, Baby Blue and Love Surrounds Me, were used for The Beach Boys' *LA* (*Light Album*) in 1979. Several others showed strong new directions, but, as Dennis let his life drift into more excesses than even he could handle, plans for the second release petered out.

Dennis Wilson drowned in 1983.

Record label:
Caribou
Produced
by Dennis Wilson and Gregg Jacobson.
Recorded
at Brother Studios, Santa Monica, California; 1976–1977.
Released:
September 16, 1977
Chart peaks:
None (UK) None (US)
Personnel:
Dennis Wilson (v, k, d); Ed Carter (g, b); Earl Mankey (g); Jamie Jamerson (b); Hal Blaine (d); Ricky Fataar (d); Curt Boettcher, Bruce Johnston, Karen Lamm Wilson, Billy Hinsche, Ed Tuleja, Gregg Jacobson, Alexander Hamilton and The Double Rock Baptist Choir (bv); Stephen Moffitt (e, m)
Track listing:
River Song; What's Wrong; Moonshine; Friday Night; Dreamer; Thoughts Of You; Time; You And I; Pacific Ocean Blues; Farewell My Friend; Rainbows
Running time:
37.25
Currently unavailable on CD
Further listening:
Beach Boys, Sunflower (1972)
Further reading:
The Nearest Faraway Place (Timothy White, 1994); www.cabinessence.com/dennis/
Like this?
Try . . . p.132

Ian Dury

New Boots And Panties

Thirty-five-year-old wordsmith and art teacher becomes roguish uncle to the nation.

As with many of the flag-bearers of the New Wave, Ian Dury was not inexperienced. He had previously combined his massively charismatic leadership of pub-rock banditti Kilburn And The High Roads, with a lecturing post at Canterbury College Of Art; and had released several records well before Punk Year Zero. After the dissolution of the Kilburns, Dury formed a songwriting team with ex-Byzantium guitarist and pianist Chaz Jankel.

"Drummer Charlie Charles and me played together in Loving Awareness, and went out as a pair for sessions," says bass-playing Blockhead, Norman Watt-Roy. "We got a call from Alvic Studios in Wimbledon to work on some demos. They were for Ian and Chaz. We clicked straight away. I just remember us laughing our heads off all the time. I'd never heard anything as funny as Clever Trevor before. We went into Workhouse Studios a few weeks later; straight in and just banged 'em out. We were given quite a free hand, everyone was throwing ideas in. Ian and Chaz were into dancey grooves, they wanted a foot-tapping feel."

Chaz and Ian's loosely-drawn manifesto was gloriously realized from the off. The lubricious, Cockney funk of Wake Up And Make Love With Me gives way, with a typical stroke of genius, to the rocking Sweet Gene Vincent – the best tribute song ever. Breezing and wheezing through a touching paean to his father, My Old Man, and the effortlessly witty, reconstructed music hall of Billericay Dickie, Dury and his posse of supremely versatile players close the album with a trio of the most complex, powerful punk tracks of the era. On Blockheads, Dury berates Essex ladism, at the same time displaying an awareness that there's a bit of Blockhead in all men. The opening 30 seconds of Plaistow Patricia (a volley of swearing removed from subsequent CD reissues) are genuinely disquieting, while Blackmail Man is two minutes of the fastest jazz-wank in the East End.

Watt-Roy: "I've played on a lot of records and this is the only one I still listen to. I remember when we all went to Blackhill's (Ian's management) to listen to it. Elvis Costello was there. Afterwards he said it was the most complete album he'd ever heard." Charles Shaar Murray of the NME described *New Boots* as "the working man's *Tubular Bells*". The public concurred, and the maverick indie label Stiff had their first Top 10 album. Ian Dury, Doctor Johnson of the Doctor Marten, had arrived.

Record label:
Stiff
Producer:
not listed.
Recorded
at Workhouse Studios, Old Kent Road, London; 1977.
Released:
September 1977
Chart peaks:
5 (UK) None (US)
Personnel:
Ian Dury (v); Chaz Jankel (g, k, bv); Davey Payne (s); Norman Watt-Roy (b); Charlie Charles (d); Laurie Latham (e); Geoff Castle (syn); Ted Speight (g)
Track listing:
Wake Up And Make Love With Me; Sweet Gene Vincent (S/UK); I'm Partial To Your Abracadabra; My Old Man; Billericay Dickie; Clever Trevor; If I Was With A Woman; Blockheads; Plaistow Patricia; Blackmail Man
Running time:
37.10
Current CD:
AHLCD57 adds: Sex And Drugs And Rock And Roll
Further listening:
Do It Yourself (1979); Laughter (1980); Mr Lovepants (1998)
Further reading:
No Sleep 'Til Canvey Island: The Great Pub Rock Revolution (Will Birch, 2000); Sex And Drugs And Rock'n'Roll (Richard Balls, 2000); www.iandury.co.uk www.blockheads.co.uk
Like this?
Try . . . p.436

Richard Hell And The Voidoids

Blank Generation

New York punk innovator belatedly makes LP. Too clever by half for most punks.

Richard Hell is placed, rightfully, at the epicentre of punk's origins. This is chiefly on account of the fact that in 1975 Malcolm McLaren noted Hell's penchant for ripped T-shirts and plundered it wholesale for his Chelsea boutique, for the Sex Pistols, and consequently for the entire punk look.

But Hell was far more important and influential than merely for his innovative fabric abuse. Changing his surname from Myers to Hell was no Tin Pan Alley star makeover, *à la* Ziggy Stardust. This was Hell's chosen life. The title track of this album revealed an agenda which was rapidly misinterpreted: rather than being a literal exhaltation of nihilism, Hell meant blank as in autonomy. But his literate lyrics were always too smart for most New Wavers. All of these songs are about identity, relationships, the transience of sex, mortality – a world where life, as the title track puts it, was "God's consolation prize".

Hell also had a great sense of rock'n'roll history, captured perfectly in a storming version of the Fogerty brothers' Walking On The Water (actually the most minimalist track on the album) recorded at a time when nobody was talking about Creedence Clearwater Revival. The other great thing about this record is guitarist Robert Quine – the balding antithesis of all the punk clones from central casting. Quine's spluttering guitar work owes more to free jazz than to the Chuck Berry-on-amphetamine histrionics of most punk. Probably the most 'punk' thing the Voidoids could have done, in fact.

Record label:
Sire
Produced
by Richard Gottehrer and Richard Hell.
Recorded
at Electric Ladyland and The Plaza, New York; 1977.
Released:
September 1977
Chart peaks:
None (UK) None (US)
Personnel:
Richard Hell, (b, v), Robert Quine (g, bv), Ivan Julian (g, bv); Marc Bell (d)
Track listing:
Love Comes In Spurts; Liars Beware; New Pleasure; Betrayal Takes Two; Down At The Rock And Roll Club; Who Says?; Blank Generation (S); Walking On The Water; The Plan; Another World;
Running time:
32.10
Current CD:
7599261372
Further listening:
The Kid With The Replaceable Head/I'm Your Man (1979)
Further reading:
MOJO 77; England's Dreaming (Jon Savage, 1992); www.richardhell.com
Like this?
Try . . . p.390

Iggy Pop

Lust For Life

Iggy's acknowledgement as punk's founding father is marked with his first Top 30 UK hit.

From the exhilarating opening groove, now familiar via the movie Trainspotting and a host of commercials, *Lust For Life* proclaims itself Iggy Pop's most effervescent, vital album – one that saw his collaborator David Bowie at a towering peak in his songwriting – accompanied by a stunningly inventive band. The album found Iggy, who'd enjoyed a modest career revival with his previous Bowie collaboration, *The Idiot*, in a newly-optimistic mood: "I was living on coke, hash, red wine and German sausages, I had my own little place with cold water showers, and I was the happiest person in the world." Where *The Idiot* had been a Bowie-influenced experimental affair, *Lust For Life* was determinedly an Iggy album, recorded in two weeks of nocturnal sessions at Hansa Studio 1 overlooking the Berlin Wall.

Practically every song was written and conceived in the studio, with Iggy revelling in his new industrious work ethic. He'd show up at the studio with vocal or instrumental snippets on his tape recorder, and argue into the night with Bowie: "There was a lot of friction going on. But on the other hand we were both really into the project, The thing was written in one day, he came down and sat at the piano and we taped about eight things like that." Bizarrely, the album's title track came from the signature oompah band theme to German public television, spotted by Bowie; Iggy's words incorporated William Burroughs references, while the whole affair was powered forward by the superb sibling rhythm section of Hunt and Tony Sales ("I put everything into those songs," says drummer Hunt. "I fooled myself into thinking it was a proper band.").

The optimism and electricity generated in the studio is exemplified by the closing fade-out of Success, where Iggy ad-libs lines about buying expensive rugs, while Bowie and the Sales brothers, singing the backing vocals live, try not to break into hysterics. Sadly, much of the confidence seemed misplaced in the subsequent months, for, following the death of Elvis Presley on August 16, 1977, RCA dedicated its pressing plants to churning out Presley material, all in-store RCA promotions were withdrawn and Presley memorial material put in its place. Iggy's greatest solo album was forgotten in his homeland, the unfortunate victim of the King's terminal event atop the commode.

Record label:
RCA Victor
Produced
by Bewlay Bros (Iggy Pop and David Bowie).
Recorded
at Hansa Tonstudios, Berlin, Germany; June 1977.
Released:
September 1977
Chart peaks:
28 (UK) 120 (US)
Personnel:
Iggy Pop (v); Carlos Alomar, Ricky Gardiner (g); Tony Sales (b); Hunt
Sales (d); David Bowie (p)
Track listing:
Lust For Life; Sixteen; Some Weird Sin; The Passenger; Tonight; Success (S); Turn Blue; Neighborhood Threat; Fall In Love with Me
Running time:
40.41
Current CD:
CDOVD278
Further listening:
The Idiot (1976)
Further reading:
MOJO 29; I Need More (Iggy Pop, 1996); www.theroc.org/mus-link/bands/i/ iggypop.htm
Like this?
Try . . . p.283

Steely Dan

Aja

Steely Dan's most sophisticated and commercially successful work, a masterpiece of session layering.

Recorded at immense cost over many months at various Los Angeles studios, with one song (Peg) added later in new York, *Aja* stands as a monument to the apparently limitless perfectionism of Steely Dan songwriters Walter Becker and Donald Fagen.

"I think because of the kind of music we were doing, it seemed to us that it should be real seamlessly put together and have a high level of polish to make it work," explains Becker. Accordingly, the album credits read like a Who's Who of '70s session players, with only their old friend Denny Dias retained from the original Steely Dan line-up – and then only as one of three guitarists on the title track, a multi-sectioned suite based on an oriental motif and boasting a sterling sax solo from Weather Report's Wayne Shorter. This was typical of the new Steely Dan, which after "dumbing down" their ambitions in order to kick-start its career, had now re-inflated them to way beyond their original expectations.

And with unprecedented expectations came unprecedented measures, with each of the album's seven songs being recorded several times over by different combinations of expensive session musicians, to allow Becker and Fagen to decide which particular accents of rhythm and style best suited a particular song. At its most absurd, this strategy resulted in a parade of no fewer than seven top guitarists being called in to try and find the right guitar solo for Peg, a search called off only when Jay Graydon came up with the elegantly pirouetting break that graces the released track. "A lot of times we didn't know what we wanted," admits Becker. "Other times, we just wanted it to be better, so we'd keep trying for another take. Many days we'd make guys do 30 or 40 takes and we'd never listen to any of them again, because we knew none of them were any good; but we just kept hoping that somehow it was just going to miraculously get good."

Along with hints about the album's jazzier style, Becker and Fagen had previously warned that, after the fuss that had been made over the previous album *The Royal Scam*'s title track (a political parable about Puerto Rican immigrants in New York), the new songs would have no social significance. They were, however, some of the most emotionally satisfying the duo ever came up with, featuring celebratory portraits of high-spirited girls (Peg and Josie), Zen-like reflections on satiety (Aja and Home At Last), and a touchingly *simpatico* tribute to bohemian losers (Deacon Blues). Fusing pop and jazz in a subtle, seamless alloy entirely at variance with the leaden jazz-rock riffing of their "fusion" contemporaries, *Aja* proved to be the band's most popular album, eventually selling in excess of five million copies.

Record label:
ABC
Produced
by Gary Katz.
Recorded
in Los Angeles and New York; 1976–77.
Released:
September 1977
Chart peaks:
5 (UK) 3 (US)
Personnel:
Donald Fagen (v, k, police whistle); Walter Becker (b, g); Denny Dias (g); Larry Carlton (g); Lee Ritenour (g); Steve Khan (g); Jay Graydon (g); Dean Parks (g); Chuck Rainey (b); Victor Feldman (k, vibes, pc); Joe Sample (k); Michael Omartian (k); Paul Griffin (k, bv); Don Grolnick (k); Paul Humphrey (d); Steve Gadd (d); Bernard Purdie (d); Rick Marotta (d); Ed Greene (d); Jim Keltner (drm, pc); Gary Coleman (pc); Tom Scott (s, lyricon); Wayne Shorter (s); Pete Christlieb (s); Clydie King King, Shirley Matthews, Venetta Fields, Rebecca Louis, Tim Schmit, Michael McDonald (bv); Roger Nichols (e)
Track listing:
Black Cow (S); Aja; Deacon Blues (S); Peg (S); Home At Last (S); I Got The News (S); Josie (S/US only)
Running time:
39.56
Current CD:
MCLD19145
Further listening:
Gaucho (1980) and comeback album Two Against Nature (2000) are comparable in terms of texture, accent and attitude.
Further reading:
www.steelydan.com
Like this?
Try . . . p.188

Johnny Thunders And The Heartbreakers

L.A.M.F.

The only punk band who could sing about the street-gang lifestyle with authority.

When heroin becomes more of an interest than music it is tough to keep your career going. Ex-New York Dolls Johnny Thunders (*né* Genzale) and Jerry Nolan managed both for a while, and their band had quite a reputation, but simply because of their music. Managed by ex-Warhol protégé Leee Black Childers, they were invited in late 1976 by Malcolm McLaren, who had briefly managed the Dolls, to fly to London and join the Sex Pistols/Damned/Clash Anarchy Tour. The tour was a mess of cancelled gigs and rescinded payments, but Childers got the band exposure through packed-out London concerts and they were soon signed to Track Records. Several singles appeared – Chinese Rocks sold 20,000 copies in its first week of release. Track asked Pete Townshend acolyte Speedy Keen (his telltale nickname marking him as the perfect Heartbreakers producer) to hurry up the album.

It took several weeks to record at two studios, six months to mix at *five* different studios and still it wasn't right. The initial sound of *L.A.M.F.* (Like A Mother Fucker) was murky; though it's likely that Track's mastering – rather than the mix – was responsible for the sonic problems. By the time *L.A.M.F.* came out, the Heartbreakers had a UK following but most of the musicians, club owners and record company people they'd dealt with hated them: it's not easy working with junkies. But the album was a rocks-off affair from start to finish; not so much punk rock as NYC toughs playing elemental rock'n'roll for dancing or pogo-ing It was like updated Eddie Cochran, noted Jake Riviera perceptively, or at least Eddie Cochran with a $125 a day habit. Some of the songs (Pirate Love, Going Steady) were leftovers from the Dolls days – yet this was classic stuff; you could bet any song's title would be repeated at least half a dozen times, welded to a riff Gene Vincent would've killed for.

Record label:
Track

Produced
by Speedy Keen and Daniel Secunda.

Recorded
at Essex Studios and Ramport Studios, London; February–March 1977.

Released:
October 3, 1977

Chart peaks:
55 (UK) 55; (US) None

Personnel:
Johnny Thunders (v, g); Walter Lure (v, g); Billy Rath (b, v); Jerry Nolan (d)

Track listing:
Born To Lose; Baby Talk; All By Myself; I Wanna Be Loved; It's Not Enough (S/UK); Chinese Rocks (S/UK); Get Off The Phone; Pirate Love; One Track Mind; I Love You; Going Steady; Let Go

Running time:
40.04

Current CD:
FREUD CD445 remixed and issued as L.A.M.F: The Lost '77 Mixes adds: Can't Keep My Eyes Off You; Do You Love Me?

Further listening:
Thunders' first solo effort So Alone (1978)

Further reading:
In Cold Blood: The Authorised Biography Of Johnny Thunders (Nina Antonia, 1987); http://home.eol.ca/~ifftay/thunders.htm

Like this?
Try . . . p.366

Electric Light Orchestra

Out Of The Blue

The least fashionable band of its day reach preposterous peak.

ELO's brand of space-age, orchestral Beatley rock had struggled in the early days to click with a mass audience, but the more band *auteur* Jeff Lynne allowed his writing to come from his pop heart, the more successful they became. Initial ELO albums had been lugubrious affairs, straining to combine a Walrus density with progressive rock weight.

Lynne: "I thought it was cool to write long songs. It took me ages to get that violin out of my arse!"

The first three albums featured brutal-toned cellos but with 1974's *Eldorado* using a full orchestra, the sound attained a lighter touch as Lynne surrendered to his Beatles instincts; John Lennon even said if The Beatles had made records in the '70s, they'd be like ELO music. Lynne loved that. *A New World Record* (1976) was an international breakthrough spawning three hit singles and the pressure was on for the follow-up. Deciding upon a double, Lynne set himself three weeks in a Swiss chalet to write two albums worth of songs. "For the first four days I couldn't get a thing. I just looked at all that equipment and thought, What a funny job I have!" The juices started flowing and though Mr Blue Sky took a week to finish ("I pounded the chord sequence for nine hours in a row one day"), he wrote 13 new songs in a fortnight. Three months in Munich with their favourite engineer Mack produced this magnificent, ridiculous smorgasbord of Beatles/Beach Boys/Bee Gees/Roy Orbison nicks, echo effects, extravagant call-and-response backing vocal hooks, monolithic slabs of Louis Clark strings and choir, and a sackful of great pop tunes.

The words meant little (Lynne was often finishing them at the vocal sessions), the mother spaceship sleeve was a thematic red herring (though the motif was adopted as a stage for the tour) and critics were scornful (Sounds: "Why does the female preying mantis eat its mate after orgasm? Why do ELO sell so many records?"). But the feel-good bounce of Mr Blue Sky (surely one of *the* great uplifting pop records) the mock-epic Standing In The Rain and the power ballads Steppin' Out and Big Wheels are the inspired work of a singular pop craftsman and have worn amazingly well. There were advance orders of four million for the album, and though their next, *Discovery* (1979), was even more successful, *Out Of The Blue* is Lynne's pinnacle.

Record label:
Jet
Produced
by Jeff Lynne.
Recorded
at Musicland Studios, Munich; May–July 1977.
Release date:
October 1977
Chart peaks:
4 (UK) 4 (US)
Personnel:
Jeff Lynne (v, g, k, a); Bev Bevan (d); Richard Tandy (k, a); Kelly Groucutt (b, v); Mik Kaminsky (v); Hugh McDowell (c); Melvyn Gale (c); Louis Clark (a, oa)
Track listing:
Turn To Stone; It's Over; Sweet Talkin' Woman; Across The Border; Night In The City; Starlight; Jungle; Believe Me Now; Steppin' Out; Concerto For A Rainy Day; Standin' In The Rain; Big Wheels-Summer And Lightning-Mr Blue Sky; Sweet Is The Night; The Whale; Birmingham Blues; Wild West Hero
Running time:
70.16
Current CD:
Epic 450885 9
Further listening:
Eldorado (1974); A New World Record (1976); Discovery (1979)
Further reading:
The Electric Light Orchestra Story (Bev Bevan, 1980)
Like this?
Try . . . p.258

Sex Pistols

Never Mind The Bollocks – Here's The Sex Pistols

Punk rock crash-lands in the mainstream, just as the Sex Pistols fall apart.

By April 1977, the Sex Pistols had been thrown off both EMI and A&M, and shunted around a succession of London recording studios. Manager Malcolm McLaren was holding back from signing to Virgin, but the Pistols were still motivated enough to finally commence the recording of their debut album. Though countless demos were recorded with their soundman, Dave "Boss" Goodman, their two A-sides thus far – Anarchy In The UK and the aborted A&M single God Save The Queen – had been produced by Chris Thomas, hired on account of Paul Cook's fondness for his work with Roxy Music. The template for Pistols recordings had thus been set, and the vast majority of tape was gleefully filled by Steve Jones' piled-up guitars.

"Phil Spector's my inspiration as a rock producer," Jones told NME. "So what I wanted to get was a new Wall of Sound."

"I was a bit bored making that album," John Lydon recalls now. "There were something like 21 guitar tracks laid down and only two tracks for vocal. I did most of the songs all the way through, one or two takes, and that's it. And I got very annoyed."

The first phase of work was halted by the Pistols' signing to Virgin on May 12, 1977. Two weeks later they released God Save The Queen, and reached the height of their infamy in the summer of Elizabeth's Silver Jubilee. This impacted on the second spurt of recording: on June 18, having worked on Holidays In The Sun, John Lydon, Chris Thomas and engineer Bill Price were attacked by a gang of irate royalists. Inevitably, it was Lydon they were after: the damage inflicted on one of his hands was permanent. Against such a background, it's amazing the record was ever finished. Also weighing against the Pistols was the ineptitude of their new bass player: Sid Vicious made no audible contribution to the album at all (though he's alleged to be buried somewhere in the mix of Bodies), leaving the playing of brutally simple, root-note bass parts to Jones.

It was late September, a month after the legendary SPOTS tour (Sex Pistols On Tour Secretly), before the LP was finalised. Its working title – God Save The Sex Pistols – was jettisoned, though confusion still surrounded the final tracklisting. So it was that 10,000 initial copies omitted Submission, slipped into the package as a one-sided single. Such hiccups mattered little: *Bollocks* was deservedly lauded as a epochal triumph. "It's all speed, not nuance," said Rolling Stone, "and the songs all hit like amphetamines or the plague, depending on your point of view."

Record label:
Virgin
Produced
by Chris Thomas.
Recorded
at Wessex Studios, London; May–September 1977.
Release date:
October 1977
Chart peaks:
1 (UK) 106 (US)
Personnel:
John Lydon aka Johnny Rotten (v); Steve Jones (g, b); Paul Cook (d); John Ritchie aka Sid Vicious (b); Bill Price (e)
Track listing:
Holidays In The Sun (S); Bodies; No Feelings; Liar; God Save The Queen (S); Problems; Seventeen; Anarchy In The UK (S); Submission; Pretty Vacant (S); New York; EMI
Running time:
38.30
Current CD:
CDVX2086
Further listening:
8LP demos on There Is No Future (1999) and Early Daze (1992); the entire Pistols canon on Kiss This (1992)
Further reading:
Classic Rock Albums: Never Mind The Bollocks (Clinton Heylin, 1998); England's Dreaming (Jon Savage, 1992); Sex Pistols: The Inside Story (Fred and Judy Vermorel, 1987)
Like this?
Try . . . p.387

Jacques Brel

Brel

Belgium's great chansonnier bids adieu.

Jacques Brel was in a bad way when he arrived in France for the sessions that would comprise his final recordings. He had been in semi-retirement for a decade, during which time his Anglophone profile had never been higher, thanks to Scott Walker (Jackie et al), Alex Harvey (Next) and Terry Jacks (who had heard The Beach Boys toying with Seasons In The Sun). But it was when he was diagnosed as having terminal cancer (he was a 100 filterless-a-day man) that the effects of mortality, a common subject of his songs, came into focus. He was 48.

From his home in the South Pacific, he wrote to old collaborator Jouannest and label boss Eddie Barclay, wondering if they would be interested in some of his "nonsense". Jouannest was the first to hear Brel's demos; the timbre of his voice had deepened, his ability with lyrics was still there, but the melodies were boring. This was no discouragement because, by tradition, *chansonniers* concentrated on the words, tunes would only distract the listener.

In the studio, Brel's enthusiasm evaporated. His fast-failing health meant he wanted as few hassles as possible and could only manage a maximum of three takes for each song. If it sounded off – and it often did – then tough. Barclay, unaware of the singer's impending death, started formulating plans for an album of duets with Streisand as a way of breaking America once again. How this would have worked is anyone's guess, as Brel still aligned himself with the French refuseniks who wanted to repel American influences – allowing, of course, for the wah-wah pedal on Les F?

As soon as recording was completed, Brel took off, determined to avoid giving any interviews and insisting on a low-key release. Nevertheless, the record company embarked on an unparalleled marketing campaign, creating an air of mystery that was only alleviated the day before release, when radio stations were finally allowed to play the album. Within 24 hours, 650,000 copies had been bought in France alone. The subject of constant intrusion by the French press, Brel himself hung on another 11 months, commenting only that he hated the sleeve.

Record label:
Barclay
Produced
by Gerhard Lehner.
Recorded
in Paris, September 1977.
Released:
November 1977
Chart peaks:
None (UK) None (US)
Personnel:
Jacques Brel (v); Gerard Jouannest (p); Marcel Azzola (accordion); Francois Rauber (o)
Track listing:
Jaures; La Ville S'Endormait; Vieillir; Le Bon Dieu; Les F?; Orly; Les Remparts De Varsovie; Voir Un Ami Pleurer; Knokke-Le-Zoute Tango; Jojo; Le Lion; Les Marquises
Running time:
48.30
Currently available CD:
810 537 2
Further listening:
Ce Gens-La (1966) – the LP that introduced Jackie, Mathilde and Tango Funèbre to the world; Quand On N'a Que L'Amour, a two-CD best of. For Brel in English, Scott Walker Sings Jacques Brel (culled from Scott 1–3) is ample proof of why Brel considered Scott the foremost interpreter of his work.
Further reading:
Jacques Brel: The Biography (1998)
Like this?
Try . . . p.233

Suicide

Suicide

Proto-punk electronic rock'n'roll; Elvis and The Seeds with the technology of tomorrow.

Alan Vega and Martin Rev were the first to use the term "punk" in a musical context, when they put on something called "A Punk Music Mass" at a New York art gallery in 1971.

"Everybody else in the world has claimed it – Richard Hell, Legs McNeil – but I don't give a shit, we were the first," says Vega. "I liked the juxtaposition of the words 'punk' and 'mass' – they just don't go with one another. It was like a poetry thing. And five or six years later, it's a movement! Whoever would have thunk it?"

When that happened, however, the punk movement's music bore little or no relation to the strange, edgy hybrid that Vega and Rev had developed, though compared to the dreary three-chord thrash-merchants, Suicide were undeniably the real punk iconoclasts. Martin Rev was a free-jazz pianist whose sonic experiments had led him to delve into primitive electronic devices by the time he hooked up with Alan Vega at the Project For Living Artists, a gallery space for which the latter served as caretaker. Influenced by garage bands like The Seeds and electronic peers such as the Silver Apples, they devised a scary new kind of pop music which used Rev's machines to generate a backdrop of electronic pulses and poignant melody lines, over which Vega would intone melodramatic tales of urban low-lifes, lovers and losers, in his feverish Presley vocal pastiche. Suicide's live shows were always tense, confrontational events, the duo being regarded as contravening punk style laws, but by the time they came to record their debut album for Marty Thau's Red Star label, they had developed a set which mixed social-realist tales of urban dystopia like the 10-minute tragic opus Frankie Teardrop with erotic dreams like Cheree.

"They're basically true stories," claims Vega. "Cheree's about a girlfriend of mine, for instance. I wrote about people I knew, and Marty did the same with the music. There was a little time for love here and there, but mostly it was a horror story!" Though their music had at least as powerful an adrenalin surge as anything thrown up by punk, they were hopelessly out of step with the era's musical fashions; accordingly, their debut album remained very much a cult item, a fate shared by their subsequent releases.

Record label:
Red Star
Produced
by Craig Leon and Marty Thau.
Recorded
at Ultima Studios, Blauvelt; New York, 1977.
Release date:
November 1977
Chart peaks:
None (UK) None (US)
Personnel:
Alan Vega (v); Martin Rev (electronics)
Track listing:
Ghost Rider; Rocket USA; Cheree; Johnny; Girl; Frankie Teardrop; Che; Cheree (remix); I Remember; Keep Your Dreams
Running time:
43.56
Current CD:
BFFP133CDL adds live tracks: Mr Ray; Las Vegas Man; 96 Tears; Keep Your Dreams; I Remember; Harlem; 23 Minutes Over Brussels
Further listening:
The Ric Ocasek-produced follow-up, Alan Vega/Martin Rev – Suicide (1980), is a smoother and sleeker variant on the same formula. Vega's solo albums (such as Collision Drive (1981) and Saturn Strip (1983)) explore techno-rockabilly territory, while Martin Rev's solo efforts are electronic instrumentals (although Cheyenne is largely backing tracks from the second Suicide album).
Further reading:
www.multimania.com/jes/music/suicide2.htm
Like this?
Try . . . p.458

Throbbing Gristle

Second Annual Report

A lo-fi blueprint from the heart of the Death Factory.

In the basement of an old East End knitting factory situated on the fringes of Hackney's London Fields parkland – once a giant burial pit for plague victims – Throbbing Gristle assembled *Second Annual Report* in the latter half of 1977. Their use of disturbing subject matter and improvised, synthesised sound, created from hand-built and customised instruments, was so uncompromising, that it took "rebelliousness" to a level undreamt-of in the punk climate and identified a new musical genre: industrial music.

"We were absolutely antithetical to rock'n'roll at that point," declares vocalist Genesis P-Orridge, "We really didn't care if anybody liked it, or if we sold any records. Mark Perry of Sniffin' Glue had famously said, 'Learn three chords now form a band.' I said, 'Learn none at all.' To play chords was to plug back into the tradition on some level."

Set against a deep ambient roar, speech samples, synth screeches and uncontrolled feedback, the barely coherent words of Slug Bait, the opening section of live excerpts that fill side one, drew from two recent murder cases, with P-Orridge assuming the role of psychopathic killer. Altogether now: "I pull out your baby/I chew its head off with my teeth/As you bleed to death I kill it."

The subject of murder wasn't new to a rock audience, but the viewpoint was. The piece wasn't *about* the event, it sounded like it *was* the event. The assortment of punks, artists, critics and politicians that saw this performance at the ICA in October 1976, stood dumbfounded afterwards. It was meant, as P-Orridge later reflected, "To confront ALL assumptions in ALL aspects of the culture. Considered mischief with a motive of evaluation and rejuvenation of the medium itself."

The headline-grabbing ICA event, called Prostitution, was to mark the transformation of Coum Transimissions, a seven-year-old performance-art collective, into Throbbing Gristle. If Coum were barely tolerated in the art world, then Throbbing Gristle would be an abomination to rock.

To their surprise, the initial 785 copies of the album sold out quickly, mostly through Rough Trade. The title reflected the band's journalistic intentions, and darkly mimicked corporate speak. Released on their own Industrial Records label, it was the model independent release: totally self-financed and recorded on a portable Sony cassette recorder with a condenser mic that was simply placed opposite the band to record their gigs or studio sessions – a financial limitation but fortuitous send-up of studio professionalism. The technique also gave the recording its volatile, nightmarish quality. "It has," says P-Orridge, "a perfect ambiguity that one cannot create consciously."

Record label:
Industrial Records
Produced
by Throbbing Gristle
Recorded
at The Death Factory, Hackney, London; May–September 1977
Released:
November 1977
Chart peaks:
None (UK) None (US)
Personnel:
Genesis P-Orridge (b, violin, v); Peter Christopherson (t, tapes, processing); Cosey Fanni Tutti (Raver and Satelite guitar); Chris Carter (k, rhythms, m)
Track listing:
Industrial Introduction; Slug Bait – ICA; Slug Bait – Live at Southampton; Slug Bait – Live at Brighton; Maggot Death – Studio; Maggot Death – Southampton; Maggot Death – Brighton; After Cease To Exist – The Original Soundtrack of the Coum Transmissions Film.
Running Time:
39.56
Current CD:
Mute TGCD2 includes: Zyclon B Zombie; United
Further Listening:
D.O.A (1978); 20 Jazz Funk Greats (1979); Journey Through A Body (1981)
Further Reading:
Wreckers Of Civilisation: The Story of Coum Transmissions and Throbbing Gristle (Simon Ford, 1999)
Like this?
Try . . . p.143

Roberta Flack

Blue Lights In The Basement

The fifth gold album by the most impassive of the great soul divas.

She has been out of the limelight for so long that it's difficult to remember that Flack was once a major figure. Her first real success came in 1972 when The First Time Ever I Saw Your Face (from her excellent 1969 debut *First Take*) belatedly became a hit after its use in the movie Play Misty For Me. Of all her records, this is the most resourceful, the most thoughtful, the best of her essays on grown-up soul.

Flack was no spring chicken – she was pushing 40 when she made this set – and if Michael Jackson was a kid setting the pace in black pop, Flack was a vanguard representative of what was happening at the other extreme, the adult soul which had been formulated in her albums and those by The Detroit Spinners, Al Green and others. She has a rather sombre voice, somewhat akin to Nina Simone and Carmen McRae; jazz-directed singers who, like Flack, often accompanied themselves on piano. Although there's some joyful music here – Fine, Fine Day and the delicious revision of The Box Tops' hit, Soul Deep – Flack suggests a comfortable kind of happiness. Why Don't You Move In With Me goes on to suggest that "we could be a family", a search for domestic bliss which fades away on the meltingly beautiful 25th Of Last December. Some of the best songwriters of the era are represented here – Gwen Guthrie, Eugene McDaniels, Rachel Perry – and there is what, unhappily, turned out to be one of the final examples of her many duets with Donny Hathaway, who died a little over a year after the album was made (he fell from a hotel room window).

Blue Lights – her last great work – is beautifully played, too. Flack began working in piano bars in the '60s, and she knew many of the best cats to hire. In its latest remastering, the record has a somewhat eccentric sound, but Flack herself had an idiosyncratic way in the studio; a perfectionist, but not technically very adept at the board, she needed assistance to get records finished, even though she is still credited – Rubina Flake is a pseudonym for Roberta Flack.

Record label:
Atlantic
Produced
by Rubina Flake, Joe Ferla and Eugene McDaniels.
Recorded:
Spring 1977.
Released:
December 1977
Chart peaks:
None (UK) 8 (US)
Personnel:
Roberta Flack (v, k); Reggie Lucas, Hugh McCracken, Jeff Mironov, John Tropea, David Spinozza (g); Michael Kamen (oboe); Harry Whittaker, Ronnie Foster, Don Grolnick, Paul Griffin, Rob Mounsey, Leon Pendarvis (k); Anthony Jackson, Will Lee, Basil Fearrington (b); Howard King, Steve Gadd, Jimmy Wong, Idris Muhammed, Allen Schwarzberger (d); Mtume, Crusher, Jimmy Maeulin, Dave Carey, Gary King (pc); Donny Hathaway (v)
Track listing:
Why Don't You Move In With Me; The Closer I Get To You; Fine, Fine Day; This Time I'll Be Sweeter; 25th Of Last December; After You; I'd Like To Be Baby To You; Soul Deep; Love Is The Healing; Where I'll Find You
Running time:
41.22
Current CD:
Warner Brothers 3282791
Further listening:
First Take (1969); Feel Like Makin' Love (1975).
Like this?
Try . . . p.93

Billy Joel

The Stranger

Italian guy with chip on shoulder finally hits the big time.

Phil Ramone made the difference. With four almost great albums behind him, Billy Joel needed the guidance of a master producer to hit the bull's-eye he'd been missing. "The band had been under the gun with other producers, having to prove themselves, and also, there were always studio players, who were good but who weren't me," Joel said in 1978. "Phil liked my guys right off the bat. He heard them play the songs and said, 'Don't play any different than you play on the road – be the rock'n'roll animals that you are.' We did songs in five takes instead of 15 or 20. He was one of the guys. We'd throw around ideas, kick the songs around, try them different ways and get them right. Sometimes we'd throw pizza at each other."

Appropriately, there was a song called Scenes From An Italian Restaurant, a McCartney-ish suite of three wildly different sections sewn tastefully together. And anywhere else you dropped the needle you found a winner: the 16-note ivory attack-ack-ack of Moving Out, the cabaret swank of Vienna, the gorgeous balladry of She's Always A Woman and the fiery acoustic rocker Only The Good Die Young (Joel on the song's banned status: "As soon as kids found out that there was some authority that didn't want them to hear it, they went out and bought it in droves and it became this big hit"). The album's most enduring song, Just The Way You Are, almost didn't make the cut.

"I didn't like it very much," Joel says. "We were in the studio listening back to it and I was not even gonna put it on the album, then Linda Ronstadt and Phoebe Snow showed up and they said, 'You've got to put that on the album!' I said, 'Yeah, you think so?' And they just pleaded with me to put it on the album. So I'm going to listen to what women say. I put it on the album."

Record label:
CBS
Produced
by Phil Ramone.
Recorded
at A&R Recording, New York, 1977
Released:
December 1977
Chart peaks:
25 (UK) 2 (US)
Personnel:
Billy Joel (p, v, k); Doug Stegmeyer (b); Liberty DeVitto (d); Richie Cannata (s, clarinet, flute, k); Phil Woods (s); Steve Khan, Hiram Bullock, Steve Burgh, Hugh McCracken (g); Dominic Cortese (acc); Richard Tee (k); Ralph McDonald (pc); Phoebe Snow, Lani Groves, Gwen Guthrie, Patti Austin (bv); Patrick Williams (oa); Jim Boyer (e)
Track listing:
Moving Out (Anthony's Song) (S); The Stranger; Just The Way You Are (S); Scenes From An Italian Restaurant; Vienna; Only The Good Die Young (S); She's Always A Woman; Get It Right The First Time; Everybody Has A Dream
Running time:
40.17
Current CD:
4911842
Further listening:
The Nylon Curtain (1982)
Further reading:
www.turnstiles.org
Like this?
Try . . . p.829

Townes Van Zandt

Live At The Old Quarter, Houston, Texas

The late legendary Texan troubadour's live masterpiece

When Townes Van Zandt died, aged 52, in 1997, he left behind a small but highly significant body of work – "aggressive folk", he called it, "poem songs" - that has never stopped attracting admirers. Neil Young, Willie Nelson, Sonic Youth, Cowboy Junkies, Tindersticks, Guy Clark, Steve Earle, Bono and Bob Dylan are among countless musicians who speak of Van Zandt with reverence. But during his lifetime, few people had any idea who he was, let alone bought his records. Hence the ironic title of his sixth Poppy Records album, 1973's *The Late Great Townes Van Zandt.* But his 'death' didn't help sell this one either. Poppy filed for bankruptcy, and Townes did what he had always done, and drifted for the next four years.

But before he left Houston, in July '73 he played a four-night residency at the Old Quarter - a 100-capacity club which, rare for the time, attracted a mixed crowd of country and hippie rock fans. Van Zandt was known for his remarkable performances - Steve Earle declared him "the most riveting solo performer I've ever seen, just closed his eyes, played and sang, and you couldn't take your eyes off him". Townes' Houston-based producer friend Earl Willis had "seen a lot of his shows", but these, he said, were "as good as he ever got." He had persuaded Van Zandt a live album might change his fortunes and offered to buy a new, top-of-the-range TEAC 3340 recorder to record his Old Quarter shows if the notoriously wayward singer (a mentally damaged alcoholic) "took it seriously. Townes stayed pretty clean for the week and really got involved and enthused. He had been working on his picking - you could tell; he was really sharp and primed."

That the album features just two shows was due to "technical difficulties" - the club's loud air conditioner. "So on the Friday and Saturday nights, even though it was July and *very* hot, we prevailed on the owner to run without air conditioning. We left the doors and windows open, so we did get some stray sounds from the street, but by having two nights we were able to get everything we needed."

The tapes sat on Willis' shelf for over three years, until .Poppy's chief returned with a new label, Tomato. Finally released in 1977, the excellent double album featured some of Townes' best-known songs - Pancho & Lefty, Mr Mudd & Mr Gold, To Live Is To Fly, Tecumseh Valley, For The Sake Of The Song - 15 from earlier albums, 11 new ones and three covers. release. No-one paid much notice.

SS

Record label:
Tomato
Produced
by Earl Willis.
Recorded
at The Old Quarter, Houston, Texas.
Released:
1977
Chart peaks:
None
Track Listing:
Disc One: Announcement, Pancho & Lefty, Mr. Mudd & Mr. Gold, Don't You Take It Too Bad, Two Girls, Fraternity Blues, If I Needed You, Brand New Companion, White Freight Liner Blues, To Live Is To Fly, She Came Around And She Touched Me, Talking Thunderbird Blues, Rex's Blues, Nine Pound Hammer. Disc Two: For The Sake Of The Song, Chauffeur's Blues, No Place To Fall, Loretta, Kathleen, Why She's Acting This Way, Cocaine Blues, Who Do You Love, Tower Song, Waiting 'Round To Die, Tecumseh Valley, Lungs, Only Him Or Me
Further listening:
A Gentle Evening with Van Zandt
Further reading:
For the Sake of the Song by Townes Van Zandt (1977)
Like this?
Try . . . p.350

Gerry Rafferty

City To City

Bolshy, reclusive songwriter's landmark of Scottish soft-rock. Immortalised by a sax motif.

Gerry Rafferty was a gifted man not cut out for fame. After cutting his teeth with comedian Billy Connolly in The Humblebums, he first tussled with the big time after forming Stealer's Wheel – self-styled "Scots version of Crosby Stills Nash And Young" – with fellow songwriter Joe Egan. Rafferty quit as their debut album, produced by Lieber and Stoller, no less, was released, only to return when Stuck In The Middle With You (1973) charted in Britain and America, but only on condition that Egan sacked the rest of the band. Two albums later they broke up, with Rafferty no longer speaking to Egan and about to embark on a three-year legal battle with their management.

But then came *City To City*, Baker Street and a further short-lived struggle with the horrors of wealth and public approbation. Never before can an album's commercial success have been built so squarely on one sax solo. As Baker Street rose to Number 3 in the UK and, after a live airing on David Frost's American TV show, Number 2 in the States, the album took off towards five million sales and even ended *Saturday Night Fever*'s six-month run at the top of the US album chart. Session star Raphael Ravenscroft's mournful plaint became an unforgettable calling card for the melancholy beauty of much of *City To City*. Yet Ravenscroft was called into the session only as an afterthought when Rafferty and co-producer Hugh Murphy – his one career-long colleague – decided mutually that the guitar line they had earmarked for the song wasn't happening.

In America, the label had big plans for Rafferty, fondly imagining that, with his gift for sensitive lyrics and radio-friendly melodies, they had found a tunesmith of Paul McCartney stature. But they swiftly discovered his reluctance to be a superstar. He resisted all overtures for a major tour there, opting instead for the studio and a quiet family life on his farm in Kent. His subsequent solo albums described the same downward parabola as Stealer's Wheel's, both commercially and, it must be said, artistically. However, the durable power of Rafferty's best soft-rock standards was acknowledged in the '90s when Quentin Tarantino revived Stuck In The Middle With You for the Reservoir Dogs soundtrack and Baker Street was covered by house crew Undercover (1992, Number 2 in the UK singles charts) and ex-Nirvana drummer Dave Grohl's Foo Fighters (1997).

Record label:
United Artists
Produced
by Hugh Murphy and Gerry Rafferty.
Recorded
at Chipping Norton Studios; September–October 1977.
Released:
January 1978
Chart peaks:
6 (UK) 1 (US)
Personnel:
Gerry Rafferty (v, k, p); Gary Taylor (v, b); Barbara Dickson (v); Jerry Donahue (g); Andy Fairweather-Low (g, d); Rab Noakes (v); Roger Brown (v); Hugh Burns (g); BJ Cole (sg); Brian Cole (Dobro, sg); Tommy Eyre (k, brass, a); Barry Hammond (e); Nigel Jenkins (g); Paul Jones (hm); Glen LeFleur (pc, d); Vivienne McAuliffe (v); John McBurnie (v); Mick Moody (g); Hugh Murphy (v, tabla); Declan O'Doherty (e); Graham Preskett (fiddle, mandolin, v); Raphael Ravenscroft (s); Henry Spinetti (d); Joanna Carlin (v); Willie Ray (acc)
Track listing:
Ark; Baker Street (S); Right Down The Line (S); City To City (S); Stealin' Town; Mattie's Rag; Whatever's Written In Your Heart (S); Home And Dry (S/US); Island; Waiting For The Day
Running time:
51.12
Current CD:
EMI CDFA3119
Further listening:
Humblebums (1969)
Further reading:
www.redstone-tech.com/gerry
Like this?
Try . . . p.539

The Adverts

Crossing The Red Sea With The Adverts

Punk pioneers leave it too late to make their mark on album, but do it anyway.

During the first months of 1977, Gaye Advert – smudged make-up, faded denims, ripped leathers – was a punk icon to rival Johnny Rotten. Stiff Records stuck her on the sleeve of One Chord Wonders, The Adverts' first 45, and lookalikes sprouted everywhere. These were different times, but not that different: the presence of a near-inanimate woman bassist quickly aroused suspicions about the band's musical abilities, doubts that were seemingly confirmed when a ragged version of Bored Teenagers turned up on an EMI various artists live album taped at the Roxy. When Gary Gilmore's Eyes (inspired by a Death Row killer's wish to leave his eyes to science) gatecrashed the UK Top 10 in August, The Adverts were poised to become New Wave heavyweights. Instead, the one-chord wonders soon began to resemble wonders of a less celebrated kind: the one-hit variety.

Had *Crossing The Red Sea* . . . made it into the shops that summer, things would have been different. Instead, it was November before the band committed their well-practised set to tape, having signed to Anchor, a subsidiary of US major ABC. Once within the unpunkish walls of Abbey Road, they recorded and mixed the album in two weeks with a minimum of overdubs. The songs, all staccato rhythms and Glam-like choruses, sparkled with unabashed energy and an endearing air of amateurism. Sophistication was provided by Smith's gallant attempt to wrestle with the dilemmas of the new punk age. It was all here: the untrained resolve (One Chord Wonders, Bored Teenagers), liberation (Bombsite Boy, New Church), confusion (No Time To Be 21) and a healthy dollop of cynicism (Safety In Numbers, The Great British Mistake). In sum it was an exemplary summation of a remarkable few months in rock, but by February 1978, when it eventually appeared, The Adverts were *passé*.

"I was writing conventional songs in an unconventional way," Smith explains, "but there was this dumbing down – Oi! bands and punk copyists who thought that punk rock was only about putting on a leather jacket and playing at 100mph." Caught in the crossfire between a new conservatism and the post-punk experimental scene, and hampered by ABC's decision to shut down Anchor prior to its release, *Red Sea* instead became the Great Lost Punk Album. After a poorly received follow-up, 1979's *Cast Of Thousands*, the group folded.

Record label:
Bright
Produced
by John Leckie.
Recorded
at Abbey Road, London; November 1977.
Released:
February 1978
Chart peaks:
38 (UK) None (US)
Personnel:
TV Smith (v); Gaye Advert (b); Howard Pickup (g); Laurie Driver (d)
Track listing:
One Chord Wonders (S); Bored Teenagers; New Church; On The Roof; Newboys; Bombsite Boy; No Time To Be 21 (S); Safety In Numbers (S); Drowning Men; On Wheels; Great British Mistake. Current CD adds earlier recordings found on two singles: Gary Gilmore's Eyes; Bored Teenagers; Safety In Numbers; We Who Wait – plus two cuts, Gary Gilmore's Eyes; New Day Dawning, taped at the album sessions but dropped from the final running order.
Running time:
32.00
Current CD:
ESMCD 451
Further listening:
The Punk Singles Collection (1997)
Further reading:
MOJO 78
Like this?
Try . . . p.410

Nick Lowe

Jesus Of Cool

Pub rocker and honorary punk crests the New Wave.

"I was never a punk. I was definitely pub rock. Bit like Paul Weller really." Thus, Nick Lowe, the Renaissance man of the snug bar defines his late '70s creative self. The former bassist with Brinsley Schwarz found himself co-opted by the punk movement when he became the first artsist to release a single on Stiff Records (So It Goes/Heart Of The City)

"Punk was really an attitude thing, and I liked that, but I was raised in playing good." Because he knew his way around a studio but wasn't averse to recording quickly and cheaply, Nick found himself in demand as a producer for arriving artists such as The Damned and Elvis Costello. His bash-it-down philosphy earned him the soubriquet "Basher" Lowe. And he applied all he'd learned from pub to punk when cutting his first solo album. "I deliberately messed things up a bit in the production," he says. "I'd put a tambourine up too loud or mix the vocals too low: generally leave things a bit undercooked, or at least cooked in a ragamuffin style. At the time I was just a frustrated music bloke, there was a lot of horrible prog rock and old singer-songwriter stuff around so anything that changed the status quo was all to the good."

I Love The Sound Of Breaking Glass encapsulates this disillusionment perfectly: "I need the noises of destruction/ When there's nothing new." The brittle piano weirdness that accompanies the loping, funky bass and the laid-back vocal captures the spirit of New Wave better than a hundred rowdier tracks. The rest of the album is a delicious jamboree bag of different "throwaway ideas", in Lowe's typically self-effacing estimation. The Beach Boys collide with Billy J Kramer on Little Hitler. No Reason adopts reggae. Shake And Pop, one of several songs to take a lyrical knife to the throat of the music biz, lurches like a drunken Chuck Berry. In complete contrast, Marie Provost is a ghoulish country-rock tale of a dead woman eaten by her dog, while Nutted By Reality begins as disco-funk and then transmogrifies into a Fab Four-styled novelty number.

"We were the first generation for whom music had gone round a full cycle. We could strike poses and play games. I suppose you could call it ironic rock." In the US, where the British title was thought to be a bit racy, they lifted the copy from a British advertisment for the album, calling it *Pure Pop For Now People.*

Record label:
Radar
Produced
by Nick Lowe.
Recorded
at Pathway and Eden Studios.
Released:
February 1978
Chart peaks:
22 (UK) None (US)
Personnel:
Nick Lowe (v, b, g); Dave Edmunds (v,g); Billy Bremner (g); John Turnbull (g); Bob Andrews (k); Andrew Bodnar (b); Norman Watt-Roy (b); Steve Goulding (d); Terry Williams (d); Charlie Charles (d)
Track listing:
Music For Money; I Love The Sounding Of Breaking Glass (S); Little Hitler (S); Shake And Pop; Tonight; So It Goes; No Reason; 36" High; Marie Provost; Nutted By Reality; Heart Of The City
Running time:
33.12
Currently unavailable on CD.
Further listening:
Labour Of Lust (1979); The Impossible Bird (1994)
Further reading:
No Sleep Till Canvey Island: The Great Pub Rock Revolution (Will Birch, 2000)
Stiff: The Story Of A Record Label (Bert Muirhead, 1983) available from
www.theturkeyzone.co.uk
www.dbd.co.uk/nicklowe
Like this?
Try . . . p.626

Buzzcocks

Another Music In A Different Kitchen

Definitive New Wave pop album: rousing hooks, race-track riffs, experimental leanings.

Catapulted into action after witnessing an early Sex Pistols performance, this Manchester-based band had virtually crumbled at the start of 1977 after frontman Howard Devoto quit. He'd regarded the release of the self-financed Spiral Scratch EP as the final realisation of an ambition. "Me and Pete decided to carry on," recalls Steve Diggle. "Pete took over the vocals, I switched from bass to guitar and we developed the twin-guitar style that became the classic Buzzcocks sound."

Two singles, Orgasm Addict and What Do I Get?, and a constant round of touring kept the band's profile high throughout 1977 but it was the punk-pop elegance of their spring 1978 debut album that sealed their reputation. "We'd toured that set for months," says Diggle, "so we knew the songs inside out. It was just ready to explode onto the tape." No punk-era album rivals *Another Music* in terms of its boundless effervescence, though Diggle acknowledges that the band's youthful enthusiasm was matched by Martin Rushent's assured approach to the production. "What you hear is what we did," he states, "but he was great to work with. We'd record three backing tracks for each song, choose the best, then add overdubs. Nothing was laboured, and there was none of this, 'We'll get it right in the mix' attitude. It wasn't overproduced yet it still sounded unique."

Being installed in a major-league studio like Olympic also had its advantages. "It was a massive room which enabled us to get a good drum sound. But we'd also bought these tiny H/H combo amps which allowed us to get a good sustain sound without having to crank up the volume levels. They were vital in obtaining that buzzsaw guitar feel."

Essentially a studio translation of the band's live set, *Another Music* was nevertheless easier on the ear than most punk-era albums. Despite being laden with hooks (I Don't Mind was just one of several potential singles), the record also hinted at greater experimentation. Moving Away From The Pulsebeat, which hung on a hypnotic John Maher rhythm and was even circulated to DJs as a club 12-inch, wasn't the only track to betray a Krautrock influence.

"Autonomy was inspired by Can. It was my attempt at impersonating a German taking off an Englishman," says Diggle. "The album had lots of influences and directions. People forget that. We weren't just about singles." The first few thousand copies were issued in carrier bags with the record's catalogue number on one side and the word "Product" on the other: a typically witty gesture from one of the most powerful and intelligent bands of the epoch.

Record label:
UA
Produced
by Martin Rushent.
Recorded
at Olympic Studios, Barnes, London; December 28, 1977–January 31, 1978.
Released:
March 1978
Chart peaks:
15 (UK) None (US)
Personnel:
Pete Shelley (g, v); Steve Diggle (g, v); John Maher (d); Steve Garvey (b); Doug Bennett (e)
Track listing:
Fast Cars; No Reply; You Tear Me Up; Get On Our Own; Love Battery; Sixteen; I Don't Mind (S); Fiction Romance; Autonomy; I Need; Moving Away From The Pulsebeat
Running time:
35.39
Current CD:
724382830924 adds Love Bites (1998) Real World; Ever Fallen In Love (With Some One You Shouldn't've?) (S); Operator's Manual; Nostalgia; Just Lust; Sixteen Again; Walking Distance; Love Is Lies; Nothing Left; ESP; Late For The Train
Further listening:
Singles Going Steady
Further reading:
Buzzcocks: The Complete History (Independent Music Press, 1995)
www.buzzcocks.com
Like this?
Try . . . p.610

Pere Ubu

The Modern Dance

Singular, uncompromising art-punk debut.

Pere Ubu were college drop-outs – five young men who saw no point in "half-assed art" – who came together in Cleveland, Ohio, where a healthy music scene had been thriving since the early 1970s. But it was, to many, the epitome of Nowheresville. They convinced themselves that the weight of history had fallen on their shoulders: they were destined to move rock music forward, but resigned themselves to anonymity. "This is a very, very powerful atmosphere to work in," says David Thomas. "The utter hopelessness of it, in that no one would know, and the knowledge that this was unique."

Tightened up by playing every week at the Pirate's Cove club in the industrial zone known as The Flats, and with two stunning singles (30 Seconds Over Tokyo and Final Solution) under their belt, Pere Ubu went for broke on their debut album. They recorded it in a couple of weeks at the out-of-town Suma Sound, with Ken Hamann, who had been working since the '40s and whose CV included engineering for The Lemon Pipers and Grand Funk Railroad. He captured the band's idiosyncratic creativity at flash-point and the finished work was as radical as they intended.

Non-Alignment Pact opens with Allen Ravenstine's unpredictable EML synthesizer emitting an uncomfortable, abrasive signal to which guitarist Tom Hermann responds with a Chuck Berry-style riff, a launch pad for a song which marries avant-garde experimentalism with rock'n'roll clout. The urban sprawl of Street Waves is typical, with the group's rolling groove and Thomas' whooping wail of a voice buffetted by toxic waves from the synth, but there are also poignant moments such as the melancholic Chinese Radiation. Critics, especially in the UK, raved. Pere Ubu were tagged "industrial", which was only partly useful; although the music was dark and intense, there was melody and absurdist humour in there too; the group never saw their environment as an industrial wasteland. "Its greatest influence on us was the notion of sound as a powerful, poetic tool," says Thomas. And far from remaining unknown, the group have produced consistently intriguing music for over two decades.

Record label:
Mercury
Produced
by Pere Ubu with Ken Hamann.
Recorded
at Suma, Cleveland, Ohio; November 1977.
Released:
April 1978
Chart peaks:
None (UK) None, (US)
Personnel:
David Thomas (v, musette); Tom Herman (g); Allen Ravenstine (EML syn, s); Tony Maimone (b); Scott Krauss (d); Ken Hamann (e); Paul Hamann, Mike Bishop (ae)
Track listing:
Non-Alignment Pact; The Modern Dance (S/US); Laughing; Street Waves (S/US); Chinese Radiation; Life Stinks; Real World; Over My Head; Sentimental Journey; Humor Me
Running time:
39.15
Current CD:
Cooking Vinyl COOKCD141
Further listening:
The quickly written, but equally impressive follow-up, Dub Housing (1978)
Further reading:
www.dnai.com/~obo/ubu/
Like this?
Try . . . p.517

Van Halen

Van Halen

Hard-rock colossus blows the competition out of the water.

By 1978, heavy metal already needed re-inventing. Fortunately, Van Halen had the blueprint. Guitarist Eddie was an alchemist, his licks influential, his virtuosity always tempered by *joie de vivre.* Frontman David Lee Roth was his perfect foil; a charismatic peacock in Spandex. After a demo financed by Kiss's Gene Simmons led to a contract with Warner's, staff producer Ted Templeman (Captain Beefheart, Montrose) took charge of the band's debut.

The lean, testosterone and Jack Daniels-fuelled performances featured few overdubs. Ostensibly, Templeman's job was to capture live performances already perfected on the Pasadena/Santa Barbara bar circuit. Most tracks hover around the three-and-a-half-minute mark, evidencing a strong pop sense, bolstered by Eddie and bassist Michael Anthony's falsetto harmonies. Roth – ever the preener – moots his sexual prowess throughout; on his cover of John Brim's Ice Cream Man, you sense the "push-ups" he's offering have little to do with dairy produce.

In a 1996 interview with Smashing Pumpkins' Billy Corgan, Eddie confided that the instrumental showpiece Eruption was an afterthought recorded in one pass at Templeman's suggestion. "And there's a mistake at the top end of it," he added. "To this day, whenever I hear it, I always think, Man, I could've played it better."

It was a flaw nobody else noticed, and Eddie – then aged 22 – dominated this record. Like Jimmy Page, he had a keen appreciation of the hook riff, evident herein a startling reworking of The Kinks' You Really Got Me, and his own Ain't Talking 'Bout Love. Two decades later, Apollo 440 would pay homage, pairing the latter song's intro with a drum'n'bass loop on Ain't Talkin' 'Bout Dub. When Van Halen toured with Black Sabbath after this album's release, the Brummie's leaden riffs suddenly seemed *passé*, and a coup by the support act was widely reported. Soon, Los Angeles would spawn a host of copycat bands, but none of them had Eddie's talent or Roth's easy wit. *Van Halen* eventually sold over six million copies.

Record label:
Warner Brothers
Produced
by Ted Templeman.
Recorded
at Sunset Sound Recorders, Hollywood; 1977.
Released:
April 1978
Chart peaks:
34 (UK) 19 (US)
Personnel:
David Lee Roth (v); Edward Van Halen (g); Michael Anthony (b); Alex Van Halen (d); Don Landee (e)
Track listing:
Runnin' With The Devil (S); Eruption; You Really Got Me (S); Ain't Talkin' 'Bout Love (S/US); I'm The One; Jamie's Cryin'; Atomic Punk; Feel Your Love Tonight; Little Dreamer; Ice Cream Man; On Fire
Running time:
35.34
Current CD:
7599273202
Further listening:
Van Halen II (1979)
Further reading:
Crazy From The Heat (David Lee Roth, 1998)
www.van-halen.com
Like this?
Try . . . p.454

Kraftwerk

The Man-Machine

The Düsseldorf Dynamos add a sardonic political overview to their romantic-realist style.

The Man-Machine was the album which ushered in the age of electronic pop, clearing the ground for everyone from The Human League and Depeche Mode to Daft Punk and Pole. Like its predecessor *Trans-Europe Express*, it was another concept album, offering a sly, ambiguous commentary on the relationship of man and machine, and the dehumanisation of man in industrial society. The group were intrigued, for instance, to learn that the Russian word for "worker" is "robotnick", although in interviews Ralf Hütter expressed an altogether more sanguine attitude to the man-machine interface.

"The dynamism of the machines, the 'soul' of the machines, has always been a part of our music," he claimed. "We are playing the machines, the machines play us, it is really the exchange and friendship we have with the musical machines which make us build a new music."

The marshalling, in revolutionary red and black, of the dynamic diagonals of the Russian constructivist El Lissitzky for the album's cover art cleverly conveyed the paradoxical Utopian promise and totalitarian threat of the early 20th-century modernist notion of "machine art" which Kraftwerk were effectively resurrecting. The album's pristine, machine-tooled presentation of tracks with titles like Neon Lights, Spacelab, The Robots and (most pertinently) Metropolis further drove home its theme of antique modernity: these are all dated, nostalgic visions of the future, polished and shiny with the awed glow of conviction, before the notion of modernism began to rust. Even the album's hit single The Model, ostensibly a hymn to unattainable beauty, deals with a woman determined to present herself to the world as object rather than subject.

The music itself was sleeker and more gracefully minimal than before, while the rhythm tracks were so infectious that Whitfield Records' Leanard Jackson, flown in from LA to mix some of the tracks, was surprised to find himself dealing with four white Germans, rather than the black musicians he imagined had laid down the grooves. Derived from hours of improvisation, the tunes were slowly chipped into shape by the group – literally, "machined" until they gleamed – while a new order of fastidious complexity was applied to the hypnotic electronic percussion: a track like the nine-minute Neon Lights might seem relentlessly repetitive on first listen, but deeper attention reveals that each of the little drum fills which punctuates its progress is different from the rest.

Provisionally entitled *Dynamo*, the album went on to sell over 100,000 copies in the UK and 200,000 in France, in the process becoming a much-beloved cornerstone of electronic pop.

Record label:
Capitol
Produced
by Ralf Hütter and Florian Schneider.
Recorded
at Kling Klang Studio, Düsseldorf; 1977–78.
Released:
May 1978
Chart peaks:
9 (UK) None (US)
Personnel:
Ralf Hütter (v, electronics); Florian Schneider (v, electronics); Karl Bartos (electronic pc); Wolfgang Flur (electronic pc); Joschko Rudas, Leanard Jackson (e)
Track listing:
The Robots (S); Spacelab (S); Metropolis; The Model (S); Neon Lights (S); The Man-Machine.
Running time:
36.10
Current CD:
CA0460392
Further listening:
The preceding Trans-Europe Express (1977) and ensuing Computer World (1981) feature the mature Kraftwerk operating on a plateau rarely approached by other electronica acts. The earlier Autobahn (1974) and Radioactivity (1975) are like preparatory sketches, while their earliest albums are more experimental and improvisatory. The later remix album The Mix (1991) re-tools their hits with new rhythmic undercarriage.
Further reading:
MOJO 41; Kraftwerk: Man, Machine And Music (Pascal Bussy 1997); Kraftwerk: From Düsseldorf To The Future (With Love) (Tim Barr, 1998) www.kraftwerk.com
Like this?
Try . . . p.678

Steve Reich

Music For 18 Musicians

American composer creates his most important crossover work.

Ask any minimalist composer about their work and the first thing they'll do is deny any allegiance to the M word. Steve Reich is no exception. He asserts that it was simply a convenient way of describing composers who, in the '60s, broke away from the rigorous complexity of modern classical composition – Reich himself, Philip Glass and Terry Riley, for example. Early on, Reich's main interests were phase and rhythm. On Come Out, two identical tapes of speech were run slightly out of phase, producing a hallucinatory effect.

A former jazz drummer, Reich later studied percussion in Ghana, and Balinese gamelan music in the US. Both styles inform works like *Drumming*. He also enjoyed the repetition and clarity of line in everything from Bach to Junior Walker's Shotgun. In 1973, Reich composed the mind-boggling sonic mesh of Six Pianos and the gamelan-like Music For Mallet Instruments, Voices And Organ. The following year, work began on what was to become his best-known instrumental work, *Music For 18 Musicians*. A composition of 12 parts all played along a basic rhythmic pulse, each discrete part, or cell, gradually mutating via augmentation. What looks dry and academic on paper is in fact sublime, with moments of stunning beauty – particularly in the multiple piano sections, and the huge arcs of bass clarinets and voices that crop up as a recurring motif.

It has become immensely influential; its rippling waveforms have found their way into DJ sets, and Reich's signature is heard on music produced by Tortoise, Pan Sonic, Alec Empire, The Orb, Aphex Twin and particularly German techno of the early '90s – a situation the composer is delighted with. "Bach and other baroque composers were writing dance forms; sarabands and gavottes that derived from the street," he notes. "This is the state of affairs until we get to Schöenberg who builds a wall between serious music and the trash out there in the street. That is totally artificial and out of kilter with the history of Western music. Now, if we can talk about what the techno groups are doing, or what they've learned from my music, I can feel inside my heart: Gee, that's great. That's the way it should be."

Record label:
ECM
Produced
by Rudolph Werner.
Exact recording
location and date unknown.
Released:
spring 1978
Chart peaks:
None (UK) None (US)
Personnel:
Shem Guibbory (vn); Ken Ishii (c); Elizabeth Arnold (v); Rebecca Armstrong (v); Pamela Fraley (v); Nurit Tilles (p); Larry Karush (p, maraccas); Gary Schall (marimba, maraccas); Bob Becker (marimba, xylpohone); Russ Hartenberger (marimba, xylophone); James Preiss (metallophone, p); Steve Chambers (p); Steve Reich (p, marimba); David Van Tieghem (marimba, xylophone, p); Glen Velez (marimba, xylophone); Virgil Blackwell (clarinet, bass clarinet); Richard Cohen (clarinet, bass clarinet); Jay Clayton (v, p); Klaus Hiemann (e)
Track listing:
Pulse; Sections I-X; Pulse
Running time:
56.31
Current CD:
8214172
Further listening:
Octet/Music For A Large Ensemble/Violin Phase (1980) took the Music For 18 Musicians style to another level of sophistication.
Further reading:
www.slis.keio.ac.jp/~ohba/Reich/srindex.html
Like this?
Try . . . p.47

Willie Nelson
Stardust

At 55, the touchstone country songwriter goes Broadway and Hollywood with smash-hit results.

Willie Nelson was the real thing. As a kid he worked in the cotton-fields near his hometown, Abbott, Texas, for $3 a day. But that didn't make him a purist. Having toiled away for years as a songwriter without himself becoming a star performer, in the early '70s he grew his hair, took to hippy hats, switched from booze to hash – and began to pick the rhinestones off the Nashville sound. In 1975, with his CBS debut *Red Headed Stranger* he defied accepted practice by insisting on creative control, secured by self-production. Commercial fears were allayed when it headed for a million sales at a time when "country hit" meant around 200,000. But label misgivings revived when he announced *Stardust* as a collection of standards drawn from writers like Hoagy Carmichael (the title track and Georgia On My Mind), Irving Berlin (Blue Skies) and the Gershwins (Someone To Watch Over Me). Columbia said he was crazy; the album wasn't country. Nelson said: "Who cares?"

He explained that, as a poor boy, radio had provided his musical education. Frank Sinatra was his favourite singer. The *Stardust* idea crystallised when Bing Crosby died in October 1977. "It was a big gamble," he acknowledged. "Until I met Booker [T Jones, of the MGs, producer, on a beach in Los Angeles] I wasn't sure how well I could do it because of my limited musical ability. These are complicated songs. They have a lot of chords in them." But with the Stax maestro arranging sparse, though warm, settings – a touch of piano, a sliver of strings – Nelson delivered the lovely essence of these honoured songs. Like Carmichael himself or Jimmy Durante, he never seemed much of a singer. But consider the aching gentleness of Moonlight In Vermont or the restrained fervour of Someone To Watch Over Me; it turns out that he hits the notes and jockeys the beat so fluently that performance becomes intimate conversation. Atlantic Records founder Jerry Wexler, who worked regularly with Aretha Franklin, wrote that Nelson, whom he produced a couple of times, shared Sinatra's "gift for incredible vocal *rubato* – prolonging one note, cutting short another, swinging with an elastic sense of time that only the finest jazz singers understand".

Stardust stayed in the American Top 200 for over two years, sold four million and, commercially, set country on the road to Garth Brooks.

Record label:
CBS
Produced
by Booker T Jones.
Recorded
at Emmylou Harris's house, southern California, on The Enactron Truck, early 1978.
Released:
June 1978
Chart peaks:
None (UK) 30 (US)
Personnel:
Willie Nelson (v, g); Bobbie Nelson (p); Paul English (d); Rex Ludwig (d); Jody Payne (g); Bee Spears (b); Chris Ethridge (b); Mickey Raphael (hm); Booker T Jones (o, p); Bradley Hartman, Donivan Cowart (e)
Track listing:
Stardust; Georgia On My Mind; Blue Skies; All Of Me; Unchained Melody; September Song; On The Sunny Side Of The Street; Moonlight In Vermont; Don't Get Around Much Anymore; Someone To Watch Over Me
Running time:
37.09
Current CD:
4952452, adds: Scarlet Ribbons; I Can See Clearly Now
Further listening:
Red Headed Stranger (1975), Nelson's country ground-breaker
Further reading:
MOJO 14; Heart Worn Memories: A Daughter's Personal Biography Of Willie Nelson (Susie Nelson, 1987); Willie Nelson Sings America (Stephen Opdyke et al, 1998); www.willienelson.com
Like this?
Try . . . p.304

Bruce Springsteen

Darkness On The Edge Of Town

After suing his manager, Springsteen rages. The cars are metaphors, the darkness is real.

Stalled for more than a year by a legal wrangle with manager Mike Appel, Springsteen achieved severance on May 28, 1977. Two days later, with the E Street Band, he walked into Atlantic Studios, New York, to start recording his fourth album. Much changed, he was determined to take total control of his career. At the same time, with *Born To Run*'s co-producer, Ivy League rock critic Jon Landau, becoming both a close friend and his new manager, Springsteen embraced a previously alien world of cultural experience, beginning with old movies. John Ford's The Grapes Of Wrath and various *films noirs*, American and French, gave him a political and emotional backdrop for his stories about "people who are going from nowhere to nowhere". At 28, in Promised Land, he sang, "Mister, I ain't a boy, no, I'm a man." Frustration off the leash, he worked fast, recording 16 songs, choosing 10.

While love and sex still seethed in his lyrics, now he acknowledged older generations too, with profound feeling for their hard lives – especially in Factory's portrait of an archetypal worker representing his own father's wasted-life bitterness. "Darkness" loomed everywhere. Springsteen noted that because Clarence Clemons' sax style was too "in-your-face" for this setting, he was given less to do this time. Guitar stood in because "it has a little more distance". But the sound of *Darkness On The Edge Of Town* is at once sombre *and* wild.

Angry rather than celebratory, it sold much less well than its predecessor. Yet it deepened Springsteen's appeal. There are conspicuously great songs: just soak in the orgasmic rush of Candy's Room followed by the slow, fathomless grief of Racing In The Streets. But *Darkness On The Edge Of Town* also touches inexplicable emotions through visceral detail, like the measured melancholy tread of Roy Bittan's piano and Springsteen's own frantic high harmonies which run almost subliminally through most tracks as if he had an anxiety-wracked second self in the studio with him. Writing and performing, he reflected on his family and their hard, poor lives as never before.

"I see my sister and her husband," he said. "These are people, you can see something in their eyes. I asked my sister, What do you do for fun? I don't have any fun, she says. She wasn't kidding." Which is part of the reason why, in a more upbeat contemporary reflection on the meaning of rock'n'roll, he concluded, "The whole idea is to deliver what money can't buy."

Record label:
CBS
Produced
by Jon Landau and Bruce Springsteen.
Recorded
at The Record Plant, New York; July–December 1977.
Released:
June 1978
Chart peaks:
16 (UK) 5 (US)
Personnel:
Bruce Springsteen (v, g, hm); Clarence Clemons (s, pc); Danny Federici (o); Roy Bittan (p); Garry Tallent (bs); Steve Van Zandt (g); Max Weinberg (d); Jimmy Iovine (e)
Track listing:
Badlands (S); Adam Raised A Cain; Something In The Night; Candy's Room; Racing In The Street; The Promised Land (S); Factory; Streets Of Fire; Prove It All Night; Darkness On The Edge Of Town
Running time:
42.31
Current CD:
CD86061
Further listening:
The familial darkness between the rock'n'roll hollering on The River, then utter societal gloom descends with the solo Nebraska. Born In The USA (1984) and Tunnel Of Love (1987)
Further reading:
MOJO 17, 62; Born To Run: The Bruce Springsteen Story (Dave Marsh, 1979); www.backstreets.com (US)
Like this?
Try . . . p.716

Talking Heads

More Songs About Buildings And Food

Itchy agit-pop angst meets Egghead.

The comparative commercial failure of Talking Heads' first album led the group's mentors to the conclusion that a less traditional production was needed to maximise the creative tension between pop-minded bassist Tina Weymouth and art-house eccentric David Byrne. They'd signed to Sire for big bucks and, as yet, they were far away from justifying the tireless press acclaim. Byrne's agit-pop storytelling had attracted an intelligent cult following and his tales of everyday tedium, crazed psychopaths and the vagaries of the business world had indicated that Talking Heads were on the verge of something quite spectacular. But if Byrne was to realise his vision of a shallow Generation X-styled America, juiced with the small-town weirdness of a David Lynch film, it wouldn't be easy.

Neither backdrop at that point even existed. Meanwhile, in a parallel universe, former Roxy Music man Brian Eno had already struggled over the same musical juxtaposition on his solo albums *Here Come The Warm Jets* and *Taking Tiger Mountain*. By '78 he'd given up on clever pop and gone ambient but he had an armoury of production techniques and a penchant for clipped rhythmic guitar and dubbed percussion that fully complemented Byrne's off-kilter worldview.

To satisfy the collision of well-grooved soul and their sense of technocratic removal, Talking Heads were wrapped in a cocoon of phased effects, looped sounds and echoey snare snaps. It was the perfect backdrop for Byrne's jerky dance and it left enough space for the rest of the group to play like a hothoused pick-up band. Even the album's cover of Al Green's Take Me To The River, which was a minor hit, managed to process a classic slice of Gospel hyperventilation into a sterilised laboratory-controlled groove. *More Songs About Buildings And Food* checks out the world from a safe distance, a sensation fully realised on the closing cut, The Big Country in which the Byrne acts like the pilot of a space capsule orbiting his former world. It's like an album of intimate and very personal songs but heard through Clingfilm.

It was a success but the delicate Weymouth/Byrne axis was rattled by the arrival of Eno. "They're like two 14-year-old boys making an impression on each other," Weymouth moaned. "By the time they finished working together for three months, they were dressing like one another... I can see them when they're 80 and all alone. There'll be David Bowie, David Byrne and Brian Eno, and they'll just talk to each other." The triad lasted one more album.

Record label:
Sire
Produced
by Brian Eno and Talking Heads.
Recorded
at Compass Point, New Providence, The Bahamas; March–April 1978.
Released:
July 1978
Chart peaks:
21 (UK) 29 (US)
Personnel:
David Byrne (v, g, pc); Chris Frantz (d, pc); Jerry Harrison (o, p, syn, g, bv); Tina Weymouth (b); Brian Eno (syn, g, pc, bv); Tina And The Typing Pool (bv on The Good Thing)
Track listing:
Thank You For Sending Me An Angel; With Our Love; The Good Thing; Warning Sign; The Girls Want To Be With The Girls; Found A Job; Artists Only; I'm Not In Love; Stay Hungry; Take Me To The River (S); The Big Country
Running time:
41.48
Current CD:
7599274252
Further listening:
The previous September's Talking Head '77 sets out Byrne's song style and the following Fear Of Music (1979) and Remain In Light (1980) refine it and develop the Eno-patented production techniques.
Further reading:
www.talking-heads.net What The Songs Look Like: The Illustrated Talking Heads (David Byrne and Frank Olinsky, 1987)
Like this?
Try . . . p.499

Blondie

Parallel Lines

Skinny-tied new Yorkers combine punk, New Wave and disco to world-beating effect.

Despite being the last act out of the original New York punk scene to be offered a record deal, the blonde ambition of ex-Playboy Bunny girl Debbie Harry and her mop-topped male colleagues paid off, when *Parallel Lines* became such a critical and commercial success that, by early 1979, Blondie had apparently become the biggest band on the planet.

Despite an early reputation as a bit of a novelty act (fellow CBGB act Patti Smith told them to "get the fuck out of rock'n'roll"), UK hits Denis and (I'm Always Touched By Your) Presence Dear (from *Plastic Letters)* showed that a bunch of punks written off in their own city could cross over into the uncertain arena of pop.

Mike "if you can't make hit singles, go chop meat somewhere" Chapman of the infamous Chinnichap production line (Sweet, Smokie, Suzi Quatro, Mud, Racey) was a risky choice for the producer's chair.

When he listened to their demos for the album, Chapman was rather taken with something called The Disco Song, a tune that had been skulking in their set since 1975 but hadn't made the cut on either their debut or *Plastic Letters*. It was played apologetically in a *faux*-reggae rhythm, but Chapman saw its potential and persuaded them to do it with a full-on funk swagger. The band really went for it, laying down a storming groove with a Roland Rhythm Machine and, according to Stein, "a bass-line copped from Goldfinger". They retitled the result Heart Of Glass.

"We didn't expect the song to be that big," Stein recalls. (This is borne out by the fact that it's buried at track four, side two on the original LP.) "[It was] a novelty item to put more diversity into the record. But it [turned out to be] a mark in history. It brought black and white music together. We weren't thinking about selling out, we were thinking about Kraftwerk and Eurodisco."

Chapman taught Blondie the importance of tightening arrangements and honing the backing tracks to a glossy perfection. Critic Lester Bangs enthused. "The thing that makes *Parallel Lines* so assuredly avant-garde is precisely that it's so airtight and multiple-choice. This is it. The masterpiece."

From the gutsy Hanging On The Telephone to the luscious Sunday Girl – a paean to Debbie's pet moggy – the success of *Parallel Lines* is down to a mixture of sweet '60s girl-group harmonies and edgy New Wave arrangements. It also spawned some enduring candy-coated punk-pop anthems in Pretty Baby, Fade Away And Radiate (featuring guitar wizard Robert Fripp) and 11:59, which many of their contemporaries would have given their skinny ties to use as singles.

Record label:
Chrysalis
Produced
by Mike Chapman.
Recorded
at the Record Plant, New York; June–July 1978.
Released:
September 1978
Chart peaks:
1 (UK) 6 (US)
Personnel:
Jimmy Destri (k); Frank Infante (g); Chris Stein (g); Nigel Harrison (b); Clem Burke (d); Deborah Harry (v); Pete Coleman (e)
Track listing:
Hanging On The Telephone (S); One Way Or Another (S/US); Picture This (S); Fade Away And Radiate; Pretty Baby; I Know But I Don't Know; 11:59; Will Anything Happen?; Sunday Girl (S); Heart Of Glass (S); I'm Gonna Love You Too (S/US); Just Go Away
Running time:
41.26
Current CD:
CCD1192
Further listening:
Eat To The Beat (1979); The Platinum Collection (1994) collects both sides of every Blondie single up to 1982, plus a handful of interesting early demos. Deborah Harry's Def, Dumb And Blonde (1989), which saw her reunited with Mike Chapman, is the sharpest of her solo albums.
Further Reading:
MOJO 63; Making Tracks: The Rise Of Blondie (Debbie Harry, Chris Stein and Victor Bockris, 1998); www.blondie.ausbone.net
Like this?
Try . . . p.690

Wire

Chairs Missing

Raising the stakes in the UK post-punk scene.

If punk came as a shock, Wire were more shocking still. Although they cut their teeth playing at the the (in)famous Roxy in London's Covent Garden, they shared as many differences as affinities with the rest of that scene. Initially the band refused to release singles, and while their 21-song, 1977 debut *Pink Flag* may have been the most brutally pared-down album of the era, it was released on Harvest courtesy of Nick Mobbs, who had also signed Pink Floyd to the label. And, horror, guitarist Bruce Gilbert was already over 30.

Gilbert admits the group learnt to play on *Pink Flag*, but they were fast learners – halfway through that album they were already experimenting in the studio and writing new songs. "A lot of material didn't survive the process of touring and the process of starting to record *Chairs Missing*," he says. "We were moving so quickly that things came and went in the blink of an eye."

By the time they were set to record the album, virtually all generic New Wave moves had been left behind. Gilbert: "We could go through lots of variations on themes and experiment with a confidence that, with a bit of practice, any structures that were unorthodox or slightly unusual we would eventually be able to handle." From the staccato chords of opener Practice Makes Perfect onwards, there was a new-found sense of dynamics and syncopation taking over from their former straight-ahead rigidity, with producer Mike Thorne's keyboards adding new textures. The ferocious Mercy clocked in at nearly six minutes, while songs like Marooned showed a more reflective approach. As an example of the band's often impenetrable humour, on Outdoor Miner they set a lyric about entomology to a gorgeous pop tune.

The album was well-received, apart from the odd sneer that it carried a Syd Barrett influence – a view Gilbert refutes totally. *Chairs Missing* is direct, powerful and bursting with ideas, and catches a group on the cusp of a journey that was to see them constantly move on throughout their on/off, 20-year course. Meanwhile, their music has exerted a widespread influence – not least on '90s Britpop.

Record label:
Harvest
Produced
by Mike Thorne.
Recorded
at Advision Studios; summer 1978.
Released:
September 1978
Chart peaks:
48 (UK) None (US)
Personnel:
Colin Newman (v, g); BC Gilbert (g); Graham Lewis (b, v); Robert Gotobed (d); Mike Thorne (k, syn); Kate Lukas (flutes); Paul Hardiman (e)
Track listing:
Practice Makes Perfect; French Film Blurred; Another The Letter; Men 2nd; Marooned; Sand In My Joints; Being Sucked In Again; Heartbeat; Mercy; Outdoor Miner; I Am The Fly (S/UK); I Feel Mysterious Today; From The Nursery; Used To; Too Late
Running time:
42.20
Current CD:
CDGO2065
Further listening:
Pink Flag (1977); 154 (1979); Behind The Curtain (1994), a collection of live tracks and early demos circa 1977–1978
Further reading:
Wire: Everybody Loves A History (Kevin S Eden, 1991)
Like this?
Try . . . p.610

The Police

Outlandos D'Amour

Unlikely stadium rock band's debut.

It was proof of Miles Copeland's managerial skill that he managed to sell The Police to A&M as a punk group. They were signed on March 22, 1978 after a gig at London's Nashville Rooms, and began a run of underachievement and ill-advised side projects: Roxanne flopped in April, and the group went their separate ways during the summer – Sting spent six weeks filming Quadrophenia, while Stewart Copeland (former drummer with Curved Air) recorded two bizarre singles under the pseudonym Klark Kent.

Their debut album was largely in the can, having been worked on since January at Surrey Sound, a rather shabby establishment in the unlikely environs of Leatherhead (since hugely upgraded): "It was a cruddy, funky place with egg cartons on the wall," remembered Sting. Copeland Sr had persuaded the Gray brothers to assist the band with its recording for little more than £1,500, and they also found themselves having to mediate with a group who were clearly not getting on (Mike Noble, then an A&R man for A&M, claims he was attracted to the band by "the incredible tension between Sting and Stewart – they loathed each other"). One incident flared up around Andy Summers' difficulty getting to grips with the guitar part for Hole In My Life. Aware that Sting fancied himself as a guitar player, he tetchily suggested that he play it himself. Sting refused, only to find Copeland offering his services.

The studio, though dingy, had its advantages – chiefly, a large sloping roof that allowed Copeland to creatively vary his drum sound. This was just one of the benefits arising from the trio's musical experience, reflected in an album which – for all the energised charge of Next To You, Peanuts and Truth Hits Everybody – had a far more varied palette than most of the New Wave dreck appearing at the time. In that sense, *Outlandos D'Amour* was instrumental in proving that virtuosic rock had a post-punk future. Most crucial of all was The Police's grasp of reggae.

"Bob Marley was the link," said Sting. "Roxanne has a real Bob Marley feel. He's half-white, so he's sort of a cultural go-between, a cornerstone. Once you get past Marley, you can get past the rest of reggae and understand it more clearly." After moderate success in America, a re-released Roxanne reached Number 12 in the UK in April 1979, and *Outlandos* was belatedly given its commercial just desserts.

Record label:
A&M

Produced
by The Police.

Recorded
at Surrey Sound Studios, Leatherhead; January–August 1978.

Released:
October 1978

Chart peaks:
6 (UK) 23 (US)

Personnel:
Sting (b, v), Andy Summers (g, v); Stewart Copeland (d, v); Nigel Gray, Chris Gray (e)

Track listing:
Next To You; So Lonely (S); Roxanne (S); Hole In My Life; Peanuts; Can't Stand Losing You (S); Truth Hits Everybody; Born In The '50s; Be My Girl – Sally; Masoko Tanga

Running time:
38.50

Current CD:
CDMID126

Further listening:
A&M box set, Message In A Box (1993)

Further reading:
Sting: Demolition Man (Christopher Sandford, 1998); www.stingchronicity.co.uk

Like this?
Try . . . p.379

Siouxsie And The Banshees

The Scream

Fiercely individualistic punks arrived late with debut album; it still sounded way ahead of its time.

Starting life as suburban Sex Pistols' acolytes dressed in fetish clothing, Sioux and Steve Severin – with guitarist Marco Pirroni and Sid Vicious on drums – improvised a debut at the 100 Club in September 1976.

Over the next 18 months, a new-look Banshees stabilised around a set of songs inspired by the Velvet Underground's atonality and Nico's bellow, a Bowie-like misanthropy and a "pure punk" antipathy towards 12-bar rock'n'roll. The mystique piled up, hastened by two extraordinary sessions for John Peel, some uncompromising interviews and a rash of "Sign The Banshees" graffiti daubed on record company walls.

"We hyped it up a lot," admits Steve Severin, "but most A&R men were too scared to come and see us because most of our shows erupted into violence. Then, out of the blue, we wrote Hong Kong Garden."

Polydor won the battle for the band's signature and, in August 1978, released Hong Kong Garden on 45. That same month, the Banshees entered RAK to record an album with rookie producer Steve Lillywhite. Severin: "We went into the sessions with a sense of relief, an arrogance that thrived on the burden of expectation, and a lot of frustration. We had this incredible sense of striving for the unattainable and we trusted no one. And we were nervous that Lillywhite would dilute the sound. He didn't understand the 'attitude' but in the end it didn't really matter – everything was in the performances."

"The album was written before going into the studio," Sioux recalls. "We had a clear idea of the sound we wanted and our set-up was very simple. All the tracks were played live with overdubs added later."

Severin adds: "Years of festering ideas and minutes of technique! Everything was bold, strong strokes. We threw away the clichés and patched together what was left."

Angular, artful and seething with contempt, *The Scream* took punk's anti-rock'n'roll rhetoric seriously: psychological breakdown (Jigsaw Feeling, Suburban Relapse), disease (Nicotine Stain) and Charles Manson (Helter Skelter) enhanced the dystopian mood. "I still think the segue from Pure into Jigsaw Feeling is one of rock's scariest moments," maintains Severin. "Here's our calling card. Get out of that!"

Blame it on suburbia, "that wonderful land of manicured lies and stifling conformity", says Sioux who, like Severin, was living in Bromley at the time. "Where else do you find such fertile breeding grounds for disparate malcontents?"

Record label:
Polydor
Produced
by Steve Lillywhite & Siouxsie And The Banshees
Recorded
at RAK, London, mixed at De Lane Lea, London, August 1978
Release date:
October 1978
Chart peaks:
12 (UK) None (US)
Personnel:
Siouxsie Sioux (v), John McKay (g), Steven Severin (b), Kenny Morris (d).
Track listing:
Pure; Jigsaw Feeling; Overground; Carcass; Helter Skelter; Mirage; Metal Postcard (Mittagessen); Nicotine Stain; Suburban Relapse; Switch
Running time:
38:26
Current CD:
839 008-2
Further listening:
The funereal follow-up, Join Hands (1979), inspired a host of gothic impersonators, none of whom matched the Banshees' dazzling run of singles, compiled on two collections, Once Upon A Time and Twice Upon A Time.
Further reading:
Entranced: The Siouxsie and The Banshees Story (Brian Johns, 1988).
www.vamp.org/Siouxsie/
Like this?
Try . . . p.411

The Jam

All Mod Cons

The Jam establish themselves as the class of '76's most popular graduates.

The first months of 1978 were hardly happy for The Jam. Their second album, *This Is The Modern World,* had been released in November 1977 to a barrage of flak, and the criticism impacted on Paul Weller's nerve. He sought comfort in his new relationship with Gill Price – but love seemed to dim his muse yet further. In February 1978, The Jam released the single News Of The World, an alarmingly weak Bruce Foxton song that betrayed the fact that the group were stalling. To cap it all, the following month saw them packed off on a US tour with Blue Öyster Cult. They returned to the UK to begin work on a third album in an understandably miserable state, and pre-production work in a country house found them atrophying further.

Their mentor, Polydor A&R man Chris Parry, heard the new material and passed judgement. "This is shit," he told his charges. Paul Weller took swift action, moving back in with his parents in Woking and re-immersing himself in some of his favourite music – The Kinks in particular. "There was a feeling we were being written off," he says now. "That pressured me into writing *All Mod Cons.* It was me proving myself."

By June, The Jam had started to rally. The scabrous Billy Hunt was recorded as their next single – but on the advice of producer/impresario Mickie Most, they instead released their reading of Ray Davies' David Watts (intended as a double A-side with A Bomb In Wardour Street, but favoured by radio). It reacquainted the trio with the charts, if hardly serving notice of a creative renaissance. Back in the studio, though, a triumph was taking shape: sharp, pop-minded but admirably innovative. "I'd like to be able to write minute-and-a-half, two-minute classics," Weller had told the NME. "If I could write a mini-opera in 1.5 minutes, that'd be great. I had an idea to write a three-minute song, where you'd got about 15 different tunes in one song. I'd just like to experiment. I've got loads of ideas." His aspirations were smeared all over the album: in the layered, effects-laden coda of In The Crowd, the shimmering ballad Fly, The Place I Love – one of Weller's best-ever compositions – and the single that proved that The Jam were now on era-defining form. Down In The Tube Station At Midnight was released on October 6, 1978 to a fiercely appreciative response. *All Mod Cons* appeared a month later, and still stands as The Jam's finest half-hour.

Record label:
Polydor
Produced
by Vic Coppersmith-Heaven.
Recorded
at RAK Studios, London; May–September 1978.
Released:
November 3, 1978
Chart peaks:
6 (UK) None (US)
Personnel:
Paul Weller (v, g, p, hm); Bruce Foxton (b, v); Rick Buckler (d, pc); Greg Jackman, Roger Bechirian (e); Chris Parry (associate producer)
Track listing:
All Mod Cons; To Be Someone (Didn't We Have A Nice Time); Mr. Clean; David Watts (S); English Rose; In The Crowd; Billy Hunt; It's Too Bad; Fly; The Place I Love; 'A' Bomb In Wardour Street (S); Down In The Tube Station At Midnight (S)
Running time:
38.20
Current CD:
537 419-2
Further listening:
In The City (1977); Sound Affects (1980)
Further reading:
A Beat Concerto (Paolo Hewitt, 1996)
Like this?
Try . . . p.322

X-Ray Spex

Germ Free Adolescents

Pointed social critique wrapped up in punky, three-minute pop.

There was a moment in the early summer of 1978 when X-Ray Spex seemed to be the punk "band most likely to". Three singles, each more accomplished and successful than the last, had taken the band from Roxy Club makeweights to Top Of The Pops regulars. And in brace-wearing Poly Styrene, dressed in brightly coloured thrift-shop chic, they featured one of the era's more engaging anti-stars. By the following spring, it had all gone wrong. All the wit with which Poly had attacked consumerism and other contemporary ills had vanished and, unable to divorce art from commerce, she quit rock-'n'roll for Krishna.

It was a far cry from the couldn't-care-less demeanour of her early performances when, with schoolgirl sax-player Lora Logic in tow, Poly and X-Ray Spex provided welcome relief from the pageant of Pistols imitators at the Roxy early in 1977. By the summer, the group had enough material for an album and, after a bidding war, signed to Virgin who released the debut 45, Oh Bondage Up Yours. One of the year's more startling singles, it was punk minimalism topped with a vocal to match the singer's idiosyncratic visual appeal. But the group were dropped, re-emerging on EMI who, rather appropriately, given Poly's lyrical concerns, offered an advertising budget that exceeded the band's advance. April 1978's The Day The World Turned Day-Glo, featuring a brass section, hinted at a growing sophistication and it worked. Identity gave the band a second Top 30 hit that summer, but by then Poly was suffering her own personality crisis.

"Get rid of the synthetic life," she advised the nation's youth through the pages of the Daily Mirror. "Go back and be natural." By the time the band's only album appeared, in November, Poly had grown bored of punk, pop and fame. Asked about the direction of her new music in the television documentary Who Is Poly Styrene?, she shrugged: "Maybe it'll turn into the sound of a Hoover."

Weeks later, she'd packed it in, leaving X-Ray Spex with a brief if memorable legacy. Lyrics like "I know I'm artificial/But don't put the blame on me/I was reared with appliances in a consumer society," epitomised Poly's dichotomy: part-fury, part-resignation, X-Ray Spex blew hot and cold between kitsch and deeper knowledge.

Record label:
Virgin
Produced
by Falcon Stuart.
Recorded
at Essex Studios. 1978
Released:
November 1978
Chart peaks:
30 (UK) None (US)
Personnel:
Poly Styrene (v); Jak Airport (g); Paul Dean (b); Rudi Thompson (s);
B.P. Hurding (d); John Mackenzie
Burns (e); Andy Pearce (ae)
Track listing:
The Day The World Turned Day-Glo (S); Obsessed With You; Genetic Engineering; Identity (S); I Live Off You; Germfree Adolescents (S); Art-I-Ficial; Let's Submerge; Warrior In Woolworths; I Am A Poseur; I Can't Do Anything; Highly Imflammable (S); Age; Plastic Bag; I Am A Cliché
Running time:
35.46
Current CD:
1704618132 adds: Oh Bondage Up
Yours! (S)
Further listening:
None of Poly's subsequent solo albums compare to this.
Further reading:
www.comnet.ca/~rina/xrayspex.html
Like this?
Try . . . p.414

Marvin Gaye

Here, My Dear

Marvin's raw soul-opera memoir. Might be his very best work.

For too many years the reputation of *Here, My Dear* rested on its stature as one of the most poisonous alimony settlements of the 20th century and it had been dismissed as an impenetrable, self-indulgent mess. But, in recent years, it has dawned on fans that in its heartbreaking honesty this double album describes love, its decline and a couple's painful separation with an intensity unique in pop.

Marvin was 20 when he married 37-year-old Anna Gordy, one of Motown-boss Berry Gordy's three sisters. She became a source of inspiration and support to him from Pride And Joy through Stubborn Kind Of Fellow and continued to be so post-bliss. He called her his "motivational force" but their marriage was stormy and childless, ending in divorce in March 1977.

Notoriously bad with money, Marvin didn't have an awful lot to offer by way of a settlement, so the judge took his lawyer's suggestion that all the proceeds of Gaye's next record should go to his former wife.

"At first I thought I'd put out a lot of garbage for the album," Marvin said later. "but it became a compulsion. All those hearings and depositions, accusations and lies . . . I knew I'd explode if I didn't get all that junk out of me."

Here, My Dear took three months in his own studio in Hollywood, a set-up which came complete with waterbedded living quarters. Marvin tended to sing in the control room, sitting at the mixing desk, overdubbing new vocal parts alongside his previous tracks until the melodies emerged. "I sang and sang until I drained myself of everything I'd lived through." When it was done, Marvin invited Anna to a playback but stayed up in the studio's apartment while she listened to it – saying almost nothing to engineer Art Stewart – and left.

With sleeve art depicting a Monopoly-type game called "Judgement" and liner notes by his lawyer, the album was released to almost universal critical disdain: it was too long, it was baffling, it was a downer. *Here, My Dear* was deleted only a few years later, the Gordy family's dismay at its bitterness towards Anna cited as a prime reason.

From this distance it can be seen as a gripping, passionate work that's full of good music; and if Marvin doesn't come out of it exactly smelling of roses, at least his candour was brave and revealing. Since Marvin's murder, Anna's opinion of the record has mellowed and, in the '90s, she sanctioned its reissue on CD. "It's taken me a while," she said, "but I've come to appreciate every form of Marvin's music, even songs written in anger."

Record label:
Motown
Produced
by Marvin Gaye; Anger co-produced by Gaye, Delta Ashby and Ed Townsend
Recorded:
Marvin Gaye's Studio, Hollywood, California. August–November 1977.
Released:
December 1978
Chart Peak:
None (UK) 26 (US)
Personnel:
Marvin Gaye (v, bv, k, syn), Nolan Smith (t), Charles Owen, Fernando Harkness (ts), Ernie Fields (as), Frank Blair (b), Bugsy Wilcox (d), Gary Jones, Elmira Collins (pc), Gordon Banks, Wali Ali (g)
Track listing:
Here, My Dear; I Met A Little Girl; When Did You Stop Loving Me, When Did I Stop Loving You; Anger; Is That Enough; Everybody Needs Love; Time To Get It Together; Sparrow; Anna's Song; When Did You Stop Loving Me, When Did I Stop Loving You (Instrumental); A Funky Space Reincarnation (S); You Can Leave, But It's Going To Cost You; Falling In Love Again; When Did You Stop Loving Me, When Did I Stop Loving You (Reprise)
Running time:
73.18
Current CD:
Motown 530 253-2
Further listening:
For an excellent overview of his career hear The Master a near-faultless 4-CD box set (1995).
Further reading:
Divided Soul (David Ritz, 1985)
Like this?
Try . . . p.369

Stiff Little Fingers

Inflammable Material

The first great UK punk record to emerge from the provinces.

With the exception of Siouxsie And The Banshees, the original cabal of '76 punk bands – Pistols, Clash, Damned, Buzzcocks, etc – had all cut records by 1977, inspiring a wave of imitators. Formed in Belfast, Stiff Little Fingers interpreted punk's received aesthetic – anti-Establishment growling, brisk tempos, barked delivery – more literally than most and, at the suggestion of journalist and mentor Gordon Ogilvie, turned to "The Troubles" in Northern Ireland for their inspiration.

Recorded in London – where the band had relocated in late 1978 – with an advance from independent record shop/label Rough Trade, *Inflammable Material* captured the bleak, violent and unpredictable mood of their strife-ridden hometown. A profoundly felt frustration and anger came across in songs like Suspect Device, State Of Emergency and Alternative Ulster, all lent a ferocious edge by singer Jake Burns throat-shredding vocals and the cauterising attack of his and Cluney's sand-blasted rhythm-lead guitar parts.

"The album was recorded in a basement in Cambridge, and took about two weeks in total," recalls Burns. "There are only a couple of guitar overdubs on the whole record – it was basically just the live set put down. Lots of it is hopelessly out of tune, but even now you can tell we meant it."

Despite its ferocious mien, the album has a musicality and subterranean humour than lifts it high above other "second-generation" punk albums. Heard in stereo, the twin guitar work is innovative, unforced and occasionally volcanic – especially on their punk-rock reworking of Bob and Rita Marley's Johnny Was (a blatant homage to The Clash's covering Junior Murvin's Police And Thieves) – while the doowop pastiche on the middle-eight of Barbed Wire Love and nimble chord changes and inauguaral open-string riff of Alternative Ulster show an instinctive understanding of pop dynamics.

Lyrically, Burns' collaborations with Ogilvie create some of the most frank and startling images to come out of the new wave: White Noise tackled racism, Suspect Device described the then seemingly insoluble political situation of Ulster and Closed Close offered a list of ironic clichés aginst a robotic art-rock groove. Two years late, perhaps, but worthy of its place among the pantheon of UK punk classics.

Record label:
Rough Trade
Produced
by Geoff Travis and Mayo Thompson.
Recorded
at Spaceward Studios, Cambridge; winter 1978–79.
Released:
February 1979
Chart peaks:
14 (UK) None (US)
Personnel:
Jake Burns (g); Henry Cluney (g); Ali McMordie (b); Brian Faloon (d)
Track listing:
Suspect Device (S); State Of Emergency; Here We Are Nowhere; Wasted Life; No More Of That; Barbed Wire Love; White Noise; Breakout; Law And Order; Rough Trade; Johnny Was; Alternative Ulster (S); Closed Groove
Running time:
41.16
Current CD:
CDP 7921052
Further listening:
All The Best (1991), 2-CD retrospective of the classic Chrysalis years
Further reading:
Record Collector 152; www.slf.com; www.murkworks.to/slf/
Like this?
Try . . . p.53

1979

Brian Eno

Music For Airports

Sound specifically devised to suit a particular space, ushered in the era of ambient music.

As the most obviously intellectual exponent of '70s British art-rock, Brian Eno found himself seriously wrong-footed by the Luddite intervention of punk, which placed a great premium on intense, non-cerebral reactions to whatever stimuli floated past its protagonist's gaze.

By comparison, Eno's musical interests had become all the more reflective as the decade had proceeded, culminating in this landmark work, the first release on his new Ambient label. As with so many of his pieces, it was partly inspired by a particular quality of another composer's work.

"My friend Peter Schmidt made me a tape of all the slow movements from the late Haydn quartets – there are six of them – arranged so there were nice shifts between them," he explains. "It was a fabulous tape to listen to, because it just pretty much stayed in the same place. I had already done *Discreet Music*, which was intended to do just that, stay in one place for a while, and *Music For Airports* was an extension of that, the idea that the new job of music could be to create a location. It didn't have to tell you anything, or guide you in any way when you got there, it just made the space for you to be there."

The space in this case was the airport, whose emotional stresses and strains Eno intended to soothe away by a kind of aural massage – much the same intention as muzak, but less patronising and less damaging to treasured musical memories. Effectively, it was the world's first chill-out album. Comprising an unhurried series of recurring piano figures (played by Robert Wyatt) suspended in an ambient haze, the gentle, non-specific, ruminative quality of *Music For Airports* owed more to the innovations of "quiet" avant-garde classical composers like John Cage and Morton Feldman than any pop or rock antecedents, and was all the more shocking for appearing in the midst of the punk *Putsch*. It has actually been employed in several airport spaces, with great success.

"A lot of things like *Music For Airports* came out of that Borgesian idea that you could invent a world in reverse, by inventing the artefacts that ought to be in it first," says Eno. "You think of what kind of music would be in that world, then you make the music and the world forms itself around the music. This American ensemble called Bang On A Can have done a live musical facsimile of *Music For Airports*, and what they've come up with is so moving: because you know it's humans playing it, it's suddenly invested with all this concentration and feeling, a tear-jerking quality that isn't really there in the original, which was originally conceived as deliberately austere and unemotional."

Record label:
Ambient
Produced
by Brian Eno.
Recorded
in London and Conny Plank's Studio, Cologne; 1978.
Released:
March 1979
Chart peaks:
None (UK) None (US)
Personnel:
Brian Eno (syn, tapes, treatments); Christa Fast, Christine Gomez, Inge Zeininger (bv); Robert Wyatt (k); David Hutchins, Conny Plank, Rhett Davies (e)
Track listing:
1/1; 1/2; 2/1; 2/2
Running time:
42.20
Current CD:
EGEDC17
Further listening:
Eno has subsequently released a varied selection of ambient-music albums, including Ambient 4: On Land (1982), Thursday Afternoon (1985), The Shutov Assembly (1992) and Neroli (1993).
Further reading:
MOJO 19; MOJO 55; www.hyperreal.org/music/artists/brian_eno/discog.html
Like this?
Try . . . p.673

The Roches

The Roches

Heady mix: the three sisters' punk-folk debut produced by King Crimson's Robert Fripp.

Late '70s New York was a good place to peddle music with a difference and The Roches certainly fitted that bill. Warner Brothers noticed them tearing up Greenwich Village clubs with a delightfully squiffy combination of folk, jazz, barbershop and girl-group harmonies – delivered with an intensity that bordered on dissonance. The company had also recently signed Fripp as a producer and in late 1978 this slightly odd pairing got hitched.

Terre Roche recollects him as "the only producer we worked with who believed in recording what came out of the artist rather than creating it in the studio. Much of that album was in fact recorded live sitting around in a semi-circle playing acoustic guitars and singing." Fripp puts it a little more technically: "To get a radio hit you mix everything to the middle. The Roches didn't need that kind of crass strength. I mixed the album so any point along a line from left to right speaker is equally valid as a listening perspective." Hence the sleeve line, "Produced In Audio Vérité".

A comparison of the first two tracks illustrates the variety and power of the collection. The opener, We, is a goofball signature tune in The Monkees Theme mould, replete with vaudevillian vocal curlicues: "We are Maggie and Terre and Suzzy/We don't give out our ages/And we don't give out our phone numbers." The quite magical Hammond Song follows. The long, close-harmony washes that drive the track recall the very best of another set of siblings, the West Coast Wilsons, but with further piquant twists. The lyrics hint at a split within the trio caused by a lover as a single voice defies the unity of the chorale. "Remember we were a family, with all the underlying heaviness," says Suzzy. "At the same time there was a lot of love on that first record." Terre concludes, "Even though our sound was softer I always felt that issuing our album in the iconoclastic climate of punk/new wave was a definite boon".

Influential New York Times critic John Rockwell made it his favourite record of the year, but, more importantly, the genre-busting inheritance of The Roches' debut lives on in the work of successful female artists from k.d. lang to Liz Phair.

Record label:
Warner Brothers
Produced
by Robert Fripp.
Recorded
at the Hit Factory, New York; September–November 1978.
Released:
March 1979
Chart peaks:
None (UK) 64 (US)
Personnel:
Suzzy Roche (v, g); Maggie Roche (v, g, syn); Terre Roche (v, g); Robert Fripp (g); Tony Levin (b); Jim Maelen (pc); Larry Fast (syn); Ed Sprigg (e); Jon Smith (ae)
Track listing:
We; Hammond Song; Mr Sellack; Damned Old Dog; The Troubles; The Train; The Married Men; Runs In The Family; Quitting Time; Pretty And High.
Running time:
39.59
Current CD:
Warner Bros. 3298-2
Further listening:
Nurds (1980); We Three Kings (1990) and Can We Go Home Now? (1995)
Further reading:
Folk Roots January–February 1996 (www.froots.demon.co.uk); Dirty Linen September–October 1995 (www.futuris.net) www.roches.com
Like this?
Try . . . p.569

Lowell George
Thanks, I'll Eat It Here
Solo jaunt for Little Feat star with a tragic outcome.

By the close of 1975, Little Feat's implied leader, Lowell George, was rapidly losing interest. "The guy was moving past the notion of a group," remembers Martin Kibbee, Lowell's former bandmate and songwriting partner in pre-Feat combo The Factory. "The idea of having a band that's a democracy with all members as business partners with artistic input; there's a downside to that if you're an artist with a unique vision, which he was."

Although he'd produced all of Feat's albums since *Sailing Shoes*, Warner Brothers were apprehensive about Lowell producing what would become *Time Loves A Hero*, possibly mindful of his rapacious cocaine use at this point. But Lowell used their reluctance to his advantage, agreeing to the appointment of producer Ted Templeman for the Feat album in return for an advance for a solo record. Thus, in early 1976, Lowell began work. Recordings would continue piecemeal over a two-and-a-half-year period, sessions slotted around increasingly fraught Little Feat tours and recordings. Lowell worked wherever he happened to be, with whomever was around to help out – the glitterati of the LA session scene or a mariachi band plucked from a local Mexican restaurant. Such a variety of players, and the numerous locations, contributed to the album's charming inconsistency, kept in check by imaginative production and George Massenberg's masterful engineering.

Lowell wanted to focus on his singing, thus there's little of his signature slide playing, although he does roll out a pretty flawless solo on his version of I Can't Stand The Rain. Only four cuts are originals, but all the elements of his musical personality are there: his unique humour and skewed vision (Cheek To Cheek – with the aforementioned mariachi band), his playfulness (Himmler's Ring), sensitivity (Find A River), tight-but-loose grooves and sincere, flowing singing. As liberating as it was, work on the album also paralleled the disintegration of his relationship with Little Feat, his failing health – which included severe backaches and hospitalisation with hepatitis – and the worsening of his bad habits which, just weeks after the album's release, ultimately led to the 34-year-old singer's fatal heart attack while on tour to promote it. Rather than exploit his demise, Warners withdrew promotion and allowed the album to fade into the background of rock history.

"The fun that we had I really haven't had since," says Kibbee. "He was a very inspiring guy. You felt you were working on something important, because he loved it so much it just rubbed off on you. It was not about money and careers, we just loved the music. The fact that we were being allowed to do this blew our minds."

Record label:
Warner Brothers
Produced
by Lowell George.
Recorded
at Sunset Sound, Sound Factory West, Hollywood Sound Recorders, at home with Wally Heider's mobile. 1976–79
Released:
April 1979
Chart peaks:
None (UK) None (US)
Personnel:
Fred Tackett (g), Ritchie Hayward, Jim Keltne, Jim Gordon, Jeff Porcaro, Mike Baird (d), Chuck Rainey (b), Bill Payne, David Foster, Nicky Hopkins, Gordon DeWitte, David Paich, Jimmy Greenspoon (k), Herb Pederson, JD Souther, Bonnie Raitt, Van Dyke Parks (v) and many others.
Track listing:
What Do You Want The Girl To Do; Honest Man; Two Trains; I Can't Stand The Rain; Cheek To Cheek; Easy Money; 20 Million Things; Find A River; Himmler's Ring
Running time:
31.34
Current CD:
2-3194 adds Heartache
Further listening:
As Time Goes By: The Very Best Of Little Feat (1995)
Further reading:
MOJO 8.
Like this?
Try . . . p.638

Sister Sledge

We Are Family

On a working sabbatical from Chic, Edwards-Rodgers wrote and produced a disco classic.

Signed by Atlantic in 1973, and by 1975 working with Bert de Coteaux and Tony Silvester, the four Sledge Sisters from Philadelphia were primed for success by the small hit Mama Never Told Me off their *Circle Of Love* album. At the time, two sisters were working their way through university, one was at art college and the fourth, lead singer Kathie, was still in high school. The Chic mainmen ensured the sisters' graduation by skilfully fashioning for them an instantly appealing pop-soul album that lit up the peaking disco market with classy ballads, infectious dance tracks and the trademarked sound of Nile Rodgers' rhythm guitar and Bernard Edwards' impossibly nimble and fluid bass playing, solidly grounded by Tony Thompson's imposing drumming.

"They came to us with a complete package they had written," said Joni Sledge, "songs they felt were what we were about from our other records and seeing us at different shows. But the song We Are Family was written after they met us." That said, the methods of Rodgers and Edwards working on Sister Sledge did not differ wildly from their preparation and recording of a Chic album. "Chic are into a strict way of doing things. For example, they'll teach you the song in the studio 'cos they feel like you shouldn't know anything about it before you record it. It's kinda strange working that way. They'll teach you line by line and say, 'OK we'll record it up to that much.' Then there are certain songs where they'll say, 'OK take it away, do what you want for the rest of the song.' They have definite ways of doing it and you have to do it that way. At first I found it kinda hard to adjust to but I learned to respect what they were doing."

Just as well, because Chic gave the Sledges their best, and best-selling album. The title track, an anthem of family, sexual and (disco) cultural solidarity; the floating, dreamy Lost In Music; the poppy Thinking Of You; the disco paean He's The Greatest Dancer; all highlight a set that, along with Chic's Greatest Hits, continue to define the best of sophisticated dancefloor pop.

Record label:
Atlantic

Produced
Bernard Edwards and Nile Rodgers.

Recorded
at the Power Station, New York; 1978

Released:
April 1979

Chart peaks:
18 (UK) 3 (US)

Personnel:
Kathie, Debbie, Kim and Joni Sledge (v); Nile Rodgers (g); Bernard Edwards (b); Tony Thompson (d); Robert Sabino, (p, clavinet); Andy Schwartz (p); Raymond Jones (Fender Rhodes); Sammy Figueroa (pc); Alex Foster, Jean Fineberg (s); Jon Faddis, Ellen Seeling (t); Barry Rogers (tb); Alex Foster (flute); Alfa Anderson, Norma Jean Wright, David Lasley, Diva Gray, Luther Vandross (bv); Karen Milne, Cheryl Hong, Marianne Carroll (strings); Gene Orloff (concert master)

Track listing:
He's The Greatest Dancer; Lost In Music; Somebody Loves Me; Thinking Of You; We Are Family; Easier To Love; You're A Friend To Me; One More Time

Running time:
40.45

Current CD:
122715872

Further listening:
Dance Dance Dance: The Best Of Chic (1991); The Very Best Of Sister Sledge 1973–93 (1993)

Like this?
Try . . . p.371

Joy Division

Unknown Pleasures

Punk's darkest forces reach Manchester and signal a new grey dawn.

Sid Vicious may have died a victim of his punk'fs-court-jester mythology, but there was nothing remotely comic-book about Joy Division's Ian Curtis, a mild misanthrope whose thin skin left him prey to life's rotten realities. This enigmatic frontman, whose "dying insect" stage act mirrored his own epilepsy, found some solace in punk's distressed aesthetic until the early hours of May 18, 1980, when he hanged himself. In this light, his work inevitably sounds like an extended suicide note. From its austere, Peter Saville-designed monochrome sleeve in *Unknown Pleasures* was an exemplary exercise in sorrow.

On the face of it, the band were four pool-playing lads from the less-fashionable parts of Manchester who'd been fired up by the Sex Pistols and taken under the wing of manager Rob Gretton and Factory boss Tony Wilson. After a ragged start as Warsaw, Joy Division were soon artfully distilling the contemporary malaise in a way that belied their untrained origins. Much of that artfulness was down to producer Martin "Zero" Hannett. Not that the band quite understood why. "When we played the album live, the music was loud and heavy. But we felt that Martin had toned it down, especially with the guitars," complained Bernard Sumner later. "The production inflicted this dark, doomy mood over the album."

Hannett, whose lifestyle later killed him, countered: "They were a gift to a producer because they didn't have a clue." Certainly, what chronicler Jon Savage described as Hannett's "shiny, waking-dream production gloss" lent a magisterial quality to the material, but *Unknown Pleasures* wasn't solely the product of a headstrong producer bullying musicians who didn't know better.

A year earlier, Joy Division had recorded an album for RCA which was scrapped after creative differences with the producers.

By April 1979, having worked with Hannett on two songs for a Factory compilation, the band had virtually perfected the album in rehearsal. What Hannett – a kind of punk Phil Spector – did was to separate the instruments and cloak the material in his customary metallic reverb. The drums, augmented by a drum machine, ran like clockwork (Disorder), the bass worked the melodies (Insight), the guitar rifts, strangely reminiscent of old Black Sabbath chord sequences (New Dawn Fades), were used for texture, and Curtis's weary, occasionally explosive vocals (She's Lost Control) added an unremittingly bleak lyricism. The singer insisted that the sessions took only four-and-a-half days; at least as much time would have been spent at the mixing-desk creating what was arguably the first post-punk album.

Record label:
Factory
Produced
by Martin Hannett.
Recorded
at Strawberry Studios, Stockport, April 1979.
Released:
June 1979
Chart peaks:
71 (UK) None (US)
Personnel:
Ian Curtis (v); Peter Hook (b); Bernard Dicken (alias Sumner) (g); Stephen Morris (d)
Track listing:
Disorder; Day Of The Lords; Candidate; Insight; New Dawn Fades; She's Lost Control; Shadowplay; Wilderness; Interzone; I Remember Nothing
Running time:
38.50
Current CD:
Factory/London 228223
Further listening:
The stakes were raised further for the follow-up, Closer, recorded weeks before Curtis's suicide. The 4-CD collection, Heart And Soul, provides the complete picture.
Further reading:
MOJO 8; Touching From A Distance: Ian Curtis And Joy Division (Deborah Curtis; 1995); www.warren.org.uk/music/joyd.html
Like this?
Try . . . p.850

The B-52's

The B-52's

Courageously-coiffeured Southerners playing toy instruments invade the New York punk scene. With hilarious results!

When producer/Island Records MD Chris Blackwell first saw The B-52's on the New York club circuit, they'd already composed virtually two albums' worth of material on the long road journeys from Athens, Georgia. Captivated by their brittle sound, rudimentary instruments and sci-fi nightmare stage clothes, he began recording them at his Compass Point Studios before he'd even signed them to the label. The contrast with their penniless life on the road was unforgettable.

"We went to Chris's house and out in his boat," Kate Pierson recalls, "and we were amazed by all the studio equipment. We had this really spare sound which was built around the style of Ricky's Mosrite guitar, a really classic surf guitar sound. He used lots of open tunings inspired by Joni Mitchell; if he broke a string he'd often work the guitar parts out just on the other five as we were so broke we couldn't afford to buy any new ones. And with all this studio gear we imagined we'd have a much fuller sound – you know, really pumped up! We were shocked when we heard the record. We thought it would sound so much better! But Chris's genius was to record us exactly as we sounded on stage, everyone playing the same parts they played live and all on the same instruments. So I played my Farfisa organ and the guitar part on Hero Worship. His genius was to decide it should stay sparse and punky and edgy and really capture the quirkiness of the band."

The album took just over three weeks to record – "the basic tracks, me and Cindy in one vocal booth, Fred in another, and then some overdubs. And once Chris had made this one decision about our sound, he basically put his feet up on the console and smoked pot. I mean he *directed* the whole thing but he was very 'mellow'. Another producer could have over-produced, got session musicians in, who knows what could have happened." Breathlessly conflating '50s kitsch and proto-New Wave garage spunk – and hingeing on the contrast between the girls' Day-Glo harmonies and Fred Schneider's declamatory camp – *The B-52's* sold over 500,000 copies worldwide, practically without radio play. Three albums later, they would find themselves in pole position in the MTV-fuelled US New Wave derby. Pierson fondly remembers one shell-shocked review of that epic first record: "They are *not* going to import their American trash aesthetic over here!"

Record label:
Island
Produced
by Chris Blackwell.
Recorded
at Compass Point Studios, Nassau, Bahamas; March–April 1979.
Released:
July 1979
Chart peaks:
22 (UK) 59 (US)
Personnel:
Kate Pierson (k, v, g); Fred Schneider (v, walkie-talkie, toy piano, k); Ricky Wilson (g, smoke alarm); Keith Strickland (d, pc); Cindy Wilson (v, bongos, g, pc); Robert Ash (e)
Track listing:
Planet Claire; 52 Girls; Dance This Mess Around; Rock Lobster; Lava; There's A Moon In The Sky (Called The Moon); Hero Worship; 6060-842; Downtown
Running time:
39.25
Current CD:
IMCD1
Further listening:
Wild Planet (1980); Cosmic Thing (1989) contains their huge comeback hit Love Shack.
Further reading:
www.b52s.net
Like this?
Try . . . p.559

AC/DC

Highway To Hell

Aussie rockers finally break the States six months before the death of vocalist Bon Scott.

Their UK success established with 1977's *Let There Be Rock* and cemented with follow-ups *Powerage* and the live *If You Want Blood, You've Got It*, AC/DC now turned their attention to the States. Two years of near non-stop touring on the "highway to hell", as Angus called the road in America, was starting to do the trick. What would finally tip the balance, their record label figured, was a more polished album, so they upped the budget and prised the band away from Australia. Next, producers Harry Vanda and (Angus and Malcolm's brother) George Young packed them off to the States with former Hendrix engineer Eddie Kramer who'd recently had hits producing Aerosmith and Kiss.

It did not go well. "We thought, We can't work with him," said Malcolm Young, "but the label were going to drop us if we didn't. It was a tricky situation. Finally our manager did a bit of wheeling and dealing and managed to get a tape to Mutt Lange, a friend of his, then known for producing New Wave acts like Graham Parker and The Boomtown Rats. We told Kramer, We're having tomorrow off, we need a break, and we went in and wrote nine songs in one day and whacked them off to Mutt. He got straight back and said he wanted to do it and the rest is history."

Lange spent three weeks with AC/DC in London's Roundhouse Studios, walking a tightrope between the simplicity that the band wanted and the polished production the label was paying for. AC/DC's first million-seller, it was stuffed with air-punching rock anthems and the band's trademark solid riffs and quickly became a staple at teenage headbangers' booze-fuelled parties on both sides of the Atlantic.

As sales grew, so did their notoriety. The album attracted the unwelcome attention of America's Moral Majority, who castigated them from pulpits and picketed their shows. It didn't help when LA serial killer Richard Ramirez, aka "the Night Prowler", was arrested in an AC/DC T-shirt, claiming that his rapes and Satanic rituals were inspired by the song Night Prowler and the band's name, which he reckoned stood for Anti-Christ/Devil's Child. Meanwhile, the song Touch Too Much proved prophetic. Early the next year, at the end of another mammoth tour, Bon Scott was found dead in a car in London. The singer, the coroner said had "drunk himself to death".

SS

Record label:
Atlantic
Produced
by Robert John "Mutt" Lange.
Recorded
at Roundhouse Studios, London; June 1979.
Released:
August 1979
Chart peaks:
8 (UK) 17 (US)
Personnel:
Bon Scott (v); Angus Young (g); Malcolm Young (g); Cliff Williams (b); Phil Rudd (d); Tony Platt (e)
Track listing:
Highway To Hell; Girls Got Rhythm; Walk All Over You; Touch Too Much; Beating Around The Bush; Shot Down In Flames; Get It Hot; If You Want Blood (You've Got It); Love Hungry Man; Night Prowler
Running time:
39.40
Current CD:
7567924192
Further listening:
Let There Be Rock (1977); Bon Scott And The Fraternity: Complete Sessions 1971–2 (1972)
Further reading:
MOJO 51; AC/DC – The Kerrang! Files! (Malcolm Dome, 1995)
Like this?
Try . . . p.538

Chic

Risque

After a clutch of hit singles, the Chic groove moves up a gear. Get down to the perfect beat.

There comes a time when all pop formulas reach a plateau of perfection. Motown did that in the '60s. James Brown nailed down the definitive "one" in the early '70s and in an 18-month period at the end of that decade Nile Rodgers and Bernard Edwards produced a clutch of albums for Chic, Sister Sledge and Diana Ross that crystallised the essence of hi-gloss funk. The state of the art sounded like this.

Magic moments abound; the climatic one note string parts on My Feet Keep Dancing courtesy of The Chic Strings, Bernard Edwards' trademark percolator bass, bubbling away under My Forbidden Lover, vocalists Alfa Anderson and Luci Martin chanting out their wish lists on Good Times like little disco haikus. That song's bass line established a legacy that ran through Queen's Another One Bites The Dust, The Sugarhill Gang's Rappers Delight, and out into soul music's pool of definitive riffs.

Risque celebrated black people moving on up, and Good Times ("Halston, Gucci, Fiorucci") was as much of a barometer of black aspirations in the late '70s as any civil rights song was in its time. The band's visual sophistication was matched by some of the leanest, yet most opulent dance music ever made. Everything as immaculate as Chic's wardrobe. Even the lyrics are styled to suit the rhythms.

Only when you glance at the lyric sheet do you notice that the sultry A Warm Summer Night has but five lines, twenty words. Such economy can be devastating – both lyric and treatment of Will You Cry (When You Hear This Song) are as achingly understated as Bacharach and David at their finest. Put Tony Thompson's crisp drumming, Bernard Edward's infectious bass and Nile Rodgers icy guitar chops together and what do you get? Grooves that defined an era.

aRecord label:
Atlantic
Produced
by Bernard Edwards and Nile Rodgers.
Recorded
at The Power Station, New York; 1979.
Released:
August 1979
Chart peaks:
29 (UK) 5 (US)
Personnel:
Nile Rodgers (g); Bernard Edwards (b); Tony Thompson (d); Raymond Jones (k); Robert Sabino (k); Andy Schwartz (k); Karen Milne, Cheryl Hong, Karen Karlsrud, Valerie Haywood (strings); Bob Clearmountain (e)
Track listing:
Good Times (S); A Warm Summer Night; My Feet Keep Dancing (S); My Forbidden Lover (S); Can't Stand To Love You; Will You Cry (When You Hear This Song); What About Me
Running time:
34.50
Curremt CD:
AMCY118
Further listening:
C'est Chic (1978); and other Bernard Edwards and Nile Rodgers productions: Sister Sledge, We Are Family (1979); Diana Ross, Diana (1980)
Further reading:
The Death Of Rhythm And Blues (Nelson George, 1988)
Like this?
Try . . . p.421

Ry Cooder

Bop Till You Drop

Cooder's flair and care has an odd covers collection singing with one sweet voice. World's first digital rock album, allegedly.

Widely regarded as a maestro following session stints with Captain Beefheart, The Rolling Stones and Little Feat, Ry Cooder tended to believe he never got anything right. In 1978, commenting on earlier endeavours to Rolling Stone, he reckoned he had strayed "right off the map" with the Hawaiian accents of his Chicken Skin Revue tour in 1976–77 and that with 1978's *Jazz* he had then fallen into sterile "archivism" by "trying to revive traditions in a cute academic way – too much of that and you get relegated as a quirk artist, somebody people can't listen to without wearing their fucking think caps all the time". Still, he felt more confident about this R&B collection: "The style of song is well suited to my weird voice. The idea is to blend warm vocal arrangements and the guitar sound so that one leans on the other."

He knew what he was about. *Bop Till You Drop* sparkled and flowed like a stream over rocks. Opening with Mort Shuman and Doc Pomus' Little Sister offered a familiar point of reference, but the priapic hustle of Elvis Presley's version was replaced by an intricate weave of guitars and the high, keening harmonies of Bobby King and friends. While this was Cooder at his most charming, he was quite willing to get down and dirty too. He performed to Oscar standards in character as the would-be stoic trying to break off an affair with his best friend's woman in Arthur Alexander's Go Home, Girl. Then he switched to bug-eyed street-corner lecher for his own hometown song Down In Hollywood ("She's showing everything she's got, mm-mm") and slapstick yarn-spinner for Shuman and Jerry Ragovoy's Look At Granny Run Run (a pre-Viagra tale of how Grandpaw got overstimulated by a new pill).

An album steeped in what one critic called "the unruffled intensity of the groove", it did quite well commercially. But Cooder remained concerned about the desultory chart action he achieved: "I've always been aware that my records didn't sell real well. At one time it didn't matter. But it's hard not to worry now. You have to try to get your numbers up." He never could and, during the 1980s, he moved on to write movie soundtracks for a living while promoting ethnic music as a passionate hobby – which eventually led to his catalysing The Buena Vista Social Club phenomenon, an improbable worldwide hit album by a group of internationally unknown Cuban pensioners.

Record label:
Warner Brothers
Produced
by Ry Cooder.
Recorded
at Warner Brothers Recording Studio, north Hollywood, California; 1979.
Released:
August 1979
Chart peaks:
36 (UK) 62 (US)
Personnel:
Ry Cooder (v, g); David Lindley (g); Ronnie Barron (g,o); Patrick Henderson (o); Jim Keltner (d); Tim Drummond (b); Milt Holland (pc); Bobby King, Herman Johnson, Chaka Khan, George "Biggie" McFadden, Randy Lorenzo, Pico Payne, Greg Prestopino (v, bv); Lee Herschberg (e)
Track listing:
Little Sister (S/UK); Go Home, Girl; The Very Thing That Makes You Rich (Makes Me Poor) (S/UK); I Think It's Going To Work Out Fine; Down In Hollywood; Look At Granny Run Run; Trouble, You Can't Fool Me; Don't You Mess Up A Good Thing; I Can't Win
Running time:
39.50
Current CD:
7599273982
Further listening:
Chicken Skin Music (1976) – Tex-Mex Hawaiian R&B and it works!
Further reading:
www.geocities.com/BourbonStreet/Delta/7969/
Like this?
Try . . . p.632

Bob Dylan

Slow Train Coming

Dylan in born-again Christian album shock!

How could the coolest man in the world undergo a conversion to fundamentalist Christianity? Chronologically, after the Rolling Thunder Revue chaos, in 1977 his wife Sara divorced him and won custody of their five children, the following year his obsessional autobiopic *Renaldo And Clara* bombed. Elvis Presley's death caused him unwonted upset. Dylanology suggests that Bob's Damascene moment occurred on November 17, 1978, in a hotel room after a show in Tucson, Arizona. His own account goes: "There was a presence in the room that couldn't have been anybody but Jesus . . . Jesus put his hand on me. . . . I felt my whole body tremble. . . I truly had a born-again experience, if you want to call it that."

At once, he began writing religious songs. Slow Train and Do Right To Me Baby (Do Unto Others) appeared in soundchecks. Then, back home in California, he joined a sect called the Vineyard Fellowship and attended daily Bible study classes for three months. In May 1979, he flew to Muscle Shoals for 11 days of recording. Inspired in every sense, his dark admonitions retrieved the cold ferocity of early protest songs like Masters Of War. Recruited after Dylan saw Dire Straits play in Los Angeles a few weeks earlier, Mark Knopfler sounded like an enraged B.B. King, while Muscle Shoals stalwart Barry Beckett on piano played brimstone from the minatory intro to Gotta Serve Somebody through to the grim Gospel precisions of When He Returns.

Some resented his going Christian as a betrayal of shared values – perhaps even worse than his going electric in 1965 – Dylan's temporary tendency to on-stage denunciation of sinners confirmed that he'd embraced all the nastier aspects of fundamentalism. "Art can lead you to God," he proclaimed. "I think that's the purpose of everything. If it's not doing that, what's it doing? It's leading you the other way."

Controversy helped *Slow Train Coming* become his second-best-selling album after *Desire*. He thumped Bible for three more albums then moved on. As Eric Clapton remarked: "Bob goes through changes. Sometimes he's a heavy drinker, sometimes dry. Sometimes he's into dope, then not. He can disappear with a carload of Mexicans. No phase is the final one."

Record label:
CBS
Produced
by Jerry Wexler and Barry Beckett.
Recorded
at Muscle Shoals, Alabama; May 1979.
Released:
August 1979
Chart peaks:
2 (UK) 3 (US)
Personnel:
Bob Dylan (v, g); Mark Knopfler (g); Tim Drummond (b); Barry Beckett (k); Pick Withers (d); Muscle Shoals Horns (horns); Carolyn Dennis, Helena Springs, Regina Havis (bv); Gregg Hamm (e)
Track listing:
Gotta Serve Somebody (S); Precious Angel; I Believe In You; Slow Train; Gonna Change My Way Of Thinking; Do Right To Me Baby (Do Unto Others); When You Gonna Wake Up; Man Gave Names To All The Animals; When He Returns
Running time:
46.39
Current CD:
Columbia 32524
Further listening:
Those who consider his "religious phase" an aberration might consider and enjoy the moral fervour of The Freewheelin' Bob Dylan (1963) and the sombre contemplation of mortality in Time Out Of Mind (1997)
Further reading:
Song And Dance Man III: The Art Of Bob Dylan (Michael Gray, 1999); www.bobdylan.com
Like this?
Try . . . p.197

Gang Of Four

Entertainment!

Clangorous, post-punk, post-Marxist masterpiece put danceability on the New Wave agenda.

Gang Of Four formed in 1977 at Leeds University, describing themselves as a "fast rivvum and blues band", but by the time they recorded *Entertainment!* they were light years ahead of that. However, there were still loud echoes of Dr Feelgood's guitarist Wilko Johnson in the choppy, abrasive stylings of Andy Gill – "Yes, I thought Wilko was brilliant. Ska and reggae were also big influences – that's where I got the ideas about dropping instruments in and out, creating spaces." On the strength of the well-received Damaged Goods EP, Gang Of Four signed to mega-corporation EMI.

"We could have hidden away on Rough Trade, say, but we wanted people to hear our music," explains Gill. "EMI gave us money and let us get on with it. The sessions were pretty fraught as we were a very argumentative band. I would try to impose certain syncopated drum patterns on Hugo, and he'd throw his sticks at me and storm off. We didn't know much about studio techniques, but I knew I wanted a dry sound. We used transistor amps as an anti-rockist gesture – trying to get away from that warm Marshall feel."

The slashing punk-funk and the half-shouted, discursive vocals succeed brilliantly in conveying the sense of anomie the group felt. "We looked at our lives and the lives of our friends and came up with a simple rather than a simplistic view of modern capitalism. I mean we didn't tell anyone to go and smash WH Smith's windows."

On the lop-sided strut of Natural's Not In It, vocalist Jon King agonises over "The problem of leisure/What to do for pleasure" before concluding "This heaven gives me migraine." The sublimely sour feedback of Anthrax opens into an equally bitter lyric: "Love'll get you like a case of anthrax." I Found That Essence Rare is almost pop, albeit in a gnarly, Buzzcocks way. The press lapped up the challenging conflation of intellect, innovation and intuition and R.E.M.'s Michael Stipe commented that "*Entertainment!* shredded everything that came before it. I stole a lot from them."

Record label:
EMI

Produced
by Andy Gill, Jon King and Rob Warr.

Recorded
at the Workhouse, Old Kent Road, London; May–June 1979.

Released:
September 1979.

Chart peaks:
45 (UK) None (US)

Personnel:
Jon King (v, melodica); Andy Gill (v, g); Hugo Burnham (d, bv); Dave Allen (b, bv); Rick Walton (e)

Track listing:
Ether; Natural's Not In It; Not Great Men; Damaged Goods; Return The Gift; Guns Before Butter; I Found That Essence Rare; Glass; Contract; At Home He's A Tourist; 5.45; Anthrax

Running time:
39.43

Current CD:
CZ 541

Further listening:
Solid Gold (1981); Songs Of The Free (1982) and 100 Flowers Bloom (1998), a 2-CD compilation. Bassist Dave Allen helped found Shriekback.

Further reading:
Booklet by Jon Savage accompanying 100 Flowers Bloom; a booklet by Greil Marcus accompanying A Brief History Of The 20th Century compilation.
www.emdac.demon.co.uk/phil/gof/gof_indx.html

Like this?
Try . . . p.738

Al Green

The Belle Album

The Reverend Al ascends the pulpit to deliver a soulful sermon on life, love and God.

For soul singers, the opposing pulls of the spiritual and the sexual, of God and get-down!, are well-chronicled fact. That this should be the case is not surprising, because gospel had been a major source of '60s soul voices and a prominent component of the singing style and song structure. From Little Richard and James Brown, whose leadership of the jail choir earned him the recommendation for parole which set in train events that ended with the development of funk, to genuine sons and daughters of the church, Sam Cooke and Aretha Franklin, it was rare to find a soul singer who did not owe at least part of his or her style to gospel.

Green was no different – his father sacked him from The Green Brothers gospel quartet when Al was caught listening to rock'n'roll – and, like Little Richard, he felt a strong and constant tug back to the church. With producer Willie Mitchell in Memphis, Green became one of the very best soul acts of the early '70s, his delicacy of phrasing and inimitable tone bringing to earthy songs such as Tired Of Being Alone, Let's Stay Together, Love And Happiness and Here I Am (Come And Take Me). But the inspiration of church was never far from the surface: "I was a plain old Baptist Pentecostal born-again in the middle of a rock'n'roll career," he admitted. Indeed, Take Me To The River, Full Of Fire and the like are clearly spirituals in all but name.

In 1976 Green bought the First Church of Full Gospel Tabernacle in Memphis, installing himself as pastor. The following year he split with Mitchell and announced his new direction with *Belle*, a perfect commingling of the sacred and the secular, the line "It's you I want, but it's Him that I need" in the title track capturing the opposing pulls on Green's emotions and reflected throughout the album by the churning I Feel Good and the gentler ripple of Feels Like Summer.

Green took an accidental fall from the stage in 1979 as a warning from his God. "I was moving towards God, but I wasn't moving fast enough. That was God's way of saying I had to hurry up." He wouldn't make another soul album until 1993.

Record label:
Hi
Produced
by Al Green.
Recorded
at American Music, Memphis; Spring/Summer 1979
Released:
September 1979
Chart peaks:
None (UK) 103 (US)
Personnel:
Al Green (v, g); Reuben Fairfax Jr (b, bell lyre); James Bass (g); Leon Thomas (clavinet, Fender Rhodes); Johnny Brown (p, Fender Rhodes); Fred Jordan (Fender Rhodes, Roland String Ensemble, Polyphonic Orchestron); John Toney (d, Syndrum); Rob Payne (Syndrum); Ardis Hardin (d); Buddy Jarrett (alto); Darryl Neely, Fred Jordan (t, flugelhorn); Ron Echols (ts, bs); Margaret Foxworth, Linda Jones, Harvey Jones (bv)
Track listing:
Belle (S); Loving You; Feels Like Summer (S/US); Georgia Boy; I Feel Good; All 'N' All; Chariots Of Fire; Dream
Running time:
41.15
Current CD:
HIL0160
Further listening:
Al Green Gets Next To You (1971); Let's Stay Together (1972); I'm Still In Love With You (1972); Call Me (1973), and the surprisingly good Don't Look Back (1993)
Further reading:
Take Me To The River (Al Green, 2000)
Like this?
Try . . . p.22

Gary Numan

The Pleasure Principle

Gary Numan's first "official" solo album, establishing him as the first international synth-pop star.

Inspired by his adolescent icons David Bowie, Lou Reed, Iggy Pop and Marc Bolan, at the end of the '70s Gary Numan fleshed out his punk band The Tubeway Army into a garagey electronic band. The alienated sci-fi drone of the single Are Friends Electric? was swiftly followed to the top of the charts by *Replicas*. However, it was the 21-year-old Londoner's completely guitar-free follow-up, *The Pleasure Principle*, which took the world by storm.

Recorded in a tiny London studio, Numan built his Moog-dominated, techno-rock sound around soaring keyboard lines, piano, strings, heavy percussion and clipped, monotone vocals.

"I concentrated on a very rich, layered, poly-Moog sound," he says. "In the late '70s, synthesizers provided an opportunity for people without any great musical training or ability to make pop music. You could rent them fairly cheaply, record them in little studios and they would sound incredibly powerful."

By sticking to one-word song titles, avoiding choruses and selling himself with an image of doleful introspection framed in the neon tubes of his promo videos and massive stage shows, Numan scored his second UK Number 1 album and single of 1979, Cars, a cold, symmetrical, electro-disco track featuring tambourine and handclaps, also made the Top 5 in the States. It was to open the floodgates to a new wave of aloof, image-conscious, British suburban synth artists like The Human League, Depeche Mode and Soft Cell, effectively signalling the end of UK punk.

This cultural shift towards synthesizers and showbiz led to a massive critical assault on Numan by a rock press who still clung to punk's "authentic" guitar-driven thrills. In spite of continued bad press, Cars kept rebounding back in to the Top 20 (its latest incarnation, Armand Van Helden's hip hop cut-up Koochy), while *The Pleasure Principle*'s lesser-known track, Films, has been credited by the likes of Afrika Bambaataa and The Beastie Boys as one of hip hop's original breakbeats.

The album's angular, rhythmic style has also been cited by techno pioneers like Moby and Juan Atkins as playing a significant role in the birth of modern dance music. According to Trent Reznor of Nine Inch Nails, "It painted an emotional place that wasn't pleasant to be in. It seemed creepy science fiction in an unpleasant way."

Reissued in 1998, *The Pleasure Principle* was hailed as a "spooky" classic, completing a gradual, 20-year critical reversal which recently inspired Spin magazine to conclude: "Against all odds, history has vindicated Numan."

Record label:
Beggars Banquet
Produced
by Gary Numan.
Recorded
at Marcus Music, London, spring 1979
Released:
September 1979
Chart peaks:
1 (UK) 16 (US)
Personnel:
Gary Numan (v, k); Paul Gardiner (b); Christopher Payne (k, va); Cedric Sharpley (d, pc); Billy Currie (v); Garry Robson (bv); Rikki Sylvian, Harvey Webb (e)
Track listing:
Airlane; Metal; Complex (S); Films; M.E.; Tracks; Observer; Conversation; Cars (S); Engineers
Running time:
41.12
Current CD
BBLO 10CD adds: Random; Oceans; Asylum; Me! I Disconnect From You (Live); Bombers (Live); Remember I Was Vapour (Live); On Broadway (Live)
Further listening:
Replicas (1979); Telekon (1980); Exile (1997)
Further reading:
Praying To The Aliens (Gary Numan and Steve Malins, 1997), plus all of Numan's catalogue features extensive sleevenotes www.numan.org
Like this?
Try . . . p.380

The Residents

Eskimo

Anonymous San Franciscan art pranksters break the commercial ice with their vision of life up North.

The Residents are perhaps best known for the giant eyeballs they wear on their heads, first used on the cover of *Eskimo*, their sixth album and the record most often credited with establishing them as emperors of experimentalism. "It's without doubt one of the most important albums ever made, if not the most important," raved MOJO's Andy Gill, then writing for the NME. An overstatement, maybe, but *Eskimo* still has the power to unsettle, amuse and enchant.

On previous records the band had given pop music a deliciously weird going-over (try their version of Let's Twist Again in German on *Third Reich And Roll*) and written a synth-driven pseudo-opera (*Not Available*). *Eskimo* purported to be an accurate representation of Inuit music and culture, supposedly made using the five-note Eskimo scale and traditional instruments.

Drummer Chris Cutler (Henry Cow, Pere Ubu) played percussion on the album. "It was all recorded in their own studio at 444 Grove St, San Francisco. There were a few roto-toms and some other bits and bobs. I was more or less given a free rein. I didn't have any music to play along to. They made me sit in a fridge and breathe Arctic air which had been brought back in Thermos flasks by their guru N. Senada." Cutler smiles. "All, none or some of the above might be true."

There is no doubt The Residents did research Eskimo life, but the piece seems as much a comment on the nature of American society. The bitter, almost constant synth swooshes (Don Preston, ex-Mothers Of Invention) which denote the Arctic wind also conjure up a sense of urban alienation, and the guttural chants which make up the vocals are quite obviously distorted English. The repeated phrase "Coke adds life" stands out in particular, while the Angakok (priest) bears a striking resemblance to a Southern US preacher. The album closes with the beautifully melodic, quasi-prog of Festival Of Death; a release from the often atonal but enthralling depiction of births, hunts and snow madness that has gone before. The first 10,000 copies were pressed in Arctic White vinyl and it went on to sell 100,000 – amazing for an own label issue at the time. The following year they put out an eight-minute edit of the album called *Diskomo*, set, unsurprisingly, to a disco beat. Cool.

aRecord label:
Ralph Records
Produced
by The Residents.
Recorded
at 444 Grove Street, San Francisco; April 1976–May 1979.
Released:
September 1979
Chart peaks:
None (UK) None (US)
Personnel:
The Residents and Snakefinger [Phil Lithman] (v, all instruments); Don Preston (s); Chris Cutler (d, pc)
Track listing:
The Walrus Hunt; Birth; Arctic Hysteria; The Angry Angakok; A Spirit Steals A Child; The Festival Of Death
Running time:
39.06
Current CD:
CD 016
Further listening:
Meet The Residents (1974); Third Reich And Roll (1976); Commercial Album (1980); 25th Anniversary Box Set, Very good 4-CD package with informative booklet (1997).
Further reading:
Meet The Residents: America's Most Eccentric Band (Ian Shirley, 1998)
www.residents.com
Like this?
Try . . . p.403

The Slits

Cut

The band nobody wanted to sign defy detractors with the most sophisticated album of 1979.

When The Slits lost drummer Palmolive in autumn 1978, it looked as if the game was up. The band had little to show for an 18-month career except a mass of (usually) bad press highlighting their shortcomings, some traumatic support slots on tours with The Clash and The Buzzcocks, and, more recently, another scotched record deal. But within a year, The Slits turned it round with an album that banished the "punk incompetents" tag forever.

The band's close ties with The Sex Pistols and The Clash initially worked in their favour, winning them press interest and prestigious gigs. Yet rock's inherent sexism soon characterised The Slits as New Wave novelties or unwelcome intruders.

An extraordinary radio session recorded in spring 1978 for John Peel was evidence of new musical muscle too. "Punk pulled everything apart," says Viv Albertine. "We dissected what we said, what we wore and how we sounded. We certainly didn't want to play 12-bar like every other band."

Through a mixture of accident and design, The Slits had become the great white hope of the post-punk avant-garde. But the band's rejection of convention drew them closer to black music – reggae in particular – which they'd discovered through Don Letts, Roxy Club DJ and, briefly, the band's manager: "They had a real affinity with the rebel aspect of the music and the culture," he says. According to Albertine, "Dub seemed to have a femininity about it; it was more fluid." After a shambolic late '78 tour with The Clash with new drummer Budgie on board, the group landed a deal with Island, and recruited Dennis "Blackbeard" Bovell as producer. The punky-reggae party was about to begin. From being the band nobody wanted to sign, The Slits became the sound of the future.

"They were way ahead of their time," insists Letts. "They took reggae's emphasis on the bassline over melody and guitars. And *Cut* used the mixing-desk as an instrument." The results were shocking – not least to the group's core following, who expected robustly recorded versions of the band's avant-punk live set. Instead, hitherto impenetrable songs like Newtown, Instant Hit and So Tough were transformed into hi-tech exercises in spatial tension with Budgie's inventive percussion centre stage. However, the group's decision to pose nude – albeit covered in mud and irony – for the album's sleeve prompted further controversy, and despite portraying themselves as prophet-like modern primitives on subsequent releases, cultural confusion eventually got the better of the band and their effectiveness dwindled. *Cut*, however, remains a vital document. One suspects that if it had been made in a less male-dominated climate it would be far more celebrated today.

Record label:
Island
Produced
by Dennis Bovell.
Recorded
at Ridge Farm Studios, London; spring 1979.
Released:
September 1979
Chart peaks:
30 (UK) None (US)
Personnel:
Ari Up (v); Viv Albertine (g, v); Tessa Pollitt (b, v); Budgie (d); Mike Dunne (e)
Track listing:
Instant Hit; So Tough; Spend, Spend, Spend; Shoplifting; FM; Newtown; Ping Pong Affair; Love And Romance; Typical Girls; Adventures Close To Home
Running time:
31:59
Current CD:
8425502
Further listening:
The Peel Sessions (1992)
Further reading:
www.comnet.ca/~rina/slits.html; Lipstick Traces: A Secret History Of The Twentieth Century (Greil Marcus, 1990)
Like this?
Try . . . p.379

Marianne Faithfull

Broken English

A '60s icon shreds her past.

After cramming enough living into the '60s to last any normal lifetime, Marianne Faithfull effectively retired for the first half of the '70s – though it's probably more accurate to say that her drug habit retired *her.* She resurfaced with a couple of pleasant but insipid country-pop sets, but these were no preparation for the emotional fireball of *Broken English.*

"Punk made the album possible," she has commented. "Vast stadium tours, crazed male ego-driven bands, pop grandiosity in general – these were not my thing at all. The hard, defiant, honest world of punk showed me where and how I fitted in, where I could be relevant."

The title track is an indictment of the Cold War superpowers' posturings – though the undercurrents of her own psychic turmoil are also pretty apparent. The closer is a torrent of foul-mouthed abuse aimed fairly obviously at inconstant lover Ben Brierley, which makes that turmoil all-too plain – though, surprisingly, she didn't write it: poet Heathcote Williams did. "I told Heathcote, 'I would *die* to sing these lyrics.'" But "sing" barely describes the haunting, ravaged keen that characterises her delivery throughout, and which contrasts so startlingly with the folkie warble of her '60s recordings. The settings, too were a departure: an understated, hypnotic mesh of synths and guitars that made her livid vocals all the more stark.

Several songs seem like attempts to dump the baggage handed to her by early media fame. Her splendid cover of Lennon's Working Class Hero trashes the (inaccurate) picture of her as privileged daughter of the aristocracy, while The Ballad Of Lucy Jordan – pre-empting the grittier narratives of her Kurt Weill period – portrays the suicide of a suburban housewife denied any taste of the glamorous life which Marianne herself experienced. "The public's preconceived image of me has always been a thorny problem," she says. "But singing those songs was not a clever, conscious, detached move on my part, it was an intensely emotional decision that I deeply felt."

The only respite from the lamentations comes with the hope/black humour of Witches' Song – "inspired by an exhibition of drawings by Goya on a visit to the Prado in 1967 with Mick Jagger". The final line runs, "Remember death is far away and life is sweet." Marianne had been to Hell and back, and knew the value of life. *Broken English* has the songs to prove it.

Record label:
Island
Produced
by Mark Miller Mundy.
Recorded
at Matrix Studios, London; May–July 1979.
Released:
October 1979
Chart peaks:
57 (UK) 82 (US)
Personnel:
Marianne Faithfull (v); Barry Reynolds (g); Steve York (b); Terry Stannard (d); Joe Maverty (k); Steve Winwood (k); Dyan Birch, Frankie Collins, Isabella Dulaney (bv); Jim Cuomo (s); Guy Humphries (g); Morris Pert (pc); Darryl Way (vn); Ed Thacker, Bob Potter (e)
Track listing:
Broken English (S); Witches' Song; Brain Drain; Guilt; The Ballad Of Lucy Jordan (S); What's The Hurry; Working Class Hero; Why D'Ya Do It
Running time:
37.46
Current CD:
IMCD11
Further listening:
Strange Weather (1987) – in which older, wiser, croakier Marianne reprises songs from earlier in her career as cabaret standards; A Secret Life (1995) – a lush collaboration with Angelo Badalamenti; Vagabond Ways (1999) includes the extraordinary Incarceration Of A Flower Child, written by Roger Waters almost three decades previously.
Further reading:
www.planete.net/~smironne – lots of detail on recording sessions.
Like this?
Try . . . p.527

Madness

One Step Beyond

Debut album from the Southern branch of the ska revival.

Many great bands emerged from the vibrant, hybrid jungle of pub rock, punk and New Wave in late '70s Britain, but few more enduring than the self-styled Nutty Boys from North London, Madness. They first leapt to prominence when their version of Prince Buster's song, The Prince, was a hit on The Specials' 2-Tone label.

"We used to go and watch Ian Dury a lot," recalls guitarist Chris Foreman. "Though we were basically ska we had a lot of other strings to our bow, just like Ian. There was a bit of a [label] feeding frenzy after The Prince was a hit, but we didn't want to be pigeon-holed as 2-Tone. We met Dave Robinson from Stiff and Clive Langer (ex-Deaf School) on the circuit, and when Clive said he wanted to produce us we were like, wow! because we really liked his band. Basically, the album was our live set. We got it all recorded in about two weeks. The production was great because Alan (Winstanley – engineer) was a bit of a perfectionist, but Clive liked things when they sounded a bit wrong – Lee's sax for example. Once it was so out of tune that it had almost come back in! I remember when Clive wanted to put strings on Night Boat To Cairo, we thought it was a bit poncey, but Clive said he'd pay for the sessions if we didn't like the result. We liked it."

The exuberance of the songs and performances on *One Step Beyond*, from the irresistibly danceable bluebeat of the title track to the cod cool jazz of Razor Blade Alley, marked Madness as more than promising newcomers. But it was the classic, faintly melancholic pop of My Girl and Bed And Breakfast Man (recalling the domestic dramas purveyed by the Fabs and Kinks) which suggested that they were a good bet for the long term. The British took the album and the group to their hearts. After the furrowed brows of punk, fun was clearly what the pop nation needed. Madness broke the ice at parties while hinting at a sophistication that would give them more chart hits than practically any other British '80s outfit.

Record label:
Stiff
Produced
by Clive Langer.
Recorded
at TW Studios, Hammersmith, London; May–June 1979.
Released:
October 1979
Chart peaks:
(UK) 2; (US) None
Personnel:
Graham "Suggs" McPherson (v); Mike Barson (k); Chris Foreman (g); Mark Bedford (b); Lee Thompson (s, v); Dan Woodgate (d, p); Chas Smash (v); Alan Winstanley (e)
Track listing:
One Step Beyond (S/UK); My Girl (S); Night Boat To Cairo (S/UK); Believe Me; Land Of Hope And Glory; The Prince (S/UK); Tarzan's Nuts; In The Middle Of The Night; Bed And Breakfast Man; Razor Blade Alley; Swan Lake; Rockin' In A Flat; Mummy's Boy; Chipmunks Are Go!
Running time:
39.00
Current CD:
Virgin CDOVS 133
Further listening:
Absolutely (1980); 7 (1981); Presents The Rise And Fall (1982)
Further reading:
www.madness.co.uk; www.outrageouscreations.com/madness
Like this?
Try . . . p.481

The Specials

Specials

Cracking debut from Coventry's punk-ska innovators and social commentators.

By 1979 punk was stagnating and this multi-racial Coventry septet – who began in 1977 as The Coventry Automatics – were about to sweep the nation with their new beat – an intensified, aggressive fusion of punk and ska they called 2-Tone. Hair worn into a suedehead crop, dressed in Fred Perry shirts, mohair and tonic three-button suits, Crombies and tasselled loafers and bearing an attitude that had zero tolerance for bullshit, their sharp political awareness, biting sarcasm and cynical humour became the voice for many of Britain's disillusioned youth.

They'd first come to public attention as The Special AKA when they supported The Clash on their On Parole tour. By this time their live performances were becoming the stuff of legend – powerful, effulgent and terrifying, it was difficult to distinguish the band from their rude-boy following and stage invasions were *de rigueur*. Their first release on their own 2- Tone label was Gangsters, a rough-hewn tip of the hat to Prince Buster's Al Capone. Incredibly, it made the Top 10. Aligning their label with Chrysalis Records they entered TW Studios in their home town to record their first album.

"Everyone was pissed," admits Jerry Dammers, "We spent most of our time in the pub over the road from the studio." Nevertheless *Specials*, produced by Elvis Costello, captures the group's raw, breathless energy immaculately. Of the 14 tracks, four are skanking standards – Prince Buster's Too Hot, The Maytals' Monkey Man, Clement Seymour Dodd's You're Wondering Now, and A Message To You Rudy which features the inimitable trombone of Rico Rodriquez, who also featured on Dandy Livingstone's original.

Eight of the remaining tracks were penned by founder member Dammers (real name Gerald Dankin) including the bitter Too Much Too Young which borrowed heavily from Lloyd Charmers' risqué Birth Control, Doesn't Make It Alright with it's call for racial harmony, "Just because you're a black boy/Just because you're a white/It doesn't mean you've got to hate him/Doesn't mean you've got to fight/It doesn't make it alright", the pro-active positivity of It's Up To You and Nite Klub, with it's instantly identifiable lyric, "I don't want to dance in a club like this/All the girls are slags and the beer tastes just like piss."

"I can only write about things that make me angry," Dammers later commented. A month after the album's release The Specials and their ska stable mates The Selecter and Madness all performed separately on the same edition of Top Of The Pops – 2-Tone's moment had clearly arrived with some force.

Record label:
2-Tone
Produced
by Elvis Costello.
Recorded
at TW Studios, Coventry; summer 1979.
Released:
October 1979
Chart peaks:
4 (UK) 84 (US)
Personnel:
Terry Hall (v); Neville Staples (v); Jerry Dammers (o); Roddy Radiation (g); Lynval Golding (g); Horace Panter (b); John Bradbury (d); Rico Rodriquez (horns); Dick Cuthell (horns); Chrissie Hynde (bv)
Track listing:
A Message To You Rudy (S/UK); Do The Dog; It's Up To You; Nite Klub (S/UK); Doesn't Make It Alright; Concrete Jungle; Too Hot; Monkey Man; (Dawning Of A) New Era; Blank Expression; Stupid Marriage; Too Much Too Young; Little Bitch; You're Wondering Now
Running time:
40.41
Current CD:
Chrysalis CCD 5001 adds: Gangsters
Further listening:
comprehensive best of The Specials Singles (1989); More Specials (1980). In The Studio (1984).
Further reading:
You're Wondering Now: A History Of The Specials (Paul Williams, 1995); The Two Tone Story (George Marshall, 1991); www.two-tone.co.uk
Like this?
Try . . . p.434

The Clash

London Calling

A seismic shift from punk recasts them as a kind of rockabilly, pop, reggae jukebox.

Something in *London Calling*'s musical scope, gush of ideas and feel-good rock'n'roll Zen brings to mind two other legendary doubles: Dylan's *Blonde On Blonde* and the Stones' *Exile On Main Street.* In fact, it's confusing to think of this as a "punk" record at all: *London Calling* was a celebration of the music The Clash enjoyed long before they became New Wave iconoclasts – blues, reggae, ska, soul, jazz, funk, rockabilly. It was, as Strummer would put it, "probably our greatest moment".

Their love affair with black American music had never been far from the surface but their interest was really re-awakened when they first toured the States in early '79, with Bo Diddley as support and a revved-up cover of Sonny Curtis' I Fought The Law in their set.

On returning to England, they donned brothel creepers and grew quiffs and work began at a Pimlico rehearsal space. Between tea breaks and football games, a torrent of material was unleashed. Strummer was particularly loquacious: his increasingly complex lyrics taking the band's socio-political interests into new areas – the Spanish Civil War, cocaine-addled US company executives, Hollywood movie stars, impending apocalypse – while sticking with staple Clash fare like tower-block alienation, other pop stars and what it's like to be in The Clash. Meanwhile, Paul Simonon challenged the Strummer/Jones writing monopoly with Guns Of Brixton, a nervy punk-reggae hybrid brilliantly arranged by Jones.

After a demo version of the album was left on the tube by roadie Johnny Green, CBS insisted that they bring in a "proper" producer – so they dug out legendary '60s DJ Guy Stevens (who'd produced Free and Mott The Hoople among others) from semi-retirement, and booked into Wessex Studios in Highbury.

The sessions kicked off with a cover of Vince Taylor's British rock classic Brand New Cadillac, which set out the band's stall as *nouveau* Teddy punks. Some songs, like Rudie Can't Fail and The Card Cheat, felt as if they were long lost Jamaican/American greats but were actually Clash originals. The *coup de grâce*, though, came in the form of Mick Jones' lightly funky Train In Vain, a touching love song inspired by The Slits' Viv Albertine, added at the last minute (and hence not listed on the original sleeve).

When it was released in December 1979, with a brilliant Ray Lowry cover pastiching Elvis's first LP from Pennie Smith's shots of the group's second US tour, *London Calling* secured The Clash's reputation. A record worthy of Rolling Stone's 'Best album of the '80s' award.

PG

Record label:
CBS
Producer:
Guy Stevens
Recorded:
Wessex, London, summer 1979
Released:
December 1979.
Chart peaks:
9 (UK) 27 (US)
Personnel:
Joe Strummer (v, g), Mick Jones (g), Paul Simonon (b), Topper Headon (d), Micky Gallagher (k), Bill Price (e)
Track listing:
London Calling (S); Brand New Cadillac; Jimmy Jazz; Hateful; Rudie Can't Fail; Spanish Bombs; The Right Profile; Lost In The Supermarket; Clampdown; The Guns Of Brixton; Wrong 'Em Boyo; Death Or Glory; Koka Kola; The Card Cheat; Lover's Rock; Four Horsemen; I'm Not Down; Revolution Rock; Train In Vain (S/US)
Running time:
65:09
Current CD:
Columbia: Clash 3
Further listening:
The On Broadway (Sony) box set provides a meaty career overview, with the bonus of some rare archive tracks; the 2-CD The Story Of The Clash (Sony) is good for beginners; otherwise you really need to digest the albums individually.
Further reading:
The Last Gang In Town by Marcus Gray (Fourth Estate); A Riot Of My Own by Johnny Green (Indigo); feature MOJO 71.
Like this?
Try . . . p.810

Pink Floyd
The Wall
Claustrophobic double concept album whose bleak themes appeared to permeate its makers.

Someone once conducted a poll among the millions who purchased *The Dark Side Of The Moon* to discover why they liked it: they found it was Pink Floyd fans' favourite album to have sex to. No-one has undertaken a survey of the equally large numbers who purchased *The Wall*, so the use they make of an album about alienation, fascism, sadomasochism and despair, inspired by a rock star's hatred of his audience, remains a matter for conjecture.

A multi-level musical, lyrical, psychological and architectural concept that became a film starring Bob Geldof and one of the most elaborate theatrical stage shows ever, featuring Gerald Scarfe's animations, *The Wall* was sparked by an incident that closed the *Animals* tour. Waters, so disillusioned by stadium shows that he spat at a fan and fantasised about dropping bombs on the audience, said he would only perform again behind a wall. It also instigated the break-up of the band – starting with Rick Wright's dismissal during recording and ending with Waters' departure after *The Final Cut*. Bob Ezrin, one of three credited producers, called the atmosphere in the studio "war" – admittedly a "very gentlemanly" war "as they're English".

But the sessions – which took place outside of Britain for the very same tax reasons that prompted the album's genesis (finding themselves bankrupt with a huge tax bill thanks to poor financial mismanagement, the band agreed to make one of the two putative solo projects Waters had been writing) – also had successful moments of what Gilmour called "the last embers of Roger's and my ability to work collaboratively together". Though most songs were Waters compositions, Comfortably Numb started out as a part-written Gilmour song which, with Waters' lyrics, became one of the album's – and the band's – most affecting and memorable numbers.

Another collaboration – this time between Waters and Ezrin, who suggested the disco beat – produced hit single Another Brick In The Wall [Part II]. Its dark themes appeared to mirror the turmoil in the lives of its creators, both in and out of the studio. "Everybody," said Ezrin, "was going through amazing stuff in their individual lives, and we all brought our pain and our weakness and our foibles and our peculiarities to the table. But in the final analysis it produced what is arguably the best work of that decade and maybe one of the most important rock albums ever made."

SS

Record label:
EMI
Produced
by Bob Ezrin, Roger Waters and David Gilmour; co-produced by James Guthrie.
Recorded
at Superbear, France.
Released:
December 1979
Chart peaks:
3 (UK) 1 (US)
Personnel:
Roger Waters (v, b); David Gilmour (v, g); Rick Wright (k); Nick Mason (d); Bruce Johnston, Toni Tennille, Joe Chemay, John Joyce, Stan Farber, Jim Haas, the children of Islington Green School (bv); James Guthrie (e); Nick Griffiths, Patrice Quef, Brian Christian, Rick Hart, John McClure (e)
Track listing:
In The Flesh?; The Thin Ice; Another Brick In The Wall [Part 1]; The Happiest Days Of Our Lives; Another Brick In The Wall [Part II] (S); Mother; Goodbye Blue Sky; Empty Spaces; Young Lust; One Of My Turns (S); Don't Leave Me Now; Another Brick In The Wall [Part III]; Goodbye Cruel World; Hey You; Is There Anybody Out There; Nobody Home; Vera; Bring The Boys Back Home; Comfortably Numb (S); The Show Must Go On; In The Flesh; Run Like Hell (S); Waiting For The Worms; Stop; The Trial; Outside The Wall
Running time:
75.83
Current CD:
8SNY68519
Further listening:
Dark Side Of The Moon
Further reading:
www.pinkfloyd.com
Like this?
Try . . . p.162

The 1980s

Elvis Costello And The Attractions

Get Happy!!

Twenty golden nuggets of Stax-influenced pop.

During preparations for *Get Happy!!* Elvis Costello was spied leaving legendary Camden record shop Rock On with armfuls of '60s soul and R&B albums. "I was listening to a lot of the music I'd loved when I was 15, such as Motown and Stax," admits Elvis, and, clad in its deliberately distressed, retro sleeve, with a packed tracklisting including a cover of obscure Sam & Dave tune I Can't Stand Up For Falling Down, *Get Happy!!* is indeed informed by the taut songwriting and muscular musicianship of the heyday of soul. Thus Booker T's Time Is Tight riff emerges on Temptation, one of the core trilogy of songs completed by Opportunity and Possession. This last was written about a waitress in a cafe near the studios in Amsterdam, and is described by Costello as "a total lust song, it has nothing to do with any art concept".

Nevertheless, artfulness abounds, from the jittery ska tones of Black And White World and Human Touch to the lovelorn country of Motel Matches and the impressionistic shadowplay of B-Movie. A frantic reading of The Merseybeats' classic I Stand Accused is complemented by such frenetic originals as Riot Act and Man Called Uncle, all of which belie the "wasted" condition of the band after two and a half years of solid touring and recording.

Rather than wearing them down, the tough schedule had produced a lean and powerfully efficient unit which left no space for the frontman to over-indulge in wordplay. It's not all retro either; Elvis drew on a range of contemporary influences too. He had just produced The Specials' debut album and had been enjoying Berlin-era Bowie on tour.

Although there's no direct musical evidence of his Bowie/Eno fascination, the album has a thoroughly modern ring, due in some part to the decision to scrap the original set of "wretched arrangements" in favour of "a more rhythmic accompaniment than the tricksy, nervy backing we'd been using", thereby marking a departure from the skinny-tied, New Wave sound associated with his first three albums. The Attractions maintain a manic pace on *Get Happy!!*'s 20 tracks, five of which are under two minutes long. In the UK the goodwill created by Costello's biggest hit to date, Oliver's Army from predecessor *Armed Forces*, helped the first single – I Can't Stand Up For Falling Down – reach number four in the charts. And in the States, the album's Top 20 status was in part due to mainstream patronage by the likes of Linda Ronstadt, who had recently included three Costello songs on her latest album. *Get Happy!!* lives up to its title as Costello's most enthusiastic and life-affirming collection.

Record label:
F Beat
Produced
by Nick Lowe.
Recorded
at Wisseloord Studios, Hilversum, Holland; October 1979. New Amsterdam recorded at Archipelago Studios, London; summer 1979.
Released:
February 1980
Chart peaks:
2 (UK) 11 (US)
Personnel:
Elvis Costello (v, g); Steve Nieve (k); Bruce Thomas (b), Pete Thomas (d)
Track listing:
I Can't Stand Up For Falling Down (S); Black & White World; 5ive Gears In Reverse; B Movie; Motel Matches; Human Touch; Beaten To The Punch; Temptation; I Stand Accused; Riot Act; Love For Tender; Opportunity; The Imposter; Secondary Modern; King Horse; Possession; Man Called Uncle; Clowntime Is Over; New Amsterdam (S); High Fidelity (S)
Running time:
48.23
Current CD:
DPAM5 adds: Girl's Talk, Clowntime Is Over (Version 2); Getting Mighty Crowded; So Young; Just A Memory; Hoover Factory; Ghost Train; Dr Luther's Assistant; Black And White World (demo); Riot Act (demo); Love For Tender (demo); Hoover Factory (demo); Ghost Train (demo).
Further listening:
Trust (1981)
Further reading:
The Big Wheel (Bruce Thomas, 1990)
Like this?
Try . . . p.324

The Cramps

Songs The Lord Taught Us

Ladies and gentlemen, please welcome psychobilly – and one of the most exciting live outfits ever.

To this day, The Cramps are one of the greatest live outfits ever to walk the planet. "At the time rock'n'roll had turned into 'rock music' and we just wanted to get it back to what it was in the beginning," says singer Lux Interior. "We wanted the same simplicity you find with a Shadows Of Knight song, an early rockabilly number or the Velvet Underground."

The band were introduced to producer Alex "Big Star" Chilton by New York photographer friend Stephanie Chernikowski and as Lux remembers – "Immediately he was fun; not snobbish or arty. He's a wild person in the true sense of the word, and a little too honest, which doesn't earn him a lot of friends." Through Chilton's Memphis connections the band booked time in Sam "He-who-discovered-Elvis" Phillips' studio. The sessions were disjointed; often due to lack of financial support from the record company or the fact that various engineers couldn't/wouldn't work with Wildman Chilton.

"Alex would get drunk. . . we'd pick him up off the console. . .!" deadpans Lux. "We just played and played – ripped through, no over-dubs, all in the same room. It was a bit Dada. If you're out of control you're bound to make new things." They captured some of the most visceral performances ever committed to vinyl. From the break-neck hillbilly boogie of The Johnny Burnette Rock'n'Roll Trio's Tear It Up, to grinding '60s garage stomps – witness their terminally sleazy manifesto Garbageman – the combo obviously knew their history and lived it as well, amalgamating their primal influences with a timeless punk swagger. The twin guitars of Rorschach and Gregory conjure up shards and shrouds of feedback and then rip them with knife-sharp single-note runs from the Link Wray How-To manual.

Over the top Lux howls paeans to outsiders everywhere: "I was a teenage werewolf/Braces on my fangs/A Mid-West monster with the highest grades."

"There's a lot more metaphor and autobiography in our songs than people realise," notes Ivy. "In Ohio (Lux's birthplace) we felt very isolated..."

Getting a satisfactory final mix proved difficult, Chilton apparently rejecting one mix "because it sounded too good". Finally Chilton, Ivy and Lux came up with what Lux calls "an engineer's nightmare!" Ivy reckons it's a little "swimmy sounding", lacking the razor edge of the band's live shows. Nevertheless, it certainly sounded like no one else at the time, the album was ecstatically reviewed, and The Cramps spawned many imitators, none of whom could match either the seriousness or the humour of the originators.

Record label:
IRS
Produced
by Alex Chilton.
Recorded
at the Sam C Phillips Recording Studio, Memphis; July–September 1979.
Released:
April 1980
Chart peaks:
None (UK) None (US)
Personnel:
Lux Interior (v); Poison Ivy Rorschach (g); Bryan Gregory (g); Nick Knox (d)
Track listing:
TV Set; Rock On The Moon; Garbageman; I Was A Teenage Werewolf; Sunglasses After Dark; The Mad Daddy; Mystery Plane; Zombie Dance; What's Behind The Mask?; I'm Cramped; Tear It Up; Fever (S/UK)
Running time:
36.55
Current CD:
EMI/Zonophone 4 93836 2 adds: I Was A Teenage Werewolf (with false start); Mystery Plane (original mix); Twist And Shout (original mix); I'm Cramped (original mix); The Mad Daddy (original mix)
Further listening:
Gravest Hits (EP, 1979); Psychedelic Jungle (1981); A Date With Elvis (1986); Flamejob (1994)
Further reading:
The Wild, Wild World Of The Cramps (Ian Johnston, 1990) www.geocities.com/thecrampspage
Like this?
Try . . . p.432

Smokey Robinson

Warm Thoughts

A soul legend grows old gracefully.

Smokey Robinson had had a difficult time of it in the '70s. His albums were still stickered with the old Motown legend, "The Sound Of Young America", but in 1980 he was turning 40, and in the eight years since quitting The Miracles he hadn't achieved a terrific amount of solo success. But the previous year had seen him hit a new vein of excellence with *Where There's Smoke*, the most vibrant album he'd yet made, climaxing with the gorgeous hit, Cruisin'. *Warm Thoughts* – though it didn't quite have the same impact – now sounds like the perfect follow-up.

What he was seeking was a synthesis of his hit-machine vitality with the romanticism that had always drenched his writing, blending it all into something which a mature black audience could identify with. He might have blueprinted Motown's pop style with the likes of Going To A Go-Go, but Tears Of A Clown was more like the real Smokey. So his songwriting began to grow darker and more pensive, even if he never gave up on the cheeky wordplay which was another of his hallmarks. Nobody else would try and get away with a title like Into Each Rain Some Life Must Fall, even if that is the darkest and most wrenching of all the tracks on offer here. There are lighter pieces too, such as the irresistible Let Me Be The Clock ("For the time of your life, I'm a cuckoo I know"), but the centrepiece is What's In Your Life For Me, a deeply considered piece of songwriting with the subtlest melodic and harmonic shifts.

After all those years of having the highest, creamiest tenor in black music, Smokey's voice was beginning to thicken, yet it still touched peaks and skipped over bar lines in ways which must have been the despair of some of his rivals. His great records of the '80s – *Being With You*, *Essar*, *Yes It's You Lady* – continued to build on what he had set out to do on this record. But despite the big hit he scored with the title track of *Being With You*, his audience continued to drift away, which must have hurt such a great artist. Today, he is more interested in golf than music.

Record label:
Motown
Produced
by Smokey Robinson.
Recorded
at Motown Studios, Hollywood; 1980.
Released:
April 1980
Chart peaks:
None (UK) 14 (US)
Personnel:
William "Smokey" Robinson (v); Sonny Burke, Roderick Rancifer (k); Marv Tarplin, Phil Upchurch, David T Walker, Melvin "Wah Wah" Ragin, L Marlo Henderson (g); Wayne Tweed, Kenneth Burke, Scott Edwards (b); James Gadson, Scotty Harris (d); James Sledge (congas); Michael Jacobsen (c); Fred Smith (f, s); Cheryl Cooper, Ivory Davis, Claudette Robinson, James Sledge, Patricia Henley Talbert (bv)
Track listing:
Let Me Be The Clock; Heavy On Pride (Light On Love); Into Each Rain Some Life Must Fall; Wine, Women And Song; Melody Man; What's In Your Life For Me; I Want To Be Your Love; Travelin' Through
Running time:
36.31
Not available on CD
Further listening:
Where There's Smoke (1979); Being With You (1981)
Further reading:
Smokey: Inside My Life (1990)
Like this?
Try . . . p.416

ngeles

s accessible and influential answer to New York and London punk.

It was believed that punk would never take off in Los Angeles. Life was too sunny, too easy. X believed otherwise.

The embryonic X was Florida native Christine Cervenka and Baltimore's John Doe (born John Dukac) who met at a poetry workshop where Doe, entranced by Cervenka's poetry, mooted the idea of putting her lyrics to music in a band.

"I'm no dummy," says Exene (who changed her first name in lapsed Catholic support for Christ having His name dumped out of Christmas, as in Xmas). "The first thing I asked was, 'What about my publishing?'"

Doe recruited rockabilly guitar whiz Billy Zoom who had played in Gene Vincent's final bands, and found drummer DJ Bonebrake at an open audition. Bonebrake won the drummer's seat when he showed up with a piccolo snare, a drum which cracks through any music like a rifle shot. The quartet's image was strong: Doe's greaser's hair fell in his face as he pummelled his bass and howled, exotic Exene sang Beat poetry lyrics against bizarre atonal melodies, Zoom stood with legs apart and a stupid grin on his boyish face wailing riff after riff, leaving Bonebrake as the straight man, the grad student who wandered into the wrong group. This first album was largely their live set. It was produced by Doors keyboardist Ray Manzarek, largely because he was the only hip name to come backstage at the Whiskey and tell Doe that his band could actually go places. They did, and they didn't.

After *Los Angeles* it all began to fragment into thrash metal, cowpunk, surf punk, hardcore, straight edge, roots rock and even spoken word. But for a brief moment the Beat-meets-punk songs of John Doe and Exene Cervenka caught lightning in a jar.

Record label:
Slash
Produced
by Ray Manzarek.
Recorded
at Golden Sound Studios, Hollywood; January 1980.
Released:
April 1980.
Chart peaks:
None (UK) None (US)
Personnel:
John Doe (b, v); Exene Cervenka (v); Billy Zoom (g); DJ Bonebrake (d); Ray Manzarek (k)
Track listing:
Your Phone's Off The Hook But You're Not; Johnny Hit And Run Paulene; Soul Kitchen; Nausea; Sugarlight; Los Angeles; Sex And Dying In High Society; The Unheard Music; The World's A Mess It's In My Kiss
Running time:
28.05
Currently unavailable on CD
Further listening:
Wild Gift (1981); More Fun In The New World (1983)
Further reading:
Make The Music Go Bang!: The Early LA Punk Scene (edited by Don Snowden, 1997); Beyond And Back: The Story Of X (Chris Morris, 1983)
Like this?
Try . . . p.392

Linton Kwesi Johnson

Bass Culture

Anglo-Caribbean dub poetry. Sounds good, kicks like a mule.

Naturally, most great albums come from people who have dedicated their lives to music – whole-heartedly, if not monastically. But Linton Kwesi Johnson always had too much on the go to make that commitment. Moving from Jamaica to Brixton, London, when he was 11, he did well academically, graduating with a sociology degree. He worked in the civil service and factories for a while, but his passion flowed through black political activism and poetry (published regularly from 1973 on). In 1977 he recorded his first album *Dread Beat An' Blood*. Initially credited as Poet And The Roots, he was so well connected culturally and politically that his backing band, assembled by Dennis Bovell, comprised the cream of British-based reggae. Between his sleek, deep speaking voice and the musicians' syncopating sensitivity a new genre, dub poetry, was created. Johnson's third album, *Bass Culture*, proved its apogee.

Mostly, it took a sparse, hard line; Street 66 pugnaciously defying a police raid on a house party and Inglan Is A Bitch angrily lamenting abuses suffered by England's first generation of West Indian immigrants. But, with the title track and Reggae Sounds – both published as poems five years earlier – Johnson took a daring leap into cultural and intellectual territory hardly ever touched on in reggae (or any other kind of pop music). He explained that these songs were "basically talking about art and experience – I don't want too much eyebrows raised now! I mean they're about how you feel and how you translate that into meaningful entertainment that inspires and motivates at the same time." Rarely can street life and academic training have blended so naturally. He wrote and spoke and played the sinuous unity of word, music, rhythm and fighting oppression. It was Gerard Manley Hopkins as militant reggae: "Shock-black bubble-doun-beat bouncing/rock-wise tumble-down sound music;/foot-drop find drum, blood story,/bass history is a moving/is a hurting black story" (Reggae Sounds); "Muzik of blood/black reared/pain rooted/heart geared; all tensed up/in the bubble an the bounce/an the leap an the weight-drop/ SCATTA-MATTA-SHATTA-SHACK!/what a beat!" (Bass Culture). But perhaps it was one of those moments when an artist shoots so high, makes it, and has nothing left to say. After *Bass Culture* Johnson devoted himself to community politics, journalism and teaching, recording only one more album of new material.

Record label:
Mango
Produced
by Linton Kwesi Johnson and Blackbeard.
Recorded
at Gooseberry Sound Studios, London, 1980.
Released:
May 9, 1980
Chart peaks:
46 (UK) None (US)
Personnel:
Linton Kwesi Johnson (v); Vivian Weathers, Floyd Lawson (b); Jah Bunny, Winston Curniffe (d); John Kpiaye (g); Dennis Bovell, Webster Johnson (k); James Danton (s); Henry Tenyue (s, t); Dick Cuthell (t); Rico (tb); Julio Finn (hm); Clinton Bailey, Everald Forrest (pc); John Caffrey, Mark Lusardy, Dennis Bovell (e)
Track listing:
Bass Culture; Street 66; Reggae Fi Peach; Di Black Petty Booshwah; Inglan Is A Bitch; Loraine; Reggae Sounds; Two Sides Of Silence
Running time:
31.08
Current CD:
RRCD 26
Further listening:
Tings An' Times (1990) – brief return to recording, ten years on but still sharp.
Further reading:
Dread Beat & Blood (Bogle-L'Ouverture, 1975), Inglan Is A Bitch (Linton Kwesi Johnson, 1980)
Like this?
Try . . . p.743

Magazine

The Correct Use Of Soap

Gloomy art-rockers' happiest hour.

Signed by Virgin on the strength of a three-track demo, Manchester's Magazine cut sombre and intellectual figure. Their 1978 debut, *Real Life* caused a considerable critical and commercial splash; the follow-up, *Secondhand Daylight* only a ripple in comparison. For the difficult third album, Devoto resolved to work quicker and to highlight the talents of McGeoch, whose impressively versatile guitar sound had been squeezed out by keyboards on the previous album. Hannett (who'd worked with Devoto on the Buzzcocks' Spiral Scratch EP) was not Devoto's first producer of choice – Tony Visconti, John Barry and Sly Stone had all been requested – but his work with Joy Division and the fact that he had shared a flat with keyboardist Dave Formula secured him the job.

Twenty years on, Devoto – who has long since quit the music business and now works at a photographic agency – regards *The Correct Use Of Soap* as his band's best studio work. The outright anger of its predecessors was smoothed out and replaced with a percolating existential irritability although, Devoto claims, "it was more hurt. I was in a spiritually difficult place at that time. My father had died when we were on tour in America for the first time the previous summer – that chucked me into a spin – and I had also fallen in love in various places in the world. I was a very confused person. Even a year later, at the end of *Magic, Murder And The Weather* [Magazine's final studio album from 1981], I was still on the same psychic curve – down, down, down."

Curiously, this presents a brighter, more uptempo Magazine, demonstrating McGeoch's creative way with the subverted Johnny B Goode riff and subtle jazz nuance, alongside their more familiar, brooding Roxy Music and Bowie inflections. The inclusion of the Sly Stone classic – which they had been playing live as a final encore for some time – helped demolish Magazine's reputation as arty and difficult depressives, despite Devoto's downbeat delivery, which he borrowed directly from the funkmeister's Thank You For Talkin' To Me Africa version.

The Correct Use Of Soap was also significantly the result of Devoto's desire "to get a bit more straightforward"; he stopped wearing make-up on stage and began to withdraw from the band's press commitments, harbouring a deep-seated feeling that the end for him was not far off. This was clinched when McGeoch quit after a European tour to join Siouxsie And The Banshees. He proved almost impossible to replace and, despite the release of another album a year later, for Magazine the writing was by now most definitely on the wall.

Record label:
Virgin
Produced
by Martin Hannett.
Recorded
on the Manor Mobile at Summa rehearsal studios, Chelsea and The Townhouse, London; December 1979 and February 1980.
Released:
May 1980
Chart peaks:
28 (UK) None (US)
Personnel:
Howard Devoto (v); John McGeoch (g, bv); Barry Adamson (b); John Doyle (d, pc); Dave Formula (k); Laura Teresa (bv)
Track listing:
Because You're Frightened; Model Worker; I'm A Party; You Never Knew Me; Philadelphia; I Want To Burn Again; Thank You (Falettinme Be Mice Elf Agin) (S); Sweetheart Contract; Stuck; A Song From Under The Floorboards (S)
Running time:
39.36
Currently unavailable on CD
Further listening:
Real Life (1978); Secondhand Daylight (1979); Devoto solo album Jerky Versions Of The Dream (1983); The Unanswerable Lust (1988), as Luxuria; box set Magazine ... Maybe It's Right To Be Nervous (2000)
Further reading:
www.buzzcocks.com/SecretPublic/SP_main/Devoto/body_devoto.html
Like this?
Try . . . p.402

Peter Gabriel

Peter Gabriel (III)

Gabriel astounds with his third and best solo album.

After leaving Genesis in 1975, Peter Gabriel had taken time off when he "grew cabbages and made babies" but continued to write songs. Following a frustrating period of trying to compose for other artists ("I was unhappy not to be in control of the arrangements"), he emerged with his debut solo album early in 1977. Over the following three years Gabriel re-established himself as a vital songwriter and uniquely charismatic performer and amazingly – given the sweeping-away-the-old-guard spirit of the times – he retained a credibility that his contemporaries must have wondered at.

That credibility was never higher than when Nick Kent in the NME gave Gabriel's third album a full-page review saying "I don't expect to hear a better record all year." From the rumbling threat of Intruder to the stone-faced outrage of Biko, *Peter Gabriel* (or *Melt*, as it's sometimes called, a reference to the striking cover and to distinguish it from the other three albums with the same title) is a model of intelligent, potent rock music. The mini presidential assassination movie Family Snapshot, the forceful And Through The Wire (featuring Paul Weller on searing rhythm guitar) and the ingenious and melodic hit Games Without Frontiers, were all decorated with disturbing, visceral textures and driven by an extraordinary cymbal-free drum track. Although producer Steve Lillywhite had been involved in notable "drum sound" albums (Siouxsie And The Banshees' *The Scream* among them), it was when Genesis pal Phil Collins was hammering out a tom-and-snare pattern and engineer Hugh Padgham was experimenting with gated reverb effects that Gabriel was inspired, writing Intruder there and then.

Gabriel: "I was certain it was a landmark drum sound. Now I get annoyed when people say I have copied Phil's sound." Collins, meanwhile, was annoyed not to be given more than "drum pattern" credit for the song itself.

The anthemic Biko was a heartfelt song of sorrow for the South African situation, some time before such things were fashionable. "I was disappointed it wasn't a hit," says Gabriel. "I had really hoped it would be an anthem against apartheid." It had its impact in time however, with Little Steven citing it as the inspiration behind his Sun City project. Gabriel went global soon after *Peter Gabriel III*, playing the rock-star-with-a-conscience with considerable artistry and dignity.

Record label:
Charisma
Produced
by Steve Lillywhite.
Recorded
at Bath with the Manor Mobile and the Townhouse, London
Released:
June 1980
Chart peaks:
1 (UK) 22 (US)
Personnel:
Kate Bush (bv); Phil Collins (d); Peter Gabriel (v, k); Larry Fast (k); Robert Fripp (g); John Giblin (g); Dave Gregory (g); Tony Levin (stick); Jerry Marotta (d); Dick Morrisey (s); Paul Weller (g); Morris Pert (pc); David Rhodes (g); Hugh Padgham (e)
Track listing:
Intruder; No Self Control; Start; I Don't Remember; Family Snapshot; And Through The Wire; Games Without Frontiers; Not One Of Us; Lead A Normal Life; Biko
Running time:
45.34
Current CD:
PGCD3
Further listening:
Peter Gabriel (1977); Peter Gabriel (1978); So (1986)
Further reading:
Peter Gabriel (Spencer Bright, 1999); www.petergabriel.com
Like this?
Try . . . p.341

AC/DC

Back In Black

With Bon Scott dead, AC/DC unleash their new frontman – and catapult to megastardom.

Twenty years on, *Back In Black* still makes the hair stand up on the back of the neck. It was recorded only weeks after vocalist Bon Scott was found dead in a parked car in London after a too-good night out on the town and – unsurprisingly given the circumstances – is a lethal combination of wild and barely suppressed emotion, anger at Bon for leaving them and a wilful determination to carry on.

"There was a nothingness around everyone," says Malcolm Young. "At the funeral Bon's dad said 'You can't stop, you've got to find someone else', and our manager came up with a list of singers – but we weren't interested. We thought, we can't replace Bon. He was unique." Material for a follow-up to the previous year's breakthrough album *Highway To Hell* had been started with Bon, who actually played drums on the demos. Finally, fed up with "sitting around moping", Malcolm and Angus got together to play and decided to keep going. The man chosen to sing was someone Bon himself had once recommended – Brian Johnson, ex-Geordie, possessor of a powerful, abrasive, drain-cleaner-gargling voice and an ebullient, down-to-earth personality. He joined them in a Bahamas studio with *Highway To Hell* producer Mutt Lange.

"We'd got the title before we'd even written a word", remembers Malcolm. "Angus said, 'Why not call it *Back In Black* and make a black album cover as a tribute to Bon?' It was a hard album to make but it had its magic moments." Matching their turbulent mood swings, the Bahamas was being hit by hurricanes and stalked by a machete-wielding killer. Inside the studio the band closed ranks and focussed on the record – they jettisoned the earlier lyrics to start from scratch with their new frontman. The result was an album stuffed with rock anthems: You Shook Me All Night Long; Rock And Roll Ain't Noise Pollution; the sombre tolling bell of opener Hell's Bells – soon to become a stage prop. Lange gave a polished, powerhouse metal production to their trademark riffs and grinding beat. "He wanted to take the sound a bit further," said Malcolm, "and he got it bang-on. That album still impresses everyone for its production." Leaving the Bahamas for the New York mixing room after a week off, the band gathered for the playback. "We thought, 'Fucking hell, this is a monster.'" It was. Over ten million people bought it in the US alone. The band were megastars.

SS

Record label:
Atco
Produced
by Robert John "Mutt" Lange.
Recorded
at Compass Point Studios, Bahamas; April and May 1980.
Release date:
July 1980
Chart peaks:
1 (UK) 4 (US)
Personnel:
Brian Johnson (v); Angus Young (g); Malcolm Young (g); Cliff Williams (b); Phil Rudd (d); Tony Platt (e)
Track listing:
Hell's Bells; Shoot To Thrill; What Do You Do For The Money Honey; Given The Dog A Bone; Let Me Put My Love Into You; Back In Black; You Shook Me All Night Long; Have A Drink On Me; Shake A Leg; Rock And Roll Ain't Noise Pollution
Running time:
40.42
Current CD:
4951532
Further listening:
Highway To Hell (1979) and Let There Be Rock (1977), featuring original vocalist Bon Scott; Flick Of The Switch (1983) and The Razor's Edge (1999) featuring Johnson.
Further reading:
MOJO 79; AC/DC – The Kerrang! Files! (Malcolm Dome, 1995)
www.acdc.rock.com
Like this?
Try . . . p.128

Echo And The Bunnymen

Crocodiles

Universally lauded debut from the group nearly called Mona Lisa And The Grease Guns who made overcoats hip.

Echo And The Bunnymen's first recordings were stiff-limbed affairs. A session for John Peel in 1979 which showcased rudimentary songs like I Bagsy Yours (later retitled Monkeys), and their debut single, Pictures On My Wall, the same year, sounded hesitant, flat and linear, bound by the restrictions of their primitive drum machine. The press initially greeted them as a substandard version of Neil Young – bad news indeed for musicians inspired by Bowie, The Velvets, The Doors and The Thirteenth Floor Elevators.

With manager Bill Drummond urging them to get a drummer, the teenage Pete De Freitas was recruited. His tough, imaginative playing had a galvanising effect. Added to Ian McCulloch's pin-up potential the effect on their popularity was spectacular. Said Rob Dickins, who signed them to Warner's new Korova imprint after seeing that show himself, "The singer looked so charismatic. He was beautiful. His voice had that Jim Morrison ring to it. The songs weren't well-formulated, but you saw 'Star' in neon above his head."

By the time the band came to record *Crocodiles*, the old untogetherness had vanished completely, replaced by an expansive, melodramatic sound. "We found we were capable of doing something good," said McCulloch, "That album just opened up possibilities." On Going Up, the supple rhythm section acted as a launch pad for guitar lift-off, before the song drifted into a delicious, spacey coda – McCulloch drolly intoned that there were not enough people with flowers in their hair, a sentiment also mischievously scratched in the run-out groove, which got them labelled in some quarters as "psychedelic", at a time when the jury was out on whether or not that was cool.

"Whoever the turd was who first said that, they should chop his head off," said McCulloch after being constantly asked about the band's drugs intake. "It doesn't mean anything, 'psychedelic'. If only rock critics could learn to be as original as we are. If the music's got a dreamlike quality, maybe it comes from dreams. It doesn't have to be drug-induced. We get drunk like once in a blue moon but that's about it."

On the title track – with its ferocious cross-cutting guitars – and the relentless on-beats of the apocalyptic All That Jazz, the band also proved they could rock, while the sublime Rescue, released as a single, became the student soundtrack to the summer. *Crocodiles*, as NME predicted, would become "one of the contemporary rock albums of the year."

Record label:
Korova
Produced
by David Balfe, Bill Drummond and Ian Broudie.
Recorded
at Rockfield and Eden Studios; summer 1979.
Released:
July 1980
Chart peaks:
17 (UK) None (US)
Personnel:
Ian McCulloch (v, g); Will Sergeant (g); Les Pattinson (b); Pete De Freitas (d); David Balfe (k); Hugh Jones (e); Rod Houison (e)
Track listing:
Going Up; Stars Are Stars; Pride; Monkeys; Crocodiles; Rescue (S/UK); Villiers Terrace; Pictures On My Wall; All That Jazz; Happy Death Men
Running time:
32.53
Current CD:
2292 42316-2
Further listening:
Heaven Up Here (1981); *Porcupine* (1983); *Ocean Rain* (1984)
Further reading:
www.bunnymen.com
Like this?
Try . . . p.550

The Soft Boys

Underwater Moonlight

Second from cult Cambridge crew led by Robyn Hitchcock, inheritor of Syd Barrett's mantle of strange.

"I went into the music business with negative expectations and they were all fulfilled," says Robin Hitchcock. The Soft Boys may have supported several of the big-hitters in the late '70s days of punk and glory, but it wasn't really their scene. "We were really a psychedelic pub-rock band, scared of getting hit by a flying audience member."

The combo put out one ill-conceived single for Andrew Lauder's trendy Radar Records before re-grouping to release the over-complicated, intermittently brilliant album *A Can Of Bees*. "You can't listen for too long without getting a migraine," sighs Hitchcock. Yet from this general gloom the absolutely scintillating *Underwater Moonlight* emerged.

"It became a simpler and happier band. Matthew (Seligman) joined and he was a far more straight-ahead player than Andy (Metcalfe) – and he liked his pop, and Kim liked his pop, and I began to feel I could write songs rather than ideas with music attached." The opening trio of tracks bears this out. The wonderfully malevolent I Wanna Destroy You sounds likes hell's Bee Gees backed by The Who. Kingdom Of Love is a melodic jewel; British Art'n'B circa '66 – lyrical oddness, held aloft by a golden guitar riff. Positive Vibrations rushes to the sea on torrents of jangling guitar, sitar and harmonies borrowed from the American West Coast.

"[Producer] Pat Collier was a graduate of the '60s school of guitar. He knew how to make a little money go a long way. Kim and I only had volume pedals but he made us sound brilliant. I remember writing the cheque for the I Wanna Destroy You session, it was £30." Rew's versatile, vigorous playing is certainly a key element in the album's success, but at the very centre stands Hitchcock: a looming, oneiric poet with a singular sense of humour – "I would ramble all through time and space/ Just to have a butcher's at your face/ You're the one I love or so it seems/ Because you've confiscated all my dreams." Whether on the Beefheart-style slash'n'burn of Old Pervert or the perfect pealing beauty of Queen Of Eyes, Hitchcock commands the ring. The album barely made a dent at the time, but since then many bands (including R.E.M.), have acknowledged its influence. Rew went on to have hits with Katrina And The Waves, while Hitchcock's solo career continues to swim against the tide and continues to delight, much like *Underwater Moonlight*.

Record label:
Armageddon
Produced
by Pat Collier (except Spaceward sessions – produced by studio staff).
Recorded
at Spaceward, Cambridge; Summer 1979; Alaska and James Morgan Studios, London; early 1980.
Released:
July 1980
Chart peaks:
None (UK) None (US)
Personnel:
Robyn Hitchcock (g, k, v); Kimberley Rew (g, b, syn, v); Morris Windsor (d, v); Matthew Seligman (b); Andy King (sitar); Gerry Hale (vn)
Track listing:
I Wanna Destroy You (S/UK); Kingdom of Love; Positive Vibrations; I Got The Hots; Insanely Jealous; Tonight; You'll Have To Go Sideways; Old Pervert; The Queen Of Eyes; Underwater Moonlight
Running time:
35.36
Currently unavailable on CD
Further listening:
A Can Of Bees (1979); Invisible Hits (1983); The Soft Boys: 1976–1981 (1993); Solo – Hitchcock: I Often Dream Of Trains (1984); Eye (1990) Rew: Tunnel Into Summer (2000)
Further reading:
MOJO 53; Ptolemaic Terrascope; March 1995 and April 1998 (www.terrascope.com) www.robynhitchcock.com www.kimber leyrew.com. Good fan sites – www.fegmania.org and www.glasshotel.net/gh
Like this?
Try . . . p.197

Dead Kennedys

Fresh Fruit For Rotting Vegetables

Baroque-punk venom from San Francisco.

Ten years after San Francisco was hippy capital of the world, a new countercultural force took root in the city, led by a band whose very name spat in the face of the previous decade's idealism. Dead Kennedys' guitarist East Bay Ray: "We were trying to restore what the hippies believed in: tolerance for experimentation, the do-it-yourself thing and the questioning of authority." Song titles such as Kill The Poor and Forward To Death, however, hardly shouted Love and Peace. "Well, Biafra was into shredding people lyrically. But basically we just wanted people to think for themselves. We wanted to wake people up with a two by four."

After building a ferocious live reputation and establishing their own groundbreaking label – Alternative Tentacles – they went in to record their debut. The band produced it themselves (producer "Norm" was actually engineer Oliver Dicicco's cat) and R. Pepperell (East Bay Ray) received a "Production Assistance" credit on the original sleeve. He attributes the record's artistic success to group discipline. "Everyone in the band had a work ethic and a craftsmanship ethic: a commitment to not letting things slide. We had a budget of about $6000 and we stuck to it. It helped that we had all been in rock bands before, and had the ability to express the musical ideas in our heads – we could stop on a dime and go off in another direction."

This facility is apparent throughout what must qualify as the most musically complex punk record ever made. When Ray starts invoking Wagner, Arabian scales and Ravel's Bolero in an explanation of the classic California Über Alles he's not bullshitting. The sudden appearance of an oompah-band waltz section in Chemical Warfare is another case in point. All these elements are welded together by vocalist Jello Biafra's human theremin impersonation, Ray's loud but startlingly variable guitar playing, a kick-corporate-ass rhythm section and a heavy dose of warped humour. "We didn't see ourselves as a Top 40 proposition," says Ray. "We thought this might be our only chance, so we just put everything in." The album was a critical and commercial success, and gave the DKs several more chances to berate the bad guys and energise the good guys, making a damn fine noise in the process.

Record label:
Cherry Red
Produced
by "Norm".
Recorded
at Mobius Music, San Francisco; Spring 1980.
Released:
September 1980
Chart peaks:
33 (UK) None (US)
Personnel:
Jello Biafra (v); East Bay Ray (g); Klaus Flouride (b, v); Ted (d); Paul Roessler, Ninotchka (k); 6025 (g)
Track listing:
Kill The Poor (S/UK); Forward To Death; When Ya Get Drafted; Let's Lynch The Landlord; Drug Me; Your Emotions; Chemical Warfare; California Über Alles (S); I Kill Children; Stealing People's Mail; Funland At The Beach; Ill In The Head; Holiday In Cambodia (S); Viva Las Vegas
Running time:
32.49
Current CD:
CDBRED10
Further listening:
Lard: The Last Temptation Of Lard (1990), Biafra's side-project with Ministry members Al Jourgenson and Paul Barker.
Further reading:
www.geocities.com/Athens/Forum/3111/dk.htm
Like this?
Try . . . p.444

Talking Heads

Remain In Light

David Byrne looks to Africa, lightens up, influences a generation of musicians and sells very few records indeed.

Things did not look good when Talking Heads assembled in the Bahamas to start recording their fourth album, *Remain In Light.* According to bassist Tina Weymouth, long-time Heads' producer Brian Eno was reluctant to become involved again, having fallen out with David Byrne during recording of their collaborative album, *My Life In The Bush Of Ghosts.* Within a week, engineer Rhett Davies quit in frustration, and Byrne has confirmed that there was tension between himself and Weymouth over the direction of the music.

He has said, for example, "We were really intrigued and excited by the formal aspects of African music." She, however, insisted, "No-one discussed with us the fact that we were going to be playing in an African style."

Nevertheless, what they created was a whole new direction, not just for Talking Heads but for '80s rock in general. With the quartet expanded by the addition of horns, extra percussion and voices, they moved away from traditional songwriting by improvising songs in the studio, diving headlong into the complexities of African polyrhythms and replacing Byrne's urban paranoia with more affirmative lyrics.

"I think the music was important in that," says Byrne. "The anxiety of my lyrics and my singing didn't seem appropriate to this kind of music. This music is more positive, though a little mysterious at the same time."

The other vital ingredient was Eno, taking a much more active part in the music here than on previous Talking Heads albums. Eno's fingerprints are everywhere, from vocal harmonies and counterpoints to layered ambient sounds, lyrics and rhythmic devices.

Guitarist Chris Frantz confirms that "The barriers between musician and producer were being broken down because we were writing the songs in the studio."

"An album of brave inventions and haunting textures," drooled NME on release, but Rolling Stone nailed it even better with "Scary, funny music to which you can dance and think, think and dance, dance and think, *ad infinitum.*"

Predictably, though, the world wasn't ready for doing two things at once. "It was the worst-selling Talking Heads album ever," points out Frantz. Tightly formatted American radio found it impossible to programme because, as Byrne recalls, "The reaction we heard was that it sounded too black for white radio and too white for black radio."

By the end of the '80s, however, *Remain In Light* featured at Number 4 in Rolling Stone's selection of the decade's greatest albums.

Record label:
Sire
Produced
by Brian Eno.
Recorded
at Compass Point, Nassau, Bahamas; Sigma Sound, New York; Eldorado, Los Angeles; 1980
Released:
October 8, 1980
Chart peaks:
21 (UK) 19 (US)
Personnel:
David Byrne (g, b, k); Adrian Belew (g); Jerry Harrison (g, b, k); Tina Weymouth (b, k); Chris Frantz (d, k); Brian Eno (k, b, v); Nona Hendryx (v); Jon Hassell (t, horns)
Track listing:
Born Under Punches (The Heat Goes On); Crosseyed And Painless; The Great Curve; Once In A Lifetime (S); Houses In Motion (S); Seen And Not Seen; Listening Wind; The Overload
Running time:
40.04
Current CD:
7599260952
Further listening:
The seeds of this new Talking Heads can be found in My Life In The Bush Of Ghosts by David Byrne and Brian Eno (1981). Although released after Remain In Light, it was recorded earlier.
Further reading:
Talking Heads (Jerome Davis, 1986). www.talking-heads.net
Like this?
Try . . . p.700

Nic Jones

Penguin Eggs

Melody Maker's Folk Album Of The Year takes the English folk revival to a new level of contemporary relevance.

There were strong clues on this magnificent album that Jones was heading into bold new territory, busy writing his own material and gleefully passing it off as traditional music to a folk scene still hung up on the niceties of history. He always was a colourful, wilful character who'd think nothing of turning his back on the audience or singing gibberish if he didn't think they were listening. "I once sang the same song twice in a row and no-one noticed!" he says with some triumph. "People didn't want me to write my own songs, they only wanted to hear traditional material, so I'd just do it and everyone would assume it was traditional. Other times I'd re-write traditional songs or stick in new verses. Nobody ever knew."

Penguin Eggs had such vitality, and Jones' modern guitar arrangements had such a contemporary feel, his appeal was surely on the verge of stretching way beyond the folk scene, which had long held him in reverence since his days running a club in Essex and his early tentative steps with the group The Halliard. But less than two years after recording the album, he was on the last leg of a long drive home from a gig in the early hours when he was involved in an appalling crash with a lorry and critically injured. It's assumed he fell asleep at the wheel, but Nic himself has no recollection of the accident. He was subsequently partly paralysed and although able to re-learn the guitar and play at home, he has not appeared on stage since.

"That's not important," he says with typical modesty. "I enjoy playing but I'm not bothered about appearing in public, I'm happy to play for my own satisfaction. There's plenty of others around to do it, they don't need me." Happily there has been a widening awareness of his influence in recent years, partly due to the rise of Kate Rusby, who cites Jones as one of her main inspirations. "I listen to him all the time and *Penguin Eggs* is a brilliant album," she says. "Sadly I never saw him play but the biggest thrill of my career was when he came to one of my gigs in York. I was so nervous but he sat in the front row and beamed all the way through and congratulated me after. Lovely man."

Record label:
Topic
Produced by
Tony Engle.
Recorded
at Livingstone Studios, London; late 1979.
Released:
October 1980
Chart peaks:
71 (UK) None (US)
Personnel:
Nic Jones (v, g, fiddle, a); Dave Burland (v); Tony Hall (melodeon); Nic Kinsey (e), Billy Kinsley (e)
Track listing:
Canadee-I-O; Drowned Lovers; Humpback Whale; Little Pot Stove; Courting Is A Pleasure; Barrack Street; Planxty Davis; Flandyke Shore; Farewell To The Gold
Running time:
45.14
Current CD:
TSCD411
Further listening:
The earlier The Noah's Ark Trap (1977) gave lots of clues to the direction Jones was heading for Penguin Eggs. For an excellent collection of obscurities and live recordings In Search Of Nic Jones (1998).
Like this?
Try . . . p.457

Motorhead

Ace Of Spades

Metal's excess and punk's attack; Lemmy's filthy, speed-propelled, biker-rock zenith.

"*Ace Of Spades*" said Black Sabbath's Ozzy Osbourne, "is a fucking killer."

The trio, formed by vicar's son Lemmy after Hawkwind threw him out (his drug intake, amazingly, too much even for them), were in Ozzy's opinion "the ultimate heavy-metal band". And their debut appeared just as the UK rock press had announced heavy metal's death at the hands of punk.

"I don't think our music has anything to do with heavy metal," Lemmy argued. "I think we sound more like punk, when you get into it, with the speed we play. And I'm a fucking cobbled-together bass player– I'm supposed to be playing rhythm guitar."

In the beginning their audience, made up mostly of Hell's Angels, was small. But, by 1979, their following had expanded into a substantial cult, which included many punks. That year had seen the release of three Motorhead albums. *On Parole* was a weak reissue, but the other two were classics. *Overkill* and *Bomber* had established their reputation as the loudest, fastest, nastiest band in rock. Thus it was a confident band who took a short break from their hectic live schedule –"I like to keep it concise," said Lemmy, "smack them in the face and split. Short, sharp shock" – to record Ace Of Spades.

"That whole time we knew that we were on a roll. I wish I could remember everything that happened – I'm sure that there's someone out there that does. I'm just fucked if I can!"

But if life in the Motorhead camp had become a blur, *Ace Of Spades* provided the perfect soundtrack to the band's endless hang-over. A combination of vodka, Jack Daniel's, Special Brew, speed and general road-dog debauchery resulted in tracks like Jailbait (complete with a pre-take belch), Love Me Like A Reptile, and Fast And Loose.

It was their biggest hit – UK Top 5. And though still not scraping the US charts, the album's influence Stateside was formidable, helping to catalyse the '80s thrash and speed-metal genres that spawned Slayer, Anthrax and Metallica. "If there wasn't a Lemmy and a Motorhead, there wouldn't be a Metallica," claimed Metallica drummer Lars Ulrich in December 1995.

The thunderous Spaghetti Western-inspired title track (itself a Top 20 single) was resurrected for use in an advert for Pot Noodles in '90s – around the same time that the critics who had dismissed Motorhead as "the worst band in the world" started mentioning their name in the same sentence as bands like The Stooges and The MC5.

Record label:
Bronze
Produced
by Vic Maile.
Recorded
at Jackson's Studios, Rickmansworth; August 4–September 15,1980.
Released:
October 1980
Chart peaks:
4 (UK) None (US)
Personnel:
Lemmy (v, b); "Fast" Eddie Clarke (g); Phil "Philthy Animal" Taylor (d)
Track listing:
Ace Of Spades (S); Love Me Like A Reptile; Shoot You In The Back; Live To Win; Fast And Loose; (We Are) The Road Crew; Fire, Fire; Jailbait; Dance; Bite The Bullet; The Chase Is Better Than The Catch; The Hammer
Running time:
36.37
Current CD:
ESMCD912 adds: Dirty Love; Please Don't Touch; Emergency
Further listening:
Hawkwind's Space Ritual (1973), featuring Lemmy, is classic UK acid rock, while Overkill (1979); Bomber (1979) and No Sleep 'Til Hammersmith (1981) capture Motorhead at their most thrilling during the post-punk years of the late '70s and early '80s.
Further reading:
The Illustrated Collector's Guide To Motorhead, (Alan Burridge and Mick Stevenson, 1999); www.imotorhead.com
Like this?
Try . . . p.451

The Jam

Sound Affects

Pop psychedelia meets the Gang Of Four: Weller's great post-punk statement is his most sophisticated album.

Between 1977 and 1980 The Jam barely had time to draw breath. How were they coping? "I came to the sessions for *Sound Affects* with only three, maybe four songs pre-written," Paul Weller admits. "Vic [Coppersmith-Heaven: long-time group producer] copped a lot of flak for the time it took to make, and it was frustrating, but if the songs weren't there. Anyway the pressure of constantly touring and recording ain't such a bad thing for a young band."

To judge by the results, released barely twelve months after the excellent *Setting Sons*, Weller was thriving on it. "*Sound Affects* is my favourite Jam record. We kept to our fundamental sound but stretched it a bit." The stretching went two ways. Firstly it involved exploring textures which moved them closer to post-punk contemporaries such as the Gang Of Four and Wire. Witness the gangly dissonance, startling dub vocal effect and French coda of final track Scrape Away. But there's also Start's obvious homage to The Beatles' Taxman ("Yeah, I know! I've always thought there was more James Brown to it though") through to gentle psych-rock experiments such as the backwards guitar interlude before Dream Time, and the bluebottle which buzzes its way between speakers before the acidic ska of Music For The Last Couple.

"Special stereophonic Japanese fly that was," recalls Weller wryly. "I think it was in the drum booth with Rick so I thought, Why not." Lyrically, Weller was on a bookish kick. "A poem by a bloke called Paul Drew inspired That's Entertainment. I was reading Geoffrey Ashe's Camelot And The Vision Of Albion and a lot of Shelley at the time too." His admiration for Percy Bysshe extended from the poet's aesthetic (That's Entertainment's reference to the "tranquility of solitude") to his politics: the repeated chant of "They know that God created all men equal" on Man In The Corner Shop. Weller, still only 22, had crafted a record of precocious maturity. The critics saw it as his *Revolver* and the British public bought it in barrowloads. The Jam's next and final offering, *The Gift*, was their only Number 1 album, but *Sound Affects* is their masterpiece.

Record label:
Polydor
Produced
by Vic Coppersmith-Heaven and The Jam.
Recorded
at Town House Studios, London; June–October 1980.
Released:
November 28, 1980
Chart peaks:
2 (UK) 72 (US)
Personnel:
Paul Weller (v, g, p); Bruce Foxton (v, b); Rick Buckler (d, pc),.
Track listing:
Pretty Green; Monday; But I'm Different Now; Set The House Ablaze; Start (S); That's Entertainment (S/Import); Dream Time; Man In The Corner Shop; Music For The Last Couple; Boy About Town; Scrape Away
Running time:
35.29
Current CD:
537 421–2
Further listening:
All Mod Cons (1978) and Setting Sons (1979) are the two other classic Jam albums.
Further reading:
The Jam: The Modern World By Numbers (Paul Honeyford, 1995); www.geocities.com/SunsetStrip/Towers/6411/links1.html
Like this?
Try . . . p.264

Phil Collins

Face Value

Genesis drummer launches solo career fuelled by marriage breakdown.

Already respected – for his early '70s Genesis work – as one of rock's most musical drummers, Phil Collins' profile had risen since 1975 when he replaced Peter Gabriel as lead vocalist; his sunny, blokeish style and commercial writing ability helped the band attain stadium status. By 1980, it was time to make a solo album. His workaholism had taken its toll on his marriage (in his absence, wife Andrea had dallied with a decorator) and Collins found himself alone, noodling angry songs in his home studio. Please Don't Ask – a remarkably vulnerable and moving separation song – had already appeared on Genesis's *Duke* but there was plenty more where that came from. If Leaving Me Is Easy and You Know What I Mean adopted a heartfelt, winningly plaintive style and I Missed Again had a jaunty frustration as expressed by the brittle Earth Wind And Fire horns. It wasn't all gloom though: The Roof Is Leaking maintained a hopeful tone in the face of poverty-stricken rural struggle and the Stephen Bishop-like This Must Be Love celebrated his new relationship with Jill Tavelman.

But the most memorable track was the opener In The Air Tonight, a brooding piece of unambiguous fury ("Well if you told me you were drowning/I would not lend a hand"), finally exploding with an apocalyptic drum fill treated to Hugh Padgham's customised concrete-room-gated-reverb effect, forever to be known as the Phil Collins Drum Sound. Collins performed it on Top Of The Pops with a paint pot on his piano, a symbol his wife took very personally; Andrea: "Implying decorator, implying affair, implying that was what happened to our marriage when that wasn't what happened at all."

Face Value went on to sell over 4 million copies, Genesis records started to sound like Phil Collins records and his solo follow-up; 1984's *Hello, I Must Be Going*, continued the revenge/catharsis-through-song theme, much to Andrea's dismay; "I didn't understand why he wasn't writing incredible love songs for Jill. To go on and on as he did was very mean." Though he and Genesis went on to do amazing business through the '80s and '90s, as Collins became housewife's choice so the music got less interesting. With his ubiquity an irritant to the impartial observer, Collins rarely recaptured that balance between creativity and the un-self-conscious expression that makes his solo debut so valuable.

Record label:
Virgin
Produced
by Phil Collins with Hugh Padgham.
Recorded
at Old Croft, the Townhouse and Village Recorder, LA; 1980.
Released:
February 1981
Chart peaks:
1 (UK) 7 (US)
Personnel:
Phil Collins (v, k, d); Darryl Steurmer, Eric Clapton (g); John Giblin (b); Alphonso Johnson (b); Ronnie Scott, Don Myrick (s); Louis Satterfield (tb); Rhamlee Michael Davis, Michael Hawis (t); Joe Partridge (sg); Shankar (vn, tamboura)
Track listing:
In The Air Tonight (S); This Must Be Love; Behind The Lines; The Roof Is Leaking; Droned; Hand In Hand; I Missed Again (S); You Know What I Mean; Thunder And Lightning; I'm Not Moving; If Leaving Me Is Easy (S); Tomorrow Never Knows
Running time:
40.36
Current CD:
CDV 2185
Further listening:
Duke (Genesis, 1980); But Seriously (1989)
Further reading:
Phil Collins (Ray Coleman, 1997)
Like this?
Try . . . p.557

Dick Gaughan

Handful Of Earth

Folk Roots magazine's 'Album of the '80s', re-established the passionate Scot as one of Britain's most committed folk singers.

"*Handful Of Earth* blew me away when I heard it, Gaughan's commitment to the songs is remarkable," said Billy Bragg. "In many ways it goes beyond folk music but everything you ever believed folk music could and should be is there. I toured East Germany with him before the Wall came down and I watched him in awe." Wherever you go on the British – and indeed more informed American – folk circuit, the reaction is the same.

"Dick gets inside a song like no-one else and proved himself a truly great singer," said June Tabor of the former member of traditional Celtic group Boys Of The Lough and folk-rock band Five Hand Reel. Even Gaughan himself, a modest man passionately opposed to any form of celebrity, knew he'd taken the traditional song form to fresh heights of intensity and stirring power on *Handful Of Earth.*

"After I made it I felt, Well that's it, I'm not going to do anything better. It was the best I could do, the best blend of songs I could find. I was fresh again after coming out of the whole Five Hand Reel band period, I'd done a record with Andy Irvine, I had a whole load of ideas to juggle about and the years and years of frustration all went into *Handful Of Earth.* After that I had to do something different, there was absolutely no point in trying to remake *Handful Of Earth.*"

So just as Paul Brady decided his *Welcome Here Kind Stranger* represented a peak for Irish traditional song and boldly spun off into a brave new career as a singer-songwriter, Gaughan's music also took on a new turn with a hard political edge and adventurous experiments with rock arrangements, even including an improvised modern-jazz album with percussionist Ken Hyder (*Fanfare For Tomorrow*). But *Handful Of Earth* remains his masterwork, turning well-known ballads like Erin-Go-Bragh and Both Sides Of The Tweed into passionate Scottish anthems and restoring politics to the front line of British folk music with Workers Song and Leon Rosselson's emotive story of the Diggers' revolt The World Turned Upside Down, which became a modern classic covered, among others, by Billy Bragg. Other songs on the album were also widely covered, including the poignant Song For Ireland, now constantly heard performed by Irish bar bands and buskers, but oddly enough written by an Englishman, Phil Colclough.

Record label:
Green Linnet
Produced
by Dick Gaughan and Robin Morton.
Recorded
at Temple Studios, Scotland; late 1980.
Released:
March 1981
Chart peaks:
None (UK) None (US)
Personnel:
Dick Gaughan (v, ag, g); John Cunningham (k, whistle); Phil Cunningham (k, whistle); Stewart Isbister (b); Brian McNeill (fiddle, b); Robin Morton (e)
Track listing:
Erin-Go-Bragh; Now Westlin Winds; Craigie Hill; The World Turned Upside Down; The Snows They Melt The Soonest; Lough Erne; First Kiss At Parting; Scojun Waltz; Randers Hopsa; Song For Ireland; Workers Song; Both Sides Of The Tweed
Running time:
43.21
Current CD:
TSCD419
Further listening:
Redwood Cathedral (1999), while Gaughan's interest in taking folk music to more intense levels is demonstrated on A Different Kind Of Love Song (1983). His most political work is True And Bold: Songs Of The Scottish Miners (1986).
Further reading:
Dick Gaughan runs his own informative website, www.dick-alba.demon.co.uk
Like this?
Try . . . p.51

The Birthday Party

Prayers On Fire

A terrifying cartoonish trip to rock's psychotic edge.

To the often uninspiring post-punk landscape of the early '80s, The Birthday Party brought a bug-eyed, lurching intensity, crooked humour and a magpie's eye for musical styles. The keynote was excess: "I write a hell of a lot of lyrics when I'm really drunk," notes Nick Cave. "When we were recording *Prayers On Fire*, I was fairly drunk the whole time."

The group had returned to their native Australia to record, after spending a miserable 10 months trying to make their mark in Britain. By all accounts the studio was an open house, but from this inebriated mayhem a perversely disciplined album emerged. Hometown band Equal Local ("They were an avant-garde outfit," remembers guitarist Rowland Howard. "They'd stand in line and tap their feet frantically all at the same time") dropped in to contribute the menacing, big-band brass riff to Nick The Stripper.

Cave's splenetic delivery displays the mixture of self-loathing and self-aggrandisement which often marks great performers; a flailing, barking, spidery Elvis brutalised by punk. The muscular cross-rhythms worked up by the band point at a stew of influences: The Velvets (Ho-Ho), Kurt Weill (Just You And Me) and Pere Ubu (Cry), with strongly flavoured scraps of country (Capers), rockabilly (A Dead Song) and jazz-blues (Yard) thrown in for good measure. Though the band deny any knowledge of Captain Beefheart before the sessions, he seems like the presiding deity. King Ink encapsulates the album's lyrical sideswipe: "King Ink feels like a bug swimming in a soup bowl/Oh! Yer! Yer! What a wonderful life – Fats Domino on the radio." This dislocation mirrors engineer Tony Cohen's memory of the time: "At the time we thought we'd made a Little River Band-style record, horrible and slick. Now, looking back, of course it's not."

Contemporary critics raved; the band went on to record the utterly feral *Junkyard*, but drug problems and personality clashes would derail them. Howard formed Crime And The City Solution while Cave went solo, and Harvey played for both. *Prayers On Fire* has moments that they've never bettered.

Record label:
4AD
Produced
by The Birthday Party.
Recorded
at Armstrong's Audio Visual Studios, Melbourne and Richmond Recorders; December 1980–January 1981.
Released:
April 1981
Chart peaks:
None (UK) None (US)
Personnel:
Nick Cave (v, k, s, d); Rowland S Howard (g, v, s); Mick Harvey (k, g, pc); Tracy Pew (b); Phil Calvert (d); Phillip Jackson (t); Mick Hunter, Stephen Ewart (brass); Tony Cohen (e)
Track listing:
Zoo-Music Girl; Cry; Capers; Nick The Stripper (S/Aus); Ho-Ho; Figure Of Fun; King Ink; A Dead Song; Yard; Dull Day; Just You And Me
Running time:
35.09
Current CD:
GAD 104 CD adds: Blundertown; Kathy's Kisses
Further listening:
Junkyard (1982); best of, Hits (1992); Live 1981–1982 (1999); Nick Cave From Here To Eternity (1984)
Further reading:
Bad Seed (Ian Johnston, 1996); www.thebirthdayparty.com
Like this?
Try . . . p.415

Journey

Escape

Former jazz-rockers deliver AOR colossus. It spent over a year in the US Top 20.

Escape was Journey's Whopper with cheese; soft-rock in a bun; histrionics with fries. It paved the way for Foreigner, Styx and REO Speedwagon, and '80s America gobbled it up. "In the heat with a blue jean girl/Burnin' love comes once in a lifetime," sang Steve Perry on Stone In Love. It was hardly Keats, but tagged to Neal Schon's stoked power-chords, even the most clichéd memory of rock-chick action seemed delicious.

The album saw Jonathan Cain replace Gregg Rolie on keyboards, and as co-writer of all ten tracks, Cain helped Journey to perfect a sound which one less-than-enamoured critic described as "advanced jukebox Muzak". On Open Arms – soppy enough to warrant a 1995 cover by Mariah Carey – they were guilty as charged, but Don't Stop Believin's update on Springsteen's Born To Run ethic proved irresistible.

Reviewing Journey's seventh album, Rolling Stone joined the dissenters, positing that they "could be any bunch of fluff-brained sessioneers with a singer who sounds like a eunuch." Perhaps they meant *unique*. Perry could be melodramatic, certainly, but on Mother Father, his easy slides from soprano to alto demonstrate an extraordinary ability. Elsewhere, former Santana member Neal Schon's performance on Still They Ride was equally impressive, the notes of his guitar solo cascading with an attack and fluidity which Eddie Van Halen was amongst the first to acknowledge.

Who's Crying Now, Don't Stop Believin' and Open Arms all went Top 10 Stateside, and *Escape* eventually sold in excess of nine million copies. Its success prompted the band to collaborate with Data Age Incorporated on the *Escape* video game, an Atari 2600 product whose plot involved escorting Journey from the stage to the Scarab Escape Vehicle pictured on the album's cover. Naturally, obstacles en route included love-crazed groupies.

Journey's 1983 follow-up *Frontiers* sold a respectable enough six million. By now, though, Perry was constantly at loggerheads with Valory and Smith, whom he eventually sacked. So, not all sweetness and light, then.

Record label:
CBS
Produced
by Mike Stone and Kevin Elson.
Recorded
at Fantasy Studios, Berkeley, California; spring 1981.
Released:
August 1981
Chart peaks:
32 (UK) 1 (US)
Personnel:
Steve Perry (v); Neal Schon (g,v); Jonathan Cain (k,g,v); Ross Valory (b,v); Steve Smith (d); Wally Buck (ae)
Track listing:
Don't Stop Believin'; Stone In Love; Who's Cryin' Now; Keep On Runnin'; Still They Ride; Escape; Lay It Down; Dead Or Alive; Mother, Father; Open Arms
Running time:
42.43
Current CD:
486662 2
Further listening:
Frontiers (1983)
Further reading:
journey.simplenet.com; www.journeythe band.com
Like this?
Try . . . p.49

The Human League

Dare

Self-conscious synth minimalism evolves into chart-topping New Romantic ear candy.

Suzanne Sulley burst into tears the day Don't You Want Me went to Number 1 in America. Not only had it knocked the mawkish Ebony And Ivory off the top, it's success also vindicated Phil Oakey's decision to replace the band's synth-whiz founders Martin Ware and Ian Craig-Marsh with a pair of unknown disco dollies. Nobody expected the League to bounce back from the split. Across two albums preoccupied with a modish synthetic brutalism, the Sheffield quartet had poised itself between post-punk experiment and chart pop. But it was Ware and Marsh's baby all the way – Oakey was just the figurehead who sounded faintly uncomfortable reciting Being Boiled, and Adrian Wright was just simply uncomfortable, before and after the split. Especially after. "He hated us," Catherall recalled. "Wouldn't even say hello in the mornings."

Under the intuitive guidance of co-producer Rushent and engineer Dave Allen, however, the animosity turned to instinctive chemistry. "When we first heard Sound Of The Crowd," Sulley told Smash Hits, "it was just thump-crash-thump-crash, and straight away we said 'definite hit'. You could dance to it." Musically, Catherall and Sulley's contributions were restricted to the deep mix harmonies which haunted half the album. But the sight of them onstage as the material took shape, Sulley "flailing like an octopus", as Oakey put it, and Catherall "completely out of time", instilled new discipline into the band's writing, and direction to their style. You could dance to all of it. Sound Of The Crowd, Love Action and Open Your Heart were hits even before Dare's Halloween release; and if Don't You Want Me distorted everything afterwards, still its enormity could not detract from the remainder of the album. Even in deadly earnestness (Seconds lamenting the death of John Lennon, the chilled paranoia of Darkness), *Dare* was riddled with infectious confections.

Record label:
Virgin
Produced
by Martin Rushent and the Human League.
Recorded
at Genetic Sound Studios, 1981.
Released:
October 31, 1981
Chart peaks:
1 (UK) 3 (US)
Personnel:
Philip Oakey (v, syn); Joanne Catherall (v); Susanne Sulley (v); Ian Burden (syn); Jo Callis (syn); Philip Adrian Wright (syn)
Track listing:
The Things That Dreams Are Made Of (S, US only); Open Your Heart (S); The Sound Of The Crowd; Darkness; Do Or Die; Get Carter; I Am The Law; Seconds; Love Action (S); Don't You Want Me (S)
Running time:
40.48
Current CD:
CDV2192
Further listening:
Love And Dancing (1982)
Further reading:
www.andwedanced.com
Like this?
Try . . . p.517

The Police

Ghost In The Machine

Truly global rock from a disintegrating group who used their frustration to create a deeply ambitious album.

"Very horrible," says Sting of the making of *Ghost In The Machine*. "Very dark. Miserable. Our marriages were breaking up, our marriage was breaking up, and yet we had to make another record." This most problematic phase of The Police's progress was enacted against an idyllic backdrop: the Caribbean island of Montserrat.

The band and newly-hired producer Hugh Padgham arrived on June 15,1981. For all his stresses, Sting in particular seemed to relish the environment – and for a reggae-inflected band, this was a perfect temporary home. Back in the UK, 2-Tone was at its peak, and ska – as evidenced by Spirits In The Material World, Hungry For You and Rehumanize Yourself – was a clear influence on the album. But Padgham's deep-pile production took the music somewhere completely new, as did Sting's increasingly ambitious lyrics. His clear socio-political stance meant that the album, named after an Arthur Koestler book, would forge his reputation as an exemplar of pretension.

On the musical side, *Ghost* saw The Police kicking back – given their problems, probably a smart move. "It was a please-yourself album," said Sting. "Our previous records were experiments in commercialism. I'd been obsessed with the idea of coming up with a commercial record. *Ghost* doesn't have that concern. It's just us." So it was that he ended up playing a quadruple-tracked saxophone part on Hungry For You, and gleefully contributing to the hilariously over-egged coda of Every Little Thing She Does Is Magic – taped not in Montserrat, but during a stopover in Quebec. Sandwiched between such tomfoolery was The Police's most serious song to date: Invisible Sun, the rumbling attempt to empathise with the IRA's hunger strikers, into which they poured all their creeping misery to stunning effect.

Lofty lyrical themes, an almost jazzy combination of relaxation and musical sophistication, and a retrospective admission that The Police were coming apart – it's not unreasonable to see *Ghost In The Machine* as the first Sting solo album. On his return to the UK, Sting played a brief solo set at a London gala for Amnesty International, during which Eric Clapton was heard to mutter: "Sting has arrived". He wasn't far wrong.

Record label:
A&M
Produced
by The Police and Hugh Padgham.
Recorded
at AIR Studios, Montserrat; Le Studio, Quebec; June–August 1981.
Release date:
October 1981
Chart peaks:
1 (UK) 2 (US)
Personnel:
Sting (v, b, k, s); Andy Summers (g, k, v); Stewart Copeland (d); Jean Roussel (k)
Track listing:
Spirits In The Material World; Every Little Thing She Does Is Magic; Invisible Sun; Hungry For You (J'Aurais Toujours Faim De Toi); Demolition Man; Too Much Information; Rehumanize Yourself; One World (Not Three); Omegaman; Secret Journey; Darkness
Running time:
41.10
Current CD:
CDMID162
Further listening:
A&M box set Message In A Box (1993)
Further reading:
Sting: Demolition Man (Christopher Sandford, 1998); www.stingchronicity.co.uk
Like this?
Try . . . p.661

Black Flag

Damaged

A US hardcore milestone, marking the vocal debut of Henry Rollins.

"As a parent... I found this an anti-parent record." The words stuck on to the first 25,000 copies of *Damaged* were lifted from a statement made by MCA's Al Bergamo, defending his company's decision not to distribute Black Flag's incendiary debut album. However, thanks to the group's own DIY sales work, MCA were already too late: the record was shipping to stores across the country. *Damaged* was out.

In his diary, Henry Rollins described Black Flag's live show as "the ultimate soundtrack to a full-scale riot". Listening to *Damaged* it's easy to see what he meant. More anti-everything than anti-parent, Black Flag's first full-length LP explodes with frustration, alienation and unrestrained rage. From the opening air-raid warning riff of Rise Above to the agonised slo-mo grind of Damaged II, they hold nothing back. Black Flag took on all-comers: Spray Paint and Police Story are anti-authority, TV Party and Six Pack satirical sideswipes at apathetic beer culture. Depression and Damaged I spill over with self-loathing, while No More and What I See spew pure malevolence.

The music itself is a riot of adrenalised, distorted metal cranked out by a group possessed, as though they'd only get the one chance to leave their mark. Greg Ginn's molten guitar combined rhythm and lead in a mangled collision, scrawling riffs across the group's runaway rhythmic blur. Rollins, then the new guy, says of Ginn: "He was relentless... he would tape the headphones to his head so they wouldn't fly off."

Henry himself had much to prove: in the audience barely two months previously, the DC punker found himself thrown into the deep end in LA by a group itching to record. He had little choice but to meet them head-on: "I would sing as hard as I could every time. I didn't know anything about pacing myself." It shows – words are spat out with a rasping, untrained aggression like punk primal-scream therapy.

Black Flag would go on to record several excellent albums and, alongside groups like Minor Threat and the Dead Kennedys, help to establish an independent touring and distribution network which would lay the groundwork for the global domination of groups like Nirvana and Green Day. But they would struggle to recapture the power and intensity of *Damaged*.

Record label:
SST
Produced
by Spot and Black Flag.
Recorded
at Unicorn Studios, Hollywood; September 1980.
Released:
November 1981
Chart peaks:
None (UK) None (US)
Personnel:
Henry Rollins (v); Greg Ginn (g); Dez Cadena (g, v); Charles Dukowski (b); Robo (d); Spot, Francis Buckley (e)
Track listing:
Rise Above; Spray Paint; Six Pack; What I See; TV Party; Thirsty And Miserable; Police Story; Gimmie Gimmie Gimmie; Depression; Room 13; Damaged II; No More; Padded Cell; Life Of Pain; Damaged I
Running time:
34.47
Current CD:
SST 007
Further listening:
The First Four Years (1984); My War (1984); Slip It In (1984); Rollins Band, Life Time (1988)
Further reading:
Get In The Van (Henry Rollins, 1994); Turned On: A Biography of Henry Rollins (James Parker, 1998)
Like this?
Try . . . p.451

Iron Maiden

Number Of The Beast

From Brit-metal hopefuls to globe-straddling concern.

Number Of The Beast is the album which succeeded in turning Iron Maiden into a household name in Britain, affording them a global reputation which they enjoy to this day. It showcases the new-found songwriting confidence exhibited by band leader and bass player Steve Harris – hook-filled metal nuggets like Run To The Hills, and the title track (resplendent alongside moments of atmospheric melodrama such as Hallowed Be Thy Name) still form the corner-stone of any Maiden set some 20 years later: testament to Harris' ability. Equally significant is the arrival of vocalist Bruce Dickinson. Recruited by ebullient manager Rod Smallwood in the beer tent at the Reading Festival, Bruce replaced the wayward Paul Di'Anno in the late summer of '81 and fittingly had his photo snapped with the band cradling a pint of Ruddles in a local boozer. Dickinson had confidence by the lungful.

"When I first joined I thought I could be the best damned singer this band had ever had," he explains. "I knew that they were ready to do things properly, that the set-up was there. It really was a case of when things were going to happen. When I heard the material for the album that they'd been working on, I knew they were ready."

The release of Run To The Hills in February 1982 confirmed Bruce's initial suspicions, smashing its way into the UK charts at Number 7. Primed by a 20-date UK tour, the album charged to the top of the charts on release. Despite the odd moment which hasn't weathered well (such as opener Invaders), *Number Of The Beast* is best viewed as an ambitious step forward which paid incredible dividends. While Maiden's peers like Angel Witch, Saxon and Diamond Head enjoyed faltering homegrown reputations, Maiden began carving out an international career which would lead to worldwide album sales in excess of 40 million.

Record label:
EMI
Produced
by Martin "Farmer" Birch.
Recorded
at Battery Studios, London; November–December 1981.
Released:
March 1982
Chart peaks:
1 (UK) 33 (US)
Personnel:
Bruce Dickinson (v); Steve Harris (b); Dave Murray (g); Adrian Smith (g); Clive Burr (d); Nigel Hewitt-Green (e)
Track listing:
Invaders; Children Of The Damned; The Prisoner; 22 Acacia Avenue; TheNumber Of The Beast (S); Run To The Hills (S); Gangland; Total Eclipse; Hallowed Be Thy Name
Running time:
44.55
Current CD:
4969180
Further listening:
Killers (1981); Powerslave (1984); the landmark double live set, Live After Death (1985)
Further reading:
Run To The Hills (Mick Wall, 1999); www.ironmaiden.com
Like this?
Try . . . p.208

Toto

IV

Muso sextet named after the dog in The Wizard Of Oz clean up at the 1982 Grammys.

Despite huge success with their 1978 single Hold The Line, *IV* found Toto with everything to prove. *Turn Back* (1981) had been dismissed as an album which favoured a self-conscious virtuosity over songs. On *IV*, they remedied this, writing strong pop melodies and making sure that most tracks were at "power-ballad" pace. For a band composed of session-musicians whose previous credits included Miles Davis and Steely Dan, this showed considerable restraint.

The recording process was anything but insular. Toto employed five engineers, six sound-recordists and a host of fellow session players. This last group included yet more Porcaro brothers. Band members Steve and Jeff were now joined by Mike Porcaro, who played cello on Good For You, and Joe Porcaro, who was responsible for the marimba hook on Africa. The final extravagance was a spell at Abbey Road to record James Newton Howard's string arrangements. By now Toto were well over budget, but they sensed they would recoup. For many, *IV* conjures little more than pony-tailed bass-players sipping Pepsi, but it's enjoyable, just as Baywatch is enjoyable. Highlights include Rosanna, written for the actress Rosanna Arquette, and I Won't Hold You Back, its production reminiscent of Richard Carpenter until Lukather's lovelorn vocal segues to a fiery guitar solo. More curious is Paich and J Porcaro's Africa, all congas and airy analogue synth. Reportedly the rest of the band were as bemused as the public by the song's lyrics : "I know that I must do what's right/ Sure as Kilimanjaro rises above the Serengeti", sings Paich, before repeatedly blessing the rain. How odd.

When *IV* won a gob-smacking six Grammys including best album, some cited nepotism, claiming that the band knew almost everybody on the voting panel. Either way, Joe Public was as taken as the Academy, and on the back of five hit singles, *IV* eventually sold over three million copies. When Hungate left before the accompanying tour, and Kimball followed suit, Toto's remaining members decided to return to their day jobs before starting on a follow-up. Lukather's next session was Michael Jackson's *Thriller*. Which was nice.

Record label:
CBS
Produced
by Toto.
Recorded
at Sunset Sound and Record One, Los Angeles; Abbey Road, London; 1981.
Released:
April 1982
Chart peaks:
4 (UK) 4 (US)
Personnel:
Bobby Kimball (v); Steve Lukather (g, v); David Paich (k,v); Steve Porcaro (k,v); Jeff Porcaro (d, pc); David Hungate (b); Lenny Castro (pc); Mike Porcaro (c); Joe Porcaro (marimba); James Newton-Howard (oa); The Martyn Ford Orchestra (strings); Al Schmitt, Tom Knox (e); Greg Ladanyi (e, m)
Track listing:
Rosanna (S); Make Believe (S); I Won't Hold You Back (S); Good For You; It's A Feeling; Afraid Of Love; Lovers In The Night; We Made It; Waiting For your Love (S); Africa (S)
Running time:
42.18
Current CD:
450088 2
Further listening:
Isolation (1984)
Further reading:
www.toto99.com
Like this?
Try . . . p.368

Marshall Crenshaw

Marshall Crenshaw

A walking encyclopedia of '50s and '60s rock and R&B, Crenshaw mounts a one-man revolution against '80s slickness.

At a time when radio meant Survivor's Eye Of The Tiger and Steve Miller's Abracadabra, Marshall Crenshaw arrived like rock'n'roll's long-lost son. "I felt at odds with what was going on," Crenshaw says of that summer of 1982. "Part of my approach on the first album was choosing certain things as influences and rejecting others. I was doing this kind of private rebellion in my mind."

He rejected what he called "throw-away pop". Instead, the singer chose sturdy golden-era influences: Buddy Holly, the pleasing dink of a Spector session glockenspiel, the "oohs" of The Beach Boys and the streamlined song design of Motown and The Beatles. Impressed by his home demos, Warner Brothers signed him and let him self-produce. But the transition from apartment to New York's Record Plant was rough.

"I was a little overwhelmed by 24-track equipment because I was used to working on 4-track," Crenshaw says. "I wasn't really getting the sounds and I was in over my head. The other thing that got to me was we were really under pressure to make a good record. There were high expectations."

The MO of cutting bass and drums together, then overdubbing guitars and vocals, captured a rough-and-ready spirit in tracks such as There She Goes Again, Rockin' Around In NYC. and She Can't Dance, while Cynical Girl benefitted from more deliberate layering.

"When I recorded that at home I had one Vox 12-string," Crenshaw recalls. "When we did it at the Record Plant, there are 14. It really gets the buzzing thing going on – like a big bees' nest."

Shortly before recording his debut, Crenshaw had been playing John Lennon in the stage show Beatlemania. "We were in the studio on December 8, 1981, which was exactly a year after John had been shot. And the day he got shot, he'd been in the Record Plant. So we all stopped working that day and sat around and talked about John Lennon. Everybody there had known him. It made me think that if he'd been alive, I probably would've met him. That was exciting for me."

Record label:
Warner Brothers
Produced
by Richard Gottehrer and Marshall Crenshaw.
Recorded
at The Record Plant, NYC; January 1982.
Released:
May 15, 1982
Chart peaks:
None (UK) None (US)
Personnel:
Marshall Crenshaw (g, v); Robert Crenshaw (d, v); Chris Donato (b, v); Tony Garnier (b); Michael Osborn (pc); Thom Panunzio (e)
Track listing:
There She Goes Again; Someday, Someway (S); Girls...; I'll Do Anything; Rockin' Around In NYC; The Usual Thing; She Can't Dance; Cynical Girl; Mary Anne; Soldier Of Love; Not For Me; Brand New Lover
Running time:
38.35
Current CD:
BSK-3673 2
Further listening:
Field Day (1983), Number 447 (1999)
Further reading:
www.marshallcrenshaw.com
Like this?
Try . . . p.804

The Cure

Pornography

Most bands are happy when they make their greatest album. The Cure broke up.

The NME review called it "Phil Spector in hell"; Robert Smith simply describes it as hell.

"I look back on it as just a crazed month, I was incredibly driven to make that album. It would be impossible for me to make an album like *Pornography* again. I was deranged, standing there screaming at people."

It *was* an intense album, even on the post-punk, proto-Goth yardstick by which the Cure were then measured. The culmination of a three-year cycle launched by 1980's *17 Seconds*, and following hard on the heels of the funereal *Faith*, *Pornography* was brutal, despairing and very, very ugly. But it was not, Smith insisted, "a violent album. If anything, it was about the inability to be violent."

The opening lyric sets the scene, Smith's vocal rising above 100 Years' crumbling castle wall of sound to insist, "It doesn't matter if we all die."

It was only later that he admitted that quite the contrary was on his mind; "I hate the idea that you'd die for your audience, [but] I was rapidly becoming enmeshed in that around the time of *Pornography*, the idea that Ian Curtis had gone first and I was soon to follow. I wasn't prepared for that to happen."

He just wasn't certain how to prevent it, and *Pornography* howls his frustration through the fractured wedding march of Siamese Twins ("I chose an eternity of this"); the numbing horror of Hanging Garden; and onto the cathartic rancour of the title track, composed the previous Christmas on a chemical vacation at Steve Severin's house.

Relentless in its density, a totalitarian battering where even the silences between tracks scream, *Pornography* is unlike any other Cure album. Childhood fancies like Bowie, Steve Harley and Alex Harvey, so vividly peeping through past (and future) Smith compositions, are nowhere to be seen; and though Smith has returned to the sounds of *Pornography* on several occasions since then (*Disintegration*, *Blood Flowers*), he has never reprised its intensity. And with good reason.

"It's like rereading old diaries. That period, I tend not to dwell on too much, because it wasn't much fun."

A few months later, Simon Gallup is thrown out after a violent quarrel on tour in Europe and Robert Smith joins Siouxsie And The Banshees. The next incarnation of The Cure, fanfared by the electropop of Let's Go To Bed in December '82 and The Walk the following year will be very different from *Pornography* – comparatively jolly, some might say. Smith, though eternally glum, will never again seem quite so serious.

Record label:
Fiction
Produced
by The Cure and Phil Thornally
Recorded
at RAK Studio One, London, Jan–Feb 1982
Release date:
May 1982
Chart peaks:
8 (UK) None (US)
Personnel:
Robert Smith (v, g, k), Simon Gallup (b,k), Laurence Tolhurst (d, k)
Track listing:
One Hundred Years; A Short Term Effect; The Hanging Garden (S); Siamese Twins; The Figurehead; A Strange Day; Cold; Pornography
Running time:
43.22
Current CD:
CD FIX 7
Further listening:
The raw, cuter beginnings on Three Imaginary Boys (1979) – released in the US as Boys Don't Cry, the darkness thickens on Faith (1981), Disintegration (1989) is cited by Smith as the second part of a Pornography trilogy with Blood Flowers (2000) as its culmination.
Further reading:
Faith (Dave Bowler and Bryan Dray, 1995)
Like this?
Try . . . p.460

John Cale

Music For A New Society

Ex-Velvet Underground man's tenth album and deliberately, the hardest sell of them all.

"I wanted to do a *Marble Index*," Cale admits, invoking Nico's most glacially bleak album, a record he also produced. "What I was most interested in was the terror of the moment." Coming down from the sonic attack of *Honi Soit* – coming down, indeed, to the point where even he had to confess, "there were some examples where songs ended up so emaciated they weren't songs any more," Cale cast an eye back over a catalogue which had already been described as psychotic, and decided to show people precisely what psychosis really was.

"The songs were very difficult. They were entrenched in a certain *ennui* or angst that a lot of people associate with John Cale." Centring everything on his voice, adapting instrumentation not because it fit the songs but because it added to the atmospheres, *New Society* was sparse, cracked and scary. In his autobiography, Cale acknowledges that the spirit of the Velvet Underground hung heavily over the proceedings, the sense of "breaking things down into their lowest common denominator and seeing how much tension can be created between the individual parts".

Disembodied whispers and laughter cut through Thoughtless Kind; ghostly orchestral snatches give wife Rise, Sam And Rimsky-Korsakov its sole hope of melody; the ironic juxtaposition of Beethoven's Ninth (Song To Joy) and Cale's Damn Life. Even Close Watch, reprised from 1975's *Helen Of Troy* and the closest thing to a beautiful love song Cale has ever admitted to, is torn apart and turned in on itself, while Changes Made, the solitary rocker – included at his label's insistence to keep the whole affair from being too wrist-slashing – has the opposite effect entirely, bursting out to remind listeners of everything the rest of the album has rejected. But even though it was bleak, Cale had no fears about its effect. "It wouldn't make people jump out of windows," he shrugs. "They just wouldn't buy the damned album."

Record label:
Island
Produced
by John Cale.
Recorded
at Skyline Studios, New York; 1982.
Released:
August 1982
Chart peaks:
None (UK) None (US)
Personnel:
John Cale (v, g, k); DJ Young (g); Alan Lanier (k); David Lichtenstein (d); Risé Cale (v); John Wonderling, Mike McLintock, Robert Elk, Pipe Major Tom FitzGibbon ("accompanying musicians")
Track listing:
Taking Your Life In Your Hands; Thoughtless Kind; Sanities; If You Were Still Around; Close Watch; Broken Bird; Chinese Envoy; Changes Made; Damn Life; Rise, Sam And Rimsky-Korsakov
Running time:
44.38
Current CD:
YMCD 003 adds In The Library Of Force
Further listening:
for its twin, Marble Index by Nico (1969); for its corollary, Sabotage (1980)
Further reading:
What's Welsh For Zen (John Cale and Victor Bockris, 2000)
Like this?
Try . . . p.298

Kate Bush

The Dreaming

From pop star to cult artist in one peculiar, brilliant album.

When Kate Bush – a white-faced, red-lipped, flyaway-haired siren squalling mystical, sexy hippy-chick lyrics in the voice of a banshee – appeared in January 1978 singing Wuthering Heights, jaws dropped. People didn't know whether to laugh or listen harder. Those who chose the latter – and by 1981 there had been enough of them to support three hit albums and ten hit singles – heard an endearingly eccentric prodigy of rare creativity and singular style. Her music had evolved from piano-driven orch-rock into adventurous and unique soundworlds which utilised her unusual vocal mannerisms and light surrealism to increasingly powerful effect, as in Breathing, a claustrophobic creation concerning post-nuclear birth.

In 1981, writing a song a night to a drum machine (inspired by Peter Gabriel) she eventually felt compelled to "sever all the links I had had with the older stuff", in order to maximise the potential of her new, rhythmically assertive material. She had felt too easily influenced by other people; that meant saying goodbye to engineer Jon Kelly and producing *The Dreaming* herself. Always driven by the artistic rather than the business impulse (finding live work an unbearable personal upheaval, she quit it in '79), it took over a year and cost a small fortune with Kate finding it the most technically, artistically and emotionally demanding project of her life. But she was proud of the finished product, a dark, imposingly sophisticated and aggressive record of thundering rhythms and ethnic textures, acrobatic vocal effects and murky lyrics, full of inventive twists – the 5/4 groove of Sat In Your Lap, the chilling screams on Pull Out The Pin, All The Love's moving parade of voices saying "goodbye" on an answerphone.

Some soon-to-be-familiar aspects of the Fairlight – the then-vogueish sampling instrument used throughout – make some of the music rather "of its time", but its commitment, its unreasonable intensity and daffy combination of Vietnam/Aboriginal/*film noir*/escapologist imagery still impresses. Press and public alike were confused. Its density was attacked as overproduction, its ambiguousness as wilful obscurity. Kate: "Maybe the album is more difficult for people than I meant it to be. It isn't intended to be complicated." Just as the mainstream were getting used to her, she made *The Dreaming* – her "she's gone mad" album; if there had been any doubt of the dichotomous pop star/artist balance, there wasn't now.

Record label:
EMI
Produced
by Kate Bush.
Recorded
at Townhouse, Abbey Road, Odyssey, Advision; 1981–82
Released:
September 1982
Chart peaks:
3 (UK) None (US)
Personnel:
Kate Bush (Fairlight, v, k, p); Jimmy Bain (b); Ian Bairnson (g); Brian Bath (g); Rolf Harris (didgeridoo); Paddy Bush (hm, mandolin, stick); Geoffrey Downs (t); Percy Edwards (sound effects, v); Stuart Elliott (d); Dave Gilmour, Gordon Farrell, Paul Hardiman, Gary Hurst (v); Preston Heyman (d, stick); Sean Keane (vn) Dave Lawson (syn), Donal Lunny (bouzouki), Alan Murphy (g), Liam O'Flynn (whistle, uillean pipes), Del Palmer (b, v), Esmail Sheikh (d), Danny Thompson (b), Richard Thornton (choir), Eberhard Weber (b)
Track listing:
Sat In Your Lap; There Goes A Tenner; Pull Out The Pin; Suspended In Gaffa; Leave It Open; The Dreaming; Night Of The Swallow; All The Love; Houdini; Get Out Of My House
Running time:
42.25
Current CD
CDP7463612
Further listening:
Never Forever (1980); Hounds Of Love (1985)
Further reading:
www.gaffa.org
Like this?
Try . . . p.31

The Psychedelic Furs

Forever Now

After critical panning of their second album, British post-punk outfit make a do-or-die plunge Stateside.

It was the dreaded "difficult third album" for The Psychedelic Furs. Having enjoyed across-the-board critical acclaim and Top 20 success in Britain with their decidedly edgy, agreeably gloomy debut in 1980, the band found the follow-up just one year later fell on hostile reviewers' ears and was greeted by a resoundingly indifferent public. Recognising that US college radio wielded serious muscle in terms of introducing leftfield music to a youthful, pre-MTV, record-hungry market, Butler and band decided to try and make a go of it in the States. Trimmed to a four-piece after the sackings of original members Roger Morris (guitarist) and saxophonist/ keyboardist Duncan Kilburn, the Furs set about moving towards a tougher, more textured sound, with greater emphasis on song structure.

"*Forever Now* was really charting new territory for us," says guitarist John Ashton. "We knew a lot of what we were doing was taking a chance, but we didn't have too much to lose. We thought, if we fail with this one, so what?" The choice of Todd Rundgren as producer – over Steve Lillywhite, who had produced the first two LPs – was a deliberate attempt to give the band an aesthetic reboot. His well-known fondness for British music was a good counter to the Furs' early love of American bands – most notably Iggy and The Stooges, MC5 and the Velvet Underground – and he had already expressed an interest in the Furs' work.

The album was recorded not in the famous Utopia Studios proper, but in a small room on Rundgren's property in Mink Hollow Road in Lake Hill in around six weeks. Remembers Ashton: "On this album, we wanted to strip the sound back, to get away from trying to make every single thing sound louder than everything else. *Forever Now* is the sound of a band finding another direction and I'd be telling a huge untruth if I said we weren't interested in hit singles – we were. That's what bands are supposed to do."

The Furs bagged an American hit, Love My Way in February 1983 but it was a revised version of Pretty In Pink (ironically, from the lambasted second album), the song which inspired a movie, which was to really make their name, three years later. *Forever Now* delivered a clutch of darkly addictive, hook-laden yet existentially uneasy pop songs (President Gas, Love My Way, Forever Now), along with the brooding, psychedelic nod to The Beatles that is the cello-decked Sleep Comes Down. Although by no means the most successful, it remains the most cohesive, assured and definitively Furs-like of their albums.

Record label:
CBS
Produced
by Todd Rundgren
Recorded
at Utopia Sound Studios, Bearsville, NY, April/May 1982
Release Date:
September 1982
Chart peaks:
20 (UK) 61 (US)
Personnel:
Richard Butler (v), John Ashton (g), Tim Butler (b), Vince Ely (d, pc), Gary Windo, Donn Adams (horns), Ann Sheldon (cello), Mark Volman, Howard Kaylan (bv), Todd Rundgren (k, s, e), Chris Andersen (e)
Track listing:
President Gas (S/US); Love My Way (S); Run And Run; Merry-Go-Round; Sleep Comes Down; Forever Now; Danger (S); You & I; Goodbye; No Easy Street
Running time:
40: 57
Current CD:
CB38261
Further listening:
The Psychedelic Furs (1980); Love Spit Love, (1994) Love Spit Love formed by Butler after the demise of the Furs
Further reading:
www.sonymusic.com/artists/ ThePsychedelic Furs
Like this?
Try . . . p.159

The Dream Syndicate

The Days Of Wine And Roses

A fanfare from California's Paisley Underground, a guitar-rock anomaly in synth-dominated times.

The Dream Syndicate invented the Californian Paisley Underground scene, which brought chiming guitars and a '60s aesthetic back into fashion in the early 1980s. Following the success of a self-released EP, the band were signed by punk label Ruby/Slash for the recording of their watershed guitar-soaked, neo-psychedelic LP. Syndicate leader Steve Wynn remembers that recording was off to a shaky start.

"We got to the studio at around 7pm for a graveyard session, and no one was there to meet us. We just sat around by the front door with our instruments in the car and took turns going to Kentucky Fried Chicken for greasy bits of bird." The entire album was knocked out from midnight till 5am. "We weren't nervous or intimidated – we were pretty carefree about what we did."

Wynn set about melding Karl Precoda's free-associative guitar assaults with his own dreamy drone-poems. "We always figured we would just push everything to an extreme, have fun, make noise and not worry about the end result," he says. But producer Chris D. had other ideas for the studio novices. "I encouraged Chris to push Karl's guitar and my harmonica on the outro of Until Lately into the extreme red, driving it to the point of white noise," says Wynn. "He finally threw up his hands and said, 'If you want your record to sound terrible you can do what you want, but it's a bad idea.' I'm glad that we held our ground and that saner minds didn't prevail."

Mercifully, level heads were also absent when it came to the construction of the unrelenting title cut, which distils the band's unwieldy essence into one tight seven-minute jam – an unthinkable act in itself in 1982. It's sloppy, but its primitive nature is what has elevated the album to legendary status in some quarters, particularly among fellow musicians: Kurt Cobain and The Black Crowes' Chris Robinson both claiming inspiration from it.

Record label:
Rough Trade
Produced
by Chris D.
Recorded
at Quad Teck Studio, Los Angeles; September 1982.
Release date:
October 1982
Chart peaks:
None (UK) None (US)
Personnel:
Steve Wynn (g,v); Karl Precoda (g); Kendra Smith (b, v); Dennis Duck (d); Pat Burnette (e)
Track listing:
Tell Me When It's Over (S); Definitely Clean; That's What You Always Say; Then She Remembers; Halloween; When You Smile; Until Lately; Too Little, Too Late; The Days Of Wine And Roses
Running time:
41.32
Current CD:
23844-2
Further listening:
The Day Before Wine And Roses, Live At KPFK (1995); Steve Wynn solo album, Kerosene Man (1990)
Further reading:
www.stevewynn.net
Like this?
Try . . . p.572

Donald Fagen
The Nightfly

Steely Dan frontman fashions affectionate tribute to his "faux-luxe" jazz-fan adolescence.

Though its sleek jazz-pop lines were not too far-removed from later Steely Dan albums like *Aja* and *Gaucho*, the subject matter of Donald Fagen's debut album marked a striking departure from his earlier work. Originally intended to be titled *Talk Radio*, it eschewed Steely Dan's usual sardonic distance in favour of autobiographical closeness, offering a sentimental view of his own childhood development. In unprecedentedly autobiographical songs like IGY (International Geophysical Year) and New Frontier he depicted the hopes and dreams of a late-'50s adolescence lived in the shadow of the Cold War, while the title track evoked the sense of cultural liberation provided by distant R&B and jazz DJs for teenagers stranded in soulless suburban developments hundreds of miles away.

The Nightfly was recorded with the usual painstaking attention to detail that had marked the later Steely Dan albums, using the same top session players. But where Dan had always striven to record the basic grooves in real time, this time Fagen, enamoured of the new 32-track digital recorder that engineer Roger Nichols had chosen to record on, opted to overdub each part separately. This introduced a whole new range of difficulties into the recording process. Apart from the usual teething problems associated with new technology, the musicians found they were being asked to accomplish the virtually impossible: pianist Michael Omartian objected strongly when asked to set the groove of the title track on his own, with nothing to play against but a soulless click-track; even worse was to come when Fagen demanded subtle timing differences between the left- and right-hand piano parts on a cover of Lieber and Stoller's Ruby Baby – eventually, the parts were recorded simultaneously by Omartian and Greg Phillinganes sitting together at the same keyboard.

The album was an immediate critical success upon its release, nominated for seven Grammy Awards including Album Of The Year. But Fagen himself regretted making it almost immediately, slipping into a bad case of writer's block which ensured there would be no follow-up album for more than a decade.

"I wanted to do an autobiographical album, and I really put everything I knew into the *Nightfly* album," he recalled later. "And after that I really wasn't inspired to do anything. I fell into a bit of a depression for a while. I think, that like a lot of artists, especially in the music business, I was young and successful, and I was basically still an adolescent. I started to address some of these things with *The Nightfly*, and I got really scared after it was done; I felt I'd exposed myself in a way that I wasn't used to doing, and I kind of retreated psychologically from that."

Record label:
Warners
Produced
by Gary Katz.
Recorded
at Soundworks Digital Audio/Video Recording Studios, New York; Village Recorders, Los Angeles.
Release date:
October 1982
Chart peaks:
44 (UK) 11 (US)
Personnel:
Donald Fagen (v, k, synth blues harp, a); Greg Phillinganes (k); Michael Omartian (k); Rob Mounsey (syn); Hugh McCracken (g); Larry Carlton (g); Dean Parks (g); Rick Derringer (g); Steve Khan (g); James Gadson (d); Jeff Porcaro (d); Ed Green (d); Steve Jordan (d); Anthony Jackson (b); Chuck Rainey (b); Marcus Miller (b); Abraham Laboriel (b); Will Lee (b); Randy Brecker (t, flugelhorn); Dave Tofani (s); Michael Brecker (s); Ronnie Cuber (s); Dave Bargeron (tb, euphonium); Valerie Simpson (bv); Zack Sanders (bv); Frank Floyd (bv); Gordon Grody (bv); Daniel Lazarus (bv); Leslie Miller (bv); Starz Vanderlocket (pc); Roger Nichols (e, pc)
Track listing:
I.G.Y. (S); Green Flower Street; Ruby Baby (S); Maxine; New Frontier (S); The Nightfly; The Goodbye Look; Walk Between Raindrops
Running time:
38.53
Current CD:
7599236962
Further listening:
Aja and Gaucho
Further reading:
www.steelydan.com
Like this?
Try . . . p.175

Michael Jackson

Thriller

A motherlode of hit singles – seven out of nine tracks. One of the biggest albums in pop history.

Off The Wall had sold 12 million copies worldwide and was on the UK charts for 173 weeks spawning five hit singles (four in the US). In the three subsequent years Jackson became a background voice for hire as he studied other acts' production and studio performance techniques. Eventually, with the same team in place and the majority of the writing from the same sources (four from Jackson; three from Rod Temperton, including the title track), recording began.

Reflecting the feeding frenzy about his private life in the press, a couple of the tracks (notably Billie Jean and opening track Wanna Be Startin' Somethin') simmered with the hurt, anger and paranoia that would set the agenda for the rest of his century's life and work.

Whereas *Off The Wall* was recorded at, for the late '70s, considerable speed with no loss of due care and attention to detail, *Thriller* was meticulous in planning and execution, to the point of obsessiveness.

Soul and R&B were downgraded and the emphasis shifted to dance pop and rock. Guitarist Eddie Van Halen was brought in to add edge to Beat It and Temperton's title track became a marvellous, comic rock-soul horror vignette with veteran thesp Vincent Price Hammering it up; the innovative, expensive videos from these tracks shattered MTV's unspoken racial barrier.

A duet with Paul McCartney (The Girl Is Mine) maintained a relationship started with *Off The Wall*'s Girlfriend. Recalling the sessions, the musicians spoke of painstaking preparations – drummer Ndugu Chancler set up in a room by himself as he did eight or nine takes of Billie Jean in three hours; Louis Johnson bringing four of his collection of basses to the party before settling on the Yamaha. To end on more stats, because that is what the exhaustively marketed album represented in the end: in the seven months to June 1983, a time when the record industry was in recession, *Thriller* sold a million copies a month. In addition to 1983's Album Of The Year, *Thriller* won eight other Grammys. It was just what the '80s needed to hear, a record that equated extravagance with success.

Record label:
Epic
Produced
by Quincy Jones.
Recorded
at Westlake Audio and Ocean Way Studios, Los Angeles.
Released:
December 1982
Chart peaks:
1 (UK) 1 (US)
Personnel:
Michael Jackson (v, bathroom stomp board, drum case beater); Greg Phillinganes (Rhodes, k, syn); Bill Wolfer (syn, k, programming); Steve Porcaro (syn, programming); Michael Boddicker (syn, emulator, vocoder); David Paich, David Foster, Rod Temperton, Brian Banks (syn); David Paich (syn, p); Tom Bahler (Synclavier); Brian Banks, Anthony Marinelli (programming); Greg Smith (Synergy, syn); David Williams, Dean Parks, Steve Lukather, Eddie Van Halen, Paul Jackson (g); Louis Johnson, Steve Lukather (b); Jeff Porcaro, Ndugu Chancler (d); Paulinho da Costa (pc); Jerry Hey, Gary Grant (t, flugelhorn); Larry Williams (s, flute)
Track listing:
Wanna Be Startin' Somethin' (S); Baby Be Mine; The Girl Is Mine (S); Thriller (S); Beat It (S); Billie Jean (S); Human Nature (S); P.Y.T. (Pretty Young Thing) (S); The Lady In My Life
Running time:
42.15
Current CD:
MILLEN4
Further listening:
Off The Wall (1979)
Further reading:
Michael Jackson: The Magic and the Madness (J Randy Taraborelli, 1992)
Like this?
Try . . . p.647

U2

War

U2's coming-of-age album, epic and compelling.

When U2 began writing their third album *War*, a pervading sense of desperation hung over them.

"The first two albums had gone well," says guitarist The Edge, "but they'd hardly taken the world by storm. We knew our future was hanging in the balance."

Alone in a seaside cottage in Howth, North Dublin, the guitarist began to stockpile ideas on a primitive Tascam 4-track while his bandmates took a holiday. He knew time was precious. Weighed down by the size of the quartet's financial debt to Island Records and suffering post-tour fatigue, The Edge briefly considered quitting the band. But gradually the bones of Sunday Bloody Sunday and Seconds appeared – and, thanks to an Adam Clayton bassline written on the road, New Year's Day was soon shaping up nicely too.

Lyrically, *War* found U2 politically charged and pre-irony, Bono's passionate beliefs colouring many of the songs. Drowning Man was full of Old Testament imagery, 40 was Psalm 40, and Sunday Bloody Sunday – famously misconstrued as a rebel song by some Irish Americans – urged both Republicans and Nationalists "to claim the victory Jesus won". No surprise, then, that booze and chemical stimulants weren't part of the recording equation – as Kid Creole's Coconuts discovered when they dropped by to sing on Surrender.

Another guest was future Waterboy Steve Wickham, invited to play on Drowning Man after a chance meeting with The Edge at a bus stop. Steve Lillywhite's production on the track is impressionistic, the chiming acoustic guitars and Wickham's fiddle awash with reverb. Elsewhere, on Like A Song and Two Hearts Beat As One the producer's raw, almost skifflish approach feeds on U2's post-punk energy.

Reportedly, '40' – a track which would close many U2 live shows on subsequent tours – was almost omitted from the final track-listing. "Steve said, 'This is a great tune, but it's not going to work without some drastic edits,'" says The Edge. Two whole sections were ditched at the 11th hour and, impressed by the results, Bono improvised his vocal on the spot.

The album topped the UK charts and peaked at Number 12 in the US. Stadium gigs beckoned, and a more generous budget from Island for 1984's *The Unforgettable Fire* yielded a far more sculpted sound.

Record label:
Island
Produced
by Steve Lillywhite and Bill Whelan.
Recorded
at Windmill Lane, Dublin; October–December 1982.
Released:
February 1983
Chart peaks:
1 (UK) 12 (US)
Personnel:
Bono (v, g); The Edge (g, p, ls, v); Adam Clayton (b); Larry Mullen Jr (d); Steve Wickham (vn); Kenny Fradley (tp); Cheryl Poirier, Adriana Kaegi, Taryn Hagey, Jessica Felton (bv); Paul Thomas (e)
Track listing:
Sunday Bloody Sunday; Seconds; New Year's Day (S); Like A Song?; Drowning Man; The Refugee; Two Hearts Beat As One (S); Red Light; Surrender; '40'
Running time:
42.10
Current CD:
IMCD 141
Further listening:
October (1981)
Further reading:
Unforgettable Fire: The Story Of U2 (Eamon Dunphy, 1988); www.atu2.com
Like this?
Try . . . p.413

Aztec Camera

High Land, Hard Rain

Aztec Camera's debut album, a romantic counterpoint to the post-punk scene.

At the age of 16, Roddy Frame announced to his English teacher he was quitting school to pursue a career as a pop star. Having learnt his chops via jazz gigs with his father in the working men's clubs of East Kilbride, near Glasgow, he'd already secured a record deal with pioneering Scottish indie label Postcard.

Label boss Alan Horne had immediately recognised the quality of Roddy's poetic ruminations on love and life, set to complex folk-jazz-pop arrangements: Bert Jansch, Neil Young and Wes Montgomery were all influences. Moving down to London after the success of singles Just Like Gold and Mattress Of Wire, Frame signed to Rough Trade and decamped to Eastbourne to record an album.

"Scritti Politti [fellow Rough Trade artists] were a big influence on me at the time," recalls Frame. "I'd hooked up with John Brand and Bernie Clarke, and they seemed dead right to me. John knew a lot about Neil Young and liked to smoke a joint. We went down and recorded the album at International Christian Communications in Eastbourne at night. We went out to the beach in the morning: it was very exciting, very intense and we stayed there for about a month. Bernie Clarke did a lot of the arrangements – there were so many complicated details."

After kicking off the flamenco-inflected Oblivious, with the enchanting lick "They call us lonely when we're really just alone", *High Land, Hard Rain* journeys through Roddy's fragile teenage psyche, from the elegiac We Could Send Letters to the rousing Walk Out To Winter, thick with melodious semi-acoustic chording and poetic observations about the bleak '80s scene. Even at its most melancholic, a spirit of optimism and romance prevails, as testified by the yearning strains of The Bugle Sounds Again ("Grab that Gretsch before the truth hits town!") and the closing off-the-cuff rag Going Down The Dip, a reference to Roddy's East Kilbride local, The Diplomat.

Listening today, the only flaws relate to the production: the flanged drums and the occasionally over-reverbed confluence of instruments – Hammond, acoustic, first-take vocals. But overall this remains a wonderful insight into a flourishing talent.

Record label:
Warner Brothers
Produced
by John Brand and Bernie Clarke.
Recorded
at International Christian Communications, Eastbourne; spring 1983.
Released:
May 1983
Chart peaks:
22 (UK) 129 (US)
Personnel:
Roddy Frame (v, g, hm); Campbell Owens (b); Bernie Clarke (o, p); Dave Ruffy (d, pc); John Brand (e)
Track listing:
Oblivious (S); The Boy Wonders; Walk Out To Winter (S); The Bugle Sounds Again; We Could Send Letters; Pillar To Post (S); Release; Lost Outside The Tunnel; Back On Board; Down The Dip
Running time:
38.40
Current CD:
4509-92849-2 adds: Haywire; Orchid Girl; Queen's Tattoos
Further listening:
Mark Knopfler-produced follow-up Knife (1984) was a disappointment, but the straight-ahead white soul pop of Love (1987) – which gave Frame his biggest hit singles – and the rockier Stray (1990) proved him an enduring tunesmith. Later albums returned to a more stripped-down approach.
Further reading:
Record Collector 244; Blue Suede Brogans: Scenes From The Secret Life Of Scottish Rock Music (Jim Wilke, 1992)
Like this?
Try . . . p.553

Billy Bragg

Life's A Riot With Spy Vs Spy

Cheaply made, budget-priced, half-a-debut launches a punk-folk hero.

"If you look at what else was in the charts in 1982–83 you can see why *Life's A Riot* proved a success," says Billy Bragg, "all that hyped-up New Romantic stuff – then this comes out and it is a true solo effort. It appealed to both the singer-songwriter crowd and the punks who couldn't relate to New Romanticism but loved the guitar sound and the minimalism."

Bragg, broke in south London, had almost despaired of ever making an album after various false starts with record companies. A homemade demo received a good notice in Melody Maker and led to a publisher offering further recordings providing they were just Billy and his guitar. He recorded solidly for three days ("There are about 15 different versions of A New England alone," says Bragg), directly onto quarter-inch tape with just in-house producer/engineer Oliver Hitch pressing the buttons and telling Billy when to start.

Masquerading as a TV repairman, Bragg then blagged his way into Charisma Records and met A&R man Peter Jenner (Pink Floyd's first manager) who liked the tapes and promised to issue them as a mini-album as there was a bit of money left over in his budget. He pressed 5,000 and got the brilliant Barney Bubbles to design the cover. "The record industry has to come to terms with the colossal scale of unemployment, especially for young people," Jenner said at the time. "Our philosophy is that it's the idea, the song, the personality, the talent that matters, not the technology, the hype or the styling. Billy's album in both price and quality is a foretaste of lots more to come."

Songs as potently bare as To Have And Have Not and The Man In The Iron Mask gave plenty of notice that here was a singer-songwriter with the charge of The Clash and the social focus of Woody Guthrie. Plugger Jeff Chegwin heard Radio 1 DJ John Peel say on air he'd do anything for a mushroom biryani. He and Bragg went straight round to the nearest curry house and drove to Radio One with Peel's dinner, asking only that he listen to *Life's A Riot* in return. It worked. The same night Peel thanked Bragg for the vegetable curry and played The Milkman Of Human Kindness. He was on his way. A Peel session followed, swiftly pursued by a string of ecstatic reviews and Bragg's own persuasively full-on live performances up and down the country did the rest. Reissued by Go-Discs, it quickly sold 110,000 copies and entered the charts.

Record label:
Utility
Produced
by Oliver Hitch.
Recorded
at Park Street Studio, London; February 1–3, 1983.
Released:
May 1983
Chart peaks:
30 (UK) None (US)
Personnel:
Billy Bragg (v, g); Oliver Hitch (e)
Track listing:
The Milkman Of Human Kindness; To Have And Have Not; Richard; A New England; The Man In The Iron Mask; The Busy Girl Buys Beauty; Lovers Town Revisited
Running time:
15.10
Current CD:
Cooking Vinyl COOKCD 060 (Back To Basics) compiles all of Riot with Brewing Up With Billy Bragg (1984) and the Between The Wars EP (1985).
Further listening:
Between The Wars EP (1985), The Internationale (1990). There's a useful best-of accompanying his album William Bloke (1996). Also outstanding is collaboration with Wilco, setting newly-discovered Woody Guthrie lyrics to music on Mermaid Avenue (1998).
Further reading:
Still Suitable For Miners: Billy Bragg, The Official Biography (Andrew Collins, 1998)
Like this?
Try . . . p.268

King Sunny Ade

Synchro System

The first African pop album to be recorded in London.

When Ade was signed to Chris Blackwell's Island label in 1982, there was a definite impetus to bring some overview of African pop to a western audience suddenly hungry for new flavours in an increasingly international dance and club scene. But was Ade a pop musician, his band a team of faithful stalwarts – or was he an overlord of dance music in the manner of Hamilton Bohannon, submerging his own personality within the groove? It was hard to tell, and that confusion was one reason why Ade and his music remained mostly within a marginalised following.

His first set for Island, *Juju Music*, was an anthemic introduction to his Nigerian sound, less about the helium-toned guitars which dominated much other African pop, and more about the choral harmonies of his many singers and the jittery polyrhythms of the talking drummers and percussionists. But the subsequent set, *Synchro System*, recorded in London under the stewardship of Martin Meissonier, was the most determined bid to shape Sunny's groove and make it amenable to foreign ears. Meissonier carefully distinguished each element in the band in his mixes, so the voices sailed over the simmering percussion below and the guitars twanged out the little trademark rifts which set each composition apart. Ade and Meissonier himself then thickened the broth with just enough keyboard colour to fill out the ensembles.

It remains an abstract, a frozen picture of what The African Beats were like rather than a celebration of their art. There could be no substitute for seeing this glorious group, but even on record the music still sounds intensely vivid. Ade's own curiously small voice, a little whispery instrument in the mix, is as singular a part of *Synchro System* as the percussive chatter of the drums, or the cheery call-and-response of the other vocalists. Island pursued their ambitions with Ade for one further record, the even groovier *Aura*, but then they let him go.

Record label:
Island/Mango
Produced
by Martin Meissonier.
Recorded
at Music Works, London.
Released:
July1983
Chart peaks:
93 (UK) None (US)
Personnel:
King Sunny Ade (g, v); Segun Mori, John Akpan, Bob Ohiri, Elder Osei (g); Demola Adepoju (steel g); Jonah Bonsu (k); Felili Lawal (b); Fatioke Abiodun (agogo); Gani Alashe (shekere); Michael Babatola (maracas); Alhaji Timmy Olaitan, Rasaki Aladokun (talking drums); Mioses Akanbi (d); Shina Abiodun (congas); Femi Owomoyela, Jacob Ajakaye, Matthew Olojede, Niyi Falaye, Tunde Demiola (v)
Track listing:
Synchro Feelings- Ilako; Mo Ti Mo; Penkele; Maajo; Synchro System; E Saiye Re; Tolongo; E Wele; Synchro Reprise
Running time:
38.56
Current CD:
1625397372
Further listening:
Juju Music (1982); Aura (1984)
Further reading:
The Rough Guide To World Music (1994)
Like this?
Try . . . p.60

R.E.M.

Murmur

Pivotal work of the '80s American rock renaissance, finding perfection in understatement.

Following gruelling but ultimately unsuccessful demo sessions with English pop producer Stephen Hague (Pet Shop Boys, Human League, New Order), which had seen R.E.M. do over 40 takes of Catapult, only to have Hague later overdub synthesizers without their knowledge, the group reassembled with Mitch Easter (who had produced their *Chronic Town* EP) and Don Dixon to make their debut album. The more easy-going mood of the sessions at Reflection Studios enabled the group to record most of the songs in one or two takes.

In contrast to the band's raucous live performances, many of the recorded versions were built around acoustic guitars, as REM discovered the breakthrough folk-rock style that would revolutionise American rock in the '80s. The track Laughing, for instance, featured Buck, Mills, Easter and Dixon strumming together, double-tracked to produce a wall of eight acoustic guitars. Much of the album's indefinable magic comes from the air of mystery that surrounds it, from the cover photograph of kudzu, a vine common to the American south, to the unusually murky, "pillowy" mix and Michael Stipe's unnaturally quiet vocals, which bear out the album's title. In some cases, this was because the lyrics were developed from sounds rather than meanings.

"I purposely did not want any of the lyrics understood," said Stipe of Radio Free Europe. "The main reason for that was that I hadn't written any of the words yet, so I just kind of blabbered over the whole single."

On 9-9, by contrast, it was a semantic strategy. "We deliberately recorded it so you would never be able to decipher any of the words except the very last phrase, which is 'conversation fear', which is what the song is about," explained Stipe. Despite the occasional inaudibility, it was still clear which kind of matters were exercising Stipe's muse: apathy and commitment (Talk About The Passion), humiliation and contempt (Laughing), cultural imperialism (Radio Free Europe) and moral proscription (Moral Kiosk).

Lighter and janglier than later R.E.M. albums, its blend of Byrdsome guitar arpeggios, contrapuntal vocal harmonies and flexible rhythms proved hugely influential over the subsequent decade. It was an immediate critical success on its release in 1983, going on to be voted Album Of The Year in Rolling Stone and placing second in the Village Voice's prestigious end-of-year critics' poll. It says much for its character that despite the band's subsequent globe-girdling fame, *Murmur* has retained all of its mystery and magic.

Record label:
IRS
Produced
by Mitch Easter and Don Dixon.
Recorded
at Reflection Studio, Charlotte, North Carolina; January 1983.
Release date:
August 1983
Chart peaks:
None (UK) 36 (US)
Personnel:
Michael Stipe (v); Peter Buck (g, k); Mike Mills (b, k, bv); Bill Berry (d, bv); Don Dixon, Mitch Easter (e)
Track listing:
Radio Free Europe (S); Pilgrimage; Laughing; Talk About The Passion (S); Moral Kiosk; Perfect Circle; Catapult; Sitting Still; 9-9; Shaking Through; We Walk; West Of The Fields
Running time:
44.11
Current CD:
CDMID129
Further listening:
Virtually all of R.E.M.'s albums are required listening for any aware listener. The follow-up Reckoning (1984) was a further refinement of the Murmur sound; the Joe Boyd-produced Fables Of The Reconstruction (1985) initiated the '80s folk-rock revival; Life's Rich Pageant (1986) and Green (1988) adopted a harder, more political tone
Further reading:
The Story Of REM (Tony Fletcher, 1993); REM Inside Out: The Stories Behind Every Song (Craig Rosen, 1997)
Like this?
Try . . . p.237

Tom Waits

Swordfishtrombones

Barfly troubadour Waits takes the weird way out of a cul-de-sac.

In the '70s, Tom Waits' vivid song world of plump-hearted street loners and five-and-dime losers had earned him critical acclaim and a healthy cult status, but there was a sense that he'd taken the Bones Howe-produced, gruffly sentimental, seedy lounge approach as far as it would go.

"I was getting lazy," Waits admitted. "I used to hear everything with a tenor saxophone, I had a very particular musical wardrobe." Halfway through scoring Francis Ford Coppola's movie One From The Heart in 1980 as a "lounge operetta about two years too late" he got in "a humbug" and left to write *Heartattack And Vine* before returning to complete the movie score.

It was a time of upheaval for Waits: he had split with girlfriend Rickie Lee Jones and moved to New York, met and married Kathleen Brennan and was keen to break the album-tour cycle of his existence. He credits his new wife with not only saving his life – there were reports that the line between himself and the drunken, broken characters in his songs was getting worryingly thin – but also with giving him the confidence to break with his old management and production team. "She knew that I was interested in a lot of diverse musical styles that I'd never explored before on my own records," Waits said. "She started playing a lot of records for me, the seminal idea for that record really came from Kathleen." That record was *Swordfishtrombones*, vocally and lyrically recognisably Waits, but musically amounting to a re-invention. Weill-esque stomps, semi-abstract instrumental vignettes, malformed minor blues all set in an extraordinary soundworld of harmonium and sledgehammers, organ and metal aunglongs, twisted electric guitar and bell plates, trombone and glass harmonica; "a kind of a demented little parade band" or "mutant dwarf orchestra" as Waits variously had it.

The music was influenced by Harry Partch – a musician inspired by the American hobo existence and maverick instrument inventor of the '30s and '40s – and assisted by Partch's gramolodium player Francis Thumm, but Waits insists on back-crediting his wife as chief inspiration. "She really co-produced that record with me, though she didn't get the credit." The disturbing, surprisingly spacious music ("I liked the holes in it as much as I liked what was in them") was tantamount, as MOJO's Barney Hoskyns pointed out, to "throwing a gigantic spanner in the works". It was too much for his record company, Asylum, who passed on it, leaving Waits free to sign with Island and exploit his new-found inspiration and sometimes official creative partnership for another seven, increasingly ambitious albums.

Record label:
Island
Produced
by Tom Waits.
Recorded
at Sunset Sound, Los Angeles; July–August 1982.
Released:
September 1983
Chart peaks:
62 (UK) None (US)
Personnel:
T Waits (syn, fiddle, g, harmonium, o, v); C Gayle (v); V Feldman (pc); S Manne (d); B Reichenbach, D Hyde (tb); P Jolly (p, accordion); J Lowe, L Morgan (wind); L Thompson (hm); R Barron (k); E Bikales (o); L Taylor (b); B Alcivar (p); R Aldcroft (tb, horn, s); D Budimir (g); L Bunker (d); A Clark (bagpipes); G Cohen (b, acoustic b); T Edwards (s); C Findley (t); R Gibbs (hm); C Guitarlos (g); S Hodges (hm, d); R Hyde (tb); J Sheldon (t); G LaVant(horn);J Porcaro (pc); E Richards (vibraphone); J Romano (tb, t); A Stewart (bagpipes); F Tackett (banjo, g); BJ Thomassie (d)
Track listing:
Underground; Shore Leave; Dave The Butcher; Johnsburg, Illinios; 16 Shells From A Thirty-Ought-Six, Town With No Cheer; In The Neighbourhood (S); Just Another Sucker On The Vine; Frank's Wild Years; Swordfishtrombone; Down, Down, Down; Soldier's Things; Gin Soaked Boy; Trouble's Braids; Rainbirds
Running time:
40.31
Current CD:
IMCD 48
Further listening:
Rain Dogs (1985)
Further reading:
www.officialtomwaits.com
Like this?
Try . . . p.244

Ruben Blades

Buscando America

The first crossover salsa album, and a calling card for a major Hispanic star.

By 1982 Ruben Blades had grown weary of prowling New Yorica's salsa ghetto. Other *salseros* might dance more slickly or dress more flamboyantly, but none was smarter than the Panamanian singer, a trained lawyer whose ambition was to become President of Panama.

Over the last five years, Blades' fruitful partnership with trombonist and producer Willie Colon had given him massive success; the pair's 1978 album *Siembra* (Seed) was a *cause célèbre*, Blades' song Pedro Navaja an anthem for Hispanic emigrants. Part of Blades' message was that North and South Americas were a continuum – "We are all Americans," he declared – yet his music remained little known outside of the *barrios.*

After falling out with Fania Records, and with Colon, Blades decided what he needed was a cross-over album. The result was *Buscando America* (Discovering America), an ambitious attempt to cross-pollinate salsa for a wider audience.

The blast of doo wop that opens the album served notice that this was no ordinary salsa record. Instead of the rich brass arrangements provided by Colon there were, gasp, synthesizers, while elsewhere Blades switched between singing and rap. The sleeve, meanwhile, carried the lyrics in both Spanish and English. Alongside typically Blades social cameos like Decisiones was El Padre Antonio, a song about the murdered El Salvadorean priest Oscar Romero, and Desapariciones, which mourns the "disappeared" of Latin America's dictatorships.

Buscando America worked for Blades in several ways. For the mainstream media an opinionated Latin singer able to articulate the Hispanic viewpoint made a good story. *Buscando America* also introduced Blades to a white music audience and even extended his appeal among Latin listeners for whom much salsa was vulgar and disreputable.

"Instead of just looking at the street corner for my subjects, I looked down the neighbouring street, then the city, then the world," he explained. Liike Blades' previous work, the record enlarged Latin music's own conception of what it was and could become, setting a precedent that artists like Gloria Estefan would later follow. The synths sound creaky today, otherwise *Buscando* still delivers.

Record label:
Elektra
Produced
by David Rodriguez and Ruben Blades.
Recorded
at Eurosound Studios, New York; May–August, 1983.
Released:
October 1983
Chart peaks:
None (UK) None (US)
Personnel:
Ruben Blades (v, g, maraccas); Mike Vinas (g); Oscar Hernandez (p); Eddie Montalvo (tumbadoros, pc, bv); Louie Rivera (pc); Ralph Irizarry (timbales, pc); Ray Adams (d)
Track listing:
Decisiones; GDBD; Desapariciones; Todos Vuelven; Caminos Verdes; Padre Antonio Y El Moniguillo; Buscando America
Running time:
39.01
Current CD:
EA60352
Further listening:
1988's English language album Nothing But The Truth featured collaborations with Lou Reed and Elvis Costello, while 1996's La Rosa de Los Vientos [The Rose of the Winds] bagged a Grammy.
Further reading:
Salsa (Sue Steward, 1999)
Like this?
Try . . . p.215

Bruce Springsteen

Born In The USA

Springsteen mingles big heart and big ideas and goes global.

Quite consciously still growing up in his early thirties, after *The River* (1980) Springsteen took time out to digest diverse issues such as the onrush of wealth and fame, his lack of a long-term girlfriend, and his encounters with political campaigners including the Vietnam Veterans Of America. Then, on January 3, 1982, at his house in Holmdel, New Jersey, on an old reel-to-reel he suddenly recorded more than a dozen songs. He thought it was a demo. But when he and The E Street Band reconvened in May at The Power Station these ferocious vignettes resisted every arrangement they came up with. Springsteen was bemused – until he decided the demo *was* an album. The solo, grim, hit-free *Nebraska* came out that September and sold sparsely, but enhanced Springsteen's reputation as an artist of integrity.

However, back in May, something seismic did happen. One day, he stood alone in the studio and began to doodle a riff around a song which had sounded feeble on the Holmdel "demo". Just then the band arrived and, forthwith, slammed out one of the iconic tracks of the decade, Born In The USA. "I said, Roy, get this riff," Springsteen recalled. "He just pulled out that sound on the synthesizer (the opening fanfare). We played it two times and our second take is the record." Over the next three weeks they recorded five more songs.

Then, with Springsteen involved in *Nebraska* and his closest friend Van Zandt leaving to go solo, the band album got sticky again. Even though Springsteen wrote 70 songs start to finish, finding the right ones was the problem. They squeezed out My Hometown in February 1983, Bobby Jean and No Surrender the following autumn – along with Cover Me, originally written for disco queen Donna Summer in spring 1982 – and Springsteen finally came up with Dancing In The Dark in March 1984 ("It was just like my heart spoke straight through my mouth without even having to pass through my brain"). The peculiarly Springsteenian dark pop smash hit completed *Born In The USA*'s enormous emotional span, from the title track's agonised roar of anger about the Vietnam aftermath to the priapic bedroom intensity of I'm On Fire, the hard-rocking blues of I'm Going Down and the quiet father-and-son intimacy of My Hometown.

But, as an event, everything about it was grand-scale. It took Springsteen to the world. He was in his pomp, the greatest blue-collar rock star ever. Also, inevitably, heading for a fall.

Record label:
CBS
Produced
by Bruce Springsteen, Jon Landau, Chuck Plotkin and Steve Van Zandt
Recorded
at The Power Station and The Hit Factory, New York; May 1982; February, August and October–November 1973; March 1974.
Released:
June 1984
Chart peaks:
1 (UK) 1 (US)
Personnel:
Bruce Springsteen (v, g); Roy Bittan (p, syn); Clarence Clemons (s); Danny Federici (k); Garry Tallent (b; Steve Van Zandt (g); Max Weinberg (d); Toby Scott (e)
Track listing:
Born In The USA (S/US); Cover Me (S); Darlington County; Working On The Highway; Downbound Train; I'm On Fire (S); No Surrender; Bobby Jean; I'm Goin' Down; Glory Days (S); Dancing In The Dark (S); My Hometown (S)
Running time:
46:19
Current CD:
Columbia CD86304
Further listening:
Nebraska (1982), Born In The USA's mirror image, and the Tracks (1998), box set of outtakes because it's very good and sets his most commercial album in a career context. Darkness On The Edge Of Town (1978) and Tunnel Of Love (1987)
Further reading:
MOJO 17, 62; Glory Days: Bruce Springsteen In The 1980s (Dave Marsh, 1987); www.backstreets.com (US)
Like this?
Try . . . p.226

The Specials

In The Studio

"Difficult" third album helped to liberate a political freedom fighter and spelled the end of 2-Tone.

"I had to write the third Specials album without The Specials. Not an easy thing to do," recalls Jerry Dammers, founder member and chief songwriter. One week The Specials were top of the singles chart with Ghost Town, soundtracking 1981's week of inner-city riots; the next they were in tatters, as vocalists Terry Hall and Neville Staples and guitarist Lynval Golding left without warning to form the Fun Boy Three. Announcing a return to the group's original name of Special AKA and recruiting singer Stan Campbell, Dammers locked himself in the studio. He emerged occasionally to release a single, but it was three years before he delivered this brave, inspired, non-ska mix of lounge-jazz muzak and dub-reggae, a record which proved that there was such a thing as a blend of politics and pop which was effective on both counts.

It was not an easy album to make, even by "difficult third album" standards. Tracks were rewritten, reworked and re-recorded over and over again. It took so long, in fact, that the Fun Boy Three's entire career was over by the time this album came out. The intense Housebound, an agoraphobic nightmare rumoured to be directed at Terry Hall, could just as easily have described Dammers himself, holed up in the control room day and night for 36 months. Day after day would be spent singing the same line repeatedly until the perfectionist Dammers was satisfied. The one exception was its best-known track, Nelson Mandela – Dammers' spontaneous freedom chant took a mere four days to complete. Produced by Elvis Costello (who'd also produced The Specials' debut), the song featured The Beat's Rankin' Roger and Dave Wakeling and the return of Lynval Golding. The brutal War Crimes ("From the graves of Belsen, to the ruins of Beirut/I can still see people dying") made for a gloomy single, but there's also a taste of Dammers' cynical humour on What I Like Most About You Is Your Girlfriend, the only Specials track to feature his deadpan lead vocals.

By the time the album was ready it was attracting attention as an expensive folly and was, unfairly, judged accordingly. It sold poorly and became the group's swansong. A combination of contractual obligations and financial ruin made it the last album Dammers has released.

Record label:
2-Tone
Produced
by Jerry Dammers, Dick Cuthell, Dick Cuthell and Jerry Dammers, Elvis Costello.
Recorded
at Woodbine Studios, Air Studios, Vineyard and Phoenix Studios, Wessex Studios, London; between September 1981–83.
Release date:
June 1984
Chart peaks:
34 (UK) None (US)
Personnel:
Jerry Dammers (p, o); Gary McManus (b); Stan Campbell (v); Rhoda Dakar (v); John Shipley (g); John Bradbury (d); Rico Rodriquez (tb); Dick Cuthell (cornet, flugel horn); Andy Aderinto (s); Egidio Newton (bv); Caron Wheeler (bv); Naomi Thompson (bv); Claudia Fontaine (bv); Horace Panter (b); Tony "Groko" Utah (congas); Roddy Radiation (g); Nick Parker (vn)
Track listing:
Bright Lights (S/UK); The Lonely Crowd; What I Like Most About You Is Your Girlfriend (S/UK); Housebound; Night On The Tiles; Nelson Mandela (S); War Crimes (The Crime Is Still The Same) (S/UK); Racist Friend (S/UK); Alcohol; Break Down The Door
Running time:
42.42
Current CD:
CCD 5008
Further listening:
The Specials Singles (1991)
Further reading:
You're Wondering Now: A History Of The Specials (Paul Williams, 1995); The 2-Tone Story (George Marshal, 1991)
Like this?
Try . . . p.229

SOS Band

Just The Way You Like It

The birth of one of the '80s' most distinctive sounds.

Jimmy Jam and Terry Lewis, respectively the keyboard player and bassist with Minneapolis funk band The Time, had just finished recording Just Be Good To Me for the SOS Band's fourth album, *On The Rise.* It was one of a number of projects in a burgeoning production career, but now they were at Atlanta airport waiting for the flight to San Antonio where they were due to link up with The Time for a gig. They got snowed in, never made the show and were sacked by Prince, The Time's keeper. It was a firing that launched Jam and Lewis' full-time production career.

Other acts – notably Janet Jackson and Alexander O'Neal – had bigger worldwide hits with Jam and Lewis, but no one better defined the producers' sound than the SOS Band. They'd created the blueprint – lush synth pads, plushly thudding drums, liquid bass – in Tell Me If You Still Care and the thundering Just Be Good To Me on *On The Rise*, which signalled a switch in focus onto Mary Davis' voice with its rich tone and slightly husky edge. Weaned on the productions of Gamble and Huff and Rodgers and Edwards, Jam and Lewis had worked with the SOS Band since their third album, 1982's imaginatively titled *III*, and by now knew the band's strong points. With thick washes of keyboard and a gentle, measured pace, opening track No One's Gonna Love You creates a ripe atmosphere and romantic mood that Davis' reading exploits to the full. Weekend Girl expands the palette and the tougher title track closes the first side of the vinyl release as the best-conceived and executed Jam-Lewis recording. The final three tracks – the uptempo dancer Body Break, the perky Feelings and the ballad I Don't Want Nobody Else – were written by the band and are much what one would expect from an experienced team (they had been Santa Monica, house band at Atlanta's Regal Room). This split of material between band and producers creates a tension, a fine balance between ballad and beat, emotion and dance, but the Jam and Lewis tracks, strongly featuring Davis, are, by some distance, the pick.

Record label:
Tabu
Produced
by Jimmy Jam and Terry Lewis with SOS Band.
Recorded
at Master Sound, Atlanta and Creation Audio, Minneapolis; 1983–84
Released:
August 1984
Chart peaks:
29 (UK) 12 (US)
Personnel:
Mary Davis (v); Jason "TC" Bryant (k, v); Abdul Raoof (t, v); Bruno Speight (g), Jerome "JT" Thomas (pc, d); John Simpson (b); Billy Ellis, Sonny Killebrew (s); Terry Lewis, Monte Moir, Leticia Peterson, Gwendolyn Traylor, Joyce Irby, Jimmy Jam (bv). Additional musicians: Jimmy Jam, Terry Lewis, Stewart Hanley, Lloyd Oby
Track listing:
No One's Gonna Love You; Weekend Girl; Just The Way You Like It; Break Up; Feeling; I Don't Want Nobody Else; Body Break
Running time:
45.58
Currently unavailable on CD
Further listening:
Check the brilliant On The Rise (1983) with its excellent side one suite; and two more commercially successful Jam and Lewis productions, Janet Jackson's Control (1986) and Alexander O'Neal, Alexander O'Neal (1985)
Further reading:
www.flytetyme.com
Like this?
Try . . . p.333

Hüsker Dü

Zen Arcade

Minneapolis trio emerge from the highly-charged early '80s US hardcore scene with winningly melodic double set.

The way Bob Mould picks his guitar *à la* A Hard Day's Night at the end of opening track Something I Learned Today provided a big clue to what Hüsker Dü intended with this record. By the time *Zen Arcade* arrived in 1984, Hüsker Dü had already forged a fearsome reputation, with their 1982 debut, *Land Speed Record* the epitome of snarling, super-fast hardcore. But come *Metal Circus* a year later, the group's love of The Beatles and The Byrds was beginning to seep through – they even released their version of the latter's Eight Miles High as a single in spring 1984. When pressed in interviews at the time, Bob Mould professed – tongue no doubt firmly in cheek – that Hüsker Dü had passed the punk test on a number of occasions. He also asserted that they knew they wrote good songs; Grant Hart maintained that their music had always had a "serious pop edge". By the time of *Zen Arcade*, the group were covering ground as if taking an idiosyncratic, high-speed overview of contemporary America.

Hart's Pink Turns To Blue and Mould's Chartered Trips showed that Hüsker Dü had two accomplished and complementary songwriters and singers – they even sang harmonies together. Harnessed to the group's formidable firepower, the combination was irresistible. Indeed, few, if any, groups have touched the concentrated ferocity of a song such as I'll Never Forget You; a howl of wounded rage set to dragster-speed riffing.

On a double album like *Zen Arcade*, you could argue a certain percentage of filler is necessary to give the listener some breathing space, but all the tracks here have a role, even Hart and Mould's piano cameos. The 14-minute, live-in-the-studio instrumental, Reoccurring Dreams – which got the group dubbed as the hardcore Grateful Dead – shows off the Hart/Norton rhythm section as a particularly propulsive unit, while Mould's guitar forays sound like entire cities being laid to waste; "No overdubs or fancy stuff", the sleevenotes proclaim. Every track is a first take – except two that they started too fast – which again saw them "passing the punk test". Hüsker Dü soon gained a reputation as one of the '80s' most influential rock groups, and although they streamlined their music later on, *Zen Arcade* captures them at their most adventurous. As to those Beatle influences, a couple of years later they were playing Ticket To Ride in concert.

Record label:
SST
Produced
by Spot and Hüsker Dü.
Recorded
at Total Access, Redondo Beach, California; October 1983.
Released:
September 1984
Chart peaks:
None (UK) None (US)
Personnel:
Bob Mould (g, v, b, pc, p); Greg Norton (b, bv); Grant Hart (d, v, pc, p, g); Spot (e)
Track listing:
Something I Learned Today; Broken Home, Broken Heart; Never Talking To You Again; Chartered Trips; Dreams Reoccurring; Indecision Time; Hare Krsna; Beyond The Threshold; Pride; I'll Never Forget You; The Biggest Lie; What's Going On; Masochism World; Standing By The Sea; Somewhere; One Step At A Time; Pink Turns To Blue; Newest Industry; Monday Will Never Be The Same; Whatever; The Tooth Fairy And The Princess; Turn On The News
Running time:
70.25
Current CD:
SST CD 027
Further listening:
New Day Rising (1985), and Flip Your Wig from later the same year.
Further reading:
world.std.com/~thirdave/hd.html
Like this?
Try . . . p.451

Lloyd Cole And The Commotions

Rattlesnakes

Glasgow University graduates plunder four decades of music and Eng. Lit. to produce clever and successful debut.

In the early and mid-'80s a gaggle of young groups emerged from the post-punk wreckage to strike a blow for songwriting craftsmanship. Scritti Politti, The Smiths and Prefab Sprout all knew their onions, but arguably Lloyd Cole And The Commotions produced the best first shot of the lot. Drummer Stephen Irvine remembers its genesis.

"Neil, Lloyd and Blair were in a soul band before I joined. With Lawrence (son of Lonnie Donegan) and myself involved it took an altogether less blue-eyed soul feel."

That feel still plays a very important part on *Rattlesnakes* however: witness the Tony Joe White-like funkiness and luxuriant strings of Speedboat, or the Philly-derived beats and falsetto vocal of Patience.

"We rehearsed a lot, refining as we went. By the time we got our deal, Paul Hardiman (producer) was exactly what we needed. We wanted to work with him after hearing *Soul Mining* by The The. He knew exactly how to get each of us to perform to the best of our abilities."

Irvine has another theory as to why *Rattlesnakes* still feels fresh today. "Thankfully we all had our eyes on vintage equipment when we signed, and didn't go for the new sounds and effects that were in vogue in 1984 but seem so dated now. Phew."

The Commotions clearly played a good team game but Cole was the star. His wavering, protean voice – a vessel of the vulnerable and the knowing, proved to be the ideal vehicle for his sour-sweet musings, "She's got cheekbones like geometry and eyes like sin/And she's sexually enlightened by Cosmopolitan."

Cole was also a compulsive and fearless namedropper: Truman Capote, Leonard Cohen, Grace Kelly and Simone de Beauvoir all rub shoulders in his songs. Forest Fire was a timeless pop-soul gem blessed with a sublime build that climaxed in howling art-rock guitar. Charlotte Street possessed the kind of riff that stiffened the backbone of the British Invasion and the undulating Byrdsian guitar figures kept several songs flying high.

It was all very knowing, and Cole's inability to resist a literary reference got up some noses, but he judged his balancing act between artifice and instinct perfectly, making *Rattlesnakes* utterly right for its time. Though he continues to produce decent albums to this day – and has subsequently made some impact in the US – Cole has never seized the moment in quite the same alluring way.

Record label:
Polydor
Produced
by Paul Hardiman.
Recorded
at The Garden, Shoreditch, London; March and June 1984.
Released:
October 12, 1984
Chart peaks:
13 (UK) None (US)
Personnel:
Lloyd Cole (g, v); Neil Clark (g); Blair Cowan (k); Lawrence Donegan (b); Stephen Irvine (d, p); Anne Dudley (a)
Track listing:
Perfect Skin (S); Speedboat; Rattlesnakes (S); Down On Mission Street; Forest Fire (S); Charlotte Street; 2CV; Four Flights Up; Patience; Are You Ready To Be Heartbroken?
Running time:
36.06
Currently unavailable on CD
Further listening:
Easy Pieces (1985); solo album Bad Vibes (1993)
Further reading:
www.lloydcole.com
Like this?
Try . . . p.539

Julian Cope

Fried

Former Teardrop's experiment in acoustic psychedelia went unappreciated in the age of The Thompson Twins.

It's the turtle shell that everyone notices first. Confirmation that, yes, drug-addled Julian Cope really is nuts! For Cope though, posing with a turtle shell on his back was a pre-emptive strike.

After The Teardrop Explodes split, Cope was aware that critics were tiring of his acid consumption, some even suggesting that he might go the same way as Syd Barrett. To a Barrett fan like Cope, though, this hardly constituted a warning. Undeterred by the critical pasting administered upon 1984's *World Shut Your Mouth*, he immediately resumed work and decamped to Cambridge in defiant mood.

"If these records have to be my *TB Sheets* or *Starsailor* [obscure gems by Van Morrison and Tim Buckley]," wrote Cope in his autobiography, "then so be it."

On arrival, his first move was to write a protest song of sorts. Bored with a climate in which every Tom, Dick and Tears For Fears was heralding their new record as "unlike anything you've ever heard before", Cope went the other way: "I decided that if it hadn't been done before, then I wasn't interested."

Drawing on a 400-year-old tradition, he wrote the primitive, pulsing Reynard The Fox (a song which he later cited as the inspiration for his archaeological tome, The Modern Antiquarian). Happy with the direction things were taking, he stuck a picture of Brian Wilson on the wall – to be consulted in times of crisis– and abandoned clothing for the remaining sessions, feeling that people would hear the nakedness. Oddly, you knew exactly what he meant. A clutch of desolate ballads, all strummed minor chords and catatonic Hammond organs, lent substance to the Syd Barrett comparisons. But such comparisons sold short the stark lucidity of Me Singing, Torpedo and Laughing Boy – performances which could induce a Glastonbury of goosepimples on the thickest of skins.

Unsurprisingly, Cope's record company hated it, not least for the turtle shell. They attempted to make a hit of its one indisputable moment of pop majesty, Sunspots. But to the public, even that conveyed something of the strangeness in which it was recorded: Cope perched atop a huge arched window attempting to hoover it clean, whilst his also-tripping producer discussed drums with the photo of Brian Wilson.

Needless to say, it tanked, and Cope was dropped. Some kind of revenge was afforded in 1987 by the successful bombast of *Saint Julian*, but it was only when Cope tapped back into his progadelic roots with 1991's *Peggy Suicide* that he truly rediscovered his form.

Record label:
Mercury
Produced
by Stephen Lovell.
Recorded
at Spaceward Studios, Cambridge; July 1984.
Released:
November 1984
Chart peaks:
87 (UK) None (US)
Personnel:
Julian Cope (v, g, b, o); Donald Ross Skinner (g); Steve Lovell (g); Brother Johnno (g); Chris Whitten (d)
Track listing:
Reynard The Fox; Bill Drummond Said; Laughing Boy; Me Singing; Sunspots (S); The Bloody Assizes; Search Party; O King Of Chaos; Holy Love; Torpedo
Running time:
42.50
Current CD:
523 370-2 adds: I Went On A Chourney; Mic Mak Mok; Land Of Fear
Further listening:
Peggy Suicide (1991); Jehovahkill (1992); Interpeter (1996); Julian Cope And The Teardrop Explodes: Floored Genius: The Best Of Julian Cope And The Teardrop Explodes (1992)
Further Reading:
MOJO 73; Head On/Repossessed – brilliant, funny autobiography chronicling the Teardrops and solo years until 1990; www.headheritage.co.uk
Like this?
Try . . . p.385

Frankie Goes To Hollywood

Welcome To The Pleasure Dome

The extravagant soundtrack to the biggest UK sensation of 1984.

"They have the wit of The Beatles, the decadence of The Rolling Stones and the wildness of the Sex Pistols." That was how one tabloid paper reacted to the Frankies back in 1984 and for once the reporting was absolutely spot-on. The Liverpudlians dominated the singles charts as no act had done since the golden age of Merseybeat. They equalled Gerry & The Pacemakers' hoary chart statistic with three consecutive chart-toppers from inception (a record since smashed by The Spice Girls, Westlife *et al*), and positively thrived on controversy. They were first glimpsed in 1982 on TV show, The Tube, cavorting to an early version of Relax in skimpy, black-leather bondage gear.

At a time when gay pop stars remained in the closet, Holly Johnson and Paul Rutherford brazenly flaunted their preferences. As Johnson accurately observed, "Frankie Goes To Hollywood might not have been part of an identifiable movement as the Sex Pistols had been, but the ideas of stylish pleasure and guilt-free sexuality perfectly matched the mood of the period." They even inspired a high-street fashion boom with their sloganeering T-shirts emblazoned with cryptic Frankie Says . . . commands. Musically, they were always operating at the sharp end of technology with studio boffin Trevor Horn and his team spending months at the Fairlight (a high-end sampling and sequencing rig) formulating their sound.

By the time this album was completed the group were the biggest-selling UK singles act in years. In order to take full advantage of their massive media profile, the record was as elaborately packaged as possible. And, prematurely for such novices, it was a double. The Frankies' talents were spread rather thinly over four sides, filler included lacklustre reworkings of Springsteen's Born To Run, Edwin Starr's War and Gerry Marsden's Ferry Cross The Mersey. Most agreed that this would have made a far better single album, but such reservations were forgotten amid the clamour to purchase the record.

On reflection, it's still the classic singles here that prove most arresting – the pulsating and erotic Relax, the awesome, dramatic Two Tribes and the sumptuous string-laden The Power Of Love. The following year they tried for a fourth Number 1 with the admittedly strong title track but by then Frankie fever had waned. What they left behind was a glowing reminder of a band burning themselves out in incandescent glory.

Record label:
ZTT
Produced
by Trevor Horn.
Released:
November 1984
Chart peaks:
1 (UK) 33 (US)
Personnel:
Holly Johnson (v); Mark O'Toole (b, v); Paul Rutherford (v); Brian Nash (g); Peter Gill (d); Anne Dudley (oa, k); Steve Lipson (e)
Track listing:
Well...; The World Is My Oyster; Snatch Of Fury; Welcome To The Pleasure Dome (S); Relax (S); War; Two Tribes (S); Ferry Cross The Mersey; Born To Run; San Jose; Wish; Krisco Kisses; Black Night White Light; The Only Star In Heaven; The Power Of Love (S); Bang
Running time:
70.11
Current CD:
CID 101
Further listening:
Liverpool (1986)
Further reading:
A Bone In My Flute (Holly Johnson, 1994)
Like this?
Try . . . p.844

The Minutemen

Double Nickels On The Dime

Ferociously articulate speed funk and political shouting from California.

Californian hardcore, like any other punk-based movement, fed on the intensity of the present, but its high-on-life buzz, distinguished it from the nihilism of UK punk-affiliated music. Some of the major players were even constructivist in their thinking. None more so than The Minutemen, whose five years of performing evolved into a kind of critique of both rock music and the real world, which D Boon's songs and playing broke down into tiny, angry fragments.

Like their SST label-mates Hüsker Dü, with whom they engaged in some friendly competition (the first edition of this set, originally a double LP, has "Take that, Huskers!" etched into the vinyl), The Minutemen were thinkers from an age when agitprop still had a foothold just outside the rock mainstream. Because they were, in most respects, a hard-playing rock three-piece, their early records were speedball deliveries of songs that often barely breached the one-minute barrier, but by the time they made *Buzz Or Howl Under The Influence Of Heat*, a 1983 EP, Boon had expanded his lyric-writing to accommodate the song form as most listeners knew it. You could hear this three-man team making themselves into tougher, less wayward players, and the subject matter and the vision was getting increasingly deadeye in its precision.

Double Nickels On the Dime is their marathon masterpiece. Cut over a pair of two-day sessions, the group nailed 45 songs. Boon's diehard leftism informs most of the lyric commentary, from bits and pieces like Shit From An Old Notebook to There Ain't Shit On TV Tonight, a miniature personal manifesto that ends on "No more lies! We are responsible." Mike Watt contributes some lighter notes, and they also do covers of Van Halen's Ain't Talkin' About Love and Steely Dan's Doctor Wu – these men were music fans as much as politicians. But Boon was a man in a hurry. "My skin keeps the storm inside," he sings on Storm In My House, and in this thin-sounding but tight and momentous record, with nothing throwaway despite the huge number of songs, he sang his epitaph. He was killed in a highway accident while the band was on tour in Arizona in December 1985, and The Minutemen were no more.

Record label:
SST
Produced
by Ethan James.
Recorded
at Radio Tokyo, California.
Released:
1984
Chart peaks:
None (UK) None (US)
Personnel:
D Boon (g, v); M Watt (b, v); G Hurley (d); E James (e)
Track listing:
D's Car Jam/Anxious Mo-Fo; Theatre Is The Life Of You; Viet Nam; Cohesion; It's Expected I'm Gone; #1 Hit Song; Two Beads At The End; Do You Want New Wave Or Do You Want The Truth?; Don't Look Now; Shit From An Old Notebook; Nature Without Man; One Reporter's Opinion; Political Song For Michael Jackson To Sing; Maybe Partying Will Help; Toadies; Retreat; The Big Foist; God Bows To Math; Corona; The Glory Of Man; Take 5, D; My Heart And The Real World; History Lesson-Part II; You Need The Glory; The Roar Of The Masses Could Be Farts; ***** Mr Robot's Holy Orders; West Germany; The Politics Of Time; Themselves; Please Don't Be Gentle With Me; Nothing Indeed; No Exchange; There Ain't Shit On TV Tonight; This Ain't No Picnic; Spillage; Untitled Song For Latin America; Jesus And Tequila; June 16th; Storm In My House; Martin's Story; Doctor Wu; Ain't Talkin' About Love; Little Man With A Gun
Running time:
79.14
Current CD
import SSTCD 028
Further listening:
Post-Mersh Vol 3 (1989)
Like this?
Try . . . p.559

Dire Straits

Brothers In Arms

The first CD to sell a million, statistics and reputation have served to obscure its artistic worth.

The sound of a voice, the sound of a guitar – what was it about *Brothers In Arms*? A receding hairline, a headband, a sweaty vest – Dire Straits *fashionable*? Never. More than any other chart phenomenon of the '80s, the album passed unexplained, inexplicable. But Knopfler had led the band's music through constant change and development from the sharp pub rock which first attracted London local radio interest in 1977. He began writing much longer pieces (notably, the 14-minute Telegraph Road from their previous studio album, 1982's *Love Over Gold*). He added keyboard players Alan Clark and, for *Brothers In Arms*, Guy Fletcher. If his growly voice and crying guitar remained the band constants, everything else was on the move.

In the winter of 1983–84, after hectic months producing albums for Bob Dylan and Aztec Camera, and getting married, he set time aside to write Dire Straits' next. With no premonitions of grandeur and rarely satisfied with his own work anyway, he would fiercely criticise the songs – Your Latest Trick he could never understand, One World was "horrible". The phrase "brothers in arms" had lodged in his brain after a conversation with his father who noted that the communist USSR supported the (then) fascist military dictatorship of Argentina in the Falklands War. But the song generalised the soldier's plight and Knopfler felt he failed to sustain the potential theme of war (what is it good for? or similar) through the album.

Yet the evidence is that, unless studio performance really did alchemise dross, he underrated his basic work. The characteristic dense melancholy of the title track – soon a favourite at funerals – and Your Latest Trick, the old-time rocking strut of Money For Nothing and Walk Of Life, the neat tonal fit of the less distinctive songs proved irresistible. The album topped charts in 24 countries, driven by Money For Nothing, Dire Straits' first American Number 1 single. It was a sour, sneery monologue transcribed, Knopfler says, almost verbatim from a New York electrical shop owner denouncing the "yo-yos" and "faggots" who played their guitars on the MTV. Even that he credited to the influence of Randy Newman: "Maybe I wouldn't have written that kind of character song but for him – you have to put yourself in other people's shoes."

Record label:
Vertigo
Produced
by Mark Knopfler and Neil Dorfsman.
Recorded
at Air Studios, Montserrat; The Power Station, New York; Air Studios, London; November 1984–April 1985
Released:
May 17, 1985
Chart peaks:
1 (UK) 1 (US)
Personnel:
Mark Knopfler (v, g); John Illsley (b, bv); Alan Clark (k); Guy Fletcher (k, bv); Omar Hakim, Terry Williams (d); Neil Dorfsman (e); Sting (bv)
Track listening:
So Far Away (S); Money For Nothing (S); Walk Of Life (S); Your Latest Trick; Why Worry; Ride Across The River; The Man's Too Strong; One World; Brothers In Arms (S)
Running time:
54.35
Current CD:
9252642
Further listening:
Their first, Dire Straits (1978), and their last On Every Street (1991) – striking entrance, graceful exit.
Further reading:
Mark Knopfler: An Unauthorized Biography (Myles Palmer, 1991); www.mark-knopfler-news.co.uk (includes link to brothersin-arms.com fan site)
Like this?
Try . . . p.456

Prefab Sprout

Steve McQueen

Majestic second album from County Durham's finest.

Prefab Sprout's *Swoon* (1983) – with its jump-cut melodies, quasi-jazz/fusion changes and oblique lyrical twists – remains a breathtakingly impressive debut. Its author, Paddy McAloon, isn't so sure: "The things that people mistook for cleverness were terrible ignorance. We were very insular and just evolved a weirdly overdeveloped, strange style, our own little world." Thomas Dolby, a pop artist at the technological cutting edge, was guesting as singles reviewer on BBC Radio One and in despair at the quality of the music until he heard Don't Sing from *Swoon* and thought, "this soulful Geordie voice over frantic acoustic guitars and harmonica was the best thing I'd heard for ages." The band, listening in, got in touch with Dolby and asked him to produce their next album.

Paddy: "I gave him a huge collection of songs and almost all the ones he picked were from 1979, long before Swoon." The resulting album was called *Steve McQueen* because "he was really good in an un-arty sort of way" (Paddy) – rather unlike the record itself – but released as *Two Wheels Good* (with extra tracks) in the USA after objections by the actor's estate. Better focused and more approachable than their debut, it was among the freshest, brightest records of the '80s, full of twisting, memorable songs, luminous textures and solid grooves. Songs like Appetite and Goodbye Lucille #1 established McAloon's reputation as one of pop's great mavericks: a lyricist of range, depth and ambition; a chordsmith and melodist of daring originality; a craftsman of fiercely individual discernment. As it happened, Paddy agreed: "I know I'm probably the best writer on the planet," he said in 1985, "who are my rivals?"

Another time, however, he was keen to acknowledge his producer's contribution to *Steve McQueen*; "I was so much in awe of what Dolby had done to shape it, I kind of thought, This is his record, he's made this really good." A modest hit was eventually achieved with the umpteenth re-release of When Love Breaks Down and the Sprouts went on to greater commercial success with *From Langley Park To Memphis* (1988) and perhaps even grander artistry with *Jordan The Comeback* (1990), but as Thomas Dolby observes, "there's something magical about the *Steve McQueen* album, an openness and expectation that none of us have touched since." Refined and sophisticated as the album appears to the listener, it's surprising that Dolby adds, "I'm sure it's partly because we didn't really know what we were doing."

Record label:
CBS
Produced
by Thomas Dolby.
Recorded
1985
Released:
June 15, 1985
Chart peaks:
21 (UK) None (US)
Personnel:
Paddy McAloon (g, v); Wendy Smith (bv); Martin McAloon (b); Neil Conti (d); Thomas Dolby (k)
Track listing:
Faron Young; Bonny; Appetite; When Love Breaks Down; Goodbye Lucille #1; Hallelujah; Moving The River; Horsin' Around; Desire As; Blueberry Pies; When The Angels
Running time:
45.22
Current CD:
Sony 466336 2
Further listening:
Swoon (1983); From Langley Park To Memphis (1988); Jordan The Comeback (1990)
Further reading:
http://users.deltanet.com/~plockton/sprout.html
Like this?
Try . . . p.484

Kate Bush

Hounds Of Love

Crowning glorious album from the UK's most influential female artist ever.

"It was my 'She's gone mad' album," said Kate Bush in the late '80s, looking back at *The Dreaming* (1982). That seemed to be the verdict from record company and public alike as the album completed her commercial decline over four albums from a million sales for *The Kick Inside* (1978) to 60,000. But her reaction to relative failure was to make complete her escape from her girlhood role as "the company's daughter" into womanly independence. From July 1983, she invested a slab of her royalties in upgrading the studio she had set up in a barn at her parents' farmhouse on the outskirts of South-East London. A 48-track desk and a Fairlight synthesizer-sampler meant she could record much of the album there.

"In music you have to break your back before you even start to speak the emotion," she said. "The way I work is very experimental and when you're in a studio that's costing a phenomenal amount every hour it puts too much pressure on you. It zaps creativity."

Freed from increasing debt to the label, she pressed ahead with the transition from writing at the piano to building from a rhythm track – something she had learned via guesting on a Peter Gabriel album. At last, she was able to blend writing, recording and production into one untrammelled creative process. From these ideal circumstances emerged an album embodying her belief that "art is a tremendous sensual-sexual expression" and "the communication of music is very much like making love".

Reflecting the last days of vinyl dominance, *Hounds Of Love* divides down the middle. The A-side's five songs are unconnected but brilliant tracks, springing vibrantly from Bush's focus on rhythm – be it the percussive gallop of Running Up That Hill (A Deal With God) or the frantic pulsing of the Medici Sextet's strings on Cloudbusting. The second side is a suite – Bush didn't mind using the unfashionable term "concept". Her imagination careens around various ideas that haunted her: the fear of being trapped beneath ice; the image of Ophelia drowning. Bush switchbacks through time, referring to witches and astronauts, drawing in traditional fiddles and all manner of Fairlight noises and effects, while the emotional tone sweeps from enervated torpor (And Dream Of Sheep), through terror (Waking The Witch) to redemptive warmth (The Morning Fog).

Throughout, perhaps more potent than any other aspect of an electrifying album, her voice is remarkable, a church organ of range and colour that still never loses the urgent intimacy of the impassioned artist.

Record label:
EMI
Produced
by Kate Bush and Jon Kelly.
Recorded
at Bush family's farmhouse studios, Kent; mixed at Windmill Lane and Abbey Road. January 1984–June 1985.
Released:
September 1985
Chart peaks:
1 (UK) 30 (US)
Personnel:
Kate Bush (k, v); Kevin McAlea (syn); Alan Murphy, Brian Bath (g); Del Palmer, Eberhard Weber, Danny Thompson (b); Stuart Elliott, Charlie Morgan (d); Johnathan Williams (c); Liam O'Flynn (uillean pipes); John Sheahan (whistles, vn); Paddy Bush (balalaika, dijeridoo); Donal Lunny (bouzouki); Morris Pert (pc); The Medici Sextet (strings); Richard Hickox Singers (v).
Track listing:
Running Up That Hill (S); Hounds Of Love (S); The Big Sky (S); Mother Stands For Comfort; Cloudbusting (S); And Dream Of Sheep; Under Ice; Waking The Witch; Watching You Without Me; Jig Of Life; Hello Earth; The Morning Fog
Running time:
47.34
Current CD:
E21S25239
Further listening:
Box set This Woman's Work (1990)
Further reading:
www.paradiseplace.org.uk
Like this?
Try . . . p.8

Dexy's Midnight Runners

Don't Stand Me Down

Chart-topping young soul rebels make their most ambitious album; sales plummet and acclaim eludes them.

Dexy's Midnight Runners had already released two best-selling albums and a couple of Number 1 singles (Geno and Come On Eileen) before embarking on their most ambitious and misunderstood project. Mainman Kevin Rowland spent an age fashioning this work but, as months passed into years, many of the group's younger fans had moved on. When the album finally appeared, the critics savaged it and Rowland effectively sabotaged its chances by initially refusing to extract a single from it. It quickly fell off the charts. All of which was a terrible injustice as the record was the most challenging and passionate of Rowland's tempestuous career.

"I stand by the work," Rowland insists. "I think it's really good. But I was a very misplaced person around *Don't Stand Me Down*. I found the success I'd achieved with Dexy's to be quite meaningless. I felt like a workhorse, working for the record company, going around the world promoting product. It just felt like it had nothing to do with me anymore. It was all very uncreative so I started searching for something with a bit more meaning. I'd been reading about Ireland around 1983 so I thought that's what I'll do – Irish Republicanism, and socialism too. I'd go on marches and walks. *Don't Stand Me Down* was originally going to be a much more political album but I think fear made me tailor it more personally in the end."

The album's centrepiece is the extraordinary This Is What She's Like, which combines a treatise on the essence of a woman with sarcastic diatribes on the ignorance of the English upper-middle classes. Musically, it merges opaque dialogue with Beach Boys' harmonies and a coda of Stax-style horns. Other tracks are equally inventive, although One Of These Things proved a bit too close to Warren Zevon's Werewolves Of London for comfort, prompting a successful copyright claim from Zevon.

Time has seen the album re-evaluated as a classic, which has prompted debate about why it failed on release. Many point to the cover which featured the remaining Dexys dressed immaculately in expensive Ivy League suits like upmarket chartered accountants. Rowland disagrees: "The real reason people didn't buy it is because they never heard it. The only song played on the radio was the butchered version of This Is What She's Like seven or eight weeks after the album came out. It was too late – and that was my mistake."

Record label:
Mercury
Produced
by Kevin Rowland, Helen O'Hara, Alan Winstanley and Billy Adams.
Recorded:
Spring 1984–July 1985, Montreux; Matrix Studios, London; Outside Studios, Reading; Selectsound, Hertfordshire; Electric Ladyland, New York.
Released:
September 1985
Chart peaks:
22 (UK) None (US)
Personnel:
Kevin Rowland (v); Billy Adams (g, rg, v); Helen O'Hara (vn, v); Nicky Gatfield (s, v); Vincent Crane (p); Tim Dancy (d); Julian Littman (mandolin); Jimmy Patterson (tb); Tommy Evans (steel g); Robert Noble (o, syn); John Edwards (b)
Track listing:
The Occasional Flicker; This Is What She's Like (S); My National Pride [previously titled Knowledge Of Beauty]; One Of Those Things; Reminisce Part Two; Listen To This; The Waltz.
Running time:
54.37
Current CD:
CRECD 154
Further listening:
For contrast, their classic debut Searching For The Young Soul Rebels (1980).
Further reading:
Essay in Love Is The Drug (John Aizlewood, 1994)
Like this?
Try . . . p.493

The Fall

This Nation's Saving Grace

Raucous, long-serving Mancunian shower add a hint of California sun, get a decent producer and hit a career peak.

At the turn of this century, The Fall had clocked up a 23-year career. Mark E Smith can claim to be not only the most credible survivor of the original punk era, but also the keeper of one of the most enduring visions in the history of rock. The Fall has always been Smith's vision; founder and sole original member, legendarily as caustic and difficult as he is dedicated, Smith's allegiance to punk was largely thanks to the galvanising power of its DIY ethic. The Fall's uniquely primitive sound (which has been expanded – but rarely departed significantly – from its original blueprint) owes more to the garage punk of '60s America, the raw attack of vintage rockabilly, and the hypnotic repetition of Can and the Velvet Underground. Smith's vocal style – the mad bark of a bellicose street hawker – is a one-off; the greatest non-singer who isn't Lou Reed.

In their eighth awesome year, many of The Fall's more conservative fans were resenting the creeping commercial influence of Mark's new American wife, guitarist and co-writer Brix. Although the new Fall were hardly about to upset Duran Duran, Brix was indeed staunchly in love with the pop history of her native California, which was reflected in the bright strum of her Rickenbacker and the accessibility of her melodies. "Even with the old songs," she said in a 1984 interview, "I think I add some shadow and light to them. I give it a lot of drive, as well as adding some 'glamour' to it all."

Still widely thought to be their finest album, *This Nation's Saving Grace* catches The Fall at a moment of thrilling congruity, playing to their strengths with great clarity. Thanks to John Leckie, their first truly skilled producer, Bombast rages harder than any previous Fall song to that point, while LA uses the group's trademarks in service of what can fairly be described as a pop song. The meeting of the marginal and the mainstream proved winning here, taking The Fall into the UK Top 30, and making them look as though they belonged there.

Record label:
Beggars Banquet
Produced
by John Leckie.
Recorded
at Music Works, London and Chapel Lane, Hereford; June–July 1985.
Released:
September 1985
Chart peaks:
54 (UK) None (US)
Personnel:
Mark E Smith (v, g); Brix Smith (lead g, v); Stephen Hanley (b); Karl Burns (d); Simon Rogers (k, g, b); Craig Scanlon (rhythm g)
Track listing:
Mansion; Bombast; Barmy; What You Need; Spoilt Victorian Child; LA; Gut Of The Quantifier; My New House; Paintwork; I Am Damo Suzuki; To Nkroachment: Yarbles
Running time:
65.56
Current CD:
BBL 67 CD adds: Vixen; Couldn't Get Ahead; Petty (Thief) Lout; Rollin' Dany; Cruisers Creek
Further listening:
458489 A Sides (1990), The Wonderful And Frightening World Of The Fall (1984); Palace Of Swords Reversed (1987)
Further reading:
www.visi.com/fall (The Official Fall Website)
Like this?
Try . . . p.485

The Waterboys

This Is The Sea

They called it "The Big Music". They were right.

The first two Waterboys albums – particularly 1984's *A Pagan Place* – had introduced what became known as "The Big Music", a sound that requires the overused adjective "widescreen". "The song The Big Music [from *A Pagan Place*] was about seeing God's hand in the world," says Scott today. "But it became this catch-all term; I've seen it used to refer to lots of groups – U2, Simple Minds – and I always took it to mean the cinematic sound of *A Pagan Place* and *This Is The Sea*." Writing for *This Is The Sea*, he was inspired – as ever – by Patti Smith's *Horses*, but also Van Morrison's *Astral Weeks* and Television's *Marquee Moon*.

Much of the pre-production was done at Seaview, Karl Wallinger's home studio. "I'd be trying out ideas; Karl would record it all and chip in with a bass part or a synthesizer part and stack up reverbs until the sound in his speakers seemed like a place to inhabit."

Opening with the heady, goosebump-inducing trumpet intro to Don't Bang The Drum – cooked up by Scott and trumpeter Roddy Lorimer under the influence of Miles' *Sketches of Spain* – *This Is The Sea* proved all the "coming and going" worthwhile. It's an epic, furiously alive record, infused with a sweeping spirituality (The Pan Within, Spirit) and an energising anger – Old England (with crowd noise from a Prince bootleg) is a scathing critique of Thatcher's Britain, Be My Enemy a rapid-fire "ode to paranoia" warning foes to expect vengeance.

The album's most famous track began its life in New York. Scott's then-girlfriend had asked him if it was easy to write songs. Answering "yes", he took an envelope and immediately wrote the first verse of The Whole Of The Moon. The rest of the lyric took months, but the finished song remains one of Scott's finest to date and his biggest hit.

The year after *This Is The Sea*, Scott moved to Ireland, where fiddler Steve Wickham and accordion virtuoso Sharon Shannon helped colour the folky "raggle-taggle" palette of *Fisherman's Blues* and *Room To Roam*. It was The Whole Of The Moon, though, which raised Scott's profile again in 1991 when ravers adopted it as a come-down anthem, prompting a re-release which won him an Ivor Novello award for songwriting in 1992.

"I think it has a lot of power," says Scott of *This Is The Sea* today. "From when I began in bands at 15 or 16, there's a progression that reaches its climax with the finishing of [that record]. The only thing I could do afterwards was do something different; all my youthful rock dreams were achieved on *This Is The Sea*."

Record label:
Ensign
Produced
by Mike Scott, Mick Glossop, John Brand and Karl Wallinger.
Recorded
at Amazon, Park Gates, Townhouse and other studios; March–July 1985 .
Released:
September 1985
Chart peaks:
37 (UK) None (US)
Personnel:
Mike Scott (v, g, p, k); Karl Wallinger (k, b, bv); Anthony Thistlewaite (s); Roddy Lorimer (tp); Chris Whitten, Kevin Wilkinson, Pete Thomas (d)
Track listing:
Don't Bang The Drum; The Whole Of The Moon (S); Spirit; The Pan Within; Medicine Bow; Old England; Be My Enemy; Trumpets; This Is The Sea
Running time:
42.37
Current CD:
CDP3215432
Further listening:
A Pagan Place (1984); The Secret Life Of The Waterboys (1994) – excellent compilation of outtakes and rarities; The Whole of The Moon – The Music Of Mike Scott And The Waterboys (1998) – useful compilation also rounds up some of Scott's stripped-down solo work; A Rock In The Weary Land (2000) – his best record since This Is The Sea.
Further reading:
www.waterboys.co.uk
Like this?
Try . . . p.473

Jesus And Mary Chain

Psychocandy

Studied rebellion from leather 'n' Ray-Ban's-clad feedback Führers.

Lauded as "the new Sex Pistols" by the music press, the Jesus And Mary Chain's blink-and-you-miss-'em live shows quickly became antagonistic affairs. One infamous North London Polytechnic gig in 1985 ended in a riot. "We really believed we could seriously change the way people made music," frontman Jim Reid explained laconically.

It was a far cry from their first appearance supporting mild-mannered jangle-merchants The Loft at Alan McGee's London club The Living Room. With heads down and backs to an audience of 15 people, there was no trace of the self-conscious abrasiveness that would soon become their trademark. By the time of Creation Records' debut single, Upside Down, the JAMC were courting controversy and the A&R men were in a frenzy.

Psychocandy was like no other debut LP. Describing themselves as "Eighties beatniks with an image that is shoddy but stylish", the Mary Chain made an exhilarating, intoxicating Wall Of Sound. Beneath that chaotic Velvet Underground-style white noise hid dark but beautifully crafted melodies worthy of Phil Spector. Recorded at Southern Studios and produced by the group – they didn't trust outsiders – all egos were left at home. It didn't matter who played what: the Reid brothers were after the perfect sound. Much swapping of instruments took place to get the parts down. As Jim explained: "Guitars look good. That's all we really care about."

Drugs were in plentiful supply. "We only take acid and speed!" the band declared, which explained in part the deranged, manic edge to their sound. The 14 tracks (all written by Jim and William on acoustic guitar – "The noise came later," admitted William) include album opener Just Like Honey, three minutes of bleak romanticism that strikes up with the opening drumbeats from The Ronettes' Be My Baby, and the angry, acidic pop of Never Understand. The Living End and In A Hole are driller-killer drones and the yearning, reflective Something's Wrong clocks in as the longest track at four minutes.

Before the album's release, Bobby Gillespie had already returned to Primal Scream. "He only played drums to help us out of our mess when Murray Dalglish left," said Jim. Although *Psychocandy* was hardly designed to set the mainstream alight, by the following August the JAMC would reach Number 13 in the singles chart with their Some Candy Talking EP.

Record label:
Blanco Y Negro
Produced
by The Jesus And Mary Chain.
Recorded
at Southern Studios, London; summer 1985.
Released:
November 1985
Chart peaks:
31 (UK) None (US)
Personnel:
Jim Reid (v, g); William Reid (g, v); Douglas Hart (b); Bobby Gillespie (d)
Track listing:
Just Like Honey (S); The Living End; Taste The Floor; The Hardest Walk; Cut Dead; In A Hole; Taste Of Cindy; Never Understand (S); Inside Me; Sowing Seeds; My Little Underground; You Trip Me Up (S); Something's Wrong; It's So Hard
Running time:
38.50
Current CD:
2292420002 adds: Some Candy Talking (S)
Further listening:
Follow-up Darklands (1987) – more mood-swing existentialism minus the feedback; Barbed Wire Kisses (1988) – assorted A- and B-sides and outtakes; Stoned And Dethroned (1993), a foray into reflective country rock with cameos from Shane McGowan and Mazzy Star's Hope Sandoval.
Further reading:
www.amniisia.com/aprilskies/net/
Like this?
Try . . . p.528

Shaun Davey And Rita Connolly

Granuaile

The most accessible of his singular folk-rock/ orchestral epics.

Born in Belfast, Shaun Davey drifted into music while studying fine art at the Courtauld Institute in the early '70s through a brief folk-rock collaboration with James Morris, who subsequently founded Windmill Lane Studios. Returning to Ireland, Davey made a living with advertising jingles while pursuing the unprecedented concept of fusing uillean pipes with orchestra.

The fruits of that vision, *The Brendan Voyage*, thrust him into prominence in the early '80s but *The Pilgrim*, an almost ruinously colossal follow-up, was less well received. *Granuaile* was a direct reaction against composing on such a scale, yet still honed further what was by then Davey's trademark fusion of traditional Irish instrumentation (principally O'Flynn's pipes) within a European classical framework (here, a particular echo of Vivaldi) and coloured with a rock sensibility.

Known in legend as Granuaile, Grace O'Malley forged a long life as a "pirate queen" – storming castles, rustling cattle and commanding the warships that dominated the west of Ireland during the socially and politically turbulent Elizabethan era. Having enjoyed Anne Chambers' biography, Davey recreated O'Malley's story as a gripping, dynamic and richly drawn song-cycle written specifically as a vehicle for Rita Connolly, who had already cameod sensationally in *The Pilgrim*. The result was both moving and dramatic, integrating orchestral instruments fully into a small group context and conjuring O'Malley's spirit of defiance and the atmosphere of time and place.

Granuaile was aired twice before its recording and several times subsequently, including an RTE televised performance at the Greenwich Festival in 1987 for which Davey had added modest revisions – notably replacing the light relief of The Dismissal with Hen's March. This track plus two further Greenwich takes, deemed superior, featured on the subsequent CD version (a policy favoured also on the eventual CD revision of *The Pilgrim*). Davey subsequently returned to large-scale orchestral works before settling into a routine of highly regarded film, television and theatrical scoring. He also wrote songs for, and produced, two Connolly solo albums; yet both the singer, who rarely performs live, and *Granuaile* – last staged in Mayo in 1992 – remain monstrously under-known.

Nevertheless, like *The Pilgrim*, revised and resurrected for the first time in 10 years for a Dublin performance in March 2000, *Granuaile* may yet enjoy a renaissance: "Rita's been muttering about it recently," says Davey. "I'm proud of it and I don't believe it's been performed enough. So, yes, if the opportunity arose I would revise it again!"

Record label:
Tara
Recorded:
Produced
by Shaun Davey.
Released:
December 1985
Chart peaks:
None (UK) None (US)
Personnel:
Rita Connolly (v); Liam O'Flynn (uillean pipes); Des Moore (g); Donal Lunny (bouzouki, bodhran); Helen Davies (harp); Carl Gerraghty (sax); Marian Doherty (harpsichord); Noel Eccles (dr, pc); Gareth Hudson (c); 22-piece chamber orchestra; Brian Masterson (e)
Track listing:
Dubhdarra; Ripples In The Rockpool; The Defence Of Hen's Castle; Free And Easy; The Rescue Of Hugh De Lacy; The Dismissal; Death Of Richard-An-Iarainn (intro); Death Of Richard-An-Iarainn; Sir Richard Bingham; The Spanish Armada; The New Age
Running time:
45.10
Current CD:
Tara CD 3017
Further listening:
The Pilgrim (1983), and the Connolly solo albums Rita Connolly (1992) and Valparaiso (1995).
Further reading:
Granuaile (Anne Chambers, 1984)
Like this?
Try . . . p.42

Robert Cray

Strong Persuader

A million-seller and Grammy-winner, the biggest blues record of the '80s.

Although Stevie Ray Vaughan was arguably a more in-demand performer, it was Robert Cray who rekindled the blues as a popular music in the '80s. He'd gone the usual route of blues artists since forming his first band in 1974 (with bassist Richard Cousins, a long-term confederate), playing the small-time live circuit and cutting records for independent labels with only a modest reach. But his 1985 triple-header with Albert Collins and Johnny Copeland, *Showdown!*, was a Grammy-winner and an album that was more widely reviewed in the rock press than most blues albums could normally hope for. On the strength of this, Cray signed to Mercury. Assisted by a shrewd press and media campaign, he was suddenly fêted as a brilliant young practitioner of the blues. *Strong Persuader* won him a second Grammy and went on to sell over a million.

Cray was fortunate in his producers, Bromberg and Walker, who also had a hand in some of the most effective songs. They made the most of Cray's lean, clear voice, untypical of the coarse-grained blues shouters which many people associated with the form; his taut and wiry guitar solos; his funky, modest but skilful band. Cray's *métier* was meanness, a cruel persona which he filtered into these songs like a brutal alter ego. But he was clever about distancing himself from his artistic self: he refers to the character as "Young Bob", the dark side of the real Robert. That makes the cold-eyed stud of Right Next Door (Because Of Me) or the homicidal cuckold of Smoking Gun into plausible fantasy figures that Cray steps inside for just long enough; I Guess I Showed Her is the other side of the coin. Though he sings the occasional 12-bar, Cray essentially put his faith in R&B as a more expansive music, and his later records found him moving towards a sort of rocking soul music, with less of the blues in it. None, though, have been as successful as this one, either critically or commercially, although the best of the follow-ups, *Don't Be Afraid Of The Dark*, does include some of his toughest material. For a period, he was successful enough to be courted by some of the biggest names in music: he even turned down an offer from Michael Jackson to appear on *Bad*.

Record label:
Mercury
Produced
by Bruce Bromberg and Dennis Walker.
Recorded
at Stage and Sound and Haywood's, Los Angeles; 1986.
Released:
January 1986
Chart peaks:
34 (UK) 13 (US)
Personnel:
Robert Cray (g, v); Peter Boe (k); Richard Cousins (b); David Olson (d); Lee Spath (pc); The Memphis Horns; Bill Dashiell (e)
Track listing:
Smoking Gun; I Guess I Showed Her; Right Next Door (Because Of Me); Nothin' But A Woman; Still Around; More Than I Can Stand; Foul Play; I Wonder; Fantasized; New Blood
Running time:
39.26
Current CD:
Mercury 830568-2
Further listening:
Don't Be Afraid Of The Dark (1988)
Further reading:
www.rosebuds.com/cray/
Like this?
Try . . . p.784

Anita Baker

Rapture

From waitress to '80s soul phenomenon and home again in eight years.

In 1980, Arista had bought the Ariola label and with it the contract of modestly successful Detroit soul band Chapter 8, which they allowed to lapse. Legend has it that the executives at Arista thought the lead singer – one Anita Baker – wasn't good enough. Returning to Detroit, Baker worked as a short-order cook, a waitress and eventually as a legal secretary.

In 1982 she got an offer from Otis Smith (who had signed Chapter 8 to Ariola) to record on his new Beverly Glenn label. The album that appeared was *The Songstress* (1983) which got her some attention, though the label's slowness in agreeing to a follow-up album resulted in Baker signing with Elektra, while still earning her living in a law firm.

Partly funding the recording herself (hence the "executive producer" credit she gets on the sleeve), she hired ex-Chapter 8 member Michael J Powell as producer and surrounded by ace sessioneers recorded *Rapture* which, from the sheen of Baker's skin on the album cover to the sensuous and precise music within, was a flawless product. When provocative new trends in black music were exploding from the street by the month, Baker kept her head and made a traditional (i.e., with its roots in the '70s) soul record with brooding, slow-burn minor tunes of romantic celebration and earthy longing. Baker's voice was an extraordinarily rich, restrained instrument that was further distinguished from many soul divas by a Sarah Vaughan-like jazz sensibility in her phrasing, the best example of which is the delightful series of improvised choruses on the fade of Been So Long.

Bolstered by the hit singles Sweet Love and Caught Up In The Rapture, the album won two Grammys and went on to sell over six million worldwide, establishing Baker as a genuine soul star of the late '80s and one of the all-time pop vocal greats. The follow-on albums did well enough but betrayed the common weakness of much glossy soul, succumbing to an under-inspired if efficient formula.

While fans of her artistry await a proper jazz album (she appeared on two tracks of pianist Cyrus Chestnut's eponymous CD in 1998), her leisurely approach to recording in the '90s bears out her famously quoted maxim; "You leave home to seek your fortune and, when you get it, you go home and share it with your family."

Record label:
Elektra

Produced
by Michael J Powell, except No One In The World; produced by Marti Sharron and Gary Skardina.

Recorded
in LA, autumn 1985.

Released:
March 1986

Chart peaks:
13 (UK) 11 (US)

Personnel:
Anita Baker (v, executive producer); Vesta Williams, Darryl Phinnessee, Natalie Jackson, Lynn Davis, Phillip Ingram, Jim Gilstrap, Alex Brown, Bunny Hull, Barry Diament (bv); Jimmy Haslip, Fred Washington, David B Washington (b); Robert Feist, Sir Gant, Randy Kerber (k); Lorenzo Brown, Paulinho Da Costa, Lawrence Fratangelo (pc); Paul Chiten, Greg Phillinganes (syn); Donald Griffin, Greg Moore, Dean Parks, Michael J Powell (g); Ricky Lawson, Arthur Marbury (d); Don Myrick (s); Warren Woods (finger snaps)

Track listing:
Sweet Love (s); You Bring Me Joy; Caught Up In The Rapture (s); Been So Long; Mystery; No One In The World; Same Old Love; Watch Your Step

Running time:
37.09

Current CD:
7559604442

Further listening:
The Songstress (1983); Giving You The Best That I Got (1988); Compositions (1990)

Further reading:
www.aub.dk/~tj/anitamain1.htm

Like this?
Try . . . p.396

The Bulgarian National Radio And Television Chorus

Le Mystère Des Voix Bulgares

World music that inspired Californian hippies then, over a decade later, topped the UK indie charts.

The Bulgarian State Radio and Television Female Vocal Choir had been assembled in 1951 by Philip Koutev, a composer whose task it was to use traditional music to advocate communism. The members of the choir brought to it their own region's folk songs, which were transformed into vehicles for six-part lead vocals and complex harmonies for 24 voices. Among the outsiders to be gripped by the new sound was Marcel Cellier, a Swiss engineer and part-time ethnomusicologist who spent 15 years in Bulgaria, much of it in the archives of the Bucharest Institute For Folklore. In 1966, Elektra's Nonesuch label released the album *Music Of Bulgaria*, and Koutev's choir struck a chord with the West Coast hippies. "They're like Angels, exceptionally pure," said Jerry Garcia, before sitting down to write Uncle John's Band, the opening track on *Workingman's Dead*, based on Bulgarian village music.

In the '80s, Cellier licensed his archives to Philips in France, entitling the resulting albums *Le Mystère Des Voix Bulgares*, the mystery, he claimed, lay somewhere between the "beauty of perfection and the perfection of beauty". A tape of the first volume found its way into the hands of Bauhaus's Peter Murphy in 1985, who played it to Ivo Watts-Russell. Ever-willing to use his label to indulge his passions (witness This Mortal Coil), the boss of 4AD then started searching for the source and discovered Cellier's LPs. 4AD released *Le Mystère Des Voix Bulgares* the following spring, while on a roll with The Cocteau Twins and Colourbox. Word-of-mouth recommendations meant the album quickly achieved cult status and Elektra took up the baton in the States. In an odd side-effect of their global success, the choir started using the album title as its recording and touring name. Though not the first Bulgarian compilation, Le Mystère took eastern European music to a level of acclaim hitherto unimaginable.

Record label:
4AD
Produced
by Marcel Cellier.
Recorded
throughout various Bulgarian villages.
Released:
April 1986
Chart peaks:
None (UK) None (US)
Personnel:
Yanka Roupkina (solo v); Kalinka Vatcheva (solo v); Stefka Sabotinova (solo v)
Track listing:
Pilentze Pee; Svatba; Kalimankou Denkou; Strati Na Angelaki Doumasche; Polegnala E Pschenitza; Messetschinko Lio Greïlivko; Breï Yvane; Erghen Diado; Sableyalo Mi Agontze; Prïtourïtze Planinata; Mir Stanke Le; Schopska Pesen; Polegnala Todora
Running time:
36.53
Current CD:
CAD603CD
Further listening:
Le Mystère Des Voix Bulgares, vols 2–4; Village Music Of Bulgaria (various artists)
Like this?
Try . . . p.400

Peter Gabriel

So

Eleven years after Genesis, his Grammy-winning world/pop/dance hit harvest.

It had been four years since Gabriel's fourth album. His head brimming with ideas, he had been working on film treatments and writing soundtrack music (*Birdy – Music From The Film* appeared on an album the year before *So*). He was also organising WOMAD, his annual festival of world music and art, which in turn led to his decision to take time off to upgrade his studio in the Wiltshire countryside and "explore this hybrid of non-European music and electronics". As the British press hailed him variously as a "pioneer" or a "cultural imperialist", Gabriel recorded a German-language version of his fourth album. Its producer, he later discovered, was having an affair with Gabriel's wife. Gabriel, meanwhile, had domestic complications of his own: an affair with actress Rosanna Arquette. Going along with a friend's advice, the Gabriels entered therapy. It was in this emotionally turbulent state – living apart from his family, seeing Arquette whenever possible – that Gabriel made his US breakthrough *So*.

One could speculate as to the cause – the combination of lust and loss, the tension between freedom and free-falling, a feeling of having to prove himself – but the quality and variety of songs on Gabriel's first album with a title was outstanding. Sledgehammer, its best-known track, was a sexy, funky tribute to the R&B bands Gabriel had loved as a teenager. Wayne Jackson of The Memphis Horns was brought in to lead the horn section; and Gabriel had even considered hiring funkmeister Nile Rodgers to produce before opting to stick with Daniel Lanois, with whom he had worked on *Birdy*.

Owning his own studio and its inherent lack of clock-watching might have been responsible for the time it took to make the album (various tracks, including In Your Eyes and Mercy Street, were completely rewritten between the album's start and end), but it can also claim credit for some fascinating experiments in electro-ethnic cross-pollination.

A highlight was the evocative, gospel-tinged duet with friend Kate Bush, Don't Give Up, the album's second hit single. The first, and even bigger, hit was Sledgehammer (UK Top 5; American Number 1). Its ubiquitous promo clip – dancing oven-ready chickens; animated fruit whirling about Gabriel's stop-motion face – was showered with awards.

WOMAD, soundtracks, charity concerts, art projects, his Real World record label and multi-media company, would occupy Gabriel for the next six years before he followed up *So* with *Us* – the album that documented his eventual separation from both Arquette and his wife.

Record label:
Virgin
Produced
by Daniel Lanois and Peter Gabriel.
Recorded
at Real World, England and Polygram Studios, Rio De Janeiro; February–December 1985.
Released:
May 1986
Chart peaks:
1 (UK) 2 (US)
Personnel:
Peter Gabriel (v, k, p); David Rhodes (g); Daniel Lanois (g); Tony Levin (b); Manu Katche (d); Kate Bush (v); Youssou N'dour (v); Laurie Anderson (v); Nile Rodgers (g); Kevin Killen (e)
Track listing:
Red Rain (S); Sledgehammer (S); Don't Give Up (S); That Voice Again; In Your Eyes (S); Mercy Street; Big Time (S); We Do What We're Told (Milgram's 37); This Is The Picture (Excellent Birds)
Running time:
46.25
Current CD:
PGCD 5
Further listening:
Peter Gabriel IV (1982)
Further reading:
Peter Gabriel, An Authorised Biography (Spencer Bright 2000); www.petergabriel.com
Like this?
Try . . . p.456

The Smiths

The Queen Is Dead

The Smiths' most rounded album saw them established as the most celebrated independent band of the decade.

Financial wrangling, management changes and a long-winded dispute with their record company, Rough Trade, were the backdrop to the recording of the Smiths' third studio album. Bassist Andy Rourke had recently been fired from the group and replaced by Craig Gannon, but was back on board by the time they entered the studio.

"My main memory is of darkness," recalls Johnny Marr. "Both literally and metaphorically. It was winter and we were in self-imposed isolation." Marr was feeling the pressure of public scrutiny and hitting the bottle.

"I felt like I was diving into a mire and [had to hold] onto the belief that I was coming out the other end. It certainly was my darkest hour, which made it bad for everybody else. We'd got over the curve which most bands don't, and I had this feeling that, if we're going to take our place among the greats then we had to get ourselves in the frame of mind that created great stuff. I knew exactly what was expected of us, which was to do something that was genuine art."

The intense, satiric title track mirrored Morrissey's mindset with a brutal and occasionally comic depiction of contemporary England plagued by moral and spiritual bankruptcy.

"I think that's my favourite Smiths lyric," says Marr, "brilliant in the true sense." It set the scene for a rich panorama of sound and colour, embracing the romantic melodrama There Is A Light That Never Goes Out, the maudlin self-absorbed I Know It's Over, the frivolous musichall romp Frankly Mr Shankly and uproariously camp, Carry On-styled Some Girls Are Bigger Than Others.

Delayed by several months due to legal injunctions, the album finally emerged in the summer of 1986 and effectively elevated the Smiths to a new creative and commercial level.

"At the end we knew that we'd done it and whether or not people were going to accept it was beside the point," notes Marr. "It was time to get back on the bus and start touring again. Job done."

The tour was a riotous affair. "There was perfect musical unity between myself, Mike and Andy," says Johnny. "It was a dream for me to play. Mike was just behind me and Andy fitted in the middle. That's the way we worked. I had something with Mike and Andy that I won't have playing with any other people."

As for Morrissey, he confirmed that beneath all the doom and drama lay a clever writer with a rich vein of comic irony. Whatever else they accused him of, critics finally acknowledged his role as one of rock's most sardonic humorists.

Record label:
Rough Trade
Produced
by Morrissey and Marr.
Released:
June 1986
Chart peaks:
2 (UK) 70 (US)
Personnel:
Morrissey (v); Johnny Marr (g, p); Andy Rourke (b) Mike Joyce (d). Stephen Street (e)
Track listing:
The Queen Is Dead; Frankly, Mr Shankly; I Know It's Over; Never Had No One Ever; Cemetry Gates; Bigmouth Strikes Again (S); The Boy With The Thorn In His Side (S); Vicar In A Tutu; There Is A Light That Never Goes Out; Some Girls Are Bigger Than Others
Running time:
37.06
Current CD:
WEA 4509918962
Further listening:
Meat Is Murder (1985), Strangeways, Here We Come (1987).
Further reading:
Morrissey & Marr: The Severed Alliance (Johnny Rogan, 1992).
Like this?
Try . . . p.535

Run DMC

Raising Hell

Rap momentarily mates with metal and is propelled overground.

In 1986, rap was little more than five years old, and still in thrall to a set of references that had been defined at the dawn of the '80s. Run DMC came out of the old world and promptly defined an altogether new one. In 1985, they were on tour with Kurtis Blow, Whodini and the Fat Boys as part of a package called "Fresh Fest"; one year later they released the album and single that revolutionised the rap form. Rubin had added metallic touches to LL Cool J's 1985 album *Radio*, but *Raising Hell* showcased the decisive melding of the two forms, when Run DMC duetted with Aerosmith on Walk This Way.

"I remember that the idea was met with some question at first," recalls Rubin, "but they listened to the song and wrote all the words down and started thinking 'We can do this.' The Aerosmith guys came down and played the guitars. Then Steven [Tyler] sang his chorus vocals first, and then Run did the rhymes and Steven joined in. We did it all in a day."

The group's account is of a rather more sceptical view of the idea than Rubin suggests ("Yo! This is hillbilly gibberish bullshit!" said McDaniels when presented with a lyric sheet), but the track's brutal brilliance was self-evident. It was one of three rock-based cuts on *Raising Hell* – there was also It's Tricky, based on a sample of The Knack's My Sharona, and the title track, on which Rubin once again scrawled his fuzz-toned musical signature. Even the more straight-laced rap songs utilised a hard-hitting aesthetic that was new to the rap milieu. The best example was My Adidas, a fantastically minimal track on which Run DMC paid tribute to their favourite brand of sneaker. It also introduced the rap world to corporate sponsorship: after the album's release, producer and manager Russell Simmons took an Adidas executive to a Run DMC show, and within seconds of the song's opening had clinched a deal.

All that apart, the importance of *Raising Hell* – which sold over five million copies in the US – lay in its destruction of the last few fences that stood in the way of rap's dominance of American pop culture. "It was important in that it brought it to the mainstream and it showed people rap was 'music,'" says Rubin. "It allowed hip hop into homes it had never been in before."

Record label:
Profile
Produced
by Russell Simmons and Rick Rubin.
Recorded
at Chung King House Of Metal, NYC.
Released:
July 1986
Chart peaks:
41 (UK) 3 (US)
Personnel:
Joseph Simmons aka Run (v); Darryl McDaniels aka DMC (v); Jason Mizell aka Jam Master Jay (DJ, k, pc); Sam Sever (programming); Daniel Shulman (b); Rick Rubin (g); Steven Tyler (v); Joe Perry (g); Steve Ett, Andy Wallace, Jay Burnett (e)
Track listing:
Peter Piper (S); It's Tricky (S); My Adidas; Walk This Way (S); Is It Live; Perfection; Hit It Run; Raising Hell; You Be Illin' (S); Dumb Girl; Son Of Byford; Proud To Be Black
Running time:
39.53
Current CD:
PCD1217
Further listening:
King Of Rock (1985); also, hear Rubin's rap/rock hybrid take shape on LL Cool J's Radio (1985)
Further reading:
The Hip Hop Years (Alex Ogg with David Upshal, 1999); www.thadweb.com/rundmc
Like this?
Try . . . p.34

Elvis Costello

Blood And Chocolate

Underrated career peak featuring the garage sound of "a band falling apart".

By 1986, life was becoming complicated for Elvis Costello. A failed marriage and two disappointing and over-produced flops – *Punch The Clock* and *Goodbye Cruel World*, both made with the production team of Clive Langer and Alan Winstanley – had directed him into a creative impasse characterised by manic name changes (he is billed here as Napoleon Dynamite). Hanging out with The Pogues as producer of their defining album *Rum Sodomy & The Lash* may not have been recommended by his doctor, but it stabilised Costello emotionally by hooking him up with Caitlin O'Riordan. She promptly gave up her duties as The Pogues' bassist and married him.

Earlier in the year, Costello had ventured outside the Attractions for an entire album, the stunning *King Of America*, which was produced by his hero T-Bone Burnett and featured a shifting cast of sessioneers, including the legendary James Burton. "*King Of America* showed me one of the problems on the records we'd done with Clive and Alan – the band was simply falling apart," says Costello. And fall apart they did, gloriously, on *Blood And Chocolate*. With old hand Nick Lowe at the helm, Costello and the rest of the Attractions convened for one last blow-out. Lowe set up the band in one room at Olympic Studios, deliberately allowing their sounds to bleed into each other.

"We set up and played as loud as we did on-stage," recalls Costello. "It was a really primitive record – just one mic in the middle of the studio. That's the only way we could achieve that low dynamic." Throughout, Costello's concerns remain constant: romantic possession, betrayal and disgust overlaid with a biting wit and surreal paranoia, as evidenced on the album's first single, the Dylanesque epic Tokyo Storm Warning, which conjures up a wealth of queasy imagery from KKK conventions to "Disney abattoirs". Described as "a protest song", Tokyo Storm Warning reached Number 73 in the charts – not surprising given its lyrical savagery and six-minute duration. Costello's shaky hand with singles was displayed when he followed up with I Want You. "Maybe releasing two six-minute singles back to back wasn't the way to do it," he says. Though certainly the high-point of the album, it is arguably the most twisted love song ever recorded, a tale of deception and all-consuming jealousy spat out over a menacing musical backdrop.

"There were quite a few scores being settled on that record," admits Costello, who adds that the crude recording technique added resonance to the songs. "On I Want You, everything you hear on the last minute is all from my vocal mic – you can hear the band only when they're bleeding through onto my voice."

Record label:
F-Beat
Produced
Nick Lowe with Colin Fairley.
Recorded
at Olympic Studios, London; February–April 1986.
Released:
September 15, 1986
Chart peaks:
16 (UK) 84 (US)
Personnel:
Napoleon Dynamite [aka Elvis Costello] (v, g); Steve Nieve (k); Bruce Thomas (b); Pete Thomas (d)
Track listing:
Uncomplicated; I Hope You're Happy Now; Tokyo Storm Warning (S); Home Is Anywhere You Hang Your Head; I Want You (S); Honey Are You Straight Or Are You Blind?; Blue Chair; Battered Old Bird; Crimes of Paris; Poor Napoleon; Next Time Round
Running time:
47.52
Current CD:
Demon DPAM 12
Further listening:
Spike (1989); Best Of (1999); the best of the Warners Years on Extreme Honey (1997)
Further reading:
The Big Wheel (Bruce Thomas, 1990); Let Them All Talk: Elvis Costello (Brian Hinton, 1999); www.elvis-costello.com
Like this?
Try . . . p.345

Paul Simon

Graceland

After a decade in the wilderness, Simon's songwriting gifts are re-invigorated with the energy of African music.

To suggest that *Graceland* contributed to the downfall of apartheid may be an overstatement but, in retrospect, it's certainly hard to rationalise the barrage of flak Paul Simon endured for working with the South African musicians who inspired this genre-busting album.

"*Graceland*'s instincts were right," he insists, "and it called into question a lot of thinking, which is good."

Even in Simon & Garfunkel, he had championed world music (cf El Condor Pasa) long before it became a *cause célèbre*, but the fusion of Western pop with township jive, *kwela* and *mbaqanga* styles on *Graceland* coincided serendipitously with the revitalising of Simon as a songwriter. "It started in 1984," Simon explained when the album was released. "A friend gave me a cassette of an album called *Gumboots: Accordion Jive Hits, Volume 2*." Surprised and impressed by how much this technically simple, happy music reminded him of the '50s rock'n'roll he'd grown up with, Simon went to Johannesburg in February 1985 to seek out the African musicians on *Gumboots*, hoping to collaborate with them on a new album. For more than a year, recording in Africa, the UK and various American locations, Simon brought together a unique combination of extraordinary musicians whose remarkable skills added texture, harmony, sound and playing technique previously unimaginable in the confines of Western pop.

For Simon, who had previously started with melodies and lyrics and then arranged them for a record, this process offered an exciting new way to create. "I thought, I have enough songwriting technique that I can reverse this process and write this song after the tracks are made. If I have a really good track and I write a good song, well then my chances of making a good record are vastly improved over the other way of working. And in the process of working in that way, I discovered different ways of turning the form around, from constantly listening to the way African guitarists and the bass players were altering what they were playing from verse to verse."

Heart-stopping moments abound – the first hit of Ladysmith Black Mambazo's vocal harmonies in Homeless, Baghiti Khumalo's mercurially slithering basslines in You Can Call Me Al – but it's the coherence and vision of *Graceland* as a whole that elevates it into the pantheon of classic rock albums. "Every groove is a small miracle," said Charles Shaar-Murray in New Hi-Fi Sound. "He has indeed made an excellent album."

Record label:
Warner Brothers
Produced
by Paul Simon.
Recorded
in Johannesburg, New York, Lafayette, Los Angeles and London; February 1985–May 1986.
Chart peaks:
1 (UK) 3 (US)
Released:
October 4, 1986
Personnel:
Paul Simon (v, g, b, synclavier); Chikapa "Ray" Phiri, Adrian Belew (g); Demola Adepoju (g); Morris Goldberg (pennywhistle); Alex Foster (as); Leonard Pickett (ts); Ronald E Cuber (bs, bass saxophone); Earl Gardmer, John Faddis, Randy Brecker, Lewis Michale Soloff, Alan Rubin (t); David W Bargeron, Kim Allan Cissel (tb); Rob Mounsey (k); Forere Motloheloa, Bagithi Khumalo (b); Vusi Khumalo, Isaac Mtshali (d); Youssou N'Dour, Makhaya Mahlangu, Babacar Faye, Assane, Thiam, Ralph McDonald (pc)
Track listing:
The Boy In the Bubble (S); Graceland (S); I Know What I Know; Gumboots; Diamonds On the Soles Of Her Shoes; You Can Call Me Al (S); Under African Skies (S); Homeless; Crazy Love Vol II; That Was Your Mother; All Around The World Or The Myth Of Fingerprints
Running time:
43.10
Current CD:
7599254472
Further listening:
Still Crazy After All These Years (1975)
Like this?
Try . . . p.632

XTC

Skylarking

The artistic and commercial renaissance of Swindon's finest.

XTC had been struggling to find their niche since main man Andy Partridge's debilitating – and, as it turned out, permanent – stage fright of 1981 had precluded touring. After the triumph of *English Settlement* of the same year, their last two albums *Mummer* (1982) and *Big Express* (1984) had seen the band's profile dip from cutting-edge craftsmen to negligible, arcane eccentrics – their psychedelic spoof project *The Dukes Of Stratosphere* (1985) had, embarrassingly, outsold both. A restless Geffen (XTC's US label) suggested Todd Rundgren produce the next album and guitarist Dave Gregory was genuinely excited by the potential of the Rundgren-Partridge meld: "What a fantastic pool of minds. Of course I'd reckoned without the ego problem."

Todd selected the demos and programmed the running order into a concept. Partridge: "He picked everything of Colin's and half of mine. And I thought, Am I that crap suddenly? Is Colin that brilliant?" In the studio, Rundgren was musically dazzling but poisonously sarcastic. Gregory: "It was just nasty and unnecessarily unpleasant. Todd got the measure of Andy's conceit and Andy rose to the bait every time."

The band rowed furiously, Colin left temporarily and, after his third attempt at mixing, Todd signed off and XTC had *Skylarking*, an album of gloriously warm, pastoral psychedelia which entirely belied the tumult of its making.

The most coherent and, perhaps, most likeable work of XTC's career, Partridge's brilliance here takes on an appealing pastel hue, while Moulding's five excellent songs are a personal triumph which balance the personality of the record beautifully; Rundgren's luscious production manages to make XTC sound both less and more like themselves. Partridge: "At the time I felt like disowning it. I thought, Jesus, this man's killed our career.' But I think he actually brought something out in us that we didn't know how to bring out, he did us a great favour."

Relegated from the album to the B-side of Grass – *Skylarking*'s first single – was an odd, angry little atheist's song of Andy's called Dear God, which Partridge regarded as a "petulant failure" but American college radio had picked up on, causing a furore in the process. "Mail was 50 per cent 'This is fantastic you've voiced what I've been thinking for years' and 50 per cent 'You're going to roast in hell.'" A Florida radio station received a bomb threat about it and a disaffected student held a New York State school secretary at knifepoint, demanding the track be played over the school PA. Dear God was hastily reinstated on *Skylarking* and XTC found a whole new audience.

Record label:
Virgin
Produced
by Todd Rundgren.
Recorded
at Utopia Sound Studios, Woodstock, NY and Soundhole Studios, San Francisco; spring 1986.
Released:
October 1986
Chart peaks:
90 (UK) 70 (US)
Personnel:
Andy Partridge (v, g); Colin Moulding (v, b); Dave Gregory (v, g, p, k, chamberlain); Prairie Prince (d)
Track listing:
Summer's Cauldron; Grass (S); The Meeting Place; That's Really Super, Supergirl; Ballet For A Rainy Day; 1000 Umbrellas; Season Cycle; Earn Enough For Us; Big Day; Another Satellite; Mermaid Smiled; Dear God (S/US); The Man Who Sailed Around His Soul; Dying; Sacrificial Bonfire
Running time:
45.42
Current CD:
CDV2399
Further listening:
English Settlement (1981); Oranges And Lemons (1989); Apple Venus Volume 1 (1999)
Further reading:
MOJO 64; XTC Song Stories (XTC and Neville Farmer, 1998) www.chalkhills.org
Like this?
Try . . . p.712

Beastie Boys

Licensed To Ill

The Never Mind The Bollocks for the '80s hip hop generation.

In 1985, Def Jam chief Russell Simmons received a call from Madonna's management. They were under the impression that he represented the Fat Boys: would they be interested in being the support act on the Like A Virgin tour? Without missing a beat, Simmons passed over the fact that he nothing to do with the corpulent rappers and instead recommended the Beastie Boys. The result was the honing of the obnoxious Beastie persona, as MCA, Mike D and Ad Rock performed to arenas of teenage girls who hated them.

In the wake of that tour, the trio completed the recording of their debut album with Simmons' Def Jam partner, Rick Rubin. To save money most of the work was done in the early hours, after the Beasties and their mentor had been partying in the New York clubs. This hedonistic mood permeates the album: The New Style, She's Crafty, No Sleep Till Brooklyn, all brim with beery hyperactivity. But for all the party-hearty atmosphere, *Licensed To Ill* was rightly acclaimed as a bold step forward for rap. Rubin had developed the rock-hip hop collision on both LL Cool J's *Radio* (1985) and Run DMC's *Raising Hell* (1986), and the Beastie Boys' debut was the pinnacle of this approach. The opening seconds of Rhymin' And Stealin', using sampled drums from Led Zeppelin's When The Levee Breaks, said it all: this was rap music that pilfered a great deal of heavy metal's brute power.

Much of the album was also knowingly funny, as the Beastie Boys revelled in gonzoid lairiness based not only on old-school rap *braggadocio*, but a clear love of rock cliché: No Sleep Till Brooklyn takes its lyrical lead from Motorhead's We Are The Road Crew. Then there was Fight For Your Right – gloriously moronic metal topped with giggle-strewn exhortations to teenage rebellion. The LP was to swiftly endear itself to every misunderstood adolescent in the Western world – and still does.

"What boggles my mind," says Mike D, "is that *Licensed To Ill* remains one of the biggest-selling catalogue records. We never envisaged the longevity and neither did Russell Simmons. He was used to rap records being big for maybe a couple of months. It still sells something like 500,000 a year. I wonder if it's people wearing out their old copies, or 14-year-old kids just getting into it now. Either way, it's too weird."

Record label:
Def Jam
Produced
by Rick Rubin and the Beastie Boys.
Recorded
in New York, 1986
Released:
November 1986
Chart peaks:
7 (UK) 1 (US)
Personnel:
Michael Diamond (v); Adam Horovitz (v); Adam Yauch (v); Kerry King (g); Rick Rubin (g, programming); Steve Ett (e)
Track listing:
Rhymin And Stealin; The New Style (S); She's Crafty (S/UK); Posse In Effect; Slow Ride; Girls (S/UK); Fight For Your Right (S); No Sleep Till Brooklyn (S); Paul Revere; Hold It Now Hit It (S); Brass Monkey; Slow And Low; Time to Get Ill
Running time:
44.33
Current CD:
527 351–2
Further listening:
Pre-rap Beasties on Some Old Bullshit (1994); The Sounds Of Science(1999)
Further reading:
Rhyming And Stealing: A History Of The Beastie Boys (Angus Batey, 1998)
Like this?
Try . . . p.702

The The

Infected

One young Londoner vents his brooding spleen at Thatcher's Britain.

Like its immediate predecessor, *Soul Mining*, *Infected* was a record fuelled by speed, vodka and Ecstasy, but its prevailing claustrophobic mood was far from euphoric. "*Infected*, to an eerie, ultimately disturbing extent is like 1986 trapped on vinyl," claimed the NME on its release.

Lyrically, the album dealt with such diverse subjects as US militarism, the male sex drive, and what mainman Matt Johnson described as the "greed culture" of Thatcherism. When he began writing the album, Johnson was just 23. Initially, he had approached Tom Waits, Brian Eno and Holger Czukay as possible producers, even spending a week in New York discussing the project with Waits over pool. Though keen, Waits was too busy but suggested that Johnson self-produce with a good engineer. Enter Livesey and Mosimann, later successful producers in their own right.

Despite the album's political edge and sleazy, often jagged arrangements, the recording sessions were anything but po-faced. "We spent a lot of time chasing around the control room with cream cakes and soda siphons," says Johnson. He also recalls that his duet with Neneh Cherry on Slow Train To Dawn came about after he got her "so drunk on vodka that she almost fell down the stairs". Heartland, featuring Steve Hogarth's gorgeous honky-tonk piano, has aged particularly well. Thanks to the now unshocking line "piss-stinking shopping centre", however, it fell foul of the censors when released as a single. Against the political backdrop of a US attack on Libya, Sweet Bird Of Truth's lyrics were also deemed unsuitable for daytime radio. To complicate matters, the title track was misconstrued as a reference to AIDS.

Shortly after its release, *Infected* gained a much-needed profile boost when Tim Pope and Peter Christopherson's promotional film of the entire album scored two Channel 4 screenings in quick succession. It had been filmed at considerable expense in Peru and Bolivia, with Johnson writing the storyboards for Heartland, Infected and The Mercy Beat. The album went on to sell around one million copies worldwide, but for Johnson, the highest accolade came years later: "I was at a party when this young, black American fighter pilot came up to me. He told me that he'd quit his job after listening to Sweet Bird Of Truth."

Record label:
Epic

Produced
by Matt Johnson, Warne Livesey, Gary Langan and Roli Mosimann.

Recorded
at Air Studios, Oxford Circus; Livingstone, North London; The Garden, Shoreditch, London; 1984–86.

Released:
November 1986

Chart peaks:
14 (UK) 89 (US)

Personnel:
Matt Johnson (v, g, k); David Palmer (d); Dan Brown (b); Jeff Cline (acoustic b); Steve Hogarth (p); Judd Lander (hm); Neneh Cherry (v)

Track listing:
Infected (S); Out Of The Blue (Into The Fire); Heartland (S); Angels Of Deception; Sweet Bird Of Truth (S); Slow Train To Dawn (S); Twilight Of A Champion; The Mercy Beat

Running time:
41.10

Current CD:
4886112

Further listening:
Soul Mining (1983)

Further reading:
www.thethe.com

Like this?
Try . . . p.502

Jane Siberry

The Walking

A singular vision explodes across an expansive canvas; Canada's secret is delivered to the world.

No one says Jane Siberry is crazy – unlike fellow Canadian Mary Margaret O'Hara; eccentric, perhaps. Her early works, this album included, all evoked a sense of vulnerability – but despite the glittering, woozy dreamscapes, Siberry wasn't soft; the experimentalism she prized was subtly focused, and she was tough enough to fight for it in dealings with the music industry. From a non-musical family, Siberry was writing songs before her feet could touch the ground from the piano stool; she would later revisit this juvenilia on *Teenager*, singing songs of innocence with the voice of experience.

As a student of microbiology in Ontario, she financed her debut, *Jane Siberry* (1981), with tips from a waitressing job, and in 1984 signed to a small Canadian label which joined with A&M/Wyndham Hill to release *No Borders Here. The Speckless Sky* (1985), went gold in Canada; her vision grew bigger still on this, her fourth album, described by Siberry as "a series of successive clearings and cinematic landscapes, each expanding into the next." While the making of 1993's *When I Was A Boy* was a three-year ordeal, *The Walking*, though profoundly introspective, was completed smartly. As a major label debut, it was a radical thing: no track less than five minutes, and two – the opener and closer – over ten. The dreamlike quality of the songs is enhanced by an array of non-musical effects and snatches of intimate dialogue; on the shiversome *tour de force* for spurned lover and Greek chorus, The Lobby, Siberry duets with a multi-tracked choir of her own voice (Chorus: 'This is your darkest hour'/Siberry: 'This is my finest moment'). What makes it spark is a mix of the seductive, intellectual and humorous, the lush meshes of swooping sound and sudden mood changes, and Siberry's clear, multi-octave voice. The sassy Red High Heels and rapturous The Walking will always be amongst her best work – so will the broken, post-relationship Goodbye: "I want a table/No just for one/But I know you do/I can see some from here/OK then say for two/But there's only one." Epic in scope, with huge emotional punch, the album is freebase poetry of an instantly accessible kind. Reviews were adoring. Siberry has said, "The saving grace for me is that record companies have never considered anything I do a 'hit'." Nevertheless, there was a certain pressure, and in 1996 she left Warner Brothers to start her own label, Sheeba.

Record label:
Reprise
Produced
by Jane Siberry and John Switzer.
Recorded
at Manta Sound Company, Toronto.
Released:
January 1987
Chart peaks:
None (UK) None (US)
Personnel:
Jane Siberry (v, g, k); Anne Bourne (k); John Switzer (b); Ken Myhr (g); Al Cross (d)
Track listing:
The White Tent The Raft; Red High Heels; Goodbye; Ingrid (And The Footman); Lena Is A White Table; The Walking (And Constantly); The Lobby; The Bird In The Gravel
Running time:
54.00
Current CD:
DSBD 31040
Further listening:
Bound By The Beauty bowls along, sometimes hymnal (The Valley), sometimes genially flaky (Everything Reminds Me Of My Dog); Summer In The Yukon collects highlights from her career up until When I Was A Boy (1993), her second masterpiece. Best of the output on her own label, Sheeba, is probably the sparse and lovely Teenager (1996) in which she revisits her earliest songs, originally recorded in her room with the sound of truck gears changing outside.
Further reading:
www.sheeba.ca to obtain One Room Schoolhouse, Siberry's engaging little book about her thoughts, computers and God.
Like this?
Try . . . p.546

U2

The Joshua Tree

Irish band imagines a mythic America of frontier spirit and spiritual quest.

U2 had only just finished touring their previous album when they set to work on their next. They had no new songs written at the time; rather, they simply got together at Adam Clayton's house at Danesmoate, and waited to see what happened. "Myself and Edge would be up at six o'clock in the morning, then Adam'd drop in, just writing songs and playing records," Bono explained, while engineer Steve Rainford told author Carter Alan, "at the beginning of [each] session, [there] was a band rehearsal. It's really the essence of how they do it – they bang around till they make it the way they like and then they record it."

Broadening the elemental nature of 1984's *The Unforgettable Fire*, *The Joshua Tree* encapsulated the band's grandiose vision of a mythic America. The videos which accompanied the singles – a Beatles-esque rooftop performance, an impromptu miming session on the streets of Las Vegas – and the ragged frontier innocence which overhangs the album reinforced *The Joshua Tree* became U2's biggest-selling album ever; it wasn't hard to see why.

"We wanted to try and capture a place as well as a mood," Mullen said. "We wanted to give each song a sense of location." From the forlorn ghost-ridden shacks of Red Hill Mining Town to the joyous apocalypse-hoedown of Trip Through Your Wires; from the killer's eye-view of Exit to the CIA training ground of Bullet The Blue Sky, *The Joshua Tree* was a panorama, the Edge said, of "the America of the great R&B and country performers, [of] civil rights people like Martin Luther King and Bobby Kennedy; [of] the new journalism of people like Truman Capote and Norman Mailer, the way they were able to bring you to a place was almost cinematic. We tried to do that on the album."

And the title? "There are many reasons for it," Bono revealed. "But it's almost impossible for me to explain that seriously, for me to take myself as seriously as that. Inevitably we're going to lie a lot." But he did admit, "Larry was too embarrassed to tell his girlfriend that we were going to call the LP after this clump of prickles in the desert."

Record Label:
Island
Produced
by Daniel Lanois and Brian Eno.
Recorded
at Danesmoate, early 1986; Windmill Lane Studios, Dublin; Spring 1986, August 1986–January 1987.
Released:
March 9, 1987
Chart peaks:
1 (UK) 1 (US)
Personnel:
Bono (v); The Edge (g, k, v); Adam Clayton (b); Larry Mullen Jr (d); Daniel Lanois (tambourine, omnichord, g, v); Brian Eno (DX7 programmes, k); Arklow Silver Band. Where The Streets Have No Name; With Or Without You; Bullet The Blue Sky and Red Hill Mining Town remixed by Steve Lillywhite.
Track Listing:
Where The Streets Have No Name (S); I Still Haven't Found What I'm Looking For (S); With Or Without You (S); Bullet The Blue Sky; Running To Stand Still; In God's Country (S); Trip Through Your Wires; One Tree Hill; Exit; Mother Of The Disappeared
Running time:
50.15
Current CD:
U2 6
Further listening:
The Unforgettable Fire (1984); Rattle And Hum (1988)
Further reading:
Outside Is America (Carter Alan, 1992)
Like this?
Try . . . p.408

Prince

Sign O' The Times

Prince's eighth album was a self-made Technicolor sprawl that netted three US Top 10 singles

Coming off the sales shrinkage of his previous albums *Parade* and *Around The World In A Day*, *Sign O' The Times* was nothing if not a calculated risk. Deeply entrenched in jazz legend Miles Davis' corpus at the time, Prince buffed his new material with tricked-out, high-sheen arrangements that pushed his New Power Soul to new heights.

But *Sign O' The Times* seemed to be trouble-plagued from the start. Prince had been bursting with ideas, he'd planned an album by his feminine alter-ego Camille, a double set to be made with sidekicks Wendy & Lisa and a triple album called *Crystal Ball* – all of these ideas were rejected by Warner Brothers as uncommercial. Then there were teething problems with his swanky new facility, Paisley Park.

"Prince hired a guy named Frank Demedi to install one of these state-of-the-art consoles in Paisley Park," recalled the album's engineer Susan Rogers. "One night he dreamt a song, which turned out to be The Ballad Of Dorothy Parker, and insisted on recording it immediately." Despite the console's total absence of high end, Prince laid it down and mixed the song that night.

"Technically it's a total mistake," says Rogers, "but he likes good mistakes if they work." The album which emerged was characterised by many happy accidents. Housequake, the album's funkiest jam, was inspired by a late-night recording session with 80's LA pop queens The Bangles, while a nocturnal studio visit from Scottish *chanteuse* Sheena Easton resulted in U Got The Look.

"Sheena came into the studio unannounced, 'cos she wanted Prince to produce her next album," says Rogers. "U Got The Look had gone through a million changes, and he was really struggling with it. It was originally a mid-tempo thing, but he had sped it up at the last minute and asked her to sing on it. I think she was a little taken aback by the sexual nature of it at first, but he convinced her to get into it, and it worked perfectly."

In the first months at Paisley Park he cut over 300 songs, many of them entirely by himself. Less ornate than predecessor *Parade* songs such as The Cross and the sparse but riveting title cut, nevertheless reverberated with an intense, soulful energy that would be missing from subsequent albums. In fact, *Sign O' The Times* was the last great Prince album. A few one-offs aside, little of his subsequent work had this much impact. A prolonged legal battle with his label Warner Brothers and a severe case of monomania sidetracked him in the '90s, and for many of his fans he has yet to reclaim his creative and commercial juice.

Record label:
Warner Brothers
Produced
by Prince.
Recorded
at Paisley Park, Chanhassen, Minnesota; Sunset Sound, Los Angeles, and Dierks Studio Mobile Tracks; summer and autum 1986.
Released:
March 1987
Chart peaks:
4 (UK) 6 (US)
Personnel:
Prince (g, d, b, k, v); Eric Leeds (s); Atlanta Bliss (t); Sheena Easton (v); Susan Rogers, Coke Johnson, Prince (e)
Track listing:
Sign O' The Times (S); Play In The Sunshine; Housequake; The Ballad Of Dorothy Parker; It; Starfish and Coffee; Slow Love; Hot Thing; Forever In My Life; U Got The Look (S); If I Was Your Girlfriend (S); Strange Relationship; I Could Never Take The Place Of Your Man (S); The Cross; It's Gonna Be A Beautiful Night; Adore
Running time:
79.59
Current CD:
7599255772
Further listening:
Prince And The Revolution, Purple Rain (1984); Around The World In A Day (1985); Parade (1986)
Further reading:
www.npgonlineltd.com/
http://users.ids.net/~dmsr/dmsr.html – an online archive of Prince history
Like this?
Try . . . p.261

Butthole Surfers

Locust Abortion Technician

Psychedelia and punk in a pre-grunge union.

The Butthole Surfers were the Merry Pranksters of '80s US indie rock. Emerging at a time when orthodox hardcore (Black Flag, Bad Brains) still reigned, they belonged to a nonconformist tradition that seemed in danger of extinction. Instead, with Big Black and Sonic Youth, they formed an influential triumvirate that reacquainted rock with an earthy dissonance, a noise that eventually went overground with grunge. Like The Grateful Dead, the Buttholes made music that existed less for itself than as the public expression of a way of life. The Dead epitomised wild drugs and communality; the Buttholes wilder drugs and a conviviality born of boredom.

There was nothing unusual in the band's formation – two high-achieving students, Gibby Haynes and Paul Leary, met at college in 1981 – but there convention ended. As the band's name suggests, Haynes, the son of a Texan children's television host, revelled in ludicrous outrage. His comic-dystopian visions spilled over into live appearances, which would often resemble freak shows, with nude dancers and films depicting all manner of depravity. "The world would be a sad place if we became a monster group," confessed drummer King Coffey. The Buttholes never quite became "monster", but after a handful of records that owed little to rock-'n'roll convention, they came of age in 1986 with *Rembrant Pussyhorse*. The record was well-received and paved the way for a successful European tour, where Haynes' debuted his "Gibbytronix", a digital delay box that enabled his voice to match the group's increasingly mangled music. The Gibbytronix was all over *Locust Abortion Technician*, the Buttholes' first record for influential UK indie Blast First, and a definitive statement of rock'n'roll grotesquery. According to Leary, the group reverted back to an 8-track for the sessions (like most things in the Buttholes' history, remain shrouded in mystery) which took place at a studio equipped with one microphone and an archaic tape-machine that weighed around 800 pounds. Disparate styles – psych, punk, electronic, ethnic, even a Black Sabbath pastiche (Sweet Loaf) – sounded strangely compatible after receiving the Buttholes treatment. Sewer blues (Pittsburg To Lebanon), queasy basslines (22 Going On 23), fuzz-guitar overload (Graveyard, USSA), even something approaching a conventional avant-rock song (Human Cannonball).

Record label:
Blast First
Producer not listed
Recorded
winter 1986.
Released:
March 1987
Chart peaks:
None (UK) None (US)
Personnel:
Gibby Haynes (v); Paul Leary (g); King Coffey (d); Theresa Taylor (d); Jeff Pinkus (b)
Track listing:
Sweat Loaf; Graveyard; Pittsburg To Lebanon; Weber; Hay; Human Cannonball; USSA; The O-Men; Kuntz; Graveyard; 22 Going On 23
Running time:
32.42
Current CD:
LBV05
Further listening:
Hairway To Steven (1988) refined the formula – and with a greater acoustic presence, too.
Further reading:
www.buttholesurfers.com/
Like this?
Try . . . p.451

Slayer

Reign In Blood

Third album by devil-bothering LA thrash metal squad sends moral majority into a tizzy.

When maverick producer Rick Rubin signed Slayer to Def Jam back in late '85 there were those who questioned his judgement. Quite what a Satanic metal band from LA had in common with the rap world was anyone's guess. "To me it made perfect sense. When I heard Slayer I just thought that I had to sign them because they were just as extreme and relevant as, say, Public Enemy," explains Rubin.

As if to introduce the band to the Def Jam family, Rubin also persuaded guitarist Kerry King to lay down the guitar tracks on the Beastie Boys keg-party anthem Fight For Your Right (To Party) on the rap brats' chart-topping *Licensed To Ill* debut. In truth it did little to prepare the world for Slayer's forthcoming album.

Reign In Blood was a short, sharp shocker, causing an immediate storm of controversy thanks to opening track, Angel Of Death. The song's principal protagonist was notorious Nazi death-camp doctor, Joseph Mengele. The band were immediately accused of being Nazi-sympathisers.

"We've had a lot of flak about that, but we are not Nazis," stated frontman Tom Araya, at the time. "The song is very graphic, but it's an observation. No more, no less. People make films about this kind of stuff so why can't you write a song about it?"

Despite the band's attempts to clear the air, Def Jam's distributors, CBS, in a knee-jerk reaction, refused to release the album in the US and Geffen stepped in to distribute the record. In the UK, however, Warner Brothers (Geffen's distributor) felt the album featured "unsuitable content" and pulled the plug. When *Reign In Blood* finally emerged on London Records in the UK, it had already attained legendary status among an audience hungry for taboo thrills.

While Angel Of Death had caused most of the brouhaha, the rest of the subject matter was no less gruesome, tracks like Piece By Piece, Necrophobic and Criminally Insane boasted all the subtle allure of The Texas Chainsaw Massacre, the graphic lyrical imagery matched by clinically savage playing. Slayer had delivered the most brutal metal album of the late '80s.

Record label:
American Recordings
Produced
by Rick Rubin and Slayer.
Recorded
'in LA'; mid-1986.
Released:
April 1987
Chart peaks:
46 (UK) 94 (US)
Personnel:
Kerry King (g); Jeff Hanneman (g); Tom Araya (v, b); Dave Lombardo (d); Andy Wallace (e)
Track listing:
Angel Of Death; Piece By Piece; Necrophobic; Altar Of Sacrifice; Jesus Saves; Criminally Insane (S); Reborn; Epidemic; Post-mortem; Raining Blood
Running time:
29.03
Current CD:
4917982
Further listening:
Hell Awaits (1985); South Of Heaven (1988)
Further reading:
www.diabolus.net
Like this?
Try . . . p.128

The Replacements

Pleased To Meet Me

Fifth album from the dishevelled, influential alternative rockers, now reduced to a trio.

In the early '80s, Minneapolis, as well as being home to the artist then known only as Prince, was the epicentre of American post-punk rock: Hüsker Dü, Soul Asylum and, wildest of the lot, The Replacements, formed in 1979 after Paul Westerberg joined brothers Bob and Tommy Stinson's and Chris Mars' garage band. Their early Twin/Tone albums were a jumble of styles – country, folk, heavy rock, blues – delivered with a punk spirit and a bar-room swagger like a ragged, budget-version Rolling Stones. By 1985 their garage-punk roots were starting to grow out, and Seymour Stein signed them to his Warner Brothers offshoot label Sire. Suddenly they were label-mates with Madonna.

"We were really young, jaded and nonchalant about the whole thing," said Tommy Stinson about the change in their fortunes. "We weren't thinking, Wow, we're on a major label, we're going to make lots of money, we were just, Who cares? We just had a real Fuck The System attitude about it all."

Though major label debut *Tim* continued their shift towards more evocative, mature material, this musical progress was offset by increasingly fraught relationships within the group, largely thanks to their self-destructive lifestyles. And as the band prepared to record their second Sire album *Pleased To Meet Me*, guitarist Bob Stinson was sacked. (Eight years later, in 1995, he would be found dead in his apartment of a suspected drug overdose.)

Despite the loss of their guitar player, they hunkered down in Memphis with producer Jim Dickinson, chosen for his Big Star connection – Alex Chilton was Westerberg's idol; his presence is felt elsewhere on the album in the tribute track named after him and in his guest appearance on closer I Can Hardly Wait. Westerberg's growth as a songwriter is highlighted on the bitter-sweet Never Mind, the acoustic Skyway and the harrowing suicide anthem The Ledge. Ironically, his mellowing approach split the band in 1990 following the mid-tempo melancholia of *All Shook Down*, a Replacements album widely viewed as the frontman's first solo effort. *Pleased To Meet Me*, however, insured that The Replacements' legacy was considerable, with the likes of Kurt Cobain and The Black Crowes claiming it as a key influence.

Record label:
Sire
Produced
by Jim Dickinson.
Recorded
at Ardent Studios, Studio B, Memphis; 1987.
Released:
May 1987
Chart peaks:
38 (UK) 131 (US)
Personnel:
Paul Westerberg (v, g); Tommy Stintson (b); Chris Mars (d); East Memphis Slim (k); Teenage Steve Douglas (bass flute, bs); Price Gabe (s); Andrew Love (ts); Ben Jr (tp); Alex Chilton (g); John Hampton, Joe Hardy (e)
Track listing:
IOU; Alex Chilton (S); I Don't Know; Nightclub Jitters; The Ledge (S); Never Mind; Valentine; Shooting Dirty Pool; Red Red Wine; Skyway; I Can Hardly Wait (S)
Running time:
33.32
Current CD:
925 557 2
Further listening:
Tim (1985); All Shook Down (1990); Paul Westerberg 14 Songs (1993); Suicaine Gratification (1999)
Further reading:
Student Matt Tomich's Skyway fan site is packed with photos and regular updates on all Replacements activity past and present: www.theskyway.com
Like this?
Try . . . p.624

LL Cool J
Bigger & Deffer

Ladies' man breaks rap wide open while manager Sean "Puffy" Combes takes notes in the wings.

Ain't nothing like the old skool, as Tupac Shakur noted, and there are few modern rappers and hip-hoppers who don't owe something to the original B-boy, the man who styled himself Ladies Love Cool James.

Just 18 years old when this dynamite album was released, James Todd Smith had already established himself as a bare-chested, gold-chained pin-up who could rap alongside the best of them. The first artist to release a single on Def Jam, he'd starred in Krush Groove and his boastful, ladykilling style made him a star of the genre's first big US tour, on which he stole the show night after night from the likes of Run DMC and Grandmaster Flash. Writer Nelson George described LL as "larger than life, almost a cartoon, a rapper as arena rock star".

Debut album *Radio* had borne the influence of Def Jam's resident hard-rock freak Rick Rubin, who had littered it with heavy metal samples in much the same way as he would with Run DMC and the Beastie Boys. But on *Bigger And Deffer*, LL emerged from Rubin's shadow, using the far funkier yet sparse electro scratching and astute sampling of Earl "Bobcat" Erving and his LA Posse colleagues Darry Pierce and Dwayne Simon. Matched with their eclectic choice of samples, from the Shaft theme on Get Down to James Brown on Kanday and Chuck Berry on Go Cut Creator Go, LL's boastful and dynamic raps and charismatic persona helped shoehorn rap into the commercial mainstream, offering an authentic alternative to the whiny white-boy posturing of the genre's other titans, the Beastie Boys.

"*Bigger & Deffer* is a concept album, and the concept is LL's ego," wrote Vibe magazine's Sia Michel. "Self-mythology is the aim of any rapper, but no one else has ever come close to such put-me-in-the-pantheon ego-tripping." The key to the album's appeal lies in his tag – ladies really did love James, particularly when he revealed his sensitive side on the landmark I Need Love, the first true love song of rap and his first UK Top 10 hit. Against the delicate and soulful bedrock of samples, LL serenades a romantic infatuation which teeters on the edge of, but never spills over into, lasciviousness. That was reserved for the ensuing Def Jam tour, when he used I Need Love as an excuse to dry-hump an onstage sofa, sparking charges of public lewdness in Columbus, Ohio.

Record label:
Def Jam
Produced
by LL Cool J and the LA Posse.
Recorded
at the Chung King House Of Metal, NYC
Released:
June 1987
Chart peaks:
54 (UK) 3 (US)
Personnel:
LL Cool J (v); Bobcat Erving (scratches); The LA Posse (samples, programming); Russell Simmons (production supervisor)
Track listing:
I'm Bad (S); Kanday; Get Down; The Bristol Hotel; My Rhyme Ain't Done; .357 – Break It On Down; Go Cut Creator Go; The Breakthrough; I Need Love (S); Aah Let's Get Ill; The Do Wop; On The Ill Tip
Running time:
45.19
Current CD:
527353-2
Further listening:
Kool Moe Dee, How Ya Like Me Now (1988); Run DMC, Raising Hell (1986); Sean "Puffy" Combes, No Way Out (1997)
Further reading:
The Vibe History Of Hip Hop (1999)
Like this?
Try . . . p.605

Def Leppard

Hysteria

Multi-platinum soft-metal Brummies dodge the worst luck of their career to produce their best album.

With the release of *Pyromania* in March 1983, Def Leppard had become the biggest-selling British hard-rock band of the '80s with sales of the album topping the eight-million mark. As the band regrouped in Ireland in early '84 with Mutt Lange to start work on *Hysteria*, the producer announced that he was suffering from exhaustion, having worked on *Pyromania*, Foreigner's *4* and The Cars' *Heartbreak City* in quick succession. Unable to wait for Lange, Leppard enlisted the services of Meat Loaf producer Jim Steinman and elected to start recording in Wisseloord, Holland. The results were nigh-on disastrous, leading to Steinman's departure.

Then, as the band took a Christmas break, drummer Rick Allen's Chevrolet Corvette Stingray spun off the road between Sheffield and his parents' home in Dronfield, severing his left arm in the process. Allen and his girlfriend Mirium Barendsen were rushed to the Royal Hallamshire Hospital, where Allen's arm was sewn back on, only for infection to set in. Three days later it had to be amputated.

In a show of solidarity, Leppard refused to contemplate life without their friend and insisted that they would wait for him.

"We intend to have Rick back on stage and participating if at all possible," stated manager Peter Mensch at the time, leading to speculation that two drummers might be involved. Instead, Leppard soldiered on with Lange back on board and started work on *Hysteria*, programming the drums on a Fairlight computer while Allen began his rehabilitation and began to develop a unique keypad drum system which would allow him to rejoin the band onstage.

After an intense period of speculation *Hysteria* emerged in the summer of '87 and astounded the critics (who'd always resented down-to-earth Leppard's success). Lange's production sounded immense, setting standards for the next generation of stadium-rock bands. A stronger record than *Pyromania*, *Hysteria* matched muscle (on tracks such as Armageddon It!, Animal, Gods Of War) with melody (on the likes of Love Bites, Love And Affection and the title track) with a stadium-sized sense of fun. Even the cheesy Pour Some Sugar On Me, Rocket and Boston-esque opener Women are delivered with a certain tongue-in-cheek charm. While Leppard continued to sell albums by the truckload, however, their on-the-road habits were starting to take their toll, most notably on guitarist Steve Clark. Following a late-night drinking session, Clark was found dead in his Chelsea apartment on January 8, 1991. For Leppard things would never be the same again.

Record label:
Bludgeon Riffola
Produced
by Robert "Mutt" Lange.
Recorded
at Wisseloord Studios, Holland; summer 1984–summer 1985.
Released:
August 1987
Chart peaks:
2 (UK) 1 (US)
Personnel:
Steve Clark (g); Phil Collen (g); Rick Savage (b); Joe Elliott (v); Rick Allen (d); The Bankrupt Brothers (bv); Mike Shipley, Nigel Green (m)
Track listing:
Women (S); Rocket (S); Animal (S); Love Bites (S); Pour Some Sugar On Me (S); Armageddon It! (S); Gods Of War; Don't Shoot Shotgun; Run Riot; Hysteria (S); Excitable; Love And Affection
Running time:
62.40
Current CD:
830 675
Further listening:
Pyromania (1983); Slang (1996)
Further reading:
Def Leppard: Animal Instinct (David Fricke, 1985); www.webnl.com/senff/leppard.html
Like this?
Try . . . p.404

Guns N' Roses

Appetite For Destruction

Full-length debut by LA guttersnipes blends the spirit of the Stones, vintage Aerosmith and the Pistols.

"I want this to be the biggest-selling debut album from a rock act ever!" was W Axl Rose's characteristically immoderate cry when Geffen released *Appetite For Destruction*.And so it was, arguably, with 15 million worldwide sales chalked up in the four years before the follow-up dual release of *Use Your Illusion I* and *II*.

Guns N' Roses came together in mid-'80s Los Angeles with a common urge to make a new noise out of their mutual interest in hard rock and punk. Their enthusiasm for drink and drugs meant they could never put an exact date to the band's formation, but Geffen's talent scouts discovered them living in vile shared accommodation off Sunset Boulevard in 1985. However, it took A&R woman Teresa Ensenat some time to fix them up with a producer because, she said, "People were very afraid of this band."

Eventually, Mike Clink, a quiet young man who had engineered for Heart and Eddie Money, agreed to take on the general misbehaviour and in particular Rose's posturing, or by some accounts, manic-depressive mood swings.

But, behind all the racket, the band had written a collection of songs fundamentally true to their collective character and, on the right day, they could play them to savage effect. A lot of their writing candidly confessed their bad habits. For example, Nightrain is a tribute to the cheap wine of that name ("It would fuck you up for a dollar. Five dollars and you'd be gone!" Rose crowed nostalgically). The scathing My Michelle refers to one of the singer's girlfriends who "led a crazy life doing drugs" and Mr Brownstone is a cautionary tale of heroin addiction. Yet Rose's commercial boast was fulfilled because they had, unwittingly it seemed, also come up with some far less abrasive material in the radio-friendly Paradise City and Sweet Child O' Mine.

Even so, Rose's voice wasn't the sweetest noise on radio and *Appetite For Destruction* took 12 months of constant touring to reach Number 1 in the US. At which, predictably enough, able to satisfy said appetite at whim, the band began to fall apart. There were endless fights: between themselves, with audience members, with policemen. And there was genuine tragedy in the death of two fans trampled to death at the 1988 Castle Donnington festival. Come 2000, with only three more albums behind them, Rose still claimed that Guns N' Roses existed – but that he was the only member.

"It was the success that screwed us up," Slash once lamented before adding with some pride, "but *Appetite* was an album we made because that's what we were about. It wasn't dictated by industry policy or business decisions, it was an honest record."

Record label:
Geffen
Produced
by Mike Clink.
Recorded
at Rumbo Recorders, Canoga Park, Los Angeles; August 1986.
Released:
August 1987
Chart peaks:
5 (UK) 1 (US)
Personnel:
W Axl Rose (v, syn, pc); Slash (g); Izzy Stradlin (g); Duff "Rose" McKagan (b); Steven Adler (d)
Track listing:
Welcome To The Jungle (S); It's So Easy (S); Nightrain (S); Out Ta Get Me; Mr Brownstone; Paradise City (S); My Michelle; Think About You; Sweet Child O' Mine (S); You're Crazy; Anything Goes; Rocket Queen
Running time:
53.50
Current CD:
GED 24148
Further listening:
Live @*?! Like A Suicide (1987)
Further reading:
Over The Top: The True Story Of Guns N' Roses (Mark Putterford, 1993)
Like this?
Try . . . p.278

The Smiths

Strangeways Here We Come

The Smiths' swansong brimmed with images of death.

"I don't think this album is what we're about to most people," says Johnny Marr. "They've decided that *The Queen Is Dead* is the better album and I don't agree. All the songs are better, it's produced better and it's got a better atmosphere. I might be wrong but I don't think I am."

By 1987, The Smiths appeared to have come full circle. Marr, having almost lost his life in a car crash, was eager to enter the studio but his priorities were changing. Andy Rourke had overcome his heroin addiction and was playing well alongside Mike Joyce. Morrissey, as ever, was being enigmatic and unpredictable, but seemed up for another album. Contrary to popular myth, the sessions were relatively stress-free. Drink flowed during the early stages and Marr appeared determined to take the group in a new direction, away from their image as indie jingle-jangle kings. As Andy Rourke observed: "A Rush And A Push And The Land Is Ours stands out because it didn't have any guitars on it at all. I thought that was a first." Morrissey was at his most characteristically maudlin and no less than seven songs were death-related, including the single Girlfriend In A Coma and Death At One's Elbow.

"My favourite memory of making *Strangeways* was putting the strings on Last Night I Dreamt That Somebody Loved Me," says Johnny, "and doing the guitars on Stop Me . . . a load of amps and a load of guitars all turned up full and I was dropping this steel knife onto the guitars and they were making these godawful huge kerrangs, so I enjoyed doing that."

If there was a problem it lay in the background, with Marr insisting on retaining his manager against Morrissey's wishes. There were also changes in attitude about what The Smiths represented. Morrissey voiced a desire to make records and go home, rather than conquer the world. Marr was also getting into dance music, which took him even further away from Morrissey's worldview.

"Sometimes it came down to Sly Stone versus Herman's Hermits," Johnny quipped afterwards, "and I knew which side I was on."

By the following summer the unthinkable had happened. Marr announced his decision to quit. The dream was over.

"It's the one Smiths record I've actually sat down and listened to since the break-up," says Johnny now. "It really was the first time that I'd listened to a Smiths record voluntarily. I found that I knew and remembered every single note. I remembered *being* every single note, and I really, really enjoyed it and thought it was a great record."

Record label:
Rough Trade
Produced
by Johnny Marr, Morrissey and Stephen Street.
Recorded
at Wool Hall, Bath; spring 1987.
Released:
September 1987
Chart peaks:
2 (UK) 55 (US)
Personnel:
Morrissey (v); Johnny Marr (g, p); Andy Rourke (b); Mike Joyce (d); Steve Williams (ae)
Track listing:
A Rush And A Push And The Land Is Ours; I Started Something I Couldn't Finish (S); Death Of A Disco Dancer; Girlfriend In A Coma (S); Stop Me If You Think You've Heard This One Before (S/US); Last Night I Dreamt That Somebody Loved Me (S); Unhappy Birthday; Paint A Vulgar Picture; Death At One's Elbow; I Won't Share You
Running time:
36.09
Current CD:
4509918992
Further listening:
Meat Is Murder (1985); The Queen Is Dead (1986)
Further reading:
Morrissey & Marr: The Severed Alliance (1992)
Like this?
Try . . . p.524

Depeche Mode

Music For The Masses

The most subversive pop group of the age finally tire of pop.

They'd begun as defiantly feeble electro-popsters under the guidance of Vince Clarke. When he departed to form, consecutively, The Assembly, Yazoo and Erasure, it seemed that they were doomed, but it turned out that they had another visionary in their midst, bubble-haired changeling Martin Gore, who took control and began to steer them down an ever-darkening path.

Last time out, on *Black Celebration*, the landscape had been bleak, the vision austere, and they'd recorded in Berlin with Daniel Miller. This time around, they went to Paris and insisted the mood would be "optimistic". And by songwriter Martin Gore's recent standards ("I don't want to start any blasphemous rumours . . .") it probably was. Just Can't Get Enough was a long way off now, and it was about to get pushed back even further.

Amid soaring pinnacles of synthi-symphonic grandeur, *Music For The Masses* emerged as an album of tight corners, dark rooms and deeply private ruminations, voiced through some of Gore's most oblique lyrics yet. New York's Village Voice condemned the militaristic lope of Never Let Me Down Again as "a metaphor for drugs or gay sex" (but omitted mention of the coy tribute to Soft Cell's Torch in the song's coda); others saw the fragile Little 15 as an open endorsement of paedophilia. The Things You Said spat betrayal through sharp, broken teeth; and the understated Behind The Wheel traced its text down similar corridors to the earlier Master And Servant – but without the whiplash smile. Gore, it appeared, was no stranger to the *demimonde* of S&M imagery and fatal attractions.

If Gore's lyrics were left wide open to interpretation, however, in the studio there was no room for manoeuvre. Even his bandmates were simply handed his demos and, according to Andy Fletcher, instructed simply to "Copy what he'd done." Only in the search for sounds and samples did Gore permit the others to contribute, and *Music For The Masses* overflows with the delirium of that freedom, a pantechnicon of clattering kitchenware, tinkling toys and somewhere, what Alan Wilder described as "a pygmy doing his wail . . . turned into something that sounds nothing like a pygmy". The first time *Music For The Masses* fell onto the turntable, that just about summed up Depeche Mode as well.

It would not be lost on them that the darker they became the more success they achieved. Indeed that proved to be a disastrous equation for them on a personal level. But by the time of *Violator*, another helping of oddly upbeat nihilism, they were one of the very biggest pop groups in the world, and the saccharine jingles of their early days were unimaginable.

Record label:
Mute
Produced
by Depeche Mode and David Bascombe
Recorded
at Studio Guillauhme Tell, Paris; Konk, London; spring 1987
Release date:
October, 1987
Chart peaks:
10 (UK) 35 (US)
Personnel:
Andrew Fletcher (k), Martin Gore (k), Alan Wilder (k), David Gahan (v)
Track listing:
Never Let Me Down Again (S); The Things You Said, Strangelove (S); Sacred; Little 15 (S); Behind The Wheel (S); I Want You Now; To Have And To Hold; Nothing; Pimpf.
Running time:
44.32
Current CD:
STUMM 47 adds: Agent Orange, Never Let Me Down Again (Aggro Mix), Spanish Taster, Pleasure Little Treasure
Further listening:
Black Celebration (1986), Violator (1990)
Further reading:
Depeche Mode: A Biography (Steve Malins 1999)
Like this?
Try . . . p.380

1987

Bruce Springsteen

Tunnel Of Love

Springsteen veers from stadium-size music and socio-political context to sing of men and women, love and fear.

Since 1984, Springsteen had been through the mill. A huge world tour. Rival American presidential contenders claiming Born In The USA as personal endorsement. Chrysler trying to buy him – or, rather, *that* song again – for $12 million. Rejecting these advances, he had nonetheless succumbed to a degree of hubris when compiling a five-LP live set.On the other hand, he had tackled one declared problem – emotional isolation – by marrying actress Julianne Phillips on May 13, 1985. About two years on, in his home studio, within three weeks he wrote and recorded most of *Tunnel Of Love* (bar One Step Up and a few E Street Band member over-dubs).

He told an interviewer he wanted to write romantic songs that "took in the different types of emotional experiences in any relationship where you are really engaging with that other person and not involved in a romantic fantasy or intoxication". His themes – explicitly in Two Faces and Brilliant Disguise – were "the twin issues of love and identity", set against an urgent sense of "the passage of time". Everything about the record reflected an awareness, unusual among artists of any sort, that his audience was "moving on as I was", rather than demanding endless remakes of *Born To Run*.

This produced a luminous honesty. He regularly had to deny that the songs were "literally autobiographical", but their essence plainly came from the bone marrow of his marriage. The Rambo figure of the *Born In The USA* tour metamorphosed into a stoic assailed by fundamental doubts. In One Step Up ("and two steps back") he just doesn't know how to resolve his "dirty little war" of a relationship; in Cautious Man he leaves the marriage bed in the middle of the night, sees "nothing but road" ahead and slips back while his wife still sleeps; in Tougher Than The Rest, despite everything, he swears he will go the real-life distance "if you're rough and ready for love"; in All That Heaven Will Allow and Valentine's Day he simply offers love in hope. *Tunnel Of Love* is one of rock's most profoundly felt albums. Every quiet, sparsely elegant song reaches to the soul of common experience.

Springsteen toured *Tunnel Of Love* with The E Street Band, then broke it up. Within a year of the album's release, he was divorced and beginning another dark night of confusion not resolved until he settled down with backing singer Patti Scialfa and, perhaps, accepted his share in "the beauty of God's fallen light" so carefully depicted by Cautious Man.

Record label:
CBS
Produced
by Bruce Springsteen, Jon Landau and Chuck Plotkin.
Recorded
at Springsteen's home, Rumson, New Jersey (except One Step Up, recorded at A&M Studios, Los Angeles); January–February and April 1987.
Released:
October 1987
Chart peaks:
1 (UK) 1 (US)
Personnel:
Bruce Springsteen (v, g); Max Weinberg (d, pc); Danny Federici (o); Garry Tallent (b); Nils Lofgren (g, bv); Roy Bittan (syn); Patti Scialfa, Clarence Clemons (bv); James Wood (hm); Toby Scott (e)
Track listing:
Ain't Got You; Tougher Than The Rest; All That Heaven Will Allow; Spare Parts (S); Cautious Man; Walk Like A Man; Tunnel Of Love (S); Two Faces; Brilliant Disguise; One Step Up (S); When You're Alone; Valentine's Day
Running time:
46.28
Current CD:
4602702
Further listening:
The Ghost Of Tom Joad (1995) – the next time he found his voice for a whole album.
Further reading:
MOJO 17, 62; www.backstreets.com.
Like this?
Try . . . p.196

George Michael

Faith

Former teen idol comes good on his solo debut, in a welter of lust and pained remorse.

George Michael is a bit of a depressive, or he was in the early '80s. The Wham! years had been rampant but not stress-free, and "I had to get away from the whole up-up-up thing because I felt so down." He and Andrew Ridgeley shook hands amicably enough but Michael remained too low to move forward, and hid out in LA getting wrecked on booze and ecstasy. It was only when Ridgeley paid a visit and, during an alcohol-soaked session, Michael poured out his woes, that he began to regroup. "I changed my mind about carrying on, about playing the game. I decided I'd do it all over again, but this time, on my terms."

Two painstaking years went into writing and producing *Faith*, which was to be seen as a turning point, replacing the image of the grinning pop idiot with that of a sophisticated adult. The chosen look was hoodlum chic: designer stubble, torn jeans and a leather jacket (on the sleeve, George has his nose stuck under his arm as if staggered by the reek of pheromones). Said Ridgeley, "I never understood why he wanted to portray that image – the brooding, macho guy. That's not him."

The music was an even bigger surprise. Michael had released two solo singles, heart-on-the-sleeve ballads Careless Whisper and A Different Corner. I Want Your Sex, *Faith*'s first single, discussed a different anatomical location. Pumping along on a testosterone-fuelled riff and punctuated by grunts, it was banned by the BBC and hammered for recklessness in the age of AIDS. There was, however, a moral logic.

Michael: "Sex in rock'n'roll is always sex with a stranger, it's the idea that there is nothing erotic at all about your boyfriend or girlfriend." I Want Your Sex was about "fucking within a relationship with someone you know and want to be with, yet you can't keep your hands off them."

The theme of swooning, mature commitment continued with the likes of Father Figure and One More Try. For anxious publisher Dick Leahy, reassurance that his boy knew what he was about came when he heard what would be the second single. "George had just a bit of an intro, the intro to the track Faith. I told him, in the '50s, all we did was: you go into a guitar lick, you go back to the bridge, and then intro the chorus. Two and a half minutes. So why not make a '50s record? Next day I went to the studio and he played me Faith. He said, 'You mean like that?' Cheeky sod."

Record label:
Epic
Produced
by George Michael.
Recorded
at Sarm West and Puk Studios, 1986.
Released:
November 14, 1987
Chart peaks:
1 (UK) 1 (US)
Personnel:
George Michael (v, b, k); Deon Estus (b); Ian Thomas (d); Lee Fothergill (g); Hugh Burns (g); Robert Ahwai (g); Danny Schogger (k); Chris Cameron (p); Shirley Lewis (bv); John Altman, Mark Chandler, Steve Waterman, Malcolm Griffiths, Jamie Talbot, Steve Sidwell, Rick Taylor (horns); Chris Porter (e)
Track listing:
Faith (S); Father Figure (S); I Want Your Sex (S); One More Try (S); Hard Day; Hand To Mouth; Look At Your Hands; Monkey (S); Kissing A Fool (S)
Running time:
58.09
Current CD:
4600002
Further listening:
Older (1996) is an assured and wistful take on personal pain. In the light of George's 1998 outing it can be seen as a landmark record about ageing, AIDS bereavement, and the friction between public and private personae. Ladies And Gentlemen (1998) gives you 30 of George's best, including collaborations with Astrud Gilberto, Elton John and Mary J Blige.
Further reading:
Bare (Tony Parsons, 1991)
Like this?
Try . . . p.829

Boogie Down Productions

Criminal Minded

The third part of hip hop's second "holy trinity": the "golden age" started here.

Alongside Public Enemy's and Eric B & Rakim's debuts, Criminal Minded ushered in an unparalleled era of cohesive creativity in hip hop. Yet it remains less widely known than it deserves.

Laurence Parker first met Scott Sterling at the Franklin Men's Shelter in the Bronx in 1985. Scott, 23, worked there; Parker, 20, was looking for a bed, and the two discovered a shared love of hip hop. The younger man adopted the name KRS-1, a contraction of Kris, itself short for Krisna, a nickname earned by his interest in world religions. Scott already called himself La Rock at his DJ gigs.

The duo's 1986 single, South Bronx, was part strident declaration, part coruscating history lesson, KRS laying down the law about rap's early years in bellicose, belligerent style. The follow-up album was no less hard-hitting, P Is Free detailing forgotten stories from crack-ravaged New York and Poetry showcasing KRS's revolutionary new style of rap, where syllables and phrases are insinuated within the song's fabric. Even more chilling is 9mm Goes Bang, the story of a crack dealer engaged in a war with competitors, the first incidence of a first person crime story on a New York rap record.

Criminal Minded relied on a drum machine-driven melange of samples mainly culled from late '60s and early '70s funk, but that's only part of the story. Dope Beat loops AC/DC's Back In Black, 9mm Goes Bang and The P Is Free betray a heavy reggae influence, and the title track finds KRS singing lyrics to the tune of Hey Jude. Credit is also due to Ced Gee of fellow Bronx group Ultramagnetic MCs, who was given "special thanks" on the sleeve but did most – of not all – of the drum machine programming.

The record became the most talked-about rap record of even that epochal year. BDP were signed to major label Jive, and by the time the duo replaced Kurtis Mantronik as in-house producers at rap indie Sleeping Bag, the "golden age" sampling aesthetic had replaced the electro stutter as hip hop's most progressive sonic format. Yet on that very day this second deal was signed Scott was shot dead in a parked car in an apparent revenge attack after BDP posse member D-Nice had been involved in an argument over a woman. KRS continued using the BDP name until 1993, and to this day his records bear the credit "overseen by Scott La Rock". The case remains unsolved.

AB

Record label:
B-Boy Records
Produced
by KRS ONE:
Scott La Rock: Ced Gee
Recorded
at
Released:
September 1987
Chart peaks:
LSR8812
Personnel:
Scott La Rock (turntables, v on Dope Beat): Blastmaster KRS ONE (v)
Track listing:
Poetry: South Bronx: 9mm Goes Bang: Word From Our Sponsor: Elementary: Dope Beat: Remix For P Is Free: The Bridge Is Over: Super-Hoe: Criminal Minded
Running time:
46 mins 37 secs
Current CD:
LSR8812
Further listening:
Boogie Down Productions – Edutainment (Jive 1990): KRS ONE – A Restrospective (Jive 2001): By All Means Necessary (Jive 1988)
Like this?
Try . . . p.581

Ultramagnetic MC's

Critical Beatdown

An unfairly neglected yet influential classic from the heyday of New York hip hop.

A victim of record business hold-ups, the debut by the apostrophically challenged Bronx rap group Ultramagnetic MC's is often denied its rightful place among the pantheon of classics of rap's golden age. As the group's lead rapper, maverick wordsmith Kool Keith, explains, delays meant others stole their thunder.

"We were in motion before Public Enemy," Keith recalls. "We were the only group out with the sound, but getting our deal together took a long time. But Def Jam beat us out and blew Public Enemy up and got behind them."

By the time Critical Beatdown arrived, it wasn't just PE who'd beaten Ultra to the dirty breakbeat-fuelled punch. Their Bronx neighbours, Boogie Down Productions, had also emerged with a strikingly similar aesthetic, ironically with Ultramagnetic's help: Ced Gee, the group's principal producer, assisted BDP with their album.

Nevertheless, the quality of the material meant that Critical Beatdown was still lauded when it finally surfaced, though its sales have never reflected its quality. Recorded in Queens after pre-production and demoing had been completed in Ced's home studio, the album was largely self-produced, but benefitted from the input of engineer Paul C. "Paul wasn't just an engineer," Keith acknowledges. "He kept pushing me to get my vocals better, and he mixed the whole album. And he had the drums..."

Paul, who was killed in mysterious circumstances shortly after Critical Beatdown was released, is credited with production on the album's standout track, Give The Drummer Some, which he built out of samples from an obscure James Brown-produced 45, The Dee Felice Trio's There Was A Time. This song, and the album's title track, would go on to have undreamed of consequences: Liam Howlett, a British DJ and Ultra fan, later incorporated samples of Keith's rhymes into two tracks, Out Of Space and Smack My Bitch Up, which became hits for his band, the Prodigy.

The rest of the album, though, is no less sparkling, samples used ranging from Joe Cocker and David Bowie to the funk of James Brown, The Meters and Jimmy Castor. Keith, who wrote some of Ced's lyrics as well as his own, is already a masterful and mysterious rapper, his acerbic wit coupled with complex rhyme schemes that often see him wrapping sentences around the ends of lines, while essaying outrageous metaphors.

"Critical Beatdown was fun to make, because we didn't have any restrictions," Keith concludes. "We just wrote it because it sounded good."

AB

Record label:
Next Plateau
Produced
by Ced Gee, Ultramagnetic MC's, Paul C (Give The Drummer Some)
Recorded
at Studio 1212, "The Ultra Lab"
Released:
1988
Chart peaks:
Personnel:
Kool Keith (v): Ced Gee (v): Moe Luv (turntables): TR Love
Track listing:
Watch Me Now: Ease Back: Ego Trippin' (MC's Ultra Remix): Moe Luv's Theme: Kool Keith Housing Things: Travelling At The Speed Of Thought (Remix): Feelin' It: One Minute Less: Ain't It Good To You: Funky (Remix): Give The Drummer Some: Break North: Critical Beatdown: When I Burn: Ced-Gee (Delta Force One)
Running time:
47 minutes 9 seconds
Current CD:
Next Plateau/Roadrunner NP 5496.2
Further listening:
Funk Ya Head Up (1992): The Four Horsemen (1994): Dr Octagon – Dr Octagonocologist (1995): Kool Keith – Sex Style (1997)
Like this?
Try . . . p.300

Leonard Cohen

I'm Your Man

Comeback which redefined the erstwhile king of the bedsit bards as a careworn, comic observer of modern mores.

By his own admission, Leonard Cohen had "lost his voice" sometime in the '70s, started to regain it on 1985's *Various Positions*, but was only really restored to full artistic vigour three years later with *I'm Your Man*, the ninth and finest album of his long and distinguished career. Apologising for his slow workrate (he took two years to write the previous album's highlight Hallelujah, for instance), he explained, "It just seems to take me a long time to bring things to completion. I generally do a book between albums."

Reflecting his peripatetic bohemian lifestyle, the album was recorded in various studios in Paris, Montreal, New York and Los Angeles, and featured the newly computer-literate songwriter's most successful forays into new music technology, with synthesizer and drum-machine replacing the acoustic guitar of earlier albums. The songs, too, seemed to reflect a new sense of resolution and self-confidence, from the opening intellectual battle-cry of First We Take Manhattan to the Zen-like equanimity of the closing Tower Of Song, one of the finest pieces ever written about the lonely predicament of the writer's existence. Throughout, Cohen's wry wit found its perfect medium in his dry, slightly sinister baritone, itself the cue for one of the album's more amusing lines, when he acknowledges sardonically that he was "born with the gift of a golden voice".

"A lot of us don't know how to sing according to certain standards," he told Q magazine, "but there is a whole tradition of music where you just want to hear the man telling a story as accurately and as authentically as you can. That's why people like me can get away with making records. There are certain times when I feel that my voice is absolutely appropriate for the song, like in Tower Of Song."

And, he might have added, in the title track, as devotedly romantic a song as this legendary ladies' man has ever written. Ultimately, the secret to *I'm Your Man*'s success may be the authentically personal ring to the material, which evokes the singer's character in a more multi-dimensional manner than before. "When [a song's] really personal, everybody understands it," Cohen explained. "There's a middle ground which is just unzipping and self-indulgence, but when you really tell the truth people immediately perceive that. Like when I wrote I Can't Forget, it started off as a kind of hymn, and I ended up sitting at this kitchen table thinking, Where am I really? What can I really tell anyone about anything? So I wrote, 'I stumbled out of bed/Got ready for the struggle ...' "

Record label:
CBS
Produced
by Leonard Cohen with Roscoe Beck, Michel Robidoux and Jean-Michel Reusser.
Recorded
at Studio Tempo, Montreal; DMS Studios, Montreal; Studio Montmartre, Paris; Soundworks, New York; Stagg Street Studio, Los Angeles; Rock Steady, Los Angeles; Studio 55, Los Angeles, 1987.
Released:
February 1988
Chart peaks:
48 (UK) None (US)
Personnel:
Leonard Cohen (v, k); Jeff Fisher (k); Larry Cohen (k); Michel Robidoux (k, d); Peter Kisilenko (b); Vinnie Colaiuta (d); Tom Brechtlein (d); Lenny Castro (pc); Bob Stanley (g); John Bilezikjian (oud); Raffi Hakopian (vn); Sneaky Pete Kleinow (ps); Jennifer Warnes (v); Anjani (v); Jude Johnstone (v); Ian Terry (e); Roger Guerin (e); Leanne Ungar (e)
Track listing:
First We Take Manhattan (S); Ain't No Cure For Love (S); Everybody Knows; I'm Your Man; Take This Waltz; Jazz Police; I Can't Forget; Tower Of Song
Running time:
41.02
Current CD:
460642 2
Further listening:
Songs Of Love And Hate (1971)
Further reading:
www.leonardcohen.com
Like this?
Try . . . p.685

Tracy Chapman

Tracy Chapman

An '80s one-off, the black female folk singer whose intimate style went global.

"I just think that people need to understand that if the person next door doesn't have enough food or is about to lose their home, that affects everyone else." This classically simple and sincere protest singer's credo was the improbable basis of Tracy Chapman's (barely six-month) ascent from coffeehouse obscurity in Massachusetts to selling millions of her self-titled debut album. All it took to convert pure intentions into unpredicted commercial bonanza was two spots on the Nelson Mandela tribute concert at Wembley Stadium, the second a lucky accident when she was pushed back on because thieves had whipped some of Stevie Wonder's keyboard programmes.

But for all the industry hand-rubbing at the time, the album remains a pristine realisation of everything burning in a young artist's heart and soul. Born in 1964, she was raised by a single mother in a Cleveland, Ohio ghetto during the latter part of the civil-rights-campaign era, the background to Across The Lines. If that forged her, she then found her musical outlets in a completely different setting. At 16, she was awarded a scholarship to a private school in Connecticut, and subsequently graduated to Tufts University in Medford, Massachusetts. There she studied anthropology and found a home for her songs on the New England coffeehouse circuit. Later, fame sometimes brought graceless questions implying she had somehow invaded a white musical neighbourhood. Naturally, she answered pithily that music had no colour bars: "Folk music comes from an Anglo and Afro tradition. People forget that blacks in this country have a folk music and a history."

Spotted busking on the street, she was quickly signed to Elektra Records and Elliot Roberts' management (he had handled Neil Young, Bob Dylan and Joni Mitchell, whose then husband Larry Klein played bass on *Tracy Chapman*).

Experienced and versatile producer David Kershenbaum accepted the integrity of a very enclosed young artist and so let the songs do the work, from the contained anger of protest and social obervation in Talkin' 'Bout A Revolution and Fast Car to the achingly restrained love song For My Lover and the pained delicacy of Behind The Wall, which concerned child abuse. As Kershenbaum said at the time, "What was difficult was holding back from adding things. What Tracy wanted was to keep the songs earthy and rootsy. I don't think many people have made a record this naked."

Record label:
Elektra
Produced
by David Kershenbaum.
Recorded
at Powertrax, Hollywood, California; 1987.
Released:
April 1988
Chart peaks:
1 (UK) 1 (US)
Personnel:
Tracy Chapman (v, g, pc); David LaFlamme (vn); Ed Black (sg); Paulinho Da Costa (pc); Danny Fongheiser (pc); Jack Holder (o, dobro, dulcimer, sitar, p, g); Larry Klein (b); Bob Marlette (k); Steve Kaplan (k, hm)
Track listing:
Talkin' 'Bout A Revolution (S); Fast Car (S); Across The Lines; Behind The Wall; Baby Can I Hold You (S); Mountains O'Things; She's Got Her Ticket; Why?; For My Lover; If Not Now . . .; For You
Running time:
35.51
Current CD:
60774-2
Further listening:
Crossroads (1989)
New Beginning (1995)
Telling Stories (2000)
Further reading:
www.elektra.com/elektra/tracychapman/index.jhtml
Like this?
Try . . . p.250

The Go-Betweens

16 Lovers Lane

UK-resident Australians return home to finally make the feelgood pop album they've threatened throughout their ten-year career.

A favourite of English undergraduates; they dropped references to Plath, Genet and Joyce in their lyrics; and one of their two frontmen wore dresses on stage. None of these things are in themselves surprising, of course. It's just that when Brisbane teenagers Robert Forster and Grant MacLennan formed The Go-Betweens, they wanted to be pop stars. "Whenever I think of The Monkees," wrote Forster on the sleeve of their 1978 debut, "it's a sunny morning, Last Train To Clarksville has been written, and we are left with our own imperfection." This didn't stop them trying to emulate it. For most of the '80s, no music press critics' poll was complete without that year's Go-Betweens offering. Fans (among them Morrissey and R.E.M.) seemed perplexed at the commercial failure of claustrophobic, lovelorn classics like Tallulah and Before Hollywood. A move to London opened a seam of emotionally tangled lit-pop (and enough interpersonnel intrigue to rival Fleetwood Mac) but it was only when Forster and MacLennan returned to Australia that they relaxed enough to write that quintessential pop album.

"There was definitely a sense of it being a big party," says MacLennan. "We were back in Australia, and thoughwe'd made so much of our best music in London, we hadn't been happy. I suppose that people think great albums should come from pain and misery but this was the opposite."

In producer Mark Wallis, the eccentric Forster had found his match. Wallis demanded that he sing the mournful Dive For Your Memory on the roof of the studio building. Drummer Lindy Morrison hated Wallis, mainly because he replaced her with a machine on five songs. In fairness though, his decision works well with the should've-been summer hit Streets Of Your Town. After touring *16 Lovers Lane* for a year, The Go-Betweens inked a new deal with Capitol, but on reflection there was nowhere to go. They'd finally completed an album full of the sort of songs they'd aspired to as teenagers.

"Normally," mused Forster, "when a band splits up and it's two songwriters you assume that it's the two songwriters who broke up, but it was Grant and I breaking away from the rest of the band. We'd just had enough of everyone else."

An embittered Lindy Morrison summed up their legacy in disparaging terms. "The only people we appealed to were a fistful of wanky journalists and some university students." She had a point, but when Forster and MacLennan reconvened in 2000 for a new Go-Betweens album, she wasn't invited.

Record label:
Beggars Banquet
Produced
by Mark Wallis.
Recorded
at Studios 301, Sydney, Australia;
May 1988.
Released:
August 1988
Chart peaks:
81 (UK) None (US)
Personnel:
Robert Forster (v, g, hm); Grant MacLennan (v, g); Lindy Morrison (d); Amanda Brown (vn, oboe, g, v); John Willsteed (b, g, Hammond organ, p)
Track listing:
Love Goes On!; Quiet Heart; Love Is A Sign; You Can't Say No Forever; The Devil's Eye; Streets Of Your Town (S); Clouds; Was There Anything I Could Do? (S); I'm Allright; Dive For Your Memory
Running time:
37.05
Current CD:
BBL 2006 CD
Further listening:
Liberty Belle And The Black Diamond Express (1986); Tallulah (1987); Go-Betweens 1978–1990 (1990); Robert Forster, Danger In The Past (1990)
Further reading:
The Go-Betweens (David Nichols, 1997)
www.go-betweens.net
Like this?
Try . . . p.140

Talk Talk

Spirit Of Eden

For their fourth album a London-based pop band travel to previously uncharted territory.

Few could have been prepared for the exquisite and extraordinary design of this music. Most listeners of the day thought of Talk Talk as purveyors of yearning synth-pop. But there were one or two clues of what was about to happen for anyone who was paying attention, such as the spare Chameleon Day on their hit album *Colour Of Spring* (1986). Following that album's success, Talk Talk frontman Mark Hollis decided he'd tired of pop music. Under the influence of producer and collaborator Tim Friese-Greene – who had developed his interest in composers like Messiaen, Stockhausen and Cage – Hollis explored the form's outer limits. But it took time to get there. The album was almost complete when Hollis decided it was too much like a rock record and opted to erase the whole thing. With the slate clean, they edged towards the new sound they'd imagined. "Working with space, the idea of the geography of sound was important," says Hollis, "and deciding that we'd treat one side of the album as one whole piece."

Focussing on subtlety and restraint, they constructed new, transparent basic tracks and invited guest musicians to embellish them. One was violin prodigy Nigel Kennedy who found it hard to break out of his virtuoso noodling. Friese-Greene made him play less by gaffer-taping together the fingers on his left hand. On another occasion that has entered into studio lore, the team spent a long and expensive day recording a large brass section and kept only the sound of a trumpeter clearing spit from his mouthpiece.

When all the guests were recorded, the tracks were montaged and sculpted for weeks until the final songs emerged. There were suggestions of Stockhausen in the fragmentary arrangements and echoes of John Lee Hooker in the expressive, percussive guitar, but overall there was a jazz ambience, something akin to Miles Davis' In A Silent Way, a palpable sense of musicians in a room, of instruments resonating against one another, of air being pushed around. The cavernous live-room at Wessex studios – a former church – was the perfect environment, and Hollis credits engineer Phill Brown, a veteran who'd worked under Hendrix/Yes maestro Eddie Kramer, with capturing its ambience. Brown had approached them after hearing *Colour Of Spring* and maintains that making *Spirit Of Eden* was one of the most intense experiences of his career, also recalling how they customised the control room for maximum atmospheric effect.

"It was very psychedelic," he remembers. "We had candles and oil wheels, strobes going, sometimes just total darkness in the studio. You'd get totally disorientated, no daylight, no time frame. I lost a year of my life to that record, but what a record!"

Record label:
Parlophone
Produced
by Tim Friese-Greene.
Recorded
at Wessex Studios, London; June 1987–August 1988.
Released:
September 1988
Chart peaks:
19 (UK) None (US)
Personnel:
Mark Hollis (v, p, o, g); Lee Harris (d); Paul Webb (b); Tim Friese-Greene (harmonium, p, o, g); Martin Ditcham (pc); Robbie McIntosh (dobro, 12-string g); Mark Feltham (hm); Simon Edwards (Mexican bass); Danny Thompson (db); Henry Lowther (t); Nigel Kennedy (v); Hugh Davies (shozygs); Andrew Stowell (bassoon); Michael Jeans (oboe); Andrew Marriner (clarinet); Christopher Hooker (cor anglais); The choir of Chelmsford Cathedral; Phill Brown (e).
Track listing:
The Rainbow/Eden/Desire; Inheritance; I Believe In You; Wealth
Running time:
41.24
Current CD:
RETALK103
Further listening:
The Colour Of Spring is a magnificent pop record and a dry run for this sound, if a little more typically '80s. Laughing Stock (1991) took the experiment even further out.
Further reading:
MOJO 51
Like this?
Try . . . p.483

Mary Margaret O'Hara

Miss America

First – and, to date, final – album of idiosyncratic avant-torch songs from a thoroughly singular artist.

Mary Margaret O'Hara appeared to have been doing fine ploughing her own low-key furrow until she put this out, and came face to face with criticism of the cruellest, most personal sort. Born in Toronto, she joined rock band Songship in 1976, later renaming them Go Deo Chorus. As lead singer, she wrote many of the songs that would appear on *Miss America*, and developed a wild stage manner of scat-style ad-libbing while flapping one arm like a flag, the other limp at her side. She quit Go Deo in '83, but a demo tape drew Virgin's attention, and she was signed in '84. She went into the studio that November, with XTC's Andy Partridge producing; he left after a day. Guitarist Rusty McCarthy explains what may have thrown him: "She might have her rhythm section switching beats, bass playing backwards or bass in 3/4 time and drums in 4/4." Only four tracks (all ballads) were accepted by Virgin, who insisted on something more marketable. There followed a lengthy stand-off, during which O'Hara wrote more, but nothing that pleased the label. Then, in October 1987, experimental guitarist and composer Michael Brook saw her live and offered to help mix and produce. The result was an album of sensuous singing, unorthodox arrangements and a brave emotional range – from the quivering nerves of Year In Song, whose broken and repeated phrases suggest a mind about to fracture, to the yearning To Cry About and the consoling lullaby You Will Be Loved Again. With elements of jazz and country, and the "troubled AOR" of Not Be Alright and Body In Trouble, the album seemed to have realised all that O'Hara intended; she chose the title "because I thought the record was so much unlike what those two words together said."

But Virgin wasn't happy. Though UK reviews were glowing, the album failed to chart. American critics, however, took badly to its audacity: one called her "Annie Hall with a lobotomy", commenting on her anxious live performance, another said "Dementia's not something a crowd expects of a singer-songwriter." Virgin gave the album little support and let it die. (It was repackaged and reissued by Koch in 1996.) Apart from a handful of guest spots, the fragile Miss O'Hara – a force of nature who can deliver with accomplishment – has tragically, but understandably, kept her distance from the record industry ever since.

Record label:
Virgin

Produced
by Mary Margaret O'Hara and Michael Brook.

Recorded
at Rockfield Studios, Monmouth, Wales; Phase One Studios, Toronto, Canada; Comfort Sound, Toronto, Canada.

Released:
October 1988

Chart peaks:
None (UK) None (US)

Personnel:
Mary Margaret O'Hara (v); Rusty McCarthy (g); Michael Brook (infinite g); Don Rooke (s); Hugh March (vn); David Piltch, Hendrik Riik (b)

Track listing:
To Cry About; Year in Song; Body's In Trouble; Dear Darling; A New Day; When You Know Why You're Happy; My Friends Have; Help Me Lift You Up; Keeping You in Mind; Not Be Alright; You Will Be Loved Again

Running time:
46.00

Current CD:
CDV2559

Further listening:
The Christmas EP (three covers, one original) came out on Virgin in 1991, and has also been reissued by Koch (KOC-CD 7935). She appears frustratingly low in the mix on Morrissey's single November Spawned A Monster (May 1990). Other than her floating membership of Toronto's The Henrys – seek out Chasing Grace (1996) and Desert Cure (1998) – and occasional contributions to soundtracks and compilations, that's it.

Like this?
Try . . . p.507

Keith Richards

Talk Is Cheap

Stone going it alone makes best Stones album in ages.

Keith Richards had never thought of making a solo album until Mick Jagger announced that he didn't want to tour *Dirty Work*, going off instead to cut his own second solo project, *Primitive Cool*. Keith killed time by producing a rip-snorting version of Jumpin' Jack Flash for Aretha Franklin and acting as chief instigator and bandleader on the superb Chuck Berry movie Hail! Hail! Rock and Roll! Richards' accomplice on these ventures was a dreadlocked New York drummer in the David Letterman house band, Steve Jordan. Richards and Jordan began hanging out in New York, jamming and writing in a little studio on Broadway.

"That's where Steve and I became real tight," says Richards. "And suddenly we had some songs. And then the idea came, y'know: let's make a record." As the writing progressed, the "cute pink room" at Studio 900 became a kind of clubhouse, and a band, the X-Pensive Winos, began to coalesce around Richards and Jordan. . "Almost without realising it, we'd put together this incredible machine, this band that was so hot nobody could believe it," says Keith. "After the first night, we looked at each other and it was like we'd been playing together ten years. And then I was hooked."

The ideas came thick and fast but they took a while to become songs. "The trouble with me is I leave songs in a sort of half-finished state till somebody grabs it and says, Yeah!" admits Richards. "I have to wait for somebody to react to something that's coming out of me. If I get enthusiasm, then that turns me on and I think, well, maybe I ain't stupid after all."

"My job up to that point had been writing songs for Mick to sing," says Richards. "Most of the songs Mick could have sung, but they wouldn't have taken such funny, quirky leaps, because I just sing differently and I hear different melodies." The album sounded to many ears like the best Stones album the Stones never made. Yes, there was filler on it – Struggle, How I Wish and Whip It Up – but the rest was the pure, unadulterated Keith many of us had longed to hear, free of Jagger's posturings. As for the extraordinary *J'accuse* of You Don't Move Me, as acerbic as Lennon's anti-Macca How Do You Sleep? it may have been, but it was also full of genuine pain at what the Stones had allowed to leak away over the decades.

"Mick's never mentioned it to me," says Richards, "but Bernard Fowler told me that when he was on tour in Australia he'd walk out of the room every time someone put the album on. And hey, I've got a couple of others in reserve if he wants more!"

BM

Record label:
Virgin
Produced
by Keith Richards, Steve Jordan
Recorded
at Air, Montserrat; Le Studio, Montreal.
Chart Peaks:
37 (UK) 24 (US)
Release date:
autumn 1988
Personnel:
Keith Richards (v, g), Steve Jordan (d, bv), Waddy Wachtel (g), Charley Drayton (b, bv), Ivan Neville (k), Sarah Dash (v, bv). Bootsy Collins (b), Bernie Worrell (o, Clavinet), Bobby Keys (s), Maceo Parker (as), Chuck Leavell (o), The Memphis Horns (horns), Stanley "Buckwheat" Dural (accordion), Patti Scialfa (bv), Sam Butler (bv), Michael Doucet (vn), Johnnie Johnson (p), Joey Stampinato (b), Mick Taylor (g)
Track listing:
Big Enough; Take It So Hard; Struggle; I Could Have Stood You Up; Make No Mistake; You Don't Move Me; How I Wish; Rockawhile; Whip It Up; Locked Away; It Means A Lot
Running time:
47.06
Current CD:
Virgin CDV2554
Further listening:
Live At The Hollywood Palladium (1991) Keef and his Winos on the get-out-of-jail free tour.
Further reading:
Keith: (Stanley Booth, Bob Gruen 1996) Keith Richards: The Unauthorised Biography (Victor Bockris, 2002); Keith Richards: Satisfaction (Christopher Sandford, 2003)
Like this?
Try . . . p.16

My Bloody Valentine

Isn't Anything

FX-laden noiseniks torch the late '80s UK independent scene.

Between 1984 and 1987, My Bloody Valentine tried everything. Having uprooted from their native Dublin, guitarist/songwriter Kevin Shields and drummer Colm O'Ciosoig, with original vocalist Dave Conway, ventured to Holland, then Berlin, where they flaunted some Birthday Party-inspired art/noise garage rock.By 1985, they were in London. By the time of the 1986 EP, The New Record By My Bloody Valentine, the band – now with bassist Debbie Goodge – had fashioned a bubblegum-like wall of fuzz sound with bowl-cut haircuts to match. A couple of singles and the *Ecstasy* mini-LP, issued on The Primitives' Lazy label during 1987, hardly suggested much had changed except, perhaps, acquiring a mild thirst for recognition.

The band's fortunes were turned around by two events. In the summer of 1987, Bilinda Butcher replaced the outgoing Conway, bringing with her a delicate singing style and an untrained but ambitious guitar technique. And Creation Records, home of contemporary retro-pop, offered them plenty of studio time to develop their ideas. The first fruit of this new liaison was the startling You Made Me Realise 12-inch, which had all the thrills of tough American avant-rockers like Sonic Youth and Dinosaur Jr., plus a willingness to mess with the textures of sound. This was achieved to even greater effect on *Isn't Anything*, a remarkable exercise in sonic disorientation where soothing voices lay deep in the mix, and guitars became disfigured by distortion, sampling and effects. Sensual yet dangerous, robust but ethereal, physical and cerebral, the album – recorded by two women and two men – made opposites collide spectacularly. "We want to go as far as possible," he said. And they did. The follow-up, *Loveless*, was astonishing – richer, stranger, even more oblique. Extraordinarily, the two singles that preceded it – Soon; the Tremolo EP – gave the band their first taste of chart success. But *Loveless* had cost a fortune to record and didn't sell well enough for Creation to fund a third album.

They signed to Island Records but Shields' obsessive working methods proved too much for the rest of the band who drifted away as the decade wore on. Tales emerged of weeks spent in the studio overdubbing feedback and engineers fleeing the sessions in fear of their hearing. In 1998 Shields reportedly delivered a series of stunning instrumentals but without Bilinda to complete them the music missed a vital component. No follow-up to *Loveless* has ever appeared. In 1999 Shields surfaced at last to work with Primal Scream, appearing on their *Exterminator* album, ironically the final release on Creation Records.

Record label:
Creation
Produced
by My Bloody Valentine.
Recorded
at Foel Studios, Wales, Time Square Studios, The Greenhouse.
Released:
November 1988
Chart peaks:
None (UK) None (US)
Personnel:
Kevin Shields (g, v); Bilinda Butcher (g, v); Colm O'Ciosoig (d); Deb Goodge (b); Dave Anderson (e); Steve Nunn (e); Alex Russell (e)
Track listing:
Soft As Snow (But Warm Inside); Lose My Breath; Cupid Come; (When You Wake) You're Still In A Dream; No More Sorry; All I Need; Feed Me With Your Kiss (S); Sueisfine; Several Girls Galore; You Never Should; Nothing Much To Lose; I Can See It (But I Can't Feel It)
Running time:
37.59
Current CD:
CRECD040
Further listening:
Loveless (1991)
Further reading:
My Bloody Valentine's Loveless (David Keenan, 2004)
Like this?
Try . . . p.154

Steve Earle

Copperhead Road

Gravel-throated country singer hits paydirt with his least country record.

Earle's biggest-selling album marked his move from MCA's Nashville division to its LA pop branch – a transfer predicated by his deeper move into rock on 1987's *Exit O*. On this record, with its skull-and-crossbones and army camouflage sleeve, country music – other than the pedal steel and mandolin on the title track and the rootsy rebel rock song Devil's Right Hand, still one of Earle's most popular – often seems only a subtext. A diverse, substantial and unpretentious rock album populated with the kind of small-town characters that made debut *Guitar Town* so compelling – from moonshining white trash to the dope-growing Vietnam vet – *Copperhead Road* includes a track with a drum machine (You Belong To Me), another with The Pogues (Johnny Come Lately), a Christmas single (Nothing But A Child) written to raise money for a children's charity and guest appearances by Telluride, Neil MacColl and ex-Lone Justice singer Maria McKee.

Seven of the 10 songs were recorded with backing band The Dukes in Memphis; Nashville, Earle said, didn't have engineers who could make rock records. The Pogues collaboration was done in London on St Patrick's Day – Earle, who had written the song for the band after befriending them on an earlier UK tour, flew over to join them (along with Joe Strummer and The Specials' horn section) for the encore at a show at London's Town And Country Club before moving the party on to Livingston Studios at the other end of the tube line.

"I wanted to make a record that rocked a lot harder than I'd been able to before, something that was a little closer to the way we sounded live," said Earle, "because I think the first two records are a little tamer than I'd have liked. *Copperhead* is almost two records – it's one of the last records where I was really thinking in terms of vinyl and having two distinct sides, that have a different tone. For that reason, and because I did several things on that record that were outside the norm, *Copperhead* is less cohesive to me as an album and I'm less proud of it and the way it hangs together than almost any other album that I've made." Three million record-buyers, however, disagreed.

SS

Record label:
MCA
Produced
by Steve Earle and Tony Brown.
Recorded
at Ardent Studios, Memphis, Tennessee; Livingstone Studios, London.
Released:
December 1988
Chart peaks:
None (UK) 45 (US)
Personnel:
Steve Earle (v, g, hm, 6-string bass, mandolin); Donny Roberts (g, b); Bill Lloyd (g); Bucky Baxter (ps, ls, dobro); Ken Moore (k); John Jarvis (p); Kelly Looney (b); Custer (d); Neil MacColl (mandolin); Maria McKee; John Cowan; Radney Foster (bv); Telluride and The Pogues (various); Joe Harvey (e)
Track listing:
Copperhead Road; Snake Oil; Back To The Wall; The Devil's Right Hand; Johnny Come Lately; Even When I'm Blue; You Belong To Me; Waiting On You; Once You Love; Nothing But A Child
Running time:
43.36
Current CD:
MCLD 19213
Further listening:
Guitar Town (1986); Train A Comin' (1995); The Mountain (1999)
Further reading:
MOJO 79; www.steveearle.net Hardcore Troubadour: The Life and Near Death of Steve Earle (Lauren St John, 2002)
Like this?
Try . . . p.243

New Order

Technique

New Order's post-acid house masterpiece revealed the potential of electronic pop to move both the soul and the feet.

The city's music scene had become synonymous with slate-grey miserablism but when Manchester went to Ibiza, strange and wonderful things occurred.

Previous album *Brotherhood* had represented something of an *impasse* and, following a glut of retrospective releases, New Order had begun looking like a spent force. But from late 1987 onwards, they'd been ingesting exciting new sounds at their own Manchester club, The Hacienda. The acid-house/ecstasy explosion they witnessed gave New Order a new lease of life.

"They're one of Europe's biggest dance-pop groups, but New Order never used to fucking dance," claimed label boss Tony Wilson at the time. "They haven't danced for ten years, and now they dance again."

Sessions began in Ibiza, although the recording was hampered by mammoth amounts of partying (with the non-abstemious likes of the Happy Mondays). Working titles for the new album – Balearic Beat, The Disco One, The Happy One – reflected their fascination with the emerging scene. On returning to England and Peter Gabriel's Real World studio, the music began taking form, encompassing equal, seamlessly joined amounts of dance and guitar rock.

"The great thing that happened," confirmed Tony Wilson, "was Alan Meyerson was able to clothe both the dance tracks and the rock tracks in the same ambient world."

From the pure pop rush of Run to the heart-rending intensity of Vanishing Point, the album underlined Sumner as one of Britain's very finest writers of coolly penetrating melody. As usual, the eventual titles were all but unrelated to tracks. Undecided about which track to release as a single, but needing a title for the sleeve production, they simply chose the title Fine Time only fitting it to the song later. Eventually chosen was the song they'd been calling Balearic Beat, its release accompanied by a video featuring a screen full of tumbling computer-generated capsules and a hilarious Top Of The Pops appearance in which Bernard showed the nation the then-unknown Bez dance.

Lyrically, *Technique* was less fun. Bernard had recently separated from wife Sue and lines like "I worked hard to give you all the things that you need" (from Love Less) have a sharply autobiographical feel far removed from the opaque *ennui* of old. The usually circumspect Sumner even admitted that the lyrical inspiration was, predominantly, "birds".

"*Technique* is held together by being Bernard's *Blood On The Tracks*," Wilson said. "I think it's their finest album to date."

Record label:
Factory
Produced
by New Order.
Recorded
at Mediterranean Studios, Ibiza and Real World Studios, Box, Wilts; summer–autumn 1988.
Released:
January 1989
Chart peaks:
1 (UK) 32 (US)
Personnel:
Bernard Sumner (v, g, k); Peter Hook (b, k); Gillian Gilbert (k); Stephen Morris (d, k); Alan Meyerson, Michael Johnson (e)
Track listing:
Fine Time (S); All The Way; Love Less; Round And Round (S); Guilty Partner; Run (S); Mr Disco; Vanishing Point; Dream Attack
Running time:
39.59
Current CD:
8573 81367-2
Further listening:
Low Life (1985); Brotherhood (1986); Substance (1987)
Further reading:
Dreams Never End (Claude Flowers, 1995)
www.neworderonline.com
Like this?
Try . . . p.430

XTC

Oranges And Lemons

Nine albums in and XTC aren't getting any worse.

Artistically and commercially rejuvenated following the cult success of *Skylarking*, XTC were happy to capitalise on their burgeoning Stateside success by returning to the US with a keen young American producer, Paul Fox, who had impressed with his Culture Club and Yes remixes. With a budget that allowed for families to accompany, XTC decamped to Los Angeles for five months.

Having been kept on a short leash during *Skylarking* by Todd Rundgren, Partridge's expansive imagination was given more room by the relatively inexperienced Fox and the sessions dragged on beyond the patience of the musicians' families (who returned to Swindon after two months), not to mention Virgin, who threatened to pull the plug as the album went £30,000 over budget. Also, the band were in dispute with their former manager and Andy was drinking heavily, morbidly dwelling on the pointlessness of future income given the ongoing litigation. Unusually, he relinquished the mix to Fox, flying home to recuperate.

In the end *Oranges And Lemons* was a startling record which, in contrast to the misleading Yellow Submarine cover, fizzes with timeless pop energy and weighty invention. From the eastern metal romp of Garden Of Earthly Delights, the effortless juggling of the baby/penis metaphor on the sly and breezy Pink Thing, the life-giving/destructive evolution of himself as a Miniature Sun to the awe-inspiring Wilson-esque achievement of Chalkhills And Children, it's Partridge's show and he fills it full of showstoppers, though Moulding's solid songs keep their customary cool among impossibly vibrant company; "I won't rock the boat," he sings significantly in One Of The Millions.

Britain, long-since allergic to XTC's vulgar prowess, virtually ignored the album but the States were more receptive, even tempting the stage-wary Partridge out on a radio tour and pre-Unplugged acoustic TV appearances. With Partridge's performing juices flowing again, Tarquin Gotch, XTC's then-manager had one last attempt to get the band on some proper, money-spinning live shows. He fabricated the idea, with Dave and Colin's connivance, of a tour as XTC with Thomas Dolby taking Partridge's place. Andy: "I had actually suggested they tour without me. But when he said, 'Look we'll get someone in who looks a bit like you and who's got a bit of a name,' that really put my nose out of joint. I said, 'Well, perhaps I could come on for a couple of numbers towards the end' and he said, 'Come on for the whole fucking set, you idiot.' Smelt of ruse." Tarquin Gotch retired gracefully, wished XTC well and left them to their cult status.

Record label:
Virgin
Produced
by Paul Fox.
Recorded
at Ocean Way and Summa Studios, Los Angeles; May–September 1988.
Release date:
February 27, 1989
Chart peaks:
28 (UK) 44 (US)
Personnel:
Andy Partridge (v, g); Colin Moulding (v, b); Dave Gregory (v, g, p, k); Pat Mastelotto (d); Mark Isham (t); Paul Fox (p)
Track listing:
Garden Of Earthly Delights; The Mayor Of Simpleton; King For A Day; Here Comes President Kill Again; The Loving; Poor Skeleton Steps Out; One Of The Millions; Scarecrow People; Merely A Man; Cynical Days; Across This Antheap; Hold Me My Daddy; Pink Thing; Miniature Sun; Chalkhills And Children
Running time:
60.51
Current CD:
CDV 2581
Further listening:
English Settlement (1981); Skylarking (1986); Apple Venus Volume 1 (1999)
Further reading:
MOJO 64; XTC Song Stories (XTC and Neville Farmer,1998)
Like this?
Try . . . p.66

De La Soul

3 Feet High And Rising

Dazzling debut from three Amityville, NY friends which turned hip hop on its head.

It's no exaggeration to claim that De La Soul's debut casually pulled the rug out from under the established hip hop scene at the time and stamped upon it the hallmark of a whole new genre. Its release marked the dawning of the self-proclaimed D.A.I.S.Y. (Da Inner Sound, Y'all) Age, which replaced the *braggadocio* of big-hitters like LL Cool J and the comedy capers of The Fat Boys with a totally new mood – soulful, downbeat and playful to the point of whimsy. The trio's self-deprecation was reflected not only in their soft-guy stage names (Trugoy invented his by reversing the name of his favourite food – yogurt), but also in the way they dressed – hippyish and bright, as opposed to their peers' suits or gold chains.

Their music was an equally radical kettle of kippers, infusing hip hop's familiar form with soul, psychedelia, pop, jazz, funk, reggae, even big band and television theme sounds, then wrapping the whole in a game-show format, complete with brief skits and pseudo-ads.

"It was us fooling around, acting like assholes when we were supposed to be getting work done," claims Jolicoeur. "Little did we know how important this fooling around would become."

Almost bewilderingly sample-heavy (Steely Dan, Hall & Oates, Funkadelic and Liberace, for starters) at a time when the practice was still in its infancy, the LP soon plunged De La Soul into seriously hot legal water. The Turtles – a sample of whose You Showed Me turns up on Transmitting Live From Mars layered with snippets of a French language lesson – sued the trio for a hefty sum, marking the end of an age of innocence for rap; no crew would ever use an uncleared sample again.

The success of *3 Feet High . . .* (it made Number One in the American R&B chart) encouraged the three to form a loose collective – The Native Tongues Posse – with like-minded souls A Tribe Called Quest, Queen Latifah, Jungle Brothers, Monie Love and Black Sheep. They went on to release three more albums before the end of the century, but none scaled the vertiginous heights of their debut, 1993's *Buhloone Mind State* marking a particularly disastrous attempt to reclaim earlier groundbreaking territory. This year saw them release a brand-new, goodtime, neo-Daisy-age album, *Art Official Intelligence: Mosaic Thump* allegedly part of a trilogy, but De La Soul's place in hip hop history has been secure since the last millennium.

Record label:
Tommy Boy
Produced
by Prince Paul.
Recorded
at Calliope, New York; 1988.
Released:
March 1989
Chart peaks:
26 (UK) 24 (US)
Personnel:
Posdnuos aka Kelvin Mercer, Trugoy the Dove aka David Jolicoeur, P.A. Pasemaster Mace aka Vincent Mason (v); The Jungle Brothers with Q-Tip (guest v); Al "Game Show" Watts (m, e)
Track listing:
Intro; The Magic Number (S); Change In Speak; Cool Breeze On The Rocks; Can U Keep A Secret; Jenifa Taught Me (Derwin's Revenge); Ghetto Thang; Transmitting Live From Mars; Eye Know (S); Take It Off; A Little Bit Of Soap; Tread Water; Say No Go (S); Do As De La Does; Plug Tunin' (Last Chance To Comprehend); De La Orgee; Buddy; Description; Me, Myself And I; This Is A Recording 4 Living In A Full Time Era (L.I.F.E.); I Can Do Anything (Delacratic); D.A.I.S.Y. Age; Plug Tunin' (original 12" version); Potholes In My Lawn
Running time:
67.25
Current CD:
TBCD1019
Further listening:
De La Soul Is Dead (1991), Art Official Intelligence: Mosaic Thump (2000)
Further reading:
http://multsanta.madvision.co.uk/dela and www.tommyboy.com
Like this?
Try . . . p.370

The Pixies

Doolittle

First, death to the Pixies was an album and a poster. Then it was a career path. Suddenly, all we were left with was the hope that none of the members would rest in peace.

With any type of music, there's always a heyday before the sound is pegged as a genre with a neat little name. In this case, think about a time before rock was alternative. For those who remember those tunes outside the mainstream before they were a genre that topped the charts, the Pixies was our Velvet Underground: limited fanbase, hugely influential, an inspiration to so many other bands, even an inspiration for its fans to start bands.

No less a groupie than Kurt Cobain himself called "Smells Like Teen Spirit" a Pixies rip-off tune. The Boston-based quartet, which released its debut Come on Pilgrim EP in 1987, perfected a song structure that was often emulated, relying on a quiet start that was then punctuated with cacophonous, jagged choruses where everybody turned everything up. While the rhythm section of David Lovering (drums) and Kim Deal (bass) laid down a perfectly sane foundation, the others (singer/guitarist Black Francis, born Charles Thompson, and lead guitarist Joey Santiago) did whatever they could to keep things insane. It might have been controlled chaos up front, but at the time, it was different enough to sound more like utter, unfiltered, mainlined chaos. Even heard today, the Pixies' brand of insanity makes of-the-moment yellers sound like they're full of stock rage, canned angst, and pickled fury.

The Pixies weren't the first to yell like rebels of rock 'n' roll; they just figured out how to do it in a way that hadn't been heard before. They gave yelling in rock 'n' roll a whole new range and, in turn, a whole new audience. The band would go on to record a handful of LPs, plus a slew of coveted B-sides. David Bowie called them "the band of the '80s." U2 asked them to support their Zoo TV tour. But the Pixies never gained the pop success that many of their contemporaries did, and it is thought to be part of the reason that the band broke up in 1991.

In the band's explosive little pop gems, they married the sacred with the profane. Shredding guitars and that screaming met with touching, odd-fellow harmonizing between Francis and Deal. English was complemented by high school French and Spanish (un chien andalusian, anyone?). Only the Pixies could make such nonsense make sense.

Here was an album that talked of waiting by boxcars for friends, sloppy love, gay love, a well-endowed man, field-hockey girls, primate space travel, levitation, Catholic guilt, and the University of Massachusetts.

It was enough to make anyone stay in school and go to college.

AD

Record label:
4AD
Produced
by Gil Norton
Recorded
at Downtown Recorders, Boston MA
Released:
April 1989
Chart peaks:
8 (UK) 98 (US)
Personnel:
Black Francis (vocals, guitar); Joey Santiago (lead guitar); Kim Deal (bass, vocals); Dave Lovering (drums)
Track listing:
Debaser, Tame, Wave of Mutilation, I Bleed, Here Comes Your Man, Dead, Monkey Gone to Heaven, Mr. Grieves, Crackity Jones, La La Love You, No. 13 Baby, There Goes My Gun, Hey, Silver, Gouge Away
Running time:
38:35
Current CD:
GAD905CD
Further listening:
Come on Pilgrim, Caribou, Bossanova, Tromp le Monde, Complete B Sides
Further reading:
www.pixieslive.com
Like this?
Try . . . p.483

Bonnie Raitt

Nick Of Time

Perennial promotion contender belatedly makes it into the big league with smooth, modern blues collection.

Bonnie Raitt was respected as one of the finest slide guitarists of her generation, and possessed of one hell of a blues-rock voice to boot.

Nonetheless, she had never really fulfilled her potential, perhaps because of well-publicised drink and drug problems. After 18 years of paying dues and producingalbums of varying quality for Warners, Raitt went straight, signed to Capitol and threw in her lot with producer Don Was.

"In many ways it was like a first album. It was for a new label, and it was my first sober album," Raitt recalls, "It was really refreshing for me to play a lot of guitar and go back to a stripped-down production".

Was's sympathetic, roomy treatment manages to apply a loving pop polish to this strong, varied collection of songs while still packing a bottom-end punch. But ultimately it's Bonnie's performances which make *Nick Of Time* special.

The title track is a self-penned slice of smooth but affecting pop-soul, which acknowledges both the ticking of the female biological clock and Raitt's own narrow escape from artistic and emotional oblivion. Her rendition of John Hiatt's Thing Called Love marries sassy vocals to her even sassier slide: a gritty shimmer of sound that comes from the core of the blues ("I don't just put on an electric guitar – I know how to ride it"). And her lustful tones on the slow-burning funk of Love Letter are hotter than Georgia asphalt. She closes with two marvellously contrasting tracks. On the emotive jazz ballad I Ain't Gonna Let You Break My Heart Again, Herbie Hancock's piano provides beautiful (and sole) accompaniment; The Fabulous Thunderbirds back Raitt's own old-fashioned R&B stomper, The Road's My Middle Name.

Raitt was as surprised as anyone by *Nick Of Time*'s four Grammy successes.

"I figured I might win Rock-Female as a sort of career nod – 'All right Bonnie, you got your shit together.' But best album? Ella Fitzgerald was reading my name! I'll never get over it as long as I live. And if I do, you can shoot me!"

Record label:
Capitol

Produced
by Don Was.

Recorded
at Oceanway and The Record Plant, LA. 1988

Released:
April 1989

Chart peaks:
51 (UK) 1 (US)

Personnel:
Bonnie Raitt (g, v, p); Michael Landau (g); Jerry Lee Schell (g); Arthur Adams (g); John Jorgensen (g); JD Maness (ps); Hutch Hutchinson (b); Chuck Domanico (b); Preston Hubbard (b); Herbie Hancock (p); Scott Thurston (k); Michael Ruff (k); Don Was (k); Ricky Fataar (d, pc); Tony Braunagel (d, pc); Paulinho da Costa (pc); Fran Christina (d); Sir Harry Bowens, Sweet Pea Atkinson, Arnold McCuller, David Crosby, Graham Nash (bv); Marty Grebb(s); Kim Wilson (hm); The Heart Attack Horns: Bill Bergman, Dennis Farias, Greg Smith and John Berry Jr (horns); Ed Cherney (e)

Track listing:
Nick Of Time (S); Thing Called Love (S/UK); Love Letter; Cry On My Shoulder; Real Man; Nobody's Girl; Have A Heart (S, US only); Too Soon To Tell; I Will Not Be Denied; I Ain't Gonna Let You Break My Heart Again; The Road's My Middle Name

Running time:
42.57

Current CD:
CDEST 2095

Further listening:
Give It Up (1972);

Further reading:
www.bonnieraitt.com

Like this?
Try . . . p.526

The Stone Roses

The Stone Roses

The album that heralded the start of the 1990s: old-fashioned psychedelia meets a newly fashionable drug – ecstasy.

"Proper good times," recalls Ian Brown. "We were in London, recording at night. We'd get a taxi back at seven in the morning and we all shared a house in Kensal Rise. They'd give us £10 a day for food, which was a load for us." The Stone Roses had signed to the nascent Silvertone label in April 1988, telling the company – according to Brown – that they had "30 or 40" songs, when in fact their repertoire contained no more than a large handful. The onus was clearly on Brown and John Squire to get writing, and in the slipstream of the deal, they frenziedly augmented older songs such as I Wanna Be Adored and Made Of Stone with the likes of Bye Bye Badman and Shoot You Down. The rush hardly impaired the quality of the material – a fact not lost on producer John Leckie, hired thanks to the Roses' admiration for his work on the XTC side-project The Dukes Of Stratosphear. "I couldn't wait to get them in the studio," he said, given that the Roses had never experienced a long recording project before, he could reasonably expect them to work with goggle-eyed enthusiasm. As evidenced by footage of the sessions (available on Silvertone's Special Edition of the album), they did just that.

Their joie de vivre also manifested itself in experimentalism: Don't Stop, Brown's favourite track on the LP, was created by running the demo of Waterfall backwards and embellishing the results in real-time; the thrilling coda of I Am The Resurrection was built piece-by-piece, and the song's trebly acoustic guitar – reminiscent of Street Fighting Man – was recorded on a Philips ghetto-blaster. Recording was interrupted for the best part of four months by the release of Made Of Stone as a single and the attendant touring and promotion. After stints at Rockfield and Konk, the Roses and Leckie finally called time on the album in early 1989: "When we'd finished," Brown recalls, "Leckie says, 'This is really good. You're going to make it.' And I remember thinking, I know."

His belief was justified. Though its initial chart-placing was fairly low, the album sold well off the back a series of increasingly successful singles and rapidly became a generational touchstone. With the Happy Mondays, the Roses signalled the first significant "alternative" music crossover since The Smiths; moreover, *après* Madchester (as the movement of similarly amiably blokeish bands came to be known) came the New Lad *deluge.*

Record label:
Silvertone
Produced
by John Leckie.
Recorded
at Battery Studios, North London; June–August 1988; Rockfield Studios, Wales and Konk Studios, London; January 1989.
Released:
April 1989
Chart peaks:
19 (UK) 86 (US)
Personnel:
Alan "Reni" Wren (d, bv); Gary "Mani" Mounfield (b); John Squire (g); Ian Brown (v); Paul Schroeder (e)
Track listing:
I Wanna Be Adored (S); She Bangs The Drums (S); Waterfall (S); Don't Stop; Bye Bye Badman; Elizabeth My Dear; (Song For My) Sugar Spun Sister; Made Of Stone (S); Shoot You Down; This Is The One; I Am The Resurrection (S)
Running time:
48.58
Current CD:
ORE CD 502
Further listening:
Non-LP cuts on Turns Into Stone (1992) and The Complete Stone Roses (1995); pre-LP tracks on Garage Flower (1996)
Further reading:
The Stone Roses And The Resurrection Of British Pop (John Robb, 1997)
Like this?
Try . . . p.275

1989

Tom Petty

Full Moon Fever

His first solo outing featured a stellar cast – and a couple of Heartbreakers.

When Tom Petty first presented *Full Moon Fever* to MCA, they rejected it. No singles, apparently. Fortunately, Plan B involved a prestigious stint with a neat little combo called The Travelling Wilburys. His blues duly chased, Petty returned to *Fever* a year later, augmenting the tracklisting with Love Is A Long Road, All Right For Now and a note-for-note cover of Gene Clark's Feel A Whole Lot Better. In the interim, there had been staff changes at MCA, so it seemed logical to play the album to the new regime. "They loved it," said Petty at the time. "Go figure."

Though billed as Petty's first "official" solo record, *Fever* featured Heartbreakers Campbell and Tench, and all of The Wilburys bar Dylan. Sadly, Roy Orbison died before the record's release: on its sleeve, Petty thanks him for "advice and support during this LP". The record's guitars are taut and muscular, its drums are Ringo-esque, and six of the songs clock-in under three minutes. As Face In The Crowd and Free Fallin' ably demonstrate, Petty's the master of a writing process akin to musical *haiku*.

Much of the record was recorded at Mike Campbell's home studio, and at "lightning speed". Day one yielded Free Fallin', day two Yer So Bad. As ever, Petty and his co-producer Lynne (who also co-wrote half the record) are up-front about their sources. Apartment Song does a cut 'n' paste job on the drum riff from Holly's Peggy Sue; Petty references Del Shannon's Runaway on Runnin' Down A Dream, then gets Del to appear on the record (he's credited with "farmyard noises"). "The album is a chance for Petty to explore, play and maybe fall on his face without having much at stake," suggested Rolling Stone's review, mindful of the new Heartbreakers album Petty was already working on. In the end *Fever* triumphed in its own right, going triple-platinum and winning him an ASCAP award for Free Fallin'. On the accompanying tour, Petty threatened to pull a New Jersey concert if the authorities didn't allow Greenpeace lobby-access, and I Won't Back Down took on a new resonance. He stood firm; they relented.

Record label:
MCA
Produced
by Jeff Lynne, Tom Petty and Mike Campbell.
Recorded
at MC (Mike Campbell's) Studios, Rumbo Studios, Sunset Sound, Devonshire Studios, Conway Studios, Sound City Studios, Los Angeles; May & November 1988
Released:
June 1989
Chart peaks:
8 (UK) 3 (US)
Personnel:
Tom Petty (v, g, k); Mike Campbell (g, sg, b, k, mandolin); Jeff Lynne (b, g, k, bv); Phil Jones, Jim Keltner (d, pc); Benmont Tench (p); George Harrison (g, bv); Roy Orbison, Howie Epstein (bv); Del Shannon ("farmyard noises")
Track listing:
Free Fallin' (S); I Won't Back Down (S); Love Is A Long Road; A Face In The Crowd; Runnin' Down A Dream (S); Feel A Whole Lot Better; Yer So Bad; Depending On You; The Apartment Song; Alright For Now; A Mind With A Heart Of Its Own; Zombie Zoo
Running time:
39.32
Current CD:
MCD 06034
Further listening:
Wildflowers (1994)
Further reading:
www.tompetty.com
Like this?
Try . . . p.226

NWA

Straight Outta Compton

Album that took gangsta rap out of the underground and onto the front pages after attracting attention from the FBI.

Hard to believe that at one time Eazy-E, Dr Dre and Ice Cube all fought for the spotlight in one powerhouse aggregation. With MC Ren and DJ Yella, Niggaz With Attitude etched the blueprint for West Coast Gangsta Rap with *Straight Outta Compton*. The album was shocking in its graphic depiction of South Central LA street life and unrelenting in its young, African-American male perspective. Without the global consciousness of Public Enemy, their closest competitors, NWA played with explicit and sexist language and freely-borrowed samples on songs set to some unusually hard, loud beats, that raged at the reality of death, crime and loss of racial pride.

From the opening, title-cut manifesto, through the "built to last" jam Gangsta Gangsta, NWA delivered the goods from the frontlines with keen reporters' eyes. Sirens screeched, gunshots rat-a-tat-tatted and cop radios interfered, adding to the documentary style. Though Express Yourself (which sampled Charles Wright & The Watts 103rd Street Rhythm Band) and Something 2 Dance 2 (cutting together Planet Rock and Dance To The Music) lightened things up, this was a record which begged to be heard at top volume. And that's how it was in the summer of '89 when it blazed from car stereos and boom boxes.

But the group had its detractors. Ruthless anthem Fuck Tha Police, which outlined police brutality in South Central Los Angeles, found attention in all the wrong places. The Parents' Music Resource Center (PMRC) – the US organisation headed by Senator Al Gore's wife Tipper that campaigned to "sticker" albums whose material they considered questionable – declared it a danger to minors, while the FBI sent the group and record retailers a written warning. Meanwhile, the band members – former drug dealer (now deceased) Eazy-E, a hot-tempered Dre and an unrepentant Cube – were not doing much to sweeten their public image. The controversy helped them notch up sales of three quarters of a million albums before they'd even set foot on tour, cracking the Top 40 in the US and almost managing the same feat in the UK. Follow-up *Efil4zaggin* went further still, topping the US charts. In Britain its release was delayed after being impounded by the Metropolitan Police's Obscene Publications Squad. The ensuing court case, with Geoffrey Robinson QC defending, was found in the band's favour, their barrister successfully arguing that it was "street journalism" and "the black equivalent of our rugby songs." NWA also found supporters in the rock press, who likened *Straight Outta Compton* to The MC5's and Sex Pistols' watershed, revolutionary battle-cries.

Record label:
Ruthless
Produced
by Dr Dre and Yella, executive producer, Eazy-E.
Recorded
and mixed at Audio Achievements, Torrance, CA; 1989.
Released:
August 1989
Chart peaks:
47 (UK) 37 (US)
Personnel:
Dr Dre (m); DJ Yella (DJ); Ice Cube (v); Eazy-E (v); MC Ren (v)
Track listing:
Straight Outta Compton; Fuck Tha Police; Gangsta Gangsta (S); If It Ain't Ruff; Parental Discretion Iz Advised; 8 Ball (Remix); Something Like That; Express Yourself (S); Compton's In The House (Remix); I Ain't Tha 1; Dopeman (Remix); Quiet On Tha Set; Something 2 Dance 2
Running time:
60.24
Current CD:
CDL57102
Further listening:
AmeriKKKa's Most Wanted, Ice Cube (1990).
Like this?
Try . . . p.566

Aerosmith

Pump

A textbook study on how to follow the rock comeback of the decade.

The sleeve shot says it all: two trucks, great hunks of road-worn metal, reared up and fucking. "I was in an elevator one day that had a seat and mirrors", said Steven Tyler of Love In An Elevator, the first of the album's five US hit singles. "It's the greatest place in the world to do it. Plus you might get caught so you come even quicker." The major advantage of their newly cleaned-up, healthy lives, according to Tyler, was that time and energy previously spent chasing the dragon could now be more carnally employed. The other advantage, of course, was an end to the drug-fuelled arguments that almost broke up the band and a new focus on their career that resulted in the unimagined success of their first substance-free album *Permanent Vacation*. Sticking with the winning formula, *Pump* found the band back in Vancouver with producer Bruce Fairbairn and song doctors Jim Vallance (Bryan Adams) and Desmond Child (Bon Jovi), who had helped co-write some of that last album's most memorable tracks. But where on the last album you could at times feel the firm hand of a record company steering the has-been rock stars in the desired commercial direction, this time the energised stars were fully in control.

"There was a lot less of other people," said Joe Perry, "and a lot more of us." With the confidence that comes with mega-platinum success, the band knew what was wanted this time. First they would cut the space between songs. "We thought, let's butt the songs up close together so there's no dead time, no air, just go right into the next song like, 'They're bored! Next song – hurry!'" said Tyler.

Next they fancied branching out a little musically, experimenting with different instruments – "Joe came in and said 'Tuba? Not on my record!'" but the Mexican horns and dulcimers stayed – and with songs like the atmospheric Janie's Got A Gun, so did the lyrics – here, about child abuse. But it was the vigorous, horny Aerosmith of the old days that dominated, as the opening track Young Lust attested – no matter that the frontman would soon celebrate his 40th birthday.

SS

Record label:
Geffen
Produced
by Bruce Fairbairn.
Recorded
at Little Mountain Sound Studios, Vancouver, Canada; 1989.
Released:
September 1989
Chart peaks:
3 (UK) 5 (US)
Personnel:
Steven Tyler (v); Joe Perry (g); Brad Whitford (g); Tom Hamilton (b); Joey Kramer (d); Mike Fraser (e)
Track listing:
Young Lust; F.I.N.E; Going Down; Love In An Elevator (S); Monkey On My Back; Water Song; Janie's Got A Gun; Dulcimer Stomp; The Other Side; My Girl; Don't Get Mad Get Even; Hoodoo; Voodoo Medicine Man; What It Takes
Running time:
47.44
Current CD:
GFLD19255
Further listening:
Rocks (1976); Get A Grip (1993); Nine Lives (1997)
Further reading:
Toys In The Attic: The Rise, Fall And Rise Of Aerosmith (Martom Huxley)
www.aerosmith.com
Like this?
Try . . . p.514

1989

The Blue Nile

Hats

Enigmatic masters of Glaswegian film noir finally deliver a masterpiece.

I Love This Life, a lone single on the RSO label in 1981, announced the arrival of a Scottish trio making minimal but evocative music using, as leader Paul Buchanan remembers, just "a bass, a borrowed drum machine, one guitar, a Farfisa organ and a little one-note synthesizer."

Two years later, on their marvellous debut album, *A Walk Across The Rooftops*, the band's ability to paint vivid pictures from such a basic palette was abundantly evident. Buchanan: "Somewhere there we'd started to think, 'If we put that sound with this other rhythm track it makes you think about a mountain or a little city' and we got very interested in that – the visual aspect – using the instruments to represent the context of the song. For example, the guitar on Tinseltown In The Rain we thought sounded like traffic, a general background hubbub outside your window. We avoided anything that the listener would think was just a guy playing a solo on a Gibson or Telecaster." On *Hats* they perfected this technique, creating a glistening cityscape, the songs like long camera pans across its vista of chimneypots, neon lights and rain-washed streets where disenchanted lovers walk at night, wondering what tomorrow will bring. It was introspective, intimate, sentimental and often profoundly sad. Its apparently effortless grace was hard won, however. In the six years since their debut, The Blue Nile had cut and discarded an entire album.

"It just wasn't a true record," says Buchanan of this lost work. "We fell back on tricks – put more reverb on that, put overdub on that. On our days off, we started to work on other things that seemed to have an authenticity about them." Legend says the band held an informal playback for this second album and wiped the tapes as they went through the machine. Buchanan doesn't recall it that way, but confirms the music was erased. "If you're struggling with something and it's just not shaping up, to erase the tape is quite liberating."

Management problems kept The Blue Nile out of the studio for almost a year; when they finally resumed work they cut much of *Hats* in the first five days. The new songs – all credited to Buchanan – concerned the bittersweetness of a life which was falling down around the band's ears, long-term relationships coming to an end, close family passing away. "It was a desperately bad time for us," Buchanan recalls. "Fundamental shifts took place in our personal lives during *Hats*. And so I'd say that record's about reassurance. That's why 'It's all right!' crops up in the lyrics so often. It's patently about someone whose circumstances are far from all right."

Record label:
Linn
Produced
by The Blue Nile and Calum Malcolm.
Recorded
at Castle Sound, Pencaitland 1985–89
Released:
October 1989
Chart peaks:
12 (UK) None (US)
Personnel:
Paul Buchanan (v, k); Robert Bell (b); Paul "PJ" Moore (g); Calum Malcolm (e)
Track listing:
Over The Hillside; The Downtown Lights (S); Let's Go Out Tonight; Headlights On the Parade (S); From A Late Night Train; Seven AM; Saturday Night (S)
Running time:
38.47
Current CD:
LKHCD2
Further listening:
A Walk Across The Rooftops (1983); the purposefully rumpled and, therefore, patchy Peace At Last (1996) which manages at least four great songs.
Further reading:
MOJO 32
Like this?
Try . . . p.760

1989

The Jungle Brothers

Done By The Forces Of Nature

A less bracing, more embracing companion for Public Enemy's Fear Of A Black Planet.

Melle Mel's immortal line, "It's like a jungle/Sometimes it makes me wonder how I keep from going under," had become part of the rap vernacular, but no one took this metaphor further than The Jungle Brothers. Hip hop rarely sounded funkier than this full-flowering of the Native Tongues' psychedelicised, Afrocentric vision. *Done By The Forces Of Nature*, with its bountifully inclusive rhymes and lushly organic samples, is a virtual concept album in which the ghetto is TransAfrikanExpressed into a fertile black Arcadia.

With their low-budget debut *Straight Out The Jungle* (released in 1988 on the minuscule Warlock label), they set out the bones of their liberal, anti-materialist, autonomous agenda, keying hip hop into the black bohemian tradition of their native Harlem. Now, with a much-expanded sound palete, they fluently and resoundingly filled in the gaps. Acknowledge Your Own History speaks proudly of their African heritage; Black Woman offers a sensual corrective to rap's burgeoning misogyny; the storming pow-wow of Doin' Our Own Dang reunited the Native Tongues collective, an idealised community of like-minded New York rappers De La Soul and A Tribe Called Quest (plus female UK rapper Monie Love) created by Afrika in the image of his namesake's Zulu Nation. Bambaataa senior later returned the compliment claiming, "The Jungle Brothers are taking music in a new direction, and now they're influencing *me*."

Musically, the entire inheritance of black music – from African guitar textures to the P-Funk snare snap – was thrown into the pot. Rolling Stone was moved to comment that "DJ Sammy B trades in mechanical beats for soulful, funky, often downright African grooves making for some of the most musical rap around." Despite its influential status, the album sold only a moderately respectable 250,000 copies thanks to Warners' half-hearted promotional efforts. After two years touring to boost sales further, the JBs ventured further into avant territory with 1993's frequently astonishing *J Beez Wit The Remedy*. But by then the Native Tongues had fragmented and no one was listening. The late '90s saw them returning as a much-reduced post-big-beat novelty act. Today, their masterpiece *Done By The Forces Of Nature* can be seen as hip hop's premier return to the source.

Record label:
Warner Brothers
Produced
by The Jungle Brothers.
Recorded
at Calliope Studios, New York; spring 1989.
Released:
November 1989
Chart peaks:
41 (UK) None (US)
Personnel:
Mike G (v); Afrika Baby Bambaataa (v); DJ Sammy B (samples); Dr Shane Faber (k, e); Red Alert, Greg Curry, Gregg Mann (e)
Track listing:
Doin' Our Own Dang (S); Beyond This World; Feelin' Alright; Sunshine; What U Waitin' 4? (S); U Make Me Sweat; Acknowledge Your Own History; Belly Dancin' Dina; Good Newz Comin'; Done By The Forces Of Nature; Beeds On A String; Tribe Vibes; J. Beez Comin' Through; Black Woman; In Days 2 Come; Kool According 2 A Jungle Broth
Running time:
59.48
Current CD:
7599-26364-2
Further listening:
Straight Out The Jungle (1988); J Beez Wit The Remedy (1993)
Further reading:
The Vibe History Of Hip Hop (1999); The Hip Hop Years: A History Of Rap (Alex Ogg with David Upshall, 1999); www.junglebrothers.com
Like this?
Try . . . p.532

Virgo

Virgo

Rare, mysterious and unfeasibly beautiful deep house.

For anyone conversant with black music's history, the story of the early Chicago house scene makes depressingly familiar reading: innovative young black artists change music forever while being comprehensively ripped off by wily businessmen. Early house artists gained neither money nor US fame from their genre-defining records. Those smart enough to cross the Atlantic and forge DJing careers on the burgeoning British rave scene survived, the rest vanished into wounded obscurity.

Such was the case with Merwyn Saunders and Eric Lewis, two Chicago producers who recorded for the legendary Trax label – home to Summer Of Love classics like Marshall Jefferson's House Music Anthem (Move Your Body), Mr Fingers' Can U Feel It? and Jamie Principle's Baby Wants To Ride. Trax was owned by Larry Sherman, who controlled Chicago's only pressing plant, Musical Products, and indulged in some highly dubious business practices, including dispensing entirely with the troublesome matter of contracts or paperwork, pressing records onto old LPs and second-hand vinyl (most original Trax releases are virtually unlistenable for this reason), and, according to Marshall Jefferson, charging aspiring producers for the pleasure of having their records released.

Whether Saunders and Lewis paid for the privilege is unknown, but the duo recorded two remarkable 12" EPs for Trax in 1988: Do You Know Who You Are under the name Virgo 4 and Ride as M.E. The music contained on them was as strange and evocative as the track titles – School Hall, In A Vision, Going Thru Life. At a time when most house music celebrated the primal, sexual urgency of the dancefloor, Saunders and Lewis' tracks sounded wistful and desperately sad. Mournful synth melodies and scattered snatches of guitar echo through the mix, simple piano lines endlessly repeat, drenched in reverb. It was thoughtful, contemplative music in an era of instant-fix, ecstasy-friendly anthems. It was, quite literally, deep house.

In the UK, the two EPs were collected onto this album, released on a short-lived offshoot of the Streetsounds label in a sleeve that looked like a cheap bootleg, and incorrectly credited to Virgo. Despite the sleeve credits, most assumed the album was the work of Marshall Jefferson who had, confusingly, recorded under the Virgo moniker. The record sold in minuscule quantities: even if it hadn't, it's doubtful whether Saunders or Lewis would have ever seen a cent.

Record label:
Radical
Produced
by Merwyn Saunders and Eric Lewis.
Recorded
in Chicago, 1988.
Release date:
1989
Chart peaks:
None (UK) None (US)
Personnel:
Merwyn Saunders (k); Eric Lewis (k)
Track listing:
Do You Know Who You Are (S); In A Vision; Going Thru Life; Take Me Higher; Ride (S); School Hall; Never Want to Lose You; All The Time
Running time:
44.27
Currently unavailable on CD
Further listening:
Various Artists The House That Trax Built (1997)
Further reading:
Altered State (Matthew Collin, 1996); Last Night A DJ Saved My Life (Bill Brewster and Frank Broughton, 1999)
Like this?
Try . . . p.163

1989

Beastie Boys

Paul's Boutique

Misunderstood and oft-overlooked, the Beasties' second album is one of hip hop's finest.

Shattered by the emotionally draining Licensed To Ill world tour, and incensed with their label's unwillingness to pay them what they felt they were due from their multi-platinum debut, the Beastie Boys made a decisive break. Moving to Los Angeles and ditching both the Def Jam imprint and producer, Rick Rubin, the clown princes of hip hop set about reinventing themselves anew.

A chance meeting at an LA club set the Beasties on a collision course with production triumvirate The Dust Brothers. Within weeks, with the Beasties freed from their Def Jam deal and re-signed to Capitol, the six men were in the studio together. But that was only the start of the story.

Both the Beasties and the Dust Brothers yearned to craft a complex, layered, sample-hungry record, but technology had yet to catch up to their imaginations. Working with samples restricted to twelve seconds, each song was assembled piecemeal across a wide number of studios. With material largely written as it was being created, including the intricate, frequently hilarious lyrics, the entire process took a gargantuan 16 months.

Throwing in everything from funk and disco staples (Sly & The Family Stone, The Commodores) through primal rap (Funky Four Plus One), rock (Black Oak Arkensas) and even country (Johnny Cash, bluegrass banjo picker Eric Weissberg), Paul's Boutique predates the "crate-digging", thrift-store-shopping, record collector aesthetic it helped inspire. Deliberately experimental, the album it most closely resembles is The Beatles' Abbey Road – partly because the Beasties sample The End, but also because both records revel in their chopped-up, unconventional structures.

Paul's Boutique, though, was doomed. There was no way it would better Licensed To Ill's multi-million sales, and its initial 800,000 sell-through was deemed a failure. The record also suffered because, at the same time on the other side of America, another trio by the name of De La Soul were also busy crafting a samplead-elic masterpiece.

"I remember buying it [Paul's Boutique] and thinking how great it was," De La's producer, Prince Paul, said. "But later I met the Beastie Boys and they said 'Man, we was mad at you when you made 3 Feet High And Rising! That's what we were doing! We really hated you guys!' "

Their thunder stolen, their genius overlooked, the Beasties had to try again. Their next record would relaunch their career and remake them in yet another iconic image. But Paul's Boutique remains their finest hour.

AB

Record label:
Capitol
Produced
by Beastie Boys: Dust Brothers (Matt Dike, John King, Mike Simpson): Mario G Caldato Jr.
Recorded
at Mario G's: The Opium Den
Released:
July 1989
Chart peaks:
44 (UK) 14 (US)
Personnel:
Ad-Rock (v): Mike D (v): MCA (v): E-Z Mike [Mike Simpson] (turntables)
Track listing:
To All The Girls: Shake Your Rump: Johnny Ryall: Egg Man: High Plains Drifter: The Sounds Of Science: 3 Minute Rule: Hey Ladies: 5 Piece Chicken Dinner: Looking Down The Barrel Of A Gun: Car Thief: What Comes Around: Shadrach; Ask for Janice: B-Boy Bouillabaisse a) 59 Chrystie Street b) Get On The Mic c) Stop That Train d) A Year And A Day e) Hello Brooklyn f) Dropping Names g) Lay It On Me h) Mike On The Mic I) A.W.O.L.
Running time:
53 mins 10 secs
Current CD:
CDP 7 91743 2
Further listening:
Licensed To Ill (Def Jam, 1986), Hello Nasty (Capitol 1998)
Further reading:
Rhyming & Stealing – A History Of The Beastie Boys by Angus Batey (IMP)
Like this?
Try . . . p.261

The 1990s

The Sundays

Reading Writing And Arithmetic

Cocteau Twins + The Smiths = startling debut from a better class of bedsit band.

Guitarist Gavurin and vocalist Wheeler met at Bristol University in the mid-'80s, formed a songwriting and personal partnership, and a four-piece band called The Sundays. They moved to London to get some live experience and a record deal. Their first gig, a support slot at Camden Town's The Falcon, saw them on the receiving end of next-big-thing reviews and feverish record company attention. "We definitely weren't complaining about the press or the music business interest in us," says Gavurin, "but we'd barely played a gig – let alone recorded a note – and we didn't want the hype to turn people off." Taking their time, in due course a single appeared – Can't Be Sure, an eventual Number 1 in John Peel's Festive Fifty – followed by *Reading Writing And Arithmetic*, a remarkable debut album which more than justified the anticipation.

A record of great beauty and imagination, *Reading* easily transcends its obvious influences: The Smiths (the callow pastiche I Kicked A Boy is the album's low point) and the Cocteau Twins. With Gavurin's jangling guitar drones serving as glittering backdrops to Wheeler's extraordinarily inventive vocal lines, her kewpie-doll, cut-glass voice – all odd pronunciations and sighing asides – spin line after memorable line. The pervading tone of the lyrics is one of the lightly ironic self-doubt of intelligent youth; the tunes – abounding with sophisticated, sometimes polytonal shapes – were composed after the music, which gives them a distinctively honed quality, but Wheeler's carefree delivery ensures the cleverness is never overbearing. Indeed, one is simply transported by the *faux-naif*-ness of it all. Successful on both sides of the Atlantic, The Sundays virtually disappeared to America for two years and by the time follow-up album *Blind* (1993) appeared (basically a more oblique – if still lovely – version of *Reading Writing And Arithmetic*), it seemed that their moment had passed.

Record label:
Rough Trade
Produced
by The Sundays and Ray Shulman.
Recorded
at Livingstone Studios, London during 1989.
Released:
January 1990
Chart peaks:
4 (UK) 39 (US)
Personnel:
David Gavurin (g); Harriet Wheeler (v); Paul Brindley (b); Patrick Hannon (d)
Track listing:
Skin And Bones; Here's Where The Story Ends; Can't Be Sure; I Won; Hideous Towns; You're Not The Only One I Know; A Certain Someone; I Kicked A Boy; My Finest Hour; Joy
Running time:
38.31
Current CD:
CDPCS7378
Further listening:
Blind (1993); Static And Silence (1997). The latter, though their most conventional work is still beguiling, and contains their biggest hit, Summertime.
Like this?
Try . . . p.594

The Cowboy Junkies

The Caution Horses

Toronto country disciples return with a second album so lonesome it could cry.

The Cowboy Junkies previous album *The Trinity Sessions*, had been a breeze, recorded during one relatively problem-free day on November 27, 1987, in Toronto's Holy Trinity Church. Brother-and-sister duo, Margo and Michael Timmins had, along with a band of like-minded Canadian country aficionados, laid down a beautiful, echo-soaked album of sparse white-soul ballads around one mic, that had brought them to the attention of an audience starved of rootsy emotion in the late '80s. Now all they had to do was follow it up.

The initial idea was to record on tour in whatever acoustically interesting settings they came to.

"It was a complete disaster," says Michael Timmins. "We've tried to wipe it out of our collective consciousness."

Next, in April of 1987, the band unwisely rented a bizarre Toronto landmark called the Sharon Temple – a freezing-cold modernist structure of wood and glass with no central heating and a resident ghost – where the band descended into a state of collective misery and all the recordings ended up as a strange eerie swirl of dead sound complete with unexplained cries, knocks and whispers. They christened the tape "Sharon", took it on tour with them and became fascinated by the ethereal ghostliness of the thing.

Back home, in the relative luxuries of Toronto's Eastern Sound Studios, they worked on a cross between the one-mic recordings of *The Trinity Session* and the multi-layered fragility of Sharon, a mix of reticence and power embodied in the eventual title of the album.

"We huddled around one mic," explains Michael, "but placed single microphones on all of our instruments so we could capture the fullness of the arrangements without losing that intimacy. But the ghosts remained. There are sounds on there we can't account for."

The result is an album of 10 hauntingly beautiful songs about relationships, slice-of-life tales about loneliness and failed romance where "all the characters are about to lose someone or they've lost someone".

But what finally makes *The Caution Horses* so compelling is that, in the soul of the production, in Michael's lyrics and Margo's voice of sensual *ennui*, the ghosts of Sharon remain. By both accident and design, this is an album occupied by the lonesome dust-choked souls of America's blue highways. Only occasionally, it seemed, did those ghosts ever come back to visit them again.

Record label:
RCA
Produced
by Peter Moore and Michael Timmins.
Recorded
at Eastern Sound, Toronto, Canada; December 1989.
Released:
March 1990
Chart peaks:
33 (UK) 47 (US)
Personnel:
Margo Timmins (v); Michael Timmins (g); Peter Timmins (d); Alan Anton (b); Jeff Bird (mandolin, hm, fiddle); Jaro Czerwinec (accordion); Kim Deschamps (ps, lap sg); David Houghton (pc); Tom Henderson (e)
Track listing:
Sun Comes Up, It's Tuesday Morning; 'Cause Cheap Is How I Feel; Thirty Summers; Mariner's Song; Powderfinger; Rock And Bird; Witches; Where Are You Tonight?; Escape Is So Simple; You Will Be Loved Again
Running time:
44.32
Current CD:
74321183572
Further listening:
The Trinity Sessions (1988); 200 More Miles: Live Performances 1985–1994; Selected Studio Recordings 1986–1995
Further reading:
their wonderful website www.cowboyjunkies.com
Like this?
Try . . . p.545

Public Enemy

Fear Of A Black Planet

The most sustained onslaught of polemic in black American music since The Last Poets.

Public Enemy called the quasi-liberal bluff that lies at the heart of rock'n'roll's limited notion of representational politics.

"Soul music is too sugary and bland," said some people in the Philly-dominated '70s. "Uh-oh now its too angry," they said when Chuck D, Flavor Flav, Terminator X, and Professor Griff, tore the roof off the sucker.

The final verse of Fight The Power, alone, where Chuck D rails against Elvis and John Wayne, convinced those who needed convincing that there was a whole other agenda going on here. Public Enemy's studio crew, The Bomb Squad (Hank and Keith Shocklee, Eric "Vietnam" Sadler, and Carl Ryder) took hip hop production methods to new levels of brutality/sophistication with a mindblowing barrage of sound which utilised anything up to 80 separate tracks in the mix. When music writers talk of sonic assault it's often critical shorthand at best, cliché at worst, but not in this case. Synth squeals, saxophone squalls, James Brown screams and funky drummer loops fight for your attention over scatter-gun lyrics that veer from focussed revolutionary fervour to incoherent rage to stream-of-consciousness Afrocentricity and rush by in a declamatory blur, namechecking every issue of importance in the rap lexicon, from murdered Black Panther Huey P Newton to Oscar-winning Uncle Tom movie Driving Miss Daisy. The film industry is decried for offering stereotypical screen roles (Burn Hollywood Burn). Policing and healthcare are condemned in the self-explanatory 911 Is A Joke. The "system" (everything from the military industrial complex to the white-dominated record industry) is decried and strategically resisted throughout.

Chuck D, the genre's most articulate and conscientious spokesperson, has called rap music "black people's CNN". In which case Gil Scott-Heron was wrong. The revolution will be televised. The track titles alone function as bulletins from the frontline.

Record label:
Def Jam
Produced
by The Bomb Squad: Hank and Keith Shocklee, Carl Ryder, Eric "Vietnam" Sadler.
Recorded
at Green Street Recording, New York and Music Palace, Long Island, New York Winter 1989.
Released:
April 1990
Chart peaks:
4 (UK) 10 (US)
Personnel:
Chuck D (v); Flavor Flav (v); Terminator X (turntables); Professor Griff (v); Branford Marsalis (s); Big Daddy Kane (bv); Ice Cube (bv)
Track listing:
Contract On The World Love Jam; Brothers Gonna Work It Out; 911 Is A Joke; Incident At 66.6 Fm; Welcome To The Terrordome; Meet The G That Killed Me; Pollywanacraka; Anti-Nigger Machine; Burn Hollywood Burn; Power To The People; Who Stole The Soul? Fear Of A Black Planet; Revolutionary Generation; Can't Do Nuttin' For Ya Man; Reggie Jax; Leave This Off Your Fuckin' Charts; B Side Wins Again; War At 33 1/3; Final Count Of The Collision Between Us And The Damned; Fight The Power
Running time:
65.04
Current CD:
5234462
Further listening:
It Takes A Nation Of Millions To Hold Us Back (1988)
Further reading:
Fight The Power (Chuck D, 1997)
Like this?
Try . . . p.537

World Party

Goodbye Jumbo

One-man repository for pop's golden moments downloads a troveful.

"I think all of *Jumbo*'s different elements worked, and when I finally finished it I slept the best I'd ever slept," says Karl Wallinger. "I was the procrastinator from hell, but Guy (Chambers) kept pushing to get things finished. He deserves credit for that."

Sessions for World Party's second album had begun at the beautiful old rectory in Woburn where Wallinger had recorded *Private Revolution*. The "trees, shrubs and pheasants" setting was inspirational, but Wallinger had bought a load of new recording gear and was fast running out of space. Tired of climbing over his bed to record a drum track, he relocated to larger premises in Islington, North London. The flit added further months to *Jumbo*'s elephantine gestation period.

When Wallinger was ensconced at Seaview (note the ironic name), his manager Steve Fargnoli paired him with Joe Blaney, a Paisley Park engineer who'd just finished working on Prince's *Lovesexy*. Wallinger – no slouch in the engineering department himself – acknowledges that lessons learned from Blaney were invaluable when recording *Jumbo*'s drum and vocal tracks. The album's inspirational touchstones are obvious: Way Down Now borrowed Sympathy For The Devil's "whoo whoos" and Show Me To The Top plundered Prince's sound-library circa *Sign O' The Times*.

Crucially, though, *Jumbo* was far more than the sum of its lifts. Wallinger's songs moved way beyond pastiche and some – Message, God On My Side – are pearls. Lyrically, the album found Wallinger further exploring the environmental themes of his breakthrough single Ship Of Fools. Message In The Box, Thank You World and When The Rainbow Comes all campaigned for wiser stewardship of the earth's resources. "I used to sing about girls, but on *Jumbo* I wanted to sing about the world," he says. "I always thought it would have been great if Otis Redding's Try A Little Tenderness had been about the planet."

The record sold around 300,000 copies – "nothing", in Wallinger's estimation. "We'd just won a Q Award for best album and we were meant to tour with Neil Young," he laments. "Ensign said, 'No, it's back in the studio for you.' That was a big mistake." Ironically, the Number 2 chart placing of the flawed follow-up *Bang!* easily eclipsed that of its predecessor."

Record label:
Chrysalis
Produced
by Karl Wallinger.
Recorded
at Seaview Studios, Woburn, Bedfordshire; Seaview Studios, London; 1987–89.
Released:
May 1990
Chart peaks:
36 (UK) 73 (US)
Personnel:
Karl Wallinger (v, k, p, g, b, d, pc); Guy Chambers (k); Jeff Trot (g); Jerod (g); Chris Whitten (d); Martyn Swain (b); Sophia Ramos (v); Sinead O'Connor (v); Steve Wickham (vn); Joe Blaney (e)
Track listing:
Is It Too Late (S); Way Down Now; When The Rainbow Comes; Put The Message In The Box (S); Ain't Gonna Come Till I'm Ready; And I Fell Back Alone; Take It Up; God On My Side; Show Me To The Top; Love Street; Sweet Soul Dream; Thank You World
Running time:
53.38
Current CD:
MDCHEN10
Further listening:
Egyptology (1997)
Further reading:
www.worldparty.net
Like this?
Try . . . p.273

Jane's Addiction

Ritual De Lo Habitual

Third – and last – studio album from the visionary alternative rockers dubbed "the thinking man's metal band".

Perry Farrell always said he would break up his band if he felt like it, and that's exactly what he did after making their brilliant third album and first chart success. The enigmatic artist-frontman – with the looks of a psychedelic Punch – formed Jane's Addiction in the mid-'80s after moving from Miami to LA. Their self-released, self-titled '87 debut was a raw, artily experimental mix of punk, folk, jazz and heavy rock that bore little resemblance to anything around them at the time – LA's holy trinity of big-hair glam metal, thrash and Guns N' Roses – and, along with its more developed follow-ups, was to have a deep and lasting effect on the '90s alternative rock scene.

Two years after first major label album *Nothing's Shocking*, the band returned to the studio with Dave Jerden – brought in for the previous record as an engineer when Farrell insisted on producing, then upgraded to co-producer. That album, though critically acclaimed, was not commercially successful: the sleeve, a tasteful depiction of naked female Siamese twins on fire which got it banned in several US outlets, didn't help. Undeterred, *Ritual* featured three nude sculptures in cod-Mexican religious pose, its lyrics printed on a tiny prayer book. The band's most melodic album, it was noisy, maniacal and brutal one minute, gentle and hypnotic the next, with long druggy jams and an off-kilter artistic vision that was neo-hippy way before people called the '90s the '60s upside-down.

"I tried to go for the big picture," said Farrell, "so there's sex and violence in there but also love and happiness" – and sometimes both in the same song. In the haunting Classic Girl, gunshots ring out while the lovers are in bed; in the exotic Of Course, the big brother who has been holding the young Perry's hand suddenly slaps his face, teaching him that "one must eat the other" while simultaneously contemplating the other's beauty. "It's a cruel world," said Farrell. "There's all these germs that are attacking you and everybody is like their own separate germ and they're all trying to eat each other."

With the album in the US Top 20 and the noise-funk single Been Caught Stealing a UK hit, Farrell announced: "I've got ideas in my head and things I want to do, and they don't include Jane's Addiction." The band Kerrang! decribed as the saviours of '80s metal, "bright, colourful, confused and just plain fucked", broke up after headlining one of those ideas, Farrell's travelling alternative rock circus Lollapalooza.

SS

Record label:
Warner Brothers
Produced
by Dave Jerden and Perry Farrell.
Recorded
at Track Record, Los Angeles; February 1990.
Released:
August 1990
Chart peaks:
37 (UK) 19 (US)
Personnel:
Perry Farrell (v); Dave Navarro (g); Eric Avery (b); Stephen Perkins (d); Ronnie S Champagne (e)
Track listing:
Stop!; No One's Leaving; Ain't No Right; Obvious; Been Caught Stealing (S); Three Days (S); Then She Did . . .; Of Course; Classic Girl (S)
Running time:
51.38
Current CD:
7599259932
Further listening:
Nothing's Shocking (1988); Porno For Pyros, Farrell's post-Addiction band.
Further reading:
Perry Farrell: The Saga Of A Hypester (Dave Thompson, 1995); http://xiola.org/
Like this?
Try . . . p.560

The La's

The La's

Charmed, '60's-influenced pop, from of a man who liked to saw at the branch he was sitting on.

Scores of rave reviews greeted The La's' eponymous debut, but one critic called it "Shit, the worst record in the world". Ironically, the dissenting voice belonged to Lee Mavers, the band's own linchpin. He'd been hailed as the lost prophet of Merseybeat, but ultimately his perfectionism made him impossible to work with.

The album was recorded over three years, during which numerous changes in the band's line-up occurred. In July 1989, some 15 months ahead of *The La's'* release, Sounds noted that five different producers had already come and gone, too. Maver's unreasonable demands must surely have contributed. He'd wanted a 1960s mixing-desk with authentic dust; a producer who could make a guitar sound like the tree it was chopped from.

Initially, the singer had rated some sessions recorded in Devon. These were conducted with producer Mike Hedges, whose equipment included ex-Abbey Road gear guaranteed to delight purists, dust or no dust. Later, however, Maver's famed contrariness kicked in. Thinking they'd finished the album, Power and then-drummer Chris Sharrock had gone to Hawaii with their respective partners. Mavers felt snubbed, and dumped the work done with Hedges, while they were away. Fearing further sabotage, Go! Discs brought in Steve Lillywhite to finish the project, but a miffed Mavers walked out, and the album was eventually released without his approval.

You wouldn't guess it, but many of Mavers' lead vocals on the record are guides. *The La's* has aged well, perhaps because it's free of stilted, date-stamping sounds like the power snare. Key constituents include Mavers' taut acoustic guitar, Power's bouncing basslines, and clever, interweaving vocal arrangements drenched in spring-reverb. There She Goes remains outstanding, its jangling intro unforgettable, the three-note hook of the title showcasing Mavers' strong falsetto. (The song has been covered by, among others, the Boo Radleys and Sixpence None The Richer.) Elsewhere, the Fabs' influence – which The La's always denied – is obvious in the Help!-like guitar sound of Feelin'. Doledrum's skiffle-feel might owe more to The Quarrymen.

Reclusive and unpredictable, Mavers made recordings in Brentford and Liverpool circa 1995, but only close friends have ever heard the results. As MOJO's Jon Bennett noted in February 2000, "PRS royalties from There She Goes alone total around £4,000 every three months, so Mavers has little financial incentive to release any fresh product." Power gained further hits – but less acclaim – when he went on to front Cast.

"They're embarrassing," commented Mavers at the time, "he's learned nothing from The La's."

Record label:
Go! Discs
Produced
by Steve Lillywhite.
Recorded
in various locations; 1987–90.
Released:
October 1990
Chart peaks:
30 (UK) 196 (US)
Personnel:
Lee Mavers (v, g); John Byrne (g); John Power (b); Paul Hemmings (g); Peter Camell (g); Neil Mavers (d); Chris Sharrock (d)
Track listing:
Son Of A Gun; I Can't Sleep; Timeless Melody (S); Liberty Ship; There She Goes (S); Doledrum; Feelin'; Way Out (S); I.O.U.; Freedom Song; Failure; Looking Glass
Running time:
35.17
Current CD:
8282022
Further listening:
Breakloose: Lost La's 1983–86 (2000)
Further reading:
MOJO 75
Like this?
Try . . . p.535

Happy Mondays

Pills 'N' Thrills And Bellyaches

Acid House decisively re-routed into rock music.

By the summer of 1990, the Happy Mondays were mutating into very unlikely pop stars. The *Rave On* EP had taken them on to Top Of The Pops in November 1989, but it was the success of their cover of Jon Kongos' He's Gonna Step On You, retitled Step On and released in April 1990, that decisively marked their commercial elevation. All of a sudden, they were – in Mondays parlance – "Armani'd up". Shaun Ryder even started to look strangely handsome.

They took off on a US tour in the summer of 1990 (documented in the long-form video Call The Cops), and then arrived in LA to record their third album. The location spoke volumes about the Mondays' newly-upmarket image: Capitol Studios was more used to sessions by Frank Sinatra than six Mancunian toerags. The choice of producers was inspired: on account of their roots in the acid house upsurge, Paul Oakenfold and Steve Osborne infused the Mondays' music with the crisp precision common to dance music, and in doing so defined the sound of state-of-the-art '90s rock.

In tandem with U2's *Achtung Baby*, *Pills 'N' Thrills* set a standard that is still respected a decade later. Oakenfold and Osborne worked 12-hour shifts, six days a week. "We'd get each individual player in to do their part," says Oakenfold. "Shaun would just come down at night and do his vocal. We'd spend time with Mark on guitar and Gary on drums, and get down the backing track before Shaun even arrived. I think he slept most of the day." That isn't to underestimate the brilliance that Ryder displays on *Pills 'N' Thrills*. Kinky Afro oozes sleaze and low-life shabbiness as coolly as any Stones song ("Son, I'm 30/I only went with your mother 'cos she's dirty"), Dennis And Lois is a brilliantly surreal paean to the perils of life on the road ("Honey, how's your breathing? If it stops for good we'll be leaving"), and the fantasy scenario in God's Cop – Ryder getting stoned with then-notoriously right-wing UK police chief James Anderton – is simply inspired.

It was after the release of this album that people started to hurl around epithets like "Dylan-esque". But within two years Ryder would be in Barbados, foregoing work on the follow-up album in favour of smoking crack. For one brief moment, however, he led an operation capable of something dangerously close to genius.

Record label:
Factory
Produced
by Paul Oakenfold and Steve Osborne.
Recorded
at Capitol Studios, Los Angeles; August–September 1990.
Released:
November 1990
Chart peaks:
4 (UK) 89 (US)
Personnel:
Shaun Ryder (v); Mark Day (g); Paul Ryder (b); Gary Whelan (d, pc); Paul Davis (k); Bez ("Bez"); Rowetta (v); Tony Castro (pc); Simon Macham (programming)
Track listing:
Kinky Afro (S); God's Cop; Donovan; Grandbag's Funeral; Loose Fit (S); Dennis And Lois; Bob's Yer Uncle; Step On (S); Holiday; Harmony
Running time:
43.57
Current CD:
3984282512
Further listening:
Bummed (Factory, 1988); Greatest Hits (London, 1999)
Further reading:
High Life 'N' Low Down Dirty (Lisa Verrico, 1998)
Like this?
Try . . . p.86

Primal Scream

Screamadelica

One of the top-five all time reasons to take ecstasy? Screamadelica.

Primal Scream's overall career may or may not earn them the title of a vital band, but there's no doubt that *Screamadelica* deserves mention as an album for an era. With chorus lines like "Come Together" and "Higher than the Sun," the Primals provided a younger generation with the anthems for its best imitations of a hippie moment. As the earliest album of success that married rock and rave sounds and sensibilities, *Screamadelica* allowed us to stumble through catatonic bliss at our own, fresh groove.

Once the party had mellowed a bit, however, came a mix of successes and critiques. The band won the first ever Mercury Music Prize on the one hand, but were criticized for only being as good as their producers on the other hand. (*Screamadelica* featured the likes of the Orb, Andy Weatherall, and Jah Wobble handling production duties, and it was the first success the Primals experienced after two previous albums with a heavy garage rock influence.) Favorites like "Movin' On Up," "Slip Inside this House," "Don't Fight It, Feel It," "Come Together," "Loaded," and "Higher Than the Sun" were each praised individually, but when viewed together some found the range in the music off-putting for a long-player, arguing that *Screamadelica* was a great collection of songs, but not a satisfying album.

The Primals, led by the Scottish-born Bobby Gillespie and featuring a revolving lineup in the years that followed, would go on to score top ten hits in England, headline at Glastonbury, and even debut a song initially called "Bomb the Pentagon" just before the events of September 11th. For most of their fans, however, they are unlikely to ever be viewed as the prophets that they seemed like in 1991.

As *Screamadelica* ages without sounding terribly embarrassing, to the band's critics we say "Don't Fight It, Feel It." And, for the hell of it, we also add a "Rama lama lama fa fa fa."

As for the fans, well, we sing, "I drift in inner space, free of time/ I find a higher state of grace, in my mind/ . . . My soul's an oasis, higher than the sun/ I'm higher than the sun."

AD

Record label:
Creation in UK and Warner Bros the US.

Produced
by Andrew Weatherall and Hugo Nicolson (tracks 3, 5–7, 9–11); tracks 1 and 8 mixed by Jimmy Miller; track 2 produced by Hypnotone and Andrew Innes; track 4 produced by The Orb (Dr Alex Paterson and Thrash).

Released:
January 1991

Chart peaks:
8 (UK) none (UK)

Personnel:
Bobby Gillespie (vocals), Andrew Innes (guitar), Robert Young (guitar), Henry Olsen (bass), Philip "Toby" Tomanov (drums), Martin Duffy (organ), Denise Johnson (backing/guest vocalist)

Track listing:
Movin' on Up, Slip Inside This House, Dont' Fight It, Feel It, Higher Than the Sun, Inner Flight, Come Together, Loaded, Damaged, I'm Comin' Down, Higher Than the Sun (A Dub Symphony in Two Parts), Shine Like Stars

Running time:
62.50

Current CD:
CRECD076

Further listening:
Vanishing Point (1997)

Further reading:
www.primalscream.net
Primal Screen: Higher Than the Sun (Grant Fleming, 1997); The Music Myths & Misbehaviour of Primal Scream (Kris Needs, 2003)

Like this?
Try . . . p.551

Massive Attack

Blue Lines

It invented trip-hop and remains the only truly great British hip hop LP.

"A lot of *Blue Lines* was recorded in what we called The Poo Room," reminisced Massive Attack DJ and songwriter, Andrew "Mushroom" Vowles. "One of the nappies that belonged to Neneh Cherry's kid got trapped in the air vent . . . I guess you could say that we've got less of a romantic memory of that album than everyone else."

Over the last decade, Massive Attack have told a number of stories like this, attempting to deflate the myth that surrounds their debut album. It's an understandable reaction: no other album to emerge from the British dance scene has been as influential as *Blue Lines*. The echoes of its slow-burning breakbeats and dub-heavy basslines can be heard everywhere from advert soundtracks to subsequent albums by U2 and Madonna.

It was a remarkable collaborative effort by a group of producers, DJs and rappers who had ruled Bristol clubland in the '80s, running a club, The Dug Out, and releasing two flop singles as The Wild Bunch. After DJ Milo elected to move to Japan and producer Nellee Hooper left to work with Soul II Soul, the remaining members recruited Tricky Kid, a rapper from Bristol's notorious Knowle West estate, and veteran reggae singer Horace Andy and pooled their resources for an album.

Grant "Daddy G" Marshall provided the reggae basslines and rimshot drumbeats that made rap tracks like Five Man Army so unlike anything else in hip hop. Rappers Robert "3D" Del Naja and Tricky Kid made no attempt to disguise their Bristol accents or their British frame of reference, rhyming about Subbuteo and Red Stripe lager. Horace Andy sang refrains from his Jamaican hits of the '70s, Skylarking and Money Money. And singer Shara Nelson brought her remarkable voice to album opener Safe From Harm and its centrepiece, the remarkable Unfinished Sympathy.

"It started out as a pretty weak track," says 3D of this classic single. "It was never meant to be this immense track. There was a string piece that Johnny [Dollar] played on the keyboard and it became obvious it would sound better with an orchestra."

Despite this trial-and-error approach, the album dripped with post-acid-house cool. It was, Daddy G claimed later, innovation borne of a beguiling arrogance.

"The whole thing was, in Bristol, we were so obsessive, there was this thing about quality control," he said. "From the early days, you couldn't wear the wrong jeans or the wrong trainers. Same with music. On that first album, we were testing each other: 'Are you down? Are you down?'"

Record label:
Circa/Wild Bunch
Produced
by Massive Attack with Johnny Dollar.
Recorded
at the Coach House, Bristol; 1990.
Released:
April 1991
Chart peaks:
13 (UK) None (US)
Personnel:
3D Del-Naja (v, k); Mushroom Vowles (k, turntables); Daddy G Marshall (v, k); Tricky Kid (v); Shara Nelson (v); Willy Wee (k); Horace Andy (v)
Track listing:
Safe From Harm (S); One Love; Blue Lines; Be Thankful For What You've Got (S); Five Man Army; Unfinished Sympathy (S); Daydreaming (S); Lately; Hymn Of The Big Wheel (S)
Running time:
45.11
Current CD:
WBRCD 1
Further listening:
Protection (1994); Mezzanine (1998)
Further reading:
MOJO 56; Straight Outta Bristol (Phil Johnston, 1997); www.massiveattack.co.uk
Like this?
Try . . . p.602

Slint

Spiderland

Slint's second, final and massively influential album has been elevated to near-mythical status since its low-key release in 1991.

Slint's first record *Tweez* slipped out without fanfare at the tail end of the '80s, attracting little press but sending excited ripples through the post-hardcore/pre-grunge scene. Brian McMahan and Britt Walford had both played with Louisville, Kentucky's impossibly young hardcore melodists Squirrel Bait in the early part of the decade. Hooking up with guitarist David Pajo and bassist Ethan Buckler they recorded *Tweez* with "some fucking derd niffer" – aka Steve Albini. The results were both obtuse and intriguing: an off-kilter collage of jazz, punk and metal; there was little, however, to suggest what was to follow.

Spiderland came out of nowhere; even years after its initial release there is little to compare it to, bar an ever-growing legion of imitators and emulators. As Lou Barlow, of Sebadoh and Folk Implosion, described it: "It was quiet-to-loud without sounding like grunge or indie-rock. It sounded more like a new kind of music."

Slint's arrangements had become more fluid, less edgy; sparse and precise, given pin-sharp clarity by engineer Brian Paulson. McMahan's younger brother thought it sounded "spidery" and inadvertently named the record. But what was most gripping was the intense emotive power that bled from this music, so much so that stories have circulated that at least one member of the band checked themselves into a mental hospital not long after the album was cut. Talking to Select magazine, Britt Walford would neither confirm or deny these rumours saying only: "[We were] definitely trying to be serious about things, pretty intense, which made recording the album kinda stressful."

McMahan's abstract, seemingly confessional narratives are delivered in a half-whisper, occasionally erupting into a searing scream. The cataclysmic climax of Good Morning, Captain apparently made McMahan physically sick as he cried to be heard over a maelstrom of raging guitars.

Slint have long since taken separate musical paths and given up trying to explain how a group who only made two albums and played perhaps 30 shows at most could've become so influential. Like many albums afforded "classic" status, *Spiderland* was a true one-off. The ever-astute Steve Albini, penning one of the few reviews at the time – for Melody Maker – correctly predicted a future of Slint-inspired bands, awarding the album "ten fucking stars". The last word, however, belongs to Dave Pajo – these days trading as Papa M – speaking to Lime Lizard magazine: "Slint was unspoken. It was about subtlety, awareness . . . the fraternal order of Louisville, Kentucky . . . We only did what happened."

Record label:
Touch And Go
Produced
by Brian Paulson and Slint.
Recorded
at River North Recorders, Chicago; August–October 1990.
Released:
April 1991
Chart peaks:
None (UK) None (US)
Personnel:
Brian McMahan (v, g); Dave Pajo (g); Todd Brashear (b); Britt Walford (d); Brian Paulson (e)
Track listing:
Breadcrumb Trail; Nosferatu Man; Don; Aman; Washer; For Dinner; Good Morning, Captain
Running time:
39.36
Current CD:
TGCD64
Further listening:
Tweez (1989); David Pajo's Papa M, Live From A Shark Cage (2000); Brian McMahan's The For Carnation, The For Carnation (2000); Palace Brothers, There Is No One What Will Take Care Of You (1993)
Further reading:
www.southern.net/southern/band/SLINT
Like this?
Try . . . p.595

Electronic

Electronic

Mancunian supersideproject produce a debut that lives up to the hype

The formation of a super-group means one of two things once it releases a record: it would either get slaughtered because of an inability to live up to unreasonable expectations; or it would be good enough-not even great-for people to lose their critical faculties. The involvement of Johnny Marr and Bernard Sumner, with more than a helping hand from those Pet Shop Boys Neil Tennant and Chris Lowe, up the stakes further. The anticipation was palpable.

And rarely as it usually is, thankfully, we had a case of the great. Though the balance has changed with later albums, the sound of the debut very much resembled that of Sumner's New Order. His vocals were sounding as young and teenage as ever, and Marr was perfectly comfortable twisting pop riffs all over and around more enchanted lyrics.

Oddly enough, the songs did not sound all that electronic, making the band name one of the worst aspects of this new project. The wordless "Soviet" seems to be a short foray into the morose, but the rest of the project came off like a celebration of life, the new-found freshness of the recording process, and possibly even the fact that each of them was in each others' company. Naturally, it wasn't too much of a stretch for listeners to fall in love with songs like "The Patience of a Saint," "Getting Away With It," and "Get the Message." Not only was this music by previously celebrated band members and guest musicians, but it was a conscience effort, it seemed, on their part to craft genuinely intelligent pop gems. Whatever was up with the name, Marr and Sumner had certifiable hits on their hands.

As the years go by, the release schedule of Electronic's albums very much indicates that this is very much a bit on the side for the personnel involved. But the evolution of their sound from album to album has made them an impressive, legitimate band rather than one of those frustrating side-projects that never gets beyond the past work and egos of its members. Electronic may never have a hit like their debut album's singles again, but at this point we can at least call them a good band that came into its own. Even if they have a terrible name, and a doubly terrible debut album title.

AD

Record label:
Factory in UK
Produced
by Bernard Sumner and Johnny Marr
Recorded
at Clear, Manchester
Released:
May 1991
Chart peaks:
2 (UK) None (US)
Personnel:
Bernard Sumner (vocals, guitar); Johnny Marr (guitar and programming); Neil Tennant (vocals); [Denise Johnson (vocals); Donald Johnson (Drums, Percussion); Chris Lowe (Keyboards); David Palmer (drums); Helen Powell (oboe)]
Track listing:
Idiot Country, Reality, Tighten Up, The Patience of a Saint, Getting Away With it, Gangster, Soviet, Get the Message, Try All You Want, Some Distant Memory, Feel Every Beat
Running time:
52:31
Current CD:
CDPRG1012
Further listening:
Twisted Tenderness (April 1999), Raise the Pressure (1996)
Like this?
Try . . . p.530

Crowded House

Woodface

Smart, brooding pop from Oz.

Bassist Nick Seymour once characterised Crowded House as a band that was hanging on by the skin of its teeth after every album. After *Temple Of Low Men* (1989) conspicuously failed to capitalise on the US success of their eponymous debut, he must have felt that skin was stretched pretty thin as songwriter Neil Finn took time out from the band to write with older brother Tim for a projected Finn brothers album. Neil had been in Tim's eccentric, arty New Wave band Split Enz and was responsible for writing their breakthrough hit I Got You.

Although they had been making music together since their childhood in Te Awamutu, New Zealand, Neil and Tim had never written together before; the writing went well but the Finn brothers' project was postponed. Unhappy with what he was producing for the next Crowded House album, Neil imported the brothers' songs onto the record along with his big brother into the band. This did not help the already uncertain band dynamics.

Nick Seymour: "It became difficult to work out what the chemistry was based on and where I fitted into it. I know Paul [Hester] felt the same way. A couple of times, Neil and Tim tried to do everything on the record."

Neil admits it must have been difficult for Seymour and Hester: "The Finn brothers may have rode in through the door and imposed ourselves, but that's just the way it happened. It gave us Weather With You, which in terms of our fortunes was a positive thing."

Weather With You was a plaintive acoustic number with *Rubber Soul* harmonies and a unison chorus that gently urged the world to sing along and most of it did. The other hit singles – Fall At Your Feet, Four Seasons In One Day, It's Only Natural – were equally attractive and represented well the warmth and richness of the album; meticulously stripped-back arrangements of classic-sounding pop songs, superficially Beatles-esque but with a considerably more elliptical, melancholy lyrical approach that Neil Finn sometimes referred to as a "Leonard & McCartney" quality – the darkness of Leonard Cohen mixed with Macca's melodiousness.

Tim Finn eventually quit in the middle of a UK tour (Tim: "We were cancelling each other out") while the album stayed in the charts for over two years. Attempting to loosen what he considered his "natural crafting instinct" for the follow-up *Together Alone* (1993), Neil reflected that *Woodface* "sounded really finicky to me, overworked and a little bit polite and overly thought out."

The charm of the album is that to most ears, it sounds like exactly the opposite. And as Paul Du Noyer rightly remarked in Q magazine at the time, "these songs sound like they're here to stay."

Record label:
Parlophone
Produced
by Mitchell Froom and Neil Finn.
Recorded
at A&M Studios, Ocean Way, Sunset Sound Factory Los Angeles and Periscope, Melbourne; spring 1991.
Released:
July 1991
Chart peaks:
34 (UK) 83 (US)
Personnel:
Paul Hester (d, v, k, p); Nick Seymour (b, v); Neil Finn (g, v, k); Tim Finn (p, v, g); Ricki Fataar (d); Chris Wilson (hm); Peter Bucknall (vln); Vince Parsonage (viola); Alex Acuna (pc); Geoffrey Hales (pc); Jack Mack (brass); David Hidalgo (accordian); Jorge Callendrelli (oa); Sharon Finn (bv); Mitchell Froom (k); Mark Hart (k); Stuart Ellison (k)
Track listing:
Chocolate Cake; It's Only Natural (S); Fall At Your Feet (S); Tall Trees; Weather With You (S); Whispers And Moans; Four Seasons In One Day (S); There Goes God; Fame Is; All I Ask; As Sure As I Am; Italian Plastic; She Goes On; How Will You Go
Running time:
48.04
Current CD:
CDEST2144
Further listening:
Temple Of Low Men (1989), Together Alone (1993); Recurring Dream – The Very Best Of Crowded House (1996)
Further reading:
MOJO 7, MOJO 38
Like this?
Try . . . p.524

Simply Red
Stars

Rapturous white soul bypasses fashion and critical opprobrium.

"I lived in England for 25 years and now I'm wreaking my revenge," said Mick Hucknall. By 1991, based in Milan rather than his native Manchester, he had a fondness for ruffling feathers – going against opinion-poll trends to speak up for the EU, or un-Englishly boasting about his vocal prowess ("I don't see anyone around who's getting near me"). But his popularity only grew. Before undertaking his fourth album, he clearly drew a deep breath. Aged 30, he exercised his puppy fat away and had the EU cross-and-stars symbol tattooed on a forearm. Further, rather against the spirit of his leftist rhetoric, he terminated Simply Red's equal-shares band status, re-engaging some of them as sidemen (albeit sumptuously waged). "It set me free as a writer," he claimed.

Oddly enough, this seemed to work. *Stars*, the first Simply Red album without a cover version, flowed with alluring warmth; not the smallest indication of simmering dissent. While the playing is as slick as ever and Hucknall generally sticks to the love-and-sauce lyrical formula, there are constant small surprises: the one-note piano "solo" closing Something Got Me Started; the suddenly spoken, argumentative "Wait a minute. This is wrong" turnaround in Your Mirror; the 45-second inner monologue sax solo that follows the opening line of How Could I Fall ("for someone so superficial?", that is).

With *Stars* Hucknall honed his ability to sing his hoarse yet pitch-perfect way around any awkwardness, including his own tendency to lumpy lyric-writing. To him, no vocal terrors lurked in gauche constructions like, "For all the jealousy I caused you/States the reason why I'm trying to hide" (Stars). Thanks, in part, he said, to his recent study of Sinatra: "The way he approaches a tune is so simple and clear. There's no, 'Hey, watch me warble for 10 minutes.' Boom! He tells you the story. I started to try that with the song Stars. I realised how it brings people in, gives them the sense you're having a conversation with them, rather than getting on your high horse and *singing*. The notion of storytelling is important; that will transcend any musical fashion."

Hucknall wasn't wrong. *Stars* sold hugely everywhere except America. By the end of the millennium, at around four million copies, it was vying with Oasis's *(What's The Story) Morning Glory?* to overtake Michael Jackson's *Bad* as the top-seller ever in the UK.

Record label:
EastWest
Produced
by Stewart Levine and co-produced by Mick Hucknall.
Recorded
at Condulmer Studios, Venice, Italy; 1991.
Released:
September 30, 1991
Chart peaks:
1 (UK) 79 (US)
Personnel:
Mick Hucknall (v); Fritz McIntyre (k, bv); Tim Kellett (k); Heitor TP (g); Ian Kirkham (s); Gota (d, pc, programming); Shaun Ward (b); Darren Klein (e)
Track listing:
Something Got Me Started (S); Stars (S); Thrill Me (S/UK); Your Mirror (S/UK); She's Got It Bad, For Your Babies (S/UK); Model; How Could I Fall; Freedom; Wonderland
Running time:
41.18
Current CD:
9031-75284-2
Further listening:
Picture Book (1985); *Men And Women* (1987); A *New Flame* (1989); *Blue* (1998) – you like one, you like nearly all of UK's most consistent and substantial white soulman.
Further reading:
Simply Mick (Robin and Rob McGibbon, 1994); www.simplyred.com (official), www.simplyred.org (unofficial)
Like this?
Try . . . p.489

Nirvana

Nevermind

It blew the '80s away and became the most influential rock album of the '90s.

A label spokesman summed it up best. Before *Nevermind* was released, Geffen thought they'd be doing well to sell a quarter of a million. A decade on, they've shifted 30 times that many, the singer is dead, the band is long gone and rock in the 21st century is still feeling the after-effects.

"It still makes me laugh," bassist Novoselic admits, "thinking about the journalists who slagged *Nevermind* when it first came out. Because now they all say they loved it from the start." He doesn't name names, but it's true – *Nevermind* was greeted with either undying love or unrelenting hatred; with an acknowledgement either that Nirvana had turned out something very special indeed, or that the Pacific NW spawned the same mud-soaked pit of sub-metallic tedium it had always had: grunge by name, grunge by nature.

Not that Nirvana disguised their roots. Smells Like Teen Spirit, the break-out first single, was born of their attempts to master Boston's More Than A Feeling, and all three musicians subsequently admitted that *Nevermind* was littered with similar ghosts. It's what Nirvana brought to the party that mattered, though, the gut-wrenching roar which would later see Cobain compared with John Lennon as both a visionary and a voice. Nirvana were indeed hard rock, but they were hard rock with a soul and sensitivity, concise in an era of excess and pop in an age of joylessness. Not for nothing did Cobain describe Nirvana's sound as "the Bay City Rollers getting molested by Black Flag." And so *Nevermind* swings from moments of skull-crushing intensity to passages of sublime beauty; from the adrenalined Lithium to the mantric Something In The Way, from the brutal Territorial Pissings to the compulsive Come As You Are and onto Polly, which combines the two with cunning passion. More than that, *Nevermind* touched a nerve which rock'n'roll had forgotten it ever possessed – but would not lose sight of again. The tragedy of Cobain's death, just three years later, ensured that.

Record label:
Geffen
Produced
by Butch Vig and Nirvana.
Recorded
at Sound City, Van Nuys, CA; May–June 1991
Release date:
September 1991
Chart peaks:
7 (UK) 1 (US)
Personnel:
Kurt Cobain (v, g); Chris Novoselic (b, v); David Grohl (d, v); Kirk Canning (c)
Track listing:
Smells Like Teen Spirit (S); In Bloom (S/UK); Come As You Are (S); Breed; Lithium (S); Polly; Territorial Pissings; Drain You; Lounge Act; Stay Away; On A Plain; Something In The Way; Endless Nameless
Running time:
59.14
Current CD:
DGCD 24425
Further listening:
Nirvana's debut, Bleach (1989); Incesticide (1992), a compilation of rare material; In Utero (1993), the band's final album.
Further reading:
Come As You Are (Michael Azerrad, 1994); www.odyssey.net/subscribers/damien/nirvana.html
Like this?
Try . . . p.533

Red Hot Chili Peppers

Blood Sugar Sex Magik

Careening out of tragedy, the thunderously funky, emotionally volcanic Peppers become stars.

Their original guitarist and lifelong friend Hillel Slovak died of a heroin overdose in 1988. In grief, singer-rapper Anthony Kiedis sank deeper into his own addiction then tried to clean up. Despite a big reputation as a live band, their fourth album, *Mother's Milk*, fell short of the American Top 50. Then on-stage and dressing-room horseplay saw bassist Flea and drummer Chad Smith arrested for sexual harrassment and Kiedis for indecent exposure. They seemed to place self-destruction unwontedly high on the group agenda.

But then they met producer Rick Rubin. He insisted they immure themselves in a Laurel Canyon *hacienda* for a couple of months and make the album they were capable of. Cleaned-up Kiedis went for it: "The band gave me something to want to get better for. I was a completely dysfunctional self-destructive drug addict and that was a huge failure for me, but what getting off it led me to was the most beautiful feelings in my life and the most beautiful creation of music in my life."

Released at the same time as Nirvana's *Nevermind*, *Blood Sugar Sex Magik* was overlooked at first, then took hold. The singles Give It Away and Under The Bridge led millions into the album's extraordinarily sustained funky intensity. Flea's bass was incendiary, Frusciante's guitar endlessly imaginative, while Smith's drums recalled John Bonham with added bootie-shaking. Kiedis belied their reputation as muscled-up, sexist "jocks" by throwing emotional caution to the wind. Under The Bridge recalled "the despair and isolation I felt as a hardcore junkie". My Lovely Man uttered a crunching valedictory to his best friend Slovak with touching tenderness and contempt for any fool who wanted to snigger when he sang, "I love you too/See my heart/It's black and blue/When I die/I will find you."

Overwhelming, a flood, *Blood Sugar Sex Magik* almost drowned its creators too. During recording Frusciante was obviously losing it (in the candid studio film Funky Monks he claimed to have watched a female ghost screwing). The following May he quit mid-tour and over the next several messy years the Red Hot Chili Peppers succumbed to drugs and diverse breakdowns – until Frusciante hauled himself back from death's door, detoxed and rejoined the band to make their second-best album *Californication*.

Record label:
Warner Brothers
Produced
by Rick Rubin.
Recorded
at Hacienda in Laurel Canyon, Hollywood Hills; May–June 1991.
Released:
September 1991
Chart peaks:
25 (UK) 3 (US)
Personnel:
Anthony Kiedis (v); John Frusciante (g); Flea (b); Chad Smith (d); Brendan O'Brien (e)
Track listing:
The Power Of Equality; If You Have To Ask; Breaking The Girl; Funky Monks; Suck My Kiss; I Could Have Lied; Mellowship Slinky In B Major; The Righteous & The Wicked; Give It Away (S/US); Blood Sugar Sex Magik; Under The Bridge (S); Naked In The Rain; Apache Rose Peacock; The Greeting Song; My Lovely Man; Sir Psycho Sexy; They're Red Hot
Running time:
75.36
Current CD:
7599-26681-2
Further listening:
Californication (1999) – Frusciante recovered, band revived.
By The Way (2002)
Further reading:
True Men Don't Kill Coyotes (Dave Thompson, 1993); www.redhotchilipeppers.com
Like this?
Try . . . p.549

Nine Inch Nails

Pretty Hate Machine

Trent Reznor's debut album teaches us how to dance and carry our angst well all at the same time.

As a high school drama student in Pennsylvania, Trent Reznor was awarded a prize for his performance in the musical *Jesus Christ Superstar*. His role? Judas.

In a sense, Reznor has been singing about sin ever since taking home the high school prize. Now Judas was hardly one to claim to be "Jesus Christ on ecstasy," like Reznor would as Nine Inch Nails, but the release of *Pretty Hate Machine* in 1989 marked the first time that electronic music with lyrically twisted verses were to create significant waves within a mainstream audience. Reznor would create more musically accomplished albums than *Pretty Hate Machine*. In fact, he would go on to record in the infamous Manson family home where Sharon Tate and so many others were killed; to win a Grammy for a song with the words "fist fuck" in it (surely a first); and to live in a New Orleans Garden District home with a manicured lawn located blocks from author Anne Rice's residence (both houses are tourist attractions of sorts in the Big Easy).

What Reznor accomplished with *Pretty Hate Machine*, however, was unlike anything done before. His music captured a doom and gloom that was both controversial and kinky enough to appeal to the kids and repulse the adults. Other bands fueled the moment's teenage angst by building on rock 'n' roll's tradition, but Nine Inch Nails borrowed from the worlds of industrial and dance music. The emotional palette was provided by keyboards and other machine-made studio favorites. Those previously synthetic, sissy, and side-lined machines of rock outfits were taking center stage, and suddenly all kinds of non-goth fans were willing to brood along with Mr Reznor, the one-time piano prodigy.

"Head Like a Hole" was the anthemic everybody's favorite, but everybody has their own personal favorite. There's the bereaving electro of "Down in it," the rigid mourning of "Something I Can Never Have," the studio wizardry of "Kinda I Want to" or "Ringfinger," the drive of "Sin," and the vampire kink of "The Only Time." It was never easy to agree on a favorite, but always easy to agree on at least one thing: Reznor's work might have sounded like controversial devil's work to adults-the stuff of bad hair, makeup, and suicides-but it had a pathos and humanity that left many a troubled teen rejoicing and dancing because, finally, they really felt alive.

Play it again, Trent: "My moral standing is lying down/ Nothing quite like the feeling of something new/ Maybe I'm all messed up. Maybe I'm all messed up in you/ But this is the only time I really feel alive. This is the only time I really feel alive/ I can't help thinking Christ never had it like this."

AD

Record label:
TVT Records
Produced
by Trent Reznor
Recorded
at
Released:
September 1991
Chart peaks:
67 (UK) 75 (US)
Personnel:
Trent Reznor (vocals, guitar, drums, keyboards, bass, programming); James Wooley (keyboards); Richard Patrick (guitar); Chris Vrenna (drums)
Track listing:
Head Like a Hole, Terrible Lie, Down in it, Sanctified, Something I Can Never Have, Kinda I Want to, Sin, That's What I Get, The Only Time, Ringfinger
Running time:
48:49
Current CD:
CID9973
Further listening:
Broken (1992), The downward Spiral (1994); Closer to God (1994), The Fragile (1999), And All That Could Have Been (2002)
Further reading:
www.nin.com
Like this?
Try . . . p.312

A Tribe Called Quest

The Low End Theory

Rap – meet jazz.

Hip hop journalist Harry Allen had claimed that "hip hop is the new jazz". The previous year, Jazz Thing (on the soundtrack of Spike Lee's Mo' Better Blues) saw Gang Starr allying with Branford Marsalis to sermonise on the lineage linking the two genres. But it was this Queens crew's second album that used the confluence to most potent effect. Even before their 1990 debut *People's Instinctive Travels And The Paths Of Rhythm*, Q-Tip's mellifluous tones had already enlivened albums by both The Jungle Brothers and De La Soul. With *The Low End Theory* he would commercially outstrip his flagging seniors with supporters spanning both "alternative" critical circles and the mainstream hip hop community. The use of the breathy horns and tumbling acoustic basslines of modern jazz introduced new heights of sampling subtlety and a smoky, after-hours ambience to hip hop. Verses From The Abstract even featured jazz veteran Ron Carter on double bass.

The lyrical mood was also distinctly Beat with Q-Tip labelling himself The Abstract Poet. His enlightened odyssey contrasted with his partner Phife's more unreconstructed worldview to form one of rap's most compelling double-acts. This dualistic approach sees dissertations on black identity rubbing weirdly against more grounded issues like the importance of skypagers. A breach of contract court case with their first agent had also seemingly burned off some of their earlier naive positivity, with the falsity of the show-business world a frequent target.

"We want to steer clear of trends," Q-Tip claimed at the time. "Even the pro-black thing has become just a trend now. A lot of it is phoney. With us, it's from the heart. We don't want to gear ourselves to anyone who isn't willing to think for themselves." Throughout, the music glowed with the confidence of those who knew they were breaking new ground. Indeed, the blunted trip-hop subgenre – taken up by labels like Mo' Wax – can in part be traced back to this album's innovative soundworld. Just as the Native Tongues collective began faltering, A Tribe Called Quest broke away from the pack.

Record label:
Jive
Produced
by Skeff Anselm and A Tribe Called Quest.
Recorded
at Battery Studios, Greene Street Studios and Soundtrack Studios, New York; spring 1991.
Released:
September 1991
Chart peaks:
58 (UK) 45 (US)
Personnel:
Q-Tip (rapping); Phife (rapping); Ali Shaheed Mohammad (samples); Ron Carter (b); Ms Vinia (v); Busta Rhymes (v)
Track listing:
Excursions; Buggin' Out; Rap Promoter; Butter; Verses From The Abstract; Show Business; Vibes And Stuff; The Infamous Date Rape; Check The Rhyme (S); Everything Is Fair; Jazz (We've Got); Skypager; What?; Scenario
Running time:
48.05
Current CD:
CHIP117
Further listening:
People's Instinctive Travels And The Paths Of Rhythm (1990); Midnight Marauders (1993)
Further reading:
The Vibe History Of Hip Hop (1999); The Hip Hop Years: A History Of Rap (Alex Ogg with David Upshall, 1999); www.algonet.se/~top/tribehr.htm
Like this?
Try . . . p.532

ew Sweet

iend

eet ditches the session players and roughens up his meaty power pop anthems for his third album.

The original title of Matthew Sweet's third album was *Nothing Lasts*, a reflection of the recently divorced singer's bleak state of mind at the outset of recording. Then he fell in love again, and retitled the album *Girlfriend*.

"He had a lot of anxiety making the record, but I never associated it with the divorce," says engineer Jim Rondinelli. "It was fear that his songs would never see the light of day, or that the label would make us stop mid-stream. But the record does work on a very personal level. Like all great songwriters, Matthew gives you a peek into the inner workings of his soul."

Before recording, Sweet, producer Fred Maher and Rondinelli formulated a sonic plan. "We had some rules we applied to the record to help keep it concise and focussed," Rondinelli says. "We didn't use any effects. There's not a bit of reverb, no digital delay, no stomp boxes – all the guitar distortion is the sound of somebody turned up all the way. Also, on previous records they'd surrounded Matthew with all these heavy-duty session singers. It had the effect of making his unique, character-filled voice sound totally disparate from all the other voices. So he did all his own backgrounds and came up with amazing parts."

There were hi-jinks to lighten the intensity of the sessions. Rondinelli says: "Madonna was upstairs making Vogue at the same time. One of Matthew's favourite hobbies was wondering if she was curious about our music and would stop down. He would slip notes upstairs through the assistant engineer, but she didn't write back."

Though the diva snubbed him, Sweet found a new audience. "The rougher sound of *Girlfriend* ended up succeeding because Nirvana had come out six weeks previously," says Rondinelli, "and blown a hole so wide through radio that people were scrambling to find music that was guitar-driven, loud and edgy. Matthew's was a great fresh record that spoke to a segment of the population that hadn't had a voice."

Record label:
Zoo Entertainment
Produced
by Fred Maher and Matthew Sweet.
Recorded
at Axis Studios, New York; 1990.
Released:
October 21, 1991
Chart peaks:
None (UK) 100 (US)
Personnel:
Matthew Sweet (g, b, p, v); Richard Lloyd (g); Ric Menck (d); Robert Quine (g); Greg Leisz (lap steel); Fred Maher (d); Lloyd Cole (g); Jim Rondinelli (e)
Track listing:
Divine Intervention; I've Been Waiting (S); Girlfriend (S); Looking At The Sun; Winona; Evangeline (S); Day For Night; Thought I Knew You; You Don't Love Me; I Wanted To Tell You; Don't Go; Your Sweet Voice: Does She Talk?; Holy War; Nothing Lasts
Running time:
60.19
Current CD:
0550072
Further listening:
100% Fun (1995)
Further reading:
www.matthewsweet.com
Like this?
Try . . . p.574

Neil Young & Crazy Horse

Weld (with Arc)

An artist of extremes celebrates the noise, power and pain of his electric guitar.

On different tours in 1991 Sonic Youth supported Neil Young, a maverick legend, and were supported by Nirvana, obscure newcomers. Then, that autumn, Nirvana released *Nevermind*, which launched grunge, while Young released the live *Weld*, which filled the bargain bins (the first time he had missed the US Top 100 since his 1969 debut). Yet, musically, the two albums were cut from the same cloth – pop tunes allied to almighty guitar noise – and retrospection illuminates *Weld* as a career crescendo.

Young had spent much of the '80s experimenting, partly in reaction to his second son Ben's sufferings with severe cerebral palsy. With his wife Pegi, he dedicated himself to the boy's care. As Young later observed, his recordings, especially 1983's "techno-pop" *Trans*, flowed from "a part of my life that practically no one can relate to".

But he insisted his style shifts flow from strong emotions, not whims – and so it was when he turned to rock again: "One morning I woke up and I just heard rock'n'roll in my head so fucking loud that I couldn't ignore it."

For the first time since 1979 he reunited with Crazy Horse. "They bring out a part of me that's very primitive," he said. The outcome was *Freedom* (1989), *Ragged Glory* (1990) and *Weld*. With sweet songs like Heart Of Gold and Only Love Can Break Your Heart off the agenda, *Weld* epitomises Young's capacity for expressing unresolved turmoil full-on. Although it repeats old favourites and chunks of its immediate predecessors, unbridled performances drawn from many different gigs make it the epitome of "fucking loud" Neil Young. In particular, Cinnamon Girl and Like A Hurricane counterpoise distortion and vocal harmony with exquisite oomph, while sardonic anger roars out through Welfare Mothers ("I'm hungry, Ma!") and Love To Burn (broken couple at war: "'Why'd you ruin my life?'/'Where you takin' my kid?'").

Arc (the one-track feedback assault originally packaged with *Weld*) might now be a separate purchase for the more resolute fanatic only. But Young's cover of Blowin' In The Wind proves the method in his cranked-up madness as he revives the much-abused old protest song via sound-effect guns, bombs, and sirens, vocals combining querulous fragility with stoic hope, and overwhelming guitar, which leaves the song ripped apart, then reconstructed, much like The Star-Spangled Banner after Jimi Hendrix had done with it.

Of course, his next move was to go acoustic again because all the racket had given him tinnitus.

Record label:
Reprise
Produced
by Neil Young and David Briggs with Billy Talbot.
Recorded
live by Remote Recording Services Silver Studio, at various concerts January–September 1991.
Released:
October 28, 1991
Chart peaks:
20 (UK) 154 (US) 154
Personnel:
Neil Young (v, g); Ralph Molina (d, v); Billy Talbot (b, v); Frank "Poncho" Sampedro (g, Univox Stringman, v); Dave Hewitt, David Briggs (e)
Track listing:
Hey Hey, My My (Into The Black); Crime In The City; Blowin' In The Wind; Welfare Mothers; Love To Burn; Cinnamon Girl; Mansion On The Hill; F*!#in' Up; Cortez The Killer; Powderfinger; Love And Only Love; Rockin' In The Free World; Like A Hurricane; Farmer John; Tonight's the Night; Roll Another Number; Arc (promo S, edited version; US only)
Running time:
115.54 (Arc 34:57)
Current CD:
7599-26671-2 Arc now issued separately; 9267692
Further listening:
Freedom (1989) and Ragged Glory (1990); studio precursors of Weld's big noise.
Further reading:
MOJO 10, 25, 44; The Complete Guide To The Music Of Neil Young (1996); Neil Young: The Rolling Stone Files (1994)
Like this?
Try . . . p.558

Teenage Fanclub

Bandwagonesque

Breakthrough album from the Glasgwegian quartet who were darlings of the early '90s indie rock scene.

Teenage Fanclub are the sort of great band who could never become icons: they care too much about songs, too little about being rock musicians. But this enduring Glasgow quartet hold a firm place in the pop pantheon.

Made up of modest, amiable music obsessives, Teenage Fanclub created a huge transatlantic buzz for their 1989 debut album, *A Catholic Education* – a buzz inversely proportionate to the time and money spent on it. Yet despite an almost comically murky tone, the strength of the record's hooks and melodies shone through. Fortunately, when the band entered the studio to record its follow-up, a fat American contract with Geffen Records looming, they decided to let its songs breathe unencumbered. Leader Norman Blake recalls that producer Don Fleming was key in coaxing the group down a purer pop path.

"We liked a lot of pop music," he says, "but we all liked Sonic Youth a lot as well, and I think we were trying to direct the band more to sound like them. And then Don said, 'Look, you really do harmonies well – why don't you do that? Be more of a pop group. It's what you're good at.'" This approach resulted in a sublime collection of classically informed guitar-pop, ambling in tempo, often lyrically irreverent (especially The Concept's great ode to a tragically hip girl scenester). *Bandwagonesque* topped Album Of The Year lists worldwide and became a considerable sales success Stateside. Dogged though it was by relentless comparisons to Big Star – "You can see why people made the comparisons," admits Blake, "and we *had* been listening to them" – no one could deny that it transcended mere tribute.

In America, TFC were parcelled up with grunge. The band's refusal to play up to their perceived allegiances with the likes of friends and labelmates Nirvana may have been their commercial undoing in the US. But *Bandwagonesque* remains one of the '90s' most appealing attempts to harness the simple beauty of The Song.

Record label:
Creation
Produced
by Don Fleming, Paul Chisholm and Teenage Fanclub.
Recorded
at Amazon Studios, Liverpool; April–May 1991.
Released:
November 1991
Chart peaks:
24 (UK) 137 (US)
Personnel:
Norman Blake (g, v); Gerard Love (b, v); Raymond McGinley (g, v); Brendan O'Hare (d) with Joseph McAlinden (b, strings); Don Fleming (occasional g and v); Dave Buchanan (handclaps)
Track listing:
The Concept; Satan; December; What You Do To Me; I Don't Know; Star Sign; Metal Baby; Pet Rock; Sidewinder; Alcoholiday; Guiding Star; Is This Music?
Running time:
42.56
Current CD:
CRECD 106
Further listening:
A Catholic Education (1990)
Further reading:
www.teenagefanclub.co.uk
Like this?
Try . . . p.159

U2

Achtung Baby

Out with the pomp and in with the irony, it's a new, dancefloor-friendly U2.

In a fleet of gaudily decorated Trabants, caked in make-up and smoking skinny cigars, U2 re-emerged after a two-year break having exchanged the achingly sincere trad-rock of *Rattle And Hum* for something very different.

"We just realised we had reached the end of a particular phase," says The Edge, who admits to having fallen under the influence of industrial acts such as KMFDM and the Young Gods at the time. "We decided to open up to what was going on musically, to soak up a lot of the great stuff which was around. The sense of rhythm and the groove being produced by the Manchester bands was also a bit of a throw-down."

That's not to say that the band's trademark graceful ballads and swollen epics are not present; to offset a noise collage such as album opener Zoo Station or the metallic funk of The Fly, there's the heartbreaking fragility of One and the rousing Who's Gonna Ride Your Wild Horses?

The sessions began at the legendary Hansa Studios in Berlin under Daniel Lanois, but the new direction soon caused ructions. "There was a fair amount of doubt and it became a little difficult," confides The Edge. "Adam and Larry weren't persuaded by some of the ideas and also had problems with Bono writing in this ironic way." Berlin was eventually abandoned for Dublin where cohort Brian Eno was drafted in.

"Part of the dynamic of my relationship with them is to ask questions, to be bloody-minded," says the man who is at other times "just the synthesizer player or the producer". Eno was keen for U2 to address the way in which the world was changing on the cusp of the '90s. "The Wall had fallen, Perestroika was kicking in, and suddenly the picture had changed," he says. "There was this feeling of new possibilities. The question was: 'What's our response to this?'"

Achtung Baby did a fine job of reinventing U2. The album's first single, The Fly, went straight to Number 1 in Britain – knocking Bryan Adams' (Everything I Do) I Do It For You off its perch after four wretched months – but the album's failure to top the UK charts suggests fans loyal to their earlier work must have been dismayed. Still, the album was a big-seller, each new single – often with remixes by the likes of Paul Oakenfold and Stereo MCs – revealing a new aspect to its charms. All proceeds from the crystalline One were donated to AIDS research. "One was one of those songs where you get a gift," recalls The Edge. "It just arrived, and we had it down within about 15 minutes. In those situations you just have to make sure you don't get your hands all over it and fuck it up."

Record label:
Island
Produced
by Daniel Lanois with Brian Eno.
Recorded
at Hansa Ton Studios, Berlin; Dog Town, STS and Windmill Lane, Dublin; 1990.
Released:
November 1991
Chart peaks:
2 (UK) 1 (US)
Personnel:
Bono (v, g); The Edge (g, k, v); Adam Clayton (b); Larry Mullen Jr (d, pc)
Track listing:
Zoo Station; Even Better Than The Real Thing (S); One (S); Until The End Of The World; Who's Gonna Ride Your Wild Horses (S); So Cruel; The Fly (S); Mysterious Ways (S); Tryin To Throw Your Arms Around The World; Ultra Violet (Light My Way); Acrobat; Love Is Blindness
Running time:
55.29
Current CD:
CIDU28
Further listening:
Zooropa (1993)
Further reading:
U2 At The End Of The World (Bill Flanagan, 1995); www.atu2.com
Like this?
Try . . . p.517

Cypress Hill
Cypress Hill

An alternative history for gangsta rap would have started here… had anyone been able to match the concept.

In any art form there are developments and there are dead ends: work that, as vital and energised as it may be, didn't change the world as much as it should have. In the history of gangsta rap, Cypress Hill's debut is one of the latter.

The group comprised Sennen "Sen Dog" Reyes and his brother, Mellow Man Ace, teenage gang member Louis "B-Real" Freeze and New York expatriate Italian-American DJ Lawrence "Muggs" Muggerud. After Ace left for a solo deal Muggs engineered Cypress' signing to the new RuffHouse label, initially only for a single.

With the differences between east and west coast hip hop becoming pronounced, Cypress Hill were an intriguing anomaly. Muggs' dusty breakbeats made the group sound more New York than Los Angeles, and when their album, recorded for the then paltry sum of $50,000, arrived in 1991, it flew in the face of the increasingly bland, smoothed-out production style prevalent in LA. B-Real's lyrics had the unmistakable tang of reality: a gang member who'd been shot in the course of his activities, his writing showed a chilling nonchalance. "How you know where I'm at when you haven't been where I've been?/Understand where I'm comin' from," he urged on standout track How I Could Just Kill A Man. "When you're up on the hill in your big home/I'm out here, riskin' my dome. Here is something you can't understand…".

They courted a new audience for rap – the fans of alternative rock who could appreciate the noise and the aggression but had no time for the sexism – by avoiding words like "bitch" which littered the recordings of their competitors. The Grateful Dead-inspired logo was designed to adorn t-shirts, a fanbase-building commercial exercise no rap group apart from Public Enemy had managed to tap into. It worked.

"When we came out the rap field was so diverse, we thought we had to do everything different," Sen Dog explained later. "If kids were wearing baseball caps on their album covers we'd wear some other type of hat. If we had it our way we'd have performed every show with hoodies so you'd never know what we looked like."

Because it stood aside from the already crippling conservative conventions of the genre, Cypress Hill's debut is one of a handful of genuine gangsta rap masterpieces. But it seems it was too complete a concept for anyone but the band themselves to follow.

AB

Record label:
RuffHouse/Columbia
Produced
by DJ Muggs
Recorded
at Image Recording, Los Angeles
Released:
November 1991
Chart peaks:
None (UK) 31 (US)
Personnel:
B-Real (v): Sen Dog (v): DJ Muggs (turntables)
Track listing
Pigs: How I Could Just Kill A Man: Hand On The Pump: Hole In The Head: Ultraviolet Dreams: Light Another: The Phunky Feel One: Break It Up: Real Estate: Stoned Is The Way Of The Walk: Psycobetabuckdown: Something For The Blunted: Latin Lingo: The Funky Cypress Hill Shit: Tres Equis: Born To Get Busy
Running time:
46.54
Current CD:
RuffHouse/Columbia 468893 2
Further listening:
Black Sunday (RuffHouse, 1993)
Further reading:
www.cypresshill.com
Like this?
Try . . . p.665

Khaled

Khaled

The first Arabic crossover album, Algerian rai with a West Coast sheen.

Five years after being crowned King of Rai in his native Oran, Cheb Khaled dropped the prefix (meaning "young", but with rebellious undertones), and planned an assault on Europe. Deciding to split the album between pop and a rootsier rai with a Western glossiness, he recruited two producers: Don Was, with whom he would record in Los Angeles, and Michael Brook, who had come to his attention via his collaborations with the Pakistani *qawwali* singer Nusrat Fateh Ali Khan.

"I had no intention of leaving rai behind, I wanted to build on it. What I wanted to do would still be folk music, but we were going to play it on non-traditional instruments. It was an evolution."

The five songs Was recorded feature guitar, bass, drums and brass, with only Moshen Chentouf and Mustapha Kada from Khaled's band contributing.

"My interest was in bringing traditional elements into a pop sound," remarks Brook, whose six tracks are constructed almost as mirror images of the Was songs. Nevertheless, Khaled's methods were anything but traditional. "When I arrived at the studio in Belgium," remembers Brook, "his band was there and knew what songs they were recording, but nothing had been worked out, that was my job. Khaled didn't even come down to the studio for the first three weeks. I liked rai but I didn't know that much about it – this may be how rai musicians always work, but not me: it was very unnerving." Fortunately, when Khaled did arrive, he immediately approved of what was already on tape, changed a few things, then added his vocals. Finally, to prove it was his album, he hung around a bit longer, recording some keyboards, accordion and *oud* (an Arabic lute). The mix worked, in France, with its sizeable North African community, the Was-produced Didi became the first Arabic single to make the Top 10; throughout North Africa, the Middle East and into India, the album sold in huge quantities – the first Arab pop star had arrived.

Record label:
Cohiba
Produced
by Don Was and Michael Brook.
Recorded
at Microplant, Los Angeles and ICP, Brussels; 1991.
Released:
January 1992
Chart peaks:
None (UK) None (US)
Personnel:
Khaled (v, k, bendir, accordion, oud); Don Was (b, k); Michael Brook (g, b, pc); Randy Jacobs (g, b); Mustapha Kada, Benjamin Muhoberac (k); Moshen Chentouf (bendir, derbouka); David Coleman (c, oud); Afid Saidi, James Pinker (d); Eric Fernandez (g); Youssef Chebaan, Abderaseque Hilal (vn); Bill Bergman (ts); Greg Smith (bs); David McMurray (s); John Berry (t); Arnold Massat (p, o); Wily N'For (b); Djoum (pc); Steve Deutsch (programming); Arnold McCuller, Sir Harry Bowens; "Sweet Pea" Atkinson (bv)
Track listing:
Didi; El Arbi; Wahrane; Ragda; El Ghatli; Liah Liah; Mauvais Sang; Braya; Ne M'En Voulez Pas; Sbabi; Harai Harai
Running time:
49.27
Current CD:
511 8152
Further listening:
Young Khaled, a compilation of raw Algerian material; N'ssi N'ssi (1993); 1, 2, 3 Soleils, (1998) a live album that proved rai had become the music of choice for young France.
Further reading:
www.sospubs.co.uk/sos/1997_articles/oct97/khaled.html
Like this?
Try . . . p.130

Pearl Jam

Ten

The stadium-rock side of the Seattle grunge explosion.

"We're not treating this band like some blockbuster film. It's more like a small film that's just really nice to come and get into. There's a magic inherent in it. It'd be really depressing to be promoted as the next big thing," said Pearl Jam vocalist Eddie Vedder back in late 1991, just as *Ten* hit the racks in the States. Twelve months later, Pearl Jam had sold in excess of two million copies of their debut album in America alone. Along with peers Nirvana, Alice In Chains and Soundgarden, Pearl Jam became unwitting Generation X figureheads. Guitarist Stone Gossard and bass player Jeff Ament were alumni of '80s Seattle bands Green River and Mother Love Bone. MLB had signed to Polydor and recorded their debut album *Apple* when singer Andrew Wood died of a heroin overdose, leaving Gossard and Ament to pick up the pieces with the help of their friends in Soundgarden, using drummer Matt Cameron, while assembling their new band with guitarist Mike McCready.

At the recommendation of ex-Red Hot Chili Peppers drummer Jack Irons, the nascent outfit made contact with San Diego surfer and would-be singer Vedder by mailing him a cassette.

"Jeff sent me a tape of three songs and I sent him back a mini-opera!" recalls Vedder. The tape included Footsteps, Once and the stirring Alive, all of which made it into PJ's set, the last two also appeared on *Ten*. Alive itself has often been misconstrued as Pearl Jam's tribute to Wood. It isn't; the *Temple Of The Dog* album – recorded with Cameron, Gossard, Ament, McCready and Soundgarden frontman Chris Cornell during one of Vedder's initial visits to Seattle – is.

An uplifting blend of intelligent hard rock and sweeping atmospherics, *Ten* emerged to rapturous reactions on both sides of the Atlantic. Propelled by singles Alive, Even Flow and Jeremy (the latter featuring a dramatic video highlighting a tale of child abuse), it established Pearl Jam as a stadium-sized phenomenon. Pearl Jam's reaction to their new-found celebrity involved refusing to make videos for their second album *Vs* and withdrawing from promotional activities in general. It wasn't enough to stop *Vs* from selling a then-record-breaking 1.3 million copies in 13 days.

Record label:
Epic
Produced
by Pearl Jam and Rick Parashar.
Recorded
at London Bridge Studios, Seattle; March–April 1991.
Released:
February 1992
Chart peaks:
18 (UK) 2 (US)
Personnel:
Eddie Vedder (v); Jeff Ament (b); Stone Gossard (g); Mike McCready (g); Dave Krusen (d); Rick Parashar (p, o, pc), Walter Gray (c); Tim Palmer (fire extinguisher, pepper shaker, mixer);
Track listing:
Once; Even Flow (S); Alive (S); Why Go; Black; Jeremy (S); Oceans; Porch; Garden; Deep; Release
Running time:
53.26
Current CD:
468884 2
Further listening:
Vs (1993); No Code (1996); Mirror Ball with Neil Young (1995)
Further reading:
Five Against One: The Pearl Jam Story (Kim Neely, 1998)
Like this?
Try . . . p.359

k.d. lang

Ingénue

Unconventional country star swaps twang for torch songs, and the world falls at her feet.

With 1988's alluring *Shadowland*, Kathryn Dawn Lang's obsession with country had reached its apotheosis, but country wasn't where she planned to stay. She and collaborator Ben Mink considered where to head next; though "overwhelmed by options", she was driven most to "explore my Peggy Lee influences" – and that's what guided *Ingénue*.

"Even as Ben and I were writing, we were thinking, oh, so this is what the record's going to sound like. Rock'n'roll and soul are only slight influences for me; I'm more and more influenced by classical music, Yma Sumac and Peggy Lee. As a singer, it was my aspiration to use the power of subtlety. Julie London was a big inspiration, Carmen McRae, all those singers who use their lower, softer register."

The title came first, then the cabaret setting. The songs fell into place, inspired by lang's personal life.

"During this time I fell in love for the first time. The theme of the record is obviously love, but it's getting to a point of love where you realise you have no control and you can't manipulate it."

As recording began, however, another aspect of control was in jeopardy. lang uses her first-rate voice with precision, but at this point "I would try to sing and my pitch was flat. To lose your pitch at 30 years old – I'm going, like, 'Please God, don't take it away. I had massages – nothing. I went to homeopaths – nothing. I saw my singing specialist – no different. As a last resort, I went to my dentist, and it turned out I had a root canal which was infected and was pushing on my Eustachian tube, so my higher frequency was cut down a little bit in my right ear, and it was taking me out of tune."

Teeth sorted, lang swept through what would become her crossover outing. *Ingénue* was sleek and dark, heavy with languor, knowing but bewildered by desire and the realisation that, having found what you want, you can't always make that thing want you. By recording's end, her affair was over, having brought her to her knees ("I'll shroud every sign of need I swear/Save me") but opened her eyes. It gave her the confidence to come out in public as a lesbian, and that summer she had the cover of Vanity Fair, getting wet-shaved by Cindy Crawford.

The post-breakup tracks – Constant Craving, a hands-down winner from its first winsome accordion cadence, and Miss Chatelaine – portrayed a lang newly in love with the world, and the album won a Grammy and sales of 1.6 million.

"When *Ingénue* came out," she has said, "I was really the thing for a year."

Record label:
Sire/Warner Bros.
Produced
by Greg Penny, Ben Mink and k.d. lang.
Recorded
at Vancouver Studios, Vancouver, BC, Canada.
Released:
March 22, 1992
Chart peaks:
3 (UK) 18 (US)
Personnel:
k.d. lang (v); Ben Mink (g, vn); Teddy Borowiecki (p, accordion); David Piltch (b); Graham Boyle (pc); Gary Burton (vibraphone); Randall Stoll (d); Sue Leonard (bv)
Track listing:
Save Me; The Mind of Love; Miss Chatelaine (S); Wash Me Clean; So It Shall Be; Still Thrives This Love; Season of Hollow Soul; Outside Myself; Tears of Love's Recall; Constant Craving (S)
Running time:
41.59
Current CD:
7599268402
Further listening:
Take in the sepia-toned Shadowland (1988), or try the smoking songs of Drag (1997). Probably best to avoid All You Can Eat (1995), which lacks vitality; its tepid reception almost derailed lang's career.
Further reading:
All You Get Is Me (Victoria Starr, 1994); official biography Carrying The Torch (William Robertson 1993); www.kdlang.com
Like this?
Try . . . p.490

P.J. Harvey

Dry

Rock's rude health in the early '90s was confirmed by the arrival of a unique voice from the West Country.

With most ears attuned to catching baggy beats from Manchester, shoegazers from the Home Counties or Seattle's grunge exports, the arrival in autumn 1991 of a diminutive, austere-looking girl from a farming community in north Dorset might easily have gone unnoticed. But, like her early hero, Captain Beefheart, Polly Harvey was a genuine maverick. Music, for Harvey, was as much a lifeline as a career, and her relationship with it was visceral: "I like something that grabs you and shakes you around," she said in 1992, something that "makes you feel sick and gets in your stomach."

Remarkably, her debut album was equal to those aspirations. Harvey had served her apprenticeship with a local band, Automatic Dlamini, fronted by long-time collaborator John Parish. After three years perfecting her guitar skills, contributing the occasional vocal and stockpiling songs, she struck out alone in 1991, taking with her two ex-Dlamini members, Rob Ellis and Ian Olliver. That summer, a demo arrived at the offices of UK indie Too Pure.

"It was completely different to anything else I was hearing," says label co-founder Paul Cox. "It was just not 'indie' at all." Island Records agreed, and after Dress was issued as a single in October, and Olliver had been replaced by Stephen Vaughan, the major invited the trio to record their debut album in a hi-tech Chiswick studio with, says Cox, "no strings attached". But the band were unhappy with the results and headed back to Head's Icehouse Studio in Somerset to re-record the album over the Christmas period.

Curiously, Harvey decided not to record some of her best songs of the period, such as stage highlights Man-size and Me Jane, and left them to the following album (by which time they sounded a little overworked). Nevertheless, *Dry* – which cost just £5,000 to record – was a remarkable achievement that prompted Rolling Stone to nominate Polly Harvey as the year's best songwriter and Island to finally prise her away from Too Pure. Harvey posed naked for the album sleeve, rejected attempts to include her among the burgeoning Riot Grrl posse, declared she wasn't a feminist and rejected the inevitable "indie Madonna" tag. Songs like Sheela-Na-Gig (about a vulva-displaying gargoyle) and Happy And Bleeding took a fiercely independent, and sometimes contradictory, take on sex and desire, love and loss. The unvarnished backings, which occasionally threatened to engulf her, were appropriately raw and edgy. A bonus disc, *Demonstration* – basically the whole of *Dry* in demo form – free with initial copies, only served to enhance the singer's *auteur* status and it was little surprise when she disbanded the trio after 1993's *Rid Of Me*.

Record label:
Too Pure
Produced
by PJ Harvey
Recorded
at Icehouse Studio, Somerset; winter 1991.
Released:
March 1992
Chart peaks:
11 (UK) None (US)
Personnel:
Polly Harvey (v, g); Rob Ellis (d, v); Stephen Vaughan (b); Lisa Comer (bv); Tom Rickman (c); Stephen Allen (bv); Mike Paine (g); Head (e)
Track listing:
Oh My Lover; O Stella; Dress (S); Victory; Happy And Bleeding; Sheela-Na-Gig (S); Hair; Joe; Plants And Rags; Fountain; Water
Running time:
35.05
Current CD:
PureCD010
Further listening:
If *Dry* was raw, the Steve Albini-produced follow-up, *Rid Of Me* (1993) was positively skin-flaying.
Further reading:
www.pjharvey.net
Like this?
Try . . . p.458

Pavement

Slanted And Enchanted

Crypto-campus alt-rock intellectuals discover songs.

Released into the maelstrom of optimism for underground rock that accompanied Nirvana's swift rise, Pavement's debut album was received as if it were a cultural and generational clarion call. Distilling at least 25 years of maverick rock gesture into 14 songs, it was thought to portend the underground's great coming-out party.

Of course, the fledgling group's intentions were considerably more modest. Pavement then consisted only of Stockton, California friends SM and Spiral Stairs (né Steve Malkmus and Scott Kannberg, respectively). Recorded for $800 in the garage studio of Gary Young, an aged casualty of the hippy dream who had become the group's drummer, *Slanted And Enchanted* was meant to fulfil little more than any American garage band's hope to make, according to Kannberg, "a cool record".

"Recording *Slanted* was our first stab at what we termed a 'classic record'," Kannberg says. "This meant we actually practised for a week before recording it. I thought the songs sounded like Dinosaur Jr, Buffalo Tom, or The Fall." Pavement had already earned something of a reputation within America's insular community of college radio listeners and fanzine readers with a trio of EPs. *Slanted*'s allure was thus greatly enhanced by the perceived enigma of its creators. The various permutations of the advance cassette, circulated without song titles or credits, actually featured in the annual critics' poll of New York's Village Voice newspaper. One such tape was reviewed by Spin magazine six months before the album's release.

Where the EPs are little more than slapdash descendents of British post-punk aesthetes Swell Maps and The Fall, *Slanted* remains an incredible collision of ideas, wholly deserving of its ecstatic praise. Despite snatches of indebtedness to the Velvet Underground's insistent strum, The Fall's skewed sense of language, or Krautrock's loose but exacting rhythms, Pavement's amalgamation of influences had no precedents. The band would soon expand to five core members (not including Young, who was gone within a year), and become no little influence themselves to legions of "indie-rock" bands, despite never receiving the commercial pay-off expected for them. "*Slanted* is still my favourite among our albums," says Kannberg. "It was Pavement in its purest form. It was punk rock then. It was raw and new and we felt like we were changing things. Surprise, surprise."

Record label:
Big Cat
Produced
by Pavement.
Recorded
at Louder Than You Think, Stockton, CA; January 1991; South Makepeace Studios, Brooklyn, NY; December 1990.
Released:
April 1992
Chart peaks:
72 (UK) None (US)
Personnel:
SM [Stephen Malkmus] (g, v, b), Spiral Stairs [Scott Kannberg] (g, b), Gary Young (d)
Track listing:
Summer Babe (Winter Version) (S/US); Trigger Cut (S/UK); Wounded Kite At :17; No Life Singed Her; In The Mouth A Desert; Conduit For Sale!; Zurich Is Stained; Chesley's Little Wrists; Loretta's Scars; Here; Two States; Perfume-V; Fame Throwa; Jackals, False Grails: The Lonesome Era; Our Singer
Running time:
39.08
Currently CD:
ABBCD034
Further listening:
Compilation of early singles and out-takes, Westing (By Musket And Sextant) (1993); Crooked Rain, Crooked Rain (1994); and mature (and final?) album, Terror Twilight (1999)
Further reading:
www.stephenmalkmus.com
Like this?
Try . . . p.451

The Black Crowes

The Southern Harmony And Musical Companion

Propelled to stardom with their massive-selling debut, the road-weary Crowes dig deeper for their follow-up.

The Atlanta band's 1990 debut on Def American label had been an enormous critical and commercial success. With its title borrowed from the old Elmore James song and its shamelessly retro Stones-meets-Faces-via-Aerosmith-and-Lynyrd-Skynyrd rock-soul sleaze, *Shake Your Money Maker* had shifted a mind-boggling six million copies. But two years of sampling both the delights and the horrors of the road had left the band in a strange state of strength and fragility. Understandable, then, that their second album was a far more profound, mature and complex record, with an elegance and musicality that the band's exuberant debut had barely hinted at.

"Your first record – same with every band – always stands apart, because you don't tour with your first record," said vocalist Chris Robinson. "We were a local band, we had these songs which we'd finally got to where we could go into a studio with them and make a record, and then you sit at home and wait for it to come out. Then once it was out suddenly we were on tour for 20 months straight. Our lives had become completely insane – and we're very sensitive people."

One casualty of the road was guitar player Jeff Cease, who was replaced by Marc Ford in the first of several line-up changes. A new keyboard player, Eddie Hawrysch, was brought in also to help fill out the sound – the task completed by female R&B backing singers. Where the swaggering, British-rock-influenced *Money Maker* was a decidedly feel-good record, the more textured *Southern Harmony* was often dark and haunted, delving deeper into the band's own Southern heritage, its raucous rock'n'roll tracks rubbing shoulders with stoned melancholia, tormented blues and a reflective, acoustic reading of Bob Marley's Time Will Tell. Though not short of accessible numbers – Sting Me, to name one – this was very much an *album*, as the paucity of big hit singles and its debut at the top of the US album charts attested. Amazingly, this embarrassment of riches took just eight days to record. "Spending six months in the studio," sniffed Robinson, "was for Springsteen." He'd eat his words when the next album came along.

SS

Record label:
Def American
Produced
by The Black Crowes and George Drakoulias.
Recorded
"in recording studios in the United States"; winter 1991–92.
Released:
May 1992
Chart peaks:
2 (UK) 1 (US)
Personnel:
Chris Robinson (v); Rich Robinson (g); Marc Ford (g); Johnny Colt (b); Steve Gorman (d); Ed Hawrysch (p); Brendan O'Brien (e)
Track listing:
Sting Me; Remedy; Thorn In My Pride; Bad Luck Blue Eyes Goodbye; Sometimes Salvation; Hotel Illness; Black Moon Creeping; No Speak No Slave; My Morning Song; Time Will Tell
Running Time:
50.37
Current CD:
9269762
Further listening:
Shake Your Money Maker (1990); Amorica (1994)
Further reading:
The Black Crowes (Martin Black, 1993); www.blackcrowes.com
Like this?
Try . . . p.835

Baaba Maal

Lam Toro

Africa goes techno. Dance remix version also released.

Baaba Maal was Senegal's No 2 star (after Youssou N'Dour) when he invited Simon Emmerson (then trading as Simon Booth of the acid-jazz pioneers Working Week) to Senegal to work on an album that would take a different course from his previous acoustic recordings."He was suspicious," recalls Emmerson, "but then he realised that adding modern dance beats involved no compromise on his part. I didn't want to dilute his traditions, but wanted him to believe that together we could empower him."

Maal was a trained musician, having attended the Ecole Des Beaux Arts in Dakar, the Senegalese capital, and both his parents had a musical background. He had also studied in Paris, where he had learnt European theory, and he had travelled widely in Africa, deliberately studying other kinds of music. He was ready for the challenge.

"He took our songs back to his band," says Emmerson, "and when he discovered that they could play them, any worries just disappeared." There was one track, Daande Lenol ("voice of the people", also the name of Maal's band), that Emmerson thought he recognised. "It definitely sounded Irish. So I asked Davy Spillane to add uilleann pipes to it." Spillane was keen to join in: he recognised the tune and told Emmerson that because of their travelling background, many Irish people feel their roots lie in Africa.

Reviews of the album were overwhelmingly positive – "the sound of Africa future" – even if purists were dismayed. Emmerson was put in sole charge of the sequel (*Firin' In Fouta*) and roped in more Celts. The result was a high-water mark for African music, garnering a Grammy nomination into the bargain and leading to the formation of the Afro-Celt Sound System, an ad hoc arrangement of European musicians and members of Daande Lenol.

"At first I did not like the phrase 'world music,'" says Maal, "but I started to think of it as meaning music for all the world. Then my interest grew."

Record label:
Mango
Produced
by Simon Booth, Baaba Maal and Eric Clermontet.
Recorded
at Studio 2000, Dakar, Senegal; 1991.
Released:
July 1992
Chart peaks:
None (UK) None (US)
Personnel:
Baaba Maal (v); Mangu El Papichulo (rap); Assane N'Daye Cisse (g, pc); Hilaire FJ Chaby-Hary (g, k); Kaow Cissoko (kora); Davy Spillane (pipes); Lester Mendez (k); Bada Seck (d, sabar, bougarabou, djembe); Massamba Diop (tama, droma, sabar, bv); Thio M'Baye (sabar); Cesar Sogbe (e)
Track listing:
Hamady Boiro (Yelle); Daande Lenol; Lem Gi; Ndelorel; Yela; Toro; Daniibe; Olel; Sy Sawande; Hamady Bogle
Running time:
52.58
Current CD:
CIDM1080
Further listening:
Firin' In Fouta (1994); Djam Leeli (1989); Baayo (1991); The Afro-Celt Sound System's Volume 1: Sound Magic (1996)
Further reading:
www.worldbeatplanet.com/baaba-maal/
Like this?
Try . . . p.700

Lemonheads

It's A Shame About Ray

Boston indie scenester's finest hour invents "bubblegrunge", accidentally.

By mid-1991 Evan Dando was 24 and tired of music. Leader and only constant member of the Lemonheads, he had thrash-popped his way through five albums in as many years, culminating with their widely unremarked major-label debut *Lovey* (1990). He had dissolved the band twice, mislaid numerous band members along the way and even got confused about his own role in the group as he intermittently took the drum stool or played guitar. In short, Dando was a stranger to his own career path.

But, while on tour in Australia, he had met local musicians Tom Morgan and Nic Dalton. "They really helped me get into music again," he says. Pure pop-music fans, they enabled Dando to find the magic mixture he had been seeking throughout his involvement in his hometown hardcore metal and punk scenes and his personal preoccupation with Gram Parsons.

With a clutch of new songs, some co-written with Morgan, the new Lemonheads set to, abetted by their producers' diverse Los Angeles contacts such as Ricky Nelson's son Gunnar, sometime Dylan studio sideman Barry Goldberg and erstwhile Doobie Brother Jeff "Skunk" Baxter.

It's A Shame About Ray's 12 songs sparkle with brilliant, caustic *noir*-pop – My Drug Buddy, Confetti and the title track perhaps the most dazzling examples. Rather a shame, then, that the song which finally brought the Lemonheads wider attention was a cover of Simon And Garfunkel's Mrs Robinson and its attendant video which turned Evan into an MTV heart-throb.

"Well, that's typical of what happens, I guess," says Dando. "It was really an accident, 'cos we recorded the song for the re-release of the The Graduate on video." The single a hit, Mrs Robinson was added to the album six months after its original release and *Ray* started climbing the charts.

Sadly, despite making two more enjoyable and inventive albums – *Come On Feel The Lemonheads* (1993) and *Car Button Cloth* (1996) – Dando's subsequent inclination was to veer sharply away from success – initially via hard drugs. As he once reflected, "Why am I so into Gram Parsons? If I stepped back and looked at myself, I'd find that a little suspicious."

By the late '90s he had disappeared, his vanishing regretted by those who'd enjoyed not only his brief musical high noon, but the sharp wit of a character who greeted his first hit thus: "I'm a pop star now. I have a voice. I want to say that violence should end. We need to redo the '60s. Make necklaces again."

Record label:
Atlantic
Produced
by The Robb Brothers with Evan Dando.
Recorded
at Cherokee Studios, LA
Released:
July 1992
Chart peaks:
33 (UK) 68 (US)
Personnel:
Evan Dando (g,v); David Ryan (d); Juliana Hatfield (b,v); Skunk Baxter (sg), The Waters Sisters (bv); Dee Robb, Bruce Robb, Joe Robb (e)
Track listing:
Rockin' Stroll; Confetti (S); It's A Shame About Ray (S); Rudderless; My Drug Buddy; The Turnpike Down; Bit Part; Alison's Starting To Happen; Hannah and Gabi; Kitchen; Ceiling Fan In My Spoon; Frank Mills
Running time:
29.33
Current CD:
7567 824602 adds Mrs Robinson (S)
Further listening:
Best Of The Lemonheads – The Atlantic Years (1998); Car Button Cloth (1996)
Further reading:
The Lemonheads: The Illustrated Story (Everett True, 1994);
Like this?
Try . . . p.564

Eric Clapton

Unplugged

The MTV format gives Clapton the biggest album of his life.

On March 20, 1991 in New York, Eric Clapton's four-year-old son Conor, fell to his death through an open window from his mother's 53rd-floor apartment. Clapton had taken him to Ringling Brothers' circus the night before. He organised the funeral in Surrey nine days later.

Afterwards he told Rolling Stone Ron Wood, "I'm not going to give in. I'm going to work, work, work." First, he tried to edit that year's 24 Royal Albert Hall shows into an album. "I hated everything I heard," he said later. "My soul went dead to music. I hated it because I thought, This was life *before*. How can I relate to this? This shouldn't be." But gradually his "absolute belief in music as a form of communicating a healing force" revived.

Recording the soundtrack to a modest movie called *Rush*, he met veteran songwriter Will Jennings and played him the first verse of a new song: "Would you know my name if I saw you in heaven?" Clapton asked for help to finish it. Jennings, whose mother had just died, proved the ideal partner.

Clapton went on to write several more songs mourning Conor, directly or otherwise, including Lonely Stranger. He considered building them into an album. But then, in January, 1992, he played MTV's Unplugged live acoustic slot and, by chance, he was able to play what needed playing. In a studio by the Thames, with his regular band – drummer Steve Ferrone had read the lesson at Conor's funeral – he recorded a set that balanced his own songs with blues standards written or immortalised by Big Bill Broonzy, Bessie Smith, Leadbelly and Robert Johnson. The naked delicacy of Tears In Heaven and Lonely Stranger was underpinned by the stoic heart of both the cottonfield and ghetto 12-bars and his own great hymns to love forlorn and then love mourned, Layla and Old Love.

Clapton could have drowned *Unplugged* in self-pity. Instead he looked up and out and the whole album rang true – so its grace readily survives fading public memory of the circumstances. For all the guitar "God" legend and, latterly, his Versace lifestyle, he had reached a point where simple, musicianly performance and honest, undemonstrative singing could honour both his son's memory and, in the manner of popular art at its best, the life of every listener. To borrow Canadian critic Robert Cushman's definitive assessment of Sinatra's greatness, on *Unplugged* Clapton didn't sing *about* himself, he sang *from* himself. Used everything he had and gave it away.

Record label:
Duck
Produced
by Russ Titelman.
Recorded
at Bray Studios, Berkshire, England;
January 16, 1992.
Released:
September 12, 1992
Chart peaks:
2 (UK) 1 (US)
Personnel:
Eric Clapton (v, g); Ray Cooper (pc); Nathan East (b); Steve Ferrone (d); Chuck Leavell (k); Andy Fairweather-Low (g); Katie Kissoon, Tessa Miles (bv); Jim Barton (e)
Track listing:
Signe; Before You Accuse Me; Hey Hey; Tears In Heaven; Lonely Stranger; Nobody Knows You When You're Down and Out; Layla (S); Running On Faith; Walkin' Blues; Alberta; San Francisco Bay Blues; Malted Milk; Old Love; Rollin' and Tumblin'
Running time:
61.47
Current CD:
9362-45024
Further listening:
Layla And Other Assorted Love Songs (1971) by Derek And The Dominos; 461 Ocean Boulevard (1974) – prime rocking (and a bit of reggae); From The Cradle – electric blues covers revisited with an academic passion; Pilgrim (1998) – his first new songs for years, still in the wake of Tears In Heaven.
Further reading:
www.claptononline.com/index.shtml (official); www.slowhand.net, www.claptononline.com (unofficial)
Like this?
Try . . . p.304

Paul Weller

Paul Weller

Solo debut heralding Weller's creative and commercial rebirth.

In 1990, Paul Weller's fortunes were at their lowest ebb. The Style Council had split soon after Polydor rejected their house-inspired final album, and Paul – 32 years old and without a record or publishing deal – entered his infamous "house-husband" phase, desperately unsure about his musical future. Contrary to popular belief, however, he didn't stop writing and recording; he even toured Japan around that time – and it was a Japanese label, Pony Canyon, that partly funded *Paul Weller*. Pieced together from various sessions, with Weller playing vocals, guitar and, on all but two tracks, bass, the album reflected Weller's quest for a fresh identity, a notion expressed directly in songs like Uh Huh Oh Yeh ("Took a trip down Boundary Lane/Try to find myself again") and Kosmos ("Who am I? What am I? Where am I to go?"), but also apparent in the constant probing and melding of different styles – jazz, soul, folk, rock – and even in the sleeve visuals (Paul with cropped hair and paisley'n'beads inside, bowl-cut and ruffled shirt on the cover).

Musically, the most striking evolution was the bucolic, hippy-ish vibe, felt most keenly in the intoxicating flute solo on Clues, and the Traffic-esque acoustic guitar on Bitterness Rising.

"I'd started to listen to people I wouldn't have previously given the time of day to," says Weller. "I dropped that blinkered thing I had as a youth where I wouldn't listen to people with beards. People like Crosby Stills And Nash, Van Morrison. But I'd always listened to black music in whatever shape or form." Melancholic and optimistic by turns, the sense of a musician determined to rediscover his muse was overwhelming, and pushed him to new creative heights on the jazzy, late-night Fender Rhodes strains of Strange Museum and psychedelic spacy grooves of late-addition Kosmos. His next album, the mega-selling *Wild Wood*, was essentially a refinement of this fascinating, back-against-the-wall triumph.

Record label:
Go! Discs

Produced
by Brendan Lynch and Paul Weller.

Recorded
at Nomis, London and Black Barn Studios, Surrey; 1991–92

Released:
September 1992

Chart peaks:
88 (UK) None (US)

Personnel:
Paul Weller (g, v, b, k, pc); Jacko Peake (s, flute); Steve White (d, pc); Dee C Lee, Dr Robert, Camelle Hinds (bv)

Track listing:
Uh Huh Oh Yeh (S); I Didn't Mean To Hurt You; Bull-Rush; Round And Round; Remember How We Started; Above The Clouds (S); Clues; Into Tomorrow (S); Amongst Butterflies; The Strange Museum; Bitterness Rising; Kosmos

Running time:
53.43

Current CD:
Island 828355-2

Further listening:
Wild Wood (1993); greatest hits package Modern Classics (1998)

Further reading:
MOJO 19, 77; Paul Weller: My Ever Changing Moods (John Reed, 1996)

Like this?
Try . . . p.109

R.E.M.

Automatic For The People

The dark, folky, muted record that made them the world's biggest band.

After the shiny-happy, chart topping *Out Of Time*, R.E.M. reined in the jangle-rock formula to record this Southern Gothic collection of sombre folk and orchestral songs. Ironically, the meditation on dead friends, celebrities and the past would become the band's biggest-selling record to date with nearly 20 million served worldwide.

Named after the slogan of an Athens soulfood kitchen, *Automatic* started as a collection of instrumental demos. Engineer John Keane recalls the pre-production sessions: "They came in and recorded 26 songs, most of them incomplete without lyrics. Then they took the tapes somewhere else and worked on them. By the time I heard the finished product, I didn't know if I was hearing the demo or if they'd redone it."

That's because tracks like Sweetness Follows, Nightswimming and Star Me Kitten retained a spartan, ghostly quality. There were bigger production numbers that wouldn't have sounded out of place on *Out Of Time*, like The Sidewinder Sleeps Tonite (with its irresistible/unintelligible Mike Mills and Stipe chorus, "Call me when you try to wake her up") and Man On The Moon (with its layer upon layer of chiming guitars from Peter Buck). And there was an R.E.M. anomaly: a straight ahead, beautiful, everyone-can-relate-to-it single, Everybody Hurts. Beginning as a rehearsal-room noodle on electric piano by drummer Bill Berry the song was given uncharacteristically simple lyrics by Michael Stipe. In 1994, Berry told MOJO when the band first played the song, Stipe stood in a corner cupping his hands over his mouth and left ear, "Which is always a good sign. And he came up with the lyrics in the time it took us to go through the song, three or four times. None of us really thought it would see the light of day. It was kind of a joke song at first . . . that song's a great example of how he polished a turd."

The political-rocker Ignoreland, a song at least one half of the band claims to dislike, pulled at the heartstrings of diehards who missed the jangle, not to mention other fan favourites like the airy acoustic numbers Try Not To Breathe, Monty Got A Raw Deal (about Montgomery Clift) and Find The River (dedicated to departed Stipe buddy, River Phoenix). Clearly, *Automatic For The People* rates because every one of its 12 songs is worthy of attention. Did we mention the creeping keyboards of New Orleans Instrumental No. 1? Done.

Record label:
Warner Brothers
Produced
by Scott Litt and R.E.M.
Recorded
at Bearsville Studio, Bearsville, New York Criteria Recording Studios, Miami, Florida; additional recording at John Keane Studio, Athens; Georgia Kingsway Studio, New Orleans; Louisiana Bosstown Recording Studios, Atlanta, Georgia;.1991–2
Released:
October 1992
Chart peaks:
1 (UK) 2 (US)
Personnel:
Michael Stipe (v); Peter Buck (g); Mike Mills (b, v); Bill Berry (d, p, v); John Paul Jones (oa); Bertis Downs (k); Clif Norrell (e, m); Scott Litt (hm, clavinet, m);
Track listing:
Drive (S); Try Not To Breathe; The Sidewinder Sleeps Tonite (S); Everybody Hurts (S); New Orleans Instrumental No. 1; Sweetness Follows; Monty Got A Raw Deal; Ignoreland; Star Me Kitten; Man On The Moon (S); Nightswimming (S); Find The River (S)
Running time:
41.40
Current CD:
9362450552
Further listening:
Out of Time (1991); Fables of the Reconstruction (1985)
Further reading:
MOJO 12; R.E.M.: Talk About The Passion, An Oral History (Denise Sullivan, 1994); www.remhq.com
Like this?
Try . . . p.383

Aphex Twin

Selected Ambient Works 85–92

Debut double collection by techno Mozart.

"Living in Cornwall, if I wanted to hear a dub record I had to make it myself," Richard James, AKA The Aphex Twin, says, explaining both his rural upbringing and musical isolation. Both have served him well.

In early interviews he told anyone who would listen that he never slept, had composed literally thousands of tracks, and customised all his own keyboards – the latter embellishment seemingly based on little more than the fact that he hot-wired his Roland 1000 mini synth when he was at school and built another synth during his brief spell at university. Gullible members of the press swallowed this wholesale in their desire to create "stars" out of otherwise anonymous keyboard *auteurs*. In James' case though, they were right – and, fanciful as it may seem to suggest of machine-made music, this record is as resonantly English as the compositions of Edward Elgar and Ralph Vaughn Williams.

Selected Ambient Works conveys a strange, exploratory beauty that is only ever present in music when nobody knows what the rules are. Some of it was recorded on a domestic tape recorder when James was in his early teens. Much of it sounds like it was recorded in a deserted underground station late at night with the wind howling through empty tunnels. The warmth of tracks like Xtal and Pulsewidth make you realise how rapidly terms like "ambient" and "electronica" became codified. As genres sprung up around these otherwise arbitrary classifications the music became less adventurous, more rule-bound. James' music on the other hand, has always resolutely defied categorisation. His hybridised track titles, part sense, part ur-language reinforce this resistance.

"I've never read any poetry," mused the modern electronic era's one true genius in 1993. "But I'm sure I'd like it if I did." He released a further double and a triple CD set over the next 18 months.

Record label:
R&S
Produced by
Richard D James.
Recorded
in Cornwall and London; 1985–92.
Released:
November 1992
Chart peaks:
11 (UK) None (US)
Personnel:
Richard James (syn, k)
Track listing:
Xtal; Tha; Pulsewidth; Ageispolis; I; Green Calx; Heliosphan; We Are The Music Makers; Schottkey 7th Path; Ptolemy; Hedphelym; Delphium; Actium
Running time:
74.22
Current CD:
3922CD
Further Listening:
Surfing On Sine Waves (1992); Selected Ambient Works Vol 2. (1994); I Care Because You Do (1995); Richard D James Album (1996)
Further Reading:
Ocean Of Sound (David Toop, 1995); www.aphextwin.nu
Like this?
Try . . . p.645

Dr Dre

The Chronic

The record that changed a genre forever

Dr Dre's The Chronic is to gangsta rap what Nirvana's Nevermind is to independent rock. Both introduced not just artists but entire genres to new audiences, and both had first singles that were surprise hits and became anthems for two huge sections of frustrated American youth.

While Smells Like Teen Spirit encapsulated the hopeless, focusless anger of provincial "white trash", Dre's Nuthin' But A "G" Thang catalogued the drinking, partying and shagging aimlessness of inner city gang affiliates. As testimony to the times they were made in, neither record claims to have any solutions.

"I'm not a political person at all," Calvin "Snoop Doggy Dogg" Broadus boasted. "Music is an art, it's made to dance to, or sit back and relax to. It ain't made to preach. I'm just tryin' to sell records."

The Chronic's gestation was painful. In 1991, NWA member Dre began to believe he wasn't seeing his share of the money from his productions for leader Eric "Eazy E" Wright's Ruthless label. Dre turned to a new friend, former American Footballer Marion "Suge" Knight, for help. Allegedly freed from his contract after Knight's baseball bat-wielding associates convinced Eazy to follow the path of least resistance, Dre signed to Knight's new Death Row Records, a label reputedly part funded by drug money, and The Chronic began to take shape.

Dre enlisted a crew of session musicians, vocalists and writers including Snoop and Texan rapper The D.O.C., who had had to give up his rap career after damaging his vocal cords in a car accident. He slowed hip hop down to suit the sun-drenched, car-centric LA listening experience, heavily utilising the laid-back sound of the Parliament-Funkadelic axis to support Snoop's languid flow.

"I've never heard the perfect hip hop album, but I'd like to make one," Dre told Rolling Stone in 1993. "The Chronic is about the closest." It is a masterpiece, but it is frequently depressing, its bleakness wearying the listener. Snoop's brilliant Lil' Ghetto Boy provides a rare moment of introspection, and there is humour; though it's usually at the expense of Eazy and NWA's manager, Jerry Heller, the "stars" of Dre Day and Bitches Ain't Shit.

More problematic is The Chronic's legacy. Its success energised thousands of wannabe "studio gangstas", artists who believed they'd sell if they were as profane, sexist and unrepentant as possible. It is to the enduring shame of the record buying public that so many of them did.

AB

Record label:
Death Row Records
Produced
by Dr Dre
Recorded
at Death Row Studios, Los Angeles
Released:
1992
Chart peaks:
None (UK) 3 (US)
Personnel:
Dr Dre (v, kbds, drum programming): Snoop Doggy Dogg (v): RBX (v): Jewell (v): Ruben (v): That Nigga Daz (v, drum programming on Rar-Tat-Tat-Tat): Nate Dogg (v): Warren G (v): BJ (v): Big Tittie Nickie (v): D.O.C. (v): Samara (v): Rage (v): Kurupt (v): Bushwick Bill (v): Emmage (v): Colin Wolfe (kbds, bass): Justin Reinhardt (kbds): Eric "The Drunk" Borders (gtr): Chris Clairmont (gtr): Katisse Buckingham (flute, sax)
Track listing
The Chronic [Intro]: Fuck Wit Dre Day [And Everybody's Celebratin']: Let Me Ride: The Day The Niggaz Took Over: Nuthin' But A "G" Thang: Deeez Nuuuts: Lil' Ghetto Boy: A Nigga Witta Gun: Rat-Tat-Tat-Tat: The $20 Sack Pyramid: Lyrical Gangbang: High Powered: The Doctor's Office: Stranded On Death Row: The Roach [The Chronic Outro]
Running time:
62 mins 52 secs
Current CD:
Death Row DROW 110
Further listening:
2001 (Interscope, 1999)
Further reading:
Have Gun Will Travel (Ronin Ro)
Like this?
Try . . . p.566

Ice Cube

The Predator

A bile-spitting monster of a record recorded in response to the 1992 LA rebellion.

In terms of the career of its creator, this album was a watershed; for its genre, it was no less pivotal. But as a historical document The Predator is almost unparalleled.

Aged just 23, the rapper born O'Shea Jackson was already a veteran. He'd been in NWA, starred in two movies, and now, in November 1992, his third solo album became the first rap LP to go enter the US chart at No.1. What he had to say, however, was something middle America wasn't ready to hear.

On April 29, following the acquittal of four police officers videotaped beating black motorist Rodney King, South Central LA erupted in six days of rioting. The causes and aftermath of these events are brilliantly and savagely dissected on this ferocious record, completed in little more than a month that autumn.

"I loved it!" Cube told June Joseph of UK magazine Hip Hop Connection of the rioting. "The only thing I didn't like was that people got hurt, but that's the only thing this country understands. I'm glad we didn't just sit back because America doesn't hear pickets and protest singing, she just hears mass destruction."

Cube had prophesied the conflagrations in earlier lyrics, but his words had been overshadowed by accusations of racism. Rounding on his critics with the vigour of the vindicated, he switches from defence to unrepentant attack in the quiver of a syllable. "I told you what would happen and you heard it, read it/But all you could call me was anti-Semitic," he growls. "Regret it? Nope. Said it? Yep."

In this brief, furious moment Cube's wonderful voice and brilliantly sculpted lyrics were allied to the perfect musical accompaniment. The scratchy drums and melodic samples set up a succulent backdrop against which his full-bodied voice flows. Now I Gotta Wet 'Cha finds Cube stalking Simi Valley, looking for the jurors, while We Had To Tear This Motherfucker Up, the album's riveting centrepiece, deals with King's attackers in shocking, graphic terms.

He returned a year later with Lethal Injection, a record that oozed visceral power but took too many musical cues from Dr Dre's The Chronic, released a month after The Predator. As Cube focussed on film, records took a back seat, and subsequent albums have found him coasting, though commercially viable. Until he truly tries to test himself on record again, The Predator will remain his defining aural achievement.

AB

Record label:
Priority
Produced
by Ice Cube, DJ Pooh, Bobcat, Torcha Chamba, DJ Muggs, Sir Jinx, Mr Woody, Rashad, Pocketts
Recorded
at Echo Sound, Glendale, CA: The Hit Factory, NY
Released:
1992
Chart peaks:
No 1 (US) No 1 R&B (US) [Note: the first album to simultaneously top the Billboard pop and R&B album charts since Stevie Wonder's Songs In The Key Of Life]
Personnel:
Ice Cube (v): Das EFX (bkg v on Check Yo Self): Bob Morse (bass on Who Got The Camera?): Max (bkg v on Say Hi To The Bad Guy):
Track listing:
The First Day Of School (Intro): When Will They Shoot?: I'm Scared (Insert): Wicked: Now I Gotta Wet 'Cha: The Predator: It Was A Good Day: We Had To Tear This Mothafucka Up: Fuck 'Em (Insert): Dirty Mack: Don't Trust 'Em: Gangsta's Fairytale 2: Check Yo Self (Featuring Das EFX): Who Got The Camera?: Integration (Insert): Say Hi To The Bad Guy Bonus tracks on 2003 reissue: Check Yo Self ('The Message' Remix): It Was A Good Day (Remix): 24 Wit An L: U Ain't Gonna Take My Life
Running time:
56 mins 34 secs (original) 72 mins 18 secs (2003 reissue)
Current CD:
72435-43339-2-7
Further listening:
AmeriKKKa's Most Wanted (1990)
Like this?
Try . . . p.348

Stereo MC's

Connected

One of the most influential records in the history of late 20th century British music.

Easily the most successful record to have emerged from the British hip hop milieu, Connected was the culmination of years of artistic development.

Originally conceived by Nottingham-born, London-based rap fans Rob Birch and Nick Hallam as a hip hop duo with a DJ, the Stereos debut was a post-Daisy Age rap album. 33 45 78 gave the group a foothold, but in promoting it they realised they wanted to make music that fell outside the purist definitions of what hip hop was. The follow-up, Supernatural, took them some of the way there, spawning a US hit with Elevate My Mind, and its more expansive sound meant the Stereos replaced their DJ with drummer Owen If and a trio of female vocalists. It was by and for this line-up that Connected was created.

Inspired as much by the "baggy" scene which had brought clubbers and gig-goers together as by anything going on in hip hop or dance music, Connected represents one of those moments where a band taps into the ether and distils their time and place perfectly. The groove-based compositions resonated with a wide range of audiences, while Rob's rapped blend of streetwise homespun philosophising and rave generation, do-for-self exhortation touched people who wouldn't have dreamed they'd ever get anything out of a hip hop album. The title track's low-slung groove and Step It Up, a bouncing, bounding, dancefloor singalong, became huge hits, and remain in heavy rotation on radio stations and in adverts today, though what strikes anyone returning to the album ten years or more on is how fresh, timeless and forward-thinking the whole thing still sounds.

Connected's impact was seismic. The Stereos swept the board at the 1993 BRIT Awards, but, if anything, the album has increased in power and importance as the years have drawn on. A raft of hip hop-derived British music emerged in its wake, and while everyone from Norman "Fatboy Slim" Cook to The Prodigy would (rightly) argue that they succeeded on their own merits, nobody can deny that it was the Stereos, and this album, that paved the way.

"I think we felt slightly out of step with what was going on," Nick reflected. "It wasn't intentional, and I'm not saying we were geniuses or anything like that. But somehow, the combination of what we were doing was what other people started doing a considerable time later."

They were ahead of their time; and, in many ways, Connected remains there.

AB

Record label:
4th & Broadway/Island
Produced
by the Stereo MC's
Recorded
at Workhouse Studios, London
Released:
October 1992
Chart peaks:
2 (UK) 92 (US)
Personnel:
Rob Birch (v): Nick "The Head" Hallam (kbds): Owen If (drums): Cath Coffey (v): Verona Davies (v): Andrea Groves (v): Jennifer Ismail (add v on Connected, Fade Away, The End): James Hallawell (add kbds on Connected, organ on Creation): Kickhorns (brass on Connected, Fade Away, Step It Up, Playing With Fire, Creation, The End): Matthew Seligman (bass on All Night Long, The End): Paul O'Kane (bass on Step It Up, Creation, guitar on Playing With Fire): Johnny T (strings on Chicken Shake): Ivan Hussey (strings on Chicken Shake): Laura Cochrane (strings on Chicken Shake): Anya Ulman (strings on Chicken Shake): Chicu Modu (sax on The End)
Track listing:
Connected: Ground Level: Everything: Sketch: Fade Away: All Night Long: Step It Up: Playing With Fire: Pressure: Chicken Shake: Creation: The End
Running time:
53 mins 27 secs
Current CD:
512 743-2 BRCD 589
Further listening:
33 45 78 (1989): Supernatural (1991): Deep Down & Dirty (2001)
Further reading:
www.stereomcs.com
Like this?
Try . . . p.619

Brad

Shame

Down-time Pearl Jam side project yields unexpected treasure.

"We've found the groove. Have a good time. Make sure your seatbelts are fastened," states vocalist Shawn Smith by way of introduction to 20th Century, the fifth track on Brad's debut album. As if to emphasise Smith's opening gambit, Brad lock into an unfeasibly funky groove which centres around Stone Gossard's percussive guitar pattern, underpinned by bass player Jeremy Toback's fluid bass and drummer Regan Hagar's backbeat. It sounds effortless and fun. Which was probably the aim of Brad as a whole.

Formed in late 1992 by Gossard following a gruelling two-year stint on the road promoting Pearl Jam's debut album, *Ten*, Brad came together when the guitarist got back to Seattle and decided to call up his old friend and former Mother Love Bone bandmate Regan Hagar for a jam. Hagar turned up with friend, ex-Bliss and Pigeonhed singer Shawn Smith in tow and, following the recommendation of LA man Toback as a suitable bass player, the quartet elected to record this off-the-cuff album for a few thousand dollars. Just over two weeks later, Shame was in the can. For Gossard it was particularly therapeutic.

"To have the opportunity to go out and explore your playing with different musicians really expands your own perspectives. Because Brad is more of a side project the pressure is probably not as great. Everyone's tolerance of one another is increased because it's not your main band," states Stone.

Shame borrows from both funk and rock, though, mercifully, it certainly isn't funk rock. The sound is lithe and easy-going, the mood set by Smith's exceptional white soul vocal and piano figures; indeed, the piano intro to the stunning opener, Buttercup, draws you immediately into its fragile atmosphere – even more remarkable, it was captured in one straight take. Tracks like Nadine and the blues-peppered ballad Screen highlight Smith's exceptional talent; the Zeppelinesque Down marks the first recorded vocal appearance by bass player Jeremy Toback, who has since gone solo.

Shame is a delicious, well-kept secret whose sophistication belies its casual inception.

Record label:
Epic
Produced
by Brad.
Recorded
at Avast Recording Co, Seattle; October 4–21, 1992.
Released:
May 1993
Chart peaks:
72 (UK) None (US)
Personnel:
Stone Gossard (g); Regan Hagar (d); Shawn Smith (v, p, o); Jeremy Toback(b); Brendan O'Brien (m); Brett Eliason (e)
Track listing:
Buttercup; My Fingers; Nadine; Screen; 20th Century (S); Good News; Raise Love; Bad For The Soul; Down; Rockstar; We
Running time:
42.44
Current CD:
ZK53600
Further listening:
Pigeonhed, Pigeonhed (1993), Smith's other band, on Sub Pop; Brad, Interiors (1997); Satchel – another band with Smith on vocals, Family (1996); Shawn Smith, Let It All Begin (2000)
Further reading:
Very little exists on Brad in print or online. www.geocities.com/SunsetStrip/Towers/1854/index.html is the best source of info
Like this?
Try . . . p.190

Aimee Mann

Whatever

Though it failed to chart, it put her on top of the suddenly much-discussed heap of American singer-songwriters.

Jon Brion joined the vaguely New-Wavish band 'Til Tuesday for its final tour, in 1990, just about when its chief songwriter and singer, Aimee Mann, was beginning to realise that getting a record contract wasn't the end of her problems, but the beginning. As all hell broke loose with her label, Epic, Mann continued to hone her latest batch of smart, witty songs, with Brion assuming a larger role as her collaborator, arranger and boyfriend.

"The guy plays every instrument under the sun," marvels Mann, who continues to have a musical relationship with him. "It's truly miraculous to see him work. He can arrange in his head on the spot." Just as importantly, Brion played DJ for Mann, re-acquainting her with the ambitious pop music she'd grown up with; The Beatles, The Kinks, Big Star and The Zombies. As she and Brion recorded the songs that would become *Whatever*, they kept those gems of '60s pop as inspiration. "There was a lot of talk about making a great record, a magical record," recalls drummer Michael Hausmann, who is now Mann's manager. "One thing Jon emphasised was working on whatever tracks excited us that day. We didn't adhere to any strict schedule."

The album wears its influences effortlessly, with Mellotrons, toy pianos and optigans weaving gracefully through Brion's sumptuous arrangements. Though in the end there is something indefinably sad about the album, *Whatever* brims with catchy hooks and melodies.

"Jon and I share this concept of perpetual melody," says Mann. "When I stop singing, something else has to take over that continues the melodic thread or a variation on it." The two also spent a lot of time discussing songwriting. One goal they agreed on was that lyrics should be either true or witty, but it was even better if they were both. The brilliant Fifty Years After The Fair uses the New York World's Fair of 1939 to explore the fact that our expectation for the future always outstrips reality. "Jon and I had this running joke that we'd like to have something we'd call the World's *Un*fair, with rides like the Vicious Cycle and the Emotional Rollercoaster," Mann says.

When *Whatever* was released in the spring of 1993, there was a lot of gossipy speculation that it was about Mann's break-up with songwriter Jules Shear, a charge Mann wearily rejected, just as she did the charge that it was bitter. "To me it's not bitter," she said, "it's wry. But you see, that's a distinction I don't think a lot of people make, probably because they don't come across the word 'wry' too often."

Record label:
Geffen Records
Produced
by Jon Brion.
Recorded
at Q Division, Boston; Capitol, LA; Clubhouse; Blue Jay; Bearsville, Woodstock, NY; Sunset Sound, LA; 1990–92.
Released:
May, 1993
Chart peaks:
39 (UK) None (US)
Personnel:
Aimee Mann (g, b, v, pump o, Mellotron, pc, dixie cup); Jon Brion (g, v, b, d, pump o, p, vibraphone, Mellotron, chamberlain, optigan, glockenspiel, tambourine, kazoo); Buddy Judge (g, v); Roger McGuinn (g, v); Michael Hausmann (d); Jim Keltner (d); Milt Sutton (d); Randy Brion (euphonium, trombone); David Coleman (electric c)
Track listing:
I Should've Known (S); Fifty Years After The Fair; 4th of July; Could've Been Anyone; Put Me On Top; Stupid Thing (S/UK); Say Anything; Jacob Marley's Chain; Mr Harris; I Could Hurt You Now; I Know There's A Word; I've Had It (S/UK); Way Back When
Running time:
52.49
Current CD:
GED24956
Further listening:
I'm With Stupid (1995)
Further reading:
www.aimeemann.com
Like this?
Try . . . p.614

Orbital

Orbital

Techno as protest song, soul music and festival crowd pick-me-up

Before the second album bearing Kent-born duo Orbital's name (but no official title – fans give it the Beatles-esque title of The Brown Album), few thought that techno could provide anything other than pounding dancefloor fodder or soothing ambient head-balm. The brothers Hartnoll, however, were unaccustomed to obeying generic rules.

"We used to have quite savage bickering matches with the record company, because we were the least conventional group they'd ever had," remembered Phil Hartnoll. After the release of their 1991 debut, they had begun playing live, an unprecedented move in a dance scene accustomed only to mimed "personal appearances" in clubs. Then they released the single Halcyon, a melancholy, mid-tempo track based around a sample from Opus 3's ravetastic cover of Edward Barton's It's A Fine Day. Inspired by their mother's addiction to banned anti-depressant Halcyon, the track was far removed from the cartoon-sampling "hardcore" then dominating the charts. Its B-side, The Naked And The Dead went even further into the darkness, sampling the vocals of Scott Walker. The album that followed (which included a radically remixed version of Halcyon) proved that techno could express sentiments deeper than "let's dance".

Overshadowed by the Conservative government's introduction of the rave-bashing Criminal Justice Act, Orbital shifted away from the bright, ecstasy-friendly optimism of their debut. Impact (The Earth Is Burning) is its centrepiece, an unlikely, but dramatic mixture of hand-raising euphoria and furious environmental concern that needed no more than a solitary snatch of spoken vocal ("It's a cry for survival!") to get its message across. Anyone who doubted its potency and ability to connect with an audience is directed to Orbital's two remarkable dusk appearances at Glastonbury in 1994 and 1995, where, backed by video footage of falling rainforests and then-Prime Minister John Major, an extended Impact drew possibly the loudest cheers of the festival.

Record label:
Internal
Produced
by Phil and Paul Hartnoll.
Recorded
at Strongroom Studios, London; 1993.
Released:
June 1993
Chart peaks:
28 (UK) None (US)
Personnel:
Phil Hartnoll (k); Paul Hartnoll (k); Kirsty Hawkshaw (v); Paul Helliwell (g); Chris Daly (k)
Track listing:
Time Becomes; Planet Of The Shapes; Lush 3–1 (s); Lush 3–2; Impact (The Earth Is Burning); Remind; Walk Now . . .; Monday; Halcyon + On + On (s); Input Out
Running time:
63.57
Current CD:
1623510262
Further listening:
The first Orbital album, Orbital (1991); Snivilisation (1994); In Sides (1996)
The Middle of Nowhere (1999)
Further reading:
http://members.aol.com/orbital101/welcome.html
www.loopz.co.uk (official site). Given site still exists, but is uninspiring
Like this?
Try . . . p.675

The Palace Brothers

There Is No-One What Will Take Care Of You

Discordant debut set of haunting back-porch insurgency from quasi-religious strummers.

When The Palace Brothers' *There Is No-One What Will Take Care Of You* sneaked out in the early '90s, it was totally unexpected, though a limited-edition seven-inch single, Ohio River Boat Song, had hinted at what they were up to. At a time when U2 were embarking on their *Zooropa* tour and "traditional roots" rock was represented by little more than The Waterboys and Neil Young when unplugged, the downhome simplicity and almost chilling atmosphere of this record was at a tangent all its own.

So who were these people? "My folks were violent atheists," singer Will Oldham admitted when quizzed about the making of The Palace Brothers. "We sang weird distorted hymns in which religious references were mutated into somehow secular ones, custom cut by my mother. We did do a lot of singing. My mother played the accordion and my father the trumpet. My sister played a guitar usually." What he omitted to mention was that at one time Oldham had been a close associate of mythical Louisville band, Slint, and took the evocative cover picture of their highly influential *Spiderland* album.

His own music was warmly greeted. Said Spin: "Not just stripped-down but damn near gutted . . . [it] glows with white-boy campfire soul..." The NME picked up on the album's unhinged qualities: "[This] is music quite unlike anything in the US indie-rock scene – insane, minimal and beautiful." Oldham had identified something that had become lost, the art of storytelling. "I like the idea of them being stories," said the always-reticent Oldham of his songs. "I think that it's more thinking of a narrative atmosphere, like a movie or something." The music sounded as if it had been recorded in a barn some years before the advent of pop music and there was a curiously religious verve infiltrating Oldham's pained, cracking vocal. But Melody Maker hit just the right note in their review: "The Palace Brothers are sad, probably mad and living in a time and place we can only take their word for."

Wherever it was from, The Palace Brothers' haunting debut managed to create a mood so potent you wanted to be there too.

Record label:
Big Cat
Produced
by Will Oldham and The Palace Brothers.
Recorded
in Kentucky, 1992.
Released:
July 6, 1993
Chart peaks:
None (UK) None (US)
Personnel:
Will Oldham, Paul Oldham; Brian McMahan (g); Britt Walford (d)
Track listing:
Idle Hands Are The Devil's Playthings; Long Before; I Tried To Stay Healthy For You; The Cellar Song; Pulpit; (I Was Drunk At The); There Is No-One What Will Take Care Of You; O Lord Are You In Need?; Merida; King Me; I Had A Good Mother And Father; Riding; O Paul
Running time:
38.44
Current CD:
Drag City DC34CD
Further listening:
The follow-up, Palace Brothers (1994) refined the back-porch, backwood feel a little.
Further reading:
http://users.bart.nl/~ljmeijer/oldham/index.htm
Like this?
Try . . . p.326

Björk
Debut

Not strictly her debut, but a new beginning for Iceland's most extraordinary export.

After the demise of avant-indie band The Sugarcubes in 1991, singer Björk spent time in her native Iceland, living "a beautiful life" but her appetite for artistic stimulation ("I wanted danger, I wanted threats") saw her relocate to London to begin her solo career. Her British DJ boyfriend Dom Thrupp introduced her to Massive Attack/Soul II Soul producer Nellee Hooper and they got on so well that her idea for using several producers for the projected *Björk's Affairs* album was scrapped.

"She would arrive, really buzzing from an idea, and we'd literally dive into it, and in a couple of hours, would have something resembling the final product," remembered Hooper. "She'd come up with an original idea, with an overall picture of the song. She liked the way I didn't take her too literally. She'd say, I want this track to sound like Stockhausen, and I'd play a Quincy Jones loop from an old film score, and she'd say, That's exactly what I meant."

Her thirst for unusual inspiration (she had written The Anchor Song on a harmonium during a cycle tour of Icelandic churches) was quenched in this period by the techno scene.

"Every night we'd go out after recording to a different club," says Hooper, "so every morning was a hangover and every evening was a party. Of course there were tears and arguments, from both sides, but that's how you make a good record."

Debut was a startlingly individual accomplishment. The girl who recorded a best-selling (in Iceland) album of standards aged 11 and had been an indie-rock star (and before leaving her homeland was considering joining a speed-metal band), finally emerged as an international leading player in cutting-edge pop. Though Björk was quick to acknowledge the album as a 50–50 duo project, the listener is held by the extraordinary mercurial personality at the centre of the music; a voice that ranges from a coquettish sigh to a guttural howl, strong thoughtful melodies juxtapose excitable improvisations, intriguingly accented ambiguous/revealing lyrics (translated from the "North Sea gibberish" she composes with, according to Hooper) and an overwhelming sense of someone whose artistic sensibilities are exploding with life. Big-time sensuality, in fact. Her visual flair only enhanced the attractiveness of her idiosyncratic style and the mainstream audience swallowed it whole. *Debut* was the first of three albums that marked Björk as one of the outstanding artists of the decade.

Record label:
One Little Indian
Produced
by Nellee Hooper with Björk, David Arnold, Danny Cannon and Tim Simenon.
Recorded
at Wild Bunch Studios, Bristol; Olympic, Townhouse, Livingstone, Matrix, Swanyard, London; Workhouse Studios, Bombay and Summa Studio, Los Angeles; spring 1993.
Released:
July 1993
Chart peaks:
3 (UK) 61 (US)
Personnel:
Björk (v, k); Marius De Vries, Paul Waller, Martin Virgo, Garry Hughes (k); Corky Hale (harp); Luis Jardim (b, pc); Bruce Smith, Nellee Hooper (d, p); Jhelisa Anderson (bv); Jon Mallison (g); Talvin Singh (tabla); Sureh Sathe (a); Oliver Lake, Gary Barnacle, Mike Mower (b)
Track listing:
Human Behaviour; Crying; Venus As A Boy; There's More To Life Than This; Like Someone In Love; Big Time Sensuality; One Day; Aeroplane; Come To Me; Violently Happy; The Anchor Song; Play Dead
Running time:
52.22
Current CD:
TPLP 31 CDX
Further listening:
Post (1995); Homogenic (1997) Vespertine (2001)
Further reading:
MOJO 48; www.björk.com
Like this?
Try . . . p.677

Smashing Pumpkins

Siamese Dream

Chicago outfit fill stadiums with their prog-tinged take on quiet/LOUD! grunge.

"At some point during the making of this record, I got tired of people telling me what to do. I ended up doing what I wanted to do, and that meant the metal, the pop and the lullabies together," stated Billy Corgan in July 1993 when this, Smashing Pumpkins' second album was released.

Corgan was a man who could always see sound reasons to assert his control, and a multiplicity of problems presented themselves around the making of Siamese Dream. Despite the stable presence of co-producer Butch Vig (who'd also had a hand in debut Gish), tension between the band members ran rampant as Wretzky and Iha's romantic relationship broke up and Chamberlin slumped into a mire of heroin addiction. Corgan, in a sticky patch with his own relationship as it happened, (over?)compensated by playing most of the others' instrumental parts himself. "There was a lot of pressure on me to stay focussed and not get fucked up," he argued. "So if I was a tyrant it was 'cos our band was expected to sell a zillion and write eight generational hits, not because I wanted to be a tyrant. It wasn't the making of Siamese Dream that pushed me into therapy, it was my relationship with my now wife."

Such stuff can break a band, but in this case Corgan's fired-up ego delivered. Opening thunderously with Cherub Rock, *Siamese Dream* adds a progressive edge to the Pumpkins' grungy origins. Moreover, it marks Corgan's coming of age as a writer. While Gish had hinted at the band's potential, tracks like the soaring Today, the semi-acoustic Disarm and the fragile Soma (featuring R.E.M.'s Mike Mills on piano) offered opulent fulfilment. When they had finished recording, Chamberlin went straight into rehab, though it didn't take long for him to get back into the habit, and he was sacked a couple of years later after touring keyboard player Jonathan Melvoin died of a heroin overdose while in his company in a New York hotel. Describing the emotional uproar of a band drawn together by musical ideas rather than existing friendships, Wretzky once said, "For me, being in Smashing Pumpkins is like being married to three people you never even wanted to date. With the exception of Iha, of course."

Corgan, meanwhile, simply pressed on: "The classic story is that we came off the road after 18 months behind *Siamese Dream* and three days later I started writing *Mellon Collie.*" His drive ensured that even their less convincing records were fired by grand conceits; exhausted, in 2000 they declared their intention to call it a day after a farewell tour.

Record label:
Hut Recordings
Produced
by Butch Vig and Billy Corgan.
Recorded
at Triclops Sound Studios, Atlanta, Georgia; late 1992
Released:
July 1993
Chart peaks:
4 (UK) 10 (US)
Personnel:
Billy Corgan (v, g, Mellotron); D'Arcy (v, b); Jimmy Chamberlin (d); James Iha (g); Eric Remschneider (c); David Ragsdale (v); Mike Mills (p); Mark Richardson, Jeff Tomei, Butch Vig (e)
Track listing:
Cherub Rock (S); Quiet; Today(S); Hummer; Rocket; Disarm (S); Soma; Geek USA; Mayonnaise; Spaceboy; Silverfuck; Sweet Sweet; Luna
Running time:
62.17
Current CD:
CDHUT 11
Further listening:
the unwieldy but impressive double album Mellon Collie And The Infinite Sadness (1995) Mary Star of the Sea (2003)
Further reading:
MOJO 37;
www.smashingpumpkins.com
Like this?
Try . . . p.376

Sheryl Crow

Tuesday Night Music Club

Belated debut reveals classic rock'n'roller, pithy in every word and note.

Tuesday Night Music Club spoke for the life of an artist who had worked her passage. Born in Kennett, Missouri (pop. 10,000), Crow took a degree in classical piano, played with St Louis bar bands, in Los Angeles sang back-ups for stars including Michael Jackson, wrote songs for Eric Clapton and Celine Dion, and made such a hash of her putative debut album that she begged A&M to withhold it and let the $250,000 costs ride on a second shot. Remarkably, they said OK.

So she was 30 when, tentatively, she joined the loose collective – the Tuesday Night Music Club – which gathered around experienced producer Bill Bottrell's Toad Hall studio. "Bill has this big coffeehouse-looking room," she recalled. "We'd play a song through three or four times, use the best take and that was it. People sitting there having a great time. What better way to make music?" Probably none. Everything about the album sits right. The surface swings and parties. It's the undertow drags you under, the laconic, barbed lines and Crow's conversational storyteller's voice cutting like cheesewire, or maybe like Hank Williams – "When Bill listened to Leaving Las Vegas he said, You're country at heart, you should dive in feet first. And that's what we did, a down-and-outer working-man's country record. Although the record company were, Don't say the C-word!" All I Wanna Do, the hit that launched the album, was typical. Sound: perfect cheery singalong. Scenario: two morning boozers in a bar mocking the "good people of the world washing their cars" while they "have some fun/ Billy likes to peel the labels/From his bottles of Bud and shred them on the bar".

But the song that meant most to Crow was the jazz-tinged We Do What We Can. It told the story of how, 20 years earlier, her father gave up playing trumpet when the sudden death of his bandmate and best friend brought a chill of mortality to his life. Significantly, she says Bottrell liberated her into writing it. He encouraged her to talk it through on tape then instructed her to bring in the song the following day. She did. Then she persuaded her father to dig out his horn, fly in from Kennett and record the wisps of muted melancholy heard down-mix on the album. It was the ultimate fulfilment of her music life, chapter one; Sheryl Crow's emergence, after all, as a musician and woman of redoubtable substance.

Record label:
A&M
Produced
by Bill Bottrell.
Recorded
at Toad Hall, Pasadena, California, 1992–3.
Released:
August 3, 1993
Chart peaks:
8 (UK) 3 (US)
Personnel:
Sheryl Crow (v, Hammond organ); Bill Bottrell (g, ps); Kevin Gilbert (d); David Baerwald (g); Dan Schwartz (b); Brian MacLeod (d); David Ricketts (b); Blair Lamb (e)
Track listing:
Run, Baby, Run (S); Leaving Las Vegas (S); Strong Enough (S); Can't Cry Anymore (S); Solidify; The Na-Na Song; No One Said It Would Be Easy; What I Can Do For You (S, UK only); All I Wanna Do (S); We Do What We Can; I Shall Believe
Running time:
49.42
Current CD:
540 126-2-18
Further listening:
Sheryl Crow (1996), The Globe Sessions (1998) – she produced and wrote them herself and they're very good too.
Further reading:
MOJO 35; www.sherylcrow.com; http://sherylcrow.dvb-labs.com/
Like this?
Try . . . p.685

The Breeders

Last Splash

An ad-hoc indie supergroup eclipse their parent bands then blow it.

The early '90s indie explosion, prompted by Nirvana's commercial breakthrough in 1991, gave new life to loud, angular guitars and maverick songwriting. Robust, no-nonsense production values became vogueish once more.

It was the perfect environment in which The Breeders, formed in 1989 by Kim Deal and Tanya Donelly as relief from their day jobs with the Pixies and the Throwing Muses, could flourish. Unfortunately, despite releasing two critically acclaimed albums (the second also commercially well received), the band eventually succumbed to their own maverick ways, and have failed to capitalise on the success of *Last Splash*.

With Deal and Donelly on guitars, and bassist Josephine Wiggs poached from modest UK indie outfit The Perfect Disaster, The Breeders (a name reclaimed from the Deal twins' teenage combo) recruited maverick producer (he says he just records things) Steve Albini, who'd produced the Pixies' *Surfer Rosa*, and emerged in 1990 with *Pod*, a thrilling, yet strangely measured affair that inevitably utilised the Pixies' dynamics and the Throwing Muses' moodiness to great effect.

It was two years before they found time to record again, re-emerging in 1992 with the excellent *Safari* EP, which upped the guitar-pop quota but provided a suitable departure point for Donelly, who quit to form Belly. Now with Kim's twin sister Kelley on guitar, and permanent drummer Jim MacPherson, The Breeders used a support slot with Nirvana to experiment with new material, before regrouping that winter to begin work on the second album.

Within hours of their arrival in San Francisco, in January 1993, news broke that Black Francis had disbanded the Pixies. Newly liberated, The Breeders partied hard on a houseboat during the sessions, and emerged in the summer with the spirited, suitably erratic, and often brilliant *Last Splash*. Kim Deal, whose songwriting came of age in 1988 with Gigantic (on the Pixies' *Surfer Rosa*), dominated the album. She wrote and sang virtually all of the songs, which ranged from the effervescent wooziness of Cannonball, and the tough but tender Do You Love Me Now?, to the irresistible simplicity of No Aloha and the dirge-like Roi. With her sensuous, cartoonish voice – the velvet glove that made the album's fearsome, twin-guitar assault approachable to a surprisingly wide audience – *Last Splash* went platinum in the States.

Record label:
4AD
Produced
by Kim Deal and Mark Freegard.
Recorded
at Coast Recorders and Brilliant Studios, San Francisco and Refraze, Dayton, Ohio and mixed at the Plant, Sausalito; early 1993.
Released:
September 1993
Chart peaks:
5 (UK) 33 (US)
Personnel:
Kim Deal (g, v, Moog); Kelley Deal (g, v); Jim MacPherson (d); Josephine Wiggs (b, d, c, v); Carrie Bradley (vn, v); Mark Freegard (e)
Track listing:
New Year; Cannonball (S); Invisible Man; No Aloha; Roi; Do You Love Me Now? (S); Flipside; I Just Wanna Get Along; Mad Lucas; Divine Hammer (S); S.O.S.; Hag; Saints; Drivin' On 9; Roi (reprise)
Running time:
39.47
Current CD:
CAD 3014 CD
Further listening:
Pod (1990), the band's debut, less frenetic and slightly less tuneful than its successor with Steve Albini's trademark claustrophobic sound.
Further reading:
http://4ad.com/artists/breeders (official); www.noaloha.com (unofficial)
Like this?
Try . . . p.595

Uncle Tupelo

Anodyne

Full of gorgeous, if cryptic, songs, it managed to reinvent American roots music while sounding absolutely timeless.

Uncle Tupelo's founding members Jeff Tweedy and Jay Farrar, who had played in a number of punky, '60s' cover bands after meeting at a suburban St Louis high school, had a crazy plan for their fourth album.

"On our first two," says Tweedy, "the producer had steered us towards overdubbing and things like that. I don't think we were purists back then, we just didn't understand [the process]. We were way more comfortable making *March 16–20, 1992* because that was playing live with minimal overdubs. With *Anodyne*, the idea was not to do *any* overdubs. None. To make a live studio record." Though the song Anodyne required 15 takes, most took just two or three.

They recorded in Austin and invited everyone they knew to drop by. Among the takers was the late Doug Sahm, who assured them, "You guys do what you do and when it comes to my part, it'll be perfect." And on Give Back The Key To My Heart, his raucous vocal was exactly that. Max Johnston, Michelle Shocked's brother, added twang with fiddle and lap steel.

"A lot of the stuff Max ended up doing came about through trying to fit these real traditional instruments into a kind of rock music he'd never heard," says Tweedy. "He'd play a little lick and we'd tell him to repeat it. That's why there are a lot of lap steel riffs that keep getting repeated, like in We've Been Had."

Although they shared songwriting credits, Tweedy and Farrar, like Lennon and McCartney at the end, did not actually write together. As a lyricist, Farrar is so tantalisingly cryptic that even Tweedy had given up asking for explanations. With hindsight, though, it's easy to read disillusion in what at first seem to be songs about failed love. In late 1993, during the tour for *Anodyne*, Farrar informed the band he was quitting. Tweedy laughs ruefully when the line "Can't seem to find common ground" from High Water is read to him.

"If I'd actually been able to understand Jay's lyrics I would have been more prepared for the demise of Uncle Tupelo," he says. "But I thought they were beautiful songs. I didn't worry about what they were about." Tweedy soon resurfaced with his new band, Wilco, only partly aware that Uncle Tupelo had quietly set the whole Americana boom of the late '90s in motion.

Record label:
Sire
Produced
by Brian Paulson.
Recorded
at Cedar Creek Recording, Austin Texas; May and June, 1993.
Released:
October 1993
Chart peaks:
None (UK) None (US)
Personnel:
Jay Farrar (g, mandolin, v); Jeff Tweedy (g, b, v); Ken Coomer (d); Max Johnston (fiddle, ls, dobro); John Stirrat (b); Doug Sahm (g, v); Lloyd Maines (ps)
Track listing:
Slate; Acuff-Rose; The Long Cut; Give Back the Key to My Heart; Chickamauga; New Madrid; Anodyne; We've Been Had; Fifteen Keys; High Water; No Sense in Lovin'; Steal the Crumbs
Running time:
43.25
Current CD:
9 45424-2
Further listening:
March 16–20, 1992 (1993) and the first album by Jay Farrar's son Volt, Trace (1995)
Further reading:
No Depression: An Introduction to Alternative Country Music. (Edited by Grant Alden and Peter Blackstock, 1998); Modern Twang: An Alternative Countrh Music Guide and Directory (David Goodman, 1999); the bimonthly alt country magazine, No Depression or its website, www.nodepression.net
Like this?
Try . . . p.477

Wu-Tang Clan

Enter The Wu-Tang (36 Chambers)

The record that changed the rap music industry.

It is no exaggeration to say that the Wu-Tang Clan's debut was one of the most important albums in hip hop history. It took the music back to its "golden age" sound when syrupy G-Funk was the norm, and changed the way the record business operated.

Cousins Robert "Prince Rakeem" Diggs and Gary "The Genius" Grice, two experienced emcees down on their luck, developed the idea for the perfect rap group in the early '90s. They renamed their Staten Island home Shaolin, and took the Wu-Tang name after a posse of renegade medieval Chinese monks whose martial arts skills were legendarily varied and lethal. Becoming The Rza and The Gza, Diggs and Grice added friends and family members to the line-up. Most had been in trouble with the law, and several were making ends meet by dealing drugs. All were hungry to succeed.

A self-financed single, Protect Ya Neck, was sold on the streets, using marketing expertise picked up in the drugs game. It sold over 20,000 copies and New York's A&R community began to take notice.

Determined to ensure they wouldn't make the same mistakes as when they'd both previously had record deals, Grice and Diggs signed the band to Steve Rifkind's new Loud imprint. The historic deal allowed every Clan member to record solo material for whatever label they chose, and ensured members could appear on each others' records. It forced Loud to market the group as a brand, and meant each member had to work extraordinarily hard.

"We could go in the studio tomorrow," Method Man explained in the autumn of 1994, "Rza could throw a beat on, and I could go in there and write something, just 'Bam!' And the shit'd be a hit. Somebody else would be writing something while I'm doing my shit, then they'd go and jump on it. And it could go on any one of our albums, Wu-Tang or solo."

Enter The Wu-Tang succeeded because of its differences. Rza's dusty breakbeat aesthetic gave the record a defiantly Spartan sound, deepened through the use of the ageing technology in his basement studio. Lyrically the record sparkled, the range of voices and flows comparable to the fighting styles used in the martial arts films the group referenced.

The Wu discography now numbers more than 25 albums, and while their fortunes have ebbed and flowed they remain the most powerful and enduring brand in rap history.

AB

Record label:
Loud/RCA
Produced
by Prince Rakeem "The Rza" (except Da Mystery Of Chessboxin': co-produced by Ol' Dirty Bastard: Wu-Tang Clan Ain't Nuthing Ta F' Wit: co-produced by Method Man)
Recorded
at Firehouse Studio, NY
Released:
November 1993
Chart peaks:
none (UK) 41 (US)
Personnel:
Prince Rakeem "The Rza" (v): The Method Man (v): U-God (v): Rebel INS (v): Shallah Raekwon (v): Ghost Face Killer (v): Ol' Dirty Bastard (v): The Genius "The Gza" (v): The 4th Disciple (turntables): Masta Killa (v – not credited on sleeve)
Track listing:
Bring Da Ruckus: Shame On A Nigga: Clan In Da Front: Wu-Tang – 7th Chamber: Can It All Be So Simple/Intermission: Da Mystery Of Chessboxin': Wu-Tang Clan Ain't Nuthing Ta F' Wit: C.R.E.A.M.: Method Man: Protect Ya Neck: Tearz: Wu-Tang – 7th Chamber – Part II: Method Man (remix) Skunk Mix (Bonus Track): Conclusion
Running time:
61 mins 29 secs
Current CD:
74321203672
Further listening:
Iron Flag (2002): Genius/Gza – Liquid Swords (1995): Raekwon – Only Built 4 Cuban Linx (1995): Ghostface Killah – Iron Man (1996: Rza – The World According To Rza (2003)
Like this?
Try . . . p.717

Ali Farka Toure With Ry Cooder

Talking Timbuktu

West Africa's leading bluesman meets a West Coast slide guitar legend.

Nothing annoys Ali Farka Toure more than being told he sounds like John Lee Hooker, or any other American bluesman. "I'd never heard American music before I started playing," he growls. "When I hear John Lee Hooker, I hear Malian music adapted for another country." The similarities are there – if anybody needed proof that the blues originated in Africa – but Toure's record company were still sceptical when the voice on the other end of the phone claimed to be Ry Cooder, wondering if he could meet up with the African guitarist. Both men were in London in the summer of 1992, where they talked about collaborating in the future.

By autumn 1993, the normally reticent Toure was prepared to take a sabbatical from his farm in Timbuktu and travel to California. During rehearsals in Cooder's home in Santa Monica, Toure revealed a loose, reflective mood, far removed from the harsh electric feel of his most recent albums. A perfect blend of California and the blues. It should have been a breeze to record, but Cooder suddenly found himself involved with some heavy juju. Things came to a head when he asked Toure to play his *n'jurkel*, a one-string lute made of cow hide, a gourd and horsehair. "Ali Farka wouldn't play fiddle in my house in Santa Monica, because it's too near the beach and he didn't want to provoke the ocean spirits. He wouldn't play in Hollywood because he thought there were hungry spirits roaming the hallways of the studio where we were working. 'Bad energy in this part of town,' he said. He seemed very happy and powerful, but there were some deep things troubling him." Unable to get to the bottom of Toure's blues, Cooder subtly took the music further, planning a more rounded LP than anything Toure had recorded previously. The tunes were more focussed, the sequence showcased Toure's development, with tribal fiddling followed by full band numbers. The rewards were a Grammy, a timely boost for Cooder's profile and international acclaim for Toure and World Circuit.

Record label:
World Circuit
Produced
by Ry Cooder.
Recorded
at Ocean Way Recording Studio, Los Angeles, California; September 1993.
Released:
March 1994
Chart peaks:
44 (UK) None (US)
Personnel:
Ali Farka Toure (v, g, njarka); Ry Cooder (g, mbira, tamboura, mandolin, marimba); Hamma Sankare (calabash); Oumar Toure (congas, bongos); John Patitucci (b); Jim Keltner (d); Clarence "Gatemouth" Brown (g)
Track listing:
Bonde; Soukora; Gomni; Sega; Amandrai; Lasidan; Keito; Banga; Ai Du; Diaraby
Running time:
60.10
Current CD:
WCD 040
Further listening:
Radio Mali (1996 compilation of sessions from the '70s); Ali Farka Toure (1988); The River (1990) and The Source (1992). Anything by John Lee Hooker.
Further reading:
http://africanmusic.org/artists/alifarka.html
Like this?
Try . . . p.700

Giant Sand

Glum

Prolific Arizona combo deliver their ill-fated masterpiece.

Glum was the album where Giant Sand got it so right that it just had to go completely wrong. Formed as Giant Sandworms by singer Howe Gelb in Tucson, Arizona in 1980, the group had spent the decade honing their beatnik lyrics, rockabilly strum and love of a dusty melody into a wind-blown version of alternative country that touched punk rock and loungecore along the way. Eternally unsettled, they shortened their name and changed line-ups on practically every record. Finally, on their 1991 album *Ramp* they seemed to have found their sound and for their next they even enlisted a proper producer in Malcolm Burn, who'd previously worked with John Mellencamp and Lisa Germano.

"It was a fine slice and dice experience thanks to Malcolm's attention and attenuation span," recalls Howe Gelb. "The man has good ears. I'd say, 'Remember that glitsch of a sound we got three days back,' and he'd go straight to it."

Guest appearances from Victoria Williams, Rainer Ptaceck, Chris Cacavas and Peter Holsapple allowed the sound to move across a number of previously uncharted regions. Burn and Gelb laboured long and hard to produce a seamless procession of songs that sounded like they'd been recorded in one take, moving through the rooms of some palatial desert dwelling, inhabited by like-minded bandoleros. There's the folky ambience of Calexico; the mariachi lounge of The Friends Of Dean Martinez; Howe Gelb's solo lonesome blues and the disturbed pop of the partnership they formed with Lisa Germano as OP8. It's a breathtaking journey that climaxes with a bar-room rendition of Hank Williams' I'm So Lonesome I Could Cry delivered by a local restaurant owner. "The closing number is Pappy Allen with his wife and daughter singing harmony." Gelb explains. "He died before the album came out and I couldn't listen to the song for about a year after." And neither could anyone else. The group had been signed to fledgling label Imago which quickly went to the wall, the album crept out and was almost immediately deleted, fated to remain an obscure gem.

Record label:
Imago
Produced
by Malcolm Burn, Howe Gelb and John Convertino.
Recorded
at Kingsway in New Orleans, plus various home locations in Tuscon, Arizona; summer 1993.
Released:
March 1994
Chart peaks:
None (UK) None (US)
Personnel:
Howe Gelb (g, p, v); John Convertino (d); Joey Burns (b); Paula Jean Brown (b); Harriet and Cheryl Allen (bv); Malcolm Burn (k, programming; Mark Walton (b); Rainer Ptaceck (dobro); Peter Holsapple (slide guitar); Trina Shoemaker (v); Lisa Germano (fiddle); Chris Cacavas (o); Pappy Allen, Victoria Williams, Indiosa Patsy Jean Gelb (v); Neil Harry (steel guitar); Sofia Albertson (intro droolery)
Track listing:
Glum; Yer Ropes; Happenstance; Frontage Road; One Helvakowboy Song; Painted Bird; Spun; Left; Faithful; Birdsong; I'm So Lonesome I Could Cry
Running time:
49.02
Currently unavailable on CD
Further listening:
following Glum's non-appearance the band recorded under many guises before getting back together for 1999's similarly inventive Chore Of Enchantment which, along with Ramp (1992), is absolutely essential.
Further reading:
www.giantsand.com
Like this?
Try . . . p.597

Morrissey
Vauxhall And I

Reining in the bitterness for the warmest, most expansive album of his solo career.

If we believe his interviews, the happiest day in Morrissey's life was May 21, 1959; the day before he was born.

If he'd ever been truly happy, heaven knows that by 1994 Morrissey had become the boy who cried "Woe!", mining such a rich vein of self-deprecatory humour from his depression that questions of veracity ceased to be important.

The truth is that *Vauxhall And I* was recorded after one of the worst periods of Morrissey's life. During the spring of 1993, three of his closest associates had died within weeks of each other. His manager, Nigel Thomas, had died of a heart attack; Tim Broad, who'd made eleven of his videos, passed away the following month. Then Mick Ronson, who had produced Morrissey's 1992 album, *Your Arsenal*, died of cancer. Thrown into shock, Morrissey locked himself away in his Primrose Hill house and slowly watched his desire for fame evaporate.

"I thought it was time to put lots of things away in their boxes," he said, "and allow age to take its natural toll. I was really tired of the past."

"He had these grand ideas that he couldn't translate musically," remembers bassist Jonny Bridgwood, "The only instructions I remember him giving anyone was that he didn't want it to be an indie album. It was so odd, circumspect. Bits we thought would become choruses became verses, it was all back to front."

As with *Your Arsenal*, Morrissey flirted with images of roughneck post-war violence, name-checking the tasty villains of Graham Greene's Brighton Rock on Now My Heart Is Full and sampling the teenage Teds of Carol Reisz's We Are The Lambeth Boys on Spring-Heeled Jim but thanks to Steve Lillywhite's production the feel was of nostalgia, lost youth and wistful melancholia.

"Steve was very good in a textural way," says Bridgwood. "People think there are orchestras on that album, strings, but there aren't. That's all Steve's sound textures."

The mood of the album was aptly summed up by Morrissey as one of "jubilant exhaustion". Possibly realising that he had made his one true masterpiece, he told William Shaw in Details in 1994, "I now feel free to do absolutely nothing at all, live in a mansion flat in Chelsea and see nobody; a perfect life."

The album went straight in at Number 1. Morrissey was mobbed at HMV. It wouldn't happen again.

"The spirit of it was great," remembers Bridgwood. "The next one [1995's *Southpaw Grammar*] was an album too far. It was a nice summer and it was never to be repeated."

Record label:
Parlophone
Produced
by Steve Lillywhite
Recorded
at Hook End Manor
June–August 1993
Released:
March 1994
Chart peak:
1 (UK) 18 (US)
Personnel:
Morrissey (v, e), Boz Boorer (g), Alan Whyte (g,v), Jonny Bridgwood (b), Woodie Taylor (d), Chris Dickie (e)
Track listing:
Now My Heart Is Full; Spring-Heeled Jim; Billy Budd; Hold On To Your Friends; The More You Ignore Me The Closer I Get; Why Don't You Find Out For Yourself; I Am Hated For Loving; Lifeguard Sleeping, Girl Drowning; Used To Be A Sweet Boy; The Lazy Sunbathers; Speedway
Running time:
39.54
Current CD:
7243 8 27797 2 8
Further listening:
Viva Hate (HMV 1988), Your Arsenal (HMV 1992), Maladjusted (Island 1997)
Further reading:
www.CemetryGates.com
Like this?
Try . . . p.393

Hole

Live Through This

Savagery, dislocation, tormented devotion; released in the month of Kurt Cobain's suicide.

Despite the fraught relationship Courtney Love had with husband Kurt Cobain, they seem to have been soulmates, matching each other in drive, taste and self-destructiveness. It's a sad but, perhaps, predictable irony that when Love finally achieved greatness, Cobain would unintentionally overshadow her. *Live Through This* was released April 12; four days earlier, Cobain had shot himself.

A self-imposed promotional blackout meant the album struggled; a divided reception saw it embraced as a legacy of Cobain but criticised for capitalising on his death and having profited from his uncredited input. No doubt there was some assistance – but Love had her style together before she met Cobain.

After carting herself round the punk globe as a hanger-on, she worked initially with Kat Bjelland, later of Babes in Toyland; moving to Seattle she assembled her own band, beginning with Eric Erlandson, whose full-bore rock chords blended perfectly with Love's jagged New Wave vocals. 1991's *Pretty On The Inside* had the band touted as the next Nirvana (*everyone* from Seattle got that); it was a raw, self-abusive, abrasive listen.

The following year, Love and Cobain married and had a daughter and, if there was turbulence, there was happiness and creativity, too. Love told Rolling Stone she was "finding a higher ground, trying to find ideal songs in myself with the kind of competition I'm up against in my own house".

She brought in a new rhythm section with Schemel and Pfaff and the sound, while still sabre-toothed, developed key ingredients – melody, counterpoint, hooks – against which the vulnerable, blood-spattered lyrics could shock satisfyingly. This they would've done anyway; more so, and with prophetic power, after the suicide, in lines like the imploring "If you live through this with me/I swear that I will die for you" and the raging "Go on, take everything/Take everything/I want you too," which would prefigure Love's distraught public haranguing of Cobain for absenting himself.

Even now, the album's energy, vitriol and anguish can make the scalp prickle.

Two months after its release, Pfaff was found dead of an overdose.

When the air had cleared, *Live Through This* went on to rack up platinum sales and win commendations in papers from Rolling Stone to the New York Times, but Love was battered. Though she toured the album rip-roaringly, her musical output has never been the same.

Record label:
Geffen
Produced
by Paul Q Kolderie and Sean Slade.
Recorded
at Triclops Studios, Atlanta; 1993.
Released:
April 12, 1994
Chart peaks:
13 (UK) 52 (US)
Personnel:
Courtney Love (v, g); Eric Erlandson (g); Kristen Pfaff (b, p, bv); Patty Schemel (drm)
Track listing:
Violet (S); Miss World (S); Plump; Asking for It; Jennifer's Body; Doll Parts (S); Credit In The Straight World; Softer, Softest; She Walks On Me; I Think That I Would Die; Gutless; Rock Star
Running time:
38.19
Current CD:
GED 24631
Further listening:
crunching debut Pretty On The Inside (1991) includes the self-explanatory Teenage Whore; My Body The Hand Grenade (1997) rounds up early singles and rarities; Celebrity Skin (1998) was a conscious attempt to make a hit record and, while it's hardly the Raspberries album Courtney had been threatening, it certainly soft by Hole standards.
Further reading:
Courtney Love: The Real Story (Poppy Z Brite, 1997) is a useful book on Love.
Like this?
Try . . . p.533

Blur

Parklife

Britpop starts here. Possibly. Even if not, it's a sneery, snotty English classic.

"We never really felt we were making another album," Damon Albarn reflects on Blur's early days. "We just recorded all the time and, at the end of the year, there it was." But what a year it had been. The heyday of grunge and the dogdays of Madchester, 1993 saw Blur barely keeping their balance on the thin line dividing great inventions from good intentions. "We were total mavericks," Albarn decides. "The country was utterly uninterested in the idea of reviving British pop music. So we just got on with it."

The seeds of *Parklife* were sown during Blur's disastrous first American tour, promoting their debut album, *Blur* (1991). "We developed a reputation as caricatures of the English stereotype," says Albarn, "and although I don't think it was very accurate then, we were more than happy to live up to the billing." The subsequent *Modern Life is Rubbish* road-tested the concept; the road itself did the rest. "Suddenly something was happening," says the singer. "There was a wonderful dialogue between us and the audience. They just started singing everything, so we started recording while we were touring, getting down the energy which we felt in ourselves and from the audience. It was a very deliberate thing. We had to find our personality as a band, so we worked on that, musically and lyrically."

The band that had been stigmatised as a stereotype reinvented whatever it was they were stereotyping to begin with; in the Mockney swagger of Parklife; in the Club Med rat-packery of Girls And Boys; in the Batley Variety Club yearning of To The End. But, most of all, Blur's original, prickly character burst through in odd lines such as "Dirty little monsters eating all the morsels" (End Of A Century). Of course, influences hang heavy in the air about Blur: the Small Faces, The Kinks, even Paul Weller make their mark. But *Parklife* was less a remembrance of the good old days than a celebration (or otherwise) of England as it is – a lazy Sunday with the stores all shut, a village green with an Asda in the middle and a tube station where it's always midnight. If *Parklife* is a time capsule, at least as a remembrance of the English 1990s it's more than fair.

Record label:
Food
Produced
by Stephen Street; To The End produced by Stephen Hague, John Smith, Blur.
Recorded
at Maison Rouge, Fulham, London; November 1993–January 1994.
Released:
April 1994
Chart peaks:
1 (UK) None (US)
Personnel:
Damon Albarn (v, Moog, Hammond organ, melodica, harpsichord recorder); Graham Coxon (g, clarinet, s, pc, v); Alex James (b, v); Dave Rowntree (d, pc); Louise Fuller (vn); Rick Koster (vn); Mark Pharoah (vn); John Metcalfe (va); Ivan McCready (cello); Phil Daniels (v); Richard Edwards (tb); Roddy Lorimer (flugelhorn, tb); Tim Sanders (ts); Simon Clarke (bs); Neil Sidwell (tb); Laetitia Sadier (v); Simon Hague (accordion)
Track listing:
Girls And Boys (S); Tracy Jacks; End Of A Century (S); Parklife (S); Bank Holiday; Badhead; Debt Collector; Far Out; To The End (S/UK); London Loves; Trouble In The Message Centre; Clover Over Dover; Magic America; Jubilee; This Is A Low; Lot 105
Running time:
52.47
Current CD:
Food CD10
Further listening:
Modern Life Is Rubbish (1992); The Great Escape (1994)
Further reading:
3862 Days: The Official History Of Blur (1999)
Like this?
Try . . . p.131

Ted Hawkins

The Next Hundred Years

One of the most soulful voices ever recorded, gained belated recognition near the end of a troubled life.

For months, Michael Penn had been raving to producer Tony Berg about the incredible street singer who worked the sidewalks of his Santa Monica neighbourhood.

"I think he is the greatest singer in the world," Penn would say, meaning exactly that. Berg didn't actually see Penn's mysterious singer until one night in 1991, when he accompanied Penn to a musicians' benefit for the homeless. Berg listened in utter amazement, then rushed backstage to meet Ted Hawkins, who, it turned out, had quite a story.

The son of an alcoholic prostitute and a father he never met, Ted had served three years at the infamous Parchment Farm while still a boy, then travelled the world as an itinerant musician. Along the way he'd made a number of albums, but none had succeeded enough to free him from having to sing on the streets. Believing it was crucial to respect Hawkins' methods, Berg recorded him alone then added overdubs.

"He was wonderfully idiosyncratic," recalls Berg. "There was a collection of props he needed to have with him in order to perform. The milk crate he sat on, his huge plastic thumbnail, his leather glove, which he used to fret the guitar, and his piece of linoleum-covered plywood on which he would tap his foot. And if anything disrupted the perfect equilibrium of those objects, he would go home."

Hawkins died of a stroke, on New Year's Day, 1995, less than a year after the release of *The Next Hundred Years*, which stands as a fitting final testament to his powers. With a voice that sounds a bit like Sam Cooke's, only rougher and more rural, he makes his way through covers like Jesse Winchester's Biloxi and some fantastic originals.

But, says Berg, "The thing that best demonstrates how extraordinary Ted was is the last cut, the John Fogerty song, As Long As I Can See The Light. Ted did that a cappella, just tapping his foot. And as I'm listening to it I realise his pitch centre didn't waver at all. That's when I realised Ted had perfect pitch. We overdubbed an entire band to Ted's a cappella performance maybe four or five months after he did it.

"Most incredibly Ted remembered I wanted a 16-bar phrase for a solo section. So in the middle of his a cappella take he led into it by saying, 'Won't you play that for me right now,' then tapped his foot for 16 bars and came back in perfectly in time and tune. It was amazing."

Record label:
Geffen
Produced
by Tony Berg.
Recorded
at Tony Berg's Home Studio, Los Angeles; April–September 1993.
Released:
May 1994
Chart peaks:
None (UK) None (US)
Personnel:
Ted Hawkins (v, g); Tony Berg (g, k); Chris Bruce (g); Pat Mastelotto (d, pc); Jim Keltner (d, pc); Greg Wells (d, pc); John Pierce (b); Guy Pratt (b); Kevin McCormick (b); Greg Leisz (Hawaiian g, ps, ls); Patrick Warren (k); Billy Payne (k); Martin Tillman (c)
Track listing:
Strange Conversation; Big Things; There Stands The Glass; Biloxi; Groovy Little Things; The Good And The Bad; Afraid; Green-Eyed Girl; Ladder of Success; Long As I Can See The Light
Running time:
37.41
Current CD:
GED24627
Further listening:
Watch Your Step (1982), Happy Hour (1987) or Rhino's career retrospective, The Ted Hawkins Story: Suffer No More (1982)
Further reading:
www.the-bunker.org/ted/ted.html
Like this?
Try . . . p.664

Everything But The Girl

Amplified Heart

A near-death experience gives the duo new life.

There's a strange medical condition known as "amplified emotions." Usually brought on by a traumatic blow to the head, it somehow causes the brain to respond irrationally to otherwise normal circumstances. For example, if a petal falls off a flower, you might burst into tears.When they were searching for a title for this lovelorn collection, Ben Watt and Tracey Thorn borrowed the idea. *Amplified Heart* is the perfect description of that volatile, uncertain state that follows a break-up – when something as innocuous as the title of a book or the way a stranger touches their hair can make you sob out loud.

In 1992, Watt contracted Churg-Strauss Syndrome, a rare auto-immune disorder that ravages the internal organs. After six months in the hospital and four life-saving operations, the formerly cherubic musician emerged 45 pounds lighter and minus most of his digestive system.Though Watt has documented his year in hell in the book, *Patient*, he told MOJO how it affected the duo's music-making: "Though I wouldn't wish it on my worst enemy, the illness was the most incredible kick-start, creatively. We'd been at our lowest creatively and imaginatively."

Thorn adds, "For the last couple of years lots of our songs have had a dynamic where you start off with this difficult situation, then the final verse wraps it up with a good conclusion – which works quite well. But it's harder for the listener to use those songs as a real release of emotion. By the end you've got nowhere to go. It wasn't exciting to me so I couldn't imagine how it was exciting anyone else."

In its initial release, *Amplified Heart* failed to ignite beyond the duo's usual cult following. Watt and Thorn were also dropped by their UK label, WEA. Then, almost two years later, one of the album's sleeper tracks, Missing, was remixed into a dancefloor thumper by Todd Terry and it topped the charts across the world. Suddenly, EBTG had a career and a new direction, which they've continued to explore on *Walking Wounded* and *Temperamental.*

As Watt told *CMJ*, "The things that we're actually borrowing from, in terms of mood and texture, they're similar to what we've always done. The dark, blunted, melancholy moods of Massive Attack are very much what our initial sound was all about."

Thorn added with a chuckle, "People are being quite respectful as well because, in the heart of all this new stuff, we haven't changed drastically. It's not like we're suddenly writing hands-in-the-air anthems, trying desperately to have hits in our sad middle age."

BDM

Record label:
Atlantic (US) / Blanco Y Negro-WEA (UK)
Produced
by Ben Watt with Jerry Boys
Recorded
at Livingston Studio, The Strongroom, Whitfield Studio, Battery Studo, Mayfair Studio, London; November 1993-February 1994
Released:
July 1994
Chart peaks:
20 (UK) 46 (US)
Personnel:
Ben Watt (g, p, k, v); Tracey Thorn (v); Danny Thompson (b); Dave Mattacks (d); Martin Ditcham (pc); Richard Thompson (g); Peter King (s); Kate St. John (cor anglais)
Track listing:
Rollercoaster; Troubled Mind; I Don't Understand Anything; Walking to You; Get Me ; Missing; Two Star; We Walk The Same Line; 25th December; Disenchanted
Current CD:
82605-2
Further listening:
Walking Wounded (1996)
Further reading:
MOJO 29, www.ebtg.com
Like this?
Try . . . p.371

Jeff Buckley

Grace

The only completed album by one of rock's most gifted practitioners.

Unfailingly charming, with a film star's looks, Jeff Buckley was a performer of unprecedented potential. Although he often sang about death – almost every song on *Grace* alludes to it – he gave every indication of loving life.

Despite a high-profile appearance at the Hal Wilner-organised Tim Buckley tribute in New York in 1991, Jeff wanted to avoid any comparisons with his father from those who came "expecting the Second Coming – I never fail to disappoint". Though he was never short of offers, before signing a record deal he went through years of honing his solo skills, academically at the Los Angeles Musicians Institute and then practically at the Sin-é, Fez and Bang On bars in New York where he would sing everything from TV themes to covers of Nusrat Fateh Ali Khan's devotional music. Because he could do anything with his voice, he did just that, trying to find the sounds he aspired to, "that spoke from the very fibre of my being".

All credit, then, to producer Andy Wallace (who had mixed Nirvana's *Nevermind*) for capturing so much of Buckley's infinite variety. In part, this depended on the producer's sensitive mood setting – for instance, he encouraged Buckley to start every session with a loosening Sin-é-style solo set.

Buckley was looking for "longevity" from the outset and Wallace recalls him constantly trying to rework the material and ever anxious to improve the vocals; a couple of years on, talking to MOJO, Buckley was still worrying about his interpretation of Leonard Cohen's Hallelujah: "I don't think I did that right. It sounded more like a child and sometimes I've sung it more like a man. I hope Leonard doesn't hear it." He was also fussy when it came to running order: "Sequence is really important. I'm an inveterate, annoying DJ at people's houses. I'm trying to get a flow, but if you're not careful it's just *your* flow."

It turned out, however, to be his only studio album because on May 29, 1997, when he was about to record his second, he drowned in the Mississippi. Not exactly unfulfilled, though. *Grace* would be enough adornment for most lifetimes in music, its particular allure perhaps captured in something he said on stage at a Meltdown festival in London. No doubt obliquely alluding to his absent father and the mother who brought him up single-handedly, he said, "You know, I love these women's songs. Men are fuck-ups and the only good thing about that is that so many wonderful torch songs have been written about what men have done to women and I love to sing them." By no means sexually ambiguous, Buckley liked to refer to himself as "a *chanteuse*".

Record label:
Columbia
Produced,
engineered and mixed by Andy Wallace.
Recorded
at Bearsville Studios, Quantum Sound and Soundtrack Studios; September 1993–April 1994.
Released:
August 1994
Chart peaks:
50 (UK) None (US)
Personnel:
Jeff Buckley (v, g, o, harmonium, dulcimer, tabla); Mick Grondahl (b); Matt Johnson (d, pc, vibes); Michael Tighe, Gary Lucas (g); Loris Holland (o); Misha Masud (tabla); Karl Berger (oa); Cliff Norell (e)
Track listing:
Mojo Pin; Grace; Last Goodbye (S); Lilac Wine; So Real; Hallelujah; Lover, You Should Have Come Over; Corpus Christi Carol; Eternal Life; Dream Brother
Running time:
51.46
Current CD:
475928 2
Further listening:
Live At Sin-é (1993)
Further reading:
Dream Brother: The Lives & Music of Jeff Buckley & Tim Buckley (David Browne, 2001).
www.jeffbuckley.com
Like this?
Try . . . p.685

Oasis

Definitely Maybe

Noisy arrival of back-to-basics pop mythologists.

It was Smiths' guitarist Johnny Marr who'd listened to the rough demo dropped through his door and got the band responsible signed to his management company Ignition. And it was Marr who loaned Oasis a vanload of amps and Rickenbackers when they decamped to Sawmills in Cornwall in an attempt to transfer the white heat of their live performance to record (though in the end they used their own "crappy knackered equipment"). Initially former Sensational Alex Harvey Band member David Batchelor was in charge.

"We met up," remembers Noel Gallagher, "and we had the same record collection and I thought, fine," but only two songs from the sessions that followed ever made it to the overdubbing stage (Slide Away and Rock'N'Roll Star). It was just an old-fashioned culture clash. "He was in his fifties," Noel points out, "and I'm like 27 and we're sitting at the mixing desk and I'm saying, 'Let's get a bit mad and push it to the fucking limits here! Turn the fucking thing up, compress the shit out of it so that the speakers blow up!' He'd go *(affects voice of whingeing old-timer)*, 'Nope 'cos this is the way we done it in our day, son.' I'd say, 'I want it to sound like an aeroplane taking off,' and he'd say, 'You mean you want a fucking Yamaha 90 backwards fucking flange-loop-snubble with an irk on it?' In the end we said it's not working. We either go with my madness or his saneness and *I'm* in charge! So our soundman Mark [Coil] operated the desk and we just set the whole band up in one room, no sound baffles, no headphones, Our Kid in the vocal booth 'cos you have to, worked out a set list and played the set over and over again, chose the best one, overdubbed it, and if you listen to the snare drum on the master tape you can hear the whole album. Nothing is separated. Volume right up. All done live! Must be the loudest album since *The Who Live At Leeds*."

Record label:
Creation
Produced
by Noel Gallagher and Mark Coyle, with Owen Morris.
Recorded
at Monnow Valley, South Wales and Sawmills, Cornwall; December 1993–March 1994.
Released:
August 30, 1994
Chart peaks:
1 (UK) 58 (US)
Personnel:
Liam Gallagher (v); Noel Gallagher (g, bv); Paul Arthurs (g); Paul McGuigan (bs); Tony McCarroll (d); Anthony Griffiths (bv on Supersonic); Anjali Dutt, Dave Scott, Roy Spong, Mark Coyle (e)
Track listing:
Rock 'N' Roll Star; Shakermaker; Live Forever; Up In The Sky; Columbia; Supersonic; Bring It On Down; Cigarettes And Alcohol; Digsy's Dinner; Slide Away; Married With Children
Running time:
52.03
Current CD:
RKIDCD006
Further listening:
(What's The Story) Morning Glory (1995); B-sides collection Masterplan (1998)
Further reading:
MOJO 14
Like this?
Try . . . p.264

Manic Street Preachers

The Holy Bible

Turbulent, seething and relentlessly dark; the Welsh ideologues' most urgent album was wilfully out of step with Britpop.

It may have marked the hedonistic birth of Britpop, but 1994 was also the year that rock music embraced chronic dysfunction: Kurt Cobain's suicide, Courtney Love's tear-drenched appearance at the Reading Festival, Richey Edwards' descent into a breakdown, and the record that resulted from his woes – arguably the most wretched, doom-laden LP in the modern rock canon.

The Manics had been dealt a cruel blow at the tail-end of 1993 when Philip Hall, the manager with whom they had a familial bond, died from cancer at the age of 34. He left them at a particularly crucial juncture: their second album, *Gold Against The Soul*, had been an anti-climax, and their love of fuzz-toned hard rock – and Guns N' Roses in particular – was beginning to pall. A song called Donkeys, one of the B-sides of Roses In The Hospital, released in September 1993, suggested a more left-field, art-punk approach might be on the cards. But their next move was still unclear. Their record company had suggested that the Manics record their third album in Barbados. Instead, they returned to their native south Wales, and a tiny Cardiff studio called Soundspace, available for the princely sum of £50 a day.

"I used to commute in on the train," said drummer Sean Moore. "Regular work: drum till six, then go home. It was like a little job."

If such words suggested comfy domesticity, the lyrics that Richey Edwards had been hyperactively scrawling into his notebooks occupied a far more angst-ridden universe. Yes was a hymn to the self-loathing that arose from the Manics' compliance with rock-biz ritual; 4st 7lb a glimpse of the anorexia from which Edwards was reportedly suffering. There was also the small matter of a song called The Intense Humming Of Evil, whose lyric arose from Edwards' near-obsession with the Nazi Holocaust.

Charged with putting Edwards and bassist Nicky Wire's words to music, James Dean Bradfield and Moore returned to the Manics' love of angular post-punk: Joy Division, Gang Of Four. The group had clearly also spent much of the previous six months listening to Nirvana's *In Utero*. The resulting album, which resolutely avoided self-pity and turned Edwards' turmoil into something deeply confrontational, was also accompanied by an image change: the Manics dressed in military apparel, like some psychotic terrorist cell.

"*The Holy Bible* was the Manics at our coolest," says Nicky Wire. "The look was brilliant, the songs were brilliant, and we were all at our thinnest. It was us against everything, really."

Record label:
Columbia
Produced
by the Manic Street Preachers. She Is Suffering produced by Steve Brown.
Recorded
at Soundspace, Cardiff; January–March 1994.
Released:
August 30, 1994
Chart peaks:
6 (UK) None (US)
Personnel:
James Dean Bradfield (v, g); Nicky Wire (b); Sean Moore (d, pc); Richey Edwards (design, g); Silva (e)
Track listing:
Yes; Ifwhiteamericatoldthetruthforonedayitsworldwouldfallapart; Of Walking Abortion; She Is Suffering (S); Archives Of Pain; Revol (S); 4st 7lb; Mausoleum; Faster (S); This Is Yesterday; Die In The Summertime; The Intense Humming Of Evil; PCP
Running time:
56.23
Current CD:
477421 2
Further listening:
Everything Must Go (1996), their first album without ideological lynchpin Richey, and arguably their last vital work.
Further reading:
Everything (A Book About Manic Street Preachers) (Simon Price, 1999); www.manics.co.uk
Like this?
Try . . . p.101

Portishead

Dummy

West Country collective's debut fuses hip hop, torch song and soul, accidentally sparking a key musical trend of the late '90s: trip-hop.

Portishead's debut *Dummy* was one of the first albums to match the pulsing, organic texture of '60s soul with the magpie sampling of hip hop. Throw in the exoticism of spy-*noir* movie scores and the formidable vocal presence of Beth Gibbons, and you had the perfect purchase for the sophisticated '90s record buyer.

After playing in "ridiculous, awful rock bands", Geoff Barrow discovered the sampler and before long joined the ranks of bedroom musicians. At 22 he found work as an apprentice engineer at Bristol's Coach House Studios, his tenure taking place as The Wild Bunch were evolving into Massive Attack. With backing from Massive Attack's manager Cameron McVey, Barrow began making demos and assembling a team to realise his own musical vision: first was vocalist Beth Gibbons, whom he met during the coffee break at an Enterprise Allowance course in February 1991. Geoff and Beth's first completed collaboration was It Could Be Sweet, the oldest track on *Dummy* by nearly three years.

"[That] was totally done when Geoff played it to me," remembers Adrian Utley, an experienced guitarist who'd made a living playing jazz with the likes of slave-driving neo-bopper Tommy Chase. "People don't mention that song when they talk about *Dummy*, but I was blown away. And still am."

"It was like a light bulb coming on," says Barrow of Utley's arrival. "Ade's not anti-sampling; it was just at that point we realised that if we could get our *own* samples, those sounds won't turn up on other records." Engineer Dave McDonald was responsible for ageing the band's own breaks and transferring them to vinyl for Barrow to manipulate. "I had to unlearn everything I'd learned about getting nice clean sounds," he laughs."

Then came "the endless amounts of pissing about in the studio", as Barrow self-deprecatingly describes it. It produced one of the decade's most distinctive, and most imitated, sounds – torchy, groovy, spooky music, deep but accessible. The key to it all was Gibbons' voice. She refused to talk about it much and was wary of praise for her singing. "I sometimes feel guilty, when I think of people like Billie Holiday and Edith Piaf, who are heroes of mine," she told Ireland's Hot Press. "I wasn't a victim of child abuse. I didn't have a dysfunctional family, and – apart from one thing which, sorry, I'm not going to tell you about – my worst teenage trauma was trying to get my homework done on time."

Dummy went on to sell millions. Portishead had created a perfect post-modern work of art. The trouble they had producing a follow-up is another story.

Record label:
Go! Beat
Produced
by Portishead with Adrian Utley.
Recorded
at State Of Art and Coach House Studios, Bristol; 1991–94.
Released:
August 1994
Chart peaks:
2 (UK) 79 (US)
Personnel:
Geoff Barrow (k, programming, d); Beth Gibbons (v); Adrian Utley (g, b, k); Clive Deamer (d); Neil Solman (k); Gary Baldwin (k); Andy Hague (t); Richard Newell (drum programming); Strings Unlimited (strings); Dave McDonald (e, nose flute)
Track listing:
Mysterons; Sour Times (S); Strangers; It Could Be Sweet; Wandering Star; Numb (S/UK); Roads; Pedestal; Biscuit; Glory Box (S)
Running time:
45.34
Current CD:
828 522-1
Further listening:
Hard-won follow-up Portishead (1997) refines the idea further; live album PNYC (1998) is an unexpectedly gripping intensification of their – by then – familiar sound. Barrow guested on Earthling's 1995 album Radar.
Further reading:
MOJO 47; www.portishead.co.uk
Like this?
Try . . . p.166

Offspring

Smash

Orange County nerds kickstart the punk-pop pick-up.

"Part of me wants to say 'Hey, we didn't jump on a punk-rock bandwagon'. If people are looking for credentials, we're pretty intact. Even my car's pretty punk rock! It's a 1989 Toyota pick-up. I've slept in it many times. We toured the country in it once," stated Dexter Holland back in December 1994, in a bid to answer his critics.

To purists the fact that Offspring had sold in excess of a million copies of their third album *Smash* within six months violated punk's self-imposed ethics.

"To a lot of people, if you're on the radio and on MTV then you're no good anymore, you must be a sell-out," offered Dexter.

Spearheaded by three singles – Gotta Get Away, Come Out And Play and Self Esteem – *Smash* possessed an infectious set of tunes which appealed directly to the post-grunge kids and new punks alike. The fact that the neo-bubblegum riffing of Gotta Get Away and Self Esteem both boasted Nirvana-ish melodies (the latter being particularly redolent of Come As You Are) helped tremendously when it came to convincing programme directors across America to add the Offspring to their all-influential playlists.

Despite their growing success, Offspring were determined to plough as much back into the US punk scene as they'd extracted from it. A prime example was their decision to cover The Didjits' Killboy Powerhead and include it on this album. As *Smash* continued to sell, eventually topping the 10-million mark, Offspring re-doubled their efforts, covering The Damned's Smash It Up for the soundtrack to Batman Forever in early 1995. Meanwhile, Holland set up his own label, Nitro, and proceeded to sign bands which he himself had idolised in his youth (The Vandals being a case in point).

By the end of 1995, *Smash* had become the biggest-selling album on an indie label of all-time. For Offspring the next step was to leave Epitaph and sign to Columbia. Whether that actually harmed the band's credibility further is debatable, although the band's first major label album, *Ixnay On The Hombré*, did seem to suffer from a genuine lack of interest despite its fiery quality. By the end of the decade, however, Offspring had returned to their commercial peak with *Americana* and their dork anthem Pretty Fly (For A White Guy).

Record label:
Epitaph
Produced
by Thom Wilson.
Recorded
at Track Records and The Hook, North Hollywood; January–February 1994.
Released:
September 1994
Chart peaks:
21 (UK) 4 (US)
Personnel:
Bryan "Dexter" Holland (v, g); Kevin "Noodles" Wasserman (g, bv); Greg K [Kriesel] (b); Ron Welty (d, bv)
Track listing:
Time To Relax; Nitro (Youth Energy); Bad Habit; Gotta Get Away, (S); Genocide; Something To Believe In; Come Out And Play (S); Self Esteem (S); It'll Be A Long Time; Killboy Powerhead; What Happened To You; So Alone; Not The One; Smash
Running time:
46.46
Current CD:
Epitaph 86432-2
Further listening:
Ignition (1992); Ixnay On The Hombré (1997)
Further reading:
Kerrang! (3/12/1994)
Like this?
Try . . . p.458

Songhai

Songhai 2

Roots music? This is roots-of-everything music.

The pedigree of *nuevo* flamenco stars Ketama stretches back through generations: the Carmonas (Juan, Antonio, Jose Luis and Jose Miguel) belong to the Habichuelas, Granada's greatest flamenco name; José Soto comes from the revered Sorderas of Jerez de la Frontera. Toumani Diabate's background is just as fine – his father had brought the 21-stringed *kora* (an African lute made of a large gourd covered in hide) to Mali and developed it as a lead instrument. But the gypsies and the *jeli* (Malian musician class) have another thing in common: breaking barriers – Ketama had recorded with Don Cherry and Ray Barreto, Diabate would go on to play blues with Taj Mahal.

"I had tried to record with other European musicians, but the results had been failures," remembers Diabate, "but perhaps Ketama were closer to the spirit of Africa."

Perhaps it has something to do with Ketama also being the name of an African town at the centre of the marijuana trade. In October 1987, after playing a London show, Ketama attended a party where Diabate played an impromptu set. A few nights later, they were invited to share an African paella with Diabate, Lucy Duran and the Hannibal label's Joe Boyd (the former Incredible String Band and Nick Drake producer). The musicians meshed intuitively, and planned to record in Spain the next spring, with Danny Thompson on bass.

The results – *Songhai* – were not just a cracking set of Afro-flamenco tunes that move seamlessly from one type of strings to another, with stunning solos that flow from every direction, but a political manifesto for the newly minted (June 1987) tag "world music". Six years later, a follow-up was released (Thompson was replaced by Javier Colina for the majority of tracks) that, in Godfather style, was better than the first. By this time, the politics of world music were better established: gypsies came west from India, stopped in West Africa, then their music either headed north with the Moors and Celts, or was shipped further west by slave traders. If "world music" had to be justified, *Songhai 2* did that and more.

Record label:
Hannibal
Produced
by Joe Boyd, Mario Pacheco and Lucy Duran.
Released:
October 1994
Chart peaks:
None (UK) None (US)
Personnel:
Sute Monebo; Niani; Pozo Del Deseo; Monte De Los Suspiros; Djamana Djana; De Jerez A Mali; Ndia; De La Noche A La Manana; Mali Sajio; Pozo Del Deseo
Track listing:
Ketama: Antonio Carmona (v, pc), Jose Miguel Carmona (g, mandolin), Juan Carmona (g, lute); Toumani Diabate (kora); Danny Thompson (b); José Soto (v, g); Javier Colina (db); Kassemàdy (v); Bernado Parrilla (vn); Keletigui Diabate (balafon); Basekou Kouyate (ngoni); Amparo Carmona (castanets); Joselin Vargas (runmeras); Djanka Diabete, Diaw Kouyate, Aurora (bv); Jose Luis Garrido, Benito Gil, Jerry Boys (e)
Running time:
50.04
Currently unavailable on CD
Further listening:
Songhai (1988); Ketama's Ketama (1987); Toumani Diabate's New Ancient Strings (1999); Toumani Diabate and Taj Mahal Kulanjan (1999); Duende, a 3-CD flamenco set.
Further reading:
www.flamenco-world.com
Like this?
Try . . . p.743

Nas

Illmatic

Perhaps the perfect debut, and a generally acknowledged hip hop classic.

A teenager from the same Queensbridge projects that Marley Marl and MC Shan had put on the rap map in the mid-'80s, Nasir Jones had rapped verses on a couple of other people's records, becoming the most talked-about newcomer amid New York rap's post-gangsta rebirth.

Snapped up for management by the former 3rd Bass rapper and Wild Pitch label A&R, MC Serch, Nas was being hailed as "the new Rakim". In Serch's estimation, Nas was "pound for pound, lyric for lyric, the best emcee I ever heard". Together, they set out to make the ultimate debut.

Legend has it that Illmatic, a remarkably concise album, was condensed from over 60 tracks submitted by some of hip hop's heaviest hitters. What remains is suitably astonishing, as if an entire lifetime's prolific and profound writing had been distilled into its nine tracks.

Queensbridge gave Jones all the material he needed. With the eye of a filmmaker and the soul of a poet he took what he saw, what he heard and what he knew, added a twist of what he could imagine, and created lyrics couched in a streetwise vernacular that had the power to touch the listener.

In Memory Lane, a DJ Premier track built around an ethereal sample from a Ruben Wilson record, Nas essays the procedure: "Check the prognosis – is it real or showbiz?/My window faces shootouts, drug overdoses/Live amongst no roses, only the drama". One Love, produced by A Tribe Called Quest's Q-Tip and featuring a memorable thumb-piano sample, is constructed as a letter home from a jailed QB foot soldier. NY State Of Mind takes the listener on a hair-raising chase around the Queensbridge staircases, the click of a jammed gun in the hands of a pre-teen drug runner almost audible in Nas's precise delivery.

An undoubted classic, Illmatic nevertheless caused problems for its creator. Had it arrived as the culmination of several years' sustained creative progress, nobody would have minded: but because of its sheer perfection, it proved as much millstone as milestone. All his subsequent albums have been fine enough, but all have been found lacking compared to this. His career hasn't suffered; he is one of rap's blue-chip brands, and is widely credited with winning his high-profile on-record battle with Jay-Z. But he has yet to fully emerge from the lengthy shadow this debut album casts.

AB

Record label:
Columbia
Produced
by DJ Premier, L.E.S., Nas, Pete Rock, Large Professor, Q-Tip
Recorded
at D&D Recording, NYC: Unique Studios, NYC: Chung King, NYC: Battery Studios, NYC: PowerPlay Studios, Long Island City, NY
Released:
April 1994
Chart peaks:
None (UK) 12 (US)
Personnel:
Nas (v): AZ (v on Life's A Bitch): Olu Dara (trumpet on Life's A Bitch): Pete Rock (bv on The World Is Yours)
Track listing:
The Genesis: NY State Of Mind: Life's A Bitch: The World Is Yours: Halftime: Memory Lane (Sittin' In Da Park): One Love: One Time 4 Your Mind: Represent: It Ain't Hard To Tell
Running time:
39 mins 43 secs
Current CD:
Columbia 475959 2
Further listening:
It Was Written (1996): Nastradamus (1999): God's Son (2002)
Like this?
Try . . . p.696

The Notorious B.I.G.

Ready To Die

A masterpiece all too often overlooked because it seemed to prophecy the death of its maker.

Although the violent demise of its creator has overshadowed the music, Ready To Die is a remarkable record. No less an authority than KRS-ONE has deemed it to be the greatest hip hop album ever made, and he certainly has a point.

According to most accounts, Christopher Wallace was a small-time crack dealer plying his trade in Brooklyn when he discovered he had an aptitude for writing and reciting compelling raps. One of his demos was passed on to Sean "Puffy" Combs, the fastest rising executive in the New York music business, who was amazed by the tape and set about getting the rapper on record.

Inking a label deal with Arista to distribute his new imprint, Bad Boy, Combs made Wallace his number one act. Together they created a concept album that told the story from birth to self-inflicted gunshot death of a murderous hoodlum in the crack-ravaged New York of the 1990s.

Throughout the album Biggie's protagonist contends with the hand life has dealt him. The opening introduction sets the life story to a musical context, songs from different eras condensing a 24-year biography into three minutes, bringing the listener up to speed for the hour that follows.

Musically, Ready To Die is consistent, punchy and hard-hitting yet the record retains a distinctly commercial flavour. The majority of the tracks were produced by Easy Mo Bee, little lauded prior to this album, and little used thereafter. There were concessions to daytime radio (Big Poppa, Juicy), street-oriented hip hop for the hardcore fans (the brilliant sci-fi beats of DJ Premier's Unbelievable), tinges of reggae (Respect) and plenty of great, unpretentious, dirty-grooved New York rap (the rest).

Throughout, Biggie's verses insinuate syllables into the music, stories intertwining and resolving as the character returns home from prison to discover that guns have replaced knives, and crack has turned small-time hoods into murderous empire-building millionaires. Each vignette is beautifully sketched, if disarmingly amoral and desperately bleak: it's as if Mike Leigh made rap records about Brooklyn dealers instead of films about depressed, impoverished Brits.

By the time his follow-up was released, Biggie had been murdered, gunned down in a scene that could have been taken from one of his chillingly observed lyrics, and Ready To Die had become both prophecy and epitaph. But removed from that tragic context it remains a work of immense power, every inch the classic its devotees claim it to be.

AB

Record label:
Bad Boy
Produced
by Sean "Puffy" Combs, Darnell Scott, Easy Mo Bee, Norman & Digga/Bluez Brothers, Carl "Chucky" Thompson, Jean "Poke" Oliver, DJ Premier, Lord Finesse
Recorded
at The Hit Factory, New York: Soundtracks Recording Studio, New York: Sound On Sound Recordings Inc, New York: Chung King House Of Metal, New York: D & D Recording Studio, New York
Released:
October 1994
Chart peaks:
None (UK) 15 (US)
Personnel:
Notorious B.I.G. (v): Carl "Chucky" Thompson ("instruments" on One More Chance): Method Man (v on The What, Me & My Bitch): Total (v on Juicy): Sybil Pennix (v on Me & My Bitch): Diana King (v on Respect)
Track listing:
Intro: Things Done Changed: Gimme The Loot: Machine Gun Funk: Warning: Ready To Die: One More Chance: #!*@ Me (Interlude): The What: Juicy: Everyday Struggle: Me & My Bitch: Big Poppa: Respect: Friend Of Mine: Unbelievable: Suicidal Thoughts
Running time:
68 mins 57 secs
Current CD:
78612730002
Further listening:
Life After Death
Further reading:
LAbyrinth – Randall Sullivan (Canongate 2003)
Like this?
Try . . . p.580

Public Enemy

Muse Sick 'N' Hour Mess Age

Oft-overlooked masterpiece by the greatest rap band of all time.

"Muse... is the high school ugly duckling who comes back to the 10 year reunion like 'Damn, who are you?'" wrote Public Enemy leader and instigator Chuck D on the band's website in 2002. "Some people never ventured to the second side or listened to it past Give it Up."

Muse Sick 'N' Hour Mess Age qualifies as possibly the most under-appreciated – or, to use the vernacular, "slept-on" – hip hop album of all time. After 1992's Greatest Misses album, Muse Sick... arrived with critics ready to dispatch the band to the rap equivalent of the knacker's yard. Gangsta rap had seemingly stolen much of Chuck's revolutionary thunder and the genre's new-found mainstream success was making PE's sales figures from the past look small beer. And this edgy, musical, defiantly unrepentant release was not the response many were expecting. But it should have been, for the only real constants in PE's career had been onward development and ceaseless change.

With the benefit of some hindsight, Muse Sick... emerges as a fine Public Enemy album and, if anything, perhaps even more prescient than anything else in their illustrious career. Context, though, is everything. We now know that, following disagreements with Def Jam, Chuck took his band independent, reinventing himself and the group in an online environment. It's all there in one of the bonus tracks, Harry Allen's Information Superhighway Phone Call To Chuck D, a discourse left on Chuck's answerphone by the band's "media assassin" on the necessity to retain copyright to take advantage of new distribution methods.

Reinvigorating the PE sound with what he would later term "ferocious soul", Chuck referenced the black power era sounds ever more blatantly. Race Against Time is an admitted homage to the Chambers Brothers' black rock anthem Time Has Come Today, both tracks speeding up and slowing down, playing on the listener's perceptions of seconds ticking away. Chuck would later go on to make more overt nods in the direction of funk and soul pioneers, in particular on his solo album, while later projects like the Fine Arts Militia would visually and aurally owe a debt to the period.

All this was merely part of the Public Enemy grand plan: always stay relevant, always go against the grain, never make the same record twice. That critics would later claim that their super-negative reviews had destroyed the band's career – as one reviewer did, on publicenemy.com's message board – was laughable. Muse Sick... was a milestone, not a tombstone.

AB

Record label:
Def Jam
Released:
August 1994
Chart peaks:
12 (UK) 14 (US)
Personnel:
Chuck D (v): Flavor Flav (v): Terminator X (turntables)
Track listing:
Whole Lotta Love Goin On In The Middle Of Hell: Theatrical Parts: Give It Up: What Side You On?: Bedlam 13:13: Stop In The Name...: What Kind Of Power We Got?: So Whatcha Gone Do Now?: White Heaven/Black Hell: Race Against Time: They Used To Call It Dope: Aintnuttin Buttersong: Live And Undrugged (Pt. 1 – 2): Thin Line Between Law And Rape: I Ain't Mad At All: Death Of A Carjacka: I Stand Accused: Godd Complexx: Hitler Day: Harry Allen's Information Superhighway Phone Call To Chuck D: Living in A Zoo Remix
Running time:
68 mins 44 secs
Current CD:
5233622
Further listening:
Fear Of A Black Planet (Def Jam 1990): There's A Poison Goin' On (Atomic Pop 1999): Chuck D – The Autobiography Of Mistachuck (Mercury 1996)
Further reading:
Fight The Power – Rap, Race And Reality by Chuck D (Payback Press 1998)
Like this?
Try . . . p.537

Leftfield

Leftism

Mega-selling dance album which set new standards.

"We basically made the album up as we went along," claimed Paul Daley on *Leftism*'s release. "Hopefully now it sounds complete, something that can be listened to in one go." *Leftism* did better than that: it essentially defined a blueprint for the successful dance album, regularly varying the tempo from the expected techno thud and bringing in a mass of guest vocalists to add local colour.

Already hailed as groundbreakers on the dance scene – Daley and partner Neil Barnes' 1991 single Not Forgotten was widely acclaimed as the first "progressive house" single, offering a dubbier British slant on a US genre – their debut album was a mammoth commercial success. Tracks continue to turn up on film and television soundtracks to this day. Essentially, *Leftism* was a summation of the duo's career to date, wildly remixing old singles Release The Pressure and Song Of Life, while paying homage to their youthful enthusiasm for reggae (roots singer Danny Red appeared on the seismic dub track Inspection) and punk with Open Up, a collaboration with John Lydon. "I'd known John since I was 19," remembered Barnes. "He was a right cunt . . . We'd wanted to do a track with him for about two years, but it took all that time to get him to commit to doing it and to get the track good enough."

Elsewhere, their choice of guest collaborators and spread of influences revealed the catholic tastes of the two former session percussionists. Toni Halliday of then-vogueish indie band Curve provided a sweetly cooing vocal on the dreamlike single Original, while African vocalist Djum Djum appeared alongside an array of ethnic samples and percussion on Afro Left. In a dance scene which loves to invent endless genres and sub-genres, *Leftism* was genuinely unclassifiable, pitched somewhere between house, techno, trip-hop and reggae. On release, its tracks could be heard everywhere from daytime Radio One to underground techno clubs, demonstrating the album's remarkable poise between commercialism and innovation, and casting a shadow over Leftfield's career: it would be four years before they followed it up, with the disappointing *Rhythm And Stealth*. Leftfield, the epitome of the faceless, characterless dance production duo, were suitably nonplussed when prompted to explain the album's groundbreaking power: "All good dance music is based on rhythm," said Daley, "and that happens to be what me and Neil are good at."

Record label:
Hard Hands/Sony
Produced
by Leftfield.
Recorded
at Rollover Studios, London; August 1993–August 1994.
Released:
January 1995
Chart peaks:
3 (UK) None (US)
Personnel:
Neil Barnes (k, pc); Paul Daley (k, pc); Papa Dee, Earl Sixteen, Djum Djum, Toni Halliday, John Lydon, Danny Red, Lemn Sissay (v); Kevin Hayes (berimbou)
Track listing:
Release The Pressure (S/UK); Afro-Left; Melt; Song Of Life (S/UK); Original (S/UK); Black Flute; Space Shanty; Inspection (Check One); Storm 3000; Open Up (S); 21st Century Poem
Running time:
69.47
Current CD:
HANDCD2
Further listening:
Rhythm And Stealth (1999)
Further reading:
www.leftfield-online.com
Like this?
Try . . . p.678

P.J. Harvey

To Bring You My Love

Woman from the West Country pitches a Wang Dang Doodle. Result: hair-raising sensuality.

Born and bred in Corscombe, Dorset (pop. 600), Polly Jean Harvey learnt to play guitar late, at 18, then graduated from The Police Songbook to writing her own songs within weeks. Yet, four years later in 1991 when she moved to London, rock life was all struggle. Cultishly notorious for her feisty debut album *Dry* (1992) and the savage follow-up *Rid Of Me* (1993), she succumbed to a breakdown, which led to recuperation back home with her parents.

Often, she spoke as if the music itself damaged her health: "I haven't got a clue how our records affect other people but they make me feel quite ill."

Nonetheless, she re-emerged declaring *Rid Of Me* "not hard enough, not uncomfortable enough" and broke up the, to all appearances, blistering trio that was P.J. Harvey. For her third album she evolved an intriguing co-production partnership with John Parish, a former colleague from Dorset band Automatic Dlamini, and the redoubtable Flood (he had worked on *Zooropa* with U2 whose manager, Paul McGuinness, had signed with Harvey after *Rid Of Me*).

"We were going to do the album pretty live," Parish recalls. "But during rehearsals she felt she was losing control of the songs, so we went back to the demos and painstakingly built everything else around them. The whole process was difficult. Polly had a clear idea of what she wanted – unfortunately it was a different idea every day."

Despite these conflicts, the end result is a triumph: an atmospheric, inventive update of blues tradition drawing on the preceding years when Harvey had listened devotedly to R&B/blues greats like Willie Dixon and Howlin' Wolf – "Every single song of theirs is about sex," she notes. "Well, I think that is the most invigorating, exciting and extreme subject I can write about."

The slow-walking guitar opening of the title track could have been played by Hubert Sumlin for one of Wolf's shamanistic spells. Long Snake Moan is a growling Led Zeppelined groove with a wink, of course, to Blind Lemon Jefferson's Black Snake Moan.

To Bring You My Love saw Harvey's voice grow into a shape-shifting wonder, all sinister mumbles and witchy ululations worthy of Diamanda Galas. The power of her elemental, often Bible-based, imagery was undiminished, but she also sounded a little more distanced than before from the psychic pain of her cast of narrators – murderous mothers, lovers dominant or wronged, herself in one guise or another perhaps. Still disturbing then, but controlled and strong enough to provoke Courtney Love's observation that Harvey was "the one rock star who makes me feel shit".

Record label:
Island
Produced
by Flood, Polly Jean Harvey and John Parish.
Recorded
at Townhouse Three, Battersea, London; September–October 1994
Released:
February 28, 1995
Chart peaks:
12 (UK) 40 (US)
Personnel:
Polly Jean Harvey (v, g, p, k, pc); John Parish (g, k, d, pc); Joe Gore (g); Mick Harvey (k, b); Jean-Marc Butty (d, pc); Flood (e, m)
Track listing:
To Bring You My Love; Meet Ze Monsta; Working For The Man; C'mon Billy (S); Teclo; Long Snake Moan; Down By The Water; I Think I'm A Mother; Send His Love To Me (S); The Dancer
Running time:
42.43
Current CD:
CID8035
Further listening:
Dry (1992); Rid Of Me (1993) – excoriating album produced by Steve Albini, presented in stripped-down, but no less brutal, form on 4-Track Demos (1993); Dance Hall At Louse Point (1996) a collaboration with John Parish; the intimate, queasy electronics of Is This Desire? (1998)
Further reading:
The Rolling Stone Book Of Women In Rock (Barbara O'Dair, 1997); www.pjharvey.net
Like this?
Try . . . p.359

Elastica

Elastica

Debut from Britpop's three-girl, one-boy sensations, owing – quite literally on some tracks – a clear debt to late '70s New Wave.

Until the release of Elastica's debut single, Stutter, in late 1993, Justine Frischmann had been a shadowy figure on the proto-Britpop scene, a member of an early Suede line-up, and partner to, consecutively, Brett Anderson and Damon Albarn. Stutter, a full-throttle power-punk anthem on 7-inch only, had wowed the indie scene with its confrontational subject matter (a boy's inability to rise to the occasion). Unleashed a little over a year later, Elastica shared a similar gender tilt, but the music had evolved into an angular attack of growling geometric basslines and trebly art-rock guitar figures. The debt to Wire, The Stranglers, The Adverts and Blondie was patently clear, to the extent that publishing wrangles – to the benefit of both Wire (Connection, the offspring of Three Girl Rhumba) *and* The Stranglers (Waking Up, ditto No More Heroes). With remarkable good humour, Frischmann commented at the time that since Wire weren't making records anymore, it was perfectly acceptable for other bands to write new Wire songs.

But Elastica had a flavour all its own: the stirring metronomic pulse of S.O.F.T. and Indian Song, the almost choral interweaving of Justine's and Donna's voices in Blue and Stutter. Despite its cohesive feel, the record had an uneasy genesis.

"My main memory is that it was a struggle to get the whole band in to the studio," recalls Frischmann. "Everyone had these, erm, hectic social lives. Donna and Justin were in the middle of a permanent party and would always arrive at the studio with a crowd of people. They weren't exactly committed. Marc [Waterman] and me were doing what we could; he knew what I wanted but it proved so hard for him that he had a nervous breakdown after it was made. He didn't work for six months after."

The album, begun with newcomer Waterman in EMI's West End demo studio before moving to Ray Davies' Konk complex, had the further fascination of peepholing the relationship of Britpop's most famous pairing. Never Here, in particular, seemed to document the shifting balance of power within Justine and Damon's relationship. It took the band five years to complete a follow-up (The Menace); by that time Matthews had quit, Holland had left and re-joined, the band had been dropped by Geffen, their American label, and become a six-piece and Justine and Damon's relationship was long over. Certainly the energy that galvanised Elastica seemed to have dissipated. "I remember Ray Davies wandering round in his white panama hat saying that it was the best debut album since The Pretenders," says Frischmann. "I think, in retrospect, it was an interesting comment."

PG

Record label:
Deceptive
Produced
by Marc Waterman and Elastica.
Recorded
at EMI demo studios, Rathbone Place and Konk, London; winter1994–95.
Released:
March 13, 1995
Chart peaks:
1 (UK) 66 (US)
Personnel:
Justine Frischmann (v, g); Donna Matthews (v, g); Annie Holland (b); Justin Welch (d); Dan Abnormal [aka Damon Albarn] (k); Marc Waterman (e); Kevin Paul (ae)
Track listing:
Line Up (S); Annie; Connection (S); Car Song; Smile; Hold Me Now; S.O.F.T.; Indian Song; Blue; All-Nighter; Waking Up (S); 2:1; Vaseline; Never Here; Stutter (S)
Running time:
40.29
Current CD:
Bluff 014CD
Further listening:
The Menace (2000), the long-awaited follow-up, which features several Peel session tracks.
Like this?
Try . . . p.400

Guided By Voices

Alien Lanes

The eighth full-length album from prolific lo-fi tune-smiths lifts them out of obscurity.

Alien Lanes was for many the first introduction to Dayton, Ohio's Guided By Voices (GBV, or Guided By Beer as Breeder Kim Deal christened them in honour of their onstage alcohol consumption), yet in reality it marked the culmination of nearly 10 years, and almost as many albums, spent in obscurity. Previous albums had steadily increased the GBV profile but it was the band's Matador debut that finally propelled them from the margins with Rolling Stone declaring them Best Indie Rock Band and the group making their US national television debut on the Jon Stewart show. They even toured overseas for the first time – playing the Reading Festival accompanied by a fridge full of beer.

Guided By Voices were born in 1986 when Fourth Grade teacher Robert Pollard decided to make real one of the many imaginary bands he shared with his brother Jim. GBV's R.E.M.-ish (and ultra-collectable) debut *Forever Since Breakfast* was followed by a series of albums found more often in the band members' basements than record stores. Gradually word-of-mouth coupled with "manager for life" Pete Jamison's surreptitious mail-out's, side-stepped Pollard's reluctance to promote his talents outside of Dayton. In 1992 *Propeller* brought GBV to the attention of Cleveland's Scat Records and two stellar albums followed: *Vampire On Titus* (1993) and *Bee Thousand* (1994). Combined with a return to playing live, kick-started by an acclaimed showcase in New York, and praise from the likes of Thurston Moore, The Beastie Boys and fellow Daytonians The Breeders, GBV were at last taking their lo-fi hook-laden mix of The Beatles, The Who and power pop beyond the Ohio state line.

Written and recorded in several weeks, *Alien Lanes* saw them attempting to cram more songs, hooks and riffs into one album than most groups manage in an entire career. Veering from fully formed pop classics to truncated song-snippets threaded together with Pollard's off-the-wall wordage. GBV albums had always been blessed with at least a handful of songs to die for but *Alien Lanes* possessed these in abundance, even if many lasted less than a minute.

Since then, many changes have occurred in GBV-land, not least the departure of all but Pollard, who now *is* Guided By Voices, and signed to Creation Records just prior to its dissolution. Several albums have followed, all of interest but none really capturing Pollard's mix of tunefulness and lo-fi intimacy as completely as this one did.

Record label:
Matador
Produced
by Guided By Voices with Jim Pollard.
Recorded
in Tobin Sprout's basement, Dayton, Ohio; 1994
Released:
March 1995
Chart peaks:
None (UK) None (US)
Personnel:
Robert Pollard (v, g); Tobin Sprout (g, v); Mitch Mitchell (g); Kevin Fennell (d); Jim Greer (b); Jim Pollard (g) Greg Demos (b, g, vn)
Track listing:
A Salty Salute; Evil Speakers; Watch Me Jumpstart; They're Not Witches; As We Go Up, We Go Down; (I Wanna Be A) Dumbcharger; Game Of Pricks(s); The Ugly Vision; A Good Flying Bird; Cigarette Tricks; Pimple Zoo; Big Chief Chinese Restaurant; Closer You Are; Auditorium; Motor Away (S); Hit; My Valuable Hunting Knife (S); Gold Hick; King And Caroline; Striped White Jets; Ex-Supermodel; Blimps Go 90; Strawdogs; Chicken Blows; Little Whirl; My Son Cool; Always Crush Me; Alright
Running time:
41.33
Current CD:
OLE 123
Further listening:
Boxset compilation of first albums Box (1995); from the rest of Pollard's huge back catalogue, try Under The Bushes, Under The Stars (1996); Mag Earwhig (1997); Do The Collapse (1999)
Further reading:
www.gbv.com
Like this?
Try . . . p.656

Radiohead

The Bends

Bruising second album proves a sleeper hit transforming the fortunes of former critics' whipping boys.

The bends – decompression sickness – is what you get when, having been near the bottom, you shoot up to the top too fast. Two years earlier Radiohead's debut album *Pablo Honey* sold one and a half million copies – a lot of them to Americans, and most of those on the back of the hit single Creep, a jagged, affecting anthem – inspired by Thom Yorke's doomed relationship – whose alienation and rejection young Americans took to heart. "Success is a weird thing." remembers Yorke. "It really isolates you. We've always as a band kind of floated along in our own bubble but when you're touring America and you're in this perpetual state of movement without really getting anywhere and everything's taken care of for you, it's so isolating. It's very lonely, but it's also very inspiring. There's this sense of being exposed to lots and lots of different, crazy stuff, and being forced to consider it in isolation – and as a band we've always worked best in isolation."

Ignoring music-biz pressure to stay in the States, where they were loved, they returned to England, where they were not and started their second album. It was a tough record to make – partly the pressure of "having so much to prove; we knew we had to do something that was brilliant" – but mostly it was studio-phobia. Hard to believe these days, but Radiohead "had never really looked at the studio as an extension of what we were doing, more as an obstacle to get around". The first recording session, which lasted two months, was spent chasing a hit single (mostly centring around the song Sulk), became fraught with difficulties and was largely abandoned. The band's management sent them on tour to work on the material some more. A second shorter session was scheduled "and we got more done in those two weeks than we had in two months. [Producer] John Leckie was very good at getting us to see the studio in a different way and taking the mystique out of it – almost making it like a musical instrument that you're learning to play."

The speed and skill with which they learned to master this new instrument was mind-boggling. The vast sweep of *The Bends*' musical vision, mature musicianship, angry, articulate lyrics and big, bleakly beautiful melodies took listeners by surprise. A UK Top 10 hit (the lack of singalong single gave it less of an impact on the US charts), by year's end *The Bends* – named after a track actually written and demoed before they finished making *Pablo Honey* and kept because "it was kind of prophetic" – topped many of the major music magazines' Best Album polls.

SS

Record label:
Parlophone
Produced
by John Leckie.
Recorded
at Rak, The Manor and Abbey Road, England; late 1994 and early 1995.
Released:
March 1995
Chart peaks:
6 (UK) 88 (US)
Personnel:
Thom Yorke (v, g, p); Jonny Greenwood (g, syn, o, p, recorder); Ed O'Brien (g, v); Phil Selway (d); John Leckie, Nigel Godrich, Chris Brown, Jim Warren (e)
Track listing:
Planet Telex; The Bends; High And Dry (S); Fake Plastic Trees (S/UK); Bones; (Nice Dream); Just (S/UK); My Iron Lung (S/UK); Bulletproof... I Wish I Was; Black Star; Sulk; Street Spirit (Fade Out)
Running time:
48.37
Current CD:
CDPCS7372
Further listening:
OK Computer (1997); Hail to the Thief (2003)
Further reading:
MOJO 46; Exit Music: The Radiohead Story (Mac Randall, 2000); www.radiohead.com
Like this?
Try . . . p.689

Pavement

Wowee Zowee

US indie darlings confound critics with their 'difficult' third album, the most diverse and eccentric of their career.

Expectations ran high when Pavement decamped to Memphis in late 1994 to make *Wowee Zowee*. Their 1991 debut, *Slanted and Enchanted*, had shaken up the underground with its infectious synthesis of practically every alternative style there had ever been, whilst its follow-up, 1993's *Crooked Rain, Crooked Rain*, had taken a more classic rock direction, albeit a markedly eccentric one. When Cut Your Hair became a hit and major labels started to circle, fans worried that the band might be about to commit the cardinal sin of selling out. They had nothing to fear, of course – Pavement remained on Matador and made an album that covered new ground without sacrificing any of their distinctive melodic and lyrical style for commercial gain. *Wowee Zowee*, then, is Pavement's *White Album* - a disjointed, fragmentary record stuffed with treasures that take time and dedication to be appreciated.

Clearly consistency of mood was not being striven for. In fact, a dizzying number of styles is represented, from lilting country (Father To A Sister Of Thought), driving psychedelia (Half A Canyon) and straight punk (Serpentine Pad) to warped blues (Rattled By The Rush), winsome pop (Motion Suggests Itself) and anthemic rock (A, T & T). There are also nods to their roots in the brief thrash of Flux + Rad as well as departures such as the much-admired pedal steel on Father To A Sister Of Thought.

Singer, lead guitarist and principal songwriter Stephen Malkmus's lyrics are as inscrutable as ever throughout. "Grounded" is apparently about his doctor's car collection, whilst he flippantly explained that Kennel District was "soundtrack music from a never-released John Hughes picture." The frequently cryptic nature of his words can perhaps be attributed to his self-confessed habit of improvising as he sang, typifying the laid-back approach underlying the entire record.

"There really was no plan, it was just sprawl", confirmed Malkmus. "The less it fitted together, the better." He even jokingly proposed that fans should listen to the album on shuffle, the better to experience its diversity. Critics, however, missed the point, choosing instead to carp about its chaotic feel. Rolling Stone, for example, called it "half-baked", clearly feeling that it would have benefited from some judicious editing. Pavement devotees, needless to say, fell deliriously on it, and would argue today that it stands not only as the band's definitive statement, but also as one of the most joyous, imaginative and unpredictable records of the decade.

Record label:
Matador
Produced
by Pavement
Recorded
by Easley Studios, Memphis, TN, Nov. 1994 / Random Falls, NY, Feb. 1995.
Released:
Spring 1995
Chart peaks:
18 (UK) None (US)
Personnel:
Stephen Malkmus (g,v) / Scott Kannberg [aka Spiral Stairs] (rg) / Mark Ibold (b) / Bob Nastanovich (d, k) / Steve West (d)
Track listing:
We Dance / Rattled By The Rush (s) / Black Out / Brinx Job / Grounded / Serpentine Pad / Motion Suggests Itself / Father To A Sister Of Thought (s) / Extradition / Best Friend's Arm / Grave Architecture / A, T & T / Flux = Rad / Fight This Generation / Kennel District / Pueblo / Half A Canyon / Western Homes
Running time:
56.11
Current CD:
REWIGCD011
Further listening:
Compilation of early singles and out-takes, Westing (By Musket And Sextant) (1993); Crooked Rain, Crooked Rain (1994); and mature (and final?) album, Terror Twilight (1999)
Like this?
Try . . . p.650

Alanis Morissette

Jagged Little Pill

"The top-selling debut by a woman ever" was, in fact, her third.

Alanis Morissette was thrown for a loop by her mid-teen life as a precocious starlet who made two pop albums and starred on Canadian children's TV. It must have been a strange existence, sowing the seeds of some powerful emotions she had no way of expressing – until she moved from Toronto to Los Angeles and, at 20, met Glen Ballard. A family man in his early forties, he had a solid CV of pop craftsmanship – the height of it writing Man In The Mirror for Michael Jackson. He was presented to her only as the latest in a line of possible writing partners, but when they sat down together something happened. "Within half an hour we were writing a song," he recalled. "I'd play a few phrases on guitar and her pen would start rolling across the paper." Morissette just called it "magic". They sat there in his home studio, no one else allowed in, and wrote song after song, "very visceral and fast", as she put it.

They had found a natural ability to bring out the best in one another. Morissette loosened up Ballard so that he could let rip the rackety grunge noise so different from the quiet civilities of the standard "sensitive" singer-songwriter album. And, crucially, he supported her in every risk taken, especially You Oughta Know. In this now-notorious lyric a raging jealous Morissette rails at her ex about his new squeeze: "Would she go down on you in a theatre? Are you thinking of me when you fuck her?" Recording it, Ballard saw her teeter on the brink of that line: "I was there to say, That's really you, that's what it should be and it's beautiful. I had a religious intensity about getting it right." She confirmed his impression: "I thought, This is exactly how I feel, but I don't want to hurt anybody. Glen just said, You have to do this."

The demo recorded at Ballard's house was spotted by 22-year-old A&R man Gary Oseary from Madonna's Maverick label. Rough rock, an inspired tumble of candid, conversational lyrics, a whooping bare-wire voice, it provided at least 80 per cent of every track on *Jagged Little Pill*. Within four months of release it was Number 1 in America and, for all its intimacy and complex emotions, on its way to demolishing every musical and cultural divide as it sold 30 million.

Morissette lived up to her individualistic ideal – "Be vulnerable unapologetically" – and the world made the connection.

Record label:
Maverick
Produced
by Glen Ballard.
Recorded
at Glen Ballard's house, San Fernando Valley, California; Westlake Studios and Signet Sound, Hollywood, February 1994–April 1995.
Released:
June 13, 1995
Chart peaks:
1 (UK) 1 (US)
Personnel:
Alanis Morissette (v, hm); Glen Ballard (g, k); Dave Navarro, Basil Fung, Michael Landau (g); Flea, Lance Morrison (b); Benmont Tench, Michael Thompson (o); Matt Laug, Rob Ladd (d); Gota Yashiki (groove activator); Victor McCoy, Rich Weingard (e); Jolie Levine (ae)
Track listing:
All I Really Want (S/UK); You Oughta Know (S); Perfect; Hand In My Pocket (S/UK); Right Through You; Forgiven; You Learn (S); Head Over Feet (S/UK); Mary Jane; Ironic (S); Not The Doctor; Wake Up; You Oughta Know (unlisted remix); Your House (hidden track)
Running time:
55.58
Current CD:
9362-45901-2
Further listening:
Supposed Former Infatuation Junkie (1998) – the less welcoming, still striking, follow-up.
Further reading:
MOJO 32; Alanis Morissette: Jagged (Paul Cantin, 1997); www.repriserec.com/alanis/
Like this?
Try . . . p.17

Oasis

(What's The Story) Morning Glory?

In the mid-'90s, the UK could sing along to every track.

As co-producer Owen Morris puts it, "*Morning Glory* was the most incredibly easy session I've ever been involved with. Apart from the fights."

When the Beatles-fanatic Mancunians' first album, *Definitely Maybe*, topped the UK album chart in 1994 it was hardly the outcome of a smooth ride. Their general rough-neighbourhood rowdiness featured the fierce sibling rivalry between songwriter Noel and singer Liam Gallagher, whiteheated by onrushing fame. The following April, with original drummer Tony McCarroll's replacement Alan White, they convened at country-house studio Rockfield. Booked for six weeks, they skimmed through the first seven days. But then the Gallaghers' private Krakatoa erupted. Liam was upset by Noel's decision to take the lead vocal on Don't Look Back In Anger. Feeling redundant, he set off for the pub. Later, he returned with a crowd of "friends" who interrupted the session. Noel hit the roof and they had a battle which led to him battering his younger brother with a cricket bat. Undaunted, Liam revived and tried to kick Noel's bedroom door down, but only managed to injure his foot.

Morris still grimaces at the memory: "The biggest fight I've ever seen. It was horrible, horrible, horrible."

Noel Gallagher drove off, swearing he had left the band because it wasn't worth the pain and uproar. Liam went home to his mother in Manchester with an arm and a leg in bandages and plaster.

Three weeks later, though, after an indirect exchange of regretful messages, Noel returned and they finished the album on schedule. The last song written was Cast No Shadow – composed on the train as Noel returned to Wales, it was an uncharacteristically gentle reflection on his difficulties with expressing any deep emotion, both personally and in his lyrics ("I asked myself why/Can I never let anyone in"). Liam sang it with aching empathy.

The ill-begotten album was brilliant, absurdly catchy throughout, rocking with a near-Phil Spector hugeness at times (Roll With It, Some Might Say, the title track), then unpredictably warm and delicate (Wonderwall, Cast No Shadow). Although Noel confidently joined critics in panning the lyrics – "I'm no Morrissey," he often said – he could turn out some nice phrases and he captured the experience for the band and enraptured, practically reborn, British pop fans with a marvellously mixed metaphor from the chorus of the final track: "you will find me/Caught beneath the landslide/in a champagne supernova/A champagne supernova in the sky".

Record Label:
Creation
Produced
by Owen Morris and Noel Gallagher.
Recorded
at Rockfield Studios, Gwent, Wales; May–June 1995.
Released:
October 2, 1995
Chart peaks:
1 (UK) 4 (US)
Personnel:
Liam Gallagher (v); Noel Gallagher (lead g, v, Mellotron, p, E bow); Paul "Bonehead" Arthurs (rhythm g, Mellotron, p); Paul McGuigan (b); Alan White (d); Paul Weller (lead g, bv on Champagne Supernova); Tony McCarroll (d on Some Might Say)
Track Listing:
Hello; Roll With It (S); Wonderwall (S); Don't Look Back In Anger (S); Hey Now; untitled instrumental; Some Might Say (S); Cast No Shadow; She's Electric; Morning Glory; untitled instrumental; Champagne Supernova
Running time:
50.00
Current CD:
RKIDCD007
Further listening:
Definitely Maybe (1994) – nearly as good as their definitive second album
Further reading:
MOJO 14, 30, 49; Getting High: The Adventures Of Oasis (Paolo Hewitt, 1997); www.oasisinet.com
Like this?
Try . . . p.207

Pulp

Different Class

The most durable dues-payers ever finally go toppermost with sardonic wit and hangdog tunefulness.

Jarvis Cocker formed Pulp as a 16-year-old Sheffield schoolboy in 1979, took on most of the *Different Class* line-up during the '80s, playing to tiny audiences and selling no records for years on end until, at long last, in 1993, Island spotted them. The following year, *His 'N' Hers* entered the UK Top 10 and suddenly Cocker strutted his stuff as a rayon-and-crimplene master of self-mockery. "Being in a band for so many years without any hint of success is pretty depressing," he explained. "What we've had to do is develop a sense of irony. It was either that or kill ourselves!"

Enlisting new producer, Chris Thomas, and giving long-time roadie/sideman Mark Webber full band membership, as ever they wrote loads of music, maybe 40 tracks' worth, before Cocker gave a thought to the words. But by April they decided most of them were naff. Except for this pungent story about a posh girl itching to get in touch with the "noble" poverty of the working class. "The first time we played Common People I realised it was significant," he says. "It fitted the mood of the times." Released as a single that June, it was a UK Number 2 hit and promptly inspired the band to knock off another eight tracks in a fortnight. They came up with a savoury stew of Barry Ryan-style pop melodrama, French *chanson*, and saucy old English musichall pop.

Pulp achieved their apotheosis even before the album was finished. At the Glastonbury Festival they late-substituted for The Stone Roses. "Everyone sang along with Common People," marvels Cocker. "That excitement, knowing for once in your life you had a mass audience, gave me confidence. If Common People hadn't been a success I don't think I would have written Mis-Shapes because that's a rallying cry. It's based on the feeling of a Sheffield Saturday night when the beer monsters want to smack you because you've got orange trousers or funny glasses or a funny haircut – and you have to run."

Subsequently, Cocker secured lasting notoriety by wiggling his bum at the posturing Michael Jackson on the 1996 BRITS show. But he and Pulp might be better credited for the way their longevity was based on sharing all income equally regardless of who did what and for camping in tents behind the stage for the whole of the Glastonbury Festival they headlined.

Record label:
Island
Produced
by Chris Thomas.
Recorded
at Townhouse, London; January–August 1995.
Released:
November 5, 1995 (UK); February 27, 1996 (US)
Chart peaks:
1 (UK) None (US)
Personnel:
Jarvis Cocker (v, ag, g, Vocoder, syn, Mellotron, Micro-Moog); Russell Senior (g, vn); Candida Doyle (Farfisa organ, Fender Rhodes piano, Mini-Moog synthesizer); Steve Mackey (b); Nick Banks (d, pc); Mark Webber (g); David "Chipper" Nicholas (e)
Track listing:
Mis-Shapes (S); Pencil Skirt; Common People (S); I Spy; Disco 2000 (S); Live Bed Show; Something Changed; Sorted For E's & Wizz (S); F.E.E.L.I.N.G.C.A.L.L.E.D.L.O.V.E.; Underwear; Monday Morning; Bar Italia
Running time:
52.04
Current CD:
CID 8041
Further listening:
His 'N' Hers (1994), This Is Hardcore (1998) – widely underrated precursor and follow-up to their big album.
Further reading:
Pulp (Martin Aston 1996); www.pulponline.com
Like this?
Try . . . p.422

The Auteurs

After Murder Park

As Britpop rages, England's most unjustly neglected songwriter quietly makes the best British rock album of the decade.

Luke Haines instantly established his reputation as one of England's finest songwriters with The Auteurs' wry, tuneful debut, 1993's *New Wave*. The album topped several 'best of year' critical lists and, though the band notoriously lost the Mercury Music Prize to Suede by a single vote, they were tipped for stardom. Inexplicably, though, 1994's *Now I'm A Cowboy* was less successful, despite containing the excellent singles 'Lenny Valentino' and 'Chinese Bakery'.

But perhaps freedom from pressure to sustain chart placings was just what Haines needed. Jaded by touring, in the summer of 1994 he jumped from a 15-foot high wall in Spain. The resultant broken ankles landed him in a wheelchair for two months, which he spent writing the extraordinary words and music of *After Murder Park*. As 1995 drew on and their contemporaries traded insults in the playground of West London, The Auteurs toiled in Abbey Road Studios. Having Steve Albini at the controls helped. Much in demand after producing Nirvana's mighty *In Utero* (whose immense power and unsettling mood is shared with *After Murder Park*), his hands-off approach ideally suited the band, who nailed the album in under a fortnight.

Spurning Britpop's retro swagger in favour of a darker, more intense atmosphere, the band rehearsed the songs to perfection,. Far removed from the jaunty commonplaces of Oasis, Blur and co., *After Murder Park* is characterised by stinging guitar, muscular drumming, menacing Hammond organ and poignant cello.

It's impossible to isolate highlights on such a consistent album. From the rousing 'Dead Sea Navigators' to the malevolent 'Buddha', from the delicate beauty of 'Fear of Flying' to the sheer spite of 'Everything You Say Will Destroy You' and the joyous riffing on 'Tombstone', there's no weak link. Lyrically Haines is at his acerbic best throughout, also proving himself an unlikely guitar hero – witness the searing solo in 'Married To A Lazy Lover'. Despite its awesome punch, *After Murder Park*'s ominous mood jarred with the times and it bellyflopped. Albini was left to persuade the world what it was missing. 'They did a job on that album that nobody has done in years', he enthused. 'They carved a sound for each song without resorting to fancy tricks.' Though Haines has recorded much since, including the extraordinary *Baader-Meinhof* album and hits with Black Box Recorder, most would agree that he has done nothing to match *After Murder Park*. But then, as the adage has it - nor has anyone else.

Record label:
Hut
Produced
by Steve Albini
Recorded
at Abbey Road Studios, London, Nov. 1995.
Released:
February 1996.
Chart peaks:
53 (UK), None (US)
Personnel:
Luke Haines (g,v, harmonium), James Banbury (cello, keyboards), Alice Readman (b), Barney C. Rockford (d).
Track listing:
Light Aircraft On Fire (s) / The Child Brides / Land Lovers / New Brat In Town / Everything You Say Will Destroy You / Unsolved Child Murder (s) / Married To A Lazy Lover / Buddha / Tombstone / Fear Of Flying / Dead Sea Navigators / After Murder Park.
Running time:
39.17
Further listening:
New Wave (1993); Now I'm A Cowboy (1994); Baader Meinhof (1996); How I Learned To Love The Bootboys (1999).
Current CD:
DGHUT33
Like this?
Try . . . p.182

Nusrat Fateh Ali Khan And Michael Brook

Night Song

The final international album by the greatest devotional singer modern Pakistan has produced.

Nusrat Fateh Ali Khan had fast become one of world music's leading lights in the '90s, with two entirely separate careers on the rise simultaneously – full-time as a Sufi, revered throughout Asia and the Asian diaspora, and part-time as a darling of the alternative crowd, idolised by Jeff Buckley and a collaborator with Perry Farrell on the soundtrack to Dead Man Walking (a phrase that actually comes from a description of *qawwali* singers in trance). Massive Attack's remix of the song Mustt Mustt had kickstarted their career and taken Pakistani *qawwali* onto British dancefloors. A series of experimental albums had followed on Peter Gabriel's Real World label, hand-in-hand with a similar line in traditional sacred LPs. *Night Song* – a nod to the way Indian *ragas* can be described as "morning" or "evening" depending on their mood – was to take meditational experimentation to extremes.

"I'd recorded backing tracks for *Mustt Mustt* that were song length," recalls Michael Brook, "this was completely alien to him, he'd only be warming up after six minutes. This time, I made very basic tracks, but they would be 22 minutes long; any chord changes would lead to completely new songs. There was a little implied melody, but most of the instruments were added afterwards. He was really only used to being accompanied by tabla, drone and harmonium."

Nusrat had changed, too; in particular, he was enthusiastic about multi-tracking, and provides either harmonies or a dialogue with his soaring tenor on most of the tracks. The album opens with a *kora* (an African harp), Lament has a percussive backing that is almost industrial, My Comfort Remains has a juddering, funky feel, and Longing could be late-period Roxy.

"He was open to experimentation," says Brook, "and saw our projects as a distinct thing, within the context that he was a *qawwali* singer." Brook worked on the resulting recordings for more than a year, editing Nusrat down into cohesive six-minute slices, strengthening the melodies. From start to release took almost three years. A year later, with his star still rising, Nusrat's liver failed, and he died on August 16, 1997.

Record label:
Real World
Produced
by Michael Brook.
Recorded
at Real World Studios, Wiltshire; 1993–94.
Released:
February 1996
Chart peaks:
None (UK) None (US)
Personnel:
Nusrat Fateh Ali Khan (v, harmonium); James Pinker (d); Jo Bruce (k, d, woodwind); Michael Brook (infinite guitar, b, k, drones); Mick Karn (b); Robert Ahwai (b); Dildar Hussain (tabla)
Track listing:
My Heart, My Life; Intoxicated; Lament; My Comfort Remains; Longing; Sweet Pain; Night Song; Crest
Running time:
48.01
Current CD:
CDRW50
Further listening:
Mustt Mustt (1990); Shahbaaz (1991); Devotional Songs (1992); Love Songs (1992)
Further reading:
www.nfak.com
Like this?
Try . . . p.567

Fugees (Refugee Camp)

The Score

They made it look easy, but becoming the biggest hip hop band in the world was anything but.

The Fugees, a New Jersey trio comprising Haitian immigrants Wyclef Jean and Prakazrel Michel and New Yorker Lauryn Hill, had released their debut, Blunted On Reality, to decent notices but poor sales in 1993. Seen as part of the "alternative hip hop" movement created by a mainstream media uncomfortable with hardcore hip hop's excesses, the group were shunned by rap fans. With these negative preconceptions to overturn, the band took time to gather momentum. The Score was far from an overnight smash.

Their breakthrough came with a cover of the Roberta Flack hit Killing Me Softly. The band had recorded a dancehall reggae revision, with Jamaican star Bounty Killer rapping as Hill sang a rewritten chorus that made the song into a sound system battle anthem. Permission to release this version was denied, and the band were persuaded to include a straightforward cover on the LP. Promoted to US radio but never released as a single, it became a massive radio hit, crossing the group over to a pop audience, and resulting in huge album sales.

The group were peaking together. Clef and Pras, often ignorantly dismissed as talentless no-marks hampering Hill's creativity, co-produced most of the record, discovering a judicious midway point between streetwise hip hop and melodic pop. Tracks like Ready Or Not, Fu-Gee-La or The Mask are hip hop of rare depth, poetic insight matched to backing tracks that convey far more than rap's lingua franca of anger, aggression and tension. It became, at the time, the highest selling hip hop album to date.

Tensions, though, existed between Wyclef and Hill. "I was definitely involved at one time with her, and that's probably half of the problem," Clef explained four years later of the band's inability to record a follow-up. "When it came to the music, we would just get down and do it – the only thing that went sour I would say was our relationship. So if anybody hears The Fugees have broken up – which they haven't – it's because of the relationship."

Hill released a stunning solo debut but has since become a virtual recluse, and Pras has yet to convince. Wyclef, though, has shown he can work in any musical discipline he chooses, his three solo LPs interspersed with producing and writing global hits for everyone from Destiny's Child and Whitney Houston to Tom Jones. But that third Fugees album seems as far off as ever.

AB

Record label:
RuffHouse/Columbia
Produced
by Wyclef, Shawn King, Lauryn Hill, Prakazrel "Pras", Jerry "Te Bass" Duplessis, Warren Riker, John Forte, Salaam Remi, Diamond D, Handel Tucker
Recorded
at The Booga Basement Studio, East Orange, NJ
Released:
1996
Chart peaks:
2 (UK) 1 (US)
Personnel:
Wyclef (v, gtr): Lauryn Hill (v): Prakazrel "Pras" (v): DJ Backspin (sctraches): J Forte (v, drum programming on No Woman No Cry): Omega (v): Diamond D (v): Pace 1 (v): Young Zee (v): Ra Digga (v): S Dunbar (drums and drum programming on Fu-Gee-La (Sly & Robbie Mix)): R Shakespeare (bass on Fu-Gee-La (Sly & Robbie Mix)): H Tucker (kbds on Fu-Gee-La (Sly & Robbie Mix)): G Parkinson (v on Fu-Gee-La (Sly & Robbie Mix)): Red Alert (v on Intro and Outro)
Track listing:
Red Intro: How Many Mics: Ready Or Not: Zealots: The Beast: Fu-Gee-La: Family Business: Killing Me Softly: The Score: The Mask: Cowboys: No Woman, No Cry: Manifest/Outro: Fu-Gee-La (Refugee Camp Remix): Fu-Gee-La (Sly & Robbie Mix): Mista Mista: Fu-Gee-La (Refugee Camp Global Mix)
Current CD:
RuffHouse/Columbia 483549 2
Further reading:
Lauryn Hill: Beyond the Fugees (Jaqueline springer 2002)
Like this?
Try . . . p.509

Underworld

Second Toughest In The Infants

Iconoclastic and arty trio create new type of intelligent, elegant – and popular – prog-techno.

Themes of urban psychosis and existential anxiety loom as large on Underworld's second album as on their debut, but stylistically, it's a smoother, lower-slung and altogether more slippery beast.

"Since day one," says Karl Hyde, "Rick and I have enjoyed bringing together sounds that are very crude with sounds that are very precise, combining electronic sounds with a human element." The pair's concern with texture, mood and emotional cohesion wins out over the visceral demands of the dancefloor and consequently *Second Toughest . . .* works better on the couch than it does in the sweaty confines of a club, the banging Rowla notwithstanding.

Underworld, though, had no more a plan as to the final desired outcome than ever they did. "I have strong feelings about albums," says Rick Smith. "To me they are not collections of tracks, they are things in themselves. They have a shape of their own. We don't lay out plans or directions for albums; they're very natural and they represent the meeting point of a load of different thoughts."

Plan or no, crucial to the overall restrained melancholia of *Second Toughest* is Hyde's lyrical and vocal input (Underworld are unique in that their vocals are not just lifted from samples). Sourced from scrapbooks filled as a result of late-night prowls around the world's major cities over the previous eight or so years, Hyde's text is frequently prescient, occasionally opaque, often unbearably poignant and always powerful.

"It wasn't automatic writing and it wasn't even surreal," he says of his lyrical work on *Second Toughest*, "it was to do with the fact that I have always believed – and still do – that we see the world as a series of fragments. I went out in various cities at night around the world, scavenging, and one's state of mind tends to not be in sunny places if that's what you're doing. But, whatever I brought back, Rick would always see the humour and the irony and the positivity and draw that out. The duality of the text then became important and enchanting to both of us. We never discuss what things mean to us; I know where they came from, Rick knows where he's taken them and when we're performing onstage, I have both those possibilities in my mind."

Subtleties of lyrical interpretation are undoubtedly far from the minds of the hordes of heaving hedonists who see Underworld play, but live, even their *Zeitgeist*-grabbing anthem Born Slippy (not included on the album because it was already finished), with its chant of "lager lager lager" was awash with a very real pathos. And tracks such as the epic in three parts that is Juanita/Kiteless/To Dream Of Love and the sepia-tinted Blueski clearly reveal the spacy, deep-rooted soul which makes Underworld tick.

Record label:
Junior Boys Own
Produced
by Underworld.
Recorded
at Rick Smith's spare bedroom studio, Romford; December 1993–November 1995.
Released:
March 1996.
Chart peaks:
9 (UK) None (US)
Personnel:
Karl Hyde (v, g); Rick Smith (samples, programming, e); Darren Emerson (DJ)
Track listing:
Juanita/Kiteless;/To Dream Of Love; Banstyle/Sappy's Curry; Confusion The Waitress; Rowla; Pearl's Girl (S); Air Towel; Blueski; Stagger
Running time:
73.08
Current CD:
JBOCD4
Further listening:
Dirty/Big Mouth (1992, 12" by Lemon Interrupt – Underworld's alter ego); dubnobasswithmyheadman (1993); Beaucoup Fish (1999)
Further reading:
www.dirty/org/underworld
Like this?
Try . . . p.608

Maria McKee

Life Is Sweet

For her third solo album, she unleashed the full force of her ferocious talent, and nobody noticed.

That this beautiful, disturbing, terrific record came and went without a tickertape parade is unfathomable. Perhaps its boiling, melodramatic intensity was too much for fans of Maria's earlier incarnation as a purveyor of twangy, country-flavoured AOR. But it was on *Life Is Sweet* that she finally blossomed into her true colours.

From as early as she can remember, this child of Hollywood was around freaky rock types. Her brother, 18 years her senior, was Brian McLean of Love. At 18, she formed Lone Justice and started the cow-punk bandwagon, before producer Jimmy Iovine decided she was a putative pop diva, and guided her towards the lush balladry of Show Me Heaven – a British Number 1 single. Her second solo album *You Gotta Sin To Be Saved* opted for a looser, more gospel-influenced style, but Maria was unhappy with it. "Once I went on the road I realised I was completely bored with the material," she admits. "I wanted to do something a bit more raw and diverse and I started to think, What if I just completely wiped away everything I've done before?"

So she began to stockpile songs that were entirely true to her moods. "I was dating a guy who would listen to Bowie all the time and I started to notice Mick Ronson and how he used guitar as a kind of extra vocal, playing a lot of back-up melody. I realised that when I picked up electric guitar I could do that. And the songs started to turn into identity stuff, about growing into my adult womanhood, as an artist and someone with a mental disorder!"

The edgy Scar Lover, exuberant Absolutely Barking Stars and feverishly uneasy I'm Not Listening – a nervous breakdown set to music – tore up all her old material, both lyrically and sonically. Best of all, perhaps, is the title track, a duct-prickling ballad of hope. "I thought it was the greatest record of all time," laughs Maria, "and I assumed everybody would feel the same way. Tony Burke, my A&R man at Geffen, bless him, took it to a marketing meeting and nearly lost his job! It got the thumbs down from 12 out of the 13 people in the meeting, all the people responsible for promoting it." Somehow, Geffen were persuaded to release the album, but it emerged to an almost audible critical shrug.

"The rejection was incredibly difficult," says Maria today. "I was nearly suicidal because people hated it so much. Talk about being silenced, that was very, very hard for me to deal with, especially when I knew how good it was. But I think I really needed to tear everything down and start over, out of that there had to be a phoenix from the flames, so I see it as a turning point in my life."

Record label:
Geffen
Produced
by Maria McKee, Bruce Brody & Mark Freegard
Recorded:
Groovemaster, Cherokee and A&M Studios, LA, 1995
Released:
May 1996
Chart peaks:
None (UK) None (US)
Personnel:
Maria McKee (v, g, ag), Bruce Brody (o, p, Moog), David Nolte (b, g), Rick Kavin (d, pc) Susan Otten (bv, pc), Martin Tillman (orchestration)
Track listing:
Scarlover; This Perfect Dress; Absolutely Barking Stars; I'm Not Listening; Everybody; Smarter; What Else You Wanna Know; I'm Awake; Human; Carried; Life Is Sweet; Afterlife
Running time:
46.13
Currently CD:
GED24819
Further listening:
The debut, Maria McKee (1987) has one or two pearls, notably Breathe. There are some good moments on You Gotta Sin To Be Saved (1992).
Further reading:
MOJO 31; www.mariamckee.net
Like this?
Try . . . p.526

RL Burnside

A Ass Pocket of Whiskey

Mississippi Delta blues king rucking in the street with Noo Yawk punks.

In 1995 Jon Spencer was looking for a new thing. From the aboriginal garage wail of his first band, Pussy Galore, to the malfeasant feedback of The Jon Spencer Blues Explosion, Spencer had spent 10 years seeking out the primitive beating heart of musical rebellion. Working on the follow-up to their 1994 album, *Orange* – complete with string sections, breakbeats and Beck Hansen – the desire was to get back to something raw and primeval. One album they'd play over and over again was RL Burnside's *Too Bad Jim* on Fat Possum Records. Burnside started recording for Matthew Johnson's Fat Possum label in 1992 but he'd already been playing music for close to 40 years.

Born in Oxford, Mississippi in 1926, Burnside learned his music directly from his neighbour, Mississippi Fred McDowell and made his recording debut in 1968 on George Mitchell's Arhoolie anthology *Mississippi Delta Blues, Vol 2* He spent the next 25 years touring Europe and the US, grinding out a strange churning mongrelisation of field blues, country church music, and 19th-century fife-and-drum bands.

Believing RL's one-measure riff-patterns to be the way back to the source, Spencer enlisted him as tour support for The Blues Explosion in 1996. Every night he'd sit in RL's dressing room as the 70-year-old bluesman entertained him with "toasts" – dirty hand-me-down tales such as Signifyin' Monkey and Stackolee ("I got a ass pocket of whiskey, front-pocket of gin/You open this motherfuckin' door or I kick the motherfucker in"). Spencer asked whether RL would consider reworking these toasts into songs for an album with The Blues Explosion.

"I said, Oh man, ain't nobody gonna buy that," remembers Burnside, "but five days after the tour the phone rang and it was John Spencer and he said, 'Hey RL, you ready to do that album?' I said, Hell yeah, come on down. We'll do it if it don't hurt me none. We rented one of them big hunting clubs 10 miles from my house and we did the album in four hours."

"He was a real task master," says Jon Spencer, thinking back, "No heat or running water, just a big Marshall stack in the front room, we were hangin' on for dear life." Fuzzed vocals, distorted guitar and filthy lyrics. The result was stark, mean-assed hill-country blues as it should to be played – rhythmic, chaotic, with all the ramshackle speed of a truck hurtling over a cliff.

Record label:
Matador
Produced
by Matthew Johnson.
Recorded
at Lunati Farms, Hollis Springs, Mississippi; June 2, 1996.
Released:
September 1996
Chart peaks:
None (UK) None (US)
Personnel:
RL Burnside (v, g); Kenny Brown (g); Judah Bauer (g, hm, v, Casio SK-1); Russell Simins (d); Jon Spencer (g, v, d, theremin)
Track listing:
Goin' Down South; Boogie Chillen; Poor Boy; 2 Brothers; Snake Drive; Shake 'Em On Down; The Criminal Inside Me; Walkin' Blues; Tojo Told Hitler; Have You Ever Been Lonely
Running time:
41.58
Current CD:
OLE 214-2
Further listening:
RL Burnside Too Bad Jim (1994); The Jon Spencer Blues Explosion, Acme (1998) and Acme Plus (1999)
Further reading:
www.fatpossum.com and Robert Palmer's excellent liner notes to Too Bad Jim
Like this?
Try . . . p.55

DJ Shadow
Endtroducing . . .
A triumph for vinyl recycling.

On November 1, 1990, Josh Davis – a 17-year-old freshman at the University of California – awoke feeling both hungover and guilty. The hangover was the result of the previous night's Halloween celebrations. The guilt crept in when Davis realised a whole day which could have been spent making music was being wasted on being wasted. It dawned on him that the college life was not one he wanted to be leading. Thus DJ Shadow was born.

Raised on his parents' '70s-biased collection the young Shadow was not interested in the bland radio rock of '80s America. Hearing The Message by Grandmaster Flash in 1982 was an epiphanic moment. "I was struck by the directness of the words and the starkness of the music." Two months later he caught another extraordinary noise: Planet Rock by Afrika Bambaataa. His fate was sealed. By late 1984, the pre-pubescent B-boy had tried his hand at break-dancing and graffiti. That Christmas he was given a set of decks and was soon practising, going over and over the rhythmic breaks, like a budding guitarist learning a Hendrix solo by rote, until he was better than the records. He was soon making his own.

"I'm very untechnological," Davis says. "I don't like anything that gets in the way of a cool vibe. When I'm working I try and shut out all other stimuli."

Some years later Davis constructed this, his debut full-length album entirely on one outmoded sampler, an AKAI MPC60. After a daily two-hour drive to his studio, he'd search through his mountain of bargain-bin LPs for samples and start stacking loops and sequences onto a digital multi-track, slowly weaving this curious masterpiece. It was a painstaking, sometimes frustrating process that ate up nine months of his life.

Strictly adhering to his "100% sampled" guarantee, he would deliberately screw up time signatures and break his own sonic rules, doing the opposite of what his instincts said.

If Shadow's methodology can be encapsulated in one stylistic flourish it is in the way that the choral themes and piano motifs (some from David Axelrod's *Songs Of Innocence*) re-occur throughout the album, give it spiritual resonance and are juxtaposed with the earthy ambience of gangster movie dialogue. "*Endtroducing*. . . was incredibly personal for me and Josh," says Mo' Wax's supremo James Lavelle. "I've never been involved in something or heard something that hit me as much since the first time I started hearing records. And I don't think I'll ever get that feeling again."

Record label:
Mo' Wax
Produced
by DJ Shadow.
Recorded
at The Glue Factory, San Fransisco; 1995.
Released:
September 1996
Chart peaks:
17 (UK) None (US)
Personnel:
DJ Shadow (e, m)
Track listing:
Best Foot Forward; Building Steam With A Grain Of Salt; The Number Song; Changeling; Transmission 1; What Does Your Soul Look Like (Part 4); Stem/Long Stem; Transmission 2; Mutual Slump; Organ Donor; Why Hip-Hop Sucks In '96; Midnight In A Perfect World; Napalm Brain/Scatter Brain; What Does Your Soul Look Like (Part 1 – Sky Blue Revisit); Transmission 3
Running time:
63.36
Current CD:
MW059CD
Further Listening:
What Does You Soul Look Like? EP (1994), a dry run for this album. Also, the brilliant Mo' Wax samplers Headz (1994) and Headz 2 1996)
Further reading:
www.djshadow.com
Like this?
Try . . . p.658

Belle & Sebastian

If You're Feeling Sinister

Fey Glaswegian indie heroes born on a college music-business course.

In January 1996, Stuart Murdoch and Stuart David met on the Stow College, Glasgow music-business course under the aegis of Alan Rankine, formerly Billy Mackenzie's partner in the Associates. Each year, college label Electric Honey Records would release a record and this year it was to be the band the two Stuarts had formed, Belle And Sebastian (named after an old French children's TV show). The album, *Tigermilk*, released in May, caused an A&R scramble, and the band were rapidly signed to new labels Jeepster Records in the UK and The Enclave in the US.

Tigermilk was a happy experience, made in a flurry of excitement – audible in the rough, buzzy sound – so it seemed natural to expect that *Sinister* would follow the same dynamic. Recording began just two months after *Tigermilk*'s release, in the same studio, on all the same gear. But things had altered. Producer Gregor Reed was unavailable and Tony Dougan stepped in and Stuart Murdoch, the group's only songwriter at that point naturally took charge of proceedings. "It was Stuart's baby," confirms Stevie Jackson, "and whatever it was, for better or for worse, is what he wanted – but I think he undersold a lot of the songs." Murdoch, though famously reticent, has also spoken of opportunities missed, times he wished he could re-make the record.

Whatever they intended, what they got – in only 10 days – was a softly beautiful, witty and sincere record full of gentle charm; happy/sad boy meets girl narratives set in endearingly mundane locations and stuffed with kitchen-sink detail. With a mystique fanned by their reluctance to be interviewed or pose for conventional band photos, Belle And Sebastian's arrival in the year of Britpop's messy demise couldn't have been better timed. Press and public welcomed them with open arms. *Sinister* drew comparisons to Felt, Love and the Smiths; Rolling Stone even claimed that "Had Nick Drake lived long enough to know how to smirk, he would have loved this band."

But the band were immune to its appeal. "I think maybe *Sinister*'s got the best songs on it, but I'd say it was a major disappointment at the time," says Stevie Jackson. "The magic just wasn't there."

"The songs are all just about buses and schoolgirls as far as I can make out," shrugs Chris Geddes.

"I don't want to be down about it, though," says Stevie. "It's growing on me now."

But there's no pleasing some people. The next album *The Boy With The Arab Strap* sold three times as many and won them a Brit award. They all seem to hate that one even more.

Record label:
Jeepster
Produced
by Tony Dougan.
Recorded
at Cava Studios; Glasgow; July 1996.
Released:
November 1996
Chart peaks:
None (UK) None (US)
Personnel:
Stuart Murdoch (v, g); Isobel Campbell (c, v, recorder); Richard Colburn (d); Chris Geddes (p, o, glockenspiel); Stevie Jackson (g, v, hm); Stuart David (b); Sarah Martin (vn, s)
Track listing:
The Stars Of Track And Field; Seeing Other People; Me And The Major; Like Dylan In The Movies; The Fox In The Snow; Get Me Away From Here, I'm Dying; If You're Feeling Sinister; Mayfly; The Boy Done Wrong Again; Judy And The Dream Of Horses
Running time:
41.18
Current CD:
JPRCD001
Further listening:
Tigermilk (1996); Lazy Line Painter Jane box Set (2000), contains first three EPs; Fold Your Hands Child, You Walk Like A Peasant (2000)
Further reading:
MOJO 50; www.belleandsebastian.co.uk
Like this?
Try . . . p.15

Supergrass

In It For The Money

Ivor Novello-award-winning Oxford trio find life beyond Britpop on bruising second album.

In 1995 Supergrass were cheeky younger brothers to the nation. They had two members still in their teens; *I Should Coco*, a rambunctious album stuffed full of Britpop fizz-bombs reached Number 1, and one of the best singles of the decade, Alright, made them household names. Despite their obvious sophistication, there was a feeling Supergrass weren't *serious* enough to stay the course; Alright was a *pop* record, after all. 1997's *In It For The Money* suggested otherwise.

"I suppose there's a grain of truth in the fact that we had something to prove," recalls bassist Mick Quinn, "but basically we just wanted to make another bloody good album. We went into Sawmills again because we knew there would be no surprises there, and we worked with John Cornfield again [engineer on *Coco*] because we'd liked him before. There were about five songs worked up beforehand, the others were just a chorus here, a riff there. The first track we got down was Richard III and that went so well it gave us a buzz that carried on all the way through." The opening salvo is a four-gun salute as fine as any in the rock armoury. The title track comes on like the Cardiacs playing Abba until the astounding, pull-the-plug edit into the Motor City-drive of Richard III ("Words were said about that cut at Parlophone, but we stuck to our guns"). Tonight feels like a punked-up Saturday Night's Alright (For Fighting), but the revelation is Late In The Day – an affecting, morose number that wouldn't sound out of place on Hunky Dory.

Mick: "It wasn't a happy, happy time. That's in the lyrics a bit, subconsciously; coming to terms with the glare of publicity. But there were moments, like recording outside [Hollow Little Reign is the only track from that session on the finished album], getting the echo off the hills. We had this little envelope of time when the tide was in when we could record."

In It For The Money finds Supergrass blending influences with a panache beyond almost all of their contemporaries; growing up in public, with intelligence and humour.

Record label:
Parlophone
Produced
by Supergrass and John Cornfield.
Recorded
at Sawmills Studio Cornwall and Konk Stusios, London May–November 1996
Released:
February 21, 1997
Chart peaks:
2 (UK) None (US)
Personnel:
Gaz Coombes (v, g); Mick Quinn (v, b); Danny Goffey (v, d); Bob Coombes (k); Satin Singh (pc); Sam Williams (theremin); Hornography and the Kick Horns (horns)
Track listing:
In It For The Money; Richard III (S); Late In The Day (S); G-Song; Sun Hits The Sky (S); Goin Out (S); It's Not Me; Cheapskate (S, US only); You Can See Me; Hollow Little Reign; Sometimes I Make You Sad
Running time:
43.09
Current CD:
CDPCS7388
Further listening:
The brash debut, I Should Coco (1995); the mellower follow-up Supergrass (1999)
Further reading:
MOJO 42; www.supergrass.com
Like this?
Try . . . p.616

Nick Cave & The Bad Seeds

The Boatman's Call

The black-clad bard strips down to bare essentials.

Despite his 15-year, 10-album career after the Birthday Party, Nick Cave's origins as a malcontent have proved tough to shake off. Hard drugs, run-ins with journalists, a ridiculously high body count in his songs and his impeccably groomed Grim Reaper persona have stoked his mordant reputation. *The Boatman's Call* might not have closed that particular chapter completely (for all its intimacy, the album's sparseness emphasises its solemnity), but it finally transmitted the ruined dignity of his later solo work to an audience beyond ageing Goths and misanthropes.

Its lyricism, drawn from the residue of at least two doomed relationships, and Cave's enduring love affair with the Bible, invites favourable comparisons with Leonard Cohen, even Dylan's *Blood On The Tracks*. The album came off the back of *The Murder Ballads* (1996), the near million-selling set that managed both to raise Cave's profile (thanks to the international hit duet with fellow Aussie Kylie Minogue on Where The Wild Roses Grow) and bring his nightmare scenarios to some kind of parodic conclusion. That success coincided with the break-up of his relationship with his Brazilian wife Vivian Carneiro and a short-term liaison with creative soulmate Polly (P.J.) Harvey. The time was somehow right for a mid-life confessional.

Cave began stockpiling material during the making of *The Murder Ballads*, but unlike that and previous albums, where the Bad Seeds would add flesh to the bare bones of his songs, Cave's *auteur*-ist touch remained largely intact with little adornment. It was, he admits, the nearest he'd come to recording a genuinely solo album. "All of the songs were written very much on my own, and I was very much absorbed in my own world at the time of writing them." Despite its long gestation period, the album was recorded quickly. "The idea was to preserve the rawness of the demos."

The band, who, says the singer, "suppressed their ego for the greater good of the record", maintained a muted presence, allowing the refined simplicity of the songs to radiate. Cave's lyrics, now largely stripped of metaphor and characters, were reduced to their elegant essentials. Into My Arms opens the record with the kind of impassioned restraint that Cave had hinted at for years, but had never managed to sustain. *The Boatman's Call* was different. Here, his seemingly unquenchable thirst for glorious melodrama was ousted for a more subtle, if no less acutely felt intoxication. Speculation that West Country Girl and Black Hair were probably about Polly Harvey seems insignificant in the face of the album's enduring qualities. It's little surprise that Cave has remained uncharacteristically silent since its release.

Record Label:
Mute
Producer not listed.
Recorded
at Abbey Road and Sarm West, London; July 1996.
Released:
March 1997
Chart peaks:
22 (UK) None (US)
Personnel:
Nick Cave (v, p, k, vibes); Blixa Bargeld (g); Mick Harvey (b, g, vibes, k); Thomas Wydler (d, pc); Conway Savage (p, b. v); Martyn P. Casey (b); Jim Sclavunos (d, bells); Warren Ellis (vn, accordion); Flood (m)
Track Listing:
Into My Arms (S); Lime Tree Arbour; People Ain't No Good; Brompton Oratory; There Is A Kingdom; (Are You) The One That I've Been Waiting For? (S); Where Do We Go Now But Nowhere?; West Country Girl; Black Hair; Idiot Prayer; Far From Me; Green Eyes
Running time:
52.12
Current CD:
CD STUMM 142
Further listening:
The Best Of Nick Cave & The Bad Seeds (1998) provides a useful summation of his solo work.
Further reading:
MOJO 40; Bad Seed: The Biography Of Nick Cave (Ian Johnstone, 1996); And The Ass Saw The Angel (Nick Cave, 1990);
Like this?
Try . . . p.478

Gorky's Zygotic Mynci

Barafundle

After much early promise, the cherished Welsh mavericks come of age.

When they began recording *Barafundle* in rural Wales, GZM's average age was just 22. Their *Tatay* and *Bwyd Time* albums had drawn together influences as disparate as The Fall, The Beach Boys, and the pastoral psychedelia of Caravan and Soft Machine. *Barafundle* – named after their local beach in Dyfed – owed more to The Incredible String Band, Medicine Head and Faust. Gorwel Owen had been the band's engineer since *Tatay* but here he stepped into the producer's chair. The result was a dazzlingly ambitious record of considerable charm and originality. Guests included the Childs' dad on *crumhorn* and *shawm*, and Owen's wife Fiona on backing vocals. Conceits included frontman Euros' lizard impression, and a Welsh language song whose entire lyric translated as "Stomach, stomach."

The album was written over a two-year period, but recorded fairly quickly. Changes of mood, pace and texture challenge the listener throughout, some songs even segueing into choral or Medieval-sounding sections. In parts it's reminiscent of The Incredible String Band, but it has a pronounced mood of its own, drawing the listener into its gentle, crepuscular world. If Patio Song – a charming ode to romance full of curious rustic images ("Isn't it a lovely day?/My patio's on fire") – typifies the album's playful side, other, darker material evidences Euros Childs' growing maturity as a lyricist. (The Barafundle Bumbler, is a comic, but ultimately poignant portrayal of a seaside Peeping Tom). Equally affecting is Sometimes The Father Is The Son, written by bass-player Richard James in the empty house his family were about to move into. The band encouraged James to sing it himself, but he demurred, and thus Childs remembers confusion over the lyrics during recording: "John and I were singing 'there's a reason to die, but where's the reason to live?', he says, "but at the mix Richard pointed out it was supposed to be 'there's a reason to die, but where's the reason to kill?' I liked our version. It was quite Charles Manson."

Barafundle eventually sold around 30,000 copies worldwide; hardly major-league, but as Euros Childs commented at the time: "Sales have never been that important for us." Mercury Records were less philosophical, dropping the band abruptly after the release of their next album, *Gorky 5*. They later signed to Mantra, and remain a *cause célèbre* for many fans.

Record label:
Fontana
Produced
by Gorwel Owen and Gorky's Zygotic Mynci.
Recorded
at Stlwdio Ofn, Llanfaelog, Wales; autumn 1996.
Released:
April 1997
Chart peaks:
46 (UK) None (US)
Personnel:
Euros Childs (v, k, p); Megan Childs (vn, bv, k); Richard James (b, g, k); John Lawrence (g, k, b, recorder,v, p); Euros Rowlands (d, pc); Gorwel Owen (p, k, e); Pete O'Connor (ae)
Track listing:
Diamond Dew (S); The Barafundle Bumbler; Starmoonsun; Patio Song (S); Better Rooms; Heywood Lane; Pen Gwag Glas; Bola Bola; Cursed, Coined And Crucified; Sometimes The Father Is The Sun; Meirion Wyllt; The Wizard And The Lizard; Miniature Kingdoms; Dark Night; Hwyl Fawr I Pawb; Wordless Song
Running time:
47.57
Current CD:
534 769 2
Further listening:
Bwyd Time (1995); Gorky 5 (1998); Spanish Dance Troupe (1999)
Further reading:
MOJO 58; www.geocities.com/SunsetStrip/Mezzanine/6707 www.gorkys.com (official site)
Like this?
Try . . . p.601

Fountains Of Wayne

Fountains Of Wayne

Sharp songwriting and exuberant production from a band who took their name from a garden shop.

"I always like first albums that have a definite, concise, clear sound to them," Adam Schlesinger says. "I think it's a good way for a band to be introduced."

In 1995, Schlesinger's musical cohort Chris Collingwood had thrown down the gauntlet for what the Fountains Of Wayne were about by writing "three stupid songs" in one afternoon.

"I thought they were great," Schlesinger recalls, "and it was inspiring that they were silly songs that were actually good. We immediately spent a week writing, sitting in this bar in New York and just making up titles to see if we could turn them into songs. We didn't think too much about making each song some kind of masterpiece, but rather taking the kind of craft that we had developed and having fun with it."

Fountains Of Wayne wasn't the duo's first attempt at pop glory. Schlesinger was part of the band Ivy and had written the title song for Tom Hanks' celebration of '60s pop life, That Thing You Do. Collingwood had been in and out of bands too and claims that, whenever he got a chance, he had a tendency to write country songs about his cat.

"But it was almost like, suddenly, after having taken songwriting seriously for a long time, we just had this licence to toss stuff off and see what happened," says Schlesinger.

"A big tendency used to be to overwork things and make it a little too busy," Collingwood adds. "But we wrote this quickly and kept it simple and spare."

Within a week, Leave The Biker, Sick Day, Radiation Vibe (a UK hit single) and other well-cut gems spilled from their pens. The duo then spent another seven days in the studio. "The plan was, let's get a Marshall," Schlesinger told Q in 1997. "So we rented this Marshall amplifier and the songs we recorded were just a kind of way to try out this amp. Afterwards, we liked the amp so much we bought it off the rental company. And we tried to make the production as unobtrusive as possible. There's not a lot of overdubbing. The background vocals are it, for the most part."

Schlesinger and Collingwood's basic blueprint was irresistible, the songs being witty without drawing attention to their smarts. Each functioned as a concise vignette of city life, making the album as rich as a book of short stories. Typical of the drooling critical response was Dave DiMartino's MOJO rave: "Almost better than anything, ever."

The follow-up *Utopia Parkway* was just as good, some say better, but neither album caught the wider public's favour and the Fountains were dropped by Atlantic in 2000.

Record label:
Atlantic
Produced
by Adam Schlesinger.
Recorded
at The Place, New York; January and April 1996.
Released:
May 1997
Chart peaks:
(UK) 67; (US) None
Personnel:
Chris Collingwood (v, g, k); Adam Schlesinger (d, g, k, v); Danny Weinkauf (b); Dominique Durand (v); Gary Maurer (e)
Track listing:
Radiation Vibe (S); Sink To The Bottom (S); Joe Rey; She's Got A Problem; Survival Car (S); Barbara H (S); Sick Day; I've Got A Flair; Leave The Biker; You Curse At Girls; Please Don't Rock Me Tonight; Everything's Ruined
Running time:
36.20
Current CD:
92725-2
Further listening:
Utopia Parkway (1999) more songs of the same quality, more slickly recorded.
Further reading:
MOJO 42; www.fountainsofwayne.com
Like this?
Try . . . p.583

Jerry Garcia Band

How Sweet It Is...

Jerry Garcia resoundingly demonstrates that there's life after the Dead.

He never quite admitted it in so many words, but Jerry Garcia hinted on many occasions that by 1990 a lot of the fun had gone out of working with The Grateful Dead. The band was too successful, was attracting the wrong audience and had become a monstrous, unwieldy, voracious corporation. As he conceded to Rolling Stone: "We've been running on inertia for quite a long time. And that's always dangling in front of me, the thing of, Shit, if I was on my own I could . . ."

The thought was never quite fully articulated, but any chance he got, Garcia worked with his own band, enjoying playing civilised venues like San Francisco's Warfield Theatre, where these performances were recorded. The Garcia Band admittedly lack the exhilarating abandon of the Dead at their peak, but one can certainly say that on the blues, Dylan and Garcia compositions that comprise this album, they sound immeasurably funkier, more soulful and tighter. Much credit for this must go to the backing singers, Gloria Jones (formerly Marc Bolan's other half) and Jackie LaBranch, and to full-throttle organist Melvin Seals. Listen to That's What Love Will Make You Do, for example, where Seals solos dramatically – and is immediately followed by Garcia responding to the challenge, launching into a fiery solo while the band rock like the clappers.

The album features two Dylan songs. "I don't feel I'm exactly the most romantic person in the world, so I can only do so many love songs without feeling like an idiot," reflected Garcia. "But Dylan has written songs that touch into places people have never sung about before, and I sing his songs because they speak to me emotionally." Indeed, Garcia's delivery of Tears Of Rage is intensely moving, his guitar wonderfully expressive. Says co-producer Steve Parrish: "This band came out of Jerry's love of music. A love so profound even The Grateful Dead couldn't contain it all."

Record label:
Grateful Dead Records
Produced
by John Cutler and Steve Parish.
Recorded
at Warfield Theatre, San Francisco; 1990.
Released:
May 1997
Chart peaks:
None (UK) None (US)
Personnel:
Jerry Garcia (g, v); Melvin Seals (k); John Kahn (b); David Kemper (d); Gloria Jones, Jackie LaBranch (bv), John Cutler (e)
Track listing:
How Sweet It Is (To Be Loved By You); Tough Mama; That's What Love Will Make You Do; Someday Baby; Cats Under The Stars; Tears Of Rage; Think; Gomorrah; Tore Up Over You; Like A Road
Running time:
77.22
Current CD:
ARI14051
Further listening:
the 2-CD set The Jerry Garcia Band (1991) has more material from the same shows.
Further reading:
Dark Star: An Oral Biography Of Jerry Garcia (Robert Greenfield, 1996)
Like this?
Try . . . p.342

Ron Sexsmith

Other Songs

The shy Canadian songsmith makes one for the ages.

Thank Elvis Costello. It was his constant trumpeting to the press in 1995 that rescued Ron Sexsmith's eponymous debut from bargain bin obscurity. Costello told *MOJO*, "It's a modest and elegant gem. I've been playing it all year and you could all be listening to it for another twenty."

Yet, despite the blessing of the bespectacled one and most music mags, Sexsmith still had to fight to make a second record. His choice of producer was the initial problem. "Mitchell Froom was the last person that the label wanted to do it," Sexsmith says. "They didn't think he knew how to make a commercial album. They were throwing all these names at me for producers, like the guy who did Hootie & The Blowfish. So I disappointed them when I said, 'I really want to do it with Mitchell again, because we felt like we were onto something on my first album and we had a lot more that we wanted to do.'"

Froom and Sexsmith spent a few weeks huddled in pre-production – arranging songs and listening to records for inspiration. "One we listened to was *Pet Sounds*," Sexsmith recalls. "It was a new album for me, not something I grew up with. I was really relieved to find it was as great as everyone had said it was. I gave a copy to Mitchell, who hadn't heard it since he was a kid. One thing we both really liked was how the songs didn't always have a beat behind them, but they were driven along by percussion. We took some ideas from that."

Recording began in November 1996 at the Magic Shop in Greenwich Village. The crisp, clear beauty of autumn in New York infused itself into the sessions, giving the tracks a romantic glow. Backed by an ace band, including Jerry Marotta on drums and Brad Jones on bass, Sexsmith breezed through live takes on his exquisite songs – Thinking Out Loud, Strawberry Blonde and the haunting Child Star (Sexsmith: "I was thinking of Dana Plato and Michael Jackson - all those kids that get messed up by early fame").

The result of what Sexsmith calls "upbeat, pleasant" sessions was a near perfect second album. While it didn't set the charts on fire, it has remained the artist's definitive statement. "There was something a bit out of step or retro about some of the stuff," Sexsmith reckons. "But the last thing we wanted to do was make a retro album. At the time I was 32, and that's where I come from - The Kinks and Harry Nilsson and all that melodic stuff. When this record came out, that wasn't really what was happening. But I like to think that we made a record that won't sound embarrassing when people listen to it ten or fifteen years from now."

BDM

Record label:
Interscope
Produced
by Mitchell Froom and Tchad Blake
Recorded
at Magic Shop, NYC; November-December 1996
Released:
June 1997
Chart peaks:
None (UK) None (US)
Personnel:
Ron Sexsmith (v, g); Mitchell Froom (k); Brad Jones (b); Don Kerr (d, v); Jerry Marotta (d, p); Larry Campbell (ps); Sheryl Crow (accordion); Dave Douglas (t); Greg Cohen (b); Chris Speed (clarinet, s); Bob Stuart (tuba); Kenny Wollesen (marimba, vibraphone); Josh Roseman (tb); Tchad Blake (e)
Track listing:
Thinking Out Loud; Strawberry Blonde; Average Joe; Thinly Veiled Disguise; Nothing Good; Pretty Little Cemetery It Never Fails; Clown in Broad Daylight; At Different Times; Child Star; Honest Mistake; So Young; While You Were Waiting; April After All
Running time:
39:51
Current CD:
Int 3P-6156
Further listening:
Cobblestone Runway (2002)
Further reading:
www.ronsexsmith.com
Like this?
Try . . . p.698

Radiohead

OK Computer

Oxford band cut unpredictable third album only to find it voted Greatest Album Ever Made.

"*The Bends* was a huge confidence boost," says Thom Yorke, "but on *OK Computer* we were trying to deal with the fact that [this time] everyone was interested in what we came up with."

The Bends had almost pulled them apart, so a less gruelling working method was sought. "We were nostalgic for the time when Jonny and I used to do 4-track stuff," says Thom, "do it when we felt like it, go round his house, write a song, tape it and fuck off home. That's what we were trying to do here." Keen to avoid being trapped in a studio, they asked Nigel Godrich to assemble, and run, a mobile recording set-up they could take wherever they fancied. After a fertile writing spell, new songs were road-tested before recording began in earnest, notably on a 13-date tour opening for Alanis Morissette. Hearing the material in these surroundings, American label Capitol thought they'd be getting a U2-scale best-seller stuffed with arena-pleasers. But as recording progressed, a totally different record took shape.

Work had begun at The Fruit Farm, the band's Oxfordshire rehearsal space, then moved to a mansion house in Bath. "We made it our own and developed this real sense of freedom," says Godrich. "We could do anything . . . play croquet in the middle of the night, if we wanted to, whatever."

"We'd been listening to Ennio Morricone and Can and lots of stuff where they're abusing the recording process. We wanted to try that," recalls Thom. "No Surprises was the first thing we recorded. We'd bought all this gear, put it together and it was literally the first time everything was plugged in: pressed the button, the red light comes on and that was No Surprises. The take on the album is exactly how we played it, bar a few small fixings. But we did *six* different versions of it afterwards – 'That bassline's not quite right' and this, that and the other – being anal. We went back to the first take in the end, because we'd discovered during recording that it's about catching the moment and fuck whether there's mistakes or not."

One by one, the putative hits that Capitol's executives had earmarked fell by the wayside. Many of the songs that remained seem to be about witnessing other peoples lives; there's a removed, refracted mood, both lyrically and sonically, with Yorke's voice at its most exploratory and explosive.

If the record company was, at first, bemused, *OK Computer* was ecstatically received by the public, topping many year-end polls in the press, and soon being hailed the Best Album Ever Made in at least one readers' vote. The band-least-likely-to in 1992 were, by the end of the century, regarded by many as the finest in the world.

Record label:
Parlophone
Produced
by Nigel Godrich with Radiohead.
Recorded
on The Canned Applause Mobile stationed at The Fruit Farm, Abingdon; Jane Seymour's House, Bath; late 1996–early 1997.
Released:
June 16, 1997
Chart peaks:
1 (UK) 21 (US)
Personnel:
Thom Yorke (g, v, k); Jonny Greenwood (g, k); Colin Greenwood (b); Ed O'Brien (g, bv); Phil Selway (d, p)
Track listing:
Airbag; Paranoid Android (s); Subterranean Homesick Alien; Exit Music (For A Film); Let Down; Karma Police (s); Fitter, Happier; Electioneering; Climbing Up The Walls; No Surprises (s); Lucky; The Tourist
Running time:
53.27
Current CD:
CDNODATA02
Further listening:
The Bends (1994)
Further reading:
MOJO 46; Exit Music: The Radiohead Story (Mac Randall, 2000); www.radiohead.com
Like this?
Try . . . p.587

The Buena Vista Social Club

The Buena Vista Social Club

Cuba's pre-revolutionary musicians strike gold in the last-chance saloon.

"The best thing I was ever involved in," said Ry Cooder after completing work on what was always likely to be a fun project. If he had known more than two million record-buyers would agree he might have been less reserved. Three years later he was able to reflect that: "Timing and luck are responsible for 80 per cent of Buena Vista's success." As for the luck, this was an album that was not meant to be recorded. Nick Gold, the head of World Circuit, had an idea for two albums – one big-band, one country-style – using Cuban and African musicians, and asked Juan de Marcos González, the leader of the band Sierra Maestra, to put together an all-star outfit. Gold then invited Ry Cooder along to play guitar and produce. By the time the American guitarist arrived in Havana, one album (*A Toda Cuba Le Gusta*) was almost finished, but the Africans were ensnared in visa hell and the tape recorder had failed. Used to such snafus, the Cubans sat around the Egrem studios – built by RCA in the '50s – discussing favourite old songs. With Cooder and Gold listening in, a new plan quickly took shape – an album of classic *son* (the precursor to salsa, but with the emphasis on the melodies and lyrics rather than rhythms), played by musicians who were around in the '30s.

"There were only about a dozen people left who could have played on *Buena Vista*," acknowledged Cooder, "and when these guys go, that's it." Among the band at the sessions were the guitarist and songwriter Compay Segundo, 87; Rubén González, a 77-year-old arthritic pianist; and Ibrahim Ferrer, a retired singer who now preferred to shine shoes for a living and had to be coaxed into the studio with $50. As much as the music, it was the way their stories captured the imagination that catapulted Buena Vista into the big league – apart from the record sales, there were international tours (from Carnegie Hall to the Royal Albert Hall), a moving Wim Wenders documentary and several spin-off solo careers. And to think it was largely thanks to a knackered tape deck.

Record label:
World Circuit
Produced
by Ry Cooder.
Recorded
at Egrem Studios, Havana; March 1996.
Released:
June 1997
Chart peaks:
48 (UK) 50 (US)
Personnel:
Ibrahim Ferrer (v); Ry Cooder (g); Eliades Ochoa (v, g); Compay Segundo (v, g); Orlando "Cachaito" López (b); Rubén González (p); Omara Portuondo (v); Jerry Boys (e)
Track listing:
Chan Chan; De Camino A La Vereda; El Cuarto De Tula; Pueblo Nuevo; Dos Gardenias; ¿Y Tú Qué Has Hecho?; Veinte Años; El Carretero; Candela; Amor De Loca Juventud; Orgullecida; Murmullo; Buena Vista Social Club; La Bayamesa
Running time:
60.08
Current CD:
WCD 050
Further listening:
Buena Vista Social Club Presents Ibrahim Ferrer (1999); Introducing Rubén González (1997); A Toda Cuba Le Gusta (The Afro-Cuban All Stars, 1997); Buena Vista Social Club Presents Omara Portuondo (2000)
Further reading:
MOJO 42, 67; Buena Vista Social Club (Wim Wenders and Donata Wenders, 2000). See also Wenders' extraordinary documentary, Buena Vista Social Club.
Like this?
Try . . . p.426

Spiritualized

Ladies And Gentlemen We Are Floating In Space

Two years in the making, their most exploratory and most commercially successful album.

"It has to be a lot larger than life. It has to deal with extremities, it can't deal with mediocrity. It's not about day-to-day stuff – it's the big picture," was Jason Pierce's explanation of the criteria applied to the music of *Ladies And Gentlemen.*

A yearning, a striving for something – even in the states of enervation Pierce sketched out in his lyrics – was something that had always run through Spirtualized's music.

It had begun with the gorgeous rock chamber music of *Lazer Guided Melodies* in 1991, a sound that was expanded four years later on the less impressive *Pure Phase.* But with *Ladies And Gentlemen* it went right off the scale: in the number of personnel involved, the number of studios used and the length of songs (Cop Shoot Cop, featuring Dr John, clocked in at 17 minutes), even up to the venues where Spiritualized promoted the album.

Pierce had regularly alluded to getting high, but the group's space-rock/soul revue was about to be taken to the world's tallest structure, the CN tower in Toronto for The Highest Show On Earth.

The music was magnificent – a stunning amalgam of rock-'n'roll, gospel, psychedelia, soul, coruscating free-jazz white-outs and stately strings. Pierce's mercurial touch ensured the music always sounds poised, despite the vast instrumental forces used. His long-standing "problem with rhythm" (in respect of drum-driven music) was resolved on songs like I Think I'm In Love, where the instruments play in gradually mutating rhythmic patterns, like a rock version of systems music.

The lyrics were not, Pierce claims, about his relationship break-up with keyboard player Kate Radley, but they sound more personal and less banal than in the past. And even at their most desolate they carry a feeling of positivity.

Ladies And Gentleman is a prime example of a wildly ambitious project that actually came off, Even the packaging of the CD – in a foil blister pack like an enormous pill, complete with dosage instructions – was stunning. Reports had been leaking out that the album was something special, and reviews from an astonished press were soon making "album of the decade" claims on its behalf. Pierce has said that he "didn't want *Ladies And Gentlemen* to adhere to a blueprint, not even a Spiritualized blueprint."

He got his wish.

Record label:
Dedicated
Produced
by J Spaceman.
Recorded
at Moles Studio, Bath; The Church, Rooster Studios and The Strongroom Studios, London; House Of Blues, Memphis; The Hit Factory, New York; A&M Studios, Los Angeles; 1995–1997.
Released:
June 1997
Chart peaks:
4 (UK) None (US)
Personnel:
J Spaceman [Jason Pierce] (v, g, p, hammer dulcimer, autoharp); Kate Radley (k, v); Sean Cook (b, hm); Damon Reece (d, pc); John Coxon (g, melodica JD800), Dr John (p, v); Alexander Balanescu, Clare Connors, Ed Coxon (vn) and Kathy Burgess (va); Sophie Harris (c); Angel Corpus Christi (acc); Andy Davis (k); Simon Clark (flute, bs); Tim Sanders, Terry Edwards (ts); Roddie Lorimer (t, flugelhorn); Neil Sidwell (tb); Tim Jones (french horn); BJ Cole (ps); The London Community Gospel Choir (v); D Allison, M Bjerke, T Curwen, D Nash (e)
Track listing:
Ladies And Gentlemen; Come Together; I Think I'm In Love (S); All Of My Thoughts; Stay With Me; Electricity (S); Home Of The Brave; The Individual; Broken Heart; No God Only Religion; Cool Waves; Cop Shoot Cop
Running time:
70.02
Current CD:
DEDCD 034A
Further reading:
MOJO 51
Like this?
Try . . . p.637

Cornershop

When I Was Born For The 7th Time

Shambling, eternally underachieving, Anglo-Indian indie also-rans surprise everyone.

A major British Asian music breakthrough had been on the cards for years. But nobody could have anticipated the extent of the eclecticism that Tjinder Singh would bring to the party: The Beatles' Norwegian Wood sung in Punjabi, a smash pop hit (Brimful Of Asha, a Number 1 on the back of Norman Cook's less than subtle remix) in homage to Indian actress Asha Bhosle, a bizarre Asian country skit Good To Be On The Road Back Home. The album quietly ridiculed a culture hang-up about roots, authenticity and political correctness.

"It's something for everyone," says Singh. "Country to brunch with hip hop, cricket on the lawn with Punjabi folk music and a square dance before dinner with the most righteous of beats." He even got Allen Ginsberg to weigh in with a vocal. Spin called Singh a "folk singer in a global village", though pundits struggled to pigeonhole a band that held credibility in dance and indie clubs, dabbled in hip hop, weren't afraid of politics and still managed to wind up on the radio.

It wasn't always this way. Cornershop began as a defiantly inept quartet (including Tjinder's brother Avtar) loosely associated with the Riot Grrl movement – who gained notoriety by burning photos of Morrissey during their first interview for the music press (in protest at the "equivocal" stance of songs such as Bengali In Platforms, Asian Rut and National Front Disco), and releasing their debut single on "curry-coloured" vinyl. Their early releases were intriguing rather than actually listenable, valuing polemic and mayhem over craft. Tjinder and Ben began to explore dance music, releasing tracks under the pseudonym Clinton (finally getting around to an album of their own, *Disco And The Halfway To Malcontent* in 1999). The mesmeric single 9am Jullandar Sheer, included on Cornershop's second album, signalled a huge leap forward; it also attracted the attention of David Byrne, who signed them to his Luaka Bop label in the States in 1995. The original quartet split soon afterwards, remaining members Tjinder and Ben opting to pursue the methods they'd learned on the Clinton releases. It's this mix of politics, humour, beats and chaos that makes *When I Was Born For The 7th Time* so rich and appealing.

Record label:
Wiiija
Produced
by Tjinder Singh and The Automator.
Recorded
at West Orange Studios, Preston; Sun Plantation, San Francisco; Eastcote Studios, London; late 1996–early 1997.
Released:
September 8, 1997
Chart peaks:
17 (UK) None (US)
Personnel:
Tjinder Singh (v, g, scratching); Ben Ayres (g, k, tamboura); Allen Ginsberg (speech); Paula Frazer (v); Anthony Saffery (harmonium, k, sitar); Nick Simms (d); Justin Warfield (rap); Robert Buller (strings); E Johnson (strings); Alan Gregson, Philip Bagenal (e)
Track listing:
Sleep On The Left Side (S); Brimful Of Asha (S); Butter The Soul; Chocolat; We're In Yr Corner; Funky Days Are Back Again; What Is Happening?; When The Light Appears Boy; Coming Up; Good Shit; Good To Be On The Road Back Home; It's Indian Tobacco My Friend; Candyman; State Troopers (Part 1); Norwegian Wood
Running time:
54.18
Current CD:
WIJCD1065
Further listening:
Woman's Gotta Have It (1995)
Further reading:
www.cornershop.com
Like this?
Try . . . p.551

Bob Dylan

Time Out Of Mind

Dylan's most compelling work in years found him wracked with romantic distress.

During his seven-year-long songwriting hiatus since 1990's disappointing *Under The Red Sky*, Dylan had re-immersed himself again in the traditional musics that first inspired him to pick up an acoustic guitar, returning to its dark portents, timeless verities and poetic language for a couple of albums of folk and blues covers, *Good As I Been To You* and *World Gone Wrong*.

"Those old songs," he acknowledged, "are my lexicon and my prayer-book." But widespread rumours of writer's block were finally dashed by the appearance of *Time Out Of Mind*, his finest work since 1975's *Blood On The Tracks*.

With Daniel Lanois again installed as producer, and employing a backing band whose members knew how to play the blues without polishing away its abrasive qualities, the album featured songs that had been written the previous winter, whilst Dylan was snowed-in at his Minnesota ranch.

"Environment affects me a great deal," he told the New York Times. "A lot of the songs were written after the sun went down . . . this one phrase was going through my head: 'Work while the day lasts, because the night of death cometh when no man can work' – it was at the forefront of my mind for a long period of time."

Accordingly, the overall tone of the album is unremittingly bleak, its songs concerned with the anger and desolation of lost love, the spectre of mortality cast across all our lives, and, in the closing 17-minute opus Highlands, the point of saying anything at all. Comparing the album to his and Lanois' previous work, the acclaimed *Oh Mercy*, Dylan said, ". . . these songs, I felt, were more all-encompassing. They were more filled with the dread realities of life."

Occasionally, as on Dirt Road Blues, these dread realities are softened slightly by a jaunty, laidback presentation that echoes JJ Cale's blues shuffles; elsewhere, the burring undertow of organ and Dylan's keening rasp brought a chill immediacy to dark pieces like Cold Irons Bound and the single Love Sick.

"I can't help those feelings," he admitted. "I'm not going to try to make a fake Pollyanna worldview. Why would I even want to? I'm not going to deny them just because they might be a little dismal."

The unflinchingly dismal portents proved a little close to home shortly after the sessions, when Dylan narrowly survived a potentially fatal heart ailment. Things improved dramatically with the release of *Time Out Of Mind*, which was acclaimed as one of his finest recordings, going on to secure Dylan his first ever Album Of The Year Grammy award.

Record label:
Columbia
Produced
by Daniel Lanois.
Recorded
at Criteria Recording Studios, Miami; 1997.
Released:
September 1997
Chart peaks:
10 (UK) 10 (US)
Personnel:
Bob Dylan (v, g, k, hm); Daniel Lanois (g, mando-gtr); Bucky Baxter (g, p); Duke Robillard (g); Robert Britt (g); Cindy Cashdollar (sg); Augie Meyers (k); Jim Dickinson (k); Tony Garnier (b); Winston Watson (d); Jim Keltner (d); David Kemper (d); Brian Blade (d); Tony Mangurian (pc); Mark Howard (e)
Track listing:
Love Sick (S); Dirt Road Blues; Standing In The Doorway; Million Miles; Tryin' To Get To Heaven; 'Til I Fell In Love With You; Not Dark Yet; Cold Irons Bound (S); Make You Feel My Love; Can't Wait; Highlands.
Running time:
72.52
Current CD:
486936 2
Further listening:
Sonically, Dylan's earlier Daniel Lanois-produced album Oh Mercy (1989) is the closest to Time Out Of Mind, and also shares something of its world-weary mien.
Further reading:
MOJO 51; 1997 interview in the New York Times.
Like this?
Try . . . p.345

Kelly Joe Phelps

Roll Away The Stone

A solo reinvigoration of the country blues tradition, as elemental as music by original masters such as Skip James.

Slide guitar virtuoso Kelly Joe Phelps' stark and dark second album is clearly rooted in country blues, yet performed with such striking originality that he's in a category of his own. One thing that makes Phelps' meticulously detailed and exquisite music so unusual is his unconventional technique of playing with the guitar flat upon his lap. "The fact I'm not holding the guitar up, nor am I fretting any chords, frees the instrument up – it's almost like playing a piano," he explains. "Also I stopped using finger picks, so I can pick the notes with different parts of the finger – deeper in the finger or on the tip or sides – which gives me more freedom in affecting the tone."

Phelps recorded most of the album in his living room. "I hung blankets across windows and mattresses against the door. Being an improviser – I didn't work out any guitar parts before I recorded them – demanded many sessions with many different mindsets and mood swings and various levels of intoxicants, and I recorded each song as many times as I could stand, trying to capture the version with the correct spirit. The primary work was in putting the emotional content on tape."

Although acclaimed mostly for his playing, Phelps' singing is just as impressive. "I try to sing as if the voice was a seventh string on the guitar – or sometimes it's like imagining a saxophone or a harmonica." The anguished version of See That My Grave Is Kept Clean is particularly acute, but throughout Phelps performs with an engrossing intensity, sounding like someone who's no stranger to the darker side of the human condition. The album's most glorious moment is the spiritual When The Roll Is Called Up Yonder, a heartrendingly beautiful song of unshakeable faith in salvation, sung in a voice that suggests brave resilience in the face of suffering. A quietly dignified expression of hope, it is profoundly moving.

Record label:
Rykodisc
Produced
by Kelly Joe Phelps.
Recorded
Nine tracks "in the living room of my apartment" in Vancouver, Washington, the rest "in an empty house in North-east Portland". Sessions spanned four months over the winter of 1996.
Released:
September 1997
Chart peaks:
None (UK) None (US)
Personnel:
Kelly Joe Phelps (g, v); Craig Carothers (m); Dave Schiffman (e)
Track listing:
Roll Away The Stone; Sail The Jordan; When The Roll Is Called Up Yonder; Hosanna; Without The Light; Footprints; Go There; See That My Grave Is Kept Clean; Cypress Grove; That's Alright; Doxology
Running time:
58.55
Current CD:
RCD-10393
Further listening:
Shine Eyed Mister Zen (1999), the follow-up to Roll Away The Stone, is also astonishingly powerful, with Phelps travelling still further from his country-blues roots.
Further reading:
www.kellyjoephelps.com
Like this?
Try . . . p.609

The Verve
Urban Hymns

Three albums in and – despite internal turmoil – The Verve find the perfect fusion of craft and feel.

In early 1996, freshly divorced from his band, Richard Ashcroft was quietly living the life of a newlywed in Bath, and writing songs at a prolific pace. Producer John Leckie was working nearby, at Real World Studios, when he got a call to drop by and hear the work: "It was a very inspiring time, this was obviously something special."

Ashcroft gathered former Verve-mates Jones and Salisbury and old Wigan friend Simon Tong (who played keyboard-mediated string parts), and worked on over 30 songs.

The sessions took place in a week at Ridge Farm, Surrey before they concluded at the Townhouse studio in Shepherd's Bush. "It was very loose," says Leckie, "Rather than finish anything off, Richard would want to do something new. I'd say, 'Let's finish three tracks,' but he would write more. What the songs needed was another musician – a Keith Richards, a George Harrison."

Approaches to guitarists Bernard Butler (ex-Suede) and John Squire (ex-Stone Roses), didn't work out. Aware that he needed to turn a corner, Ashcroft and the band began working with Youth at Olympic Studios. "I veered him away from influences like the Roses towards a more universal, classic approach," he says. The routine was almost office-like: a 10am start, and the promise of returning home while it was still light. Here, the final versions of the *Urban Hymns* songs took shape, notably Bitter Sweet Symphony. It had been honed by Leckie, who'd heard Ashcroft singing along to Andrew Loog Oldham's version of The Last Time, and encouraged him to work with the results. Ashcroft later considered dumping the track, but Youth urged him not to. It wasn't until early 1997 that the sessions neared the end. Aware that he was still missing that vital musical foil, Ashcroft put 1995's ructions behind him and telephoned former Verve guitarist Nick McCabe.

McCabe's re-entry allowed The Verve to re-form and finally glean their commercial just deserts. But it also placed them in dire danger of yet another split. It finally came in the summer of 1998 – long after *Urban Hymns* had sold seven million copies – and this time engulfed the whole band. When the dust had cleared, only Pete "Sobbo" Salisbury was left at Ashcroft's side.

Perhaps the most fascinating chunk of debris from The Verve's tempestuous years are the Leckie tapes for *Urban Hymns*, which contain different versions of released songs and a clutch of compositions – Misty Morning June, Lord I've Been Trying, Little Bit Of Love, Fly To The Sun, at least half a dozen others – that may never enter the public domain.

"They're all unheard, and they're great stuff," says Leckie. "They stand up as finished recordings." Roll on the box set.

Record label:
Hut
Produced
by Chris Potter, Youth and The Verve.
Recorded
at Olympic Studios, Barnes; October–December 1996; Metropolis Studios, Chiswick; January–August 1997.
Released:
September 1997
Chart peaks:
1 (UK) 63 (US)
Personnel:
Richard Ashcroft (v, g); Nick McCabe (g); Simon Tong (g, k); Simon Jones (b); Peter Salisbury (d)
Track listing:
Bitter Sweet Symphony (S); Sonnet (S); The Rolling People; The Drugs Don't Work (S); Catching The Butterfly; Neon Wilderness; Space And Time; Weeping Willow; Lucky Man (S); One Day; This Time; Velvet Morning; Come On; Deep Freeze (hidden track)
Running time:
76.00
Current CD:
CDHUT45
Further listening:
A Northern Soul (1995)
Further reading:
The Verve: Crazed Highs And Horrible Lows (Martin Clarke, 1998)
Like this?
Try . . . p.84

Alabama 3

Exile On Coldharbour Lane

Maybe you had to be there …

With hindsight, perhaps it wasn't the easiest sell: a mass of south London-based left-wingers adopting appalling American accents, claiming they'd met in rehab and were out to save the soul of Country music. Alabama 3's image has overshadowed their art, which is a crying shame: because, as this debut shows, the music was magnificent.

The other problem was that to understand Alabama 3 you had to understand Brixton. The humming heart of south London, the area was where Rastas, rappers and Rizla-rollers rubbed shoulders with punks, police and politicos, while radical agendas were espoused over pints in pubs that hadn't been decorated since the '60s. Alabama 3's music was inspired as much by the jukeboxes in Brixton's Irish boozers as it was by the sounds pumping out of cars slouching down the district's clogged thoroughfares.

If you lived in Brixton in 1997, the idea of a band melding harmonicas to Happy Mondays-style low-slung techno and pushing a working class anti-drugs message in a country & western style seemed so obvious it was a wonder nobody else had done it sooner. They were their heirs of the area's musical miscegenators, from Mick Jones of The Clash and Big Audio Dynamite, through punk/rap punsters Carter USM and the Stereo MC's, and their record ought to have forced followers to similarly challenge generic musical conventions.

The songs were honed in gigs across the SW2 and SW9 postal districts that made local heroes out of Jake "Rev. Dr D. Wayne Love" Black and Rob "Larry Love" Spragg. If you were there, every track here will be accompanied by its own personal mental slide show. Sadly, A3's music was so site-specific it seemed that anyone who *didn't* live in Brixton was unable to get their head around it.

Until, that is, TV producer David Chase heard Woke Up This Morning while driving home in his car in New Jersey, and realised he'd just found the perfect theme tune for the series he was working on about a neurotic Mafia boss and his family. Inspired by the true-life story of a woman who shot her abusive husband, Woke Up … contains all the elements that make this album such a treat – it feels real, true and vital, but taps into several traditions simultaneously in a way that makes it sound current yet timeless. The band have made two albums since, but will struggle to make a more important or visionary record than this one.

Record label:
Elemental
Produced
by Matthew (Boss Hogg) Vaughan & The Ministers At Work
Recorded
at The Dairy, Brixton, London: The Steamrooms, London
Released:
1997
Chart peaks:
Personnel:
L Love (v): The Very reverend Dr. D Wayne Love (v): The Mountain Of Love (harmonica, jaws harp, v): Sir Real "Congaman" Love L.S.D., O.P.T. (perc, acc gtr): Mississippi Guitar Love (gtr): L. B. Dope (drums), Lady Love, Little Eye Tie (D. Wayne's Ladies): The Street Angels [Debra, Milton, Ray, Charita] (v): T Bowden (banjo): C McGoldrick (dbl bass): B.J. Cole (pedal steel gtr): DJ Manuel Dex & Shifta (turntables): J Mehrin (accordion): J Smith (acc gtr): E Thompson (v): B. Atwell & T Maxim (v)
Track listing Converted:
Speed Of The Sound Of Loneliness: Woke Up This Morning: U Don't Dans 2 Tekno: Bourgeoisie Blues: Ain't Goin' To Goa: Mao Tse Tung Said: Hypo Full Of Love (The 12 Step Plan): The Old Purple Tin (9% Of Pure Heaven): The Night We Nearly Got Busted: Sister Rosetta: Peace In The Valley
Running time:
62 mins 40 secs
Current CD:
ELM-40 CD
Further listening:
La Peste
Further reading:
www.alabama3.co.uk
Like this?
Try . . . p.597

Rakim

The 18th Letter / The Book Of Life

A remarkable comeback album and hits package from the greatest emcee of all time.

Ask any long-term hip hop fan or artist to name the best rapper of all time, and you'll quickly find a consensus. Wyndarch, Long Island, native William "Rakim" Griffin is the emcees' emcee.

From his emergence as a teenager alongside DJ Eric Barrier, through a stuttering career of four albums spread over seven years before their 1993 split, he produced a volume of work unparalleled in the hip hop canon.

His solo debut should have arrived in '95, but masters were leaked from the studio and bootlegged. The sessions were scrapped; Rakim started again, and The 18th Letter was the eventual result.

Interpreted by some as the work of a fallen great playing catch-up, The 18th Letter received a lukewarm response. It definitely made concessions to a hip hop mainstream, but there was no hip hop mainstream when Rakim had last recorded, so that was entirely understandable.

"People used to think that some of my tracks was a little too abstract, so this time I wanted to feed the world," he explained. "I wanted the beats to hit 'em right away, and I wanted the lyrical content to hit 'em right away. I wanted to make 'em understand. Immediately."

The title track – his favourite – is a breathtaking swoop through human history, Rakim metaphorically declaring that his art is something historical, cultural and religious that he's not so much creating as channelling. The DJ Premier-produced New York (Ya' Out There) captures the sound of the city better than any music since Gershwin's Rhapsody In Blue, and When I'm Flowin' is a masterclass in the art of lyricism. "When I'm flowin', theoretically speaking like a drummer," he rhymes, "I take you through the streets to the parks in the summer/Or illustrate a time or place you never been in/Make you focus on the future after seein' the beginning". The Mystery (Who Is God?) is the spellbinding centrepiece, three verses that find Rakim delving into the mystical symbolism of the 5% Nation Of Islam religion, rewriting the creation story from a hip hop perspective.

Unsure that enough of rap's new fans would be aware of his catalogue, Universal chose to package initial quantities of The 18th Letter with the 15-track Book Of Life. Culled from his four albums with Eric B, it's filled with gems of insightful, incisive, poetically driven hip hop, tracks that still yield revelations to the listener hundreds of plays later. Either CD would grace a catholic collection; the double is a must-buy.

AB

Record label:
Universal
Produced
by Father Shah, DJ Premier, DJ Clark Kent, Pete Rock, Nick Wiz, Naughty Shorts (The 18th Letter); Eric B & Rakim (The Book Of Life)
Recorded
at Track Factory Studios, NY
Released:
November 1997
Chart peaks:
72 (UK) 4 (US)
Personnel:
Rakim (v): Eric B (DJ on The Book Of Life)
Track listing:
The 18th Letter
The 18th Letter (Always And Forever): It's Been A Long Time: Remember That: The Saga Begins: Guess Who's Back: Stay A While: New York (Ya' Out There): Show Me Love: The Mystery (Who Iss God?): When I'm Flowin': It's Been A Long Time (Suave House Remix)
The Book Of Life
I Know You Got Soul: Follow The Leader: Eric B Is President: Microphone Fiend: I Ain't No Joke: Lyrics Of Fury: My Melody: Know The Ledge: Move The Crowd: Let The Rhythm Hit 'Em: Mahogany: In The Ghetto: Casualties Of War: The Punisher: Paid In Full
Running time:
Current CD:
UD2-53111
Further listening:
The Master (1999)
Like this?
Try . . . p.696

Stina Nordenstam

People Are Strange

Allusive, Swedish songstress finds herself laid bare in other people's songs.

Gil Scott-Heron in songs like Is That Jazz has teasingly nudged those who believe in the easy classification of music. Anyone who tries to categorise Stina Nordenstam will be similarly elbowed. On her journey beginning in 1991 with her debut album *Memories of a Colour* and followed two years later by *And She Closed her Eyes* she has attracted the flotsam of comparison and become the twisted, melancholic sister of Tori Amos, Bjork and PJ Harvey. On hearing her first album, critics fused her with Ricky Lee Jones. These are not directions to find Stina Nordenstam but arrows on a very large map.

The cover versions on *People Are Strange* lead on from her own compositions that evoke her introverted response and the not always pleasant experiences she feels she has had to endure. She does not want to be photographed, refuses to give concerts and is rarely interviewed. "I want to be invisible and private" she has stated and the blurred ever changing, self-photographed images on the sleeve of *People Are Strange* add to the enigmatic quality of the music itself. Here are the songs of Prince, Roy Orbison, Leonard Cohen and The Doors amongst others and they are not simply covered but vacuumed of recognisable traits and imbued with a fragile originality that seems personal despite her reticence to reveal a biographical narrative.

Perhaps this album has been easier to discuss and publicise than previous ones. When she is asked about the lyrics on And She Closed Her Eyes, the brittle but passionate voice can be heard. " I have a strong resentment of hanging myself out like that. But I think that's rather understandable. If you're a depressive person, you don't sit and laugh at jokes. Just like it feels right now, that I have to make up half lies about the lyrics."

Not so for the cover versions on *People Are Strange*, here she seems happy to describe the elliptical or direct influences on the interpretation of well known songs like Purple Rain. "One rainy morning an Arab came by playing his clarinet backwards and Ian[Caple, keyboardist] showed me another of those second-hand store microphones for me to try out and the rain turned to hail and we all became at the same time absent-minded and concentrated." This distractedly personal influence on time-honoured compositions enshadows the songs with a paradoxical yet illuminating glare.

TD

Record Label
EastWest
Produced
by Ian Caple and Stina Nordenstam
Recorded
at Sweet Silence Studios, Copenhagen, 1997
Released:
January 1998
Chart Peaks:
Personnel:
Stina Nordenstam (v,g,piano); Robin Key (g, b,); John Tonks (d, programming); Ian Caple (k, programming)
Track Listing:
Sailing, I Dream of Jeannie, Love Hurts, Bird on a Wire, Purple Rain, Swallow Strings, Like a Swallow, Reason to Believe, I came so Far for Beauty, Come to Me, People are Strange
Running Time:
36.45
Current CD:
3984 24506-2 EastWest
Further Listening:
Memories of a Colour (1996), And She Closed Here Eyes (1996), This is Stina Nordenstam (2002)
Further Reading:
www.stinaonline.com
Like this?
Try . . . p.812

Air

Moon Safari

Faux-naïf aural bubble-bath spearheading the late '90s French invasion of the British charts.

Each year in Britain one album becomes inescapable in the nation's clubs, boutiques and cafes and ever-present as background music on TV. In 1998 that album was *Moon Safari*, ubiquitous to such a degree that many of its initial fans soon become immune to its abundant charms. But time will come to judge it as a fascinating record that was seized upon with good reason: it captured exquisitely the mood of its time – pre-millennial retro-futurist nostalgia for a simpler tomorrow – using a perfectly judged synthesis of lounge music, progressive rock and disco (pop's most "modern" manifestations in their respective times) to represent a cool sexy sound.

Nicolas Godin and Jean-Benoît Dunckel were 15 years old when they first met in the music room at a school in Versailles for maverick children. Godin intended to be an architect, Dunckel a mathematician. After college, the two friends dodged French National Service and formed a band called Orange which went nowhere. Then, in 1996, they began working together in a little studio in Versailles and recorded an unremarkable dance groove called Modular Mix, which was picked up by Mo'Wax records. It attracted enough positive attention to spur them on in this mode, though they credit their meeting with local engineer Stéphane Briat – nicknamed Alf – as the genesis of the signature style they developed on this album. With Alf at the controls, they cut a string of quirky instrumental singles (subsequently collected as *Premiers Symptomes*); some of these melodies would be further refined for *Moon Safari*.

The duo consider themselves composers rather than pop stars. "We like playing," says Nicolas. "We get up in the morning and want to play music. But we spend most of our time looking for the right chords." Indeed, though the recording was fairly swift, a great deal of time, they claim, was spent on the writing. Tending to disagree on most things, they realised they were onto something good whenever they found common ground. They concurred on the melodic sophistication of Bacharach, some folksy colouring, a little disco and a touch of ELO. The use of classic electronic keyboards like the Wurlitzer electric piano, Vocoder and Mini-Moog, and the distinctive, dry '70s bass sound, all aided the comforting, retrospective feel, and allowed listeners a Proustian rush back to a dream past.

"Emotions guide us, it's very instinctive," remarks Dunckel. "We try for strong, pure composition."

"It's very shy music," adds Godin. "And it's optimistic, but it's optimism that you don't believe."

Record label:
Source
Produced
by Jean-Benoît Dunckel and Nicolas Godin.
Recorded
at Around The Golf, Versailles; Gang Studios, Paris and Abbey Road; London, 1997.
Released:
January 1998
Chart peaks:
6 (UK) 41 (US)
Personnel:
Jean-Benoît Dunckel (o, p, elec p, MS20 synthesizer, Solina string ensemble, miniMoog, mellotron); Nicolas Godin (b, g, ag, Moog, v, o, d, pc, ha) with Beth Hirsh (v); P. Woodcock (ag, tuba); Marlon (d), David Whittaker (oa), Stéphane Briat (e)
Track Listing:
La Femme D'Argent; Sexy Boy (S); All I Need (S); Kelly, Watch The Stars! (S); Talisman; Remember; You Make It Easy; Ce Matin La; New Star In The Sky (Chanson Pour Solal); Le Voyage De Penelope
Running time:
43.47
Current CD:
CDV2848
Further listening:
The sound takes shape on Premiers Symptomes (1997, reissued in 1999 with extra tracks). The film soundtrack The Virgin Suicides (2000) is more functional, but still beautiful in places.
Further reading:
www.fuzzie.freeserve.co.uk
Like this?
Try . . . p.584

Madonna

Ray Of Light

Commercial and cool, danceable, moving: her lucky 13th album made Madonna hip again.

"I'm trying to affect people in a quieter way," said Madonna of *Ray Of Light*'s release in 1998 and, in relative terms, she was. Until then her decade had been far from quiet: her conceptual art/postmodern coffee-table porn book Sex, and accompanying album *Erotica*, had received a noisy kicking from the world's media. The remorse-free follow-up, *Bedtime Stories* (accompanying look: ruffled, post-coital diva) had a lukewarm reception. Then came her most successful foray into the movies with the Rice/Lloyd Webber *Evita*, during which she finally resolved a media-driven mother fixation by becoming one herself. It is possibly this that prompted the spiritual rebirth of *Ray Of Light*. The opening lines, "I traded fame for love without a second thought" (from the poignant Drowned World/ Substitute For Love), say a lot about her state of mind.

Madonna's singles have always been remixed for a club airing but *Ray of Light* is her first album geared specifically to the dance-floor: "I think the whole record would sound great on drugs," she noted helpfully. Indeed, the psychedelic swirl of the title track or Sky Fits Heaven are as trancey as anything played on the beaches in Goa that year. Madonna had found the perfect producer in British dance veteran William Orbit. Orbit's career began in the band Torch Song but struck gold in 1990 with Bassomatic's lithe hit Fascinating Rhythm; he also had some success with his Guerilla ("progressive house") and *N*-Gram (largely ambient) labels. The electronic burble that characterises his work here (and elsewhere) were far-removed from his next job – Blur's *13*; conversely, the single he produced for All Saints (Pure Shores) seemed a concerted attempt to replicate the *Ray Of Light* sound.

Madonna's legendary drive was in no way affected by her new inner peace: "You can sleep when you're dead," she told Orbit during the recording. Early in the sessions, they worked on the vocal for Mer Girl, a whirling effects-drenched monologue in which Madonna recounts a family gathering in the Detroit suburbs, where she grew up. "She stepped out of the vocal booth and everyone was rooted to the spot," Orbit recalls. "It was just one of those moments, really spooky."

Ray of Light (the title track was an adaptation of a song by obscure '70s British duo Curtis/Muldoon) may be an intensely personal album and special for that reason, but it's also Madonna doing what she does best; identifying an already popular genre – in this case trancey, psychedelic dance music – and reclaiming it in the name of million-selling pop. Something she has an unerring knack for.

Record label:
Maverick/Warner Brothers
Produced
by Madonna and William Orbit, with Marius De Vries and Pat Leonard.
Recorded
at Larrabee Studios North, Universal City, CA; 1997.
Released:
February 1998
Chart peaks:
1 (UK) 1 (US)
Personnel:
Madonna (v); Fergus Gerrand (d, pc); Marius De Vries (k); Craig Armstrong, Pat Leonard (oa); Pat McCarthy, David Reitzas, Jon Englesby, Matt Silva (e)
Track listing:
Drowned World/Substitute For Love(S); Swim; Ray Of Light (S); Candy Perfume Girl; Skin; Nothing Really Matters (S); Sky Fits Heaven; Shanti-Ashtangi; Frozen (S); The Power Of Goodbye (S); To Have And Not To Hold; Little Star; Mer Girl
Running time:
66.52
Current CD:
9362-46847-2
Further listening:
The Immaculate Collection (1990); Like A Prayer (1989); Something To Remember (1991) – ballads compilation
Further reading:
I Dream Of Madonna: Dreams Of The Goddess Of Pop (Edited by Kay Turner, 1993); Alex Keshishian's film, In Bed With Madonna: Truth Or Dare (1991); and, of course, the tabloid press
www.madonna.com
Like this?
Try . . . p.371

The Handsome Family

Through The Trees

Breakthrough album from U.S country gothic husband-wife team

Urban, polluted and with a distinct lack of tumbleweeds, Chicago seems an odd place for alt. country to have such a powerful hold. But its thriving scene has produced a number of bands with a strong U.K following, chief among them The Handsome Family. When the husband-wife duo's third album *Through The Trees* appeared in 1998 - an American gothic country classic: dark, twisted, blackly comic tales of death and decay, drink, desperation and dead dogs - few outside their adopted hometown (they originate from Texas and New York) had heard of them. By the year's end that had changed, as their album topped the critics' Best Of polls and their increasingly frequent U.K shows drew bigger and bigger crowds.

It was a home-made album, recorded on equipment borrowed from Jeff Tweedy of Wilco. Tweedy, Chicago's biggest alt. country star ("It's scary, people follow him around the supermarket looking to see what he's buying", said Rennie Sparks) also guests on backing vocals and guitar. Just about everything else is played by Rennie and Brett. The band who played on their debut album - reduced to a trio on their second - had become a duo on *Through The Trees* following their drummer's departure. "He kept saying, " Bret explained, "'Why don't you stop writing all those damn sad songs?' He wanted to have fun. Drum machines drink less and get paid less too." Added Rennie, "A good drum machine sounds like that Edgar Allen Poe story The Tell-Tale Heart, where the thump, thump, thump just gets louder and louder. Really scary."

You can see why they were dubbed the Gomez and Morticia Addams of country. Rennie's captivating lyrics read like American gothic short stories (of which she is a published author). Her music historian husband's melodies, sung in a rich, deep baritone, sound like Johnny Cash writing a spaghetti western soundtrack, or David Lynch and Poe rewriting Ghost Riders In The Sky in an abandoned bar. Old and elemental. "We don't think of ourselves as a reaction against Nashville", said Brett. "We don't give a shit about Nashville. I stopped listening to modern country or folk around the 1960s or so. We're definitely more into the real old stuff."

"Old songs", added Rennie, "are so wonderfully gloomy."

The Handsome Family have since left Chicago for the less concrete-laden New Mexico, where they continue to make acclaimed albums. Greil Marcus has called them The Beatles of the folk world, and Beatle Ringo Starr named them as a favourite band.

SS

Record label:
Loose VJCD 105
Producer:
Brett Sparks and Dave Trumfio
Recorded:
In the Sparks' and Trumfio's living rooms and bathrooms
Released:
April 6, 1998
Chart Peaks:
None (UK) None (US)
Personnel:
Brett Sparks and Rennie Sparks (voc, gtr, bs, pno, banjo, dobro, melodica, autoharp, drum machine). Guests: Jeff Tweedy (bk voc and occasional gtr). Dave Smith and Dave Winer (horns). Jessica Billey (violin)
Track listing:
Weightless again; My sister's tiny hands; Stalled; Where the birch trees lean; Cathedrals; Down in the ground; Giant of Illinois; Down in the valley of hollow logs; I fell; The woman downstairs; Last night I went out walking; Bury me here; My ghost
Running time:
44.05
Current CD:
VJCD105
Further listening:
Down in the Valley (compilation, 1999); Twilight (2001)
Further reading:
www.handsomefamily.com
Like this?
Try . . . p.716

Boards of Canada

Music Has the Right to Children

Cerebral, laid back electronica with a soul rooted in the past

"We love the sound of music that seems to be barely under control. We love music that's out of tune in a beautiful way, or dissonant or damaged." So says Mike Sandison, one half of Boards of Canada. It could be a clarion call for a particular seam of music that lays claim to being emotional but BOC's 1998 album, *Music Has The Right To Children* on the legendary electronica label Warp is a startlingly moody convergence of blips, beats and svelte melodies.

The album's origins and influences along with the bands name itself are rooted in the past. Sandison and Marcus Eoin spent time in Canada as children and from an early age they were curious about the jerky, lo-fi documentaries released by The National Filmboard of Canada. They were inspired enough by the rough quality of the soundtracks to create their own compositions as children and record them using audio tapes with ropey playback quality. That quality may have been digitised and remastered on the album but the essence of why they recorded it is still there. As Sandison says, "... imperfections are where the magic is. To us the tunes we write are imperfect, the sounds are imperfect, even the artwork."

There is more than a graphic link to the 70s /early 80s childhood of the duo. Songs like The Colour of the Fire and Aquarius have the singsong undulation of children's voices mixing with the electronic beats layered alongside the sustained resonance of simple melodies. And while they are not about reconstructing a period feel by any means, there is a sense of Budd and Eno type ambience to their music and above all there is space. Just as they live sufficiently distant from the urban sprawl of Edinburgh, they refuse to clutter their music with an over-produced sound that can synthesise a kind of electronic claustrophobia and which can epitomise the worst of off the shelf and in the sampler electronic music. As Sanidson says, "I don't think its easy to be truly independent as an artist at the same time as being part of an urban community. I'm not saying its impossible but it just doesn't suit us. Besides, when I'm faced with the choice of hanging out with my friends round a bonfire where we live or being squashed in a London tube with some suit's elbow in my face, its an easy choice to make."

Its perhaps ironic but not surprising that BOC should have built up strong and loyal following in cityspace both prior and since their signing to Warp. People living in that urban sprawl don't always want to hear music that simply reverberates their foundations or lulls them with predictable rhythms. Even and maybe especially in the city you need the sense of peace, of resurging memory that Boards of Canada soulful, thoughtful music provides.

TD

Record Label:
Warp
Produced
By Michael Sandison and Marcus Eoin
Recorded
At Hexagon Studio, Scotland 1997
Released:
April, 1998
Chart Peaks:
None (UK) None (US)
Personnel:
Michael Sandison & Marcus Eoin
Track Listing:
Wildlife Analysis, An Eagle on your mind, the color of the fire, telephasic workshop, triangles and rhombuses, sixtyten, turquoise hexagon sun, kaini industries, bocuma, roygbiv, rue the whirl, aquarius, alson, pete standing alone, smokes quantity, open the light, one very important thought
Running Time:
62:58
Current CD:
WARPCD055
Further Listening:
Peel Session (1998), In a Beautiful Place Out in the Country (2000), Geogaddi (2002)
Further Reading:
www.boardsofcanada.com
Like this?
Try . . . p.675

Plastikman

Consumed

Forget snapping the glow-sticks and listen up. It's Richie Hawtin, but you can't dance to it.

Here was the Ontario man who had given us so many killer dancefloor moments courtesy of his stadium-style techno sets, his Plastikman releases, and his hyper-creative mix discs. Here he was releasing his first full-length since United States immigration banned Richie Hawtin from his beloved Detroit and the rest of the country for eighteen months. Here he was calling it *Consumed.* Surely a sonic boom was in order.

Instead, Hawtin's 1999 masterpiece resembled a dance track only in the low buzz that one hears outside a club when waiting in line to get in. *Consumed* was the distant memory of the faint remnant of the ghost of Hawtin's dance-friendly tracks released under the Plastikman alias. *Consumed*'s rumble runs throughout the album, but it's the industrious bassline of machinery instead of any trance-inducing sort. Echos of sounds slowly and even casually develop, oftentimes looped and washed with the pace a dub producer might prefer. Synthetic washes are few and far between, but each one of them is deliberate and even meditative in its development. The sum total is a long-player to be heard start to end with the kind of attention you might pay at an art installation.

Hawtin has said that his inspirations for the album were the textures in the colored swatches of Rothko paintings, plus the curves and cavities of Anish Kapoor sculptures. In the past, he has also noted that techno can be viewed as a genre of music "closest to a contemporary art form." As an extension of his desire to have techno music and its spirit of music-making taken more seriously than a series of dancefloor ditties, *Consumed* is his most successful work to date in terms of matching his conceptual goals with seductive, engaging sounds. Tracks like Ekko, Locomotion, and even Consume and Consumed are oftentimes indistinguishable, but the album's development as time passes is unquestionable. In fact, when listened to with great attention, Hawtin's album succeeds in suspending our sense of time—a feeling that oftentimes overcomes certain revelers on a dancefloor for a very different set of reasons.

Consumed was certainly an unexpected release at the time, but it has helped cement our understanding of the other side of Hawtin that is eager to see the music that he loves gain a more subtle, art-oriented context. Hawtin himself has also collaborated with the painter Jason Martin on a project taped by the BBC, and even created an installation that sat alongside the work of Anish Kapoor in a group show for the French Millennium Exhibition. Should any of this prove disconcerting for those who just want to dance, Hawtin reminds us, "Beats are the placeholders of silence."

AD

Record label:
Novamute
Produced
by Richie Hawtin
Recorded
at The Building, Windsor, Ontario, Canada
Released:
May 1998
Chart peaks:
N/A
Personnel:
Richie Hawtin (Engineer, Producer); Nilz (Mastering)
Track listing:
Contain, Consume, Passage (In), Cor Ten, Convulse, Ekko, Converge, Locomotion, In Side, Consumed, Passage (Out)
Running time:
73:40
Current CD:
NOMU065CD
Further listening:
Sheet One (1993), Recycled Plastik EP (1994), Musik (1994), Richie Hawtin—Decks, EFX & 909 (1999)
Further reading:
www.m-nus.com
Like this?
Try . . . p.670

Gillian Welch

Hell Among The Yearlings

Old-style country music with dirt under its fingernails and murder in its heart.

On the sleeve of her second album, American neo-traditionalist country singer Gillian Welch has the air and appearance of a '40s war bride: tough yet sensual, and more than able to take care of herself. It's a demeanour borne out in her music, which has the authentic sound and style of earlier times: when she sings lines like "Rocks in my pocket and the devil on my back", you could be listening to some long-lost cousin of Robert Johnson, though her singing reflects more the poor-white traditions of Appalachian Mountain music, particularly when she flats and sharps notes as effectively as on the opener Caleb Meyer, a song of violation in which the eponymous rapist suffers immediate retribution.

It's typical of the brusque, unflinching worldview of Welch and her partner David Rawlings' songs, which cover the hardships and moral ambiguities of the underside of life with a commendable lack of sentimentality. There's a gripping apprehension of mortality in songs like Rock Of Ages and I'm Not Afraid To Die, made all the more compelling by the austerity of her delivery and the sparseness of the settings, which reinforce the antique feel of the album.

Welch derived her love of bluegrass and old-time music from the liberal grade school her parents – themselves songwriters – had her attend as a child. "The kind of music they do is pretty different from what I do," she reckons. "Musically, it's as if they found me in a basket on the doorstep!" She was especially influenced by The Stanley Brothers, and in 1992 moved to Nashville to pursue a career in country music, despite her anachronistic style being completely out of kilter with current country fashions – although the duo dispute that their sound is truly traditional. "There's more ninths and open intervals in the real traditional stuff, especially in the harmonies," explains Rawlings, "than there were when it got put into folk and got squared off, when the college kids of the '60s were singing it." They do, however, liberally employ country music's three thematic staples of God, sex and death, a tendency Welch excuses by asking, "What else can happen in the third verse? You either have to make an appeal to God, or you die!"

The album, whose title derives (via a fiddle tune) from an old cattle-driving phrase referring to the easy spookability of yearling calves, was written and recorded quickly, while "we were still figuring out what the songs meant". As a result, they're peculiarly raw and exposed, bereft of the cosy blandishments of modern country music, which fits their bleak subject matter perfectly. "We were in a very private space when we wrote them," acknowledges Welch, "and I think that comes across."

Record label:
Almo Sounds
Produced
by T-Bone Burnett.
Recorded
at Sound City, Van Nuys; Ocean Way Recording, Hollywood; MCA Music, Sound Emporium and Nevada Studios, Nashville, Tennessee; 1997–98.
Release date:
July 1998
Chart peaks:
None (UK) None (US)
Personnel:
Gillian Welch (v, g, banjo, b, d); David Rawlings (v, g, d, e); T-Bone Burnett (k); Rick Will (e); Roger Moutenot (e)
Track listing:
Caleb Meyer; Good Til Now; The Devil Had A Hold Of Me; My Morphine; One Morning; Miner's Refrain; Honey Now; I'm Not Afraid To Die; Rock Of Ages; Whiskey Girl; Winter's Come And Gone
Running time:
39.04
Current CD:
ALMCD 60
Further listening:
Revival, Welch and Rawlings' 1996 debut.
Further reading:
MOJO 58
Like this?
Try . . . p.602

Lauryn Hill

The Miseducation Of Lauryn Hill

The album which fulfilled all of Hill's promise with The Fugees made her the most successful female Grammy winner in history.

Listening to Hill, you might imagine a streetwise rapper with a dysfunctional background. In fact, she comes from a comfortable New Jersey family and was groomed for stardom from an early age.

She began at 13, charming the crowd at the Harlem Apollo's amateur night with Smokey Robinson's Who's Loving You. While still at school she was a prolific poet, founded a gospel choir, played on the basketball team and was a cheerleader and homecoming queen – in her spare time, that is, when not acting in daytime TV soap As The World Turns, the Whoopi Goldberg movie *Sister Act 2* or playing with The Fugees (Haitian immigrant Pras Michel was a classmate of hers and Wyclef Jean his cousin). The trio released their first album, *Blunted On Reality* in 1994 when she was 19, but initially she balanced this burgeoning musical career with history studies at Columbia University, New York and the formation of The Refugee Project to help underprivileged kids.

She finally gave up her studies when the cover version singles Killing Me Softly and No Woman No Cry broke through and propelled *The Score* (1996) towards worldwide sales of more than 17 million. However, after lengthy touring, The Fugees fragmented into solo projects, though denying permanent dissolution.

Hill served notice of her emergence with her part in creating the title track of Aretha Franklin's 1998 album *A Rose Is Still A Rose*; she co-wrote and produced it, then directed the video too. ("She was right on target with the message," said Franklin. "It was two powerful sisters working together.") Since, on-stage, in a display of conspicuous versatility The Fugees would all swap instruments throughout their set, it was then no great surprise that Hill was responsible for almost every aspect of her own album, released four months after Franklin's.

The Miseducation Of Lauryn Hill – a title adopted from Carter G Woodson's book The Miseducation Of The Negro – is the fruition of all her energy and talent, using a fairly orthodox soul/hip hop musical idiom to pungently relate her own experiences, from racist abuse to childbirth. Some of her more caustic rants about the evils of stardom have been interpreted, despite her denials, as a swipe at Wyclef Jean; one of the album's more profound highlights is a graphic ode to the birth of her son Zion (the father, her partner, is Bob Marley's son Rohan). It incorporates a vitriolic put-down of industry figures who were appalled when a second pregnancy coincided with the making of the album – her daughter, Selah, was born two months after its release – and tried to convince her that motherhood would destroy her career. Wrong, quite clearly.

Record label:
Columbia
Produced
by Lauryn Hill.
Recorded
at Museum Studio, Jamaica and Quad Studio, New York.
Released:
August 25, 1998
Chart peaks:
1 (UK) 1 (US)
Personnel:
L Hill (v, g, a); E Robinson, S Thunder, S Johnston (v); L Holland (o, clarinet, p, k); T Barney (b); B Beadle (s, flute); MJ Blige (v); R Byrd (pc); D'Angelo (v); F Dunnery (g); Don E (k, p, o); P Fakhourie (b), J Poyser (p, k, syn, celeste, harpsichord); K Robinson (tp, flugelhorn); N Robinson (tb); C Smith (v, g); A Smith (g); E Stockley (v); F Virji (tambourine); D Frasier (s); E Valletti (harp); J Marley, C Santana, R Browne (g); G Paradise (harp); DJ Supreme (DJ); J Newton (g); T Newton (p); V Nobles (drum programming); T Wilksons, R Wilson, J McNeil (v); S Zender (b); L Randolph, Kio Pugh
Track listing:
Intro; Lost Ones; Ex-Factor; To Zion; Doo Woop; Superstar; Final Hour; When It Hurts So Bad; I Used To Love Him; Forgive Them Father; Every Ghetto Every City; Nothing Even Matters; Everything Is Everything; Miseducation Of Lauryn Hill; Can't Take My Eyes Off You; Tell Him
Running time:
77.45
Current CD:
4898432
Further listening:
The Score (1996)
Like this?
Try . . . p.337

Fatboy Slim

You've Come A Long Way, Baby

The most successful British dance album in the world . . . ever?

For an album that sounds so effortless and freewheeling, former Housemartin Norman Cook's second foray under the most successful of his many aliases (he's also been Pizzaman, The Mighty Dub Katz, Feelgood Factor, Fried Funk Food and a mover in Beats International and Freakpower) had a long, difficult gestation period. The problem wasn't so much a lack of inspiration but his penchant for partying and a gargantuan drug intake. Matters came to a head in the summer of 1998, when he was interviewed live in Ibiza on future wife Zoë Ball's Radio One breakfast show. In response to a query about the whereabouts of his new album, an audibly refreshed Cook giggled "Who cares?" The incident led to furious rows with his major label backers, but the attitude – I'm on drugs, I'm having fun, *who cares?* – runs through the record.

Most albums informed by chemicals have their dark, sinister side, but this is simply a long, Day-Glo party, packed with dumb jokes and druggy non-sequiturs: a track called You're Not From Brighton (because Cook isn't), a vocodered refrain of "California is druggy, druggy, druggy" (because Cook has "a lot of friends on the West Coast who take a lot of drugs"), the recording of a caller to Boston's WBCN radio station, enthusing that Fatboy Slim is the "band of the 90s, if you can call him a band" and Fucking In Heaven, where a taped message from unwitting American producer Freddy Fresh ("If you could do me a Fatboy Slim remix, I'd be fucking in heaven") is chopped up into the track's refrain of "Fatboy Slim is fucking in heaven."

Recorded in the tiny, equipment-stuffed back bedroom of Cook's former Brighton home, pictured on the inside cover, *You've Come A Long Way, Baby* owes its power to Cook's canny ability to meld unlikely samples together. The album's biggest hit, The Rockafeller Skank, mixes The Just Brothers' Northern Soul instrumental Sliced Tomatoes with The John Barry Seven's pre-Beatles exploitation thriller theme Beat Girl and throws in a snatch of a hip hop MC. The UK Number One Praise You manipulates a sample from Camille Yarborough's Take Yo Praise. Its slow, soulful tones were a response to the slew of inferior copies of Cook's trademark fast, breakbeat-heavy sound; big beat.

"Tzant's Sounds Of The Wickedness was a turning point," said Cook. "I thought, 'It sounds like me so I'm going to do something else.' I wasn't very flattered."

He needn't have worried. While Tzant are one-hit wonders now consigned to the rummage bin of history, *You've Come A Long Way, Baby* established Cook as an international star. Will it be seen as an important record in years to come? Who cares?!

Record label:
Skint
Produced
by Fatboy Slim.
Recorded
at House Of Love, Brighton; summer 1998.
Released:
October 1998
Chart peaks:
1 (UK) 34 (US)
Personnel:
Norman Cook (k, v, programming)
Track listing:
Right Here, Right Now (S); The Rockafeller Skank (S); Fucking In Heaven; Gangster Tripping (S); Build It Up – Tear It Down; Kalifornia; Soul Surfing; You're Not From Brighton; Praise You (S); Love Island; Acid 8000
Running time:
62.06
Current CD:
BRASSIC11CD
Further listening:
Better Living Thru Chemistry (1996); On the Floor At The Boutique – mix album (1998) Halfway between the gutter and the stars (2000).
Further reading:
www.normancook.net; www.skint.net
Like this?
Try . . . p.839

Ravi Shankar

Live At Monterey

Cultural melting pot reaches boiling point.

"I had played Carnegie Hall in 1958," says Ravi Shankar, "but it was only after George Harrison became my student that I became a superstar in a pop sense." By the time Shankar arrived in California in 1967, he was a big deal. Impressed by the hippies' interest in Eastern spirituality, he accepted a lucrative invitation to play Monterey, despite reservations about the way that the Age of Aquarius equated India with drugs. He arrived on the Friday, determined to find out as much as he could about rock. Simon & Garfunkel, Otis Redding and Janis Joplin all received the thumbs-up, but he found The Grateful Dead too loud, and Jimi Hendrix's sexuality and guitar-burning shocked him. After he had witnessed The Who destroying all their instruments, Shankar was distraught and threatened to leave, claiming it was impossible for him to play in such an atmosphere.

"I was bothered by the drugs and the mixing-up of tantra, mantra, sex and hashish. Some people say I criticised Jimi Hendrix and The Who, but I did not criticise their music. They did not show respect to their instruments, breaking them, kicking them, burning them. We do not do that in my culture." A compromise was reached to stop Shankar walking out: he would play on the Sunday afternoon, before any other acts, and nobody would follow directly after him. Shankar had got over his shock by the time he took to the orchid-strewn stage along with Alla Rakha, a long-time collaborator. It had been raining all day, but the skies cleared for the two-and-a-half-hour set. After two days of over-indulgence, the blissed-out audience were prepared to sit and listen – even, in their addled enthusiasm, applauding the tuning-up. "They were concentrating on the music, it was a wonderful atmosphere, really beautiful. And this inspired me, it was a very good concert that day. I played other festivals after that, but I often wondered why; they were always the wrong conditions for listening to my music. Back in India, I was accused of jazzifying my music for playing to the hippies. They thought I was a goner."

Record Label:
EMI/Angel
Produced
by Richard Bock.
Recorded
at Monterey Pop Festival, California; June 1967.
Released:
October 1998
Chart peaks:
None (UK) None (US)
Personnel:
Ravi Shankar (sitar); Alla Rakha (tabla)
Track Listing:
Raga Bhimpalasi; Tabla Solo In Ektal; Dhun (Dadra And Fast Teental)
Running time:
53.29
Current CD:
CDM5669192
Further listening:
In Celebration (4-CD box set that proves Shankar's virtuosity and adaptability); West Meets East LPs 1 and 2; the 1967–68 sessions with Yehudi Menuhin is, disrespectful this might sound, serious head music. Another Live At Monterey with different tracks was released on the Ravi Shankar Music Circle label in 1967.
Further Reading:
My Music, My Life (Ravi Shankar, 1995)
Like this?
Try . . . p.257

Beck

Mutations

The wild card in Beck's far-from-orthodox pack.

So anxious was Geffen UK about the reception here of the follow-up to the enormously successful paragon of hipster cool which was *Odelay*, that advance PR claimed at the time it wasn't a "proper" Beck album, but rather some kind of aberrant creative interlude. In truth, it was far from that. The aptly titled *Mutations* was an album Beck simply had to make. Many of its mellow, thoughtful and downright sweet songs were years old by the time he came to record them, but as a body of work they expose a touching fragility, replacing his by now familiar post-modernist savvy with a genuine, heartfelt romanticism.

It was recorded remarkably quickly – less than two weeks – in the legendary studios where Ray Charles put down I Can't Stop Lovin' You and Brian Wilson fiddled with the impossibly fine details of Good Vibrations, with Nigel Godrich at the controls. Right from the off, his and Beck's was a happy and harmonious working relationship. "Some producers play around and twiddle with knobs forever; that can definitely squelch any creative energy happening in the studio," claimed Beck later. "Nigel was great; he'd have the microphones up in 15 minutes and by that time, everybody had learned their part. We'd play it two or three times and then that'd be it. We almost felt guilty – it was too easy."

Unfairly perceived by some as a calculated exercise in retro indulgence, *Mutations* is in fact the natural confluence of several elements: Beck's desire to allow The Classic Song its own life, rather than simply instil it with that of its singer; the myriad stylistic influences crammed into the record's grooves; and the fact that Ocean Way's mixing desk was an analogue mono model from the '60s which made panning impossible. True, there are inflections picked up from The Beatles' *Revolver* and White Album, alongside those of Pink Floyd, The Doors, Yes and even Chick Corea, but Beck has his peers – Static has the bereft beauty of a Folk Implosion tune, while the spirit of Nirvana's On A Plain hovers over Runners Dial Zero. Tropicalia, however, throws a crucial stylistic curveball. Named after Brazil's populist music movement of the '60s and undoubtedly connecting Beck with the Latino district where he grew up, this track is a vibrant fusion of western and African sounds, something he is clearly addicted to.

"This music is extremely contagious," Beck has said. "It has enormous happiness and it's genuine and human. We're not allowed to broach similar happiness in rock; to us, it isn't allowed. It's why I play this music." It was Tropicalia which pointed the way forward for Beck's next album, the vastly different, effervescently good-time *Midnite Vultures*.

Record label:
Geffen
Produced
by Nigel Godrich and Beck Hansen.
Recorded
at Ocean Way Studios, Los Angeles; March 19–April 3, 1998.
Released:
November 1998
Chart peaks:
24 (UK) 13 (US)
Personnel:
Beck Hansen (v, g, syn, hm, glockenspiel); Smokey Hormel (g); Justin Meldal-Johnsen (b); Roger Joseph Manning Jr (k, harpsichord); Joey Waronker (d, pc); Elliott Caine (t); David Ralicke (flute, tb); Nigel Godrich (e)
Track listing:
Cold Brains; Nobody's Fault But My Own (S); Lazy Flies; Cancelled Check; We Live Again; Tropicalia (S); Dead Melodies; Bottle Of Blues; O Maria; Sing It Again; Static; Diamond Bollocks; Runners Dial Zero (S)
Running time:
52.26
Current CD:
GED 25184
Further listening:
Stereopathetic Soul Manure (1997), a compilation of Beck's home recordings 1988–93
Further reading:
MOJO 61; www.beck.com
Like this?
Try . . . p.383

Bonnie "Prince" Billy

I See A Darkness

Blues-styled testaments on life and the world's short-comings from a former Palace brother.

Having already examined the rural roots of Kentucky and his strange upbringing, first as The Palace Brothers, and then simply Palace, Will Oldham adopted another persona to delve deeper into the underbelly of Americana. As Bonnie "Prince" Billy he set out his stall as a spooky storyteller, unfolding the mysteries of dark corners and darker ideals. The 11 songs touched on everyday loss, unquenchable sadness and a subdued vision of new beginnings. On its release, MOJO described the album as "harrowing gothic-folk at its darkest. A quiet gem for those chill, midwinter evenings", while folk magazine Dirty Linen opined, "There is a chilling, quasi-minimalist quality to these songs." Indeed, Oldham's assembled team stripped the music to its bare bones. The focus lies instead on Will's double-tracked vocals, which stray in and out of harmony and discord; they provide *I See A Darkness* with a disturbing ambience, something Oldham – who is often reticent to the point of coma in interviews – seemed keen to play up when asked where these songs were heading. "Towards death," he replied, "it becomes more pleasant and laughable every day." The well-disguised playfulness of Oldham's songs and their almost nursery-rhyme sub-melodies turned the eerie button to 11, making this an unnerving festival of sadness.

"I don't think of myself as a downer," Oldham countered when quizzed for a Las Vegas local paper, "I like myself; I enjoy myself. There is no pity in my music, for myself or any other fuckhead. Most of the music I love makes me feel happy. But even unhappiness makes me happy."

I See A Darkness may be uplifting for some, unbearable for others. Therefore, like a horror movie in grainy black and white, it's every bit the cult epic you'd expect.

Record label:
Domino
Produced
by Paul Oldham.
Released:
January 19, 1999
Chart peaks:
None (UK) None (US)
Personnel:
Bob Arellano; Colin Gagon; Paul Oldham; Will Oldham; Peter Townsend
Track listing:
A Minor Place; Nomadic Revery (All Around); I See A Darkness; Another Day Full Of Dread; Death To Everyone; Knockturne; Madeleine-Mary; Song For The New Breed; Today I Was An Evil One; Black; Raining In Darling
Running time:
37.58
Current CD:
WIG 59
Further listening:
single/mini-album Blue Lotus Feet (1998); earlier Palace Brothers' fare Viva Last Blues (1995) or There Is No-One What Will Take Care Of You (1993); as Will Oldham, Arise Therefore (1996) and Lost Blues And Other Songs (1997)
Further reading:
http://users.bart.nl/~ljmeijer/oldham/index.htm
Like this?
Try . . . p.796

Steve Earle & The Del McCoury Band
The Mountain

Steve Earle comes with a lot of baggage. No matter that he cleaned up his act in 1995 after long, degenerative spells addicted to crack and heroin, or that his madcap days of girls (six ex-wives at the last count) and guns were apparently behind him. His post-detox records – *I Feel Alright, El Corazon, Transcendental Blues* – sometimes seemed dragged down by the wreckage of his past.

The Mountain – on the other hand – arrived mercifully free of all weighty biographical concerns. Devised as a tribute to the late, great bluegrass king Bill Monroe, the album was an unselfconscious nod to the man who had long inspired Earle and whom Earle finally met and played with just a few months before Monroe's death in 1996: "It was the thrill of my life," Earle recalled. "*The Mountain* is my interpretation, to the best of my ability and with all of my heart, of the music Bill Monroe invented."

It was a stunningly boisterous exercise. The instruments may have all been acoustic, but the record abounded with furious, visceral music. The songs - all Earle originals, written quickly and assuredly to order – instantly assumed the gravitas of age-old Appalachian standards, while their author had the good sense to recruit the Del McCoury Band, undisputably the best in the business when it came to capturing the maverick Monroe spirit. "They're the best bluegrass band working today," Earle remarked at the time. "Great friends and wonderful teachers."

The band's ear-poppingly intricate ensemble-playing was the perfect foil for Earle's cracked voice, as they dipped into pockets of peace before erupting into spinning fiddle or mandolin solos of merciless precision. The lack of biographical context also brought out the best in Earle's narrative flair: the craggy workingman's rasp of *Leroy's Dustbowl Blues* sat beside the heartbreaking miner's waltz of *The Mountain*, while the puffed up, sexual boasts of *Graveyard Shift* grinned wolfishly at the lovelorn *Carrie Brown*. Elsewhere, the fur really flew on *Connemara Breakdown, Dixieland* and *Texas Eagle*.

"My primary motive in writing these songs was both selfish and ambitious," Earle admitted later. "I wanted to write just one song that would be performed by at least one band at every bluegrass festival in the world long after I have followed Mr. Bill out of this world." With *I'm Still In Love With You* – a keening, clever duet with Iris Dement – and the closing *Pilgrim* – written on the morning of former bandmate Roy Juskey Jr's funeral and featuring a whos-who of Nashville aristocracy on backing vocals – Earle could rest satisfied that he had delivered his aim.

GT

Record Label:
E-Squared
Produced
by Twangtrust and Ronnie McCoury
Recorded
at Room & Board, Nashville, TN
Released:
February 1999
Chart Peaks:
51 (UK) None (US)
Personnel:
Steve Earle (g, v); Del McCoury (g, v); Ronnie McCoury (mandolin, v); Rob McCoury (banjo); Jason Carter (fiddle); Mike Bub (b); Iris Dement (v); Jerry Douglas (dobro); Stuart Duncan (fiddle); Gene Wooten (dobro); Dan Gillis (tin whistle); Emmylou Harris et al (backing v)
Track Listing:
Texas Eagle; Yours Forever Blue; Carrie Brown; I'm Still In Love With You; The Graveyard Shift; Harlan Man; The Mountain; Outlaw's Honeymoon; Connemara Breakdown; Leroy's Dustbowl Blues; Dixieland; Paddy on the Beat; Long Lonesome Highway Blues; Pilgrim
Running Time:
45.50
Current CD:
GRACD252
Further Listening:
Guitar Town (MCA 1986), El Corazon (Warners 1997), Jerusalem (E-Squared 2002)
Further Reading:
Hardcore Troubadour: the Life & Near Death of Steve Earle – Lauren St. John, Fourth Estate
Like this?
Try . . . p.599

XTC

Apple Venus Volume 1

XTC record again after a seven-year pause, creating a resplendent compositional triumph.

Following a five-year strike, XTC were finally free of Virgin Records and keen to record their stockpile of songs in two volumes. Volume Two was to feature songs that "were more easy, rather idiotic in places, electric guitars making a bit of a racket" while Volume One would explore the non-standard, orchestral areas Andy Partridge had been threatening on 1992's *Nonsuch* with esoterica such as Rook and Omnibus. An acrimonious misunderstanding involving payment for use of Chris Difford's studio put the project a further two months behind but found Haydn Bendall, an Abbey Road veteran with extensive experience in recording and editing orchestras. Eventually, the band and producer settled down around a keyboard and a computer to arrange the songs by committee, later adjourning to Chipping Norton to record rhythm tracks with drummer Prairie Prince. Guitarist Dave Gregory already felt alienated by the reliance on editing and orchestral expense and Andy, increasingly regarding Dave as a negative presence, blew.

Partridge: "I was just telling him to pull his weight and get into it a bit more. I don't think he ever forgave me."

Dave resigned and Partridge and Moulding moved on with a frantic one-day orchestral session at Abbey Road, a couple of overnight arrangements by Mike Batt (Green Man, I Can't Own Her) and months of editing. Losing Haydn Bendall after six months to a Peter Greenaway project, Nick Davies – who had mixed *Nonsuch* – helped Partridge and Moulding complete the album.

English through and through – from the pagan overtones of Andy's Green Man to Colin's Lionel-Bart-meets-Ray-Davies charmer Frivolous Tonight and the romantic schoolroom ache of Harvest Festival – *Apple Venus Volume 1* is a ravishing record.

Moulding: "What we wanted to do was make a more cohesive album. We were little bit jealous of Todd Rundgren's production skills on *Skylarking*. A lot of songs were chosen with that flow in mind."

Full of joy (I'd Like That), pain (Your Dictionary) and whimsical rage (River Of Orchids), the craftsmanship and care in this majestic music showed up much of Britpop to be the callow work it was; MOJO called them a "pair of 40-something March hares who could show many a 25-year-old how a great album should be constructed." If the song credit ratio (Andy's nine to Colin's two) made it look like a Partridge solo album, he had an answer: "Most of them have been."

A heartening indicator of undiminished – not to say evolving – capabilities, the story of this valuable pop *auteur* and his under-productive pal continues.

Record label:
Cooking Vinyl
Produced
by Haydn Bendall and Nick Davis.
Recorded
at Chipping Norton, Haydn Bendall's place, Colin Moulding's place and Abbey Road.
Released:
February 1999
Chart peaks:
42 (UK) 106 (US)
Personnel:
Andy Partridge (v, g); Colin Moulding (v, b); Gregory (g, p, k, v); Prairie Prince (d); Guy Barker (t); London Session Orchestra
Track listing:
River Of Orchids; I'd Like That; Easter Theatre; Knights In Shining Karma; Frivolous Tonight; Green Man; Your Dictionary; Fruit Nut; I Can't Own Her; Harvest Festival; The Last Balloon
Running time:
50.02
Current CD:
COOKCD172
Further listening:
English Settlement (1981); Skylarking (1986); Oranges And Lemons (1989), Wasp Star (Apple Venus Volume 2) (2000)
Further reading:
MOJO 64; XTC Song Stories (XTC and Neville Farmer, 1998)
Like this?
Try . . . p.596

The Roots

Things Fall Apart

The coming of age of a hip hop institution.

The list of puns available to the hack writing about Philadelphia hip hop band The Roots and their career-vindicating fourth LP Things Fall Apart is lengthy. Whether one tries to ignore the time they spent growing underground, before this record took their budding success to full bloom, or instead examines the fertile soil of hip hop culture in which their music germinated, the seeds for potential wordplay have already been sown.

Yet, despite the joshing, the notion of the band being somehow organic is fundamental. The Roots ended up using bass, drums and keyboards because their early gigs were not played in clubs over PA systems, but busked out of doors where acoustic instruments were more use. They came at hip hop from a different direction and helped change elements of the music's sound. At the same time, they discovered that a live band could do anything a sampler could do, and more: the 'Hip Hop 101' routine, a medley of classic rap hits, became a much-loved part of their live show.

Yet all this meant that, to many listeners, The Roots were little more than a novelty hip hop jukebox – capable of spitting out entertaining versions of everyone else's hits, but without a definable style of their own. Illadelph Halflife, their 1997 album, had gone some way to addressing this concern, but it was their next album – the band's fourth – that first showed the wider world what The Roots were really about.

Instead of basing tracks on sampled loops, the band build up mantra-like musical phrases that lead rapper Tariq "Black Thought" Trotter sprays his word pictures over. The key is that the band acknowledge no constraint on their creativity: whether the song needs is a sample, a string section or a female chorus, then that's what the song gets. Nothing here is partially successful or partially realised, and there are no moments where the listener is left to feel "if only…".

The album deservedly won the band a Grammy, but that was never going to go to their heads. "We went from virtual obscurity to having the world's attention," their drummer and leader Ahmir "?uestlove" Thompson told Mojo on the eve of the release of the follow-up, Phrenology. "For so long we've been ignored and under the radar that I'm virtually shocked any time anyone shows us any love."

AB

Record label:
MCA
Produced
by The Grand Wizzards
Recorded
at Ivory Productions (Sigma Studios), Philadelphia, PA
Released:
March 1, 1999
Chart peaks:
None (UK) 4 (US)
Personnel:
A Thompson (drums): T Trotter (v): Malik B (v): L Hubbard (b): K Gray (kbds, acc gtr): Jazzy Fatnastees (bkg v): F Dantzler (v): Lady B (bkg v): Dice Raw (v): Eve Of Destruction (bkg v): S Storch (kbds): J Poyser (kbds)Mos Def (v): Common (v): I Szwec (violin): E Kumrow (violin): D Garnet (viola): L Gold (viola) M Daulne (bkg v): B Siegal (v) E Badu (v): A Tidd (gtr): W Wimbly (gtr): B Powers (synth)
Track listing
Act Won: Table Of Contents : The Next Movement: Step Into The Relm: The Spark: Dynamite!: Without A Doubt: Ain't Sayin' Nothin' New: Double Trouble: Act Too: 100% Dundee: Diedre Vs Dice: Adrenaline!: 3rd Acts: You Got Me: Don't See Us: The Return To Innocence Lost
Running time:
70 mins 26 secs
Current CD:
MCD 11948 / 111 948-2
Further listening:
Illadelph Halflife (1996): Phrenology (2002)
Like this?
Try . . . p.591

Blur

13

Damon's heartbreak confidential – Graham's nervous breakdown

Blur's 6th album is almost entifrely a reflection on the break-up of Damon Albarn's relationship with Justine Frischmann. This bodes well. Albarn is never better than when he puts the Cunning New Ideas book to one side, opens up his veins and lets the sadness and sheer disappointment of life seep out. Behind that cheeky nu-pop sheen, Blur have often hinted at a world-weary muse (This Is A Low, The Universal). On *13* the melancholia is cranked up a notch, and then some. No Distance Left To Run, the draining fatigue of loss trembling through Albarn's cracked vocals, is an aubade of brokenhearted intensity. This is what it sounds like when you simply give up.

But it's not about giving in. If *13* is bruised, it's wise and subtle too. It's about learning your lessons and moving on. The opening track Tender, full of gospel-infused soul, sets the tone:

"Come on, come on – get through it. Come on, come on – love is all we need."

Counterpointing Damon's raw confessional, Graham Coxon weighs in with querulous vocals on two tense and spiky songs that tell out his own mounting dissatisfaction. The edgy paranoia of Coffee & TV says everything about the madness of fame – of having celebrity thrust upon you to an extent that it starts to feel dangerous. This is the song that tells the world Blur's stopped being fun for introspective Graham.

Produced with lush (and sometimes overbearing) textures by William Orbit, *13* will remain crucial as an album of songs of loss and longing, and as a key signpost in the life and times of one of the UK's greatest bands.

TS

Record label:
Food
Produced
by William Orbit
Released:
March 1999
Chart peaks:
1 (UK) 80 (US)
Personnel:
Damon Albarn (vocals); Graham Coxon (guitars, vocals); Alex James (bass, vocals); Dave Rowntree (drums)
Track listing
Tender; Bugman; Coffee & TV; Swamp song; 1992; B.L.U.R.E.M.I.; Battle; Mellow Song; Trailerpark; Caramel; No distance left to run; Trimmtrabb; Optigan 1
Current CD:
FOODCD29
Further listening:
Parklife (1994); Blur (1997); Think Tank (2003). Also Gorillaz (2001). Coxon side projects – The Sky is Too High (1998)
Further reading:
3862 Days: The Official History of Blur (Stuart Maconie, 1999)
Like this?
Try . . . p.688

Low

Secret Name

Breakthrough album for Minnesota lo-folk trio

Low, with us for 10 whole years now, say this about themselves:

"Low is a trio from Duluth, Minnesota who make very slow music. Low play songs stripped to their bare essentials: slow tempos, quiet voices, powerful lyrics and minimal instrumentation."

"Quiet" and "slow" only begin to give a feel for Low's haunting lo-folk, their sinuous ballads made all the more devastating by their sense of restraint. Amid the eerie spacings and slow builds, there lives a sense of wonder in Low's hushed hymns. *Secret Name* is the band's fifth album, and takes its name from perhaps its most beautiful entry, Weight of Water.

Secret Name is the band's first collaboration with Lord of Lo, Steve Albini. Recorded in New York over 9 days in late 1999, this sounds and feels like a record where everything just came together. They set up, they recorded – that's it. The opening track I Remember sets their stall out with trademark tranquility, yet with ever-building power and an ever-present sense of threat. For a full minute there's the funereal beat of a pedal drum, a persistent audio crackle in the foreground and one foreboding bass coda before Alan Sparhawk's plaintive vocal seeps into the song. This, and the sepulchral Don't Understand, are timeless, everlasting tracks from a band coming into their prime. Wolves in sheep's clothing? Oh yes.

Sparhawk alternates vocals with Mimi Parker, whose understated pain reverberates through Days Of… and the awesome Weight of Water. The sense of loss in Days Of…, delivered with a voice, a cymbal and the laconic strum of a guitar, could not be more affecting at Volume 11. As it is, you have to strain to hear each bittersweet moment, and it breaks your heart.

Low are one of those rare groups that seem to be a product of their environment – their place, their skies and surroundings and memories are as much a part of their songs as the notes and timbres. On Missouri there's a spirit of bowed regret for a time and place gone by, while Sparhawk laments the mystic night skies of his youth on the sparse and tender Starfire.

Secret Name is the album that brought Low to their still-tiny constituency, but the legend is building.

KS

Record label:
Kranky (US) Tugboat (UK)
Produced
by Steve Albini
Recorded
at Electrical Audio, November 20–28, 1999
Released:
April 1999
Chart peaks:
None (UK) None (US)
Personnel:
Alan Sparhawk (vocals, guitar); John Nicholas (bass); Mimi Parker (vocals, drums); Ida Pearle (violin), Tresa Ellickson (viola), Kera (cello)
Track listing
I Remember; Starfire; 2-step; Weight for Water; Missouri; Don't understand; Soon; Immune; Lion – Lamb; Days of Will the night; Home
Current CD:
TUGCD007
Further listening:
The Curtain Hits the Cast (1996); Things we lost in the fire (2001); Trust (2002)
Further reading:
www.chairkickers.com (Low's own site). For articles: www.chairkickers.com/low/articles
Like this?
Try . . . p.651

Ben Folds Five

The Unauthorized Biography of Reinhold Messner

The piano-based power trio goes out with a CinemaScopic bang.

Ben Folds was thinking big, in a *Journey to the Center of the Earth* kind of way. While he stops short of calling it a concept album, he envisioned the heart of *Messner* as a thirty-minute suite that revolved around themes of courage, rites of passage and mortality, "I was having an early mid-life crisis".

There was even more worry after the first week in the studio. "I had the feeling of how it would sound, but I was extremely slack in getting the songs written," admits Folds. "I realized that we had enough stuff to feed the beast for just a couple of days. I had all these ideas in my head, but I was like, 'Man, what are we gonna play? I don't know what this song is called. I don't have any words for it. It doesn't have a chorus.' A little bit like a Miles Davis experience. The guys were pissed off. They would leave and I would sit by myself, trying to fill in the blanks." As the suite started to take shape, Folds was urged to reconsider his vision. "I had everybody involved take me aside and beg me not to write an album that was one long song. Robert and Darren both asked me to please consider doing what it is that I actually do, which is write pop songs. In the end, the record was dissected. But when it was a suite, it was actually done well. But everyone was against the idea. Everyone wanted singles."

And so Army was pulled from the suite, injected with jaunty horns and souped up with a catchy chorus. Ditto the makeover for Don't Change Your Plans, a seven-minute wandering piece that was sliced and diced down to four minutes of Bacharach-esque pop. Some wildly experimental moments remained, such as Your Most Valuable Possession, a trippy phone message from Folds' dad, set to a jazzy groove ("A happy accident - the tracks that you hear beneath it were being played simultaneously when he left the message," Folds laughs). The result - a winning collection of ambitious pop songs.

The album (Reinhold Messner was the first man to climb Mt. Everest without oxygen support) was considered a commercial disappointment, and probably sounded the death knell for the group. But Folds says, "I think I knew it would be the last album. I had been thinking about the band being over for a while. The record sounds like a last record. There are hints throughout the lyrics. What I like about it is it's really old-fashioned, intense record-making. It's one of the last records I know of that was recorded in such a naive way. We were all upset, we go into the studio, we put it down that way, things get mixed up, argued over and we have to figure it out."

BDM

Record label:
Sony/550 Music
Produced
by Caleb Southern; Mixed by Andy Wallace
Recorded
at Sound City, Los Angeles; Grandmaster, Los Angeles; Water Music, Hoboken, NJ; RPM Studios, New York; November 1998-January 1999
Released:
April 1999
Chart peaks:
22 (UK) 35 (US)
Personnel:
Ben Folds (v, p, k); Robert Sledge (b, v); Darren Jessee (d, v); Jane Scarpantoni (c); Antoine Silverman, Mark Feldman, Lorenza Ponce (vn); John Mark Painter (fluegelhorn, valve trombone); Tom Maxwell, Paul Shapiro (ts); Ken Mosher (bs, as); Frank London (t);
Track listing:
Narcolepsy; Don't Change Your Plans; Mess; Magic; Hospital Song; Army; Your Redneck Past; Your Most Valuable Possession; Regrets; Jane; Lullabye
Running time:
40:37
Current CD:
COL69808
Further listening:
Whatever and Ever Amen (1997), Rockin' The Suburbs (2001)
Further reading:
www.benfolds.com, www.benfoldsfive.com
Like this?
Try . . . p.382

Moby

Play

No escape in the summer of '99 as Moby is played everywhere

Depending on your view and perhaps your musical tastes, the use of samples has either revolutionised or sounded the death knell of original, contemporary music. From the wholesale plundering of James Brown's vocal yips to entire string sections being lifted from John Barry soundtracks; sampling, love it or hate is here to stay.

Moby ran into criticism over his use of samples on his 1999 release *Play,* mostly after the album went platinum over and over again in country after country and became *the* unavoidable sound of the year as it seemed everyone from summer lovers to elevator operators hummed along to the mix-up of ambient, soul, gospel and hiphop. In addition to the 18 songs on the album, Moby has said, there are another 200 written that were never used. How many of these used the field recordings of Alan Lomax who painstakingly recorded indigenous black music from the 1920s and 30s, we may never know but Moby was forthright about his use of these moving, heart-rending vocals. "My main interest in these old vocals was more my emotional response to them as opposed to where they came from. They appealed to me on a very subjective level." The result is a long album which carefully creates layers of spiritual ambience, filling it out with soft break beats before spiking the listener with an upbeat track like BodyRock.

Moby's journey from early techno cult hits like Go which famously sampled the Twin Peaks theme through the metallic thrash of Animal Rights to the lush territory of Play, has been marked by his well-documented commitment to veganism, Christianity and socio-economic reforms. Moby, whatever else he has been accused of, is hardly the nouveau-riche rock star with a guilty conscience. Just as his attitude towards the treatment of animals influenced Animal Rights; so has his spiritual beliefs through the use of religious accapellas given the album some sincerity.

Moby has shown himself to be very much an intelligent user of technology and he has mused long and hard about the future influence such technology might have. "People in the future will be able to drive down the road, and through voice commands, take the drums from a Led Zeppelin song and put Billie Holiday's vocals on top of them and then play the whole thing backwards and twice as fast but at the original pitch." The trick then has to be more than simply being clever with buttons but rather to use source material in a creative and personal way. Moby, unsurprisingly, has something to say about that too. "If you create something that contains fragments from other songs but sounds nothing like any of these songs, have you written a new song ?"

TD

Record Label:
Mute
Produced
by Moby (Honey mixed by Mario Caldato Jnr; Natural Blues mixed in Sheffield by I Monster)
Recorded
at own Studio, New York, January 1999
Released:
May 1999
Chart Peaks:
1 (UK) 38 (US)
Personnel:
Moby and samples
Track Listing:
Honey, Find My Baby, Porcelain, Why Does My Heart Feel So Bad, South Side, Rushing, Bodyrock, Natural Blues, Machete, 7, Run On, Down Slow, If Things Were Perfect, Everloving, Inside; Guitar, Flute & Strings, The Sky is Broken, My Weakness
Running Time:
1.03
Current CD:
Mute B00063JBY
Further Listening:
18 (2002); Animal Rights (1999)
Further Reading:
www.moby.org; www.mute.com
Like this?
Try . . . p.584

Groove Armada

Vertigo

An album which restored a sense of fun and spontaneity to dance music

Playing live for electronic bands can be a complicated and fraught affair. Any band can suffer technical hitches live but for music which relies heavily on a mass of audio and digital cables coiled round a cockpit of synthesisers, one jack in the wrong place or a computer crashing in the humid jungle of a smoke shrouded stage and…

But playing live for Groove Armada is the essence and the origin of their sound. Perhaps its because Andy Cato and Tom Findlay the duo who are Groove Armada are not simply knob twiddlers but accomplished 'real' musicians in their own right and certainly this love of varied instrumentation as well as for a wide range of musical influences comes across in their appearances at festivals in the late 90s and early 2000s. As Findlay recalls, "We both sort of grew up with that whole kinda rave scene in the 90s, the kind of informative years before Thatcher stepped in and ruined it all" [The Criminal Justice Bill is widely cited as the reason why illegal gatherings over a certain number of people playing repetitive beats fizzled out or mutated into ticketed commercial gatherings.]

At the 2002 Gatecrasher event they astounded dance audiences and confounded preconceptions of dance events by playing with a full live band. As Cato points out, " A lot of people haven't seen the dynamic of horns and percussion and live bass and guitar and MCs and vocalists before. Its basically like a traditional funk band wound up with some 21st Century technology."

The soul influences can be heard right the way through *Vertigo*. From the halcyon days feel of At The River to the full on, no nonsense jam down of I See You Baby (Shakin' That Ass) the album reverberates with a sense of party, the best of times encapsulated. Like Massive Attack who collaborated with vocalists like Tracy Thorn and Horace Andy, Groove Armada add another layer to their sound by merging vocalists and live instrumentation with programmed beats. Along the way they have worked with artists as diverse as rapper Jeru the Damaja and soul vocalist Richie Havens. The result is a very modern sound freshened by a live feel that defies the listener not to tap toes or sing along.

Being experienced DJs, both Cato and Findlay have embraced the opportunity to record a much more diverse sound than they can usually mix when playing a set where everyone expects consistent, meat and two veg house music. This, as Cato mentions is changing and the eclectic samples and shifting pace of Vertigo are testament to their experiences of playing live. " We spent a lot of weekends playing up and at 'em house sets. I think at the moment we're in the situation that when people ask for a Groove Armada remix they can either get a house tune or an ambient adventure."

TD

Record Label
Pepper Records
Produced
By Andy Cato and Tom Findlay
Recorded
At Battery Studios 1999
Released:
May 1999
Chart Peaks
23 (UK)
Personnel:
Keeling Lee (g); M.A.D.(v); Kick Horns (horns); Simon C Clarke (flute, alto sax, baritone sax) ; Roddy Lorimer (trumpet, flugelhorn); Tim Sanders (tenor sax); Gram'ma Funk (v); Dominic Betmead (scratching); Sophie Barker (v);
Track Listing:
Chicago, Whatever, Whenever, Dusk You and Me, Pre 63, If Everybody Looked the Same, Serve Chilled, I See You Baby, A Private Interlude, At the River, In My Bones, Your Song, Inside My Mind (Blue Skies)
Running Time:
65.09
Current CD
0530332
Further Listening
Goodbye Country (Hello Nightclub) (2001); Lovebox (2003)
Further Reading
www.groove-armada.com
Like this?
Try . . . p.641

The Flaming Lips

The Soft Bulletin

More than 15 years into their career: an accessible, commercial, brilliant record.

Large, lush and beautifully orchestrated, *The Soft Bulletin* is a far cry from The Flaming Lips' self-confessed "amateur punk rock" days in Oklahoma City. Formed by Wayne Coyne and his brother Mark in 1983, the fledgling Lips couldn't play instruments or sing but they boasted the only PA system on the local scene, and thus supported every passing punk band from Black Flag and Hüsker Dü to The Butthole Surfers. After a self-titled debut in 1984, the band recorded a further four albums with the LA-based Restless label. Early on, their fluctuating line-up included a stint on second guitar by soundman Jonathan Donahue – who eventually went on to pursue a side project, Mercury Rev – before settling upon the core of Wayne Coyne, Michael Ivins and multi-instrumentalist Steven Drozd.

A series of spoof calls to Warner Bros. (mostly as Perry Farrell!) eventually paid off, and with major label bucks behind them, the Lips began a series of albums that would eventually culminate in *The Soft Bulletin*.

"I think [*The Soft Bulletin*] was the result of an accumulative effect," says Wayne. "After everything we'd done from being the worst punk-rock band to the experimental concerts [at the time of *Zaireeka*], [the album's] come to mean something more than if it stood on its own."

In fact, much of the material on *The Soft Bulletin* came from the sessions for *Zaireeka*, their ambitious album consisting of four CDs designed to be played simultaneously, for quadraphonic thrills.

"I think we've realised that we do like making big-budget records," muses Wayne. "Sometimes I feel like we're given these Steven Spielberg budgets, only we're only going to be playing in the art houses to a handful of people".

Nonetheless, *The Soft Bulletin* is without a doubt their most accessible album. Produced by long-time friend Dave Fridmann (Mercury Rev, Jane's Addiction, Delgados), though not dissimilar in feel to their three previous albums (*Hit To Death In The Future Head*, *Transmissions From The Satellite Heart* and *Zaireeka*), the elaborate sonic collage of instruments, effects and Wayne's fragile vocals gel more tunefully than ever. And there's less clamour; the usual guitars, gongs and radar blips blend seamlessly with piano, harps, vibes and grand orchestration (What is the Light/The Observer particularly).

"We're lucky if we sound at all conventional," decides Wayne. "If we do it's by mistake. We simply do what we like and if that comes into the popular music realm, then good, maybe someone can make some money out of it and we hope we're first in line."

Record label:
Warner Bros.
Produced
by The Flaming Lips, Dave Fridmann, Scott Booker
Recorded
at Cassadaga, New York April 1997–February 1999
Release date:
May 17, 1999
Chart peaks:
39 (UK) None (US)
Personnel:
Wayne Coyne (v,g), Steven Drozd (d, v, g, k), Michael Ivins (b, v, g), Scott Bennett (b), Peter Mokran (p, m)
Track listing:
Race for the Prize; A Spoonful Weighs A Ton; The Spark That Bled; Slow Motion; What Is The Light?; The Observer; Waitin' for a Superman; Suddenly Everything Has Changed; The Gash; Feeling Yourself Disintegrate; Sleeping on the Roof; Race for the Prize (Mokran mix); Superman (Mokran mix); Buggin'
Running Time:
58.17
Current CD:
9-46876-2
Further listening:
Transmissions From The Satellite Heart (1993)
Further reading:
www.flaminglips.com
Like this?
Try . . . p.549

Travis

The Man Who

Change of direction transforms Scottish pop hopefuls into soul-baring success.

At the end of Travis's retro-poppy debut album, *Good Feeling*, there's a song called Funny Thing, an altogether darker, moodier number than anything that preceded it. And, as Travis mainman Fran Healey has pointed out, that was the starting point for *The Man Who*. Much of *Good Feeling* had been Healey adopting a pop-star guise that he hoped would take him to the top and, good as the songs were, it wasn't until he really started exploring his inner feelings on *The Man Who* that Travis connected with a huge audience. Squeezing out material for *The Man Who* was almost as agonising for Healey as his lyrics suggest. "I don't know what I'm going to write about or what the tune's going to be. I just sit there with a dictaphone going, 'Fuck, fuck, fuck, this is shite.' And then I go and watch the telly for three weeks, then come back and maybe do another two minutes."

This process, with Healey continually prodded along by Independiente Records boss Andy McDonald, nevertheless resulted in songs as tuneful as they were emotional, drawn from a well of experiences that included being bullied at school and growing up without a father. There's an extraordinary enveloping warmth to the music, partly accounted for by the fact that some tracks were recorded on the same mixing desk as Pink Floyd's *Dark Side Of The Moon* (famed for its warm sounds), but mostly it's down to the gentle intimacy in Healey's voice, the delicacy of the instrumentation and the uplifting tenderness of the tunes.

It didn't, however, always seem that way to Healey. "Halfway through the recording, I was thinking, Shit, this is all quite mellow and down. Then I thought, Well, fuck it."

Musical inspirations such as John Lennon, Radiohead, Simon & Garfunkel and John Barry are barely disguised, but the quality of the writing transcends its influences; the songs take up residence in heart and head very quickly. On release, many critics agreed that it was overloaded with ballads, but Melody Maker realised that "the energy and inspiration here is harnessed into something classy and bordering on classic." Quality will eventually out though, because a full 13 weeks after release *The Man Who* hit Number 1 in the UK, and has subsequently walked off with a brace of BRITS, a Q award and a clutch of album-of-the-year placings in music press year-end roundups.

Record Label:
Independiente
Produced
by Nigel Godrich, Mike Hedges.
Recorded
at Rak Studios, London, and Mike Hedges' studio, Normandy; September 1998.
Chart peaks:
1 (UK) 135 (US)
Released:
May 24, 1999
Personnel:
Fran Healey (g, v); Dougie Payne (b); Andy Dunlop (g); Neil Primrose (d)
Track Listing:
Writing To Reach You (S); The Fear; As You Are; Driftwood (S); The Last Laugh Of The Laughter; Turn (S); Why Does It Always Rain On Me? (S); Luv; She's So Strange; Slide Show; (unlisted: The Blue Flashing Light)
Running time:
47.35
Current CD:
ISOM 9CD
Further listening:
Although markedly different, Good Feeling (1997), remains an impressive pop debut.
Further reading:
www.travisonline.com
Like this?
Try . . . p.230

The Beta Band

The Beta Band

Maverick Scots' debut in "not as bad as they said it was" shock.

Before they made this full-length debut, The Beta Band were feted by the British music press, favourably compared to Beck, and regarded as possible inspirers of a new breed. Three four-track EPs had served notice that here, at last, was an iconoclastic band unable and unwilling to churn out derivative, cliched indie pap. By the time this self-titled album came out, however, something rather more than the usual British music press backlash had begun.

Problems arose when the group gave what appeared to be a disarmingly frank interview to the NME ahead of the album's release. "It's definitely the worst record we've ever made, and it's probably one of the worst records that'll come out this year," de facto front man Steve Mason said. "It's got some terrible songs on it. None of them are fully realised or even fully written."

His band mate Robin Jones additionally revealed that a 30-minute ambient track inspired in part by The KLF's Chill Out album had been dropped from the record by EMI, their Regal imprint's parent company. The band's manager and Regal boss Miles Leonard added to the furore, noting that "They wanted to record each side in a different continent, one in Tokyo, one in Mexico, and so on. It would have cost three-quarters of a million pounds."

If this was a brilliantly conceived strategy to set the Betas apart from the then vogue "we're the best band in the world" posturing everyone post-Oasis seemed to want to adopt, it was only a partial success. Many reviewers seemed to side with the band's "it's rubbish" sentiments, and buyers stayed away.

There had, admittedly, been some real problems. The Hard One had to be completely re-recorded after clearance to sample the Bonnie Tyler hit Total Eclipse Of The Heart had been first denied, then later given, by the songwriter Jim Steinman. The six-week studio schedule had already proved tight after the band arrived to begin work with their "songwriting" for the album comprising a single sheet of A4 with ideas for each song in note form.

Yet The Beta Band is a far from poor record. Rather than portray them as adherents to Beck's slacker school of thought, it revealed the group as a dreamy-eyed cross between the Boys Beach and Beastie, intuitively able to adopt breakbeats, samples and drum loops on the one hand with harmonies, introspective lyrics and sunkissed melodies on the other.

AB

Record label:
Regal
Produced
by Chris Allison and the Beta Band
Recorded
at Sawmills: Rockfield: Jacobs
Released:
June 21, 1999
Chart peaks:
18 (UK) None (US)
Personnel:
Steve Mason (vocals, percussion, drums); John MacLean (turntable, sampling); Richard Greentree (bass); Robin Jones (drums, percussion)
Track listing:
The Beta Band Rap: It's Not Too Beautiful: Simple Boy: Round The Bend: Dance O'er The Border: Broken Up Acingoong: Number 15: Smiling: The Hard One: The Cow's Wrong
Running time:
62.02
Current CD:
Reg 30 CD 7243 520016
Further listening:
The 3 EPs (1998) Hot Shots 2 (2001)
Further reading:
www.betaband.com
Like this?
Try . . . p.692

Mos Def

Black On Both Sides

"Speech is my hammer/Bang the world into shape/ Now let it fall..."

A rapper, actor and activist, Dante "Mos Def" Smith announced his place at the vanguard of hip hop's new world order with the 1999 release of this stunning debut.

Though he'd appeared in ER among other US TV shows, by the mid-'90s Mos had concentrated on rapping. After releasing his first single independently he and the New York independent label Rawkus came across one another. It was a mutually fortuitous match. The label was to New York's hip hop underground of the '90s what Def Jam had been to the same scene a decade earlier. Rawkus provided an outlet for a new breed of rapper who, in the post-Biggie, post-gangsta environment, craved something of the intellectual and musical satisfaction hip hop was once synonymous with. And Mos became their biggest star.

A hip hop renaissance man, Mos not only rapped and occasionally sang, but was an accomplished multi-instrumentalist who could even scored strings. By the time he made this album he had guested with De La Soul and A Tribe Called Quest, released several singles and collaborated with label-mate Talib Kweli on the NY underground's startling manifesto album, Mos Def And Talib Kweli Are Black Star. Still, the consistency, quality and power of Black On Both Sides was something of a shock.

Consciously referencing not only hip hop's late '80s "golden age" – a time of lyrical ingenuity, innovative sampling and politicised, often revolutionary lyrical content – Black On Both Sides is also a record that is open and inclusive enough to entice listeners who don't know the first thing about rap history. Mos had roped in jazz legend Weldon Irvine to help shape this musical landscape, and with a clutch of eminent hip hop producers peaking together, the sound is at once organic yet technologically savvy.

The songs, though, are the biggest asset. Rewriting rap codes and playing with conventional roles, Ms Fat Booty is a role-reversal tale, Mos falling for the curvaceous honey only for her to prove unwilling to commit, then, five tracks later, he's warning of incipient privatisation of the planet's water supplies on New World Water. Hip Hop is a thunderous acclamation of his chosen art form, didactic but empowering, a "medicine for loneliness" that "reminds me of Thelonius/and Dizzy", while Rock 'N' Roll pointedly notes that white music has thirstily drunk from the wellspring of black musical creativity, and suggests that now's as good a time as any for payback.

AB

Record label:
Rawkus
Produced
by Mos Def, Diamond, 88 Keys, Ayatollah, Mr Khaliyl, Ali Shaheed Muhammed, David Kennedy, Psycho Les, Etch-A-Sketch, Ge-Ology, D-Prosper, DJ Premier,
Recorded
at Sony Music Studios, NYC: Chung King, NYC: D&D Studios, NYC
Released:
October 11, 1999
Personnel:
Mos Def (v, bass, congas, perc, kbds, drums, string arrangement on Climb, vibraphone on May-December): Weldon Irvine (kbds, Hammond Organ on Umi Says, kbds arrangement on Climb and Habitat, string arrangement on Climb, piano on May-December): Etch-A-Sketch (turntables): Busta Rhymes (v on Do It Now): Will I Am (Fender Rhodes on Umi Says): Johnny Why (gtr on Rock N Roll): Talib Kweli (v) on Know That): Vinia Mojica (v on Climb): Q-Tip (v on Mr Nigga):
Track listing:
Fear Not Of Man: Hip Hop: Love: Ms Fat Booty: Speed Law: Do It Now feat Busta Rhymes: Got: Umi Says: New World Water: Rock N Roll: Know That feat Talilb Kweli: Climb feat Vinia Mojica: Brooklyn: Habitat: Mr Nigga feat Q-Tip: Mathematics: May-December
Running time:
Current CD:
rawkus P2-50141
Further listening:
Mos Def & Talib Kweli Are Black Star (Rawkus, 1997)
Like this?
Try . . . p.806

Paul Westerberg

Suicaine Gratification

Former Replacement articulates depression of the heart

Having apparently become used to a career of diminishing commercial returns, the ex-Replacement finally ran out of steam with his second solo album, Eventually, in 1996. Stodgy, uninspired and lacking in heart, the album was conceived with one eye and both hands on the record store tills. Having quit his vices in the early 1990s after a decade of alcoholic and narcotic frolics turned into acute dependency, it seemed that Westerberg had grown up a little too much. It didn't work. The record still bombed.

Sober, severely depressed and sick of the "vaudevillian circus" of rock'n' roll, he retreated to his basement in Minneapolis and began to write, without any concern for his dwindling market. "I just started expressing," he recalled, "like I did when I was younger. Without a band, you tend to come up with stuff that's for yourself. That's what this record is."

If this was indeed Westerberg writing for himself, then he really was in bad shape. The songs that emerged were essays in melancholia, fear and hurt, based around fragile piano melodies and raw acoustic guitars. Despite moving to various studios with producer Don Was (Quincy Jones was first choice but politely declined), Westerberg retained most of his self-played basement demos and augmented subtle overdubs: a french horn on Self Defense, a vocal duet with Shawn Colvin on the aching Born For Me, acoustic bass and pedal steel on others. But essentially, the home cooked flavour was retained.

Kicking off with the a wry ode to mid-life depression ("I wake up from a dream and look for rain/take an amphetamine and a crushed rat's brain...") the downbeat theme of *Suicaine Gratification* was quickly established. Even the rockers - I'm The Best Thing That Never Happened and Whatever Makes You Happy ("I'm pretty sure/It isn't me..") – were stripped bare of all sheen and painfully self lacerating.

"One of the reasons I'd avoided making a record like this in the past is that you then have to discuss it," Westerberg admitted at the time. "If you want to really dissect it, there's something to be uncomfortable about in every song. That's why I'm almost welcoming the notion of a grand depression at its heart, as a kind of blanket explanation: 'Yeah, I was depressed, could see no hope. Now go away.'" Once again, the record buying public took his advice literally, as he surely knew – perhaps even hoped – that they would. It was the final nail in the coffin of his major label career, so he simply went back to the basement, emerging with two schizoid albums in 2002. They were just fine, but an album packed with this kind of skewed loveliness only happens once in an artist's lifetime.

GT

Record Label:
Capitol
Produced
by Don and Paul WASterberg
Recorded
in Minneapolis, New York City and Los Angeles
Released:
October 1999
Chart Peaks:
None (UK) None (US)
Personnel:
Paul Westerberg (v, g, piano, b, drums, melodica, keyboards, percussion,); Suzie Katayama (cello, accordion); Richard Todd (French horn); Don Was (b); Jim Keltner (drums); Josh Freese (drums); Benmont Tench (keyboards); Shawn Colvin (v); Abe Laboriel Jr. (drums); Dave Pirner (v); Laura Kanani (v); Steve Ferrone (drums); Greg Leisz (pedal steel);
Track Listing:
It's A Wonderful Lie; Self Defense; Best Thing That Never Happened; Lookin' Out Forever; Born For Me; Final Hurrah; Tears Rolling Up Our Sleeves; Fugitive Kind; Sunrise Always Listens; Whatever Makes You Happy; Actor In the Strret; Bookmark; Copenhagen (hidden track)
Running Time:
48.53
Current CD:
7243 4 99145 2 0
Further Listening:
All For Nothing – The Best of The Replacments (Warners 1997) Stereo (Vagrant 2002)
Further reading:
http://members.aol.com/paulspage/
Like this?
Try . . . p.474

Cut Chemist & DJ Shadow

Brainfreeze

Two mad vinyl scientists change the way people thought about funk singles.

A collage symphony that set a new standard for DJ mix tapes, Brainfreeze wasn't just a piece of music – it became a phenomenon.

Californian turntablists Shadow and Cut Chemist were approached to headline a DJ festival in San Francisco. Wanting to create a special, one-off piece for the event, Cut suggested to Shadow that they should only use 45rpm singles.

"In the process of getting the set together I was just going through my collection and going, 'This is kind of funny, let's check this out,'" Shadow recalled. "There were records all over our floor, and that's how the set was gleaned. Dance The Slurp was just in my collection."

The conceptual centrepiece of the mix, Dance The Slurp was a record given away by convenience store chain 7-Eleven. A ridiculous affair, the song adds a rumbustious funky marching band to a chorus of people noisily sucking the chain's Slurpee Slush ice drink through straws. "I just became fascinated with this thing, and because it had a breakbeat it was just hilarious," Shadow remembers. "So I played it for Cut Chemist, and it was his idea to mix Kraftwerk underneath it."

The remainder of the mix comprises often obscure but always very funky segments of a wide range of 45s, with the DJs beat-mixing, scratching and playing with the music, twisting the sounds into new shapes, and throwing things together in ways that are humorous, inventive and entertaining. As an exercise in the art of the DJ, it's peerless.

Shadow and Cut were overwhelmed by the response when they debuted their mix. They decided to manufacture a limited run of 1000 CDs, having recorded one of their final rehearsals to DAT. This sold out immediately, and soon the CD was commanding prices in excess of some of the sums being paid for the original records they'd used, which themselves had all rocketed in price from their previous levels. Rufus Thomas, Eddie Bo and Lou Courtney were among the artists whose records shot up in value due to the so-called "Brainfreeze effect".

Since then, the mix has been extensively bootlegged, both on CD and vinyl, and in 2002 Shadow and Cut Chemist repeated the trick with the Product Placement mix, which they took on world-wide tour.

"What could be better than DJ-ing and the collector world merging together?" Shadow reflects. "Those are our two greatest passions – records and the spinning thereof – so it was just meant to be."

AB

Record label:
Seventy7
Produced
by DJ Shadow, Cut Chemist
Recorded
at Released: 1999
Chart peaks:
none
Personnel:
DJ Shadow (turntables):
Cut Chemist (turntables)
Track listing:
Brainfreeze Part 1:
Brainfreeze Part 2
Running time:
52 mins 19 secs
Current CD:
currently unavailable
Further listening:
Product Placement (One Twenty Seven, 2001)
Further reading:
http://uwu.8m.com/bf/
Like this?
Try . . . p.265

Iggy Pop

Avenue B

In which the Naughty Little Doggie gets divorced

"It was in the winter of my fiftieth year", murmurs Iggy Pop over the dark, David Lynchy music of the title track, *"when it hit me: I was really alone."*

A lot of changes had gone down in Iggy Pop's life since his1996 album *Naughty Little Doggie.* An eventful three years, personally and professionally, that saw Pop transformed - through cult films Trainspotting and Velvet Goldmine and a special guest spot on the Sex Pistols reunion tour - into a new generation rock icon at the very same time that his ten-year marriage was falling apart. In November 1998, Iggy moved out of the apartment on Avenue B in New York City where he and his wife Suki had lived, and relocated to Miami. Before leaving town he recorded this album named after his marital home in a rehearsal space - a former ice cream factory and meat packaging plant - in the East Village, his band supplemented by cool jazz trio Medeski, Martin and Wood.

A remarkably different Iggy Pop album, its ten songs and three spoken word pieces were mostly slow, stripped-down and reflective. "Someone at the record company put out a circular saying it's a 'divorce record'", said Iggy. "But it's not. It's a post-marriage record, about a guy on his own, figuring out what he's going to do with what is left of his life."

Hence the graphically personal lyrics, in which the priapic punk boasts on the one hand of Fraulein floor-fucking and *"sleeping with someone new every night and in the morning politely saying 'bye"*, and on the other cynically pondering if he might be *"better off being a fag"*. Like Pop said, he had "a fuck of a subject". Though not one his record company would have much liked, had they known what was going on. They would have been happier, with his Superpunk profile at an all time high, with something more juvenile and delinquent. But Pop , "well aware that I could have become someone you trot out for nostalgia festivals", decided to "do something chancey." His reason for hiring a "big rock producer" was to keep the record company at bay. "If I'd have called them and said, 'Listen, this is Iggy Pop and what I want to do is go into this little room under an ice cream factory with portable equipment and record this song I've written about a Nazi girl and I've got this bit in the middle where I whistle, you'll love it!' there might have been trouble. Don (Was) put a positive spin on everything."

Serious and funny, filthy and cruel, *Avenue B* is an utterly compelling album - and a one-off. Pop's follow-up album was classic 'cartoon Iggy'.

SS

Record label:
Virgin 7238 4821623
Producer:
Don Was
Recorded:
In a former factory in New York, Daniel Lanois' studio in Ventura, California and two Hollywood studios
Released:
September 1999
Chart peaks:
None (UK) None (US)
Personnel:
Iggy Pop (guitar, keyboards, vocals); Chris Wood (bass); Billy Martin (drums); Peter Marshall (guitar); David Mansfield (viola, violin); Lenny Castro (percussion); Michael Chaves (keyboards); Larry Mullins (drums, tabla, vibraphone); Hal Cragin (bass); Michael Chaves (keyboards)
Track listing:
No shit; Nazi girlfriend; Avenue B; Miss Argentina; Afraid to get close; Shakin' all over; Long distance; Corruption; She called me daddy; I felt the luxury; Espanol; Motorcycle; Façade
Running time:
49.26
Current CD:
CDVUS163
Further listening:
The Idiot (1977); Lust for Life (1977); Nude & Rude: the best of Iggy Pop (1996)
Further reading:
Biopic: Iggy Pop (Gavin Evans, 2003); Neighbourhood Threat: On Tour with Iggy Pop (Alvin Gibbs, 2000)
Like this?
Try . . . p.307

Coldplay, Oslo, Norway by Alessio © Corbis

The 2000s

Shelby Lynne

I Am Shelby Lynne

New musical direction that reaches heights previously hidden

Shelby Lynne has the kind of back story cynical publicist's dream about. Born in Virginia in 1968 and raised in Alabama, at the age of 17 her estranged father shot her mother dead and then killed himself. Lynne still refuses to talk about it, on the basis that "it has nothing to do with my music." It's best – perhaps - to listen to songs like *Leavin',* *Life Is Bad* and *Thought It Would Be Easier* and make up one's own mind. A year after the tragedy she married briefly, then moved to Nashville in the early 90s where she cut a trio of big-hair country albums which set nobody's house on fire. Then – as if out of nowehere – came *I Am Shelby Lynne.*

Of course, it only *appeared* to have come from nowhere. The reality was more prosaic. Having fallen for Sheryl Crow's *Tuesday Night Music Club* in 1997, Lynne had a major rethink about her musical direction. She contacted Bill Bottrell, Crow's producer, and they starting work on the songs that would eventually become *I Am Shelby Lynne.* "It was all spur of the moment, not a planned thing," she recalled. "We never sat down and planned to write any of the songs, they just came naturally." She seemed equally at a loss to explain the sudden burst of inspiration. "People change and songs are meant to be written when they are. I don't think you can force them. It takes me living it first."

Although Bottrell took a huge amount of credit for shaping the musical landscape, the songs had Lynne's life and voice stamped all over them. Recorded in San Francisco and Lynne's native Alabama, with tugging strings added in Memphis, each of the ten tracks was drenched in loss – for family, for men, for some other time and place. "There's an emptiness," agreed Lynne, "a real hollow feeling that just feels good."

The record's highpoint - *Where I'm From,* a heartsore yearning for home - evoked nothing less than the understated majesty of *Georgia on My Mind*: "Crickets spreading rumours by the shore-line/where the lonesome lady whine…"

Still, Lynne found it hard to escape the easy Sheryl Crow comparisons. The album's opener *Your Lies* may have taken Crow's rock-chick blueprint and infused it with a hundred times the energy and exhiliration, but there the similarities ended. "We're just not the same," sighed Lynne when questioned. "I just don't get it, and I'm sure it pisses her off too. I don't like comparisons, I don't feel the need to make them." Quite right too. This was something different, a classic blend of country-soul music which stood eyeball to eyeball with Dusty Springfield, Aretha Franklin and Patsy Cline and didn't take a beating. No mean feat.

GT

Record label:
Mercury
Produced
by Bill Bottrell
Recorded
at Camp House & Firehouse, Alabama; The Old Schoolhouse & William's Place Studio, California; House of Blues Studio, Memphis.
Released:
February 2000
Personnel:
Shelby Lynne (v, g); Bill Bottrell (v, d, keyboards, g, organ, b, harmonica, pedal steel); Grey D'Augelli (b, keys, caspar horns); Roger Fritz (g, mandolin, dobro); Bill Coulson (caspar horns); Jay Joyce (g, b, keys, organ); Dorothy Overstreet (d);
Track listing:
Your Lies; Leavin'; Life Is Bad; Thought it Would be Easier; Gotta Get Back; Why Can't You Be?; Lookin' Up; Dreamsome; Where I'm From; Black Light Blue
Running time:
36.07
Current CD:
ADD 546 177-2
Further listening:
Love, Shelby (Island 2001)
Like this?
Try . . . p.31

Air

The Virgin Suicides

Moody, melancholic soundtrack that became the definitive album for the Air sound.

It is probably a wild claim to say that Air saved modern French music but it is a cliché given some weight when you start to list the limited success French music has achieved beyond its boundaries. As French music moved away from self-reflection –sincere, ironic or otherwise and embraced the multicultural and electronic influenced sound that swept through Europe in the 90s suddenly Etienne de Crecy, DJ Cam, The Mighty Bop and St Germain truly evoked Peter Gabriel's adage 'music sans frontieres.'

Air's debut album, *Moon Safari*, released in 1998, seamlessly merged the filtered and resonant sounds so predominant in electronica with melodic tunes given both texture and pathos through ethereal ballads or city scaped, vocoded narratives.

In 2000, Air recorded the soundtrack for Sofia Coppola's debut film *The Virgin Suicides*. Unlike *Moon Safari*, this album was made to a specific brief but like another French soundtrack nearly two decades before it stood out beyond the images it was designed to soundtrack. Vladimir Cosma's soundtrack for the cult film Diva released in 1982 set the tone for a decade by creating mood with opera and solo piano then jarring it purposefully with 80s beats. The mid seventies feel to Jeffrey Eugenides novel on which the film is based is similarly evoked by Air and indeed for those who had loved *Moon Safari*, it truly felt like a follow up album.

As Nicolas Godin, one half of Air, reflects, "Just when we were trying to get away from the seventies, too." He jokes. "We call this record Dark Side of the Moon Safari! But a lot of the soundtracks we have grown up with have stuck in our heads and that shows. We wanted to get that dark feeling of teenagers growing up in the suburbs."

Air's take on what makes a soundtrack album flew in the face of Hollywood cash-in tie-ins where a whole slew of songs would be cobbled together and act as a accompaniment rather than a soundtrack designed to add a another layer to the film's narrative. Godin is dismissive of the lure of commercial soundtrack honeypot.

"We don't want to work with names. We want to work with artistic and creative people, whoever they may be. It was good to work with Sofia because it was her first film as well as out first soundtrack, so we were all virgins."

The result is one of the most distinctive soundtracks in years. It uses motif like most true soundtracks but layers the melodies, initialising the mood with sweepings orchestral pads then stripping it down with minimal tones and creating a mood so dark yet sublime which resonates with or without the film.

TD

Record Label:
Source/Virgin France
Produced
by Air
Released
February 2000
Chart Peaks:
14 (UK) None (US)
Personnel:
Nicolas Godin (composing, programming); Jean Benoit Dunckel (composing, programming); Gordon Tracks (v,d); Hugo Ferran (sax.); Brian Reitzell (d)
Track Listing:
Playground Love, Clouds Up, Bathroom Girl, Cemetary Party, Dark Messages, The Word 'Hurricane', Dirty Trip, Highschool Lover, Afternoon Sister, Ghost Song, Empty House, Dead Bodies, Suicide Underground.
Running Time:
40.31
Current CD:
Source/Astralwerks 10332
Further Listening:
Moon Safari (1998), Premieres Symptomes (2000), 10 000 Hz Legend (2002) Air/Baricco (2003),
Further Reading:
www.fuzzie.freeserve.co.uk
Like this?
Try . . . p.678

Badly Drawn Boy

The Hour of Bewilderbeast

Genius, pure genius

People were shocked when this album came out. Really, they were knocked sideways by its brilliance. No one should have doubted The Boy, but by the time of *The Hour Of Bewilderbeast's* summer 2000 release Damon Gough had been written off as an urban myth. Whispers emanating from the Manchester underground through 1998 had it that here was, by anybody's standards, a unique talent. That was borne out to an extent by the winsome track I Need A Sign on B.D.B's debut e.p, but it was the follow-up release *It Came From The Ground* (1999) that had punters and reviewers reaching for the smelling salts. There hadn't been anything this sly and thrilling since Happy Mondays. *Bewilderbeast* didn't so much follow up on that promise as blow it aside in an avalanche of insight, melody, poetry and infectious Folk Soul. Yet prior to the album, Damon Gough had all but poleaxed his soaring reputation with a series of wilfully shambolic live appearances. The conventional wisdom went that The Boy was a piss-head blessed with sidekicks and studio masters who were making silk out of his silt. What tosh that turned out to be.

The Hour Of Bewilderbeast, all 18 tracks of it, is a glorious collection of songs. From The Shining right through to Epitaph this is a record you play from start to finish. Really, there are no 'skip' moments, only sections that dazzle you more than others. Stand-out tracks include Magic In The Air (a song that captures summer love as beautifully as any) and Pissing In The Wind, but the moments that encapsulate B.D.B's funky joie de vivre are the fuzz-infused opening bars of Once Around The Block. Just irresistible. Genius, pure genius.

KS

Record label:
Twisted Nerve/XL
Released
June 2000
Chart peaks:
13 (UK) None (US)
Personnel:
Damon Gough (vocals, guitar)
Track listing:
The shining; Everybody's stalking; Bewilder; Fall in a river; Camping next to water; Stone on the water; Another pearl; Body rap; Once around the block; This song; Bewilderbeast; Magic in the air; Cause a rockslide; Pissing in the wind; Blistered heart; Disillusion; Say it again; Epitaph
Current CD:
TNXL133CD
Further listening:
About a boy (2002); Have you fed the fish? (2002)
Further reading:
www.badlydrawnboy.co.uk
Like this?
Try . . . p.284

2000

Coldplay

Parachutes

From Yellow to gold to multi-platinum

The chronicle behind Coldplay is decidedly atypical for a rock band whose seminal LP would go on to staggering worldwide success. Here is the story of four boys who meet at London University College, preoccupied by studies ranging from maths and astronomy to ancient world history—boys who play hockey of all things. Alas, out of a shared a love of music said boys start a band (whose name they borrow from a friend's defunct musical outfit), and put out a couple EPs. The EPs end up piquing the admiration of the press and major labels alike, and said boys go on to become rock superstars. But not, that is, before first finishing their studies.

As it was four university grads suddenly found themselves unwittingly complicit in a mounting British rock movement, thrown in by comparison with the likes of Verve, Radiohead and Travis. It was a tenuous era, preceding that in which the British press would set their collective gaze abroad and lavish laurels on rawer incarnations like the Strokes, the White Stripes, and the Vines. Transience is the nature of the business, however, and it did nothing to hinder the breakout achievement of *Parachutes*. The album entered the British charts at number one and was nominated for the coveted Technics Mercury Music Prize. While it didn't get the nod, *Parachutes* did eventually go on to bag the 2002 Grammy for Best Alternative Music. The single Yellow became nothing less than a household institution in the UK as well as in the States when ABC selected it as the official theme song for its promo spots.

Parachutes was produced with Ken Nelson of Gomez and Badly Drawn Boy fame, with an acknowledged eye toward the organic character of the music. Most of the album was laid down on analog, some of the tracks were recorded live, and little was later compressed. It took over six months to complete, but only because minimal technical manipulation was invoked, thus necessitating a multitude of takes.

The seeming effortlessness of the album, coupled with its admittedly clean and youthful origins, earned it as much ire as it did praise, and some critics dismissed it as wan, spineless and apologetic. Alan McGee, former head of Oasis's label Creation, used the term "bedwetters" (a compliment compared to the repeated scorn of Noel Gallager himself.) And while the album is not exactly as daring as, say, any activity involving an actual parachute, it is undeniably honest and terribly melodic and shot through with the type of effusive vocals that made commercial stars of Jeff Buckley and Dave Matthews. Such inspirations are patent, yet, as Matt Diehl of Rolling Stone stated, "*Parachutes* ultimately rises above its influences to become a work of real transcendence."

DW

Record label:
Parlophone
Released
July 2000
Chart peaks:
1 (UK) 51 (US)
Personnel:
Chris Martin (vocals, piano); Jon Buckland (guitar); Guy Berryman (bass); Will Champion (drums)
Track listing:
Don't panic; Shiver; Spies; Sparks; Yellow; Trouble; Parachutes; High speed; We never change; Everything's not lost
Current CD:
5277832
Further listening:
A rush of blood to the head (2002)
Further listening:
www.coldplay.com
Like this?
Try . . . p.611

Harold Budd

The Room

Open a Budd and chill . . .

The term ambient music (like minimalist music) can conjure up a number of possibilities – most of them unattractive. From the soft, synthesised pads soothing elevator riders to the blissed out, beatless sugar of dawn in 'Ibitha', ambient music is considered wallpaper. Followers of Harold Budd's four decade career would disagree. Like Brian Eno with whom he collaborated on the 1980 album *Plateaux of Mirrors*, Budd comes from a sensibility, a sensitivity towards abstraction – of emotion, the physical environment, the whole gamut of life experience. As Budd recalls, he was influenced by the abstract expressionist painter Mark Rothko, describing his work as 'brilliant blasts of colour that engulfed you." adding that "One shatters glass in a vacuum then finds the art part among the shards." That statement in itself could be the calling card of many a creative person. It allows the possibility of discovery while understanding that it can be and should be a personal journey.

Budd's 2000 release represents not just this concept but the overall direction of his music since his first release *The Pavilion of Dreams* in 1978. *The Room* builds on the track first initialised on the 1988 album *The White Arcades* and each of the thirteen pieces represent a certain space, each one different from the last yet still reverberating with Budd's signature decorative and attractive sound. It is possible that ambient music in all its forms encourages introspection but what Budd does not allow is for that introspection to be easy. There is an edge to the warmth; a chilled draught that winds its way through the layered tones of the music. There are warm memories in the rooms evoked by the simple but evocative piano, but the tonal drones indicate an uneasiness that memory can produce. Like Erik Satie, *The Room* provokes a sense of melancholy that is both reassured and challenged.

The problem that some critics have applied to ambient music is that it is too far abstracted to have emotional resonance. Sometimes the emphasis has been on soulless experimentation that has alienated all but the most ardent of listeners. Budd says himself that back in the sixties he became too bound up in the cold aesthetics of distance listening. As he recalls, " I nearly minimalised myself out of a career !" But his inherent desire to involve himself in the emotion of music no matter how minimal propelled him in a different direction from that of mentors such as John Cage. *The Room* is about involvement ultimately; of observation and characterisation of a life led. There are not easily accessible narratives here necessarily and perhaps that is the reasons why *The Room* has a lasting effect.

TD

Record label:
Atlantic
Produced
By Harold Budd
Recorded
At Orangewood Studios, Mesa, Arizona, March 2000
Released:
August 2000
Personnel:
Harold Budd(all instruments except); Chas Smith (pedal steel guitar, metal crotales); Terrence Budd (acoustic guitar)
Track Listing:
The Room of Ancillary Dreams; The Room of Oracles; The Room of Stairs; The Room of Corners; The Room Alight; The Candied Room; The Room of Mirrors; The Room Obscured; The Room of Forgotten Children; The Room of Accidental Geometry; The Room of Secondary Light; The Flowered Room; The Room
Running Time:
54.55
Current CD:
Atlantic 7567 83382-2
Further Listening:
The Pavilion of Dreams (1978); The Plateaux of Mirrors (1980); The White Arcades (1988)
Further Reading
www.atlantic-records.com
Like this?
Try . . . p.678

Ryan Adams

Heartbreaker

Visionary rock troubadour stripped bare

Having watched his wayward band of contenders – Whiskeytown – collapse under the time honoured weight of record company disputes, non-stop touring, hard drinking and internecine squabbles, Ryan Adams followed his heart to New York from his native North Carolina in 1999 to be with his girlfriend Amy. He fell head over heels in love – both with his girl and the city. He trawled the Museum of Modern Art. He even bought a cat. Then he got his heart smashed to smithereens.

"I tend to be an easy heart," Adams recalls, "and I snapped just like that. I had to get the hell out of New York. I was scared. I was breaking up with my girl and I had no money. It wasn't good." Retreating first to his mother's house in Jacksonville, NC, then to Nashville, he eventually scraped himself up off the floor long enough to write some deeply personal, cathartic songs, suffused with shades of the deepest blue. Recorded in a mere two weeks, *Heartbreaker* utilised the talents of some of the best of Nashville's bloodline: Emmylou Harris, David Rawlings, Gillian Welch and Kim Richey among them. Producer and co-musician Ethan Johns – son of legendary Rolling Stones knob twiddler Glyn Johns – was a major influence in pushing Adams to the very edge of his capabilites as a songwriter. "Ethan is the most talented, thought-provoking, most inspiring and most bluntly critical person I've ever met," Adams says. "He knew I was only half trying."

Under the demanding gaze of Johns and using primarily acoustic textures soaked in harmonica and pedal steel, *Heartbreaker* was a bruising document of hard times in New York. Bleak yet beautiful, it recalled nothing so much as an alt.country bookend to Bob Dylan's end-of-the-affair classic *Blood on the Tracks*, standing as an enduring document of that rare and glorious moment in time when an audaciously gifted singer and songwriter finally comes of age.

Much of *Heartbreaker* sounded timeless, like it could have been written at any point during the last half century. Woody Guthrie, Gram Parsons, Hank Williams and country-fried Stones were all in there, but the final essence was unique. Kicking off with the atypically rollicking To be Young, the record soon slowed to a mesmerising crawl through the heart-sick wastelands of the self-explanatory AMY, My Winding Wheel, Call Me On Your Way Back Home, Come Pick Me Up and In My Time of Need. Greeted rapturously, it announced Adams as the boy-most-likely-to. He followed it up in 2001 with the glossier, rockier *Gold*, at which point Ryan Adams became the boy-who-just-did. But it is *Heartbreaker* that will surely endure.

GT

Record Label:
Bloodshot Records/Cooking Vinyl
Produced
by Ethan Johns
Recorded
at Room A, Woodland Studios, Nashville, Tennessee
Released:
September, 2000
Chart Peaks:
None (UK) None (US)
Personnel:
Ryan Adams (v, g, piano, harmonica, banjo); Ethan Johns (drums, bass, chamberlin, glockenspeil, B-3, vibes); David Rawlings (v, g, banjo, tambourine); Gillian Welch (v, banjo, g, bass); Pat Sansone (p, chamberlin, organ); Emmylou Harris (v); Kim Richey (v); Allison Pierce (v)
Track Listing:
(Argument with David Rawlings concerning Morrissey); To Be Young; My Winding Wheel; AMY; Oh My Sweet Carolina; Bartering Lines; Call Me On Your Way Back Home; Damn, Sam; Come Pick Me Up; To Be The One; Why Do They Leave?; Shakedown on 9th Street; Don't Ask For the Water; In My Time of Need; Sweet Lil' Gal (23rd/1st)
Running Time:
52.03
Current CD:
COOKCD205
Further Listening:
Gold (Lost Highway 2001); Demolition (Lost Highway 2002); Whiskeytown – Pneumonia (Lost Highway 2001)
Further reading:
www.ryan-adams.com
Like this?
Try . . . p.529

Afterlife

Simplicity 2000

Ibitha uncovered . . .

Take a moment to probe beyond the glamour, chaos and brazen vulgarity of Ibiza's dance culture and what are you left with? Huge interrupted stretches of devastating coastline, tear jerking sunsets and a handful of hillside villages that allow life to loaf by, seamlessly, simply. Afterlife's debut, *Simplicity 2000* manages to capture the islands hidden alter ego and translate it into an emotional vinyl oil painting. The driving force behind Afterlife, Steve Miller, who was born in the same hood as Tolkein and produced the album from his current home in Cheshire, has used the landscape and native inhabitants of Ibiza as a working metaphor.

"Jose Padilla asked me to write something specific for his compilation Café del Mar 3. I went over to Ibiza and was deeply affected by the powerful vibe of the island – the people, the scenery, the way of life. The album is a reflection of my time spent there."

Miller felt that Ibiza had not only opened him up on an emotional level, "I made the album to reflect how I felt inside and how I was changing as a person," but exposed him to a more liberal way of producing music. He no longer felt constricted by the need to preempt fashions in the UK. The result is a very honest album, which ventures way beyond the sentimental expectations of popular Chill Out. It's mission statement is not so much one of sedating but rather emoting. Track One, *Dub in Ya Mind*, sung by Rachel Lloyd – voice of a fallen angel, juxtaposes strings and sensual melodies with quirky trip hop beats slowed to a pulse. The effect is more invigorating than 'chilling.' Tack two, *Never Before,* pushes the pulse that little bit faster with it's flamenco driven rhythms and track seven, *Borneo* is *Burning,* in spite of its lullaby appeal, causes you to sit up and think. Whether the track is laden with deft political undertones or it is something entirely innocent, it is a gorgeous feat of melancholy that has you reaching for the tissues. All twelve of the tracks flow seamlessly into a beautifully executed narrative, which pays homage to the pure ethereal resin of native Ibiza. Miller's favourite track is *Dub in Ya Mind.*

"I wrote it immediately upon my return from Ibiza having worked with José and Lenny Ibizarre. We used to have small private parties at Cap des Falco on the southern tip of the island. The track perfectly encapsulates my feelings about that place."

And it's worth taking a trip to Cap des Falco for a snapshot of the landscape and ambience that has inspired Miller. Forget your pay per view communal sunsets at the Café del Mar, *Simplicity 2000* really is Ibiza uncovered.

HW

Record label:
Hedkandi
Produced
Steve Miller
Recorded
Delta Quadrant
Released:
September 2000
Personnel:
Steve Miller
Track listing:
Dub in ya mind (Blue Water mix); Never before; Show you something; Cry (Brown Bear mix); 5th and Avenida; Deeper (into places); Borneo is burning; Glide; Breather (original version); La Nina; Blue bar; Cry (original mix); Dub in ya mind (ibizzares insatiable mix); Falling; Show you something (Chris Coco Balaric beats mix); Lo delta; Breather (Arithunda mix); Cry (Factor 15 sunset dream remix); Cry (Spoon Wizard mix); Show you something (ambient mix)
Current CD:
HEDK013
Like this?
Try . . . p.405

Esbjörn Svensson

Good Morning Susie Soho

Swedish trio maps out a possible future sound of jazz

Its says a lot about the sickly state of jazz music that while this 2000 album topped critics' polls and set the trio on course for packed European tours, it did little to spread the name of the pianist Esbjörn Svensson into wider public consciousness (in Britain at least).

In Svensson's native Sweden the album reached 15 in the pop charts and the group became the first jazz outfit to feature on European MTV. The trio, who had been recording since 1993, began as a pretty orthodox unit, much influenced by Keith Jarrett. Good Morning Susie Soho marks the consolidation of "the EST sound", a style firmly rooted in jazz improvisation but which takes in rhythms from rock and electronica and melodies from pop and Scandinavian folk. Svensson was listening to classical music and Radiohead when the record was conceived. Bassist Dan Berglund was as much a fan of early Black Sabbath as Charlie Mingus and Magnus Oström had become a dab hand at reproducing beatbox sounds acoustically. The trio had also played many rock clubs – partly because Sweden's jazz scene is scarcely huge – partly in an attempt to break out of the jazz ghetto.

By the group's standards Good Morning Susie Soho was a relaxed project. Usually they got a couple of days in the studio; this time they had five. And when they weren't happy with the results they were able to go in again and re-record. "It was a help. It gave us the chance to experiment a lot more, and we added some new tunes," says Svensson.

The title track was written while the group was gigging in London and for a while was called merely London. During a sunny outdoor breakfast in the capital the name was changed to Good Morning Soho. "Then Magnus who is the one who normally names the tunes added the name Susie just because he liked the way it sounded," says Svensson.

The album convincingly explores wide stylistic territory – from the spacey techno of The Wraith to the funky swing of Do The Jangle and the cool groove of the title track, powered by Berglund's wah-wah bass. A hidden track at the end clatters straight into rock territory. Warm press reviews followed. The German Der Spiegel hailed Svensson as "the future of jazz piano". The New York Times declared the EST sound to be "not what jazz was but a vision of what it can be". At any rate for those who thought that the most progressive jazz was now coming out of Europe, not America, the album was powerful evidence.

JBL

Record label:
Act
Released:
October 2000
Personnel:
Esbjörn Svensson; Dan Berglund (bass); Magnus Öström (drums)
Track listing:
Somewhere Else Before; Do The Jangle; Serenity; The Wraith; Last Letter From Lithuania; Good Morning Susie Soho; Providence; Pavane: Thoughts of a Septuagenarian; Spam-Boo-Limbo; The Face of Love; Reminiscence of a Soul
Current CD:
ACT90092
Further listening:
Winter in Venice (1999); Esbjorn Svensson Trio plays monk (2001); Strange Place for Snow (2002)
Further reading:
www.esbjornsvenssontrio.com
Like this?
Try . . . p.24

P.J Harvey

Stories From The City, Stories From The Sea

Big love, raw sex

Polly Harvey's 6th album simply blows you away with its raw power – even in its reflective moments. From the jagged, controlled violence of *Big Exit* right through to the lush and elegiac *We Float*, this is P.J Harvey in complete control, working us over from the inside out.

All the pulsating aggression is still there, but this time Polly is the onlooker, the detached narrator rather than the accused or the victim. On the smouldering blues of *The Whores Hustle And The Hustlers Whore*, her voice croaks with ennui and disappointment, but more than anything she radiates a so-fucking-what stance that's more impervious than angry. That sense of inevitable disillusionment is realised with ineffable and effortless beauty on the duet with Thom Yorke, *The Mess We're In*. It's an impossibly lovely song, its chorus lilting out the disconsolate refrain:

"*The city sun sets over me*"

But ***Stories From The City…*** is an album that throbs with heart and soul and sex and, yes, *hope*. On *Good Fortune* we find Polly celebrating the moment, asking no more and trying merely to crystallise it, preserve it in time and say This Happened And It Was Good. Inevitably that optimism comes hand in glove with the P.J Harvey compulsion that all good things, if not intrinsically false, will of necessity fade away – but on this album she seems fine with that. It's the same on *You Said Something* and the quietly poetic *Place Called Home*, these are blistering and beautiful songs by a woman who has seen it all.

All that love and hope and fury, all the seething and soaring and waning emotions that tug and pull beneath the surface of these songs finally explode with the ballistic and anthemic *This Is Love*. This is the song that characterises ***Stories From The City, Stories From The Sea*** . It's intensely heavy soul - abrasive, seductive, unflinchingly sexual.

KS

Record label:
Island
Produced
by Rob Ellis, PJ Harvey, Mick Harvey
Released
October 2000
Chart peaks:
23 (UK) 42 (US)
Personnel:
Polly Harvey (vocals, bass, guitar, keyboards); Rob Ellis (drums, keyboard, piano, backing vocals); Mick Harvey (bass, drums, percussion, backing vocals)
Track listing:
Big exit; Good fortune; A place called home; One line; Beautiful feeling; The whores hustle and the hustlers whore; This mess we're in; You said something; Kamikaze; This is love; Horses in my dreams; We float; This wicked tongue
Current CD:
CID8099
Further listening:
Rid of Me (1993); To Bring You My Love (1995); Dry (1999)
Further reading:
www.pjharvey.net
Like this?
Try . . . p.612

Jeff Mills

Metropolis

Techno heavyweight thrusts the future of the future music into realms far beyond the dancefloor by creating an original score and edit to Fritz Lang's silent-film classic.

After more than a decade of touring the world as one of the world most in-demand DJs, after spinning with three turntables at once, and after releasing a slew of influential dancefloor tracks, the tireless one they called the Wizard began wondering about the future of techno. A musical form that had been born out of continual innovation was stagnating in its repetitive sounds, drug culture, and new-found commercial appeal. For Mills and others who think of techno's emotional content beyond the pace of its beats, dance music was in danger of being ghettoized to the clubs, appreciated as limited musical form capable of only soundtracking the happiest, most ecstatic points in one's life. The focus on innovation and evolution had been blurred by a pursuit of fun for fun's sake.

DJs like Mills and Richie Hawtin, supremely skilled jockeys who were always looking to do something unheard of first, turned to other artforms to find a different purpose for their electronic music. While Hawtin collaborated with British painter Jason Martin on a project for the BBC, Mills decided to make his own installations along with tackling the giant project of soundtracking Fritz Lang's *Metropolis*.

The silent film had already been subject to fifteen different soundtracks, including ones by Giorgio Moroder and Phillip Glass. For this reason, and also because the film's themes were thought to be so well-suited for a first-time techno project of this kind, Mills went about not only composing music for what he wanted to achieve, but also creating a whole new edit of the film to work with his idea for the score. No matter how skilled a DJ he was before, this was a whole new mix and match, an unprecedented cut and paste.

In the autumn of 2000, Paris' Centre de Pompidou debuted Mills' *Metropolis*. In an hour-long screening and soundtrack, Mills accomplishes a dramatic execution of so many of his desires. The music was playful, frenetic, timid, and more-much more than what one was accustomed to hearing in techno. From the cerebral meandering of "Entrance to Metropolis" (used for Lang's long shots of the cityscape) to the pulsating "Keeping of the Kept" (played during the factory interior scenes), Mills injects studio equipment with a rare range of functionality.

Metropolis is not yet the music that Mills is best known for. But in terms of its scope, intentions, and emotive execution, it'll be the kind of thing that others-maybe even the next generation of techno artists-will fondly remember him by.

AD

Record label:
Axis Records
Produced
by Jeff Mills
Released:
October 2000
Chart peaks:
None
Personnel:
Jeff Mills
Track listing:
Entrance to Metropolis, Perfecture: Somewhere Around Now, They Who Lay Beneath, Convicted to Paradise/Maria, Keeping of the Kept, Landscape, Blue Print, Transformation A, Transformation B, Robot Replica, Revolt, Flood, Storm Among Us, Silence, New Beginning
Running time:
59:06
Current CD:
56155 (IMPORT)
Further listening:
Waveform Transmission Vol. 1 (1992), Mix-Up Vol. 2 Featuring J. Mills 1995), Purposemaker Compilation (1998), At First Sight (2002)
Further reading:
www.axisrecords.com
Like this?
Try . . . p.675

Mary J Blige
Mary

One thing Mary. J has never tired of is lamenting the imperfections of love and relationships. The cheating-lying good-for-nothing-brother is a recurring leitmotif throughout M.J's work and the latter half of her self-titled album, *Mary* struts in a similar direction. So while she's treading familiar ground here, M.J's vocals lend a raw candour to even the most clichéd of her lyrics. When she offers up well-worn lines such as:

"She said it was your child. And it really messed me up. How could you deny your own flesh and blood?" it's still delivered with such staggering emotional conviction that you are half willing to buy into all the cynicism - again.

Mary is MJ's fourth album, nurtured over the course of a three-year studio break then honed to perfection by a dazzling entourage of producers and writers. Lauren Hill, Burt Bacharach, Stevie Wonder and Baby Face have all left their imprint, yet it's the purity and passion of Mary J's voice that soars above everything and everyone. *Mary* lacks the melodic belligerence of its predecessors, and apart from the finger clicking dance floor classic, *Let No Man Put Asunder,* works best as a pool side, soaking up the sun -sipping on Martinis affair. It swoons with sugared melancholy, thrives on sensual melodies and M.J works her voice through the full range of its instrumental potential. While some of her joint efforts work well – Stevie Wonder's contribution to track Seven, *Time,* is a beautifully philosophical take on the lunge and surge of time – others undoubtedly dilute the overall integrity of the album. Her duet with George Michael, *As*, for example, is a crude stab at 'crossover' friendliness, while *Not Looking,* featuring K-Ci Hailey, is just bland and pleading to be skipped.

It's a measure of M.J's diva status that the great and the good now queue up for the kudos of collaboration, but the one burning beacon that sears through this record is Mary's voice. She transmits an emotional intensity that bears no comparison and it's here, on *Mary,* that it's gift-wrapped in all its spectrum of shades and subtleties. Forget the cohorts – feel the voice.

HW

Record Label:
MCA Records
Produced
by Mary J. Blige and Kirk Burrows
Released:
April 2000 (first release September 1999)
Chart peaks:
5 (UK) 2 (US)
Personnel:
Mary J. Blige (vocals)
Track listing:
All that I can say; sexy; Deep inside; Beautiful ones; I'm the love; As; Time; Memories; Don't waste your time; Not looking'; Your child; No happy holidays; Love I never had; Give me you; Let no man put asunder; Give me you (nino radio edit)
Current CD:
1122552
Further listening:
What's the 411? (1992); Share my world (1997); No more drama (2001)
Further reading:
www.mjblige.com
Like this?
Try . . . p.497

2000

y

…s sound filled with folksy samples continues
… …itish tradition of musical eccentricity.

For the LemonJelly duo, Fred Deakin and Nick Franglen, making music came relatively late in life. Not until their early thirties did they start producing the sound that would epitomise a very British slant on chilled electronica. Deakin and Franglen carefully if eclectically built the experience that is LemonJelly- the music, the graphics, the website.

Franglen after a stint as a gardener wrote music for multinationals like Sega and Sony before going on to program for Pulp, amongst others. Deakin eager to carry on his teenage love for music established weird and wonderful club nights like Thunderball in Edinburgh and Impotent Fury in London. As he says, "I was completely obsessed with music and I was really desperate for some kind of creative interface with it. So I started Djing and I've been doing that for 20 years now." These strange and at the time highly original club nights would demonstrate, Deakin's love of the eccentric and fly in the face of po-faced musos. "We'd have cake nights that would invariably end in food fights. We'd stage nights in castles, ice rinks and art galleries. Just lots of really stupid stuff to try and make people have a good time, to leave their cool baggage at home."

Deakin's enthusiasm for interacting with his audience is legendary as is his love of the amiably eccentric and both factors have influenced their music and can be heard on their debut EP. The album essentially collects together their Eps the first of which Bath was released in 1998. While many downbeat outfits like Kruder and Dorfmeister sample like there was no tomorrow – and no litigation – it's the way in which LemonJelly use their quirky samples that counts. DJ Shadow on his masterful release, Endtroducing, uses sampling as an instrument, a tool which used well can create not just another layer to the music but an original voice. There are samples from an incredible range of sources – from Teach Yourself Folk Guitar used on ' The Staunton Lick to the field recordings of Dr.William Brook. Everything and not even excluding the kitchen sink is in there but while Bond, Middle-Eastern samples can be found by anyone it is way there are used and fused with jazzy riffs, folky progressions that makes *Ky* such an original album.

Above all it is the humour that stands out. So much of electronica tends towards the impersonal and Deakin and Franglen have challenged this. There is a sense of origin as well, a very British sound that is evoked by obscure TV programmes and stuffy RP voices. On the track 'Page One' stoned beats help us listen to the self-help samples. Ironically in such a new form of music, there is a sense of nostalgia, of popular cultural history to this electronica. There is a sense of history sampling itself.

TD

Record label:
Impotent Fury
Released:
October 2000
Personnel:
Fred Deakin; Nick Franglen
Track listing:
In the bath; Nervous tension; Tune for Jack; His majesty King Raam; Staunton lick; Homage to Patagonia; Kneel before your God; Page one; Come
Current CD:
IFXLCD139
Further listening:
Lost Horizons (2002)
Further reading:
www.lemonjelly.ky
Like this?
Try . . . p.261

Roni Size Reprazent

In The Mode

A neglected masterpiece that should fulfilled all the grand promises drum and bass had made.

Two months before its release, Roni Size was pondering the as-yet untitled follow-up to New Forms, the Mercury Music Prize-winning album from his collective Reprazent which had put drum and bass on the British musical map.

"I'm still young in making albums, I'm still learning, but this time around I've learned so much," he enthused. "And I know about trying to actually get into a piece of music, so deep into it that you're ignorant to everything around you. I'm in that mode at the moment."

In The Mode turned out to be a tighter, leaner, more relentless work than its often sprawling predecessor: a clearer, more accessible, yet even more uncompromising record. In The Mode saw Size and fellow producers Krust, Die and Suv take drum and bass's, ahem, new forms, match them to punk's energy, hip hop's attitude and rock's volume, and kick the resultant explosions out of the speakers.

Reprazent's lives had been changed by New Forms' success. Size donated the £25,000 Mercury winnings to The Basement, a youth centre in his native Bristol where he'd first learned to program a drum machine, and victory helped bring the band more live bookings. In The Mode was conceived in rehearsals and jam sessions, the four producers' technology and samples meshing with live bass, drums and, in particular, vocals.

In addition to Reprazent's own singer, Onallee, and emcee, Dynamite, Size looked outside the group. Wu-Tang Clan rapper Method Man and Rage Against The Machine's Zack De La Rocha both turned in ferocious performances while Rahzel, the human beatbox best known for his work with The Roots, allowed Size to record him in full experimental flow. To "produce" the resulting In Tune With The Sound, Size had merely to press the "record" button.

Yet In The Mode, clearly a superior record to its predecessor, didn't receive anything like the acclaim. The mainstream media had already found drum and bass passe, and the music had slipped back underground. Reprazent became probably the best live rock band in the world, but sets at the Essential Festival in the summer of 2001 seem to have proved their swan song.

Since then, while Size, Die and Krust and Dynamite have recorded plenty, Reprazent seem dead in the water. It's as if Size, disheartened by the muted response to this musical direction, had decided to try something different, even when, creatively, his work was touching new, uncharted peaks.

AB

Record label:
Talkin' Loud
Produced
by Roni Size except Ghetto Celebrity (with Krust and Die), Lucky Pressure (with Suv), Balanced Chaos, Who Told You, Heavy Rotation (with Die), In Tune With The Sound (with Rahzel) and Snapshot (additional production by Krust and Die).
Recorded
at Channel House, Bristol
Released:
2000
Chart peaks:
18 (UK) None (US)
Personnel:
Roni Size (kbds): Krust (kbds): Die (kbds): Suv (kbds): Onallee (v): Dynamite MC (v): B Watt (gtr) Spry (perc): R Merrill (drums) Si John (bass): A Byron-Collins (piano): J Allen (bass): Method Man (v): Z De La Rocha (v)
Track listing:
Railing Pt 2: In + Out: System Check: Ghetto Celebrity feat. Method Man: Lucky Pressure: Balanced Chaos: Switchblade: In Tune With The Sound feat. Rahzel: Who Told You: Heavy Rotation: Staircase: Mexican: Dirty Beats: Out Of The Game: Centre Of The Storm feat. Zack De La Rocha: Idi Banashapan: Snapshot: Play The Game
US version has different track-listing and sequence. Balanced Chaos is omitted, Play The Game and In + Out are in different versions
Running time:
79 mins 41 secs
US version running time: 76 mins 0 secs
Current CD:
5481762
(US 314 548 201-2)
Further listening:
New Forms (1997)
Like this?
Try . . . p.703

OutKast

Stankonia

Rap reinvented as P-Funk by a Georgia duo constantly duelling between the musically sacred and the secularly profane.

OutKast's fourth LP is an acknowledged masterpiece of a genre that seemed, at the dawn of the new millennium, to have finally come to terms with its past and begun to realise its potential. It was only its makers who seemed unable to extricate themselves from the record's contradictions.

Andre "Dre"/"Andre 3000" Benjamin and Antoine "Big Boi" Patton had a US rap No 1 single before they were out of their teens. The group worked predominantly with live instruments, though the music they produced was less the rustic, soul-inspired grooves of bands like The Roots than a futuristic take on funk that owed a debt to George Clinton and Prince. Mr DJ, a partner with Dre and Big Boi in the production unit Earthtone III, explained the process to www.alphabeats.com:

"Sometimes we go to clubs and watch the bands and pick out who we want to play for us," he said. "Of course, we got people that we always use. And we just all hook up and have big vibe sessions. We sit around, smoke a few, drink a few. Sometimes it's good and sometimes it ain't so good." Yet what ended up on Stankonia fell uniformly into the former category.

Lyrically OutKast mixed and matched tales of strip clubs, gang banging and sex with meditations on spirituality, love and politics. In an earlier encapsulation of their duality, civil rights veteran Rosa Parks sued them after they titled a song in her name, her action partially motivated by the group's language. On Stankonia, though, all the elements gelled.

"You don't feel one way all the time," Dre would later explain. "Some days you wake up on one side of the bed, and all you wanna do is party. And some days you got somethin' to say. So we put both of them together."

Stankonia took their sound supernova. Ms Jackson became a worldwide pop hit, and there are standouts throughout, though first single BOB – Bombs Over Baghdad – is an obvious head-turner. "At the time hip hop was kind of relaxed. Everybody was getting paid, so it wasn't as hungry. We wanted that song to sound fierce, to sound urgent," explained Dre of BOB's blitzkrieg power and blistering pace, inspired by hearing drum & bass. Yet the message behind that provocative title, that people shouldn't talk the talk if they can't walk the walk, remained decidedly, decisively ambiguous.

AB

Record label:
LaFace/Arista
Produced
by Earthtone III (Mr DJ, Andre 3000, Big Boi): Organized Noize: Antonio "LA" Reid
Released:
November 2000
Chart peaks:
10 (UK) 2 (US)
Personnel:
Andre 3000 (v); Big Boi (v): Khujo Goodie from Goodie Mob (v on Gasoline Dreams): Killer Mike (v on Snappin' & Trappin'): J-Sweet (v on Snappin' & Trappin'): Gangsta Boo (v on I'll Call Before I Come): Eco (v on I'll Call Before I Come): B-Real (v on Xplosion): Back Bone (v on We Luv Deez Hoez): Big Gipp from Goodie Mob (v on We Luv Deez Hoez): Erykah Badu (v): Slimm Calhoun (v): C-Bone (v): T-Mo Goodie from Goodie Mob (v): Cee-Lo Goodie (v): Big Rube (v): S Brown (v)
Track listing:
Intro: Gasoline Dreams: I'm Cool (Interlude): So Fresh, So Clean: Ms. Jackson: Snapin' & Trappin': D.F. (Interlude): Spaghetti Junction: Kim & Cookie (Interlude): I'll Call Before I Come: B.O.B.: Xplosion: Good Hair (Interlude): We Luv Deez Hoez: Humble Mumble: Drinkin' Again (Interlude): ?: red Velvet: Cruisin' In The ATL (Interlude): Gangsta Sh*t: Toilet Tisha: Slum Beautiful: Pre-Nump (interlude): Stankonia (Stanklove)
Running time:
73 mins 17 secs
Current CD:
73008 26072 2
Further listening:
Aquemeni (1998)
Like this?
Try . . . p.367

Lambchop

Nixon

Lo-fi Americana collective's big production hit

Soul and country might not sound on the surface the most compatible of bedfellows (although music historians will beg to differ), but it's a marriage that Lambchop have kept alive through their extraordinary career with neither side hogging the duvet. Until the Nashville collective's sixth album, *Nixon*. Here singer-writer Kurt Wagner's passion for soul - earlier evident on the Curtis Mayfield and Frederick Knight covers, Gimme Your Love and I've Been Lonely So Long, on 1998's *What Another Man Spills* - was given its fullest rein.

And also its biggest production. Previously lumped with alt. country's lo-fi acts, more through necessity than choice - fiercely independent, the collective has always refused to take record company money; each member has a day job, so that whatever the band makes subsidises the next record and tour - *Nixon* was, in Wagner's words, their "full-on lush monster. I liked the lo-fi thing fine, but I wanted to see what would happen, taking our kind of wacky content and the way we are, and use all the technology people are using now and see if we could pull it off, and still keep our souls intact."

Which is how Nashville's least mainstream band came to dip its big toe into Establishment waters. Stretching the shoestring near to breaking point, they squashed a string orchestra, a gospel choir and a team of engineers who had worked with country' music's Big Boys into a small studio already packed with Lambchop's 14 card-carrying members plus three guests.

The gospel singers were let loose on the celebratory Up With People, but not before they'd quizzed Wagner on the meaning of the song. Kurt's lyrics here, as always, were a mix of candour and poetry. "I was very careful with the choir director not to get them too deep into what was going on in the lyrics, because I was afraid they would freak out. I did have to go through what 'progeny' meant, to make sure it wasn't about the Devil. Once they knew what it was, one woman went 'Amen!'" Elsewhere, songs like The Distance From Here To There, sung in an intimate, whispered falsetto, had a delicacy that belied the extravagant size of the band.

Nixon - which had as little to do with the disgraced ex-President as Lambchop has with the glove puppet they stole the name from - was a critical and commercial success. "Not that it was Britney Spears," said Wagner, "but a modest jump of people actually knowing who the fuck we are." And it terrified him. Hence the quiet, low-key sound of 2002's follow-up *Is A Woman*.

SS

Record label:
City Slang 20152-2
Producer
by Mark Nevers/ Kurt Wagner
Recorded
by Sound Emporium, Beech House and Studio 19, Nashville
Released:
February 2000
Chart peaks:
60 (UK) None (US)
Personnel:
Paula James Booker (guitar); Ken Coomer (percussion); Dennis Cronin (cornet, trumpet, vocals); Tony Crow (Piano); John Delworth (Hammond Synth, juno, Hammond organ, piano); Allen Lowrey (drums); Jonathan Marx (trumpet, vocals); Alex McManus (guitar) Nashville String Machine (strings); Mark Nevers (guitar); Paul Niehaus (Fender Telecaster, pedal steel, vocals); Matt Swanson (bass); Deanna Varagona (sax, vocals); Kurt Wagner (guitar, juno, vocals)
Track listing:
The Old Gold Shoe/ Grumpus/ You Masculine You/ Up With People/ Nashville Parent/ What Else Could It Be/ The Distance From Her To There/ The Book I Haven't Read/ The Petrified Florist/ The Butcher Boy
Current CD:
201522
Further listening:
How I Quit Smoking (1996); Hank (1996); What another man spills (1998)
Further reading:
www.lambchop.net
Like this?
Try . . . p.477

Rachid Taha

Made In Medina

Forget chronology: Led Zeppelin knew nothing about North African music until they heard this

Having started out in a French-Algerian punk band that attacked the racism faced by immigrants from North Africa, Taha had spent the 1990 looking at ways to fuse his Arabic roots with rock and pop. *Diwan*, his previous album, had lifted him out of the roots ghetto with modern interpretations of songs whose authors came from traditional musical backgrounds. But *Made In Medina* took rock'n'roll as its base camp and then fitted the roots into the cracks.

The opening tracks, Barra Barra and Foqt Foqt (sounds salacious, but actually refers to *human relationships diverted from their nobler impulses* according to Taha), were recorded with the help of a New Orleans rock group and, in a climate where corporate-pussy nu metal rooled, Taha crunched through the skulls of the opposition like they were papier mache. By Aie Aie Aie, the guitars were out and Maghrebi and Egyptian percussion drove the songs on ‹ the heaviness, however, was provided by a string section clearly under the influence of Zep. You didn't need to be too alert, though, to notice the electronic dance beats: Medina and Hey Anta are straightforward house cum disco tunes, albeit, in the latter case, with a great Bo Diddley riff.

Once Taha had lured you in, the facade came down for the home straight: En Retard is the most rootsy of all the tracks, a rai tune in the style of Algerian street singers from the 1930s. The rhythm is bass-heavy, backing vocals come from B'net Marrakesh, a group of Berber women whose forte is working themselves up into a trance and bashing their heads with metal percussion instruments. The closer, Garab, is an apocalyptic funk stew that builds in intensity until becoming a Sympathy For The Devil (or I Am The Resurrection if you so choose) for the new millennium.

So how do you sell something that covers Led Zeppelin, The Clash, Bo Diddley, The Stones Rose, The Stones and house, but does it in Arabic' You embark on two years on the road, including a two tours of America (one in the wake of 9/11 the other as war with Iraq was looming), playing with a balls-on-the-line, take-no-prisoners force that reaches out to teen rockers and world music fans alike. 'I am not world music,' Taha always insists. 'Half my band, maybe, the oud and percussion. But the guitars, bass and drums are rock.' So how rock is Taha really? Well, he owns a Parisian lesbian bar. QED.

DH

Record label:
Barclay/Universal
Produced
by Steve Hillage
Recorded
by A-Wave Records, London; American Sector, New Orleans; Studio De Belleville, Paris
Chart peaks:
None (UK) None (US)
Release date:
October 2000
Personnel:
Rachid Taha (voc), Steve Hillage (programming, guitar), Stanton Moore (drums), Robert Mercurio (bs), Hakim Hamaduche (oud), Hassan Lachal (perc), Hossam Razy (perc), Jeff Raines (gtr), Rich Vogel (keyboards), B?Net Marrakesh (vocs),
Track listing:
Barra Barra/Foqt Foqt/Medina/Ala Jalkoum/Aie Aie Aie/Hey Anta/Qalantiqa/En Retard/Verite/Ho Cherie Cherie/Garab
Release date:
February 6, 2001
Running time:
63:54
Current CD:
5439952
Further listening:
Carte Blanche (2000); 123 Soleils (2000); Rachid Taha Live (2002)
Further reading:
http://kabish.com/adrian/rachid_taha/
Like this?
Try . . . p.257

Rufus Wainwright

Poses

Oscar Wilde meets Mozart in this lush diary of a boy's coming of age in NYC.

"I think one of the most important things a songwriter can do sometimes is not write songs," Rufus Wainwright told *Performing Songwriter* in 2001. "Sometimes you need to store up your creative juices. Before my second record, I just needed some real-life experiences in order to have some things to write about that were different from everyday stuff." Towards that end, Wainwright checked into the Chelsea Hotel in New York. Like a character from an Oscar Wilde play - or Wilde himself - he went on a months-long wanton tear through the city, from penthouse party to club rave, binge-ing on carnal and chemical pleasures.

"As I sort of woke up from the haze, the song Poses came to me," Wainwright says. The gorgeous plum of a ballad, ripe with melody and poetry ("In the green autumnal parks conducting all the city streets / A wondrous chorus singing all these poses") became the starting point for the album.

Wainwright says, "I had a style that I wanted go on with for the rest of the album. It's about the experience of a young man in the city - both wonderful and terrible. I try to walk that fine line between debauchery, death and sanity."

The 26-year old hunkered down into the writing process - "My usual style is to take months and months on the songs, just pondering them" - then teamed up with Canadian producer Pierre Marchand.

"My first record was very exclamatory," Wainwright told *Salon*. "It was kind of saying, 'I am a great force arriving here with my orchestra and 80 xylophones. Look out!' The basic idea for this album was that it should be less demanding and easy to listen to. I still think it's pretty intense at times, but we wanted it to be something you could play loudly or softly, or your headphones, or as background music."

From the Nilsson-esque bounce of Cigarettes and Chocolate Milk to the stately grandeur of The Tower Of Learning to the smoky French amour of Rebel Prince, the collection is so bountiful in melody and invention that it makes Wainwright's singer-songwriter contemporaries look like so many Salieris.

While *Poses* never broke through to the masses, you get the sense that Wainwright is going to be around for a while. "One of my main goals is the same as some of my biggest heroes - like Sibelius, Verdi and Wagner, who are the composers that I love. They only got better as they got older and wrote their best material just before they died. I would like to go in that same track. I don't want to go in that pop way, where you have to do your best in your first two records, then you do a string of mediocre shit."

BDM

Record label:
Dreamworks
Produced
by Pierre Marchand; "Shadows" produced by Alex Gifford
Recorded
at Ocean Way, Los Angeles; BJG, London; The Magic Shop, NYC; Rocket Carousel, Los Angeles;
Released:
June 2001
Chart peaks:
117 (US)
Personnel:
R Wainwright (v, p, k, g, dobro); P Marchand (b, p); A Gifford (b, p, g, bass clarinet); E Johns (g, b, d); A McErlain (g); M Vincent Chaves (g); G Arreguin (g); J Hill (b, v); P Wilson (b); M Auf De Maur (b); R Causon (k); D Legassick (k, programming); B Tench (k); K Hupp (d); P Thomas (d); J Keltner (d); A Sood (d); V Indrizzo (d); S Sidelnyk (programming); Y Desrosiers (banjo, g, mandolin); A Srinivasan, S Allard, J-M LeBlanc, M Belair, G Beaudry, I Rathbone, R Ware (vn) J Dupras, W Hos, V Potuin, G Hay (va); C Antoun, C Guigere, H Skewes, L Fairhurst (c); J Paquin, P Savoie (french horn); N Forget (oboe)
Track listing:
Cigarettes and Chocolate Milk; Greek Song; Poses; Shadows; California; The Tower of Learning; Grey Gardens; Rebel Prince; The Consort; One Man Guy; Evil Angel; In a Graveyard; Cigarettes and Chocolate Milk (Reprise)
Running time:
53:26
Current CD:
0044-50237-2
Further listening:
Rufus Wainwright
Further reading:
www.rufuswainwright.com
Like this?
Try . . . p.243

Nitin Sawhney

Prophesy

Transcending the Asian Underground tag, Sawhney's fifth album is the most global-aware, all-encompassing LP you've ever heard

The idea that it might be difficult for an underground artist to follow an album that had been nominated for a Mercury Music Prize and won a South Bank award clearly never troubled Nitin Sawhney. For others, *Beyond Skin* might have seemed the pinnacle, but it was only the base camp for the next stage in a career that had encompassed stand-up comedy, acid jazz and the first new wave of British-made Indian music. Furthermore, Sawhney was adamant that he was bored with 'writing songs about nothing' and determined that *Prophesy* would mean something to all who heard it.

The recording process took in six continents, with Sawhney offering the microphone to anybody he felt had something to say, whether powerful or dispossessed: a New York cabbie explained his fears about being excluded from the technology-driven new order ('I'm a low-tech man in a high-tech world ... maybe I don't wanna change?); Nelson Mandela offered the advice, 'We are free to be free'; and Yothu Yindi's leader Mandawuy Yunupingu gave advice ('Development should be a right, not something that is forced down our throats'). This is world music without the ghettoising that label often implies.

Yes, it is a concept album: one that looks at perspectives of the future through the voices of those ignored at G7 or G14 summits, like Brazilian street children or Native American shamen. Speeches and news bulletins pepper the rhythm tracks, ideas fill the gaps. 'Development is not just about material progress, but about spiritual development. People like the Native Americans and Aborigines have a feeling for the land. They know that things are out of tune and want to retune them.'

Musically, unsurprisingly, it covers all bases. The opening four tracks are almost symphonic in their horizons, segueing from a Prince-like soul track to ghostly Indian instrumentals so that you never notice the join. It's not until Cheb Mami's spiralling Algerian wail opens Moonrise that you notice how far you have come. The digeridoo of Developed subversively slides into a South African school choir on Footsteps. Even tunes that are ostensibly instrumental, such as the flute and drum'n'bass Breathing Light, contain Asian percussion vocals, highlighting how integral human participation is. Most importantly, the polemic is anything but heavy-handed: Sawhney collected as stellar a cast of musicians and singers as he could. As a result, you are free to disagree with every word of it, but you are certain to be seduced by the music.

DH

Record label:
(V2)
Producer:
Nitin Sawhney
Recorded:
Chart
Release date:
June 2001
Personnel:
Nitin Sawhney (gtr, kbds, programming), Cheb Mami (voc), Natacha Atlas (voc), Trilok Gurtu (perc), Steve Shehan (perc), Jose Miguel Carmona (flamenco gtr), Rishile Primary School Choir (voc), London Community Gospel Choir (voc), English Chamber Orchestra, Orquesta Nationale De Brasilica, Mandawuy Yunupingu (voc), Terry Callier (voc), Pinky Tusadero (voc), Jeff Jacobs (rant), Nina Miranda (voc), Jayanta Bose (tabla), Tina Grace (voc), Eska (voc), Nelson Mandela (voc)
Track listing:
Sunset/Nothing/Acquired Dreams/Nothing More/Moonrise/Street Guru (Part One)/The Preacher/Breathing Light/Developed/Footsteps/Walk Away/Cold & Intimate/Street Guru (part Two)/Ripping Out Tears/Prophesy
Running time:
52:10
Current CD:
VVR1015912
Further listening:
www.nitinsawhney.com
Like this?
Try . . . p.700

The White Stripes
White Blood Cells

As *White Blood Cells* was released, the White Stripes found themselves occupying an era populated by a marked number of other bands prefixed by 'the' (the Strokes, the Vines, the Hives), all of whose music seem to be stamped with the description 'stripped down,' and whose success was heralded as a rebirth of rock.

Their breakthrough LP, *White Blood Cells* established the Detroit duo as the best of the bunch—the most genuine and the most endowed with talent. The album was the band's third full-length in as many years, and that *White Blood Cells,* released by the independent label Sympathy for the Record Industry, landed the duo on MTV and onto the covers of shrink-wrapped glossy magazines is probably owing as much to its timing as to its musical genius. 2001 was nothing if not the year of garage rock revival.

The White Stripes' breakout success was latent in their first two records, *The White Stripes* (1999) and *De Stijl* (2000), all it took was the colossal swell in the popularity of a subculture and the subsequent perked eyebrows of a record industry for things to really turn around for Jack and Meg White. Rumors abounded about their relationship—they claimed outwardly to be siblings, but a marriage certificate surfaced proving that they had actually once been married. Despite the tabloid-esque chatter, the real query seemed to be just how two otherwise quietly humble kids managed to make so much noise, churning out sweat-drenched, crunchy numbers mined from so diverse a collection of influences.

The record evokes an encounter of delta blues, rocking chair country, Motor City rock, and punk, with esoteric bents as diverse as the show tune. The album was recorded in Memphis, appropriately enough, and is infused with not a little Southern sway. Of working in the South, Jack White told *the Onion*, that what was important was "just the confinement, for us to go to places where we're forced to work. We made a mistake with our second album, recording it in my living room. It's too distracting to be at home and do that kind of thing. You're better off when you're away from town, and you've got no choice but to get down to brass tacks."

The result of the focus is 16 tracks consisting mostly of guitar and drums, with the odd organ thrown in, minimally produced with a primal, cathartic rawness reminiscent of the Stripes' most oft-cited influences: old time blues crooners Son House, Robert Johnson and Blind Willie McTell. The lyrics are, by turns, gentlemanly and antagonistic, their sentiment either juxtaposed with or propelled by the crackling, raunchy assault of the music behind them.

DW

Record label:
Sympathy for the Record Industry
Produced
by Jack White
Recorded
At Easley-McCain Memphis, Tennessee
Released:
July 2001
Chart peaks:
58 (UK) None (US)
Personnel:
Jack White (Guitar, Piano, Vocals, Producer, Mixing); Meg White (drums, background vocals)
Track listing:
Dead Leaves and the Dirty Ground; Hotel Yorba; I'm Finding it Harder to be a Gentleman; Fell in Love with a Girl; Expecting; Little Room; The Union Forever; The Same Boy You've Always Known; We're Going to be Friends; Offend in Every Way; I Think I Smell a Rat
Current CD:
XLCD151
Further listening:
The White Stripes (1999); De Stijl (2000); Elephant (2003)
Further reading:
www.whitestripes.com
Like this?
Try . . . p.451

Starsailor

Love Is Here

Wigan boys wear their hearts on their sleeves

It began and ended with the voice. Actually, it began in Wigan, but that shouldn't detract from the fact that there was genuine grace on Starsailor's debut. Mostly, it flowed from James Walsh's voice, which displayed trace elements of Tim Buckley, Bono and Robert Plant, but which ended up being the band's undefinable and unique calling card and a thing of beauty in its own right.

Starsailor convened at college in Wigan, when all four members found themselves on the same bill at an end-of-year concert. "The others were quite a bit older and keen to pass on their musical knowledge," remembers Walsh, who became obsessive in his pursuit of rock classicism. "I'd say the Charlatans. They'd say Bob Dylan. It was older people who persuaded me to dig deeper into music and trace it back, like a treasure hunt."

They played their first gig in April 2000; within a year were signed to a major label and gazed out resplendent from the cover of the NME, hailed – as is normal in these matters – as the "the best new band in Britain". The hype could easily have killed them before they had really begun. "We were getting a lot of media attention even before we had worked out how we really wanted the band to sound," admitted Walsh. "That could have damaged us, but I think it drove us, so that when we came to make the record we knew we had to raise our game. We knew we had to make an album ten times better than if there hadn't been all the hype."

When the debut eventually arrived, it did not disappoint. The band and producer Steve Osborne deliberately steeped the record in simple, uncluttered grandeur to create a direct, emotional sound that would endure far beyond the latest production fads. "We just went into the studio and played it on basic instruments," recalled Walsh. "We wanted to do it the way people did it in the Sixties. We didn't say, 'Show us what your machines and boxes can do'. So on that level I suppose it is retro."

While there may be some truth in Walsh's later claim that "we had a few great songs and a few OK ones," it wasn't just about the voice; there were enough timeless, killer songs on *Love Is Here* to confound most critics: Alcoholic, Lullaby, Way to Fall and the hit single Good Souls all displayed a vital emotional ebb and flow well beyond Walsh's 20 years. As an opening salvo from a band that looks destined to go the distance, *Love Is Here* was an exceptional statement of intent.

GT

Record label:
Chrysalis
Produced
by Mark Aubrey and Steve Osborne
Recorded
at Rockfield Studios
Released:
August 2001
Chart Peaks:
2 (UK) None (US)
Personnel:
James Walsh (v,g); James Stelfox (b); Ben Byrne (d); Barry Westhead (keyboards)
Track Listing:
Tie up My Hands; Poor Misguided Fool; Alcoholic; Lullaby; Way to Fall; Fever; She Just Wept; Talk Her Down; Love is Here; Good Souls; Coming Down
Running Time:
57.49
Current CD:
5353502
Further Listening:
Further Reading:
www.starsailor.net
Like this?
Try . . . p.101

Mercury Rev

All Is Dream

Baroque'n'roll as ideas and orchestration meet in an album of sobering beauty

Great things were expected of this follow-up to the sublime *Deserters Songs*, and with the sweeping orchestration and the uniquely sweet and sumptuous Mercury Rev sound, *All Is Dream* delivered. Subdued & mature, the album illustrates the band's imagination in full flight, and if there is a mild sense of anti-climax upon first listen, especially when compared to their previous release, it soon is to disappear.

The record starts promisingly with the pomp and craft of The Dark Is Rising, a song that plunges us right into the dream-theme of the album. To the backdrop of the lonesome piano, following a booming timpani and Western movie strings opening, frontman songwriter Jonathan Donodue's whispered and wistful intonations tell a tale of fleeting love:

"I dreamed of you on my farm/I dreamed of you in my arms/In my dreams/I'm always wrong."

It is a thing of beauty in an album of granduer.

Donohue's is a seductive dreamworld, a place inhabited by snakes and spiders, and where stories of Greek mythology and ancient Hindu texts are quoted. Reality comes in the appearance of ex-lovers. And all with a luscious accompaniment, Stephen Sondheim-like arrangments and evocations of Hollywood melodrama. By the time of Lincoln's Eyes we are swirling in a vortex of sopranos, violins, musical theatre with fangs, sharks and the kitchen sink being introduced. It can get preposterous. But ambition always begets the absurd And what's wrong with that?

Record label:
V2
Produced
by Dave Fridmann and Jeff Mercel
Released:
August 2001
Chart peaks:
11 (UK) None (US)
Personnel:
Jonathan Donahue (vocals, guitar); Sean 'Grasshopper' Mackiowiack (guitar); Jeff Mercel (drums, piano); Adam Snyder (keyboards); Dave fridmann (bass); Suzanne Thorpe (woodwind); Jimy Chambers (drums); Sarah Adams (viola); Amy Helm (vocals); Gregor Kitzis (violin); Maxine Neuman (cello); Larry Packer (violin); Laura Seaton (viola); Tony Visconti (flute, mellotron, orchestration, string arrangements)
Track listing:
The dark is rising; Tides of the moon; Chains; Lincoln's eyes; Nite and fog; Little rhymes; A drop in time; You're my queen; Spiders and flies; Hercules
Current CD:
VVR1017528
Further listening:
Yerseld is Steam (1991); See you on the other side (1995); Deserter's Songs (1998)
Further reading:
www.mercuryrev.net
Like this?
Try . . . p.760

The Strokes

Is This It

Impossible glamour that starts in a basement and ends in huge acclaim. It is "it".

Depending on which side of the fence you sat in 2002, the Strokes were either a shameless cookie-cutter rehash of any number of New York rock bands from the 70s, or the greatest thing to happen to rock and roll in two decades. There seemed to be one consensus amongst the polemic, however: those who considered *Is This It*, the band's first LP, to be anything less than an outstanding album, were simply lying to themselves.

The hype generated by 2001's *The Modern Age* EP, had major labels tripping over themselves. Ultimately it was RCA who landed the deal, the only company who tolerated the group's vow never to make a video (the band has since capitulated, making three videos thus far). After an initial recording attempt with former Pixies producer Gil Norton, whose vision proved too polished for the band's wishes, the Strokes rediscovered the gritty resonance they had harnessed with *The Modern Age* with still then-unknown producer Gordon Raphael at Transporterraum Studio.

Recorded in a diminutive basement in New York's Lower East Side, *Is This It* was subsequently imbued with the stylish dissent that pervades the subculture's stomping grounds. Calculatedly mussed hair, threadbare denim, leather jackets and skinny ties were forever preserved for posterity on vinyl. Coming just weeks on the heels of September 11, 2001, the US CD release of the album was forced to leave behind the track New York City Cops, whose overt questioning of the intelligence of New York's finest was seen by the label as a bit too insensitive.

Read anything ever written about the Strokes and you will invariably come across allusions to the Velvet Underground, Television, the Stooges, the Ramones, et al. While the influences are patent, *Is This It* revises the stripped-down garage rock of Gotham's past with a uniquely current catchiness and dance sensibility. It is above all, an undeniably fun record. The typical review by notoriously cynical indie rock critics went something like, As much as I want to hate the Strokes for all their blatant hipness, I can't help but love this album.

Julian Casablancas told Rolling Stone Magazine, "I feel like sometimes great artists—it won't politically affect anything, but it can make a crack in the ceiling and you can see a bit of light. You don't know what's gonna come, but you try. I think eighty-five percent of the fun is just going for it." With *Is This It*, the Strokes managed to cultivate the perfect grouping of accessible subversion and rock 'n' roll pose with an unconscious yet impeccable cultural timing—elements whose seemingly mutual exclusivity lent their melding a vigor that could crack ceilings indeed.

DW

Record Label:
RCA
Produced
by Gordon Raphael
Recorded
at Transporterraum, New York, New York;
Released:
27th August 2001 (UK); 11th September 2001 (US Vinyl); 9th October 2001 (US);
Chart peaks:
2 (UK) 74 (US)
Personnel:
Julian Casablancas (vocals); Nick Valensi, Albert Hammond, Jr. (guitar); Nikolai Fraiture (bass); Fab Moretti (drums).
Track listing:
Is This It; The Modern Age; Soma; Barely Legal; Someday; Alone Together; Last Night; Hard To Explain; NYC Cops; Trying Your Luck; Take It Or Leave It
Running time:
Current CD:
RTRADECD030
Further reading:
www.thestrokes.org
Like this?
Try . . . p.610

Spiritualized

Let It Come Down

The Spaceman, out in a place of his own

When you live for music, as we all must do to be visiting these pages, it's easy to get excited about the things you love. At other times in this guide, reviewing other records, I've found myself thrilled by Mull Historical Society for example, and Blur and PJ Harvey. I can't help myself – I love these artists and I rave on about their music. But I want to reserve some special space, some higher plane of appreciation for Jason Pierce. Maybe it's because he's never quite realised the success his swooning orchestrations merit, maybe it's because of the transcendental nature of the pieces themselves but I do, I see Spiritualized out there on a level and in a place of their own.

From the astral ballads of Spaceman 3, through *Ladies And Gentlemen We Are Floating In Space* and *Lazer Guided Melodies* to *Let It Come Down*, Jason Pierce has offered a whole new take on strung-out, drugged-up space hymns. For starters, here is an artist who has never 'experimented' with drugs. He doesn't 'use' drugs. The drugs use him – use him up, use him out and still he comes back for more. Jason Pierce takes drugs and the music he makes – stoned, blissful, unstructured, exhilarating - is as much a product of his altered states as it is a result of any formal and considered creative process. If anybody can say their songs "just come", it's him. *Let It Come Down* is instantly classic comedown rock, Pierce's sauce material never far from the surface. He embraces his narcotic journeys on *Twelve Steps* and on *The Straight And Narrow* laments:

"The trouble with the straight and narrow is, it's so thin I keep sliding off the side."

Let's hope he doesn't slide too far.

KS

Record label:
Spaceman/Arista
Produced
by Jason Pierce and John Coxon
Released:
September 2001
Chart peaks:
3 (UK) None (US)
Personnel:
Jason Pierce
Track listing:
On fire; Do it all over again; Don't just do something; Out of sight; The twelve steps; The straight and the narrow; I didn't mean to hurt you; Stop your crying; Anything more; Won't get to heaven (the state I'm in); Lord can you hear me
Running time:
63.01 (US)
Current CD:
74321882242
Further listening:
Lazer guided melodies (1992); Pure phase (1995); Ladies and gentlemen we are floating in space (1997); Complete works volume 1 (2003)
Further reading:
www.spiritualized.com
Like this?
Try . . . p.396

Mull Historical Society

Loss

Startlingly inventive debut from Tobermory's finest

This amazing collection from Colin McIntyre is, in every sense, a classic debut album. The thing that makes the best first albums truly wonderful is that feeling that every single great idea, every great lyric, every great tune that's ever slipped through the composer's fields of thought in his life to date are represented there on that first record. The debut album is a filter and a mission statement of the writer's accumulated brilliance – so far. Imagine then, if you will, that your inspiration and observations have been gleaned from a remote-ish isle off the Western Highlands of Scotland.

The legend surrounding Mull Historical Society is that teenage Colin grew up in Tobermory listening to his uncle's cabaret band playing Eagles and U2 cover versions. The pure romance of the guitars, the amps, even the look and feel of the sheaves of song-sheets sealed his destiny. He scribbled and noted and recorded, building up an archive of 300-odd songs but never quite having the conviction or the confidence to play any of them live. He just carried on writing, collating, collecting and jotting down. He didn't really think that the type of incisive observational songs he was writing could possibly matter to anyone but himself. Then a trickle of bands started breaking through – Travis, Badly Drawn Boy, Belle & Sebastian – making music that had some things in common with some of his own songs. He decided what the heck, why not.

Having presumably passed over approximately 290 odes in making his final selection, ***Loss*** is a superbly inventive collection, covering all the shades and nuances of the McIntyre muse. There's humour here, there's ire and irony, and of course there's loss in all its forms – loss of youth, loss of innocence, loss of cultural identity and the grief and sadness of personal loss.

Some of the songs have the upbeat dancehall shindig verve of a mutant Beach Boys or E.L.O. There's a buoyant *joie de vivre* about Animal Cannabus and This Is Not Who We Said We Were that's belied by acidic lyrics. Watching Xanadu has a big-beat swoon and swoop, but once again its vivacious sheen only partly masks a maudlin heart.

Other songs – the wistful I Tried and the Hammond-tinged Barcode Bypass are more at home with their tristesse, while the gorgeous Only I is an acoustic ballad stripped bare. Loss is layered with ideas and complexities, each new listening coaxing out things we may have left behind last time. This is Pet Sounds from The Hebrides, and it's only just the beginning.

KS

Record label:
Blanco Y Negro
Produced
by Colin McIntyre
Released:
October 2001
Personnel:
Colin McIntyre
Track listing:
Public service announcer; Watching Xanadu; Instead; I tried; This is not who we were; Barcode bypass; Only I; Animal cannabus; Strangeways inside; Mull Historical Society; Paperhouses
Current CD:
0927413072
Further listening:
Us (2003)
Further reading:
www.mullhistoricalsociety.com
Like this?
Try . . . p.385

Saul Williams

Amethyst Rock Star

Spoken word meets rap and rock, with Rick Rubin manning the boards: but it's not that straightforward...

Raised on avant garde jazz, rap and Paul Robeson, Williams was studying philosophy and drama in New York when he discovered the "poetry slam" scene. These performance-based events mixed poetry with the hip hop generation's sensibility: and this bohemian son of what he terms "culturally middle class" parents had found his spiritual home.

After starring in the 1998 movie Slam, a poetry precursor to Eminem's 8 Mile, Williams' careers all began to blossom. MTV published a volume of his poetry, and, as this debut was released in the autumn of 2001, he was also starring alongside Kevin Spacey in the movie K-Pax. But, while widely acclaimed, the commercial response to this album was muted.

Signed by Rick Rubin on the strength of his performance in Slam, Williams deeply understood the cultural forces that were working through him. He was an outspoken critic of mainstream hip hop's tired diet of machismo and misogyny, and felt that Rubin, who had helped take the genre overground as both producer and label head, was responsible for developments both positive and negative.

"Rick was looking for a hip hop album, whatever hip hop means to him," said Williams, explaining his partnership with Rubin. "And although he helped formulate in my mind through his career what hip hop is, I think my mind grew in directions that he couldn't have planned. I ended up saying to him, 'Rick, you abandoned hip hop, you're that absent father that abandoned your child, and I'm that child coming back to you and saying, Look, this is the type of shit I've gotten into now. You're karmically responsible for a lot of the bullshit now, and you have debts to pay, through me'."

As Williams admits, this made the sessions for Amethyst Rock Star "interesting". Over the jaw-dropping range of textures and sounds – squalls of deconstructed Hendrix-at-Woodstock guitar (Om Nia Merican), drum & bass scattershots ruthlessly marshalled by Roni Size cohort Krust (Coded Language) – Williams lashes out at nihilism and negativity in the music he loves. He saw rap as an art form that had reneiged on its revolutionary promise and turned traitor, repackaging the worst in reactionary values in rebel outfits and doling the resultant slop out to an all-but uncritical media and audience. It was medicine that proved too strong for most to stomach, but is an infusion the genre has never needed a shot of more urgently.

AB

Record label:
American/Columbia
Produced
by Rick Rubin: Saul Williams (co-producer): Musa Bailey (add prod on Penny For A Thought): Krust (add prod on Coded Language)
Recorded
at
Released:
August 2001
Chart peaks:
Personnel:
Saul Williams (v): Jerome Jordan (gtr, bck v): Maximina Juson (b): Chris Eddleton (d): Mayram Blacksher (viola): Nioka Workman (cello): Musa Bailey (DJ, add. programming): Kwame Brandt-Pierce (kbds): Esthero (v on Tao Of Now): Chad Smith (d on Om Nia Merican)
Track listing:
La La La: Penny For A Thought: Robeson: Tao Of Now: Fearless: Untimely Meditations: Om Nia Merican: 1987: Coded Language: Our Father: Wine
Running time:
58 mins 26 secs
Current CD:
501593 2
Further listening:
Not in My Name (2003)
Further reading:
She (MTV, 1999); Said the shotgun to the head (MTV, 2003); www.saulwilliams.com
Like this?
Try . . . p.24

Cesaria Evora

Sao Vicente Di Longe

Grandmother from Cape Verde gets to record in Rio De Janeiro and Havana, but still manages to sound heartbroken

Ignoring a brief and disillusioning recording career when she was younger, Evora's career really began in her late forties, when her future producer heard her singing to some Cape Verdean expats in a Lisbon cafe. It was her first time away from the rocky archipelago where she made her name, and the island whose name was given to this, her eighth album (*Saint Vicente From A Distance*). It does her no disservice, even when she can fill concert halls worldwide, to call Evora a bar singer (well, so was Sinatra). 'My home town was an important port. Boats from Africa would stop on their way to America, ships from Brazil would stop on their way to Portugal. The bars were full of sailors and fishermen who wanted to hear Frank Sinatra, Elvis and Nat King Cole, but I would sing them our music.'

Our music was morna, the Cape Verdean ballad equivalent of Portugal's fado and coladero, faster but hardly happier, both of which are sung in the Portuguese creole of the islands. Sailors cried into their beer while Evora sang, smoked and swigged cognac and whisky. It was a living but no career; not, at least, until Jose Da Silva heard her and realised the whole world liked to cry into its beer too.

Her first three albums were released in France to increasing acclaim, but 1992's *Miss Perfumado* caught everyone by surprise as the French critics invoked Billie Holiday, tours sold out and a quarter of a million bought the disc. The next two albums, *Cesaria* and *Cabo Verde* refined the sound and increased sales. *Cafe Atlantico* went even further, capitalising on the contemporary enthusiasm for Cuba by positing Cape Verde as an ocean crossroads where African and Cuban music first entwined.

For *Sao Vicente*, her producers treated to her to the big-band, all-star treatment. It moved her out of the bar environment, but still worked, because Evora is a peerless singer of particular song styles: the environment hardly matters if you have an empty heart and full glass. In fact, the duets with Raitt (whom she'd never met), Guerra (a young Spanish songwriter) and Caetano Veloso (they had worked together before) are among the highlights. And then, when the Cuban pianist Chucho Valdes stepped forward on the Brazilian standard Negue, it was crying time again. In her mid-fifties, Evora was simply getting better.

DH

Record label:
(RCA)
Produced
by Jose Da Silva
Recorded
at Studio Plus XXX, Paris; Studio Abdala, Havana; Studio De Mega, Rio de Janeiro
Chart peaks:
None (UK) None (US)
Release date:
April 2001
Personnel:
Cesaria Evora (voc), Fernando Andrade (pno), Joao Pina Alves (gtr), Antonio Alves (cavaquinho), Aderito Goncalves (side gtr), Virgilio Julio Duarte (acoustic bs), Carlos Monteiro (drms), Antonio Domingos Gomes (sax), Chucho Valdes (piano), Caetano Veloso (voc), Bonnie Raitt (voc), Teofilo Chantre (voc), Pedro Guerra (voc), Orquesta Aragon
Track listing:
Sao Vicente Di Longe, Homem Na Meio Di? Homem, Tiempo Y Silencio, Sabor De Pecado, Dor Di Amor, Nutridinha, Regresso, Esperanca Irisada, Ponta De Fi, Crepuscular Solidao, Linda Mimosa, Negue, Bondade E Maldade, Fada, Pic Nic Na Salamansa
Running time:
64.26
Current CD:
74321836682
Further listening:
Cafe Atlantico (Lusafrica, 1999), Cabo Verde (RCA, 1997) Miss Perfumado (1992); The Best of Cesaria Evora (2003)
Further reading:
www.cesaria-evora.com
Like this?
Try . . . p.215

Orlando Cachaito Lopez

Cachaito

Debut album from the only person to have appeared on every single track recorded under the umbrella of the Buena Vista Social Club

Bass players? solo albums are usually hideous vanity-pampering affairs. A quick look at the band used by the Cuban bassist, seems to confirm this: a double bassist and four percussionists jamming together in a studio, oh joy. Well, prepare to have your expectations confounded, this was the most exciting album to come out of Cuba in years.

"I knew what I wanted to do," Cachaito explains. "My first love has always been jazz and I wanted to take the African influences that run through Cuban music, remove the European influences we were accustomed to and add some others, like DJ Dee Nasty from France and Bigga Morrison's Hammond organ."

It turned into a labour of love for Nick Gold, the boss of World Circuit, whose plan it was to give the bassist his turn in the spot-light. For a start, although organs are common in Jamaican reggae, there wasn't a single Hammond on Cuba. Strings and horns were easy to get hold of, but such was the cache of Buena Vista, that Pee Wee Ellis, Hugh Masekela, Tony Remy and Junior Dan were up for the sessions. Then there was the matter of finding a Cuban guitarist. Tres players are ten-a-penny, but Manuel Galban was an altogether different kind of axeman, described by Ry Cooder as the "Cuba's Duane Eddy". He had risen to fame in the 1960s as musical director for Los Zafiros, Havana's greatest doo-wop group. But music had turned sour for the guitarist when he watched three of his compadres drink themselves into early graves.

The man at the heart of it all was unperturbed by the pressure. Not only had he played in jazz, Latin and classical ensembles all his life, he was from Cuba's premier bass dynasty, his father (Israel) and uncle (Cachao) being the acknowledged masters of both the mambo and the descarga jam session. "My earliest memories are of my father playing with the Havana Symphony Orchestra by day and with a dance band at night. He knew what he wanted me to do when I grew up, so he made sure I was always surrounded by music."

So a group of Class A musicians sat down together in a studio in Havana and jammed. A recipe for disaster in some hands, but after five or six decades of descargas, these guys knew exactly what they were doing. Then some hip fairy dust was sprinkled over the mix in the form of scratching, loops and samples. Result: the coolest jazz album in years. Crazy, man, crazy.

DH

Record Label:
World Circuit
Produced
by Nick Gold
Recorded
at Egrem, Havana; Livingston Studios, London
Did not chart
Release date:
April 2001
Running time
48:09
Current CD:
WCD061
Personnel:
Orlando Cachaito Lopez (bs), Miguel Anga Diaz (congas), Amadito Vales (timbales), Carlos Gonzalez (bongos), Alejandro Pichardo (guiro, claves), Bigga Morrison (Hammond), Manuel Galban (gtr), Tony Remy (gtr), Pee Wee Ellis (tenor sax), Hugh Masekela (flugelhorn), Junior Dan (electric bs)
Track listing:
Siempre Con Swing/Redencion/Mis Dos Pequenas/A Gozar El Tumbao/Cachaito In Laboratory/Tumbao No 5/Conversacion/Tumbanga/Oracion Lucumi/Wahira/Anais/La Negra
Further listening:
Buena Vista Social Club (World Circuit), Cachao Master Sessions (Crescent Moon)
Further reading:
Buena Vista Social Club (Thames and Hudson, 2000)
Like this?
Try . . . p.632

Jay-Z

The Blueprint

A modern milestone in the increasingly blanded-out world of mainstream rap.

Shaun "Jay-Z" Carter was a late convert to rap. Deciding his life expectancy wasn't too great if he carried on being a drug dealer, he decided to make his hobby into his career at a fortuitous point in hip hop's history.

By 1995 the emergence of a new New York school of rappers, led by Nas and Carter's Brooklyn neighbour The Notorious BIG had established a template that allowed the city's lyricists to talk about the lifestyles of the rich and infamous rather than glorying in the gory detail.

Carter rechristened himself Jay-Z and, allegedly using money from his prior occupation, funded a debut, Reasonable Doubt. He made up for lost time, interspersing what became annual albums with frequent guest appearances and ghost-wrote hits for everyone from Will Smith to Dr Dre.

Yet the degree of critical and commercial success his sixth album generated still came as a surprise. Sonically, Jigga and his producers steered hip hop away from millennial digital experimentation into a primordial musical stew of lush soul and roughneck breakbeats, making it OK once again for the music's creators to embrace sampling after years of record company pressure to do otherwise.

Just Blaze and Kanye West, both virtually unknown before The Blueprint, produced the lion's share, Blaze's technique of speeding up samples from old soul records giving hip hop its first startlingly new sonic twist since Public Enemy's Bomb Squad first brought their noise over a decade earlier. Lyrically, Jay was magisterial, Heart Of The City weaving biographical anecdotes into a timeline of pop groups breaking up while Takeover sparked one of hip hop's most entertaining on-record feuds, Jigga landing seemingly unprovoked blows on Nas. The verbal tussle helped both men sell records, but also showed that the genre could generate controversy without resorting to physical violence.

"I wanted to present this music as the blueprint," Jay told interviewer Andrew Panos. "I wanted to say who I am and say these are the things that shaped me. I grew up on soul music. My mum would play it loud on a Saturday. That's what was in the house. So The Blueprint is taking it back, to soul, to MC battles, to all of that, break it down then build it up again." That he succeeded in this considerable aim is as remarkable as it is indubitable.

AB

Record label:
Roc-A-Fella
Produced
by Bink, Kanye West, Just Blaze, Poke & Tone, Timbaland, Eminem
Recorded
at Baseline Studios, NYC: Manhattan Center, NYC
Released:
September 2001
Chart peaks:
30 (UK) 1 (US)
Personnel:
Jay-Z (v): Eric "E-Bass" Johnson (bass on The Ruler's Back): Keyamo (strings on The Ruler's Back): Bink (Programming on The Ruler's Back): Josey Scott of Saliva (add v on Takeover): Q-Tip (add v on Girls, Girls, Girls): Slick Rick (add v on Girls, Girls, Girls): Biz Markie (add v on Girls, Girls, Girls): Stephanie Miller (add v on Jigga That N***a): Michelle Mills (add v on Jigga That N***a): Eminem (add v on Renegade): Bo (organs on Blueprint (Momma Loves Me)): Victor Flowers (live organs on Blueprint (Momma Loves Me)): Schevise Harrell (background v on Blueprint (Momma Loves Me)): Luren Leek (background v on Blueprint (Momma Loves Me))
Track listing:
The Ruler's Back: Takeover: Izzo (H.O.V.A.): Girls, Girls, Girls: Jigga That N***a: U Don't Know: Hola' Hovito: Heart Of the City (Ain't No Love): Never Change: Song Cry: All I Need: Renegade (feat. Eminem): Blueprint
Running time:
63 mins 48 secs
Current CD:
586 396-2
Further listening:
Blueprint 2 – The Gift And The Curse (2002)
Like this?
Try . . . p.513

Gillian Welch

Time (the Revelator)

Third album, first own-label release, from acclaimed L.A.ppalachian

The surging popularity of bluegrass and old-time mountain music as the 21st century rolled in had less to do with any Millennial longing for simple, rural pleasures than the mighty success of the Coen Brothers' *O Brother Where Art Thou?* (the comedy in which George Clooney and his fellow chain gang escapees find redemption as early radio stars The Soggy Bottom Boys). Welch was associate producer and show-stealer of the movie's soundtrack, as well as that of the spin-off concert documentary *Down From The Mountain.*

The young singer-writer from Los Angeles had previously released just two full albums of minimalist mountain music. These were enough to gain her the respect of fellow musicians – from old-timers like Ralph Stanley to peers like Alison Krauss – and the veneration of fans. "Wearing the producer's hat for the first time" on *O Brother* . . . inspired Welch "to go it alone" on her follow-up to 1998's *Hell Among The Yearlings*. Completely. Not only was this album self-produced, it was released on her own label.

Although as spare, acoustic and stark as its predecessors, *Time (the Revelator)* is a more complex album. The 'time' Welch is interested in here is not a linear and diachronic but circular and overlapping. The *O Brother...* experience had prompted her interest in time's amorphousness, how she could walk past "a ten year old boy" on the street with a hi-tech Walkman on,"singing Man Of Constant Sorrow," for instance

Recurring musical and lyrical themes loop in and out, round and around. April 14th Part 1 and Ruination Day Part 2 are essentially the same song deconstructed and rearranged – first as a lovely ballad, then as chilling gospel-blues. And old instruments (banjo, acoustic guitar) accompany contemporary tales (the ex-boyfriend in My First Lover who put her down while his Steve Miller records played in the background). As always there is that strangely seamless blend of her partner David Rawlings' gently amiable flat-picking and the intense, sombre, mournful austerity of Welch's voice. The most remarkable tracks are its longest - six-and-a-half minute opener Revelator, and near-15 minute closer I Dream A Highway, both of them gently trance-inducing and powerfully emotive, with a sense of time stretched out into something endless and circular and yet at the same time too short. Welch bends her notes like a blues harmonica on Elvis Presley's Blues, in which she namechecks the "country boy" whose favourite studio - Nashville's legendary RCA Studio B - was reopened especially for the recording of this excellent album.

SS

Record label:
Acony ACNY 0103
Producer:
Gillian Welch and David Rawlings
Recorded:
RCA Studio B, Nashville
Released:
2001
Personnel:
Gillian Welch (voc), David Rawlings (gtr)
Tracklist:
Revelator/ My First Lover/ Dear Someone/ Red Clay Halo/ April The 14th Part 1/ I Want To Sing That Rock And Roll/ Elvis Presley Blues/ Ruination Day Part 2/ Everything Is Free/ I Dream A Highway
Current CD:
0190103
Further listening:
Revival (1998); Soul Journey (2003)
Further reading:
www.gillianwelch.com
Like this?
Try . . . p.585

Brendan Benson

Lapalco

Power pop wonderboy gets dropped from the majors only to return five years later with an indie gem.

"We don't hear a single" – five words that can paralyze an artist faster than the Vulcan nerve pinch.

In 1997, Brendan Benson was recording the follow-up to his critically adored debut, *One Mississippi.* When he turned over the tapes to his label, Virgin, they went all Spock on him.

A year-long deep freeze of self-doubt and depression followed. When Benson emerged, he was a changed man. "I got a little wiser and less naive, and a lot more ambitious and pro-active. Before, the deal had been handed to me. I never even asked for it. I do things now because I want it more."

For his sanity's sake, he also moved from L.A. back to Detroit, where he'd spent most of his youth. "I didn't have a whole lot of friends in L.A. Mostly I was at home fretting over stuff related to the music business. I kind of collapsed under the pressure. In Detroit, I'm closer to family and friends. It's healthy and creative."

This all set the stage for the making of his bedroom masterpiece, *Lapalco.* With its swirl of hook-heavy melodies, pumped-up guitars and caramel harmonies, the sound is pure power pop. But repeated plays reveal something more emotionally fragile at work. Dark undercurrents pulse beneath the songs, especially in their lyrically honest assessment that most relationships are fleeting and bound to fail.

Like other great homemade albums - think of *McCartney* and Rundgren's *Something / Anything* as *Lapalco's* bunkmates- there are plenty of rough edges in the sound. An amplifier buzz here, a voice crack there. Benson: "I love moments like those - little mistakes and happy accidents and bits that were left in. My favourite records have loads of mistakes in them. You could say that it blows the mystique or brings it down to earth. But I think it does the opposite somehow. It makes it that much more personal."

Co-producing with ex-Jellyfish guitarist Jason Falkner gave Benson an extra boost when his confidence wavered. "Where I fall short or leave off, Jason picks up," Brendan says. "He's very focused and he helped create a lot of the atmosphere and sound of the record."

Lapalco (also the name of the street where Benson grew up) has been received with even more critical applause than Benson's first record. *Rolling Stone* called it "timeless music that takes multiple listens to unfold." But more meaningful to him is that he's grabbed the reins of his artistic destiny. "Being on a small label, I get to see the results of my work," he says. "It might only be 5,000 records sold rather than 50,000, but the difference is that I worked for it and I helped sell those records."

BDM

Record label:
Startime International
Produced
by Brendan Benson & Jason Falkner
Recorded
at Brendan's home studio
Released:
February 2002
Chart peaks:
None (US),
Personnel:
Brendan Benson (v, g, b, k, d, pc); Jason Falkner (g, b, k, d, pc); Emma J. (v)
Track listing:
Tiny Spark; Metarie; Folk Singer; Life In The D; Good To Me; You're Quiet; What; Eventually; I'm Easy; Pleasure Seeker; Just Like Me; Jetlag
Running time:
42:26
Current CD:
ST-006
Further listening:
One Mississippi (1996, out of print)
Further reading:
www.brendanbenson.com, MOJO 108
Like this?
Try . . . p.657

Salif Keita

Moffou

The golden voice of Mali gets back on track after years in the wilderness

It would be a cruel exaggeration to say Salif Keita's career was a shambles before he recorded this, but it certainly wasn't looking healthy. His previous album, Papa, released on Blue Note and produced by Living Color's Vernon Reid, sounded as if it had been recorded for a New York audience and was panned by western critics. "It was not liked in America or Europe," Keita admits, "but it sold very well in Africa. People wanted to hear their musicians sound like the outside world." It was five years before we would hear from Keita again, and it is perhaps telling that the best song on *Papa*, Ananamin, would reappear in a more traditional - and better – guise, Ana Na Ming, on *Moffou*.

"As a boy, I could not play in the fields with the others because I was albino. Some people were scared of me, and the sun was too strong for my skin. So I would sit under a tree and play a moffou, a small flute, we used to scare birds. I wanted to go back to that simple life again, make that kind of music." Such is the apparent simplicity of *Moffou*, it feels almost timeless, every track sounds as if it could have been made specifically for children, but there is a complexity at the heart of each song. Yamore begins with n'goni and guitar playing off each other quietly, but when the female vocals come in, the backing effortlessly turns to accordeon, countless guitars and their African equivalents and a metallic percussion. You won't notice this unless you concentrate, because Keita's impassioned vocals dominate every second.

Other songs sounds even simpler, as if Keita and his guitar are making up a nursery rhyme on their own, playing around with melodies until they find something they like. Utterly mesmeric. But the standout track, Madan, is a different beast, with everything bursting into life over a belting bassline and frantic percussion, while Keita and his backing singers trade lines. On *Papa*, it might have been swamped with keyboards and programmers' brainstorms, but here you feel right in the heart of Africa. As the percussion grows more frenetic, Keita's voice disappears into the mix, almost in a dub fashion; when it returns he seems to have been taken over by the spirit of Elvis in 1968, singing as if his very life depends on it. This is that rare thing of beauty, an album where not a single second feels like filler.

DH

Record label:
Universal
Produced
by Salif Keita, Jean Lamoot, Freddy Zerbib
Release date:
April 2002
Running time:
60:42
Personnel:
Salif Keita (voc), Kante Manfila (acoustic gtr), Djelly Moussa Kouyate (gtr), Jean-Louis Solans (gtr), Harouna Samake (camele n?goni), Sayon Sissoko (n?goni), Mamadou Kone (calabash), Benoit Urbain (accordeon), Mino Cinelu (perc), Mehdi Haddad (lute)
Track listing:
Yamore/Iniagige/Madan/Katolon/Souvent/Moussolou/Baba/Ana Na Ming/Koukou/Here
Running time:
52:10
Current CD:
0169062
Further listening:
Soro (1997)
Further reading:
www.salifkeita.net
Like this?
Try . . . p.684

Afel Bocoum, Damon Albarn, Toumani Diabate And Friends

Mali Music

Blur man takes time out, goes to Africa, makes record. Gallagher brothers not particularly impressed

In the summer of 2000, Oxfam invited Blur's frontman, then taking a break from the group and working with Gorillaz, on a trip to Mali. "I said yes, but I had no idea what they wanted me to do, I didn't want them to expect anything of me." With Britpop all but dead, its former king was no longer content with rewriting The Kinks' back catalogue. "Blur was so far removed from me, really. I'd grown up listening to Indian music, Arabic music, flamenco, and seeing the Buena Vista Social Club and Ibrahim Ferrer in concert had been one of the most emotional nights of my life. But I'd also been listening to African music, and I knew about Toumani Diabate."

When Albarn arrived in Bamako, the capital city, arrangements had been made to meet with Diabate, the young king of the kora (a 21-string harp), and Afel Bocoum, the protege of Ali Farka Toure, king of the African blues guitarists. "That was how it started, I met Toumani, they laughed at my melodeon, we went to his home and jammed." Feeling that music was part of the unavoidable atmosphere wherever he went in Mali, Albarn taped everything. The song titles are more like geographic pointers than keys to the music: Ko Kan Ko Sata Doumbia On River was a recording of one of the very few female ngoni players while she was sitting in a boat; 4am At Toumani's speaks for itself.

When he returned to London, Albarn had 40 hours of snippets, riffs, jams, snatches of melodies and, most importantly, ideas. However, the Gorillaz project was nearing fruition, business called, and the tapes sat waiting his return. Months went into editing the fragments, while Gorillaz cohorts such as bassist Junior Dan were brought in to add something that British record buyers could recognise. Reggae, dub, electronic effects and some laidback guitar turn the tracks into an identifiably west London world music, although the Malian roots are never lost.

Having completed his edit, Albarn had no idea what to do with the results. Then, during a conversation with the owners of his favourite London record shop, Honest Jons, he asked them why they didn't start their own imprint. After that, things just fell into place: a label was born, some new African musicians were discovered, Albarn brought fans of two separate strands of music together, and Oxfam got the column inches and proceeds they'd been looking for in the first place. Oh, and the record was great listening. A success then, all told.

DH

Record label:
Honest Jon's
Produced
by Studio 13
Recorded
by Mali
Release date:
April 15, 2002
Track listing:
Afel Bocoum (voc, gtr), Damon Albarn (voc, melodeon, kbds, kalimba), Toumani Diabate (kora), Junior Dan (bs), Cass Browne (drms), Simon Burwell (kbds), Nabintou Diakite (voc, ngoni), Lobi Traore (gtr) Spoons/Bamako City/Le relax/Nabintou Diakite/Makelekele/The Djembe/Tennessee Hotel/Niger/4am At Toumani?s/Institut National Des Arts/Kela Village/Griot Village/Le Hobon/Sunset Coming On/Ko Kan Ko Sata Doumbia On River/Les Ecrocs
Running time:
57.45
Current CD:
5384402
Further listening:
Afel Bocoum Alkibar (World Circuit); Toumani Diabate Jarabi: The Best Of (Hannibal)
Further reading:
www.astralwerks.com/mali_music/default.html
Like this?
Try . . . p.699

Tom Waits

Alice

Balladeer pulls influences from his career to create something new

Although not recorded and released until well into the new millennium, the seeds for *Alice* were sown with Waits' collaboration with avant-garde theatre director Robert Wilson a decade earlier. Wilson had already bashed heads with Waits on the dark, difficult *Black Rider* project and had had an invigorating affect on the slurring troubadour. "When I met him I felt like I was with an inventor, Alexander Graham Bell or one of those guys," said Waits. "He's a deep thinker. In theatre, he's developed a whole language for himself and those he works with."

The songs on *Alice* were originally co-written in by Waits and his wife Kathleen Brennan in 1992 for Wilson's stage production (described as 'an avant-garde opera'), which was performed at the Thalia Theatre, Hamburg in December 1992. The theatre piece focused on the relationship between the Reverend Charles Dodgson (aka Lewis Carroll) and Alice Liddell, the inspiration for Alice In Wonderland. Frankly, the listener need know none of this to savour the beauty of the record. "The songs aren't really a linear narrative," said Waits in 2002. "They might have been part of the theatre piece to begin with but if you're going to do a record it has to stand alone.You have to get beyond the original concept; it's like making a movie out of a book."

Few could argue that Alice wasn't an immense achievement in its own right. While effortlessly pulling together the disparate strands of Waits career - the mesmerising, eponymous opening ballad could have sneaked onto Blue Valentines, while the rollicking Vegas pastiche Table Top Joe and the crazed Germanic stomp of Kommienezuspadt and Reeperbahn sounded like the last word in Waits' long time obsession with those bizarre stylistic forms – Alice also sounded staunchly unlike anything he had done before. Warm, blurred, reflective and mournful, laced with cello and pump organ, the heart of the record lay deep in some of Waits's greatest ever balladry: Lost In the Harbour ("Everybody's hiding their tears/but they're crying inside"), No One Knows I'm Gone, Flowers Grave and I'm Still Here.

What made Alice all the more remarkable was that Waits was making another record at the same time, the angry, dissonant and dark Blood Money. "It was hard recording the two albums at the same time," he later admitted. "Using a lot of the same musicians and trying to keep them sounding completely different." It was a balancing act only an artist as precocious and focused as Waits could have pulled off. As Chris Roberts remarked in his (UNCUT) review: "Everything on Alice is on the verge of crying. At every corner he makes the correct aesthetic move and gets it absolutely right." GT

Record Label:
Anti, Inc.
Produced
by Tom Waits & Kathleen Brennan
Recorded
at The Pocket Studio, Forestville, California
Released:
May 2002
Chart Peaks:
20 (UK)
Personnel:
Tom Waits (v, p, mellotron, pump organ, pod, stomp, violin, chamberlin, toy); Eric Perney (b), Colin Stetson (sax, clarinet); Gino Robair (d, percussion); Ara Anderson (muted trumpet, baritone horn, trumpet); Larry Taylor (b, g, percussion); Matt Brubeck (cello, b); Bent Clausen (swiss hand bells, p); Bebe Risenfors (violin, viola, clarinet, baby bass, fiddle); Nik Phelps (french horn, trumpet); Dawn Harms (violin); Andrew Borger (oil drums, frame drum, percussion); Tim Allen (scraper)
Track Listing:
Alice; Everything You Can Think; Flowers Grave; No One Knows I'm Gone; Kommienezuspadt; Poor Edward; Table Top Joe; Lost In the Harbour; We're All Mad Here; Watch Her Disappear; Reeperbahn; I'm Still Here; Fish & Bird; Barcarollie; Fawn
Running Time:
48.23
Current CD:
ANTI 6632-2
Further Listening:
Swordfishtrombones (1983)
Further Reading:
Wild Years: The Myth & Music of Tom Waits – Jay S Jacobs (ECW Press)
Like this?
Try . . . p.68

Eminem

The Eminem Show

If it ain't broke, don't fix it: but while The Eminem Show is a repeat, the next episode will be worth tuning in for.

Arriving at Difficult Third Album time as arguably the biggest male solo vocalist since Elvis Presley, Marshall Mathers III was in no mood to buck any of his own immensely successful trends. So the album he made was less a forward-looking exercise than an attempt to put his numerous houses into some sort of order. That it went on to sell in stupendous quantities – 7.6 million in the US in 2002 alone – was a given.

The reason a troubled white boy from working class Detroit became the fulcrum of a black music form may never be fully explained, but inevitably much ink has already been spilt trying. The single most important factor, though, is that the motor-mouthed kid from the trailer park was possessed of one of the quickest minds in popular culture, and a gift for expressing it. A natural at winding up his enemies while delighting his fans, Eminem elevated trash talk to art, and turned his life into soap opera, seeming to delight in provoking outrage yet unable to stop dramas at home eroding his confidence.

What's most striking about this album is how little confidence Eminem seems to have in his own considerable abilities as a rapper and lyricist. Time after time he gets close to a moment of revelation or introspection, only to flee before he allows anyone close. Say Goodbye Hollywood touches on what appears to be a raw nerve, Mathers admitting that "All I wanted was to give Hailie [his daughter] the life I never had/Instead, I forced us to live alienated". Acknowledging responsibility for his own dysfunction, though, is as close as he comes to healing his self-inflicted wounds.

Sing For The Moment achieves some perspective, an impassioned defence of rap as free speech that succeeds in sounding righteous where other songs seem only self-pitying. Yet, knowing, as Mathers does, that his position at the eye of a media storm is as much the result of his own choices as anything else, he gives himself scant room for manoeuvre.

Not a classic, The Eminem Show is clearly an important record, but the fervent hope is that Mathers' next studio foray will yield the masterpiece he is clearly capable of. This will only happen, though, when Eminem allows himself to use his own eyes to look at the world, instead of writing defensively about the Show he presents to the watching world.

AB

Record label:
Aftermath/Interscope
Produced
by Dr Dre: Eminem: Jeff Bass: Timbaland: Denaun Porter
Recorded
at
Released:
May 27, 2002
Chart peaks:
1 (UK)
Personnel:
Eminem (v): Obie Trice (v on Drips): Paul D Rosenberg (v on Paul Rosenberg): Dina Rae (v on Superman): Steve Berman (v on Steve Berman): D-12 (v on When The Music Stops): Dr. Dre (v on Say What You Want To Say): Nate Dogg (v on 'Till I Collapse): Hailie Jade (v on My Dad's Gone Crazy): Ken Kaniff (v on Curtains Close): Joe Perry (gtr): Jeff Bass (bass, gtr, kbds): Steven King (gtr, kbds, voiceover)L Luis Resto (kbds): Barbara Wilson (bck v): Conesha Owens (bck v): Mike Elizondo (bass, gtr, kbds)
Track listing:
Curtains Up: White America: Business: Cleaning Out My Closet: Square Dance: The Kiss: Soldier: Say Goodbye Hollywood: Drips: Without Me: Paul Rosenberg: Sing For The Moment: Superman: Hailie's Song: Steve Berman: When The Music Stops: Say What You Say: 'Till I Collapse: My Dad's Gone Crazy: Curtains Close
Running time:
77 mins 19 secs
Current CD:
493290
Further listening:
The Slim Shady LP (1999): The Marshall Mathers LP (2001)
Further reading:
Angry Blonde (HarperCollins, 2002); www.eminem.com
Like this?
Try . . . p.663

Ms. Dynamite

A Little Deeper

Suddenly a Briton had something to say to the Americans about keeping it real.

"I am not here to be a stereotypical feisty young girl. I'm actually here with what I believe is something important to say. I just want people to think more," declared a 21-year-old Ms Dynamite in 2001. Hardly the stuff of successful twenty-first century r&b and hip-hop artists either Stateside or in the UK, yet Dynamite-who famously rapped to her compatriots "Now who gives a damn/ About the ice on your hand?/ If it's not too complex/ Tell me how many Africans died/ For the buggettes on your Rolex"-was determined to make a run for the top by promoting an anti-bling platform.

More amazing than her stance, however, was just how quickly that run to the top took place. Despite dabbling in all kinds of trouble as a teen, and only finally grabbing a microphone in her late teens, Dynamite needed just two years to vault from obscurity to UK garage diva to a hip-hop and r&b artist with a Mercury Music Prize for her debut album. Dynamite's positive, challenging, and street-savvy rhymes helped her become the first woman of colour to win Britain's top music prize, and made her the first legitimate English player in the American-style hip-hop game. By calling urban music artists out on all their posturing, materialism, and supposed sexual prowess, Ms Dynamite effectively asked, how is that keeping things real?

"In my life generally," she says, "I've been lucky to have a lot of intelligent, loving people around me who will take out five minutes to teach me things about myself without preaching at me, just showing me naturally."

These lessons, along with all the soul, roots, and reggae music that her mother played for her, laid the foundations for an album with a message that said much to today's urban dwellers.

AD

Record label:
Polydor/Interscope
Produced
by Bloodshy and Avant
Released:
June 2002
Chart peaks:
1 (UK)
Personnel:
Ms. Dynamite (vocals); Van Gibbs (bass); Thomas Lindberg (bass); Arthur Smith Trio (keyboards); Eddison Electrik (drums, fender rhodes, guitar); Chris Gibbs (vocals); Danny Harrison (keyboards); Vincent Henry (horn); Bruce Purse (horn)
Track listing:
Natural High (interlude), Dy-na-mi-tee, Anyway U Want It (feat. Keon Bryce), Put Him Out, Brother, It Takes More (Bloodshy Main Mix), Sick 'n' Tired, Afraid 2 Fly, Watch Over Them, Seed Will Grow (feat. Kymani Marley), Krazy Krush, Now U Want My Love, Too Experienced (feat. Barrington Levy), Gotta Let U Know, All I Ever, A Little Deeper
(UK listing): It Takes More (Bloodshy Main Mix); Natural High (Interlude); Afraid 2 Fly; Sick 'n' Tired; Anyway U Want It (feat Keon Bryce); Now U Want My Love; Seed Will Grow (feat. Kymani Marley); Dy-Na-Mi-Tee; All I Ever Wanna Do; Gotta Let U Know; Put Him Out; Crazy Crush; Brother, A Lil Deeper; Watch Over Them; Get Up Stand Up (hidden track)
Current CD:
5899552
Further reading:
www.msdynamite.co.uk

Sonic Youth

Murray Street

NY's finest return with best work in over a decade

After a tenure as producer for Sonic Youth's two previous full-lengths, *Goodbye 20th Century* (1999) and *NYC Ghosts and Flowers* (2000), prolific musician, producer and ubiquitous auteur Jim O'Rourke somehow managed to find time in his schedule between working with the likes of Wilco and Smog, as well as on four solo projects to join the band as a full-time musician for *Murray Street.*

While the previous collaborations between O'Rourke and the foursome toyed with an experimental inaccessibility, Murray Street was, upon its release, hailed as the most clear-cut, conventionally melodic collection Sonic Youth had put together since their days as cult rock heroes in the late 80's.

The addendum of O'Rourke and his patented tuneful improvisation proved a welcome catalyst for a group who otherwise may have run out of avant investigational directions. While hardly a compromise, *Murray Street* roots instances of dissonance and feedback for which Sonic Youth was known in a landscape of clean riffs and ambling hooks.

The album takes its name from a street in downtown Manhattan tucked away unassumingly beneath the auspices of the towering financial district. Murray Street was the birthplace of Lionel Trains, was once part of Queen's Farm, was the initial location of Columbia College in 1787, and remains the name of Sonic Youth's studio on the block. It is, like the album itself, invested with a storied history. Shortly after the band began recording in the summer of 2001, an airplane engine from one of the planes that struck the World Trade Center, just blocks away, landed on the street. The group continued to record during the months following the attack, as the city on the streets around them repaired and rebuilt itself.

Thurston Moore said in Res Magazine, "The area was so desolated while we recorded through the winter. Our soundtrack was the streets, particularly Murray Street, being torn up and patched down a hundred times—and the rigs hauling off destroyed building relentlessly through the night. We were of the mind to create music as a holistic, positive activity amidst the wreckage." And he told Interview Magazine, "Concurrent with us making this record, they would dig up the street, then they would patch it; then they would dig it up again and they would patch it. They kept changing and rearranging conduits of water and electricity. To me, it was like they were working on their own record."

Surrounded by the process of reinvention, Sonic Youth did not so much retool its own identity, but rediscovered an approach devoid of pretense that allowed for one their most affecting albums to date.

DW

Record label:
Smells Like Records
Produced
by Sonic Youth
Recorded
at Murray Street. Recorded and Mixed by Jim O'Rourke at Echo Canyon NYC, August 2001–March 2002
Released:
June 2002
Personnel:
Kim Gordon (vocals), bass); Lee Ranaldo (vocals, guitar), Steve Shelley (drums), Thurston Moore (vocals, guitar), Jim O'Rourke; Jim Sauter and Don Dietrich (horns on radical adults)
Track listing:
The Empty Page; Disconnection Notice; Rain on Tin; Karen Revisited; Radical Adults Lick Godhead Style; Plastic Sun; Sympathy for the Strawberry
Running time:
45.37
Current CD:
4933192
Further listening:
Bad Moon Rising (1985); Evol (1986); Sister (1987); Daydream Nation (1988); Goo (1990); Dirty (1992); Washing Machine (1995); Goodbye 20th Century (1999)
Further reading:
www.sonicyouth.com; www.smellslikerecords.com
Like this?
Try . . . p.359

Idlewild

The Remote Part

Scottish boys return with hands-in-air anthem

Having come high-tailing out of Edinburgh in 1997 with a sound accurately described as "a flight of stairs falling down a flight of stairs", by 2000 Idlewild had softened their edges to the extent that *100 Broken Windows*, their second full length record, had made the US market sit up and take notice. Spin voted it The Best Album You Didn't Hear in 2000, while Rolling Stone raved about "the great British tradition of cheerfully art-damaged lyrical pretension". Suddenly, America became rather excited about Idlewild, so when the band reconvened in the summer of 2001 it was with the expectation that they would finally deliver the goods.

They began recording the album in New York, where they were encouraged to experiment by mentor Lenny Kaye of the Patti Smith Group. Those six days in the studio helped the band find the musical self-assurance and lyrical focus to make a more ambitious record. "One of the things that made The Remote Part a better album was that the lyrics were much more specific," said vocalist Roddy Woomble. "I was confident enough to push myself forward so people could understand what I was singing about."

From those embryonic sessions in New York, the band decamped to a remote studio in Inchnadamph, Sutherland in the far north of Scotland. The geographical extremes in many ways encompassed the extremities of Idlewild's sound. At once both tender and tough, the new songs refined their melodic-meets-thrashy signature to a fine art, while at the same time reaching new heights of lyricism. In Inchnadamph, the record began to come together. "We'd work all day on songs and ideas and then at night we'd drink," recalls Woomble. "We could do exactly what we wanted."

The album may have spawned the anthemic UK singles You Held The World In Your Arms and American English, but the ambitious self-assurance at its heart peaked with the closing epic In Remote Part/Scottish Fiction, a collaboration with Glaswegian poet Edwin Morgan. "It showed how much we've moved on from where we began," agreed Woomble. "It's a song I'm hugely proud of, and it's the one that has made people take us seriously."

The Remote Part did the trick. Idlewild appeared on Letterman and Leno in the US, their videos went into heavy rotation on MTV. But more importantly, the record showed that – like their kissing cousins REM – they were capable of walking the commerical/artistic tightrope with grace and aplomb.

GT

Record label:
Parlophone/EMI
Produced
by Dave Eringa; Dave Eringa & Guy Massey; Stephen Street
Recorded
at Intervals throughout the year 2001
Released:
July 2002
Chart Peaks:
3 (UK)
Personnel:
Bob Fairfoul (b); Rod Jones (g); Colin Newton (d); Roddy Woomble (v); PLUS: Jeremy Mills (p); Allan Stewart (g); Edwin Morgan (v); Sally Herbert (strings)
Track listing:
You Held The World in Your Arms; A Modern Way of Letting Go; American English; I Never Wanted; (I Am) What I Am Not; Live In A Hiding Place; Out of Routine; Century after Century; Tell Me Ten Words; Stay the Same; In Remote Part/Scottish Fiction
Running time:
38.18
Current CD:
7243 540243 0 6
Further listening:
100 Broken Windows (Capitol 2000)
Further reading:
www.idlewild.co.uk
Like this?
Try . . . p.692

The Flaming Lips

Yoshimi Battles the Pink Robots

Their most accessible album yet . . . excepting the Sony titles

Events surrounding the recording of the Flaming Lips' previous album, the critically acclaimed *The Soft Bulletin* (1999), had been fraught with life-threatening mishaps that seemed to randomly plague band members, including spider bites, car accidents and head wounds. For *Yoshimi Battles the Pink Robots*, the trio returned to the studio with producer Dave Fridmann, content with not having had to avert near tragedy just to get there.

The album was recorded at Fridmann's studio near Buffalo. But while the geographical distance from the distractions of the big city may have allowed for some degree of focus, the project was just one of three in which the Lips were involved at the time. Also in the works was the soundtrack to the documentary film "Okie Noodling" by filmmaker friend Bradley Beesley, as well as production of a full-length feature movie "Christmas on Mars," starring front man Wayne Coyne as a Martian who teaches human cosmonauts about the true meaning of the season.

In his notes on the bands website, Coyne says of juggling the three endeavors, "The 'Okie Noodling' batch [of songs] had a decidedly un-moralizing bent...while the 'Pink Robots' batch were of an optimistic and philosophical spirit, and...the 'Christmas On Mars' score being melancholy and sometimes crushingly depressing dirges with religious textures and spacey sound effects." The three separate ventures had each distinct airs, and the respective immersion in each, it turned out, fueled clarity for the other two.

It was to Fridmann's technical mastery that much of the sonic brilliance of *The Soft Bulletin* was owed. So when it came time to record the eleven tracks that would constitute *Yoshimi*, the decision of whom to turn to was an easy one. Coyne said of the relationship in *Rolling Stone*, "[Fridmann] is really on—I hate to use words like this—but the cutting edge of where ideas and music and production can be. And if people hear that on our record, a lot of that can be attributed to him, because we're still just the weirdos sitting on the couch going, '*Make it louder!*'"

The result is an album whose multi-layered atmospheric soundscapes are the arena for segmented narratives about robots, hypnosis and love. And while not a concept record, *Yoshimi* bookends a pleasantly authored journey. Its lyrical substance comprises profound considerations on existence, morality and death paradoxically couched in a lighthearted, whimsical disposition—an absurdity that is classic Lips. Fans and critics have, over the years, questioned the sanity of Coyne and some of his harebrained artistic decisions, but often a lack of conventional sense is required for the realization of such poignant contradictions.

DW

Record label:
Warner Bros.
Produced
by Dave Fridmann
Recorded
at Tarbox Road Studios, Buffalo, New York
Released:
July 2002
Chart peaks:
13 (UK)
Personnel:
Wayne Coyne (vocals); Michael Ivins (bass); Steven Drozd (drums)
Track listing:
Flight Test; One More Robot/Sympathy 300-21; Yoshimi Battles The Pink Robots, Pt. 1; Yoshimi Battles The Pink Robots, Pt. 2; In The Morning Of The Magicians; Ego Tripping At The Gates of Hell; Are You A Hypnotist??; It's Summertime; Do You Realize?; All We Have Is Now; Approaching Pavonis Mons By Balloon
Current CD:
9362481412
Further listening:
Oh my Gawd!!! . . . The Flaming Lips (1987); Transmissions from the satellite heart (1993); Clouds taste metallic (1995); Zaireeka (1997); The Soft Bulletin (1999)
Further reading:
www.flaminglips.com
Like this?
Try . . . p.423

The Vines

Highly Evolved

The future of rock . . . ?

After six years of little-known existence playing only a handful of gigs at local pubs in their hometown of Sydney Australia, the Vines eventually managed to pique the interest of A&R reps, land a few important opening acts—including two with Aussie alterna-legends You Am I—and secure funding for a record.

What was to be *Highly Evolved* began at the renowned Sunset Sound Studios in Los Angeles, with the help of Rob Schnapf who had previously lent his polishing talents to the likes of Beck, Guided By Voices, Foo Fighters and Elliott Smith. Following some fits and starts, the first single, Factory, was released on XL Recordings in November 2001, and the hype machine that would surround everything the Vines touched in the year to come was begun.

It seemed the Vines embodied much of what the recording industry was looking to get its hands on in the waning months of that year (see the Strokes, the White Stripes). And if they didn't, one could certainly be fooled by the reaction of the British press. NME couldn't come up with enough superlatives to describe the group, calling them "a perfect synthesis of the Beatles and Nirvana," immediately bestowing "Single of the Week" status to the cut, and later saying of their first headlining performance at Sydney's Vic on Park in February 2002, "This band are the future of rock. In ten years time, 10,000 people will claim to have been at this gig."

Not surprisingly, a fierce bidding war between major labels ensued, honors eventually going to Capitol in the US, Heavenly in the UK, and EMI in Australia. When *Highly Evolved* finally hit the shelves, it landed at number three on the UK charts behind Oasis and The Red Hot Chili Peppers, making the Vines the first Australian band to gain a top-five spot on the UK charts with a debut.

The sound that emerged with *Highly Evolved* was quick to be dubbed post-grunge and earned the group not a few comparisons to Nirvana. But the album is also notably diverse in scope, especially for a debut, moving deftly from sneering guitar-driven anthems to syncopated pop ditties to up-strummed numbers reminiscent of the Specials. What binds the miscellany is out-and-out punk intensity. Speaking with Juice Magazine, front man Craig Nicholls described it thusly: "There is an intensity to our music that may sound like negativity sometimes, but mostly I see the music as optimistic. I'm certainly an optimistic person; I don't see much point in being alive if you're not. Music helps you feel that way. It has certainly lifted me. Before music, there wasn't much in the world for me to do. It gave me a reason to go outdoors."

DW

Record label:
Capitol Records (US), Heavenly Recordings (UK), EMI (Japan), EMI (Europe), EMI (AUST)

Produced
By Rob Schnapf

Recorded
at Sunset Sound Studios, Los Angeles, California

Released:
July 2002

Chart peaks:
3 (UK)

Personnel:
Craig Nicholls (Guitar, Percussion, Piano, Vocals); Patrick Matthews (organ, bass, piano); Roger Manning (keyboards); Stephen Rhodes (percussion, engineer); Joey Waronker (drums); Ethan Johns (percussion); Victor Indrizzo (drums)

Track listing:
Highly Evolved; Autumn Shade; Outtathaway!; Sunshinin'; Homesick; Get Free; Country Yard; Factory; In the Jungle; Mary Jane; Ain't No Room; 1969

Current CD:
HVNLP36CD

Further listening:
Only one album so far

Further reading:
www.thevines.com

Like this?
Try . . . p.387

Bruce Springsteen

The Rising

Bruce articulates post 9/11 America

Having ditched his crack squad of New Jersey rabble rousers following the huge commercial triumph of 1984's *Born in the USA*, Springsteen attempted to cut loose from his self-created grandiose musical mythology with subsequent studio recordings. *Tunnel of Love* (1987) and *The Ghost of Tom Joad* (1995) worked well as quiet, reflective solo albums, but the tougher *Lucky Town* and *Human Touch* (both 1992) were clearly poorer for the lack of the snap and crackle of the E-Street Band ensemble. So it was that after re-uniting the band for a few dates in 1999, Springsteen brought the whole shebang back into the studio in 2001 for *The Rising*. The reunion was not without rancour. "When I parted with the band in 1988, I think some guys took it harder than others," he admitted. "Some guys were angry. But I called everybody, told them what I was doing, and it really worked as a unit."

Written and recorded with uncharacteristic urgency in the aftermath of the World Trade Center bombings, the songs came quickly. "The body of the record was written between September [2001]," recalls The Boss, "and we finished up in May [2002]. About 5 or 6 months." Springsteen roped in producer Brendan O'Brien in a conscious attempt to update the trademark E-Street Band sound for the new millennium. "I felt it had to live up to the history of work we'd done," he said. "Brendan is a musician himself, he's very musical and had a lot of good ideas, so we went down south to Georgia and went into the studio."

Although the shadow of 9/11 hangs over the record, it is rarely explicit. Only on the clumsy Worlds Apart does he falter. Elsewhere, Springsteen homes in on the minutiae of loss, with the result that the focus is on the personal rather than the political: witness the dignified Into the Fire, the resigned Nothing Man and the touching litany of mundanity that made up You're Missing: "Coffee cup's on the counter/jacket's on the chair/Papers on the doorstep/ but you're not there."

Muscially, The Rising was a mixture of restrained, downbeat folk melodies and angry, biting rockers with guitars that crackled and crunched like never before. The mood was predominantly sombre, shot through with dark portents and religious imagery. Only on Waitin' On a Sunny Day and Mary's Place did the music and lyrics finally meld together in a truly joyful manner. Elsewhere, it was the sound of a 53-year old man – filled with both hope and despair – holding out both hands to his natural constituency: the firefighters, the blue collar workers, essentially the people Springsteen had always written about and for, but rarely with this amount of compassion. They heard him.

GT

Record Label:
Columbia
Produced
by Brendan O'Brien
Recorded
at Southern Tracks Recording, Atlanta, Georgia
Released:
July 2002
Chart Peaks:
UK 1, US 1
Personnel:
Bruce Springsteen (v, g, harmonica); Roy Bittan (keyboards, p, mellotron, kurzweil; organ; korg M1; crumar); Clarence Clemons (sax, v); Danny Federici (keyboards); Nils Lofgren (g, dobro, slide, banjo, v); Patti Scialfa (v); Garry Tallent (b); Steven Van Zandt (g, v, mandolin); Max Weinberg (d) PLUS: Soozie Tyrell (violin, v,); Brendan O'Brien (hurdy gurdy, glockenspiel, bells); Larry Lemaster (cello); Jere Flint (cello); Jane Scarpantoni (cello); Nashville String Machine; Asif Ali Khan and Group.
Track Listing:
Lonesome Day; Into the Fire; Waitin' On a Sunny Day; Nothing Man; Countin' On A Miracle; Empty Sky; Worlds Apart; Let's Be Friends; Further on (Up the Road); The Fuse; Mary's Place; You're Missing; The Rising; Paradise; My City Of Ruins.
Running Time:
72.57
Current CD:
COL 508000 2
Further Listening:
Born to Run (Columbia 1975).
Further Reading:
Bob Dylan, Bruce Springsteen and American Song – Larry David Smith, Greenwood Press.
Like this?
Try . . . p.69

Solomon Burke

Don't Give Up on Me

The King of Soul & Rock is in exile no more.

The 21st century has been mighty kind to the hibernating—and slightly forgotten—soul legend Solomon Burke. In 2001, he was inducted into the Rock & Roll Hall of Fame. The following year he was enjoying all kinds of praise for his album *Don't Give Up on Me*—both before and after it was released. That same year, he was given his own day in his native town when Philadelphia mayor John Street declared July 19 Solomon Burke Day (Burke was born in Philly on March 21, 1940). Finally, the start of 2003 saw the Hall of Famer win his first Grammy ever.

The underappreciated crooner cemented his reputation as one of the soul greats thanks to his legendary Atlantic recordings in the 1960s. Atlantic Records co-founder Ahmet Ertegun, who released Burke's earliest recordings, has called him "a great soul singer—probably the greatest." For the man also known as the Bishop and the Reverend, however, the real triumph, is that he is alive and kicking it in 2002.

Burke is still active running his own ministry, and tending to the 21 children he has fathered (there's also 68 grandchildren to check in on). With a few of his children, he also continues to run an independent mortuary chain out of his home, where the 300-plus pound King of Rock & Soul can oftentimes be found sitting on a throne, dressed in a cape, wooden staff in hand. Both blessed and cursed with a killer money-making instinct, in the past, the Bishop has run a limousine service; raced back to Philadelphia from late-night NYC recording sessions in order to plow snowy streets in the morning for $4/hour; and was even rumored to have run a sandwich service on an all-star soul singers' tour bus that raised its prices as they all traveled deeper and deeper into the then-segregated South.

In celebration of this life and this unparalleled voice, songwriters like Bob Dylan, Tom Waits, Van Morrison, Joe Henry, and Brian Wilson all gave Burke original songs for *Don't Give Up on Me*. Burke proves he's still the one you want singing to you as you fall asleep; his voice is controlled and tamed and reassuring—warm and soothing as soup when he's singing about heartache, redemption, loss, and all kinds of other classic soul themes. The effect of songs like "Don't Give Up on Me," "Soul Searchin'," "The Judgement," and "None of Us Are Free" (with the Blind Boys of Alabama) in today's world of over-sung, over-falsettoed, strained ballads is a pleasant reminder of what a genuinely powerful voice can achieve.

AD

Record label:
Fat Possum Records
Produced
by Joe Henry
Recorded
at Sunset Sound Factory, Hollywood, CA
Released:
July 2002
Personnel:
Solomon Burke (vocals), Jay Bellerose (drums and percussion), Chris Bruce (guitar), David Palmer (piano and keyboards), David Piltch (bass), Rudy Copeland (organ), Niki Harris (backing vocals), Jean McClain (backing vocals), Bennie Wallace (tenor saxophone), Daniel Lanois (electric guitars on "Stepchild"), The Blind Boys of Alabama (backing vocals on "None of Us Are Free")
Track listing:
Don't Give Up on Me, Fast Train, Diamond in Your Mind, Flesh and Blood, Soul Searchin', Only a Dream, The Judgement, Stepchild, The Other Side of the Coin, None of Us Are Free, Sit This One Out
Current CD:
5035820129
Further listening:
Soul Meeting—the Soul Clan (1968), Proud Mary: The Bell Sessions (1969), Take Me, Shake Me (1983), Change is Gonna Come (1986), Home in Your Heart: The Best of Solomon Burke (1992)
Further reading:
www.thekingsolomonburke.com
Like this?
Try . . . p.57

Aimee Mann

Lost In Space

Desolation never sounded so gorgeous.

In space, no one can hear you scream. The tagline from the sci-fi classic *Alien* could do double-duty for Mann's fourth solo album. The space is more inner than outer and the slimy monster here is one with four heads – isolation, depression, compulsion and addiction. As in the movie, the characters in the songs are preyed upon and harvested as vessels for the continuation of more dark emotions.

"For me, it's all about trying to understand people," Mann explains. "People are pretty fucked up, and I'm right there along with them. If my songs give people the impression that I'm emotionally disturbed – well yeah, you're right. Over the last few years, I've also done a lot of reading about psychology and personality disorders, and I incorporate that into what I'm writing about. These things are out there and they're not that unusual. I don't know anyone who I can describe as 100% normal and happy."

If this all sounds like too much gravity to endure, Mann makes it just the opposite by matching her inner-galactic explorations with pop melodies to die for. You can float through songs such as "Humpty Dumpty" and "Pavlov's Bell" on a purely surface level, buoyed by the retro-rocket guitars and big choruses. Even the minor key dirges are so tuneful and colorful in their arrangements (Mann credits producer Michael Lockwood with creating the compelling "space noises") that you'll be humming along as you enter another black hole in the lyric.

Mann says this dark-light contrast is something she's admired in Elliot Smith's albums, especially *XO*. "That's the main inspiration for my record. It's a record that I listened to over and over when it first came out, and then I went through recently a phase of trying to listen to newer stuff, or the radio, and then one day, I stuck in *XO* again. I thought, 'This is just amazing!' He's courageous enough to share things that are difficult and painful."

Free from the major labels that tied her in knots for years, Mann released this record, like its predecessor, *Bachelor No. 2*, on her own SuperEgo label. She says, "A major label would've had a problem with the theme of the record anyway. *Lost in Space* is a real old-fashioned long-playing album. It's not just because I grew up with that – records that were good from beginning to end, records that people cared about, rather than one or two singles with a bunch of filler. I think it's a rip-off to the public, who pay a lot of money for a CD and should get something more for it. As it is, this record has a really consistent flavor from song to song, and it's nice not to have to compromise that."

BDM

Record label:
SuperEgo
Produced
by Michael Lockwood (with Ryan Freeland and Mike Deneen)
Recorded
at Stampede Origin Studio, Sonora Recorders, Henson Recording Studios, Q Division, Kampo, Los Angeles; October 2000-March2002
Released:
August 2002
Chart peaks:
35 (US)
Personnel:
A Mann (v, g, b, p, pc); M Lockwood (g, chamberlin, theremin); J Falkner (b); D Palmer (k); M Deneen (p, k); P Warren (k); J Bruni (p, k); J Sands (d, pc); J Bellerose (d); M Penn (loops); B Judge (v); D Sahanaja (v); M Randle (v); R Squeezebox (v); J Quarmby (ar); S Katayama (conductor); J Derouin, P Kent, B Garabedian, M De Leon, J Wittenberg, N Leggett, A Garabedian, S Chatman, D Campo, M Richards (v); D Buffum, C Mukogawa (va); L Corbett, D Smith, S Richards, D Stone (c)
Track listing:
Humpty Dumpty; High on Sunday 51; Lost in Space; This Is How It Goes; Guys Like Me; Pavlov's Bell; Real Bad News; Invisible Ink; Today's the Day; The Moth; It's Not
Running time:
43:05
Current CD:
SE-007
Further listening:
Bachelor No. 2
Further reading:
www.aimeemann.com
Like this?
Try . . . p.614

Coldplay

A Rush of Blood to the Head

Coldplay cement their position as the biggest British band in the world.

Following the overwhelming success of their first LP, *Parachutes*, it would have been easy, expected—commercially acceptable, even—for Coldplay to fall back on formula, fire up the songwriting Xerox machine, churn out a veritable carbon copy of the previous effort, and watch the cheques roll in again. As it turned out, *A Rush of Blood to the Head* was a defiant follow-up born of self-imposed standards imminently aware of such probabilities.

If the year following the release of *Parachutes* was kind to the band in terms of good old fame and fortune, it was nothing if not taxing in its intensity. Near constant touring had left the group emotionally and creatively spent, and rumours circulated that Coldplay would soon be no more; that they were allegedly not up to the challenge of besting their debut. Drummer Will Champion told the Observer, "I think we all found that first year in Coldplay, with all the success and acclaim and criticism, bewildering. We didn't lose it, but we lost our bearings, probably [front man] Chris [Martin] most of all. Now we've got a handle on it and we're confident about who we are. We all feel very excited about what we can do."

In addition to the weathering tolls entailed by practical demands, Coldplay had to learn to roll with the punches of criticism that accompanied their rise. As Martin sings in The Scientist, "Nobody said it was easy/No one ever said it would be this hard." Much of *A Rush of Blood to the Head* feels like little answers to challenges, both overt and implicit, that were levied on the band during their time in the spotlight. At times the foursome wishes to remind their audience they can indeed rock; there are moments of sweeping, atmospheric scope only hinted at on the first album; and there is Martin's by then infamous voice and its markedly increased stylistic range.

In the effort to avoid the trappings that over-production can impose the group elected to move the recording process out of London and into a small studio in Liverpool. Chris Martin told Rolling Stone that the initial attempt "was just sounding a bit like a band who had loads of money and could afford to make any expensive record, and it didn't really have any passion or soul. And that's what we wanted to get...You have to rely on the tunes and the emotions, rather than the heavy technology." Teaming up once again with co-producer Ken Nelson, the band sought once more to achieve emotive intensity via the most organic means possible. Thus, while *A Rush of Blood to the Head* is sonically more complex than *Parachutes*, it manages to retain, and build upon, the melodic authenticity for which the band was praised.

DW

Record label
Parlophone
Produced
by Ken Nelson and Coldplay
Released:
August 2002
Chart peaks:
1 (UK)
Personnel:
Guy Berryman (bass), Jon Buckland (guitar), Will Champion (drums, percussion), Chris Martin (vocals, guitar)
Track listing:
Politik; In My Place; God Put A Smile Upon Your Face; The Scientist; Clocks; Daylight; Green Eyes; Warning Sign; a Whisper; A Rush of Blood to the Head; Amsterdam
Running time:
54.08
Current CD:
5405042
Further listening:
Parachutes (2000)
Further reading:
www.coldplay.com; www.arushofbloodtothehead.co.uk
Like this?
Try . . . p.407

Roddy Frame

Surf

Low-key acoustic album reaffirms Frame's songwriting alchemy and revives ailing critical fortunes.

Roddy Frame, the boy wonder who'd wowed the critics with his early recordings for the Scottish indie Postcard in the early '80s, was by the late '90s clearly running out of creative steam. After several years at Warner Brothers, he had signed to Andy MacDonald's hip post-Go! Discs label Independiente, delivering *The North Star*, a pristine-sounding but uneventful album of soulful MOR ballads whose lack of success left him feeling disillusioned and frustrated with the music business. With his career now in commercial decline for over a decade, he acknowledged that discretion was the better part of valour and disappeared from view.

That *Surf*, the record he resurfaced with on an obscure indie four years later, was everything its '90s forebears were not may have a had a lot to do with the sobering blow of *The North Star*'s failure. Since 1987's *Love*, Frame's records had leaned heavily on slick, hi-tec productions and arrangements – this time, however, the record featured just Roddy's voice and guitar, and was recorded at home on his Apple Mac computer via a couple of pre-amps. In keeping with the stripped-bare feel, the songs were stark and confessional, suggesting a man whose flair for romantic meditations and clever poetic conceits had been amplified rather than dulled by his experience of four years in the wilderness.

The major inspiration for the record was Paul Westerberg's mostly acoustic *Suicaine Gratification*, which had hogged Roddy's turntable throughout the previous summer. Armed with a rhyming dictionary and his computer, the singer pieced together the new songs over many months: the result was a huge well of 30something heartache, spilling out over complex, lightly jazzy chord progressions and exquisite folk picking. Lyrically, Frame's poetic weaponry was set to stun, as evidenced by lines such as "I know this is not just some irrational belief/Floats with the logic of a falling leaf/Sailing on the wind/Must logic end where love begins again?" (from the title track).

Elsewhere, a strong sense of London streetlife permeates the songs, from references to Frame's hanging with the "twilight" crowd in the East End to namechecks for Big Ben and SW3. "I was so caught up in getting the words and melodies right that I hadn't noticed that London crept through between the cracks. I've been living here for 20 years, my girlfriend's from London and it comes out. I love London, it's such a great city, it's a very inspiring place."

Surf was not a commercial success, but those who recognised Frame's quiet genius could see he was back on form.

PG

Record label:
Redemption
Produced
by Roddy Frame
Recorded
by Hannah Grace Dellar in Frame's home studio 2002
Release date:
September 2002
Chart peaks:
None (UK) None (US)
Personnel:
Roddy Frame (v, g)
Tracklisting:
Over You;Surf;Small World; I Can't Start Now; Abloom; Tough; Big Ben; High Class Music; Turning The World Around; Mixed Up Love; For What It Was
Running time:
35.44
Current CD:
RRUK2
Further Listening:
Aztec Camera's High Land Hard Rain (Warner Brothers, 1983)
Further reading:
www.killermontstreet.com
Like this?
Try . . . p.671

Orchestra Baobab

Specialists In All Styles

The kings of old-timey West African Cuban music make a triumphant return of fifteen years in the wilderness

Sometimes, the story behind the album is so good that you can overlook the faults in the actual product. Fortunately, this one has a killer tale and cuts to match. In the 1970s, Orchestra Baobab were one of the biggest bands in West Africa, their story being the very essence of rock'n'roll and involving curses, deaths, kidnapped musicians and foreign tours that ended in desperate straits. The music they played was a lightly Africanised form of Cuban son, a sophisticated sound that had been brought to Senegal by sailors, and popular through the twin virtues of being both acceptably African and enticingly exotic. By the early 1980s, however, younger musicians, led by Youssou N'Dour, had decided it wasn't African enough and drifted away from the scene. The old guard were hard pressed to find enough work to survive.

In 1982, Baobab organised one final session. That should have been the end of the matter, but those final recordings developed a life of their own. In Paris, where expats were less interested in N'Dour's newfangled mbalax, imported tapes were bootlegged and bootlegged again. By the time they reached Britain, they were probably sixth or seventh generation. That didn?t stop World Circuit spotting their potential and arranging to release them as the *Pirates Choice* LP in 1986.

The band were all in full-time employment by then and unaware of the extent of their cult. Ten years on, fresh from the success of the *Buena Vista Social Club* reunion, World Circuit had other ideas and wondered if they would be interested in going back into the studio' Tracking the original members down was no easy task. Barthelemy Attiso, for example, was now a lawyer in Togo and had not played guitar in 15 years, but the spirit was willing. Youssou N'Dour, remembering what he had learnt from the band, was eager to help out.

The result just sings with the joy of being able to do what they always wanted to do. There's one bona fide Cuban classic, El Son Te Llama, a guest vocal from another class Cuban, Ibrahim Ferrer, perhaps the definitive take of On Verra Ca, the band's theme tune, and a killer piece of faux Latin in Hommage A Tonton Ferrer. The interplay between Attiso's guitar and Issa Cissokho's sax is a delight, the massed vocals are very heaven, and the laidback ambience makes this a must for any sunny day. A story with a happy ending.

DH

Record label:
World Circuit
Produced
by Nick Gold with Youssou N'Dour
Recorded
in Livingston Studios, London
Chart peaks:
None (UK) None (US)
Release date:
September 2002
Personnel:
Balla Sidibe (voc), Rudy Gomis (voc), Ndiouga Dieng (voc), Assane Mboup (voc), Medoune Diallo (voc), Barthelemy Attiso (voc, gtr), Issa Cissokho (sax), Thierno Koite (sax), Latfi Ben Geloune (gtr), Charlie Ndiaye (bs), Montaga Koite (drm)
Track listing:
Bul Ma Min, Sutukun, Dee Moo Woor, Jiin Ma Jiin Ma, Ndongoy Daara, On Verra Ca, Hommage A Tonton Ferrer, El Son Te Llama, Gnawoe
Running time:
50.08
Current CD:
WCD064
Further listening:
Pirates Choice (World Circuit)
Further reading:
Mojo 96
Like this?
Try . . . p.274

Beck

Sea Change

Where was his dance machine and his music? Mourning-and we're all that more blessed because of it.

When Beck released his album *Sea Change* in 2002, many let out a collective yawn. *Sea Change* was a very quiet album, and most hoped that he had gotten that phase out of the way with 1998's *Mutations*. The hope? On with the freaky party that allowed us all to be losers and funny-looking dancers, the same one that was Grammy-certified in '99 with the release of *Midnite Vultures*.

Sea Change was hardly a party. Instead, it was Beck's unflinching meditation on loss, with an assist by hotshot contemporary artist Jeremy Blake's artwork, prompted by his breakup with a longtime girlfriend. Beck was free of irony, and free of satire, and free of anthems. Instead, he offered us sincerity and honesty, all given a long, deliberate look after the end of a nine-year relationship. And as the album grew upon each listen, *Sea Change* emerged as a headphone favorite and Mr Hansen's most courageous album to date. What we had in front of us was the purest Beck we'd never known-and for a while, as it often does, that made us feel uneasy.

Whereas Beck has sounded anything from loud and jagged to quiet but spare in the past, this was full and orchestral.It proved to be a sound that kept giving. Beyond these arrangements, the song order rewards the patient listener with a loose narrative and thematic development of his loss. Early songs like "The Golden Age," in which Beck laments about days where he barely gets by and doesn't even feel like trying, focus on the early feelings of emptiness and purposelessness that come with loss. He is tired and restless. Eventually, his songs hint at a desire to get out, to try the different things that we do to take our mind off of loss, to make an attempt to fill the recent void with soul-searching activity. By the orchestral end of the album, Beck's deliberate meditation on his loss has yielded the best one can hope for: for the listener, a complete, astonishing album to be played start to finish; and for the artist, some semblance of healing as he sings, "Looking for a satellite/ In the rays of the heaven again/ . . . Yesterdays are mending."

In typical Beck fashion, his next album is said to be very different from *Sea Change*, with Dan the Automator manning the production table. Beck has always embarked on the courageous process of reinventing himself from album to album, but *Sea Change* was an alarming arrival even for those who knew to expect the unexpected. As an album that is both the most surprising of his career and the best example of how he likes to reinvent his career, *Sea Change* is his masterpiece. In "Little One," the song from which Beck's latest takes its album title, he sings, "In a sea change, nothing is safe." It's a lyric for the album, the career, and the ages.

AD

Record label:
Interscope
Produced
by Nigel Godrich
Recorded
at Ocean Way Studios
Released:
September 2002
Chart peaks:
20 (UK)
Personnel:
Beck Hansen (vocals, acoustic guitar); Justin Meldal-Johnsen (electric bass); Roger Manning, Jr; (clavinet); Smokey Hormel (acoustic slide guitar); James Gadson (drums); Joey Waronker (percussion); Nigel Godrich (keyboards)
Track listing:
The Golden Age, Paper Tiger, Guess I'm Doin' Fine, Lonesome Tears, Lost Cause, End of the Day, It's All in Your Mind, Round the Bend, Already Dead, Sunday Sun, Little One
Running time:
48.55
Current CD:
4933932
Further listening:
Odelay (1996), Mutations (1998), Midnite Vultures (1999)
Further reading:
www.beck.com
Like this?
Try . . . p.204

Jurassic 5

Power In Numbers

Most successful album – commercially as well as musically – from a band dedicated to reminding rap what it's lost.

Formed in the mid-'90s in Los Angeles when two rap groups merged, Jurassic 5 set about reclaiming hip hop from those who had taken the music away from its roots. The moniker was a joke, one of the sextet's girlfriends remarking that they were obsessed with prehistoric rap, but there was always more to J5 than that.

The group's two DJs, Nu-Mark and Cut Chemist, shared an obsession with unearthing, devouring and re-using obscure sample material. Any group with these two making its beats was bound to hark back to a time before sample clearance worries sent the music's mainstream into a stew of syrupy synths and turgid programming.

But it was the rappers who really captured the attention: the first '90s rap group to overtly reference the genre's old school, J5's interlocking wordplay and unison chorus rapping marked a deliberate attempt to return the music to its party-centric past. Or, as Chali 2na put it on Break, "we're trying to take rap back to its primitive state", a state where the form may sound familiar but innovation remains paramount.

Throughout, this album gleams with verbal ingenuity and musical exuberance, allowing the emcees to spread a message as well as an attitude. Freedom entreats without preaching, while Sum Of Us finds the rappers admitting mistakes in their cautionary stories. But it's when it's revelling in hip hop as a varied, vivacious musical form where Power In Numbers scores heaviest. What's Golden, an affirmation of their musical mission statement, has Chali 2na making like "the verbal Herman Munster" over the cheesy organ sample, while Break, a hymn to the DJ, finds the emcees quoting Rakim lyrics. A Day At The Races was a beat Cut Chemist had made in homage to the speed-rappers of the late '80s and had been holding on to for some time: four verses in, you're convinced the only thing that could make it any better would be if Big Daddy Kane to be up next. And, of course, he is.

Power In Numbers consolidated what had always been an enthusiastic audience in Europe, but its impact back home was just as conclusive, breaking into the Billboard Top 20 in its first week and earning J5 a spot on the 2003 Lollopalooza tour. Suggesting that it wasn't just a retro-obsessed underground but the commercial mainstream too that needed an injection of old school rap values.

AB

Record label:
Interscope

Produced
by Cut Chemist: DJ Nu-Mark: JuJu of The Beatnuts: SA-RA Creative Partners

Recorded
at Red October Chemical Storage Facility: Log Cabin Studios: Mad Hatter Studios: Ameraycan Studios:

Released:
October 7, 2002

Personnel:
Akil (v): Chali 2na (v): Zaakir (Soup) (v): Marc 7 (v): Cut Chemist (turntables): DJ Nu-Mark (turntables): Big Daddy Kane (v on A Day At The Races): Percy P (v on A Day At The Races): Nelly Furtado (v on Thin Line): Kool Keith (v on DDT): "Boy Wonder" (v on Hey)

Track listing
This Is: Freedom: If You Only Knew: Break: React: A Day At The Races: Remember His Name: What's Golden: Thin Line: After School Special: High Fidelity: Sum Of Us: DDT: One Of Them: Hey: I Am Somebody: Acetate Prophets

Running time:
56.11

Current CD:
493 437-2

Further listening:
Jurassic 5 EP (Play It Again Sam 1998)

Further reading:
www.jurassic5.com

Like this?
Try . . . p.532

Johnny Cash

American IV: The Man Comes Around

Cash does covers and makes them his own

In 1993, rap-metal producer Rick Rubin invited veteran country maverick Johnny Cash to make a stripped-down, back-to-basics record in Rubin's LA living room. The record that followed - *American Recordings* - went on to win a Grammy. In the years between his 60th and 70th birthdays, Cash completed the trilogy with two further albums reflecting increasingly upon religion and mortality. Still, nobody was quite ready for *The Man Comes Around.*

Beset by a desperately debilitating illness – misdiganosed first as Parkinson's Disease, then as Shy-Drager Syndrome, and now defined as Autonomic Neuropathy ("I think it means you're getting old and shaky," he smiled) – Cash dredged the record from his frail frame by sheer force of will. "I found strength to work on this album just to spite this disease," he said. "I came to the studio sometimes with no voice, when I could have stayed at home and pouted, but I couldn't let that happen. I recorded when that was the last thing in the world I thought I could do. And there's a great deal of strength coming out of that weakness."

Like the three previous installments in the Cash-Rubin axis, *The Man Comes Around* was recorded with sparse acoustic instruments, mainly in Rubin's LA home, but also augmented by sessions at Cash's home studio in Tennessee and a tumultuous version of Danny Boy cut in two hours at St. James Church Episcopal cathedral in LA. The singer, his producer, friends and family all contributed ideas for songs to record, but the final cuts clearly represented the apogee of Cash's career-long obsession with God, death and redemption. Although most of the songs were covers, Cash's versions left the originals looking redundant. By discarding what he felt was irrelevant, he turned each performance into something dark, mysterious and haunted.

This approach was best exemplified in his bone-bare readings of Nine Inch Nails' Hurt and Depeche Mode's Personal Jesus: "Hurt is a song about a man's pain and what we're capable of doing to ourselves," Cash reflected. "I could relate to that from the very beginning. Personal Jesus [is] probably the most evangelical gospel song I ever recorded. I don't know that the writer meant it to be that, but that's what it is."

Elsewhere, in the title track Cash contribued his best self-penned song for years, a brooding gem studded with apocalpytic menace. "I firmly believe that it's the best record we've done," he said upon its release. "It reaches out even farther than the others did, it goes in so many different directions. We take no prisoners, we do it the way we want to. And we look forward to the work to be done." Defiant to the last.

GT

Record label:
American Recordings/Lost Highway
Produced
by Rick Rubin
Recorded
at Cash Cabin Studio, Nashville, TN.
Released:
November 2002
Personnel:
Johnny Cash (g, v); Randy Scruggs (g); Smokey Hormel (g, slide); Benmont Tench (p, organ, mellotron, harmonium, wurlitzer, vibes); Mike Campbell (g); Fiona Apple (v); Roger Manning Jr. (chamberlin, mellotron, p, bells); Marty Stuart (g); John Frusciante (g); Billy Preston (p); David Ferguson (ukelele); Don Henley (v); Jeff Hannah (g); Kerry Marx (g); Nick Cave (v); Laura Cash (fiddle); Joey Waronker (d); Thom Bresh (g); 'Cowboy' Jack Clement (dobro); Terry Harrington (clarinet); The Whole Cash Gang (v)
Track listing:
The Man Comes Around; Hurt; Give My Love to Rose; Bridge Over Troubled Water; I Hung My Head; First Time Ever I Saw Your Face; Personal Jesus; In My Life; Sam Hall; Danny Boy; Desperado; I'm So Lonesome I Could Cry; Tear Stained Letter; Streets Of Laredo; We'll Meet Again; Big Iron
Running time:
55.59
Further listening:
American Recordings (1994),
Further reading:
Cash – Johnny Cash, (Harper Collins)
Like this?
Try . . . p.81

Common

Electric Circus

Sprawlingly eclectic masterpiece that demands a re-evaluation of what hip hop is.

The irony is inescapable. Chicago rapper Lonnie Rashid Lynn was known as Common Sense until the existence of a rock group of the same name meant he had to lose the "Sense" part. That this most erudite and philosophical of rappers has to label himself as everyday seems grotesque. Worse, his career journey had seen him move from slinging street slang as Common Sense to espousing complex social and spiritual visions as Common, the name change the reverse of the artistic evolution.

Electric Circus caught flak from hip hop fans who felt that Common had abandoned his "traditional" rap past. Instead, Electric Circus indelibly inks hip hop into the history of black American music, showing both how the art form is the product of manifold influences, yet can encompass all that has gone before.

Though recorded across the US, the bulk of the work was done at New York's Electric Lady studios, and that facility's most noted patron looms large over the manifold textures and sounds. Jimi Was A Rock Star, the only track completely recorded and mixed at Electric Lady, ignores the tug of war over Hendrix's cultural legacy and attempts to place him simultaneously in his black and white musical contexts for the first time. Over a squall of grinding guitars and a reverberating rhythm section, Common and Erykah Badu intone a weird bass-and-soprano duet, the lyrics seeking to understand what drove this most iconic of musical figures. Noting that Jimi "played the streets like an instrument", they describe him as "searching for that magic place/that he could touch/in the sky/Just to get his people high". Arriving late in the track listing, this is the album's focus, an intense, if awkward-sounding peak.

The rest of the record is united only in its eclecticism and diversity. Guests including Prince, Mary J Blige and Stereolab's Laetitia Sadier drop in and out of the ever-changing soundscape. At one end of the spectrum is I Am Music, a vivid recreation of Cotton Club-era jazz. At the other is I Got A Right Ta, a simple, brilliant slice of Neptunes-produced blues-hop, Common's lyrics riding a harmonica-strewn beat. Yet even as he gets back to rap basics he's explaining why he shouldn't be constrained by any limits placed on the music he theoretically makes: "Hip hop is changing," he notes, asking, "Y'all want me to stay the same?" No, sir: that would make no sense at all.

AB

Record label:
MCA

Produced
by Ahmir "?uestlove" Thompson: James Poyser: Dilla: Pino Palladino: Karriem Riggins: The Neptunes: Jeff Lee Johnson: The Soulquarians: Jay Dee

Recorded
at Axis Studios, Philadelphia, PA: Electric Lady Studios, New York, NY: The Studio, Philadelphia, PA: Studio A, Dearborn Heights, MI: Chicago Recording Company, Chicago, IL.

Released:
December 2003

Personnel:
Common (v): VMojica (v): M Daulne(v): James Poyser (kbds piano): A Thompson (drums handclaps): J Lee Johnson (gtr): P Palladino (bass): Dilla (d, b, elec gtr): Bilal (v); E Breezy (bkg v;: F Walker (perc); T Tribbett (bkg v); Omar (v); D Chillz (v); M J Blige (v); P Williams (bkg v, v); L Sadier (v); Prince (kbds and gtr); B Humphrey (flute); D Bennett (flute); Larry Gold (string arrangement); Cee-Lo (v) J Scott (v); E Badu(v);

Track listing:
Ferris Wheel: Soul Power: Aquarius: Electric Wire Hustler Flower: The Hustle: Come Close: New Wave: Star *69 : I Got A Right Ta: Between Me, You & Liberation: I Am Music: Jimi Was A Rock Star: Heaven Somewhere: The Light

Running time:
77 mins 19 secs

Current CD:
113 163-2

Further listening:
Resurrection (Relativity 1997)

Further reading:
www.okayplayer.com/common

Like this?
Try . . . p.591

Royksopp

Melody A.M

The finest music to have come out of Norway since . . . well, ever actually.

Just when you thought electronic music had crossed every boundary, bleeped every bleep and messed with every last effect in the soundscape, Royksopp come up with the freshest and most enchanting slice of electronica for many a midnight sun.

Hailing from Tromso – wintry even by Norweigian standards – Royksopp's sound is perfectly Scandic. Cute, svelte and minimalist, *Melody A.M* is the post-ironic soundtrack to modern post-clubbing. Picking up and pushing on from the point where Air and Groove Armada ran out of puff, Royksopp major in Downbeat – that ambient space embracing spectral backbeats, wryly referenced humour, 70s synths, dreamy vocals, trip-hop loops and, when the part demands, a spangling Nordic harp or two. *Melody A.M* offers all of the above , and more.

Setting the tone with their sly and ethereal take on Burt Bacharach in the breezy opener *So Easy*, Royksopp exercise an artful mastery of their genre. They're good – and they know they are. The pearls just keep on coming, track after rippling track. Worldwide smash hit *Eple* is irresistibly hypnotic electro; *Poor Leno* is metronomic synth-disco, while *Royksopp's Night Out* is a throbbing Krautrock epic worthy of Can.

All good things are here: moody horns and bubbling bass on *She's So*, tripped out planet rock on *In Space*, warped and loopy feedback on *Remind Me* and fuzzy chicanery on *40 Years Back*. Its guile as well as its title invites us to file ***Melody A.M*** under Easy Listening, but it's too clever for that. If there's such a thing as Northern Lite Disco then Royksopp are it.

HW

Record Label:
Wall of Sound
Produced
by Royksop
Released:
August 2002
Chart peaks:
9 (UK)
Personnel:
Anneli Marian Drecker (vocals); Erland Oye (vocals); Ole Vedard Skauge (bass); Craig Morrison (remixing); Graeme Reedie (remixing); Ernest Saint Laurent (instrumentation mixing)
Track listing:
So easy; Eple; Sparks; In Space; Poor Leno; Higher place; Royksopp's night out; Remind me; She's so; 40 Years back/Come
Running time:
46.27
Current CD:
WALLCD027
Further reading:
www.astralwerks.com/royksopp
Like this?
Try . . . p.312

HKB Finn

Vitalistics

A journey of self-discovery and enlightenment through music, HKB Finn's debut is an as yet buried treasure.

Although operating within the parameters of the much-maligned British hip hop milieu, Andrew "HKB Finn" Ward's solo debut was so much more. Collaborating with Tunde Jegede, a composer and musician trained in both the Western classical and Gambian traditional realms, as well as working with contemporaries from the jazz and rap worlds, Finn created a record that adds rich layers to all the genres he encounters.

Although best known as lead rapper with UK rap group Katch 22, Ward had always made it his business to understand music from outside the often closeted environment of British hip hop. During his upbringing in Jamaica he was introduced to Mento singing, and, along with the rock, pop and reggae he heard, would later fuse these disparate traditions. After Katch split Ward almost got a major deal as part of a rock-rap outfit called Band Substance, rapped with a jazz quintet called No Flags, played gigs with drum & bass act JB Rose and even ended up rapping with the Royal Philharmonic Orchestra. All of this impacts on Vitalistics.

"There's an old saying that once you've learned something you can't unlearn it," Ward explained. "I'd learned all this stuff from the classical end – how to influence emotion with chords, and standing on stage with 40 other players, thinking, 'An orchestra's just a band with lots of people! Instead of just one guitarist you've got ten violinists all playing the same thing.' And I thought, 'Damn! This is what my music's missing'. So I set about trying to work on an album that brought in all these influences, all these different shapes, until it ended up as this thing."

Vitalistics, which took almost five years to complete, does all Ward wanted, and more. The journey begins with Spirit Of The Nomad, Ward examining notions of self over Jegede's warm, emotive kora, and travels, via the penultimate Epiphany, on to the closing I Remember, in which all the lessons learned are laid bare. "Be not afraid of who you are," he intones. "Be strong, be what you've always wanted to be . . . And always remember who you are". A sleeve note by Onyekachi Wambu maps out Finn's musicological heritage, tracing his lineage back to the Jalis of West Africa, just in case the music hadn't made that clear. A magnificent, memorable album that, at the time of writing, is still to reach the size of audience it merits.

AB

Record label:
Son Records
Produced
by Tunde Jegede: Lotek: Tom Szirtes: HKB Finn: Shur-I-Kan: Wayne Bennett: Don Jose
Recorded
at Gateway Studios, Kingston Upon Thames, London: "The Secret Lotek Sonic Lab": The Discerning Ear Dojo, London: RMS Studios, London: Bridge Studios, Birmingham: Intimate Studios, London: Milo Studios, London: SAE Studios, London: Odessa Studios, London
Released:
2002
Chart peaks:
None (UK) None (US)
Personnel:
HKB Finn (Andrew Ward) (v, b): T Jegede (cello, kora, log drum, bugorabou, percussion, pizzicato cello, cello, vibraphone): Stephen Hussey (violin): Jo Archard (violin): Mandy/Amanda Drummond (viola, chorus v): Tatiana Mais (v); Sophia Walker (v); Mary Mzumara (v)
Track listing
Spirit Of The Nomad: Bladow!: Bananaz: Cool: Be: Motion Fitness: Vitalistics: In The Stillness: Y?: What If?: The Ballad Of Marie Celeste: Epiphany: The Path To Inner Peace: I Remember
Running time:
69 mins 29 secs
Current CD:
SONCD021
Further listening:
Katch 22 – Dark Tales from Two Cities (Kold Sweat 1993)
Further reading:
www.sonrecords.com
Like this?
Try . . . p.551

Missy Elliott

Under Construction

One of rap's most futuristic visionaries goes back to the old school, and finds that understanding your history means you function better in the present.

There's reinvention, and there's reinvention. And when Missy Elliott reinvented herself, the results could hardly have been more surprising.

The Virginia Beach rapper, producer and music executive had spent the second half of the '90s carving out a unique niche for herself. In the company of production cohort Tim "Timbaland" Mosley, she released three albums that found favour both with hip hop devotees and people who wouldn't normally touch the genre with a barge pole. The reasons for this were two-fold: firstly, Missy and Timbaland's soundscapes were like no other: spacey, minimal, flavoured with Eastern spice and loaded with bass-heavy bounce, they were what a listener in 1985 might have hoped *all* hip hop would sound like in the 21st century. The second factor, though, was that Missy herself was an instantly likeable anti-star. She flaunted her larger-than-life figure in space-age videos and became an icon for feminists and the politically correct, an unconventionally attractive woman proving that you didn't have to be white, blonde, cute and size 6 to cut it as a pop star.

So Under Construction was something of a shock. On the sleeve and in her coinciding media appearances, Missy had clearly shed several stone and glammed up her look, shortening the distance between her and some of her less credible peers. And the response she and Timbaland had crafted to the dominance of their Virginia Beach neighbours The Neptunes (whose production style, clearly owing a tad to Missy and Tim, adorned records by everyone from Common and N.O.R.E. to Britney Spears and Justin Timberlake) was decidedly unexpected. Instead of rewriting hip hop's sonic rule-book, they instead began to look back.

The first single, Work It, lifted the same Bob James sample that Run DMC used for Peter Piper, and across it Missy raps lasciviously about her own sexuality. Still daring to flout all conventions, it boasted a chorus in which the hookline was played backwards: a $1m prize was offered to the first person to unravel its meaning. Elsewhere, Jay-Z guests on the hip hop reminiscences of Back In The Day, and Wu-Tang Clan's Method Man drops by to help re-make his own Bring The Pain.

This acknowledgement of hip hop's past made Under Construction the most consistently satisfying LP of Missy's career. It's also the most joyous, as if the lifting of the burden of constant innovation freed her and Mosley to simply get on with making the music they wanted to make.

AB

Record label:
Elektra
Produced
by Missy Elliott: Timbaland: Craig Brockman:
Released:
November 2002
Chart peaks:
23 (UK)
Personnel:
Missy Elliott (v): Method Man (v on Bring The Pain): Ludacris (v on Gossip Folks): Jay-Z (v on Back In The Day): Ms Jade (v on Funky Fresh Dressed): Beyoncé Knowles (v on Nothing Out There For Me): TLC [Tionne "T-Boz" Watkins, Rozonda "Chilli" Thomas] (v on Can You Hear Me): Lisa Crawford (bkg v): Tweet (v)
Track listing:
Go To The Floor: Bring The Pain: Gossip Folks: Work It: Back In The Day: Funky Fresh Dressed: P***ycat: Nothing Out There For Me: Slide: Play That Beat: Ain't That Funny: Hot: Can You Hear Me: Work It
Running time:
59 mins 12 secs
Current CD:
62813
Further listening:
Supa Dupa Fly (1997): Miss E... So Addictive (2001)
Further reading:
www.missyelliott.co.uk
Like this?
Try . . . p.20

Youssou N'Dour

Nothing's In Vain (Coono Du Reer)

The biggest name in African music returns to his roots majestically

If N'Dour's rise had been spectacular since 1984 – the word-of-mouth success of *Immigres*, singing on *Graceland*, Peter Gabriel tours, the mammoth sales of the single Seven Seconds – his inability to actually establish himself as an artist of international significance remained apparent to all of those who were watching closely. He might have been the most famous African singer on the planet, but what did that mean when a string of good albums had come and gone, along with contracts at several major labels? The good stuff was easy to find, even if you didn't make the trip to a market in Senegal, where cassettes of his rootsiest mbalax sell by the barrowload, but so were numerous failed attempts at crossing over to the pop market, usually involving Gabriel, Sting or even Wyclef Jean. The plain, unpalatable truth was that nobody in Europe or America wanted to buy an African singing dodgy Motown covers, however well he performed them. *Nothing In Vain*, N'Dour's first album for Nonesuch, followed close on the heels of *Joko*, which itself had taken six years to come out after the success of the million-selling *The Guide: Wommat*. The quick turnaround raised all sorts of fears, but the truth was simple: N'Dour had spotted what was wrong, regrouped with his close associates in his Dakar club and studio, and gone even further back than back to basics.

It takes only a couple of bars before his new sound becomes apparent. After a quarter of a century of frantic percussion and all-out dance numbers, Tan Bi (Heat, Breeze, Tenderness) arrives on a kora (21-string harp) riff that sounds like a Celtic folk number. Even the unusual Senegalese fiddle that joins in is reassuringly laid-back. As the full band arrives, it becomes apparent that some of the things N'Dour has learnt from pop have been beneficial: the sound is immaculate, the production expansive. And so this new maturity went on, even on the polyrythmic mbalax dance tracks.

N'Dour's recent career had been based around playing western music in an African style, all the better (supposedly) to catch two markets, but the guitars, bass, drum kits and keyboards that were typical of this approach had gone, or, at least, become subordinated to African instruments. Even in a year that saw other African artists adopt this approach (Baaba Maal, Salif Keita and Kandia Kouyate, for example), it was great to hear the king of them all rising above the bedlam.

DH

Record label:
Nonesuch
Produced
by Youssou N'Dour and Habib Faye
Recorded
at Xippi, Dakar
Chart peaks:
None (UK) None (US)
Released:
October 2002
Personnel:
Youssou N'Dour (voc), Habib Faye (guitar), Edouard Manga (kora), Thiama Sy (xalam), Barou Sall (xalam), Mbaye Ndiaye (riti), Al-Seyni Camara (balafon), Babacar Faye (Perc), Jaco Largent (perc) Assane Thiam (tama)
Track listing:
Tan Bi/Moor Ndaje/Li Ma Weesu/Genne/La Femme Est L'Avenir De L'Amour/Mbeggeel Noonu La/Il N'Y A Pas D'Amour Heureux/Sagal Ko/C?est L'Amour/Doole/So many men/Yaru/Africa, Dream Again
Running time:
53:15
Current CD:
7559796542
Further listening:
Wommat (The Guide) (Sony, 1994); Immigres (Earthworks, 1994)
Further reading:
www.youssou.com
Like this?
Try . . . p.649

Calexico

Feast Of Wire

Acclaimed fourth album (twice that number counting tour-only CDs) from desert rock duo and guests

If they should ever make a Calexico pinball machine, you can just picture how it would look. The ball drifting up the long, straight desert highway towards an impossibly distant horizon and ricocheting, fatalistically, towards the bright lights of a dusty bar or the dark of a roadside cafe, getting waylaid in some forgotten ghost town before breaking out and making a desperate sprint across the border. The sound would be snippets of Spaghetti Western and Mariachi, music that to anyone raised on cowboy films instinctively evokes big skies, open spaces, man against nature, man against man. "It's the West", is how Joey Burns, who, with John Convertino, comprises the core of Arizona-based Calexico, explained their music. "There's something about these bands that come from out here that take these traditional styles and twist them and make them completely their own."

All of Calexico's albums have that Western movie feel; all at times sound like the lost soundtrack to a film. Those elements we've come to associate with them – the accomplished instrumental soundscapes with their Mexican horns, propulsive cowboy-picture drums and string arrangements – are all present and correct here, if occasionally given a more urban, experimental touch (Attack El Robot! Attack!'s zombie dance beat and garotted, spacey keyboards). But this time there's less sprawl and distance to the music, a willingness on the part of the 16 songs to stay in one place, hang out a while and enjoy themselves.

Though the lyrics remain for the most part dark and bleak – suiting the album's theme of "someone on the other side of the border wanting to come north and risking their life to do it" - the music is often sensuous and sparkly. The modern-day desperado in Quattro gets an upbeat song with an unusual-for-Calexico clattering-twinkling rhythm and a smouldering fire of horns. The poignant Across The Wire (Widescreen) is set to rich, stirring, and horn-happy Tex Mex-country. And the bitter homeless man in opener Sunken Waltz wallows in a warm song saturated with accordion, sturdy drums and Burn's trembling, delicate, compelling vocals (which on this album often brings to mind a young Neil Young). Seductive, stirring songs about crushed hope and the corruption of beauty, excellent musicianship and some of their most ambitious arrangements made *Feast Of Wire* Calexico's most fully-realised and accomplished album to date. Postscript: shortly after the album's release, Calexico played at a wedding; the couple said they'd proposed to each other while listening to the song Not Even Stevie Nicks. (Initial pressings included a bonus disc featuring covers of songs by Link Wray, François Breut and The Minutemen.)

SS

Recold label:
City Slang LC06853
Produced
by Joey Burns, John Convertino, Craig Schumacher
Recorded
by Wavelab, Tucson, Arizona
Released:
February 2003
Personnel:
John Convertino (drums, vibraphone, marimba, percussion, accordian, piano [9]); Joey Burns (upright bass, cello, guitar, loops, mandolin, voice, percussion, accordian & organ); Martin Wenk (trumpet [7,11], accordian [4,7]); Paul Niehaus (pedal steel); Jacob Valenzuela (trumpet [2,7,10,11,15]); Nick Luca (synthesiser, piano, guitar); Volker Zandar (bass); Craig Schumacher; (synthesiser [2,16], trumpet [2])
Track listing:
Sunken waltz; Quattro (world drifts in); Stucco; Black heart; Pepito; Not even Stevie Nicks; Close behind; Woven birds; The book and the canal; Attack El Robot! Attack!; Across the wire (widescreen); Dub latina; Guero Canelo; Whipping the horse's eyes; Crumble; No doze
Running time:
45.28
Current CD:
202132
Further listening:
The Black Light (1998); Hot Rail (2000)
Further reading:
www.casadecalexico.com
Like this?
Try . . . p.487

Willie Nelson

Crazy: The Demo Sessions

Fifteen of Nelson's earliest demos from 1961-66, digitally restored and remastered.

Hillbilly music had barely got used to its new name 'country' before the hit-making machinery stepped in, suffocating it in cloying layers of rhinestones and strings. Even its greatest outlaws, Johnny Cash and Willie Nelson, suffered prettification by their producers. "My demos were always better than the records that came out", said Nelson. "(With) all the voices and the strings... it wasn't me. I wasn't comfortable doing it. And it didn't sell." And yet while Cash found musical redemption in recent years through his Rick Rubin collaborations, Nelson (his 1996 self-produced, stripped-down masterpiece *Spirit* aside) made some less fortunate choices. His last album prior to *Crazy: The Demo Sessions* - 2001's bloated, guest star-stuffed *The Great Divide* - was over-produced, over-played, emotionally unengaging.

Seriously sparse, the first eight cuts here are simply voice and guitar (a mournful drizzle of pedal steel aside). You hear Nelson's fingers squeak on the guitar neck, his every intake of breath. The clear, unswerving vocals are so intimate that if you leave the room and come back, it sounds disconcertingly like you forgot you'd left Willie Nelson on your sofa, singing. Though the next seven tracks have a honky-tonk band - distinguished session men: Hargus 'Pig' Robbins, Buddy Emmons, Roy 'Junior' Husky - they're still understated. As you'd expect from demos, especially ones made 40 years ago when neither equipment nor artists called for more than basics. Yet these don't sound in the least incomplete - in fact sound a good deal better than after the Nashville producers got to them. Check Nelson's earliest version of Crazy, from 1961 - the very same recording Patsy Cline listened to before making the song a hit. Some songs are less familiar, one - I'm Still Here - getting a first-time release. It's one of the few uptempo tracks. Most are Nelson's trademark ballads: Are You Sure; Three Days; A Moment Isn't Very Long; an angst-ridden I've Just Destroyed The World - the song Ray Price made a top 20 single in 1962 and Willie included on *Teatro* 26 years later.

That they survived at all is a miracle, since demo tapes were ordinarily recycled until worn out. They were found in a box marked "Pamper" - the publishing company for whom Nelson became a staff writer soon after arriving in Nashville. (Further information in the CD's bonus video). "In my mind", recalled Nelson, "I wasn't trying to cut demos, I was just trying to get the best sound that I could with the musicians that we had there, and we had some good ones." Relaxed, unforced, unadorned, these one-take versions show Nelson at his finest.

SS

Record label:
Sugar Hill SUGCD 1073
Produced
by Steve Fishell, Willie Nelson
Released:
February 2003
Personnel:
Willie Nelson (vocals, guitar); Floyd Chance (bass); Jimmy Day (guitar); Ray Edenton (guitar); Buddy Emmons (guitar); Buddy Harman (drums); Bob L. Moore (bass); Hargus "Pig" Robbins (piano); Pete Wade (guitar)
Track Listing:
Opportunity to cry; Three days; Undo the right; What do you think of her now; I've just destroyed the world; Permanently lonely; Are you sure; Darkness on the face of the earth; Things to remember; A moment isn't very long; Crazy; The local memory; I gotta get drunk; Something to think about; I'm still here
Running time:
40.15
Current CD:
SH1073
Further listening:
Red headed stranger/To lefty from Willie (1999)
Further reading:
The facts of life and other dirty jokes (Metro, 2003); www.willienelson.com
Like this?
Try . . . p.716

Sigur Ros

Agaetis byrjun

Spellbinding other-worldly symphonies from Icelandic soundbenders

Sigur Ros dripped into the mainstream subconscious – if not exactly smack bang into full focus – their ethereal *Svefn-G-Englar* was included on Cameron Crowe's *Vanilla Sky* soundtrack. The soaring majesty of the track invited lazy comparisons with Enya. Sigur Ros are more complex, more taxing, much, much weirder – though undoubtedly there is a mellifluous aspect to their queer symphony. And after a short, beguiling intro burst it's *Svefn-G-Englar* – a prolonged and soothing workout in mellow techno – that's first up on this astonishing debut record from Jon Por Birgisson's Icelandic experimentalists.

Agaetis byrjun is astonishing for the sheer variety of its sonic landscaping – from the bleak and elemental *Hjartao Hamast* to the gut wrenching and near religious onslaught of *Ny Batteri*. Each track has a sensuality of its own, each making quixotic use of a whole range of instrumentation (a Sigur Ros stable is to play guitar with a violin bow, creating a caustic, yet hypnotic sound-drag). Grandiose trip-hop loops skitter beneath the melancholy electronica of *Flugufrelsarinn*, while *Staralfar* is majestic in the gently intensifying opera of its build. Birgisson likes to bend his vocal delivery into a near-dissonant wail that often acts as another and alienating wall of sound. Then just as the siren (painting the songs in an imaginary language the band call Hopelandic) threatens to sweep away all who listen, tracks like *Viorar Vel* and *Olsen Olsen* are spellbinding – impossibly lovely, bewitchingly simple acoustic honey.

Aegetis byrjun an album of staggering tonal contrast, defying classification and utterly deserving of its New Classic tag.

KS

Record label:
Fat Cat
Released:
March 2003
Personnel:
Jon Thor Birgisson (guitar, vocals); Orri Páll DýRason (drums); Georg Holm (bass, vocals); Kjartan Sveinsson (keyboards)
Track listing:
Intro; Svefn-g-englar; Staralfur; Flugufrelsarinn; Ny Batteri; Hjartao Hamast (bamm bamm bamm); Viorar Vel Til Loftarasa; Olsen olsen; Agaetis Byrjun; Avalon
Running time:
70.49
Current CD:
FATCD011
Further listening:
(untitled) (2002)
Further reading:
www.sigur-ros.co.uk
Like this?
Try . . . p.586

The White Stripes

Elephant

Forward to the past as the Stripes go lo-fi

When the White Stripes entered the studio this time round they were a considerably different band than that which had laid down the 16 tracks of *White Blood Cells* in Memphis the year before.

It wasn't that the Detroit duo had shifted styles or altered their already slim personnel, but since the release of *White Blood Cells* and its subsequent consideration as the seminal album of the garage rock revival, Jack and Meg White had played just about every late night network television show, graced the cover of innumerable slick magazines, and accepted shiny metallic moonmen statuettes at the MTV Video Music Awards. For any band whose identity is inextricably tied to notions of independence and authenticity, inordinate amounts of fame are a tough thing to reconcile. In the NME, Jack White noted, "I like things as honest as possible, even if sometimes they can only be an imitation of honesty." As it turned out, the Stripes managed to weather the media blitzkrieg with manifest poise, always retaining the upper hand by being deceptively coy about their personal lives and even throwing a wrench in the works here and there by purposefully spreading untrue rumors.

When the time came to record *Elephant*, the band seemed determined to preserve the air of authenticity for which they had been celebrated, or at least an imitation thereof. They again chose to record in a remote location, this time setting up shop in Liam Watson's Toe Rag studio in Hackney, London, a facility characteristically devoid of production bells and whistles. No equipment in the place dated past 1963. As the credits on the *Elephant* CD jacket plainly declare, "No computers were used during the writing, recording, mixing or mastering of this record." The entire album was recorded on an eight-track reel-to-reel in just ten days.

Elephant is the product not only of an obsessive allegiance to authenticity, but also of a strict adherence to some clearly delineated rules and conventions. As Jack told the New York Times Magazine, "We're white people who play the blues, and our problem was how do we do that and not be fake? Our idea was to strip away everything unnecessary, to put ourselves in a box, to make rules for ourselves...I'm disgusted by artists or songwriters who pretend there are no rules. There's nothing guiding them in their creativity."

The album itself is 'dedicated to the death of the sweetheart,' a requiem for lost innocence in a world of dissolving conventions—a world unfettered by a false sense of liberation and consumed by ephemeral, materialistic concerns. It may seem counterintuitive for the White Stripes, at heart a punk rock band, to be concerned with the dissolution of convention in the modern world, but Jack and Meg White seem to make it their business to defy intuition.

DW

Record label:
V2/Third Man (US); XL/Third Man (Europe)
Produced
by Jack White
Recorded
at Toe Rag Studios, London, UK
Released:
April 2003
Chart peaks:
1 (UK)
Personnel:
Jack White (Guitar, Piano, Vocals, Producer, Mixing); Meg White (drums, vocals); Holly Golightly (vocals)
Track listing:
Seven Nation Army; Black Math; There's No Home for You Here; I Just Don't Know What To Do With Myself; In The Cold, Cold Night; I Want To Be The Boy To Warm Your Mother's Heart; You've Got Her In Your Pocket; Ball And Biscuit; The Hardest Button To Button; Little Acorns; Hypnotize; The Air Near My Fingers; Girl, You Have No Faith In Medicine; It's True That We Love One Another
Running time:
47.47
Current CD:
XLCD162
Further listening:
White Stripes (2001); White Blood Cells (2001); De Stijl (2002)
Further reading:
www.whitestripes.com
Like this?
Try . . . p.83

Nick Cave and the Bad Seeds

Nocturama

Cave struggles through the emotions once again

From early Birthday Party rock n' roll thrashings to melancholic and murderous ballads, there has always been something in Nick Cave's voice that seemed emblematic; lamenting, passionate words and evocative music that seemed to capture the moment.

In any long music career there are bound to be moments of crossroading and dead-ending; an artist travel-weary on a road so well worn that it becomes like a perpetual blur with all that is passed and all that is ahead similarly smooth and featureless. *Cave* has lasted perhaps because he has recognised that a creativity surviving on automatic is no creativity at all. When the Birthday Party split up, the Bad Seeds 1983 album *From Her To Eternity* was a violent jolt in the ears of listeners full of expectation of what they might hear. Eleven albums and twenty years later, *Nocturama* feels as though Cave has carried on up the road, remembering every thrash, every gentle chord to make an album that seems to be panoramic in its view. In a musical world filled with transience, Cave proves that it is not the destination that counts but the journey.

Nocturama can be seen as Cave and his fellow *Bad Seed's* response to a manufactured method of making music. Not just in other bands but in their own. The previous album, *No More Shall We Part*, seemed craftsmanlike and meticulously layered but did not have the verve of spontaneity. During a tour of Australia in 2002, they took some time out and recorded the album in a week. As Cave says, "The idea was to take some of the preciousness about the making of the record away and possibly create records more like they did in the old days where there was a faster turn around."

The last track seems to encompass this rekindled interest in recorded spontaneity, an attempt to approach the charged intensity of his live appearances. Babe, I'm on Fire has 43 verses and lasts for fifteen minutes. Here, Cave the eclectic and moody band leader is cast as ringmaster, dramatically – or perhaps that's melodramatically – trying to contain the wild animals who are let loose on the songs, all the time trusting that he will not be mauled, his straining voice still tautly controlling the raucous rabble around him.

Composition has never come easy to Cave: "It always feels really difficult - it never feels healthy." *Nocturama* has the feel of being alive, of displaying a verve, a need to embrace a whole swathe of emotions evoking past, present and future. *Nocturama* might not have been healthy for Cave but is truly nourishment for the soul. His struggle is part of our process.

TD

Record label:
Mute
Produced
by Nick Cave and Noick Launay
Released:
February 2003
Chart peaks:
20 (UK)
Personnel:
Nick Cave (vocals, piano, Hammond); Mick Harvey (guitar, bass, backing vocals); Blixa Bargeld; (guitar, pedal steel, backing vocals); Thomas Wydler (drums, percussion); Martyn P Casey (bass); Conway Savage (backing vocals); Jim Sclavunos (drums, backing vocals); Warren Ellis (violin); The Blockheads (backing vocals)
Track listing:
Wonderful Life; He wants you; Right out of your hand; Bring it on; Dead man in my bed; Still in love; There is a town; Rock of Gibraltar; She passed by my window; Babe, I'm on fire
Running time:
56.23
Current CD:
CDSTUMM207
Further listening:
The best of Nick Cave and the Bad Seeds (1998)
Further reading:
And the Ass saw the Angel (Nick Cave's novel, Penguin, 2001); www.nick-cave.com
Like this?
Try . . . p.594

The Easy Life

Lounging. And collecting the music it spawned.

The complex history of the whole process goes like this. Stop me if I'm getting too technical. In the late-1940s the LP record came into being. Soon afterwards people began throwing them out. The end.

Sales charts concentrate on point-of-purchase transactions. But we all know, don't we, that a record's life is infinite, and things only get interesting once the record becomes disposable. Just look at all those gimmicky, functional, craze cash-in records that littered the post-war American Dream: Music for your barbecue, music to accompany home movies, music to strip for your husband by, etiquette instruction records, how-to-fight-tooth-decay records, armed-forces recruitment records, teach-yourself-hypnosis records, sound-effects records, records to test out your hi-fi. No subject was ever too bizarre or too banal for vinyl.

Yes, when Mr Life met Miss Style they spawned a curious baby called . . . well, a host of names have sprung up to define the undefinable. There's Easy Listening (which immediately prompts the question, how hard should listening have to be?), Mood Music (which never, of course, means bad mood music), Light Music (which assumes that music can be weighed like gas), Light Classical (a hybrid classification which was invented by the BBC in the 1920s in its attempt to create a middlebrow form that would entice the popular audience towards more high-brow fare), Background Music (which is so vague as to be nonsensical – all music becomes background music at the flick of a volume switch) and the ubiquitous trademark Musak. In Brave New World, Aldous Huxley imagined a dystopian future where people listened to "synthetic music" which piped out "hyper-violin, super-cello, and oboe-surrogate". George Owen Squier, the inventor of Musak, thought this sounded jolly nice. He put together the word "music", and the phonetically and graphically pleasing "Kodak" and designed sounds to improve industrial efficiency. According to author Joseph Lanza: "the rhythms [were meant] to create a feeling of well-being and eliminate stress. Programmes were tailored to workers' peak periods, as measured on a Musak mood-rating scale ranging from 'Gloomy-minus three' to 'Ecstatic-plus eight'." Yet another musical area concerns the easily digestible music that has sprung from the jazz idiom: cocktail jazz, light jazz, and what Frank Sinatra, approvingly, called polite jazz. But none of these terms really do the job, do they?

Clearly there's a problem with any catch-all tag that tries to reign in this stuff. Stressing its camp value or disposability doesn't do justice to artists like Mantovani, Percy Faith, Bert Kaempfert, Ray Conniff, and Liberace, whose albums have sold in their millions. Relegating it all to a lower cultural form is grossly insulting to artists such as Henry Mancini, Gordon Jenkins, Nelson Riddle and Michel Legrand, who are all highly accomplished soundtrack composers. Until he was reclaimed by modern ironists Burt Bacharach suffered from this syndrome too. It must be galling for a man who studied under Darius Milhaud and who invests even the simplest pop tune with subtlety to be lumped in with the Lawrence Welks and Geoff Loves.

To many record collectors, for many years, it was simply the stuff that you filed under Miscellaneous – until one day, if you're like me, you suddenly realised that the Miscellaneous section of your record collection seemed to have swelled to about 200 LPs – none of which I'd ever knowingly paid more than £1 for. Not so much a collection as the legacy of a lifetime's casual accumulation. A junk-shop and car-boot plunderer who watched in disdainful amusement as grown men fought each other to a standstill just to secure that scratched to bits, dog-eared, 1971 LP of dubious prog-vintage on some crap "Underground" label. ("It's £30 in the book." "Yeah maybe. But it's also unplayable.") I was one of those who just exchanged mysterious "invasion of the bodysnatchers"-style looks with others Who Knew Differently as we went about our business, gathering up any LP featuring a balding man playing a sitar on the cover or a teenage girl throwing ill-advised dance shapes while flashing the kind of grin that made you doubt her sanity. Our mental health, on the other hand, even as we staggered away from a stall clutching our fifteenth 20p bargain of the morning, was never in question.

While Middle America concentrated on its patio furniture, its brown shoes, and its tooth decay, the hipsters' take on the 1950s was best exemplified by Ken Nordine.

In 1957 he recorded the first of four "Word Jazz" LPs. Slightly surreal, stream-of-consciousness ramblings accompanied by *simpatico* jazz backing. The best are *Word Jazz* and *Son Of Word Jazz* (Dot Records 1957). Rhino Records have re-issued these on CD, while Asphodel have re-issued another classic, *Colors on CD* (1995). Nordine's tendencies first became apparent when he worked on NBC Radio on the 1950s. "I suggested that I read the news with a blues background," he says. "The idea (for *Colors*) came from a series of commercials I did for the Fuller Paint Company. They said, 'Do whatever you want – just mention our name.' So I wrote, 'The Fuller Paint Company invites you to stare with your ears at Yellow.'"

Exotic perceptions of other cultures have been on the Western agenda since Marco Polo came back from his holidays and proclaimed that Japan was the new Constantinople. Eastern influences on Western music existed long before Easy Listening came on the scene. Everyone from Claude Debussy to Duke Ellington incorporated Japanese and East Asian motifs into their art in the early part of the century. Exotica first hits Easy Listening with the post-World War Two craze for all things Hawaiian and Polynesian. Steel guitars, tiki bars and Hula dancing were the most obvious manifestations of this in the 1950s and for a short time the exotica trend pervaded everything from cocktails to dress sense to home furnishings. The best-known exponents of musical exotica are Martin Denny, Arthur Lyman and Les Baxter. In this respect *Exotica Suite* (composed and arranged by Les Baxter and performed by Cy Zentner and Martin Denny (Liberty, 1962)) represents a veritable supergroup of smooth. Equally seminal are Denny's own *Exotica Vols 1–3* (Liberty, 1958, 1959, 1960). "My music is a combination of the South Pacific and the Orient, what a lot of people imagined the islands to be like." Denny told RE:Search magazine, "It's pure fantasy though. The exotic bird calls began quite accidentally. One night we were playing a certain song and I could hear the frogs going 'rivet rivet rivet'. When we stopped playing, the frogs stopped croaking, a little while later I said 'Let's repeat that tune' and sure enough the frogs started croaking again. As a gag, some of the guys spontaneously started doing these bird calls . . . the following day one of the guests came up and said, 'Mr Denny, you know that song you did with the birds and the frogs? Can you do that again?' . . . he'd thought that was part of the arrangement."

Former Denny band member Arthur Lyman made notable additions to this strand with *Taboo Vols 1* and *2* (Vocalion,1959 & 1960). The sleeve of *Vol 2* was infamously adorned with a brace of shrunken death-heads. Other examples where the Western colonial gaze exoticised a culture are the late-1950s revival in Latin American music (lots of sleevenotes talking of "wild, untamed rhythms") and the "lost world of the Incas" vibe that was applied to much South American music (regardless of whether it originated in the remote mountains of Peru, or the fully industrialised cities of Brazil and Argentina). Probably the two most extraordinary talents to emerge from this strand are Juan Garcia Esquival and Yma Sumac. Each adds a new level to the cultural conundrum by offering their own highly idiosyncratic take on American appropriations of their own respective cultures. Esquivel was a Mexican-born bandleader, composer and arranger who dismantled Hollywood soundtrack structures and reassembled them on Mars. His genuinely exotic use of unorthodox instrumentation and sound technology and his fragmentary approach to vocal arranging, which predates dub reggae by 20 years, can be best heard on *Other Worlds Other Sounds* (RCA, 1958) *and Exploring New Sounds In Stereo* (RCA, 1959) The best tracks from these and other Esquivel albums are rounded up on *Cabaret Manana* (RCA CD, 1995). Outer space is a frequent destination for Easy explorers, but stranger even than Esquivel was St Louis-born Lucia Pamela. Her 1969 album *Into Outer Space With Lucia Pamela* (Arf Arf CD re-issue, 1992) is a compelling travelogue of journeys to other planets all delivered with fetchingly unhinged conviction and an attention to local detail ("I see people. Must be the Moon people") which convinces the listener that she is speaking from personal experience. She has also published a colouring book of her drawings.

However, Peruvian-born Yma Sumac is, quite simply, the high priestess of the exotic. Possessing (or perhaps possessed by) an extraordinary four-octave voice which ranged from an unearthly scream to frequencies so low you would swear that the tape is running slow, the best of her albums are the Les Baxter-produced *Voice Of The Xtabay*, *Legend Of the Jivaro* and *Legend Of The Sun Virgin*. The best of them are rounded up on the 1995 Rev-ola CD *Voice Of The Xtabay*. Sumac said that when her music first appeared people didn't know whether they were "classical or mumbo-jumbo. We chose the title, *The Voice of the Xtabay* and let people judge for themselves whether the record was classical, semi-classical or contemporary. When I say classical I don't mean opera by Puccini or Verdi or Wagner; I mean classical Incan music."

A European, middle-aged swinger's variant on the exotic was perfected in the faintly African lilt of *A Swinging Safari* by Bert Kaempfert & his Orchestra (Polydor, 1962).

Of all the sub-categories in the realm of nether-music, TV theme tunes are the most naggingly pervasive. Because pop history is so fixated with sales figures, theme tunes rarely get considered in their proper context. They enter the public domain surreptitiously, lodge themselves in the subconscious mind and remain there forever. They can usually be recalled as evocatively and fondly as any hit single, even though they rarely enter any pop chart. Indeed, in many cases they achieve the kind of longevity denied to all but the biggest-selling pop singles. One definition of a cultured man is someone who can listen to the William Tell Overture without thinking of The Lone Ranger. Count me out then, kemo-sabe.

The commissars of this category are Nelson Riddle and Henry Mancini. *Route 66 And Other TV Themes* (Capitol, 1962) contains Riddle's classic arrangements for The Untouchables, Naked City and Sam Benedict, among others. *This Is Henry Mancini* (RCA 2LP, 1971) rounds up the great man's scores for Peter Gunn, The Pink Panther, Moon River, The Brothers Go To Mothers, Baby Elephant Walk, and 15 others. *This Is Cult Fiction Royale* (Virgin 2CD, 1997) and *The Avengers And Other Top Sixties TV Themes* (Sequel 2CD, 1998) are the two most comprehensive CD reissues of theme tunes. *Cult Fiction*'s 47 tracks span everything from Lalo Schifrin's main title themes for Bullitt and Dirty Harry through the Gerry Anderson puppetry of Thunderbirds, Fireball XL5 and UFO, to Hill Street Blues and Twin Peaks. The 60 tracks on the Sequel double offer as comprehensive a selection of '60s themes as you'll find on one CD (everything from Dr Finlay's Casebook to Peyton Place).

In recent years the German-born bandleader Pete Thomas has become the highest-profile European soundtrack composer. His music for the Jerry Cotton crime films (gathered together on *100% Cotton* (Crippled Dick Hot Wax CD, 1996) and the seven-part German TV series *Raumpatrouille* [Space Patrol] (Bungalow CD, 1996), are as deservedly well-known and as epoch-defining as Laurie Johnson's music for The Avengers or Ron Grainer's for The Prisoner. And thanks to Pulp sampling one of the *Raumpatrouille* tracks, Bolero On The Moon Rocks, for the title track to their *This Is Hardcore* LP, Thomas has found a ready-made audience among the contemporary loungecore crowd. *Warp Back To Earth* (Bungalow CD 1999) combines unreleased Thomas tracks and incidental fragments from the 1960s with a CD full of remixes by kindred spirits such as Stereolab, Coldcut, Tipsy, and Stock, Hausman, and Walkman. A good introductory taster to all the above is the 1995 Polydor CD compilation *Pete Thomas – Twenty Easy Listening Classics*.

For anyone who measured out their TV childhood in the 1960s and 1970s, one of the most evocative programmes ever made must be the small-screen adaptation of The Adventures Of

Robinson Crusoe, with music by Robert Mellin & Gian Piero Reverberi (Silva Screen CD 1997). This was a 13-part Franco-English co-production with a beautifully haunting theme tune and some very creative incidental music, some of it quite surprising for 1963. The series was first shown on British TV in late 1965 and repeated during every subsequent summer holiday 'til the mid 1970s. Scheduling of the 13 episodes dictated that we usually missed the final episode because it nearly always seemed to be shown the week we went back to school. The plot may have been lost to eternity, then, but the music remains a vivid and pleasant memory.

One of the great lost genres of the late 1950s and early 1960s is what we might loosely call Music For Swingers. The term conveniently covers everything from adult humour records to out-and-out porno soundtracks. Many of these records were distributed via mail order and they sold in their thousands. Indeed "Swinger" as a demographic category appeared in most American market-research reports of the period. 1950s albums such as *How To Stay Sexy Tho' Married* and *Here's Looking Up Your Hatch* by innuendo queen Ruth Wallis and *Knockers Up* and *Banned In Boston* by "sinsational" Rusty Warren give you a fair idea of their content by title alone. "Those records were not sold in stores," noted Warren. "After the show people would come up and I'd sell them an album, take a card and put them on a mailing list. You never sat alone and listened with earphones like people do today. It was a 'party album' concept. You shared my records with friends at a barbecue or party."

These much overlooked nightclub entertainers struck a blow for anti-censorship with their risqué material. In the '60s the torch passed to film-maker Russ Meyer. The original motion-picture soundtracks to such Meyer bra-busting epics as Faster Pussycat Kill Kill, Vixen, Supervixen and Beyond The Valley Of The Ultravixens are all available on CD (Laserlight). The series of 13 German teensploitation films initiated by the 1970 feature Schulmaden Report (Schoolgirl Report) were as popular as, and contemporaneous to, the Confessions Of series in the UK. The best of Gert Wilden & His Orchestra's soundtracks for these movies – currently enjoying renewed cult status on German satellite TV – has been gathered together on the Crippled Dick Hot Wax compilation *Schoolgirl Report & More Music From Sexy German Films (*1968–72). Another essential social document of our times on the same label is Manfred Hubler and Siegfried Schwabs soundtrack to the lesbian skinflick Vampyros Lesbos: *Sexadelic Dance Party* (CD 1995) The music is more varied than that on *Schoolgirl Report* with throbbing hard-rock guitars and some of the most out-of-tune sitar playing you're ever likely to hear. Quentin Tarantino used, er, snatches of Vampyros Lesbos on the Jackie Brown soundtrack.

The best recent round-up of Italian erotica is the self-explanatory 20-track *Erotica Italia* (Bistro/Arista CD, 1997) compiled by Martin Green and Patrick Whitaker, the "curators" responsible for *The Sound Gallery Vols 1 & 2* (Studio 2 Stereo CD, 1995 & 1996), two of the first compilations to acknowledge the growing interest in Easy Listening and incidental music. Martin Green's bargain-bin maxim "thou shalt always purchase the album with a track called LSD Party on it" has held many of us in good stead down the years as we pluck out buried gems from damp boxes on foggy mornings.

As anyone reared on 1950s and 1960s sci-fi movies will tell you, in the future (ie 1972) technology was going to be big. Huge monolithic banks of computers would line every laboratory wall. Transport, on the other hand, would be lithe and fuel-less. We would all have our own personal jet pack or monorail and get all the nutrition we needed from a little silver pill. The future in music was best explored with the theremin. The soundtracks to Spellbound and The Lost Weekend showcased its ethereal ambience. The ubiquitous Les Baxter was, all too briefly, a pioneering Easy explorer and exponent of theremin records with his *Music Out Of The Moon* (Capitol). *Man In Space With Sounds* by Attileo "Art" Mineo (Subliminal Sounds, CD 1997) is a masterful fusion of eerie orchestration and analogue electronica, originally composed for the

Seattle State's World Fair in 1963. Available on CD with or without the creepy commentary.

When Robert Moog unveiled his synthesizer in the mid-'60s he opened up a whole new world of sonic possibilities. While fringe avant-gardists explored the instrument's atonal options, most Moog twiddlers in the popular entertainment field preferred to go "Eeeeeeeeeoooooow." Everyone from Emerson, Lake and Palmer to Chicory Tip in fact. The golden age of Eeeeeeeeeoooooow was 1968–73, coincidentally the golden age of the space race. Arguably it was the sheer mundanity of the American moon landings (black-and-white pictures of astronauts goofing off) that gave added cachet to these records. Suddenly, the synth-dominated Easy Listening of anonymous session men sounded more exploratory than the Apollo missions. The sleevenotes of *Switched On Rock – The Moog Machine* (CBS, 1969) namecheck the album's producer and engineers among others but make no direct mention of who actually wielded the mighty Moog, as it eeeeooooowed its way through versions of Get Back, Jumpin' Jack Flash, Aquarius/Let The Sun Shine In and Spinning Wheel among others (every Moog album of this period had to contain a version of Spinning Wheel. It was the law).

The best British exponent of session Mooging was John Keating. His albums *Space Experience* and *Space Experience 2* (Studio 2 Stereo, 1972 & 1975) feature the mighty VCS3 on an adventurous mixture of covers (Rocket Man, Star Trek, Jesus Christ Superstar, etc) and cleverly crafted Keating originals. Keating's yearning and strangely soulful sonic vistas capture the sleazy decadence of the early '70s so well that these albums should probably have been called Emmanuelle Goes To The Moon.

Hugo Montenegro was best known as a straightforward interpreter of Hollywood film scores before his cover of Morricone's The Good The Bad & The Ugly gave him a worldwide Top 10 single. His *Moog Power* album (RCA, 1969) is a masterpiece of the genre. Aided by Paul Beaver (of Beaver and Krause fame and the man who programmed the original Moog prototype), *Moog Power* has a title track that was later sampled to good effect by De La Soul. Probably the portion of the album best known to British audiences is a short snippet of Montenegro's version of MacArthur Park. Does the phrase ba-ba ba-ba ba-ba ba-ba ba-ba ba-ba-ba ring any bells? It should do. It is from here that Pearl and Dean took the theme music that became synonymous with British cinema advertising – insert name of local curry house here – during the 1960s and 1970s.

Meanwhile in the parallel universe of the easy-zone Jean Jacques Perrey and Gershon Kingsley were forging a new kind of bubbly bleepertronics with their albums *The In Sound From Way Out* and *Kaleidoscopic Vibrations* (Vanguard 1971). Kingsley has described the former album "as both fun and painful" to make. "Each piece took a solid week of tape splices to prepare. What we did preceded sampling; we recorded the sounds and spliced them together. Nowadays you just record the sound and digitise it." The later album contains a mixture of Perrey-Kingsley originals like The Savers and Fallout and synthed-up interpretations of Winchester Cathedral, Mas Que Nada, Moon River and One Note Samba. Perrey's 1973 Vanguard solo effort *The Amazing New Electronic Pop Sounds Of Jean Jacques Perrey* is also recommended. As well as the Moog, both albums feature the Ondes Martonet and the highly distinctive burble of the mini-electronic keyboard known as the Jenny Ondioline.

The entire notion of highly skilled Musicians' Union session men knocking out cover versions of selections from the acid-rock canon playfully undermines rock music's tenuously constructed notion of authenticity. This is where the easy ethos is at its most subversive. Many of these albums were made by balding guys called Geoff or Johnny (and a disproportionate number of them were called Johnny) in the studio downtime between doing the score for the new Rowntree's Fruit Gums ad and nipping down to the BBC to peel off a swift strict-tempo version of Have You Seen Your Mother Baby (Standing In The Shadows)? for some lunchtime show on the Light Programme.

John Schroeder was Pye Records' in-house producer/composer, and along with pianist Johnny Pearson, one half of Sounds Orchestral, whose 1965 hit Cast Your Fate To The Wind endures as an Easy classic. Schroeder's *Dolly Catcher* album (Pye, 1967) is state-of-the-art lounge-prog. Arranged and conducted by John Cameron, it features the cream of British session men. Versions of Lucy In The Sky With Diamonds, Up Up And Away, and Donovan's Epistle To Dippy bed down next to distinctive and quirky Schroeder Orchestra originals such as Explosive Corrosive Joseph, But She Ran The Other Way, and the marvellous title track. The featured session vocalist is Uriah Heep man David Byron.

Pye was also responsible for another classic of the genre, The Harry Roche Constellation's 1973 album *Spiral*, featuring versions of Stevie Wonder's Superwoman, Bob Dylan's Lay Lady Lay, Henry Mancini's Ludmilla's Theme. And Pete Moore's EMS synthesizer sure plays a mean solo on Pinball Wizard. The album's *magnum opus*, Pete Moore's 10-minute title track, showcases among others the vocals of Claire Torry, best known now for her appearance on Pink Floyd's *Dark Side Of The Moon* singing on Great Gig In The Sky.

Hip session men probably don't come much hipper than Bob Thiele. As in-house producer at ABC-Impulse he was responsible for many of John Coltrane's most immortal recordings. Allowed to cut loose with a budget what did Bob do? Naturally he whipped out his Selmer Varitone Clarinet and got together with some of California's finest (Tom Scott, Bill Plummer, Gabor Szabo, Carol Kaye) to indulge in hip Easy Listening versions of Light My Fire (another easy staple), Eight Miles High, and an unbelievably jaunty version of Dylan's Rainy Day Women on *Light My Fire, Bob Thiele And His New Happy Times Orchestra* (ABC Impulse, 1967).

Pop Goes The Electric Sitar by Vincent "Vinnie" Bell (Decca, 1967) showcases the Coral Electric Sitar as heard on Traffic's Paper Sun, The Box Tops' Cry Like A Baby, and countless other hits of the period and, more recently, Belle & Sebastian's Legal Man. Vinnie utilises the instrument on versions of Little Antony's Going Out Of My Head, Lennon-McCartney's Eleanor Rigby, and Les Baxter's Quiet Village among others.

American arranger/composer/producer/conductor Johnny Harris specialised in complex arrangements and lengthy and luxuriant orchestration. *Movements* (Warner Bros., 1970) contains great covers of Give Peace A Chance, Light My Fire, Wichita Lineman and Paint It Black, and a smattering of Harris's own equally inventive compositions.

Had you tried to engage the average rock fan in conversation about any of this stuff in the '70s they would have just sneered and gone back to their Yes LPs. But, gradually, something had happened to this music. Our perception of all music mutates and renews itself periodically but, 40 years on from their original release, some of those light orchestral and space-age bachelor-pad records sounded so straight they sounded weird – much weirder than most rock music. Down among the anthropologists, Genesis P. Orridge of avant-industrialist beat combo Throbbing Gristle had probably been the first artist to publicise the murky backwaters of easy listening. Throbbing Gristle's ironically titled 1979 LP *20 Jazz Funk Greats* included a track called Exotica and Porridge himself networked extensively with musicians and artists on the west coast of America who were also drawn to the voodoo magic of Martin Denny, Les Baxter, and Arthur Lyman. When the Mike Flowers Pops went to Number 2 in the UK singles chart during the winter of 1995 with an Easy Listening version of the Oasis song Wonderwall, the wider public realised that something was going on. But the real revolution was happening among experimental acts like Stereolab and the less House-bound spirits of dance music who immediately sensed – and sampled – the sonic possibilities of Easy Listening's extraordinarily rich textures. *Trip Tease* by Tipsy (Asphodel, 1996) *Schizophonic* by Combustible Edison (Sub Pop, 1996) and *Soundtracks For Living by The Gentle People* (Rephlex, 1997) are all contemporary albums made "in the style of" by kindred Easy spirits. And they are 100 times more playful and adventurous than most dance albums of the period.

After Flowers, the media were desperately playing catch-up, clearly befuddled by the whole phenomenon. One Music Week article suggested to its readers that critics have been so bemused by the Easy Listening "trend" that they have had to invent terms like "loungecore" to explain it. This brought me particular joy as I invented the term in the first place. Compiling a CD called *The Easy Project* for Castle in 1995, I was asked at the last minute to come up with a catchy subtitle that would encompass the genre. With more than a nod to Throbbing Gristle's penchant for ironic juxtaposition, I came up with "20 Loungecore Favourites". Right now, somewhere on the internet, you can be sure that some earnest spod will be arguing over the precise definition of loungecore, carefully placing records in, or outside, a category that was coined to subvert the categorisation of music in the first place. And which I made up in about five seconds.

Perhaps the best illustration of how all of this upends and subverts our sense of musical hierarchies was provided when Radio One got in on the act in 1996 and devoted an entire night to Easy Listening. Going for the easy, kitsch option, no pipe-and-slippers pun was left unexplored, no cocktail left unsipped, no crap Peters And Lee and Carpenters record left unplayed. In fact, such was their desire to appear fashionably ironic that Radio One's all-embracing definition of the genre included everything from Burt Bacharach's finest compositions to Benny Hill and Dana. However, a far greater irony appeared to be lost on the show's hosts. Many of the records they were now upholding as kitsch classics, would in their day have provided the bedrock of Radio One's daytime schedules, playlisted, and played *ad infinitum*, without a trace of irony. Quack quack oops.

Further reading:

The books that did more to publicise the whole phenomenon than any other were V. Vale and Andrea Juno's Incredibly Strange Music Volumes I and II (published by RE:Search in 1993 and 1994 respectively). Volume One features interviews with, among others, Martin Denny, Gershon Kingsley, and Jean Jacques Perrey, as well as long-time collectors/obsessives such as The Cramps, Phantom Surfers and Untamed Youth. Volume II features Yma Sumac, Rusty Warren, Ken Nordine, Korla Pandit and Robert Moog, among others, while former Dead Kennedy, Jello Biafra gives the comprehensive anthropological lowdown on collecting these 50-cent gems. Joseph Lanza's Elevator Music (Quartet 1995) has also been influential. Subtitled A Surreal History Of Musak, Easy Listening, and Other Moodsong, Elevator Music prioritises the author's own tastes; Ray Conniff, Frank Chacksfield, Robert Farnon, Norrie Paramor, 101 Strings etc. Slightly more tangential, but no less compelling to read are David Toop's Ocean Of Sound (Serpents Tail, 1995) and Exotica (Serpents Tail, 1999). Finally for a visual feast of the sleeves that adorned these neglected gems, try the ultimate antidote to tasteful coffee-table books, Album Covers From The Vinyl Junkyard (Booth-Clibborn Editions, 1997).

Written by Rob Chapman.

The Single Life

Reggae, the music that didn't believe in the album.

Reggae doesn't fit. Never has done. Whether in the guise of ska, rock steady, JA boogie or anything else, most Jamaican music has lurked obstinately outside rock's marketing rules. Even after the success of Bob Marley, when outside interests had retooled reggae to uphold the same values as Anglo-American pop music, dancehall reggae still didn't conform, neither did ragga or new roots. For nearly 50 years, with a few notable exceptions – Bob Marley; the internationally-oriented Black Uhuru or Third World and British acts such as Steel Pulse and Matumbi – the reggae album has been a misnomer.

This has nothing to do with public perception either. Given most record companies' priorities, Jamaican music's international impact has been enormous, sales figures remain much more than respectable and most megastores' reggae sections occupy a serious amount of floor space. Reggae's removal from Rock's Big Lists isn't a matter of elitism, it's all about rationale.

Reggae exists in its own world because the motivation behind the establishment of an endemic Jamaican music industry, around 45 years ago, as unique to that island. Although there are parallels to the USA's delta blues or New Orleans jazz, Jamaica's particular cultural parochialism could only have happened where and when it did. An island environment – spiritually as well as physically – and a special set of economic circumstances combined to produce an indigenous music business before there was any indigenous music, and a market in which the actual mass-production and selling of records was originally no more than a by-product. That market continues to dominate the way reggae is made today, regardless of advancing technology, corporate pressures or geographic location.

The chief factor behind this singular state of affairs was the "sound system".

Fifty-odd years ago these enormous mobile disco set-ups – mountainous stacks of hand-crafted speaker cabinets powered by amplification with intercontinental reach – boomed out across open-air dances known, for obvious reasons, as "lawns", an exclusively downtown Kingston phenomenon. Originating in the ghettos, where electrification was minimal and domestic ownership of radios or record players rare, lawns were one of the very few ways the desperately poor could enjoy professionally performed American R&B, the fashionable form back then. And as the British-franchised, state-endorsed radio station, Radio Jamaica Redifussion, was modelled on the BBC Light Programme – aimed at Jamaica's middle classes and specialising in the likes of Brook Benton and Bing Crosby – the sound systems were the only way Jamaicans could experience the more extreme ends of contemporary black music: Roscoe Gordon, Wynonie Harris, Bill Doggett, The Moonglows and Jesse Belvin (though, oddly, Elvis' It's Now Or Never was a huge sound-system favourite).

The sound systems soon became community focal points, with the bigger operators assuming Don-like status. To keep their systems on top they needed a continual supply of "killer cuts", tunes nobody else owned. Hot, imported US R&B singles were fiercely guarded, often literally, and all information would be scratched off the labels and new names scrawled on. But, as styles changed in America, so the sources of these records started to dry up and the enterprising second wave of sound men drew upon Jamaica's indigenous musical talent (there were many big bands entertaining the mostly American tourists in the large hotels) and started cutting their own records at the end of the 1950s, which is when the extraordinary relationship between Jamaican music, its consumers and its producers was set in place.

This new generation of operators, led by Clement "Coxsone" Dodd and Duke Reid, recorded local musicians in faithful imitations of R&B, a musical wave which became known as JA Boogie. When they first became record producers it was in the most literal sense – they were the money men who'd rent the studios, organise and pay the musicians, pick the material and ultimately own the recording. Leslie Kong, who recorded Desmond Dekker, The Wailers and Jimmy Cliff, only got into production because he needed records to sell in his shop. Arrangements were left up to the bandleader and as Jamaican studios of that era made those Make Your Own Record booths that used to be found on railway stations look sophisticated, there wasn't a great deal of engineering skill involved.

As the whole point was to have music nobody else's dance had, the finished product was usually a one-off, an acetate or soft wax disc that would be road-tested immediately on the producer's own sound system, and if it moved the crowd it would be kept, if not destroyed or maybe sold on to a less illustrious operation. Successful records' styles and patterns would be repeated in subsequent sessions, whichever aspects were obviously pleasing the audience would be played up.

Since then, Jamaican sound system crowds have been the most important consideration in the country's music business and the operators have called the shots. When Prince Buster changed the beat to greater reflect the indigenous population and Coxsone began to mass-produce records for sale, everything was lawn-tested first. Crowd reaction was dictating style, speed, *riddim* and release schedule. Even now, nearly 50 years on, many of the top producers still own sound systems, or have arrangements with big sets allowing them to try out new recordings. It's the same throughout the Jamaican cultural diaspora too – Dennis Bovell, Aswad, Smiley Culture and Maxie Priest all had strong UK sound system connections, and in the USA New York's vibrant dance-hall reggae industry is rooted in the Brooklyn sound systems. Such connections are why, unless it's something as carefully approached as, say, Bob Marley's later work, so many of reggae's big stars fail at home with music they've recorded for international consumption.

More importantly, this is why so little Jamaican music has been recorded with albums in mind and why the producer is, in most cases, more important than the artist. Sound systems don't need albums, they need a continuous and plentiful flow of singles, therefore reggae has always been treated by its artistic and business communities as a singles medium. And although the producer is now far more likely to be hands-on creative than in those early days, the hierarchy remains the same: he creates or procures backing tracks and selects the right singer or MC to front them. Artists were (still are among Jamaica's myriad of tiny record labels) paid a flat fee for singing a song – "voicing a tune" is the term – perhaps a little more if they brought their own song in and all the house band had to do was arrange it. As copyright laws weren't applied to music in Jamaica until the early 1990s, ownership of a song rested on who owned the particular recording of it, and if the producer had sponsored the session he owned the soft wax. Long contracts were unheard of and deals were done on a song by song basis with singers voicing for several different producers, often in the same day and sometimes even the same song, which served to perpetuate the singles mentality as singers' piece-rate deals meant the more money they wanted, the more records they cut. Producers weren't investing in careers, although there were plenty of artist/producer relationships that were fruitful and long-lasting, the resultant albums were always a collection of sides recorded over several years rather than a whole work cut from start to finish in one period.

Which is why most of the music discussed below has been subdivided by producer rather than artist.

SKA

Ska represents the first period of modern Jamaican music, from the end of the 1950s until the middle of the following decade. A period during which the island gained independence from Great Britain (August 6, 1962) and the search for a genuinely Jamaican cultural expression intensified. Therefore the music of that period evolved from a slavish imitation of American music (larger New Orleans and Miami radio stations could be picked up in Jamaica) to something far more proprietary.

The three most significant ska producers, Duke Reid, Clement "Coxsone" Dodd and Prince Buster, were also Kingston's biggest sound-system owners. But while they were all essentially pulling in the same direction – the pool of players used being so small they were almost using the same band under different names – each producer had their own idiosyncrasies that brought the ska era a far wider musical spectrum than is immediately obvious.

Various

TROJAN TRLS 275

Shufflin' On Bond Street – Jamaican R&B And Ska Instrumentals

Produced by Duke Reid **Recorded** between 1959 and 1966, at Federal Studios, RJR and Treasure Isle Studios, Kingston, Jamaica **Personnel include:** Roland Alphonso (tenor s); Lloyd Brevett (b); Baba Brooks (t); Drumbago (d); Don Drummond (t); Jerry Hines (g); Tommy McCook (tenor s); Herman Marquis (alto s); Johnny Moore (t); Rico Rodriguez (t); Ernest Ranglin (g); Lynn Taitt (g) **Track listing:** Watermelon Man – Baba Brooks Band; Duck Soup – Drumbago's Orchestra; Green Door – Roland Alphonso; What Makes Honey – The Duke Reid Group; Joker – The Duke Reid Group; Blackberry Brandy – Roland Alphonso; The Rude Boy – The Duke Reid Group: Country Town – Baba Brooks Band; Thunderball – Tommy McCook And His Supersonics; Rain Fall – Baba Brooks Band; Cotton Tree – Tommy McCook and The Skatalites; Nuclear Weapon – Tommy McCook and The Skatalites; Western Flyer – Baba Brooks Band; Froggy – Baba Brooks Band; Mad World – Baba Brooks Band; Storm Warning – Lynn Taitt And The Comets

Running more or less in chronological order, this album plots a course from JA Boogie through ska to prototype rock steady (Storm Warning is rock steady in everything but tempo) and clearly shows how, as ska matured, it allowed the musicians the same sort of flourishes that marked their big-band and jazz incarnations and points the way forward to a more indigenous way of doing things by stirring *burru*-style drumming into Ducksoup.

Various

HEARTBEAT HB 105

Ska After Ska After Ska

Produced by Duke Reid **Recorded** between 1962 and 1966, at Federal Studios and Treasure Isle Studios, Kingston, Jamaica Personnel include: Roland Alphonso (tenor s); Frank Anderson (t); Gladstone Anderson (p); Lloyd Brevett (b); Baba Brooks (tr); Charlie Cameron (hm); Dennis Campbell (tenor s); Drumbago (d); Don Drummond (tb); Winston Graham (t); Aston Henry (d); Sammy Ismay (tenor s); Lloyd Knibb (d); Tommy McCook (tenor s); Stanley "Ribs" Notice (tenor s); Ernest Ranglin (g); Rico Rodriguez (tb); Lloyd Spence (b); Lester Sterling (alto s); Lynn Taitt (g); Ron Wilson (t); Winston Wright (o) **Track listing:** Thoroughfare – Don Drummond and the Skatalites; Magnificent Ska – Lynn Tait and The Baba Brooks Band; It's Real – The Silvertones; Strongman Sampson – Eric "Monty" Morris; Alley Cat Ska – Treasure Isle All-Stars; When You Are Wrong – The Techniques; Carry Go – Bring Come – Justin Hinds And The Dominoes; Street Corner – Don Drummond and the Skatalites; True Confession – The Silvertones; When I Call Your Name – Stranger Cole and Patsy Todd; Musical Storeroom – Frank Anderson and The Skatalies; Words – Owen and Leon Silvera And The Skatalites; Duke Reid Speaks; Burial – Duke Reid And His Group; Guns Fever – Derrick Morgan And The Skatalites; Oh Little Girl (Take 2) – Lloyd & Glen; Get Your Feet Moving – Eric "Monty" Morris; Only Suffering – Funny Man And The Boys; Storm Warning – Lynn Taitt And His Comets; Rough And Tough – Stranger Cole; Nuclear Weapon – The Baba Brooks Band

This album is remarkable in that it provides one of the very few examples of Duke Reid as a physical presence. Duke Speaks finds him berating his players for not putting the bass and drums far enough to the fore – he had a speaker in his office at the back of his liquor store, connected on a open line to the studio which had been constructed out of wood on top of the building – and every time he heard something he wasn't happy with he'd run upstairs to let his displeasure be known. When working with singers, Reid's ska had a more soulful, mellow quality, with musical subtlety taking over from technical manoeuvring, as he always seemed more at home with love songs rather frantic, shuffling jolly ups. It's in this area that the links between R&B and ska are most noticeable – no coincidence the Duke was a big R&B fan who sponsored and personally hosted an R&B radio show before he built his sound system.

Various

HEARTBEAT HBCD 86/87

Ska Bonanza: The Studio One Ska Years

Produced by Clement "Coxsone" Dodd **Recorded** between 1961 and 1965, at Federal and Studio One, Kingston, Jamaica. **Personnel include:** Aubrey Adams (p); Roland Alphonso (tenor s); Frank Anderson (t); Gladstone Anderson (p); Lloyd Brevett (b); Baba Brooks (t); Don Drummond (tb); Winston Graham (t); Lloyd Knibbs (d); Cecil Lloyd (o); Tommy McCook (tenor s); Johnny "Dizzy" Moore (t); Ernest Ranglin (g); Rico Rodriguez (tb); Lester Sterling (alto s); Lynn Taitt (g); Winston Wright (o) **Track listing:** Nimble Foot Ska – The Skatalites; Spred Satin – The Skatalites; Arte Bella – Ken Boothe and Stranger Cole; Streets of Gold – Roland Alphonso And The Soul Vendors; Ah De Pon Dem – Rita Marley Anderson And The Wailers; Black Sunday – The Skatalites; Don't Want Your Loving – Cornell Campbell; Old Fowl Ska – Roland Alphonso; Enna Bella – Eric "Monty" Morris; Jezebel – Owen Grey with Clue J And His Blues Blasters; Always On A Sunday – Frank Anderson And Tommy McCook; Sugar Bag – Lee Perry; Settle Down – Lester Sterling – Johnny Moore And Tommy McCook; Turn Me On – The Checkmates; When The Well Runs Dry – Bunny & Skitter; Wheel And Turn – Frank Anderson And Tommy McCook; Oceans 11 – Cecil Lloyd and Roland Alphonso; Over The River – The Jiving Juniors; My Heaven – Alton Ellis and Eddie Parkins with Aubrey Adams And The Dew Droppers; Set Back (Just Cool) – Roland Alphonso And Carroll McLaughlin; Du Du Wap – Chuck Josephs And Dobby Dobson With Aubrey Adams; Man In The Street – Don Drummond; Simmer Down – Bob Marley And The Wailers; Shining Light – Toots And The Maytals; Push Wood – Jackie Opel; Wonder No More – Andy And Joey; Bongo Tango – Roland Alphonso; Sucu Sucu – Roland Alphonso; 20.75 – Roland Alphonso; Stop Making Love – The Gaylads; How Many Times (Do You Remember) – Bob Marley And The Wailers; Roll On Sweet Don (Heaven And Hell); Sit Down Servant – Jackie Opel; Go Jimmy Go – Bob Marley And The Wailers; Stew – Peas And Cornflakes – Aubrey Adams And Rico Rodriguez; Answer Me My Darling – Derrick Harriot; River Jordan – Clancy Eccles With Hersand & The City Slickers; Salt Lane Shuffle – Clue J And His Blues Blasters; Jeannie Girl – The Charmers; Lonely Moment – Lascelles Perkins with Clue J And His Blues Blasters

Coxsone was a long-time jazzman, his first forays into DJing coming when, as a teenager, he'd draw crowds to his mother's liquor store by playing selections from his large collection of jazz albums on the shop's gramophone. And these roots show up on this collection, a comprehensive cross-section of his work that grew enormously in depth and intricacy after he opened his own recording facility, Studio One in Brentford Road. Not only was it the first black-owned studio in Jamaica, but he became the first studio boss to put the house band (essentially The Skatalites) on wages instead of paying them per side, in order to encourage experimentation and greater musical quality. Although his vocal productions are not to be sniffed at, it's in the instrumentals that his jazz instincts make for some remarkable music, notably when Don Drummond, Jamaica's premier trombonist, was involved.

Prince Buster

SEQUEL NEXCD 253

Prince Buster Fabulous Greatest Hits

Produced by Prince Buster

Recorded between 1960 and 1966, at RJR Studios and West Indies Studios, Kingston, Jamaica, and Advision Studios, London, England **Personnel include:** Gladstone Anderson (p); Val Bennett (tenor s); Lloyd Brevett (b); Baba Brooks (t); Dennis Campbell (tenor s); Drumbago (drums); Georgie Fame (o); Junior Nelson (trm); Red Price (s); Ernest Ranglin (g); Rico Rodriguez (trm) **Track listing:** Madness; Al Capone; Wash Wash; God Son; It's Burke's Law; 10 Commandments; Blackhead Chineman; 30 Pieces Of Silver; Hard Man Fe Dead; Earthquake; Ghost Dance; Take It Easy; Too Hot; My Girl; This Is A Hold Up; Shaking Orange Street; Big Five; Rough Rider; Wreck a Pum Pum; Julie On My Mind; Pharaoh House Crash; Tie The Donkey's Tail; Finger Further ska listening: The Maytals: Sensational Ska Explosion (Jamaica Gold JMC200112); The Best Of Desmond Dekker (Music Collection International MCCD115); Various Artists: Ska Boogie – Jamaican R&B, The Dawn Of Ska (Sequel NEXCD254); Tommy McCook And The Skatalites: The Birth Of Ska (Trojan TRL274)

This is the work of a man determined to experiment. This collection concentrates on his work as a singer rather than his productions, it therefore misses out on such ground-breaking moments as Oh Carolina, They Got To Go and Humpty Dumpty, when he began building songs around rhythm patterns that involved Rasta drumming and so wrenched things away from Coxsone and Reid's identifiable R&B clones. However, what shines out here is the exuberance of music that at last truly belonged to the people who were making it. Tracks like Madness, Shaking Up Orange Street and It's Burke's Law are celebratory tracks that became the benchmark for ska around the world. And speaking of internationalism, Wash Wash was cut in London during 1963 and features Georgie Fame on the organ.

Outside of Reid, Coxsone and Buster, the other important ska producers were Leslie Kong (Jimmy Cliff, Desmond Dekker, The Wailers, Derrick Morgan and Joe Higgs), Byron Lee (The Maytals and his own group The Dragonnaires) and Vincent Chin whose Randy's operation had most success with John Holt and Alton Ellis and a series of instrumentals, the best of which were led by trombone players Rico Rodriguez and Don Drummond.

ROCK STEADY & EARLY REGGAE

Ska's mutation into rock steady in the mid-1960s came about for a number of reasons, the most prominent being that ska was too one-paced to allow for a well-rounded dancehall experience. Another suggestion is that the island's unnaturally hot summer of 1966 required a less frantic soundtrack. But overriding everything else is the pattern that has run through four decades of Jamaican music – every few years a sound system owner looking to revitalise his appeal will carefully reinvent the beat. Rock steady, which pretty quickly mutated into reggae, came out of a soul boom that swept the island in 1964–65 as a knock-on from R&B evolving into soul in the US. The musician given most credit for moving the music on at this point is guitarist Lyn Taitt, who, significantly, isn't Jamaican but Trinidadian and had travelled extensively, assimilating many musical influences. He hired himself out, with his group The Jets, to most Kingston producers but made the deepest impact as Duke Reid's in-house arranger. His guitar-led sessions slowed the beat down and created a far mellower, soulful sound. The new style was exactly what Reid felt comfortable with, as it lent itself so perfectly to American-style (eg Impressions) harmonising, and for several years hits streamed out of Treasure Isle Studios with the rest of the industry following suit.

Various Artists CDHB 95/96

Duke Reid's Treasure Chest: Treasure Isle Rock Steady

Produced by Duke Reid **Recorded** between 1964 and 1970, at Treasure Isle Studios, Kingston, Jamaica. Tommy McCook's Supersonics: Gladstone Anderson (p); Drumbago (d); Neville Hinds (o); Hugh Malcolm (d); Herman Marquis (s); Tommy McCook (tenor s); Ernest Ranglin (g); Lynn Taitt (g); White Rum Raymond (v); Winston Wright (o) **Track listing:** We Are In The Mood (take two) – The Royals; Come On Little Girl (take two) – The Melodians; Things You Say You Love – The Jamaicans; The Tide Is High – The Paragons; You Don't Need Me – The Melodians; Rock Steady – Phyllis Dillon; Soul Style – The Duke Reid Group; Can't Stand It – Alton Ellis & Lloyd Williams; Queen Majesty – The Techniques; Heartaches – Vic Taylor; Midnight Hour – the Silvertones; Midnight Hour – U-Roy; My best Girl – The Paragons; Loving Pauper – Dobby Dobson; I'll Get Along Without You – The Melodians; I'll Never fall In Love – The Sensations; Travelling Man – The Techniques; Don't Stay Away – Phillis Dillon; LaLa Means I Love You – Alton Ellis; Hey Leroy – Honey Boy Martin; No Good Rudie (take three) – Justin Hinds & The Dominoes; Everybody Bawling – U-Roy; Ba Ba Boom – The Jamaicans; Cry Tough – Alton Ellis; You Have Caught Me – The Melodians; Perfidia – Phyllis Dillon; Those Guys – The Sensations; Ranglin On Bond Street – Ernest And Tommy; Girl I've Got A Date (alternate version); How I Wish It Would Rain – The Techniques; It's Raining – The Three Tops; Love Is A treasure – Freddy McKay; You Done Me Wrong – Tyrone & The Slickers; Right Track – Phyllis Dillon and Hopeton Lewis; Everyday Is A Holiday – The Sensations; Holiday Version – Winston Wright; (False Start) Come Back Darling – Girl Stachmo; Mother's Tender Care (take two) – The Ethiopians; My Girl – The Techniques; Moonlight Lover – Joya Landis

The ultimate rock steady collection, cool, silky music with singing back as the focal point. It shows off Reid's complete understanding of the style, and the establishment of the classic Jamaican-style harmony singing – three-part, but with a democracy that finds the voices swapping the lead throughout songs, occasionally mid-line.

U-Roy & Friends

TROJAN CDTRL 359

Your Ace From Space

Produced by Duke Reid **Recorded** during 1969 and 1970 at Treasure Isle Studios, Kingston, Jamaica **Personnel:** Tommy McCook And The Supersonics, including Gladstone Anderson (p); Drumbago (d); Neville Hinds (o); Hugh Malcolm (d); Herman Marquis (s); Tommy McCook (s, f); "White Rum" Raymond (v); Winston Wright (o) **Track listing:** Tide Is High – U-Roy & The Paragons; On The Beach – U-Roy & The Paragons; Flashing My Whip – U-Roy & The Paragons; Wear You To The Ball – U-Roy & The Paragons; Happy Go Lucky Girl – U-Roy & The Paragons; Same Song – U-Roy & The Paragons; Merry Go Round – U-Roy & John Holt; Drive Her Home – U-Roy & Hopeton Lewis; Tom Drunk – U-Roy & Hopeton Lewis; Rock Away – U-Roy & The Melodians; Super Boss – U-Roy & The Melodians; Everybody Bawlin' – U-Roy & The Melodians; Version Galore – U-Roy & The Melodians; Words Of Wisdon – U-Roy; My Girl – U-Roy & The Techniques; Ruler Of The Nation – U-Roy; Ain't That Loving You – U-Roy & Alton Ellis; Wake The Town – U-Roy; Hot Pot – U-Roy; Peace And Love – U-Roy & The Jamaicans; Things You Love – U-Roy & The Jamaicans; Treasure Isle Skank – U-Roy; True Confessions – U-Roy & The Silvertones; Do It Right – U-Roy & The Three Tops; True True – U-Roy & Ken Parker; Big Boy & Teacher – U-Roy; Behold – U-Roy; Don't Stay Away – U-Roy & Phillis Dillon; Honey Come Forward – U-Roy; Your Ace From Space – U-Roy

It was Reid who first started recording "toasting" singles when he cut his sound system deejay U-Roy on top of rudimentary dub versions of some rock steady classics. By dropping the deejay into the holes left in the mix, U-Roy was able to almost converse with the vocalist while scatting and whooping in his live dancehall style. Although these may seem somewhat clunky compared with today's toasting, at the time they were a sensation and represent the origination of the art of studio deejaying.

Various

TROJAN TRL270

Jumping With Mr Lee 1967–1968

Produced by Bunny Lee **Recorded** during 1967 and 1968 in Kingston, Jamaica **Personnel include** Bobby Aitken (g); Gladstone Anderson (p); Mr Bassie (b); Val Bennett (tenor s); Vin Gordon (tb); Winston Grenan (d); Johnny Moore (t); Lester Sterling (alto s); Lynn Taitt (g) **Track listing:** Long Time Me No See You Girl – The Sensations; Love And Devotion – The Uniques; Jumping With Mr Lee – Val Bennett & The Bunny Lee All-Stars; Hold You Jack – Derrick Morgan; Bangarang – Lester Sterling and Stranger Cole; Little Boy Blue – Pat Kelly; Story Of Love – The Uniques; A Change Is Gonna Come – Ken Parker; Jumping With Val – Val Bennett; Girls Like Dirt – The Uniques; Tribute To King Scratch – Lester Sterling; Somebody's Baby – Pat Kelly; Sounds And Soul – Vin Gordon; My Conversation – The Uniques; Sir Lee's Whip – Lester Stirling; The Beatitude – Slim Smith & The Uniques

Although Prince Buster and Coxsone both made entirely creditable rock steady, they were never in Duke Reid's class and were overshadowed by newcomer Bunny Lee, a former Treasure Isle record plugger. Lee was one of the first big-time producers not to own a sound system and although he'd still try his recording out at other people's dances he looked for an audience beyond the sound system lawns and focused on selling records to the increasingly prosperous Jamaican working classes and to expats in the UK. Because of this there was usually more emphasis on the artist on Bunny Lee-produced records as he knew that meant more to the consumer who wasn't a dancehall regular. And as *Jumping With Mr Lee* shows, he was equally at home with vocal or instrumental, one of the facets of his work that kept him on top as, at the end of the 1960s, rock steady became "reggae as we know it".

Lee Perry & The Upsetters HEARTBEAT CD 7601

The Upsetter Shop Volume 2

Produced by Lee Perry **Recorded** between 1968 and 1973, at Randy's Studio, WIRL, Dynamics and Studio One, Kingston, Jamaica **Personnel** include: Glen Adams (o); Gladstone Anderson (p); Aston "Family Man" Barrett (b); Carlton Barrett (d); Val Bennett (s); Lynford Brown (g); Winston Grennan (d); Jackie Jackson (b); Denzil Laing (pc); Alva Lewis (g); Hugh Malcolm (b); Lee Perry (pc); Linval Martin (b); Scully Sims (pc); Ranford Williams (g); Winston Wright (o) **Track listing:** Check Him Out – the Bleechers; Uncle Charlie – The Mellotones; Uncle Charlie (version) – Dillinger; Sunshine Rock – The Upsetters; who Tell All – David Isaacs; Can't Take It Any More – Pat Satchmo; Caught You Red Handed (take 3) – Eric Donaldson & The West Indians; Caught You Red Handed (take 4) – Eric Donaldson & The West Indians; Water More Than Flour – Al & The Vibrators; X-Ray Vision – Glen Adams & The Upsetters; People Sokup Boy – Lee Perry; Gee – Al & The Vibrators; Some Sympathy – Dave Barker; Tender Love – The Inspirations; Creation – The Upsetters; Cloud Nine – Carl Dawkins & The Wailers; Tighten Up – The Inspirations; Tighten Up Skank – Dillinger; Sweets For My Sweet – Rehearsal – The Silvertones **Further rock-steady listening:** The Ethiopians: Original Reggae Hitsound (Trojan TRL228); The Heptones: The Heptones (Studio One SOCD9002); Various Artists: Joe Gibbs Mood (Trojan TRL394); Derrick Harriot & The Crystalites: For A Fistful Of Dollars (Jamaican Gold JMC200211)

The Bunny Lee collection shows the development of rock steady into "reggae" as an organic state of affairs, brought about by the electric bass reasserting the rhythm section's position while electric organ took over from the piano. However, one man who lit a rocket under the idea of a new style was Lee Perry. Having been around sound systems for several years, he understood the Kingston audiences, but, as he claims, brought a vital ingredient to the table – he was a country boy with a rural Jamaican sensibility. Today he'll claim his aim was, after years of rock steady's Americanisation, to reintroduce a Jamaican feel. *The Upsetter Shop Volume 2* is a collection of Perry's early productions that gives far more away about what he wanted to do than the gimmicky *Return Of Django* stuff that sold so well at the time. Reggae's sequences and signatures are all there, albeit in raw form, and the jerkiness of the guitar and the stabbing, arched finger approach to the ivories conjures up the banjo and drum patterns of *mento*, Jamaica's best-known folk music. Also present and correct are elements of the eccentricity that would become Lee Perry's trademark in years to come.

ROOTS REGGAE

Roots reggae was, according to Big Youth, the movement's premier deejay, the reaction of a younger group of performers who had grown up with reggae and for whom Jamaican independence wasn't working: "The people had enough of pure *dibidibidabidoo* at the dances, without some alternative that represent how they feel. That's where the new generation of deejays, younger guys, came in because we could really see where it should be coming from. And on the sound systems we are much closer to the people than so many of the big record producers."

For the first time musicians began to open their own recording set-ups, allowing a new wave of players greater autonomy. As Rastafarianism swept Jamaica, singers and players began to show their devotion to Jah with hymn-like lyrics and minor chord melodies. Rhythms slowed down, while righteousness and social/political comment became fairly universal. This phase of reggae was when, spearheaded by Bob Marley, the music truly went international, and thanks to the expectations of foreign markets the stars began to shine from behind the producers' shadows.

Big Youth

TROJAN TRL61

Screaming Target

Produced by Gussie Clarke Recorded 1972, Kingston, Jamaica **Personnel:** N/A **Track listing:** Screaming Target (Version 1 & 2); Concrete Jungle; Tippertone Rock; The Killer; Pride And Joy Rock; Honesty; Be Careful; One Of These Fine Days; Solomon Grundy; I'm Alright; Lee A Low

Screaming Target became something of a yardstick for roots style, both on and away from the mic. With a raw, instinctive energy, Big Youth yanked the whole idea of toasting on from the U-Roys and Dennis Alcapones by addressing issues instead of just the dancehall crowd, and put in place a more narrative method of delivery. Youth and producer Gussie Clarke were not yet 20 years old when they cut *Screaming Target* and had all the respect for the established way of doing things you'd expect from a couple of spiky teenagers. But just as he was the new sound of the streets, Big Youth was also the look – the first performer to flash his dreadlocks on stage, the baby dreads he shows off on this album's sleeve were one of the earliest examples. Burning Spear had not yet locksed up, Bunny was the only Wailer to do so and there are very few dreadlocks on display in The Harder They Come. It made this album a very cool accessory to carry around in 1973.

Augustus Pablo

SECHANIE MESSCD1007

King Tubby Meets Rockers Uptown

Produced by Augustus Pablo **Recorded** between 1972 and 1975 at Randy's Studio, Kingston, Jamaica; mixed by King Tubby, in 1976, at King Tubby's Studio, Kingston, Jamaica **Personnel:** Aston "Family Man" Barrett (b); Carlton Barrett (d); Bobby Ellis (t); Vin Gordon (tb); Richard "Dirty Harry" Hall (tenor s); Augustus Pablo (o, p, clavinet, melodica); Robbie Shakespeare (b); Earl "Chinna" Smith (g) **Track listing:** Keep On Dubbing; Stop Them Jah; Young Generation Dub; Each One Dub; 555 Dub Street; Braces Tower Dub; King Tubby Meets Rockers Uptown; Corner Crew Dub; Say So; Skanking Dub; Frozen Dub

Dub as an end in itself rather than merely an accompaniment had been threatening for a while by this time, but it was during the roots era that it really came into its own. Of course, the new studio technology helped, but the ideas behind it concerned themselves with creating something genuinely dread rather than just dropping out bits of the original tune to allow toasting or, as it was first used, for the dancehall crowds to take over the vocals themselves. And there is probably no better example of the high art of dub, the craft of the remixer, than this album. Sound system operator, disc cutter and remix engineer King Tubby was simply the most technically adventurous, stylistically imaginative and musically daring of his genre. And as Augustus Pablo's music was never less than intricate, delicate and deftly layered, having King Tubby pick it apart and gently put it back together in a different order was always going to be definitive.

Burning Spear

MANGO RRCD20

Marcus Garvey

Produced by Jack Ruby **Recorded:** in 1974 at Randy's Studio, Kingston, Jamaica **Personnel include:** Aston Barrett (b); Tony Chin (g); Tyrone Downie (o); Bobby Ellis (t); Vin Gordon (tb); Richard "Dirty Harry Hall (tenor s); Bernard Harvey (p, o, clavinet); Delroy Hines (bv); Herman Marquis (alto s); Carlton Samuels (f); Robbie Shakespeare (b); Earl Smith (g); Leroy Wallace (d); Rupert Willington (bv) **Track listing:** Marcus Garvey; Slavery Days; The Invasion; Live Good; Give Me; Old Marcus Garvey; Tradition; Jordan River; Red, Gold & Green; Resting Place.

In the rush of excitement that accompanied the mainstream embracing dub and deejay styles as the most potent expressions of roots culture, it's sometimes easy to overlook singers other than Bob Marley. But roots singing was a vibrant strand and Burning Spear and Horace Andy show how, respectively, it encompassed the almost mystically spiritual and the lovers' rock element without either end losing sight of what it was supposed to be doing. *Marcus Garvey* was cut when Burning Spear (aka Winston Rodney) still operated as a trio with regular backing singers Rupert Willington and Delroy Hines and the album is a stunning example of the classic Jamaican three-part harmony being subverted by minor chords, slowed down rhythms and dread sentiment. It pulls no punches as regards expecting listener commitment.

Horace Andy

BLOOD & FIRE BAFCD006

In The Light

Produced by Horace Andy and Everton DaSilva **Recorded** during 1976 and 1977, at Harry J Studio, Kingston, Jamaica **Personnel:** Noel Alphonso (d); Bernard Harvey (k); Wayne Jarett (bv); Bobby Kalphat (k); Augustus Pablo (k); Leroy Sibbles (b); Michael Taylor (b, k); Leroy Wallace (d) **Track listing:** Do You Love My Music; Hey There Woman; Government Land; Leave Rasta; Fever; In The Light; Problems; If I; Collie Herb; Rome **Further listening:** Keith Hudson: Pick A Dub (Blood & Fire BAFCD003); Culture: Two Sevens Clash (Sachanie SHANCD44001); Dennis Brown: Wolves & Leopards (Blue Moon CDBM046); Lee Perry: Super Ape (Upsetter ILP3 9417) The Congoes: Heart Of the Congoes (Blood & Fire BAFCD009) The Mighty Diamonds: Right Time (Sechanie SHANCD43014)

Practically the opposite of *Marcus Garvey*. True, most of the subject matter is equally righteous, but Andy's falsetto, the much lighter production and frequent lapses into the secular make this dancehall as much as classroom fare.

DANCEHALL AND BEYOND

It would be easy to say the roots movement died with Bob Marley in 1981, but the truth is it had been staggering somewhat for a couple of years by then. The idea of reggae going international in the wake of Marley's success was forcing it to re-address its reasons for doing what it did; computerised studio technology was changing the way music was made; and, as has been the case in so many of the music's shifts, a new generation of musicians just wanted to try something different. But rather than have peace and love on their minds, this new set were responding to a shift in black American culture post-1970s, sex and violence became the order of the day. What began as "slackness", the bawdy, Carry On-ish subject matter that has always had a place in Caribbean music, mutated into a quite nasty misogyny, homophobia and fascination with crime and, by the 1990s, dancehall reggae wasn't a very nice place to be.

Although there were many producers willing to make these "gun and *punani*" records – the recently opened-up US market hoped to sit them alongside gangsta rap – and mainstream critics willing to endorse them as a "raw expression of the ghetto soul" or "reality", there were as many in the Jamaican music business horrified at what was passing itself off as music. It was only a matter of time before it became clear that a blind alley was being explored – the music had long lost its shock value and international record companies turned away as it began to go too far – and some manner of righteousness, or just plain old enjoyment of music began to resurface.

Buju Banton

LOOSE CANNON 534 135-2

'Til Shiloh

Produced by: Buju Banton; Bobby Digital; Donovan Germain; Sylvester Gordon; Dave Kelly; Steely & Clevie Recorded during 1994 and 1995 at Digital B, Penthouse Studios, Cecil Black Recording Studios, Cell Block Recording Studios, and Studio 2000, all in Kingston, Jamaica **Personnel:** Danny Browne; Glen Browne (ac g); Dalton Brownie (g); Junior Chin (t); Clevie (d); Sly Dunbar (d); The Firehouse Crew; Dean Fraser (s); Dave Kelly (d); Robbie Lyn (k); Mafia & Fluxy; Steely (b, k); Handel Tucker (k, d); Andre Tyrell (d); Lloyd Willis (k) **Track listing:** Shiloh; 'Til I'm Laid To Rest; Murderer; Champion; Untold Stories; Not An Easy Road; Only Man; Complaint (featuring Garnett Silk); Chuck It So; How Could You; Wanna Be Loved; It's All Over; Hush Baby Hush; What Ya Gonna Do? (featuring Wayne Wonder); Rampage; Champion (remix)

Buju Banton's turnaround was among the more graphic illustrations of how modern Jamaican music returned to its roots. In 1992, as a hugely successful ragga deejay, he achieved international notoriety with the single Boom Bye Bye, a tasteful ditty endorsing the shooting of homosexuals. The next year his friend, the deejay Panhead, was shot dead in the street and, by 1994, Buju had grown dreadlocks, seen the error of his ways and cut one of the new roots scene's landmark albums *'Til Shiloh*. He rounded up some of the top producers in Jamaica and turned his gruff toasting style to the reflective and overtly righteous, and in doing so turned many people – players and fans – on to the prospect of marrying the modern dancehall excitement to old-style roots values.

Sizzla

GREENSLEEVES GRELCD243

Black Woman & Child

Produced by Bobby "Digital" Dixon **Recorded** 1997 at Digital B, Kingston, Jamaica **Personnel:** Bongo Herman (conga); Paul Crossdale (k); Donald Dennis (b,k); Dish (conga); Sly Dunbar (d); Dean Fraser (s); Paul Henton (d,b,p); Jazwad (d,b,k); Barry O'Hare (d,b,k); Melbourne Miller (d); Benjy Meyers (b,k); Nambo (tb); Robbie Shakespeare (b); Ernie Wilks (g) **Track listing:** Black Woman & Child; Hard Ground; More Guidance; Make It Secure; Oh What A Joy; Love Is Divine; One Away; Guide Over Us; Give Them The Ride; Babylon Use Dem Brain; No Time To Gaze; Too Much To Bear; Mi Lord; Give Them The Ride (Morgan Heritage remix)

'TIL SHILOH provided a template for this album three years later, in which the young Bobo Dread (an orthodox Rastafarian sect) berates all manner of Babylonianism over music and rhythms lovingly sculptured by Bobby Digital, one of the most innovative producer/engineer/sound system operators of recent times. Digital refashions some old rock steady rhythms as well as crafting a few new ones of his own and manages to soften Sizzla's sometimes abrasive ranting without dulling its edge.

Luciano

ISLAND JAMAICA IJCD 3001

Where There Is Life

Produced by Phillip "Fattis" Burrell **Recorded** during 1994 and 1995 in Kingston, Jamaica **Personnel:** Cat Coore (g); Donald Dennis (g,k); Sly Dunbar (d); Dean Fraser (s, bv); Leba Hibbert (bv); Robbie Lyn (k); Robbie Shakespeare (b); Nicky Tucker (bv) Track listening: It's Me Again Jah; Lord Give Me Strength; Who Could It Be; He Is My Friend; Your World And Mine; Just Like The Wind; He; Good God; There's No Love In The World; Where There Is Life; Heaven Help Us All; In This Together **Further listening:** Garnett Silk: It's Growing (Vineyard VYCD4); Yellowman: Zungguzungguguzungguzeng (Greensleeves GREL57); Shabba Ranks: Just Reality (Vineyard VYCD6); Prince Jammy (Various Artists): Sleng Teng Extravaganza (Melodie 792909-2); Capleton: Alms House (Greensleeves GREL182); Junior Delgado: Fearless (Big Cat ABB1002862)

Next to the late Garnett Silk, Luciano is the premier new roots singer, and by the time he cut *Where There Is Life* he'd been singing long enough – first on sound systems, then making singles – to underscore his agreeable, pleading tone with enough confidence to really stretch himself. Burrell was exactly the right producer for such advancements, as well as being technically correct he has a vision of internationalism that, while willing to take chances, is firmly rooted in its home environment. Together on this album they've proved the new roots movement has genuine substance and that modern reggae can structure itself as accessible songs and remain as esoteric as most people expect it to be.

Required reading (in general): Bass Culture: When Reggae Was King (Lloyd Bradley, 2000); Bob Marley: A Rebel Life (Dennis Morris, 1999); The Rough Guide To Reggae (Steve Barrow & Peter Dalton, 1997); Born Fi Dead (Laurie Gunst, 1995)

Written by Lloyd Bradley.

100 Great Soundtracks

Music to watch films by

There has always been a link between film and music. Even the most *bijou* of silent screen theatres usually employed a pianist to underline the onscreen action, to heighten the tension in chase scenes or provide the hearts and flowers whenever romance blossomed. There were even attempts made to accompany certain features with the sounds of phonograph recordings, a silent short featuring a British variety act, Little Tich And His Big Boots, was marketed in 1900 with an accompanying gramophone disc.

Epic features merited sounds worthy of their importance. Director DW Griffith and composer Joseph Carl Briel pieced together a full orchestral score for the premiere of Birth Of A Nation in 1915, while other scores found such celebrated composers as Milhaud and Shosktakovich providing the settings for later silent movies.

And when, in 1927, Al Jolson sang Dirty Hands, Dirty Face, in the film The Jazz Singer, and spontaneously yelled "Wait a minute, wait a minute. You ain't heard nothin' yet," he could hardly have been aware of the fuse he was lighting. Hailed, somewhat inaccurately, as the first major talking picture, this low-budget production not only earned Warner's $3 million but also resulted in a spin-off, double-sided smash single for Jolson My Mammy/Dirty Hands, Dirty Face, marking the first significant symbiosis between movies and music sales.

From then on, many films would come linked to record releases. And, oddly, many of the biggest money-spinning hits stemmed not from musicals but from scores created for dramas. During the early '50s Anton Karas' zither theme to The Third Man topped the US sales listings for 11 straight weeks, while Percy Faith's recording of the title song to Moulin Rouge retained pole position for 10. Melodies like The Dream Of Olwyn were remembered long after their films had been forgotten.

The arrival of the long-playing record in 1948 sparked the birth of the soundtrack album as we know it today. No longer did musical memories of a cinematic experience have to be purchased in three-minute portions. Whole scores could be placed on a disc. Not that there was a headlong rush into soundtrack albums by record and film companies. It took several years for the public to make the switch from 78rpm shellac discs to the better-quality, but expensive, 33rpm long-player. Gradually, the breakthrough came. During 1955 the soundtrack to Oklahoma! topped the US charts. It would eventually retain a chart position for 229 weeks. The following year, pianist Carmen Cavallaro's album of music culled from the biopic The Eddy Duchin Story, went to Number 1 in the States, while The King And I soundtrack became a best-seller, as did Elmer Bernstein's powerful score for The Man With The Golden Arm.

Though rock'n'roll movies proliferated during this period – in the wake of Bill Haley's Rock Around The Clock thundering over the titles at the start of Richard Brooks' The Blackboard Jungle – they provided little in the way of soundtrack albums. Even The Girl Can't Help It (1956), the first rock film anyone could own up to seeing without embarrassment, failed to arrive in album form at the time. Likewise, Rock Around The Clock, a box-office smash that was, in reality, a feeble excuse for Bill Haley to exhibit his limited wares. Those movies that did provide soundtrack albums, like Rock All Night and Rock Pretty Baby, sold poorly and deservedly so. It took Elvis Presley's Jailhouse Rock and King Creole to shove chart doors open. In Britain, Cliff Richard also demonstrated that doing it for the kids could result in soundtrack sales. But when album charts were first compiled, the biggest sellers were undoubtedly things like Rogers and Hammerstein's score to South Pacific – which topped the UK album charts for 96 weeks between 1958 and 1961 – and the Bernstein/Sondheim score to West Side Story which topped US and UK charts for months in both stage and film versions.

But once the beat boom arrived, the reign of the soundtrack was over. The success of pop was also clearly going to influence the creation of movie tie-in albums. It was Easy Rider, basically a compilation album, which demonstrated that intelligent programming plus an understanding of the culture could add up to something memorable and thoroughly commercial. A chart album that followed quickly in the wake of The Graduate (Simon & Garfunkel's monster release – albeit one that only contained one new track in Mrs Robinson), Easy Rider delineated the way to go. Slam a few tracks together and shazam! No Max Steiner, David Raskin or Bernard Herrmann need apply for a scoring chore ever again. At least, that was the theory. And certainly it paid off in the case of American Graffiti, (1973) where director George Lucas merely sorted through his collection of golden oldies from his teen years to shape an unbeatable, nostalgic 41-song soundtrack.

Others took the ploy a stage further. If the chosen tracks could be pieced together from new material, featuring existing or up-and-coming stars on a certain company's books, then the film itself could act as a launching pad for those acts. Again, this worked in the case of Footloose, which sold nine million copies worldwide and spawned several major hits. Equally, this approach resulted in some of the most dim-witted compilations ever to grace the soundtrack scene, and some odd anomalies too. The soundtrack to John Hughes' Some Kind Of Wonderful took a bunch of existing hits or album tracks and, apparently pointlessly, got the original artists to re-cut them.

Thankfully, Hollywood and Europe's big-screen composers never faded away. Though often bested chartwise by such singles-oriented soundtracks as *Saturday Night Fever*, *Top Gun*, *Dirty Dancing* and *The Bodyguard* (some of the biggest selling albums, of any kind, of all time), the likes of John Barry, Bill Conti, Thomas Newman, Ennio Morricone, John Williams and Quincy Jones continued to enhance and enchant. And some pure soundtrack albums – like *Rocky* and *Star Wars* – have simply never stopped selling.

All this however, is simply scratching the surface. Soundtrack is an all-encompassing genre, with countless factions. The blaxploitation movies alone provided a mine of music, as have reggae, country, rap, blues, jazz and concert releases. Providing a pointer to the best or most important 100 releases in such a widespread area might be considered at best foolhardy, at worst an impossible task. But that's what we've attempted to do here; we've concentrated on music (or a soundtrack) that was influential in its day, music that has withstood the test of time and soundtrack albums that are enjoyable in their own right, away from the screen. We've not ranked them but, like the main body of the book, have run them chronologically.

"You ain't heard nothin' yet?"

No prediction was ever more accurate.

Various Artists TURNER SOUNDTRACKS

Cabin In The Sky

Current CD: 8 21562 2 **Available on video, Release date:** 1943 **Chart peaks:** None **Track listings:** Main Title, Foreword, But The Flesh Is Weak, The Prayer, The First Revelation, Saint Petunia, Beside The Still Waters, The Meek And The Mild, Petunia In The Wilderness, Love Me Tomorrow, Sweet Petunia, The Third Revelation, Little Joe Throws Snake Eyes, Amen – MGM Studio Orchestra; Li'l Black Sheep, Happiness Is A Thing Called Joe – Ethel Waters; Dat Suits Me – Ethel Waters with Butterfly McQueen; Cabin In The Sky, Taking A Chance On Love – Ethel Waters with Eddie Anderson; Honey In The Honeycomb – Ethel Waters; Ain't It The Truth – Lena Horne; Life's Full O' Consequences – Lena Horne with Eddie Anderson; Honey In The Honeycomb – Lena Horne; Things Ain't What They Used To Be, Going Up, Down At Jim Henry's – Duke Ellington And His Orchestra; Shine – Duke Ellington & His Orchestra with John Bubbles; Ain't It The Truth – Louis Armstrong; Old Ship Of Zion – Kenneth Spencer And The Hall Johnson Choir **Further listening:** Stormy Weather, the soundtrack to the follow-up film, featuring the talents of Lena Horne, Fats Waller, Cab Calloway and Bill Bojangles Robinson. **Further reading:** A Separate Cinema, 50 Years Of Black Cast Posters (John Kisch and Edward Mapp, 1992)

The first film adaptation of an all-black Broadway musical, Cabin In The Sky originally appeared onscreen in 1943. MGM, who made the film, had no record company at that point but some of the songs became hits for performers on other labels, Benny Goodman notching a US Top 20 single with the title number. The film was a fantastical affair, bound around a good woman's attempts to keep her husband's soul from falling into Lucifer's clutches. But the songs, penned by such as Vernon Duke, Harold Arlen and Yip Harburg, were all of superior quality and performed by many of America's premier black entertainers. Taking A Chance On Love won an Oscar nomination.

Doris Day with Harry James And His Orchestra COLUMBIA

Young Man With A Horn

Current CD: ACL 582 **Release date:** March 1950 **Chart peaks:** None **Track listing:** I May Be Wrong; The Man I Love; The Very Thought Of You; Pretty Baby; Melancholy Rhapsody; Would I Love You; Too Marvellous For Words; Get Happy; I Only Have Eyes For You; Limehouse Blues; With A Song In My Heart; Lullaby Of Broadway **Further listening:** Duet (Sony) a further jazz-inclined outing for the former Doris Von Kappelhoff, this time in the company of André Previn.

The film was based around Dorothy Baker's excellent book of the same title, which supposedly (but almost unrecognisably) was inspired by the career of legendary jazz trumpeter Bix Beiderbecke. Doris Day, one of the biggest recording stars in the world during the early '50s, made ideal casting as the singer with Kirk Douglas' (ghosted by James) jazz outfit, having worked long-term with Les Brown's big band. Some of the material heard in the film, What Is This Thing Called Love, Sweet Georgia Brown, is omitted from the album, which only features four tracks including both the singer and Harry James; even so it remains one of Day's more rewarding recordings. Incidentally, the film's title had to be changed for UK consumption, arriving here as Young Man Of Music. I wonder why.

Joseph Gershenson And The Universal-International Orchestra

MCA

The Glenn Miller Story

Current CD: MCLD19025 **Available on video, Release date:** 1954 **Chart peaks:** 12 (UK) None (US) Track listening: Moonlight Serenade, Tuxedo Junction, Little Brown Jug, St Louis Blues, In The Mood, A String Of Pearls, Pennsylvania 6-5000, American Patrol, Otchi-Tchor-Ni-Ya – Joseph Gershenson & The Universal-International Orchestra; Basin Street Blues – Louis Armstrong All-Stars **Further listening:** Glenn Miller's Orchestra Wives and Sun Valley Serenade soundtracks. Available in different versions but those featuring the world's greatest dance team, The Nicholas Brothers, are superior.

Studio recreations of the Miller clarinet-and-sax sound that dominated virtually every World War II film ever to emerge from Hollywood. The film itself was fairy-story stuff and had little to do with the real Glenn Miller tale. But the music is fine, scoring over the original Miller soundtracks in terms of recording quality.

Peggy Lee, Ella Fitzgerald

DECCA

Pete Kelly's Blues

Current CD: WSCCM 0055-2 **Available on video and DVD, Release date:** July 1955 **Chart peaks:** None **Track listing:** Oh Didn't He Ramble; Sugar; Somebody Loves Me; I'm Gonna Meet My Sweetie Now; I Never Knew; Bye Bye Blackbird; What Can I Say After I Say I'm Sorry; Hard Hearted Hannah; Ella Hums The Blues; He Needs Me; Sing A Rainbow; Pete Kelly's Blues **Further listening:** Lady And The Tramp, the Disney classic has a score penned and performed by Lee.

The plot, set in 1927, involved a jazz band that played in a Kansas City speakeasy and its problems with strong-arm racketeers. All very melodramatic, but with a keen sense of period and featuring an inspired performance, as a band singer driven to madness, from Lee – who was nominated for an Oscar as Best Supporting Actress. Musically, the soundtrack's of high quality, linking two of the finest jazz singers of the period, Harold Mooney directing Lee's mainly Dixieland accompaniments while Ella, less inhibited by the restrictions of '20s sounds, performing with a knowing trio headed by pianist Don Abney. The honours work out about even; Ella's performance of Hard Hearted Hannah initially inspired cinema audiences to applaud her on-screen image, while Peggy Lee had the advantage of performing two songs penned by Arthur Hamilton, the songwriter best known for Cry Me A River, One, He Needs Me, becoming a mild hit for Lee, while Sing A Rainbow, many years later, helped provide The Dells (and Cilla Black) with chart success.

Elmer Bernstein

MCA

The Man With The Golden Arm

Current CD: MCA MVCM 168 (Japanese import) **Available on video, Release date:** February 1956 **Chart peaks:** None (UK) 2 (US) **Track listing:** Clark Street: The Top, Homecoming, Anteks; Frankie Machine; The Fix; Molly; Break Up: Flight, Louie's, Burlesque; Sunday Morning; Desperation; Audition; The Cure; Finale **Further listening:** Elmer Bernstein By Elmer Bernstein (Denon)

The film was an ideal challenge for Bernstein. A gritty storyline about Frankie Machine (convincingly portrayed by Frank Sinatra), a drummer attempting to quit a drugs habit and ditch the "40-pound monkey on his back" allowed plenty of scope for jazz sequences – and Bernstein called upon the best from the West Coast – musicians such as trumpet stars Shorty Rogers and Pete Candoli, trombonists Milt Bernhardt and Frank Rosolino, plus saxophonists Bud Shank and Bob Cooper, along with drummer Shelly Manne, who taught Sinatra all he needed to know around a drum kit. The great, pounding theme, proved a more than adequate bonus.

George Duning

MCA

Picnic

Current CD: MCAD 31357 **Available on video**. **Release date:** March 1956 **Chart peaks:** None (UK); 6 (US) **Track listing:** Love Theme; Hal's Theme; The Owens Family; Flo And Madge; Hal's Boots; Moonglow and Theme From Picnic; It's A Blue World – Torn Shirt; Torn Shirt (concluded) – Hal's Turmoil; Rosemary Pleads – Rosemary Alone; Culmination – Hal's Escape; That Owens Girl – Millie; You Love Me – Madge Decides **Further listening:** Various Artists: Billboard Top Movie Hits 1955–1959

Duning had a lengthy career as film composer, his work spanning The Devil's Mask (1946) through to The Man With Bogart's Face (1980) and encompassing a huge array of movies including Jolson Sings Again, From Here To Eternity, Bell, Book And Candle and The Devil At Four O'Clock. But Picnic remains Duning's most loved creation, his string-laden love theme being merged with a rhythmic version of the 1934 hit Moonglow to supply the musical backdrop to Kim Novak and William Holden's legendary slo-mo dance routine.

"The most formidable soundtrack I've heard in my time at the movies," reckoned The New Yorker's film critic. Duning received his due Oscar nomination but it was Morris Stoloff – an award-winning film composer in his own right, who conducted the orchestra throughout the film – who copped the hit single with the title song.

Various Artists

EMI

The Girl Can't Help It

Current CD: CDP 7 990993 2 **Release date:** May 1992 **Available on video**. **Chart peaks:** None **Track listing:** The Girl Can't Help It – Little Richard; Tempo's Temp – Nini Tempo; My Idea Of Love, I Ain't Gonna Cry No More, Ready Teddy, She's Got It – Little Richard; Cool It Baby, Cry Me A River – Julie London; Be-Bop-A-Lula – Gene Vincent; Twenty Flight Rock- Eddie Cochran; Rock Around The Rockpile, Rockin' Is Our Business – The Treniers; Blue Monday – Fats Domino; You'll Never Never Know, Ev'rytime, The Girl Can't Help It – Little Richard **Further listening:** Rock Pretty Baby, on which The Ding-A-Lings vie with Henry Mancini's big rock band; and Rock All Night, a pathetic AIP quickie, that boasted music by The Platters and The Block Busters, further illustrate the sound of rock's big screen birth pangs.

The film originally emerged in 1956 and was the first of its kind to boast colour and decent production values. The sketchy plot, about a gangster who sought to make his curvaceous, but talentless girlfriend into a singing star, served mainly to allow various rockers of the era to engage in on-stage performances, though it was Julie London, seen only as a hallucinatory haze singing Cry Me A River, that remains the film's most potent image. There was never a soundtrack album at the time of the film's release but, in the wake of countless poor-quality bootlegs, this array of songs, culled from studio takes (and omitting tracks by Abbey Lincoln and The Chuckles) appeared 36 years later. Both historically important and aurally satisfying, with the big-band offerings of Ray Anthony (once a Glenn Miller trumpet star) illustrating what passed for rock with some elements of the music biz.

Johnny Green And The MGM Studio Symphony Orchestra And Chorus

MGM

Raintree County

Current CD: Entr'acte PRCD 1781 **Release date:** 1957 **Chart peaks:** None **Track listing:** Overture; Prologue (Song Of Raintree County); Neil And Johnny's Graduation Gifts; Johnny's Search For The Raintree; Flash Perkins' Theme; Johnny And Susanna's First Meeting; July Picnic; Johnny's Farewell To Nell; River Wedding Night; Burned-Out Mansion; Susanna's Obsession; Lament For Henrietta; Carriage Ride; Return To Raintree County; Susanna's Madness; War Begins; Flash Joins Up; Little Jeemiels Born; Susanna's Secret; Susuanna And Jeemie Disappear; Johnny Leaves For The Front; Act One; Prologue – Act Two; Battle Montage; Atlanta Destroyed; Johnny And Flash at Fairweather; Jeemie Is Found; The Ambush; Flash Dies; Johnny's Escape; War's End; Reunion With Susanna; Lincoln's Funeral Train; Susanna's Tragic Decision And Her Death; Nell, Johnny And Jeemie Together; Finale

Johnny Green, the composer whose songs includes Body And Soul and I Cover The Waterfront, contributed some outstanding scores during his 10 years at MGM, none more remarkable than that for The Raintree County, a studio blockbuster in Gone With The Wind tradition, starring Elizabeth Taylor and Montgomery Clift. Green's music, which spans two CDs here, is lush and suitably broad in scope containing a theme (Song Of Raintree County), with a lyric by Paul Francis Webster, that was memorably sung on the film's soundtrack by Nat King Cole, who recorded it separately for Capitol.

Elvis Presley

RCA

King Creole

Current CD: 67454-2 **Release date:** August 1958 **Chart peaks:** 4 (UK) 2 (US) **Track listing:** King Creole; As Long As I Have You; Hard Headed Women; Trouble; Dixieland Rock; Don't Ask Me Why; Lover Doll; Crawfish; Steadfast Loyal And True; New Orleans; Danny **Further listening:** GI Blues, another of the Elvis soundtracks from an era when Las Vegas jaunts seemed a long way away. **Further reading:** The Films and Career Of Elvis Presley (Steven and Boris Zmijewsky, 1997)

Not the most successful Elvis soundtrack LP – though the *King Creole Vol.1* EP topped the US EP chart and remained there for 23 weeks – the album is, nevertheless, a better kind of Presley collection and represents a period when it seemed that the Memphis Flash might be capable of piecing together a screen career of some potency. Based on Harold Robbins' pulp novel, A Stone For Danny Fisher, it contained a couple of solid Lieber and Stoller rockers plus Claude DeMetrius' Hard Headed Women, other material came with Dixieland trimmings, reflecting the New Orleans connection. The song Danny, once considered as a title number, was initially rejected and never appeared on the original soundtrack album but was reinstated for the reissue.

Johnny Mandel

MGM

I Want To Live!

Current CD: Ryko RCD 10743 **Release date:** November 1958 **Chart peaks:** None **Track listing:** Main Title; Poker Game; San Diego Party; Henry Leaves; Stakeout; Barbara Surrenders; Trio Convicted; Trip To Corona; Peg's Visit; Gas Chamber Unveiling; Nightmare Sequence; Preparations For Execution; Letter Writing Sequence; The Last Mile; Death Scene; End Title **Further listening:** *Gerry Mulligan and The Concert Big Band At The Village Vanguard* (Verve)

The film, based around the true story of Barbara Graham, a prostitute framed for murder and sentenced to visit the gas chamber, garnered six Oscar nominations, none of which was for the score which broke all the rules by being formed of pure, undiluted jazz. Mandel, a superb arranger, worked with Gerry Mulligan on the soundtrack – Mulligan being a favourite of Graham's, who played his records while on death row. Very percussive, the big band alternating with Mulligan's smaller combo, the soundtrack stills sounds scintillating today, tracks such as Barbara Surrenders linking the Mulligan baritone sound to something close to Gil Evans; similar tonal qualities are also employed on the beautiful Peg's Visit. And virtually every classy jazz musician on the West Coast got involved somewhere along the way, the names including Bill Holman (sax), Jack Sheldon (trumpet), Frank Rosolino, Milt Bernhardt (trombone), Red Mitchell (bass), Pete Jolly (piano), Shelly Manne (drums).

Various

GREAT MOVIE THEMES

Jazz On A Summer's Day

Current CD: 60039 **Release date:** July 1999 **Chart peaks:** None **Track listing:** All Of Me – Dinah Washington; George In Brazil – George Shearing; Sweet Little Sixteen – Chuck Berry; Jimmy And Bobby – Jimmy Giuffre; Sweet Georgia Brown; Tea For Two – Anita O'Day; Thelonious, Henry And Roy – Thelonious Monk; All Night Long – Big Maybelle; Chico's Chiquitas – Chico Hamilton; Everybody's Talkin'; Didn't It Rain, The Lord's Prayer – Mahalia Jackson; Mulligan's Crow – Gerry Mulligan; Muskrat Ramble, Hold That Tiger, Ole Rockin' Chair, When The Saints Go Marching In – Louis Armstrong; Stitt & Sal – Sonny Stitt **Further listening:** Various Artists: Jazz On A Summer's Day (Castle)

The 1958 Newport Jazz Festival provided some of the finest live jazz to emerge on a major film release, with Jimmy Giuffre and Bob Brookmeyer's contrapuntal wonder The Train And River heading a memorable array of music, that included two highly personalised standards by ex-Kenton and Krupa singer Anita O'Day, a predictably edgy Blue Monk from Thelonious Monk, a great tear-'em-up blues delivered by Big Maybelle, and a wealth of other material that had cinema audiences actually applauding the screen. Unfortunately, the sound recording of this particular release is of variable quality and the list of contents pathetic – Tiger Rag is titled Hold That Tiger, Blue Monk becomes Thelonious, Henry And Roy, while the Giuffre-Brookmeyer track is named Jimmy And Bobby and so forth – presumably because the people who released the CD hadn't got a clue about what they were dealing with. Even so, after years with no release at all, this moderately priced issue remains something to be grateful for.

Jerome Moross

UNITED ARTISTS

The Big Country

Current CD: Silva Screen SSD 1048 **Available on video** **Release date:** 1958 **Chart peaks:** None **Track listing:**: Main Title; Julie's House; The Welcoming; Courtin' Time; Old Thunder; The Raid And Capture; Major Terrill's Party Dance Suite: Dance 1, Dance 2, Waltz, Polka; McKay's Ride; McKay Is Missing; The Old House; Waiting; The Big Muddy; McKay Alone; Night At Ladder Ranch; The Fight; Cattle At The River; Attempted Rape; The War Party Gathers; McKay In Blanco Canyon; The Major Alone; The Duel; The Death Of Buck Hannassey; End Title **Further listening:** The Valley Of Gwangi – The Classic Film Music Of Jerome Moross (Silva Screen)

As far as music for the Western was concerned, *The Big Country* changed everything. After Moross fashioned his score there was simply no going back. Bernstein listened and learned. As did numerous others. The thing about Moross' approach was that it really was city music. Mountains equated with skyscapers on a Moross chart. There was Copland in there somewhere but perhaps a touch of Gershwin too, as befitting a composer born in Brooklyn, especially one who, at Gershwin's behest, worked as a pianist in a touring production of Porgy And Bess. His name is rarely among those that readily surface when movie music is discussed today. But Moross is up there among the giants – not bad for a composer who only went to Hollywood to pay the bills.

Luis Bonfa and Antonio Carlos Jobim

VERVE

Black Orpheus

Current CD: 830783-2 **Release date:** 1958 **Chart peaks:** None **Track listing:** Main Title, Manha De Carnival, Macumba Scenes, Drum Schools – Luis Bonfa And Antonio Carlos Jobim; A Felicidade – AC Jobim And V De Moraes: Frevo – AC Jobim; Nosso Amor, Sunrise, A Felicidade, Manha De Carnival; Samba De Orfeo; Bola Seta Medley: And – Luis Bonfa; Samba De Orfeo – Luis Bonfa And A Maria **Further listening:** Antonio Carlos Jobim, AntonioBrasiliero (Sony)

The jazz-samba explosion of the '60s virtually began here. The soundtrack to a film that placed the Orpheus legend in a Rio carnival setting, it captured much attention after the parent movie took the Grand Prize at the Cannes Film Festival of 1959, Bonfa's main themes Samba de Orfeu and Manha de Carnaval (better known as A Day In The Life Of A Fool) and Jobim's A Felicidade becoming the kind of songs that turn up on *Best Of Brazil* compilations with considerable regularity.

Bernard Hermann

MERCURY

Vertigo

Current CD: 422106-2 **Available on video** **Release date:** 1958 **Chart peaks:** None **Track listing:** Prelude And Rooftop; Scotty Trails Madelaine; Carlotta's Portrait; The Bay; By The Fireside; The Forest; The Beach; The Dream; Farewell And The Tower; The Nightmare And Dawn; The Letter; Goodnight And The Park; Scene D'Amour; The Necklace, The Return And The Finale **Further listening:** *Bernard Hermann: The Film Scores* (Sony)

Though *Psycho* is the first Hermann score that anyone recalls – mainly due to the shower-scene shriek – *Vertigo* arguably represents the composer's finest hour. That Hermann and Hitchcock were perfect soulmates, there's no doubt. Sometimes it seemed that the music enhanced the onscreen action while there were moments when such action was only there to provide the score with a focal point. In truth, one would certainly have suffered without the other. Vertigo represented the perfect synthesis – a serpentine plot set against intriguing melodies that remained in the mind as long as the film's memorable twists.

Duke Ellington And His Orchestra

COLUMBIA

Anatomy Of A Murder

Current CD: CK65569 **Available on video** and on US DVD **Release date:** 1959 **Chart peaks:** None **Track listing:** Main Title – Anatomy Of A Murder; Flirtibird; Way Early Subtone; Hero To Zero; Low Key Lightly; Happy Anatomy; Midnight Indigo; Almost Cried; Sunswept Sunday; Grace Valse; Happy Anatomy; Haupe; Upper and Outest **Further listening:** Duke's Paris Blues soundtrack (Rykodisc)

Duke could write for anything – a ballet, a floor show, a church meeting – anything. And his few forays into film were totally rewarding, as exemplified by this score for an Otto Preminger courtroom drama. Though Duke's pieces perfectly fitted the onscreen situations, each of them could be lifted from the score and presented onstage as a showcase for the musicians featured, the main theme eventually acquiring a set of Peggy Lee lyrics to become the much-covered I'm Gonna Go Fishin'. Orchestra featured Clark Terry, Cat Anderson, Shorty Baker, Ray Nance (trumpets), Paul Gonsalves, Jimmy Hamilton, Russell Procope, Johnny Hodges, Harry Carney (reeds).

The Modern Jazz Quartet

UNITED ARTISTS

Odds Against Tomorrow

Current CD: Blue Note CDP 7 93415-2 **Available on video** **Release date:** 1959 **Chart peaks:** None **Track listing:** Skating In Central Park; No Happiness For Slater; A Social Call; Cue No.9; A Cold Wind Is Blowing; Odds Against Tomorrow **Further listening:** Django, the MJQ's second album and the one that established the group as a world-beater. Not a soundtrack, though the gorgeous title track turned up in the Dutch short Gyromorphosis and doubtless elsewhere.

John Lewis, the MJQ's pianist, had fashioned scores for two films, No Sun In Venice and a United Nations short, before turning his talents to this thriller involving a compulsive gambler who hooks up with some unlikely allies in order to rob a bank. On the original studio soundtrack the MJQ, with Lewis' piano and Milt Jackson's vibes to the fore, were heard in settings provided by a 23-piece orchestra and coloured by contributions from a guitarist, harpist and cellist, though the sprightly Cue No.9 came untarnished, being a piece heard on a bar-room jukebox. A Social Call was fleshed out for quartet performance on disc, the original piece in the film being a piano solo. Like many soundtracks, this release is not entirely what tantalised ears in the cinema. Even so, it rates among the MJQ's best albums.

André Previn

MGM

Elmer Gantry

Current CD: Rykodisc RCD 10732 **Available on video** **Release date:** 1960 **Chart peaks:** None **Track listing:** Main Title; Long Distance; Mr Babbitt; Lulu's Room; Do You Believe?; Under The Pier; Shall We Gather At The River?; Kiss Me Goodbye; Stand Up For Jesus; Elmer and Lulu; End Title; Orchestral Suite; Onward Christian Soldiers; I'm On My Way – Burt Lancaster **Further listening:** Original soundtrack The Subterraneans (Signature/Sony Special Products)

Previn doesn't always make it easy – only rewarding. Sheer Americana's at the base of things – like Aaron Copland in dissonant mode. It fits well with the storyline of a man turned preacher who leaves a trail of ruined lives in his wake. There's old-time jazz, dance-band, some revival fare and, as one of the bonus tracks on the CD – Burt Lancaster's pivotal rendering of Mahalia Jackson's I'm On My Way. Some rate this as Previn's finest.

Henry Mancini

RCA

Breakfast At Tiffany's

Current CD: 743216987782 **Available on video** **Release date:** September 1961 **Chart peaks:** None **Tracks:** Moon River; Something For Cat; Sally's Tomato; Mr Yunioshi; The Big Blow-Out; Hub Caps And Tail Lights; Breakfast At Tiffany's; Latin Golightly; Holly; Loose Caboose; The Big Heist; Moon River Cha Cha **Further listening:** The soundtrack to Charade, a Mancini score much in Breakfast At Tiffany's mould.

Much of this score is unashamedly romantic, string-laden with vocal sounds oooh-ed in best Mancini cocktail fashion. But Something For Cat is pretty good for Hollywood mambo, Sally's Tomato a relaxed slice of Latin jazz and Latin Golightly shaped as the amiable kind of thing that inspired Audrey Hepburn – cast indelibly as the dotty Holly Golightly – to write to Mancini and thank him for providing a score that contained "so much imagination, fun and beauty". It won both Best Score and Best Song (Moon River) for Mancini at the 1962 Oscars, Moon River providing lyricist Johnny Mercer with the sobriquet "Huckleberry Friend" for the rest of his life.

Cliff Richard

EMI

The Young Ones

Currently unavailable on CD **Available on video** **Release date:** December 1961 **Chart peaks:** 1 (UK) None (US) **Track listing:** Friday Night; Just Dance – ABS Orchestra And The Mike Sammes Singers; Got A Funny Feeling, The Young Ones, Lessons In Love, We Say Yeah – Cliff Richard And The Shadows; Peace Pipe, The Savage – The Shadows; Nothing's Impossible – Cliff Richard And Grazina Frame; All For One – Cliff Richard And The Mike Sammes Singers: No One For Me But Nicky – Grazina Frame; What D'You Know We've Got A Show And Vaudeville Routine, Have A Smile For Everyone You Meet, Tinkle, Tinkle, Tinkle, The Eccentric, Algy The Piccadilly Johnny, Captain Ginjah, What D'You Know We've Got A Show, Living Doll, When The Girl In Your Arms Is The Girl In Your Heart – Cliff Richard; Mood Mambo – ABS Orchestra **Further listening:** Cliff Richard Summer Holiday, the follow-up musical – again a three-hit wonder.

Hailed by critics at the time as "the best musical that Britain has ever made" (which can only have upset Jesse Matthews), Cliff Richard's third feature film was proclaimed by its distributors "the first film ever to have three hits in the Top 10". That the plot – a "let's do the show right here" variant – was tissue-thin hardly mattered. Everything was handled with youthful enthusiasm and teen was the name of the game, even if, in fact, it amounted to not much more than good old family entertainment, right down to the inclusion of musichall songs. Important, nevertheless.

Original Film Cast

CBS

West Side Story

Current CD: Sony 467506-2 **Available on video and DVD** **Release date:** March 1962 **Chart peaks:** 1 (UK) 1 (US) **Track listing:** Prologue; Jet Song; Something's Coming; Dance At The Gym; Maria; America; Tonight; Gee Officer Krupke; I Feel Pretty; One Hand One Heart; Quintet; The Rumble; Cool; A Boy Like That; I Have A Love; Somewhere (Reprise) **Further listening:** Stan Kenton's West Side Story, a powerhouse big band's interpretation of the score.

Arguably the greatest of all Broadway musicals and one that spanned generations, appealing to both My Fair Lady ravers and those who merely raved. Link Wray's Rumble was named after the West Side Story track, while even today, tracks such as Cool inspire would-be-trendy TV ads. Fashioned by writers Leonard Bernstein and then up-and-coming Stephen Sondheim in a 15 sq ft room that looked out on a airshaft, this relocation of Romeo and Juliet to the tenements of New York, ran for over 700 performances in New York and over 1,000 in London, but it was the film soundtrack that proved ultra-sensational in terms of sales, remaining in the UK charts for 154 weeks. Not bad for a musical that contained songs discarded from an earlier show (Candide) and onscreen featured only one member of the stage cast, Russ Tamblyn, who actually sang, the rest of the voices being provided by studio session singers.

Billy May

MGM

Johnny Cool

Current CD: Rykodisc RCD 10744 **Release date:** January 1964 **Chart peaks:** None **Track listing:** The Lizard; Window Washer; Dare's Affair; Borrow A Knife; Johnny Cool Theme; Morning In Balboa's; Nice Quiet Saloon; Green Tables Blues; The Coolest Pad; Juan Coolisto; Bee Boom, The Ballad Of Johnny Cool – Sammy Davis **Further listening:** Billy May, Sorta May/Sorta Dixie (Creative World)

The writer of TV's Naked City theme, arranger with Glenn Miller, Frank Sinatra, Peggy Lee, Nat Cole and many others, the trumpet-playing Billy May had little opportunity to provide a full score for motion pictures. But Johnny Cool, a gangster flick which had strong Rat Pack connections – it was produced by Peter Lawford, starred Sammy Davis and featured such other Sinatra hangarounds as Joey Bishop and Henry Silva – provided the ebullient music-maker the chance to create a big-band score that expressed his outgoing personality. Oddly, amid all the roaring riffs, high-flying trumpet solos and suchlike, it's tracks like the lightly-swinging Morning In Balboa's and Nice Quiet Saloon – half-Shearing, half-Neal Hefti stylistically – that impress most. Sammy Davis is provided with two spots to demonstrate his vocal prowess, the best being Bee Bom, which owes its all to the British TV theme for Gurney Slade, a series that starred Anthony Newley, whose songs Davis always admired.

John Barry

UNITED ARTISTS

Goldfinger

Current CD: EMI Premier CZ 557 **Available on video and DVD** **Release date:** October 1964 **Chart peaks:** 14 (UK) 1 (US) **Track listing:** Teasing The Korean; Main Title; Alpine Drive; Auric's Factory; Oddjob's Pressing Engagement; Bond Back In Action Again; Gassing The Gangsters; Goldfinger (instrumental version); Dawn Raid On Fort Knox; Arrival Of The Bomb And Countdown; Death Of Goldfinger; End Titles **Further listening;** John Barry Diamonds Are Forever soundtrack (EMI Premier); Themeology: The Best Of John Barry (Sony).

The two previous James Bond soundtracks had only achieved moderate sales but the advent of *Goldfinger* aptly resulted in gold records. "It was the first time that I was allowed to do the theme song and the entire score," explained composer John Barry.

Lyric-wise help came from singer-actor Anthony Newley who recorded a demo of the Goldfinger theme – though this remained unreleased until 1992. Instead, Shirley Bassey was brought in to provide an ultra-dramatic rendering of the all-important song which would not only establish Bond as an important factor in terms of music sales but also provide the Welsh diva with her only major US hit. Barry, of course, would go on to compose some of the most evocative and enduring film themes of the age.

Henry Mancini

RCA

The Pink Panther

Current CD: BMG Camden 74321 660472 **Available on video** **Release date:** 1964 **Chart peaks:** None **Track listing:** The Pink Panther Theme; It Had Better Be Tonight (instrumental); Royal Blue; Champagne And Quail; The Village Inn; The Tiber Twist; It Had Better Be Tonight (vocal); Cortina; The Lonely Princess; Something For Sellers; Piano And Strings; Shades of Sennett **Further listening:** Henry Mancini The Blues And The Beat (RCA)

The Pink Panther theme is probably one of the most well-known aural ID cards of all. Thanks to its use in a long-running cartoon series, everybody over the age of four can hum it and relate it to a dubious pink cat. Which is all a bit crazy considering the Pink Panther was really the name of a jewel in the original film. Apart from the famous theme, the soundtrack is filled with the tuneful throwaways that Mancini always seemed to have up his sleeve for comedy epics, one, It Had Better Be Tonight, eventually making its way into the songbooks of various easy-listening troubadours.

The Camden issue now comes as part of a two-on-one, which also features the score to The Return Of The Pink Panther.

Elmer Bernstein
RYKODISC

The Magnificent Seven

Current CD: RCD 10741 **Available on video** **Release date:** 1999 (the first Magnificent Seven soundtrack on United Artists was not what it purported to be. It contained only the main theme plus 11 other tracks not from the film) **Chart peaks:** None **Track listing:** The Magnificent Seven; Council; Quest; Strange Funeral – After The Brawl; Vin's Luck; And Then There Were Two; Fiesta; Stalking; Worst Shot; The Journey; Toro; Training; Calvera's Return; Calvera Routed; Ambush; Petra's Declaration; Bernardo; Surprise; Defeat; Crossroads; Harry's Mistake; Calvera Killed; Finale **Further listening:** The Great Escape (Intrada), another, quite different bundle of Bernstein, but one that reiterates the composer's way with a main theme – in this instance a sprightly march.

Again, it's that main theme that almost anyone can hum, a gorgeous, stirring affair that, like some of Aaron Copland's work, evokes the spirit of the West (all right, so the film's set in Mexico) and conjures visions of mountains, canyons and dusty trails. But that's not the whole *tamale*, for this score covers all the bases, with flamenco-inflected themes rubbing shoulders with blaring action moments to form a satisfying album without the listener wondering what the hell was going on onscreen.

Various Artists
EMI

Ferry Cross The Mersey

Current CD: 7243 8 56567-2 **Release date:** January 1965 **Chart peaks:** 19 (UK) 12 (US) **Track listing:** It's Gonna Be All Right, Why Oh Why, Fall In Love, Think About Love, This Thing Called Love, Baby You're So Good To Me, I'll Wait For You, She's The Only Girl For Me, Ferry Cross The Mersey – Gerry And The Pacemakers; All Quiet On The Mersey Front – George Martin Orchestra; Is It Love? – Cilla Black; I Love You Too – The Fourmost **Further listening:** Catch Us If You Can (aka Having A Wild Weekend) a soundtrack from a John Boorman film set amid Brit-Beat scene of 1965 and featuring the Dave Clark Five.

The first feature film to be set in Liverpool in the wake of Merseybeat, Ferry Cross The Mersey proved to an enjoyable experience for those into views of such landmarks as the Cavern Club and the Locarno Ballroom. Cast as a band competing in a European beat contest, The Pacemakers looked and sounded fine, Gerry Marsden obviously relishing the task of providing the band's material, writing nine songs in eight days, the nostalgic title number proving the pick of the bunch. But not all the material performed in the film made it onto record, the missing tracks being The Black Knights' I Got A Woman, Earl Royce And The Olympics' Shake A Tail Feather and The Blackwells' Why Don't You Love Me? The US version of the album differed from that released in Britain, while the CD edition that appeared in 1997 contained all the tracks from the original album in mono and stereo.

Burt Bacharach

UNITED ARTISTS

What's New Pussycat?

Current CD: Rykodisc RCD 10740 **Available on video** **Release date:** August 1965 **Chart peaks:** None (UK) 14 (US) **Track listing:** What's New Pussycat? – Tom Jones; My Little Red Book – Manfred Mann; Here I Am – Dionne Warwick; School For Anatomy/Bookworm, High Temperature, Low Resistance; Downhill And Sandy, Stripping Really Isn't Sexy, Is It?, Marriage French Style, Pussy Cats On Parade, A Walk On The Wild Wharf, Chateau Chantel, Catch As Catch Can – Burt Bacharach **Further listening:** Burt Bacharach, Make It Easy OnYourself (A&M)

The weirdo waltz that comprises the title song revealed immediately that nothing normal was going on in Bacharach-land, thanks probably to an involvement in a film that was Woody Allen's first feature as an actor and writer. But if nutty sounds were required, then, at least in the '60s, nobody did it better. So there's a cool jazz waltz in High Temperature, some real bluesville in Downhill And Shady, a kazoo-headed march that answers to the name of A Walk On The Wild Wharf and, well, a miscellany of sounds that are both loveable and laughable – in a nice way.

Elmer Bernstein

MGM

Walk On The Wild Side

Current CD: Mainstream MDCD 604 **Release date:** 1966 **Chart peaks:** None **Track listing:** Walk On The Wild Side; Somewhere In The Used To Be; Hallie's Jazz; Rejected; Doll House; Teresina; Night Theme; Walk On The Wild Side Jazz; Furnished Room; Kitty; Oliver; Comfort Southern; Finale **Further listening:** Baby The Rain Must Fall (Mainstream), a fine example of lesser-known Bernstein.

Again, a main theme that's been around and managed to stay the course, remaining as invigorating and compelling as it did when Bernstein (with a little help from an onscreen prowling cat) first employed it as the intro to the film about life in easy-come, easy-go bars and pleasure-houses of 1930s New Orleans. There's some attractive string-laden themes – Somewhere In The Used To Be proving a melody for a song waiting to happen – while Teresina is pure *cantina* music – but it's the riff-happy jazzier themes that allow Bernstein's array of superb but uncredited West Coast MU members to strut out. The Mainstream release – the first-ever CD version of the score – also features five bonus tracks from other Bernstein film ventures.

Quincy Jones

MGM

In The Heat Of The Night

Current CD: Rykodisc RCD 10712 **Available on video**. **Release date:** August 1967 **Chart peaks:** None **Track listing:** In The Heat Of The Night – Ray Charles; Peep-Freak Patrol Car, Cotton Curtain; Where Whitey Ain't Around; Whipping Boy; No You Won't; Keep Cool*; Nitty Gritty Time; It Sure Is Groovy – Gil Bernal; Bowlegged Polly – Glen Campbell; That's Enough For Me*; Shag Bag, Hounds And Harvey; Chief's Drive To Mayor; Give Me Until Morning; The Wrong Man*; On Your Feet Boy; Blood And Roots; Mama Caleba's Blues – Ray Charles; Foul Owl – Boomer And Travis; Mister Tibbs* (*Dialogue) **Further listening:** Such Quincy scores as The Hot Rock, The Pawnbroker, Dollars, etc.

The film's theme, rendered throatily by Ray Charles over the opening credits, augured well. The South, racial oppression, the weariness of the fight for equality, were all wrapped up in that musical sequence. All that remained was for Sidney Poitier, memorable as black detective Virgil Tibbs, to solve a murder despite resentment from all round. The Norman Jewison-directed classic deserved an equally meritorious score, which is what Quincy Jones provided. The band is terrific. Roland Kirk squawks, moans and screams on flute. Billy Preston contributes funky organ, while the rest of the stellar line-up – the listing includes Bobby Scott (p), Ray Brown (b), Don Elliott (t, mellophone) and Carol Kaye (b) – all play as though they're up for individual Oscars. In the event, no black contributor won an award. Quincy missed out on Hollywood's score plaudits and even Poitier failed to lift an Oscar – Rod Steiger, cast as an initially bigoted police chief, won everything in sight. Rykodisc's CD version is superb, with extra tracks, enhanced CD visuals and even Quincy's complete score to They Call Me Mr Tibbs, the mildly disappointing sequel.

Various Artists

ISLAND

Here We Go Round The Mulberry Bush

Current CD: Rykodisc RCD 10717 **Release date:** December 1967 **Chart peaks:** None **Track listing:** Virginal's Dream, Waltz For Caroline, Possession, Looking Back, Every Little Thing, Taking Out Time, Pictures Of Her, Just Like Me – The Spencer Davis Group; Utterly Simple, I Am What I Was Or What I Am, Here We Go Round The Mulberry Bush – Traffic; It's Been A Long Time – Andy Ellison **Further listening:** Smiling Phases, the definitive Traffic compilation.

Newtown Mod seemed a very desirable subject to film during the '60s. Especially in this instance, when director Clive Donner was available and Hunter Davies was providing a screenplay. So Stevenage and mini-skirts provided something to view onscreen while two of the hottest bands in the universe, one which Stevie Winwood had just quit (The Spencer Davis Group) and the one he'd just joined (Traffic) provided the kind of sounds that matched the young actors' psychedelic shirts. Time was when it was very unhip not to have a copy stuck under your arm.

Various Artists — MGM

Blow Up

Current CD: Turner Classics 8 52280 2 **Release date:** 1967 **Chart peaks:** None **Track listing:** Main Title, Verushka, The Naked Camera, Bring Down The Birds, Jane's Theme, The Thief, The Kiss, Curiosity, Thomas Studies Photos, The Bed, End Title – Herbie Hancock; Stroll On – The Yardbirds; Am I Glad To See You, Blow Up – Tomorrow **Further listening:** Tonite Let's All Make Love In London. Same place, same time but with Pink Floyd, The Small Faces and Chris Farlowe.

Antonioni's brilliantly observed study of Swinging '60s London gained a soul-jazz soundtrack worthy of its cinematography through Herbie Hancock, then known primarily as a former Miles Davis sideman. The director hoped to entice the Velvet Underground to London to appear in the club scene. Then hot psych up-and-comers Tomorrow were duly commissioned and recorded. But even they failed to make it to the final print. The Yardbirds, with Jeff Beck on guitar, eventually grabbed a meagre few minutes of onscreen fame.

Burt Bacharach — RCA VICTOR

Casino Royale

Varese Sarabande VSD 5265 **Available on video** **Release date:** 1967 **Chart peaks:** 35 (UK) 22 (US) **Track listing:** Casino Royale Theme – Herb Alpert And The Tijuana Brass; The Look Of Love – Dusty Springfield; Money Penny Goes For Broke, LeChiffre's Torture Of The Mind, Home James, Don't Spare The Horses, Sir James' Trip To Find Maya, The Look Of Love, Hi There Miss Goodthighs, Little French Boy, Flying Saucer: First Stop Berlin, The Venerable Sir James Bond, Dream On James, We're Winning, The Big Cowboys And Indians Fight At Casino Royale – Burt Bacharach **Further listening:** Burt Bacharach, What's New Pussycat? (Rykodisc)

A different kind of 007. Bonkers Bond in fact. And Bacharach's score reflected the daftness of a plot peopled by various Bonds and would-be world dominator Woody Allen. Actually, Bacharach was not as comfortable with the demands of film-scoring as one might imagine and there were some heated exchanges about the editing of his music. Even so, everything is totally melodic, the theme is as chirpy as they come and Look Of Love remains as gorgeous as it was on the day it was nominated for an Oscar.

Johnny Williams/André And Dory Previn — PHILLIPS

The Valley Of The Dolls

Current CD: 3145368762 **Available on video** **Release date:** January 1968 **Chart peaks:** None (UK) 11 (US) **Track listing:** Theme From The Valley Of The Dolls; It's Impossible; Ann At Lawrenceville; Chance Meeting; Neeley's Career Montage; Come Live With Me – Tony Scott; I'll Plant My Own Trees; The Gillian Girl Commercial; Jennifer's French Movie; Give A Little More; Jennifer's Recollection; Theme From The Valley Of The Dolls (Reprise) **Further listening:** André Previn, Goodbye Charlie (20th Century Fox)

The soundtrack was pieced together when André and Dory Previn were working as a team and writing pop songs worthy of the Brill Building pairings. The theme itself was one of those things that everyone insists Bacharach wrote, purely because (a) it sounded that way, and (b) Dionne Warwick recorded it and notched a hit that went to Number 2 in the US charts, remaining in that spot for four weeks in a row. Come Live With Me is another fine song, as is It's Impossible, while Chance Meeting pans out as a choice soft samba. Pity about the film. But the sleeve's decorative enough.

Ennio Morricone

UNITED ARTISTS

The Good, The Bad And The Ugly

Current CD: EMI-Manhattan 748408-2 **Available on video** **Release date:** February 1968 **Chart peaks:** 2 (UK) 4 (US) **Track listing:** The Good, The Bad And The Ugly; The Sundown; The Strong; The Desert; The Carriage Of The Spirits; Marcia; The Story Of The Soldier; Marcia Without Hop; The Death Of A Soldier; The Ecstasy Of Gold; The Trio (Main Title) **Further listening:** Ennio Morricone, *A Fistful Of Dollars/For A Few Dollars More* (Camden) There are literally hundreds of excellent Morricone scores and several good compilations of his most famous themes. Try *Anthology: A Fistful Of Film Music* (Rykodisc)

The best of Morricone's spaghetti western scores, an evocative aural landscape that reflects both the awe and the desolation of the desert setting to the third part of Sergio Leone's Dollars triology. Unique at the time, Morricone's sound, fashioned from an array of unorthodox instruments, was later seized upon by lesser talents attempting to make cactus interesting and has become clichéd.

Manfred Mann

HMV

Up The Junction

Current CD: RPM 189 **Release date:** May 1968 **Chart peaks:** None **Track listing:** Up The Junction (vocal); Sing Songs Of Love; Walking Round; Up The Junction (instrumental); Love Theme (instrumental); Up The Junction; Just For Me; Sheila's Dance; Belgravia; Wailing Horn; I Need Your Love **Further listening:** Manfred Mann, Soul Of Mann (EMI), a collection of instrumentals by the band.

Another film that defined '60s London, Up The Junction may have been a somewhat glossy reworking of Nell Dunn's controversial semi-documentary TV play about working-class life in Clapham. Even so, it still pulled few punches and part of its continuing appeal lies in the fact that Manfred Mann and Mike Hugg shaped a very fine score to accompany the onscreen shenanigans of Dennis Waterman, Suzy Kendall and co. with touches of pop, psychedelia, and jazz. The Mann band only appeared *in toto* on the title track, while Sing Songs Of Love was actually performed by Cherry Smash, a band headed by Mike Hugg's brother. Manfred would also fashion a score for a lesser-known soft-porn film Swedish Fly Girls. But we won't go into that here!

Various Artists

CAPITOL/SIDEWALK

Psych-Out

Currently unavailable on CD **Available on video** **Release date:** June 1968 **Chart peaks:** None **Track listing:** The Pretty Song From Psych-Out, Psycho-Out Sanctorum, Beads Of Innocence, The Love Children, Psych-Out – The Storybook; Rainy Day Mushroom Pillow, The World's On Fire, The World's On Fire (Long Version) – Strawberry Alarm Clock; Two Fingers Pointing At You – The Seeds; Ashbury Wednesday – Boenzee Cryque **Further listening:** The Trip (Edsel), another dose of LSD on a silver platter.

Though the soundtrack achieved virtually zilch in terms of cash registers, it did register a musical vote on behalf of San Francisco's hippy generation. The film itself dealt with the activities of a teenage girl who travelled to 'Frisco to seek her brother who had become a religious fanatic. Needed was a series of sounds that related to the hallucinogenic experiences of those involved and bands such as Strawberry Alarm Clock and The Seeds proved ideal choices to convey the smell of incense and tripped-out goings-on.

Quincy Jones
PARAMOUNT

The Italian Job

Currently unavailable on CD **Available on video** **Release date:** October 1969 **Chart peaks:** None **Track listing:** On Days Like These – Matt Monro; Something's Cookin'; Hello Mrs Beckerman; Brittania and Mr Bridger; If You Please; Trouble For Charlie; On Days Like These; It's Caper Time; The Italian Job; Meanwhile Back At The Mafia; Smell That Gold; Greensleeves And All That Jazz; Get A Bloomin' Move On **Further listening:** Sonny Rollins Alfie original soundtrack (Impulse)

The most in-demand cult album of recent years, at the time of writing, *The Italian Job* has never been reissued on CD, though a vinyl version appeared on the Bande Sonore label some time ago. For a film that's extremely British in content and feel, it's surprising that Quincy Jones was responsible for the soundtrack. But maybe it was a trend at the time, for US jazzman Sonny Rollins was brought in to provide the score for Alfie, another Michael Caine classic that had "made in Britain" stamped all over it. Even so, The Italian Job boasts a highly likeable, diverse score, easing in with Matt Monro's ultra-smooth version of On Days Like These, a song Q co-wrote with British lyricist Don Black, hitting the funk button on It's Caper Time and, best of all, introducing the joyously daft singalong Get A Bloomin' Move On, which virtually everyone in the UK knows and loves as The Self Preservation Society.

Michel Legrand
MGM

The Thomas Crown Affair

Current CD: Rykodisc RCD 10719 **Available on video and DVD** **Release date:** December 1968 **Chart peaks:** None **Track listing:** Whose Head Are You After; Room Service; Think You'll Get Me?; A Man's Castle; Chess; The Chess Game; Cash And Carry; His Eyes, Her Eyes (vocal version); Playing The Field; Something Else; Moments Of Love; The Boston Wrangler; Doubting Thomas; Please Come With The Money; The Crowning Touch; Theme From The Thomas Crown Affair; His Eyes, Her Eyes: Theme From The Thomas Crown Affair (The Windmills Of Your Mind) – Noel Harrison **Further listening:** Michel Legrand, Michel Plays Legrand (Laserlight)

Romance? Legrand can do romance. Witness the lush sounds he concocted for some of his early French films. So he knew what to do when scoring his first American film, on the surface a caper movie but basically a love affair between Steve McQueen and Faye Dunaway with a robbery attached. Okay, so everyone hones in on The Windmills of Your Mind, with its naive, but charm-filled vocal by Rex Harrison's son Noel. But there was more to this Affair than that. The music that set the scene for the camera-circled chess game was superb, ripe with sensual promise befitting the moment when Dunaway suggestively caresses the head of her bishop! Then there's Legrand the singer, scatting his way through Cash And Carry and providing his own romantic thing on His Eyes Her Eyes. Jazz. Playing The Field is an apt demonstration of what the composer learnt in New York studying the ways of Miles and Coltrane. Bud Shank's the altoist. But who is that incredible bassist?

Lalo Schifrin

WARNER BROTHERS

Bullitt

Current CD: 9362-45008-2 **Available on video** **Release date:** 1968 **Chart peaks:** None **Track listing:** Bullitt (Main Title); Room 26; Hotel Daniels; The Aftermath Of Love; Music To Interrogate By; On The Way To San Mateo; Ice Pick Mike; A Song ForCathy; Shifting Gears; Cantata For Combo; The First Snowfall; Bullitt (End Title) **Further listening:** Cool Hand Luke (MCA Japan) a Schifrin score that was good enough for Academy Award nomination.

Ex-Dizzy Gillespie keyboardist Schifrin produced a score befitting a movie that's best recalled for it's hills-of-San Francisco car chase. Accordingly, the music comes generally jazzy and high-octane, though such tracks as dotty boogaloo Music To Interrogate By and the sophisticated trombone-led amble Aftermath Of Love ensure that nothing's one-dimensional. And if the array of top-flight musicians (Howard Roberts – guitar, Bud Shank – flute, Mike Melvoin – piano, Ray Brown – bass, Milt Bernhart – trombone, Larry Bunker – drums etc.) sometimes emerge with things mildly Latin, then that's to be expected. After all, Schifrin was born in Argentina.

The Association

WARNER BROTHERS

Goodbye Columbus

Current CD: WPCR 10195 **Available on video** **Release date:** May 1969 **Chart peaks:** None **Track listing:** Goodbye Columbus; It's Gotta Be Real; So Kind To Me: Goodbye Columbus (instrumental version); How Will I Know You – Charles Fox; Dartmouth/Dartmouth; A Moment To Share; Love Has A Way; A Time For Love; Ron's Reverie **Further listening:** The Association's Greatest Hits (Warner Bros)

A soundtrack akin to The Graduate – just a modicum of fine originals from a strong '60s harmony group amid an array of instrumental tracks. Fox's score bears many similarities to Burt Bacharach in its use of quirky melodies. Only Ron's Reverie, an Ohio University chorale piece that comes linked to dialogue relating to the resident football squad detracts from the overall appeal.

Various Artists

UNITED ARTISTS

Midnight Cowboy

Current CD: EMI PRMCD 6 **Release date:** August 1969 **Chart peaks:** (UK) None (US) 19 **Tracks:** Joe Buck Rides Again, Fun City, Midnight Cowboy, Florida Fantasy, Science Fiction – John Barry: Everybody's Talkin' – Harry Nilsson (S); Old Man Willow; Jungle Gym At The Zoo – Elephant's Memory; Tears And Joys, A Famous Myth – The Groop; He Quit Me – Leslie Miller **Further listening:** Cinderella Liberty (20th Century), a John Williams soundtrack filled to the gills with the gorgeous sound of Toots Thielmans.

Memories of John Schlesinger's film about a Texan hustler who believes he can find easy pickings by selling his body around New York come permanently affixed to Nilsson's version of Fred Neil's Everybody's Talkin'. But the soundtrack is good throughout, from the yearning harmonica of Barry's title theme, played by jazz genius Toots Thielmans to the chunk of rhythmic sunshine known as Florida Fantasy, once utilised as a TV sporting theme.

Various Artists

STATESIDE

Easy Rider

Current CD: MCA MCLD 19153 **Available on video and DVD** **Release date:** September 1969 **Chart peaks:** 2 (UK) 6 (US) **Track listing:** The Pusher, Born To Be Wild – Steppenwolf; Kyrie Eleison Mardi Gras – Electric Prunes; I Wasn't Born To Follow, The Ballad Of Easy Rider – The Byrds; I Wasn't Born To Follow – Roger McGuinn; If You Want To Be A Bird – Holy Modal Rounders; The Weight – A Band Called Smith; Don't Bogart Me – Fraternity Of Man; If Six Was Nine – Jimi Hendrix Experience **Further listening:** The Byrds, Ballad Of Easy Rider (Columbia)

It's difficult to describe the impact that Easy Rider had when it first made it into a small London West End cinema which remained packed-out for weeks once the word got around. The first thing that patrons did after viewing was head for the record shops to look for a soundtrack album. Eventually they arrived in droves. The Road Movie to end all Road Movies, Easy Rider also contained the ultimate road music, the ease-on-down I Wasn't Born To Follow allied to the ton-up thrills of Born To Be Wild. Additionally, there were a couple of tunes for getting high to. Only the fact that The Band's original version of The Weight couldn't be used on the record marred things. Otherwise this was a memorable use of material originally recorded for other reasons. God Bless Captain America. And so say all of us.

Arlo Guthrie

WARNER BROTHERS

Alice's Restaurant

Current CD: Ryko RCD 10737 **Available on video** (US) **Release date:** October 1969 **Check peaks:** None **Track listing:** Travelling Music; Alice's Restaurant Massacre; The Let Down; Songs To Aging Children – Tigger Outlaw; Amazing Grace; Trip To The City; Crash Pad Improvs; You're A Fink – Al Schackman; Harps and Marriage **Further listening:** Arlo (Rising Son), another Guthrie album from the same period and one that contains his classic but equally dotty Motorcycle Song.

Unbelievably, the film was based around a song that began as a jingle for a hippy-owned restaurant that somehow acquired a life of its own when Woody's son added a considerable amount of verbiage concerning dumping garbage, police interest in such activities and Arlo's eventual encounter with the draft board. Both the film and soundtrack, which contains a version of the title song that runs for over 15 minutes, caught the imagination of the Easy Rider generation. Today, it seems too hippy-dippy to be allowed out on its own. But once it seemed important – which is why it's here. The Ryko issue contains additional material to the UA original, predominantly three tracks featuring Pete Seeger, along with the original 25-second Alice's Restaurant radio commercial.

Burt Bacharach

A&M

Butch Cassidy And The Sundance Kid

Current CD: 393 159-2 **Available on video** **Release date:** November 1969 **Chart peaks:** None (UK) 16 (US) **Track listing:** The Sundance Kid; Raindrops Keep Falling On My Head – BJ Thomas; South American Getaway; Raindrops Keep Falling On My Head; On A Bicycle Built For Joy – BJ Thomas; Come Touch The Sun; The Old Fun City; Not Goin' Home Anymore (Reprise) **Further listening:** Bacharach's soundtrack Lost Horizon, a musical panned by the world's movie pundits but one that nevertheless contains its fill of the composer's quirky songs.

Many soundtracks are merely incidental fare, melodic cushions for onscreen action. But Bacharach's Butch Cassidy score is far more than that; the opening track's a pure joy, an offbeat, out-of-kilter tango for sophisticates, then there's the Swingle-styled mainly 6/8 of South American Getaway, with its equally unexpected tempo switches, the rooty-toot sax of Old Fun City and the ever-sunny, ukelele-driven bit of hokum, Raindrops Keep Falling On My Head, a track for which BJ Thomas will ever be grateful.

Roy Budd

Get Carter

Current CD: Cinephile CIN CD 001 **Available on video** **Release date:** 1998 **Chart peaks:** None **Track listing:** Intro; Carter Takes A Train; Looking For Someone; Something On My Mind; Getting Nowhere In A Hurry; The Girl In The Car; Love Is A Four-Letter Word; Livin' Should Be This Way; Manhunt; Goodbye Eric; Goodbye Carter; Hallucinations; Plaything; How About You **Further listening:** The Italian Job, another in-demand, Caine-connected soundtrack.

It can be argued that soundtracks to Michael Caine films of the '60s and early '70s achieve a certain patina of desirability merely because they evoke memories of Caine at his sharpest, dealing with dolly birds, ruminating with Russians, or surrounded by a zillion bloodthirsty Zulus. All of which is true. Even so, keyboardist Budd's score to Get Carter makes it on its own terms via sounds that veer from pop gospel (Looking For Someone) and organ-ized 4am blues (Something On My Mind) to almost psychedelic soul (Livin' Should Be That Way). "Roy Budd's finest hour" suggests the insert note. A lot of people know that.

Various Artists

UNITED ARTISTS

Zabriskie Point

Current CD: Turner Classics R2 72462 **Available on video** **Release date:** March 1970 **Chart peaks:** None **Track listing:** Heart Beat Pig Meat, Come In Number 51, Your Time Is Up, Crumbling Land – Pink Floyd; Brother Mary, Mickey's Tune – The Kaleidoscope; Dark Star (Excerpt) – The Grateful Dead; Tennessee Waltz – Patti Page; Dance Of Death – John Fahey; I Wish I Was A Single Girl Again – Roscoe Holcomb; Love Scene – Jerry Garcia; Sugar Babe – The Youngbloods **Further listening:** Pink Floyd, Obscured By Clouds (Harvest)

Antonioni's successor to Blow Up was to have been the director's crowning triumph – a study of the new age of America, with youth at the helm, destroying all that had gone before and seeking fresh freedoms. Easy Rider with that added ingredient, maybe. A vast canvas affair, with Death Valley as the main star, it sported a soundtrack culled from both "borrowed" and previously unheard material by an oddball collection of artists, ranging from a song by easy-listening queen Patti Page, through to The Grateful Dead, who are heard via a brief clip of concert material. The main attraction of the soundtrack, however, was Pink Floyd's involvement, which is even more in evidence on the Turner Classics reissue, which includes a bonus disc featuring not only several improvisations by Jerry Garcia but also Country Song by the Floyd, along with an unnamed piece by the band and two additional versions of Love Scene (one a blues jam, the other a slice of piano-lounge jazz) – part of the complete score that Pink Floyd originally penned for the movie. A fascinating document.

Various Artists

UNITED ARTISTS

The Landlord

Currently unavailable on CD **Release date:** August 1970 **Chart peaks:** None **Track listing:** Brand New Day, The Axe, Love Theme, Lainie's Theme, Elgar's Fantasy, Walter G's Boogaloo – Al Kooper; Brand New Day, God Bless The Children – Staple Singers; Doin' Me Dirty, Let Me Love You – Lorraine Ellison; Rent Party – Joe Farrell; Soul Hoedown, The Landlord – The Landlords; Croquet Game – Manny Green **Further listening:** Al Kooper, Act Like Nothing's Wrong (One Way)

A flop for director Hal Ashby, the film, about a rich man's son who buys a ghetto tenement and then develops a conscience, at least boasted a solid soundtrack. Dylan sidekick and Blood Sweat & Tears founder Al Kooper roped in some of the singers he loved most (The Staples and Lorraine Ellison) along with a classy rhythm section, Chuck Rainey (bass), Paul Griffin (keyboards), Eric Gale (guitar) and Bernard Purdie (drums) and then took it from there. The music was penned in a bungalow that would later house John Belushi on the last night of his life. The sleeve featured a picture of two doorbells arranged in a curiously erotic way . . . or is that just me?

Various Artists

ATLANTIC

Woodstock

Current CD: 260001 **Available on video** in an extended director's cut **Release date:** August 1970 **Chart peaks:** 35 (UK) 1 (US) **Track listing:** I Had A Dream, Rainbows All Over Your Blues – John B Sebastian; Going Up The Country – Canned Heat; Freedom – Richie Havens; Rock And Soul Music, The Fish Cheer, I-Feel-Like-I'm-A-Fixin'-To-Die-Rag – Country Joe And The Fish; Coming Into Los Angeles – Arlo Guthrie; At The Hop – Sha-Na-Na; Drug Store Truck Drivin' Man, Joe Hil – Joan Baez; Suite, Judy Blue Eyes – Crosby, Stills And Nash; Sea Of Madness, Wooden Ships – Crosby, Stills, Nash And Young; We're Not Gonna Take It – The Who; With A Little Help From My Friends – Joe Cocker; Soul Sacrifice – Santana; I'm Going Home – Ten Years After; Volunteers – Jefferson Airplane; Medley – Dance To The Music, Music Lover, I Want To Take You Higher – Sly And The Family Stone; Star Spangled Banner, Purple Haze, Instrumental Solo – Jimi Hendrix **Further listening;** Woodstock Two (Atlantic) – tracks that didn't make it onto the original album, including some by Mountain, Melanie and The Butterfield Blues Band.

Maybe it wasn't the greatest festival ever – but it's still the one that most MOJO readers will think of first. Country Joe never had it so good, Ten Years After never played it so long and Santana never played it so unknown. Pick your own favourite moment – there are plenty to choose from. Then give a thought to acts like Bert Sommer, who never made it onto disc. Or Procol Harum, who turned down the chance to play there. Most of the rest became huge stars, not least because this sprawling set actually topped the US album charts.

Various Artists

WARNER BROTHERS

Performance

Current CD: 7599-26400-2 **Release date:** September 1970 **Chart peaks:** None **Track listing:** Gone Dead Train – Randy Newman; Performance, Poor White Hound Dog – Merry Clayton; Get Away, Powis Square – Ry Cooder; Rolls Royce And Acid, Natural Magic, Harry Flowers – Jack Nitzsche; The Hashishin – Buffy Sainte-Marie And Ry Cooder; Dyed Dead Red – Buffy Saint-Marie; Memo From Turner – Mick Jagger; Wake Up Niggers – The Last Poets; Turner's Murder – Merry Clayton Singers **Further listening:** One Flew Over The Cuckoo's Nest, a rewarding Nitzsche score.

During the late '60s Jagger was involved in the production of several soundtracks – Invocation Of My Demon Brother, Ned Kelly, Gimme Shelter etc. He also produced a single, Sister Morphine, for Marianne Faithfull, which featured contributions by Nitzsche and Cooder. All of which slotted in alongside his work for Donald Cammell and Nicholas Roeg's creepy masterpiece Performance. Nitzsche wrote and arranged most of the music on display, with Randy Newman conducting. Which, on reflection, doesn't seem a bad combination.

Booker T Jones

STAX

Up Tight

Current CD: 29667 08242 **Release date:** 1970 **Chart peaks:** None **Track listing:** Johnny I Love You; Cleveland Now; Children Don't Get Away – Judy Clay; Tank's Lament; Blues In The Gutter; We've Got Johnny Wells; Down At Ralph's Joint; Deadwood Dick; Run Tank Run; Time Is Tight **Further listening:** Green Onions (Atlantic) by Booker T & The MGs, an album headed by one of the most-heard singles in soundtrack history – memorably in American Graffiti but proving equally rewarding in at least two dozen other Hollywood productions.

Surprise, surprise, the album opens with a Booker T blues-ballad vocal. And it's good enough to make you wonder why he'd never got around to creating a vocal album up to that point. Then, his band, The MGs were the kind of unit that sounded so superb instrumentally that the lack of larynx never really mattered. Here again, Jones (keyboards), and his cohorts Duck Dunn (bass), Steve Cropper (guitar) and Al Jackson Jr (drums) provide an array of sounds that illustrate why they were never out of work during Stax's heyday. The film, a ghetto-set remake of John Ford's The Informer, with black militants depping for the IRA, was okay, but it's the soundtrack that's really lasted the course, with Time Is Tight (which also forms part of Tank's Lament) forever being utilised on other multi-artist soundtracks and TV ads.

Various Artists

Vanishing Point

Not available on CD **Available on video** **Release date:** June 1971 **Chart peaks:** None **Track listing:** Super Soul Theme, Freedom Of Expression -The JB Pickers; The Girl Done Got It Together – Bobby Doyle; Where Do We Go From Here – Jimmy Walker; Welcome To Nevada – Jerry Reed; Over Me, Dear Jesus God – Segarini And Bishop; You Got To Believe – Delaney And Bonnie; Love Theme – Jimmy Bowen Orchestra; So Tired – Eve; Mississippi Queen – Mountain; Sing Out For Jesus – Big Mama Thornton; Nobody Knows – Kim And Dave **Further listening:** Electra Glide In Blue (UA) another early '70s soundtrack covered in tarmac.

A road movie about a car-delivery man racing across America and attempting to avoid police traps, it featured a soundtrack of music mainly played by Stevie Wonder look-alike DJ Super Soul (portrayed by Cleavon Little). An amalgam of country, heavy rock, gospel and funk, it somehow worked, though neither the film nor the soundtrack managed to emulate the success of Easy Rider, which was probably the whole point of the exercise.

Isaac Hayes

STAX

Shaft

Current CD: CDSXD 021 **Available on video** **Release date:** August 1971 **Chart peaks:** 17 (UK) 1 (US) **Track listing:** Theme From Shaft; Bumpy's Lament; Walk From Regio's; Ellie's Love Theme; Shaft's Cab Ride; Caf? Regio's; Early Sunday Morning; Be Yourself; A Friend's Place; Soulsville; No Name Bar; Bumpy's Blues; Shaft Strikes Again; Do Your Thing; The End Theme **Further listening:** *Tough Guys; Truck Turner* (Stax) double helping of other Hayes soundtracks

Though Sweet Sweetback's Baaadassss Song sparked the superfly genre, it was Shaft that not only followed up but also cleaned up, thanks in part to Hayes' breathtakingly funky theme. The double-album soundtrack, released by Stax, became the fastest-selling album in the label's history. The Theme single sold a million in virtually no time at all. And, come Oscar time, Sammy Davis introduced "My man, Isaac Hayes, to sing his nominated theme song from Shaft." When the awards came up, Hayes became the first black man to win the Best Song category, giving thanks to his grandmother: "In a few days it'll be her eightieth birthday and this is her present."

Various Artists
CBS

The Strawberry Statement

Current CD: Sony AT 52419 **Release date:** 1971 **Chart peaks:** None **Track listing:** The Circle Game – Buffy Saint-Marie; Our House, Helpless, Long Time Gone – Crosby, Stills, Nash & Young; Something In The Air – Thunderclap Newman; Fishin' Blues – Red Mountain Jug Band; Down By The River, The Loner – Neil Young; Cyclatron, Coit Tower, Concerto In D Minor, Pocket Band – Ian Freebairn-Smith And The MGM Studio Orchestra; Also Sprach Zarathustra – Karl Bohn And The Berlin Philharmonic Orchestra; Give Peace A Chance – The Cast Of The Film **Further listening:** Kent State (RCA) the soundtrack to a TV documentary spanning a similar area.

The backdrop to a dramatised version of Columbia University's student riots. A great sense of period seeps from the music. Jan Stacy and Ryder Syvertsen's book Rockin' Reels observes: "This documents a unique time in college life when it was fun to go to college. The music and the period have never been equalled." Certainly worth owning for some vintage Neil Young and a couple of classics from the period in Something In The Air and Our House, if not for the ultra-corny Fishin' Blues, on which kazoo, washboard and banjo rule.

Various Artists
WARNER BROTHERS

A Clockwork Orange

Current CD: 7599-27256-2 **Available on video** **Release date:** February 1972 **Chart peaks:** 4 (UK) 34 (US) **Track listing:** Title Music From A Clockwork Orange – Walter Carlos; The Thieving Magpie; Theme From A Clockwork Orange – Walter Carlos; Beethoven's Ninth Symphony: Second Movement; March From A Clockwork Orange – Walter Carlos; William Tell Overture; Pomp And Circumstance March No.1; Pomp And Circumstance March No. IV; Timesteps – Walter Carlos; Overture To The Sun; I Want To Marry A Lighthouse Keeper – Erika Eigen; Suicide Scherzo – Walter Carlos; Beethoven's Ninth Symphony: Fourth Movement; Singing In The Rain – Gene Kelly **Further listening:** Wendy Carlos, Switched On Bach (Sony)

There was a time, albeit brief, during the late '60s and early '70s, when classical music and rock joined hands without either losing ground. The advent of Walter Carlos' electronic explorations via his Switched On Bach album and Charisma's admirable Classical Heads release best exemplified the trend. That Carlos (later reborn as Wendy Carlos) should turn his attention to A Clockwork Orange, Stanley Kubrick's still-controversial creation, made the soundtrack one of the year's great musical events, his Moog movie mode perhaps working best on the re-creation of the fourth movement from Beethoven's Ninth, with its near-psychedelic aura.

Curtis Mayfield
BUDDAH

Superfly

Current CD: Charly CPCD 8039 **Available on video** **Release date:** July 1972 **Chart peaks:** 26 (UK) 1 (US) **Track listing:** Little Child Runnin' Wild; Pusherman; Freddie's Dead; Junkie Chase; Give Me Your Love; Eddie You Should Know Better; No Thing On Me (Cocaine Song); Think; Superfly **Further listening:** Short Eyes (Charly), Curtis, Mayfield's first No.1 solo album. Across 110th Street (Ace), Bobby Womack's excellent venture into soundtracks.

Mayfield's vocally superb throughout, while songs such as Pusherman and Freddie's Dead tell you most of the things you need to know about the horrors that follow in the path of drug addiction. From the first black movie to be entirely financed by black producers – even though BANG (Blacks Against Narcotic Genocide) picketed cinemas screening the film, claiming that it glorified drug dealing.

Various Artists
ISLAND

The Harder They Come

Current CD: RRCD 11 **Available on video** **Release date:** September 1972 **Chart peaks:** None **Track listing:** You Can Get It If You Really Want, Many Rivers To Cross, The Harder They Come, Sitting In Limbo – Jimmy Cliff; Draw Your Brakes – Scotty; Rivers Of Babylon – Melodians; Johnny Too Bad – The Slickers; Pressure Drop – The Maytals; Shanty Town – Desmond Dekker **Further listening:** *The Best Of Jimmy Cliff* (Island)

Music from the first Jamaican feature film, in which Jimmy Cliff, almost typecast, portrayed a young singer who heads for a career in Kingston, Jamaica only to become involved in music-biz rip-offs and a battle against authority. His songs boast a commercial and artistic quality that would only be matched later by peak-period Bob Marley.

Nino Rota
MCA

The Godfather

Current CD: MCLD 19022 **Available on video** **Release date:** 1972 **Chart peaks:** None (UK) 21 (US) **Track listing:** Main Title (The Godfather Waltz); I Have But One Heart; The Pickup; Connie's Wedding; The Halls Of Fear; Love Theme From The Godfather; Appollonia; The New Godfather; The Baptism; The Godfather Finale **Further listening:** Nino Rota, Amarcord and A Tribute To Fellini (Rykodisc)

Again, it's one of those unshakable themes. Mention The Godfather to any film buff and the mandolin-strummed love theme immediately accompanies any memory of the movie that comes to mind. Not only buffs. There can hardly be anyone in the world, at least among those who watch TV re-runs, who doesn't connect with Rota's music. In truth, much of the music is simplicity itself, the evocative main theme (The Godfather Waltz) with its lonesome trumpet somehow proving atmospheric enough to sell the onscreen visuals in the manner intended. There are one or two other things around – the neatly crooned non-Rota song I Have But One Heart, plus Carmine Coppola's music for the wedding scene – and even if the listener feels short-changed – the original album only runs to 32 minutes – there's no denying that Rota's score is impressive. Unfortunately, it wasn't impressive enough for those who hand out Oscars. After Nino Rota received the plaudit for The Godfather II score in 1974, he was asked to return the award when someone pointed out that the composer had employed some of the self-same music for earlier Italian movies.

Ennio Morricone
RCA

Once Upon A Time In The West

Current CD: 74321 61976 2 **Available on video** **Release date:** 1972 **Chart peaks:** None **Track listing:** Once Upon A Time In The West; As A Judgement; Farewell To Cheyenne; The Transgression; The First Tavern; The Second Tavern; Man With A Harmonica; A Dimly Lit Room; Bad Orchestra; The Man; Jill's America; Death Rattle; Finale **Further listening:** Ennio Morricone, Anthology: A Fistful Of Film Music (Rykodisc)

Morricone made his name through music to Westerns. But nothing he did – not even The Good, The Bad And The Ugly – encompassed the scope and imagination of his score to Sergio Leone's sprawling epic set in Monument Valley. From the soothing yet uplifting main theme through to the edgier, haunting Man With A Harmonica, Morricone delivers music that is more than mere background throughout.

Marvin Gaye

MOTOWN

Trouble Man

Current CD: 5308842 **Release date:** December 1972 **Chart peaks:** None (UK) 14 (US) **Track listing:** Main Theme From Trouble Man; T Plays It Cool; Poor Abbey Walsh; The Break-In (Police Shoot Big); Cleo's Apartment; Trouble Man; Theme From Trouble Man; T Stands For Trouble; Life Is A Gamble; Deep-In-It; Don't Mess With Mister T; There Goes Mister T **Further listening:** Marvin Gaye, What's Going On (Motown)

It was Gaye's jazz album – the move he'd wanted to make for years. One of only two albums on which he wrote everything himself, it was, by necessity, virtually an instrumental outing, with Marvin's keyboards at the helm, the main support stemming from Trevor Lawrence's alto, tenor and baritone sax playing. A whole army of arrangers and orchestrators was ferried in to provide all the right sounds – JJ Johnson, Gene Page, Dale Oehler, Jerry Long, James Carmichael, Jack Hayes and Leo Shuken. Little was left to chance. There was just one song – Trouble Man – and that was a hit. Swinging, urban, pulsating with life, it still sounds vital. "My favourite work," Gaye claimed at one point. Understandable.

Various Artists

MCA

American Graffiti

Current CD: MCLDD19150 **Available on video** **Release date;** May 1973 **Chart peaks:** 37 (UK) 10 (US) **Track listing:** (We're Gonna) Rock Around The Clock – Bill Haley And The Comets; Sixteen Candles – The Crests; Runaway – Del Shannon; Why Do Fools Fall In Love ? – Frankie Lymon And The Teenagers; That'll Be The Day, Maybe Baby – Buddy Holly; Fannie Mae – Buster Brown; At The Hop, She's So Fine – Flash Cadillac And The Continental Kids; The Stroll, Little Darlin' – The Diamonds; See You In September – The Tempo's; Surfin' Safari – The Beach Boys; The Great Imposter – The Fleetwoods; Almost Grown, Johnny B Goode – Chuck Berry; Smoke Gets In Your Eyes, The Great Pretender – The Platters; Peppermint Twist – Joey Dee And The Starlighters; Barbara Ann – The Regents; Book Of Love – The Monotones; YaYa – Lee Dorsey; Ain't That A Shame – Fats Domino; I Only Have Eyes For You – The Flamingos; Get A Job – The Silhouettes; To The Aisle – The Five Satins; Do You Wanna Dance? – Bobby Freeman; Party Doll – Buddy Knox; Come Go With Me – The Del-Vikings; You're Sixteen – Johnny Burnette; Love Potion No.9 – The Clovers; Since I Don't Have You – The Skyliners; Chantilly Lace – The Big Bopper; Teen Angel – Mark Dinning; Crying In The Chapel – Sonny Til And The Orioles; A Thousand Miles Away – The Heartbeats; Heart And Soul – The Cleftones; Green Onions – Booker T And The MGs; Well It's Time To Go – The Spaniels; All Summer Long – The Beach Boys **Further listening:** More American Graffiti (MCA)

A Francis Ford Coppola production with direction from George Lucas, it was the rock'n'roll film that had everything – high-school hops, Saturday-night cruising, a giant jukeboxful of the best that early rock could supply, plus a guest spot from Wolfman Jack. Soundtrack-wise the result was unbeatable, only the lack of an Elvis track detracting from the feeling that the buyer need never purchase a pre-Beatles rock compilation ever again.

James Brown

POLYDOR

Black Caesar

Current CD: 5171352 **Release date:** June 1973 **Chart peaks:** None **Track listing:** Down And Out In New York City; Blind Man Can See It; Sportin' Life; Dirty Harri; The Boss; Make It Good To Yourself; Mama Feelgood; Mama's Dead; White Lightning (I Mean Moonshine); Chase; Like It Is, Like It Was **Further listening:** Slaughter's Big Rip Off (Polydor) another portion of funky sounds for big screen consumption fashioned by Brown.

A mildly less-violent-than-usual blaxploitation flick (a final scene depicting Fred Williamson getting kicked to death was cut just before release), this one featured a strong score fashioned by the self-styled Godfather Of Soul plus Fred Wesley, singer Lynn Collins chipping in a torrid Mama Feelgood with the help of the JB's. And it's not all pure funk, James emoting in best rip-your-heart-out fashion on Mama's Dead: "I wish I had made her proud to call me son." He's good at that kind of thang.

George Martin

EMI

Live And Let Die

Current CD: EMI Premier CZ553 **Available on video** **Release date:** September 1973 **Chart peaks:** None (UK) 17 (US) **Track listing:** Bond Meets Solitaire, Whisper Who Dares, Snakes Alive, Baron Samedi's Dance Of Death, San Monique – George Martin; New Orleans, Harlem – Fillet Of Soul; Bond Drops In, If He Finds It, Kill Him, Trespassers Will Be Eaten, Solitaire Gets Her Cards, Sacrifice, James Bond Theme (Composed By Monty Norman): Live And Let Die – Paul McCartney & Wings; Live And Let Die – BJ Arnau; Just A Closer Walk With Thee – Harold A "Duke" Dejan & The Olympia Brass Band; New Second Line **Further listening:** George Martin: In My Life (EMI)

One of the more adventurous Bond soundtracks, thanks to the Beatle connection. Martin's backdrop is fine, original and exciting, with The Olympia Brass Band adding a New Orleans marching-band flavour to the proceedings. But the hit theme by McCartney nearly never made it as a Wings track. When George Martin played it to Harry Saltzmann, the film producer thought it was merely a demo and suggested that it should be performed by Thelma Houston.

Various Artists

UNITED ARTISTS

Electra Glide In Blue

Currently unavailable on CD **Release date:** 1973 **Chart peaks:** None **Track listing:** Most Of All – The Marcels; Meadow Mountain Top, Song Of Sad Bottles – Mark Spoelstra; Free From The Devil – Madura; Morning/Prelude, Overture, Jolene's Dance, The Chase, Monument Valley, Tell Me – James William Guerico. **Further listening:** Chicago Transit Authority (Columbia)

The film was about a short cop who was long on brainpower. "Did you know that me and Alan Ladd were exactly the same height?" he was pictured claiming on the original front sleeve, he being Robert Blake, one-time star of the Baretta TV series. That gatefold sleeve was quite a deal, containing a six-foot Electra Glide poster and a 24-page book with scenes from the film. Most of the music came courtesy of Chicago's producer James Guerico, his association with the band being underlined by the cast line-up, which included Chicago members Peter Cetera, Bob Zemko and Terry Kath, the latter plus trombonist James Pankow and saxophonist Walter Parazaider also being employed on the soundtrack alongside a full orchestra that features such names as Larry Carlton, Paul Beaver, Conti Condoli and other top-raters. Madura are heard in concert, delivering a thrash boogie. Forgotten Elektra folky Mark Spoelstra emerges with a couple of songs while The Marcels track is the obligatory oldie.

Slade

POLYDOR

Slade In Flame

Current CD: 8491822 **Available on video** **Release date:** November 1974 **Chart peaks:** (UK) 6 (US) None **Track listing:** Standin' On The Corner; Them Kinda Monkeys Can't Swing; How Does It Feel?; Far Far Away; OK Yesterday Was Yesterday; This Girl; Heaven Knows; Summer Song (Wishing You Were Here); So Far So Good; Lay It Down **Further listening:** Feel The Noize – The Very Best Of Slade (Polydor)

Look at it this way. Noddy Holder had one of the best rock voices in the country and, over the years, things Slade have become more valuable, more highly regarded – and not just at Christmas-time. So it's not unreasonable that *Slade In Flame* has acquired a more pleasing patina over the years, and, in many ways, sounds better now than it did when the band were seemingly fighting off such pretenders as the Bay City Rollers. Summer Song still sounds the kind of thing that British beach parties should be made of, How Does It Feel? is solo Holder at his most Lennonesque, Far Far Away remains an ever-amiable amble while Them Kinda Monkeys Can't Swing almost predicts the coming of punk. Yes, years on, this has become one of the good 'uns. Even the slightly creaky movie looks charming from this distance.

The Staple Singers

STAX

Let's Do It Again

Currently unavailable on CD **Release date:** 1975 **Chart peaks:** None (UK) 20 (US) **Track listing:** Let's Do It Again; Funky Love; A Whole Lot Of Love; New Orleans; I Want To Thank You; Big Mac; After Sex; Chase **Further listening:** The Staple Singers: Beatitude – Respect Yourself (Stax)

Let's Do It Again was a later, more humourous example of the blaxploitation genre, the dotty plot involving Sidney Poitier and Bill Cosby's attempt to raise money for a church fund by hypnotising a boxer. Happily, the music was in excellent hands, Curtis Mayfield's tunes, arranged by Rich Tufo and Gil Askey, arriving superglued to the vocals of The Staple Singers. A situation that never did a songwriter any harm. As the title tune's US chart position confirmed.

Bernard Hermann

ARISTA

Taxi Driver

Current CD: 07822-19005-2 **Available on video and DVD** **Release date:** August 1976 **Chart peaks:** None Tracks: Main Title; Thank God For The Rain; Cleaning The Cab; I Still Can't Sleep; They Cannot Touch Her; Phone Call; I Realise How Much She Is Like The Others; Strange Customer; Watching Palantine On TV; You're Gonna Die In Hell; Betsy's Theme; Hitting The Girl; 44 Magnum Is A Monster; Getting Into Shape; Listen You Screwheads; Gun Play; Dear Father And Mother; Card Soap Opera; Sport And Iris; $20 Bill; Target Practice; Assassination Attempt; After The Carnage; Reluctant Hero; Betsy; End Credits **Further listening:** Original soundtrack to the 1991 version of Cape Fear (MCA) another Hermann/DeNiro linking, albeit Hermann's music is arranged and conducted by Elmer Bernstein.

Veteran composer Hermann completed this, his final score, on the very day he died. A brooding, sometimes jazz-tinged affair, Hermann's music terminates with the famous scream chord from Psycho, perhaps equating the violent rampaging of DeNiro's psychotic New York cab driver with the motel madness of Norman Bates. The track listing is that of the re-mastered version of the soundtrack, which appeared during the late '90s and is vastly different from – and superior to – that originally issued by Arista.

Rose Royce

MCA

Car Wash

Current CD: MCD 11502 **Available on video** **Release date:** November 1976 **Chart peaks:** 59 (UK) 14 (US) **Track listing:** Car Wash; Zig Zag; Water; Doin' What Comes Naturally; I'm Going Down; Put Your Money Where Your Mouth Is; I Wanna Get Next To You; Daddy Rich; Yo Yo; Sunrise; You Gotta Believe – Pointer Sisters **Further listening:** The soundtrack to Cooley High (Motown) another Michael Schultz film made around the same time.

You can imagine the pitch: "I wanna do a movie about black kids goofing off at a car wash!"

"NEXT!!!"

But, as occasionally happens, the most unlikely ingredients turned the movie and its soundtrack into a smash. In fact, this was one of the first times where a hit single actually promoted the film, rather than the other way round. The music, written and produced by the irascible, but hugely gifted Norman Whitfield, is slickly funky but, as with all his work, inventive and witty too. Rose Royce (not the name of the singer by the way, that was Gwen Dickey) were a fine act who deserve more acclaim than they've been given by music chroniclers, as, in fact does Whitfield. The film, on the other hand, isn't much cop.

Bill Conti

LIBERTY

Rocky

Current CD: Silva Screen 460812 **Available on video and DVD** **Release date:** April 1977 **Chart peaks:** None (UK) 4 (US) Tracks: Philadelphia Morning; Going The Distance; Reflections; Marine's Hymn; Yankee Doodle; First Date; Fanfare For Rocky; Butkis; Alone In The Ring; The Final Bell; Rocky's Reward; Take You Back – Valentine; You Take My Heart Away – Deetta Little And Nelson Pigford; Gonna Fly Now (Theme From Rocky) – Bill Conti **Further listening:** Rocky 3 (EMI) which contains Survivor's Eye Of The Tiger hit.

Like Vangelis' theme to Chariots Of Fire, Bill Conti's We're Gonna Fly has become something of an anthem, forever linked to scenes of sporting triumph. The rest of the score too is generally "up", paying deference to the achievement of Rocky Balboa, the boxer from nowhere who, in film after film, would overturn all odds to become an improbable world champion.

Tangerine Dream

MCA

The Sorcerer

Currently unavailable on CD **Release date:** June 1977 **Chart peaks:** 25 (UK) None (US) **Track listing:** Main Title; Search; The Call; Creation; Vengeance; The Journey; Grind; Rain Forest; Abyss; The Mountain Road; Impressions Of Sorcerer; Betrayal (Sorcerer Theme) **Further listening:** Tangerine Dream's Phaedra (Virgin)

Edgar Froese, Peter Baumann and Christoph Franke who comprised Tangerine Dream at the time of recording, never viewed the remake of Clouzot's classic The Wages Of Fear before emerging with a score. What was presented, after a reading of the script, was merely an impression of what might have happened onscreen. Not that director William Friedkin minded. He'd loved the trio's super-ambient *Phaedra* album and just wanted more of the same. Which is how things turned out, the results launching the Dream on a highly lucrative career as musical backdrop providers on such films as Wavelength, Risky Business, Miracle Mile, Rainbow Drive and countless others.

Various Artists

RSO

Saturday Night Fever

Current CD: Polydor 8000682 **Available on video** **Release date:** November 1977 **Chart peaks:** 1 (UK) 1 (US) **Track listing:** Stayin' Alive, How Deep Is Your Love, Jive Talkin', Night Fever, More Than A Woman, You Should Be Dancing – The Bee Gees; K-Jee – M.F.S.B.; Calypso Breakdown – Ralph McDonald; Disco Inferno – The Trammps; Boogie Shoes – KC And The Sunshine Band; More Than A Woman – Tavares; If I Can't Have You – Yvonne Elliman; Manhattan Skyline, Night On Disco Mountain, Salsation – David Shire; A Fifth Of Beethoven – Walter Murphy; Open Sesame – Kool & The Gang **Further listening:** Tales From The Brothers Gibb (Polydor)

The success of the film was really down to three things – the Bee Gees, disco and images of John Travolta, either strutting down the sidewalk or making like a '70s Valentino on the dance floor, all sex and energy. The soundtrack simply had to sell and did. Originally released in double-album form, it spawned hit singles, including three consecutive US Number 1s for the Bee Gees, a total that would be expanded to six, when the trio released such non-soundtrack material as Too Much Heaven, Tragedy and Love You Inside Out. When Yvonne Elliman's If I Can't Have You also topped the charts, it meant that that four Number 1s had emanated from the soundtrack, an unprecedented feat that may never be repeated. A Grammy winner as 1978's Album Of The Year.

John Williams

20TH CENTURY FOX

Star Wars

Current CD: VCD4720 (reissued with The Empire Strikes Back and Return Of The Jedi) **Available on video and DVD** **Release Date:** November 1977 **Chart peak:** 21 (UK) 2 (UK) **Track listing:** Princess Leia's Theme; The Millennium Falcon; Imperial Cruise Pursuit; Destruction of Alderaan; The Death Star – The Stormtroopers; Wookie Prisoner; Detention Black Ambush; Shootout In The Cell Bay; Dianoga; The Trash Compactor; The Tractor Beam; Chasm Crossfire; Ben Kenobi's Death; The Fighter Attack; The Battle Of Yavin – Launch from The Fourth Moon; X-Wings Draw Fire; Use The Force; The Throne Room; End Title **Further listening:** Schindler's List: The Classic Film Music Of John Williams (Silva Screen)

There can hardly be a moviegoer, either here or in a galaxy far away, who hasn't heard John Williams' Star Wars theme. There was even a disco hit version by Meco. And if the rest of the score doesn't rate whistling by milkmen, it is, nevertheless, hugely impressive, like a kind of hip Holst. Such elements as The Fighter Attack and the Death Star battle music proving edge-of-the-seat stuff even devoid of the visuals.

The Band

WARNER BROTHERS

The Last Waltz

Current CD: 7599273462 **Available on video** **Release date:** March 1978 **Chart peaks:** None **Track listing:** Theme From The Last Waltz; Up On Cripple Creek; Stagefright; It Makes No Difference; The Night They Drove Old Dixie Down; Shape I'm In; Orphelia; Life Is A Carnival; The Well; The Last Waltz Refrain; Theme From The Last Waltz; Who Do You Love – Ronnie Hawkins; Helpless – Neil Young And Joni Mitchell; Coyote – Joni Mitchell And Dr John; Such A Night – Dr John; Mystery Train – Paul Butterfield; Mystery Train – Muddy Waters; Further On Up The Road – Eric Clapton; Down South In New Orleans – Bobby Charles And Dr John; Tura Lura Lura (That's An Irish Lullaby), Caravan – Van Morrison; Baby Let Me Follow You Down; I Don't Believe You (She Acts Like We Have Never Met); Forever Young; Baby Let Me Follow You Down (Reprise) – Bob Dylan; I Shall Be Released – Bob Dylan, Neil Young, Joni Mitchell, Ronnie Hawkins, Dr John, Neil Diamond, Paul Butterfield, Bobby Charles, Eric Clapton, Ringo Starr, Ron Wood And Van Morrison: Evangeline – The Band With Emmylou Harris; The Weight – The Band And The Staples Singers **Further listening:** The Band: Music From Big Pink (Capitol)

The film, mainly shot at The Band's farewell show, held at Bill Graham's Winterland, San Francisco on Thanksgiving Day, 1976, featured an engrossing array of music by one of the hottest cast lists ever to be assembled. Everyone was on form, providing a soundtrack that undoubtedly had director Martin Scorsese rubbing his hands with glee, The Band's summit with the Staples (actually filmed and recorded on an MGM sound stage) on The Weight is a fittingly memorable closer to this triple LP set, and The Band's career in its original incarnation.

Popol Vuh

EGG

Nosferatu

Currently unavailable on CD **Release date:** November 1978 **Chart peaks:** None **Track listing:** Mantra 1; Morning Sun Rays; Venus Principle; Mantra II; On The Way; Through Pains To Heaven II; To A Little Way; Zwiesprache Der Rohrfloete Mit Der Saengerin; Die Nacht Der Himmel; Der Ruf Der Rohrfloete **Further listening:** Popol Vuh's soundtrack Aguirre, The Wrath Of God, another Herzog creation.

Nothing keyboardist Florian Frick ever produced has been less than interesting, which is why director Werner Herzog employed his band Popol Vuh on his visionary view of the Dracula story. Ethereal beauty, minimalist electronic sounds, folksy acoustic sorties, Eastern drones and misty chants, as befitting a band that took its name from the Mayan Book of the Dawn Of Life.

Various Artists

VIRGIN

Jubilee

Current CD: Editions EG CD 34 **Release date:** 1978 **Chart peaks:** None **Track listing:** Deutscher Girls – Adam And The Ants; Plastic Surgery, ParanoiaParadise – Wayne County And The Electric Chairs; Right To Work – Chelsea; Nine To Five – Maneaters; Rule Britannia, Jerusalem – Suzi Pinns; In Pornotopia – Amilcar Wargasm; Slow Water/Dover Beach – Brian Eno **Further listening:** Brian Eno: Music For Films (penned for hypothetical films though some of the music was used in Jarman productions).

No, the music to this Derek Jarman cult hit hardly rates soundtrack Valhalla status. Nevertheless, as the first real punk score and one that has remained in print for a considerable number of years, the album deserves its position in this listing. Adam Ant's Deutscher Girls has aged tremendously well and now sounds like a kitsch killer, while Chelsea's Right To Work chant is one of those tracks that you always imagine was an indie chart hit until a check through the listings proves otherwise. Those seeking the more ethereal are ably catered for by Eno's minimalistic but often engaging backdrop sounds.

Various Artists
SIRE

Banjoman

Currently unavailable on CD **Release date:** February 1979 **Chart peaks:** None **Track listing:** Lonesome Ruben, T For Texas, Foggy Mountain Breakdown – The Earl Scruggs Revue; Battle Of New Orleans, Diggy Liggy Lo – The Nitty Gritty Dirt Band; You Ain't Goin' Nowhere, The Night They Drove Old Dixie Down, Blowin' In The Wind – Joan Baez; Roll Over Beethoven, Mr Tambourine Man – The Byrds; Freight Train Boogie, Black Mountain Rag – Doc And Merle Watson; Me And Bobby McGee – Ramblin' Jack Elliott **Further listening:** Earl Scruggs: Family And Friends (Columbia) a TV show soundtrack on which the friends prove to be Bob Dylan, Joan Baez and The Byrds **Further reading:** Earl Scruggs And The 5-String Banjo (Earl Scruggs, 1980)

The film wasn't all that wonderful – an uninspired tribute to banjoist Earl Scruggs that came kitted out with concert clips and interviews. But the music documented the best in the kind of country music that appealed to the youth of the period. Even then, not all the music allocated screen time could be fitted into the confines of the single album, several songs being omitted, including all the contributions by Mother Earth, Tracy Nelson and David Bromberg. To date, the album, which sported a sleeve designed by Dean O Torrence (of Jan and Dean fame) has not been reissued on CD in either the US or Europe.

Various Artists
CHRYSALIS

Babylon

Currently unavailable on CD **Available on video** **Release date:** October 1980 **Chart peaks:** None **Track listing:** Deliver Me From My Enemies, Free Africa – Yubby U; Turn Me Loose – Michael Prophet; Whap'n Bap'n – I-Roy; Thank You For The Many Things You've Done – Cassandra; Hey Jah Children, Warrior Charge – Aswad; Beefy's Tune/Manhunter/Jazterpiece – Dennis Bovell **Further listening:** Aswad Live And Direct (Island)

Originally intended as a BBC TV play but shelved as being too inflammatory, Babylon starred Aswad guitarist Brinsley Forde as a young Brixton-based Jamaican encountering various pressures as he and friends attempt to win a London sound-system contest. Bovell's score is superb, as is most of the other music, Aswad's Hey Jah Children an engaging slice of dub, while their instrumental Warrior Charge is something of a jazz-reggae milestone.

Vangelis
POLYDOR

Chariots Of Fire

Current CD: 825 384 **Available on video** Release date; March 1981 **Chart peaks:** 5 (UK) 1 (US) **Track listing:** Titles; Five Circles; Abraham's Theme; Eric's Theme; 100 Metres; Jerusalem; Chariots of Fire; Jerusalem – Ambrosian Singers **Further listening;** Vangelis, Themes (Polydor)

As far as TV producers are concerned no one can participate in athletics anymore without being accompanied by the sound of Vangelis. In some ways the initial concept for this ground-breaking score was completely wrong and shouldn't have made it beyond the starter's pistol: synth music? For a film about the Olympics set in the early '20s? But the ploy worked brilliantly, the main title proved to be one of those mind worms that lodge in the brain forever and when the Oscars were handed out at LA's Dorothy Chandler Pavilion in March, 1982, it was this Greek composer who picked up the Original Score award.

Tom Waits And Crystal Gayle
CBS

One From The Heart

Current CD: Sony 467609-2 **Release date:** February 1983 **Chart peaks:** None **Track listing:** Opening Montage: Tom's Piano Intro/Once Upon A Time/ The Wages Of Love; Is There Any Way Out Of This Dream?; Picking Up After You; Old Boyfriends; Broken Bicycles; I Beg Your Pardon; Little Boy Blue; Instrumental Montage: The Tango/Circus Girl; You Can't Unring A Bell; This One's From The Heart; Take Me Home; Presents **Further listening:** Tom Waits The Asylum Years (Asylum)

A Coppola fantasy set in a brightly lit but cardboard Las Vegas. It was an expensive flop that bankrupted him and is not held in particularly high-esteem these days, but at least the soundtrack has proved enduring. It's Waits doing his wee-small-hours jazz thing (pretty much for the last time, as it turned out), with Crystal Gayle in nightclub-diva mode. All the songs are penned by Waits. Little Boy Blue is a heated Hammond stomp, with Waits leering wonderfully over the top. I Beg Your Pardon presents the unshaven hero in romantic guise, with altoist Teddy Edwards and the world's most underrated jazz trumpet player, Jack Sheldon in support. Broken Bicycles is a moving, nostalgic lament. Huddled together, as they are on Picking Up After You and the title song, the unlikely pairing of Waits and Gayle sound unbeatable. A fine release with nary a spare note or dud track in sight.

Ryuichi Sakamoto
VIRGIN

Merry Christmas Mr Lawrence

Current CD: CDV 2276 **Release date:** October 1983 **Chart peaks:** 36 (UK) None (US) **Track listing:** Merry Christmas Mr Lawrence; Batavia; Germination; A Hearty Breakfast; Before The War; The Seed And The Sower; A Brief Encounter; Ride Ride Ride (Celliers' Brother's Song); The Fight; Father Christmas; Dismissed; Assembly; Beyond Reason; Sowing The Seed; 23rd Psalm; Last Regrets; Ride Ride Ride (Reprise); The Seed; Forbidden Colours – David Sylvian **Further listening:** Ryuichi Sakamoto, Snowflakes Are Falling (RCA)

Bowie's most wooden screen hour (actually two), this dismal movie did boast a wonderfully textured score by Sakamoto, an Easternised answer to Vangelis' Chariots Of Fire score. The insistent title theme would, unfortunately, be converted into a disco hit (Heart Of Asia) by Watergate in 2000.

Various Artists

CBS

Footloose

Current CD: 4930072 **Available on video** **Release date:** January 1984 **Chart peaks:** 7 (UK) 1 (US) **Track listing:** Footloose, I'm Free (Heaven Helps The Man) – Kenny Loggins; Dancing In The Sheets – Shalamar; Let's Hear It For The Boy – Deneice Williams; Almost Paradise – Mike Reno And Ann Wilson; Holding Out For A Hero – Bonnie Tyler; The Girl Gets Around – Sammy Hagar; Somebody's Eyes – Karla Bonoff **Further listening:** Kenny Loggins, Yesterday, Today, Tomorrow: The Greatest Hits (Columbia)

Footloose was a remarkable display of synergism – the action of fitting the right film to the right music for public consumption, then marketing it in a way that utilises both movie and music. Dean Pitchford, who readied the film's screenplay, claimed the score was "a rock video in reverse – the idea being to mould the music to the visual images." From 47 possible tracks, nine were chosen. Rarely was a soundtrack so calculated, so aimed at the charts. Right from the opening shot of dancing feet, moving to the sound of the Kenny Loggins-performed theme, it was one of those films where the audience mentally noted each song in readiness to leap from the cinema seat after the end titles and head for the nearest record store. The result was a pure pop goldmine that sold nine million copies and spawned two US Number 1 singles. Not bad for a film based around the dog-eared story of old fogies who run a town and put the kibosh on teenage activities before bowing to the inevitable.

Vangelis

EAST WEST

Blade Runner

Current CD: 4509-96574-2 **Available on video and DVD** **Release date:** June 1994 **Chart peaks:** None **Track listing:** Main Titles; Blush Response; Wait For Me; Rachel's Song; Love Theme; One More Kiss, Dear; Blade Runner Blues; Memories Of Green; Tales Of The Future; Damask Rose; Blade Runner (End Titles); Tears In Rain **Further listening:** 1492: Conquest Of Paradise (Atlantic), another soundtrack on which Vangelis brings synth sounds to the age of Columbus. On the appropriate label, of course.

Despite the mention of a soundtrack album in the 1982 sci-fi epic's onscreen credits, the original score was not released until 1994, though the New American Orchestra did provide a re-recorded version on Warner Bros shortly after the film's original release. Even the recent version is something of a compromise, Vangelis claiming "Some of the pieces will be known from the Original Soundtrack, whilst others are appearing for the first time." Virtually all electronic, and featuring dialogue from the film, it's a spaced-out affair with many superb moments, like the lush sax-headed Wait For Me (featuring Dick Morrisey) and haunting Rachel's Song, with Mary Hopkin providing the wordless vocal.

Prince

WARNER BROTHERS

Purple Rain

Current CD: 7599-25110-2 **Available on video and DVD** **Release date:** July 1984 **Chart peaks:** 7 (UK) 1 (US) **Track listing:** Let's Go Crazy (S); Take Me With U (S); The Beautiful Ones; Computer Blue; Darling Nikki; When Doves Cry (S); I Would Die 4 U (S); Baby I'm A Star; Purple Rain (S) **Further listening:** Parade (Warner) – more of Prince's soundtrack wares, this time from Under The Cherry Moon.

The success of this movie spelt a Rocky-style triumph for the underdog musican, Prince Rogers Nelson from Minneapolis. William Blinn, executive producer of the Fame TV series first came up with the idea of the Prince movie. He drafted the plot involving The Kid, a bandleader attempting to resolve horrendous parental problems and a romance forever in peril. Then Blinn was forced to quit but maintained to the end that the film's title should be 'Purple'-coloured. Apart from some stunning concert sequences, the movie was fairly ropey. Prince was not a great thespian. But the soundtrack hoisted his career, spawning several chart singles, some of which had been recorded before filming got underway. And the album proved a dominator, remaining at Number 1 in the US for 24 weeks and selling over 15 million copies.

John Cafferty And The Beaver Brown Band

SCOTTI BROTHERS

Eddie And The Cruisers

Current CD: SB 320122 **Release date:** July 1984 **Chart peaks:** None (UK) 9 (US) **Track listing:** On The Dark Side; Mockingbird; Runaround Sue; Down On My Knees; Hang Up My Rock And Roll Shoes; Runaway; Boardwalk Angel; Betty Lou's Got A New Pair Of Shoes; Those Oldies But Goodies (Remind Me Of You); Season In Hell (Fire Suite) **Further listening;** Eddie And The Cruisers II – Eddie Lives! (Scotti Brothers)

Director Michael Davidson claimed he wanted a band that had the assets of Dion, The Doors and Springsteen's E-Streeters. But it's the latter influence that's well to the fore on this soundtrack by East Coast bar band Beaver Brown. Did Eddie Wilson, the working-class Rimbaud from New Jersey really drive his car off the bridge? The album reveals nothing – except that Cafferty and Co. are ringers for Springsteen, Clemons and their mates. And really that's enough, as America's record buyers attested.

Talking Heads

EMI

Stop Making Sense

Current CD: 5224532 **Available on DVD** **Release date:** October 1984 **Chart peaks:** 37 (UK) 41 (US) **Track listing:** Psycho Killer; Heaven; Thank You For Sendng Me An Angel; Found A Job; Slippery People; Burning Down The House; Life During Wartime; Making Flippy Floppy; Swamp; What Day That Was; Naïve Melody (This Must Be The Place); Once In A Lifetime; Genius Of Love; Girlfriend Is Better; Take Me To The River; Crosseyed And Painless **Further listening:** Talking Heads: True Stories, fresh versions of the songs heard in the film True Stories.

Another day, another filmed concert album. Except that this is not just any filmed concert album but a recording that captures David Byrne and his art-school gang at the height of their powers. Now available in a version that contains seven additional tracks to those that graced the original release, the album proves conclusively that men in ill-advised trousers, or in this case, an expandable suit, can be trusted to concoct music that can, at once, be funky, fun-filled and more than functional. For confirmation, check out the joyous, energetic rendition of Al Green's Take Me To The River which allows P-Funk keyboardist Bernie Worrell to operate on homeground as the band heads forever upwards at this 1983 Hollywood Pantages gig.

Various

MCA

Repo Man

Current CD: MCAD39019 **Release date:** 1984 **Chart peaks:** None **Track listing:** Repo Man – Iggy Pop; TV Party – Black Flag; Institutionalized – Suicidal Tendencies; Coup D'Etat, When The Shit Hits The Fan – The Circle Jerks; Hombre Secreto (Secret Agent Man), El Clavo Y Cruz, Reel Ten – The Plugz; Pablo Picasso – Burning Sensations; Let's Have A War – Fear; Bad Man – Juicy Bananas **Further listening:** Urgh! A Music War soundtrack (A&M) – the way New Wave was back in 1981.

The film seemingly had a lot of things going for it. A script by then-hot British director Alex Cox, who also directed. A cast that included Harry Dean Stanton and Emilio Estevez and a production team headed by Michael Nesmith. All that was needed was an integrated, off-kilter, energetic soundtrack, which was duly delivered by such as Iggy, Henry Rollins and Black Flag and other California punks, most of whom seemed to also turn up in Penelope Spheeris' epic Decline Of Western Civilisation movie. Come Oscar time, nobody got handed that all-important trophy, despite The Circle Jerks delivering a deliberately sedate, acoustic, version of When The Shit Hits The Fan or Cox himself supplying a lyric for Juicy Banana's Bad Man rap.

Ennio Morricone
MERCURY

Once Upon A Time In America

Current CD: Mercury 822 334-2 **Release date:** 1984 **Chart peaks:** None **Tracks:** Once Upon A Time In America; Deborah's Theme; Poverty; Childhood Memories; Amapola; Friends; Prohibition Dirge; Cockeye's Song; Amapola Part 2; Childhood Poverty; Photographic Memories; Friends 2; Friendship And Love; Speakeasy; Deborah's Theme 2; Once Upon A Time In America 2; Poverty 2 **Further listening:** The Untouchables (A&M), another soundtrack on which Morricone meets the Mob and makes all the right kind of offers.

The opening theme sits oddly – with Pan flute to the fore and the suggestion that the track was maybe shaped for one of Morricone's more exotic scores. But soon it develops into one of the composer's own Italian jobs, redolent of Sicily transplanted into the tenements of New York, where the sound of mandolins and the smell of pasta fills the air, and, not far away, a local jazz outfit reiterates the liaison between Mafia and clubland melody-makers. A warm and frequently sensuous affair, on which Morricone's score comes punctuated with the strains of Amapola, a 1934 hit for The Catillians.

Various Artists
MCA

Beverly Hills Cop

Current CD: MCLD 19087 **Available on video** **Release date:** January 1985 **Chart peaks:** 24 (UK) 1 (US) **Track listing:** New Attitude – Patti Labelle; Don't Get Stopped In Beverly Hills, Stir It Up – Shalamar; Do You Really Want My Love – Junior; Emergency – Rockie Robbins; Neutron Dance – Pointer Sisters; The Heat Is On – Glenn Frey; Gratitude – Danny Elfman; Rock'N'Roll Me Again – The System; Axel F – Harold Faltermeyer **Further listening:** Beverly Hills Cop II (MCA)

The film is now so associated with Eddie Murphy that it's hard to believe that it was first offered to Sylvester Stallone. Easier to recall that Harold Faltermeyer and Ken Forsey were brought in to write and produce original material for the score, the former's synth-happy Axel F theme, used extensively throughout the picture, being the thing that registered most, next to Murphy's volatile performance, though Frey's The Heat Is On, penned by Faltermeyer and Forsey, has continued to lead a life of its own, forever turning up on various soundtracks and TV commercials.

Ry Cooder
WARNER BROTHERS

Paris, Texas

Current CD: 7599-25270-2 **Release date:** February 1985 **Chart peaks:** None **Track listing:** Paris, Texas; Brothers; Nothing Out There; Cancion Mixteca; No Safety Zone; Houston In Two Seconds; She's Leaving The Band; On The Couch; I Knew These People; Dark Was The Night **Further listening:** Alamo Bay (London), an evocative Cooder soundtrack and one that boasts assistance from such as John Hiatt, Van Dyke Parks, David Hidalgo and others.

An atmospheric landmark, with Ry Cooder's slide invoking desert visions, sagebrush caught in the wind and Harry Dean Stanton drifting in from nowhere to spark Wim Wenders slo-mo imagery. A *cantina* concerto and a Blind Willie Johnson blues, Dark Was The Night, slot in to the score, which is otherwise played pretty much in solo mode by Cooder, though Jim Dickinson and David Lindley provide minimalist support. A sound that launched a zillion imitators.

Dave Grusin

The Fabulous Baker Boys

Current CD: GRP 2000-2 **Available on video** **Release date:** October 1986 **Chart peaks:** None **Track listing:** Main Title (Jack's Theme); Welcome To The Road; Suzie And Jack; Shop Till You Bop; Soft On Me; The Moment Of Truth; Makin' Whoopee – Michelle Pfeiffer; My Funny Valentine; Do Nothin' Till You Hear From Me – Duke Ellington Orchestra; Lullaby Of Birdland – Earl Palmer Trio; Moonglow – Benny Goodman Quartet **Further listening:** Dave Grusin: Home To Duke (GRP)

Of course if this had been interactive CD, things would have been even more attractive – Michelle Pfeiffer's rendition of Makin' Whoopee loses something without the sight of the actress making out with the top deck of a grand piano. Even so, both this and her version of My Funny Valentine are delicious enough, while Grusin's originals, particularly the sax-moody Suzie And Jack, are engaging throughout, the only truly "borrowed" track on board being the Goodman Quartet's 1936 recording of Moonglow, which comes replete with the appropriate sound of a 78rpm run-in groove. Love it!

Herbie Hancock

CBS

Round Midnight

Current CD: Sony CD70300 **Release date:** November 1986 **Chart peaks:** None **Track listing:** Round Midnight; Body And Soul; Berangere's Nightmare; Fair Weather; Una Noche Con Francis; The Peacocks; How Long Has This Been Going On?; Rhythm-A-Ning; Still Time; Minuit Aux Champs-Elysees; Chan's Song (Never Said) **Further listening:** Dexter Gordon, The Other Side Of Round Midnight (Blue Note)

It was tenor star Dexter Gordon's film really. He not only starred as an alcoholic American in Paris, but also helped provide a fine jazz soundtrack, appearing on several of the album's tracks, he and pianist Hancock being supported by an array of superb fellow jazzmen that includes Chet Baker, Tony Williams, Bobby McFerrin, Wayne Shorter, Billy Higgins and John McLaughlin.

John Barry

UNITED ARTISTS

Somewhere In Time

Current CD: Beat Goes On BGOCD 222 **Available on video** **Release date:** 1986 **Chart peaks:** **Track listing:** Somewhere In Time; The Old Woman; The Journey Back In Time; A Day Together; Rhapsody On A Theme Of Paganini; Is He The One; The Man Of My Dreams; Return To The Present; Razor; Total Dismay; Coin; Whimper; Near To The Lake; Rowing: Theme From Somewhere In Time – Roger Williams **Further listening:** John Barry, Out Of Africa (MCA)

One for those who prefer things tender. This gorgeous Barry score decorated a film about time-travel romance that flopped horribly upon release but has since become something of a cult item, with the soundtrack reputedly going platinum over the long term. The inclusion of Rachmaninoff's lovely Rhapsody On A Theme Of Paginini only enhances the tears-to-tunes ratio.

Various Artists ISLAND

The Big Easy

Current CD: IMCD 31 **Available on video**. **Release date:** August 1987 **Chart peaks:** None **Track listing:** Iko Iko – The Dixie Cups; Tipitina – Professor Longhair; Ma'Tite Fille, Nouvelle Jole Blon – Buckwheat Zydeco; Colinda – Zachary Richard; Tell It Like It Is – Aaron Neville And The Neville Brothers; Zydeco Girls – Beausoleil; Oh Yeh Yai – Terrence Simien And The Mallet Playboys; Hey Hey – The Wild Tchoupitoulas; Closer To You – Dennis Quaid; Saviour, Pass Me Not – The Swan Silvertones; Pine Grove Blues – Dewey Balfa **Further listening:** Various Artists, *Cajun Hot Sauce* (Ace)

The best in New Orleans music, with Cajun capers and zydeco riffs, all pieced together by one-time NME scribe Danny Holloway to accompany the onscreen activities of a local detective (Dennis Quaid) and a shapely special prosecutor (Ellen Barkin) as they take on the Mob between romantic interludes.

Joe Jackson A&M

Tucker: The Man And His Dream

Currently unavailable on CD **Available on video** **Release date:** November 1988 **Chart peaks:** None **Track listing:** Captains Of Industry; The Car Of Tomorrow, Today; No Chance Blues; (He's A) Shape In A Drape; Factory; Vera; Lone Bank Loan Blues; Speedway; Marilee; Hangin' In Howard Hughes' Hangar; Toast Of The Town; Abe's Blues; The Trial; Freedom Swing; Tucker Jingle; Rhythm Delivery **Further listening:** Joe Jackson, Jumpin' Jive (A&M)

Jackson, initially perceived as a would-be Elvis Costello, eventually moved on to become the Jools Holland of the early '80s, a jump'n'jive merchant who hung pictures of Louis Jordan and Cab Calloway on his walls. His music for Tucker is much in that tradition, as peppy and full of verve as Jeff Bridges' interpretation of the film's lead character. Unfortunately, the soundtrack, an invigorating mixture of big-band swing and jump, replete with bootin' sax sounds, emulated Tucker's ahead-of-its-time car in that, despite being excellent, its sales proved restricted.

Vladimir Cosma MILAN

Diva

Current CD: CH 061 **Available on video** Date: 1988 **Chart peaks:** None **Track listing:** Promenade Sentimentale; Voie Sans Issue; Gorosih; Le Zen Dans L'Art De La Tartine; La Wally; Lame De Fond; Metro Police; Le Cure Et L'Antillais; L'Usine Désaffectée – Wilhelmenia Fernandez; La Wally **Further listening:** Vladimir Cosma, Les Plus Belles Musique De Films Vol. 1 (Milan)

If the whole point of owning the record was possessing Cosma's haunting solo piano version of Promenade Sentimentale, then that would surely be enough. Happily, there are other joys to be located amid the score to what must rank as one of the most stylish films ever to emerge from France. Voie Sans Issue sounds like early Can, while elsewhere, amid the operatics, Cosma creates the kind of electronic visions that probably fill Brian Eno's dreams. Even so, it's Promenade Sentimentale, with its 4am Debussy blues appeal that calls for an instant reprise.

Various Artists

ANTILLES

The Hot Spot

Current CD: ANCD 8755 **Release date:** October 1990 **Chart peaks:** None **Track listing:** Coming To Town; Empty Bank; Harry's Philosophy; Dolly's Arrival; Harry And Dolly; Sawmill; Band Robbery; Moanin'; Gloria's Story; Harry Sets Up Sutton; Murder; Blackmail; End Credits **Further listening:** John Lee Hooker, The Healer (Silvertone)

The Hot Spot was concerned with a drifter who moved into a Texas town and planned a bank heist. More importantly, it was directed by Dennis Hopper, a friend of Miles Davis since his teen days: "Miles punched out the heroin dealer and said he would kill me if I ever did it again." One reason why the opening blues features Miles backing a vocal by John Lee Hooker – as good a start to a soundtrack album as anyone can recall. From there on in, it's the blues and little else but the blues, with the Hook humming his way from track to track with Miles screwing everything down tight. Original music by Jack Nitzsche played by John Lee Hooker, Miles Davis, Taj Mahal, Roy Rogers, Tim Drummond, Earl Palmer and Bradford Ellis.

Various Artists

ELEKTRA

The Mambo Kings

Current CD: 7559-61240-2 **Release date:** 1991 **Chart peaks:** None (UK) 50 (US) **Track listing:** La Dicha Mia – Celia Cruz; Melao De Cana (Moo La Lah), Guantanamera, Ran Kan Kan, Cuban Pete, Para Los Rumberro – Tito Puente; Mambo Caliente – Arturo Sandoval; Quiereme Mucho, Perfidia – Linda Ronstadt; Sunny Ray, Tea For Two, Accidental Mambo, Tanga, Rumba – Afro-Cubana-Mambo All-Stars; Como Fue – Beny More; Beautiful Maria Of My Soul – Mambo All Stars Featuring Antonio Banderas; Beautiful Maria Of My Soul – Los Lobos **Further listening:** Perez Prado, King Of Mambo (RCA)

The Mambo Kings thankfully removed any lingering memories of a terrible movie called Salsa from the mind, and, pretty much, did justice to Oscar Hijuelos fine novel. The soundtrack also sparks reminders of what it must have been like at New York's Palladium when mambo dropped in during the early '50s.Okay, so there's no Perez Prado here, and he was the original mainman. But Tito Puente's around and Celia Cruz, just to keep things authentic, while the Mambo All-Stars make the kind of healthy noise that was once Machito's trademark. And Arturo Sandoval's also on hand to prove that Cuban trumpet players are on a par with Brazilian soccer stars when it comes to high-register playing. There are probably small countries that could be lit by the power and electricity emanating from this album.

Various

EPIC

Singles

Current CD: EPC 471438-2 **Release date:** August 1992 **Chart peaks:** (UK) None (US) 6 **Track listing:** Would? – Alice In Chains; Breath, State Of Love And Trust – Pearl Jam; May This Be Love – Jimi Hendrix; Seasons – Chris Cornell; Waiting For Somebody, Dyslexic Heart – Paul Westerberg; Nearly Lost You – Screaming Trees; Drown – Smashing Pumpkins; Battle Of Evermore – The Lovemongers; Chloe Dancer, Crown Of Thorns – Mother Love Bone; Overblown – Mudhoney; Birth Ritual – Soundgarden **Further listening:** Kids (MCA)

For once, the critics were unanimous, Rolling Stone adjudging the soundtrack "excellent", Spin hailing it as "the Seattle music anthology, thoughtful and near perfect", while others labelled it "impressive" and "cohesive". And it really was all of those things, diverse enough – the folksy, mandolin propelled version of Led Zep's Battle Of Evermore contrasting with such as Alice In Chains' heavy but far from heartless Would? and Paul Westerberg's jaunty Dyslexic Heart. But somehow everything gels to provide a rewarding view of Seattle rock at its peak. Only the absence of Nirvana is disappointing.

Angelo Badalamenti

WARNER BROTHERS

Twin Peaks: Fire Walk With Me

Current CD: 9362450192 **Release date:** July 1992 **Chart peaks:** None **Track listing:** Theme From Twin Peaks: Fire Walk With Me; The Pine Float; Don't Do Anything (I Wouldn't Do); A Real Indication (Thought Gang); The Black Dog Runs At Night (Thought Gang); Best Friends; Moving Through Time; Montage From Twin Peaks: Girl Talk/Birds In Hell/Laura Palmer's Theme/Falling; Sycamore Trees – Jimmy Scott; Questions In A World Of Blue – Julee Cruise **Further listening:** Music From Twin Peaks (Warner Bros) – in truth, the better of the two soundtracks, this one emanating from the TV series.

Badalamenti's quirky, hazy jazz-techno-rock music for the original TV series was reiterated for the film score, though only Laura Palmer's Theme and Falling stemmed from the small screen presentation. Both veteran jazzman Scott and *chanteuse* Cruise contribute suitably smoky vocal selections, while Badalamenti himself is heard in a vocal role, delivering, rather than actually singing, four lyrics by director David Lynch that almost scream "file me under bizarre". Which is all as you might expect.

Various Artists

MCA

Pulp Fiction

Current CD: MCASD11103 **Available on video** **Release date:** August 1994 **Chart peaks:** 5 (UK) 21 (US) **Track listing:** Pumpkin And Honey Bunny – (dialogue); Miserlou – Dick Dale & His Deltones; Royale With Cheese – (dialogue); Jungle Boogie – Kool & The Gang; Let's Stay Together – Al Green; Bustin' Surfboards – The Tornadoes; Lonesome Town – Ricky Nelson; Son Of A Preacher Man – Dusty Springfield; Zed's Dead, Baby – (dialogue); Bullwinkle Part II – The Centurians; Jack Rabbit Slim's Twist Contest – (dialogue); You Never Can Tell – Chuck Berry; Girl, You'll Be A Woman Soon – Urge Overkill; If Love Is A Red Dress (Hang Me In Rags) – Maria McKee; Bring Out The Gimp – (dialogue); Comanche – The Revels; Flowers On The Wall – The Statler Brothers; Personality Goes A Long Way – (dialogue); Surf Rider – The Lively Ones; Ezekiel 25:17 – (dialogue) **Further listening:** Reservoir Dogs (1993); Urge Overkill Saturatin* (1993); Maria McKee Life Is Sweet (1996)

Suddenly all his dreams came true and Quentin Tarantino was the very hottest thing in Hollywood for a couple of years. While movie pundits debated whether he was a saviour of the medium or merely an Orson Welles-style talented-flash-in-the-pan, one thing became clear: he had a cool taste in music. The *Reservoir Dogs* soundtrack set the agenda: unusual oldies, great bits of surf music, vintage funk, but this set – and the movie it accompanied – consolidated his style and became a massive best-seller. It has all the twists and turns of the film and all its stylish tattiness too, with some great moments by such unsung artists as Maria McKee and Urge Overkill.

Various Artists
INTERSCOPE

Natural Born Killers

Current CD: IND92460 **Available on video** **Release date:** March 1995 **Chart peaks:** 10 (UK) 20 (US) **Track listing:** Waiting For The Miracle – Leonard Cohen; Shitlist – L7; Moon Over Greene County – Dan Zanes; Rock N Roll Nigger – Patti Smith; Sweet Jane – Cowboy Junkies; You Belong To Me – Bob Dylan; The Trembler – Duane Eddy; Burn – Nine Inch Nails; Route 666 – Robert Downey, Jr and Brian Berdan; Totally Hot (Interlude); Back In Baby's Arms – Patsy Cline; Taboo – Peter Gabriel and Nusrat Fateh Ali Khan; Sex Is Violent (Interlude); History (Repeats Itself) – **Track listing:** A.O.S.; Something I Can Never Have – Nine Inch Nails; I Will Take You Home – Russel Means; Drums A Go-Go – Hollywood Persuaders; Hungry Ants (Interlude); The Day The Niggaz Took Over – Dr Dre; Born Bad – Juliette Lewis; Fall Of The Rebel Angels – Sergio Cervetti; Forkboy – Lard; Batonga In Batongaville (Interlude); Warm Place, A – Nine Inch Nails; Allah, Mohammed, Char, Yaar (Interlude); The Future – Leonard Cohen; What Would U Do? – Tha Dogg Pound **Further listening:** Leonard Cohen *The Future*, Nine Inch Nails *The Downward Spiral.*

Oliver Stone's crazed collage of cinema styles for this Tarantino-scripted killing spree called for a challenging score to match. Stone hired Trent Reznor of Nine Inch Nails who compiled this superb album in the same spirit as the film. Moods swing violently between songs, as Reznor mixes his own crunching sonics with Leonard Cohen, Patsy Cline and Dr Dre. Patti Smith's raging Rock N Roll Nigger is placed next to The Cowboy Junkies' Sweet Jane for maximum contrast and many tracks run together with uncredited samples and dialogue from the film. It all provides a narrative force that makes this album an engrossing, almost movie-length entertainment without the need for visuals. Notable highlights include the otherwise unavailable Bob Dylan rendition of You Belong To Me – spookily poignant – and actress Juliette Lewis singing Born Bad. Better than all the "inspired by" soundtrack albums, this set a standard that few have risen to since.

Various Artists
EMI

Trainspotting

Current CD: 7243 8 37190-2 **Available on video and DVD** **Release date:** February 1996 **Chart peaks:** 12 (UK) 48 (US) **Track listing:** Lust For Life – Iggy Pop; Deep Blue Day – Brian Eno; Trainspotting – Primal Scream; Atomic – Sleeper; Temptation – New Order; Nightclubbing – Iggy Pop; Sing – Blur; Perfect Day – Lou Reed; Mile End – Pulp; For What You Dream Of – Bedrock Featuring Kyo; 2.1 – Elastica; A Final Hit – Leftfield; Born Slippy – Underworld; Closet Romantic – Damon Albarn **Further listening:** Shallow Grave (EMI), the soundtrack to a previous Danny Boyle directed box-office success.

Both the film and the soundtrack struck a chord amid the Britpop boom of '96. Pulp, Damon Albarn and Leftfield wrote material especially for inclusion. Elsewhere there was an established punter-puller in New Order's Temptation, a lesser one in Underworld's Born Slippy, which would re-emerge as a major hit through inclusion in the film, plus what sounded like an intriguing proposition in Sleeper's remake of the old Blondie hit Atomic but turned out to be a dud. Those who took a seat in the circle recalled that Deep Blue Day accompanied visuals of Tim Renton's life literally going down the toilet, while Perfect Day, later to be resurrected as an all-star anthem for the BBC, equated with another of Renton's heroin-induced fantasies. Virtually every sound provoked a talking point and, as '96 came to a close, the record finished up on many Best Of The Year listings. These days it's easy to snap one up from the second-hand racks.

Written by Fred Dellar.

The Best Of The Best Ofs

100 Great Compilations

Today, the rock and pop compilation has a modicum of coolness about it. Once it was all rag-bag collections of last year's chart sensations. Or, worse, pale imitations of the songs performed by unconvincing "soundalikes". ("Can YOU tell the difference between these and the original sounds?" Yes, thanks. A deaf baboon with its head in a bucket of sand could tell the difference.) Or ubiquitous, TV-advertised 20 Golden Greats that now clutter up Oxfam shops.

These days, though, hits collections are sometimes so up to date that they include hits that are yet to be released. And while endless Ministry Of Sound and Ibiza collections are the modern equivalent of the K-Tel cash-in, DJs are no longer the only celebrity compilers; cult novelists and painters are just as likely to be asked. But it was the advent of the CD in the mid-'80s, and the new format's Year Zero approach to rock history, combined with an ever-growing scholarship about the subject, which helped transform the much-maligned compilation into an object of respectability.

The idea of putting different performers together on disc is almost as old as the recording industry itself; early 78rpm albums might feature assorted light-opera stars tackling Puccini's Golden Greats, or some such. By the '50s, as the rise of the solo singer began to transform popular music, it wasn't unusual for major labels like Decca and Philips to pair seemingly unlikely artists – Winifred Atwell! Dickie Valentine! – on EPs called something like All Star Hit Parade. The album, still a rare commodity back then, was usually reserved for more esoteric fare, providing – in its 10" format – an introduction to *The Great Blues Singers* or a *Dictionary Of Jazz.*

A sign of things to come arrived at Christmas, 1958 in the form of *Oh Boy!*, ostensibly an album companion to the popular British TV show but one which featured studio recordings by the best of the new crop of singers, including Cliff Richard – a hot, sexy little number at the time. This TV tie-in format was repeated, with less success, during the early months of the beat boom, when Decca unveiled its latest stars on albums like *Thank Your Lucky Stars*, *Ready, Steady, Go!* and *Saturday Club.*

The enormous success of The Beatles and Merseybeat gave labels considerable scope. A title like Decca's *At The Cavern* might not have been all it seemed (applause was lifted from a Billy Fury live album) but at least it offered bona-fide Scousers like Beryl Marsden and The Big Three. On the other hand, while the Embassy label's *Liverpool Beat* (1964) boasted an impressive track-listing of beat-era standards, the group names were largely figments of the producer's imagination masking the fact that the album was recorded by session players who wouldn't have recognised a plate of Scouse even if were conducting the session.

Although compilations carried a whiff of opportunism, the R&B-fuelled thirst for the sounds of black America gave the genre some kudos, with Pye subsidiaries Pye International and Marble Arch providing budget-price introductions to the coveted Chess catalogue.

Pye were also pioneers of the budget album available in outlets that didn't usually stock records, like post offices, newsagents and branches of Woolworths. After striking a deal with an American music-by-the-yard provider named Dave Miller of Somerset Records, Pye came up with the notion of a cheap series that would undercut labels who were paying recording costs. Most of Miller's music was recorded by a German orchestra and was filed under names like101 Strings. *Gypsy Campfires* and *Down Memory Lane To Drury Lane* were massive sellers for Pye's Golden Guinea series which, indeed, retailed at 21 shillings (£1.05).

It was only a matter of time before someone cottoned-on to the idea of supplying facsimiles of current hits for the undiscerning punter. Woolworths started their own range of "fake hit" singles via the Top Six and Embassy labels. But the phenomenon really got underway in the early

’60s when entrepreneur Paul Hamlyn initiated Music for Pleasure (MfP), with a little help from EMI Records and the Daily Mirror. (Other lines in his quest to mass-market culture included Books for Pleasure and Prints for Pleasure.) MfP albums were originally priced at an amazing 7/11d (39p), and displayed in corner shops and electrical stores on carousels. To access the widest range of material without encountering licensing problems, labels like MfP and Hallmark re-recorded the hits of the day with hastily assembled and cheaply hired session musicians. Among such impoverished young guns available for vocal hire during the late ’60s were Rod Stewart and Elton John, the latter – bizarrely – even covering a few tunes by Nick Drake on one occasion.

The first notable chart incursion with built-in disappointment for any purchasers who’d expected to hear the real thing was *Beatlemania!*, issued by Top Six in 1964, though towards the end of the decade, titles like *Hits ’67* and *Chartbusters Of ’68* were hoodwinking young pop enthusiasts on a grand scale. By 1970, though, two series, *Hot Hits* and *Top Of The Pops*, both retailing at 12/6d, triumphed over the competition and, despite subsequent ineligibility for the charts, continued to sell well into the decade, even into the punk era – which threw up some of the genre’s most laughable fakes.

Covers of soul hits were also good for a giggle. Anyone in search of the real thing during the soul boom of the mid-’60s were probably pointed at the influential compilations aimed at the mohair suit brigade, most notably *This Is Sue!* assembled for Island Records by legendary club loon and DJ Guy Stevens. Sensing that the success of black American music in the mid-’60s was largely based on hit singles, both Atlantic and Tamla Motown began a series of Various Artist compilations as a way of breaking into the album market and source of extra revenue. The competitively priced *Solid Gold Soul*, *Midnight Soul* and *This Is Soul* did well for the former, while *A Collection Of 16 Tamla Motown Hits*, its similarly titled successors, and the long-running *Motown Chartbusters* series were virtually forerunners of the TV-advertised album.

In contrast to these hit-filled sets were the progressive and underground rock compilations designed to introduce the album-buying audience to new music at pocket-money prices (initially for around 12/6d). One of the earliest to make an impact was 1969’s *You Can All Join In*, the first in a series of Island Records samplers that also included *Nice Enough To Eat*, *Bumpers* and the lavishly packaged *El Pea*. The idea was instantly picked up by the majors, with Decca launching its *World Of . . .* series, CBS its *Rock Machine . . .* titles, Atlantic’s *Age Of Atlantic*, Polydor’s *Supergroups* and EMI’s progressive subsidiary Harvest (*Picnic*, *A Harvest Bag*). Smaller fry like Buddah (*Buddah In Mind*) and Vertigo (*Suck It And See*) also used the “loss-leader” compilation as a promotional device to break its acts.

Although newer labels like Charisma and Virgin continued with the format into the ’70s, the days of the cheap and cheerful label compilation were numbered when, late in 1971, it was announced that budget-price LPs would no longer be eligible for chart inclusion. This diminished the importance of the Various Artist compilation, although the wave of nostalgia that swept through the new decade, together with tighter record company budgets, meant that the search for new music was less crucial than it had been during the late ’60s.

The “no-budget albums” chart ruling had been prompted by an extraordinary week in August 1971 when no less than five compilations featuring anonymous session musicians appeared in the British charts, two of them, *Hot Hits 6* and *Top Of The Pops Vol. 18*, reaching Number 1. This landmark edict had another side effect: two aggressive new players arrived on the scene peddling the real thing. K-Tel and Ronco revolutionised the market by offering recent hits by the original artists on full-price, TV advertised sets like *20 Dynamic Hits* and *20 Star Tracks*. And unlike the single label compilations of the previous decade, there was remarkably little filler, hence K-Tel’s incredible success during 1972–73 when four of its first six titles topped the album chart. Inevitably, others like the Warwick, Ronco and Arcade labels soon followed with similar products.

The market for retrospective material began to flourish during the early '70s, with film soundtracks for That'll Be The Day and Stardust inspiring a host of other compilations like *The Beat Merchants* and *Hard-Up Heroes* (a trawl through the pre-fame work of'70s legends such as David Bowie and Rod Stewart), that dissected various aspects of '50s and '60s rock.

The arrival of punk didn't harm the compilation at all. In fact, the new bands' paucity of material, and the threadbare resources of the rapidly growing independent labels, actively encouraged their growth. EMI's *The Roxy, London, WC2* was one of the first and best, capturing some of the era's biggest names in their infancy at the notorious central London punk dive, while Virgin's *Short Circuit – Live At The Electric Circus*, did a similar job for the Manchester punk scene. Other big-name titles, like the double set recorded at the Hope and Anchor in Islington, or Stiff Records' *Live Stiffs Live*, were toe-in-the-water exercises in pub rock for those wary of messing with undiluted punk rock.

By 1979, even punk had its own K-Tel-styled hits collection, *20 Of Another Kind*, though with limited licensing capabilities (and, legend has it, some deliberately subversive misinformation from one of the compiler's young advisors), this and the similar *New Wave* were more an exercise in what one critic called "plastic Polydor punk". Independents like Chiswick, Beggars Banquet, Cherry Red and Fast all rushed in with sets introducing their rosters, though none with quite the kudos of Rough Trade's *Wanna Buy A Bridge?* which, as its title suggests, was essentially directed at the US market.

By the early '80s, K-Tel had run out of steam and the majors stepped in by joining forces on the *Now! That's What I Call Music* series, which invariably result in instant No. 1 albums to this day (the series has also just taken off in the US). Genre titles, too, became increasingly popular with disco, country and romantic ballads seemingly the easiest route to chart success. But the key development during that confused musical decade was a crop of specialist labels dedicated solely to the art of reissuing out-of-print titles. Ace, Beat Goes On, Charly, Demon and See For Miles paved the way for today's buoyant reissue market, which received its biggest boost when the CD arrived, its whole marketing ethos centred around re-buying your favourite music in a format that would offer "perfect sound forever". Since the late '80s, dozens of specialist labels have emerged, invariably run by enthusiasts, which lovingly assemble compilations of everything from long-lost psychedelic 45s to incidental music from barely remembered British television series.

During the '90s, majors like EMI, Universal and Sony have been rather less inclined to sub-license material to these independent outfits, developing instead their own catalogue departments with good resources and a licensing power capable of assembling expansive retrospectives like Universal's *1-2-3-4 Punk And New Wave 1976–1979* box set. However, the market for such specialist collections is limited, and it's likely that similar fabulous indulgences will be the exception rather than the rule. Perhaps the days of the expert compilation are numbered entirely. The future is, most likely, creating your own custom-made compilations via the internet. With almost any track ever recorded potentially at your disposal, websites such as Napster and Gnutella are like infinite, on-going compilation albums that you can tap into at any point to access exactly the music you want. Is that the same as being presented with a skilfully compiled collection? Maybe not, but complaining about the arrival of bottomless choice would be futile. Pop music, by definition, is in a constant state of flux and we should no more expect to undo the incredible arrival of a new age of music via the internet than we should bemoan the departure of Winifred Atwell or 101 Strings.

What follows is our selection of multi-artist compilations and greatest hits collections that best complement the main body of this book. These are mostly artists, or genres, ill-represented by the album form, that made an important contribution to pop history. In some cases, we've also chosen collections by artists who appear in the main section but whose singles merit separate attention, for example, The Beatles, James Brown and Madonna.

We've run them in roughly chronological order, though some of the multi-artist sets, in particular, may cover long periods of time. Some of these are new collections, some are contemporary compilations, chosen for their impact at the time of issue, which may have been superseded by a more thorough CD version subsequently. But most of these choices should still be available.

Once again, this is a personal selection which couldn't hope to cover every cranny of pop history and shouldn't be seen as a stand-alone list but, taken along with the other components of this book, it should provide you with a reasonable overview of pop's sprawling pageant.

Various Artists

American Folk Music

SMITHSONIAN FOLKWAYS RECORDINGS; 1997

Henry Lee – Dick Justice; Fatal Flower Garden – Nelstone's Hawaiians; The House Carpenter – Clarence Ashley; Drunkard's Special – Coley Jones; Old Lady And The Devil – Bill and Belle Reed; The Butcher's Boy – Buell Kazee; The Wagoner's Lad – Buell Kazee; King Knog Kitchie Kitchie Ki-Me-O – Chubby Parker; Old Shoes And Leggins – Uncle Eck Dunford; Willie Moore – Richard Burnett and Leonard Rutherford; A Lazy Farmer Boy – Buster Carter And Preston Young; Peg And Awl – The Carolina Tar Heels; Ommie Wise – GB Grayson; My Name Is JohnJohanna – Kelly Harrell; Bandit Cole Younger – Edward L Crain; Charles Giteau – Kelly Harrel; John Hardy Was A Desperate Little Man – The Carter Family; Gonna Die With My Hammer In My Hand – The Williamson Brothers and Curry; Stackalee – Frank Hutchison; White House Blues – Charlie Poole and The North Carolina Ramblers; Frankie – Mississippi John Hurt; When That Great Ship Went Down – William and Versey Smith; Engine 143 – The Carter Family; Kassie Jones – Furry Lewis; Down On Penny's Farm – The Bently Boys; Mississippi Boweavil Blues – The Masked Marvel; Got The Farm Land Blues – The Carolina Tar Heels; Sail Away Lady – Uncle Bunt Stephens; The Wild Wagoner – Jilson Setters; Wake Up Jacob – Prince Albert Hunt's Texas Ramblers; La Danseuse – Delma Lachney and Blind Uncle Gaspard; Georgia Stomp – Andrew and Jim Baxter; Brilliancy Medley – Eck Robertson; Indian War Whoop – Hoyt Ming And His Pep-Steppers; Old Country Stomp – Henry Thomas; Old Dog Blue – Jim Jackson; Saut Crapaud – Columbus Fruge; Arcadian One-Step – Joseph Falcon; Home Sweet Home – The Breux Frères; Newport Blues – The Cincinnati Jug Band; Moonshiner's Dance Part One – Frank Cloutier and the Victoria Cafe Orchestra; You Must Be Born Again – Rev JM Gates; Oh Death Where Is Thy Sting – Rev JM Gates; Rocky Road – Alabama Sacred Harp Singers; Present Joys – Alabama Sacred Harp Singers; This Song Of Love – Middle Georgia Singing Conv. No. 1; Judgement – Sister Mary Nelson; He Got Better Things For You – Memphis Sanctified Singers; John The Baptist – Rev Moses Mason; Dry Bones – Bascom Lamar Lunsford; John The Revelator – Blind Willie Johnson; Little Moses – The Carter Family; Shine On Me – Ernest Phipps And Holiness Singers; Fifty Miles Of Elbow Room – Rev FW McGee; In The Battlefield For My Lord – Rev DC Rice and Congregation; The Coo Coo Bird – Clarence Ashley; East Virginia – Buell Kazee; Minglewood Blues – Cannon's Jug Stompers; I Woke Up One Morning In May – Didier Hvzbert; James Alley Blues – Richard "Rabbit" Brown; Sugar Baby – Dock Boggs; I Wish I Was A Mole In The Ground – Bascom Lamar Lunsford; Mountaineer's Courtship – Ernest and Hattie Stoneman; The Spanish Merchant's Daughter – The Stoneman Family; Bob Lee Junior Blues – The Memphis Jug Band; Single Girl, Married Girl – The Carter Family; Le Vieux Soulard Et Sa Femme – Cleoma Breaux And Joseph Falcon; Rabbit Foot Blues – Blind Lemon Jefferson; Expressman Blues – Sleepy John Estes And Yank Rachell; Poor Boy Blues – Ramblin' Thomas; Feather Bed – Cannon's Jug Stompers; Country Blues – Dock Boggs; 99 Year Blues – Julius Daniels; Prison Cell Blues – Blind Lemon Jefferson; See That My Grave Is Kept Clean – Blind Lemon Jefferson; C'est Triste Sans Lui – Cleoma and Ophy Breaux and Joseph Falcon; Way Down The Old Plank Road – Uncle Dave Macon; Buddy Won't You Roll Down The Line – Uncle Dave Macon; Spike Driver Blues – Mississippi John Hurt; KC Moan – The Memphis Jug Band; Train On The Island – JP Nestor; The Lone Star Trail – Ken Maynard; Fishing Blues – Henry Thomas

Bob Dylan, Jerry Garcia, Eric von Schmidt, Jim Rooney and John Fahey, count themselves among people whose lives were changed by the 84 tracks, collected on six LPs, that the late Harry Smith dubbed from his collection of old 78s in 1952 and declared an Anthology of American Folk Music. Divided into three two-record sets – Ballads, Social Music, and Songs – they mix black and white, folkie and show-biz, professional and amateur performers who recorded from 1927, when electrical recording made a higher fidelity possible, to about 1930, when the Depression halted the recording of marginal musics in America.

Ancient voices filter ancient ballads through their daily lives, sing about Christianity, dance long-forgotten dances, and fill songs with imagery that seems to come from another, slightly familiar, planet. Assembling such an anthology today, would anyone leave off Robert Johnson or Bill Monroe? Or include such one-shot obscurities as Bill and Belle Reed, Edward L Crain, or Richard "Rabbit" Brown? But Brown, with James Alley Blues, recorded a song as chilling as anything in Robert Johnson's repertoire, and the Reeds' Old Lady And The Devil is as goofy today as it ever was.

Hear the Carter Family picking banjo-flailing Cajun music, and Blind Lemon Jefferson begging that his grave be kept clean for the first time. Although our ears aren't as virgin to this music as they once were – thanks to the legion of folklorists unleashed by the Anthology – both the sequencing and the selections are the work of a mind that didn't see things in a nice, linear, academic fashion. It's not just the music, it's being guided through it by an eccentric visionary (Smith was also an expert in string games and Ukrainian Easter eggs), who, upon being given a special Grammy for the Anthology, said, "I'm glad to say that my dreams came true. I saw America changed through music."

Robert Johnson

CBS 1961

King Of The Delta Blues

Crossroads Blues; Terraplane Blues; Come On In My Kitchen; Walking Blues; Last Fair Deal Gone Down; 32–20 Blues; Kindhearted Woman Blues; If I Had Possession Over Judgement Day; Preaching Blues; When You Got A Good Friend; Rambling On My Mind; Stones In My Passway; Traveling Riverside Blues; Milkcow's Calf Blues; Me And The Devil Blues; Hellhound On My Trail

In the early '60s Robert Johnson was another little-known singer in what was then called the "country blues" idiom. In 1961, a CBS collection assembled by Frank Driggs would become a huge influence on the emerging British beat boom and help cement Robert Johnson as a legend – and a prototype rock star.

Johnson made great copy, thanks to the "Crossroads Myth": the belief that he traded his soul with the devil in order to acquire his fiendish guitar expertise. Johnson's death in mysterious circumstances – poisoned, according to his contemporary David Honeyboy Edward, or a victim of syphilis, according to his death certificate – added to the legend.

The music was recorded in two sessions by engineer Don Law, who set up portable disc-cutting apparatus in a makeshift studio in a hotel in San Antonio, Texas on Nov 23, 26 and 27, 1936. There was a further session the following year on June 19 and 20, 1937.

Not all of the music they recorded was released at the time. Johnson wasn't particularly celebrated in his day, enjoying only one minor hit with Terraplane Blues, which sold because it referred to a popular brand of car. There were plenty of other bluesmen who were much more famous. "He did have a style that wasn't executed much," noted contemporary player Henry Townsend, when asked how he felt about Johnson's subsequent elevation to King Of The Delta Blues Singers. "I'm not criticising, but they put him up on a pedestal which he don't belong."

Johnson's legend exploded after his death. Yet it wouldn't have done so without the songs. He used some well-worn themes, but assembled them into concise tunes, and was perhaps the first musician to package all his fears, hopes and humour into perfectly realised three-minute epics. His masterful, versatile guitar accompaniment and supernaturally intense singing soon transfixed a whole new generation via this CBS collection. Keith Richards was one of many who found themselves haunted by Johnson's example: "I still remember the first time I heard it. Brian Jones bought it. Amazing. Still is. I still put that record on to frighten myself."

The CBS collection and its 1970 sequel were packed with what would become standards, including Crossroads (covered by Cream), Love In Vain (recorded by The Rolling Stones), Dust My Broom (a staple for Elmore James) and Sweet Home Chicago – a bar-room standard for everybody and their mama.

In 1990, 62 years after his death, Robert's own recordings entered the US album charts via a 2-CD compilation, *The Complete Recordings* (Columbia). The original separate volumes are still available via Columbia/Legacy's Master Sound series.

Hank Williams

POLYGRAM, 1978

40 Greatest Hits

Move It On Over; A Mansion On The Hill; Lovesick Blues; Wedding Bells; Mind Your Own Business; You're Gonna Change (Or I'm Gonna Leave); Lost Highway; My Bucket's Got A Hole In It; I'm So Lonesome I Could Cry; I Just Don't Like This Kind Of Living; Long Gone Lonesome Blues; My Son Calls Another Man Daddy; Why Don't You Love Me; Why Should We Try Anymore; They'll Never Take Her Love From Me; Moanin' The Blues; Nobody's Lonesome For Me; Cold Cold Heart; Dear John; Howlin' At The Moon; I Can't Help It (If I'm Still In Love With You); Hey, Good Lookin'; Crazy Heart; I Heard That (Lonesome Whistle); Baby, We're Really In Love; Ramblin' Man; Honky Tonk Blues; I'm Sorry For You My Friend; Half As Much; Jambalaya (On The Bayou); Window Shopping; Settin' The Woods On Fire; You Win Again; I'll Never Get Out Of This World Alive; Kaw-Liga; Your Cheatin' Heart; Take These Chains From My Heart; I Won't Be Home No More; Weary Blues From Waitin'; I Saw The Light.

There is no way Hank Williams could have won. No way. Even if the man they now call The Hillbilly Shakespeare could've survived his alcoholism, his incredibly domineering mother, two violent marriages, chloral hydrate as well as morphine abuse due to chronic back pain which also manifested itself through incontinence, his personal and professional finances were a goddamn mess and his self-esteem was so low he became both a champion inverted snob and a man with a chip on his shoulder so sizeable it's a wonder he didn't walk with a tilt.

Hank is, without doubt, the towering giant of country music, a singer who could break hearts with his nasal tenor and a songwriter whose work has been reinterpreted by countless artists outside the country music penumbra, from The Grateful Dead (You Win Again) and George Thoroughgood (Move It On Over) to Cassandra Wilson (I'm So Lonesome I Could Cry). This amazing body of songs proves that he was one of pop music's great pioneers, helping fashion the template that country music still uses today.

"Hank Williams' ultimate triumph was that, in trying to conjure up something that would sell a few records tomorrow, he defined the vernacular of contemporary country music, and provided a soundtrack for other people's lives without being halfway in control of his own," says his biographer, Colin Escott.

Williams died of a heart attack in the back seat of a car on the way to a show, on January 1, 1953. He was 29.

Various Artists

RHINO, 1990

Sentimental Journey: Pop Vocal Classics Vol. 3 1950–54

Hold My Hand – Don Cornell with Jerry Carr And His Orchestra; (Why Did I Tell You I Was Going To) Shanghai – Doris Day with Paul Weston And His Orchestra; My Heart Cries For You – Guy Mitchell with Mitch Miller And Orchestra/Chorus; Wish You Were Here – Eddie Fisher with Hugo Winterhalter And His Orchestra; Because Of You – Tony Bennett with Percy Faith And Orchestra; Cry – Johnnie Ray And The Four Lads; Lover – Peggy Lee And Gordon Jenkins And His Orchestra; Come On-A My House – Rosemary Clooney; Kiss Of Fire – Georgia Gibbs with Glenn Osser And Orchestra; I Apologize – Billy Eckstine with Pete Rugolo And Orchestra; The Song From Moulin Rouge (Where Is Your Heart) – Percy Faith And His Orchestra with Felicia Sanders; You Belong To Me – Jo Stafford with Paul Weston And His Orchestra; Wheel Of Fortune – Kay Starr with Harold Mooney And Orchestra; I Get Ideas – Tony Martin with Henri Ren? And His Orchestra; Little Things Mean A Lot – Kitty Kallen; That's Amore – Dean Martin with Dick Stabile And His Orchestra; Here In My Heart – Al Martino with Monty Kelly And Orchestra; How High The Moon – Les Paul And Mary Ford

Various Artists

RHINO, 1990

Sentimental Journey: Pop Vocal Classics Vol. 4 – 1954–59

Fascination – Jane Morgan And The Troubadors; I Could Have Danced All Night – Sylvia Syms with Jack Pleis And Chorus/Orchestra; Just In Time – Tony Bennett with Percy Faith And His Orchestra; That Old Black Magic – Sammy Davis Jr with Morty Stevens And Orchestra; Mack The Knife – Bobby Darin with Richard Wess And Orchestra; Fever – Peggy Lee with Jack Marshall's Music; Tammy – Debbie Reynolds with Joseph Gershenson And Orchestra; Let Me Go Lover – Joan Weber with Jimmy Carroll And Orchestra; What A Diff'rence A Day Makes – Dinah Washington; On The Street Where You Live – Vic Damone with Percy Faith And His Orchestra And Chorus; Singing The Blues – Guy Mitchell with Ray Conniff And His Orchestra; Chances Are – Johnny Mathis with Ray Conniff And His Orchestra; Whatever Will Be – Will Be (Que Sera Sera) – Doris Day with Frank De Vol And His Orchestra; The Wayward Wind – Gogi Grant with Buddy Bregman And Orchestra; Memories Are Made Of This – Dean Martin with Dick Stabile And Orchestra; Old Cape Cod – Patti Page with Vic Schoen And His Orchestra; The Man That Got Away – Judy Garland with Ray Heindorf And Orchestra.

Before Elvis – and the soul shouters he borrowed from – turned the youth of America into jive-talking delinquents, radio was dominated by romantic singers like Tony Bennett, Patti Page and Peggy Lee, who usually were credited as performing "with" some orchestra or other. Among the most important hits in this style were Singing The Blues by Guy Mitchell, Mack the Knife by Bobby Darin and Theme from 'A Summer Place' by Percy Faith each of which spent a staggering nine weeks atop the American charts. These collections focus more on the great standards singers like Bennett, Lee and Rosemary Clooney (mother of George) and Hollywood stars like Judy Garland, Doris Day and Dean Martin, largely avoiding popular pre-rock hokum by the likes of Frankie Laine.

Various Artists

RHINO, 1993

Doo Wop Box: 101 Vocal Group Gems

It's Too Soon To Know – The Orioles; Count Every Star – The Ravens; The Glory Of Love – The Five Keys; Gee – The Crows; Crying In The Chapel – The Orioles; Money Honey – Clyde McPhatter And The Drifters; Golden Teardrops – The Flamingos; A Sunday Kind Of Love – The Harp-Tones Featuring Willie Winfield; I – The Velvets; Goodnite Sweetheart, Goodnite – Spaniels; Sh-Boom – The Chords; Gloria – The Cadillacs With Jesse Powell Orchestra; Hearts Of Stone – The Jewels; Earth Angel (Will You Be Mine) – The Penguins; Sincerely – TheMoonglows; Mary Lee – The Rainbows; Close Your Eyes – The Five Keys; (Will You) Come Back My Love – The Wrens; Story Untold – The Nutmegs; Only You (And You Alone) – The Platters; Why Don't You Write Me? – The Jacks; When You Dance – The Turbans; At My Front Door- The El Dorados; The Great Pretender – The Platters; Lily Maebelle – The Valentines; Speedoo – The Cadillacs with Jesse Powell Orchestra; Why Do Fools Fall In Love – The Teenagers Featuring Frankie Lymon; I'll Be Home – The Flamingos; Devil Or Angel – The Clovers; Church Bells May Ring – Willows; Little Girl Of Mine – The Cleftones With Jimmy Wright And His Orchestra; I Want You To be My Girl – Frankie Lymon And The Teenagers With Jimmy Wright And His Orchestra; In The Still Of The Nite – The Five Satins; The Closer You Are – The Channels; Oh What A Nite – The Dells; A Thousand Miles Away – The Heartbeats; Please Say You Want Me – The Schoolboys With Leroy Kirkland Orchestra; Come Go With Me – The Dell-Vikings; I'm So Happy (Tra-La-La-La-La-La) – Lewis Lymon And The Teenchords; Walking Along – The Solitaires; Little Darlin' – The Gladiolas; Don't Ask Me To Be Lonely – The Dubs; Florence – Paragons; Deserie – The Charts; Whispering Bells – The Dell-Vikings featuring Krips Johnson; Tonite, Tonite – The Mello-Kings; Long Lonely Nights – Lee Andrews And The Hearts; Baby Oh Baby – The Shells; Tell Me Why – Norman Fox And The Rob-Roys; Buzz-Buzz-Buzz – Hollywood Flames; Tear Drops – Lee Andrews And The Hearts; Been So Long – The Pastels; Get A Job – The Silhouettes; Book Of Love – The Monotones; Maybe – The Chantels; I Wonder Why – Dion And The Belmonts; One Summer Night – Danleers; For Your Precious Love – Jerry Butler And The Impressions; You Cheated – The Shields; I'm So Young – The Students; Everyday Of The Week – The Students; Little Star- The Elegants; Tears On My Pillow – The Imperials; Trickle, Trickle – The Videos; Ten Commandments Of Love – Harvey And The Moonglows; 16 Candles – The Crests; So Fine – The Fiestas; Lovers Never Say Goodbye – The Flamingos; Since I Don't Have You – The Skyliners with Lenny Martin And The Orchestra; Pizza Pie -Norman Fox And The Rob Roys with Sid Bass And His Orchestra; Sorry (I Ran All The Way Home)- The Impalas with LeRoy Holmes Orchestra; A Teenager In Love – Dion AndThe Belmonts; Who's That Knocking – The Genies; I Only Have Eyes For You – The Flamingos; Hushabye – The Mystics; Rockin' In The Jungle – The Eternals; Mope-Itty Mope – Boss-Tones; Oh Rose Marie – The Fascinators With Jesse Stone Orchestra; Just To Be With You – The Passions; Shimmy-Shimmy-Ko-Ko-Bop – Little Anthony And The Imperials; The Wind – The Jesters; Stay – Maurice Williams And The Zodiacs; There's A Moon Out Tonight – The Capris; Blue Moon – The Marcels; Tonight I Fell In Love – The Tokens with Fields-Madera Orchestra; Daddy's Home – Shep And The Limelites; Barbara-Ann – The Regents; Rama Lama Ding Dong – The Edsels; Tonight (Could Be The Night) – The Velvets featuring Virgil Johnson; My True Story – The Jive Five With Joe Rene And Orchestra; Nag – The Halos; Lookin' For My Baby – The Earls; Imagination – The Quotations; Coney Island Baby – The Excellents; Remember Then – The Earls; Never Let You Go – The Five Discs; Denise -Randy And The Rainbows; Unchained Melody – Vito And The Salutations; I Do – The Marvelows; Morse Code Of Love – The Capris; My Juanita (Live) – Johnny Maestro And The Brooklyn Bridge.

Doo wop wasn't known as such in its day. It was simply part of rock'n'roll or R&B. The vocal group sound was common enough in all forms of pop in the '50s. Elvis, remember, included the Jordanaires on many of his sides of the period. But as the "solo" voice became dominant in white rock'n'roll – and the anodyne, processed sound of Frankie Avilon and Bobby Vee began to dominate the US pop charts – black music clung to the excitement and community of the group sound.

Undoubtedly born of harmony acts like The Mills Brothers and The Ink Spots – with some of the theatrical grandstanding of R&B pioneers Louis Jordan and Cab Calloway – black vocal-group music of the '50s and early '60s became identified with sumptuous four and five-part arrangements of wistful ballads, uptempo street operas of teenage yearning and finger-clicking, jivey bits of hokum that staked a street-corner claim ("They often call me Speedoo but my real name is Mr Earl"). Of course, many of the form's most famous examples predate white rock-'n'roll's breakthrough sides. Sixty Minute Man and The Glory Of Love date from1951, The Orioles' original of Crying In The Chapel is from 1953, The Chords' eternal Sh'Boom was a huge hit in 1954.

This was the sensual end of rock'n'roll – more likely to be about The Still Of The Night or Earth Angels than Great Balls Of Fire – but many of these songs still had only one thing on their mind: sex. This was the soundtrack to a population boom, remember. Whether this often dreamy music was born on sodium-lit New York street corners, as legend insists, is open to debate, but certainly the explosion of little labels – Jubilee, Dootone, Gee, a million of 'em – proves it was a form which grew from the street. And the true stuff is black. (Anyone who's ever enquired in an oldies shop about the CrewCuts' version of Sh'Boom will know the meaning of the word "humiliation".) However, it quickly became popular in other New York communities, notably among Italians. And one or two white groups turned in creditable sides – The Mello-Kings, for example. There were even some integrated groups, like the Del Vikings or the black'n'Italian Norman Fox And The Rob Roys, who once cut a single called "Pizza Pie".

To succeed, a doo wop group needed a great falsetto singer or at least a soprano, able to sing swoony, lachrymose stuff that came with an emotional edge which set it apart from mawkish Tin Pan Alley schlock. A song like Daddy's Home by Shep And The Limelights is certainly sentimental but their rendition makes it sound much more like the song of a young man coming home from war or prison than Cliff Richard's cover in the '80s, which sounded like a particularly creepy parent popping home for his tea. A prepubescent lead singer wasn't too uncommon – though it could be construed as odd, considering what they were usually given to sing. The "doo wop" or "bop-bop-sh'diddle-ip" element was, naturally, voices making do for missing musicians, providing rhythm as well as harmony. The term "doo wop" didn't stick until the revival radio shows of the early '70s. The notes in this superb box credit DJs Gus Gossert and Wayne Sierle with popularising the term.

Since then, doo wop has become the province of the most obsessive collectors and rock'n'roll archaeologists. There are some highly prized obscurities that are so rare only a handful of potentates have ever heard them. Thankfully, almost everything one needs to appreciate the music's essence is contained in this box. And if that don't get ya, then there's an equally fine Volume 2 as well.

Elvis Presley

RCA, 1987

The Sun Sessions

That's All Right; Blue Moon Of Kentucky; Good Rockin' Tonight; I Don't Care If the Sun Don't Shine; Milkcow Blues Boogie; You're A Heartbreaker; Baby, Let's Play House; I'm Left, You're Right, She's Gone; Mystery Train; I Forgot to Remember to Forget; I Love You Because; Blue Moon; Tomorrow Night; I'll Never Let You Go (Little Darlin'); Just Because; Trying to Get to You; Harbor Lights; I Love You Because [take 2]; That's All Right; Blue Moon of Kentucky; I Don't Care If The Sun Don't Shine; I'm Left, You're Right, She's Gone (My Baby's Gone) [take 9]; I'll Never Let You Go (Little Darlin'); When It Rains, It Really Pours; I Love You Because [take 3]; I Love You Because [take 5]; I'm Left, You're Right, She's Gone (My Baby's Gone) [take 7]; I'm Left, You're Right, She's Gone (My Baby's Gone) [take 12]

For years Sun Records' proprietor Sam Phillips had been telling anyone who'd listen that if he could find "a white man who had the Negro sound and the Negro feel", he'd make a billion dollars. In the summer of 1953, Phillips got his wish, when a nervous, 18-year-old named Elvis Aron Presley walked into the tiny waiting room of Sun, hoping to pay $3.98 for the privilege of making a birthday record for his mother. When the receptionist, Marion Keisker, asked him who he sounded like, he answered, "I don't sound like nobody."

He was right about that: *The Sun Sessions* are the Rosetta Stone for popular music, preserving the incendiary moment when country and blues, black music and white, collided with a big bang, all of it amplified by Phillips' own contribution, the slapback echo. It would take Phillips a year to find the right material for the young singer (on one of whose early tries he'd made the notation, "good ballad singer"), but when he did, music changed forever.

With a band that included Scotty Moore on lead guitar and Bill Black on bass, Presley cut *The Sun Sessions* in six incredible months starting July of 1954. They include Because I Love You – the first song they caught on tape – and their version of Arthur Crudup's That's All Right, the first one released, on July 19, 1954, a scant two weeks after it was recorded.

Hearing something as perfect as Trying To Get To You, it's staggering, all these years later, to realise how confident and willing to experiment this 19-year-old delivery boy was. With his wide vocabulary of gulps, squeals, hiccups and growls, Presley would never sound better or fresher. But don't underestimate the production genius of Phillips, who, when he at last found the man he was looking for, knew exactly what to do with him. That he let Presley – and this music – go to RCA for$35,000 (a very nice price at the time but nothing compared with the millions of dollars they would generate subsequently), should not cloud our judgement of *his* judgement. It was Sam's vision that lit the fuse to the rock'n'roll explosion.

Chuck Berry

MCA 1985

The Great Twenty Eight

Maybellene; 30 Days; You Can't Catch Me; Too Much Monkey Business; Brown-Eyed Handsome Man; Roll Over Beethoven; Havana Moon; School Days; Rock And Roll Music; Oh Baby Doll; Reelin' And Rockin'; Sweet Little Sixteen; Johnny B Goode; Around And Around; Carol; Beautiful Delilah; Memphis; Sweet Little Rock And Roller; Little Queenie; Almost Grown; Back In The USA; Let It Rock; Bye Bye Johnny; I'm Talking About You; Come On; Nadine; No Particular Place To Go; I Want To Be Your Driver

From the day in 1955 when he cut his first single, Maybellene, for Chicago's Chess Records, Berry retained an innate gift for definitive rock songwriting. Chuck is *the* great poet of American rock. Though many of his lyrics are essentially lists – of car accessories, say, or US cities – they express perfectly a deep-rooted American tension: between the freedom implied by the country's vast stretches of land and its population's love of material things that compromises that freedom.

Berry's only worldwide Number 1, a rotten, ribald ditty called My Ding-a-Ling, came in 1972, long after his late '50s peak, when he churned out one iconic three-chord gem after another. He may be a weird loner – truculent, tight-fisted and peculiar about sex, who for years has been content to piss-off friends and enemies alike – but, nonetheless, he turned the next generation of guitarists into Berry wannabes and cannot be overlooked in any self-respecting overview of rock.

Little Richard

RHINO, 1985

18 Greatest Hits

Tutti Frutti; Long Tall Sally; Slippin' and Slidin'; Rip It Up; Everyday; Heebie-Jeebies; She's Got It; The Girl Can't Help It; All Around the World; Lucille; Send Me Some Lovin'; Jenny, Jenny; Miss Ann; Keep A-Knockin'; Good Golly Miss Molly; Ooh! My Soul; Kansas City/Hey Hey Hey; Bama Lama Bama Loo

Richard Penniman was born black, poor and gay in Macon, Georgia, and while that is hardly an auspicious résumé in the Deep South, Little Richard not only overcame these potential obstacles, he celebrated them with abandon, performing splits and leaps, sporting piled-high hair, mascara and eye-liner. His music was a riot of conflicting tensions, the kind perhaps only a deeply-religious homosexual black man might suffer.

Though he never enjoyed a chart-topping hit, four of his frenetic piano-pounders cracked the Top 10, led by Long Tall Sally, which reached Number 6 in 1956. In 1957, at his commercial peak, he retired from pop to become a minister. Fortunately for music fans, he couldn't stay away, and in 1986 was in the inaugural class elected to the Rock and Roll Hall of Fame.

Jerry Lee Lewis

RHINO, 1993

All Killer, No Filler: The Anthology

It'll Be Me; All Night Long; In The Mood (With The Hawk); Money (That's What I Want); Please Don't Talk About Me When I'm Gone; No Headstone On My Grave; Drinking Wine Spo-Dee O-Dee; Meat Man; Crazy Arms; End Of The Road; Whole Lot Of Shakin' Going On; You Win Again; Great Balls Of Fire; Down The Line; Breathless; High School Confidential; Break-Up; I'm On Fire; Another Place Another Time; What's Made Milwaukee Famous (Has Made A Loser Out Of Me); She Still Comes Around (To Love What's Left Of Me); To Make Love Sweeter For You; Don't Let Me Cross Over (Jerry Lee Lewis And Linda Gail Lewis); One Has My Name (The Other Has My Heart); Invitation To Your Party; She Even Woke Me Up To Say Goodbye; One Minute Past Eternity; I Can't Seem To Say Goodbye; Once More With Feeling; There Must Be More To Love Than This; Touching Home; Would You Take Another Chance On Me; Chantilly Lace; Sometimes A Memory Ain't Enough; He Can't Fill My Shoes; Let's Put It Back Together Again; Middle Age Crazy; Come On In; I'll Find It Where I Can; Over The Rainbow; Thirty Nine And Holding; Rockin' My Life Away

"If I'm going to hell, I'm going there playing the piano," Jerry Lee Lewis once said, and while the Killer's personal problems have indeed obscured his musical talents at times – marrying your 13-year-old cousin will do that – it would be hard to name anyone who has straddled two types of music, rock'n'roll and country, so long and so well. A fiery and unpredictable showman who anticipated Jimi Hendrix by using assorted body parts to pound his piano keys, Lewis never had a Number 1 hit, but in 1957 Whole Lot Of Shakin' and Greats Balls Of Fire went to three and two in quick succession.

"I never considered myself the greatest, but I'm the best," he once said, and who in their right mind would wish to contradict him?

Fats Domino

EMI AMERICA 1990

My Blue Heaven: The Best of Fats Domino

My Blue Heaven; The Fat Man; Please Don't Leave Me; Ain't That A Shame; I'm In Love Again; When My Dreamboat Comes Home; Blueberry Hill; Blue Monday; I'm Walkin'; Valley Of Tears; The Big Beat; Yes, My Darling; Whole Lotta Loving; I'm Ready; I'm Gonna Be A Wheel Someday; I Want To Walk You Home; Be My Guest; Walking To New Orleans; Let The Four Winds Blow; What A Party.

The other great piano rocker.

From the age of 14, Antoine "Fats" Domino was a regular on the New Orleans bar scene, where he learned stride and barrelhouse piano from giants like Fats Waller and Professor Longhair. He joined trumpet player Dave Bartholomew's band in the mid-'40s and the pair ended up co-writing many of the songs that made Fats a constant presence in the charts from 1955 – when his first hit, Ain't That A Shame, reached Number 10 – until 1964 when the arrival of the beat group changed the face of the charts. His biggest hits were Blueberry Hill, which reached Number 2 in the US, and I'm Walkin', which got to Number 4. In fact, walkin' showed up as a regular theme in Fats' music, though not, apparently, in his life.

See also . . .

Various Artists

EMI 1996

Crescent City Soul: The Sound Of New Orleans

Mardi Gras In New Orleans – Professor Longhair; The Fat Man – Fats Domino; Mighty, Mighty Man – Ray Brown with Earl M Barnes And his Orchestra; Lawdy Miss Clawdy – Lloyd Price; The Things That I Used To Do – Guitar Slim And His Band; I Didn't Want To Do It – The Spiders; Jock-A-Mo – Sugar Boy Crawford And His Cane Cutters; I Hear You Knocking – Smiley Lewis; Tutti Frutti – Little Richard; Ain't That A Shame – Fats Domino; Let The Good Times Roll – Shirley And lee; Ain't Got No Home – Clarence "Frogman" Henry; Let The Four Winds Blow – Roy Brown; The Monkey – Dave Bartholomew; Don't You Just Know It – Huey "Piano" Smith And The Clowns; Ooh Poo Pah Doo (part 1) – Jessie Hill; Walking To New Orleans – Fats Domino; Mother In Law – Ernie K Doe; She Put The Hurt On me – Prince La La; It Will Stand – The Showmen; I Like It Like That – Chris Kenner; I Know You Don't (Love Me No More) – Barbara George; It's Raining – Irma Thomas; Working In The Coal Mine – Lee Dorsey; Tell It Like It Is – Aaron Neville; Cissy Strut – The Meters; Right Place Wrong Time – Dr John; Lady Marmalade – Labelle; Boogie Woogie Mama – Tommy Ridgley; Detroit City Blues – Fats Domino; 3X7=21 – Jewel King; That's How You Got Killed Before – Dave Bartholomew; Tee-Rah-Rah – Smiley Lewis; Stackalee – Archibald; Poppa Stoppa Theme Song – Dave Bartholomew; Jumpin' Tonight (Midnight Rockin') – Joe Turner; Ain't Gonna Do It – Dave Bartholomew; Every Night About This Time – Fats Domino; Shake Shake Baby – Archibald; Good Ax Boogie – Dave Bartholomew; I'm Gone – Shirley And Lee; Looped – Tommy Ridgley; The Bells Are Ringing – Smiley Lewis; Who Drank My Beer While I Was In The Rear? – Dave Bartholomew; Going Home – Fats Domino; Julie Mae – Smiley Lewis; Great Big Eyes (Those Little Reds) – Archibald; Little Girl Sing Ding-a-Ling – Dave Bartholomew; Bon Ton Roulet – Clarence "Bon Ton" Barlow; You Gotta Reap – Lowell Fulson; Going To The River – Fats Domino; Baby's Gone – Bobby Mitchell and the Toppers; Blue Monday – Smiley Lewis; You're The One – The Spiders; Sittin' And Wonderin' – Jesse Allen; ABCs (parts 1 and 2) – Smilin' Joe; Toy Bell – The Bees; I'm Slippin' – The Spiders; Single Life – Billy Tate; Runnin' Wild – Pee Wee Clayton; Four Winds – Dave Bartholomew; Feel So Good – Shirley And Lee; Travellin' Mood – Wee Willie Wayne; Would You – Dave Bartholomew; Witchcraft – The Spiders; I'm In Love Again – Fats Domino; One Night – Smiley Lewis; Try Rock'n'Roll – Bobby Mitchell; I Feel Good – Shirley And Lee; Someday – Smiley Lewis; Rockin' At Osmo's – Lee Allen; Chicken Shack Boogie – Amos Milburn; Please Believe Me – Charles Brown; Shame, Shame, Shame – Smiley Lewis; Sick And Tired – Chris Kenner; Sister Jenny – Johnny Fuller; I'll Be The Bee – Ruth And Al; I'm Walkin' – Fats Domino; Keeper Of My Heart – Faye Adams; I'm Gonna Be A Wheel Someday – Bobby Mitchell; I Want To Walk You Home – Fats Domino; Ooh Poo Pah Doo (part 2) – Jesse Hill; Tiddle Winks – Allen And Allen; Over You – Aaron Neville; Whip It On Me – Jesse Hill; Hello My Lover – Ernie K-Doe; I Just Want You – Bobby Charles; It Keeps Rainin' – Fats Domino. Tain't It The Truth – Ernie K-Doe; Come On – Earl King; Heavenly Baby – Allen And Allen; True Love Never Dies – Allen Orange; New Orleans Twist – Blazer Boy; Cry On – Irma Thomas; It Won't Be Me – Joe Diamond; Let's Live – Aaron Neville; Grumblin' Fussin' Nag Bag – The Del Royals; I Cried My Last Tear – Ernie K-Doe; Country Fool – The Showmen; Te-Ta-Te-Ta-Ta – Ernie K-Doe; I Done Got Over – Irma Thomas; Oogey Moo – Jesse Hill; A Certain Girl – Ernie K-Doe; Fate Planned It This Way – The Showmen; I Want Somebody – Tommy Taylor And The Five Knights; Searching For Olive Oil – The Senors; Help Yourself – Diamond Joe; The Blues – Al Robinson; Always A First Time – Earl King; Fortune Teller – Beby Spellman; Valley Of Tears – Calvin Lee; Trick Bag – Earl King; Every Now And Then – Benny Spellman; Never Again – Eskew Reeder; Lipstick Traces (On A Cigarette) – Benny Spellman; Ruler Of My Heart – Irma Thomas; 39-21-46 Shape – The Showmen; Take A Look – Irma Thomas

This is a stunning capsule guide to one American city's contribution to rock, and also a fascinating example of why early rock'n'soul was so potent and can still thrill today.

Take something like Shirley And Lee's Let The Good Times Roll. It is not an expert record on any level, but, boy, does it cook. It feels like a party, an invocation to ward off the Devil, a call to crawl beneath the sheets, whatever you need. "Come on baby this is this/This is something that I just can't miss," coos Lee to the lady of his choice. Shirley's shaky retort, though sung behind the beat and totally flat, is as vital to the brew as spice in a gumbo. Then the drums kick up a gear and the saxman arrives to sear your ears. It's punk rock – with sex appeal – and utterly irresistible.

There's s ton of similarly good stuff here: Guitar Slim, the languid splendour of Irma Thomas, Benny Spellman; by the time Aaron Neville's pleading us to Tell It Like It Is – one of the finest vocals ever recorded by anyone – you should be dancing, shagging, singing, crying ... something elemental, anyhow. There's plenty from the funky, fertile pens of Dave Bartholomew, Naomi Neville and Allen Toussaint – all in all, a fantastic reminder of why rock music mattered.

Lonnie Donegan

SEQUEL 1999

Talking Guitar Blues: The Very Best Of

Lost John; Stewball; Railroad Blues; Bring A Little Water, Sylvie; Dead Or Alive; Wabash Cannonball; Nobody's Child; Frankie And Johnny; Don't You Rock Me Daddy-O; Cumberland Gap; Gamblin' Man; Puttin' On The Style; My Dixie Darling; Jack O'Diamonds; On A Monday; Mule Skinner Blues; The Grand Coulee Dam; Sally, Don't You Grieve; Betty, Betty, Betty; Lonesome Traveller; Light From The Lighthouse; Lonnie's Skiffle Party Medley (Part 1); Tom Dooley; Does Your Chewing Gum Lose Its Flavour; Fort Worth Jail; Battle Of New Orleans; Sal's Got A Sugar Lip; Take This Hammer; You Pass Me By; San Miguel; Talkin' Guitar Blues; My Old Man's A Dustman; I Wanna Go Home; Lorelei; Sorry But I'm Gonna Have To Pass; Lively!; Virgin Mary; Have A Drink On Me; Michael Row The Boat; Lumbered; The Comancheros; The Party's Over; I'll Never Fall In Love Again; Pick A Bale Of Cotton; This Train; Noah Found Grace In The Eyes Of The Lord; Beans In My Ears; She Was T-Bone Talking Woman; Farewell (Fare Thee Well); World Cup Willie

"I was the catalyst for it all," Lonnie Donegan has often claimed (meaning the British rock business), and with some justification. The unexpected success of his Rock Island Line (originally tucked away on a Chris Barber album) unleashed the 1956–57 skiffle boom in Britain that enabled teenagers to augment their Elvis impersonations with their own music fashioned from simple household instruments. Donegan notched up over 30 hits between 1956 and 1962, though the inspiration for his workingmen's songs increasingly shifted from Leadbelly and Woody Guthrie to the British music-hall tradition. Ironically, it was the alumni of a bunch of skiffle-crazed protégés, The Quarrymen, who would unseat him. When John Lennon and Paul McCartney arrived in the hit parade it marked the end of Donegan's run.

Buddy Holly

MCA 1985

From The Original Master Tapes

That'll Be The Day; Oh, Boy!; Not Fade Away; Tell Me How; Maybe Baby; Everyday; Rock Around With Ollie Vee; It's So Easy; I'm Lookin' For Someone To Love; Peggy Sue; I'm Gonna Love You Too; Words Of Love; Rave On; Well All Right; Listen To Me; Think It Over; Heartbeat; Reminiscing; It Doesn't Matter Anymore; True Love Ways

In the three short years of his recording life, Buddy Holly effortlessly paraded the wide range of influences he'd absorbed while growing up in Lubbock, Texas, including rockabilly, Tex-Mex, big-band ballads and country. Not only was he one of rock's first singer-songwriters, but under the guidance of manager/producer Norman Petty, he varied his arrangements brilliantly, using a basic guitar, bass and drums line-up on some songs to entire string sections on others. Holly's only US Number 1 was That'll Be The Day, which hit the top in September 1957. He died on February 2, 1959,when the small plane carrying him and other musicians on the Winter Dance Party tour – notably the Big Bopper and Richie Valens – crashed into an Iowa cornfield. Holly was just 22 years old, and it's an inevitable, if sad, exercise to wonder what he might have done with an entire career.

Muddy Waters

LONDON 1959

The Best Of Muddy Waters

I Just Want To Make Love To You; Long Distance Call; Louisiana Blues; Honey Bee; Rollin' Stone; I'm Ready; Hoochie Coochie Man; She Moves Me; Standing Around Crying; Still A Fool; I Can't Be Satisfied

Muddy Waters and Otis Spann toured Britain in October 1958 and Muddy famously upset his earnest audiences with the howl of his amplified slide guitar. If this album had been released before March 1959, they'd have been better prepared. Muddy brought the Mississippi country blues of Rollin' Stone and I Can't Be Satisfied to Chicago, recruited a band with Little Walter and Jimmy Rogers in its ranks and with songwriter Willie Dixon's help created the pugnacious, strutting style that revitalised the city's clubs. Hoochie Coochie Man, I'm Ready and I Just Want To Make Love To You, along with Got My Mojo Working and Mannish Boy (not present here), provided blues boom bands, including the Stones and The Yardbirds, with a muscular repertoire that ultimately helped them to change pop's direction.

The Everly Brothers

RHINO, 2000

All-Time Original Hits

Bye Bye Love; Wake Up Little Susie; All I Have To Do Is Dream; Bird Dog; Devoted To You; Problems; Take A Message To Mary; ('Til) I Kissed You; Let It Be Me; When Will I Be Loved; Cathy's Clown; So Sad (To Watch Good Love Go Bad); Ebony Eyes; Walk Right Back; That's Old Fashioned (That's The Way Love Should Be); Crying In The Rain.

Harmony singing ran in Don and Phil Everly's family. Their father and his two brothers had sung together for years, and when Don was just seven years old, he had his own 15-minute radio show each day in Iowa, The Little Donnie Show. All grown up, the Everly Brothers scored three Number 1 hits, starting with Wake Up Little Susie in 1957 and continuing with All I Have To Do Is Dream and Cathy's Clown. Their tight, perfectly blended harmonies set the mark for just about every vocal group that followed them, from The Beatles to Simon & Garfunkel.

Various Artists

LONDON, 1961

Roots Of The Blues

Jim And John – Lonnie Young, Ed Young And Lonnie Young Jr.; The Wild Ox Moan – Vera Hall; Been Drinkin' Water Out Of A Hollow Log – Fred McDowell; All Night Long – Miles And Bob Pratcher; Levee Camp Reminiscence – Forest City Joe; Chevrolet – Oree – Lonnie Young, Ed Young And Lonnie Young Jr.; Levee Camp Holler – Johnnie Lee Moore; Eighteen Hammers – Johnny Lee Moore And 12 Mississippi Penitentiary convicts; Train Time – Forest City Joe; Freight Train Blues – Fred McDowell; Drink On Little Girl – Forest City Joe

When the seven volumes of Alan Lomax's "Southern Folk Heritage Series" were issued in March 1961, they gave the lie to those who thought all blues singers were either dead or living in Chicago. This was Volume Three, introducing to the world harmonica player Forest City Joe Pugh, the Young brothers, a fife and drum band from Como, MS and, most importantly, their neighbour, bottleneck guitarist Fred McDowell. Volume Seven, *The Blues Roll On*, with a lugubrious portrait of McDowell on its cover, contained further material by all three artists. The impact of these albums sent other researchers into the Southern states to rediscover older men like Sleepy John Estes, Mississippi John Hurt and Bukka White and brought deserved international fame to McDowell.

Various Artists

COLUMBIA 1961

The Blues

Coming Home – Elmore James; Hands Off – Priscilla Bowman; You Don't Have To Go, Ain't That Lovin' You Baby – Jimmy Reed; Just A Little Bit – Rosco Gordon; Dimples – John Lee Hooker; You Can Make It If You Try – Gene Allison; I Wish You Would – Billy Boy Arnold; Mess Around – Memphis Slim; Do What I Say – JB Lenoir; Crying For My Baby – Harold Burrage; Kansas City – Jimmy Witherspoon

Unless you bought LPs direct from America, there wasn't much blues to be found in British record racks at the start of the '60s.That was until 1961, when EMI acquired Vee-Jay and issued this comprehensive survey of the Chicago label's blues catalogue. It became a useful source of material for the nascent British R&B bands: the Stones chose Gene Allison's You Can Make It If You Try, The Yardbirds selected Billy Boy Arnold's I Wish You Would, the Animals tried on John Lee Hooker's Dimples, while Elmore James' Coming Home gave budding slide guitarists something to think about. Other luminaries to be heard were Jimmy Reed, Rosco Gordon, Memphis Slim, JB Lenoir and Jimmy Witherspoon. Nevertheless, Alexis Korner's sleevenote tried to make these blues appeal to a wider audience when he asserted, "This is music to which you can really twist!"

Little Anthony And the Imperials

RHINO 1989

Best of Little Anthony And the Imperials

It's Not For Me; The Diary; I'm Alright; Traveling Stranger; Tears On My Pillow; Two People In The World; So Much; Wishful Thinking; A Prayer And A Juke Box; Shimmy, Shimmy, Ko-Ko-Bop; My Empty Room; I'm Taking A Vacation From Love; Please Say You Want Me; I'm On The Outside (Looking In); Goin' Out Of My Head; Hurt So Bad; Take Me Back; I Miss You So.

Slightly to the right of doo wop were this unusual group who pre-figured soul. "Little" Anthony Gourdine grew up in Brooklyn and formed the group that would become the Imperials in 1957, when he was just 17 and stood 5' 4". Perfectly capturing the close harmony doo-wop style, the group's first hit was also their biggest, Tears On My Pillow, which sold over a million copies in 1958. The group then waited six years for its next Top 10 song, Goin' Out Of My Head.

Jackie Wilson

ACE 1993

The Very Best of Jackie Wilson

Reet Petite (The Finest Girl You Ever Want To Meet); Lonely Teardrops; To Be Loved; That's Why (I Love You So); I'll Be Satisfied; Doggin' Around; Lonely Life; Night; You Better Know It; Talk That Talk; Am I The Man; I'm Comin' On Back To You; A Woman, A Lover, A Friend; Baby Workout; Squeeze Her, Tease Her (But Love Her); No Pity (In The Naked City); Whispers (Gettin' Louder); I Get The Sweetest Feeling; Since You Showed Me How To Be Happy; Love Is Funny That Way; Just Be Sincere; (Your Love Keeps Lifting Me) Higher And Higher; You Got Me Walking; This Love Is Real (I Can Feel Those Vibrations).

Before he was a singer, Detroit's Jackie Wilson was a Golden Gloves boxing champion, and when he took up his new trade, he poured all of his energy into his stage show, which rivalled even James Brown's in its slick gyrations. But Wilson was a better romantic singer than Brown. "Jackie Wilson opened his mouth and out poured that sound like honey on moonbeams, and it was like the whole room shifted on some weird axis," said his A&R man, Dick Jacobs. Nevertheless, he worked harder than anyone at his shows. "Wilson would kiss all the women, especially the ugly ones," one audience member recalled, "because he knew if he did they'd be with him forever." Alas, forever wasn't very long: Wilson collapsed on stage at the Latin Casino outside Philadelphia in 1975 and died eight years later, having never come out of his coma. His urgent, almost operatic soul style had kind of collapsed with him, no one else ever took up the flame.

The Shadows

EMI 1997

The Very Best Of The Shadows

Apache; Man Of Mystery; F.B.I.; Frightened City; Kon-Tiki; The Savage; Wonderful Land; Guitar Tango; Dance On; Foot Tapper; Atlantis; Shindig; Geronimo; Theme For Young Lovers; The Rise And Fall Of Flingel Bunt; Genie With The Light Brown Lamp; (The Next Time I See) Mary Anne; Stingray; Don't Make My Baby Blue; War Lord

It's sometimes difficult to see why the world fell for The Shadows' neatly trimmed instrumental hits during the first half of the '60s, especially when you consider the awful dance routines (or rather, routine) the band accompanied them with.

"We've tried to make our tunes simple," insisted lead guitarist Hank Marvin at the peak of their career. "What's the point in playing instrumentals if you can't tap your feet or hum the melody?" But the main point of The Shadows, at least for a generation of aspiring musicians, was to place the guitar centre-stage. They may have started life as Cliff Richard's backing group, and been regarded in the US as pale imitators of The Ventures, but Marvin – who, with his Buddy Holly face-furniture, gave hope to four-eyed nerds all over Britain – was the nation's first bona-fide guitar hero.

Johnny Kidd And The Pirates

EMI GOLD 1995

25 Greatest Hits

Shakin' All Over; Some Other Guy; Please Don't Touch; Whole Lotta Woman; You Got What It Takes; Your Cheatin' Heart; Restless; You Can Have Her; Linda Lu; I Just Wanna Make Love To You; A Shot Of Rhythm And Blues; I Can Tell; I'll Never Get Over You; I Know; Hungry For Love; If You Were The Only Girl In The World; Always And Ever; Feelin'; Oh Boy; Yes Sir, That's My Baby; The Fool; The Birds And The Bees; Send Me Some Lovin'; Doctor Feelgood; Let's Talk About Us

Worth the price of entry alone for Shakin' All Over, the haunting 1960 hit which established the group's name, this extensive collection includes Kidd's only other major hit, I'll Never Get Over You, plus a mix of moody R&B and ballads that were his forte during the early '60s. Ironically, although the band's earthy style anticipated the beat boom by a couple of years, they were swiftly cast aside in the wake of Merseybeat, and though Kidd soldiered on with his theatrical live performances, he was killed in a car crash in October 1966 on the way home from a gig. The Pirates, led by ace guitarist Mick Green, reformed during the late '70s and found favour on the New Wave circuit with a meaty, beaty trio style that still packed an incredible punch. More recently Green showed up on Paul McCartney's spirited evocation of this period, *Run Devil Run*.

Various Artists
RHINO 1992

Troubadors Of The Folk Era

John Henry – Odetta; Wasn't That A Mighty Storm – Eric Von Schmidt; I'll Fly Away – Carolyn Hester; Mean Old Frisco – John Hammond; This Land Is My Land – Woody Guthrie; Silver Dagger – Joan Baez; Tomorrow Is A Long Time – Ian And Sylvia; Violets Of Dawn – Eric Andersen; Reno Nevada – Mimi And Richard Faria; Four In The Morning – Jesse Colin Young; The Universal Soldier – Buffy Sainte-Marie; Cocaine Blues – Dave Von Ronk; Morning Dew – Bonnie Dobson; San Francisco Bay Blues – Ramblin' Jack Elliott; Well, Well, Well – Bob Gibson And Bob Camp, with Dick Rosmini And Herb Brown; The First Time Ever I Saw Your Face – Ewan MacColl And Peggy Seeger; Mister Spaceman – The Holy Modal Rounders; Catch The Wind – Donovan; The Bells – The Modern Folk Quartet; Gotta Travel On – Au Go-Go Singers; I'll Roll In My Sweet Baby's Arms – The New Lost City Ramblers; River Come Down – The Journeymen; Goodnight Irene – The Weavers; Tom Dooley – The Kingston Trio; Hard Ain't It Hard – The Limeliters; Walk Right In – The Rooftop Singers; Stewball – Greenbriar Boys; Michael – The Highwaymen; Take Your Fingers Off It – The Even Dozen Jug Band; Greenfields – The Brothers Four; Silver Threads And Golden Needles – The Springfields; The Banana Boat Song – The Tarriers; Green, Green – The New Christy Minstrels; Linin' Track – "Spider" John Koerner, Dave "Snaker" Ray And Tony "Little Sun" Glover; Rider – The Big Three; Mobile Line – Jim Kweskin And The Jug Band.

The American folk-music movement began with Woodie Guthrie, upon whose guitar were inscribed the words "This machine kills fascists", and flourished in the '50s as a rallying point for the Left, beleaguered in Joe McCarthy's America. Hard as it is to believe now, folk albums routinely topped the charts in the '50s and early '60s. Tom Dooley was a Number 1 single for the Kingston Trio in 1958, and Peter, Paul and Mary actually stood 1-2-6 in the album charts for Nov. 2, 1963! The civil rights and anti-war movements brought in more conscripts until it seemed every left-leaning kid with an ounce of musical talent was strumming an acoustic guitar, readying ears and minds for a folk messiah named Dylan.

Bob, of course, quickly abandoned and out-grew traditional folk, but here's a useful primer of the sound he left behind.

John Lee Hooker
STATESIDE 1962

The Folklore Of John Lee Hooker

Tupelo; I'm Mad Again; I'm Going Upstairs; Wanted Blues; Five Long Years; I Like To See You Walk; The Hobo; Hard Headed Woman; Wednesday Evening Blues; Take Me As I Am; My First Wife Left Me; You're Looking Good Tonight

Ironically, the first Hooker album issued in Britain was an acoustic session cut for Riverside in 1959. It reflected Hooker's recent adoption by a folk fraternity that preferred blues to be intense and thoughtful rather than rampant. Deprived of amplification, Hooker's guitar work became a bland accessory rather than the competing voice that's so much a feature of his earlier recordings. That was remedied by this straight transfer of a 1962 Vee-Jay album that shrewdly spread its appeal by combining a pair of acoustic songs from the 1960 Newport Folk Festival with six further solo – but amplified – numbers and four titles with a band including labelmate Jimmy Reed. These last, alternately rhythmic and threatening, laid the groundwork for his 1964 British Top 30 hit, Dimples.

Various Artists

101 Greatest Country Hits K-TEL 1995

El Paso – Marty Robbins; Stand By Your Man – Tammy Wynette; Make The World Go Away – Eddy Arnold; Flowers On The Wall – The Statler Brothers; Crazy – Patsy Cline; It Was Almost Like A Song – Ronnie Milsap; I Was Country When Country Wasn't Cool – Barbara Mandrell; Walk On By – Leroy Van Dyke; Coal Miner's Daughter – Loretta Lynn; There Goes My Everything – Jack Greene. Country Sunshine – Dottie West; Misty – Ray Stevens; (Hey Won't You Play) Another Somebody Done Somebody Wrong Song – BJ Thomas; Delta Dawn – Tanya Tucker; All The Gold In California – Larry Gatlin/The Gatlin Brothers Band; Kiss An Angel Good Mornin' – Charley Pride; Heaven's Just A Sin Away – Kendalls; I Loved 'Em Every One – TG Sheppard; Don't All The Girls Get Prettier At Closing Time – Mickey Gilley; Louisiana Woman, Mississippi Man – Conway Twitty/Loretta Lynn; Rose Garden – Lynn Anderson; Abilene – George Hamilton IV; 9,999,999 Tears – Dickey Lee; The End Of The World – Skeeter Davis; Almost Persuaded – David Houston; The Happiest Girl In The Whole USA – Donna Fargo; For The Good Times – Ray Price; Tippy Toeing – Harden Trio; Oh, Lonesome Me – Don Gibson; Teddy Bear Song – Barbara Fairchild.; You And I – Eddie Rabbitt/Crystal Gayle; I Believe In You – Don Williams; He'll Have To Go – Jim Reeves; The Tennessee Waltz – Patti Page; It's Such A Pretty World Today – Wynn Stewart; I'm Not Lisa – Jessi Colter; I Can Help – Billy Swan; Why Me – Kris Kristofferson; Still – Bill Anderson; San Antonio Rose – Floyd Cramer; Waterloo – Stonewall Jackson; Please Help Me, I'm Falling (In Love With You) – Hank Locklin; Hello Walls – Faron Young; Down Yonder – Del Wood; Big Bad John – Jimmy Dean; Wings Of A Dove – Ferlin Husky; The Wild Side Of Life – Hank Thompson; It Wasn't God Who Made Honky Tonk Angels – Kitty Wells; The Bridge Washed Out – Warner Mack; Skip A Rope – Henson Cargill; The Battle Of New Orleans – Johnny Horton; Indian Love Call – Slim Whitman; Sixteen Tons – Tennessee Ernie Ford; Your Cheatin' Heart – Hank Williams; Big Midnight Special – Wilma Lee/Stoney Cooper; Ring Of Fire – Johnny Cash; Don't Let Me Cross Over – Carl Butler/Pearl Butler; I Dreamed Of A Hillbilly Heaven – Tex Ritter; I Don't Believe You've Met My Baby – Charlie Louvin; Foggy Mountain Breakdown – Lester Flatt/Earl Scruggs; Don't It Make My Brown Eyes Blue – Crystal Gayle; In The Misty Moonlight – Jerry Wallace; Right Or Wrong – Wanda Jackson; You've Never Been This Far Before – Conway Twitty; Mr Sandman – Emmylou Harris; Don't Touch Me – Jeannie Seely; Let's Think About Living – Bob Luman; Once A Day – Connie Smith; He Stopped Loving Her Today – George Jones; Satin Sheets – Jeanne Pruett; I Love A Rainy Night – Eddie Rabbitt; The Sweetest Thing (I've Ever Known) – Juice Newton; Before The Next Teardrop Falls – Freddy Fender; Help Me Make It Through The Night – Sammi Smith; Luckenbach, Texas (Back To The Basics Of Love) – Waylon Jennings; Lookin' For Love – Johnny Lee; I Will Always Love You – Dolly Parton; Young Love – SonnyJames; Behind Closed Doors – Charlie Rich; My Special Angel – Bobby Helms. Harper Valley PTA – Jeannie C Riley; Wolverton Mountain – Claude King; Tennessee Birdwalk – JackBlanchard/Misty Morgan; Country Bumpkin – Cal Smith; From A Jack To A King – Ned Miller; Take This Job And Shove It – Johnny Paycheck; The Carroll County Accident – Porter Wagoner; Put Your Hand In The Hand – Sandy Posey; Hey, Good Lookin' – Ace Cannon; May The Bird Of Paradise Fly Up Your Nose – Little Jimmy Dickens; On The Road Again – Willie Nelson; Ode To Billie Joe – Bobbie Gentry; When You're Hot, You're Hot – Jerry Reed; Okie From Muskogee – Merle Haggard; Convoy – CW McCall; Rhinestone Cowboy – Glen Campbell; King Of The Road – Roger Miller; Queen Of The House – Jody Miller; Detroit City – Bobby Bare; Six Days On The Road – Dave Dudley; Girl On The Billboard – Del Reeves.

Somebody once described country music as "blues for white people". OK, both are "people's music", but surely there is a difference: the blues don't usually revel in the self-conscious campiness and bathos that make so many country lyrics so quotable. Collected here are songs about work, love, home, heartbreak and driving, mostly taken from the heyday of country music – the '50's,' 60's and '70's – when Nashville's Grand Ole Opry was the most famous music hall in the country and country music's everyday operas were just grand.

Bo Diddley

CHESS 1997

His Best (Chess 50th Anniversary Collection)

Bo Diddley; I'm A Man; You Don't Love Me (You Don't Care); Diddley Daddy; Pretty Thing; Bring It To; I'm Lookin' For A Woman; Who Do You Love?; Hey Bo Diddley; Mona (AKA I Need You Baby); Before You Accuse Me; Say Man; Dearest Darling; Crackin' Up; The Story Of Bo Diddley; Road Runner; Pills; I Can Tell; You Can't Judge A Book By Its Cover; Ooh Baby.

"I play the guitar as if I was playing the drums," said Bo Diddley once. As the late critic Robert Palmer noted, Bo'd be a spectacularly rich man if the law permitted you to copyright a rhythm, for the shuffle that bears his name (also known as "Shave and a haircut: two bits") is everywhere in pop. Not that he invented it, of course. A consummate showman and tireless self-mythologizer, Diddley built his own exotically shaped guitars and choked their strings to produce a distorted roaring sound. "It's mixed up with spiritual, sanctified rhythms," he explained, "and the feeling I put into it when I'm playing, I have the feeling of making people shout."

Various Artists

ABKCO 1991

Back To Mono (1958–69) Hits of Phil Spector

To Know Him Is To Love Him – The Teddy Bears; Corrina, Corrina – Ray Peterson; Spanish Harlem – Ben E King; Pretty Little Angel Eyes – Curtis Lee; Every Breath I Take – Gene Pitney; I Love How You Love Me – The Paris Sisters; Under The Moon Of Love – Curtis Lee; There's No Other Like My Baby – The Crystals; Uptown – The Crystals; He Hit Me (It Felt Like A Kiss) – The Crystals; He's A Rebel – The Crystals; Zip-A-Dee-Doo-Dah – Bob B Soxx And The Blue Jeans; Puddin' 'N' Tain – The Alley Cats; He's Sure The Boy I Love – The Crystals; Why Do Lovers Break Each Other's Hearts – Bob B Soxx And The Blue Jeans; (Today I Met) The Boy I'm Gonna Marry – Darlene Love; Da Doo Ron Ron – The Crystals; Heartbreaker – The Crystals; Why Don't They Let Us Fall In Love – Veronica; Chapel Of Love – Darlene Love; Not Too Young To Get Married – Bob B Soxx And The Blue Jeans; Wait Til My Bobby Gets Home – Darlene Love; All Grown Up, Be My Baby – The Ronettes; Then He Kissed Me – The Crystals; A Fine, Fine Boy – Darlene Love; Baby, I Love You – The Ronettes; I Wonder – The Ronettes; Girls Can Tell – The Crystals; Little Boy – The Crystals; Hold Me Tight – The Treasures; (The Best Part Of) Breakin' Up – The Ronettes; Soldier Baby Of Mine – The Ronettes; Strange Love – Darlene Love; Stumble And Fall – Darlene Love; When I Saw You – The Ronettes; So Young – Veronica; Do I Love You? – The Ronettes; Keep On Dancing – The Ronettes; You, Baby – The Ronettes; Woman In Love (With You) – The Ronettes; Walking In The Rain – The Ronettes. You've Lost That Lovin' Feelin' – The Righteous Brothers; Born To Be Together – The Ronettes; Just Once In My Life – The Righteous Brothers; Unchained Melody – The Righteous Brothers; Is This What I Get For Loving You? – The Ronettes; Long Way To Be Happy – Darlene Love; (I Love You) For Sentimental Reasons – The Righteous Brothers; Ebb Tide – The Righteous Brothers; This Could Be The Night – The Modern Folk Quartet; Paradise – The Ronettes; River Deep, Mountain High – Ike And Tina Turner; I'll Never Need More Than This – Ike And Tina Turner; A Love Like Yours (Don't Come Knockin' Everyday) – Ike And Tina Turner; Save The Last Dance For Me – Ike And Tina Turner; I Wish I Never Saw The Sunshine – The Ronettes; You Came, You Saw, You Conquered – The Ronettes; Black Pearl – Sonny Charles and the Checkmates, Ltd; Love Is All I have To Give – The Checkmates, Ltd; White Christmas – Darlene Love; Frosty The Snowman – The Ronettes; The Bells Of St Mary – Bob B Soxx And The Blue Jeans; Santa Claus Is Coming To Town – The Crystals; Sleigh Ride – The Ronettes; Marshmallow World – Darlene Love; I Saw Kissing Santa Claus – The Ronettes; Rudolph The Red-Nosed Reindeer – The Crystals; Winter Wonderland – Darlene Love; Parade Of The Wooden Soldiers – The Crystals; Christmas (Baby Please Come Home) – Darlene Love; Here Comes Santa Claus – Bob B Soxx And The Blue Jeans; Silent Night – Phil Spector/Various Artists.

Phil Spector called his productions "little symphonies for the kids", and it was that level of grand ambition that made him the first producer to look beyond mere commercial goals and on towards a real sonic philosophy. He wanted to sell records, but it was more important to gratify his own ear.

Spector grew up in the Bronx, but moved with his mother to Los Angeles at 12 following his father's suicide. His first hit, The Teddy Bears' To Know Him Is To Love Him, was inspired by the epitaph on his father's gravestone, and his work always had a touch of dark brooding beneath the little girls' voices. Spector's Wall of Sound – his practice of overdubbing countless musicians so that drums sounded like sonic booms and guitars like thunder – was, in his words, a "Wagernian approach to rock and roll". He co-wrote Stand By Me with Jerry Lieber, produced John Lennon's Imagine, and was described by Tom Wolfe as the "first tycoon of teen". After the spectacular failure in the US of River Deep, Mountain High, the Ike And Tina Turner single he considered his masterpiece, he stepped off the treadmill, contented himself recording with The Beatles for a few years, then largely retired to a life of epic weirdness, secluding himself in his Hollywood mansion for years on end.

Four CDs of his work is much more than you need in one sitting, but this beautiful set is a treat for anyone who loves that strange, sad, pillowy thing that he does. The last disc is *A Christmas Gift To You*, one of the few "compilation" albums actually created as a whole piece and, as such, probably deserving of a place in the body of this book. One of pop's most evocative and mood-altering works – and most elaborate confections – it merits a prime place in any serious collection.

Roy Orbison

MONUMENT 1988

For The Lonely: 18 Greatest Hits

Ooby Dooby; Rockhouse; Up Town; Only The Lonely (Know How I Feel); Blue Angel; I'm Hurtin'; Running Scared; Crying; Candy Man; Dream Baby (How Long Must I Dream); Leah; Workin' For The Man; In Dreams; Mean Woman Blues; Blue Bayou; Pretty Paper; It's Over; Oh, Pretty Woman.

There have been many fine voices in rock'n'roll, but few as singular as Roy Orbison's quavering tenor. Growing up in the wonderfully named Texas town of Wink, Orbison's first influence was country and western. It was Pat Boone, his college pal at North Texas State, who persuaded Orbison to move towards pop. He recorded for Sam Phillips at Sun then moved to Nashville, where, between 1960 and '64, he scored nine Top 10 singles for Monument Records, including two Number 1s, Running Scared and Oh, Pretty Woman. Orbison was experiencing a career renaissance thanks to his work with The Travelling Willburys when he died of a sudden heart attack in 1988.

Various Artists

POLYGRAM, 1996

Growin' Up Too Fast: The Girl Group Anthology

My Boyfriend's Back – The Angels; Remember (Walkin' In The Sand) – The Shangri-Las; My Best Friend Barbara – Connie Francis; Navy Blue – Diane Renay; She Don't Deserve You – The Honeybees; Please Don't Talk To The Lifeguard – Diane Ray; It Comes And Goes – Sadina; Maybe I Know – Lesley Gore; It's Gonna Take A Miracle – The Royalettes; The Boy Next Door – The Secrets; I Wish I Knew What Dress To Wear – Ginny Arnell; 442 Glenwood Avenue – The Pixies Three; Johnny's Back in Town – Ann D'Andrea; Stay Awhile – Dusty Springfield; So Soft, So Warm – The Nu-Luvs; Look Of Love – Lesley Gore; Beatles, Please Come Back – Gigi Parker and TheLonelies; Summertime USA – The Pixies Three; Can't He Take A Hint? – Kenni Woods; Wow Wow Wee (He's The Boy For Me) – The Angels; Always Waitin' – The Paris Sisters; Watch Out Sally! – Diane Renay; Wonder Boy – Lesley Gore; Hey, Big Boy – The Secrets; The Sweet Sounds Of Summer – The Shangri-Las. Leader Of The Pack – The Shangri-Las; I Only Want To Be With You – Dusty Springfield; Dumb Head – Ginny Arnell; Cold, Cold Winter – The Pixies Three; Don't Ever Leave Me – Connie Francis; You're Welcome Back – The Sham-ettes; I Want That Boy – Sadina; I Adore Him – The Angels; One Wonderful Night – The Honeybees; Sometimes I Wish I Were A Boy – Lesley Gore; Dream Lover – The Paris Sisters; Kiss Me Sailor – Diane Renay; Back With My Baby – Kenni Woods; I Can Never Go Home Anymore – The Shangri-Las; Everybody Loves A Saturday Night – Beverly Washburn; The Other Side Of Town – The Secrets; Birthday Party – The Pixies Three – I Want To Meet Him – The Royalettes; Why Did You Go? – The Bobbi-Pins; What's So Sweet About Sweet Sixteen? – Carole Quinn; Nightmare – The Whyte Boys; That's The Way Boys Are – Lesley Gore; Footsteps On The Roof – The Shangri-Las; Growin' Up Too Fast – Diane Renay; Thank You And Goodnight – The Angels

Descended from doo wop through acts like The Chantels and The Shirelles, the girl-group explosion was just what Tin Pan Alley needed. Malleable song-hungry acts are every writing or production team's favourite kind and the craze called for mildly daring, disposable, sometimes topical fare that was pre-Beatle pop's very *raison d'être.*

By no means a definitive survey of the magic of girl groups, this set nevertheless provides an excellent picture of how widespread and prolific the pop machine was in the early '60s, being just a small sample of one label's output. Among evergreens like Leader Of The Pack, I Can Never Go Home Anymore and It's My Party you'll find great mislaid ditties such as Can't He Take A Hint; Beatles, Please Come Back and What's So Sweet About Sweet Sixteen? These, of course, represented the burning issues of the day – and every day – for the '60s teen. We shall not hear their like again.

Various Artists

RHINO 1995

Cowabunga! The Surf Box

Bulldog – The Fireballs; Moon Dawg! – The Gamblers; Church Key – The Revels, with Barbara Adkins; Underwater – The Frogmen; Mr Moto – The Belairs; Let's Go Trippin' – Dick Dale And His Del-Tones; Surfer's Stomp – The Mar-Kets; Surfin' – Beach Boys; Paradise Cove – The Surfmen; Latin'ia – The Sentinals; Bustin' Surfboards – The Tornadoes; Miserlou – Dick Dale And His Del-Tones; Surf Beat – Dick Dale And His Del-Tones; Cheater Stomp – The Fabulous Playboys; Pipeline – Chantay's; Surfer Joe (long version) – The Surfaris; Wipe Out (long version) – The Surfaris; The Rising Surf – Richie Allen And The Pacific Surfers; Surf Rider – The Lively Ones; Shoot That Curl – Chris And Kathy; KFWB Jingle (live) – Beach Boys; Surfin' USA – Beach Boys; Jezebel – The Illusions; Body Surf – Aki Aleong And The Nobles; Surf Bunny – Gene Gray And The Stingrays; Soul Surfer – Johnny Fortune; Shoot The Curl – The Honeys; Baja – The Astronauts; Pintor – The Pharos; Cat On A Hot Foam Board – The New Dimensions; Surf City – Jan And Dean; Breakfast At Tressels – Rhythm Rockers; King Of The Surf Guitar – Dick Dale And His Del-Tones; Surfin' At Mazatland – The Centurians; Surfin' Hootenanny – Al Casey, with The K-C-Ettes; The Lonely Surfer – Jack Nitzsche; Surfer Girl – The Beach Boys; Beaver Patrol – The Blazers; Fiberglass Jungle – The Crossfires; Mr Rebel – Eddie And The Showmen; Penetration – The Pyramids; Bombora – The Surfaris; Heavies – The Rotations; Moment Of Truth – Dave Myers And The Surftones; My Little Surfin' Woodie – The Sunsets; Let There Be Surf – The Chevell's; Surfin' Bird – The Trashmen; Ski Storm – The Snow Men; Disintegration – The Ready Men; Beach Party – Annette; Theme From Endless Summer – The Sandals; New York's A Lonely Town – The Trade Winds; K-39 – The Challengers; Tell 'Em I'm Surfin' – The Fantastic Baggys; On The Run – The Rondels; Walk Don't Run '64 – The Ventures; I Live For The Sun – The Sunrays; Malibu Run – The Fender IV; Misirlou (live) – Bobby Fuller Four; Hit The Surf – The Sea Shells; Storm Dancer – Jon And The Nightriders; Goin' To Malibu – The Malibooz; Wave Walk'n – The Surf Raiders; Night Of The Living Wedge – The Wedge; My Beach – Surf Punks; Tan Punks On Boards – Corky Carroll And The Cool Water Casuals; The Rebel – The Cruncher; Polaris – Insect Surfers; Chumming – The Halibuts; Save The Waves – The Surfdusters; Desert Bound – The Looney Tunes; Pier Pressure – Teisco Del Reyra; A Night In Tunisia – Laika And The Cosmonauts; Reverb 1000 (live) – Man Or Astro-Man?; Banzai Run – The Phantom Surfers; Spanish Blue – The Aqua Velvets; XKE! – The Boss Martians; Killer Dana – The Chantays; Honeybomb (live), Punta Baja – The Eliminators; Wingnut's Theme – The Sandals; Esperanza – Dick Dale.

Why do skateboarders supposedly listen to Green Day? Who knows? Why did surfers apparently dig twangy instrumentals? We don't feel this has ever been properly explained. Whatever, surf music probably began with Dick Dale's late 1961 single, Let's Go Trippin'. While the song was only a regional hit in southern California, it spawned countless imitators and launched a surf revolution that engulfed the whole country once Jan And Dean and then The Beach Boys added vocals. Still, surf music in its purest form is instrumental, as practised by bands like The Surfaris (whose pounding single, Wipe Out, went to Number 2 in 1963) and The Ventures (who have cut dozens and dozens of albums). Never before had a style been so closely tied to a specific technology – in this case, spring reverb, which brought the twangy "wet" sound nearly all these tracks share.

The Beatles

APPLE 1988

Past Masters Vol 1

Love Me Do; From Me To You; Thank You Girl; She Loves You; I'll Get You; I Want To Hold Your Hand; This Boy; Gib Mir Deine Hand; Sib Liebt Dich; Long Tall Sally; I Call Your Name; Slow Down; Matchbox; I Feel Fine; She's A Woman; Bad Boy; Yes It Is; I'm Down

The Beatles

APPLE 1988

Past Masters Vol 2

Day Tripper; We Can Work It Out; Paperback Writer; Rain; Lady Madonna; The Inner Light; Hey Jude; Revolution; Get Back; Don't Let Me Down; The Ballad Of John And Yoko; Old Brown Shoe; Across The Universe; Let It Be; You Know My Name (Look Up The Number)

These essential volumes of non-album hits, B-sides and EP tracks wouldn't be necessary today, when singles are little more than prompts for album sales. In the '60s, though, The Beatles were constantly recording stand-alone 45s, partly to satisfy demand, partly due to the sheer pace of their musical development. Barely seven years separate Love Me Do and Let It Be, but these chronologically ordered compilations plug all the gaps on that journey from lovelorn innocents to creative exhaustion.

The Kinks

CASTLE 1997/8

The Definitive Collection

Long Tall Sally; You Still Want Me; You Really Got Me; All Day And All Of The Night; Tired Of Waiting For You; Everybody's Gonna Be Happy; Set Me Free; See My Friends; Till The End Of The Day; Where Have All The Good Times Gone; Dedicated Follower Of Fashion; Well Respected Man; Sunny Afternoon; Dead End Street; Waterloo Sunset; Death Of A Clown; Autumn Almanac; David Watts; Susannah's Still Alive; Wonderboy; Days; Plastic Man; Victoria; Lola; Apeman; plus bonus disc "Waterloo Sunset": The Shirt unreleased demo); Rock And Roll Fantasy (live); Mr Pleasant; Celluloid Heroes; Voices In The Dark (remix); Holiday Romance; Art Lover (remix); Still Searching; Return To Waterloo (unreleased demo/remix); Afternoon Tea; The Million-Pound-Semi-Detached (unreleased demo); My Diary (unreleased demo); Drivin'; Waterloo Sunset (stereo mix); Scattered

"You can say everything in three minutes . . . it's the ultimate song structure," says Ray Davies. Andon the evidence of this well packaged survey of The Kinks' Pye singles, covering the years 1964–71, it's difficult to argue with him. The group's original R&B sound was given a metal twist as early as 1964's You Really Got Me, but by the mid-'60s, it was Davies' quintessentially English musical postcards (Sunny Afternoon, Waterloo Sunset) that marked him out as one of the decade's leading and most successful songwriters. The Kinks made several fine albums, too, but it was the single that inspired Davies' greatest works. "I hope it will never die," he says.

Howlin' Wolf

CHESS 1964

Moanin' In The Moonlight

Moanin' At Midnight; How Many More Years; Smokestack Lightning; Baby, How Long; No Place To Go; All Night Boogie; Evil; I'm Leavin' You; Moanin' For My Baby; I Asked For Water (She Gave Me Gasoline); Forty Four; Somebody In My Home

There was something elemental about the Wolf's music, a frontal assault on the senses that bludgeoned audiences into stunned submission. He blew harmonica like a ship's foghorn, played slide guitar like Rambo laying into his arsenal and was well served by a series of musicians that included Otis Spann, Jimmy Rogers, Willie Johnson and the ubiquitous Hubert Sumlin. As Muddy's great rival for the title of King of Chicago Blues, he racked up a succession of hits, How Many More Years, Moanin' At Midnight, Smokestack Lightning, Forty Four and Evil, all included here. Poorly served by British labels – a 1956 EP, another EP and single in 1961 – it wasn't until 1964 that this long-anticipated album arrived in the racks. Fortuitous then that this was the year the Stones took their interpretation of his Little Red Rooster to the top of the charts.

The Four Seasons (Featuring Frankie Valli)

RHINO 1988

Anthology

Sherry; Big Girls Don't Cry; Walk Like A Man; Candy Girl; Marlena; Dawn (Go Away); Stay; Ronnie; Rag Doll; Silence Is Golden; Save It For Me; Big Man In Town; Bye, Bye, Baby (Baby GoodBye); Girl Come Running; Let's Hang On!; Don't Think Twice (as The Wonder Who?); Working My Way Back To You; Opus 17 (Don't You Worry 'Bout Me); I've Got You Under My Skin; Tell It To The Rain; Beggin; Can't Take My Eyes Off You (as Frankie Valli); C'mon Marianne; Will You Love Me Tomorrow; Who Loves You; December, 1963 (Oh, What A Night)

Yes, he had the most alarming falsetto in the business, a shrill thing that made it laughingly ironic when he sang Walk Like A Man, but it is hard to argue with Frankie Valli's success. Between 1962, when his band, The Four Seasons, scored their first Number 1 hit with Sherry, and 1975, when December, 1963 (Oh, What A Night) topped the charts, Valli and his bubblegum doo-wop group from Newark, NJ, had a total of five Number 1s, plus eight other Top 10 songs. This neat collection of their peaks unfortunately omits the UK Northern Soul smash, The Night, which turned up originally on Motown's short-lived Mowest imprint. Talking of which . . .

Various Artists

MOTOWN 1992

Hitsville USA: The Motown Singles Collection (1959–1971)

Money (That's What I Want) – Barrett Strong; Shop Around – The Miracles; Please Mr Postman – The Marvelettes; Jamie – Eddie Holland; One Who Really Loves You – Mary Wells; Do You Love Me – The Contours; Beechwood 4-5789 -The Marvalettes; You Beat Me To The Punch – Mary Wells; Stubborn Kind Of Fellow – Marvin Gaye; Two Lovers – Mary Wells; You've Really Got A Hold On Me – The Miracles; Come And Get These Memories – Martha And The Vandellas; Pride And Joy – Marvin Gaye; Fingertips – Pt 2 – Stevie Wonder; (Love Is Like A) Heat Wave – Martha And The Vandellas; Mickey's Monkey – The Miracles; Leaving Here – Eddie Holland; Way You Do The Things You Do – The Temptations; My Guy – Mary Wells; Devil With The Blue Dress – Shorty Long; Every Little Bit Hurts – Brenda Holloway; Baby I Need Your Loving – The Four Tops; Dancing In The Street – Martha And The Vandellas; Mickey's Monkey – The Miracles; My Smile Just a Frown (Turned Upside Down) – Carolyn Crawford; Needle In A Haystack – The Velvelettes; Baby Love – The Supremes; Come See About Me – The Supremes; How Sweet It Is (To Be Loved By You) – Marvin Gaye; My Girl – The Temptations; He Was Really Sayin' Somethin' – The Velvelettes; Ask the Lonely – The Four Tops; Shotgun – Jr Walker And The All Stars; Nowhere To Run – Martha And The Vandellas; When I'm Gone – Brenda Holloway; Ooo Baby Baby – The Miracles; I Can't Help Myself (Sugar Pie – Honey Bunch) – The Four Tops; First I Look at the Purse – The Contours; Tracks Of My Tears – The Miracles; It's The Same Old Song – The Four Tops; Love (Makes Me Do Foolish Things) – Martha and the Vandellas; Take Me In Your Arms (Rock Me A Little While) – Kim Weston; Uptight (Everything's Alright) – Stevie Wonder; Don't Mess With Bill – The Marvelettes; Darling Baby – The Elgins; This Old Heart Of Mine (Is Weak For You) – The Isley Brothers; Greetings (This Is Uncle Sam) – The Monitors; Function At The Junction – Shorty Long; (I'm A) Road Runner – Jr Walker And The All Stars; Ain't Too Proud to Beg – The Temptations; What Becomes Of The Brokenhearted – Jimmy Ruffin; How Sweet It Is (To Be Loved by You) – Jr Walker And The All Stars; Love's Gone Bad – Chris Clark; You Can't Hurry Love – The Supremes; Beauty Is Only Skin Deep – The Temptations; Heaven Must Have Sent You – The Elgins; Reach Out (I'll Be There) – The Four Tops; (I Know) I'm Losing You – The Temptations; Standing In The Shadows Of Love – The Four Tops; It Takes Two – Marvin Gaye And Kim Weston; Hunter Gets Captured By The Game – The Marvelettes; Jimmy Mack – The Marvelettes; Bernadette – The Four Tops; Ain't No Mountain High Enough – Marvin Gaye And Tammi Terrell; More Love – Smokey Robinson And The Miracles; I Heard It Through The Grapevine – Gladys Knight And The Pips; I Second That Emotion – Smokey Robinson And The Miracles; I Wish It Would Rain – The Temptations; I Can't Give Back The Love I Feel For You – Rita Wright; Does Your Mama Know About Me – Bobby Taylor And The Vancouvers; Ain't Nothing Like The Real Thing – Ashford And Simpson; Love Child – Diana Ross And The Supremes; For Once In My Life – Stevie Wonder; Cloud Nine – The Temptations; I Heard It Through The Grapevine – Marvin Gaye; Baby Baby Don't Cry – Smokey Robinson And The Miracles; Twenty-Five Miles – Edwin Starr; My Whole World Ended (The Moment You Left Me) – David Ruffin; What Does It Take (To Win Your Love)? – Jr Walker And The All Stars; I Can't Get Next to You – The Temptations; Baby – I'm for Real – The Originals; Up The Ladder To The Roof – The Supremes; I Want You Back – The Jackson Five; The Bells – The Originals; Get Ready – Rare Earth; ABC – The Jackson Five; Ball of Confusion (That's What The World Is Today) – The Temptations; Love You Save – The Jackson Five; Signed, Sealed, Delivered (I'm Yours) – Stevie Wonder; War – Edwin Starr; It's A Shame – The Spinners; Ain't No Mountain High Enough – Diana Ross; Still Water (Love) – Four Tops; I'll Be There – The Jackson Five; Tears Of A Clown – Smokey Robinson And The Miracles; Stoned Love – The Supremes; If I Were Your Woman – Gladys Knight And The Pips; Just My Imagination (Running Away With Me) – The Temptations; What's Going On? – Marvin Gaye; Never Can Say Goodbye – The Jackson Five; Nathan Jones – The Supremes; I Don't Want To Do Wrong – Gladys Knight and the Pips; Smiling Faces Sometimes – The Undisputed Truth; Mercy Mercy Me (The Ecology) – Marvin Gaye; I Just Want To Celebrate – Rare Earth

When The Beatles hit America in 1964 – followed by The Kinks, the Stones, Hermits and other foot-soldiers in the "British Invasion" – the only homegrown artists to provide any real competition were those at Motown, Berry Gordy Jr's Detroit-based soul-lite label. A former prize-fighter with a fantastic eye for talent and an even greater determination to turn it into profit, Gordy insisted that his acts be polished in every way, going so far as to require etiquette and elocution lessons. The key word was crossover. And indeed The Beatles helped popularise the music with white listeners by covering Money and Please Mr Postman.

The Motown acts toured together and were lucky to be able to avail themselves of the superb songwriting and production talents of Smokey Robinson, the Midas-like team of Brian Holland, Lamont Dozier and Eddie Holland and the psychedelic soul visionary, Norman Whitfield. Starting with The Marvelettes' original of Please Mr Postman, which topped the US charts on Dec. 11, 1961, Gordy's label racked up an astonishing 20 No. 1 hits in its '60s heyday. Motown understood the three-minute rush of great pop like almost no other label. So much so that it suffered when the demand for the single slackened, the ascendance of the album as the market's dominant form marked the start of the label's slow but inevitable decline, hastened by Gordy's decision to up sticks from Detroit and relocate in LA. Inadvertently, he'd yanked out and killed off his label's roots.

Various Artists

RHINO, 1997

Beg, Scream And Shout

That's How It Feels – The Soul Clan; La-La-Means I Love You – The Delfonics; The Whole World Is A Stage – The Fantastic Four; Stand By Me – Ben E King; You're The Best (That Ever Did It) – The Precisions; Eight Men, Four Women – OV Wright; Every Little Bit Hurts – Brenda Holloway; Nothing Takes The Place Of You – Toussaint McCall; Private Number – Judy Clay And William Bell; I Don't Want To Lose Your Love – The Mad Lads; Who's Lovin You – The Jackson 5; Cry Baby – Garnet Mimms; Dry Your Eyes – Brenda And The Tabulations; Yes, I'm Ready – Barbara Mason; The Love I Saw In You Was Just A Mirage – Smokey Robinson And The Miracles; When Something Is Wrong With My Baby – Sam And Dave; That's How It Is When You're In Love – Otis Clay; Sweet Inspiration – The Sweet Inspirations; Baby, I'm Yours – Barbara Lewis; It Tears Me Up – Percy Sledge; I Had A Talk With My Man – Mitty Collier; Love Makes The World Go Round – Deon Jackson; Back Up Train – Al Green And The Soul Mates; Choice Of Colours – The Impressions. Ice Cream Song – The Dynamics; I've Been Loving You Too Long (To Stop Now) – Otis Redding; Stay In My Corner – The Dells; Selfish One – Jackie Ross; Hey There Lonely Girl – Eddie Holman; Every Day Will Be Like A Holiday; Funny – Joe Hinton; Wrong Number (I Am Sorry, Goodbye) – Aaron Neville; The Entertainer – Tony Clarke; It's Got To Be Mellow – Leon Haywood; Can I Change My Mind – Tyrone Davis; Sunny – Bobby Hebb; Cowboys To Girls – The Intruders; Don't Make Me Over – Dionne Warwick; Oh No Not My Baby – Maxine Brown; Fly Me To The Moon – Bobby Womack; I Do Love You – Billy Stewart; Voice Your Choice – The Radiants; I'm Your Puppet – James And Bobby Purify; Release Me – Esther Phillips; Rainbow – Gene Chandler; Sad Girl – Jay Wiggins; Wish Someone Would Care – Irma Thomas; In The Heat Of The Night – Ray Charles; Stay With Me – Lorraine Ellison; Function At The Junction – Shorty Long; Memphis Soul Stew – King Curtis; The "In" Crowd – Dobie Gray; I Sold My Heart To The Junkman – The Starlets (originally credited as The Blue Bells); Love Makes A Woman – Barbara Aklin; Lipstick Traces (On A Cigarette) – The O'Jays; Make Me Yours – Bettye Swann; She Shot A Hole In My Soul – Clifford Curry; You're No Good – Betty Everett; I'm Blue (The Gong-Gong Song) – The Ikettes; 7 Rooms Of Gloom – Four Tops; (Sweet Sweet Baby) Since You've Been Gone – Aretha Franklin; Wack Wack – The Young Holt Trio; Got To Get You Off My Mind – Solomon Burke; You've Been In Love Too Long – Martha And The Vandellas; Pouring Water On A Drowning Man – James Carr; Rescue Me – Fontella Bass; Show Me – Joe Tex; Friendship Train – Gladys Knight And The Pips; Temptation 'Bout To Get Me – The Knight Bros; Snatching It Back – Clarence Carter; Dead End Street Monologue/Dead End Street – Lou Rawls. Out Of Sight – James Brown; Get On Up – The Esquires; Only The Strong Survive – Jerry Butler; Teasin' You – Willie Tee; Backfield In Motion – Mel And Tim; Piece Of My Heart – Erma Franklin; I Don't Want To Cry – Chuck Jackson; Girl Watcher – The O'Kaysions; I Was Made To Love Her – Stevie Wonder; B-A-B-Y – Carla Thomas; You Are The Circus – C And The Shells; I'm In Love – Wilson Pickett; Searching For My Love – Bobby Moore And The Rhythm Aces; He Was Really Sayin' Somethin' – The Velvelettes; The Chokin' Kind – Joe Simon; Seesaw – Don Covay; 39-21-46 – The Showmen; A Fool In Love – Ike And Tina Turner; Bye Bye Baby – Mary Wells; The Oogum Boogum Song – Brenton Wood; Just One Look – Doris Troy; Time Is Tight – Booker T And The MG's; Sweet Soul Music – Arthur Conley; Cissy Strut – The Meters; Tighten Up – Archie Bell And The Drells; Harlem Shuffle – Bob And Earl; Are You Lonely For Me – Freddie Scott; Stop – Howard Tate; The Funky Judge – Bull And The Matadors; Some Kind Of Wonderful – Soul Brothers Six; The Monkey Time – Major Lance; Love Is Like An Itching In My Heart – The Supremes; Twine Time – Alvin Cash And The Crawlers; Tainted Love – Gloria James; My Pledge Of Love – The Joe Jeffrey Group; Sock It To 'Em JB (Part One) – Rex Garvin; Can I Get A Witness – Marvin Gaye; I Want You To Have Everything – Lee Rogers; The Real Nitty Gritty – Shirley Ellis; She's Looking Good – Rodger Collins; The Horse – Cliff Nobles And Co; Who's Making Love – Johnnie Taylor; TCB Or TYA – Bobby Patterson; Grits Ain't Groceries (All Around The World) – Little Milton; It's Your Thing – The Isley Brothers; Open The Door To Your Heart – Darrell Banks; I Can't Stand It – Soul Sisters; We Got More Soul – Dyke And The Blazers. Baby Workout – Jackie Wilson; Agent Double-O-Soul – Edwyn Starr; Barefootin' – Robert Parker; I Do – The Marvelows; Mustang Sally – Sir Mack Rice; Expressway Your Heart – Soul Survivors; Cool Jerk – The Capitols; But It's Alright – JJ Jackson; Tell Mama – Etta James; Nothing But A Heartache – The Flirtations; (I Know) I'm Losing You – The Temptations; The Memphis Train – Rufus Thomas; Last Night – Mar-Keys; Shake A Tail Feather – The Five Du-Tones; First I Look At The Purse – The Contours; Big Bird – Eddie Floyd; The Cheater – Bob Kuban And The In-Men; Danger Heartbreak Dead Ahead – The Marvelettes; Shake And FingerPop – Jr Walker And The All Stars; Boogaloo Down Broadway – The Fantastic Johnny C; Soul Finger – Bar-Kays; Take Me In Your Arms (Rock Me A Little While) – Kim Weston; Leaving Here – Eddie Holland; My Whole World Ended (The Moment You Left Me) – David Ruffin; Ain't Nothin' But A House Party – The Show Stoppers

You'll notice rather a lot of Rhino collections in this list. This quirky, characterful American imprint has excelled at creating definitive box sets, usually pregnant with annotations, rare pictures and a general sense of loving care. Rhino began 25 years ago as a store and distribution company who later got into licensing, started releasing their own compilations and eventually struck a major deal with Warner Brothers giving them access to all the treasures of that superb archive.

Which is why they can pull-off something like this: nothing less than the best pop-soul collection ever, crammed with terrific music and presented with jaw-dropping attention to detail – and a nice sense of humour, too. Rather than recycle all the obvious hits and most overdropped names – there are a million Atlantic collections that do that – *Beg, Scream And Shout* opts to mix the familiar with some of the lesser-known but equally strong cuts from soul's golden era. They've stepped out of the Warner archive too. There are Motown, Imperial and Chess sides here too. Everyone gets one shot each.

Housed in a facsimile of a 7" carrying box, each of the six CDs comes in plastic, single-shaped mounts in replica 7" bags, designed with the feel of Atlantic and Stax logos of the '60s. The neatest twist, however, is the presentation of the notes. Each track is represented by a bubblegum card with the artist's picture on the front and the requisite recording info and biog on the back. The stack of cards slot neatly into a recessed area inside the case. It's bliss on toast for any serious box freak. And a one-stop shop for anyone still asking "What is soul?" You'll need to take out a mortgage to afford it, but we couldn't leave it out of our collection.

Various Artists — KENT 1997

Dave Godin's Deep Soul Treasures (Taken FromThe Vaults) – Vol 1

I'm Never Gonna Live It Down – The Knight Brothers; Easy As Saying 1-2-3 – Timmy Willis; Lights Out – Zerben Hicks And The Dynamics; Anyone Who Knows What Love Is (Will Understand) – Irma Thomas; Have A Little Mercy – Jean Wells; Try Love – Dori Grayson; I Can't Make It Without Him – Brendetta Davis; Showdown – Kenny Carter; I'm Not The One – Larry Banks; The Turning Point – Jimmy Holiday; Standing Here Crying – The Incredibles; She Broke His Heart – The Just Brothers; You're On Top – The Untouchables; It's Not That Easy – Reuben Bell And The Casanovas; Cry Baby Cry – Van And Titus; I Still Love You – Jean Stanback; Try To Leave Me If You Can (I Bet You Can't Do It) – Bessie Banks; Songs To Sing – Raw Spit; How Much Longer (Must I Wait) – Lee Moses; Nothing's Too Much (Nothing's Too Good) – Billy Young; I Feel Like Cryin' – Sam And Bill; I'm Goin' For Myself – Eddie And Ernie; Tried So Hard To Please Her – The Knight Brothers; The Love Of My Man – Pearlian Gray And The Passengers; You Got Me – Jaibi

While we're on the subject of soul, this is a peerless collection compiled by the man who coined the term Deep Soul to describe the vein of black '60s music that went to the very edge of emotional expression. Sometimes churchy, sometimes melodramatic, these are performances that fearlessly lunge for the heartstrings. Godin, a famed columnist for Blue & Soul magazine for many years, enthused about the rawest, richest voices and collected "a lifetime's worth" of his discoveries – little-known but big-sounding singers – on this and a subsequent volume. It's quite exquisite stuff, if at times exhausting and not for the faint-hearted, the contented or the partyseeker. As Godin notes: "Generally Deep Soul manifests itself through slow tempoed numbers . . . in this genre, an uptempo pace symbolises rage and confusion rather than soul's usual invocation to happiness and a good time."

The Hollies

EMI 1993

The Air That I Breathe: The Very Best Of The Hollies

The Air That I Breathe; Bus Stop; Just One Look; Yes I Will; Look Through Any Window; He Ain't Heavy, He's My Brother; I Can't Let Go; We're Through; Searchin'; Stay; I'm Alive; If I Needed Someone; Here I Go Again; Stop Stop Stop; On A Carousel; Carrie-Anne; King Midas In Reverse; Jennifer Eccles; Listen To Me; Sorry Suzanne; I Can't Tell The Bottom From The Top; Gasoline Alley Bred; Hey Willy; Long Cool Woman In A Black Dress; The Day That Curly Billy Shot Down Crazy Sam McGee; The Woman I Love

Manchester's answer to The Beatles never quite managed consistently strong albums, but 17 UK Top 10 hits (all on this collection) ably confirm their reputation as a singles outfit. "To a certain extent there was a formula to our writing," said guitarist Tony Hicks, who often wrote the choruses, while Graham Nash and Allan Clarke handled the verses and middle-eights respectively. But it was the three-part harmonies, jangly, folk-rock guitars and quirky, infectious hooks on which The Hollies' success was based. Nash's departure in 1968 was a blow, but despite a slow descent into cabaret, a flurry of early '70s singles maintained the quality threshold.

Various Artists

RHINO 1986

Nuggets – Classics From The Psychedelic Sixties

Dirty Water – The Standells; Pushin' Too Hard – The Seeds; Psychotic Reaction – The Count Five; Let's Talk About Girls – The Chocolate Watchband; Friday On My Mind – The Easybeats; I See The Light – The Five Americans; Why Pick On Me – The Standells; Little Girl – The Syndicate of Sound; Pleasant Valley Sunday – The Monkees; Lies – The Knickerbockers; Laugh, Laugh – The Beau Brummels; Wild Thing – The Troggs; Heaven And Hell – The Easybeats; Valerie – The Monkees; Open My Eyes – The Nazz; Just A Little – The Beau Brummels; Can't Seem To Make You Mine – The Seeds; Journey To The Center Of The Mind – The Amboy Dukes.

It was Lenny Kaye, a music journalist who would go onto be Patti Smith's guitarist, who decided in 1972 to dip into the not-so-distant past and salvage a small, warped piece of it for posterity. *Nuggets* is a fantastic compilation of what's come to be known as garage music – whacked-out, twisted songs by bands that knew they had nothing to lose. Some sound eager, some sullen. Psychedelic drugs were certainly part of the mix. But the real key may have been that they were not perceived as commercial or valuable enough to be "helped" by record company front-office types and so could follow their own warped path. It was beat music that was left alone to fester and mutate.

Garage was a national movement: Los Angeles had the Music Machine, each member of whom wore one black glove; Chicago had the Shadows of Knight; and San José had Count Five, whose twangy guitar-driven Psychotic Reaction summed the whole thing up nicely: "I can't get love/I can't get satisfaction/I only get a psychotic reaction."

This set is the original double album version that defined the form. Rhino released a superb expanded 4-CD boxed version in 1998.

Sandie Shaw

VIRGIN 1996

Nothing Less Than Brilliant: The Best Of Sandie Shaw

(There's) Always Something There To Remind Me; Long Live Love; Girl Don't Come; Message Understood; Nothing Less Than Brilliant; Hand In Glove; Are You Ready To Be Heartbroken?; A Girl Called Johnny; I'll Stop At Nothing; Heaven Knows I'm Missing Him Now; You've Not Changed; Monsieur Dupont; I Don't Owe You Anything; Anyone Who Had A Heart; Comrade In Arms; Hello Angel; Strange Bedfellows; Words; Ev'rytime We Say Goodbye; Your Time Is Gonna Come; Frederick; Please Help The Cause Against Loneliness; Tomorrow; Nothing Comes Easy; Puppet On A String

Despite a brief resurgence during the 1980s, after being championed by Smiths singer Morrissey, it's difficult not to think of Sandie Shaw as the quintessential British Invasion girl-made-good, the punch-card operator from Dagenham, talent-spotted by Adam Faith, who walked barefoot onto the Top Of The Pops stage and into the singles charts. She had the ice-cool look and, for a time, the Chris Andrews-penned songs. But when the hits began to dry up in 1966, efforts to make her an all-round entertainer culminated in her 1967 Eurovision hit, Puppet On A String. Marriage and obscurity soon beckoned, and when she returned for her brief stint as an indie icon, Shaw displayed a particularly jaundiced view of her early pop puppetry. This curious round-up runs from the earliest hits to the covers of Smiths, Waterboys and Lloyd Cole. Her thoroughly unique career has taken another unexpected turn. She is a now a counsellor for pop stars who are finding fame a strain.

The Move

CRIMSON 2000

The Complete Singles Collection And More

Night Of Fear; Flowers In The Rain; I Can Hear The Grass Grow; (Here We Go Round) The Lemon Tree; Cherry Blossom Clinic; Vote For Me; Fire Brigade; Useless Information; The Girl Outside; Wild Tiger Woman; Omnibus; Blackberry Way; Curly; Beautiful Daughter; Hello Susie; Feel Too Good; Brontosaurus; When Alice Comes Back To The Farm; Tonight; Chinatown; Do Ya; California Man

Despite much intra-band rancour, several line-up changes and a legal battle with Prime Minister Harold Wilson, between 1966 to 1972, The Move were Britain's most consistent hit makers. Their songwriter was Roy Wood, a shy man who hid behind a forest of hair, and strove to become a one-man Lennon-McCartney. Wood's ambition sometimes got the better of him (The Move's albums were often patchy affairs), but when restricted to three-minute songs, he could transform good-time rock'n'roll (Fire Brigade), ballads (Curly), hard rock (Brontosaurus) and even the odd Beatles pastiche (Blackberry Way) into chart gold.

Manfred Mann

POLYGRAM TV 1993

Greatest Hits

5-4-3-2-1; Pretty Flamingo; Do Wah Diddy Diddy; Sha La La; If You Gotta Go Go Now; Oh No Not My Baby; Come Tomorrow; My Name Is Jack; The One In The Middle; I Put A Spell On You; Just Like A Woman; Poison Ivy; Mighty Quinn; Semi-Detached Suburban Mr James; Ha Ha Said The Clown; Ragamuffin Man; Hubble Bubble Toil And Trouble; There's No Living Without Your Loving; You Gave Me Somebody To Love; Got My Mojo Working; With God On Our Side; Fox On The Run

Representing a particular kind of publisher-driven pop that flourished in Britain in the '60s, here's one of its most successful practitioners. Manfred Mann was a keyboard-playing jazz enthusiast whose band became better known for the irregular assaults on the singles chart with uptempo R&B anthems and, later, Dylan-inspired pop, with much of the focus on pretty-boy frontman Paul Jones (replaced in 1966 by Mike D'Abo). Jones' departure was not the fatal blow many had expected and, while his solo career had dried up by the end of the decade, Mann's thirst for musical sophistication compelled him to split the band on a high note after 1969's Top 10 hit Ragamuffin Man to form the progressively inclined Earth Band.

There are, of course, dozens of various artist '60s hit collections that we might have recommended, but few of them felt definitive, and many only seem to last in the racks for a few months. Readers interested in the form might like to seek out other stand-alone sets by The Herd, The Move, The Marmalade, The Tremeloes, The Spencer Davis Group, The Troggs, Blue Mink and, last but least, Dave Dee Dozy Beaky Mick And Tich.

Various Artists

ATLANTIC 1990

Atlantic Soul Classics

Soul Man – Sam And Dave; In The Midnight Hour – Wilson Pickett; Respect – Aretha Franklin; I've Been Loving You Too Long (To Stop Now) – Otis Redding; Green Onions – Booker T And The MG's; Sweet Soul Music – Arthur Conley; Tighten Up – Archie Bell And The Drells; On Broadway – The Drifters; Yakety Yak – The Coasters; What'd I Say – Ray Charles; Just One Look – Doris Troy; Make Me Your Baby – Barbara Lewis; Stand By Me – Ben E King; When A Man Loves A Woman – Percy Sledge; Shake, Rattle And Roll – Joe Turner.

As the son of the Turkish ambassador to the US, Ahmet Ertegun could have become just about anything he wanted. Fortunately for music lovers, he followed his passion for black American music and in 1947 founded Atlantic Records with a New York jazz aficionado named Herb Abramson. For some years, the label scraped by, helped by the fact that its offices doubled as Ertegun's apartment on West 56th Street. In 1949 they signed Ruth Brown, promoting her as "Miss Rhythm". But the label's big break came in 1953 when Ertegun had the good fortune to be sought out by a young blind pianist named Ray Charles. It was Charles who boosted Atlantic to a major player, opening the doors for a stream of superb R&B talents, many recruited during Ertegun's field trips in the South. It helped that Ertegun surrounded himself with great talent like producers Jerry Wexler and Tom Dowd and arranger Jesse Stone. Certainly it had worthy rivals, but Atlantic, with giants like Aretha, Otis Redding, Ray Charles and Wilson Pickett, can fairly claim to be the home of soul.

The Rascals
ATLANTIC 1968

Time Peace: The Rascals' Greatest Hits

Groovin'; How Can I Be Sure; Lonely Too Long; In The Midnight Hour; I Ain't Gonna Eat Out My Heart Anymore; Good Lovin'; You Better Run; Come On Up; Mustang Sally; Love Is A Beautiful Thing; Girl Like You; It's Wonderful; Easy Rollin'; It's A Beautiful Morning

The Rascals, for whom the label "blue-eyed soul" was supposedly coined, first met in the early '60's, as members of Joey Dee and the Starliters, the house band at the Peppermint Lounge in New York City. They struck out on their own in the winter of 1964–65 and the following year notched the first of three Number 1 hits with a spirited cover of The Olympics' Good Lovin'. Though The Rascals' sound was immediately identifiable by Felix Cavaliere's organ and Eddie Brigati's warm, soulful voice, the band ranged widely from their R&B roots, from the breezy jazz-tinged Groovin' to the joyful People Got To Be Free, which Atlantic balked at releasing until the band insisted, and turned out to be a Number 1 US hit.

Various Artists
PHILIPS 1968

Tropicalia Ou Panis Et Circencis

Miserere N—bis – Gilberto Gil; Cora Materno – Caetano Veloso; Panis Et Circenses – Os Mutantes; Lindonea – Nara Le‹o; Parque Industrial – Gilberto Gil – Caetano Veloso – Gal Costaand Os Mutantes; Gelia Geral – Gilberto Gil; Baby – Gal Costa and Caetano Veloso; Tres Caravelas – Caetano Veloso and Gilberto Gil; Enquanto Seu Lobo N‹o Vem – Caetano Veloso; Mam‹e – Coragem – Gal Costa; Bat Macumba – Gilberto Gil; Hino Do Senhor Do Bonfim – Caetano Veloso – Gilberto Gil – Gal Costa and Os Mutantes

Shortly after Hendrix ignited the Monterey Festival, Brazil's music makers split in two, most supporting a bizarre march against the electric guitar. In spite of their love of the bossa nova of Joao Gilberto and Tom Jobim, the Tropicalistas went on a mission to update the sound of Rio, using electricity, bad taste, bizarre lyrics, art, poetry and whatever else came to hand. Their modernist left-wing stance alienated both the right-wing military government and patriotic socialists. In their favour, however, were the extraordinary pop abilities of Caetano Veloso and Gilberto Gil, two singer-songwriters from the northeastern region of Bahia. Thirty years on, the eight songs they wrote for this still sound like classic Beatles-esque vignettes in Portuguese, with plenty of 1960s inventiveness. Os Mutantes, on the other hand, are geniuses of the baroque, trapped inside schizoid production excesses, more out-there than Syd Barrett. So good, the leading lights were imprisoned within a year.

Booker T And The MGs

STAX 1968

Best Of

Hip Hug-Her; Slim Jenkin's Place; Green Onions; Soul Dressing; Jelly Bread: Groovin'; Mo' Onions; Summertime; Boot-Leg; Can't Be Still; Tic-Tac-Toe; Red Beans and Rice

Formed in Memphis in 1961, seven years before Martin Luther King was assassinated there, Booker T And The MGs were a rare study in racial equality, with two black men (organist Booker T Jones and drummer Al Jackson) harmonising with two white men (guitarist Steve Cropper and bass player Donald "Duck" Dunn). As the house band for the legendary Stax label, the MGs played back-up – and wrote – on countless hits by Sam And Dave, Otis Redding and Wilson Pickett. On their own they whipped up some of the leanest, funkiest instrumentals ever recorded, though an honourable mention must also go The Meters.

Sam And Dave

ATLANTIC 1969

Best Of Sam And Dave

A Place Nobody Can Find; Good Night Baby; I Take What I Want; Sweet Home; You Don't Know Like I Know; Hold On, I'm Comin'; Said I Wasn't Gonna Tell Nobody; You Got Me Hummin'; When Something Is Wrong With My Baby; Small Portion Of Your Love; Soothe Me; Soul Man; May I Baby; I Thank You; Wrap It Up; Still Is The Night; You Don't Know What You Mean To Me; This Is Your World; Can't You Find Another Way (Of Doing It); Soul Sister, Brown Sugar; Come On In

Off-stage they barely spoke to one another. But so electrifying were Sam Moore and Dave Prater's live performances that when they backed Otis Redding on one tour the headliner grumbled that they were showing him up. Nicknamed "double dynamite" for their onstage gyrations and leaps, the Stax duo never reached Number 1 in the charts, though their biggest hit, Soul Man, went to Number 2 and was the definitive example of a style of boastful soulmanship. Following their peak years (1966–68), the duo experienced more trouble than hits, with both members fighting serious drug problems and feuding over their legacy.

Diana Ross And The Supremes

MOTOWN 1974

Anthology

Let Me Go The Right Way; Breath Taking Guy; When The Lovelight Starts Shining Through His Eyes; Standing In The Crossroads Of Love; Run Run Run; Where Did Our Love Go; I'm Gonna Make You Love Me [with The Temptations]; I'm Livin' In Shame; The Composer; I'll Try Something New [with The Temptations]; No Matter What Sign You Are; Someday We'll Be Together; Baby Love; Ask Any Girl; Come See About Me; Stop! In The Name Of Love; Back In My Arms Again; Nothing But Heartaches; A Hard Day's Night; Funny How Time Slips Away; You Send Me; Falling In Love With Love; I'm The Greatest Star. I Hear A Symphony; My World Is Empty Without You; Love Is Like An Itching In My Heart; You Can't Hurry Love; You Keep Me Hangin' On; Love Is Here And Now You're Gone; The Happening; Reflections; In And Out Of Love; Forever Came Today; Some Things You Never Get Used To; Love Child.

From The Andrew Sisters to Phil Spector and The Spice Girls the vocal girl group has been a constant – but curiously, not often spectacularly successful – pop presence. But here was one female combo who, like The Spice Girls, really count as a phenomenon. The Supremes, three young black women from Detroit, were the one group that could point to a success in the '60s that rivalled The Beatles'. Between the summer of 1964, when they scored their first Number 1, Where Did Our Love Go, and the fall of 1969, the Supremes had 12 Number 1s in the US. And in one stretch of just 11 months, they had five straight singles top the charts.

The group were well named, for they were Berry Gordy's supreme creation, not just because of the money they brought into the Motown coffers, but because they were the apotheosis of Motown style: clean, classy, poised and meticulous. Taking cues from her boss, Diana Ross pushed her bandmates, Florence Ballard and Mary Wilson, to look as good as they sang. "Flo had the pipes, but Diana had the poise," said one Motown staffer. As Ross knew, that could be just as important. "Style," she told them, "is a real important expression of self."

James Brown

POLYDOR 1991

20 All-Time Greatest Hits!

I Got You (I Feel Good); Get Up (I Feel Like Being A) Sex Machine, Pt.1; I Got The Feelin'; Mother Popcorn, Pt.1; Give It Up Or Turnit A Loose; Make It Funky, Pt.1; Papa's Got A Brand New Bag, Pt.1; Think; It's A Man's Man's Man's World; Try Me; Night Train; Cold Sweat, Pt.1; Get On The Good Foot; Papa Don't Take No Mess, Pt.1; The Payback; Say It Loud (I'm Black And I'm Proud), Pt.1; Super Bad, Pts.1And 2; Hot Pants, Pt.1; Get Up Offa That Thing; Please, Please, Please.

"When you talk about James Brown and his music you're almost automatically talking about drums," said Brown's one-time road manager, Alan Leeds. "Like all great classical black music, it's built around rhythm first... And James sang like a drummer. He was playing drums with his larynx, okay?" That's about as good a summation as you'll get of what James Brown has meant to popular music. He may well be the hardest-working man in show business, and he may run the tightest, funkiest band in the business; but what Brown imprinted on American music of the past 40 years was an unswerving loyalty to the beat. Forget the capes, the grandiose introductions, and the affectation of naming his songs in "parts". That's all good fun, but it's hardly essential. What Brown did was to reach all the way back past European constructs like melody and harmony to that primal, unassailable beat, then to take it beyond the impetus to "get down" and turn it into an assertive political weapon. Though he turned out as many as eight or nine singles a year throughout the '60s, he never had a Number 1, his highest charting song being I Got You (I Feel Good), which reached Number 3 in 1965. Doesn't matter: if R&B and rock are first and foremost celebrations of rhythm, James Brown has given us the beat in its purest, most exalted form.

The Fifth Dimension

BMG/ARISTA 1972

Greatest Hits On Earth

(Last Night) I Didn't Get To Sleep At All; Stoned Soul Picnic; One Less Bell To Answer; Medley: Aquarius/Let The Shine In (The Flesh . . .); Wedding Bell Blues; Save The Country; Love's Lines, Angels And Rhymes; Puppet Man; Up, Up And Away; Never My Love; Together Let's Find Love.

Representing the rise of that glossy confection now being dubbed Sunshine Pop, The Fifth Dimension's ultra-smooth pop-soul sound – "Muzak with voices", as one critic described it – was dominated by lead singer Marilyn McCoo's honeyed vocal. A former winner of the talent award at the Miss Bronze California competition, McCoo was working as a model when she hooked up with the singers who would become the Fifth Dimension. The group was the most successful interpreter of Laura Nyro's work, one example of which, Wedding Bell Blues, they took to Number 1. Still, The Fifth Dimension's biggest hit was Aquarius/Let the Sunshine In, which topped the charts for six weeks in the spring of 1969.

Sunshine pop might also include artists on an axis from The Mamas And The Papas and The Turtles to The Partridge Family, with dozens of lesser-known acts like The Ballroom, The Sunshine Company and The Free Design providing the spur for collectors. In that it was often the work of session musicians backing clean harmony acts, it also has links with the development of bubblegum, best found in a recent series on the Varese Sarabande label, *Bubblegum Classics Vols 1–3*.

Various Artists

CBS 1969

The Story Of The Blues

Yarum Praise Songs – Fra-Fra Tribesmen; Stack-O-Lee Blues – Mississippi John Hurt; Travelin' Blues – Blind Willie McTell; Stone Pony Blues -Charley Patton; Black Snake Moan – Blind Lemon Jefferson; Pig Meat Papa – Leadbelly; Broken Yo Yo – Texas Alexander; Broke And Hungry Blues – Peg Leg Howell. It Won't Be Long Now – Barbecue Bob; Georgia Crawl – Henry Williams; Dangerous Woman – Mississippi Jook Band; Gator Wobble – Memphis Jug Band; In The House Blues – Bessie Smith; Shake It Down – Lillian Glinn; Pratt City Blues – Chippie Hill; What It Takes To Bring You Back – Butterbeans And Susie; Midnight Hour Blues – Leroy Carr; East St Louis Blues – Faber Smith; Good Whiskey Blues – Peetie Wheatstraw; WPA Blues – Casey Bill Welson; Sorry Feeling Blues – Bo Carter; Little Queen Of Spades – Robert Johnson; Parchman Farm Blues – Bukka White; Me And My Chauffeur – Memphis Minnie; I Want Some Of Your Pie – Blind Boy Fuller; Million Lonesome Women – Brownie McGhee; Wild Cow Moan – Big Joe Williams; All By Myself – Big Bill Broonzy; Roll 'Em Pete – Joe Turner; Bloody Murder – Otis Spann; Sunnyland – Elmore James; I Don't Know – Johnny Shines

In *Blues Fell This Morning* (1960) and *Conversations With The Blues* (1965), Paul Oliver explained and analysed the music and then let musicians talk for themselves. This double album was issued to coincide with a book of the same name guiding newcomers to the music through a concise but informative history of the music's many components. Each of the four sides was themed: The Origins Of The Blues, Blues And Entertainment, The Thirties – Urban And Rural Blues and World War II And After. Ranging from Ghanaian tribesmen via Blind Lemon Jefferson, Leadbelly, Bessie Smith, Leroy Carr and Robert Johnson to Joe Turner, Elmore James and Johnny Shines, these 32 examples gave some idea of the breadth of the subject, providing the inquisitive with an incentive to explore further. The presentation may have seemed a little dry but the music was unusual and fascinating.

Various Artists

ISLAND 1969

You Can All Join In

A Song For Jeffrey – Jethro Tull; Sunshine Help Me – Spooky Tooth; I'm A Mover – Free; What's That Sound – Art; Pearly Queen – Tramline; You Can All Join In – Traffic; Meet On The Ledge – Fairport Convention; Rainbow Chaser – Nirvana; Dusty – John Martyn; I'll Go Girl – Clouds; Somebody Help Me – The Spencer Davis Group; Gasoline Alley – Wynder K Frog

Island were early masters of the budget-priced rock compilation, a late '60s phenomenon that did much to introduce the world to its roster of underground acts who otherwise would have found it difficult to gain national exposure. Boss Chris Blackwell had clearly left his reggae beginnings behind in favour of the hottest young blades in London. For under a quid, cash-strapped music fans could hear the plucky label's thrilling new mix of proto-prog and psychedelic R&B. This gambit was so successful they repeated the trick with *Nice Enough To Eat* and the ambitious double sets *Bumpers* and *El Pea*. Many other labels followed suit.

Santana

COLUMBIA 1974

Greatest Hits

Evil Ways; Jingo; Hope You're Feeling Better; Samba Pa Ti; Persuasion; Black Magic Woman; Oye Como Va; Everything's Coming Our Way; Se S Cabo; Everybody's Everything.

Until the staggering, new-millennium success of *Supernatural*, Mexican-born guitarist Carlos Santana's greatest success had come at the start of the '70s, when he had two straight Top 10 singles, Evil Ways and Black Magic Woman. The band Santana was formed in the summer of 1968, when Carlos hooked up with keyboardist Gregg Rolie at a San Francisco jam session. The music was a kind of Latin soul-fusion, featuring Santana's superb guitar work and a heavy dose of percussion. Surprisingly under-explored by other combos, Latin music is a rich seam that is certainly making a comeback. There are currently a dozen or so very good compilations that explore the raw and rootsy end of the music. Notably *Nu Yorica Vols 1 & 2* on the Soul Jazz label and *Latin Break Beats* on Harmless Records.

Various Artists

EMI 1999

Harvest Festival

Evil – Edgar Broughton Band; It Didn't Work Out – Michael Chapman; Wring That Neck – Deep Purple; Tom Tiddler's Ground – Roy Harper; Morning Call – Pete Brown And His Battered Ornaments; Stone Circle – Third Ear Band; Real Cool World – Greatest Show On Earth; Octopus – Syd Barrett; Round And Round Panama – Limited Jug Band; Mother Dear – Barclay James Harvest; Maybe My Mind – With Egg – Tea And Symphony; Postcards Of Scarborough – Michael Chapman; A Glade Somewhere – Forest; Out Demons Out – Edgar Broughton Band; Living Life Backwards – Pete Brown And Piblokto; Black Sheep Of The Family – Quarter Mass; Big Fearfolly – Bakerloo; The Good Mr Square – The Pretty Things; The Lady Rachel – Kevin Ayers; A Foresaking: Our Captain Cried Shirley And Dolly Collins; Speed King – Deep Purple; Things May Come And Things May Go But The Art School Dance Goes On Forever – Pete Brown And Piblokto; Apache Drop Out – Edgar Broughton Band; Everyday – the Climax Chicago Blues Band; Butterfly Dance – Kevin Ayers; Mocking Bird – Barclay James Harvest; Kodak Ghosts – Michael Chapman; The Words Of Aaron – The Move; Fireball – Deep Purple; 10538 Overture – the Electric Light Orchestra; Breathe – Ron Geesin And Roger Waters; Medicine Man – Barclay James Harvest; Stranger In Blue Suede Shoes – Kevin Ayers And The Whole World; Fennario – Michael Chapman; The Same Old Rock – Roy Harper; Hotel Room – Edgar Broughton Band; Effervescing Elephant – Syd Barrett; Song From The Bottom Of A Well – Kevin Ayers; Money – Pink Floyd; South Africa – Roy Harper; Interview – Kevin Ayers; The Mexican – Babe Ruth; Do Ya – The Move; Something Said – Southern Comfort; Adventures In A Yorkshire Landscape – Be-Bop Deluxe; Dear Elaine – Roy Wood; Take Me To Tahiti – Kevin Ayers; Things On My Mind – Edgar Broughton Band; Hombre De La Guitarre – from Amar Caballero – Babe Ruth; Another Day – Live – Roy Harper; Roll Over Beethoven – the Electric Light Orchestra; Maid In Heaven – Be-Bop Deluxe; You Make Me Sick – Climax Chicago; Showdown – the Electric Light Orchestra; Ball Park Incident – Wizzard; I'll See You Again – Roy Harper; Poor Old Horse – The Albion Band; Old Hug Or None – Martin Carthy; Hopping Down In Kent – The Albion Dance Band; Postmans Knock – Ashley Hutchings; Spring Song – Gryphon; Have You Ever Seen The Rain? – Unicorn; Fair Exchange – Be-Bop Deluxe; Ballad Of A Salesman Who Sold Himself – Kevin Ayers; Electric Language – Be-Bop Deluxe; Short And Sweet – David Gilmour; When An Old Cricketer Leaves The Crease – Roy Harper; Erotic Neurotic – The Saints; Reuters – Wire; This Perfect Day – The Saints; Lonely Android – The Shirts; Little Girl – The Banned; I Should Have Known Better – Wire; Swing For The Crime – The Saints; Revolt Into Style – Bill Nelson's Red Noise; A Touching Display – Wire; Black Night – Deep Purple; Flying Hero Sandwich – Pete Brown And Piblokto; California Man – The Move; Magic Woman Touch – Greatest Show On Earth; Caribbean Moon – Kevin Ayers; The Calendar Song – Trinidad Oil Company; Rock – Matumbi; I Am The Fly – Wire; Life In A Scotch Sitting Room Vol 2 – Excerpt – Ivor Cutler; The Young Ones – Vivian Stanshall And Kilgarron; Sabre Dance – Spontaneous Combustion; Ships In The Night – Be-Bop Deluxe; Breathless – Bombadil; Dancing In The City – Marshall Hain; Radar In My Heart – Bill Nelson's Red Noise; Child Of The City – Strapps; Hallalujah – Deep Purple; Wells Fargo – Babe Ruth; Mess Around – Professor Longhair; Golden Hair – Syd Barrett; Up Yours – Edgar Broughton Band

The dawn of the '70s was disastrous for music in many ways. It heralded a period of great indulgence which allowed some genius to flourish but an awful lot of nonsense to find an outlet its equivalent would not receive today. Artists who sold very few records enjoyed surprisingly long careers. This set is an object lesson in all that was good and bad about the period: extravagant packaging housing five CDs of wildly hit'n'miss music – an apt tribute to an age of folly.

"What's a company like EMI doing starting an underground label?" was Melody Maker's response to the formation of Harvest Records in 1969. Whatever, the onset of the Third Ear Band and Edgar Broughton Band – two of the most unlistenable/challenging combos ever to be given studio time – certainly showed that the label's "heads" weren't going to be half-hearted about it.

Harvest's affiliation with the underground was put under considerable strain in 1973, when the success of Pink Floyd's *Dark Side Of The Moon* hid the fact that the rest of the roster was in disarray. While persevering with loss-making hangovers from the late '60s, Harvest also inveigled its way into the singles market, scoring respectable hits from the likes of Deep Purple, The Move and ELO. But any last vestiges of label identity were blown out of the water in 1977 by the arrival of punk acts like Wire and The Saints.

Few other compilations capture the compelling naffness of the decade's rock so well, though Castle's *Dawn Anthology* – a round-up of Pye's ill-starred own underground imprint – is a fascinating glimpse of a sound that seems more archaic than much older music.

Various Artists

APPLE 1972

Concert For Bangladesh

Bangla Dhun; Wah-Wah; My Sweet Lord; Awaiting On You All; That's The Way God Planned It; It Don't Come Easy; Beware Of Darkness; While My Guitar Gently Weeps; Medley: Jumpin' Jack Flash – Youngblood; Here Comes The Sun; Hard Rain's Gonna Fall; It Takes A Lot To Laugh, It Takes A Train To Cry; Blowin' In The Wind; Mr Tambourine Man; Just Like A Woman; Something; Bangla-Desh

One last, belated crack at the '60s ideal and the first great superstar benefit concert. The two shows for Bangladesh, held in Madison Square Garden on August 1, 1971, were organised by George Harrison, and supported by Ringo Starr, Eric Clapton, Bob Dylan, Ravi Shankar and a cast of rock notables. Unfortunately, despite raising significant funds (there was a movie, too), tax demands from the US and UK governments ensured that not all of the cash ended up fighting famine in the Indian subcontinent – a fact that wasn't lost on Live Aid and Farm Aid organisers years later.

Elton John

ROCKET 1990

The Very Best Of

Your Song; Rocket Man (I Think It's Going To Be A Long, Long Time); Honky Cat; Crocodile Rock; Daniel; Goodbye Yellow Brick Road; Saturday Night's Alright For Fighting; Candle In The Wind; Don't Let The Sun Go Down On Me; Lucy In The Sky With Diamonds; Philadelphia Freedom; Someone Saved My Life Tonight; Pinball Wizard; The Bitch Is Back; Don't Go Breaking My Heart; Bennie And The Jets; Sorry Seems To Be The Hardest Word; Song For Guy; Part Time Love; Blue Eyes; I Guess That's Why They Call It The Blues; I'm Still Standing; Kiss The Bride; Sad Songs; Passengers; Nikita; I Don't Wanna Go On With You Like That; Sacrifice; Easier To Walk Away; You Gotta Love Someone

Here's all the desperate "glamour", fragile talent and superficial worth of the '70s in a (golden) nutshell. At one point Elton John apparently accounted for 25 per cent of all US record sales! Though undoubtedly gifted, Elton, much as Madonna would in the '80s and '90s, primarily sold us his peculiar soul. "I'm Elton, buy me!" was the cry behind the sparkly shades, flyaway green hair and the humiliating costumes. (Why didn't anyone twig he was homosexual?) The marketing was the message.

The ultimate Elton John record remains this sturdy, 2-CD, chronological haul through his McHits. At the start of the'70s, stuff like Your Song was singer-songwriter music for people who were scared of the radical thrust of James Taylor. Elton came closest to greatness on the songs that came closest to his real self, Don't Let The Sun Go Down On Me and Someone Saved My Life Tonight retain a real, rousing power, in fact anything motivated by true feeling, like Song For Guy, works beautifully. Anything motivated by an album to fill, like Island Girl (not included here) or The Bitch Is Back, reveals Elton as the worst (or perhaps most honest) kind of pop tart.

Despite his very best efforts, Elton has brought a kind of dignity to the craft of pop stardom, if only by being so unreachably weird and accessibly likeable, sad, mad, bad and hilarious all at once.

Various Artists
SONY 1997

The Philly Sound

Expressway To Your Heart – The Soul Survivors; Cowboys To Girls – The Intruders; I Can't Stop Dancing – Archie Bell And The Drells; Only The Strong Survive – Jerry Butler; One Night Affair – The O'Jays; (We'll Be) United – The Intruders; Silly Silly Fool – Dusty Springfield; Don't Let The Green Grass Fool You – Wilson Pickett; Slow Motion (Part One) – Johnny Williams; Me And Mrs Jones – Billy Paul; Regina – Bunny Singler; The Bells – Laura Nyro And Labelle; Drowning In The Sea Of Love – Joe Simon; If You Don't Know Me By Now – Harold Melvin And The Blue Notes; 992 Arguments – The O'Jays; You're The Reason Why – The Ebonys; I Miss You – Harold Melvin And The Blue Notes; When The World's At Peace – The O'Jays; That's How Long I'll Be Loving You – Bunny Sigler; Back Stabbers – The O'Jays; Love Train – The O'Jays; The Love I Lost – Harold Melvin And The Blue Notes; Now That We Found Love – The O'Jays; Yesterday I Had The Blues – Harold Melvin And The Blue Notes; I'll Always Love My Mama – The Intruders; For The Love Of Money – The O'Jays; Bad Luck – Harold Melvin And The Blue Notes; Don't Call Me Brother – The O'Jays; Zach's Fanfare (I Hear Music) – MFSB; Love Is The Message – MFSB; Am I Black Enough For You – Billy Paul; Sunshine – The O'Jays; When Will I See You Again – The Three Degrees; TSOP (The Sound Of Philadelphia) – MFSB; Livin' For The Weekend – The O'Jays; Wake Up Everybody – Harold Melvin And The Blue Notes; Enjoy Yourself – The Jacksons; I Could Dance All Night – Archie Bell And The Drells; I Love Music – The O'Jays; Love Epidemic – The Trammps; Stairway To Heaven – The O'Jays; Show You The Way To Go – The Jacksons; Do It Any Way You Wanna – People's Choice; My One And Only Love – MFSB; Rich Get Richer – The O'Jays; Hope That We Can Be Together Soon – Harold Melvin And The Blue Notes; Ooh Child – Dee Dee Sharp; Love Train – Bunny Sigler.

Elton John once famously tried to make a Philly album, but couldn't/wouldn't finish it. The shiny allure of the sound for a chap like Elt is obvious, but, as he discovered, getting the correct balance between sharp performance and smooth setting was harder than it seemed.

Thom Bell and the team of Leon Huff and Kenny Gamble were the team responsible for a steady stream of sophisticated hits by The Delfonics, The Intruders, The Stylistics, Harold Melvin And The Blue Notes and The O'Jays in the late 60's and early 70's. All three men had worked together in a Philadelphia vocal group called The Romeos, and when they moved on to writing and production work, they remained friendly rivals, all working at Philly's Sigma Sound Studios and relying on the same pool of studio talent. Gamble and Huff's first national hit was the Soul Survivors' Expressway To Your Heart in 1967, but it was their resuscitation of Jerry Butler's flagging career with Only The Strong Survive in 1969 that really opened eyes and ears. Gamble and Huff founded their own label, Philadelphia International, in 1971. Their trademark sound used lush arrangements and unconventional instruments like vibraphones to create an aura of liquid sensuality. Their biggest hits were Billy Paul's Me and Mrs Jones, The O'Jays' Love Train and TSOP (The Sound of Philadelphia) by MFSB And The Three Degrees.

Cat Stevens
ISLAND 1990

The Very Best Of

Where Do The Children Play; Wild World; Tuesday's Dead; Lady D'Arbanville; The First Cut Is The Deepest; Oh Very Young; Rubylove; Morning Has Broken; Moonshadow; Matthew And Son; Father And Son; Can't Keep It In; Hard Headed Woman; (Remember The Days Of The) Old School Yard; I Love My Dog; Another Saturday Night; Sad Lisa; Peace Train

To his parents, he was Steven Georgiou. To his associates in the Muslim world, which he embraced in 1979, he remains Yusef Islam. But even as Cat Stevens ("I needed a name people wouldn't forget," he says), he's not been averse to change. Early hits like Matthew And Son and I'm Gonna Get Me A Gun were intelligently crafted psych-era pop, but after a career-threatening bout of tuberculosis, Stevens returned in 1970 just as the singer-songwriter boom was hitting its stride. Albums like *Tea For The Tillerman* and *Teaser And The Firecat* became international hits, but by the late '70s, the genre had become deeply unfashionable and Stevens' retirement was noteworthy only for the wrong reasons.

The Eagles

ASYLUM 1976

Their Greatest Hits (1971–75)

Take It Easy; Witchy Woman; Lyin' Eyes; Already Gone; Desperado; One Of These Nights; Tequila Sunrise; Take It To The Limit; Peaceful, Easy Feeling; Best Of My Love

One critic argued recently that this album's sound is the sound of cocaine, the fuel that propelled life in the Los Angeles fast lane in the 1970s. The Eagles, a group of LA studio pros who'd served as Linda Ronstadt's backing band, used sumptuous harmonies and layered guitars to tell moral tales of seduction, betrayal and the peaceful, easy feelings that elude us. Kicking off with the anthemic Take It Easy, this album contains no filler, just big hits. It topped the album charts for five weeks in 1976 and has continued to sell astonishingly well. In January 1999 US sales topped 25 million, and it has since passed Michael Jackson's *Thriller* as nothing less than the best-selling American album of all time.

Coca-country: it's the real thing.

T. Rex

EDSEL 1994

Great Hits: The A-Sides

Telegram Sam; Metal Guru; Children Of The Revolution; Solid Gold Easy Action; 20th Century Boy; The Groover; Truck On (Tyke); Teenage Dream; Light Of Love; Zip Gun Boogie; New York City; Dreamy Lady; London Boys; I Love To Boogie; Laser Love; To Know You Is To Love You (To Know Him Is To Love Him); The Soul Of My Suit; Dandy In The Underworld; Celebrate Summer

"Let's face it, the majority of pop hits that make it are a permutation on the twelve-bar blues and I've found one that works," said T. Rex mainman Marc Bolan in 1971. The Boppin' Elf was no musical sophisticate – it was his voice and face that set him apart – but with producer Tony Visconti he concocted a string of stylised, three-minute pop symphonies that lit up the early '70s. Visconti bowed out after Teenage Dream, and Bolan's career nosedived, but this collection proves that the Glam King was still capable of pulling out the occasional gem (Dreamy Lady, I Love To Boogie, Dandy In The Underworld) right up to his death in 1977. Let's hear it for the girly boys . . .

Various Artists

VIRGIN 1998

The Best Glam Rock Album In The World . . . Ever!

Killer Queen – Queen; Blockbuster – The Sweet; All The Young Dudes – Mott The Hoople; John, I'm Only Dancing – David Bowie; Virginia Plain – Roxy Music; The Passenger – Iggy Pop; Stay With Me – the Faces; Children Of The Revolution – T Rex; Elected – Alice Cooper; Mama Weer All Crazee Now – Slade; This Town Ain't Big Enough For The Both of Us – Sparks; Let's Stick Together – Bryan Ferry; Radar Love – Golden Earring; The Man Who Sold The World – Lulu; Judy Teen – Steve Harley And Cockney Rebel; Perfect Day – Lou Reed; 10538 Overture – Electric Light Orchestra; Ball Park Incident – Wizzard; Rock On – David Essex; Sebastian – Steve Harley And Cockney Rebel; See My Baby Jive – Wizzard; All The Way From Memphis – Mott The Hoople; 20th Century Boy – T Rex; Ballroom Blitz – The Sweet; Tiger Feet – Mud; Devil Gate Drive – Suzi Quatro; All Because Of You – Geordie; Gudbuy T'Jane – Slade; Personality Crisis – the New York Dolls; Do The Strand – Roxy Music; Once Bitten Twice Shy – Ian Hunter With Mick Ronson; Motor Bikin' – Chris Spedding; Seven Deadly Sins – Brian Eno; Cherry Bomb – The Runaways; Solid Gold Easy Action – T Rex; Standing In The Road – Blackfoot Sue; Dyna-Mite – Mud; Angel Face – The Glitter Band; Dance With The Devil – Cozy Powell; New York Groove – Hello; I Love Rock And Roll – Arrows; Can The Can – Suzi Quatro

The term "Glam Rock" was coined in spring 1971 after Marc Bolan appeared on Top Of The Pops with glitter on his cheeks, three-chord rock'n'roll simplicity on his agenda and stardom on his mind. Soon everyone from Mick Jagger to Bob Dylan was wearing sequins and make-up, though glam was essentially a British singles chart phenomenon that made little impact in America. Back-to-basics bands like Slade, The Sweet and Mott The Hoople were perfectly poised to join in; Roxy Music, David Bowie and Sparks sought to elevate the genre into art; Gary Glitter and Mud arguably turned it into farce. And what are Geordie doing in here? All that glitters is not necessarily glamorous.

Slade

POLYDOR 1997

Greatest Hits

Get Down And Get With It; Coz I Luv You; Look Wot You Dun; Take Me Bak 'Ome; Mama Weer All Crazee Now; Gudbuy T'Jane; Cum On Feel The Noize; Skweeze Me Pleeze Me; My Friend Stan; Everyday; Bangin' Man; Far Far Away; How Does It Feel; In For A Penny; We'll Bring The House Down; Lock Up Your Daughters; My Oh My; Run Run Away; All Join Hands; Radio Wall Of Sound; Merry Xmas Everybody

Originally promoted as the antithesis of glam rock decadence, this hard-working band went on to become the early '70s' most successful hit machine notching up 11 UK Top 3 hits between 1971and 1974, including six Number 1s. The recipe, according to songwriter Jim Lea, was simple: "Right from the beginning, Noddy had that raw voice and we had this big, heavy sound." But it was the promotional acumen of ex-Hendrix manager Chas Chandler, who dressed the band up as boot boys and was instrumental in creating Slade's foot-stomping wall of sound. Lack of US success and punk's iconoclasm threatened the group's existence, and after a brief resurgence in the early '80s, Slade parted acrimoniously. But with Merry Xmas Everybody the UK's favourite seasonal song, they're rarely away for long.

Various Artists

RHINO 1991

Rebel Rousers: Southern Rock Classics

Statesboro Blues – The Allman Brothers Band; Jim Dandy – Black Oak Arkansas; Funk #49 – Travis Wammack; Keep On Smilin' – Wet Willie; Fooled Around And Fell In Love – Elvin Bishop; Heard It In A Love Song – The Marshall Tucker Band; Jackie Blue – The Ozark Mountain Daredevils; Freeborn Man [Live Version] – The Outlaws; Coming Home – Johnny Van Zant Band; Caught Up In You – .38 Special; Don't Misunderstand Me – Rossington Collins Band; Free Bird [Live Version] – Lynyrd Skynyrd.

While we were slapping on the lippy, tottering on the platforms and blocking poor Buster, the Americans were getting back to basics. Sniffing the arrival of limey sissyhood, bands like The Allman Brothers struck a blow for bad ol'-fashioned family values. With hard liquor.

Southern rock was built on brotherhood, both literal and figurative. Along with Duane and Gregg, there were Toy and Tommy Caldwell of The Marshall Tucker Band and the Van Zant brothers, Ronnie who was the lead singer for Lynyrd Skynyrd; Johnny who took Ronnie's place after he was killed in a plane crash; and Donnie, who was lead singer with .38 Special. But there was a bond deeper than blood. Southern men didn't really need Neil Young to piss them off: He was just a convenient rallying point for a region that has had a chip on its shoulder for generations. "The South's gonna do it again," vowed the Charlie Daniels Band, while Lynyrd Skynyrd saluted Sweet Home Alabama.

Propelled by Southern Comfort, twin lead guitars and a mix of bitterness and defiance, Southern rock rose with the Allmans and peaked in the mid-'70s when it was hailed, mostly by folks who couldn't dance, as a worthy antidote to disco. For a glorious few years, the Allman Brothers were the most admired band in the country, thanks largely to the incendiary guitar work of Duane Allman and Dickey Betts. First Duane died, then bass player Berry Oakley. The 1977 plane crash that killed Ronnie Van Zant and two other members of Lynyrd Skynyrd cut the swaggering heart out of Southern rock. Pop music has failed to be a proper macho pursuit ever since.

KC And The Sunshine Band

RHINO 1990

The Best Of KC And The Sunshine Band

Do You Wanna Go Party; I Like To Do It; Shotgun Shuffle; Wrap Your Arms Around Me; Sound Your Funky Horn; Get Down Tonight; I'm Your Boogie Man; (Shake, Shake, Shake) Shake Your Booty; Queen Of Clubs; That's The Way (I Like It); Keep It Comin' Love; Please Don't Go; Boogie Shoes; Let's Go Rock And Roll; Give It Up; All I Want.

Completely unconflicted about their partying agenda, KC And The Sunshine Band scored a string of horn-driven dance hits between 1975 and '80, including five Number 1s. The band was formed in Miami by two session men at TK Studios, keyboardist and singer Harry "KC" Casey and bass player Richard Finch. The pair, both white, surrounded themselves with black singers and backing musicians, shook in some of the Latino rhythms they heard on the streets of Miami and made a fortune by delivering danceable chants like Get Down Tonight, That's The Way (I Like It) and (Shake, Shake, Shake) Shake Your Booty. Of the latter KC once said, "To some it was a nonsense song, but to me it had a lot more meaning and depth. There were several connotations to Shake Your Booty. It could mean to get off your can and get out there and do it, in every area, not necessarily dancing – in your whole life."

Casey and Finch also composed superb hits for other TK artists such as George McCrae, and great overlooked album cuts like I'm A Pushover. Nevertheless, they remain among the most underrated pop craftsmen of our times.

Various Artists CASTLE COMMUNICATIONS; 1996

The Electric Muse: The Story Of Folk Into Rock

Robbery With Violins – Steeleye Span; Tail Toddle (extract) – Ian Campbell Folk Group; Ril Gan Ainm – Dave Swarbrick; Spencer The Rover – The Copper Family; The Twa Corbies – Ray & Archie Fisher; The Shoals Of Herring – Ewan MacColl; Pretty Saro – Shirley Collins & Davey Graham; Rocky Road To Dublin/Drops Of Brandy – Ian Campbell Folk Group; The Mason's Apron – The Dubliners; O'Carolan's Concert – The Johnstons; Rattlin' Roarin' Willy – Sweeney's Men; Colonel Fraser – Finbar & Eddie Furey; Kemp's Jig – Gryphon; Medley – Fairport Convention; Greensleeves – Morris On Band; Eibbli Ghalil Chium Ni Chearbhail – John Martyn; Angi – Davey Graham; She Moved Through The Fair – Davey Graham; Veronica – Bert Jansch; Better Git It In Your Soul – Davey Graham; Waltz – John Renbourne; Waltz – Pentangle; Scarborough Fair – Martin Carthy; Sweet Thames How Softly – The Johnstons; John The Baptist – John & Beverly Martyn; Blackwaterside – Bert Jansch; The Fox Hunt – The Young Tradition; Bransle Gay – John Renbourn; Our Captain Cried All Hands – Martin Carthy & Dave Swarbrick; Let No Man Steal Your Thyme – Pentangle; The Wedding Song – Shirley Collins; Nottamun Town – Fairport Convention; Tam Lin – Fairport Convention; Gypsy Davey – Sandy Denny/Fotheringay; John Barleycorn – Traffic; Lord Marlborough – Fairport Convention; The Weaver And The Factory Maid – Steeleye Span; Rise Up Jock – Bob & Carole Pegg; The Gay Goshawk – Mr Fox; Bruton Town – Sandy Denny; Turn A Deaf Ear – Lindisfarne; The Third Millennium – Jack The Lad; Nobody's Wedding – Richard Thompson; The Spirit Of Christmas – Steve Ashley; The Magical Man – Mike & Lal Waterson; The New St George/La Rotta – Albion Country Band. Once I Loved A Maiden Fair – Dave Swarbrick; The Fool's Song – Robin & Barry Dransfield; Tae The Beggin' – Batterfield Band; House Of Cards – Richard & Linda Thompson; The Shame Of Doing Wrong – Richard Thompson; Wild Mountain Thyme – Bert Jansch; Both Sides The Tweed – Dick Gaughan; The Scarecrow – June Tabor; The Keel Row – Martin Simpson; Brenda Stubbert's Set/Jenny Dang The Weaver/Willie Smith's Reel – Capercaillie; Two Left Feet – Richard Thompson; Wasps In The Woodpile – Andrew Cronshaw; Susie Clelland – June Tabor & The Oyster Band; Bells Of Rhymney – The Oyster Band; Another Irish Rover – Four Men And A Dog; The Star Of The County Down – Energy Orchard; Out The Gap – Sharon Shannon; Blind Fiddler – Eliza Carthy; Phoebe – Lal Waterson & Oliver Knight

Though folk rock is well represented in the main body of the book, what the hell, here's a splendid one-stop shop that traces the development of this particularly misunderstood and marginalised British form. It was originally issued in 1975 as a 58-track joint venture between the Island and Transatlantic labels, respected folk writer Karl Dallas compiled it and felt at the time that he could get almost everything that was good into those four albums. He did, almost. Basically, if nothing on this 3-CD set gets to you, you're never going to get folk rock. But if you've fallen for it, then this is a true box of delights with all the very best in the genre represented somewhere. "The honeymoon with rock may be over, but the story isn't," Dallas declared in his original notes. It turned out it was, the following year punk would send folk scuttling underground again.

Various Artists

RHINO, 1990

The Disco Years

Car Wash – Rose Royce; More, More, More (Pt. 1) – Andrea True Connection; Dance With Me – Peter Brown; Miss Broadway – Belle Epoque; The Hustle – Van McCoy And The Soul City Symphony; Shame, Shame, Shame – Shirley And Company; Never Can Say Goodbye – Gloria Gaynor; That's The Way (I Like It) – KC And The Sunshine Band; Disco Inferno – The Trammps; (Shake – Shake – Shake) Shake Your Booty – KC And The Sunshine Band; Love Hangover – Diana Ross; Don't Leave Me This Way – Thelma Houston; Turn The Beat Around – Vicki Sue Robinson; Boogie Oogie Oogie – A Taste Of Honey; You Make Me Feel (Mighty Real) – Sylvester; Shake Your Groove Thing – Peaches And Herb; Disco Nights (Rock-Freak) – GQ; On The Beat – The BB And Q Band; Forget Me Not – Patrice Rushen; Love And Desire (Pt 1) – Arpeggio; I Want Your Love – Chic; Ring My Bell – Anita Ward; I Will Survive – Gloria Gaynor; Ain't No Stoppin' Us Now – McFadden And Whitehead; Funkytown – Lipps Inc.; Celebration – Kool And The Gang; YMCA – Village People; Heart Of Glass – Blondie; This Time Baby – Jackie Moore; Like What You're Doin' To Me – Young And Company; Last Night A DJ Saved My Life – Indeep; Got To Be Real – Cheryl Lynn; Get Off – Foxy; Young Hearts Run Free – Candi Staton; Soul Makossa – Manu Dibango; Dance (Disco Heat) – Sylvester; Rock The Boat – The Hues Corporation; Get Down Tonight – KC And The Sunshine Band; Boogie Fever – The Sylvers; Doctor's Orders – Carol Douglas; I Love The Nightlife (Disco 'Round) – Alicia Bridges; Macho Man – Village People; Dancing Machine – The Jackson 5; Love Machine (Pt 1) – The Miracles; Hot Shot – Karen Young; Le Freak – Chic; We Are Family – Sister Sledge; The Glow Of Love – Change; Knock On Wood – Amii Stewart; Bad Girls – Donna Summer.

Disco did not suck. Not the best of it, anyhow. A magical confluence of optimistic worldview and irresistible rhythm, it provided the perfect complement to the nihilistic thrill of punk, which peaked – in the UK at any rate – at roughly the same time. In the summer of 1977 it was possible to hear people bellowing along to both "Do what you wanna do, be your judge and your jury too" (T Connection) and "No future for you, and me" (Sex Pistols) at the same parties, with the same lusty enthusiasm. But disco's origins were American and much earlier, coming out of the gay dance clubs of New York City. The genre's first Number 1s were George McCrae's Rock Your Baby and The Hues Corporation's Rock The Boat, which both topped the charts in the summer of 1974. From there it grew in several directions – from the taut Latinate pop of KC And The Sunshine Band to the massively extended mechanical symphonies of Giorgio Moroder's productions for Donna Summer – into the most commercially successful pop music of the'70s and early '80s. Of course, in hindsight, with the onset of AIDS and the fall-out of the cocaine storm, disco came to represent a free-spirited pursuit of pleasure that might never be feasible again.

Bad Company

ELEKTRA 1999

The "Original" Bad Company Anthology

Can't Get Enough; Rock Steady; Ready For Love; Bad Company; Movin' On; Seagull; Superstar Woman; Little Miss Fortune; Good Lovin' Gone Bad; Feel Like Makin' Love; Shooting Star; Deal With The Preacher; Wild Fire Woman; Easy On My Soul; Whiskey Bottle; Honey Child; Run With The Pack; Silver, Blue And Gold; Do Right By Your Woman; Burnin' Sky; Heartbeat; Too Bad; Smokin' 45; Rock And Roll Factory; Evil Wind; Oh Atlanta; Rhythm Machine; Untie The Knot; Downhill Ryder; Tracking Down A Runway; Ain't It Good; Hammer Of Love; Hey, Hey

Rock supergroups notoriously lasted little longer than one album or tour and, in truth, Bad Company's legacy might have been better served had they called it quits in the mid-'70s rather than drag themselves into the '80s with diminishing returns. It all began so well, when ex-Free vocalist Paul Rodgers was joined by various Mott The Hoople and King Crimson members, with the backing of Led Zeppelin's management team. With an earthy debut album, and mid-'70s singles like Can't Get Enough and Feel Like Makin' Love sending jets of testosterone up the singles chart, Bad Company briefly rescued cock-rock from an ignominious death. Then along came . . .

Various Artists RHINO 1993

Blank Generation – The New York Scene (1975–78)

Blitzkrieg Bop – Ramones; (I Live For) Cars And Girls – The Dictators; Ask The Angels – Patti Smith Group; All For The Love Of Rock'N'Roll – Tuff Darts; Max's Kansas City 1976 – Wayne County And The Back Street Boys; X Offender – Blondie; Blank Generation – Richard Hell And The Voidoids; See No Evil – Television; In The Flesh – Blondie; Spanish Stroll – Mink DeVille; Venus – Television; Sonic Reducer – Dead Boys; Chinese Rocks – The Heartbreakers; Sheena Is A Punk Rocker – Ramones; Crocodile Tears – Mumps; Love Comes In Spurts – Richard Hell And The Voidoids; Born To Lose – The Heartbreakers; Cheree – Suicide.

In 1974 future punk historian Legs McNeil walked into CBGB on the Lower East Side of Manhattan and got his first glimpse of the Ramones: "Four really pissed-off guys in black leather jackets. It was like the Gestapo had just walked into the room. These guys were definitely not hippies." Based around a couple of downtown clubs – Hilly Kristal's Bowery dive, CBGB, in particular – the New York punk scene tapped into a strange hybrid of influences, from Andy Warhol's cool pop art to heroin, transvestism and rock's old standby, teenage nihilism. With varying degrees of self-consciousness, bands like The Ramones, Dictators and Richard Hell And The Voidoids traced their lineage back through Iggy Pop, the MC5 and the New York Dolls. As much as anything, they were purists, returning the music to its roots. Many years later, Joey Ramone would explain that whatever else his band stood for, they were a reaction to the self-indulgent songs that were popular at the time. "We grew upon the three-minute song – The Kinks, The Ronettes, The Beach Boys," he explained. "By the time we made our first album, one song would fill an entire album. Everything was this egomania, basically, with keyboard solos, drums solos, guitar solos and you-name-it-solos. And what the Ramones really did was kind of like, disassemble it, cut it back down to the bone and reassemble it, putting the excitement and fun and spirit and spark back in."

Various Artists

UNIVERSAL 1999

1-2-3-4: Punk And New Wave 1976–1979

Complete Control – The Clash; Anarchy In The UK – Sex Pistols; New Rose – The Damned; The Blitzkrieg Bop – Ramones; Shadow – The Lurkers; Thinkin' Of The USA – Eater; Ain't Bin To No Music School – The Nosebleeds; Borstal Breakout – Sham 69; I Hate School – Suburban Studs; GLC – Menace; One Chord Wonders – The Adverts; Right To Work – Chelsea; Johnny Won't Get To Heaven – The Killjoys; Bone Idol – The Drones; Where Have All The Boot Boys Gone – Slaughter and The Dogs; CID – UK Subs; I Can't Wait 'Til '78 – The Wasps; Ambition – Subway Sect; – I'm Stranded The Saints; Orgasm Addict – Buzzcocks; In The City – The Jam; Your Generation – Generation X; First Time – The Boys; Get A Grip On Yourself – The Stranglers; Don't Dictate – Penetration; In A Rut – The Ruts; Big Time – Rudi; Don't Ring Me Up – Protex; Justa Nother Teenage Rebel – The Outcasts; Solitary Confinement – The Members; Emergency – 999; 19 And Mad – Leyton Buzzards; I'm In Love With Margaret Thatcher – Not Sensibles; Romford Girls – Riff Raff; Sick Of You – The Users; Gabrielle – The Nips; Where Were You? – The Mekons; Murder Of Liddle Towers – Angelic Upstarts; Oh Bondage Up Yours! – X-Ray Spex; Sweet Suburbia – the Skids; Television Screen – The Radiators From Space; Alternative Ulster – Stiff Little Fingers; Teenage Kicks – The Undertones; Teenage Depression – Eddie And The Hot Rods; Rich Kids – Rich Kids; Baby Baby – The Vibrators; Suffice To Say – Yachts; Roadrunner – Jonathan Richman And The Modern Lovers; Don't Care – Klark Kent; Nervous Wreck – the Radio Stars; Up Against The Wall – the Tom Robinson Band; So It Goes – Nick Lowe; Police Cars – Larry Wallis; Hard Lovin' Man – Johnny Moped; Love And A Molotov Cocktail – The Flys; Where's Captain Kirk? – Spizz Energi; Sonic Reducer – Dead Boys; Search And Destroy – The Dictators; Born To Lose – The Heartbreakers; Modern Dance – Pere Ubu; Fuck Off – The Electric Chairs; California Über Alles – Dead Kennedys; I Belong To The Blank Generation – Richard Hell And The Voidoids; 10:15 Saturday Night – The Cure; Rip Her To Shreds – Blondie; I Can't Stand My Baby – The Rezillos; All I Want – Snatch; Looking After No. 1 – The Boomtown Rats; Take Me I'm Yours – Squeeze; Sex And Drugs And Rock And Roll – Ian Dury And The Blockheads; Spanish Stroll – Mink Deville; Is She Really Going Out With Him? – Joe Jackson; Whole Wide World – Wreckless Eric; Part Time Punks – Television Personalities; Safety Pin Stuck In My Heart – Patrik Fitzgerald; You Can't Put Your Arms Round A Memory – Johnny Thunders; Psycle Sluts (Part 1) – John Cooper Clarke; Jilted John – Jilted John; Kill – Alberto Y Los Trios Paranoias; Paranoid – The Dickies; Public Image – Public Image Ltd; Warsaw – Joy Division; The Staircase (Mystery) – Siouxsie And The Banshees; Damaged Goods – Gang Of Four; You – Au Pairs; How Much Longer – Alternative TV; Read About Seymour – Swell Maps; Young Parisians – Adam And The Ants; The Monochrome Set – The Monochrome Set; We Are All Prostitutes – The Pop Group; Typical Girls – The Slits; Mannequin – Wire; Shot By Both Sides – Magazine; Science Friction – XTC; Do The Standing Still – The Table; Another Girl, Another Planet – The Only Ones; Young Savage – Ultravox; Puppet Life – Punishment Of Luxury; Jocko Homo – Devo; Marquee Moon – Television

Too much is made of punk, largely because many of the generation that runs the media were so taken with it in their teens. But if it did nothing else it declared that pop – or rather a succinct blast of music, preferably in a nice picture bag – was a good thing. Punk just did not work on album.

You might think five CDs of the stuff was a bit much, but this collection is surprisingly entertaining and gripping too. And if you lived through and loved the period this is perfect for an evening of armchair pogoing, poignancy and hilarity.

Genre anthologies are notoriously difficult to do, not least because of the licensing problems involved, but *1-2-3-4* set a standard that will be difficult to surpass. All musical wings of the New Wave are covered – first generation big names (Sex Pistols, the Clash) and mavericks (Siouxsie And The Banshees, The Slits), jokers (Jilted John, the Albertos) and radicals (Pop Group, Au Pairs), boot boys (Sham 69,Angelic Upstarts) and retro-rockers (The Jam, Rich Kids), pub-rock punks (Larry Wallis, Nick Lowe) and pop-punks (Blondie, The Rezillos). Snotty New York bohos (Richard Hell,Television) and weirdies from the American backwoods (Pere Ubu) get a look in too.

Various Artists

CHRYSALIS 1993

Best Of 2-Tone

Ghost Town – The Specials; On My Radio – The Selecter; Too Much Too Young – The Special AKA; Tears Of A Clown – The Beat; Do Nothing – The Specials; People Do Rocksteady – The Bodysnatchers; Stereotype – The Specials; The Prince – Madness; Rat Race – The Specials; The Boiler – Rhoda With The Special AKA; Gangsters – The Special AKA; I Can't Stand Up For Falling Down – Elvis Costello And The Attractions; Nelson Mandela – The Special AKA; Missing Words – The Selecter; A Message To You Rudy – The Specials Featuring Rico; The Selecter – The Selecter

Nostalgia was rarely far away during the late '70s, whether it be for Carnaby Street (The Jam) or the Velvet Underground (countless cult punk acts), but the Prince Buster-inspired ska revival fashioned by the Coventry-based The Specials (later The Special AKA) was one of the more unlikely eruptions of musical archaeology. During 1979 and 1980, the bands' 2-Tone label was a model independent, combining commercial success with a strong identity (rude-boy suits, multi-racial message). But when bands like Madness and The Beat found other homes, and The Specials were torn apart after a trio of influential members split to form Fun Boy Three, 2-Tone collapsed, leaving mainman Jerry Dammers to spend more time pursuing political causes.

Rod Stewart

WARNER BROS 1989

The Best Of Rod Stewart

Maggie May; You Wear It Well; Baby Jane; Da Ya Think I'm Sexy?; I Was Only Joking; This Old Heart Of Mine; Sailing; I Don't Want To Talk About It; You're In My Heart; Young Turks; What Am I Gonna Do (I'm So In Love With You); The First Cut Is The Deepest; The Killing Of Georgie (Parts I And II); Tonight's The Night; Every Beat Of My Heart; Downtown Train

"I never thought I'd find myself writing songs like that – those dirty, rude, shagging songs," remembers the man who would be Sam Cooke. And despite the advancing years, he's still making a good fist of it (as it were.) It's his '70s work, though, that this CD largely focuses on, though the non-chronological approach spoils that moment when Rod eschewed rough'n'ready Faces-era hits like Maggie May and You Wear It Well for those smooth, mid-Atlantic, mid-'70s productions like Tonight's The Night and You're In My Heart.

Status Quo

POLYGRAM TV 1997

Whatever You Want: The Very Best Of

Pictures Of Matchstick Men; Ice In The Sun; Down The Dustpipe; In My Chair; Paper Plane; Mean Girl; Caroline; Break The Rules; Down Down; Roll Over Lay Down; Rain; Mystery Song; Wild Side Of Life; Rockin' All Over The World; Again And Again; Whatever You Want; Living On An Island; What You're Proposing; Lies; Don't Drive My Car; Something About You Baby I Like; Rock'n'Roll; Dear John; Ol Rag Blues; A Mess Of The Blues; Marguerita Time; Going Down Town Tonight; The Wanderer; Rollin' Home; Red Sky; In The Army Now; Dreamin'; Ain't Complaining; Burning Bridges; Anniversary Waltz Part 1 (Medley); Anniversary Waltz Part2 (Medley); I Didn't Mean It; When You Walk In The Room; Fun Fun Fun (featuring The Beach Boys); Don't Stop; All Around My Hat (with Maddy Prior)

Which cod-psychedelic combo became the favourite boogie band of Prince Charles? Who opened up Live Aid? Who the hell were Status Quo? God knows, but boy did we buy their records.

Here they are, representing all kinds of pop phenomena: the workaday, glamourless groups that provide easily assimilated, entry-level rock for tyros and princes; the public faves who can never be cool; and the groups who have survived the test of time by adapting shamelessly.

"There are a lot of people out there who want that old Status Quo . . ." And Francis Rossi, who's steered the band from Pictures Of Matchstick Men through the ear-bashing lurch of Caroline to the hypnotic blandness of In The Army Now (and a cover of All Around My Hat??!!) has rarely veered from a kind of public-bar-pleasing formula patented in 1970 with Down The Dustpipe. Quo today are as anachronistic and useful as a shire horse.

In truth, the perfect Quo collection would run rather shorter than this one, but even if the band, who at their mid-'70s peak were irresistible, no longer find an outlet on Radio One, that doesn't prevent them taking their music direct to the people via regular sell-out tours.

Earth, Wind & Fire,

SONY 1978

The Best of Earth, Wind & Fire, Volume 1

Got To Get You Into My Life; Fantasy; Can't Hide Love; Love Music; Getaway; That's The Way Of The World; September; Shining Star; Reasons; Sing A Song; Megamix 2000; Megamix (Radio Edit).

George Clinton of P-Funk mocked them as "Earth, Hot Air and No Fire", and there is something annoying about a group that refers to themselves as "the Creator's band." But there was probably more than a little jealousy in Clinton's comment too, for Earth, Wind And Fire were the most successful soul-funk group of the late '70s. Their only Number 1 was Shining Star, but their slick, undeniably commercial sound brought them a string of Top 10 hits. Named for the three elements in founder Maurice White's astrological sign, Earth, Wind And Fire saw music as part of a larger spiritual quest, but in their sensational live shows they weren't above using magicians, costumes and extensive props.

Billy Joel

COLUMBIA 1985

Greatest Hits, Vol. 1 & 2 (1973–1985)

Piano Man; Captain Jack; The Entertainer; Say Goodbye To Hollywood; New York State Of Mind; The Stranger; Scenes From An Italian Restaurant; Just The Way You Are; Movin' Out (Anthony's Song); Only The Good Die Young; She's Always A Woman. Disc 2: My Life; Big Shot; You May Be Right; It's Still Rock And Roll To Me; Don't Ask Me Why; She's Got A Way; Pressure; Allentown; Goodnight Saigon; Tell Her About It; Uptown Girl; The Longest Time; You're Only Human (Second Wind); The Night Is Still Young.

Bob Seger

CAPITOL 1994

Greatest Hits

Roll Me Away; Night Moves; Turn the Page; You'll Accomp'ny Me; Hollywood Nights; Still the Same; Old Time Rock And Roll; We've Got Tonight; Against the Wind; Mainstreet; The Fire Inside; Like a Rock; C'est La Vie; In Your Time

Two solid dudes representing the kind of solo-male pop America loved in the '70s and '80s. Billy Joel grew up in middle-class Hicksville, Long Island, and followed a long, arduous path to stardom. For three years he was an amateur boxer, winning 22 of 28 fights, and that pugnacity would come in handy in a career marked by many lawsuits. Joel spent more time than he'd have liked playing local nightclubs and cocktail bars, including six months in Los Angeles in 1972 when, to escape a reckoning with his record company, he performed under the name Bill Martin. His breakthrough came in 1977, when the ballad Just The Way You Are made Number 3.The song, which nearly didn't make it onto its parent album *The Strange* because no one in the band cared for it much, won two Grammy Awards and probably managed to surpass Chicago's Colour My World as America's most popular wedding song. Joel's piano-bar roots show through in his ballads, but the first of his three Number 1s was 1980's It's Still Rock And Roll To Me, in a slick disco rockabilly style.

Bob Seger specialised in a kind of heartland rock that celebrates the resilience of ordinary folk. Seger grew up poor in Ann Arbor, Michigan, and after forming a number of moderately successful local bands throughout the '60s and early '70s, he finally hit it big in 1976, with the release of the multi-platinum *Night Moves*, which climbed to Number 8, thanks in part to Seger's exhausting touring schedule. Over the next dozen years, Seger was a steady presence in the charts, notching seven Top 10 songs, capped by his only Number 1, Shakedown, from the film Beverly Hills Cop II.

We find these guys to be eminently preferable to the likes of Huey Lewis or Rick Springfield, who might also have laid claim to the same audience.

Queen

EMI, 1981

Greatest Hits (Vol. 1)

Bohemian Rhapsody; Another One Bites The Dust; Killer Queen; Fat Bottomed Girls; Bicycle Race; You're My Best Friend; Don't Stop Me Now; Save Me; Crazy Little Thing Called Love; Somebody To Love; Now I'm Here; Good Old Fashioned Lover Boy; Play The Game; Flash; Seven Seas Of Rhye; We Will Rock You; We Are The Champions

The non-chronological nature of this, the first of two essential singles compilations, masks the group's development from mid-'70s post-glam art-rockers to the hardy all-rounders of the early '80s who'd artfully survived punk and disco. In other words, they covered all bases, did a bit of everything, pleased everyone. It's a bloody good trick if you can do it.

Despite starting life as an album band, singles were Queen's real forte. They stretched the three-minute format with a series of meticulously arranged 45s that ranged from the opulence of Bohemian Rhapsody to the funk simplicity of John Deacon's Another One Bites The Dust, each delivered in the band's unique style. "Freddie wrote in strange keys, so as a guitarist you're forced to find new chords," explains Brian May.

It's unlikely that a band quite so inventive, bizarre and maddening will ever happen again. The suspension of disbelief Queen required to function probably wouldn't be granted them today.

Various Artists

STRUT 2000

Larry Levan Live At The Paradise Garage

Bourgie Bourgie – Ashford And Simpson; It's Music – Damon Harris; At Midnight – T Connection; Put Your Body In It – Stephanie Mills; Dreaming A Dream – Crown Heights Affair; By The Way You Dance – Bunny Sigler; Right In The Socket – Shalamar; Take Me Home – Cher; Pick Me Up, I'll Dance – Melba Moore; Get On The Funk Train – Munich Machine; Here We Go Again – People's Choice; Bad Mouthin' – Motown Sounds; Let Yourself Go – the Supremes; Angel In My Pocket – Change; Smack Dab In The Middle – Janice McClain; Sun Sun Sun – Jakki; Trinidad – John Gibbs And The US Steel Band; My First Mistake – Chi-Lites; Erucu – Jermaine Jackson.

There isn't a fan of underground disco alive that doesn't possess at least a handful of incredibly bad-quality cassettes of Shep Pettibone's Mastermixes on New York's Kiss, or Frankie Knuckles live at the Warehouse, Power Plant or CODs (delete as applicable). Or even, the Holy Grail itself, Larry Levan in his pomp at the Paradise Garage. Levan used to give tapes to friends and make them promise they would never copy them for everyone. And they never did. "This is for you," he would tell them. Brooklyn DJ Danny Tenaglia once described Larry Levan as the Jimi Hendrix of DJing and he wasn't far wrong. He died in November 1992, the result of a lifelong heart condition, but undoubtedly exacerbated by his prolonged and excessive drug abuse.

There are several disco veterans with stocks of ageing reel-to-reels of America's pioneers gathering dust in lofts and garages, but this is the first time one has ever been legitimately licensed and released. It contains the usual disco staples like Shalamar's Right In The Socket and Damon Harris's It's Music, the odd underground classic (Chi-Lites' My First Mistake) and the simply odd (the re-edit of Jermaine Jackson's Erucu). The mixing is ropey in parts – but then Levan's appeal came from his personality and programming skills rather than any specific technical ability – but it merely adds a touch of gritty, secular realism. The truth is, it's the nearest most will ever get to experiencing the lost days of seventies gay hedonism.

Various Artists

PAUL WINLEY RECORDS 1977

Super Disco Brakes Vol. 1–6

Take Me To The Mardi Gras – Bob James; Work Song – Pat Lundy; I Can Understand It – New Birth; Blow Your Head – JBs; Scorpio – Dennis Coffey; Gotta Get A Knutt – New Birth; Corazon – Creative Source; Scratchin' – Magic Disco Machine.

Paul Winley has been around forever. As a young songwriter in the '50s, he wrote for the likes of Ruth Brown (Smooth Operator) and by 1956 he had launched his first record label, Winley Records (the first release was by a doo-wop group called The Duponts, featuring a singer called Little Anthony). He also has the distinction of releasing the first-ever rap record, Vicious Rap by Sweet Tee, whose real name was Tanya Winley, Paul's daughter. Winley swiftly saw the commercial possibilities of the nascent hip hop scene and, in any case, rhyming over the top of records wasn't so far removed from the radio DJs, like Jocko Henderson, that he had grown up with. With DJs now searching for breaks on records, the prices of sought-after albums soared. *Volume 1* came out in 1977 and includes some of the most popular early breaks records, like Bob James' Take Me To The Mardi Gras (employed most famously on LL Cool J's Rock The Bells), Dennis Coffey's Scorpio and Work Song by Pat Lundy. It's doubtful whether any of the tracks on the Super Disco Brakes series were ever properly licensed since the cuts are clearly mastered direct from vinyl (replete with pops) and pressed on what sounds like digestive biscuits. (The liberally sprinkled spelling mistakes on the sleeves and labels – including the title! – merely add to their charm.) As a pleasurable home-listening experience, they're hopeless, but as a document of one of New York's most exciting eras, they're priceless (or $8 a pop if you ever bump into Winley on 125th Street).

The Pretenders

REAL/WEA 1987

The Singles

Stop Your Sobbing; Kid; Brass In Pocket; Talk Of The Town; I Go To Sleep; Day After Day; Message Of Love; Back On The Chain Gang; Middle Of The Road; 2000 Miles; Show Me; Thin Line Between Love And Hate; Don't Get Me Wrong; Hymn To Her; My Baby

"I tried to get a band together with almost everyone in the punk scene," recalls Chrissie Hynde. Eventually, The Pretenders emerged in 1979 with a trio of classic singles, Stop Your Sobbing, Kid and the chart-topping Brass In Pocket, and a self-titled debut album sealed their old-wave-meets-New-Wave pop reputation the following year. The deaths of guitarist James Honeyman-Scott and bassist Pete Farndon in 1982 and 1983 curtailed the band's activities, though the resourceful Hynde ("I have the vision and the songs") has kept the band going without fundamentally altering her trademark style.

Various Artists

SANCTUARY 2000

Metal For Muthas

Sanctuary – Iron Maiden; Sledgehammer – Sledgehammer; Fighting For Rock And Roll – EF Band; Blues In A – Toad The Wet Sprocket; Captured City – Praying Mantis; Fight Back – Ethel The Frog; Baphomet – Angelwitch; Wrathchild – Iron Maiden; Tomorrow Or Yesterday – Samson; Bootliggers – Nutz

With the arrival of the altogether more abrasive punk, heavy metal took a knocking in the late '70s, though the fightback wasn't long in coming. 1980's *Metal For Muthas* confirmed that the New Wave Of British Heavy Metal – snappily abbreviated to NWOBHM – was more than a grass-roots movement centred on the Midlands. "Hard rock is an expression of emotion, heartfelt and sincerely delivered," claimed influential metal DJ Neil Kay in the sleevenote. "This album is the proof. Metal is for Muthas – it is here to stay so the whole world had better get used to the idea!" He was right: metal was reborn, though of this handful of untarnished, Sabbath-inspired prime movers, only Iron Maiden managed to last the course.

Various Artists

RHINO, 1996

Youth Gone Wild: Heavy Metal Hits of the '80s

Never Enough – LA Guns; Summertime Girls (studio version) – Y&T; Rock You Like A Hurricane – Scorpions; Talk Dirty To Me – Poison; The Last In Line – Dio; Lay It Down – Ratt; Parental Guidance – Judas Priest; Blind In Texas – WASP; Ace Of Spades – Motorhead; Balls To The Wall – Accept; Street Of Dreams – Rainbow; Screaming In The Night – Krokus; We're Not Gonna Take It – Twisted Sister; Cum On Feel The Noize – Quiet Riot; Gotta Let Go – Lita Ford; Dreams In The Dark – Badlands; Rock Me – Great White; Heaven Tonight – Yngwie J. Malmsteen's Rising Force; The Final Countdown – Europe; Over My Head – King's X; Goin' Crazy! – David Lee Roth; It's Not Love – Dokken; Seventeen – Winger; Poison Ivy – Faster Pussycat; I Want Out – Helloween; I'm Onto You – Hurricane; Edge Of A Broken Heart – Vixen; Wild Thing – Sam Kinison; Say What You Will – Fastway; Heavy Metal Love – Helix; Still Of The Night – Whitesnake; Gypsy Road – Cinderella; Sleeping My Day Away – DAD; Wait – White Lion; Someone Like You – Bang Tango; Don't Dog Me – Raging Slab; Get It On – Kingdom Come; Rock Queen – Love/Hate; Scared – Dangerous Toys; Smooth Up In Ya – Bulletboys; Girlschool – Britny Fox; Addicted To That Rush – Mr Big

History shows that every generation of American parents needs a musical style to fear and loathe, and until gangsta rap came along in the early '90s, that role was ably and inventively played by heavy metal. Brainwashing, satanic references, weird hair and clothes: what were the kids getting up to in their bedrooms?

Heavy metal – a phrase first bandied about in the Steppenwolf song BornTo Be Wild – was never popular with pundits, who tended to dismiss many of the above as "hair bands". But with legions of fans – most of them disaffected mall-rat boys – groups like Poison, Great White, Twisted Sister and Quiet Riot offered something approaching an identity.

Various Artists

RHINO 1992

Street Jams: Hip Hop From The Top

Rapper's Delight – the Sugarhill Gang; The Breaks – Kurtis Blow; Sucker DJ's (I Will Survive) – Dimples D; Request Line – Rock Master Scott And The Dynamic Three; What People Do For Money – Divine Sounds; Adventures Of Super Rhyme (Rap) – Jimmy Spicer; King Of The Beat – Pumpkin; The Message – Grand Master Flash And The Furious Five; Friends – Whodini; One For The Treble (Fresh) – Davy DMX; The Pure – Captain Rock Scorpio – Grand Master Flash And The Furious Five; It's Like That – Run D.M.C; The Roof Is On Fire (Club DJ) – Rock Master Scott And The Dynamic Three; Five Minutes Of Funk – Whodini; 8 Million Stories – Kurtis Blow; A Fly Girl – Boogie Boys; Can You Feel It – Fat Boys; Basketball – Kurtis Blow; Big Mouth (Beat Box Mix) – Whodini; Roxanne, Roxanne – UTFO (The Kangol Kid, Dr Ice, And The Educated Rapper); The Real Roxanne – Roxanne with UTFO; Rappin' Duke – Shawn Brown; Genius Rap – Dr Jekyll And Mr Hyde.

"What you hear is not a test/ I'm rappin' to the beat/ And me, the groove, and my friends/ Are going to try to move your feet." So rapped the Sugarhill Gang over an infectious guitar riff borrowed from the Chic song, Good Times. It was 1979, and hip hop was still just about dancing and having a good time. In fact, large portions of Rapper's Delight were about going over to the house of a friend whose mother is a lousy cook: "The beans are hard and the chicken tastes like wood!" The hard, street-won edge of gangsta rap was still years away, though Grandmaster Flash spared no detail in The Message, his angry warning from the ghetto.

The music began in the Bronx, where DJs like Kool Herc would roll up to a playground, unload a massive sound system and play booming party music for the assembled masses. A key part of Herc's show were the vocal ad libs of his friend, Coke La Rock, who did not exactly rap, but acted as a kind of cheerleader and crowd-rouser.

Following a lull after the breakthrough of Flash and Co, rap suddenly exploded. By the time Run DMC, from Hollis, Queens, were teaming up with Aerosmith on Walk This Way, (which reached Number 4 in the charts and helped the album it was on, *Raisin' Hell*, become the first hip hop album to go platinum), hip hop had become as revolutionary and controversial as early rock'n'roll and as American as apple pie. Unlike rock, however, total white appropriation of the music was avoided and the rise of the black music business was swift and impressive. This box focuses on the B-boy, breakdance and "sucker MC" beginnings of the music. The harder, harsher West Coast manifestation of rap is generally less well collected. British series *The Hip Hop Don't Stop Vols 1–3* is also highly recommended.

Hall And Oates

RCA 1983

Rock 'n' Soul, Part 1

Say It Isn't So; Sara Smile; She's Gone; Rich Girl; Kiss On My List; You Make My Dreams; Private Eyes; Adult Education; I Can't Go For That (No Can Do); Maneater; One On One; Wait For Me (Live Version)

Soft Cell

SOME BIZZARE 1986

The Singles

Memorabilia; Tainted Love; Bed Sitter; Say Hello Wave Goodbye; Torch; Loving You, Hating Me; What; Where The Heart Is; Numbers; Soul Inside; Down In The Subway

Eurythmics

RCA 1991

Greatest Hits

Love Is A Stranger; Sweet Dreams; Who's That Girl?; Right By Your Side; Here Comes The Rain Again; There Must Be An Angel (Playing With My Heart); Sisters Are Doing It For Themselves; It's Alright (Baby's Coming Back); When Tomorrow Comes; You Have Placed A Chill In My Heart; Miracle Of Love; Sex Crime (1984); Thorn In My Side; Don't Ask Me Why; Angel; Would I Lie To You?; Missionary Man; I Need A Man

Wham!

EPIC 1986

The Final

Wham Rap (Enjoy What You Do); Young Guns (Go For It!); Bad Boys; Club Tropicana; Wake Me Up Before You Go Go; Careless Whisper; Freedom; Last Christmas (Pudding Mix); Everything She Wants (Remix); I'm Your Man; A Different Corner; Battlestations; Where Did Your Heart Go?; The Edge Of Heaven

And so we come to a selection representing the great pop practitioners of the '80s.

The top-charting duo in American rock'n'roll history, blue-eyed-soulmen Daryl Hall and John Oates, first met in 1967, when the two shared a freight elevator to escape a fight at an all-too-literal battle of the bands in Philadelphia. Before joining forces with his new friend, Hall would sing back-up for a number of legendary Philly soul groups like The Delfonics, The Stylistics and The Intruders. After a sticky start on Atlantic – where they did cut one of the greatest white soul records ever made, She's Gone – they switched to RCA and had scored seven Number 1 singles between 1977 and 1984, including three in 1981 alone. Their crisp productions and use of drum machines and synth with guitar did much to define the sound of the '80s. Whether this merits brickbats or applause is a matter for the jury to decide.

"We were just two nobodies people thought would never get a Number 1 in a million years," said Marc Almond. The enormous success Soft Cell had in 1981 with their cover of an old Northern Soul club hit, Tainted Love, has overshadowed the many charms of the first and, arguably, best of the '80s synth duos. That Almond oozed post-punk's fascination for kitsch and sleaze only served to detract from the group's witty, streetwise melodramas that, by 1983's *The Art Of Falling Apart*, had acquired much darker hues. Inevitably, the strain of holding onto a young dancefloor audience with distinctly adult material proved too much, and the pair parted, leaving Almond to pursue his private obsessions on a tide of variable solo releases.

Formed from the ashes of powerpop unfashionables The Tourists, Eurythmics' specialised in soulful electro-pop, packaged in studied cool. After a long gestation period, the duo finally broke with their sixth single, 1983's Sweet Dreams, ushering in a two-year period that saw a further six Top 10 hits, with MTV-friendly videos that, initially, emphasised singer Annie Lennox's not-particularly-striking androgyny. But a woman in a suit seemed to freak out the Americans anyhow. In world terms they were probably the most successful example of British electro-pop until Depeche Mode struck a major blow for the New Romantic clan. However, a change of direction on the rock-oriented *Revenge* album, issued in 1986, broke the spell, and the duo never quite recaptured their early success.

Wham!'s blend of infectious, floor-filling pop and pin-up visuals provided a neat escape from the bitter social climate early in the decade, a fact that wasn't lost on the duo's creative half, George Michael. Club Tropicana was, he admitted, a "dream club that couldn't possibly be true". Much the same could be said about his relationship with partner Andrew Ridgeley, and after a string of hits, breaking America and being the first Western group to perform live in China, the singer broke a generation of teenage hearts when, after testing the water with Careless Whisper (a Number 1), he pulled the plug on Wham! to go solo.

Various Artists

NME/ISLAND/TTED 1986

Good To Go

Good To Go – Trouble Funk; Meet Me At The Go Go – Hot, Cold Sweat; Still Smokin' – Trouble Funk; Make 'Em Move – Sly Dunbar And Robbie Shakespeare; EU Freeze – EU; Keys (The Chemist's Theme) – Wally Badarou; War On The Bullshit – Osiris; Sho' Nuff Bump – EU; We Need Money – Chuck Brown And The Soul Searchers; Status Quo – Donald Banks; Drop The Bomb – Trouble Funk; Riot Zone (Call The Police) – Ini Kamoze; I Like It – Trouble Funk; Movin' And Groovin' – Redds And The Boys; Good To Go (Reprise) – Trouble Funk; In The Mix (Don't Touch That Stereo) – Trouble Funk; Drop The Bomb – Trouble Funk.

It's hard to imagine now that the whole world has been subsumed by the relentless kick drum of house music that, in the mid-'80s, the industry's hot tip for global domination was go go. Muscular drum-heavy music inspired by James Brown, gestated by Chuck Brown and born in Washington DC's ghettoes, UK clubs went gaga for gogo. Island signed DC's most likely Trouble Funk and then promptly ruined them with a dreadful attempt at a crossover album, the prophetically titled Trouble Over There. Though there were several other compilations (Go Go Crankin') and live sets – notably by Chuck Brown and Experience Unlimited – Good To Go is the best of the bunch. Released via a voucher offer in the NME, it was the soundtrack album to an Island-backed feature film (starring, of all people, Art Garfunkel) and, with the possible exception of Little Benny's Who Comes To Boogie, contains go go's finest moments: We Need Money, Drop The Bomb, War On The Bullshit, Status Quo.

Looking back, it seems pretty obvious that go go, essentially a live music form, could never have had the impact that house and techno have had (not least because the '80s drug of choice in DC was angel dust). But, for a short while at least, bands like Trouble Funk and EU were among the most incendiary live groups in the world. Sadly, the tight-knit scene collapsed into in-fighting after its mid-'80s heyday, the result of bad business deals (Trouble Funk's debut album on Sugarhill went gold: they never saw a penny) and even badder drugs. Go go went went.

Various Artists

EARTHWORKS 1986

The Indestructible Beat Of Soweto

Awungilobolele – Udokotela Shange Namajaha; Holotelani- Nelcy Sedibe; Qhude Manikiniki – Umahlathini Nabo; Indoda Yejazi – Elimnyama – Amaswazi Emvelo; Emthonjeni Womculo – Mahlathini – Nezintombi – Zomgqashiyo And The Makgona TsohleBand; Sobabambo – Udokotela Shange Namajaha; Qhwayilahle – Moses Mchunu; Thul'ulalele – Amaswazi Emvelo; Sini Lindile – Nganeziyamfisa NoKhambalomvaleliso; Ngicabange Ngaqeda – Mahlathini Nezintombi Zomgoashiyo; Joyce No. 2 – Johnson Mkhalali; Nansi Imali -Ladysmith Black Mambazo

Released the same year as Paul Simon's *Graceland*, this was a drop of the hard stuff. Although world music (the term was yet to be adopted as a handy catch-all) had been available for decades – if you were prepared to seek it out – for many people 1986 was Year Zero. On Radio One, John Peel was an early evangelist, won over by guitarists who tore up rule books they never knew existed, the a cappella (*iscathamiya*) group Ladysmith Black Mambazo and vocalists such as the incomparable Mahlathini, a singer who made Barry White sound like Jimmy Somerville. Although the bands saw what they were doing as Africanising black American styles and modernising traditional Sotho and Zulu music, it still sounded completely new to an audience raised on rock. Fittingly, in 1989, Rolling Stone voted it one of the 100 greatest albums of the previous decade.

Madonna

SIRE 1990

The Immaculate Collection

Holiday; Lucky Star; Borderline; Like a Virgin; Material Girl; Crazy For You; Into The Groove; Live To Tell; Papa Don't Preach; Open Your Heart; La Isla Bonita; Like a Prayer; Express Yourself; Cherish; Vogue; Justify My Love; Rescue Me.

Like Elvis's hips and Mick Jagger's lips, Madonna's body parts have inspired outrage in all quarters. Beneath the sharpened bustiers and ripped fishnets, well, over the years we've been party to all of it, from the before-she-was-famous static nudes to the almost gynaecological candour and variety of her Sex coffee-table tome. Madonna was one of the first pop stars to blatantly make herself the product. "Manipulating people, that's what I'm good at," she once said, though she was also good at turning it all into fabulous riches.

Madonna Ciccone grew up in a lower-middle-class family in Bay City, Michigan, and after studying dance at the University of Michigan, moved to New York, where she danced briefly with the prestigious Alvin Ailey Dance Company. Soon she drifted over to the club scene, and though she was dismissed at first as a hanger-on, she proved to be an ambitious one, with a stronger knack for self-promotion than any other artist of her time. Since her first Number 1, Like A Virgin in 1984, only one of her 40-plus UK singles has failed to make the Top 10 (Take A Bow in 1994, which peaked at 11).

"I've always known this was going to happen to me," she once said. "My success was something that was meant to be."

Whatever you think of her or her music, no survey of pop over the last 20 years would dare exclude her. She may be, in fact, the biggest pop star there has ever been.

Various Artists

10 RECORDS 1988

Techno! The New Dance Sound Of Detroit

No UFOs – Model 500; Just Another Chance – Reese; Freestyle – Mayday; The Dance – Rhythim Is Rhythim; R-Theme – R-Tyme; Clear – Cybotron; Rock To The Beat – Reese; First Bass – Separate Minds; When We Used To Play – Blake Baxter; Let's Go – X-Ray; The Groove That Won't Stop – Kevin Saunderson; Strings of Life – Rhythim Is Rhythim

Few albums can claim to have given birth to an entire genre of music, but *Techno! The New Dance Sound Of Detroit* can. Although the name "techno" was little more than a convenient marketing ploy, its roots were certainly distinct from near neighbour Chicago and its own offspring house. While house was simply, as veteran A&R man Mel Cheren describes it, disco on a budget, techno's roots were more firmly in the European tradition with acts like Depeche Mode, Visage and Kraftwerk hugely influential. The compilation was the brainchild of an obsessive British Northern Soul fan, Neil Rushton, who was drawn to the growing number of releases on Transmat, KMS and Metroplex bearing the area code 313. An album was quickly put together to capitalise on the interest in nearby Chicago. The late delivery of a track by Juan Atkins – Techno Music – may have tipped the balance from its working title: The House Sound Of Detroit (the word "techno" was already a commonly used adjective among Detroit's main players).

It was while on a press junket in Detroit to promote the album that journalist Stuart Cosgrove elicited those evocative quotes that subsequently set up techno as the genre of choice for the overeducated music critic. "The music is just like Detroit, a complete mistake. It's like George Clinton and Kraftwerk stuck in an elevator," said Derrick May, while Juan Atkins told him: "Berry Gordy built the Motown sound on the same principles as the conveyor-belt system at Ford's. Today their plants don't work that way – they use robots and computers to make the cars. I'm probably more interested in Ford's robots than in Berry Gordy's music." And lo, techno was born.

Various Artists

WORLD CIRCUIT 1989

Cumbia Cumbia

La Colegiala – Rodolfo Y Su Tipica RA7; La Subienda – Gabriel Romero; LaZenaida – Armando Hernandez Y Su Conjunto; Amancienda – Adolfo Echevierra Y Su Orquesta; Navidad Negra – Pedro Laza Y Su Pelayeros; Cumbia Cienaguera – Conjunto Tipico Vallenato; Tabaco Y Ron – Rodolfo Y Su Tipica; La Piragua – Gabriel Romero; La Pollera Colora – Los Immortales; Se Me Perdio La Cadenita – La Sonora Dinamita; ElPescador – Los Warahuaco; Cumbia Sampuesina – Conjunto Tipico Vallenato

Starting out on Colombia's African-dominated Caribbean coast, *cumbia* was a percussive dance music rooted in the dances slaves would perform while wearing leg irons. It wasn't hard to do, in other words, and soon became a generic term for Colombian pop. The influence of Havana's big bands changed the music around entirely, however. Where once it was the original drum'n'bass (the bass being a large box with pluckable metal teeth), it suddenly became a vibrant, brassy and thoroughly modern form of indigenous mambo.This compilation gathers some of the greatest big bands from the Discos Fuentes label from 1950 onwards, and proves beyond a shadow of a doubt that Latin doesn't necessarily mean Cuban. Yes, there are nods to salsa, but Colombia can claim some of the credit for the global success of that particular style. And, crucially, its simplicity means you don't need to approach with trepidation: anyone can dance to it. Even you.

Various Artists

DMC/1991

Mixmag Live! Vol. 1 Mixed by Carl Cox & Dave Seaman

Carl Cox: Atomic Bass – Rhythm Section; Devil In Us All – The Warrior; I Want You – Carl Cox; Yeah Yeah Yeah – Tech Noise; Up Tempo – Tronic House; Lock-Up – Zero B; Compression – BetweenThe Grooves; Mental Techno – Tronic House; Dreamaster – Strategy And DJ Fresh; Sensory Deception – MK 13. Dave Seaman: Metropolis – Evolution; Brass Disk – Dupree; I'm Coming Hardcore – MANIC; Angels Of Love – Cocodance; Locomotion – Chocolate Fudge; It's Easy – Tamsin; Livin' For The Night – Underground Resistance featuring Yolanda; Dance No More – E-Lustrious; Get Out On The Dancefloor – DOP; You Keep The Love – G-Love featuring Jayne Casey.

DJs were huge stars a long time before the record industry realised it. In the early '90s, Camden Market in London and Affleck's Palace in Manchester were just two of the places flooded with illegal mix tapes. Shaggy-haired entrepreneurs either cajoled unknown DJs to do them at home or, more usually, they were taped direct from DAT machines in clubs (often without the DJ's prior consent). Mixmag introduced its Mixmag Live! series in 1991 with a cassette release featuring Carl Cox on one side and Dave Seaman on the other. Two other independent labels, React and Music Unites, also launched similar volumes around the same time, MU's Journeys By DJs set, beginning with a mix by techno DJ Billy Nasty. Cox's mix is an interesting timepiece, caught in a period when the brand of breakbeat house he was playing had split from the mainstream, but before it had crystallised into what subsequently became Jungle. These days some of it sounds a tad comical, almost ugly; the difference between looking at a chrysalis and a butterfly, but it still has a charm that comes from affectionately remembering the records rather than critically appraising them. Among the raucous and loosely programmed sets are tunes like Italo-house favourite Cocodance, early progressive-house staples like DOP and Lock-Up by Zero B, so Wagnerian in its approach it sounds like a phalanx of Prussian soldiers marching across the dance floor. Somehow it still sounds great. In years to come, academics with far too much time on their hands will look to LPs like this for guidance of how we got to there from here. This, then, if you will, is house music's Piltdown Man.

The Beach Boys

CAPITOL 1993

Good Vibrations: Thirty Years Of The Beach Boys

Surfin' USA (Demo Version); Little Surfer Girl (Previously Unreleased); Surfin' (Rehearsal) (Previously Unreleased); Their Hearts Were Full Of Spring (Demo) (Previously Unreleased); Surfin' Safari; 409 Punchline (Instrumental) (Previously Unreleased); Surfin' USA; Shut Down; Surfer Girl; Little Deuce Coupe; In My Room; Catch A Wave; The Surfer Moon; Be True To Your School; Spirit Of America; Little Saint Nick (45 RPM); Things We Did Last Summer (Previously Unreleased); Fun, Fun, Fun; Don't Worry Baby; Why Do Fools Fall In Love; The Warmth Of The Sun; I Get Around; All Summer Long; Little Honda; Wendy; Don't Back Down; Do You Wanna Dance; WHen I Grow Up (To Be A Man); Dance, Dance, Dance; Please Let Me Wonder; She Knows Me Too Well; Radio Station Jingles (Previously Unreleased); Concert Promo/Hushabye (Live) (Previously Unreleased); California Girls; Help Me, Rhonda; Then I Kissed Her; And Your Dreams Come True; The Little Girl I Once Knew (45 Version); Barbara Ann (45 Version); Ruby Baby (Outtake) (Previously Unreleased); Koma (Radio Promo Spot) (Previously Unreleased); Sloop John B; Wouldn't It Be Nice; You Still Believe In Me; God Only Knows; Hang On To Your Ego (Alternate Version) (Previously Unreleased); I Just Wasn't Made For Theses TImes; Pet Sounds; Caroline, No; Good Vibrations (45 Version); Our Prayer; Heroes And Villains (Sections) (Previously Unreleased); Wonderful (Previously Unreleased); Cabinessence; Wind Chimes (Previously Unreleased); Heroes And Villains (Intro) (Previously Unreleased); Do You Like Worms (Previously Unreleased); Vegetables (Previously Unreleased); I Love To Say Da Da (Previously Unreleased); Surf's Up (Previously Unreleased); With Me Tonight. Heroes And Villains (45 Version); Darlin'; Wild Honey; Let The Wind Blow; Can't Wait Too Long (Alternate Version); Cool Cool Water (Previously Unreleased); Meant For You; Friends; Little Bird; Busy Doin' Nothin'; Do It Again; I Can Hear Music; I Went To Sleep; Time To Get Alone; Breakaway; Cotton Fields (The Cotton Song) (45 Version); San Miguel; Games Two Can Play (Previously Unreleased); This Whole World; Add Some Music; Forever; Our Sweet Love; HELP Is On The Way; 4th Of July; Long Promised World; Disney Girls; Surf's Up; 'Til I Die; Sail On Sailor; California; Trader; Funky Pretty; Fairy Tale Music; You Need A Mess Of Help To Stand Alone; Marcella; All This Is That; Rock And Roll Music; It's OK; Had To Phone Ya; That Same Song; It's Over Now (Previously Unreleased); Still Dream Of It (Previously Unreleased); Let Us Go On This Way; The Night Was So Young; I'll Bet He's Nice; Airplane; Come Go With Me; Our Team (Previously Unreleased); Baby Blue; Good Timin'; Goin' On; Getcha Back; Kokomo; In My Room (Demo); Radio Spot; I Get Around (Track Only); Radio Spot; I Get Around (Track Only); Radio Spot; Dance, Dance, Dance (Tracking Session); Hang On To Your Ego (Sessions); God Only Knows (Tracking Session); Good Vibrations (Sessions); Heroes And Villains (Track Only); Cabinessence (Track Only); Surf's Up (Track Only); Radio Spot; All Summer Long (Vocals); Wendy (Vocals); Hushabye (Vocals); When I Grow Up (To Be A Man) (Vocals); Wouldn't It Be Nice (Vocals); California Girls (Vocals); Radio Spot; Concert Intro/Surfin' USA – Live 1964; Surfer Girl – Live 1964; Be True To Your School – Live 1964; Good Vibrations; Good Vibrations – Live 1966; Surfer Girl – Live In Hawaii Rehearsals – 1967

The Boys have several entries in the Collection, but this is simply here to represent the rise of the archival box set – one of the better consequences of the CD age – because it's our favourite; a nigh-perfect example of how to lay out a long and varied career in a way that's appealing to the connoisseur. This box rightly assumes that a Beach Boys nut with 40 quid to spend is going to want a mix of stuff they know and outtakes they've dreamed about, well-presented and properly annotated. They're also going to want to hear as much as possible of the fabled *Smile* sessions, and there's a good half-hour of fascinating material here, probably all you really need of that particular folly – quite lovely. The thing about most archival boxes is that you're unlikely to sit down and listen to them all the way through, but you can with this one, the career unravels nicely and there are enough surprsies to make a hefty price tag worthwhile.

Actually there are lots of boxes we like. Space prohibits including them all, but among the best we've not noted elsewhere are:

The Byrds *The Byrds* Columbia 1990
Bob Dylan *The Bootleg Series Vols 1–3* CBS 1991
The Who *30 Years Of Maximum R&B* 1994
Marvin Gaye *The Master* Motown 1994
The Zombies *Zombie Heaven* Ace 1998
The Isley Brothers *It's Your Thing* Sony 1999

(While we're on the subject, decent all-career boxes on The Rolling Stones; Sly & The Family Stone and Stevie Wonder would be nice. In your own time, people!)

New Order

LONDON 1994

(The Best Of) New Order

True Faith '94; Bizarre Love Triangle '94; 1963–94; Regret; Fine Time; The Perfect Kiss; Shell Shock; Thieves Like Us; Vanishing Point; Run 2; Round And Round '94; World (Price Of Love); Ruined In A Day; Touched By The Hand Of God; Blue Monday '88; World In Motion

Thrown into disarray by the death of singer Ian Curtis, the remaining members of Joy Division recruited keyboard player Gillian Gilbert, scoured their Third Reich history books for a new name, and gorged on late '70s electronic disco music. Taking much of their old audience with them, New Order soon found chart success without damaging their indie credibility, and despite spending much of the '90s pursuing solo projects,the growth of the dance market has only served to enhance the group's reputation.

Various Artists

MUSIC UNITES/1994

Journeys By DJ: Coldcut – 70 Minutes Of Madness

Bola – Philorene; Street Beats Vol 2 – The Truper; One Blood – Junior Reid; Jam On Revenge (The Wikki Wikki Song) – Newcleus; Extreme Possibilities – 2 Player; King Ashabanapal – Funki Porcini; Noddi Holder – Jedi Knights; Fuk – Plastic Man; Mo Beats – Coldcut; Manganese In Deep Violet – Bedouin Ascent; African Drug – Bob Holroyd; If There Was No Gravity – Air Liquide; Beats and Pieces – Coldcut; Greedy Beat – Coldcut; Music Maker – Coldcut; Find Away (Acapella) – Coldcut; King Of The Beats – Mantronix; Mag – Gescom; Blood Vibes – Masters @ Work; Trumpet Riff – Raphael Corderdos; Grace – Luke Slater's 7th Pain; First Time Ever I Saw Your Face – Joanna Law; Balthus Bemused By Colour – Harold Budd; Into The 90's – Photek; Bridge Is Over – BDP; Nu Blud – DJ Food; Friendly Pressure – Jhelisa; Freshness – Hookian Minds; Message From Our Sponsor – Jello Biafra; Unify – Pressure Drop; Again Son – Love Lee; Hot Flush – Red Snapper; Theme from Dr Who – Ron Granier; Free – Moody Boys; The Dusk – DJ Food

Coldcut's contribution to the Journeys By DJs series is the great album Grandmaster Flash and Double D and Steinski never made. Matt Black was just one of many whose idea of pop was challenged by Flash's Adventures On The Wheels Of Steel. "It just completely blew apart conceptions of what a song should be like," he recalls. "It was like, well, how's this guy done this?" The album subtitle – *70 Minutes Of Madness* – was a sly reference to their own genre-bending remix of Eric B and Rakim's Paid In Full: Seven Minutes Of Madness, which was reconstructed during a marathon 39-hour session using only records, turntables and copious cups of coffee. Thirty-four tracks were employed to make *70 Minutes Of Madness*, incorporating everything from drum and bass, hip hop, house, electro, techno, reggae, jazz and even the Theme From Dr Who. "Very important iconically were the Double D and Steinski Lesson records, because they actually were lessons," says Black. "This is how you can go about taking a bunch of old stuff and making it into something new, and it was like (clicks fingers), Yeah! I get it." William Burroughs would have been proud.

The Beautiful South

GO! DISCS 1994

Carry On Up The Charts: The Best Of

Song For Whoever; You Keep It All In; I'll Sail This Ship Alone; A Little Time; My Book; Let Love Speak Up Itself; Old Red Eyes Is Back; We Are Each Other; Bell Bottomed Tear; 36D; Good As Gold (Stupid As Mud); Everybody's Talkin'; Prettiest Eyes; Our Last Love Song

Despite their underachiever demeanour and appetite for unfussy songwriting, The Beautiful South became one of the '90s' unlikely success stories, a feat sealed by this three million-selling compilation. Formed in 1989 when two ex-Housemartins, Paul Heaton and Dave Hemingway, teamed up with songwriter/guitarist Dave Rotheray and vocalist Brianna Corrigan, the group enjoyed instant success with Song For Whoever. Their trademark – Heaton's doleful, slice-of-life storytelling, backed by easy-on-the-ear arrangements – may be disarmingly simple, a fact backed up by Rotheray's claim that they spend just one week a year writing songs, but it's a formula that has proved remarkably durable. And to think, it only took 40 years to get from Presley to this!

Various Artists

EMI 1995

The Sound Gallery

Oh Calcutta – The Dave Pell Singers; Black Rite – Mandingo; Punch Bowl – Alan Parker; The Night Rider – Alan Hawkshaw; The Riviera Affair – Neil Richardson; Jet Stream – John Gregory; Half Forgotten Daydreams – John Cameron; Jaguar – John Gregory; Life Of Leisure – Keith Mansfield; Girl In A Sportscar – Alan Hawshaw; Young Scene – Keith Mansfield; It's All At The Co-Op Now – Alan Hawkshaw; Funky Fever – Alan Morehouse And His Bond Street Brigade; Shout About Pepsi – Denny Wright And The Hustlers; The Headhunter – Mandingo; Blarney's Stoned – Alan Hawkshaw; The Earthmen – Paddy Kingsland; I Feel The Earth Move – John Keating; The Penthouse Suite – Syd Dale; The Snake Pit – Mandingo; Boogie Juice – Brian Bennett; The Detectives – Alan Tew; Jesus Christ Superstar – Johnny Keating; Music To Drive By – Joe Loss Concertium

The '80s underground's thirst for so-called "Incredibly Strange Music" was picked up by a handful of UK-based club DJs in the early '90s prompting a rash of compilations. *The Sound Gallery*, a collection of long-forgotten mood music, was the first and probably the best, much of the material recorded by ace session players at EMI's Abbey Road studios between 1968 and 1976. "Tired myopic tastemakers of yesteryear had long dismissed these records, but time has now gone full circle and I am very happy to see that these legendarily fabulous recordings are once more available for all to enjoy," chirruped the sleevenotes with tongue only partially in cheek.

The Beatles

APPLE 1996

Anthology II

Real Love; Yes It Is; I'm Down; You've Got To Hide Your Love Away; If You've Got Trouble; That Means A Lot; Yesterday (rehearsal); It's Only Love; I Feel Fine; Ticket To Ride; Yesterday; Help!; Everybody's Trying To Be My Baby; Norwegian Wood (This Bird Has Flown); I'm Looking Through You; 12-Bar Original; Tomorrow Never Knows; Got To Get You Into My Life; And Your Bird Can Sing; Taxman; Eleanor Rigby; I'm Only Sleeping (rehearsal); I'm Only Sleeping (Take 1); Rock And Roll Music; She's A Woman; Strawberry Fields Forever (demo); Strawberry Fields Forever (Take 1); Strawberry Fields Forever (Take 7); Penny Lane; A Day In The Life; Good Morning, Good Morning; Only A Northern Song; Being For The Benefit Of Mr Kite; Being For The Benefit Of Mr Kite (Take 7); Lucy In The Sky With Diamonds; Within You, Without You (Instrumental); Sgt Pepper's Lonely Hearts Club Band; You Know My Name (Look Up The Number); I Am The Walrus; Fool On The Hill (demo); Your Mother Should Know; Fool On The Hill (Take 4); Hello Goodbye; Lady Madonna; Across The Universe

We've included this as an example of how skilfully music was marketed in the '90s. The *Anthology* series represented a brilliant exercise is packaging the potato peelings of the pop process as if they were some impossibly rare delicacy. And, boy, did we lap 'em up. As Round The Horne's Fanny Haddock once breathed: "One man's leftovers is another man's rissoles."

This is the best of the three *Anthology* volumes by some distance. It's as if a sophisticated X-ray process has exposed the evolution of the Mona Lisa, and you can now buy posters of what's beneath the surface – in one she's clearly winking, in another she sports a striking blue hat. Or notebooks reveal that King Lear briefly had a fourth daughter who eloped with a vegetable salesman.

To the world at large this might be mildly engaging. To an obsessive admirer of the artists in question it is truly, madly and deeply fascinating. Any detail, any faint suggestion of context or intent, anything at all that might shed a little light on the creative process, assumes an incalculable worth. If you're the type whose pulse quickens on learning that Lennon began A Day In The Life with two bars of "sugarplum fairy sugarplum fairy", or that McCartney concludes a version of I'm Down with the words "plastic soul, man, plastic soul", then this is very heaven.

The archive rock'n'roll tracks on *Anthology I* are a curio you might dust down and admire occasionally, like a sepia snap of the band at the Star Club, while the early outtakes tend to be ragged versions of what was eventually released, songs that arrived in the studio fully rehearsed, recordings with precious few layers of experiment to strip away and scrutinise. And amid a frenzied level of marketing and expectation there was the added distortion of Free As A Bird, the focus of much worldwide hand-wringing. But this second instalment serves its purpose, and generously so. The period under the microscope, the *Help!* album to Across The Universe, is particularly ripe for excavation, full of ever-denser creations whose development often took place with the tape running.

Hear Taxman with the faintest adjustment to the backing vocal and you come over all peculiar. Got To Get You Into My Life minus the brass is shockingly underdressed. The early I'm Looking Through You is practically naked. There's a real sense of narrative to Strawberry Fields: the original demo ends on a note of despair – "I cannae do it!" – as alone in his home studio Lennon attempts to fit this extravagant vision to a finger-picked acoustic. Soon there's a guitar-driven studio working model and by Take 7 the vast superstructure is almost complete. And there's a dramatic stroll through the architecture of A Day In The Life, scaffolding still firmly in place, alarm clock and full Mal Evans bar count in evidence, as John and Paul's vocals strive for the perfect counterbalance. And most extraordinary of all – this is April '66! – an early sketch of Tomorrow Never Knows, a dense tract of "atmosphere" full of ambient noise, flailing cymbals, plastic organ and a pale disembodied vocal.

But never once does an early attempt seem anything other than a beguiling diversion. It's never heading towards anything better than the form in which it was eventually released. You're left with renewed respect for the production skills of George Martin and marvelling at the fragile chemistry of The Beatles, aware that, however they resolved their disputes, that decision was unquestionably right.

Various Artists

FFRR 1998

Essential Mix 98/01: David Holmes

Contact – Brigitte Bardot; An Elephant Called Slowly – Howard Blake; California Soul – Marlena Shaw; Lesson 6 – Jurassic 5; Smokey Jo's La La – Googie Rene Combo; My Mate Paul (Skylab Remix) – David Holmes; Higher Ground – Ellen McIlwaine; Guru Vin – Don Sebesky; There's No Vibration But Wait – Edgar Broughton; Scoobs In Columbia – Plaid; Shhh For A Little While – James Brown; East – Billy Paul; First Light – Percy Faith; Get Ready – Rare Earth; Jumpin' Jack Flash – Ananda Shankar; Cat Woman – Abaco Dream; I Just Want To Celebrate – Rare Earth; Dancing Drums – Ananda Shankar; 101 Strings – Karma Star; Knickers Of A Girl – Skylab; Little Short One Pt 1 – David Holmes; My Mate Paul (Major Force Remix) – David Holmes; Skylab – Bite This

Conceived as a credible spin-off from FFRR's hugely successful (and largely disposable) Essential Selection series, the *Essential Mix* is a chance for some of the world's more talented DJs to stretch out from the restrictions imposed by having a dance floor to fill. Holmes' mix, effectively a reprise of his contributions to Radio One's late-night mix show, is a more dancefloor-friendly take on Coldcut's turntable tricknology and an unashamed homage to the '60s. The Modtastic Googie Rene Combo's Smokey Joe's La La (on which Holmes' own My Mate Paul is based) is included, alongside rare-groove staples like Marlena Shaw's California Soul and East by Billy Paul. Bizarre cover versions abound: Ellen McIlwaine's folk-soul reading of Stevie Wonder's Higher Ground and Ananda Shankar's Jumpin' Jack Flash are both eyebrow-raisers, while Edgar Broughton's *Sing Brother Sing!* album was raided for the sublimely twisted There's No Vibration But Wait. It's all quite a contrast from his early '90s excursions, when his reputation as a DJ was made with hammer-hard techno and unyielding progressive house. Pete Tong, who A&Rs the series, likes the contrast between his own mass-market compilations and the Essential Mix series. "I'm operating in the end of the market where the sales are gigantic," he says, "but I'm not really expecting them to be dug up five years later. I still really get off on doing the sort of artistic ones, like David Holmes because they're different." If Austin Powers really had been defrosted in the year 2000, it's entirely possible he would be listening to this.

Written by Mark Paytress, Merrell Noden and Jim Irvin with Bill Brewster, David Hutcheon, Neil Slaven, Ed Ward, Sid Griffin, Mark Ellen and Paul Trynka.

Index